NEW
ENCYCLOPEDIA
OF SPORTS

NEW ENCYCLOPEDIA OF SPORTS

·

RALPH HICKOK

McGRAW-HILL BOOK COMPANY

NEW YORK   ST. LOUIS   SAN FRANCISCO   AUCKLAND   BOGOTÁ
DÜSSELDORF   JOHANNESBURG   LONDON   MADRID   MEXICO   MONTREAL
NEW DELHI   PANAMA   PARIS   SÃO PAULO   SINGAPORE
SYDNEY   TOKYO   TORONTO

Library of Congress Cataloging in Publication Data

Hickok, Ralph.
  New encyclopedia of sports.
  Bibliography: p.
  1. Sports—North America—Dictionaries. I. Title.
GV567.H52   796′.097   76-45633
ISBN 0-07-028705-8

1234567890 VHVH 786543210987

*The editors for this book were Robert A. Rosenbaum and Patricia A. Allen,
the designer was Richard Roth, and the production supervisor was
Teresa F. Leaden. It was set in VIP by University Graphics, Inc.*

Printed and bound by Von Hoffmann Press, Inc.

Contents

Preface   vii

Acknowledgments   xi

New Encyclopedia of Sports   1

Directory of Sports Organizations and Associations   541

Bibliography   545

Preface

This book is meant to be a true encyclopedia of sports—an easy-to-use reference book that contains a great deal of information about all North American competitive sports.

There are basically three types of entries, arranged alphabetically:

1. Each sport has a separate entry. These entries vary greatly in length, depending partly on the relative importance of the sport and partly on its complexity. Each entry begins with a history of the sport and includes a summary of its rules and a list of results and records. Many entries also include biographical sections and glossaries.

2. There are many entries that cut across the boundaries between sports. These are basically historical essays; among subjects covered are Amateurism and Black Athletes.

3. For quick, easy reference, there are a number of short entries on specialized subjects: the various field events of track and field, for example, and the basic implements of fencing. These define the subject and refer the reader to the entry on the specific sport for further information.

As further aids to the reader, this encyclopedia also contains a large number of cross references, bibliographies, and a directory of sports associations, organizations, and leagues.

Selection of Sports. The first step in writing an encyclopedia of this sort is to decide what a "sport" is. My basic assumption is that a sport must require some physical ability. Therefore, games such as bridge, checkers, and chess, which require no such ability, are not included.

Children's games—marbles, for instance—are also omitted, although I have included some information on the children's versions of adult sports—Little League Baseball, for example—largely because of popular interest. (Those people, including many sportswriters, who are fond of referring to professional athletes as "men playing a boys' game" have it the wrong way around, incidentally: Even a brief perusal of the history of sports reveals that virtually every sport included in this volume was "invented" by adults, for adults.)

Those sports employing animals introduce a complication of sorts. Thoroughbred racing and harness racing involve jockeys and drivers; but what about dog racing, where human beings are no longer involved once the animals are in the starting gate? Or field trials? I have included both, along with briefer entries on such animal sports as pigeon racing and horse shows—if for no other reason than that their results are customarily carried on the sports pages of newspapers. However, cat shows and dog shows are not included.

One final note: As mentioned above, only North American competitive sports are included. Sports unknown to North America are not included; nor are sports in which sheer participation, not competition, is the vital element. (Even here, however, I have hedged somewhat. There are entries for fishing and hunting, which are basically participant sports, but the entries are justified by the fact that there are trophy competitions, and world records, in both sports.)

Glossaries. Where included, glossaries are not complete; I have generally omitted terms which are clearly explained in the text, and "inside" terms which would be used only by people already deeply involved in the sport. The intent is to help the person who may come across unfamiliar terms when reading about the sport in another book or publication.

Rules. The official rules are not included for any sport, since they are written in a quasilegal language intended for coaches and officials who have time for deep study. I have substituted my own summaries and explanations of the rules, and though they are quite complete, within space limitations, they are not substitutes for the official rules. Again, the intent is to help the general reader, fan, or casual player to understand the rules.

Diagrams. Much the same may be said of the diagrams, which are my own adaptations of the official diagrams. The intent is to help the reader understand the text and the rules, not to show exactly how to lay out a playing field or court. Diagrams are not to scale.

Techniques. For many sports, there is some discussion of techniques. This is not meant to be an all-sports instruction book. For those sports a person might take up as casual recreation—badminton, for example—I have tried to write what might be called a player-oriented explanation of basic techniques.

This would be impossible, however, for a great many sports in which hours of practice and coaching are required. For those sports, my discussion of techniques is more general and is aimed at the spectator rather than the player, with the intent that a person watching such a sport might be able to understand better some of the finer points.

Research. In an introduction to a previous book, I commented that sports research, particularly in the historical area, is difficult and sometimes frustrating. I consulted many people and associations in assembling information, and inspected numerous books and periodicals.

In many cases, where historical accounts differ, I have opted for one version or another, either because the source seemed to me more authoritative or because that version seemed more logical or likely. Because of the wide range of sports covered, I have depended almost entirely on secondary sources. In many perplexing cases, however, I have attempted to go to primary sources, usually of a general nature—microfilm of old newspapers and magazines, for example, history books, and almanacs.

Names from the early era of sports present an especially difficult problem, because so often there are variances in spelling and in many cases the last name only, or the last name and initials only, have come down in the official lists. In many such cases, newspaper microfilm, almanacs, and the like helped me to choose between two or more variant spellings, or to present full names.

I am certain that I have perpetuated many errors; and, in a book of this scope, it is likely that I have added some errors of my own. I hope that those who notice such errors, and who can correct them, will do so, in the interest of greater accuracy in a later edition.

RALPH HICKOK

Acknowledgments

A book of this nature can be completed only with a good deal of help from a large number of people. First, I feel compelled to single out two men whose assistance was absolutely invaluable: W. R. "Bill" Schroeder of the Citizens Savings Athletic Foundation, who sent me copious material on many sports; and Clement F. Trainer of Wynnewood, Pennsylvania, who graciously allowed me to use his carefully prepared, authoritative lists of billiards champions.

I am also grateful to the following people for their assistance: Bill Amick, racing publicity manager, American Motorcycle Association; Dr. Pedro A. Baccalao, executive director, U.S. Fronton Athletic Association; Norman Barnes, advertising manager, the Nissen Corporation; Ervin W. Belt, executive secretary, National Field Archery Association; Irwin F. Bernstein, secretary, Amateur Fencers League of America; Robert A. Brown, American Platform Tennis Association; William F. Brown, editor, the American Field Publishing Company; Kay A. Brick, executive director, the Ninety-Nines.

Jack Carr, executive vice president, U.S. Table Tennis Association; Ray Cote, vice president, Formula One, Professional Race Pilots Association; J. E. Cooper, executive secretary, National Steeplechase and Hunt Association; Margaret C. Davenport, executive director, U.S. Track and Field Hall of Fame; John I. Day, director, Thoroughbred Racing Associations' Service Bureau; John W. Deist, secretary, American Lawn Bowls Association; John Dustin, national sports administrator, Amateur Athletic Union of the United States.

Murray Geller, president, U.S. Paddle Tennis Association; George Girsch, managing editor, *Ring Magazine;* Roger A. Godin, executive director, U.S. Hockey Hall of Fame; Jean Goertner, the American Whitewater Affiliation; Loretta Jean Gragg, executive secretary, the Ninety-Nines; Rodney J. Grambeau, director, U.S. Paddleball Association; Herbert H. Gross, secretary, U.S. Squash Racquets Association; Robert H. Grossberg, executive director, U.S. Amateur Jai Alai Players Association.

Thomas C. Hardman, editor and publisher, *The Water Skier;* Richard E. Harkin, secretary, Amateur Athletic Union of the United States; Glenn Helgeland, editor, *Archery World;* Frederick J. Herzog, C.A.E., managing director, Billiard Congress of America; Dave Hill, public relations director, Amateur Softball Association; Ruth-Anne Hugo, public relations, National Rifle Association of America; Ford W. Hubbert, Jr., editor, *Skeet Shooting Review;* Kay Hutchcraft, program coordinator, Division for Girls' and Women's Sports, Association for Intercollegiate Athletics for Women.

Paul N. Jones, executive secretary, American Casting Association; A. W. "Augie" Karcher, public relations manager, Women's International Bowling Congress; Bill Kiser, Darlington International Raceway; C. J. Landrey, assistant secretary, the Badminton Association of England; Mrs. Ruthe Larson, assistant secretary, U.S. Polo Association; Charles P. Leach, Jr., executive secretary, National All-Terrain Vehicle Association; Edmund W. Lee, secretary, Eastern Rugby Union of America, Inc.; Ray Leverton, curator, National Ski Hall of Fame; Morris Levitsky, metropolitan New York chairman of handball for the Amateur Athletic Union; James Lupher, secretary-manager, World Championship Cutter and Chariot Racing Association; Virginia B. Lyon, administrative secretary, American Badminton Association.

Elaine E. Mann, director, National Museum of Racing; Jack L. Martin, Sr., director of public affairs, U.S. Auto Club; Evelyn Masbruch, office manager, U.S. Ski Association; Frank Micalizzi, assistant to the executive secretary, National Duckpin Bowling Congress; Jerry A. Miles, director of public relations, National Collegiate Athletic Association; Cynthia J. Molburg, editor and publisher, *Team and Trail;* Ray Nelson, press relations manager, American Bowling Congress; Leah "Ping" Neuberger, historian, U.S. Table Tennis Association.

Valerie Petrie, managing editor, *Air Racing* magazine; Philip A. Pines, director, Hall of Fame of the Trotter; Bruce Pluckhahn, manager, public relations department, American Bowling Congress; Mrs. C. Frank Pollen, president, U.S. Women's Curling Association; William F. Rick, Jr., public information director, Babe Ruth Baseball; George Rickard, executive director, Roller Skating Rink Operators Association; John E. Roberts, administrative assistant, National Federation of State High School Associations; Charles W. Ryan, director of publications, U.S. Parachute Association.

C. A. Saunders, Saunders Archery Company; Iris Sindelar, editor, *American Whitewater Affiliation;* Doyle Smith, director, sports information office, U.S. Intercollegiate Lacrosse Association; Harry Smith, Jr., executive secretary, American Power Boat Association; Marcia Smoke, American Canoe Association; Alexander Solomon, historian, Amateur Fencers League of America; William A. Spencer, secretary, committee for biathlon, U.S. Olympic Committee; Stanley A. Sprague, executive secretary, U.S. Revolver Association; J. Anthony Studdy, president, Philadelphia Rugby Club.

G. N. Thiel, secretary-treasurer, U.S. Intercollegiate Lacrosse Association; Ted C. Tow, director, NCAA Publishing Service; Van Buskirk, secretary, Underwater Society of America; Joe Whitlock, director of communications, National Association for Stock Car Auto Racing; George M. Wilson, president, U.S. Modern Pentathlon and Biathlon Association; Jean C. Winder, assistant secretary, U.S. Figure Skating Association.

I must also thank my friend and colleague at Southeastern Advertising Agency, John Kurgan, for turning my very rough drawings into lucid diagrams. My two older daughters, Holly and Stephanie, helped on many occasions with filing and proofreading; and Deirdre, while too young to assist with such chores, was the source of considerable cheer during the whole project.

R. H.

NEW
ENCYCLOPEDIA
OF SPORTS

AIRPLANE RACING—The movie *Those Magnificent Men in Their Flying Machines* must have reminded many people that air racing was a craze in the days when airplanes were a novelty, reaching a peak of popularity in the prosperous 1920s, when it was commonly believed that the private plane might soon replace the automobile as a means of transportation. "The fastest sport in the world" can no longer draw the crowds it could command in the past, but it is certainly not extinct.

Types of Competition. There are basically two types of air races: point-to-point, in which planes start at one place and race to another, and closed-circuit, in which they travel around a course marked by pylons, tall, skinny pyramids that are usually checkered in contrasting colors for easy visibility. In closed-circuit racing, planes must go around the pylons; cutting a pylon by traveling inside it results in disqualification, unless the pilot immediately turns back and goes around it properly.

Within those basic classifications, there are several subgroups. Point-to-point races may be based on actual time—meaning that time spent on the ground for refueling or repairs counts, just as pit stops count in most auto races—or on elapsed time, meaning that only actual flying time counts, so there is no rush about refueling and pilots may take time out to rest during ground stops.

In early races there was free-for-all competition, with no regard to the type of plane or its weight or horsepower, since the basic purpose was to improve the breed and find which kinds of planes could travel fastest, climb highest, or stay in the air longest. But as planes improved, conditioned races entered the picture. Probably the first was the Schneider Trophy race, for seaplanes, since early seaplanes were rather clumsy vehicles that couldn't compete with land-based planes on equal terms. Many other types of conditions have been used, most of them based on horsepower or weight, tending to make the pilot more important than the plane and thus, it might be argued, making air racing more sporting.

The most sophisticated type of conditioned race is a handicap, in which each plane is rated at a par average speed, and the pilot who comes closest to his plane's par, or exceeds it by the greatest margin, is the winner. Thus, a pilot who averages 201 mph in a plane rated at 210 would beat a pilot who averages 230 mph in a plane rated at 250.

Early Racing. Air racing was at first closely linked with technical progress in aviation. There was no head-to-head competition; instead, planes were flown singly in attempts to reach the highest possible speeds, altitudes, or distances, usually for trophies or cash prizes offered to spur progress in the field.

Such competition usually took place at air meets, where a large number of pilots could congregate to show what their planes could do, and to compare notes. The first major air meet was held in August, 1909 at Reims, France. Thirty-eight planes and twenty-eight pilots were there. Cash prizes were given in six categories: longest flight, highest altitude, most passengers carried around the course, fastest daily lap, fastest two laps, and fastest three laps. The prize for the fastest two laps was the James Gordon Bennett Trophy, donated by the publisher of the New York (and Paris/International) *Herald Tribune*. Glenn H. Curtiss, a young designer who had once been a builder and racer of motorcycles, won both the Bennett Trophy and the Prix de la Vitesse (prize for speed) for the fastest three laps. His average speed was 47.65 mph.

The first important air meet in the United States was held in Los Angeles early in 1910. At that meet, Curtiss established a world speed record of 55 mph, with a passenger. A few months later, he won the *New York World* prize of $10,000 for a flight down the Hudson River from Albany to New York City. He covered the 150 mi in 2 hr, 51 min.

The Bennett Trophy competition for 1910 was the feature of America's first international air meet, held October 22–31 at Belmont Park, New York, better known for horse racing. Bennett Trophy races continued through

Ray Cote won seven consecutive national Formula One championships in "Shoestring." (*Courtesy of Ray Cote, Professional Race Pilots Association.*)

1913, and after World War I there was one final race, in 1920. The 1912 winner, Jules Vedrines of France, was the first pilot to average more than 100 mph in a flight of any distance.

The second major trophy in air racing was the Schneider Trophy, donated by French industrialist Jacques Schneider, for seaplane races over open water. The first Schneider race took place at Monaco on April 16, 1913. A Frenchman, Maurice Prevost, won the 280-km race—the only pilot to finish. His official average speed of 45.75 mph is misleading. Prevost landed before reaching the finish line and crossed it on pontoons. Nearly an hour later, someone remembered that the rules specified a plane had to *fly* across the line. Prevost hurried out, took off again, and flew back across the line to make his victory official, but the period spent on the ground was included in his total time.

World War I forced a temporary halt to air racing, but it also alerted many nations to the potential importance of air power. After the war, many governments became actively involved in developing better planes, and racing offered a good way to try them out.

After World War I. The typical postwar air meet was like a carnival. It usually began with aerial acrobatics and parachute jumping to attract crowds. Then spectators would be offered rides, for a price. Sometimes the events included balloon ascensions or races. The airplane races usually came last, as the climax to the whole program. It was also the period of barnstorming fliers, air-crazy people who performed at state fairs and air meets; their stunts included power dives, wing-walking, and other forms of aerobatics. Some of them did brief trapeze routines while suspended from a plane in flight. One of the barnstormers was Charles A. Lindbergh, whose interesting recollections of that part of his life are part of his autobiography *We*. The Wright brothers and Glenn Curtiss sponsored barnstorming troupes to promote their own engines and planes.

Schneider Trophy racing resumed in 1919, though the race that year was declared no contest when it was discovered that the only pilot to finish in the heavy fog had flown around the wrong marker. The French won their third Bennett Trophy in 1920, the first postwar race in the series—and the last, since the trophy then became the permanent possession of the French.

In 1920, too, Ralph, Joseph Jr., and Herbert Pulitzer, publishers of the *New York World* and the *St. Louis Post-Dispatch*, offered a trophy for a series of international air races to be held in the United States. The first Pulitzer Trophy race was held at Mitchel Field, near Garden City, Long Island, New York, and was won by an American, Corliss Moseley, with an average speed of 156.5 mph. In subsequent years, the race was held in Omaha, Detroit, St. Louis, and Dayton before returning to Mitchel Field in 1925, its final year. The Army and Navy both produced special racing planes and pursuit prototypes for the Pulitzer competition. The government's decision to stop spending money on air racing marked the end of the event.

National Air Races. The 1924 and 1925 Pulitzer races were run at meets called the National Air Races, which continued after the Pulitzer Trophy was withdrawn. Until 1929, the major event was the John L. Mitchell Trophy Race. The trophy was donated by Brig. Gen. "Billy" Mitchell in memory of his brother, who had been killed in

World War I. Only pilots belonging to the Army's First Pursuit Group could enter.

The Mitchell races were generally more exciting than the better-known Pulitzer races, because the planes were quite evenly matched. And twice, in 1924 and 1926, a diving start was used. In this crowd-pleasing start, the planes circle for altitude and then dive down to the starting line at evenly spaced intervals. In the 1926 race, the nine planes entered came diving across the starting line together, side by side—a so-called horse-race start. This genuine head-to-head competition, with planes very close together in their turns around the pylons, stirred more spectator excitement than the usual type of race, in which the basic competition was against time.

The National Air Races really came of age in 1929, when more than 500,000 people bought tickets to see 27 closed-circuit races, for planes of all classes, and the finishes of 9 point-to-point races, at Cleveland Municipal Airport. Most of the closed-circuit races used the horse-race start. In addition, there was a special race for women pilots, and for the first time in seven years, military and civilian planes competed against one another. The races remained in Cleveland, except for two visits to Los Angeles, until World War II ended the event.

The feature attraction in 1929 was a race for the Thompson Cup, donated by Charles Thompson of Thompson Products, Inc., for a free-for-all closed-circuit race. Douglas Davis won the cup with an average of 194.9 mph, in a plane of his own design that completely outflew a field consisting mostly of Army and Navy craft. The cup was renamed the Thompson Trophy in 1930. Military planes largely dominated Thompson competition for the next several years, but in 1936 a number of commercially produced planes were entered, and they dominated through the last prewar race, in 1939.

Another major event was added to the national schedule in 1931, when Vincent Bendix, president of the Bendix Aviation Corporation, donated a trophy for free-for-all transcontinental flights. Since the races were usually held in Cleveland, the Bendix Trophy portion of the race was actually from California to Cleveland, but winners and other competitors generally went on to the East Coast in attempts to set transcontinental records. In 1933 and 1936 the National Air Races were held in Los Angeles, and the Bendix Trophy event in those years was a true transcontinental race, from New York to Los Angeles.

After World War II. Following World War II, the renewed National Air Races were welcomed with great enthusiasm. The war had produced planes that could travel at previously unheard-of speeds. Some war-trained pilots bought surplus fighters for racing. The P-38 Lightning and the P-51 Mustang were especially popular. The Mustang, which could reach 487 mph, was the fastest of the propeller-driven planes. But there were also the jets. The Germans and British had used jet planes late in the war. The United States put the F-80 (F, for "fighter," replaced P, for "pursuit," after the war) into production in 1946, and it was available for the first postwar races. The Bendix and Thompson trophies were offered in two divisions, R for regular craft and J for jet, from 1946 through 1949. In the 1949 Thompson R Trophy race, pilot Bill Odom, in a P-51, flew off the course, stalled when he tried to get back, and crashed into a house. A woman and child were killed, as was Odom. This tragedy brought a reaction against air racing, particularly against high-speed, closed-circuit competition near residential areas, and the 1950 races were canceled. There was a Detroit Air Fair, however, at which one race, for "midget" planes, was conducted. This race, restricted to fixed-propeller planes with 190 in³ of displacement, was for the Continental Trophy, which had been introduced in 1948 at the Miami Air Maneuvers.

The National Air Races were revived in modified form in 1951, as the National Air Show, for military planes only—except for the Continental Trophy race, for civilian midget planes. That format prevailed until 1957, when the U.S. Department of Defense refused to let military craft take part, a ruling whose effect was to kill the show.

Air Racing Today. Military planes still set out to break records, but true air racing is now restricted to a handful of events in which a small but enthusiastic group of civilian pilots compete in propeller-driven planes. The P-38 and P-51 are still popular in long-distance and unlimited closed-circuit races. Most racing planes, however, are smaller craft that fly at speeds of around 200 mph. Formula One planes are usually specially built for racing. Important meets also offer races for sport biplanes and for the At-6, a fighter–trainer of World War II vintage.

Under the leadership of the Professional Race Pilots Association, the sport has been making something of a comeback in recent years. The biggest annual event, the Reno National Championship Air Races, was inaugurated in 1964 and has drawn more and more competitors and spectators every year. This features closed-circuit races in the Unlimited, Formula One, AT-6 SNJ, and Sport Biplane categories.

Powder Puff Derby. Women won surprisingly early acceptance in aviation and in air racing. Their own race, the Powder Puff Derby, is now the only air race that still attracts national attention. Established in 1947 by the Ninety-Nines, an international organization of women pilots whose first president was Amelia Earhart, the event was formally named the International Air Race for Women. But the name Powder Puff Derby, originally meant as male-chauvinist sarcasm, is now accepted proudly by the women who organize the race.

The takeoff and landing points vary from year to year. The distance is usually about 2,500 air mi. The derby is an elapsed-time race, with night flying and instrument flying forbidden, and is handicapped on par speed figures. In recent years, it has usually been a four-day race, with entrants required to stop at three designated airports for overnight stays. At six points they have to descend to 200 ft to be checked in at observation towers. The formula for determining the winner is so complicated that it used to take a day or two for judges to decide the results, but computers have since solved that problem.

Organizations. Most formal racing in the United States is conducted by the Professional Race Pilots Association, under the general supervision of the competition committee of the National Aeronautic Association. The Fédération Aeronautique Internationale (FAI), based in Paris, is the international body that supervises records in all forms of aviation.

Powder Puff Derby Winners
(P indicates Pilot, CP Copilot)

Year	Start and Finish	Winners
1947	Palm Springs, Calif., to Tampa, Fla.	Carolyn West—P Beatrice Medes—CP
1948	Palm Springs, Calif., to Miami	Frances Nolde—P
1949	San Diego to Miami	Laurette F. Savort—P Sue Kindred—CP
1950	San Diego to Greenville, S.C.	Jean P. Rose—P "Boots" Seymour—CP
1951	Santa Ana, Calif., to Detroit	Claire Walters—P Frances Bera—CP
1952	Santa Ana, Calif., to Teterboro, N.J.	Shirley Froyd—P Martha Baechle—CP
1953	Lawrence, Mass., to Long Beach, Calif.	Frances A. Bera—P Marcella Duke—CP
1954	Long Beach, Calif., to Knoxville, Tenn.	Ruth Deerman—P Ruby Hayes—CP
1955	Long Beach, Calif., to Springfield, Mass.	Frances A. Bera—P Edna Bower—CP
1956	San Mateo, Calif., to Flint, Mich.	Frances A. Bera—P Edna Bower—CP
1957	San Mateo, Calif., to Philadelphia	Alice Roberts—P Iris Critchell—CP
1958	San Diego to Charleston, S.C.	Frances A. Bera—P Evelyn Kelly—CP
1959	Lawrence, Mass., to Spokane, Wash.	Aileen Saunders—P Jerelyn Cassell—CP
1960	Torrance, Calif., to Wilmington, Del.	Aileen Saunders—P June Douglas—CP
1961	San Diego to Atlantic City, N.J.	Frances A. Bera—P
1962	Oakland to Wilmington, Del.	Frances A. Bera—P Edna Bower—CP
1963	Bakersfield, Calif., to Atlantic City, N.J.	Virginia Britt—P Lee Winfield—CP
1964	Fresno, Calif., to Atlantic City, N.J.	Mary Ann Noah—P Mary Aikins—CP
1965	El Cajon, Calif., to Chattanooga, Tenn.	Mary Ann Noah—P Mary Aikins—CP
1966	Seattle to Clearwater, Fla.	Bernice T. Steadman—P Mary E. Clark—CP
1967	Atlantic City, N.J., to Torrance, Calif.	Judy Wagner—P
1968	Van Nuys, Calif., to Savannah, Ga.	Margaret Mead—P Billie Herrin—CP
1969	San Diego to Dulles, Wash., D.C.	Mara K. Culp—P
1970	Monterey, Calif., to Bristol, Pa.	Margaret Mead—P Susan Oliver—CP
1971	Calgary, Canada, to Baton Rouge, La.	Gini Richardson—P
1972	San Carlos, Calif., to Toms River, N.J.	Marian Banks—P Dottie Sanders—CP
1973	Carlsbad, Calif., to Elmira-Corning, N.Y.	Marian Burke—P Ruth Hildebrand—CP
1974	No competition	
1975	Riverside, Calif., to Boyne Falls, Mich.	Trina Jarish—P
1976	Sacramento, Calif., to Wilmington, Del.	Trina Jarish—P

Bibliography. Kinert, Reed: *Racing Planes and Air Races*, Aero, Fallbrook, Calif., 1968; Vorderman, Don: *The Great Air Races*, Doubleday, New York, 1969.

ALL-AMERICAN TEAMS—The first All-American foot-ball team, chosen in 1889, was the idea of Caspar W. Whitney, part owner of a magazine called *This Week's Sport*. He turned to a friend, Walter Camp, for expert advice, and they collaborated on choosing teams in 1889 and 1890. The magazine then went out of business and Whitney joined *Harper's Weekly*, for whom he selected teams from 1891 through 1896. Camp chose the 1897 team for *Harper's*, and the following year he began selecting the *Collier's* All-American teams. He also listed the nine previous teams, without giving Whitney any credit, thus starting the idea that Camp himself had originated the All-American idea. Camp continued picking *Collier's* All-Americans until his death in 1925, when Grantland Rice took over the job.

Today, All-American teams are named by a number of magazines, newspapers, wire services and others for both football and basketball, and All-Americans are also selected for such other college sports as hockey, lacrosse, field hockey, and baseball. All-league, all-pro, and all-star teams are selected for many professional sports, as well.

For listings of various "all" teams, see entries for spe-cific sports.

ALL-TERRAIN VEHICLES—*See* OFF-ROAD RACING.

AMATEUR ATHLETIC UNION—In a sense, the Amateur Athletic Union (AAU) was an outgrowth of the athletic–club idea. Athletic clubs knew their own members were amateurs, but it was difficult to check on the amateurism of other athletes who might enter their meets. Athletes who had accepted prize money were known to change their names and travel long distances to compete, and in some cases, unscrupulous promoters held "amateur" meets, offering trophies and then buying back the tro-phies from the winners in order to offer them at yet another meet.

The first attempt to solve the problem was through the National Association of Amateur Athletes of America (NAAAA), formed in 1879, under the leadership of the New York Athletic Club, in order to take over jurisdiction of the national track and field championships. The NAAAA was reorganized as the AAU in 1887. The origi-nal idea was to have an organization of athletic clubs. An amateur would have to belong to a club and, through the club, to the AAU, so that it would be easy to check his credentials.

The founders had underestimated the number of ath-letic clubs in the country, and it soon became obvious that the organization would be unwieldy. In 1889 a reor-ganization plan was proposed by A. G. Mills, who later became the third president of the National Baseball League and who was the man who decided that Abner Doubleday had invented baseball. Mills's plan for the AAU was to divide the country into districts. Each district would have an association made up of all the clubs in the district, and the AAU would be a kind of federation of the associations. The plan worked, and has had great impact on international sports, most of which are now ruled by federations set up much like the AAU.

Originally comprising less than 3,000 athletes, most of them in track and field events, the AAU gradually took a number of amateur sports under its umbrella, among them bobsledding, boxing, gymnastics, handball, swim-ming, tobogganing, volleyball, water polo, and wrestling. The AAU at one time represented the United States on the international federations that control most of these sports. In addition, the AAU has worked closely with a number of allied members, organizations ruling sports over which the AAU has no direct control, including bicycling, bil-liards, casting, fencing, skiing, soccer, and others.

Two famous names have been connected with the AAU. James E. Sullivan was its president from 1906 through 1909, and served as secretary-treasurer before and after that period. He did a great deal to spread the AAU idea of amateurism—the "simon-pure" idea that has come under attack in recent years—and he greatly expanded the organization's activities, adding new sports to its jurisdiction and new national championships to its sponsorship. Since 1930, the AAU has given the James E. Sullivan Memorial Trophy to an amateur athlete "who, by performance, example, and good influence did the most to advance the cause of good sportsmanship during the year."

Daniel J. Ferris, originally a secretary to Sullivan, was secretary–treasurer for more than 30 years and was an inexhaustible worker and a remarkable public relations representative, well liked by most sportswriters. Even after his retirement, in 1957, Ferris continued to work, raising funds for a new AAU building and promoting competition, especially in track and field, between the United States and Russia.

Beginning about the mid-1950s, the AAU became involved in a continuing series of disputes with the National Collegiate Athletic Association (NCAA) over which group is to control certain sports. The "war" has been sometimes hot, sometimes cold, but generally luke-warm. At times, both groups have refused to let athletes under their control compete in certain meets sponsored by the other group. This has often become a major issue in track and field. There was a particularly violent flare-up before the 1964 Olympic Games. A truce was arranged, with Gen. Douglas MacArthur as mediator, in time for the United States to put together teams for the games. But other disputes have followed.

The AAU lost some of its power in recent years because of the NCAA-backed "federation" movement, through which separate national federations were organized for a number of sports, including track and field, gymnastics, and wrestling. The U.S. Gymnastics and Wrestling Feder-ations have won recognition from the International Olympic Committee; in addition, the IOC removed bas-ketball from AAU jurisdiction after the 1972 Olympics.

Largely because of the AAU-NCAA dispute, the Amer-ican federal government has seriously considered inter-vening in amateur athletics on several occasions. In 1974, the Senate passed the so-called Stearns bill, which would establish a Federal Amateur Sports Board to oversee a number of sports organizations in this country.

See also AMATEURISM; ATHLETIC CLUBS; NCAA; SULLIVAN AWARD.

AMATEURISM—When the Austrian Skier Karl Schranz was banned from the 1972 Winter Olympics for profes-sionalism, it was perhaps the loudest shot in a long, difficult, and often confusing battle to decide where the line between amateur and professional should be drawn. Some people wonder whether the line is really needed.

A major difficulty is that there is no genuine international definition of amateurism. Indeed, the definition varies from country to country and from sport to sport. In golf, a player may be able to regain amateur standing after having played as a professional. Hundreds of thousands of bowlers compete in leagues for prize money every week, but are considered amateurs. On the other hand, there was a time when a tennis player could lose amateur standing merely by competing against a professional.

"Amateur" is a French word, derived from the Latin amátòr ("lover"). It originally meant a connoisseur—one who loves the fine arts, appreciates them, and knows something about them, without being a professional artist. In that sense, the word was first used in English about 1784. It was first applied to sports in 1801, when it was used to describe gentlemen spectators at prize fights, opposed to the ungentlemanly rabble. It was fashionable then for gentlemen to learn something about boxing, and to attend professional fights to make gentlemanly bets based on their knowledge of the sport.

Through the first half of the nineteenth century, the difference between an amateur and a professional in England was basically a class distinction. A professional made his living from a sport, or at least competed primarily for cash prizes. An amateur might make a friendly bet on himself in, say, a sculling race, but the very act of making the bet implied that he had enough money to be able to afford to lose some if he lost the race. (The British could push this kind of class distinction even further. They did it as recently as 1920, when John B. Kelly, Sr. was barred from the Diamond Sculls event at the Henley Rowing Regatta because he made his living as a bricklayer and therefore could not be an "amateur"—meaning "gentleman.")

Oddly enough, it was in rowing, where English amateurs often won or lost sizable bets, that the rather strict American view of the amateur–professional issue first developed. In 1872, the Schuylkill Navy, a Philadelphia rowing association, sponsored a major regatta. Races were to be open to amateurs only. All the oarsmen in the area submitted entries, but half the applicants were rejected. That caused an uproar. After the races were run, the committee explained to protesting oarsmen that an amateur was someone who didn't benefit financially through sport, and that even winning a friendly bet was a way of benefiting financially. Some oarsmen then complained that, although they had made bets on themselves, they had never won any. So the committee extended its definition: Anyone who competed *in hope* of monetary gain was a non-amateur.

Two men, William B. Curtis and James Watson, were appointed to study the subject further, and they came up with pretty much the same answer: An amateur rowed for fun, a non-amateur (carefully avoiding the word "professional") in the hope of a cash reward. That has been pretty much the American rule ever since.

Other countries have different views, however, and the differences always leap into prominence in leap year, when the Olympics are held. Australia and some other countries allow "broken-time" payments to amateur athletes; that is, if they have to spend time away from work to train or to take part in competition, they can be paid the amount of money they would have earned had they not missed work. Broken-time payments to amateurs were approved by the International Olympic Committee for the first time in 1974, and were sanctioned for Olympic competition in 1976.

Russia and many other countries have state-subsidized athletes. And the United States has a large number of college-subsidized athletes. Both classes are considered amateurs by the IOC.

The American view, generally accepted by the IOC under the leadership of its long-time president Avery Brundage, has led to some striking paradoxes. An amateur can win a trophy, but may not sell or pawn it. An amateur is permitted to accept expense money, but not prize money. An amateur is not allowed to make money by writing or reporting on his or her sport even if the athlete in question is a trained journalist or broadcaster. On the other hand, AAU basketball, the long-time bastion of amateur basketball in the United States, was largely made up of teams sponsored by companies who put the players on their payrolls, sometimes at inflated salaries, and often let them practice on company time. Such teams furnished many players for American Olympic teams.

The strict line between amateur and professional is gradually fading. Open tennis competition, pitting amateur against professional, is now common, although lawn tennis leaders used to be among the most adamant upholders of the strict line.

When John B. Kelly, Jr. became president of the AAU in 1971, he spoke out against "shamateurism" and the hypocrisy it so often leads to, and he urged relaxation of some of the rules. He suggested, for example, that an athlete like Bob Hayes should be allowed to compete as an amateur in track and field, even after having become a professional football player. The AAU formally proposed this rules change to the International Amateur Athletics Federation, but it was rejected.

The National Collegiate Athletic Association did adopt that policy in 1974, however. The first players to take advantage of it were student-athletes who signed professional baseball, football, or basketball contracts early in the year, then competed in track and field or other sports during the spring.

See also AMATEUR ATHLETIC UNION.

AMERICA'S CUP—The 110-ft yacht *America*, owned by a syndicate of New York Yacht Club members, won the Royal Yacht Squadron's Hundred-Guinea Cup in a race around the Isle of Wight on August 22, 1851. In 1857 the cup was deeded to the NYYC as a trophy for which any foreign yacht could challenge. The first challenge was in 1870, when James Ashbury's English schooner *Cambria* raced against 14 American yachts, finishing eighth. Since Ashbury's second challenge, in 1871, the race has been a competition between two yachts, a challenger and a defender. By the mid-1970s, the United States had defended successfully 22 times.

For further details and results, *see* YACHTING.

ANGLING—*See* CASTING; FISHING.

ARCHERY—Because of its former military importance, archery is one of the oldest organized sports. Indeed, it was for a long time the only sport permitted in England;

These archers are competing in one of the newest major tournaments, the Desert Inn Classic. Long metal rods protruding from the fronts of the bows are stabilizers. (*Courtesy of Glenn Helgeland, Archery World.*)

from 1330 to 1414, all other sports were banned because they took time away from archery practice. Long before their use in warfare, however, the bow and arrow were important to man's survival because they permitted him to hunt, at a distance, animals which he couldn't outrun. It is likely that men were practicing archery more than 10,000 years ago, and practicing leads easily to friendly competition. It is known that the Chinese had archery contests 3,000 or more years ago.

Though the bow was used in warfare for centuries, for a long time it was not considered a very important weapon, except in certain countries, most of them in the Orient. Persian archers were mainly responsible for the defeat of the Greek army in 484 B.C. The ancient Greeks used bows—according to Homer, Odysseus killed the rival suitors with arrows from his enormous bow when he finally returned from his odyssey—but the later Greeks and Romans, when they wanted archers, usually hired mercenaries from other countries.

Nevertheless, a couple of Roman emperors adopted archery as a hobby and achieved legendary skill. Domitian (51–96) supposedly staged exhibitions in which a slave would hold up his hand, fingers spread, and the emperor would fire arrows through the spaces between his fingers. The distance is not recorded. Commodus (161–192) showed off his archery skills in the arena. One of his stunts was to decapitate ostriches as they ran by at top speed.

Archery was late coming to western Europe, and even in eastern Europe and most Asian and North African countries it was not of great importance in warfare during the early Middle Ages. Most armies during the period used a small bow, because their archers rode on horseback. The bow was used for ambushes, for guerrilla warfare, for sharpshooting during sieges, and, in open-field combat, for directing a crossfire from the flanks against a charging or retreating enemy.

The Norse changed that. They used longer bows, which shot arrows in high trajectories for much greater dis-

tances. The standard defense against the bow in the Middle Ages was to hold up a line of shields to turn away the arrows. The longer bow, however, could drop arrows behind this line of defense. William the Conqueror's victory over Harold II in 1066 was largely due to the longer bow: Arrows killed Harold and many of the English nobles.

After the Conquest, the English longbow developed. By the fourteenth century, it was 6 ft long, and the English began to use it as a strategic weapon, much like modern artillery. At the Battle of Crécy in 1346, English arrows slaughtered the French cavalry. The English bowman could launch seven arrows a minute. At Crécy, at least 6,000 archers were deployed. When the French horsemen attacked, they were showered by 42,000 arrows a minute, when they were still 250 yd away. Crécy was a major victory for the English, and they won similar victories over the French at Poitiers and Agincourt.

Ironically, another great British victory marked the beginning of the end for the bow as a major military weapon. When the Spanish Armada attempted to invade in 1588, firearms were issued to 10,000 British troops as an experiment. They were so successful that the British began replacing bows with guns. The guns then in use had a much shorter effective range; they were not as accurate and were slower in operation, but the psychological effect of the flash and the explosion made them effective weapons.

Crossbows. The crossbow is a sort of hybridization of the ordinary bow and the slingshot. The bow is held horizontally, in front of the archer, and the string is "wound up" by a mechanical device. This permits much more energy to be stored up than when the archer has to draw the string back himself, with a single pull. The crossbow is also very accurate, because it is aimed like a gun and fired by pulling a trigger. Its greatest disadvantage is that it takes much longer to load than an ordinary bow.

Competitive Archery

The first known formal competition among archers was the Ancient Scorton Arrow Contest, held in 1673 in Yorkshire, England. The sport rapidly caught on, often under royal sponsorship, throughout Europe. In 1790 the Society Royal Toxopholite (from the Greek for "bow lover") was formed in England to advance competitive archery. It was succeeded in 1844 by the Grand National Archery Association, which held the first national championship that year. The association still rules the sport in England.

The first archery club in the United States was the United Bowmen of Philadelphia, founded in 1828. The National Archery Association was organized in 1879, and the first national championship event was held that year.

Two brothers, Maurice and Will Thompson, were largely responsible for the revival of archery as a sport in the United States after the Civil War. As veterans of the Confederate Army, they were not allowed to possess firearms. They moved to what was then the Florida wilderness and, with the help of Indians, they learned to make and use archery equipment. The brothers wrote a best-selling book, *The Witchery of Archery,* and Maurice Thompson was a founder of the national association. Will won many championships in the organization's early years.

Additional impetus—especially for bow hunting—

came from Dr. Saxton Pope, who learned the sport from the last survivor of a primitive Indian tribe in California. Pope wrote a very readable account of his experiences, *Hunting with the Bow and Arrow*, which was popular among outdoorsmen in the 1920s.

Target Archery. The regulation outdoor archery target is a circular disk made of straw, at least 4 ft in diameter and 6 in thick. Its face, made of oilcloth or canvas, has five concentric circles. The inner circle, with a 9.6-in diameter, is gold. Each of the other four rings is 4.8 in wide, and the colors, reading from the center outward, are red, blue, black, and white. A hit on the gold bull's-eye scores 9 points; red scores 7, blue 5, black 3, and white 1 point. An arrow that goes all the way through the target or bounces off without sticking scores 5 points.

Competition is made up of one or more rounds; a round consists of a certain number of arrows shot from certain established distances. Most commonly used rounds are:

York: 72 at 100 yd, 48 at 80, 24 at 60.
"900": 30 each at 60, 50, and 40 yd.
Men's Metropolitan: 50 each at 100, 80, 60, 50, and 40 yd.
American: 30 each at 60, 50, and 40 yd.
Columbia: 24 each at 50, 40, and 30 yd.
National: 48 at 60 yd, 24 at 50.
Women's Metropolitan: 30 each at 60, 50, 40, and 30 yd.

Each archer shoots six arrows at a time—an end—and is then scored. In the scoring, the number of bull's-eyes is given first, followed by the point total for the end. A perfect end of six bull's-eyes at 9 points each, for example, would be scored "6-54."

World championships have been held since 1931, when the Fédération Internationale du Tir a l'Arc (FITA) was formed. For the world title, the FITA round is used: 36 arrows each at 90, 70, 50, and 30 m.

Target archery was an Olympic event in 1904, 1908, and 1920, and was restored to the Olympic program in 1972. A major reason for the long hiatus was that no distinction was made between the amateur and the professional.

Layout of a typical indoor archery range. (*Courtesy of Glenn Helgeland,* Archery World.)

Professional Archery. The Professional Archers Association was formed in 1961 to manage a tour for professional archers. Established in 1963 with 10 tournaments offering about $20,000 in prize money, the PAA tour has now grown to more than 20 major tournaments. Prize money peaked at $86,500 in 1970 and has since leveled off at between $70,000 and $80,000. There are nearly 500 members of the PAA, including coaches, tournament officials, and businessmen, in addition to competitors.

The PAA established its own rounds, for increased spectator appeal. The PAA outdoor round consists of 60 arrows, 6 each shot at 10 different targets, ranging from 20 yd to 65 yd distant. The targets are spread across the field in a V pattern, with 20-yd targets at the extreme left and right and 65-yd targets in the center. A competitor begins at the left, shooting 3 arrows at a 20-yd target, then moves to the right to shoot 3 arrows at a 25-yd target, and so on, until finishing by shooting 3 arrows at a 20-yd target at the extreme left-hand side of the shooting line.

The targets have white center circles, scoring 5 points, and 2 black rings delineated in white, scoring 4 and 3 points. A perfect score is 300. The annual PAA outdoor tournament now consists of four rounds.

Indoor Archery. Because of problems relating to space, indoor archery uses a much smaller target, 16 in across, with a 3-in bull's-eye that counts 5 points, and the range is only 20 yd. The PAA round is 60 arrows from that distance.

There are two indoor rounds recognized for international competition. Each consists of 30 arrows, shot in 10 ends of 3 arrows each. The Indoor Short Round is shot from 18 m (19 yd, 1 ft, 9 in) at a target with a 40-cm (15.7-in) face. The Indoor Long Round is shot from 25 m (27 yd, 1 ft, .029 in) at a target with a 60-cm (23.6-in) face. The targets are marked with 10 rings, proportional in size to those on the large outdoor target, and the scoring is the same as in outdoor competition.

A match consists of four rounds. In a combined match, two short and two long rounds are shot. In larger indoor areas, the "900" round is used.

Flight Archery. In flight archery, only distance counts. Competition is conducted in five classes: 1. Bows up to and including 50 lb; 2. Bows up to and including 65 lb; 3. Bows up to and including 80 lb; 4. Bows of any weight; 5. Freestyle.

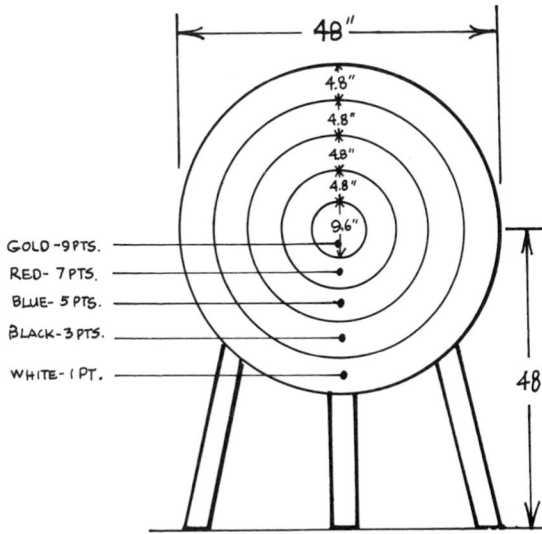

GOLD - 9 PTS.
RED - 7 PTS.
BLUE - 5 PTS.
BLACK - 3 PTS.
WHITE - 1 PT.

Archery target

The modern target bow is a remarkably complex instrument—a far cry from the yew bows of Robin Hood's era. (*Courtesy of Glenn Helgeland,* Archery World.)

The "weight" of a bow is not its actual weight, but the number of pounds of force required to pull the string back 28 in. In freestyle shooting, the archer lies on his back. His feet are strapped to the bow and he draws the string with both hands. In other classifications, the archer uses approximately the same stance as in target shooting.

Field Archery. This sport undoubtedly grew out of roving, a popular pastime among bow hunters, in which they rove through woodlands, practicing shots at whatever targets appear—twigs, rocks, bits of paper, and the like. Field archery is a formalized version. A field round consists of 14 targets, ranging in size from 6 to 24 in and in distance from 20 ft to 80 yd. Each target has a white bull's-eye surrounded by a black ring whose width is half the diameter of the bull's-eye. Thus, the 6-in target has a 3-in bull's-eye with a ring 1½ in wide. In the center is a 1½-in black circle, used only for aiming, not for scoring. A bull's-eye scores 5, and a hit on the black ring 3 points.

There is also an animal round, in which targets represent animals of various sizes, and a hunter's round, in which 36 arrows are shot at 6 targets from 6 different distances, with a 45-sec time limit for each end of 6 arrows.

Clout Shooting. At the annual national tournament, the clout is a 48-ft circle drawn on the ground, with a white flag at the center. The clout is divided into 5 concentric circles in the same proportion as that of the usual upright target, and scoring is the same—9 points for a bull's-eye, and so on. A round consists of 36 arrows; men shoot from 180 yd, women from 120.

Wand Shooting. There is a legend that Robin Hood once split a willow wand from 100 paces. It's evidence, at least, that shooting at wands was probably an archer's pastime in the Middle Ages. And it has led to another kind of modern competition. The wand is a white pole, with a 2-in diameter and 6-ft height, that sticks from the ground. Men shoot 36 arrows from 100 yd, women 36 arrows from 60 yd.

Hunting. Many bow hunters feel that theirs is the most ethical of hunting sports because, instead of being able to kill an animal from 300 or 400 yd away with a high-powered weapon, a bow hunter must get to within 80 yd of the prey, and usually closer than that. However, there have been attempts to ban bow hunting in some areas; its critics say that an animal shot with an arrow is likely to suffer a painful but not immediately fatal wound. *See* Hunting.

Archery Golf. Originally played on a real golf course, archery golf pitted archers against golfers. It is now a minor type of archery competition, using targets with 4-in bull's-eyes at distances similar to those confronting a golfer, and the archer is scored on the number of shots he takes to hit a target. As in golf, distance and accuracy are both important, so archery golf, in a sense, is a combination of flight and target archery.

Popinjay Shooting. In parts of Europe, particularly the Low Countries, crossbows are used for an unusual form of target shooting. The targets are small figures of birds, mounted on poles ranging from 80 to 100 ft high, and shots are taken almost vertically. A form of the sport was on the Olympic program early in this century.

Equipment

Bows. The traditional bow of wood—yew, orange, lemon, hickory and other species—has been largely replaced by the modern composite bow, made of laminated wood backed and faced with fiberglass. Steel, aluminum and all-fiberglass bows are also used. Both tips of the bow have grooves or notches to hold the string, which is attached by permanent loops. Strings, formerly made of linen, are now usually of artificial fibers. Slightly below the bow's halfway point is a grip, fitted to the hand, like a pistol grip. At the bottom of the grip is a small shelf, the arrow rest, which holds the arrow in place while it is being drawn back and guides it when the string is released. The "back" of the bow is the side farthest from the archer; the inner side is called the "belly."

Arrows. Pine and cedar woods, birch, aluminum alloys and fiberglass are used for arrows. The pile, a metal cap, protects the point of the arrow and gives it more penetrating power. For hunting, a wide, sharp, steel-bladed broadhead is used. The fletching may be of actual feathers, but plastic vanes shaped approximately like feathers are now more common.

Accessories. Among the archer's accessories are the quiver, for holding the arrows; an arm guard, to protect the arm from the slap of the string after release; and finger tabs and shooting gloves, for the drawing hand.

There are separate competitive categories for bows with

sights (freestyle) and bows without sights (bare bow). The bow sight, attached just above the grip, has a bead or pin that can be moved up or down to adjust elevation and from side to side to make allowances for wind.

Mechanical Releases. Controversy has arisen in recent years over the use of releases in competition. A release is a mechanical device that replaces the fingers in holding the bowstring. There are two basic types. One is a cylinder holding a nylon cord that fits around the bowstring and is held by finger pressure. The other uses a hook, which releases the bowstring when it is gently turned.

The mechanical release allows most archers to improve their scores, because it holds just one small section of string and lets it go all at once, eliminating the slight oscillation that usually arises when the archer uses three fingers to hold and release the string in the conventional way. The oscillation is caused by the fact that three sections of the string are held by the fingers, and there are always tiny variations in the times at which they are actually released.

Results of the U.S. Open Indoor Archery Tournament show what releases can do. There was no perfect 300 round shot in the competition until 1967, and there were only four more shot in the next two years. In 1970, when use of releases became more common, there were 7 perfect rounds, and the number went up to 30 in 1971.

The Professional Archers Association has banned the use of releases in its tournaments, but they are allowed in freestyle amateur competition.

Technique

The right-handed archer faces at right angles to the direction in which he or she is going to shoot, like a golfer or baseball hitter, with the target at the left. The archer holds the grip in the left hand and engages the string with the tips of the first three fingers of the right hand. The nock of the arrow is fitted to the string and, as the bow is raised to a vertical position, the archer draws the string and turns the head toward the target without moving the rest of the body. The right elbow is high, on a line with the arrow, and the string at full draw touches the chin.

If a sight is not used, the archer usually aims at a point on the target somewhere above the bull's-eye. This point of aim is, in effect, the front sight, and the point of the arrow the back sight. The greater the distance, the higher the point of aim will be. The archer adjusts aim by bending the body slightly at the waist, not by moving the bow. When all is in readiness for release, the archer draws the string a fraction of an inch farther and then straightens the three fingers simultaneously, to loose the string smoothly.

The archer's misnamed "follow-through" merely consists of holding his or her position, with the arm up and hand at release point, for a moment after letting go. This follow-through simply ensures that the archer doesn't make any out-of-the-way move before or at release that will send the arrow off course.

With a sight, the archer aims directly at the bull's-eye, adjusting the sight if necessary. If a sight is not being used, the point of aim is adjusted to increase accuracy.

Glossary

anchor—The point on an archer's face where he or she holds the string fingers at full draw.

back—The side of the bow farthest from the archer.

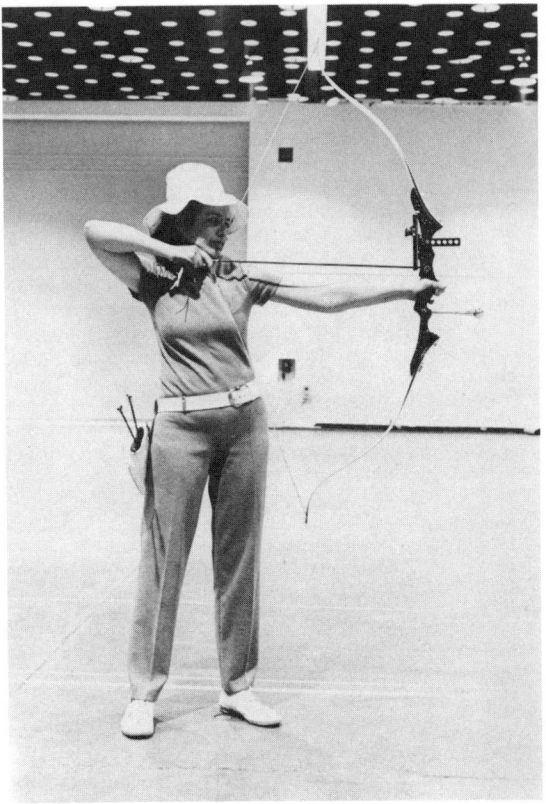

Archery was one of the first sports in which women were fully accepted as competitors. (*Courtesy of Glenn Helgeland,* Archery World.)

backing—Reinforcing on the back of the bow.

belly—The side of the bow nearest the archer.

bracing—Bending the bow to place the string in the notches.

broadhead—Sharpened steel point used in hunting.

center-shot—A cutout section above the grip that permits the arrow to be shot through the center of the bow, rather than from one side.

cock feather—The feather that is placed at right angles to the string when the arrow is nocked.

creeping—Slight forward movement of the arrow point before actual release.

cresting—Distinctive color markings on an arrow to identify the owner in scoring.

eye—End loop of a string.

fletching—Arrow's feathers or similar material.

flu-flu—An arrow with oversized feathers, usually used for bird hunting.

footed shaft—A shaft with a hardwood section on its front end.

hanging arrow—An arrow that hasn't penetrated deeply enough to project from the target at the proper angle.

jar—Failure of the bow to have smooth action after release.

kisser button—A device attached to the bowstring that touches the lips when the string is at full draw.

loose—Release.

matt—Straw disk behind the target face.

overbowed—Said of an archer using too heavy a bow.

perfect end—Six straight bull's-eyes in an end.

quarrel—A crossbow arrow.

quiver—Container for holding and carrying arrows.

recurve—A bow whose tips curve away from the archer.

release—Act of letting go the drawstring to send the arrow on its way.

self bow—Bow made of a single piece of wood.

serving—Wrapping of thread around the bowstring to prevent wear.

skirt—Part of the target outside the scoring area.

spent arrow—An arrow that has traveled too far to be effective.

spine—Stiffness of the bow.

tackle—Archery equipment.

timber—Cry of warning to announce that an arrow has been, or is about to be, released.

U.S. Champions

Men's Target

1879	Will H. Thompson	1921	J. S. Jiles
1880	L. L. Peddinghaus	1922	Robert P. Elmer
1881	F. H. Walworth	1923	W. H. Palmer, Jr.
1882	H. S. Taylor	1924	J. S. Jiles
1883	R. Williams, Jr.	1925	P. W. Crouch
1884	Will H. Thompson	1926	S. F. Spencer
1885	R. Williams, Jr.	1927	P. W. Crouch
1886	W. A. Clark	1928	W. H. Palmer, Jr.
1887	W. A. Clark	1929	E. H. Roberts
1888	Will H. Thompson	1930	Russ Hoogerhyde
1889	L. W. Maxson	1931	Russ Hoogerhyde
1890	L. W. Maxson	1932	Russ Hoogerhyde
1891	L. W. Maxson	1933	R. Miller
1892	L. W. Maxson	1934	Russ Hoogerhyde
1893	L. W. Maxson	1935	Gilman Keasey
1894	L. W. Maxson	1936	Gilman Keasey
1895	No record	1937	Russ Hoogerhyde
1896	D. F. McGowan	1938	Pat Chambers
1897	W. A. Clark	1939	Pat Chambers
1898	L. W. Maxson	1940	Russ Hoogerhyde
1899	M. C. Howell	1941	Larry Hughes
1900	A. R. Clark	1942–1945	No competition
1901	Will H. Thompson	1946	G. Wayne Thompson
1902	R. Williams, Jr.	1947	Jack Wilson
1903	W. Bryant	1948	Larry Hughes
1904	G. Philip Bryant	1949	Russ Reynolds
1905	G. Philip Bryant	1950	Stan Overby
1906	No record	1951	Russ Reynolds
1907	H. B. Richardson	1952	Robert Larsen
1908	Will H. Thompson	1953	Bill Glackin
1909	G. Philip Bryant	1954	Robert J. Rhode
1910	H. B. Richardson	1955	Joe Fries
1911	G. Philip Bryant (York)	1956	Joe Fries
	Robert P. Elmer (American)	1957	Joe Fries
		1958	Robert Bitner
		1959	Bert Vetrovsky
1912	G. Philip Bryant (York, American)	1960	Robert Kadlec
		1961	Clayton Sherman
1913	J. W. Doughty (York)	1962	Charles Sandlin
	Robert P. Elmer (American)	1963	James Yoakum
		1964	David Keaggy Jr.
1914	Robert P. Elmer (York, American)	1965	George Slinzer
		1966	Lester Gervais
1915	Robert P. Elmer	1967	Ray Rogers
1916	Robert P. Elmer	1968	Hardy Ward
1917–1918	No competition	1969	Ray Rogers
1919	Robert P. Elmer	1970	Joe Thornton
1920	Robert P. Elmer	1971	John C. Williams
1972	John C. Williams		
1973	Darrell O. Pace		
1974	Darrell O. Pace		
1975	Darrell O. Pace		
1976	Darrell O. Pace		

Women's Target

1879	Mrs. S. Brown	1920	Cynthia Weston
1880	Mrs. T. Davis	1921	Dorothy Smith
1881	Mrs. A. H. Gibbs	1922	Dorothy Smith
1882	Mrs. A. H. Gibbs	1923	N. Peirce
1883	Mrs. M. C. Howell	1924	Dorothy Smith
1884	Mrs. G. S. Hall	1925	Dorothy Smith
1885	Mrs. M. C. Howell	1926	Dorothy Smith
1886	Mrs. M. C. Howell	1927	Mrs. R. Johnson
1887	Mrs. A. M. Phillips	1928	Mrs. B. Hodgson
1888	Mrs. A. M. Phillips	1929	Mrs. A. Grubbs
1889	Mrs. A. M. Phillips	1930	Mrs. A. Grubbs
1890	Mrs. M. C. Howell	1931	Dorothy Smith Cummings
1891	Mrs. M. C. Howell		
1892	Mrs. M. C. Howell	1932	Ilda Hanchett
1893	Mrs. M. C. Howell	1933	Mildred Taylor
1894	Mrs. A. S. Kern	1934	Mrs. G. D. Mudd
1895	Mrs. M. C. Howell	1935	Ruth Hodgert
1896	Mrs. M. C. Howell	1936	Gladys Hammer
1897	Mrs. J. S. Barker	1937	Jean A. Tenney
1898	Mrs. M. C. Howell	1938	Jean A. Tenney
1899	Mrs. M. C. Howell	1939	Belvia Carter
1900	Mrs. M. C. Howell	1940	Ann Weber
1901	Mrs. C. E. Woodruff	1941	Rea Dillinger Dietrich
1902	Mrs. M. C. Howell	1942–1945	No competition
1903	Mrs. M. C. Howell	1946	Ann Weber
1904	Mrs. M. C. Howell	1947	Ann Weber
1905	Mrs. M. C. Howell	1948	Jean Lee
1906	E. C. Cooke	1949	Jean Lee
1907	Mrs. M. C. Howell	1950	Jean Lee
1908	H. Case	1951	Jean Lee
1909	H. Case	1952	Ann Weber Corby
1910	J. V. Sullivan (National)	1953	Ann Weber Corby
	L. M. Witwer (Columbia)	1954	Laurette Young
		1955	Ann Clark
1911	Mrs. J. H. Taylor (National, Columbia)	1956	Carole Meinhart
		1957	Carole Meinhart
1912	Mrs. W. Taylor (National, Columbia)	1958	Carole Meinhart
		1959	Carole Meinhart
1913	Mrs. P. S. Fletcher (National)	1960	Ann Clark
		1961	Victoria Cook
	Mrs. L. C. Smith (Columbia)	1962	Nancy Vonderheide
		1963	Jewel Hamilton
1914	Mrs. B. P. Gray (National, Columbia)	1964	Victoria Cook
		1965	Nancy Pfeifer
1915	Cynthia Weston	1966	Evelyn Goodrich
1916	Cynthia Weston	1967	Ardelle Mills
1917–1918	No competition	1968	Victoria Cook
1919	Dorothy Smith	1969	Doreen Wilber
		1970	Nancy Myrick
		1971	Doreen Wilber
		1972	Janet Craig
		1973	Doreen Wilber
		1974	Doreen Wilber
		1975	Irene Lorensen
		1976	Luann Ryon

PAA Tournament Champions

Men		Women	
1963	William Bednar	1963	Margaret Tillberry
1964	William Partin	1964	Margaret Tillberry
1965	William Bednar	1965	Margaret Tillberry
1966	William Bednar	1966	Marie Stotts
1967	Victor Berger	1967	Evelyn Goodrich
1968	Steve Robinson	1968	Gwen Learn
1969	Victor Berger	1969	Ann Butz
1970	No competition	1970	No competition
1971	Jim Riley, Jr.	1971	Ann Butz
1972	Victor Berger	1972	Ann Butz
1973	Sherm Winter	1973	Ann Butz
1974	Frank Gandy	1974	Ann Butz
1975	John C. Williams	1975	Ann Butz
1976	John C. Williams	1976	Marion Rhodes

National Archery Association Hall of Fame

(Established in 1972, the Hall of Fame is in temporary quarters at Bear Archery in Grayling, Mich.)

Fred Bear
Dorothy Smith Cummings
Harry Drake
James "Doug" Easton
Dr. Robert P. Elmer
Howard Hill
Russ Hoogerhyde
Ann Weber Hoyt

Karl Palmatier
Ben Pearson
Dr. Saxton Pope
Rube Powell
Clayton B. Shenk
Art Young
John Yount

Bibliography. Elmer, Robert P.: *Target Archery,* Knopf, New York, 1946; Lewis, Jack, ed.: *Archer's Digest,* Digest Books, Northfield, Ill., 1974.

ARTIFICIAL TURF—The "mod sod," as some sportswriters have christened it, first took root in the Houston Astrodome, which opened in 1965. The artificial turf in Houston, AstroTurf, is a product of Monsanto Chemical Company. Two competitors quickly entered the field: Minnesota Mining and Manufacturing, with Tartan Turf, and American Bilt-Rite, with Poly-Turf. By 1972 artificial turf was in use on 11 of the 26 fields used by professional football teams, and on more than 80 college football fields.

There are essentially three layers to an artificial turf installation: a gravel-sand base, a pad, and the surface itself, which is usually bonded to the pad. AstroTurf and Poly-Turf both have "blades" of synthetic grass; Tartan Turf resembles a carpet with a coarse, thick pile. Astro-Turf and Tartan Turf are both made of nylon; Poly-Turf is of polypropylene.

Artificial turf spread so rapidly that it seemed for a while that a whole new era of domed, all-weather, all-sports stadiums was beginning. The advantages of mod sod seemed obvious: less upkeep, better traction, fewer injuries, fewer worries about weather. By 1972, however, the National Football League Players Association was asking for a moratorium on new installations of artificial turf, pending a study of its actual effect on injuries; a number of stadium officials were taking a long, hard second look at the man-made playing surfaces, and there was even a congressional investigation.

There were several complaints. Synthetic turf increases temperatures by as much as 30 degrees; on the Poly-Turf in Miami's Orange Bowl, players suffered in 130-degree heat during some afternoon games. The surfaces are supposed to be safer, because cleats cannot catch in them as they can in real turf, but it appears that artificial turf causes its own kinds of injuries. "It's like putting a throw rug over a driveway," one pro football coach commented after his quarterback banged his head against an artificial surface and left a game with a concussion. Other players suffered severe "rug burns," and it was suggested by some doctors that such abrasions might be easily infected because of unusually high bacteria counts on artificial surfaces.

Artificial turf doesn't need weeding or fertilizer or sprinkling—but cleaning can be difficult; mustard stains from hot-dog wrappers, bubble gum, and cigarette burns have turned out to be problems.

There was even controversy about traction. Some players say artificial turf is too slippery; others that traction is good. But there is no controversy about the Orange Bowl surface; it gets very slippery in the afternoon heat. Poly-Turf, on the other hand, is not slippery when wet, whereas AstroTurf is.

There was less controversy about synthetic surfaces for baseball fields. Primarily because of costs, the trend is toward artificial infields, with natural turf in the outfields. Weather is a bigger factor in baseball than in football, of course, and a heavy pregame rain that might normally force a postponement will not particularly affect play on artificial turf. The livelier surface does change the game. A sharply hit ball gets through the infield faster, but infielders don't have to contend with bad bounces—except when the ball hits a seam between sections of the surface. Many managers feel that synthetic infields will virtually kill the bunt as an offensive weapon, while the hit-and-run play and the stolen base will become more important.

Other sports, notably tennis and track, have adapted to the new artificial surfaces with little difficulty.

A more recent development is the artificial surface for basketball courts. Tartan surfacing material, a relative of 3M's Tartan Turf, is used for basketball as well as for track and tennis. The first basketball installation was made in 1965, and there were about 100 such installations by the mid-1970s. Many coaches feel that the floors are better than the traditional wood because they have no "dead spot" and because falls are less likely to result in serious floor burns.

The Tartan surface can be applied either by wet-pouring or by the installation of prefabricated rolls of material. 3M also manufactures a cheaper Highland surfacing, which comes in tiles made from rubber particles in a resinous binder. Seams are sealed with resin, and the surface is covered with urethane, for sealing and leveling, and an all-weather skid-retarding layer composed of granules of Tartan surfacing material mixed with urethane. A similar urethane surface, developed by Pro-Turf, was installed on the Munich tracks used in the 1972 Olympics.

See also STADIUMS AND ARENAS.

ATHLETIC CLUBS—The oldest athletic clubs in the United States were devoted to rowing. The Detroit Boat Club (1830) is the oldest still in existence. However, those formally called "athletic clubs" or "athletic associations" usually began as organizations devoted to a wider range of sports, especially the track and field events.

The San Francisco Olympic Club, organized in 1860, grew out of a small group of friends who worked out in a backyard gymnasium starting about 1855. From gymnastics, the club branched out into other sports, including track and field and boxing. "Gentleman Jim" Corbett's boxing career began when he joined the Olympic Club and won its championship.

Probably the most important club in American sports history is the New York Athletic Club, founded by William B. Curtis—known for writing the first formal definition of amateurism and for introducing the spiked shoe into track and field—Henry E. Buermeyer, and John C. Babcock, who later invented the sliding seat for rowing shells. These three organized the club in 1866, but its official founding is dated 1868, when officers were first elected. The NYAC staged the country's first indoor track meet in 1868 and in 1876 began holding the national outdoor track and field championships.

The club was the leader in the formation of the National Association of Amateur Athletes of America, which took over the national meet from 1879 through 1888. The NAAAA was not particularly effective; out of it, however, grew the Amateur Athletic Union.

The NYAC also compiled the first amateur rules for wrestling, boxing, and swimming, in 1879, and in 1883 conducted the first national cross-country championships. The NYAC teams have, through the years, won national championships in cross-country, fencing, gymnastics, sculling, squash, swimming, track and field, water polo, and wrestling. The club also established national championship events in amateur boxing, swimming, and wrestling, and has frequently been host to national trapshooting contests and the Eastern clay-court tennis championships.

Two other athletic clubs based in New York had great success in the early national track and field championships. The Manhattan Athletic Club won 11 team titles in the 13 years from 1880 through 1892. The Irish-American Athletic Club won team titles in 1906, 1908–09, 1911, and 1913–15. This club was particularly strong in weight events; its "Irish whales" won many Olympic weight championships for the United States.

As the range of formal competitive sports has grown, and the number of events has expanded, the trend has been back toward the specialized club, though major cities still have athletic clubs devoted to a number of sports. The number of track and field clubs alone has expanded dramatically; many of the newer clubs are informally associated with colleges, and provide a chance for the college's athletes to continue training after the school year has ended or after graduation.

See also AMATEUR ATHLETIC UNION.

AUSTRALIAN FOOTBALL—"Invented" in the 1850s, when a group of Australian gold miners began kicking a rugby ball around in Victoria, Australian football has remained a game that emphasizes kicking. Formal rules were codified in 1874. The game is played on an oval field, 120–170 yd at its greatest width and 150–220 yd at its greatest length. At each end of the field are four posts, 7 yd apart. The ball is shaped roughly like a rugby ball, but is considerably larger, 29½ in at its longest axis and 22½ at its shortest. There are 18 players on each team; 15 of them are assigned to relatively fixed positions, while the other 3 are permitted to roam all over the field. The ball may be punched or kicked, but a player may not run with it unless he bounces it every 10 yd.

If the ball is punched or kicked between the two inner posts without being touched by a defender, it scores 6 points. If it is touched by a defender, or if it passes between an inner post and an outer post, it scores 1 point.

AUTOMOBILE RACING—Whenever a new vehicle appears, human beings seem compelled to use it for racing. From chariots to snowmobiles, the history of racing has been part of the history of transportation, but most types of vehicle racing have died as the vehicles either became obsolete (like chariots) or lost their novelty value (like airplanes).

Auto racing, however, has been with us all along,

despite some bad years, probably because the car has become such an important part of our lives and our civilization. It's easy for someone who does 75 in a 60-mph zone to identify with skilled professional drivers traveling around an oval course at speeds of over 200 mph.

In the beginning, auto racing had two basic purposes: to find ways of improving cars, and to publicize them. Those two purposes are still inherent in the sport, but auto racing has transcended them with a bewildering maze of classifications for exotic, specially built cars that cannot be found in a showroom, and that are often operated on fuel that cannot be bought in a service station.

Early Cars. There is nothing new about the idea of a self-propelled vehicle. A wind-propelled carriage was built in Holland as early as 1420, and Leonardo da Vinci envisioned power-driven vehicles, but there were no sources of power available in his time. Sir Isaac Newton in 1680 suggested that a carriage could be propelled by a jet of steam. The first true automobile, built in 1769 by a French army captain, Nicholas Cugnot, was a steam-powered three-wheeler that could travel about 2 miles an hour. The electric automobile arrived in 1839, the crude invention of Scotsman Robert Anderson, but it was not very successful until the invention of the storage battery, about 1880. The first gasoline-powered auto was built by Etienne Lenoir in France about 1860, but the first really successful cars were built in 1886, independently, by Karl Benz and Gottlieb Daimler, both Germans. Benz built a three-wheeler with a one-cylinder, four-stroke engine; Daimler also had a four-stroke engine, the first high-speed internal-combustion engine, which could develop 1 hp at 900 rpm, as opposed to $^8/_{10}$ hp at 300 rpm for the Benz engine.

In the United States the first steam carriage was built in 1825 by Thomas Blanchard, and Frank and Charles E. Duryea designed and built the first gasoline-powered vehicle in 1892, when they put a small one-cylinder engine into a carriage with large wooden wheels. They called it a "buggyaut." They made 13 automobiles from the same basic design, thus establishing the automobile industry in the United States.

Early Racing. Since the battle of one automobile against the clock is a special form of racing, it might be said that racing began with the earliest cars; almost all of them were timed for various distances even if they were traveling only 2 mph. But the first recorded competitive race was held in 1894, between Paris and Rouen, about 78 mi. More than 100 cars entered, but only about 20 of them actually started, and 15 finished. First prize was split between a Peugeot and a Panhard-Levassor; they averaged about 11 mph for the run.

The first recorded race in America was sponsored by the *Chicago Times Herald* on November 28, 1895. The distance was 54.36 mi, a round trip from the center of Chicago to a suburb and back. Frank Duryea won with an average of 7.5 mph. Only one other car, a Benz, finished.

The first major international series of races was for the James Gordon Bennett Trophy, 1900–05. Each country was allowed to enter a team of three cars. French manufacturers chafed at this restriction and, in 1906, the French Grand Prix was launched, which marked the end of the Bennett series.

In 1904, William K. Vanderbilt established the Vanderbilt Cup Race, 300-mi event run over a road course on Long Island. The first race drew 18 starters and about 30,000 spectators; it was won by A. L. Campbell in a Mercedes. The Vanderbilt race was held annually until halted by World War I, and it was not resumed after the war, partly because speeds had increased so much that there were many dangers involved, and partly because only one American car had ever won.

Also in 1904, the International Association of Recognized Automobile Clubs was organized to supervise international racing. It has since become the Fédération Internationale d'Automobile (FIA). Most countries are represented in the FIA by a national auto club; until 1955, the American Automobile Association was the United States representative. In that year, the United States Auto Club (USAC) was formed to supervise competitive events in place of the AAA.

Because there are a number of sanctioning bodies involved in auto racing in this country, but there can be only one national representative to the FIA, the Automobile Competition Committee for the United States (ACCUS) was formed to serve that purpose, representing several United States racing organizations.

In 1905 Charles Glidden set up a long-distance road tour over public highways, open only to American cars. The main purpose of these races was durability, not speed, and cars had become durable enough by 1914 so that the Glidden tour seemed unnecessary. In addition, a number of states and cities were banning racing on public ways, and for many years afterward racing followed quite different courses in North America and in Europe.

Indianapolis Speedway. American people still wanted to watch cars race, so closed-circuit racing developed in this country, while road racing was continuing to develop in Europe. The famous Indianapolis Motor Speedway was built in 1909. It was a macadam-surfaced, 2½-mi oval track for its first two years; then it was paved with brick, and the first 500-mi race was held on Memorial Day, 1911. Memorial Day weekend has been the standard race date ever since, except during the two World Wars, when the race was not held.

A Marmon, built in Indianapolis and driven by Ray Harroun, won the first Indy 500, but for several years afterward European cars won most of the races. As competition increased, specialization increased; European companies, which had been hoping to capitalize on the American market through Indianapolis publicity, began to drop out and concentrate on road racing, because American companies were building special race cars for Indianapolis.

The early Indy cars were usually two-seaters, and a mechanic accompanied the driver. But during the late thirties and after World War II, a new type of roadster, generally called "the Indy car," was developed: a long, heavy, powerful one-seater with most of the weight of the engine and power train on the left, to help keep it low going through the turns. An Indy car was built with just one purpose—to race in the Indianapolis 500.

But a revolution began at Indianapolis in 1961, when an Australian Grand Prix driver, Jack Brabham, qualified a flimsy-looking, rear-engined car, designed by John Cooper of England and powered by a Coventry Climax engine. The Cooper-Climax drew laughter from many spectators, but it finished a respectable ninth, and it

Barney Oldfield, whose name was once synonymous with speed, always drove with a cigar clenched between his teeth. (*Courtesy of Indianapolis Motor Speedway.*)

started some thinking. Dan Gurney, one of the few American Grand Prix racers, kept the revolution going. He entered a rear-engine car in 1962, but had to quit after 92 laps, placing twentieth. In 1963, Gurney was back, this time in a Lotus-Ford designed by Colin Chapman, designer of the Lotus Grand Prix cars, and powered by a Ford 255-in³ racing engine. Two Lotus-Fords ran. Jimmy Clark, a Grand Prix veteran but a rookie at Indy, finished second in one of them and Gurney placed seventh. Another rear-engine car, one of two Mickey Thompson Specials entered in the race, placed ninth. In 1964, 12 rear-engine cars started in the 33-car field. In 1965, there were 27 rear-engine cars and, since then, virtually every car entered at Indy has been of rear-engine design.

Meanwhile, another potential revolution had been nipped in the bud. In 1967 Andy Granatelli entered a radical design, a car with a turbine engine and four-wheel drive. It was a strange-looking car, with the driver on the right-hand side and the engine next to him, on the left. But the turbine engine had few moving parts, which made it more likely to last through the grueling 500-mi— and it was fast. Parnelli Jones drove it and was winning easily after 490 mi. Then a transmission bearing, worth $6, gave way, and he was out.

The United States Auto Club moved quickly, reducing the allowable air-intake area from 23,999 in² to 15,999. Granatelli entered three turbine cars meeting the requirement in the 1968 Indy. One of them, driven by Joe Leonard, was leading near the end of the race, but a fuel-pump shaft failed with about 22½ miles to go. USAC then reduced the allowable intake area to 11,999 in and Granatelli dropped his idea. The club also limited the width of wheel rims on four-wheel-drive vehicles to 10 in, as opposed to the 14-in rims on conventional cars, and that knocked four-wheel drive out of the Indy picture.

Other major changes were made after the 1973 Indy race, in which two drivers were badly burned—one of them, David "Swede" Savage, died more than a month later—and spectators were sprayed with burning fuel (a dozen of them were injured). Within a week after the

Wilbur Shaw won three Indianapolis 500-mi races, two in a row (1939 and 1940), in this Boyle Special Maserati. *(Courtesy of Indianapolis Motor Speedway.)*

race, fuel capacity of Indy cars was cut from 75 to 40 gal, with fuel to be contained in the left side of the car only. In 1974, the total fuel allotment for the race was cut from 375 to 340 gal. There were predictions that the increased number of pit stops might lead to more accidents, but the 1974 race was run off without a major accident.

The track itself was also changed considerably as a result of the 1973 accidents. The outside barrier was raised from 20 in to 34 in, about 140 boxes of 8 seats each were removed from along the main straightaway, and pit entrances and exits were widened and marked more clearly.

The present-day Indy car must weigh at least 1,350 lb, without fuel or driver; the minimum wheelbase is 8 ft, the maximum length 16 ft, and the maximum width 6 ft, 8 in. Piston displacement is limited, varying with the type of engine. Present maximum displacements are 161.703 in³ for supercharged engines with overhead cams, 256.284 in³ for non-supercharged engines with overhead cams, 203.400 for supercharged stock-block engines, and 320.355 in³ for stock-block engines.

Virtually every modern Indy engine is supercharged, with overhead cams. Supercharged engines have a blower that forces more air—and therefore more fuel—into the engine than it could normally take in, stepping up effective horsepower. The engines are usually either eight-cylinder Fords or four-cylinder Offenhausers, which burn a mixture of methanol and nitromethane.

Championship Circuit. Philip Morris Inc. sponsors a series of 12 races, the Marlboro Championship Trail, for Indy cars. The Indy 500 is easily the most famous and most important of the 12. A point system is used to determine the champion driver of the year.

All championship races are run counterclockwise ("keep turning left") on paved oval courses, at distances ranging from 150 to 500 mi.

Besides the Indianapolis Motor Speedway, major championship tracks are Ontario, in southern California, and the Pocono Inernational Raceway in Pennsylvania, both of which have 500-mi races; and tracks at Bryan, Texas; Cambridge Junction, Michigan; Milwaukee; Phoenix; and Trenton, New Jersey.

Purses and Prizes. The total amount of award money given out at Indy alone is now over $1 million a year, about one-fifth of it put up by manufacturers of automotive and non-automotive products. Total prizes at other championship races range from $25,000 to about $100,000. They go higher when television money is involved. A promoter usually guarantees a certain amount to the drivers, paying 40 percent of the gate if that's higher than the guarantee.

Qualifying. Indy and other championship races may draw as many as 70 entries, of which only 33 (fewer in some races) will start. The 33 are chosen through qualifying runs. At Indianapolis the first day of qualifying is the important one. Cars qualify by running 3 laps, and are then lined up in the famous "grid"—11 rows of 3 cars each—according to their average speed. The fastest wins the honored pole position, as the inside car in the front row; the two next fastest are on its right; the fourth fastest is on the pole in the second row, and so on.

The 33 fastest cars on that first day qualify, and the grid is set. But qualifying continues. The thirty-third car is said to be "on the bubble"; if someone turns in a faster qualifying time, the bubble bursts, the car is "bumped" from the grid and replaced by the new qualifier. By the end of qualifying, as many as five or six cars might have been bumped from their starting positions, but the front rows remain intact. Even if a later qualifier sets a record, the first day's fastest qualifier remains in the pole position and the new qualifier will be well back in the grid.

Dirt Tracks. USAC set up a separate dirt-track division in 1971 and is trying to revive this form of the sport, on 1-mi tracks. On a 1-mi track, dirt cars are similar to the old Indy roadsters, with front-mounted engines and heavier chassis. Sprint cars and midget cars also sometimes run on dirt, the midgets being especially popular on ¼-mi dirt tracks.

Many fairgrounds throughout the United States still have dirt tracks. A good deal of dirt-track racing, along with some sprint, midget, and stock-car racing, is sanctioned by the International Motor Contest Association (IMCA), a nonprofit organization that was formed in 1915 to serve state fairs throughout the Midwest.

Sprint Cars. Once known as the "big car," to distinguish it from midget racers, the sprint car is what most people probably have in mind when they think of a racing car. It, too, is similar to the old Indy roadster, but is somewhat smaller. The minimum wheelbase is 7 ft, the minimum tread 3 ft, 11 in.

USAC has a separate sprint-car division, but much of the racing is conducted at state fairs or small local tracks under sanction of the IMCA, United Racing Club, Big Car Racing Association, or California Racing Association.

Sprints may be run on dirt or paved tracks, usually ½ mi or more in length. Because of the size of the cars on such small tracks, it's perhaps the most dangerous version of auto racing. There are many different varieties, because rules and specifications vary somewhat from one sanctioning organization to another.

Midget Cars. USAC midget cars are cut-down versions of the dirt car. Wheelbases range from 5 ft, 6 in to 6 ft, 4 in, and engines are either 155 in³, stock-blocks, or 114 in³ with overhead cams. Again, there are a number of sanctioning bodies and therefore a number of different kinds of midget racing.

Stock-Car Racing

Al Smith, running for President in 1928, said that "Bootlegging begat the racketeer." It also begat stock-car racing. Moonshiners and bootleggers, in order to avoid federal agents, tinkered with their engines to get the most speed possible out of them. In the Southeast, because of the many winding back roads and hills, suspensions also had to be adjusted to take the rigors of power skids, treacherous high-speed turns in hilly country, and sudden U-turns at police roadblocks. Even after prohibition ended, making and transporting moonshine remained a way of life for many people in the Southeast, and some very sophisticated "stock" cars were produced. Naturally, some of the drivers with souped-up cars began to get into match races for money.

The sport became formal—and legal—in 1947, with the formation of the National Association for Stock Car Auto Racing (NASCAR) in a hotel in Daytona Beach, Florida. NASCAR was the idea of a former service-station attendant who made some extra money in racing, William H. G. "Bill" France, long-time president of the organization.

Stock cars are steel-bodied cars manufactured in the United States. "Stock" is something of a misleading term; you cannot buy one of these cars from your friendly neighborhood auto dealer. The first step in preparing a car for racing is to get rid of every ounce of unnecessary weight. The second step is to strengthen everything, for safety, endurance, and performance. And then there is the special racing engine, which usually costs more than $6,000, for a Grand National or Grand American car.

The prestigious stock-car events are run on "super speedways," tracks of 1 mi or more in length. Daytona Beach, Florida, at one time used for runs at the land speed record, was used for stock-car racing as early as 1936, on a 3.2-mi course. Daytona International Speedway, built in 1959, is now a 2.5-mi course, the same as Indy.

Other major "super speedways" are at Darlington, South Carolina, a 1⅜-mi track opened in 1950, and the Alabama International Motor Speedway at Talladega, a 2⅗-mi track opened in 1969.

NASCAR conducts races in several different divisions. They are listed in order of importance below.

Grand National. This is the stock-car equivalent of the USAC's championship races. The cars are no more than three years old, and they are powered by engines with up to 430 in³ of displacement, using 4-barrel carburetors and two pushrod-operated valves per cylinder. Minimum wheelbase is 115 in; minimum weight is 3,900 lb.

The Grand National cars can now do about 200 mph on a straightaway. In the late 1960s, car speeds began to increase tremendously, largely because of more efficient engines that could produce more horsepower without more size. It seemed to NASCAR—particularly to Bill France—that the whole thing was getting out of hand. In 1970, NASCAR adopted a rule requiring carburetor restrictor plates on certain types of engines. The plates restrict air intake and therefore cut speeds. In addition, cars with certain types of aerodynamic bodies are restricted to engines of 305 in³ or less.

Grand American. Originally called Grand Touring, the Grand American division was established in 1968. It is for smaller, sportier sedans, such as the Barracuda, Camaro, Challenger, Firebird, and Javelin. Minimum wheelbase is 100 in, minimum weight 3,200 lb. Fenders can be reshaped to take racing tires. Stock-block engines are restricted to 305 in³ or less.

Late-Model Sportsman. Cars in this division range from 4 to 13 years old. Minimum wheelbase is 115 in, maximum engine displacement 430 in³; minimum weight is 9 lb for each cubic inch of displacement.

Modified. These cars range from four years old, all the way back to 1935 models. There are virtually no restrictions on what can be done to the engine.

Hobby. This division is for amateur drivers and novices. Cars are 10 years old or older; multiple carburetors and fuel injection are prohibited.

Other Sanctioning Bodies. The Stock Car Division of USAC uses just about the same specifications as NASCAR's Grand National Division, and USAC's Sports Sedan class is similar to the Grand American. The Sports Car Club of America has a Trans-American class, also similar to the Grand American.

The Automobile Racing Club of America (ARCA), originally the Midwest Association for Race Cars, was formed in 1952 to sanction stock-car races in Ohio, Michigan, Indiana, Kentucky, and Tennessee. The change in name reflects a broader scope. ARCA races in four divisions: National Championship, similar to NASCAR's Grand National; Late-Model Sportsman, similar to the same NASCAR division; Hobby Stock, similar to NASCAR's Hobby division; and Figure Eight, in which the cars run on a Figure 8-shaped course that intersects itself.

The International Motor Contest Association sanctions about 30 stock-car events annually at Midwestern fairground tracks. Cars are generally Late-Model Sportsman types.

Road Racing

While American auto racing, before World War II, was almost entirely confined to closed-circuit tracks, Europe was developing its Grand Prix racing circuit, the pinnacle of road racing. Most of the original Grand Prix races were

Richard Petty, who has won more major races than any other stock-car driver in history, rounds a curve at the Daytona International Speedway. *(NASCAR Photo.)*

run on public streets, closed to other traffic for the occasion. However, racing on public roads was banned in England, and that country developed the closed-circuit road course, irregularly shaped tracks meant to simulate the kind of race run on roads on the Continent. Most Grand Prix races are now run on closed courses.

But Grand Prix racing—to which we shall return—is only a small part of road racing. Road racing cuts across many divisions. The USAC, for example, sponsors a series of road races for cars of the Indy type. The road cars, however, burn gasoline or methanol or a combination, but cannot use nitromethane. Minimum wheelbase is 92 in, maximum tread 80 in, and maximum body height 32 in. Even stock cars occasionally run on road tracks.

In the United States, road racing is primarily the business of the Sports Car Club of America (SCCA), which conducts a bewildering number of races in a baffling complex of divisions and classes. The SCCA, which has more than 18,000 members, takes credit for more than 300 weekends of racing every year, with each weekend including anywhere from 6 to 20 races. Many of these are amateur events. The SCCA does sanction 3 series of professional competition, totaling about 35 races a year, that pay about $2 million in purses and prizes.

Canadian-American Challenge Cup. The Can-Am series, which began in 1966, is for sports-racing cars that belong to a classification called Group 7. These are two-seaters with practically no restrictions on engine size or anything else.

Some remarkable cars have run in the Can-Am. You can climb into one of them, get up to 100 mph, and bring it to a complete stop in the grand total of 10 sec. Most of them have lightweight chassis, of aluminum-magnesium alloy, and fiberglass bodies. Almost all of them use Chevrolet V-8 engines that produce up to 700 hp—for cars that weigh only about 1,500 lb!

A team headed by designer-driver Bruce McLaren dominated the Can-Am series for four years, 1967–1971, threatening its future. McLaren was killed in 1970, testing a Can-Am car, just before the series began, but Denis Hulme and Dan Gurney drove his cars to the championship. Hulme and Peter Revson won another title for Team McLaren in 1971. In 1972–1973, the Porsche took over, first in a 917/10 model, then in a 917/30 model, winning most of the races easily so that the series again seemed endangered. After the 1974 season, the Can-Am races were discontinued because the high cost of building the cars had discouraged most manufacturers.

Trans-American Championship. The Trans-Am is for small, sporty sedans. Maximum wheelbase is 116 in and maximum displacement is 305 in³. There are two classes, over 2.5 liters (152.5 in³) and under 2.5 liters. The larger cars are primarily American-made, the smaller ones are usually imports.

This is similar to a stock-car category; indeed, the SCCA also uses the NASCAR rule for Grand American cars, that the manufacturer must produce 2,500 of the cars, or a quantity equivalent to 1/250th of his total production in the preceding year, whichever is greater. Preparation of the Trans-Am car is quite similar to the preparation that goes into a car for a major NASCAR race.

L & M Championship. Known as the Continental Championship until 1971, when L&M cigarettes took over sponsorship, this is a three-formula series of races. The

Formula A cars are limited to 305 in³ of displacement, in a stock-block engine. No supercharging is allowed, and there are very specific limitations on what can be done to the engine. Minimum weight is 1,350 lb, and fuel capacity is limited to 30 gal of everyday gasoline.

Two other types of engines are permitted—both commonly used in Grand Prix racing: an overhead-cam engine with a 3,000-cm³ (183-in³) displacement, and a supercharged engine with a displacement of 1,500 cm³ (91.5 in³). If either of these engines is used, minimum car weight is 1,105 lb and fuel capacity is only 26 gal.

The Formula B car has a minimum weight of 750 lb and a maximum displacement of 1,100 cm³.

Club Racing. The SCCA has a remarkably sensible approach to the question of amateurism. It ignores it. Or, rather, it doesn't call anyone an amateur driver. It recognizes professional events, those which carry purses, and nonprofessional events, those which don't carry purses. The nonpurse races are called club races; they culminate each November in the American Road Race of Champions.

There are two classes of club races, regionals and nationals. Regional races are for drivers with limited racing experience; nationals, for advanced drivers. About 400 point leaders from the 60 national races qualify for the American Road Race of Champions. They compete in 22 different classes of cars, spread across 7 divisions.

Production Cars. These are ordinary, commonly seen sports cars, for the most part, with very few adaptations for racing purposes. (Most of the adaptations allowed are meant to increase safety.) The cars are graded, from A to H, on the basis of lap-speed potential, thus emphasizing driver skill rather than the car's performance.

Sports Racing. Like the cars that race in the Can-Am series, these are so-called Group 7 cars—racing machines, pure and simple. The SCCA recognizes four classes, based on displacement: Class A is unlimited; Class B, 1,301–2,000 cm³; Class C, 851–1,300 cm³; Class D, 850 cm³ or less.

Sedan. Cars in this category are much the same as those that run in the Trans-Am, but the division is also subdivided into four classes: Class A, 2,501–5,000 cm³; Class B, 1,301–2,500 cm³; Class C, 1,001–1,300 cm³; Class D, 1,000 cm³ or less.

Formula SCCA. The formulas in this division are the same as the formulas for the L&M Championship, with one difference: Formula A also includes cars with a 5,000-cm³ stock-block engine.

Formula Vee. "Vee" is for Volkswagen; take a pre-1968 VW, turn it into a single-seat, open-wheel racing car, and you're all set for a Formula Vee race. Minimum weight is 825 lb, wheelbase is 81.5-83.5 in, and the engine is the standard (pre-1969) 1,192-cm³ VW engine.

Formula Super Vee. In 1969, Volkswagen increased engine capacity of cars sold in the United States to 1,600 cm³, and the SCCA quickly established the Super Vee class for those engines.

Formula F. As in the two previous classes, the idea here is to make everyone use the same engine. In this case, it is a 1,600-cm³ engine from the English Ford Cortina. Again the car is a single-seat, open-wheel racing machine. Engine preparation rules are strict.

Grand Prix Racing. Now we return to what may well be auto racing at its most glamorous, on the road courses of

Europe. Actually, there are only about a dozen real Grand Prix races during a year, and several of them are now held outside Europe, but the term is often used to describe road racing in general.

The Grand Prix races are all for Formula One cars, which are similar to the cars that run in the L&M Championship series. The exact formula changes frequently. Currently, engine size is limited to 183 in³, and only half of that if supercharged. Minimum weight is 1,166 lb. Almost all of the fastest Formula One cars now use a Ford-Cosworth engine, a V-8 which turns out 425-450 hp. The engine was developed for Ford of Britain by Cosworth Engineering. The bodies are all rather similar, too, looking somewhat like cigars flattened into wedge shapes at the front. The engines are rear-mounted, and most of the cars carry a small airfoil mounted securely to the chassis, just behind the driver's head. Formula Ones run on ordinary automotive gasoline, and they develop top speeds of about 190.

The basic point of Grand Prix races is to determine the winner of the prestigious World Drivers' Championship. Drivers get 9 points for each victory, 6 for each second place, 4 for each third place, down to 1 for a sixth-place finish. The circuit ranges over three or four continents and perhaps a dozen countries: Austria, Britain, Canada, France, Italy, the Netherlands, South Africa, Spain, West Germany, the United States, and sometimes others.

The winner of the championship is really *crème de la crème*; in any given season, only about 30 drivers are "classified" by the FIA, which gives them the unrestricted right to compete in FIA-sanctioned races in any country in the world, and only a classified driver can win the championship.

The Manufacturers' Championship. Closely allied with Grand Prix racing are a number of other races, involving sports cars, prototypes, and grand touring cars, for the World Championship of Manufacturers. The most famous of these races is the 24-hr endurance trial at Le Mans.

All the races are long ones, emphasizing endurance as well as speed. Minimum distance is 1,000 km, or 620 mi, and there are at least two drivers per car. A number of different types of cars run, as in many SCCA races, with Prototypes (Group 6), limited to 183 in³ displacement; Sports Cars (Group 5), limited to 305 in³; and Special Grand Touring Cars (Group 4), of unlimited displacement.

In many races, special classifications are set up. For example, Group 2 Special Touring Cars, not eligible for championship points, might be admitted. These are basically similar to the cars that run in the SCAA Trans-American Championship. Sometimes special prizes are awarded for cars of under 2 liters (122 in³) in the Prototype and Sports Car categories.

Other Formulas. Grand Prix drivers serve their apprenticeships by driving cars similar to, but smaller than, the Formula Ones. Under current regulations, a Formula Two car is limited to 97.6 in³ displacement, and minimum weight is 924 lb. The Formula Three displacement limit is 61 in³, and the engine block must be from a line produced at the rate of 1,000 or more during the 12 preceding months.

European-Style Rallies. The American sports-car rally is a rather leisurely event. The European-style rally is not. Drivers are judged on how close they stick to a schedule,

Richard Petty, winner of six NASCAR Winston Cup Grand National Championships, displays just one of his many trophies. *(NASCAR Photo.)*

not on all-out speed, but the schedule calls for high speeds, usually over rugged territory. The East Africa Safari, the most grueling of these rallies, covers 3,000 mi; among the hazards are virtually nonexistent roads, wild animals, dry river beds, and enormous potholes.

Other Grand Prix. In the strictest sense the only real Grand Prix races are those that count toward the World Drivers' Championship, but there are other races given the name, some of them rather interesting. There is, for example, the Tasman Series, of seven races in New Zealand and Australia, for Formula 5,000 cars—similar to the SCCA Formula A cars. Other countries with a "Grand Prix" or two are Japan, Macao, and Yugoslavia.

The Fastest Cars

The world's fastest cars don't race against one another, except in a very abstract way. They race against the clock, in search of new land speed records. It began in 1898, when a young French count, Chasseloup-Laubat, made the first recorded "flying mile" run—traveling a measured mile from a flying start. His electric car averaged 39.24 mph.

Most of the early records were set on straight stretches of ordinary pavement. But in 1904 William K. Vanderbilt set the world record at 92.307 mph on the sands of Daytona Beach, Florida, and that was where many attempts at

Stock-car racing features machines that look like standard production models, traveling at high speed and in tight quarters. (NASCAR Photo.)

the land speed record were made through the first half of 1935.

The mile record is actually set in 2 mi of travel. In 1910 the FIA, realizing that wind might assist a car, ruled that a record would be recognized only if it was an average speed for two runs, in opposite directions, within a one-hour period.

The record was pushed over 100 mph in 1904 and over 200 in 1927, by British Maj. H. O. D. Seagrave, during a long period of British supremacy in the field. Seagrave, Sir Malcolm Campbell, John Cobb, and Capt. George E. T. Eyston were among the Englishmen who ruled this branch of the sport for more than 20 years.

On September 3, 1935, Campbell became the first man ever to travel more than 300 mph on land. His record was set at the Bonneville, Utah, Salt Flats, where most such record attempts have been made ever since. The record has been pushed rapidly higher during the last 10 years—Craig Breedlove cracked the 400-mph barrier in 1963, and pushed beyond the 600-mph mark just two years later. The present record is 622.407 mph, set by Gary Gabelich in 1970.

The cars used are the most extreme example of specialization—they can be used for absolutely nothing but attempting to break the land speed record. You could drive to the supermarket in an Indy car, if you had to, but not in one of these jet-propelled monsters. They look somewhat like airplanes with stubby wings. The drivers virtually lie down in them, and have to wear oxygen masks. The engines are loaded with just enough fuel to carry them through the run, to minimize the risk of fire in the event of a crash.

The Bonneville course is 80 ft wide, and the drivers guide themselves by following a 6-in strip of tar down the center of it. The course is 13 mi long, and they use 3 or 4 mi to pick up speed, 5 mi or so to stop. The speed is measured, by electric eye, between mileposts 6 and 7. After passing milepost 7, the driver pushes a button that pops parachutes which act as brakes.

Because of the great speeds achieved by the jet-propelled cars, a separate set of records is now kept for nonjet cars, but sheer speed is the point of the whole thing, and

the jet-propelled record is unquestionably the glamorous one.

Other Forms of the Sport

Sports Car Rallies. It's hard to say whether or not a rally should be called a race. Speed is unimportant; indeed, traveling too fast is just as bad as traveling too slow. The winner of a rally is, basically, the driver who follows instructions best.

Each car has a driver and a navigator. A few minutes before the start of the event, the team is given a set of instructions, using standard abbreviations, to conduct them along a course. Each leg is to be traveled at a certain average speed. At unannounced places along the way there are checkpoints where volunteer workers log in the cars. Each checkpoint is to be reached at a certain specific time; a team is penalized a point for each hundredth of a minute it is early or late. A 5-min error (500 penalty points) can knock a team out of contention.

The driver's job is to stay on course and maintain a certain exact speed for each leg; the navigator, often working with sophisticated calculators, odometers, and stopwatches, keeps the driver informed of what his average speed is, advising him to speed up or slow down a bit to get closer to the average.

Some rallies are just for fun; others are championship events, counting for points toward the national rallying championship of the SCCA.

There is one SCCA-sanctioned rally that is more like the rugged, European variety, a real test of car and driver: the Press on Regardless, in which cars travel for four nights along 1,200 mi of logging trails in Michigan.

Gymkhana. Sometimes called an autocross or slalom, a gymkhana is also an event that emphasizes precision rather than speed. A course, usually about 3,000 ft long, is marked out with traffic-control pylons. It always includes a circle, a figure-8, and a slalom run. Runs are timed to the thousandth of a second. There is a penalty of from 3 to 5 sec for knocking over a pylon.

Ice Racing. When clouds form in the winter sky and travelers' warnings are issued and most people wonder how they're going to get to wherever they want to go, a small number of amateur drivers in the northern United States rub their hands and smile with glee at the prospect of their favorite sport: ice racing.

It's not quite as bad as it sounds. Ice racing is usually conducted on frozen lakes or fields with no obstructions, or on road courses protectively fenced in by bulldozed snowbanks. And, if cars do collide, the very fact that they are on ice makes the impact less damaging and less dangerous, because the cars simply tend to slide away from one another.

Ice races are usually organized by local auto clubs and are similar to the SCCA club racing events. Cars fall into two major classes, those with studded tires and those without. There are also ice races for motorcycles, often on frozen-over oval tracks that are used for ordinary motorcycle racing during warmer months.

Hill Climbs. Hill climbing was very popular in the days when no one knew whether or not a given car could make it to the top. The sport has declined in popularity since those early days, but it still has its enthusiasts. There is one professional hill climb, held at Pikes Peak under USAC auspices about the Fourth of July. The other climbs are amateur events, usually sanctioned by the SCCA.

One of the biggest of them is held at Mt. Equinox, near Manchester, Vermont. The mountain itself is 3,835 ft high; the course is 5.2 mi long, and it features 41 turns, including 9 hairpins. John V. N. Meyer, who is called "Mr. Equinox," has won the race nine times, and holds the record for the average speed, at 75.241 mph.

See also DRAG RACING; MOTORCYCLE RACING; OFF-ROAD RACING.

Glossary

autocross—Gymkhana; sometimes used to mean a gymkhana that allows greater speed than usual.

back off—To slow down.

banked turn—A turn that is inclined so that the outside portion is higher than the inside portion.

big banger—An engine with a large volume of displacement; usually used to mean more than 305 in³.

black flag—The signal for a driver to come into the pits, usually so race officials can inspect damage to determine if his car can run safely. It may also mean that officials have already decided his car is too slow or too dangerous to continue running.

blend—A racing fuel mixture of methanol and nitromethane.

block—The cylinder block of an engine.

blower—Supercharger.

blown engine—1. A supercharged engine. 2. A major engine failure.

bore—The diameter of a cylinder bore.

box—Transmission.

brake fade—Loss of effectiveness in braking, caused by overheating.

Brickyard—Indianapolis Motor Speedway.

bubble—The last position on the starting grid while qualifying is still going on.

cc—Cubic centimeter(s), abbreviated cm³; the standard measure of displacement in Europe. A liter, 1,000 cm³, equals 61 in³.

checkered flag—A flag of black and white squares used to signal the end of a race.

chicane—A man-made corner deliberately set up to reduce speed at a certain point on a track.

chute—A straightaway.

cm³—cubic centimeter(s).

cubes—Cubic inches (in³) of displacement; as in, "My engine has 305 cubes."

dicing—The British term for close, exciting driving.

displacement—Piston, or engine, displacement is a measure of an engine's size. It is the difference between the volume contained in the cylinders when the pistons are at the bottom of the stroke and the volume contained when the pistons are at the top of the stroke—i.e., the amount of gas displaced by the pistons. It can be calculated by multiplying the bore times the stroke times 0.785 times the number of cylinders.

draft—To follow another car very closely, taking advantage of decreased air resistance. Sometimes called "slipstreaming."

drift—A four-wheel controlled slide through a turn, used to get a car lined up to start down a straightaway without much use of the steering wheel.

fishtail—An unhappy situation in which the rear end of the car moves from side to side.

flat out—At top speed; with the accelerator to the floor.

fuel—In racing, usually a fuel other than commercial gasoline; most often some blend of methanol and nitromethane.

fueler—A car that uses special racing fuels.

full bore—At full speed; flat out.

GT—Grand Touring (Italian, *gran turismo*; French, *grand tourisme*), meaning a sedan, built in limited quantities, and meant to provide quick, comfortable travel over fairly long distances.

grid—The arrangement of cars in the starting lineup; at Indianapolis, the grid is 11 rows with 3 cars per row.

groove—The quickest route through a turn or around the entire course.

gymkhana—A type of competition in which drivers take their cars around a twisting course, executing certain prescribed maneuvers, against the clock.

hairpin—A turn that carries a car through 180 degrees.

hairy—Hair-raising; frightening.

hauler—A very fast car.

heel and toe—A technique by which a driver operates the accelerator with his right heel and the brake pedal with his right toes.

IMSA—International Motor Sports Association.

in³—cubic inch(es).

juice—A racing fuel blend.

jump—To start before given the signal; usually in drag racing.

lap—One trip around a racing circuit. As a verb, one driver laps another when he gets so far ahead of him that he passes him, thus going more than a lap ahead of him.

leadfoot—An aggressive driver who always goes for the lead.

Le Mans start—A type of start in which the drivers, at the starting signal, run to their cars, start their engines, and begin racing.

liter—Used to measure displacement in Europe, the liter is 1,000 cm³, about 61 in³, a little more than a quart.

loud pedal—Accelerator.

nerf—To bump lightly against another car, usually from behind and usually on purpose, as a warning or a bit of psychology. Very common in stock-car racing.

nitro—Nitromethane, used in exotic racing-fuel blends.

normally aspirated—An engine that "breathes" without the help of a supercharger.

Offy—The Offenhauser racing engine.

pace car—A non-racing car that leads the competitors around the course before the race begins.

paced start—A flying start led by a pace car.

pace lap—The lap just before the official start; the cars travel in formation, building up speed, so that they will be near top speed when they reach the starting line.

pacer—A driver who travels at a predetermined speed throughout a race, conserving his car in the hope that those traveling faster will drop out with irreparable problems.

PDA—Professional Drivers Association, an organization of NASCAR drivers.

pit—An area beside the track where a race car stops for servicing and fuel. Each car has its own pit.

pit stop—The act of leaving the course for a stop for repairs, refueling, tire changes, or the like.

pole—The best position in the starting grid, usually given to the driver with the fastest qualifying time. In oval-track racing, it is the first spot on the left. In a road race in which the first turn is to the right, it is the first spot on the right.

pop—Exotic fuel blend.

production—A production car or engine is one that is made in quantity, presumably on an assembly line.

prototype—A sports car that is not production; either a car especially built for racing, in limited numbers, or an experimental model.

qualifying—Preliminary sessions in which cars race against time to win places in the starting field.

rev—To gun an engine; increase the revs (revolutions per minute).

riding the rails—To take the outside line around a turn.

roll bar—A frame of tubular steel that protects the driver if the car rolls.

roll cage—A structure of tubular steel, padded with foam rubber, that surrounds the driver. Used primarily in stock cars.

rpm—Revolutions per minute.

sandbag—To hold back on a car's performance, usually during qualifying, in order to keep other drivers from realizing its potential.

shoes—Tires.

shut the gate—To block a competitor who is trying to pass on the inside of a turn.

shut-off—A point before a turn where a driver has to slow down in order to negotiate the turn.

slicks—Wide, flat tires used on the rear wheels of dragsters.

slingshot—A drag racer in which the driver sits behind the rear wheels.

slingshotting—Passing a car by first drafting in order to conserve power and then suddenly moving out of the slipstream and using the reserve power.

spin—Also "spin out"; to lose control so that the car revolves around its own vertical axis.

spoiler—An air deflector, usually mounted on the front end, to keep a car from lifting off the ground at high speeds.

sports car—A not quite definable vehicle; generally, one that handles better, brakes better, and is more maneuverable than the ordinary passenger car.

sportsman—A stock car with a light body and an engine modified in certain limited ways.

stock—An unmodified car, almost exactly as the manufacturer produced it. In this sense, however, many stock cars are not stock at all.

stock block—A mass-produced engine block.

stroke it—To drive slower than maximum speed, usually to conserve the car when it holds a safe lead near the end of a race.

switchback—See *hairpin*.

tachometer—An instrument that measures revolutions per minute.

T-bone—To hit another car broadside.

ten-tenths—Going all out; commonly used, among Grand Prix racers, to describe the impossible feat of going through a turn at exactly maximum speed.

tread—In race specifications, the tread is a car's width, measured between the center lines of its tires.

turbocharger—A supercharger driven by a turbine that is, in turn, driven by the engine's exhaust gases.

wheelbase—The distance between the front and rear axles of a car.

windmill—A supercharger.

wires—Wire wheels.

X-car—Experimental car.

yellowtail—A rookie NASCAR driver, so called because rookies are identified by yellow bumpers.

yellow flag—The flag that signals caution because of dangerous track conditions; under the yellow flag, a driver is not allowed to improve his position. In some races, this means that a driver is not supposed to gain any ground; in others, it means that he can't pass anyone, but he can otherwise gain ground on the cars in front of him.

Halls of Fame

(Halls of fame for Indy-type auto racing are maintained by Citizens Savings Hall and by the United States Auto Club. In the following biographies, C indicates Citizens Savings, A indicates USAC.)

J. C. Agajanian—Owner and sponsor of racing cars for more than 25 yr; his cars won Indianapolis 500 races in 1952 and 1963. C

James A. Allison—An Indianapolis businessman who helped finance the building of the Indy Motor Speedway. A

Melvin E. "Tony" Bettenhausen—USAC national driving champion in 1951 and 1958; killed in a 1961 crash. His son Gary is currently a top USAC driver. A, C

Jimmy Bryan—USAC national champion in 1954, 1956, and 1957, and winner of the 1958 Indy 500; killed in a 1960 crash. A, C

Bob Burman—Winner of the first featured race at the Indianapolis Speedway in 1909, Burman set a land speed record of 141.732 mph at Daytona Beach in 1911; killed in a 1916 crash. A, C

Gaston and Louis Chevrolet—Both natives of France, the Chevrolet brothers came to the United States when they were very young and both became race drivers. Gaston won the Indy 500 in 1920, in a Frontenac car built by Louis, who also designed the first Chevrolet passenger car in 1911. Louis was an outstanding road racer in 1909 before getting into design and building. One of his Frontenacs, driven by Tommy Milton, also won the 1921 Indy 500. A

Floyd Clymer—The author of many historical books about automobiles, including racing cars, Clymer founded the Clymer Publishing Company, a Los Angeles firm which is the world's largest publisher of books on automobiles and motorcycles.

Earl Cooper—As a member of the Stutz racing team, Cooper won the national championship in 1913 and 1915 and won it again, in his own Stutz, in 1917. He also designed and built some successful race cars. A, C

"Wild Bill" Cummings—Winner of the Indy 500 in 1934, Cummings also finished third, fifth, and sixth in nine starts. He was killed in a 1939 highway crash. A, C

Ralph DePalma—A native of Italy, DePalma entered 10 Indy races and six times finished in the top seven; he won in 1915. He was national champion in 1912 and 1914. A, C

Peter DePaolo—DePalma's nephew began as a riding mechanic for his uncle, then became a driver. He won the national championship in 1925 and 1927, the Indy 500 in 1925; he was the first driver to average more than 100 mph at Indianapolis. A, C

Bert Dingley—One of the early greats; cowinner of the national championship in 1909. A

Augie and Fred Duesenberg—These brothers developed

one of the first famous American racing cars, the only one ever to win the French Grand Prix (1920). A Duesenberg won the Indy in 1922, and Duesenbergs took seven of the next nine places. They also won in 1924, 1925, and 1927. The luxury passenger cars, manufactured until 1937, gave rise to the expression, "That's a Doozy!" A

Harvey Firestone—Founder and president of the Firestone Tire & Rubber Company, 1900–1932, Firestone developed the nonskid tread and other safety features for tires. He sponsored campaigns for good roads and driving safety, and also supported auto racing, vocally and financially, as a means of helping develop safe cars and tires. A, C

Carl G. Fisher—A prominent Indianapolis businessman, Fisher was one of the founders and the first president of the Indianapolis Motor Speedway, and was active in the promotion of auto racing in this country. A

Henry Ford—A firm believer in publicizing his cars by racing, Ford was his own race driver early in the century. He won his only competitive race, in 1901, and set a world land speed record of 91.37 mph in 1904 over a frozen lake in Michigan. Ford's interest in racing lapsed somewhat during the 1920s, but the company's flathead V-8, introduced in 1932, was a successful road-racing engine in other chassis.

Dan Gurney—The most versatile of American race drivers, Gurney finished second in the 1961 World Drivers' Championship, won the French Grand Prix in 1962, and entered his first Indy 500 the same year. He won the Riverside 500-mi stock-car race in 1963–1966 and 1968, and he was instrumental in introducing the rear-engined car to Indy. In 1964 he and Carroll Shelby founded All-American Racers; Gurney became sole owner in 1967. His Eagle in 1967 was the first American car with an American driver to win a Grand Prix race since 1921 and, in the same year, he became the first driver to win major races in all four major automobile categories: Formula One, Sports, Stock, and Indy. He retired from driving in 1970 but continued to build cars. C

Samuel Hanks, Jr.—National midget champion in 1941 and 1949, Hanks was national big-car champ in 1953; he won at Indy in 1957 and retired immediately afterward. C

Ray Harroun—National driving champion in 1910, Harroun came out of retirement to win the first Indy 500, in 1911; he is often credited with inventing the first rearview mirror for use in that race, since he was the only driver without a riding mechanic. He designed race cars for several years. A

Harry Hartz—An easy winner of the national driving championship in 1926—he won five races and finished second seven times—Hartz finished fourth or better at Indy five straight years, but never won. He was seriously injured in a 1927 accident and forced to retire. A, C

Eddie Hearne—A fine driver on a variety of tracks, Hearne won the national championship in 1923; he finished in the top seven at Indy five times in nine tries, but never won. A, C

Harry "Cotton" Henning—Considered one of the finest mechanics in the history of auto racing, beginning in the mid-twenties, Henning entered a number of cars at Indy through the years. He entered the winning Boyle Products Special in 1934; his cars also finished third in 1935, fourth and sixth in 1937, third and fifth in 1947, and fourth in 1948. A

Ralph Hepburn—Hepburn finished second in the closest Indy 500 in history, losing to Wilbur Shaw in 1937 by only 2.16 sec. He also had one third-, one fourth-, and one fifth-place finish in the event, in 15 tries. In 1947 he set one-lap and four-lap speed records on the track in a Novi Special. A

E. T. "Ted" Horn—The only man ever to win three national championships in a row (1946–1948), Horn won the third title posthumously, having been killed in his eleventh race in 1948; he had won two and finished fourth or better in the other eight. He also finished in the top four in nine consecutive Indy races without winning. A, C

Anton "Tony" Hulman, Jr.—After World War II, the Indianapolis Speedway, which had been unused since 1941, was in poor condition. Hulman bought it from Eddie Rickenbacker, restored it to shape, and proceeded to reinvest profits to improve it further. Under his leadership, prize money for the race went over the $1 million mark in 1970. A, C

Parnelli Jones—United States sprint-car champion in 1960–1962 and USAC stock-car champion in 1964, Jones won the Indy 500 in 1963, placed second in 1965, and seventh in 1967. After retiring from driving, he became a car owner. C

Frank Lockhart—Lockhart won the 1926 Indy 500 by nearly 5 mi, in a race shortened by rain to 400 mi; in 1927, he broke the Indy qualifying record by nearly 7 mph with an average of 120.1. He was killed in a 1928 crash while attempting to set a land speed record. A

Jean Marcenac—A highly respected mechanic, Marcenac is especially known for his work with the powerful Novi cars that were plagued by bad luck at Indy. He was the entrant of record for two Novis in 1951—they finished 10th and 25th—and was chief mechanic for the Novi team for several years. A, C

Rex Mays—A charging driver, Mays never won at Indy, though he was the fastest qualifier four times. He won two straight national championships, 1940–1941, and was Midwest sprint champion twice, 1936–1937. He was killed in a dirt-track crash in 1949. A, C

Louis Meyer—The first man to win three Indy 500s, Meyer did it in 1928, 1933, and 1936 and was national driving champion in 1928, 1929, and 1933. In 1939 he and Dale Drake bought the Offenhauser engine plant, and the "Offie" powered every winning car at Indy for 18 years, 1947–1964. Meyer then developed the Ford V-8 racing engines. A, C

Harry Miller—The first famous American racing cars were built by Miller, starting in 1916. In 1920, Jimmy Murphy won the Indy 500 and four other major races in a Miller to take the national title. A Miller car won the 1923 Indy 500, and five others finished in the top seven, and between 1926 and 1929 Millers completely dominated American racing and set a number of land speed records. They also won every Indy 500 from 1930 through 1938. A

Tommy Milton—Though born without sight in his left eye, Milton was the first driver to win two consecutive national championships (1920–1921) and two Indy 500s (1921, 1923); he set a land speed record at Daytona Beach in 1920 (156.046 mph). A, C

Lou Moore—Just before and just after World War II, the most successful Indy cars were designed, built, and owned by Moore. Moore cars won at Indy in 1938 and

1941—even though the Moore car that won the pole position in 1941 failed to finish. His Blue Crown Spark Plug Specials finished one-two in both 1947 and 1948 and one-two-three in 1949. In 1950 Moore's cars finished second, sixth, and eighth at Indy. A

Ralph Mulford—After several successes in early 24-hr races, Mulford won the national championship in 1911, when he finished second in the first Indy 500; five other times he finished in the top 10 at Indy, and he repeated as national champion in 1918. A, C

Jimmy Murphy—A riding mechanic for three years, Murphy became a driver in 1919. He was the first American to win a major European race, the 1921 French Grand Prix. With his own car, he won the 1922 Indy 500, and he won the national championship in 1922 and 1924; he was killed in a dirt-track crash late in 1924. A, C

T. E. "Pop" Myers—Myers became general manager of Indianapolis Motor Speedway in 1914, treasurer in 1915, and served as a vice-president of the Speedway Corporation from 1927 until his death in 1954. A, C

Berna Eli "Barney" Oldfield—Originally a bicycle racer, Oldfield learned to drive in Henry Ford's first racing car, in 1902, and won a 5-mi race. The following year he became the first man to travel a mile a minute. Most of his racing was done on barnstorming exhibition tours, so his name doesn't appear in many lists of champions, but he won the national title in 1903. A, C

Johnny Parsons—After winning the Midwest midget championship in 1948, Parsons moved up to big cars and won the national title in 1949, when he finished second at Indy. He won at Indy in 1950; in 1956, he was Pacific Coast midget champion. C

Jim Rathmann—His real name is Richard, but he borrowed his brother Jim's birth certificate to begin driving in 1946 because he was underage, and he's used the name ever since. In 14 Indy 500s, he won once, in 1960, after having finished second three times. He retired after the 1963 season. C

Dario Resta—The only foreign driver ever to win the American national championship, the Italian-born Resta came to this country in 1915 after some successes in Europe. He won the Grand Prize and the Vanderbilt Cup that year and finished second in the Indy 500. In 1916, he repeated in the Vanderbilt Cup and won at Indy, capturing the national title. He was killed in a 1924 crash in England. A

Eddie Rickenbacker—The most famous flying ace of World War I, Rickenbacker had earlier been a race driver. He set a world record at Daytona Beach in 1915 by reaching 136 mph and in 1916 he won $80,000 in races. After the war, he founded an automobile company that failed. In 1927 he bought Indianapolis Motor Speedway and operated it until 1941, when it was closed for the duration of the war. He sold it to Tony Hulman in 1945. A, C

Mauri Rose—Although a part-time driver, Rose took part in 15 consecutive Indy 500s, winning in 1941, 1947, and 1948; he also finished second once, third twice, and fourth once. He was national driving champion in 1936. A, C

Wilbur Shaw—Because of a succession of bad luck, Shaw didn't win the Indy 500 until he was 35, in 1937; then he won it twice more, in 1939 and 1940. He also finished second three times and fourth once. He was national champion in 1937 and 1939. Shaw was president

and general manager of the Indianapolis Motor Speedway from 1945 until his death, in a plane crash, in 1954. A, C

Harry C. Stutz—The Stutz Bearcat was one of America's first famous sporting cars, and Stutz was a pioneer in the use of auto racing for publicity. He put together a factory driving team in 1912, with basically a stock model of a Bearcat; in 1915 he developed a special racing car, three of which ran in major events. One driver, Earl Cooper, won the 1915 national championship; another, Gil Anderson, finished third; and Stutz won the makes championship. Stutz sold his company in 1922, and it continued in racing under other ownership for several years. A

William K. Vanderbilt—Although best known in the sports field for his yachts and horses, Vanderbilt sponsored the first major auto race in the United States, for the Vanderbilt Trophy in 1904. The race continued through 1908. Vanderbilt also drove to land speed records in 1902 and 1904. A, C

Bill Vukovich—"The Mad Russian," so called because of his charging tactics, was national midget champion in 1950. After leading for most of the 1952 Indy 500, he was forced out with only 20 mi to go. He became the second man to win at Indy two years in a row, 1953–1954, but was killed in a crash in 1955, while leading after 57 laps in a bid for his third straight victory. A, C

Fred Wagner—The starter for the first two Indy 500 races, Wagner was a major official almost from the beginning of auto racing. He was the starter for virtually every major AAA race until his retirement in the 1930s. A

Rodger Ward—A World War II fighter pilot, Ward became a race driver in 1946. He won both the Indy 500 and the national championship in 1959 and 1962; he also finished second twice, third once, and fourth once. In 1951 he was the USAC stock-car champion. A, C

Howard "Howdy" Wilcox—An early dirt-track star, Wilcox set a record by competing in the first 11 Indy 500 races, winning in 1919 and serving as relief driver for winner Tommy Milton in 1923. He was national champion in 1919. Wilcox was killed in a 1924 crash. A

NASCAR Hall of Fame

(The Stock-Car Racing Hall of Fame, housed at Darlington, South Carolina, Raceway, is named for Joe Weatherly, one of its members.)

E. G. "Cannonball" Baker—An outstanding early motorcycle racer, Baker set 143 cross-country speed records on motorcycles and in automobiles. He was the first commissioner of NASCAR.

Robert "Red" Byron—Byron began stock-car racing on dirt tracks in the 1930s and won the first Grand National championship in 1949.

Robert E. Colvin—Colvin was president of Darlington Raceway for 15 years, until his death in 1967. He made it a major stock-car track, for the annual Southern 500 and for the Rebel 300, for stock-car convertibles—now a 400-mi race on the Grand National Circuit.

T. Fontello "Fonty" Flock—Flock won the Modified championship in 1947 and 1949. He also won the Grand National Southern 500 in 1952 and finished second the following year.

Tim Flock—The brother of Fonty, Tim was Grand National Champion in 1952 and 1955 and had a total of 40 Grand National victories.

Ned Jarrett—Jarrett won the Late-Model Sportsman championship in 1957 and 1958, then moved into Grand National competition to win titles in 1961 and 1965. He had a total of 50 Grand National victories.

Junior Johnson—Though he never won a national title, Johnson compiled 50 Grand National race victories; tied for fifth place on the all-time list with Jarrett.

Paul McDuffie—The only mechanic in the hall, McDuffie prepared many outstanding stock cars before his death in 1960, including the Bob Welborn car that set a record of 142 miles an hour in the 1959 Daytona race. He also prepared many cars for "Fireball" Roberts and, later, for Joe Lee Johnson, who won the first World 600 in 1960.

Billy Myers—The 1955 Late-Model Sportsman champion, Myers also won two Grand National races. He managed his own race team and was a fine mechanic. He died of a heart attack during a 1958 race.

Cotton Owens—Owens, who finished second in the 1959 Grand National standings, had nine Grand National wins during his career.

Lee Petty—The first man to win three Grand National driver championships, in 1954, 1958, and 1959, Petty also finished in the top six the other nine years of his career. He won a total of 54 Grand National races, and has also prepared cars for his son, Richard.

James A. "Pat" Purcell—A onetime newspaperman and promoter, Purcell was field manager and vice-president of NASCAR for 14 years, until his death in 1966.

Glenn "Fireball" Roberts—At the time of his death in an accident in 1964, when he was 35, he was the biggest winner in NASCAR history, with 32 late-model victories and an estimated $400,000 in winnings.

Marshall Teague—A mechanic as well as a driver, Teague had seven Grand National victories before switching to Indy-type cars in 1952. He finished seventh in the Indy 500 in 1957. He was perhaps best known, though, for preparing the "Teaguemobile," a Hudson Hornet that won many NASCAR races in 1951 and 1952, driven by Teague, Herb Thomas, and Dick Rathmann.

Herb Thomas—Grand National champion in 1951 and 1953, Thomas won a total of 49 Grand National races in only seven seasons, including three wins in six starts in the Southern 500.

Joe H. Weatherly—Weatherly took the Modified championship in 1953 and then went on to win two consecutive Grand National titles, in 1962 and 1963. He won a total of 24 Grand National races, after an earlier successful career as a motorcycle racer.

Rex White—White was Grand National champion in 1960 and runner-up the following year. He had a total of 26 Grand National race victories.

Indianapolis 500 Winners

Year	Driver	Car	Av. Speed
1911	Ray Harroun	Marmon	74.59
1912	Joe Dawson	National	78.72
1913	Jules Goux	Peugeot	75.933
1914	Rene Thomas	Delage	82.47
1915	Ralph DePalma	Mercedes	89.84
1916	Dario Resta	Peugeot	83.26[a]
1917–18	No competition		
1919	Howard Wilcox	Peugeot	88.05
1920	Gaston Chevrolet	Monroe	88.16
1921	Tommy Milton	Frontenac	89.62
1922	Jimmy Murphy	Murphy Special	94.48
1923	Tommy Milton	H.C.S. Special	90.95
1924	L. I. Corum-Joe Boyer	Duesenberg Special	98.23
1925	Peter DePaolo	Duesenberg Special	101.13
1926	Frank Lockhart	Miller Special	95.904[b]
1927	George Souders	Duesenberg Special	97.545
1928	Louis Meyer	Miller Special	99.482
1929	Ray Keech	Simplex Piston Ring Special	97.585
1930	Billy Arnold	Harry Hartz Special	100.448
1931	Louis Schneider	Bowes Seal Fast Special	96.629
1932	Fred Frame	Miller-Hartz Special	104.144
1933	Louis Meyer	Tydol Special	104.162
1934	William Cummings	Boyle Products Special	104.863
1935	Kelly Petillo	Gilmore Speedway Special	106.240
1936	Louis Meyer	Ring Free Special	109.069
1937	Wilbur Shaw	Shaw-Gilmore Special	113.580
1938	Floyd Roberts	Burd Piston Ring Special	117.200
1939	Wilbur Shaw	Boyle Special	115.035
1940	Wilbur Shaw	Boyle Special	114.277
1941	Floyd Davis-Mauri Rose	NocOut Hose Clamp Special	115.117
1942-45	No competition		
1946	George Robson	Thorne Engineering Special	114.820
1947	Mauri Rose	Blue Crown Spark Plug Special	116.338
1948	Mauri Rose	Blue Crown Spark Plug Special	119.814
1949	Bill Holland	Blue Crown Spark Plug Special	121.327
1950	Johnny Parsons	Kurtis-Kraft Synns Special	124.002[c]
1951	Lee Wallard	Belanger Special	126.244
1952	Troy Ruttman	Agajanian Special	128.922
1953	William Vukovich	Fuel Injection Spec.	128.740
1954	William Vukovich	Fuel Injection Special	130.840
1955	Robert Sweikert	Zink Special	128.209
1956	Pat Flaherty	Zink Special	128.490
1957	Sam Hanks	Belond Exhaust Special	135.601
1958	Jimmy Bryan	Belond Exhaust Special	133.791
1959	Rodger Ward	Leader Card Special	135.856
1960	Jim Rathmann	Ken-Paul Special	138.767
1961	A. J. Foyt	Bowes Special	139.130
1962	Rodger Ward	Leader Card Special	140.293
1963	Parnelli Jones	Agajanian Special	143.137
1964	A. J. Foyt	Sheraton-Thompson Special	147.350
1965	Jim Clark	Lotus-Ford	150.686
1966	Graham Hill	Red Ball Lola-Ford	144.317
1967	A. J. Foyt	Sheraton-Thompson	151.207

1968	Bobby Unser	Rislone-Eagle-Offenhauser	152.882
1969	Mario Andretti	STP-Hawk-Ford	156.867
1970	Al Unser	Johnny Lightning Colt-Ford	155.749
1971	Al Unser	Johnny Lightning Colt-Ford	157.735
1972	Mark Donohue	McLaren-Offenhauser	163.465
1973	Gordon Johncock	Eagle-Offenhauser	159.014[d]
1974	Johnny Rutherford	McLaren-Offenhauser	158.589
		Jorgensen Eagle	149.213[e]
1975	Bobby Unser	McLaren-Offenhauser	
1976	Johnny Rutherford	Offenhauser	144.499[f]

[a]300 miles
[b]400 miles
[c]345 miles
[d]332.5 miles
[e]435 miles
[f]255 miles

United States Auto Club Champions
(AMERICAN AUTOMOBILE ASSOCIATION UNTIL 1956)

National Champions

1902	Harry Harkness	1938	Floyd Roberts
1903	Barney Oldfield	1939	Wilbur Shaw
1904	George Heath	1940	Rex Mays
1905	Victor Hemery	1941	Rex Mays
1906	Joe Tracy	1942–45	No competition
1907	Eddie Bald	1946	Ted Horn
1908	Louis Strang	1947	Ted Horn
1909	Bert Dingley, George Robertson (tie)	1948	Ted Horn
		1949	Johnny Parsons
1910	Ray Harroun	1950	Henry Banks
1911	Ralph Mulford	1951	Tony Bettenhausen
1912	Ralph DePalma	1952	Charles Stevenson
1913	Earl Cooper	1953	Sam Hanks
1914	Ralph DePalma	1954	Jimmy Bryan
1915	Earl Cooper	1955	Bob Sweikert
1916	Dario Resta	1956	Jimmy Bryan
1917	Earl Cooper	1957	Jimmy Bryan
1918	Ralph Mulford	1958	Tony Bettenhausen
1919	Howard Wilcox	1959	Rodger Ward
1920	Tommy Milton	1960	A. J. Foyt
1921	Tommy Milton	1961	A. J. Foyt
1922	Jimmy Murphy	1962	Rodger Ward
1923	Eddie Hearne	1963	A. J. Foyt
1924	Jimmy Murphy	1964	A. J. Foyt
1925	Peter DePaolo	1965	Mario Andretti
1926	Harry Hartz	1966	Mario Andretti
1927	Peter DePaolo	1967	A. J. Foyt
1928	Lou Meyer	1968	Bobby Unser
1929	Lou Meyer	1969	Mario Andretti
1930	Billy Arnold	1970	Al Unser
1931	Lou Schneider	1971	Joe Leonard
1932	Bob Carey	1972	Joe Leonard
1933	Lou Meyer	1973	Roger McCluskey
1934	Bill Cummings	1974	Bobby Unser
1935	Kelly Petillo	1975	A. J. Foyt
1936	Mauri Rose	1976	Gordon Johncock
1937	Wilbur Shaw		

National Association for Stock Car Auto Racing
(NASCAR)

Grand National Champions

1949	Red Byron
1950	Bill Rexford
1951	Herb Thomas
1952	Tim Flock
1953	Herb Thomas
1954	Lee Petty
1955	Tim Flock
1956	Buck Baker
1957	Buck Baker
1958	Lee Petty
1959	Lee Petty
1960	Rex White
1961	Ned Jarrett
1962	Joe Weatherly
1963	Joe Weatherly
1964	Richard Petty
1965	Ned Jarrett
1966	David Pearson
1967	Richard Petty
1968	David Pearson
1969	David Pearson
1970	Bobby Isaac
1971	Richard Petty
1972	Richard Petty
1973	Benny Parsons
1974	Richard Petty
1975	Richard Petty
1976	Cale Yarborough

Sports Car Club of America Champions

Trans-American Champions

1966	Ford Mustang
1967	Ford Mustang
1968	Chevrolet Camaro
1969	Chevrolet Camaro
1970	Ford Mustang
1971	AMC Javelin
1972	AMC Javelin
1973	Porsche Carrera
1974	Porsche Carrera
1975	Chevrolet Corvette
1976	Porsche Turbo-Carrera

L & M Formula 5000 (Continental Championship until 1971)

1967	Gus Hutchison, Lotus-Ford
1968	Lou Sell, Eagle-Chevrolet
1969	Tony Adamowics, Eagle-Chevrolet
1970	John Cannon, Starr-Chevrolet
1971	Peter Revson, McLaren M10B-Chev.
1972	Graham McRae, STP McRae-Chevrolet
1973	Jody Scheckter, Trojan T101-Chevrolet
1974	Brian Redman, Lola-Chevrolet
1975	Brian Redman, Lola-Chevrolet
1976	Brian Redman, Lola-Chevrolet

U.S. Road Racing Championship

1963	Robert Holbert, Porsche RS-61/Cobra
1964	James Hall, Chaparral II
1965	George Follmer, Lotus-Porsche
1966	Charles Parsons, Genie-Chev/McLaren-Chev.
1967	Mark Donohue, Lola-Chevrolet
1968	Mark Donohue, Sunoco Special-Chev.
	(Discontinued)

International Champions

World Championship of Drivers

1950	Guiseppe Farina, Italy
1951	Juan Manuel Fangio, Argentina
1952	Alberto Ascari, Italy
1953	Alberto Ascari, Italy
1954	Juan Manuel Fangio, Argentina
1955	Juan Manuel Fangio, Argentina
1956	Juan Manuel Fangio, Argentina
1957	Juan Manuel Fangio, Argentina
1958	Mike Hawthorn, England

1959 Jack Brabham, Australia
1960 Jack Brabham, Australia
1961 Phil Hill, United States
1962 Graham Hill, England
1963 Jim Clark, Scotland
1964 John Surtees, England
1965 Jim Clark, Scotland
1966 Jack Brabham, Australia
1967 Denis Hulme, New Zealand
1968 Graham Hill, England
1969 Jackie Stewart, Scotland
1970 Jochen Rindt, Austria
1971 Jackie Stewart, Scotland

1972 Emerson Fittipaldi, Brazil
1973 Jackie Stewart, Scotland
1974 Emerson Fittipaldi, Brazil
1975 Niki Lauda, Austria
1976 James Hunt, England

Bibliography. Ash, David: *Automobile Almanac,* 6th annual ed., Automobile Almanac, Ltd., New York, 1972; Engel, Lyle K. et al.: *The Indianapolis 500;* rev. ed., Four Winds Press, New York, 1972; Georgano, G. N., ed.: *The Encyclopedia of Motor Sport,* Viking, New York, 1971; *NASCAR Record Book,* NASCAR News Bureau, Daytona Beach, Fla., 1974 (annual); Pritchard, Anthony and Keith Davey: *The Encyclopedia of Motor Racing,* McKay, New York, 1969.

B

BABE RUTH BASEBALL—This is a national organization, founded in Hamilton Township, New Jersey, in 1951, as a baseball league for boys aged 13–15. In 1966 the organization added a program for the 16–18 age group. More than 300,000 youngsters play Babe Ruth baseball in all 50 states, Canada, Puerto Rico, and Mexico and in European and Asian countries. Games are played on regulation diamonds and under standard baseball rules, except that a regulation game lasts seven, instead of nine, innings. World tournaments are conducted in each group—the World Series for the 13–15 age group and the Tournament of Champions for the 16–18 age group.

BADMINTON—It is quite likely that badminton developed from an ancient game called battledore and shuttlecock, in which two players toss a feathered cork back and forth with tiny rackets. Ancient Greek drawings show people playing that type of game, and versions of battledore and shuttlecock have been popular in Japan, India, and Siam for at least 2,000 years.

Many sources say that British army officers serving in India added the net to the game, making it a truly competitive sport. But it is possible that the Indians themselves had a form of the sport that required a net, and that the British simply copied the idea. In any event, British officers were playing the game—then called Poona—in the late 1860s, and some of them brought the equipment to England in the early 1870s.

A group of them played it at an 1873 party given by the Duke of Beaufort at his country place, which was called Badminton, and for some time the new sport was called "the game at Badminton" or "the Badminton game." (It's interesting to note that Poona is also a place name—a city in India.)

Rules were first formalized by the Bath Badminton Club in 1887, and they have changed little since then. The Badminton Association of England was organized in 1893 and the first All-England championship was held in 1899, for men; a women's division was officially added in 1904, although unofficial women's tournaments had been held since 1900.

Badminton became popular in Canada in the 1890s, but didn't reach the United States, except for some sporadic play, until about 1929, and it gained great popularity in

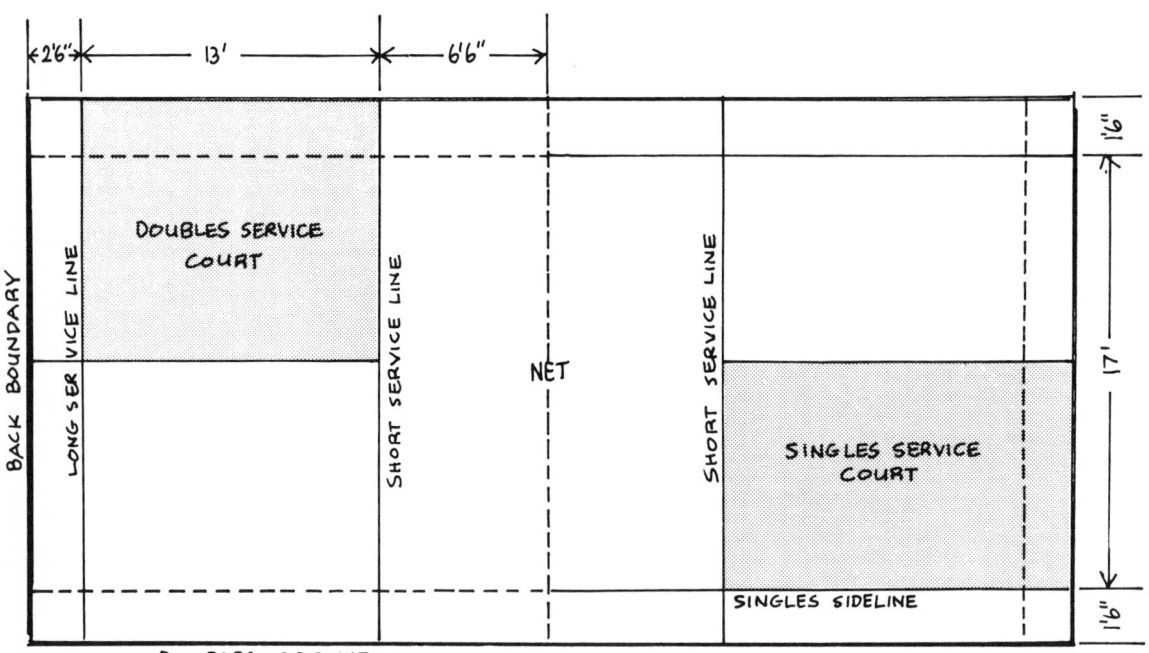

Badminton court

the mid-1930s. The American championships date from 1937.

International Competition. The International Badminton Federation was formed in 1934, and in 1939 its president, Sir George A. Thomas, offered a trophy for international team competition—badminton's equivalent of the Davis Cup. World War II postponed that idea until 1949, however. Thomas Cup competition is now held every three years, and it follows the former Davis Cup format, with preliminary zonal tournaments and then an interzonal tournament to determine a challenger, who meets the defending champion.

Mrs. H. S. Uber of England donated a trophy for similar competition among women's teams. Uber Cup play began during the 1956–1957 season.

The All-England championship still holds much the same place in badminton as the tradition-laden Wimbledon tournament does in tennis. (The Wimbledon event is also officially called the All-England tournament.)

Equipment. The shuttlecock, or "bird," is a cork hemisphere, 1 to 1⅛ in, in diameter, surmounted by a short cylindrical crown in which are embedded 14 to 16 feathers, 2¼ to 2¾ in long and with a top spread of from 2⅛ to 2½ in. It weighs between 73 and 85 grains (about 1⅙ oz).

The racket, or bat, has a nearly round face, about 7 in across, and a long thin handle. Overall length is about 27 in and weight is about 8 oz.

Rules. The badminton court is 17 by 44 ft for singles, 20 by 44 for doubles, and the net is 5 ft high.

Players begin by tossing a racket to decide which of them serves first. The server stands anywhere in his or her own right-hand service court and serves diagonally across into the opponent's right-hand service court; the serve must go beyond the short service line, 6½ ft beyond the net. The players then continue hitting the bird back and forth until one of them makes a fault. If it is the server's fault, no point is scored, but the other player wins the right to serve. Only the server can score. A player serves from the right-hand service court when the number of points is even, and from the left-hand court when there is an odd number of points.

Game is generally 15 points in men's tournament play, 11 in women's. However, men sometimes play a 21-point game. In men's play, if the score is tied at 13, the first player to reach that number has the option of "setting" the game at 5 points; that is, he declares that the first player to score 5 points (for a total of 18) will be the winner. At 14-all, the first player to reach 14 can "set" the game at 3 points. If he elects not to set the game, game remains at 15 points.

In women's play, game may be set at 3 when the score is tied at 9, or at 2 when the score is tied at 10. In a 21-point game, game may be set at 5 when the score is 19-all or at 3 when the score is 20-all.

Doubles. The doubles court is 3 ft wider, the 1½ foot alleys on either side of the court coming into play. The service court is 1½ ft wider by 2½ ft shorter than in singles. The first time a team serves, only one player serves, with service then passing to the other team. After that, both players on a team get a chance to serve before the team loses the service. To explain further: Team A serves, loses the point, and Team B then serves. Its first server, B-1, loses the point; but it is now B-2's turn to serve, and B-2 continues until that team loses the point. A-2 now serves, followed by A-1.

Dr. David G. Freeman won seven national singles titles and one All-England singles championship between 1939 and 1953. (*Courtesy of American Badminton Association.*)

Faults. The serve must be made underhand; the bat must contact the shuttlecock below the server's waist, and it must not be higher than his hand at the moment of contact. It is a fault if the server touches one of the lines enclosing the service court, and the server is not allowed to fake a serve. A server gets only one chance to make a proper serve. The player returning service must remain stationary until the serve is on its way.

It is a fault if the shuttlecock: 1. Hits the ground before it is returned; 2. falls outside the court boundaries; 3. fails to go over the net; or 4. goes through the net. If it strikes the net but falls over to the other side, it is in play.

It is also a fault if a player hits the shuttlecock before it crosses the net, touches the net with the body or the racket, or commits a "carry"—that is, if the shuttlecock is momentarily stationary on the player's racket before the player hits (actually, throws) it back.

Other special rules worth noting: If the server swings and misses, it is not a fault. It is a fault if the shuttlecock touches a player before being hit, if a player strikes it twice, or if both players on the same doubles team strike it.

Fundamentals of Play. Because of the size of the court, the height of the net, and the nature of the shuttlecock, badminton is a very fast sport. The shuttlecock may have an initial speed of 110 mph, but it slows down and begins to fall very quickly.

Fundamental striking positions and strokes are similar to those of tennis, but the lighter, longer badminton racket makes wrist action much more important, and permits some shots that would be impossible in tennis.

The most basic badminton shot is the "clear," so called because it is meant to clear the opponent's head. It is an overhead shot, similar to a tennis serve.

The drive is very similar to ordinary tennis ground strokes, either forehand or backhand. It is a flat, hard shot hit at about waist level, with the player standing approximately at right angles to the line of flight.

The overhead smash, very similar to the overhead clear, is another shot apparently borrowed from tennis. The smash is an attacking shot, usually hit from closer to the

Judy Devlin Hashman won 12 national singles and 10 All-England singles championships. *(Courtesy of American Badminton Association.)*

net than the clear, with a downward trajectory; instead of clearing an opponent's head, it is generally hit almost directly at, or in front of, the opponent.

The drop shot is meant to look like a drive, but it is a finesse shot that should just barely clear the net before it begins to drop sharply to the court. There is little backswing or follow-through, and the racket is tilted slightly upward to ensure that the bird clears the net.

The hairpin shot is unique to badminton; its name describes the shuttlecock's line of flight. It is likely to be a return of a drop shot. Hitting the shuttlecock from within 2 or 3 ft of the net, the player gives it just enough upward momentum for it to clear the net, whereupon it begins to fall to the court on the other side. It should clear the net by as small a margin as possible.

The block is another shot hit from close to the net. It is more commonly seen in doubles than in singles. It is sometimes called a "push shot"—there is hardly any swing at all, just enough to get the shuttlecock going in the other direction and across the net.

The overhead drop shot resembles the clear or smash, but the racket is tilted slightly backward and little force is used.

Another shot unique to badminton is the "around-the-head." It is, in a way, a technique of avoiding the backhand. When the shuttlecock is headed toward the player's backhand, the player moves toward it and slightly toward the net. The swing resembles that for an overhead smash, but the shuttlecock is struck at a point above the left shoulder, rather than above the head. This is difficult to visualize at first: The racket comes up as for a smash, but it is tilted to the left in order to make contact, and the follow-through carries the racket back to the right. Depending on the exact angle and the amount of force applied, this may result in a half-smash, a clear, or a drop shot.

Singles Strategy. Badminton is a sport that emphasizes change of pace and deception. The good player varies and disguises shots well. Such a player might hit three consecutive clears to the right corner of an opponent's territory, and then come up with an overhead drop shot to the left. As in tennis, a basic aim is to keep the opponent moving as much as possible, until you finally have the opponent out of position.

Doubles Strategy. In terms of strategy, doubles is more complicated than singles, because the players have to stay out of each other's way. The simplest doubles formation is the side-by-side, which is just what it sounds like: Each partner takes one side of the team's court.

The up-and-back system is also simple. One partner stands in the middle of his side of the court, at just about the short service line, while the other straddles the line dividing the left and right service courts, about halfway back.

The combination system is more complicated. When a team is on the defensive—generally speaking, when they have hit the ball high to the other team—they play side by side. But when one of them has a chance for an attacking shot, especially a smash, the other advances quickly to the net because the other team's return is likely to be high.

The most advanced and most difficult is the rotation system, generally used only by expert players. Members of a team keep circling counterclockwise. The player on the right moves toward the net; if the shuttlecock goes beyond him, his partner is able to take it on his forehand. The first player then moves back to the left corner while the second player comes to the net. The chief advantage of this system is that it virtually eliminates the backhand.

U.S. Champions

(O denotes Open, meaning foreign players admitted; C denotes Closed, for U.S. citizens only. All tournaments were open until 1970, when there were Closed and Open divisions. There was no closed tournament in 1973, no open tournament in 1974 or 1975.)

Men's Singles

1937	Walter R. Kramer	1957	Finn Kobbero
1938	Walter R. Kramer	1958	James Poole
1939	David G. Freeman	1959	Tan Joe Hok
1940	David G. Freeman	1960	Tan Joe Hok
1941	David G. Freeman	1961	James Poole
1942	David G. Freeman	1962	Ferry Sonneville
1943–1946	No competition	1963	Erland Kops
1947	David G. Freeman	1964	Channarong
1948	David G. Freeman		Ratanaseangsuang
1949	A. Marten Mendez	1965	Erland Kops
1950	A. Marten Mendez	1966	Tan Aik Huang
1951	Joe Alston	1967	Erland Kops
1952	A. Marten Mendez	1968	Channarong
1953	David G. Freeman		Ratanaseangsuang
1954	Eddie B. Choong	1969	Rudy Hartono
1955	Joe Alston	1970	Stan Hales (C)
1956	Finn Kobbero		Junji Honma (O)

1971	Stan Hales (C)	1973	Sture Johnsson (O)
	Muljadi (O)	1974	Chris Kinard (C)
1972	Chris Kinard (C)	1975	Mike Adams (C)
	Sture Johnsson (O)	1976	Paul Whetnall (O)

Women's Singles

1937	Mrs. Del Barkhuff	1960	Judith Devlin
1938	Mrs. Del Barkhuff	1961	Judy Devlin Hashman
1939	Mary E. Whitemore	1962	Judy Devlin Hashman
1940	Evelyn Boldrick	1963	Judy Devlin Hashman
1941	Thelma Kingsbury	1964	Dorothy O'Neil
1942	Evelyn Boldrick Howard	1965	Judy Devlin Hashman
1943–1946	No competition	1966	Judy Devlin Hashman
1947	Ethel Marshall	1967	Judy Devlin Hashman
1948	Ethel Marshall	1968	Tyna Barinaga
1949	Ethel Marshall	1969	Miss Minarni
1950	Ethel Marshall	1970	Tyna Barinaga (C)
1951	Ethel Marshall		Etsuko Takenaka (O)
1952	Ethel Marshall	1971	Diane Hales (C)
1953	Ethel Marshall		Noriko Takagi (O)
1954	Judith Devlin	1972	Pam Stockton (C)
1955	Margaret Varner		Eva Twedberg (O)
1956	Judith Devlin	1973	Eva Twedberg (O)
1957	Judith Devlin	1974	Cindy Baker (C)
1958	Judith Devlin	1975	Judianne Kelly (C)
1959	Judith Devlin	1976	Gillian Gilks (O)

Citizens Savings Badminton Hall of Fame

Joseph C. Alston	A. Marten Mendez
Lois Alston	John R. Mitchell
Bertha Barkhuff Cunningham	Dr. Donald C. Paup
Dr. David G. Freeman	James R. Poole
Helen L. Gibson	Donald Richardson
Chester Goss	T. Wynn Rogers
Judith Devlin Hashman	T. M. Royce
Evelyn Boldrick Howard	Loma Moulton Smith
Thelma Kingsbury	Helen Noble Tibbetts
Walter R. Kramer	Margaret Varner
Hamilton B. Law	Janet Wright
Carl Wickham Loveday	Richard O. Yeager
Ethel Marshall	Zoe Smith Yeager
Beatrice Massman	

Bibliography. Davidson, Kenneth, and Lealand R. Gustavson, *Winning Badminton,* Ronald, New York, 1953.

BALANCE BEAM—A gymnastic event for women in which competitors perform on a wooden beam, 4 in wide, about 20 ft long, and 47.2 in above the floor.

See GYMNASTICS.

BALLOON RACING—Man's centuries-old dream of being able to fly was made real by the balloon, 120 years before the Wright brothers flew the first heavier-than-air craft. The first successful large-scale balloon launching took place on June 5, 1783, when the Montgolfier brothers, Joseph and Étienne, filled a spherical balloon with hot air and released it at Annonay, France. The balloon, 110 ft in circumference, rose to about 6,000 ft and landed 1½ mi away after a 10-min flight.

Oddly, the Montgolfiers apparently never realized why their hot-air balloons could fly; Joseph, the older brother and the leader in their experiments, believed that various substances, when burned, produced various lighter-than-air gases, and came to the conclusion that a mixture of damp straw and chopped wool produced the lightest kind of gas. Later he added old shoes and decomposed meat to his formula for fuel, which tended to keep spectators at a distance.

Actually, a hot-air balloon rises because air (or any gas) expands when it is heated, thus becoming less dense, and therefore "lighter than air"—lighter than cooler air, that is.

After the successful launching of a balloon carrying a sheep, a duck, and a rooster, the Montgolfiers announced that they were going to build a man-carrying balloon. King Louis XVI agreed that the flight could take place, if two condemned criminals were the passengers. If they returned safely, they would be given pardons. This shocked a 26-year-old member of the French Academy, Francis Pilatre de Rozier—not for humane reasons, but because he felt it would be a disgrace to allow two criminals to have the honor of being the first men to fly. Pilatre de Rozier volunteered for the ascent, along with the Marquis d'Arlandes. The king finally agreed.

The Montgolfiers came up with a new design for their manned balloon—a design still used for hot-air balloons. It had a 16-ft-diameter neck surrounded by a wickerwork gallery, held in place by small cords sewn into the fabric. A wrought-iron fire basket hung from the neck by chains. The balloon weighed 1,600 lb and had a capacity of about 79,000 ft³, giving it a lifting power of about 1,700 lb.

There were trial ascents, with the balloon held captive, on October 15, and several more on October 19, when de Rozier and d'Arlandes ascended to 324 ft. The free launching took place on November 21 in Paris. The two men went up in the balloon in early afternoon and traveled 9,000 yd in 25 min, reaching a top altitude of about 3,000 ft, according to some accounts.

Meanwhile a young French physicist, Jacques Charles, had begun experimenting with hydrogen balloons. He developed a remarkably advanced balloon—a sphere of rubberized silk, with an open neck, or appendix, at the bottom and a valve at the top, controlled by a cord that passed down through the center of the balloon into the passenger basket. The appendix was a safety valve; as a balloon rises, decreased air pressure and, at times, the heat of the sun cause the gas inside to expand. If there is no opening to let the expanding gas escape, the balloon will eventually explode. The valve at the top enabled a pilot to let gas out at a safe rate when he wanted to descend.

Charles and Aine Robert made the first manned ascent in a hydrogen balloon on December 1, 1783, watched by a crowd estimated at 400,000. Hydrogen has much more lifting power than hot air; their balloon quickly leaped to 1,800 ft. After a flight of nearly 2 hr, they landed in Nesle, 27 mi from Paris. Robert got out and Charles ascended alone, flying to Tour du Lay, another 3 mi, in 35 min.

The history of ballooning could fill a book—indeed, several books have been written on the subject. In any real sense of the term, however, balloon racing didn't actually start until more than a century after the first manned ascent. Ballooning as a sport became remarkably popular starting about 1895. The Aero Club de France was organized to regulate the sport in that country in 1898, and similar clubs were soon established in other countries. In 1905 the International Aeronautical Federation (FAI) was organized in Paris to provide international regulation and government.

Like airplane racing, balloon racing began as a series of rallies at which balloonists attempted to win trophies for duration, distance, and accuracy—that is, coming as close as possible to a predesignated spot. The distance flights stirred the greatest public interest. Among the most famous were the annual races of the Aero Club of France. The Comte de la Vaulx won the first two races, in 1899 and 1900, with record-setting performances. In 1900 he flew from Vincennes, France, to near Kiev, Russia, a straight-line distance of 1,193 mi, in 35 hr and 45 min.

Bennett Trophy Races. In 1906 James Gordon Bennett, publisher of the *New York Herald,* put up a trophy for an annual international balloon race, to be organized by the FAI. It's likely that Bennett, who had previously offered a trophy for an international auto race and who later established another for an international airplane race, was trying to spur the development of powered lighter-than-air craft, but the FAI restricted the race to free balloons. The first race started from Paris, but the stipulation was that each year the winning country would take the trophy home and be host to the following year's race. The first Bennett trophy race was won by Frank P. Lahm, an American.

The Bennett Trophy race for balloons, oddly enough, long outlasted those for autos and airplanes. Except for a six-year interruption for World War I and a one-year hiatus in 1931, it remained an annual event through 1938. One balloonist, Henri Demuyter of Belgium, won six of the races, including three in a row, 1922–1924.

Balloon Racing Today. Under the leadership of the United States, ballooning has again become surprisingly popular in recent years. As of 1973, there were about 250 licensed pilots and about 200 hot-air balloons in the United States, more than in all the other countries in the world put together.

There are two reasons for the growth in popularity— development of a propane burner, which can easily be controlled to make the balloon climb or descend, and the development (by Edward Yost of Sioux Falls, South Dakota in 1961) of a durable but lightweight nylon envelope that allows a balloon to be used over and over. Yost and Donald Piccard in 1963 became the first men to cross the English Channel in a hot-air balloon.

The modern hot-air balloon still uses the old-fashioned wicker basket, because wicker is both strong and shock-absorbent. One of the modern balloon's greatest conveniences is a "rip panel," invented by John Wise of the United States, who made one of the first great long-distance flights, traveling 800 mi in less than 20 hr in 1859. The rip panel is a long section of the balloon which can be quickly ripped open on landing, deflating the balloon quickly. One big problem with early balloons was that they couldn't be deflated quickly, and therefore they often bounced along the ground and were severely damaged after landing.

Modern Racing. The most common kind of race today is a "hare and hounds" event. A race official takes off first in a "hare" balloon and the competitors try to follow him and land as close to him as possible. Thus, a balloon race really has nothing to do with speed; it is essentially a test of the balloonist's skill in piloting his craft by adjusting altitude to find favorable wind currents.

A national race is held annually under the auspices of the Balloon Federation of America (BFA).

In 1973 the BFA was host to the world's first World Hot Air Balloon championship, at Albuquerque, New Mexico. Invitations were sent to all 54 member nations of the FAI, with each country invited to send up to four balloon pilots. A total of 28 balloonists came from 13 countries to compete; in addition, 49 Americans took part in an elimination contest to pick this country's four entries.

There were four kinds of competition at Albuquerque, with the winner determined on points gathered in all four events. After one traditional hare-and-hounds race, there were three barograph tests.

The barograph is an instrument that measures altitude by measuring barometric pressure, tracing a graph on a revolving drum to preserve a permanent record. It was used in flight profile, rapid climb and level-off, and climbing and descent control tests at Albuquerque.

In the flight-profile test, a pattern was drawn on the drum and pilots attempted to stay as close as possible to the pattern. In the rapid climb and level-off test, they climbed to a predetermined height and then tried to keep the barograph tracer between two marked lines on the drum. In the climbing and descent control test, they ascended to 1,000 ft, dropped back down to within 10 ft, without allowing the balloon to touch, then went back up to 1,000 ft and down to the ground. This test was based on elapsed time. Dennis Floden of Flint, Michigan, won the overall title in the first championship.

Bibliography. Clarke, Basil: *History of Airships,* St. Martin's, New York, 1964.

BARREL JUMPING—Ice skating's version of the broad jump, barrel jumping apparently was practiced by Dutch skaters some 300 years ago. But in its more modern form, it may have developed out of obstacle races in which barrels were placed at various locations along a speed-skating course. These races became popular in Denmark about 1850.

Although a very minor form of sport, barrel jumping enjoyed a certain vogue in the United States during the 1930s and again during the early 1950s, when the event was often featured in newsreels or movie short subjects, along with such emerging sports as water skiing and surfing. It has also been shown recently on anthology-type television sports shows, because of its often spectacular nature.

The first world championship was held in 1951 at Grossinger's Country Club in upstate New York. The first United States championship was held the same year.

The barrels are laid on their sides along the ice, and the skater has to leave the ice at a scratch mark and clear the series of barrels. The total distance of the jump, not merely the number of barrels cleared, determines the winner. If the skater so much as touches one of the barrels, however, the jump doesn't count.

Rubber-coated barrels, made especially for the sport, have replaced wooden barrels, for safety's sake.

BASEBALL—The legend that Abner Doubleday invented baseball in Cooperstown, New York, in 1839 is enshrined as gospel in American folklore. But it is nothing more than folklore, despite the fact that the Baseball Hall of Fame was established at Cooperstown in baseball's "centennial" year, 1939.

The Doubleday legend began to take shape in 1904, when a committee was appointed to investigate baseball's origins. Albert G. Spalding, a pioneer baseball player, sports equipment manufacturer, and publisher, had been having a feud with Henry Chadwick, a British-born expert on baseball. Chadwick, writing in one of

Spalding's own publications, had insisted that baseball was derived from rounders, a boys' game of English origin. Spalding's patriotism was wounded by such an idea, and he insisted that baseball must be a purely American sport.

It was Spalding's idea that a commission should be appointed, and a good friend of his, Abraham G. Mills, who had been the third president of the National League, was named chairman. The commission existed for more than three years, but apparently didn't do much work or gather much evidence. When its report was issued in 1907, it was written by Mills alone, and Mills came up with the Doubleday-Cooperstown theory.

The sole evidence for the theory was a statement by one Abner Graves, who had been a schoolboy in Cooperstown in 1839. Unfortunately, Doubleday himself had been a West Point cadet in 1839, and didn't even get the summer off to go home to Cooperstown. Even more telling evidence against Graves's statement and Mills's report is the fact that Doubleday never even mentioned baseball in any of his existing letters or in his memoirs.

But the commission report was accepted. Late in the 1930s, Organized Baseball (that is, the hierarchy of professional leagues) dug out the report and decided to stage a centennial celebration—at Cooperstown, of course, where the Baseball Hall of Fame would be established as part of the festivities. Even as plans were being made for the centennial, the Doubleday theory was attacked by two people. One was a librarian, Robert W. Henderson, who demonstrated that the English game of rounders and the original game of baseball were identical. The other was Bruce Cartwright, who said he could prove that his uncle, Alexander Cartwright, had invented baseball.

Baseball's Ancestors. In his interesting book *The Man Who Invented Baseball,* Harold Peterson traces the sport's origins all the way to a game played as part of fertility rites by a New Stone Age tribe—about 6,000 B.C. Many games similar in some ways to baseball have been played in many countries through the centuries. Tracing derivations from one to another is impossible. Similar games do spring up independently in different parts of the world—lacrosse and field hockey, for example. There are only so many patterns on which a sport can be based. But it is certain that baseball descended from rounders.

Rounders is played on a field with 4 stones or posts, 12 to 20 yd apart, forming a square. A "pecker" or "feeder" throws the ball to a striker, who attempts to hit it. If successful in the attempt, the striker runs the bases clockwise—that is, going to third base first, so far as we are concerned. The striker is out upon missing the ball three times or upon hitting a foul ball; the striker is also out upon hitting a ball caught on the fly or upon being hit by a thrown ball between bases. A team remains at bat until all of its players are put out.

Henderson discovered this: In 1829, *The Boy's Own Book,* printed in both England and America, explained the rules for rounders. In 1834 the rules were copied in an American volume, *The Book of Sports*—but the heading was changed to "Base, or Goal Ball" because, the author said, those names were generally used in the United States. So a game called baseball, which was really rounders, was being played at least as early as 1834.

Like most children's games, baseball had many varia-

tions. Among the most popular were those known as town ball, round ball, and the Massachusetts game, which remained popular in New England until well into the 1850s. This was a unique version: The batter stood halfway between home plate and first base, in effect. Bases were 60 ft apart, so, upon hitting the ball, the batter would run only 30 ft to first base, and would score a run by ending up 30 ft from the starting point of the circuit. In the Massachusetts game, one out meant the team was out. According to one set of rules, the first team to score 100 runs was the winner.

In New York City a different game had developed, based on a diagram drawn in 1842. This game was played on a lopsided field, with 45 ft between the batter's box and first base, 60 ft between first and second bases, 72 ft

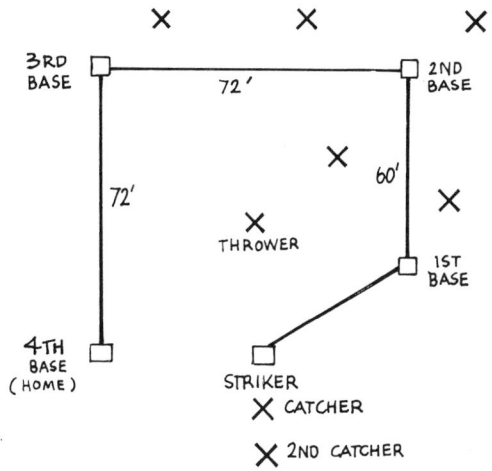

Diagram 1

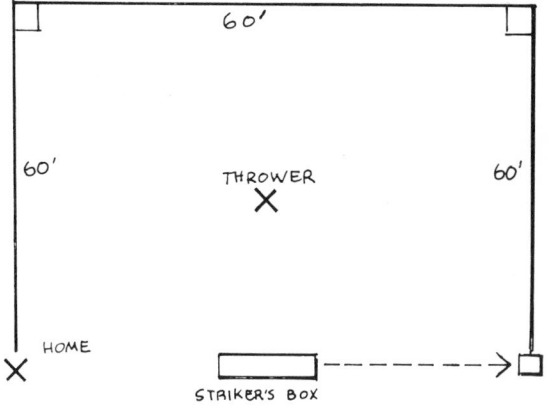

Diagram 2

Evolution of the baseball diamond

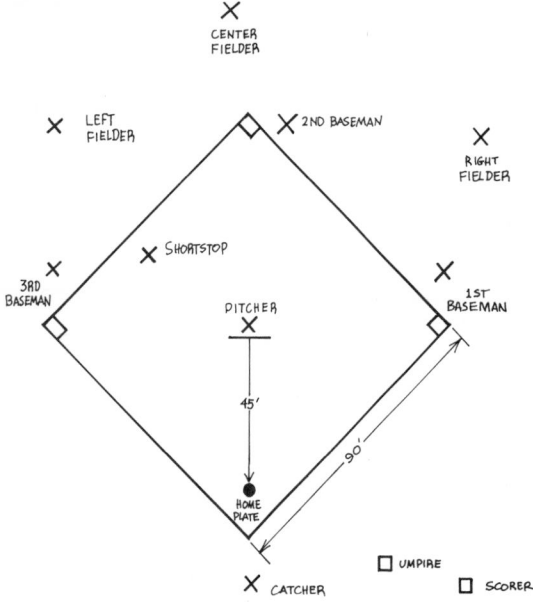

Alexander Cartwright's diagram of the baseball diamond

between second and third, and 72 ft between third and home—which was not where the hitter started out. This was the game played by a lot of fairly well-to-do young men, including many volunteer firemen. One of them was Alexander Cartwright.

The Invention. Alexander Cartwright was born April 17, 1820, in New York City. In 1842 he married—and he also joined a group of young men who got together a couple of times a week to play the New York game. Cartwright was a bank teller, an important and well-paid position for a young man in those days. He was also a member of the volunteer Knickerbocker Engine Company until it was dissolved in 1843. Many of the volunteers were young men with good occupations. It was not unusual for an entire engine company to battle a nighttime fire in full evening dress.

In the autumn of 1845, Cartwright suggested to his friends that they should organize a club. So the Knickerbocker Base Ball Club came into existence, on September 23, 1845, complete with constitution, bylaws, and a new set of rules, drawn up by Cartwright himself.

The rules specified three canvas bases, with flat, circular iron disks representing home plate and the pitcher's plate. Base lines were 90 ft long. Three outs constituted an inning. A base runner could no longer be put out by being hit by a thrown ball, but would have to be tagged or forced out. There were nine players to a side—and Cartwright's diagram located them almost exactly where they take their positions now.

There were a number of differences from modern baseball, not surprisingly. The pitcher was only 45 ft from home plate, and the pitcher's job was to let the batter hit the ball; the pitched ball had to be delivered gently,

underhand, as close to the plate as possible. Game was 21 "aces," or runs, but Cartwright allowed for equal innings, so if the first team to bat scored 21, it would continue to bat, scoring as many runs as possible, since the other team would then be given a final chance to bat. A hitter was out if the ball was caught on the first bounce or on the fly.

From this beginning in 1845, baseball spread rapidly across the country. One reason for its spread was probably Cartwright's departure for California during the 1849 gold rush. He left a long journal of his trip, which mentions teaching baseball to people at various stops along the way. He settled in Hawaii, where baseball has been popular for a long time, largely because of his early influence.

But there were many baseball missionaries. Other New Yorkers who joined the gold rush brought the sport to California. During the Civil War, Confederate prisoners learned it from Union soldiers. New Englanders moving west also brought baseball with them.

Still, the mere fact that a game spreads rapidly doesn't guarantee that it will last. Baseball's continuing popularity, in much the form that Cartwright invented, is a real tribute to him. The rules that he established made it the remarkably well-balanced game that it is. The 90-ft base lines, especially, represented a stroke of genius.

The Amateur Years. The Knickerbockers began by playing intraclub games every Monday and Thursday. The club president would pick two captains, who would choose up sides. Nonmembers were allowed to play only if there were fewer than 18 Knickerbockers on hand. They originally played at an area called the Elysian Fields in Hoboken, New Jersey.

The first recorded game was played on October 6, 1845. Only 14 Knickerbockers were there, so they played 7 to a side, and the game was limited to 11 aces instead of 21. They played at least 13 more games between then and November 18.

One June 19, 1846, the Knickerbockers played another team, in what was probably the first match ever contested under the new rules. A team called simply "New York" in the box score beat the Knickerbockers, 23–1, Cartwright umpired, and the Knickerbockers apparently used nine of their worst players. It has been suggested that the New York club was made up largely of former Knickerbockers who found it inconvenient to go to Hoboken for the games.

Other clubs quickly took shape in New York. Most of the members were "gentlemen"—bank tellers, insurance salesmen, merchants, and the like—and there was a distinctly social atmosphere to the clubs. But in 1856 two baseball clubs of workingmen were formed, the Eckfords of Greenpoint and the Atlantics of Jamaica. The game was simply too much fun to be confined to the upper classes, as the Knickerbockers and others probably would have preferred.

In 1858 an annual series between all-stars from Brooklyn and New York was inaugurated. And in 1860 the New York Excelsiors went on a tour that took in upstate New York, Pennsylvania, Maryland, and Delaware.

A group called the National Association of Base Ball Players, actually an organization of 22 clubs, had been formed in New York on March 10, 1858. It was strictly an amateur group; its bylaws stipulated that no player could be paid. The association also changed the rules a bit, calling for seven-inning games. This was soon altered to nine innings. The changes probably indicate that defenses were becoming better, and it was taking too long for a team to score 21 runs (which was "game" according to the original rules).

By 1867 there were more than 300 member clubs, and the association decided to limit membership to state associations, except in states with fewer than 10 teams.

But baseball couldn't remain a strictly amateur sport much longer. It had become too popular.

Professional Baseball

The First Professionals. Competition became so keen as early as 1860 that at least one team, the Brooklyn Excelsiors, was paying a star pitcher, Jim Creighton, under the table, making him the first known professional player. By 1866 the Philadelphia Athletics were accused of having three paid players. Much more widespread was the practice of giving a player a job in a town so that he could play for the local team.

In addition, admission was being charged at one Brooklyn park as early as 1862, and by 1864 the teams involved were getting a share of the gate receipts. (It was at this park, incidentally, that the national anthem was first played before a game, on May 15, 1862). One of the top teams of the period, the New York Mutuals, was controlled by the infamous "Boss" Tweed of Tammany Hall, who put the players on the city payroll, usually as street cleaners.

There were two other major problems: "revolving" and gambling. Certain players became known as "revolvers" because they moved from club to club, often accepting advance money at each stop before moving on. Gambling was even worse. The first real scandal occurred in a game between the Mutuals and the Eckfords on September 28, 1865, won by the Eckfords, 28-11. Three members of the Mutuals were barred for throwing the game, but all three were reinstated by 1870.

The association was being badly split. One group wanted pure amateurism; the other felt the association should recognize a group of pure professionals.

By 1869 the question was moot. In that year the Cincinnati Red Stockings were organized as an all-professional club, with no shame or hypocrisy about it. The team was put together by Harry Wright, who had come to Cincinnati in 1865 as a paid player and instructor for the Union Cricket Club. Wright assembled a 10-man squad that included only one Cincinnatian. The team toured the East and even played some games on the West Coast, winning 56 games and tying 1. They played before an estimated 200,000 people that year.

The First Pro League. The Red Stockings started a trend. Chicago fans raised $20,000 to start a team, and advertised for players. Other cities began similar efforts. Teams that had pretended to be amateur shed the hypocrisy and became full-blown professional teams.

In March of 1871, 10 professional clubs formed the National Association of Professional Base Ball Players. The teams were the Philadelphia Athletics, Washington Olympics, Washington Nationals, New York Mutuals, Troy Unions, Boston Red Stockings, Forest Citys of Rockford, Forest Citys of Cleveland, Chicago White Stockings, and the Fort Wayne Kekongas. This organization was not, strictly speaking, a league. One of its major purposes was to arrange tours. But the new association did arrange a championship competition, which a club could enter by paying $10. There was no formal schedule; the teams made arrangements among themselves for games.

The association had problems. Teams were scattered and not evenly matched, and many of them had financial difficulties. Everything was a little too haphazard. Revolving and gambling still plagued the game.

Nevertheless, this new professionalism improved the sport. The bunt was invented, as a way of getting on base. Fielders discovered they could drop flies intentionally with runners on base, in order to get double plays—

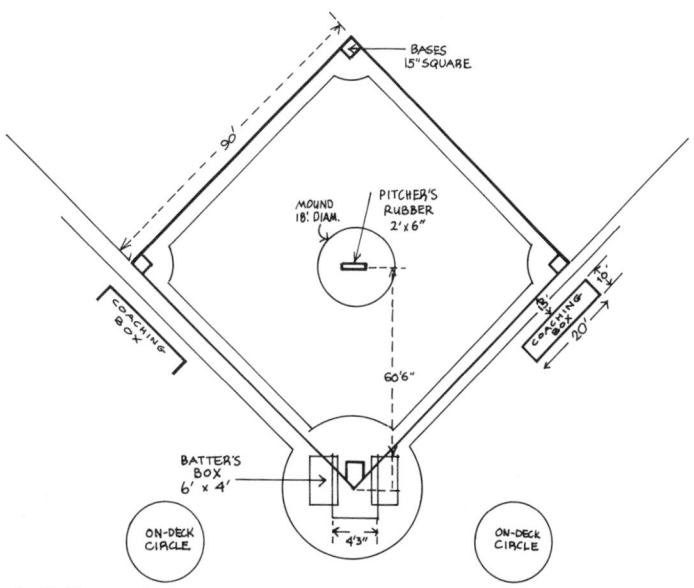

Dimensions of the baseball diamond

leading to the adoption of the infield fly rule. A fingerless glove was developed to protect infielders' hands. The catcher's mask was invented. And professionals learned a lot about "inside baseball"—the arts of position play, base running, the proper use of relay throws and cutoffs.

Two major rules changes had been made. A batter could no longer stand there indefinitely, waiting for his pitch. The umpire was empowered to call a strike if he felt the batter should have swung at a pitch. And it was decided that a ball would have to be caught on the fly, not on one bounce, to put the hitter out.

The National League. William A. Hulbert was an officer of the Chicago team in the National Association. He was also a good businessman, and he was convinced that baseball could be a good business if it were properly set up. He wanted a new kind of league. Late in the 1875 season, Hulbert persuaded four members of the Boston Red Stockings that they should join the Chicago team in 1876. They were Al Spalding, Cal McVey, James "Deacon" White, and Ross Barnes. The Red Stockings were about to win their fourth straight championship, primarily because of these four players. Hulbert also arranged to pirate Adrian C. "Cap" Anson from the Philadelphia Athletics. Hulbert was trying to strengthen his team. More important, he was trying to precipitate a crisis that would wreck the association so he could shape something else.

Late in 1875, Hulbert spoke to representatives of the St. Louis club of the National Association and of two strong independent teams, Louisville and Cincinnati, about forming a new league. A constitution was drawn up. Then four Eastern clubs, all association members, were contacted. The four were Hartford, Boston, New York, and the Philadelphia Athletics. Delegates of the eight teams, four Eastern and four Western, met in New York on February 2, 1876, and the National League of Professional Baseball Clubs was organized—the real beginning of major league baseball.

This was something new: an organization of professional clubs, not of players. Each club was given exclusive control of its own city and all territory within a radius of 5 mi. To determine the league championship, each club would play five games at home and five away with each other club. When a team signed a player, the league office was to be informed, to prevent "revolving." And the league constitution prohibited any team from signing a player who had been discharged or expelled from any other club; in effect, a blacklist was established.

The new league faced many problems in its early years. Few clubs, if any, made money. The Philadelphia Athletics and New York Mutuals were thrown out for not completing their schedules in 1876; St. Louis, Hartford, and Louisville dropped out after the 1877 season and were replaced by Indianapolis, Milwaukee, and Providence. Milwaukee and Providence lasted only one season, but Buffalo, Syracuse, Cleveland, and Troy joined in 1879, making it an eight-team league again.

Gambling and rumors of fixes hurt the league in the eyes of fans. And the 50-cent admission charge, forced by a gentleman's agreement among club owners and then, after 1880, by the league constitution, also kept a lot of fans away.

Team owners began complaining about high salaries as early as 1878. The main reason, of course, was competition among teams for the better players. In the fall of 1879,

owners adopted a policy that any team could keep five players "reserved"; that is, no other league team could attempt to sign any of those five. By 1887 a team could reserve 14 players, and the reserve clause was specifically written into the standard player's contract. As almost any baseball fan knows by now, the reserve clause states that, when a player signs a contract with a team, his services are reserved to that team even after the contract expires. A team can release a player from his contract, but the player can't release the team.

This move made players, in effect, property—it made it possible for teams to trade or sell players (that is, their contracts). The practice has been defended as the cornerstone of baseball and attacked as legalized slavery. It has led to a number of legal battles, the most celebrated being the recent Curt Flood case before the United States Supreme Court.

The American Association. Though the National League was more or less acknowledged as a "major league" by 1880, there were many other leagues and many other teams. St. Louis, Cincinnati, and Louisville were just three of many cities that loved baseball but weren't represented in the league. Philadelphia and New York, like Cincinnati, had been expelled.

On November 2, 1881, a new league was formed at a meeting in Cincinnati. The charter members were the Brooklyn Atlantics, Cincinnati Reds, Louisville, the Pittsburgh Alleghenys, and St. Louis. Brooklyn was later replaced by Baltimore, and the Philadelphia Athletics joined before the first season opened, in 1882.

The new league, the American Association, had a lot going for it. It permitted Sunday baseball and selling liquor on the grounds; teams were allowed to charge 25 cents for admission, instead of the National League's 50 cents; and the six cities represented actually had a larger total population than the National League's eight cities.

During the summer of 1882 the association signed a number of National League players, leading to some court fights. Cincinnati won the first pennant, and began to play a postseason series with the Chicago White Sox, who had won the National League pennant, but the president of the association threatened to expel Cincinnati if the series continued, so it was stopped.

The interleague war heated up in 1883. The American Association added teams in New York and Columbus. The National League quickly got rid of two weak franchises, in Troy and Worcester, and added Philadelphia and New York, which would go head-on against the association teams in those cities. Before the season opened, however, committees representing the two leagues met in a "harmony conference" in New York and worked out an agreement to honor one another's contracts. This was the first National Agreement (a third party to the pact was the Northwestern League, a minor league), which created the structure of Organized Baseball much as it exists today.

The Union Association. No sooner was that settled, however, than a new league was being organized. The Union Association, established late in 1883, quickly announced its opposition to the reserve clause, as a form of slavery. And its clubs began to go after players from the National League and the American Association. They had some success raiding the two major leagues, but they were much more successful in luring players from the weaker Northwestern League.

Organized Baseball's reply was to establish a blacklist. Any National Agreement player jumping to the Union Association would be forever (theoretically) ineligible to play for a National Agreement team. Both the National League and the American Association were hurt, but the Union Association wasn't strong enough to last more than a season. There were just too many teams (34, in all) for the number of potential fans available. Eight cities had two competing teams and Philadelphia had three.

Henry V. Lucas, whose St. Louis team had easily won the Union pennant, was allowed to enter a St. Louis team in the National League, and the league agreed to remove the blacklisting of Union players. These unilateral moves angered the American Association, and touched off another dispute between the two remaining leagues. However, everything was settled at an 1885 meeting at which a new National Agreement was written.

The First ''World Series.'' In 1884 the Providence Greys of the National League and the New York Metropolitans of the American Association decided to play three postseason games to see which was the better team. Providence won all three games. It set a precedent for postseason play between the pennant winners for the next six years. There was no formal arrangement for the series. For example, in 1887, Detroit of the National League challenged St. Louis of the American Association to a postseason series of 15 games, to be played in 10 different cities. Two of the series, including the last one, in 1890, are listed as undecided, because of tie games and disputed forfeits.

But it was a beginning. Many club owners saw the value of a real championship series, in terms of gate receipts and widespread publicity for baseball in general.

Rules Changes, 1876–1890. Baseball as played in 1876 would be rather confusing to the modern spectator. Although all the essentials of today's game were there, there were also many differences. The pitcher was still only 45 ft from home plate, and had to throw the ball underhand. And a batter could request a high or low pitch, through the umpire. A batter, in effect, had to get nine balls for a walk, and was allowed four strikes. There was no formal strike zone: an ''unfair ball'' by the pitcher was a pitch not to the batter's specifications. If the batter had two strikes and let a good pitch go by, the umpire would warn him; if he let another good pitch go, he would be called out.

The first 15 years of the National League saw an almost constant and bewildering succession of rules changes, as baseball experimented to try to find the right balance between offense and defense. A summary of the changes:

1880—Eight balls give batter first base.
1881—Pitching distance lengthened to 50 ft; seven balls give batter first base; third good ball is called strike.
1884—Six balls give batter first base; pitchers allowed to throw overhand or sidearm.
1885—Bats with one flat side permitted.
1886—Five balls give batter first base; pitcher's box enlarged from 6 by 4 ft to 7 by 4.
1887—Batters can no longer ask for high or low pitch; four strikes allowed; seven balls or being hit by a pitch gives batter first base; walk counts as hit; pitchers no longer allowed to take a run and jump before throwing the ball.
1888—Three-strike rule restored; walk no longer counts as hit.
1889—Four balls give batter first base.

The Brotherhood War. After the 1885 season, nine players from the New York Giants organized the Brotherhood of Professional Base Ball Players and elected John Montgomery Ward as president. Ward, once a fine pitcher, had become a fine shortstop after suffering an arm injury. He was a college graduate and was later to become a lawyer.

The Brotherhood soon expanded to other cities. The players were organizing what amounted to a union, for several reasons: They didn't like the blacklist; they didn't like the reserve clause; they felt that, when a player was sold, he should get part of the purchase price; and they especially objected to the 1885 Limit Agreement, under which club owners had agreed to a maximum player salary of $2,000. (The agreement was often circumvented; for example, in 1887 ''King'' Kelly was paid $3,000 ''for the use of his picture,'' in addition to his $2,000 salary.)

After the 1888 season, club owners went even further, adopting a Classification Plan, under which players were to be grouped according to skill, with specific salaries paid to each classification, ranging from $2,500 for Class A to $1,500 for Class E. Players objected and discussed striking. Instead they appointed a grievance committee to try to get the owners to throw out the classification and to forbid player sales. Nothing came of the confrontation.

When the 1889 season was still under way, the players moved. They met with Albert L. Johnson, brother of Cleveland's major. The Johnsons operated two streetcar lines in Cleveland, and they were interested in having a baseball park on one of their lines. By October, groundwork for a new league had been laid; many players had signed and Johnson had rounded up financial support. At a Brotherhood meeting on November 4, 1889, the Player's National League of Base Ball Clubs was formally organized.

The new league gave all players three-year contracts, at the same salaries they had received in 1889. It was governed by a senate of 16 players, 2 from each team, and each team paid $2,500 into a $20,000 prize fund, to be paid to teams after the season, with $7,000 going to the first-place team. It was also agreed that, if a team made a profit of more than $10,000, the excess profits would be split up equally among all league players. Teams were located in Boston, Brooklyn, Buffalo, Chicago, Cleveland, New York, Philadelphia, and Pittsburgh.

The 1890 season was a disaster for everybody. The Players' League outdrew the National League, but suffered an estimated loss of $340,000; the National League may have lost as much as $500,000. Backers of the Players' League, despite Brotherhood protests, negotiated a peace settlement with the National League, providing that all players should return to the teams they had played for in 1889. Most of the backers simply agreed to merge their teams with the National League teams in the same cities.

Another War. A new war quickly broke out when the owner of the Pittsburgh National League team, J. Palmer O'Neill, signed two American Association players, Harry Stovey and Louis Bierbauer. He was entitled to do so—because of a technicality, they were free agents—but the Pittsburgh team immediately became known as the Pirates: the association protested, but the new three-member National Board ruled that the players could stay with Pittsburgh. So the association repudiated the National Agreement and decided to establish a team in Cincinnati, in opposition to the National League team there.

This Boston club won three consecutive National League pennants, 1891 through 1893. Hall of Fame players on the team were Kid Nichols, standing at center; Hugh Duffy, kneeling in front; John Clarkson, seated behind Duffy; and King Kelly, the large, moustached player next to manager Frank Selee. *(Boston Public Library.)*

The result was a fight in which each league raided the other for players. The competition created more problems for teams already drained financially by the Brotherhood war. The American Association was in especially bad shape, and peace feelers began early. However, during what was supposed to be a truce, King Kelly jumped from the association to the Boston National League team, and association owners were angry all over again. But an agreement was signed on December 15, 1891, creating a new 12-team league. Baltimore, Washington, St. Louis, and Louisville joined the eight National League teams; the other four association clubs were bought out.

The new one-league monopoly would last for almost 10 years.

Outstanding Teams Before 1900. The Chicago White Sox were baseball's first dominant team, winning 6 pennants in the first 11 years of the National League. They won the league's first pennant, in 1876, and then, under the leadership of "Cap" Anson, they won three in a row, 1880–1882, and two more in 1885 and 1886. Anson was a playing manager, a slashing hitter who is sometimes credited with inventing the hit-and-run play. He was the game's first great star—the first to write an autobiography. Other outstanding White Sox players were shortstop Fred Williamson, whose 27 home runs in 1884 constituted the record until 1919; Larry Corcoran, the first pitcher to

throw three no-hitters; and John Clarkson, who won 52 games in 1885.

Providence and Boston also had strong teams. Boston won pennants in 1877, 1878, and 1883, and Providence won in 1879 and 1884. The Providence team was led by "Old Hoss" Radbourne, a rubber-armed pitcher who won 60 games and lost 12 in 1884. In his career, Radbourne started 503 games and completed all but 14 of them. Although that was rather unusual, even for the era, it points up one of the major differences between baseball then and now. Relief pitchers were almost unheard off, partly because rosters were much smaller.

After Detroit won the 1887 pennant and New York won two in succession, in 1888 and 1889, Boston became the dominant team, challenged only by Baltimore. The Boston club won three straight, 1891–1893, and then two more, 1897–1898, while Baltimore won the three in between, 1894–1896. Boston, managed by Frank Selee, was led by the outfielders Hugh Duffy, who hit .438 in 1894, and Tom McCarthy, and by "Kid" Nichols, a pitcher. All are members of the Hall of Fame. Outfielder Bobby Lowe was the first man ever to hit four home runs in a game. Jimmy Collins, another Hall of Fame member, became the club's third baseman in 1896. The Baltimore club was a kind of nineteenth-century Gas House Gang, led by third baseman John McGraw, shortstop Hughie Jennings, outfielder "Wee Willie" Keeler, who believed in hitting them "where they ain't," and catcher-captain Wilbert Robinson, later famous as a manager, along with McGraw and Jennings.

One of the American Association's problems was that

the St. Louis Browns were so good. They won four pennants in a row, 1885–1888, and barely missed in 1883 and 1889. The team was captained by Charles Comiskey, a first baseman, and led at the plate by Tip O'Neill, who hit .492 in 1887—the year that walks counted as hits.

The Modern Era Begins

A New Challenge. The National League monopoly was supreme through the end of the nineteenth century. But there was trouble brewing. Owners could now cut salaries, but the wrangling of 1890 had soured many fans, and gate receipts were sharply down in the early 1890s. Betting by owners, managers, and even some players didn't help public confidence in the game. Besides those problems, owners were squabbling with one another about gate receipts and other matters, and there was no real central authority to settle disputes.

Another problem was that, in a 12-team league, there were too many tail-end teams, and public interest was not very high when those teams played. They were a drag on everyone's gate receipts. Several of the teams, especially the St. Louis Browns, were in serious trouble.

By the end of the century the National League presented a confusing picture. The Browns were bought in 1899 by the owner of the Cleveland team, and he moved most of his best players to St. Louis. The owners of the Baltimore and Brooklyn teams merged their interests, but not their teams—in 1899, Ned Hanlon was manager of the Brooklyn team, but president of the Baltimore team! And there were other, similar incestuous relationships among ownerships of other teams. In 1900, Barney Dreyfuss of the Louisville team bought the Pittsburgh team and took most of Louisville's best players with him, including the young Honus Wagner.

By the 1900 season there were only eight teams in the National League—Boston, Brooklyn, Chicago, Cincinnati, New York, Philadelphia, Pittsburgh, and St. Louis.

Then Ban Johnson entered the picture—but not in the National League. Johnson, a former Cincinnati sportswriter, had become president of the Western League, a minor league, in 1894. Late in 1899 the circuit was renamed the American League, and it established teams in Chicago and Cleveland. The Chicago team was headed by Charles Comiskey. Other cities represented were Detroit, Indianapolis, Kansas City, Milwaukee, and Minneapolis. The league had a good season, financially speaking, in 1900. One of its strong points was Johnson, who really ruled the league, and gave his umpires strong, forthright backing—something National League umpires didn't get.

Meanwhile the National League players were organizing again: They formed the Protective Association of Professional Baseball Players in mid-1900. The association wanted some limitations on the reserve clause, protection against unjust salary cuts and fines, and a restriction on trading or selling a player without his approval. The league met with a committee of players, but rejected all demands.

Johnson made his move into the East, setting up franchises in Baltimore, Boston, Philadelphia, and Washington, while Indianapolis, Kansas City, and Minneapolis were dropped. He persuaded Connie Mack to accept part ownership in Philadelphia, while John McGraw headed the Baltimore club.

Once again the National League was losing players to another league. The new league honored contracts but ignored the reserve clause. At least 70 players jumped to the new league, which quickly went ahead in the box-office battle, drawing more than 2,000,000 fans in 1902, against less than 1,700,000 for the National.

The National League did score one coup. John McGraw, suspended by Johnson for his many run-ins with umpires, sold a majority interest to Andrew Freedman of the New York Giants, who promptly transferred the best Baltimore players to the National League team. Johnson countered by moving the Baltimore franchise to New York after the 1902 season.

Tired of two years of financial losses, National League owners decided to sue for peace.

A New National Agreement. National League leaders proposed consolidation into a 12-team league, the same strategy that had ended the American Association, but Johnson wouldn't have any part of it. So the two leagues worked out a peace settlement. Contract claims were settled, with the American League allowed to keep most of the players who had jumped from the National League, and the leagues agreed to honor each other's contracts and reserve rights. The league presidents and the president of the minor league organization also worked out a new National Agreement to govern Organized Baseball.

Under the agreement, a three-man National Commission was established. The major-league presidents were members, and they were to select a third party to serve as chairman. The new agreement protected the minor leagues in several ways, establishing their territorial rights, granting them reserve rights in players, and setting up a system by which major-league teams could draft players from the minors, paying minor-league teams for their contracts.

Baseball had already succeeded pretty well as entertainment. It had developed fans across the country, and it already had a collection of folk heroes. The National Agreement of 1902 gave it a new, solid foundation as a business, consolidating all the gains the game had already made and paving the way for further progress.

August "Garry" Hermann, president of the Cincinnati team, was named chairman of the National Commission. He was to serve until 1920, when the three-man commission was replaced by one virtually all-powerful commissioner.

The Modern World Series. There was no formal agreement between the leagues for a championship playoff, but in 1903 the two pennant winnners, Boston of the American League and Pittsburgh of the National, agreed to play a nine-game series for the world championship. Boston won five of the nine games.

In 1904, however, owner John T. Brush of the New York Giants, not happy with the American League—primarily because the league had a rival team in New York—refused to let his pennant winners play Boston. Ironically, it was Brush who, in 1905, proposed a set of rules for the World Series. The Brush plan was accepted, and the National League voted to make participation in the World Series mandatory for its pennant-winning team. Brush's Giants needed only five games to beat the Athletics that year, and the World Series has been an annual fixture ever since.

Teams and Players, 1901–1920. In the first 20 years of what is called the modern era of baseball, the National League had three dynasties. The Pittsburgh Pirates won the first three pennants of the century, led by Honus Wagner, a shortstop who could do everything. Wagner won eight batting titles, five times led the league in stolen bases, and had great range in the field, along with a strong, accurate arm. Like most dynastic teams, the Pirates also had good pitching, primarily from "Deacon" Phillippe and Jack Chesbro. After a five-year drought, the Pirates won again in 1909.

The outstanding team of the era, though, was John McGraw's New York Giants, who won pennants in 1904–1905, 1911–1913, and 1917. McGraw had many stars during the period, and later, but one of the brightest was Christy Mathewson, a Bucknell University graduate who used his head as well as his arm. Mathewson had a pitch called a fadeaway—what we now call a screwball, one that breaks in the opposite direction from a curve—and another called a "dry spitter," which may have been a knuckle ball, palm ball, or fork ball. He had exceptional control—he once went 68 consecutive innings without issuing a walk—and he made a real art of pitching, throwing to hitters' weaknesses and working to set them up for unexpected pitches.

Joe "Iron Man" McGinnity was another outstanding pitcher on the early Giant teams. In the 1905 World Series,

Mathewson pitched three shutouts against the Athletics and McGinnity threw a shutout for the fourth Giant win. (The Giants lost just one game in that series—when they were shut out by "Chief" Bender.) In 1903, McGinnity set a record by pitching and winning complete games in both ends of a double-header three times, all during August. Other Giant leaders were Roger Bresnahan, who arrived as a center fielder but became an outstanding catcher, and Bill Dahlen, a fine shortstop who stole 547 bases during his career.

The Chicago Cubs won four National League pennants in five years, 1906–1908 and 1910, managed by Frank Chance, "the Peerless Leader" and the first baseman in the famous Tinkers-Evers-Chance double-play combination. The Cubs had a legendary pitcher, "Three-Finger" Brown, whose throwing hand had been badly mutilated in two childhood accidents. He won 20 or more games in 6 consecutive seasons. Ed Reulbach, Carl Lundgren, Jack Pfiester, and Orval Overall were also good starting pitchers, and the Cubs had a fine catcher in Johnny Kling and an outstanding power hitter in "Wildfire" Schulte. In 1906 the team won 116 games, still a record for a single season, and in 1907 they scored the first World Series sweep in history, over Detroit.

Their 1908 pennant was controversial. Late in the season the Cubs and Giants were playing in New York, with the score tied 1-1 in the last of the ninth inning. The Giants had runners on first and third bases when Al Bridwell singled to center field, apparently winning the

The Chicago Cubs won three consecutive National League pennants, 1906 through 1908, under the leadership of player-manager Frank Chance (10). Other outstanding players were "Three-Finger" Brown (3), Johnny Evers (12), Ed Walsh (16), and Joe Tinker (18). *(Boston Public Library.)*

game. But Cub second baseman Johnny Evers called for the ball. The Giant runner on first, Fred Merkle, had run to the clubhouse without touching second base. Evers got the ball and touched second for a forceout on Merkle, nullifying the run. By now, jubilant Giant fans were all over the field and most of the Giants were in the clubhouse, so the game wasn't resumed. The league president, after a dispute, ruled that the game was a tie. The Cubs and Giants finished the season in a tie for first place and the Cubs won a replay of the tie game. The play has gone down in baseball history as "Merkle's boner," but actually it was commonplace then for a runner to leave the field without advancing when the winning run scored. Evers was probably one of the few players of the time who knew that a runner could be forced out in that situation.

The Giants resumed dominance with three consecutive pennants, 1911–1913. Rube Marquard had now joined Mathewson as a pitching ace. They won 49 games between them in 1911, 50 in 1912, and 49 again in 1913. Their catcher was "Chief" Meyers, an American Indian and a Dartmouth graduate. Two other stars were center fielder Fred Snodgrass and second baseman Larry Doyle.

That was the last National League dynasty of the 1901–1920 period. In the next seven years, six different teams won pennants. Only Brooklyn won two, in 1916 and 1920.

During the American League's first 20 years, only 4 teams won pennants more than once—Boston, Chicago, Detroit, and Philadelphia. A Chicago team led by pitcher Clark Griffith and Fielder Jones, a .311 hitter, won the first pennant in 1901. The White Sox did it with pitching and speed, leading the league in team earned-run average and stolen bases. Connie Mack's Philadelphia Athletics, boasting two great left-handed pitchers in Eddie Plank and the eccentric Rube Waddell, won in 1902. They repeated in 1905, after adding another fine pitcher, "Chief" Bender.

Despite the As' fine pitching staff, they finished second in earned-run average to Chicago in 1905, and excellent pitching carried the White Sox' "Hitless Wonders" to the 1906 pennant. The White Sox hit only .230 as a team and their top hitter batted .277. Nick Altrock won 21 games, Ed Walsh and Frank Owen 19 apiece, and Doc White, who led the league in earned-run average, won 18. The White Sox then beat the Cubs in a six-game World Series.

Boston was the first team to win back-to-back American League pennants, in 1903 and 1904. Bill Dineen, who won three games in the first World Series in 1903, and Cy Young were the pitching aces. Young won 28 games in 1903 and 26 in 1904, and Dineen won more than 20 both seasons. Hall-of-Famer Jimmy Collins played third base and managed the club, and outfielder Buck Freeman led the league in home runs and RBIs (runs batted in) in 1903 and was runner-up in both categories in 1904.

The Detroit Tigers, led by Ty Cobb, the first real American League superstar, won three pennants in a row, 1907–1909. Cobb, one of the candidates for the title of greatest player of all time, led the league in hitting all three years and for the following six years. Cobb was just as dazzling and as dangerous on the base paths as in the batter's box, stealing bases almost at will, stretching singles into doubles, advancing two bases on bunts and three bases on singles. Cobb was the epitome of the all-out competitor who cannot bear to lose, and he built a reputation for

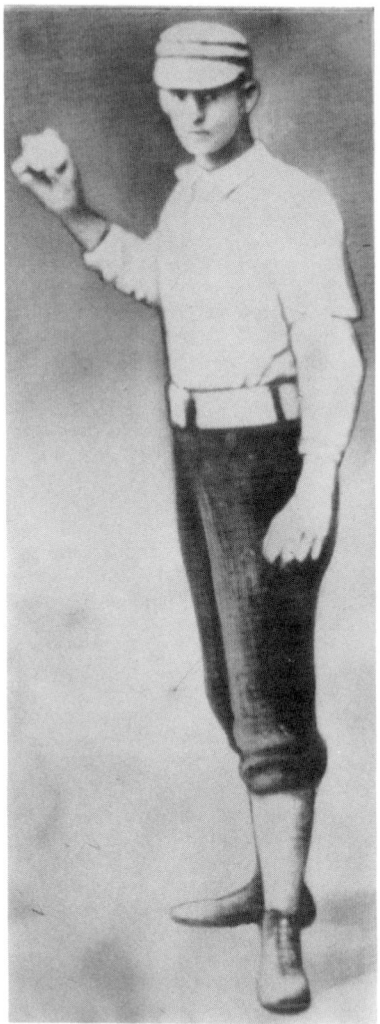

Connie Mack (originally Cornelius MacGillicuddy) arrived in the major leagues in 1886 and remained for more than 50 years as a player, manager, and owner.

dirty play—perhaps not entirely justified—that often intimidated opposing basemen.

The Tigers also had "Wahoo" Sam Crawford, whose 312 career triples is the all-time record; "Germany" Schaefer, a colorful infielder who once stole first base from second, inspiring a rule change; and a pitching staff led by George Mullin, who won 66 games during the 3-year reign. The Tigers, however, lost all three World Series.

The Athletics came back with pennants in 1910–1911 and 1913–1914. Mack had put together his "$100,000 infield" of Stuffy McInnis at first base, Eddie Collins at second, "Home Run" Baker at third, and Jack Barry at shortstop. The team also had strong pitching: Bender, Plank, and Jack Coombs in the first two pennant years, Bender, Plank, "Bullet Joe" Bush, and Bob Shawkey in the next two.

Though his last season was 1928, Ty Cobb holds at least two records that will probably never be broken: He hit over .300 in 23 consecutive seasons, and had a career batting average of .367.

The Boston Red Sox had the last dynasty of the pre-1920 era. Their key was a great outfield, led by Tris Speaker in center. Speaker, an outstanding hitter, was also a great defensive player, as were left fielder Duffy Lewis and right fielder Harry Hooper. The Red Sox won pennants in 1912, when Smoky Joe Wood won 34 games; in 1915, with fine pitching from Rube Foster, Eddie Shore, and a youngster named Babe Ruth; and in 1916, when Ruth won 23 games. Speaker was with Cleveland in 1916, but Ruth led a staff of 5 who won 14 or more games apiece.

The end of the second decade of the century was, in several ways, the end of one era in baseball and the beginning of another. The Red Sox won one more pennant, in 1918, with Ruth playing left field as well as pitching. In 1919 he spent most of his time in the outfield and hit the incredible total of 29 home runs, a major-league record at the time. However, the White Sox, who had won the 1917 pennant, also won in 1919, but lost the World Series to the Cincinnati Reds, who were heavy underdogs.

In 1920, Babe Ruth was with the New York Yankees as a full-time outfielder. And a scandal was brewing.

The Federal League. The last real challenge to organized baseball from an "outlaw" league came in 1913, when the Federal League was formed with teams in Chicago, Cincinnati, Cleveland, Indianapolis, Pittsburgh, and St. Louis. In its first season, the league hired only free agents, but in 1914 it expanded to eight teams and lured some major-league players from their teams—among

them Joe Tinker, Harry Stovall, Bill Killefer, and Mike Doolan.

In 1915 the new league stepped up its raids and signed more than 80 established major leaguers. But the league couldn't compete head-to-head in most cities where it faced competition from American or National League teams, and in December, 1915 a peace treaty was signed. Organized baseball paid $600,000 to the Federal League, which agreed to disband, and two Federal League owners were permitted to buy established teams.

The Golden Age

The Black Sox. Even during the 1919 World Series, there were rumors that the Chicago White Sox were losing dishonestly. Eddie Cicotte, their ace, lost the opener, 9-1, and the Cincinnati Reds won five out of eight. Cicotte, who had a 29-7 record during the regular season, lost two games; Claude "Lefty" Williams, 23-11 during the year, lost the other three. In the fourth game of the series, Cicotte pitched well, but committed two errors in one inning to let both Cincinnati runs score in a 2-0 defeat.

In September, 1920 a grand jury was empaneled in Chicago to investigate gambling on baseball. Many stories suddenly began to emerge, before the grand jury and in the newspapers. Cicotte admitted having accepted $10,000 to throw the series. Eventually, seven other White Sox were implicated: Williams, "Shoeless Joe" Jackson, Chick Gandil, Swede Risberg, Fred McMullin, Happy Felsch, and Buck Weaver. All eight players were indicted. They became known collectively as "Black Sox."

The action opened floodgates; suddenly there were many other stories about previous fixes and attempted fixes. It was revealed that two players, Hal Chase and Heinie Zimmerman, had been banned from baseball in 1919 for being involved in fixed games. Chase, a fine first baseman, had a long history of periodic "indifferent play" and of attempts to bribe teammates. Chase was one of the 11 gamblers also indicted by the Chicago grand jury, along with Abe Attell, a former featherweight boxing champion, who allegedly acted on behalf of gambler Arnold Rothstein to initiate the fix.

The "Black Sox" scandal was the last straw. The National Commission had not been doing its job properly. The World Series fix gave additional impetus to the growing feeling that baseball needed a new kind of government. Club owners drew up plans for a new commission, with three impartial members who would have no financial interest in the sport. After a long controversy, one commissioner was named, Judge Kenesaw Mountain Landis, and the owners decided to let him rule the sport as "czar," with no associate commissioners.

Landis was named on November 12, 1920; a new National Agreement was approved on January 12, 1921, giving the commissioner a free hand in investigating questionable acts and meting out necessary punishment. Landis' first step was to make clear that the eight "Black Sox," who had not yet been tried, wouldn't be welcomed back to major league baseball.

Ruth to the Rescue. The tarnished national pastime needed more than an iron-handed commissioner. It needed a hero who could capture the imagination of the public and make fans forget the "Black Sox." It got him.

George Herman "Babe" Ruth was a gargantua. In 6 seasons with the Boston Red Sox, he was primarily a left-handed pitcher, an exceptionally good one who set a World Series record of 29⅔ consecutive scoreless innings in the 1918 series—a record that stood until 1961. As an outfielder and home-run hitter, however, Ruth became the biggest attraction in baseball. His 29 home runs in 1919 was a record; in 1920 he nearly doubled the figure with 54, then followed with 59 in 1921 and 60 in 1927. He earned $70,000 in 1927—a year in which the average baseball salary was about $8,000.

Ruth was acquired by the New York Yankees from the Red Sox in one of a series of strange deals; the purchase price was $125,000, plus a $300,000 loan from the Yankees to Boston owner Harry Frazee. Fenway Park, home of the Red Sox, was the collateral. With that loan hanging over his head, Frazee systematically sent a whole parade of stars from Boston to New York, helping the Yankees establish and maintain a remarkable dynasty that won six pennants in eight years during the 1920s and five more pennants, including an unprecedented four in a row, in the 1930s.

The Yankee teams of both decades were loaded with stars. The 1927 club is considered by many the greatest in baseball history. In addition to Ruth, the Yankees that year had first baseman Lou Gehrig, who hit 47 home runs

Voted baseball's greatest player in 1971, the centennial year of the major leagues, Babe Ruth began as an outstanding pitcher and then became the game's first great slugger—helping to wipe out the shame of the "Black Sox" scandal in the process. (Wide World.)

Honus Wagner may have been the most versatile player of all time. A sure-handed shortstop with a remarkably strong arm, he led the National League in hits twice, in doubles seven times, in triples twice, in runs scored twice, in runs batted in five times, in stolen bases five times, and in hitting eight times.

and led the league in RBIs with 175. They had 5 starting players who hit over .300 and 4 starters with more than 100 RBIs. Two men, Bob Meusel and Tony Lazzeri, ranked among the top four in stolen bases. Gehrig and Earle Combs finished the season with more than 200 hits. Pitchers Waite Hoyt and Urban Shocker finished one-two in earned-run average, and a rookie relief pitcher, Wilcy Moore, won 19 games.

The Yankees won pennants in 1921–1923 and 1926–1928. They did it against some strong competition, including two mini-dynasties. The Washington Senators won in 1924–1925 and the Philadelphia Athletics in 1929–1931. The Senators for years had had the great pitcher Walter Johnson, and little else. In 1924, Johnson was 36, but he was still a 23-game winner, and the Senators had two Hall of Fame outfielders in Sam Rice and Goose

Goslin. In 1925, Johnson and Stan Coveleskie won 20 apiece; the Senators stole 134 bases to lead the league, and gave up only 699 runs to lead the league in that department again, while Rice hit .350 and Goslin had 113 RBIs.

The Athletics who won three consecutive pennants were also loaded with stars, including Hall-of-Famers Jimmy Foxx, Al Simmons, Mickey Cochrane, and Lefty Grove. Meanwhile the Yankees were in transition. Ruth and Gehrig were still homering and driving in runs, but they were getting older, and other former stars were gone or near the ends of their careers. The Yankee pitching was not what it had been. However, the dynasty was to be re-established.

The National League in the 1920s. The National League had somewhat better balance during the decade. The New York Giants won four pennants in a row, 1921–1924, and beat the Yankees in two out of three World Series. John McGraw's club was not loaded with great names, but it had balance and it was instilled with McGraw's fighting spirit, personified by second baseman Frankie Frisch, the Fordham Flash, who hit for average, stole bases, drove in key runs, and fielded sensationally. Frisch and shortstop Dave "Beauty" Bancroft formed a formidable double-play combination. The pitching was solid but not spectacular. In 1923 the Giants didn't have a pitcher who won more than 16 games; but they had a pair at that figure, a pair who won 13 each, and a 15-game winner.

The Giants typified the National League pennant winners of the 1920s. The home run had not assumed the importance it had in the American League. The Pittsburgh Pirates won the pennant in 1925 by hitting just 77 home runs as a team—but they stole 159 bases. Outfielders Kiki Cuyler and Max Carey were one-two in that department; Cuyler hit .357 and led in runs scored and triples. The Pirates repeated in 1927 with Paul and Lloyd Waner replacing Cuyler and Carey. Paul led in hitting with .380 and in RBIs with 131; Lloyd hit .355. As a team the Pirates hit only 54 home runs—6 fewer than Babe Ruth hit that season—but they led the league in runs scored.

It was the St. Louis Cardinals' "Gas House Gang" that gave a name to that kind of baseball. The Cardinal pennant team of 1926 was built pretty much on hitting from Rogers Hornsby, "Sunny Jim" Bottomley, and others. But in 1928 the Cardinals had added Frisch, in a controversial trade for Hornsby, and little Rabbit Maranville was playing beside him at shortstop. They also had two solid starting pitchers and good relief pitching. The Cardinals didn't really become the "Gas House Gang," though, until the next decade.

The 1930s. The St. Louis Cardinals won three of the first five pennants of the next decade. They had a rather nondescript lineup in 1930, although Frisch and Bottomley were still on the right side of the infield. Their best pitcher won only 15 games, but four others won 12 or more. In 1931 a rookie named "Pepper" Martin arrived to play center field. He hit .349, the Cardinals had four of the top five base stealers in the league, and six pitchers won 11 games or more. This was the "Gas House Gang," and Martin, who hitched rides on freight trains to get to spring training and was famous for his belly-flopping, uniform-dirtying slides, was their spiritual leader. They slumped to seventh in 1932, but won again in 1934, with a young Leo Durocher at shortstop, Joe Medwick in left field, and Martin playing third base, where he usually

stopped the ball with his chest before picking it up and throwing to first. Dizzy Dean won 30 games and his brother Paul won 19. Although Leo Durocher did give the "Gas House Gang" nickname to the team in 1934, it has often been applied retroactively, so to speak, to the 1931 team as well.

The Chicago Cubs won pennants in 1932, 1935, and 1938. Their top stars were first baseman Charlie Grimm, second baseman Billy Herman, catcher Gabby Hartnett, and pitcher Lon Warneke in 1932; in 1935, Phil Cavaretta had taken over at first base and Stan Hack became a star at third.

Bill Terry's New York Giants were the pennant winners in 1933, 1936, and 1937. They had one of the best pitchers in baseball, "King" Carl Hubbell, who baffled hitters with his screwball, and Mel Ott led the league in home runs in 1936 and 1937. The decade ended with the Cincinnati Reds on top, as they also were in 1940. The Reds, under Bill McKechnie, did it primarily on the pitching of Bucky Walters and Paul Derringer; they won 52 games between them in 1939, 42 in 1940.

The New York Yankees, despite a constantly changing cast, were still the dominant team in baseball in the 1930s. They won five American League pennants and five World Series. After the Philadelphia Athletics won their three consecutive pennants, 1929–1931, the Yankees won in 1932 with an aging team that still had many of the 1927 stars, including Ruth, Gehrig, and Lazzeri. Then Joe McCarthy did some rebuilding. In 1936, Gehrig and Lazzeri were still starters, but Ruth was gone, and young Joe DiMaggio was in center field. Frank Crosetti was now the shortstop and Red Rolfe was at third base. Red Ruffing was the club's top pitcher; he won 20 games or more four years in a row, and the Yankees won four pennants in a row, the first American League team ever to do so. They also won four World Series in succession. By 1939, Gehrig and Lazzeri had been replaced by Babe Dahlgren and Joe "Flash" Gordon, and Charlie "King Kong" Keller had taken over an outfield post. DiMaggio was now the team leader and one of the game's brightest stars.

Other teams to win pennants during the thirties were Washington, led by shortstop-manager Joe Cronin, in 1933, and Detroit, in 1934 and 1935. The Detroit lineup included home-run hitter Hank Greenberg at first base, Charlie Gehringer at second, Goose Goslin in the outfield, Mickey Cochrane behind the plate, and pitchers Tommy Bridges and "Schoolboy" Rowe. Cochrane managed the club.

World War II. The Detroit Tigers won another American League pennant in 1940, and then the Yankees took over again; 1941 began a 24-year period in which the Yankees were to win 18 pennants and 12 World Series. They won three in a row, 1941–1943. The Yankees' power—they led the league in home runs in all three years—almost obscured their great defense, anchored by DiMaggio and shortstop Phil Rizzuto.

World War II brought some discussion about whether major-league baseball should be suspended for the duration. By 1944 there was a serious shortage of manpower, but the teams struggled on with raw youngsters and long-in-the-tooth veterans. The St. Louis Cardinals, who had built up the first real farm system in baseball under the guidance of Branch Rickey, were least affected by the war. They finished second to Leo Durocher's Brooklyn Dodgers in 1941, then won pennants in 1942–1944 and in 1946.

The Cardinals had the balance so typical of top National League teams—the hitting of Stan Musial, the hustle of Enos Slaughter, the defense of shortstop Marty Marion, and the pitching of Mort Cooper, who won 65 games during the first three pennant years.

The war produced a couple of unlikely champions in the American League, however. The St. Louis Browns won their only pennant in 1944. The Tigers won in 1945 with a somewhat better lineup; Hal Newhouser won 25 games and Dizzy Trout 18. But Detroit's starting center fielder was the 39-year-old Doc Cramer. Talent was so scarce that the 1945 All-Star game was canceled.

Postwar Progress

From 1901, the beginning of the modern era, through 1945, baseball had changed surprisingly little, except for the home-run revolution led by Babe Ruth. Branch Rickey, first at St. Louis and then at Brooklyn, had developed to its fullest the idea of a farm system composed of minor-league teams, and other clubs were following suit. Lights had been installed in the Cincinnati park in 1935, but the baseball establishment was slow to accept the idea of night baseball. Teams still traveled by train. They could do so, because the "national pastime" didn't have a major-league franchise farther west than St. Louis. Not only that, but the sport had systematically excluded a sizable segment of the American population from its teams.

In some ways Judge Landis had probably prevented progress. He didn't like the farm system and had held it back by declaring a number of players free agents. He didn't like the night baseball and only reluctantly gave Cincinnati permission to play seven night games during the 1935 season.

A new era began—or began to begin—in 1944, when Landis died of a coronary thrombosis at the age of 78. He was replaced in 1945 by A. B. "Happy" Chandler, formerly governor of Kentucky. When the war ended, Americans were eager to begin enjoying themselves again, and baseball—along with other sports—was one of the chief beneficiaries.

The end of the war also released a large reserve of talent, including many young baseball players who weren't yet committed to any major league team—and the teams went after them with offers of bonus money for signing. The situation was complicated by the formation of the Mexican League, which sought established players with bonus offers, too. Several stars went to Mexico, despite Chandler's warning that they would be suspended for five years if they dared to jump.

The postwar prosperity, the bonuses, and the minor war with the Mexican League all helped to boost player salaries to new heights. Most important to baseball's future, however, was the announcement in 1942 by Branch Rickey that a new Negro baseball league was being formed; among its members was to be a Brooklyn team called the Brown Dodgers. The announcement was a smoke screen.

Jackie Robinson. Rickey merely wanted an excuse for scouting and signing black players before revealing his real intentions. He revealed them to Jackie Robinson, a former football star at the University of California, Los Angeles (UCLA) and a shortstop with the black Kansas City Monarchs, in 1945, when he signed Robinson for the Brooklyn organization. Robinson was going to play with the Dodgers, not the Brown Dodgers. He led the International League in hitting with the Dodgers' Montreal farm club in 1946. The following year, he moved to the Dodgers and, at an unfamiliar position, first base, he was named Rookie of the Year. In 1949, at second base, he was named the league's Most Valuable Player.

Once Robinson had demonstrated his ability, not only to play the game but to provide inspirational leadership and to withstand the tremendous pressures of being a door-opener, other teams began to sign black players. But the Dodgers had been first, and, partly for that reason, they were the dominant team in the National League from 1947 through 1956. In that period the Dodgers had the league's Most Valuable Player five times, the Rookie of the Year eight times—and, in every case, the player was black. They also won six pennants, led by such black stars as Robinson, catcher Roy Campanella, infielder Junior Gilliam, and pitchers Don Newcombe and Joe Black, along with white stars Peewee Reese, Duke Snider, Carl Furillo, Gil Hodges, and Carl Erskine.

Yankees and More Yankees. Other sports have had their dynasties, but there has never been, and probably never will be, any dynasty comparable to the Yankees' postwar one. The great Yankee teams of those years were largely built on money accumulated from previous dynasties. The Yankees, more than any other team, could attract young players with bonus offers. They were able to pay for a far-flung scouting system. And, when necessary, they were able to buy established players from less successful teams that needed the money.

Casey Stengel was also a big part of the Yankee postwar story. His unique brand of double talk made him seem like a clown to many; he was called a push-button manager by those who thought the Yankees had so much talent that anyone could win a pennant with the club. But dynasties are built on more than sheer player talent. As Vince Lombardi, John Wooden, and Red Auerbach are credited for building other great teams, Stengel must receive some credit for the Yankee juggernauts of the 1950s.

In 1949, Stengel had much the same team that had finished third in 1948. He made the most of it. He juggled lineups, pinch-hit frequently, platooned right-handed hitters against left-handed pitchers and vice versa, and showed other managers what a good relief pitcher could do, as Joe Page appeared in 60 games, won 13, and saved 27. The Yankees won the first of an unprecedented five consecutive pennants. After losing in 1954, they won four more in a row. Then they won another five in a row, 1960 through 1964—but they had three managers during that period, Stengel managing only in 1960.

The talent was there, of course—in abundance. In 1951 the Yankees had Jerry Coleman at second base, Bobby Brown at third, and Joe DiMaggio in center field. In 1952, Gil McDougald took over at third, Billy Martin became the second baseman, and Mickey Mantle replaced DiMaggio. And the Yankees won the pennant again, with the help of pitcher Johnny Sain and first baseman–pinch hitter John Mize, both purchased from National League teams to help out. In 1955 the Yankees had three new infielders, including Bill Skowron at first, and they didn't have a 20-game winner. But they led the league in shutouts with 18 and won a pennant.

Starting in 1957, strange things began to happen to the

Yankees. They began to lose to National League teams in the World Series. In eight years from 1957 through 1964, the National League won five World Series, with four different teams. Seven times the Yankees were in the Series, and four times they lost. Three times they discharged a pennant-winning manager who lost the World Series; Stengel was the victim in 1960, Ralph Houk in 1963, Yogi Berra in 1964.

Other American League Teams. There were some other American League pennant winners between the end of the war and the mid-1960s. The Boston Red Sox seemed to have a powerhouse in 1946 when they won their first pennant since 1918. Ted Williams hit .342, with 38 home runs and 123 RBIs, shortstop Johnny Pesky hit .355, and Ted Hughson and Boo Ferris won 45 games between them. In 1948 the Red Sox tied the Cleveland Indians for first place, but the Indians won the one-game playoff for the pennant. The Indians had the first black player in the American League, center fielder Larry Doby. They also got 26 shutouts from their pitching staff, as Bob Lemon and Gene Bearden won 20 apiece, while Bob Feller won 19. Cleveland repeated in 1954, with even better pitching: Lemon and Early Wynn each won 23, Mike Garcia won 19, Art Houtteman 15, and Feller 13. Second baseman Bobby Avila led the league in hitting, with a .341 average, and Doby led in home runs and RBIs.

In 1959, Early Wynn won 22 games for the Chicago White Sox, and they won the pennant. The White Sox resembled a National League team: They hit only .253, but stole 113 bases—the next highest team total in the league was 68—and played good defense, with Luis Aparicio at shortstop, Nellie Fox at second, and Jim Landis in center field.

The next time a team other than the Yankees won the American League pennant, baseball had entered a new era.

Movement and Expansion

For 50 seasons, major-league baseball was made up of the same 16 teams in the same 11 cities—meaning that there were five cities with two teams. Postwar prosperity had also brought inflation, and the weaker teams were having trouble surviving. Two teams in particular that faced serious financial problems were the St. Louis Browns of the American League and the Boston Braves of the National League. In 1952 there were rumors that both teams wanted to move to Milwaukee, where a new stadium was being built. In the spring of 1953, National League owners gave the Braves permission to make the move. After 13 games in their new stadium, the Braves surpassed their entire 1952 home attendance.

The Braves' move set a precedent—not only for moves by established franchises, but for major-league expansion into many cities, like Milwaukee, that wanted teams. Several factors came into play. Most existing major-league parks were near downtown areas, where parking was a problem. Many fast-growing cities were without major-league baseball, while several cities simply couldn't support two teams. Congress had investigated baseball in 1951 and had urged that the sport consider expansion into some of the cities that were waiting for it. Cities and counties were building new fields and stadiums, often in suburban areas that could draw on metropolitan populations and provide extensive parking for those who came by car.

In 1954 the St. Louis Browns became the Baltimore Orioles, and the following year the Philadelphia Athletics moved to Kansas City. Baseball became a truly national sport in 1958, when two metropolitan New York franchises moved all the way to the Pacific Coast—the Brooklyn Dodgers to Los Angeles and the New York Giants to San Francisco.

By 1960 there were many cities clamoring for teams, and not enough teams to go around. Branch Rickey, now out of baseball, announced that he was involved in organizing a third major league, the Continental League. Major-league baseball responded to the threat quickly by announcing plans for expansion. In 1961 the Washington Senators became the Minnesota Twins, to be replaced in Washington by a new Senators franchise, and the American League also established a new team in Los Angeles (now the California Angels, in Anaheim). The National League moved into Houston and back into New York with new franchises in 1962.

The National League, 1947–1964. Branch Rickey's old team, the St. Louis Cardinals, and his new team, the Brooklyn Dodgers, had to meet in a playoff to decide the 1946 pennant; the Cardinals won, then went on to beat the Boston Red Sox in the World Series. The Dodgers won in 1947 and 1949; in between, it was the Boston Braves, with the pitching of Warren Spahn and Johnny Sain. In 1950 the upstart "Whiz Kid" Philadelphia Phillies won the pennant, largely on the strength of pitching by Robin Roberts and Curt Simmons. Then, in 1951, came a pennant race that overshadowed the World Series in drama.

Leo Durocher had left the Dodgers in mid-1948 to manage the Giants. It took him a while to build his kind of team, but the acquisition of shortstop Al Dark and second baseman Eddie Stanky helped. In 1951 the Giants brought up a center fielder named Willie Mays. It took a couple of months for Mays to hit his stride. On August 11, 1951, the Giants were 13½ games behind the Dodgers. In the last game of the year, the Giants beat the Braves to tie the Dodgers for first place, having won 37 of their last 44 games. The Giants met the Dodgers in a three-game playoff for the pennant. The teams split the first two games. In the third, the Giants were losing, 4-1, in the ninth inning. They scored a run and had men on second and third with one out. Then Bobby Thomson hit a three-run home run off Ralph Branca for a 5-4 victory and the pennant, in one of the most dramatic moments in sports.

The Dodgers survived; they won the pennant in 1952 and 1953. In 1954 it was the Giants again, and they beat Cleveland in four consecutive games in the World Series. In 1955 the Dodgers not only won the pennant; they finally won a World Series for the first time in eight tries. The Dodgers of those years didn't fit the usual National League pattern. They were a power team, aided by a small park. In 1953, Duke Snider hit 42 home runs, Roy Campanella 41, Gil Hodges 31, and Carl Furillo 21. In 1955, Snider again hit 42, Campanella 32, Hodges 27, and Furillo 26.

The 1955 Dodger victory marked the first time the Yankees had lost a World Series since 1942, and the first time the National League had won two in succession since 1933–1934. The Yankees came back to beat the Dodgers in 1956, but in 1957 they lost to the Milwaukee Braves, who had the pitching of Warren Spahn and Lew Burdette—Burdette beat the Yankees three times—and power hitting from Henry Aaron, Ed Mathews, and Joe Adcock. In 1958, however, the Yankees beat the Braves.

In one of baseball's most famous games, Bobby Thomson hits the three-run homer (dotted line) that won the National League play-off for the Giants over the Dodgers in 1951. *(Public Broadcasting Service.)*

The World Series went to the West Coast for the first time in 1959, when the Dodgers won the pennant in their second year in Los Angeles. They met the Chicago White Sox. Neither team was really very impressive. The Dodgers had beaten the Braves in a playoff, but the Braves seemed much the better team. The White Sox had an aging team with a couple of marginal younger players. But they had fine pitching and they stole a lot of bases. The Dodgers won the series; the following year, they slumped to fourth place, the White Sox to third.

Two years later, expansion came; despite critics who said it represented a watering-down of the sport, expansion actually seemed to produce a more exciting form of baseball. Players who might otherwise have languished in the farm systems of better teams became starters with expansion teams. And, whether expansion had anything to do with it or not, the Yankee dynasty died, never to return, and it became hard for a National League team to win even two successive pennants.

After Pittsburgh beat the Yankees in the 1960 World Series, Stengel was "retired" and replaced by Ralph Houk, who won two World Series in a row. In 1963, though, the Dodgers beat the Yankees four games in a row—the first time that had happened to the Yankees since 1922—and Houk moved to the front office, to be replaced by Yogi Berra. Under Berra the Yankees won a fifth straight pennant, but lost the World Series to St. Louis, and Berra was fired. His replacement was Johnny Keane, who had managed St. Louis. But Keane inherited an aging team that no longer had the capability to bring up outstanding youngsters from the farm system or buy veterans from teams that needed the money.

In 1965 the Yankees finished sixth in the 10-team league. The Minnesota Twins won the American League pennant. They had been the Washington Senators before moving to Minneapolis–St. Paul in 1961, to be replaced in Washington by a new franchise. They lost to Los Angeles in a seven-game World Series in which Sandy Koufax, who had won 26 games during the season, pitched two shutouts and struck out 29 men in 24 innings.

The Dodgers lost to Baltimore in 1966, when the Yankees finished dead last in the American League. Baltimore seemed to have the makings of a dynasty, but slumped to sixth place in 1967, when the Boston Red Sox won an exciting three-team race on the last day of the season, but lost to St. Louis in the World Series. The Red Sox were led to the pennant by outfielder Carl Yastrzemski, who won the triple crown, and by pitcher Jim Lonborg, who won 22 games and lost 9. The Cardinals had good balance. Lou Brock stole 52 bases in the regular season and 7 in the World Series, Orlando Cepeda led the league with 111 RBIs, and Bob Gibson, who had missed much of the season with a broken leg, pitched 3 complete-game victories in the series. St. Louis won another pennant in 1968, but lost to Detroit in the World Series.

Playoffs. Both leagues added two more teams in 1969. The American League put teams in Kansas City—the Athletics had moved to Oakland—and in Seattle. Seattle lasted just one year before the team moved to Milwaukee in 1970. The National League added teams in San Diego and in Montreal—the first franchise outside the United States.

Because 12-team pennant races don't encourage good attendance, each league was split into two 6-team divisions, with division champions meeting in a best-of-five playoff to determine the pennant winners.

The new system immediately brought a "miracle"—not that the system gets the credit. The New York Mets, who had set new records for futility in their early years, even with Casey Stengel managing them, won the National League's Eastern Division title, then beat the Atlanta Braves (formerly of Boston and Milwaukee) for the pennant and then—miracle of miracles—beat the powerful Baltimore Orioles in the World Series. Even though their ace, Tom Seaver, lost the first game, the Mets beat the Orioles four out of five.

A year later the Orioles were being called "the best damn team in baseball." After beating Minnesota in the American League playoff, they won the World Series from Cincinnati in five games. The Orioles had great pitching from Jim Palmer, Dave McNally, and Mike Cuellar; good hitting from Frank Robinson and Boog Powell; and an inspired defense, led by third baseman Brooks Robinson, who was named the most valuable player in the series for a number of spectacular defensive plays and timely hitting.

There were those who thought the Orioles were a new baseball dynasty; they won their third straight pennant by beating Oakland in the 1971 playoff, but lost to Pittsburgh in the World Series. The Pirates had a free-swing-

ing team led by a long-underrated right fielder, Roberto Clemente, who was killed in a plane crash the following New Year's Eve.

The real dynasty was being built in Oakland. The Athletics won not only three consecutive pennants, 1972–1974, but all three World Series as well, beating Cincinnati, the Mets, and the Dodgers, in that order. The A's had everything: four good starting pitchers, led by Jim "Catfish" Hunter, and a strong bullpen; all-around great play from right fielder Reggie Jackson; the base running of shortstop Bert Campaneris; clutch hitting from third baseman Sal Bando and left fielder Joe Rudi; and all-around fine defense. Their balance was displayed by their 1972 World Series victory, despite the absence of superstar Jackson, who had suffered a leg injury in the league playoffs.

However, a surprising young Boston Red Sox team beat Oakland in three straight games in the 1975 playoffs. Boston center fielder Fred Lynn was the first player ever to be named rookie of the year and most valuable player in the same season, and outfielder Jim Rice finished second to Lynn in rookie of the year balloting.

Cincinnati's "Big Red Machine," a National League power for several seasons, finally won a world championship by beating the Red Sox in one of the most exciting World Series in history. Five of the seven games were won by one-run margins, and the final game was in doubt until Cincinnati second baseman Joe Morgan singled home the winning run with two outs in the 9th inning.

Morgan was his league's most valuable player and third baseman Pete Rose was named most valuable player in the Series. The Reds had outstanding hitting throughout the lineup, and four fine relief pitchers continually rescued a starting staff that had three pitchers with 15 victories apiece.

The Designated Hitter. Oakland owner Charles Finley upset a large segment of the baseball establishment by suggesting a whole series of changes to enliven the game at a time when it seemed that pro football was replacing baseball as the national pastime, in terms of attendance and television viewership.

Most of Finley's suggestions—using an orange baseball for better visibility, for example, and giving the batter a walk on three balls instead of four—were laughed at. But one Finley idea did bear fruit. In the first really significant rule change since the outlawing of the spitball in 1920, the American League in 1973 adopted the designated-hitter rule, allowing a team to use a ninth hitter to replace the pitcher in the batting order. The designated hitter doesn't play in the field, although he can be inserted defensively after he has started the game as the DH. If he is used on defense, the team no longer has a designated hitter and the pitcher must then bat for himself, in the spot in the batting order vacated by the player who was replaced in the field.

The National League refused to go along with the rule, but most minor leagues did. Many observers thought the American League would be severely hampered in the World Series, where the rule would not be used. But, oddly enough, Oakland pitchers hit well in the 1973 and 1974 World Series, even though they had not had a time at bat during either regular season.

Finley also suggested a designated-runner rule, but without receiving much support.

The Player Strike. Although each player has an individual contract, many provisions of the contract are standardized in the Basic Agreement, which is similar to a contract between a union and an employer. It is signed by representatives of the Major League Players Association and by the league presidents and the 24 club officials.

The Basic Agreement, among other things, sets a minimum player salary, establishes the length of the season and certain rules that must be followed in scheduling, and makes provisions for expense allowances, severance pay, and the division of championship and World Series receipts. Like other such contracts, the Basic Agreement is in effect only for a certain term—usually three years—and must then be renegotiated.

Players have a separate agreement with the major leagues covering pension benefits. In 1972, when this agreement came up for renewal, the players sought an increase in benefits. Owners were opposed. After long negotiations that accomplished little, the players voted on April 1 to go on strike. The season was scheduled to begin on April 5. It actually didn't begin until April 15, after the players got approximately what they wanted, except that the pension contract was extended only one year so that it could be renegotiated along with the Basic Agreement, which would also expire in 1973.

The Reserve Clause. There have been several disputes over baseball's reserve clause through the years. Its most serious challenge came in a suit filed in 1970 by Curt Flood, a center fielder for the St. Louis Cardinals who refused to report to Philadelphia after being traded. The reserve clause binds a player to the team with which he signs a contract. Even a one-year contract binds the player indefinitely; the team can sell or trade his contract to another team, but the player can't move to another team on his own initiative.

In 1972 the U.S. Supreme Court, in a 5-3 decision, rejected Flood's challenge, largely on the grounds that previous decisions had given baseball an exemption from the antitrust laws and that Congress had never acted to remove that exemption. There was some speculation that the players' association would attempt to have the reserve clause modified in 1973, when the Basic Agreement was due for renewal. The players did win some minor changes in the clause. The most important gave any 10-year major-league veteran the right to decide whether he will agree to his trade to another team. Another change provided that a five-year veteran cannot be sent to the minor leagues without his consent.

The players also won a major victory in the form of salary arbitration. If a player has two years of major-league service, and major-league service in three different seasons, he can submit his salary to arbitration when he and his team can't agree on a figure. "Either-or" arbitration is used: The arbitrator must accept either the team's final offer or the player's demand, and no figure in between. The arbitration is binding on both player and team.

More extreme changes were made in 1976, after a court ruled that pitcher Andy Messersmith had a right to play for any team he chose after having played out his reserve year with the Los Angeles Dodgers in 1975 without having signed a new contract. The new agreement specifies that a player becomes a free agent after having played out his reserve year, but it places a limit on the number of teams a player can bargain with and on the number of free agents

a team can sign. A 6-year veteran is given a 15-day period after the World Series when he can become a free agent by simply notifying his team of his intention. A 5-year veteran can demand to be traded, and can designate six teams to which he will not accept a trade. If not traded by March 15 before the next season, he becomes a free agent.

Baseball Rules

Equipment. The baseball is 9–9¼ in, in circumference, and 5–5¼ oz in weight. It is made of wool and twine wrapped around a rubber-covered cork center, then covered with two strips of white leather, stitched together. The bat must be no more than 42 in long and 2¾ in thick at its greatest diameter. It must be made of one solid piece of wood, generally circular in cross section.

The catcher wears a mask, chest protector, shin guards, and a leather glove, or mitt, of any size or weight. The first baseman may use a leather glove no more than 12 in long and no more than 8 in wide, with leather or lacing between the thumb and palm. Other fielders may wear leather gloves of the same maximum dimensions, but they must be finger-type gloves, not trapping mitts of the type used by the first baseman.

Playing Field. The baseball "diamond" is actually a square, 90 ft on a side. Home plate is a five-sided slab of white rubber, set flush with the ground; its pointed angle fits into one corner of the diamond. The plate is 17 in wide on its longest side, which is parallel to the pitcher's rubber. At each of the other three corners of the diamond is a base, a stuffed canvas bag 15 in square.

Base paths are marked by chalked lines. The lines between home plate and first base and between home plate and third base are extended beyond the bases to the outfield fences, forming a large V which is "fair territory."

The pitcher's mound is a circular area of dirt, 18 ft in diameter, built up to no more than 10 in at its highest point. At its center is the pitcher's plate, or rubber: a white rubber slab set flush with the ground. It is 2 ft long and 6 in wide. The front edge of the rubber is 60 ft, 6 in from the farthest portion of home plate.

Defensive Positions. There are nine players in each starting lineup. Two of them, the pitcher and catcher, form the "battery"; they are the only players who must take a definite spot on the field. The pitcher, before beginning the delivery, must have one foot on the rubber and, once the pitching motion is begun, the foot must remain there until the ball is released. The catcher must stay in the catcher's box, a rectangle 8 ft long and 43 in wide, from the moment the pitcher's motion is begun until the ball leaves the pitcher's hand.

Other defensive players may take up any positions they wish, but they must be in fair territory when the pitcher delivers the ball.

Progress of Play. The game begins with the visiting team at bat and the home team in the field. After three outs, the visiting team is retired and the home team comes to bat. Once both teams have had a turn at bat, an inning is completed. A regulation game consists of nine innings.

The object of the game is to score runs by advancing runners around the bases, in sequence; each runner who reaches home plate scores a run. The team with the most runs at the end of nine innings wins the game. If the score is tied after nine innings have been played, the game continues until, at the end of an inning, one team is ahead. If, at the end of eight and a half innings, the home team is ahead, the game is over. If, at any point after eight and a half innings, the home team goes ahead, the game ends immediately.

The Batter. The batter must stand in a chalk-lined box, to the left or right of home plate. Once this position is taken, and the ball is in possession of the pitcher while on the rubber, the batter can't leave the box without asking the umpire to call time out. Time out cannot be called once the pitcher's motion has begun.

The batter may swing or not at any delivery by the pitcher. If the batter swings and fails to hit the ball, it is a strike. If the batter hits the ball into foul territory, it is also a strike, unless the count is already two strikes. If, with a count of two strikes, the batter bunts the ball foul, or foul-tips the ball directly into the catcher's mitt, it is a third strike.

It is also a strike if the batter doesn't swing at a pitch that passes through the strike zone, a space defined by the width of the plate and by the knees and armpits of the batter when the batter is in a normal stance. If the pitch does not pass through the strike zone and the batter doesn't swing at it, it is a "ball."

After three strikes, the batter is out. (However, the catcher must catch the third strike to retire the batter. If the catcher doesn't catch it, the batter can attempt to go to first base, and the catcher must then tag or throw out the batter. This exception doesn't apply if first base is occupied, and there are fewer than two outs.) After four balls, the batter is entitled to go to first base.

The batter is also out if:

■ The batted ball, fair or foul, is caught by a fielder before it touches the ground or any other object.
■ The third strike hits the batter.
■ The batted fair ball hits the batter before it touches a fielder.
■ The batter hits the ball in fair territory and it is held by a fielder on first base before the batter reaches the base, or if the batter is touched by the ball, in possession of a fielder, before reaching the base.
■ The batter deliberately drops, throws, or otherwise uses the bat to touch a fair ball.

The batter is awarded first base if:

■ The batter is hit by a pitch, unless the batter swung at it.
■ The batter is interfered with, by the catcher or any other fielder, when swinging or when attempting to run to first base.
■ The batted fair ball hits an umpire before it touches or passes a fielder other than the pitcher.
■ The batted fair ball hits a runner before touching or passing a fielder other than the pitcher. (The runner is out, and no other runner may advance, unless forced to advance.)

If the batter hits a fair ball over the fence, it is a home run, and the batter is entitled to advance around the bases. (Each base must be touched in turn.) If the ball bounces over the fence, the batter is normally awarded two bases (a ground-rule double), and each runner also advances two bases.

The Runner. The basic rules involving runners are:

■ Once a runner has gained a base, that runner alone is entitled to the base, unless required to advance.
■ However, the batter who hits a fair ball becomes a runner and is entitled to first base, and the runner originally on first base must advance to second. If there is also a runner on second, there

must be a corresponding advance to third; if there is also a runner on third, that runner must advance to home plate.

■ A runner is out if tagged by a fielder with the live ball while the runner is off base.
■ If a runner is required to advance, the runner is awarded the next base when the batter is awarded first base.
■ A runner who is required to advance doesn't have to be tagged out; the runner is out when the base is tagged before the runner reaches it. However, if the runner following the first one is put out, the force is removed. (For example, there is a runner on first base. The ball is hit to the pitcher, who throws the batter out at first base. The force is now removed and the runner who was on first base must be tagged out; that runner may now return to first base.)
■ To score, a runner must touch the bases in their proper order.
■ A runner starting from a given base cannot advance on a caught fly ball unless he or she first retouches that base after the catch.
■ A runner, when required to retouch, must retouch all bases in reverse order.
■ If two runners are on the same base, the first runner to reach it is entitled to it, unless required to advance. The second runner must return to the previous base before being tagged, or before the previous base is tagged.
■ If the batter hits a home run, all runners are entitled to advance around the bases to home plate, but they must touch each base in the proper order.

The runner is entitled to advance:

■ One base, if a fielder, after catching a fly ball, falls into a bench or a stand.
■ One base if, when the runner is attempting to steal, the batter is interfered with.
■ Two bases if a fielder deliberately touches a thrown ball with glove, cap, mask, or any other part of the uniform while such an item is not in its usual place. (If, for example, a fielder attempts to use cap or mask to catch the ball, or if the fielder throws a glove at the ball.)
■ Two bases if a thrown ball goes into the stands or a bench, or through a fence or screen, or if it is caught in the meshes of a screen. (However, the runner gets only one base if this occurs on a pitch, or on a throw by the pitcher in an attempt to pick a runner off base.)
■ Three bases, if a fielder deliberately touches a batted ball with glove, cap, mask, or another part of the uniform while it is not in its usual place.

Interference and Obstruction. Interference is usually the act of a batter or runner that makes it difficult for a fielder to make a play. The player interfering is usually called out. Obstruction is the act of a defensive player that impedes a runner's attempt to advance. The runner is awarded one or more bases.

It is interference when:

■ A runner deliberately interferes with a thrown ball, or with a fielder trying to make a play on a batted ball. (If, in the umpire's judgment, the interference prevented a double play, both runners are called out.)
■ A runner is hit by a batted ball before it passes or is touched by a fielder. (The batter is awarded first base.)
■ A runner deliberately kicks a batted ball, even after it has passed or been touched by a fielder.
■ A coach physically assists a runner by touching the runner.

Obstruction plays arise rarely; it is important to note that the fielder who is making a play has the right of way, and it is up to the runner to avoid the fielder. However, if a fielder who is not involved in the play stands in a runner's path, it is obstruction. If a play is being made, or is about to be made, on the obstructed runner, the runner is awarded at least one base. If no play is being made on the runner, play continues; when it is complete, the umpire can impose penalties to nullify the obstruction, by awarding as many additional bases to the runner as the umpire feels the obstruction cost the runner.

Appeal Plays. On certain plays, it is up to the fielding team to point out a violation of rules to an umpire before the umpire can take any action. If a runner misses a base, for example, the umpire cannot simply call the runner out. Before the next pitch to the batter, or the next play (such as an attempted pick-off), a member of the fielding team must throw the ball to that base, tag the base, and appeal to the umpire, who then rules on whether or not the runner did miss the base.

It is also an appeal play if the runner leaves base before a fly ball is caught; if the runner misses home plate while sliding in an attempt to score; or if the runner overruns or overslides first base and doesn't return immediately.

Dead Balls. Normally, a runner may attempt to advance at his own peril whenever the ball is alive (in play). If the ball is dead, however, runners may not advance, nor may they be put out. The ball is dead when:

- The batter is interfered with.
- The ball strikes an umpire or a runner before it is touched by or passes a fielder.
- A pitched ball hits the batter.
- A runner or the batter commits interference.
- The ball goes out of the field or into the crowd or a bench.
- The ball is hit into foul territory, unless it is caught on the fly.
- An umpire has called time out.
- The plate umpire interferes with the catcher's attempt to throw.
- The pitcher commits a balk.

The ball becomes live again when the pitcher has the ball on the rubber and the plate umpire calls "play."

The Pitcher. Once the pitcher has reached the mound to begin an inning or to replace another pitcher, eight practice pitches are allowed. (However, if the previous pitcher was forced out of the game by illness or injury, the replacement is entitled to as many pitches as may be needed for warming up.)

The pitcher is allowed to pitch from either of two positions. In either case, the pivot foot (the right foot for a right-handed pitcher) must be in contact with the pitcher's plate from the moment the pitcher begins pitching motion until the moment the ball is released.

In the windup position, usually used when the bases are not occupied, the pitcher approximately faces the batter; once the pitching motion begins, the pitcher may take one step backward and one step forward with the free foot; aside from that, the pitcher must not raise either foot from the ground.

In the set position, usually used when the pitcher wants to hold runners close to their bases, the pitcher begins with the free foot in front of the rubber, and the ball is held in both hands at the waist or chest. From that position, the pitcher may "stretch"—bring the ball up over the head and back down—but must return to the set position, stopping the pitching motion, before delivering the ball. From the set position, the pitcher may also throw to a base or step backward, off the rubber, with the pivot foot.

If the pitcher makes an illegal pitch with the bases unoccupied, it is called a ball, unless the batter reaches base on the ensuing play.

The pitcher may not bring the pitching hand into contact with the mouth while anywhere on the mound. Each violation results in a called ball. The pitcher may not apply any foreign substance to the ball; spit on the ball, on the pitching hand, or on the glove; or deface the ball in any way. For such violations the pitcher can be ejected from the game.

If, in the umpire's judgment, the pitcher intentionally throws at a batter, the pitcher is warned; if there is a repetition of such an act at any time during the game, the pitcher is ejected.

With runners on base, it is a balk if the pitcher:

- Makes any motion associated with the delivery but does not pitch.
- Fakes a throw to first base while on the rubber.
- Throws to a base without stepping directly toward that base, while on the rubber.
- Makes an illegal pitch.
- Makes any motion associated with the normal pitching motion, while *not* on the rubber.
- Fakes a pitch when not in possession of the ball.
- From the set position, removes one hand from the ball without pitching or throwing it.
- Drops the ball while on the rubber.
- Pitches when the catcher is not in the catcher's box.
- Throws from the set position without having come to a stop.

On a balk, each base runner is awarded one base. However, if the batter reaches base on the play that results from the balk, and each runner advances one base or more, the play stands.

Infield Fly Rule. The infield fly rule applies only with fewer than two out and runners on first and second bases or on first, second, and third. If the ball is hit into the air and, in the judgment of the umpire, it can be caught by an infielder with ordinary effort, it is an infield fly. The batter is automatically out.

The intent of the rule is to prevent an infielder from deliberately dropping the ball, or letting it drop, in order to get a double play by forcing out two runners. A similar rule states that the batter is automatically out if a fielder intentionally drops a fly ball or a line drive with a runner on first base.

Fair or Foul? When the ball remains in the infield, it is fair only if it comes to rest, or is touched by a fielder, in fair territory. If it is hit to the outfield, it is a fair ball if it touched fair territory in the infield and was on, or over, fair territory when it left the infield; or if it lands, on the fly, in fair territory. Thus a ball that bounces directly over third base, but lands in foul territory in the outfield, is a fair ball. But if it is hit on the fly over third base, and lands in foul territory, it is a foul ball.

If an infield fly lands in foul territory, or is not caught and bounces into foul territory while still in the infield, it is a foul ball and the infield fly rule no longer applies.

Substitutions. A substitute may enter the game at any time the ball is dead. The manager must announce the substitution to the umpire. Once the manager has announced it, the substitution is made. Once replaced by a substitute, a player may not return to the game.

A pinch hitter entering the game may be removed immediately for another pinch hitter; but the first pinch hitter has been in the game, and may not re-enter.

If a substitute pitcher enters the game, the newcomer must finish pitching to the batter then at the plate, or to

Mickey Mantle was the American League's most valuable player in 1956, 1957, and 1962. He spent all of his 18-year major-league career with the New York Yankees and was elected to the Hall of Fame in 1974. *(New York Yankees.)*

any pinch hitter for that batter.

A player who enters the game must bat in the same spot in the batting order as that occupied by the person replaced. However, if two or more players enter the game at the same time, the manager may choose which spots they bat in; the manager must announce this decision to the umpire when they enter. If, for example, the manager brings a relief pitcher and a new catcher into the game at the same time, the new pitcher may bat in the former catcher's spot in the batting order, with the new catcher batting in the former pitcher's spot.

Strategy and Tactics

Pitcher vs. Batter. Although managerial and coaching decisions play a major part in baseball, the game's basic tactical duel is the continual contest between pitcher and batter. A pitcher cannot depend on sheer speed, or sheer "stuff," to defeat the hitters. Control is important, not merely in the sense of getting the ball over the plate, but in pitching to specific spots.

Almost any hitter has a weakness, and the pitcher wants to exploit that weakness. The pitcher cannot, however, just keep throwing the same pitch to the same spot. Pitching strategy is designed to set up the hitter, so that the pitch to the weakness, when it finally comes, catches the hitter off balance. A pitcher works on a hitter in two ways: by varying the speed or the type of pitch thrown,

and by "moving the ball around" from one spot to another. For example, a fast ball may be used to set up a hitter for an off-speed pitch, a curve or "change-up." Or the pitcher may use high, inside pitches to set up the batter for a low, outside pitch.

The batter, on the other hand, will usually take one of two approaches. The batter may wait for the pitch that he or she hits best—the "batter's pitch." Or the batter may wait for the "pitcher's pitch"; if the pitcher is primarily a fast-ball pitcher, the batter will be looking for the fast ball on every pitch.

Defensive Strategy. Aside from positioning defensive players according to each hitter's tendencies, the most important aspects of defensive strategy are backing up plays and getting into cutoff positions.

Backing up a play is just what it sounds like: A player gets behind the base at which a play may be made, in order to stop the ball if it gets past the primary fielder. This is quite often the pitcher's job. For example, if there is a runner on first base and a ball is hit to the outfield, the pitcher should immediately get into foul territory behind third base to back up the play there. With a runner on second base, if a fly ball is hit, the pitcher should back up third in case the runner tries to advance; if the batter gets a hit, the pitcher should back up home plate, in case the runner from second tries to score. When there are no runners, the catcher should usually back up the play at first base on an infield grounder.

A cutoff player does the opposite, getting between the ball and the place where a play is likely to be made, in case the throw is late or off target. For example, with a runner on second base, on a ball hit safely to the outfield, the first baseman or third baseman will get into position, about 30 ft from home plate and in line with the outfielder who comes up with the ball. That player is a target—the outfielder should throw the ball directly over the player's head to home plate. If the throw is off target, the cutoff player can catch it (cut off the throw) and then throw the ball to home plate; if the throw from the outfield is late, the cutoff player can catch it to keep the hitter from advancing to second base.

In many cases the player in the cutoff position is actually a "relay man," and the throw from the outfield should come to him, so he can relay it to the proper place. For example, on a ball hit to deep right-center field, the second baseman will go into the outfield to take the throw from the outfield and relay it to second or third base.

The Catcher. Because the entire field is in front of the catcher, this player serves as the team's defensive quarterback. The catcher gives the pitcher signals, specifying what kind of pitch to throw and where to throw it. The catcher has a great deal to say about this; the catcher plays virtually every day, whereas a pitcher performs only every fourth or fifth day, and consequently the catcher is likely to know the hitters better.

In a situation where the catcher suspects the other team may be attempting to steal, or to hit and run, or even to bunt, the catcher may call for a pitchout, a pitch deliberately thrown wide of the plate to give the catcher a good chance to make a throw to a base.

On many plays, it is also up to the catcher to decide which player should field the ball—especially on bunts or pop-ups—or to tell a cutoff player whether or not to cut off a throw. On bunts, the catcher will usually decide at which base the play should be made, and yell instructions.

With Runners on Base. A base runner changes the ordinary defensive alignment in several ways. With a runner on first base, the first baseman will normally play right on the base, ready to take a throw from the pitcher or catcher, to hold the runner close. The second baseman or shortstop may also have to "cheat"—play a little closer to second base than usual, to cover the base in case of a steal or a possible double play. The third baseman may play somewhat closer to home plate, if it seems likely that the batter may attempt a bunt; or in some cases, the third baseman will be stationed deep and close to the foul line, so a hit can't get past and go into the left-field corner, where it might score the runner.

With none out, when a bunt is likely, the first and third basemen will charge with the pitch to field the bunt. The second baseman will have to cover first base. The shortstop will cover second but will have to be ready to cover third as well, if the third baseman handles the ball and the runner is going to make it safely to second. Outfielders should be alert to move in to back up plays, possibly even to cover bases.

The pitcher will also have to charge, usually somewhat to the third-base side, upon completing the follow-through of the delivery. With a runner on second base, the pitcher should move even farther toward the line and attempt to handle the bunt, so the third baseman can cover for a possible play at third.

When the hit-and-run play is a possiblity, the shortstop and second baseman have to decide, before each pitch, which of them will cover second base on an attempted steal. The shortstop ordinarily signals the second baseman, either verbally or by a movement of the glove.

With a runner on third base, and fewer than two outs, the defense will sometimes play the infield in to make the play at the plate on a ground ball. All infielders will be on the infield grass. In a crucial situation—when the runner on third represents the potential winning run in the ninth inning, for example—the outfielders will also play well in, to have a play at the plate on a short fly that would otherwise drop in for a hit.

Offense. The type of offense a team uses will depend in part on the team's personnel and in part on the game situation. A team with a good deal of speed but few power hitters will often employ the bunt and hit-and-run and base stealing, and will usually play for one run at a time—especially if the team also has good pitching. A team with strong hitters is more likely to play for the big inning, trying to get runs in bunches. If a game is tied in the late innings, any team will play for one run. On the other hand, when a team is several runs behind, it will have to play for the big inning.

The bunt is a basic offensive weapon. It is usually a sacrifice—an attempt by the batter to advance a runner by tapping the ball a short distance, with the batter being thrown out at first base. A runner on second base is considered to be in scoring position, since such a runner will probably score on a hit to the outfield. The successful bunt also eliminates the possibility of the easy double play.

Some hitters use the bunt as a way of getting on base, especially if the infielders are playing deep. On a drag bunt the batter bunts the ball rather hard, in an attempt to

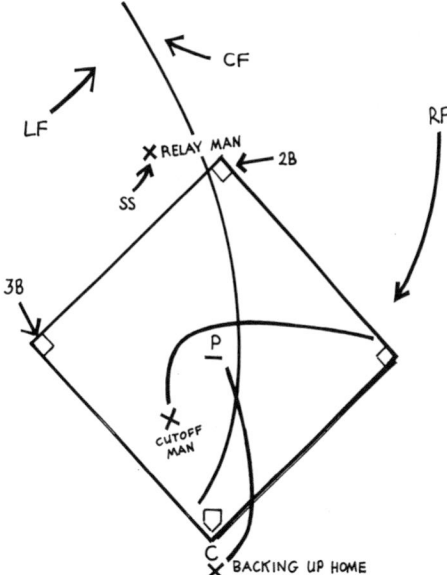

Defensive moves: runner on first, ball hit to deep left-center field

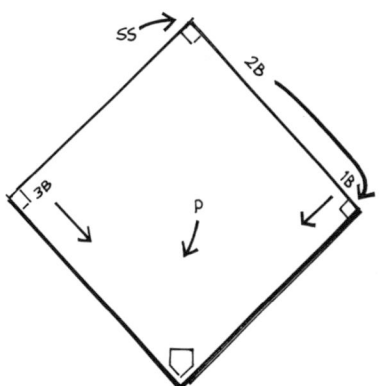

Defensive moves: runner on first, bunt expected

push it past the pitcher, toward the second baseman or shortstop.

There are times when a bunt seems likely but isn't used. That situation arises when a manager feels his next batter will be intentionally walked, and he would rather have the batter get a chance to swing.

The hit-and-run is another basic way of advancing a runner, with a good chance of also getting the hitter on base. It is usually used with a runner on first base or with runners on first and second. The runner starts with the pitch, as in a steal, but the batter must make contact with the ball. The batter usually will try to hit behind the runner—toward right field. However, a hitter with very good bat control may hit the ball to left field upon seeing that the shortstop is moving over to cover second base.

A smart hitter will try to hit behind the runner even when the hit-and-run play isn't on, because it's much harder to make a double play on a ball hit between first and second than on a ball hit to the left side of the infield. Further, if the ball goes through into right field, the runner has a good chance to go all the way to third base, whereas he would probably have to stop at second on a hit to left field.

Batting Order. A manager's most important job is probably determining the team's batting order. The first hitter should be a fast runner who is able to get on base pretty often, in one way or another; the second hitter should be a good bunter or hit-and-run artist; the third batter is usually the best hitter on the team, for average; the fourth batter is the "clean-up man," the team's best power hitter and most capable of driving in runs; the fifth batter should also be able to hit with power. The poorest hitters on the team usually bat eighth or ninth; many managers believe in always having the catcher bat eighth. In the National League the pitcher always bats ninth.

Pinch Hitters. In many situations a manager will send a pinch hitter to bat for one of his team's weaker hitters. Sometimes the manager simply wants to use the best hitter available, but in some cases the aim will be to use a left-handed hitter against a right-handed pitcher, or vice versa. The reasoning is that a left-handed batter should have more success hitting a right-hander's curve ball, since the pitch breaks toward the batter. The other manager may counter by bringing in a left-handed relief pitcher, whereupon a right-handed pinch hitter may now bat for the left-handed pinch hitter.

See also BABE RUTH BASEBALL; MINOR LEAGUE BASEBALL.

Glossary

around the horn—A double play started by the third baseman.

assist—A fielder is credited with an assist when the fielder's throw results in a putout, or should have resulted in a putout except for an error by a teammate. Any fielder who touches the ball on a play resulting in an out is credited with an assist, except for the player who makes, or should have made, the putout.

Baltimore chop—A batted ball that hits near home plate and bounces high into the air.

bases loaded—Three runners on base.

bean ball—A pitch thrown at the batter's head.

blank—To shut out.

bleeder—A lucky hit.

blooper—A short fly that drops in front of an outfielder.

bobble—Momentary fumble.

book—Accepted rules of strategy and tactics; a manager who orders a sacrifice bunt with a runner on first base and none out is "playing it by the book." Also, the assessment of a player's strengths and weaknesses; as, "the book on John Jones says he can hit the high, inside fast ball."

break—The sudden change in direction of a curve, slider, or screwball. A right-handed pitcher's curve breaks away from a right-handed hitter.

bullpen—The area where relief pitchers and other players warm up when not in the game; by extension, a team's staff of relief pitchers.

bush league—A low minor league; actions supposedly typical of that level of baseball.

cellar—Last place.

change up—A pitch thrown slower than usual.

cheap—Anything undeserved; a bleeder is a cheap hit.

Chinese home run—A cheap home run, either over a fence closer to home plate than is usual, or a wind-blown fly that barely clears a fence.

choke—To play poorly under pressure.

choke up—To grip the bat above the lower end.

circuit clout—A home run.

circus catch—A spectacular catch, usually involving a leap or a dive.

clothesline—A low, hard-hit line drive.

clutch—A crucial situation; a player who gets a hit when it is badly needed has "come through in the clutch."

clutch hitter—A hitter who is likely to come through in the clutch.

clutch play—An outstanding play in a clutch situation.

crowd the plate—To stand close to the plate when hitting.

cut—Swing; also, to put some spin on a fast ball, making it break somewhat.

cycle—A player who gets a single, double, triple, and home run in a game has "hit for the cycle."

double—A two-base hit.

double-header—Two consecutive games played by the same teams in a single day.

double play—A play on which two outs are made.

dugout—A recessed shelter for players who are not on the field at the moment.

duster—A pitch deliberately thrown near a hitter.

error—A muff, fumble, or poor throw by a fielder that permits a batter to reach base or a runner to advance one or more bases, or that prolongs a hitter's turn at bat.

fan—To swing and miss, or strike out; also, from "fanatic," an enthusiastic rooter.

fat pitch—A pitch that's easy to hit.

fielder's choice—A play on which a fielder has a choice between throwing the batter out or retiring another runner. When a batter reaches base on a fielder's choice, it counts as a time at bat but not as a hit.

fungo—A practice fly ball hit by a player or coach who throws the ball into the air and then hits it.

fungo bat—A bat with a flattened side, used for hitting fungoes.

garden—The outfield.

gardener—An outfielder.

gopher ball—A pitch that is hit for a home run.

grand slam—A home run with the bases full.

grandstander—A player who shows off for the fans.

Grapefruit League—Preseason series of games played by teams training in Florida.

ground-rule double—A batted ball that bounces into the stands; the batter is awarded second base.

grounder—A ball hit on the ground.

hit—A batted ball on which the hitter reaches base safely without an error being made or another runner being retired.

hit the dirt—To slide; or to drop to the ground to avoid being hit by a pitch.

hot box—When a runner is trapped between bases and being run down by fielders, the runner is said to be in the hot box.

hot corner—Third base.

keystone—Second base.

lead—When a runner moves a short distance off a base, the runner is taking a lead.

lead-off man—The first batter in the lineup.

no-hitter—A game in which a team gets no hits.

on deck—The player who is due to bat after the present hitter is on deck in the on-deck circle.

pass—A walk.

passed ball—A pitch that the catcher should have caught but that eludes the catcher, enabling a runner to advance.

perfect game—A game in which the pitcher retires 27 consecutive hitters, allowing no one to reach base.

pivot man—The second baseman or shortstop, when in the act of making a putout at second base and then throwing to first for a double play.

pop-up—A short, high fly ball.

portsider—A left-hander.

pull hitter—A right- or left-handed hitter who pulls the ball and hits consistently to opposite field.

putout—A fielder is credited with a putout when the fielder puts a player out by catching a fly, by tagging a base, or by tagging a runner. The catcher gets a putout by catching a third strike.

rally—A scoring outburst.

rhubarb—An argument that involves several players, coaches, and managers with one or more umpires.

rookie—A first-year player.

rosin bag—A small bag of powdered rosin, used by a player to get an improved grip on a bat or ball.

round-tripper—A home run.

rubber arm—A pitcher who can pitch frequently or for long periods without apparent strain has a rubber arm.

run batted in (RBI)—A batter is credited with an RBI when a run scores as the direct result of the batter's hit, base on balls, being hit by a pitch, sacrifice fly, or ground-out. An RBI is not awarded if a run scores when the batter grounds into a double play or when the score is the result of an error.

sack—A base.

sacrifice fly—A fly ball that allows a runner to score after the ball is caught; not a time at bat.

sacrifice hit—A bunt on which the batter deliberately gives up the chance to get on base safely, in order to advance a runner; not a time at bat.

screwball—A pitch that breaks in the wrong direction; a right-handed pitcher's screwball breaks toward a right-handed hitter, while the pitcher's curve breaks away.

shake off—A pitcher who doesn't want to throw the pitch signaled by the catcher will "shake off" the catcher by a shake of the head or by giving some other sign.

shoestring catch—A catch of a fly ball made down around a player's shoestrings.

shutout—A game in which a team is held scoreless.

single—A one-base hit.

southpaw—A left-handed pitcher; occasionally, a left-handed hitter.

spray hitter—A batter who consistently hits the ball to any field.

squeeze play—A play on which the batter bunts in an attempt to score a runner from third base. In a "safety" squeeze, the runner takes a short lead and makes sure the ball is bunted before starting for home. In a "suicide" squeeze, the runner starts with the pitch and the batter must bunt the ball, wherever it's pitched, to protect the runner.

switch hitter—A batter who can hit either left- or right-handed.

tag up—To touch a base after a fly ball is caught, before attempting to advance.

take a pitch—To allow a pitch to go by without attempting to hit it.

Texas leaguer—A blooper.

triple—A three-base hit.

triple crown—A designation for a player who leads the league in batting average, home runs, and RBIs in a single season.

triple play—A play on which three outs are made.

waste pitch—A pitch deliberately thrown outside the strike zone, either to set up the batter or in the hope that the batter will swing wildly.

whitewash—A shutout.

wild pitch—A pitch that cannot be handled by a catcher, allowing a runner to advance.

Championship Teams

National League

Year	Team (Manager)	Won	Lost
1876	Chicago (Al Spalding)	52	14
1877	Boston (Harry Wright)	42	18
1878	Boston (Harry Wright)	41	19
1879	Providence (George Wright)	59	25
1880	Chicago (Cap Anson)	67	17
1881	Chicago (Cap Anson)	56	28
1882	Chicago (Cap Anson)	55	29
1883	Boston (John Morrill)	63	35
1884	Providence (Frank Bancroft)	84	28
1885	Chicago (Cap Anson)	87	25
1886	Chicago (Cap Anson)	90	34
1887	Detroit (Bill Watkins)	79	45
1888	New York (Jim Mutrie)	84	47
1889	New York (Jim Mutrie)	83	43
1890	Brooklyn (Bill McGunnigle)	86	43
1891	Boston (Frank Selee)	87	51
1892	Boston (Frank Selee)	102	48
1893	Boston (Frank Selee)	86	43
1894	Baltimore (Ned Hanlon)	89	39
1895	Baltimore (Ned Hanlon)	87	43
1896	Baltimore (Ned Hanlon)	90	39
1897	Boston (Frank Selee)	93	39
1898	Boston (Frank Selee)	102	47
1899	Brooklyn (Ned Hanlon)	101	47
1900	Brooklyn (Ned Hanlon)	82	54
1901	Pittsburgh (Fred Clarke)	90	49
1902	Pittsburgh (Fred Clarke)	103	36
1903	Pittsburgh (Fred Clarke)	91	49
1904	New York (John McGraw)	106	47
1905	New York (John McGraw)	105	48
1906	Chicago (Frank Chance)	116	36
1907	Chicago (Frank Chance)	107	45
1908	Chicago (Frank Chance)	99	55
1909	Pittsburgh (Fred Clarke)	110	42
1910	Chicago (Frank Chance)	104	50
1911	New York (John McGraw)	99	54
1912	New York (John McGraw)	103	48
1913	New York (John McGraw)	101	51
1914	Boston (George Stallings)	94	59
1915	Philadelphia (Pat Moran)	90	62
1916	Brooklyn (Wilbert Robinson)	94	60
1917	New York (John McGraw)	98	56
1918	Chicago (Fred Mitchell)	84	45
1919	Cincinnati (Pat Moran)	96	44
1920	Brooklyn (Wilbert Robinson)	93	61

Year	Team (Manager)	W	L
1921	New York (John McGraw)	94	59
1922	New York (John McGraw)	93	61
1923	New York (John McGraw)	95	58
1924	New York (John McGraw)	93	60
1925	Pittsburgh (Bill McKechnie)	95	58
1926	St. Louis (Rogers Hornsby)	89	65
1927	Pittsburgh (Donie Bush)	94	60
1928	St. Louis (Bill McKechnie)	95	59
1929	Chicago (Joe McCarthy)	98	54
1930	St. Louis (Gabby Street)	92	62
1931	St. Louis (Gabby Street)	101	53
1932	Chicago (Charlie Grimm)	90	64
1933	New York (Bill Terry)	91	61
1934	St. Louis (Frankie Frisch)	95	58
1935	Chicago (Charlie Grimm)	100	54
1936	New York (Bill Terry)	92	62
1937	New York (Bill Terry)	95	57
1938	Chicago (Gabby Hartnett)	89	63
1939	Cincinnati (Bill McKechnie)	97	57
1940	Cincinnati (Bill McKechnie)	100	53
1941	Brooklyn (Leo Durocher)	100	54
1942	St. Louis (Billy Southworth)	106	48
1943	St. Louis (Billy Southworth)	105	49
1944	St. Louis (Billy Southworth)	105	49
1945	Chicago (Charlie Grimm)	98	56
1946	St. Louis (Eddie Dyer)	98	58
1947	Brooklyn (Burt Shotton)	94	60
1948	Boston (Billy Southworth)	91	62
1949	Brooklyn (Burt Shotton)	97	57
1950	Philadelphia (Eddie Sawyer)	91	63
1951	New York (Leo Durocher)	98	59
1952	Brooklyn (Charlie Dressen)	96	57
1953	Brooklyn (Charlie Dressen)	105	49
1954	New York (Leo Durocher)	97	57
1955	Brooklyn (Walter Alston)	98	55
1956	Brooklyn (Walter Alston)	93	61
1957	Milwaukee (Fred Haney)	95	59
1958	Milwaukee (Fred Haney)	92	62
1959	Los Angeles (Walter Alston)	88	68
1960	Pittsburgh (Danny Murtaugh)	95	59
1961	Cincinnati (Fred Hutchinson)	93	61
1962	San Francisco (Alvin Dark)	103	62
1963	Los Angeles (Walter Alston)	99	63
1964	St. Louis (Johnny Keane)	93	69
1965	Los Angeles (Walter Alston)	97	65
1966	Los Angeles (Walter Alston)	95	67
1967	St. Louis (Red Schoendienst)	101	60
1968	St. Louis (Red Schoendienst)	97	65
1969	E—New York (Gil Hodges)	100	62
	W—Atlanta (Lum Harris)	93	69
1970	E—Pittsburgh (Danny Murtaugh)	97	65
	W—Cincinnati (Sparky Anderson)	102	60
1971	E—Pittsburgh (Danny Murtaugh)	97	65
	W—San Francisco (Charlie Fox)	90	72
1972	E—Pittsburgh (Bill Virdon)	96	59
	W—Cincinnati (Sparky Anderson)	95	59
1973	E—New York (Yogi Berra)	82	79
	W—Cincinnati (Sparky Anderson)	99	63
1974	E—Pittsburgh (Danny Murtaugh)	88	74
	W—Los Angeles (Walter Alston)	102	60
1975	E—Pittsburgh (Danny Murtaugh)	92	69
	W—Cincinnati (Sparky Anderson)	108	54
1976	E—Philadelphia (Danny Ozark)	101	61
	W—Cincinnati (Sparky Anderson)	102	60

Playoff Winners
1969 New York over Atlanta, 3 out of 4
1970 Cincinnati over Pittsburgh, 3 out of 3
1971 Pittsburgh over San Francisco, 3 out of 4
1972 Cincinnati over Pittsburgh, 3 out of 5
1973 New York over Cincinnati, 3 out of 5
1974 Los Angeles over Pittsburgh, 3 out of 4
1975 Cincinnati over Pittsburgh, 3 out of 3
1976 Cincinnati over Pittsburgh, 3 out of 3

American League

Year	Team (Manager)	W	L
1901	Chicago (Clark Griffith)	83	53
1902	Philadelphia (Connie Mack)	83	53
1903	Boston (Jimmy Collins)	91	47
1904	Boston (Jimmy Collins)	95	59
1905	Philadelphia (Connie Mack)	92	56
1906	Chicago (Fielder Jones)	93	58
1907	Detroit (Hughie Jennings)	92	58
1908	Detroit (Hughie Jennings)	90	63
1909	Detroit (Hughie Jennings)	98	54
1910	Philadelphia (Connie Mack)	102	48
1911	Philadelphia (Connie Mack)	101	50
1912	Boston (Jake Stahl)	105	47
1913	Philadelphia (Connie Mack)	96	57
1914	Philadelphia (Connie Mack)	99	53
1915	Boston (Bill Carrigan)	101	50
1916	Boston (Bill Carrigan)	91	63
1917	Chicago (Pants Rowland)	100	54
1918	Boston (Ed Barrow)	75	51
1919	Chicago (Kid Gleason)	88	52
1920	Cleveland (Tris Speaker)	98	56
1921	New York (Miller Huggins)	98	55
1922	New York (Miller Huggins)	94	60
1923	New York (Miller Huggins)	98	54
1924	Washington (Bucky Harris)	92	62
1925	Washington (Bucky Harris)	96	55
1926	New York (Miller Huggins)	91	63
1927	New York (Miller Huggins)	110	44
1928	New York (Miller Huggins)	101	53
1929	Philadelphia (Connie Mack)	104	46
1930	Philadelphia (Connie Mack)	102	52
1931	Philadelphia (Connie Mack)	107	45
1932	New York (Joe McCarthy)	107	47
1933	Washington (Joe Cronin)	99	53
1934	Detroit (Mickey Cochrane)	101	53
1935	Detroit (Mickey Cochrane)	93	58
1936	New York (Joe McCarthy)	102	51
1937	New York (Joe McCarthy)	102	52
1938	New York (Joe McCarthy)	99	53
1939	New York (Joe McCarthy)	106	45
1940	Detroit (Del Baker)	90	64
1941	New York (Joe McCarthy)	101	53
1942	New York (Joe McCarthy)	103	51
1943	New York (Joe McCarthy)	98	56
1944	St. Louis (Luke Sewell)	89	65
1945	Detroit (Steve O'Neill)	88	65
1946	Boston (Joe Cronin)	104	50
1947	New York (Bucky Harris)	97	57
1948	Cleveland (Lou Boudreau)	97	58
1949	New York (Casey Stengel)	97	57
1950	New York (Casey Stengel)	98	56
1951	New York (Casey Stengel)	98	56
1952	New York (Casey Stengel)	95	59
1953	New York (Casey Stengel)	99	52
1954	Cleveland (Al Lopez)	111	43
1955	New York (Casey Stengel)	96	58
1956	New York (Casey Stengel)	97	57
1957	New York (Casey Stengel)	98	56
1958	New York (Casey Stengel)	92	62
1959	Chicago (Al Lopez)	94	60
1960	New York (Casey Stengel)	97	57
1961	New York (Ralph Houk)	109	53
1962	New York (Ralph Houk)	96	66
1963	New York (Ralph Houk)	104	57
1964	New York (Yogi Berra)	99	63
1965	Minnesota (Sam Mele)	102	60
1966	Baltimore (Hank Bauer)	97	63
1967	Boston (Dick Williams)	92	70
1968	Detroit (Mayo Smith)	103	59
1969	E—Baltimore (Earl Weaver)	109	53
	W—Minnesota (Billy Martin)	97	65
1970	E—Baltimore (Earl Weaver)	108	54
	W—Minnesota (Billy Martin)	98	64

1971	E—Baltimore (Earl Weaver)	101	57							
	W—Oakland (Dick Williams)	101	60							
1972	E—Detroit (Billy Martin)	86	70							
	W—Oakland (Dick Williams)	93	62							
1973	E—Baltimore (Earl Weaver)	97	65							
	W—Oakland (Dick Williams)	94	68							
1974	E—Baltimore (Earl Weaver)	91	71							
	W—Oakland (Alvin Dark)	90	72							
1975	E—Boston (Darrell Johnson)	95	65							
	W—Oakland (Alvin Dark)	98	64							
1976	E—New York (Billy Martin)	97	62							
	W—Kansas City (Whitey Herzog)	90	72							

Playoff Winners

1969 Baltimore over Minnesota, 3 out of 3
1970 Baltimore over Minnesota, 3 out of 3
1971 Baltimore over Oakland, 3 out of 3
1972 Oakland over Detroit, 3 out of 5
1973 Oakland over Baltimore, 3 out of 5
1974 Oakland over Baltimore, 3 out of 4
1975 Boston over Oakland, 3 out of 3
1976 New York over Kansas City, 3 out of 5

World Series Results

(First team listed for each year won world championship; game-by-game scores are listed across.)

1903	Boston (AL)	3	3	2	4	11	6	7	3
	Pittsburgh (NL)	7	0	4	5	2	3	3	0
1904	Not Held								
1905	New York (NL)	3	0	9	1	2			
	Philadelphia (AL)	0	3	0	0	0			
1906	Chicago (AL)	2	1	3	0	8	8		
	Chicago (NL)	1	7	0	1	6	3		
1907	Chicago (NL)	3	3	5	6	2			
	Detroit (AL)	3	1	1	1	0			
1908	Chicago (NL)	10	6	3	3	2			
	Detroit (AL)	6	1	8	0	0			
1909	Pittsburgh (NL)	4	2	8	0	8	4	8	
	Detroit (AL)	1	7	6	5	4	5	0	
1910	Philadelphia (AL)	4	9	12	3	7			
	Chicago (NL)	1	3	5	4	2			
1911	Philadelphia (AL)	1	3	3	4	3	13		
	New York (NL)	2	1	2	2	4	2		
1912	Boston (AL)	4	6	1	3	2	2	4	3
	New York (NL)	3	6	2	1	1	5	11	2
1913	Philadelphia (AL)	6	0	8	6	3			
	New York (NL)	4	3	2	5	1			
1914	Boston (NL)	7	1	5	3				
	Philadelphia (AL)	1	0	4	1				
1915	Boston (AL)	1	2	2	2	5			
	Philadelphia (NL)	3	1	1	1	4			
1916	Boston (AL)	6	2	3	6	4			
	Brooklyn (NL)	5	1	4	2	1			
1917	Chicago (AL)	2	7	0	0	8	4		
	New York (NL)	1	2	2	5	5	2		
1918	Boston (AL)	1	1	2	3	0	2		
	Chicago (NL)	0	3	1	2	3	1		
1919	Cincinnati (NL)	9	4	0	2	5	4	1	10
	Chicago (AL)	1	2	3	0	0	5	4	5
1920	Cleveland (AL)	3	0	1	5	8	1	3	
	Brooklyn (NL)	1	3	2	1	1	0	0	
1921	New York (NL)	0	0	13	4	1	8	2	1
	New York (AL)	3	3	5	2	3	5	1	0
1922	New York (NL)	3	3	3	4	5			
	New York (AL)	2	3	0	3	3			
1923	New York (AL)	4	4	0	8	8	6		
	New York (NL)	5	2	1	4	1	4		
1924	Washington (AL)	3	4	4	7	2	2	4	
	New York (NL)	4	3	6	4	6	1	3	
1925	Pittsburgh (NL)	1	3	3	0	6	3	9	
	Washington (AL)	4	2	4	4	3	2	7	
1926	St. Louis (NL)	1	6	4	5	2	10	3	
	New York (AL)	2	2	0	10	3	2	2	
1927	New York (AL)	5	6	8	4				

	Pittsburgh (NL)	4	2	1	3			
1928	New York (AL)	4	9	7	7			
	St. Louis (NL)	1	3	3	3			
1929	Philadelphia (AL)	3	9	1	10	3		
	Chicago (NL)	1	3	3	8	2		
1930	Philadelphia (AL)	5	6	0	1	2	7	
	St. Louis (NL)	2	1	5	3	0	1	
1931	St. Louis (NL)	2	2	5	0	5	1	4
	Philadelphia (AL)	6	0	2	3	1	8	2
1932	New York (AL)	12	5	7	13			
	Chicago (NL)	6	2	5	6			
1933	New York (NL)	4	6	0	2	4		
	Washington (AL)	2	1	4	1	3		
1934	St. Louis (NL)	8	2	4	4	1	4	11
	Detroit (AL)	3	3	1	10	3	3	0
1935	Detroit (AL)	0	8	6	2	1	4	
	Chicago (NL)	3	3	5	1	3	3	
1936	New York (AL)	1	18	2	5	4	13	
	New York (NL)	6	4	1	2	5	5	
1937	New York (AL)	8	8	5	3	4		
	New York (NL)	1	1	1	7	2		
1938	New York (AL)	3	6	5	8			
	Chicago (NL)	1	3	2	3			
1939	New York (AL)	2	4	7	7			
	Cincinnati (NL)	1	0	3	4			
1940	Cincinnati (NL)	2	5	4	5	0	4	2
	Detroit (AL)	7	3	7	2	8	0	1
1941	New York (AL)	3	2	2	7	3		
	Brooklyn (NL)	2	3	1	4	1		
1942	St. Louis (NL)	4	4	2	9	4		
	New York (AL)	7	3	0	6	2		
1943	New York (AL)	4	3	6	2	2		
	St. Louis (NL)	2	4	2	1	0		
1944	St. Louis (NL)	1	3	2	5	2	3	
	St. Louis (AL)	2	2	6	1	0	1	
1945	Detroit (AL)	0	4	0	4	8	7	9
	Chicago (NL)	9	1	3	1	4	8	3
1946	St. Louis (NL)	2	3	0	12	3	4	4
	Boston (AL)	3	0	4	3	6	1	3
1947	New York (AL)	5	10	8	2	2	6	5
	Brooklyn (NL)	3	3	9	3	1	8	2
1948	Cleveland (AL)	0	4	2	2	5	4	
	Boston (NL)	1	1	0	1	11	3	
1949	New York (AL)	1	0	4	6	10		
	Brooklyn (NL)	0	1	3	4	6		
1950	New York (AL)	1	2	3	5			
	Philadelphia (NL)	0	1	2	2			
1951	New York (AL)	1	3	2	6	13	4	
	New York (NL)	5	1	6	2	1	3	
1952	New York (AL)	2	7	3	2	5	3	4
	Brooklyn (NL)	4	1	5	0	6	2	2
1953	New York (AL)	9	4	2	3	11	4	
	Brooklyn (NL)	5	2	3	7	7	3	
1954	New York (NL)	5	3	6	7			
	Cleveland (AL)	2	1	2	4			
1955	Brooklyn (NL)	5	2	8	8	5	1	2
	New York (AL)	6	4	3	5	3	5	0
1956	New York (AL)	3	8	5	6	2	0	9
	Brooklyn (NL)	6	13	3	2	0	1	0
1957	Milwaukee (NL)	1	4	3	7	1	2	5
	New York (AL)	3	2	12	5	0	3	0
1958	New York (AL)	3	5	4	0	7	4	6
	Milwaukee (NL)	4	13	0	3	0	3	2
1959	Los Angeles (NL)	0	4	3	5	0	9	
	Chicago (AL)	11	3	1	4	1	3	
1960	Pittsburgh (NL)	6	3	0	3	5	0	10
	New York (AL)	4	16	10	2	2	12	9
1961	New York (AL)	2	2	3	7	13		
	Cincinnati (NL)	0	6	2	0	5		
1962	New York (AL)	6	0	3	3	5	2	1
	San Francisco (NL)	2	2	2	7	3	5	0
1963	Los Angeles (NL)	5	4	1	2			
	New York (AL)	2	1	0	1			

1964	St. Louis (NL)	9	3	1	4	5	3	7
	New York (AL)	5	8	2	3	2	8	5
1965	Los Angeles (NL)	2	1	4	7	7	1	2
	Minnesota (AL)	8	5	0	2	0	5	0
1966	Baltimore (AL)	5	6	1	1			
	Los Angeles (NL)	2	0	0	0			
1967	St. Louis (NL)	2	0	5	6	1	4	7
	Boston (AL)	1	5	2	0	3	8	2
1968	Detroit (AL)	0	8	3	1	5	13	4
	St. Louis (NL)	4	1	7	10	3	1	1
1969	New York (NL)	1	2	5	1	5		
	Baltimore (AL)	4	1	0	1	3		
1970	Baltimore (AL)	4	6	9	5	9		
	Cincinnati (NL)	3	5	3	6	3		
1971	Pittsburgh (NL)	3	3	5	4	4	2	2
	Baltimore (AL)	5	11	1	3	0	3	1
1972	Oakland (AL)	3	2	0	3	4	1	3
	Cincinnati (NL)	2	1	1	2	5	8	2
1973	Oakland (AL)	2	7	3	1	0	3	5
	New York (NL)	1	10	2	6	2	1	2
1974	Oakland (AL)	3	2	3	5	3		
	Los Angeles (NL)	2	3	2	2	2		
1975	Cincinnati (NL)	0	3	1	4	6	6	4
	Boston (AL)	6	2	0	5	2	7	3
1976	Cincinnati (NL)	5	4	6	7			
	New York (AL)	1	3	2	2			

Statistical Leaders

Batting—National League

1876	Ross Barnes, Chicago	.403
1877	Jim White, Boston	.385
1878	Abner Dalrymple, Milwaukee	.356
1879	Cap Anson, Chicago	.407
1880	George Gore, Chicago	.365
1881	Cap Anson, Chicago	.399
1882	Dan Brouthers, Buffalo	.367
1883	Dan Brouthers, Buffalo	.371
1884	Jack O'Rourke, Buffalo	.350
1885	Roger Connor, New York	.371
1886	Mike Kelly, Chicago	.388
1887*	Cap Anson, Chicago	.421
1888	Cap Anson, Chicago	.343
1889	Dan Brouthers, Boston	.373
1890	Jack Glasscock, New York	.336
1891	Billy Hamilton, Philadelphia	.338
1892	Dan Brouthers, Brooklyn	.335
	Cupid Childs, Cleveland	.335
1893	Hugh Duffy, Boston	.378
1894	Hugh Duffy, Boston	.438
1895	Jesse Burkett, Cleveland	.423
1896	Jesse Burkett, Cleveland	.410
1897	Willie Keeler, Baltimore	.432
1898	Willie Keeler, Baltimore	.379
1899	Ed Delahanty, Philadelphia	.408
1900	Honus Wagner, Pittsburgh	.381
1901	Jesse Burkett, St. Louis	.382
1902	Ginger Beaumont, Pittsburgh	.357
1903	Honus Wagner, Pittsburgh	.355
1904	Honus Wagner, Pittsburgh	.349
1905	Cy Seymour, Cincinnati	.377
1906	Honus Wagner, Pittsburgh	.339
1907	Honus Wagner, Pittsburgh	.350
1908	Honus Wagner, Pittsburgh	.354
1909	Honus Wagner, Pittsburgh	.339
1910	Sherry Magee, Philadelphia	.331
1911	Honus Wagner, Pittsburgh	.334
1912	Heinie Zimmerman, Chicago	.372
1913	Jake Daubert, Brooklyn	.350
1914	Jake Daubert, Brooklyn	.329

*Walks counted as hits

1915	Larry Doyle, New York	.320
1916	Hal Chase, Cincinnati	.339
1917	Edd Roush, Cincinnati	.341
1918	Zack Wheat, Brooklyn	.335
1919	Edd Roush, Cincinnati	.321
1920	Rogers Hornsby, St. Louis	.370
1921	Rogers Hornsby, St. Louis	.397
1922	Rogers Hornsby, St. Louis	.401
1923	Rogers Hornsby, St. Louis	.384
1924	Rogers Hornsby, St. Louis	.424
1925	Rogers Hornsby, St. Louis	.403
1926	Bubbles Hargrave, Cincinnati	.353
1927	Paul Waner, Pittsburgh	.380
1928	Rogers Hornsby, Boston	.387
1929	Lefty O'Doul, Philadelphia	.398
1930	Bill Terry, New York	.401
1931	Chick Hafey, St. Louis	.349
1932	Lefty O'Doul, Philadelphia	.368
1933	Chuck Klein, Philadelphia	.368
1934	Paul Waner, Pittsburgh	.362
1935	Arky Vaughan, Pittsburgh	.385
1936	Paul Waner, Pittsburgh	.373
1937	Joe Medwick, St. Louis	.374
1938	Ernie Lombardi, Cincinnati	.342
1939	Johnny Mize, St. Louis	.349
1940	Debs Garms, Pittsburgh	.355
1941	Pete Reiser, Brooklyn	.343
1942	Ernie Lombardi, Boston	.330
1943	Stan Musial, St. Louis	.357
1944	Dixie Walker, Brooklyn	.357
1945	Phil Cavaretta, Chicago	.355
1946	Stan Musial, St. Louis	.365
1947	Harry Walker, St. Louis-Philadelphia	.363
1948	Stan Musial, St. Louis	.376
1949	Jackie Robinson, Brooklyn	.342
1950	Stan Musial, St. Louis	.346
1951	Stan Musial, St. Louis	.355
1952	Stan Musial, St. Louis	.336
1953	Carl Furillo, Brooklyn	.344
1954	Willie Mays, New York	.345
1955	Richie Ashburn, Philadelphia	.338
1956	Henry Aaron, Milwaukee	.328
1957	Stan Musial, St. Louis	.351
1958	Richie Ashburn, Philadelphia	.350
1959	Henry Aaron, Milwaukee	.355
1960	Dick Groat, Pittsburgh	.325
1961	Roberto Clemente, Pittsburgh	.351
1962	Tommy Davis, Los Angeles	.346
1963	Tommy Davis, Los Angeles	.326
1964	Roberto Clemente, Pittsburgh	.339
1965	Roberto Clemente, Pittsburgh	.329
1966	Matty Alou, Pittsburgh	.342
1967	Roberto Clemente, Pittsburgh	.357
1968	Pete Rose, Cincinnati	.335
1969	Pete Rose, Cincinnati	.348
1970	Rico Carty, Atlanta	.366
1971	Joe Torre, St. Louis	.363
1972	Billy Williams, Chicago	.333
1973	Pete Rose, Cincinnati	.338
1974	Ralph Garr, Atlanta	.353
1975	Bill Madlock, Chicago	.354
1976	Bill Madlock, Chicago	.339

Batting—American League

1901	Napoleon Lajoie, Philadelphia	.422
1902	Ed Delahanty, Washington	.376
1903	Napoleon Lajoie, Cleveland	.355
1904	Napoleon Lajoie, Cleveland	.381
1905	Elmer Flick, Cleveland	.306
1906	George Stone, St. Louis	.358
1907	Ty Cobb, Detroit	.350
1908	Ty Cobb, Detroit	.324

1909	Ty Cobb, Detroit	.377
1910	Ty Cobb, Detroit	.385
1911	Ty Cobb, Detroit	.420
1912	Ty Cobb, Detroit	.410
1913	Ty Cobb, Detroit	.390
1914	Ty Cobb, Detroit	.368
1915	Ty Cobb, Detroit	.369
1916	Tris Speaker, Cleveland	.386
1917	Ty Cobb, Detroit	.383
1918	Ty Cobb, Detroit	.382
1919	Ty Cobb, Detroit	.384
1920	George Sisler, St. Louis	.407
1921	Harry Heilmann, Detroit	.394
1922	George Sisler, St. Louis	.420
1923	Harry Heilmann, Detroit	.403
1924	Babe Ruth, New York	.378
1925	Harry Heilmann, Detroit	.393
1926	Heinie Manush, Detroit	.378
1927	Harry Heilmann, Detroit	.398
1928	Goose Goslin, Washington	.379
1929	Lew Fonseca, Cleveland	.369
1930	Al Simmons, Philadelphia	.381
1931	Al Simmons, Philadelphia	.390
1932	Dale Alexander, Detroit-Boston	.367
1933	Jimmie Foxx, Philadelphia	.356
1934	Lou Gehrig, New York	.363
1935	Buddy Myer, Washington	.349
1936	Luke Appling, Chicago	.388
1937	Charlie Gehringer, Detroit	.371
1938	Jimmie Foxx, Boston	.349
1939	Joe DiMaggio, New York	.381
1940	Joe DiMaggio, New York	.352
1941	Ted Williams, Boston	.406
1942	Ted Williams, Boston	.356
1943	Luke Appling, Chicago	.328
1944	Lou Boudreau, Cleveland	.327
1945	George Stirnweiss, New York	.309
1946	Mickey Vernon, Washington	.353
1947	Ted Williams, Boston	.343
1948	Ted Williams, Boston	.369
1949	George Kell, Detroit	.343
1950	Billy Goodman, Boston	.354
1951	Ferris Fain, Philadelphia	.344
1952	Ferris Fain, Philadelphia	.327
1953	Mickey Vernon, Washington	.337
1954	Bobby Avila, Cleveland	.341
1955	Al Kaline, Detroit	.340
1956	Mickey Mantle, New York	.353
1957	Ted Williams, Boston	.388
1958	Ted Williams, Boston	.328
1959	Harvey Kuenn, Detroit	.353
1960	Pete Runnels, Boston	.320
1961	Norm Cash, Detroit	.361
1962	Pete Runnels, Boston	.326
1963	Carl Yastrzemski, Boston	.321
1964	Tony Oliva, Minnesota	.323
1965	Tony Oliva, Minnesota	.321
1966	Frank Robinson, Baltimore	.316
1967	Carl Yastrzemski, Boston	.326
1968	Carl Yastrzemski, Boston	.301
1969	Rod Carew, Minnesota	.332
1970	Alex Johnson, California	.329
1971	Tony Oliva, Minnesota	.337
1972	Rod Carew, Minnesota	.318
1973	Rod Carew, Minnesota	.350
1974	Rod Carew, Minnesota	.364
1975	Rod Carew, Minnesota	.359
1976	George Brett, Kansas City	.333

Home Runs—National League

1876	George Hall, Philadelphia	5
1877	George Schaffer, Louisville	3
1878	Paul Hines, Providence	4
1879	Charlie Jones, Boston	9
1880	Jim O'Rourke, Boston	6
	Harry Stovey, Worcester	6
1881	Dan Brouthers, Buffalo	8
1882	George Wood, Detroit	7
1883	Buck Ewing, New York	10
1884	Ed Williamson, Chicago	27
1885	Abner Dalrymple, Chicago	11
1886	Hardy Richardson, Detroit	11
1887	Roger Connor, New York	17
	Bill O'Brien, Washington	17
1888	Roger Connor, New York	14
1889	Sam Thompson, Philadelphia	20
1890	Mike Tiernan, New York	13
	Tommy Burns, Brooklyn	13
1891	Mike Tiernan, New York	16
	Harry Stovey, Boston	16
1892	James Holliday, Cincinnati	13
1893	Ed Delahanty, Philadelphia	19
1894	Hugh Duffy, Boston	18
	Bobby Lowe, Boston	18
1895	Bill Joyce, Washington	17
1896	Ed Delahanty, Philadelphia	13
	Sam Thompson, Philadelphia	13
1897	Napoleon Lajoie, Philadelphia	10
1898	Jimmy Collins, Boston	14
1899	Buck Freeman, Washington	25
1900	Herman Long, Boston	12
1901	Sam Crawford, Cincinnati	16
1902	Tommy Leach, Pittsburgh	6
1903	Jimmy Sheckard, Brooklyn	9
1904	Harry Lumley, Brooklyn	9
1905	Fred Odwell, Cincinnati	9
1906	Tim Jordan, Brooklyn	12
1907	Dave Brain, Boston	10
1908	Tim Jordan, Brooklyn	12
1909	John Murray, New York	7
1910	Fred Beck, Boston	10
	Frank Schulte, Chicago	10
1911	Frank Schulte, Chicago	21
1912	Heinie Zimmerman, Chicago	14
1913	Gavvy Cravath, Philadelphia	19
1914	Gavvy Cravath, Philadelphia	19
1915	Gavvy Cravath, Philadelphia	24
1916	Davey Robertson, New York	12
	Cy Williams, Chicago	12
1917	Gavvy Cravath, Philadelphia	12
	Davey Robertson, New York	12
1918	Gavvy Cravath, Philadelphia	8
1919	Gavvy Cravath, Philadelphia	12
1920	Cy Williams, Philadelphia	15
1921	George Kelly, New York	23
1922	Rogers Hornsby, St. Louis	42
1923	Cy Williams, Philadelphia	41
1924	Jacques Fournier, Brooklyn	27
1925	Rogers Hornsby, St. Louis	39
1926	Hack Wilson, Chicago	21
1927	Cy Williams, Philadelphia	30
	Hack Wilson, Chicago	30
1928	Jim Bottomley, St. Louis	31
	Hack Wilson, Chicago	31
1929	Chuck Klein, Philadelphia	43
1930	Hack Wilson, Chicago	56
1931	Chuck Klein, Philadelphia	31
1932	Chuck Klein, Philadelphia	38
	Mel Ott, New York	38
1933	Chuck Klein, Philadelphia	26
1934	Rip Collins, St. Louis	35
	Mel Ott, New York	35
1935	Wally Berger, Boston	34
1936	Mel Ott, New York	33

1937	Mel Ott, New York	31
	Joe Medwick, St. Louis	31
1938	Mel Ott, New York	36
1939	Johnny Mize, St. Louis	28
1940	Johnny Mize, St. Louis	43
1941	Dolph Camilli, Brooklyn	34
1942	Mel Ott, New York	30
1943	Bill Nicholson, Chicago	29
1944	Bill Nicholson, Chicago	33
1945	Tommy Holmes, Boston	28
1946	Ralph Kiner, Pittsburgh	23
1947	Ralph Kiner, Pittsburgh	51
	Johnny Mize, New York	51
1948	Ralph Kiner, Pittsburgh	40
	Johnny Mize, New York	40
1949	Ralph Kiner, Pittsburgh	54
1950	Ralph Kiner, Pittsburgh	47
1951	Ralph Kiner, Pittsburgh	42
1952	Ralph Kiner, Pittsburgh	37
	Hank Sauer, Chicago	37
1953	Eddie Mathews, Milwaukee	47
1954	Ted Kluszewski, Cincinnati	49
1955	Willie Mays, New York	51
1956	Duke Snider, Brooklyn	43
1957	Henry Aaron, Milwaukee	44
1958	Ernie Banks, Chicago	47
1959	Eddie Mathews, Milwaukee	46
1960	Ernie Banks, Chicago	41
1961	Orlando Cepeda, San Francisco	46
1962	Willie Mays, San Francisco	49
1963	Henry Aaron, Milwaukee	44
	Willie McCovey, San Francisco	44
1964	Willie Mays, San Francisco	47
1965	Willie Mays, San Francisco	52
1966	Henry Aaron, Atlanta	44
1967	Henry Aaron, Atlanta	39
1968	Willie McCovey, San Francisco	36
1969	Willie McCovey, San Francisco	45
1970	Johnny Bench, Cincinnati	45
1971	Willie Stargell, Pittsburgh	48
1972	Johnny Bench, Cincinnati	40
1973	Willie Stargell, Pittsburgh	44
1974	Mike Schmidt, Philadelphia	36
1975	Mike Schmidt, Philadelphia	38
1976	Mike Schmidt, Philadelphia	38

Home Runs—American League

1901	Napoleon Lajoie, Philadelphia	13
1902	Ralph Seybold, Philadelphia	16
1903	Buck Freeman, Boston	13
1904	Harry Davis, Philadelphia	10
1905	Harry Davis, Philadelphia	8
1906	Harry Davis, Philadelphia	12
1907	Harry Davis, Philadelphia	8
1908	Sam Crawford, Detroit	7
1909	Ty Cobb, Detroit	9
1910	J. Garland Stahl, Boston	10
1911	Frank Baker, Philadelphia	9
1912	Frank Baker, Philadelphia	10
1913	Frank Baker, Philadelphia	12
1914	Frank Baker, Philadelphia	8
	Sam Crawford, Detroit	8
1915	Robert Roth, Chicago-Cleveland	7
1916	Wally Pipp, New York	12
1917	Wally Pipp, New York	9
1918	Babe Ruth, Boston	11
	Clarence Walker, Philadelphia	11
1919	Babe Ruth, Boston	29
1920	Babe Ruth, New York	54
1921	Babe Ruth, New York	59
1922	Ken Williams, St. Louis	39
1923	Babe Ruth, New York	41

1924	Babe Ruth, New York	46
1925	Bob Meusel, New York	33
1926	Babe Ruth, New York	47
1927	Babe Ruth, New York	60
1928	Babe Ruth, New York	54
1929	Babe Ruth, New York	46
1930	Babe Ruth, New York	49
1931	Babe Ruth, New York	46
	Lou Gehrig, New York	46
1932	Jimmie Foxx, Philadelphia	58
1933	Jimmie Foxx, Philadelphia	48
1934	Lou Gehrig, New York	49
1935	Jimmie Foxx, Philadelphia	36
	Hank Greenberg, Detroit	36
1936	Lou Gehrig, New York	49
1937	Joe DiMaggio, New York	46
1938	Hank Greenberg, Detroit	58
1939	Jimmie Foxx, Boston	35
1940	Hank Greenberg, Detroit	41
1941	Ted Williams, Boston	37
1942	Ted Williams, Boston	36
1943	Rudy York, Detroit	34
1944	Nick Etten, New York	22
1945	Vern Stephens, St. Louis	24
1946	Hank Greenberg, Detroit	44
1947	Ted Williams, Boston	32
1948	Joe DiMaggio, New York	39
1949	Ted Williams, Boston	43
1950	Al Rosen, Cleveland	37
1951	Gus Zernial, Chicago-Philadelphia	33
1952	Larry Doby, Cleveland	32
1953	Al Rosen, Cleveland	43
1954	Larry Doby, Cleveland	32
1955	Mickey Mantle, New York	37
1956	Mickey Mantle, New York	52
1957	Roy Sievers, Washington	42
1958	Mickey Mantle, New York	42
1959	Rocky Colavito, Cleveland	42
	Harmon Killebrew, Washington	42
1960	Mickey Mantle, New York	40
1961	Roger Maris, New York	61
1962	Harmon Killebrew, Minnesota	48
1963	Harmon Killebrew, Minnesota	45
1964	Harmon Killebrew, Minnesota	49
1965	Tony Conigliaro, Boston	32
1966	Frank Robinson, Baltimore	49
1967	Carl Yastrzemski, Boston	44
	Harmon Killebrew, Minnesota	44
1968	Frank Howard, Washington	44
1969	Harmon Killebrew, Minnesota	49
1970	Frank Howard, Washington	44
1971	Bill Melton, Chicago	33
1972	Dick Allen, Chicago	37
1973	Reggie Jackson, Oakland	32
1974	Dick Allen, Chicago	32
1975	George Scott, Milwaukee	36
	Reggie Jackson, Oakland	36
1976	Graig Nettles, New York	32

Runs Batted In—National League

1907	Honus Wagner, Pittsburgh	91
1908	Honus Wagner, Pittsburgh	106
1909	Honus Wagner, Pittsburgh	102
1910	Sherry Magee, Philadelphia	116
1911	Frank Schulte, Chicago	121
1912	Heinie Zimmerman, Chicago	98
1913	Gavvy Cravath, Philadelphia	118
1914	Sherry Magee, Philadelphia	101
1915	Gavvy Cravath, Philadelphia	118
1916	Hal Chase, Cincinnati	84
1917	Heinie Zimmerman, New York	100
1918	Fred Merkle, Chicago	71

1919	Hi Myers, Brooklyn	72
1920	George Kelly, New York	94
	Rogers Hornsby, St. Louis	94
1921	Rogers Hornsby, St. Louis	126
1922	Rogers Hornsby, St. Louis	152
1923	Emil Meusel, New York	125
1924	George Kelly, New York	136
1925	Rogers Hornsby, St. Louis	143
1926	Jim Bottomley, St. Louis	120
1927	Paul Waner, Pittsburgh	131
1928	Jim Bottomley, St. Louis	136
1929	Hack Wilson, Chicago	159
1930	Hack Wilson, Chicago	190
1931	Chuck Klein, Philadelphia	121
1932	Frank Hurst, Philadelphia	143
1933	Chuck Klein, Philadelphia	120
1934	Mel Ott, New York	135
1935	Wally Berger, Boston	130
1936	Joe Medwick, St. Louis	138
1937	Joe Medwick, St. Louis	154
1938	Joe Medwick, St. Louis	122
1939	Frank McCormick, Cincinnati	128
1940	Johnny Mize, St. Louis	137
1941	Dolph Camilli, Brooklyn	120
1942	Johnny Mize, New York	110
1943	Bill Nicholson, Chicago	128
1944	Bill Nicholson, Chicago	122
1945	Dixie Walker, Brooklyn	124
1946	Enos Slaughter, St. Louis	130
1947	Johnny Mize, New York	138
1948	Stan Musial, St. Louis	131
1949	Ralph Kiner, Pittsburgh	127
1950	Del Ennis, Philadelphia	126
1951	Monte Irvin, New York	121
1952	Hank Sauer, Chicago	121
1953	Roy Campanella, Brooklyn	142
1954	Ted Kluszewski, Cincinnati	141
1955	Duke Snider, Brooklyn	136
1956	Stan Musial, St. Louis	109
1957	Henry Aaron, Milwaukee	132
1958	Ernie Banks, Chicago	129
1959	Ernie Banks, Chicago	143
1960	Henry Aaron, Milwaukee	126
1961	Orlando Cepeda, San Francisco	142
1962	Tommy Davis, Los Angeles	153
1963	Henry Aaron, Milwaukee	130
1964	Ken Boyer, St. Louis	119
1965	Deron Johnson, Cincinnati	130
1966	Henry Aaron, Milwaukee	127
1967	Orlando Cepeda, St. Louis	111
1968	Willie McCovey, San Francisco	105
1969	Willie McCovey, San Francisco	126
1970	Johnny Bench, Cincinnati	148
1971	Joe Torre, St. Louis	137
1972	Johnny Bench, Cincinnati	125
1973	Willie Stargell, Pittsburgh	119
1974	Johnny Bench, Cincinnati	129
1975	Greg Luzinski, Philadelphia	120
1976	George Foster, Cincinnati	121

Runs Batted In—American League

1907	Ty Cobb, Detroit	116
1908	Ty Cobb, Detroit	101
1909	Ty Cobb, Detroit	115
1910	Sam Crawford, Detroit	115
1911	Ty Cobb, Detroit	144
1912	Frank Baker, Philadelphia	133
1913	Frank Baker, Philadelphia	126
1914	Sam Crawford, Detroit	112
1915	Sam Crawford, Detroit	116
1916	Wally Pipp, New York	99
1917	Bobby Veach, Detroit	115
1918	George Burns, Philadelphia	74
	Bobby Veach, Detroit	74
1919	Babe Ruth, Boston	112
1920	Babe Ruth, New York	137
1921	Babe Ruth, New York	170
1922	Ken Williams, St. Louis	155
1923	Tris Speaker, Cleveland	130
	Babe Ruth, New York	130
1924	Goose Goslin, Washington	129
1925	Bob Meusel, New York	138
1926	Babe Ruth, New York	155
1927	Lou Gehrig, New York	175
1928	Lou Gehrig, New York	142
	Babe Ruth, New York	142
1929	Al Simmons, Philadelphia	157
1930	Lou Gehrig, New York	174
1931	Lou Gehrig, New York	184
1932	Jimmie Foxx, Philadelphia	169
1933	Jimmie Foxx, Philadelphia	163
1934	Lou Gehrig, New York	165
1935	Hank Greenberg, Detroit	170
1936	Hal Trosky, Cleveland	162
1937	Hank Greenberg, Detroit	183
1938	Jimmie Foxx, Boston	175
1939	Ted Williams, Boston	145
1940	Hank Greenberg, Detroit	150
1941	Joe DiMaggio, New York	125
1942	Ted Williams, Boston	137
1943	Rudy York, Detroit	118
1944	Vern Stephens, St. Louis	109
1945	Nick Etten, New York	111
1946	Hank Greenberg, Detroit	127
1947	Ted Williams, Boston	114
1948	Joe DiMaggio, New York	155
1949	Ted Williams, Boston	159
	Vern Stephens, Boston	159
1950	Vern Stephens, Boston	144
	Walt Dropo, Boston	144
1951	Gus Zernial, Chicago-Philadelphia	129
1952	Al Rosen, Cleveland	105
1953	Al Rosen, Cleveland	145
1954	Larry Doby, Cleveland	126
1955	Ray Boone, Detroit	116
	Jackie Jensen, Boston	116
1956	Mickey Mantle, New York	130
1957	Roy Sievers, Washington	114
1958	Jackie Jensen, Boston	122
1959	Jackie Jensen, Boston	112
1960	Roger Maris, New York	112
1961	Roger Maris, New York	142
1962	Harmon Killebrew, Minnesota	126
1963	Dick Stuart, Boston	118
1964	Brooks Robinson, Baltimore	118
1965	Rocky Colavito, Cleveland	108
1966	Frank Robinson, Baltimore	122
1967	Carl Yastrzemski, Boston	121
1968	Ken Harrelson, Boston	109
1969	Harmon Killebrew, Minnesota	140
1970	Frank Howard, Washington	126
1971	Harmon Killebrew, Minnesota	119
1972	Dick Allen, Chicago	113
1973	Reggie Jackson, Oakland	117
1974	Jeff Burroughs, Texas	118
1975	George Scott, Milwaukee	109
1976	Lee May, Baltimore	109

Stolen Bases—National League

1901	Honus Wagner, Pittsburgh	48
1902	Honus Wagner, Pittsburgh	43
1903	Jimmy Sheckard, Brooklyn	67
	Frank Chance, Chicago	67
1904	Honus Wagner, Pittsburgh	58

1905	Bill Maloney, Chicago	59
	Art Devlin, New York	59
1906	Frank Chance, Chicago	57
1907	Honus Wagner, Pittsburgh	61
1908	Honus Wagner, Pittsburgh	53
1909	Bob Bescher, Cincinnati	54
1910	Bob Bescher, Cincinnati	70
1911	Bob Bescher, Cincinnati	80
1912	Bob Bescher, Cincinnati	67
1913	Max Carey, Pittsburgh	61
1914	George Burns, New York	62
1915	Max Carey, Pittsburgh	36
1916	Max Carey, Pittsburgh	63
1917	Max Carey, Pittsburgh	46
1918	Max Carey, Pittsburgh	58
1919	George Burns, New York	50
1920	Max Carey, Pittsburgh	52
1921	Frankie Frisch, New York	49
1922	Max Carey, Pittsburgh	51
1923	Max Carey, Pittsburgh	51
1924	Max Carey, Pittsburgh	49
1925	Max Carey, Pittsburgh	46
1926	Kiki Cuyler, Pittsburgh	35
1927	Frankie Frisch, St. Louis	48
1928	Kiki Cuyler, Chicago	37
1929	Kiki Cuyler, Chicago	43
1930	Kiki Cuyler, Chicago	37
1931	Frankie Frisch, St. Louis	28
1932	Chuck Klein, Philadelphia	20
1933	Pepper Martin, St. Louis	26
1934	Pepper Martin, St. Louis	23
1935	Augie Galan, Chicago	22
1936	Pepper Martin, St. Louis	23
1937	Augie Galan, Chicago	23
1938	Stan Hack, Chicago	16
1939	Stan Hack, Chicago	17
	Lee Handley, Pittsburgh	17
1940	Lonnie Frey, Cincinnati	22
1941	Danny Murtaugh, Philadelphia	18
1942	Pete Reiser, Brooklyn	20
1943	Arky Vaughan, Brooklyn	20
1944	Johnny Barrett, Pittsburgh	28
1945	Red Schoendienst, St. Louis	26
1946	Pete Reiser, Brooklyn	34
1947	Jackie Robinson, Brooklyn	29
1948	Richie Ashburn, Philadelphia	32
1949	Jackie Robinson, Brooklyn	37
1950	Sam Jethroe, Boston	35
1951	Sam Jethroe, Boston	35
1952	Pee Wee Reese, Brooklyn	30
1953	Billy Bruton, Milwaukee	26
1954	Billy Bruton, Milwaukee	34
1955	Billy Bruton, Milwaukee	25
1956	Willie Mays, New York	40
1957	Willie Mays, New York	38
1958	Willie Mays, San Francisco	31
1959	Willie Mays, San Francisco	27
1960	Maury Wills, Los Angeles	50
1961	Maury Wills, Los Angeles	35
1962	Maury Wills, Los Angeles	104
1963	Maury Wills, Los Angeles	40
1964	Maury Wills, Los Angeles	53
1965	Maury Wills, Los Angeles	94
1966	Lou Brock, St. Louis	74
1967	Lou Brock, St. Louis	52
1968	Lou Brock, St. Louis	62
1969	Lou Brock, St. Louis	53
1970	Bobby Tolan, Cincinnati	57
1971	Lou Brock, St. Louis	64
1972	Joe Morgan, Cincinnati	58
1973	Lou Brock, St. Louis	70
1974	Lou Brock, St. Louis	118

1975	Davey Lopes, Los Angeles	77
1976	Davey Lopes, Los Angeles	63

Stolen Bases—American League

1901	Frank Isbell, Chicago	48
1902	Topsy Hartsel, Philadelphia	54
1903	Harry Bay, Cleveland	46
1904	Elmer Flick, Cleveland	42
	Harry Bay, Cleveland	42
1905	Danny Hoffman, Philadelphia	46
1906	Elmer Flick, Cleveland	39
	John Anderson, Washington	39
1907	Ty Cobb, Detroit	49
1908	Pat Dougherty, Chicago	47
1909	Ty Cobb, Detroit	76
1910	Eddie Collins, Philadelphia	81
1911	Ty Cobb, Detroit	83
1912	Clyde Milan, Washington	88
1913	Clyde Milan, Washington	74
1914	Fred Maisel, New York	74
1915	Ty Cobb, Detroit	96
1916	Ty Cobb, Detroit	68
1917	Ty Cobb, Detroit	55
1918	George Sisler, St. Louis	45
1919	Eddie Collins, Chicago	33
1920	Sam Rice, Washington	63
1921	George Sisler, St. Louis	35
1922	George Sisler, St. Louis	51
1923	Eddie Collins, Chicago	49
1924	Eddie Collins, Chicago	42
1925	Johnny Mostil, Chicago	43
1926	Johnny Mostil, Chicago	35
1927	George Sisler, St. Louis	27
1928	Buddy Myer, Boston	30
1929	Charlie Gehringer, Detroit	27
1930	Marty McManus, Detroit	23
1931	Ben Chapman, New York	61
1932	Ben Chapman, New York	38
1933	Ben Chapman, New York	27
1934	Billy Werber, Boston	40
1935	Billy Werber, Boston	29
1936	Lyn Lary, St. Louis	37
1937	Billy Werber, Philadelphia	35
	Ben Chapman, Washington-Boston	35
1938	Frank Crosetti, New York	27
1939	George Case, Washington	51
1940	George Case, Washington	35
1941	George Case, Washington	33
1942	George Case, Washington	44
1943	George Case, Washington	61
1944	George Stirnweiss, New York	55
1945	George Stirnweiss, New York	33
1946	George Case, Cleveland	28
1947	Bob Dillinger, St. Louis	34
1948	Bob Dillinger, St. Louis	28
1949	Bob Dillinger, St. Louis	20
1950	Dom DiMaggio, Boston	15
1951	Minnie Minoso, Cleveland-Chicago	31
1952	Minnie Minoso, Chicago	22
1953	Minnie Minoso, Chicago	25
1954	Jackie Jensen, Boston	22
1955	Jim Rivera, Chicago	25
1956	Luis Aparicio, Chicago	21
1957	Luis Aparicio, Chicago	28
1958	Luis Aparicio, Chicago	29
1959	Luis Aparicio, Chicago	56
1960	Luis Aparicio, Chicago	51
1961	Luis Aparicio, Chicago	53
1962	Luis Aparicio, Chicago	31
1963	Luis Aparicio, Baltimore	40
1964	Luis Aparicio, Baltimore	57
1965	Bert Campaneris, Kansas City	51

1966	Bert Campaneris, Kansas City	52		
1967	Bert Campaneris, Kansas City	55		
1968	Bert Campaneris, Oakland	62		
1969	Tommy Harper, Seattle	73		
1970	Bert Campaneris, Oakland	42		
1971	Amos Otis, Kansas City	52		
1972	Bert Campaneris, Oakland	52		
1973	Tommy Harper, Boston	54		
1974	Bill North, Oakland	54		
1975	Mickey Rivers, California	70		
1976	Bill North, Oakland	75		

Won-Lost Percentage—National League

1876	Al Spalding, Chicago	47	13	.783
1877	Tom Bond, Boston	40	17	.702
1878	Tom Bond, Boston	40	19	.678
1879	John M. Ward, Providence	46	19	.708
1880	Fred Goldsmith, Chicago	21	3	.875
1881	Larry Corcoran, Chicago	31	14	.689
1882	Larry Corcoran, Chicago	27	13	.675
1883	Jim McCormick, Cleveland	27	13	.675
1884	Charles Radbourn, Providence	60	12	.833
1885	Mickey Welch, New York	44	11	.800
1886	John Flynn, Chicago	23	6	.683
1887	Charlie Ferguson, Philadelphia	24	10	.683
1888	Tim Keefe, New York	35	12	.745
1889	John Clarkson, Boston	49	19	.721
1890	Tom Lovett, Brooklyn	31	11	.738
1891	John Ewing, New York	21	8	.724
1892	Cy Young, Cleveland	36	10	.783
1893	Gus Weyhing, Philadelphia	24	9	.727
1894	Jouett Meekin, New York	36	10	.783
1895	Bill Hoffer, Baltimore	29	8	.784
1896	Bill Hoffer, Baltimore	26	7	.788
1897	Jeremiah Nops, Baltimore	19	5	.792
1898	Ed Lewis, Boston	25	8	.758
1899	Jim Hughes, Brooklyn	26	6	.813
1900	Joe McGinnity, Brooklyn	29	9	.763
1901	Jack Chesbro, Pittsburgh	21	9	.700
1902	Jack Chesbro, Pittsburgh	28	6	.824
1903	Sam Leever, Pittsburgh	25	7	.781
1904	Joe McGinnity, New York	35	8	.814
1905	Sam Leever, Pittsburgh	20	5	.800
1906	Ed Reulbach, Chicago	19	4	.826
1907	Ed Reulbach, Chicago	17	4	.810
1908	Ed Reulbach, Chicago	24	7	.774
1909	Howard Camnitz, Pittsburgh	25	6	.806
	Christy Mathewson, New York	25	6	.806
1910	Leonard Cole, Chicago	20	4	.833
1911	Rube Marquard, New York	24	7	.774
1912	Claude Hendrix, Pittsburgh	24	9	.727
1913	Bert Humphries, Chicago	16	4	.800
1914	Bill James, Boston	26	7	.788
1915	Grover Alexander, Philadelphia	31	10	.756
1916	Tommy Hughes, Boston	16	3	.842
1917	Ferdie Schupp, New York	21	7	.750
1918	Claude Hendrix, Chicago	20	7	.741
1919	Dutch Ruether, Cincinnati	19	6	.760
1920	Burleigh Grimes, Brooklyn	23	11	.676
1921	Art Nehf, New York	20	10	.667
1922	Pete Donohue, Cincinnati	18	9	.667
1923	Dolph Luque, Cincinnati	27	8	.771
1924	Emil Yde, Pittsburgh	16	3	.842
1925	Willie Sherdel, St. Louis	15	6	.714
1926	Remy Kremer, Pittsburgh	20	6	.769
1927	Larry Benton, New York	17	7	.708
1928	Larry Benton, New York	25	9	.735
1929	Charlie Root, Chicago	19	6	.760
1930	Freddie Fitzsimmons, New York	19	7	.731
1931	Jesse Haines, St. Louis	12	3	.800
1932	Lon Warneke, Chicago	22	6	.786
1933	Ben Cantwell, Boston	20	10	.667

1934	Dizzy Dean, St. Louis	30	7	.811
1935	Bill Lee, Chicago	20	6	.769
1936	Carl Hubbell, New York	26	6	.813
1937	Carl Hubbell, New York	22	8	.733
1938	Bill Lee, Chicago	22	9	.710
1939	Paul Derringer, Cincinnati	25	7	.781
1940	Freddie Fitzsimmons, Brooklyn	16	2	.889
1941	Elmer Riddle, Cincinnati	19	4	.826
1942	Larry French, Brooklyn	15	4	.789
1943	Mort Cooper, St. Louis	21	8	.724
1944	Ted Wilks, St. Louis	17	4	.810
1945	Harry Brecheen, St. Louis	15	4	.789
1946	Murry Dickson, St. Louis	15	6	.714
1947	Larry Jansen, New York	21	5	.808
1948	Harry Brecheen, St. Louis	20	7	.741
1949	Preacher Roe, Brooklyn	15	6	.714
1950	Sal Maglie, New York	18	4	.818
1951	Preacher Roe, Brooklyn	22	3	.880
1952	Hoyt Wilhelm, New York	15	3	.833
1953	Carl Erskine, Brooklyn	20	6	.769
1954	Johnny Antonelli, New York	21	7	.750
1955	Don Newcombe, Brooklyn	20	5	.800
1956	Don Newcombe, Brooklyn	27	7	.794
1957	Bob Buhl, Milwaukee	18	7	.720
1958	Warren Spahn, Milwaukee	22	11	.667
	Lew Burdette, Milwaukee	20	10	.667
1959	Elroy Face, Pittsburgh	18	1	.947
1960	Ernie Broglio, St. Louis	21	9	.700
1961	Johnny Podres, Brooklyn	18	5	.783
1962	Bob Purkey, Cincinnati	23	5	.821
1963	Ron Perranoski, Los Angeles	16	3	.842
1964	Sandy Koufax, Los Angeles	19	5	.792
1965	Sandy Koufax, Los Angeles	26	8	.765
1966	Juan Marichal, San Francisco	25	6	.806
1967	Dick Hughes, St. Louis	16	6	.727
1968	Steve Blass, Pittsburgh	18	6	.750
1969	Tom Seaver, New York	25	7	.781
1970	Bob Gibson, St. Louis	23	7	.767
1971	Steve Carlton, St. Louis	20	9	.690
	Al Downing, Los Angeles	20	9	.690
1972	Gary Nolan, Cincinnati	15	5	.750
1973	George Stone, New York	12	3	.800
1974	Andy Messersmith, Los Angeles	20	6	.769
1975	Don Gullett, Cincinnati	15	4	.789
1976	Steve Carlton, Philadelphia	20	7	.741

Won-Lost Percentage—American League

1901	Clark Griffith, Chicago	24	7	.774
1902	Bill Bernhard, Phil.-Cleveland	18	5	.783
1903	Earl Moore, Cleveland	22	7	.759
1904	Jack Chesbro, New York	41	12	.774
1905	Rube Waddell, Philadelphia	27	10	.730
1906	Ed Plank, Philadelphia	19	6	.760
1907	Bill Donovan, Detroit	25	4	.862
1908	Ed Walsh, Chicago	40	15	.727
1909	George Mullin, Detroit	29	8	.784
1910	Chief Bender, Philadelphia	23	5	.821
1911	Chief Bender, Philadelphia	17	5	.773
1912	Joe Wood, Boston	34	5	.872
1913	Walter Johnson, Washington	36	7	.837
1914	Chief Bender, Philadelphia	17	3	.850
1915	Ernie Shore, Boston	19	8	.704
	George Foster, Boston	19	8	.704
1916	Harry Coveleski, Detroit	23	10	.697
1917	Reb Russell, Chicago	15	5	.750
1918	Sam Jones, Boston	16	5	.762
1919	Ed Cicotte, Chicago	29	7	.805
1920	Jim Bagby, Cleveland	31	12	.721
1921	Carl Mays, New York	27	9	.750
1922	Joe Bush, New York	26	7	.788
1923	Herb Pennock, New York	19	6	.760
1924	Walter Johnson, Washington	23	7	.767

1925	Stan Coveleski, Washington	20	5	.800
1926	George Uhle, Cleveland	27	11	.711
1927	Waite Hoyt, New York	22	7	.759
1928	Alvin Crowder, St. Louis	21	5	.808
1929	Lefty Grove, Philadelphia	20	6	.769
1930	Lefty Grove, Philadelphia	28	5	.848
1931	Lefty Grove, Philadelphia	31	4	.886
1932	Johnny Allen, New York	17	4	.810
1933	Lefty Grove, Philadelphia	24	8	.750
1934	Lefty Gomez, New York	26	5	.839
1935	Eldon Auker, Detroit	18	7	.720
1936	Monte Pearson, New York	19	7	.731
1937	Johnny Allen, Cleveland	15	1	.938
1938	Red Ruffing, New York	21	7	.750
1939	Lefty Grove, Boston	15	4	.789
1940	Schoolboy Rowe, Detroit	16	3	.842
1941	Lefty Gomez, New York	15	5	.750
1942	Ernie Bonham, New York	21	5	.808
1943	Spud Chandler, New York	20	4	.833
1944	Tex Hughson, Boston	18	5	.783
1945	Hal Newhouser, Detroit	25	9	.735
1946	Dave Ferriss, Boston	25	6	.806
1947	Allie Reynolds, New York	19	8	.704
1948	Jack Kramer, Boston	18	5	.783
1949	Ellis Kinder, Boston	23	6	.793
1950	Vic Raschi, New York	21	8	.724
1951	Bob Feller, Cleveland	22	8	.733
1952	Bobby Shantz, Philadelphia	24	7	.774
1953	Ed Lopat, New York	16	4	.800
1954	Sandy Consuegra, Chicago	16	3	.842
1955	Tommy Byrne, New York	16	5	.762
1956	Whitey Ford, New York	19	6	.760
1957	Dick Donovan, Chicago	16	6	.727
	Tom Sturdivant, New York	16	6	.727
1958	Bob Turley, New York	21	7	.750
1959	Bob Shaw, Chicago	18	6	.750
1960	Jim Perry, Cleveland	18	10	.643
1961	Whitey Ford, New York	25	4	.862
1962	Ray Herbert, Chicago	20	9	.690
1963	Whitey Ford, New York	24	7	.774
1964	Wally Bunker, Baltimore	19	5	.792
1965	Jim Grant, Minnesota	21	7	.750
1966	Sonny Siebert, Cleveland	16	8	.667
1967	Joel Horlen, Chicago	19	7	.731
1968	Denny McLain, Detroit	31	6	.838
1969	Jim Palmer, Baltimore	16	4	.800
1970	Mike Cuellar, Baltimore	24	8	.750
1971	Dave McNally, Baltimore	21	5	.808
1972	Jim Hunter, Oakland	21	7	.750
1973	Jim Hunter, Oakland	21	5	.808
1974	Mike Cuellar, Baltimore	22	10	.688
1975	Dennis Leonard, Kansas City	15	7	.682
1976	Bill Campbell, Minnesota	17	5	.773

Earned-Run Average—National League

1901	Jesse Tannehill, Philadelphia	2.18
1902	Jack Taylor, St. Louis	1.33
1903	Sam Leever, Pittsburgh	2.06
1904	Joe McGinnity, New York	1.61
1905	Christy Mathewson, New York	1.27
1906	Mordecai Brown, Chicago	1.04
1907	Jack Pfeister, Chicago	1.15
1908	Christy Mathewson, New York	1.43
1909	Christy Mathewson, New York	1.14
1910	George McQuillan, Philadelphia	1.60
1911	Christy Mathewson, New York	1.99
1912	Jeff Tesreau, New York	1.96
1913	Christy Mathewson, New York	2.06
1914	Bill Doak, St. Louis	1.72
1915	Grover Alexander, Philadelphia	1.22
1916	Grover Alexander, Philadelphia	1.55
1917	Grover Alexander, Philadelphia	1.85
1918	Jim Vaughn, Chicago	1.74
1919	Grover Alexander, Chicago	1.72
1920	Grover Alexander, Chicago	1.91
1921	Bill Doak, St. Louis	2.58
1922	Rosy Ryan, New York	3.00
1923	Dolph Luque, Cincinnati	1.93
1924	Dazzy Vance, Brooklyn	2.16
1925	Dolph Luque, Cincinnati	2.63
1926	Remy Kremer, Pittsburgh	2.61
1927	Remy Kremer, Pittsburgh	2.47
1928	Dazzy Vance, Brooklyn	2.09
1929	Bill Walker, New York	3.08
1930	Dazzy Vance, Brooklyn	2.61
1931	Bill Walker, New York	2.26
1932	Lon Warneke, Chicago	2.37
1933	Carl Hubbell, New York	1.66
1934	Carl Hubbell, New York	2.30
1935	Cy Blanton, Pittsburgh	2.59
1936	Carl Hubbell, New York	2.31
1937	Jim Turner, Boston	2.38
1938	Bill Lee, Chicago	2.66
1939	Bucky Walters, Cincinnati	2.29
1940	Bucky Walters, Cincinnati	2.48
1941	Elmer Riddle, Cincinnati	2.24
1942	Mort Cooper, St. Louis	1.77
1943	Howie Pollet, St. Louis	1.75
1944	Ed Heusser, Cincinnati	2.38
1945	Hank Borowy, Chicago	2.14
1946	Howie Pollet, St. Louis	2.10
1947	Warren Spahn, Boston	2.33
1948	Harry Brecheen, St. Louis	2.24
1949	Dave Koslo, New York	2.50
1950	Jim Hearn, St. Louis-New York	2.49
1951	Chet Nichols, Boston	2.88
1952	Hoyt Wilhelm, New York	2.43
1953	Warren Spahn, Milwaukee	2.10
1954	John Antonelli, New York	2.29
1955	Bob Friend, Pittsburgh	2.84
1956	Lew Burdette, Milwaukee	2.71
1957	Johnny Podres, Brooklyn	2.66
1958	Stu Miller, San Francisco	2.47
1959	Sam Jones, San Francisco	2.82
1960	Mike McCormick, San Francisco	2.70
1961	Warren Spahn, Milwaukee	3.01
1962	Sandy Koufax, Los Angeles	2.54
1963	Sandy Koufax, Los Angeles	1.88
1964	Sandy Koufax, Los Angeles	1.74
1965	Sandy Koufax, Los Angeles	2.04
1966	Sandy Koufax, Los Angeles	1.73
1967	Phil Niekro, Atlanta	1.87
1968	Bob Gibson, St. Louis	1.12
1969	Juan Marichal, San Francisco	2.10
1970	Tom Seaver, New York	2.81
1971	Tom Seaver, New York	1.76
1972	Steve Carlton, Philadelphia	1.98
1973	Tom Seaver, New York	2.08
1974	Buzz Capra, Atlanta	2.28
1975	Randy Jones, San Diego	2.24
1976	John Denny, St. Louis	2.52

Earned-Run Average—American League

1901	Cy Young, Boston	1.62
1902	Ed Siever, Detroit	1.91
1903	Earl Moore, Cleveland	1.77
1904	Addie Joss, Cleveland	1.59
1905	Rube Waddell, Philadelphia	1.48
1906	Doc White, Chicago	1.52
1907	Ed Walsh, Chicago	1.60
1908	Addie Joss, Cleveland	1.16
1909	Harry Krause, Philadelphia	1.39
1910	Ed Walsh, Chicago	1.27
1911	Vean Gregg, Cleveland	1.81
1912	Walter Johnson, Washington	1.39
1913	Walter Johnson, Washington	1.09
1914	Hub Leonard, Boston	1.01
1915	Joe Wood, Boston	1.49

1916	Babe Ruth, Boston	1.75
1917	Ed Cicotte, Chicago	1.53
1918	Walter Johnson, Washington	1.28
1919	Walter Johnson, Washington	1.49
1920	Bob Shawkey, New York	2.46
1921	Red Faber, Chicago	2.48
1922	Red Faber, Chicago	2.81
1923	Stan Coveleski, Cleveland	2.76
1924	Walter Johnson, Washington	2.72
1925	Stan Coveleski, Washington	2.84
1926	Lefty Grove, Philadelphia	2.51
1927	Wilcy Moore, New York	2.28
1928	Garland Braxton, Washington	2.52
1929	Lefty Grove, Philadelphia	2.82
1930	Lefty Grove, Philadelphia	2.54
1931	Lefty Grove, Philadelphia	2.33
1932	Lefty Grove, Philadelphia	2.84
1933	Monte Pearson, Cleveland	2.33
1934	Lefty Gomez, New York	2.33
1935	Lefty Grove, Boston	2.70
1936	Lefty Grove, Boston	2.81
1937	Lefty Gomez, New York	2.33
1938	Lefty Grove, Boston	3.07
1939	Lefty Grove, Boston	2.54
1940	Bob Feller, Cleveland	2.62
1941	Thornton Lee, Chicago	2.37
1942	Ted Lyons, Chicago	2.10
1943	Spud Chandler, New York	1.64
1944	Dizzy Trout, Detroit	2.12
1945	Hal Newhouser, Detroit	1.81
1946	Hal Newhouser, Detroit	1.94
1947	Spud Chandler, New York	2.46
1948	Gene Bearden, Cleveland	2.43
1949	Mel Parnell, Boston	2.78
1950	Early Wynn, Cleveland	3.20
1951	Saul Rogovin, Detroit-Chicago	2.78
1952	Allie Reynolds, New York	2.07
1953	Ed Lopat, New York	2.43
1954	Mike Garcia, Cleveland	2.64
1955	Billy Pierce, Chicago	1.97
1956	Whitey Ford, New York	2.47
1957	Bobby Shantz, New York	2.45
1958	Whitey Ford, New York	2.01
1959	Hoyt Wilhelm, Baltimore	2.19
1960	Frank Baumann, Chicago	2.68
1961	Dick Donovan, Washington	2.40
1962	Hank Aguirre, Detroit	2.21
1963	Gary Peters, Chicago	2.33
1964	Dean Chance, Los Angeles	1.65
1965	Sam McDowell, Cleveland	2.18
1966	Gary Peters, Chicago	1.98
1967	Joel Horlen, Chicago	2.06
1968	Luis Tiant, Cleveland	1.60
1969	Dick Bosman, Washington	2.19
1970	Diego Segui, Oakland	2.56
1971	Vida Blue, Oakland	1.82
1972	Luis Tiant, Boston	1.91
1973	Jim Palmer, Baltimore	2.40
1974	Jim Hunter, Oakland	2.49
1975	Jim Palmer, Baltimore	2.09
1976	Mark Fidrych, Detroit	2.34

Strikeouts—National League

1901	Noodles Hahn, Cincinnati	233
1902	Vic Willis, Boston	226
1903	Christy Mathewson, New York	267
1904	Christy Mathewson, New York	212
1905	Christy Mathewson, New York	206
1906	Fred Beebe, Chicago-St. Louis	171
1907	Christy Mathewson, New York	178
1908	Christy Mathewson, New York	259
1909	Orval Overall, Chicago	205
1910	Christy Mathewson, New York	190
1911	Rube Marquard, New York	237

1912	Grover Alexander, Philadelphia	195
1913	Tom Seaton, Philadelphia	168
1914	Grover Alexander, Philadelphia	214
1915	Grover Alexander, Philadelphia	241
1916	Grover Alexander, Philadelphia	167
1917	Grover Alexander, Philadelphia	200
1918	Jim Vaughn, Chicago	148
1919	Jim Vaughn, Chicago	141
1920	Grover Alexander, Chicago	173
1921	Burleigh Grimes, Brooklyn	136
1922	Dazzy Vance, Brooklyn	134
1923	Dazzy Vance, Brooklyn	197
1924	Dazzy Vance, Brooklyn	262
1925	Dazzy Vance, Brooklyn	221
1926	Dazzy Vance, Brooklyn	140
1927	Dazzy Vance, Brooklyn	184
1928	Dazzy Vance, Brooklyn	200
1929	Pat Malone, Chicago	166
1930	Bill Hallahan, St. Louis	177
1931	Bill Hallahan, St. Louis	159
1932	Dizzy Dean, St. Louis	191
1933	Dizzy Dean, St. Louis	199
1934	Dizzy Dean, St. Louis	195
1935	Dizzy Dean, St. Louis	182
1936	Van Lingle Mungo, Brooklyn	238
1937	Carl Hubbell, New York	159
1938	Clay Bryant, Chicago	135
1939	Claude Passeau, Phil.-Chicago	137
	Bucky Walters, Cincinnati	137
1940	Kirby Higbe, Philadelphia	137
1941	John Vander Meer, Cincinnati	202
1942	John Vander Meer, Cincinnati	186
1943	John Vander Meer, Cincinnati	174
1944	Bill Voiselle, New York	161
1945	Preacher Roe, Pittsburgh	148
1946	Johnny Schmitz, Chicago	135
1947	Ewell Blackwell, Cincinnati	193
1948	Harry Brecheen, St. Louis	149
1949	Warren Spahn, Boston	151
1950	Warren Spahn, Boston	191
1951	Warren Spahn, Boston	164
	Don Newcombe, Brooklyn	164
1952	Warren Spahn, Boston	183
1953	Robin Roberts, Philadelphia	198
1954	Robin Roberts, Philadelphia	185
1955	Sam Jones, Chicago	198
1956	Sam Jones, Chicago	176
1957	Jack Sanford, Philadelphia	188
1958	Sam Jones, St. Louis	225
1959	Don Drysdale, Los Angeles	242
1960	Don Drysdale, Los Angeles	246
1961	Sandy Koufax, Los Angeles	269
1962	Don Drysdale, Los Angeles	232
1963	Sandy Koufax, Los Angeles	306
1964	Bob Veale, Pittsburgh	250
1965	Sandy Koufax, Los Angeles	382
1966	Sandy Koufax, Los Angeles	317
1967	Jim Bunning, Philadelphia	253
1968	Bob Gibson, St. Louis	268
1969	Ferguson Jenkins, Chicago	273
1970	Tom Seaver, New York	283
1971	Tom Seaver, New York	289
1972	Steve Carlton, Philadelphia	310
1973	Tom Seaver, New York	251
1974	Steve Carlton, Philadelphia	240
1975	Tom Seaver, New York	243
1976	Tom Seaver, New York	235

Strikeouts—American League

1901	Cy Young, Boston	159
1902	Rube Waddell, Philadelphia	210
1903	Rube Waddell, Philadelphia	301
1904	Rube Waddell, Philadelphia	349
1905	Rube Waddell, Philadelphia	286

1906	Rube Waddell, Philadelphia	203
1907	Rube Waddell, Philadelphia	226
1908	Ed Walsh, Chicago	269
1909	Frank Smith, Chicago	177
1910	Walter Johnson, Washington	313
1911	Ed Walsh, Chicago	255
1912	Walter Johnson, Washington	303
1913	Walter Johnson, Washington	243
1914	Walter Johnson, Washington	225
1915	Walter Johnson, Washington	203
1916	Walter Johnson, Washington	228
1917	Walter Johnson, Washington	188
1918	Walter Johnson, Washington	162
1919	Walter Johnson, Washington	147
1920	Stan Coveleski, Cleveland	133
1921	Walter Johnson, Washington	143
1922	Urban Shocker, St. Louis	149
1923	Walter Johnson, Washington	130
1924	Walter Johnson, Washington	158
1925	Lefty Grove, Philadelphia	116
1926	Lefty Grove, Philadelphia	194
1927	Lefty Grove, Philadelphia	174
1928	Lefty Grove, Philadelphia	183
1929	Lefty Grove, Philadelphia	170
1930	Lefty Grove, Philadelphia	209
1931	Lefty Grove, Philadelphia	175
1932	Red Ruffing, New York	190
1933	Lefty Gomez, New York	163
1934	Lefty Gomez, New York	158
1935	Tommy Bridges, Detroit	163
1936	Tommy Bridges, Detroit	175
1937	Lefty Gomez, New York	194
1938	Bob Feller, Cleveland	240
1939	Bob Feller, Cleveland	246
1940	Bob Feller, Cleveland	261
1941	Bob Feller, Cleveland	260
1942	Bobo Newsom, Washington	113
	Tex Hughson, Boston	113
1943	Allie Reynolds, New York	151
1944	Hal Newhouser, Detroit	187
1945	Hal Newhouser, Detroit	212
1946	Bob Feller, Cleveland	348
1947	Bob Feller, Cleveland	196
1948	Bob Feller, Cleveland	164
1949	Virgil Trucks, Detroit	153
1950	Bob Lemon, Cleveland	170
1951	Vic Raschi, New York	164
1952	Allie Reynolds, New York	160
1953	Billy Pierce, Chicago	186
1954	Bob Turley, Baltimore	185
1955	Herb Score, Cleveland	245
1956	Herb Score, Cleveland	263
1957	Early Wynn, Cleveland	184
1958	Early Wynn, Chicago	179
1959	Jim Bunning, Detroit	201
1960	Jim Bunning, Detroit	201
1961	Camilo Pascual, Minnesota	221
1962	Camilo Pascual, Minnesota	206
1963	Camilo Pascual, Minnesota	202
1964	Al Downing, New York	217
1965	Sam McDowell, Cleveland	325
1966	Sam McDowell, Cleveland	225
1967	Jim Lonborg, Boston	246
1968	Sam McDowell, Cleveland	283
1969	Sam McDowell, Cleveland	279
1970	Sam McDowell, Cleveland	304
1971	Vida Blue, Oakland	301
1972	Nolan Ryan, California	329
1973	Nolan Ryan, California	383
1974	Nolan Ryan, California	367
1975	Frank Tanana, California	269
1976	Nolan Ryan, California	327

Most Valuable Players

(Chalmers Award 1911–14; league awards given in American League 1922–28, National League 1924–29; *Sporting News* award in American League 1929–30, National League 1930 only; Baseball Writers Association Award since 1931 in both leagues.)

National League

1911	Frank Schulte, Chicago	
1912	Larry Doyle, New York	
1913	Jake Daubert, Brooklyn	
1914	Johnny Evers, Chicago	
1915–23	No selections	
1924	Dazzy Vance, Brooklyn	
1925	Rogers Hornsby, St. Louis	
1926	Bob O'Farrell, St. Louis	
1927	Paul Waner, Pittsburgh	
1928	Jim Bottomley, St. Louis	
1929	Rogers Hornsby, Chicago	
1930	Bill Terry, New York	
1931	Frankie Frisch, St. Louis	
1932	Chuck Klein, Philadelphia	
1933	Carl Hubbell, New York	
1934	Dizzy Dean, St. Louis	
1935	Gabby Hartnett, Chicago	
1936	Carl Hubbell, New York	
1937	Joe Medwick, St. Louis	
1938	Ernie Lombardi, Cincinnati	
1939	Bucky Walters, Cincinnati	
1940	Frank McCormick, Cincinnati	
1941	Dolph Camilli, Brooklyn	
1942	Mort Cooper, St. Louis	
1943	Stan Musial, St. Louis	
1944	Marty Marion, St. Louis	
1945	Phil Cavaretta, Chicago	
1946	Stan Musial, St. Louis	
1947	Bob Elliott, Boston	
1948	Stan Musial, St. Louis	
1949	Jackie Robinson, Brooklyn	
1950	Jim Konstanty, Philadelphia	
1951	Roy Campanella, Brooklyn	
1952	Hank Sauer, Chicago	
1953	Roy Campanella, Brooklyn	
1954	Willie Mays, New York	
1955	Roy Campanella, Brooklyn	
1956	Don Newcombe, Brooklyn	
1957	Henry Aaron, Milwaukee	
1958	Ernie Banks, Chicago	
1959	Ernie Banks, Chicago	
1960	Dick Groat, Pittsburgh	
1961	Frank Robinson, Cincinnati	
1962	Maury Wills, Los Angeles	
1963	Sandy Koufax, Los Angeles	
1964	Ken Boyer, St. Louis	
1965	Willie Mays, San Francisco	
1966	Roberto Clemente, Pittsburgh	
1967	Orlando Cepeda, St. Louis	
1968	Bob Gibson, St. Louis	
1969	Willie McCovey, San Francisco	
1970	Johnny Bench, Cincinnati	
1971	Joe Torre, St. Louis	
1972	Johnny Bench, Cincinnati	
1973	Pete Rose, Cincinnati	
1974	Steve Garvey, Los Angeles	
1975	Joe Morgan, Cincinnati	
1976	Joe Morgan, Cincinnati	

American League

1911	Ty Cobb, Detroit	
1912	Tris Speaker, Boston	

1913 Walter Johnson, Washington
1914 Eddie Collins, Philadelphia
1915–21 No selections
1922 George Sisler, St. Louis
1923 Babe Ruth, New York
1924 Walter Johnson, Washington
1925 Roger Peckinpaugh, Washington
1926 George Burns, Cleveland
1927 Lou Gehrig, New York
1928 Mickey Cochrane, Philadelphia
1929 Al Simmons, Philadelphia
1930 Joe Cronin, Washington
1931 Lefty Grove, Philadelphia
1932 Jimmie Foxx, Philadelphia
1933 Jimmie Foxx, Philadelphia
1934 Mickey Cochrane, Detroit
1935 Hank Greenberg, Detroit
1936 Lou Gehrig, New York
1937 Charlie Gehringer, Detroit
1938 Jimmie Foxx, Boston
1939 Joe DiMaggio, New York
1940 Hank Greenberg, Detroit
1941 Joe DiMaggio, New York
1942 Joe Gordon, New York
1943 Spud Chandler, New York
1944 Hal Newhouser, Detroit
1945 Hal Newhouser, Detroit
1946 Ted Williams, Boston
1947 Joe DiMaggio, New York
1948 Lou Boudreau, Cleveland
1949 Ted Williams, Boston
1950 Phil Rizzuto, New York
1951 Yogi Berra, New York
1952 Bobby Shantz, Philadelphia
1953 Al Rosen, Cleveland
1954 Yogi Berra, New York
1955 Yogi Berra, New York
1956 Mickey Mantle, New York
1957 Mickey Mantle, New York
1958 Jackie Jensen, Boston
1959 Nellie Fox, Chicago
1960 Roger Maris, New York
1961 Roger Maris, New York
1962 Mickey Mantle, New York
1963 Elston Howard, New York
1964 Brooks Robinson, Baltimore
1965 Zoilo Versalles, Minnesota
1966 Frank Robinson, Baltimore
1967 Carl Yastrzemski, Boston
1968 Denny McLain, Detroit
1969 Harmon Killebrew, Minnesota
1970 Boog Powell, Baltimore
1971 Vida Blue, Oakland
1972 Dick Allen, Chicago
1973 Reggie Jackson, Oakland
1974 Jeff Burroughs, Texas
1975 Fred Lynn, Boston
1976 Thurman Munson, New York

Cy Young Award Winners

(For outstanding pitcher in each league, 1967–present; just one award given annually, 1956–1966.)

1956 Don Newcombe, Brooklyn (NL)
1957 Warren Spahn, Milwaukee (NL)
1958 Bob Turley, New York (AL)
1959 Early Wynn, Chicago (AL)
1960 Vern Law, Pittsburgh (NL)
1961 Whitey Ford, New York (AL)
1962 Don Drysdale, Los Angeles (NL)
1963 Sandy Koufax, Los Angeles (NL)

1964 Dean Chance, Los Angeles (AL)
1965 Sandy Koufax, Los Angeles (NL)
1966 Sandy Koufax, Los Angeles (NL)

National League
1967 Mike McCormick, San Francisco
1968 Bob Gibson, St. Louis
1969 Tom Seaver, New York
1970 Bob Gibson, St. Louis
1971 Ferguson Jenkins, Chicago
1972 Steve Carlton, Philadelphia
1973 Tom Seaver, New York
1974 Mike Marshall, Los Angeles
1975 Tom Seaver, New York
1976 Randy Jones, San Diego

American League
1967 Jim Lonborg, Boston
1968 Denny McLain, Detroit
1969 Mike Cuellar, Baltimore
       Denny McLain, Detroit
1970 Jim Perry, Minnesota
1971 Vida Blue, Oakland
1972 Gaylord Perry, Cleveland
1973 Jim Palmer, Baltimore
1974 Jim Hunter, Oakland
1975 Jim Palmer, Baltimore
1976 Jim Palmer, Baltimore

Rookies of the Year

(Just one award annually, 1947–48.)

1947 Jackie Robinson, Brooklyn (NL)
1948 Alvin Dark, Boston (NL)

National League
1949 Don Newcombe, Brooklyn
1950 Sam Jethroe, Boston
1951 Willie Mays, New York
1952 Joe Black, Brooklyn
1953 Junior Gilliam, Brooklyn
1954 Wally Moon, St. Louis
1955 Bill Virdon, St. Louis
1956 Frank Robinson, Cincinnati
1957 Jack Sanford, Philadelphia
1958 Orlando Cepeda, San Francisco
1959 Willie McCovey, San Francisco
1960 Frank Howard, Los Angeles
1961 Billy Williams, Chicago
1962 Ken Hubbs, Chicago
1963 Pete Rose, Cincinnati
1964 Dick Allen, Philadelphia
1965 Jim Lefebvre, Los Angeles
1966 Tommy Helms, Cincinnati
1967 Tom Seaver, New York
1968 Johnny Bench, Cincinnati
1969 Ted Sizemore, Los Angeles
1970 Carl Morton, Montreal
1971 Earl Williams, Atlanta
1972 Jon Matlack, New York
1973 Gary Matthews, San Francisco
1974 Greg Gross, Houston
1975 John Montefusco, San Francisco
1976 Pat Zachry, Cincinnati
       Butch Metzger, San Diego

American League
1949 Roy Sievers, St. Louis
1950 Walt Dropo, Boston
1951 Gil McDougald, New York
1952 Harry Byrd, Philadelphia
1953 Harvey Kuenn, Detroit

1954	Bob Grim, New York	
1955	Herb Score, Cleveland	
1956	Luis Aparicio, Chicago	
1957	Tony Kubek, New York	
1958	Albie Pearson, Washington	
1959	Bob Allison, Washington	
1960	Ron Hansen, Baltimore	
1961	Don Schwall, Boston	
1962	Tom Tresh, New York	
1963	Gary Peters, Chicago	
1964	Tony Oliva, Minnesota	
1965	Curt Blefary, Baltimore	
1966	Tommie Agee, Chicago	
1967	Rod Carew, Minnesota	
1968	Stan Bahnsen, New York	
1969	Lou Piniella, Kansas City	
1970	Thurman Munson, New York	
1971	Chris Chambliss, Cleveland	
1972	Carlton Fisk, Boston	
1973	Al Bumbry, Baltimore	
1974	Mike Hargrove, Texas	
1975	Fred Lynn, Boston	
1976	Mark Fidrych, Detroit	

Major-League Individual Records

(In some cases, three records are listed in a single category: An all-time record set before 1901, a modern record, and the record for the league in which the modern record was not set.)

Batting Average

Highest, lifetime—.367, Ty Cobb, 1905–1928; .359, Rogers Hornsby, 1915–1932 (National League career only).

Highest, season—.492, Tip O'Neill, St. Louis, American Association, 1887 (walks counted as hits); .438, Hugh Duffy, Boston, NL, 1894; .424, Rogers Hornsby, St. Louis, NL, 1924; .422, Napoleon Lajoie, Philadelphia, AL, 1901.

Most years, .300 or better—23, Ty Cobb, 1906–1928.

Most years leading league—12, Ty Cobb, AL, 1907–1915, 1917–1919; 8, Honus Wagner, NL, 1900, 1903–1904, 1906–1909, 1911.

Longevity

Most seasons—26, Deacon McGuire, 1884–1888, 1890–1908, 1910, 1912; 25, Eddie Collins, AL, 1906–1930; 23, Rabbit Maranville, 1912–1933, 1935.

Most games—3,298, Henry Aaron, 1954–1976; 3,033, Ty Cobb, AL, 1905–1928.

Most consecutive games—2,130, Lou Gehrig, AL, June 1, 1925, through April 30, 1939; 1,117, Billy Williams, NL, Sept. 22, 1963, through Sept. 2, 1970.

Hitting

Most at-bats, career—12,364, Henry Aaron, NL, 1954–1976; 11,429, Ty Cobb, AL, 1905–1928.

Most at-bats, season—698, Matty Alou, Pittsburgh, NL, 1969.

Most hits, career—4,191, Ty Cobb, AL, 1905–1928; 3,771, Henry Aaron, NL, 1954–1974; AL, 1975–76.

Most hits, season—257, George Sisler, St. Louis, AL, 1920; 254, Lefty O'Doul, Philadelphia, NL, 1929, and Bill Terry, New York, NL, 1930.

Most hits, game—9, John Burnett, Cleveland, AL, July 10, 1932 (18 innings).

Most consecutive hits—12, Frank Higgins, Boston, AL, June 19–21, 1938, and Walt Dropo, Detroit, AL, July 14–15, 1952.

Most consecutive games hit safely—56, Joe DiMaggio, New York, AL, May 15–July 16, 1941; 44, Willie Keeler, Baltimore, NL, April 22–June 18, 1897.

Runs

Most career—2,244, Ty Cobb, AL, 1905–1928; 2,174, Henry Aaron, NL, 1954–1974, AL, 1975–1976.

Most, season—196, Billy Hamilton, Philadelphia, NL, 1894; 177, Babe Ruth, New York, AL, 1921; 158, Chuck Klein, Philadelphia, NL, 1930.

Most, game—7, Guy Hecker, Louisville, American Association, Aug. 15, 1886; 6, by four players (Mel Ott twice).

Runs Batted In

Most, career—2,297, Henry Aaron (2174 in NL, 1954–74, 95 in AL, 1975–76); 2,209, Babe Ruth (2,197 in AL, 1914–34, 12 in NL, 1935).

Most, season—190, Hack Wilson, Chicago, NL, 1930; 184, Lou Gehrig, New York, AL, 1931.

Most, game—12, Jim Bottomley, St. Louis, NL, Sept. 16, 1924.

Home Runs

Most, career—755, Henry Aaron (733 is NL record, 1954–1974; Aaron also hit 22 in AL, 1975–76); 714, Babe Ruth (708 is AL record, 1914–1934; Ruth also hit 6 in NL, 1935).

Most, season—61, Roger Maris, New York, AL, 1961 (162-game schedule); 60, Babe Ruth, New York, AL, 1927 (154-game schedule); 56, Hack Wilson, Chicago, NL, 1930.

Most, game—4, by many players.

Most, consecutive—4, by many players.

Triples

Most, career—312, Sam Crawford, NL, 1899–1902, Detroit, 1903–1917; 297, Ty Cobb, AL, 1905–1928; 252, Honus Wagner, NL, 1897–1917.

Most, season—36, Owen Wilson, Pittsburgh, NL, 1912; 26, Joe Jackson, Cleveland, AL, 1912, and Sam Crawford, Detroit, AL, 1914.

Doubles

Most, career—793, Tris Speaker, AL, 1907–1928; 725, Stan Musial, NL, 1941–1944, 1946–1963.

Most, season—67, Earl Webb, Boston, AL, 1931; 64, Joe Medwick, St. Louis, NL, 1936.

Singles

Most, career—3,052, Ty Cobb, AL, 1905–1928; 2,426, Honus Wagner, NL, 1897–1917.

Most, season—199, Willie Keeler, Baltimore, NL, 1897; 198, Lloyd Waner, Pittsburgh, NL, 1927; 182, Sam Rice, Washington, AL, 1925.

Total Bases

Most, career—6,856, Henry Aaron, NL, 1954–1974, AL 1975–1976; 5,863, Ty Cobb, AL, 1905–1928.

Most, season—457, Babe Ruth, New York, AL, 1921; 450, Rogers Hornsby, St. Louis, NL, 1922.

Most, game—18, Joe Adcock, Milwaukee, NL, July 31, 1954; 16, by several players in both leagues.

Stolen Bases

Most, career—933, Billy Hamilton, American Association, 1888–1889, NL, 1890–1901; 892, Ty Cobb, AL, 1905–1928; 865, Lou Brock, NL, 1961–1974 (still active in 1977).

Most, season—156, Harry Stovey, American Association,

1888; 118, Lou Brock, St. Louis, NL, 1974; 96, Ty Cobb, Detroit, AL, 1915.

Games Started, Pitcher

Most, career—818, Cy Young, NL, 1890–1900, 1911, AL 1901–1911; 666, Walter Johnson, AL, 1907–1927; 665, Warren Spahn, NL, 1942, 1946–1965.

Most, season—74, William White, Cincinnati, NL, 1879; 51, Jack Chesbro, New York, AL, 1904; 48, Joe McGinnity, New York, NL, 1903.

Complete Games

Most, career—751, Cy Young, NL, 1890–1900, 1911, AL 1901–1911; 560, James Galvin, NL, 1879–1885, 1887–1889, 1891–1892 (also had 79 complete games in other major leagues for a total of 639); 531, Walter Johnson, Washington, AL, 1907–1927; 440, Grover Alexander, NL, 1911–1930.

Most, season—74, William White, Cincinnati, NL, 1879; 48, Jack Chesbro, New York, AL, 1904; 45, Vic Willis, Boston, NL, 1902.

Most consecutive—37, Bill Dinneen, Boston, AL, April 16–Oct. 10, 1904; 23, John Taylor, St. Louis, NL, April 15–July 30, 1904.

Innings Pitched

Most, career—7,377, Cy Young, NL, 1890–1900, 1911, AL 1901–1911; 5,924, Walter Johnson, Washington, AL, 1907–1927; 5,246, Warren Spahn, NL, 1942, 1946–1965.

Most, season—683, William White, Cincinnati, NL, 1879; 464, Ed Walsh, Chicago, AL, 1908; Joe McGinnity, New York, NL, 1903.

Earned-Run Average

Lowest, season—0.90, Ferdie Schupp, New York, NL, 1916 (140 innings); 1.01, Hubert Leonard, Boston, AL, 1914 (222 innings); 1.12, Bob Gibson, St. Louis, NL, 1968 (305 innings).

Games Won

Most, career—511, Cy Young, NL, 1890–1900, 1911, AL, 1901–1911, 416, Walter Johnson, AL, 1907–1927; 373, Christy Mathewson, NL, 1900–1916, and Grover Alexander, NL, 1911–1930.

Most, season—60, Charles Radbourn, Providence, NL, 1884; 41, Jack Chesbro, New York, AL, 1904; 39, Ed Walsh, Chicago, AL, 1908.

Most consecutive—24, Carl Hubbell, New York, NL, 1936–1937; 17, Johnny Allen, Cleveland, AL, 1936–1937, Dave McNally, Baltimore, AL, 1968–1969.

Most consecutive, one season—19, Tim Keefe, New York, NL, 1888; and Rube Marquard, New York, NL, 1912; 16, Joe Wood, Boston, AL, 1912; Walter Johnson, Washington, AL, 1912; Lefty Grove, Philadelphia, AL, 1931; Schoolboy Rowe, Detroit, AL, 1934.

No-Hit Games

Most, career—4, Sandy Koufax, Los Angeles, NL, 1962, 1963, 1964, 1965; Nolan Ryan, California, NL, 1973 (2), 1974, 1975.

Most, season—2, several players, including John Vander Meer, Cincinnati, NL, who had two in succession in 1938.

Perfect games—John Richmond, Worcester, NL, June 12, 1880; John Ward, Providence, NL, June 17, 1880; Cy Young, Boston, AL, May 5, 1904; Addie Joss, Cleveland, AL, Oct. 2, 1908; Ernie Shore, Boston, AL, June 23, 1917; Charlie Robertson, Chicago, AL, April 30,

1922; Don Larsen, New York, AL, Oct. 8, 1956 (in World Series); Harvey Haddix, Pittsburgh, NL, May 26, 1959 (for 12 innings, lost game in 13th); Jim Bunning, Philadelphia, NL, June 21, 1964; Sandy Koufax, Los Angeles, NL, Sept. 9, 1965; Jim Hunter, Oakland, AL, May 8, 1968.

Most consecutive hitless innings—23, Cy Young, Boston, AL, 1904; 21⅔, John Vander Meer, Cincinnati, NL, 1938.

Shutouts

Most, career—113, Walter Johnson, Washington, AL, 1907–1927; 90, Grover Alexander, NL, 1911–1929.

Most, season—16, Grover Alexander, Philadelphia, NL, 1916; 13, Jack Coombs, Philadelphia, AL, 1910.

Most consecutive—6, Don Drysdale, Los Angeles, NL, 1968; 5, Doc White, Chicago, AL, 1904.

Strikeouts by Pitcher

Most, career—3,508, Walter Johnson, Washington, AL, 1907–1927; 3,118, Bob Gibson, St. Louis, NL, 1959–1975.

Most, season—505, Matt Kilroy, Baltimore, American Association, 1886 (pitcher's mound was only 50 feet from home plate); 383, Nolan Ryan, California, AL, 1973; 382, Sandy Koufax, Los Angeles, NL, 1965.

Most, game—21, Tom Cheney, Washington, AL, Sept. 12, 1962 (16 innings).

Most, nine-inning game—19, Steve Carlton, St. Louis, NL, Sept. 15, 1969, Tom Seaver, New York, NL, April 22, 1970, and Nolan Ryan, California, AL, Aug. 12, 1974.

World Series Records

Most hits, game—4, by many players.

Most hits, series—13, Bobby Richardson, New York, AL, 1964, and Lou Brock, St. Louis, NL, 1968.

Most home runs, game—3, Babe Ruth, New York, AL, twice, in 1926 and 1928.

Most home runs, series—4, in a 4-game series by Lou Gehrig, New York, AL, 1928; in a 7-game series by several other players.

Most stolen bases, game—3, by Lou Brock, St. Louis, NL, twice, in 1967 and 1968; Willie Davis, Los Angeles, NL, in 1965; Honus Wagner, Pittsburgh, NL, in 1909.

Most stolen bases, series—7, by Lou Brock, St. Louis, NL, twice, in 1967 and 1968.

Most RBIs, game—6, Bobby Richardson, New York, AL, 1960.

Most RBIs, series—12, Bobby Richardson, New York, AL, 1960.

Most complete games, series—4, Deacon Phillippe, Pittsburgh, NL, 1903.

Most victories, series—3, by many pitchers.

Most shutouts, series—3, Christy Mathewson, New York, NL, 1905.

Most strikeouts, game—17, Bob Gibson, St. Louis, NL, 1968.

Most strikeouts, series—35, Bob Gibson, St. Louis, NL, 1968.

Baseball Hall of Fame

(Established in 1939 at Cooperstown, New York, the Hall of Fame is maintained by Organized Baseball. Recent players are elected by ballot of the Baseball Writers' Association; old-timers and players from the former Negro major leagues are chosen by special committees.)

Grover Cleveland Alexander—Pitcher; he and Christy Mathewson share the record for most National League victories, 373. Pitched for Philadelphia 1911–1917 and 1930, Chicago 1918–1926, and St. Louis 1926–1929; ten times he won 20 or more games, three times 30 or more.

Adrian "Cap" Anson—First baseman-manager; played in the old National Association 1871–1875, for Chicago in the National League 1876–1897; managed Chicago 1879–1897. Hit over .300 in 20 seasons, led the league four times; lifetime average, .339.

Luke B. Appling—Shortstop; played for the Chicago White Sox of the American League 1930–1950. Holds league record for highest batting average for a shortstop, .388 in 1936; hit over 300 in 16 seasons; lifetime average, .310.

H. Earl Averill—Outfielder; played in the American League for Cleveland 1929–1939 and Detroit 1939–1940, in the National League with Boston 1941. Hit over .300 eight times, including .378 in 1936, when he led league in hits (232) and triples (15). Lifetime average .318.

Frank "Home Run" Baker—Third baseman; played in the American League with Philadelphia 1908–1915, and New York 1916–1922. Led league in home runs four times; lifetime average, .307. In six World Series, hit .363.

David J. "Beauty" Bancroft—Shortstop; played in the National League with Philadelphia, 1915–1920, New York, 1920–1923 and 1930, Boston, 1924–1927, Brooklyn, 1928–1929. Twice led league in fielding average; lifetime batting average, .279.

Edward G. Barrow—Manager-executive; as manager of the Boston Red Sox, 1918–1920, converted Babe Ruth from pitcher to outfielder. Business manager of the New York Yankees, 1921–1939, president, 1939–1945.

Jacob P. Beckley—First baseman; played in the National League with Pittsburgh 1888–1889 and 1891–1896, New York 1896–1897, Cincinnati 1897–1903, St. Louis 1904–1907, and for Pittsburgh in the Players' League, 1890. Lifetime average, .309.

James "Cool Papa" Bell—Outfielder; played 29 years in Negro major leagues, the Mexican League, Cuba, and the Dominican Republic. In 1933 he stole 175 bases in about 200 games; once hit .480 for a season.

Charles A. "Chief" Bender—Pitcher; played with Philadelphia in the American League 1903–1914, Baltimore in the Federal League 1915, Philadelphia in the National League 1916–1917. Won 208 and lost 112; pitched a no-hitter in 1910.

Lawrence P. "Yogi" Berra—Catcher; played for the New York Yankees 1946–1964, New York Mets in 1965. Hit 358 home runs and had a lifetime average of .285; holds record for most consecutive errorless games by a catcher, 148. In 14 World Series, hit .274. Was Most Valuable Player three times.

James L. "Sunny Jim" Bottomley—First baseman; played in the National League with St. Louis 1922–1932, Cincinnati 1933–1935; with St. Louis in the American League 1936–1937. Lifetime average, .310; once had 12 RBIs in a game, a record. Hit .345 in the 1926 World Series.

Louis Boudreau—Shortstop-manager; played in the American League with Cleveland 1938–1950, Boston 1951–1952. Led league in hitting in 1944; lifetime average .295.

Roger P. Bresnahan—Catcher; played with Baltimore in

the American League 1901–1902; in the National League with Chicago, 1900, and New York, 1902–1915. Lifetime average, .279.

Dennis "Dan" Brouthers—First baseman; played in the National League with Troy, 1879–1880, Buffalo, 1881–1885, Detroit, 1886–1889, Brooklyn, 1892–1893, Baltimore, 1894–1895, Louisville, 1895, and Philadelphia, 1896; in the Players' League with Boston, 1890, in the American Association with Boston, 1891. Lifetime average, .349; six times led league in hitting.

Mordecai P. "Three-Finger" Brown—Pitcher; played in the National League with Chicago 1904–1912 and 1916, with Cincinnati 1913, in the Federal League with St. Louis and Brooklyn 1914, and Chicago 1915; won 208, lost 111.

Morgan G. Bulkeley—First president of the National League, 1901.

Jesse C. Burkett—Outfielder; played in the National League with Cleveland 1891–1898, St. Louis 1899–1901, and in the American League with St. Louis 1902–1904, and Boston 1905. Hit over .400 three times; lifetime average .342.

Roy Campanella—Catcher for the Brooklyn Dodgers, 1948–1957. National League's Most Valuable Player three times. Lifetime average, .276; hit 242 home runs. Previously played in the Negro major leagues.

Max G. Carey—Outfielder; played in the National League with Pittsburgh, 1910–1926, and Brooklyn, 1926–1929. Stole 738 bases and 10 times led the league in that department; hit .458 in 1925 World Series.

Alexander J. Cartwright—Invented modern baseball and organized first baseball club in 1845.

Henry Chadwick—Edited the first newspaper devoted exclusively to baseball, in 1867; compiled the first rule book and invented the first system of scorekeeping.

Frank L. Chance—First baseman-manager; played in the National League with Chicago, 1898–1912, in the American League with New York, 1913–1914. Lifetime average, .297; stole 405 bases. In four World Series, hit .310. Managed Chicago to pennants in 1906–1908 and 1910.

Oscar Charleston—Outfielder-first baseman; played in the Negro major leagues 1915–1940, managed ca. 1930–1950. Hit .396 in 1929.

John D. "Jack" Chesbro—Pitcher; played in the National League with Pittsburgh 1899–1902, in the American League with New York 1903–1909, and Boston, 1909. Won 198, lost 127; won 41 in 1904, the modern record.

Fred C. Clarke—Outfielder-manager; played in the National League with Louisville-Pittsburgh, 1894–1915, and managed, 1897–1915. Lifetime average .315; won pennants 1901–1903 and 1909.

John G. Clarkson—Pitcher; played in the National League with Chicago 1884–1887, Boston 1888–1892, and Cleveland 1892–1894. Won 327, lost 176; won 53 in 1885.

Roberto W. Clemente—Outfielder for the Pittsburgh Pirates 1955–1972; Most Valuable Player in 1966. Hit over .300 in 13 different seasons, four times led league; lifetime average .316.

Tyrus R. Cobb—Outfielder; played in the American League with Detroit 1905–1926, and Philadelphia 1927–1928. Hit over .300 in 23 consecutive seasons, over .400 three times, including twice in succession. Led league in hitting 12 times, including nine times in a row. Lifetime average .367, a record; had 892 stolen bases, 2,244 runs, 4,191 hits and 1,954 RBIs.

Gordon S. "Mickey" Cochrane—Catcher; played in the American League with Philadelphia 1925–1933, and Detroit 1934–1937. Most Valuable Player 1928; lifetime average, .320.

Edward T. "Cocky" Collins—Second-baseman; played in the American League with Philadelphia 1906–1914 and 1927–1930, and Chicago 1915–1926. Lifetime average .333; hit .328 in six World Series. Twice stole six bases in a game.

James J. Collins—Third baseman; played in the National League with Louisville 1895, Boston 1895–1900, and in the American League with Boston 1901–1907 and Philadelphia 1907–1908. Lifetime average, .294.

Earle B. Combs—Outfielder with the New York Yankees, 1924–1935. Lifetime average, .325; hit .350 in four World Series.

Charles A. Comiskey—First baseman-manager-owner. Played in the American Association with St. Louis, 1882–1889, 1891; in the Players League with Chicago, 1890; and in the National League with Cincinnati, 1892–1894. Lifetime average, .270; managed 1883, 1885–1900; president of Chicago White Sox, 1900–1931.

John B. "Jocko" Conlan—National League umpire, 1941–1964; worked six All-Star Games and six World Series.

Thomas H. Connolly—American League umpire, 1901–1931; chief of staff, 1931–1954.

Roger Connor—First baseman; played in the National League with Troy 1880–1882, New York 1883–1889, 1891, 1893–1894, Philadelphia 1892, St. Louis 1894–1897, in the Players League with New York 1890. Lifetime average .317; led league with .371 in 1885.

Stanley Coveleski—Pitcher; played in the American League with Cleveland 1916–1924, Washington 1925–1927, and New York 1928. Won 214, lost 141; six times won 20 games or more.

Samuel E. Crawford—Outfielder; played in the National League with Cincinnati, 1899–1902, in the American League with Detroit, 1903–1917. Lifetime average .308; holds record for most career triples, 312.

Joseph E. Cronin—Shortstop-manager; played in the National League with Pittsburgh, 1927, in the American League with Washington, 1928–1934, and Boston, 1935–1945. Lifetime average, .302; managed Washington, 1933–1934, and Boston, 1935–1947.

William A. "Candy" Cummings—Pitcher, 1866–1878; credited with inventing the curve ball.

Hazen S. "Kiki" Cuyler—Outfielder; played in the National League with Pittsburgh 1922–1927, Chicago 1928–1935, Cincinnati 1935–1937, and Brooklyn 1938. Lifetime average, .321.

Jay Hanna "Dizzy" Dean—Pitcher, a member of the St. Louis Cardinals, 1930, 1932–1937; Chicago Cubs, 1938–1941; and St. Louis Browns, 1947. Five times won 20 or more games; won 30 in 1934.

Edward L. Delahanty—Outfielder who played in the National League with Philadelphia, 1888–1889, and 1891–1901; in the Players' League with Cleveland, 1890; and in the American League with Washington, 1902–1903. Lifetime average, .346; three times hit .400 or better.

William M. Dickey—Catcher who played for the New York Yankees, 1928–1943, 1946. Lifetime average, .313.

Joseph P. DiMaggio—Outfielder for the New York Yankees, 1936–1942, 1946–1951. Lifetime average, .325. Most Valuable Player three times; hit safely in 56 consecutive games, a record.

Hugh Duffy—Outfielder; played in the National League with Chicago 1888–1889, Boston 1891–1900, Philadelphia 1904–1906; in the Players' League with Chicago 1890; in the American Association with Boston 1891; in the American League with Milwaukee 1901. Lifetime average, .330; hit .438 in 1894.

William G. Evans—American League umpire, 1908–1927.

John J. Evers—Second baseman; played in the National League with Chicago 1902–1913, Boston 1914–1917, Philadelphia 1917; briefly with the Chicago White Sox in 1922, the Boston Braves in 1929. Lifetime average, .270; hit .316 in four World Series.

William B. "Buck" Ewing—Catcher-outfielder; played in the National League with Troy 1880–1882, New York 1883–1889 and 1891–1892, Cleveland 1893–1894, Cincinnati 1895–1897; in the Players' League with New York in 1890. Lifetime average, .311.

Urban C. "Red" Faber—Pitcher; played for the Chicago White Sox 1914–1933. Won 254, lost 212; six times won 20 or more games. Won three and lost one in the 1917 World Series.

Robert W. A. Feller—Pitcher with the Cleveland Indians 1936–1941, 1945–1956. Won 266, lost 162; six times won 20 or more games. Pitched three no-hitters.

Elmer H. Flick—Outfielder; played in the National League with Philadelphia 1898–1901, in the American League with Philadelphia 1902, Cleveland 1902–1910. Lifetime average, .315.

Edward C. "Whitey" Ford—Pitcher with the New York Yankees, 1950 and 1953–1967. Won 236, lost 106; in 11 World Series, won 10 and lost 8, with a 2.71 earned-run average.

James E. Foxx—First baseman; played in the American League with Philadelphia 1925–1935, Boston 1936–1942; in the National League with Chicago 1942 and 1944, Philadelphia 1945. Four times led league in home runs; lifetime average, .325; hit 534 career home runs. In three World Series, hit .344, with 11 home runs.

Ford C. Frick—President of the National League, 1934–1951; baseball commissioner, 1951–1965.

Frank F. Frisch—Second baseman; played in the National League with New York 1919–1926, St. Louis 1927–1937. Lifetime average .316; in eight World Series, hit .294.

James F. "Pud" Galvin—Pitcher; played in the National League with Buffalo 1878–1885, with Pittsburgh 1887–1889, 1891–1892, and with St. Louis 1892; in the American Association with Allegheny 1885–1886; in the Players' League with Pittsburgh 1890. Won 361, lost 309, with 57 shutouts.

H. Louis Gehrig—First baseman with the New York Yankees 1923–1939; holds record with 2,130 consecutive games. Most Valuable Player four times; lifetime average, .340, with 493 home runs, 1,990 RBIs. In seven World Series, hit .361 with 10 home runs, 35 RBIs.

Charles L. Gehringer—Second baseman with the Detroit

Tigers 1924–1942; lifetime average, .321. Most Valuable Player in 1937.

Josh Gibson—Catcher in the Negro major leagues 1930–1946; hit 278 home runs in one four-season period, twice hit more than .400.

Vernon L. "Lefty" Gomez—Pitcher for the New York Yankees 1930–1942, Washington Senators 1943. Won 189, lost 102; four times won 20 or more games. In five World Series, won six games without a loss and compiled a 2.86 earned-run average.

Leon A. "Goose" Goslin—Outfielder; played in the American League with Washington 1921–1930, 1933, and 1938, St. Louis 1930–1932, Detroit 1934–1937. Lifetime average .316.

Henry B. "Hank" Greenberg—First baseman with the Detroit Tigers 1933–1941, 1945–1956, Pittsburgh Pirates 1947. Most Valuable Player 1935, 1940. Lifetime average .313; in four World Series hit .318 with 22 RBIs.

Clark C. Griffith—Pitcher; played in the National League with Chicago 1893–1900, Cincinnati 1909–1910, and in the American League with Chicago 1901–1902, New York 1903–1907, Washington 1912–1914. Won 240, lost 140. Managed Chicago 1901–1902, New York 1903–1908, Cincinnati 1909–1911, Washington 1912–1920. President, Washington Senators, 1920–1955.

Burleigh A. Grimes—Pitcher; played in the National League with Pittsburgh 1916–1917, 1928–1929, and 1934, Brooklyn 1918–1926, New York 1927, Boston 1930, St. Louis 1930–1931, 1932–1933, Chicago 1932–1933; in the American League with New York 1934. Won 270, lost 212.

Robert M. "Lefty" Grove—Pitcher in the American League with Philadelphia 1925–1933, Boston 1934–1941. Won 300, lost 140; won 16 consecutive games in 1931, 14 consecutive in 1928. In three World Series, won four and lost two.

Charles J. "Chick" Hafey—Outfielder in the National League with St. Louis 1924–1931, Cincinnati 1932–1937. Lifetime average, .317.

Jesse J. Haines—Pitcher for the St. Louis Cardinals, 1929–1937; won 210, lost 158. In four World Series, won three and lost one, with a 1.67 earned-run average.

William R. Hamilton—Outfielder in the National League with Philadelphia 1890–1895, Boston 1896–1901. Lifetime average .344; stole 937 bases, the all-time record; three times stole more than 100 bases in a season.

Will Harridge—American League president, 1931–1958.

Stanley R. "Bucky" Harris—Second baseman-manager; played in the American League for Washington 1919–1928, Detroit 1929, 1931; Lifetime average .274. Managed Washington 1924–1928, 1935–1942, Detroit 1929–1933, 1950–1954 and 1955–1956, Boston (AL) 1934, Philadelphia (NL) 1943, New York (AL) 1947–1948. Won pennants 1924–1925, 1947, world championships 1924 and 1947.

Charles L. "Gabby" Hartnett—Catcher for the Chicago Cubs 1922–1940, New York Giants 1941. Lifetime average, .297.

Harry E. Heilmann—Outfielder with the Detroit Tigers 1916–1929, Cincinnati Reds 1930, 1932. Lifetime average, .342; hit over .300 in 12 seasons, once over .400.

William J. B. "Billy" Herman—Second baseman; played in the National League for Chicago 1931–1941, Brooklyn 1941–1943, 1946, for Boston 1946, Pittsburgh 1947. Lifetime average .304; led league in hits (227) and doubles (47) in 1935.

Harry B. Hooper—Outfielder with the Boston Red Sox 1909–1920, Chicago White Sox 1920–1925. Lifetime average .281.

Rogers Hornsby—Second baseman; played in the National League with St. Louis 1915–1926 and 1933, New York 1927, Boston 1928, Chicago 1929–1932, in the American League with St. Louis 1933–1937. Hit over .300 in 20 different seasons, three times over .400.

Waite C. Hoyt—Pitcher; played in the American League with Boston 1919–1920, New York 1921–1930, Detroit 1930–1931, Philadelphia 1931; in the National League with Brooklyn 1932 and 1937–1938, New York 1932, Pittsburgh 1933–1937. Won 237, lost 182. In seven World Series, won six games and lost four, with a 1.83 earned-run average.

Robert "Cal" Hubbard—American League umpire 1938–1951, supervisor of umpires 1951–1969. Hubbard is the only man ever named to both the Baseball Hall of Fame and the Pro Football Hall of Fame.

Carl O. Hubbell—Pitcher for the New York Giants 1928–1943; won 253, lost 154; won more than 20 games in five straight seasons. In three World Series, won four games and lost two, with a 1.79 earned-run average.

Miller J. Huggins—Second baseman-manager; played in the National League with Cincinnati 1904–1909, St. Louis 1910–1916. Managed St. Louis 1913–1917, New York Yankees 1918–1929; won pennants 1921–1923, 1926–1928.

Montford M. Irvin—Outfielder in the National League with New York 1949–1955, Chicago 1956; lifetime average .293. In two World Series, hit .394. Previously played in the Negro major leagues for more than 10 years.

Hughie Jennings—Shortstop-manager; played in the American Association with Louisville 1891, in the National League with Louisville-Baltimore 1892–1899, Brooklyn 1899–1900 and 1903, Philadelphia 1901–1902; in the American League with Detroit 1907–1909, 1912, 1918. Lifetime average .314. Managed Detroit 1907–1920, won pennants 1907–1909.

Byron Bancroft "Ban" Johnson—President of the American League 1894–1927; turned it into a major league.

William J. "Judy" Johnson—Third baseman; played in the Negro major leagues ca. 1918–1937. He hit .341 for Hilldale in the first Negro World Series in 1924, and averaged .340 for the 9 seasons in which official statistics were kept.

Walter P. Johnson—Pitcher with the Washington Senators 1907–1927; won 416, lost 279. Holds record for most shutouts, 113, and league record for most victories; Most Valuable Player in 1913 and 1924.

Timothy J. Keefe—Pitcher; played in the National League with Troy 1880–1882, New York 1885–1889 and 1891, Philadelphia 1891–1893, in the American Association with the Metropolitans 1883–1884, in the Players' League with New York 1890. Won 344, lost 225; eight times won 20 or more games, twice more than 40.

William H. "Wee Willie" Keeler—Outfielder; played in the National League with New York 1892–1893 and 1910; Brooklyn 1893 and 1899–1902, Baltimore 1894–1898; in the American League with New York 1903–1909. Lifetime average, .345.

Joseph J. Kelley—Outfielder; played in the National League with Boston 1891 and 1908, Pittsburgh 1891–1892, Baltimore 1892–1898, Brooklyn 1899–1901, Cincinnati 1902–1906; in the American League with Baltimore 1902.

Lifetime average, .321; once made nine hits in nine times at bat in a doubleheader.

Michael J. "King" Kelly—Outfielder-catcher; played in the National League with Cincinnati 1878–1879, Chicago 1880–1886, Boston 1887–1889 and 1891–1892, New York 1893; in the Players' League with Boston 1890; in the American Association with Cincinnati and Boston 1891. Lifetime average, .313.

Ralph McP. Kiner—Outfielder; played in the National League for Pittsburgh 1946–1953, Chicago 1953–1954, in the American League for Cleveland 1955. Led league in home runs seven straight seasons, twice with more than 50; led in slugging 3 times, in RBIs once; lifetime average .279 with 369 home runs.

William J. Klem—Umpire in the National League 1904–1941; worked 18 World Series.

Sanford "Sandy" Koufax—Pitcher with the Brooklyn-Los Angeles Dodgers 1955–1966; won 165, lost 87. Pitched four no-hitters, a record, including a perfect game; in four World Series, won 4, lost 3 with an earned run average of 0.95.

Napoleon "Larry" Lajoie—Second baseman; played in the National League with Philadelphia 1896–1900, in the American League with Philadelphia 1901–1902, 1915–1916, with Cleveland 1902–1914. Lifetime average .339; hit .422 in 1901, an American League record.

Kenesaw Mountain Landis—First commissioner of baseball, 1920–1944.

Robert G. Lemon—Pitcher; played in the American League with Cleveland 1946–1958; seven times won 20 or more games, led league in shutouts with 10 in 1948. Won 207, lost 128, career ERA 3.23.

Walter F. "Buck" Leonard—First baseman in the Negro Leagues 1933–1950, in Mexican leagues 1951–1955; usually hit in the high .300s, sometimes over .400.

Fred C. Lindstrom—Third baseman-outfielder; played in the National League with New York 1924–1932, Pittsburgh 1933–1934, Chicago 1935, Brooklyn 1936. Lifetime average .311; led league in hits in 1928 with 231; hit .333 in 1924 World Series.

Theodore A. Lyons—Pitcher for the Chicago White Sox 1923–1942, 1946; won 260, lost 230. Once went 42 consecutive innings without issuing a walk.

Connie Mack—Catcher-manager; played in the National League with Washington 1886–1889, Pittsburgh 1891–1896, in the Players' League with Buffalo 1890. Lifetime average .251; managed Philadelphia Athletics 1901–1950.

Mickey C. Mantle—Outfielder for the New York Yankees 1951–1968; lifetime average .298; 536 home runs, 1,509 RBIs. Most Valuable Player three times.

Henry E. "Heinie" Manush—Outfielder; played in the American League with Detroit 1923–1927, St. Louis 1928–1930, Washington 1930–1935, Boston 1936; in the National League with Brooklyn 1937–1938, Pittsburgh 1938–1939. Lifetime average .330.

J. Walter V. "Rabbit" Maranville—Shortstop; played in the National League with Boston 1912–1920, 1929–1933, 1935, Pittsburgh 1921–1924, Chicago 1925, Brooklyn 1926, St. Louis 1927–1928. Lifetime average .258; hit .308 in two World Series.

Richard W. "Rube" Marquard—Pitcher; played in the National League with New York 1908–1915, Brooklyn 1915–1920, Cincinnati 1921, Boston 1922–1925. Won 201, lost 177; once won 19 consecutive games, a modern record.

Christopher Mathewson—Pitcher for the New York Giants 1900–1916, Cincinnati Reds 1916; won 373, lost 188, tied with Grover Alexander for most victories in league. Won 30 or more 1903–1905; no-hitters in 1901 and 1905. In four World Series, won 5 and lost 4 with a 1.15 earned run average; pitched three shutouts in the 1905 Series.

Joseph V. McCarthy—Manager of the Chicago Cubs 1926–1930, New York Yankees 1931–1946, Boston Red Sox 1948–1950; won nine pennants and seven World Series.

Thomas F. McCarthy—Outfielder; played in the National League with Boston 1885, 1892–1895, Philadelphia 1886–1887, Brooklyn 1896; in the American Association with St. Louis 1888–1891. Lifetime average .294.

Joseph J. McGinnity—Pitcher; played in the National League with Baltimore 1889, Brooklyn 1900, New York 1902–1908, in the American League with Baltimore 1901–1902. Five times pitched both games of a double-header.

John J. McGraw—Third baseman-manager; played in the American Association with Baltimore 1891, in the National League with Baltimore 1892–1899, in the National League with St. Louis 1900, in the American League with Baltimore 1901–1902, in the National League with New York 1902–1906. Lifetime average .334. Managed Baltimore 1899, 1901–1902, New York 1902–1932; won 10 pennants, three World Series.

William B. McKechnie—Managed Newark of the Federal League, 1915; in the National League managed Pittsburgh 1922–1926, St. Louis 1928–1929, Boston 1930–1937, Cincinnati 1938–1946. Won four pennants with three different teams.

Joseph M. "Ducky" Medwick—Outfielder; played in the National League with St. Louis 1932–1940, 1947–1948, Brooklyn 1940–1943, 1946, New York 1943–1945, Boston 1945. Lifetime average .324; holds league record for doubles, 64 in 1936. Most Valuable Player 1937.

Stanley F. Musial—Outfielder-first baseman with the St. Louis Cardinals 1941–1944, 1956–1963; lifetime average .331. Most Valuable Player three times.

Charles A. "Kid" Nichols—Pitcher; played in the National League with Boston 1890–1901, St. Louis 1904–1905, Philadelphia 1905–1906. Won 360, lost 202; seven times won more than 30 games in a season.

James H. O'Rourke—Outfielder; played in the National Association 1872–1875; in the National League with Boston 1876–1878, 1880, Providence 1879, New York 1885–1892, 1894, Washington 1893; in the Players' League with New York 1890. Lifetime average .314.

Melvin T. Ott—Outfielder with the New York Giants 1926–1947; lifetime average .304 with 511 home runs.

Leroy R. "Satchel" Paige—Pitcher in the Negro major leagues, the Mexican leagues, and with his own barnstorming team, 1926–1950; with the Cleveland Indians 1948–1949, St. Louis Browns 1951–1953 and the Kansas City Athletics 1956.

Herbert J. Pennock—Pitcher; played in the American League with Philadelphia 1912–1915, Boston 1915–1922 and 1934, New York 1923–1933. Won 240, lost 162; in five World Series, won 5 and lost none, with a 1.95 earned run average.

Edward S. Plank—Pitcher; played in the American League with Philadelphia 1901–1914, St. Louis 1916–1917, in the Federal League with St. Louis 1915. Won 305, lost 181, with 64 shutouts.

Charles "Old Hoss" Radbourn—Pitcher; played in the National League with Buffalo 1880, Providence 1881–1885, Boston 1886–1889, Cincinnati 1891; in the Players' League with Boston 1890. Won 308, lost 191; holds record for most victories in a season, 60, in 1884.

Edgar C. "Sam" Rice—Outfielder in the American League with Washington 1915–1933, Cleveland 1934; lifetime average .322; in three World Series, hit .302.

Branch W. Rickey—Executive with the St. Louis Browns 1916, St. Louis Cardinals 1917–1942, the Brooklyn Dodgers 1942–1950, the Pittsburgh Pirates 1956–1959; is credited with developing the farm system idea to its fullest potential. He broke the color barrier by signing Jackie Robinson.

Eppa Rixey—Pitcher in the National League with Philadelphia 1912–1920, Cincinnati 1921–1933; won 266, lost 251.

Robert E. "Robin" Roberts—Pitcher; played in the National League with Philadelphia 1948–1961, Houston 1965–1966, Chicago 1966, in the American League with Baltimore 1962–1965. Won 20 games or more six consecutive seasons, twice led league in shutouts; won 286, lost 245, career ERA 3.41.

Jack R. Robinson—Infielder; the first black to play major-league baseball, with the Brooklyn Dodgers 1947–1956. Rookie of the Year 1947, Most Valuable Player 1949; lifetime average, .311.

Wilbert "Robby" Robinson—Catcher-manager; played in the American Association with the Athletics 1886–1890, Baltimore 1890–1891; in the National League with Baltimore 1892–1899, St. Louis 1900; in the American League with Baltimore 1901–1902. Lifetime average .280. Managed Baltimore part of 1902, Brooklyn Dodgers 1914–1931; won two pennants.

Edd J. Roush—Outfielder; played in the Federal League with Indianapolis 1914, Newark 1915; in the National League with New York 1916, 1927–1930, Cincinnati 1916–1926, 1931. Lifetime average .325.

Charles H. "Red" Ruffing—Pitcher; played in the American League with Boston 1924–1930, New York 1930–1942, 1945–1946, Chicago 1947. Won 273, lost 225; in seven World Series, won 7 and lost 2 with a 2.63 earned run average.

George H. "Babe" Ruth—Pitcher-outfielder; played in the American League with Boston 1914–1919, New York 1920–1934, in the National League with Boston 1935. Lifetime average .342 with 714 home runs, 2,209 RBIs, 2,174 runs; once scored 177 runs in a season, a record, and his 60 home runs in 1927 is a record for a 154-game season. As a pitcher, won 94 and lost 46 with a 2.28 earned run average. In 10 World Series, hit .326 with 15 home runs and 33 RBIs; won 3 games and lost none, with an 0.87 earned run average.

Raymond W. Schalk—Catcher with the Chicago White Sox 1912–1928, New York Giants 1929; lifetime average .253. Holds record for most career assists by catcher, 1,810.

Aloysius H. Simmons—Outfielder; played in the American League with Philadelphia 1924–1932, 1940–1941, 1944, Chicago 1933–1935, Detroit 1936, Washington 1937–1938, Boston 1943; in the National League with Boston and Cincinnati 1939. Lifetime average .334; in four World Series, hit .329 with 15 runs scored and 17 RBIs.

George H. Sisler—First baseman with the St. Louis Browns 1915–1927, Washington Senators 1928, Boston Braves 1928–1930; lifetime average .340. His 257 hits in 1920 is a major-league record.

Warren E. Spahn—Pitcher with the Boston-Milwaukee Braves 1942, 1946–1964, the New York Mets and San Francisco Giants 1965; won 363, lost 245. Won 20 or more games in 13 different seasons; holds record for most wins by a left-hander.

Albert G. Spalding—Pitcher with Boston in the National Association 1871–1875, Chicago in the National League 1876–1877; won 254, lost 69. Managed Chicago in the National League 1876–1878, owned the team 1882–1891; founded sporting goods company in 1876.

Tristram Speaker—Outfielder with the Boston Red Sox 1907–1915, Cleveland Indians 1916–1926, Washington Senators 1927, Philadelphia Athletics 1928; lifetime average .344. Holds records for most putouts and most assists by an outfielder. In three World Series, hit .306.

Charles D. "Casey" Stengel—Outfielder-manager; played with the Brooklyn Dodgers 1912–1917, Pittsburgh Pirates 1918–1919, Philadelphia Phillies 1920–1921, New York Giants 1921–1923, Boston Braves 1924–1925. Lifetime average .284; in three World Series, hit .393. Managed Brooklyn Dodgers 1934–1936, Boston Braves 1938–1943, New York Yankees 1949–1960, New York Mets 1962–1965. Won 10 pennants, 7 World Series.

William H. Terry—First baseman-manager; played with the New York Giants 1923–1936. Lifetime average .341. Managed Giants 1932–1941; won three pennants.

Samuel L. Thompson—Outfielder; played in the National League with Detroit 1885–1888, Philadelphia 1889–1898, in the American League with Detroit in 1906. Lifetime average .336; twice hit over .400.

Joseph B. Tinker—Shortstop; played in the National League with Chicago 1902–1912, 1916, Cincinnati 1913; in the Federal League with Chicago 1914–1915. Lifetime average .264.

Harold J. "Pie" Traynor—Third baseman with the Pittsburgh Pirates 1921–1935, 1937; lifetime average .320.

Arthur C. "Dazzy" Vance—Pitcher with the Brooklyn Dodgers 1922–1932, 1935, St. Louis Cardinals 1933–1934, Cincinnati Reds 1934; won 197, lost 140.

Lloyd J. Waner—Outfielder; played in the National League with Pittsburgh 1927–1940, 1944–1945, Boston and Cincinnati 1941, Philadelphia 1942, Brooklyn 1944. Lifetime average .316.

Paul G. Waner—Outfielder; played in the National League with Pittsburgh 1926–1940, Boston 1941–1942, Brooklyn 1941, 1943–1944, in the American League with New York 1944–1945. Lifetime average .333.

John Montgomery Ward—Pitcher-shortstop; played in the National League with Providence 1878–1882, New York 1883–1889, Brooklyn 1891–1892, New York 1893–1894, in the Players' League with Brooklyn 1890. Lifetime average .283; as a pitcher, won 158, lost 102. Pitched a perfect game in 1880.

George M. Weiss—As farm director for 16 years and general manager for 13 years with the New York Yankees, Weiss was involved with a team that won 19 pennants and 17 World Series; as president of the New York Mets 1961–1967, he helped mold the team that won the world championship in 1969.

Michael F. "Mickey" Welch—Pitcher in the National League with Troy 1880–1882, New York 1883–1892; won 311, lost 207.

Zachary D. Wheat—Outfielder with the Brooklyn Dodgers 1909–1926, Philadelphia Athletics 1927. Lifetime average .317.

Theodore S. Williams—Outfielder with the Boston Red Sox 1939–1942, 1946–1960. Lifetime average .344; hit .406 1941. Most Valuable Player twice.

George Wright—Shortstop; played for the first professional team, 1869–1870, in the National Association 1871–1875, in the National League with Boston 1876–1878, 1880–1881, Providence 1879, 1882.

William H. "Harry" Wright—Known as the "Father of Professional Baseball" for organizing the first all-professional team, the Cincinnati Red Stockings, in 1869.

Early Wynn—Pitcher with the Washington Senators 1939, 1941–1948, Cleveland Indians 1949–1957, 1963, Chicago White Sox 1958–1962; won 300, lost 244. Cy Young Award in 1959.

Denton T. "Cy" Young—Pitcher; played in the National League with Cleveland 1890–1898, St. Louis 1899–1900, Boston 1911, in the American League with Boston 1901–1908, Cleveland 1909–1911. Won 511, an all-time record, lost 313. Once pitched 23 consecutive hitless innings, in 1904.

Royce "Ross" Youngs—Outfielder with the New York Giants 1917–1926. Lifetime average .322.

Bibliography. Allen, Lee: *The American League Story*, Hill and Wang, New York, 1962; ———: *The National League Story*, Hill and Wang, New York, 1961; ———: *One Hundred Years of Baseball*, Bartholomew House, New York, 1950; Daley, Arthur: *Times at Bat: A Half Century of Baseball*, Random House, New York, 1950. Danzig, Allison, and Joe Reichler: *The History of Baseball*, Prentice-Hall, Englewood Cliffs, N.J., 1959; Lieb, Fred: *The Story of the World Series*, Putnam, New York, 1965; MacFarlane, Paul, and Leonard Gettleson, eds: *Daguerrotypes of Great Stars of Baseball*, The Sporting News, St. Louis, 1968; Peterson, Harold: *The Man Who Invented Baseball*, Scribner's, New York, 1973; Seymour, Harold: *Baseball: The Early Years*, Oxford, New York, 1960; ———: *Baseball: The Golden Age*, Oxford, New York, 1971; Smith, Robert, *Baseball's Hall of Fame*, Bantam, New York, 1965; Turkin, Hy and S. C. Thompson, *The Official Encyclopedia of Baseball*, A. S. Barnes, New York, 1965.

BASKETBALL—One of the few deliberately invented sports to achieve any popularity, basketball is an American game that has spread around the world in 80 years, which demonstrates that Dr. James Naismith accomplished what he set out to do.

Naismith was a physical education instructor at the International Young Men's Christian Association Training School in Springfield, Massachusetts. The school, now Springfield College, trained men to work in YMCAs across the country. During winter, their only physical education consisted of marching, calisthenics, and gymnastics, and the students didn't enjoy any of those indoor "sports." So Dr. Luther S. Gulick, head of the physical education department, assigned Naismith to come up with something better. Naismith felt that recreation should be enjoyable, as well as re-creating, and he tried various children's indoor games, but the students were too old to enjoy them. Then he tried creating indoor versions of Rugby, soccer, and lacrosse. All three turned out to be much too rough for indoor play. Naismith knew what he didn't want: He didn't want a game where the players could run with the ball, since that implied tackling; he didn't want a game where any implements were

In 1891, Dr. James Naismith, trying to find a way of combining indoor recreation with competitive fun, invented basketball in Springfield, Massachusetts. *(Basketball Hall of Fame.)*

needed to strike the ball; and he didn't want a game where force was needed to propel a ball into a goal.

So he invented his own game. It would have a ball large enough to be handled and passed easily, and a high horizontal goal, which would emphasize accuracy rather than force. Naismith originally wanted to use boxes, but he couldn't find any of the right size, so he substituted peach baskets, suspended from the balconies at either end of the gym. The first game was played in mid-December 1891. Since there were 18 men in the class, there were 9 players to a side, and the original ball was a soccer ball. The new sport, which didn't have a name yet, was an instant success.

During Christmas vacation, many of Naismith's students introduced the game in their home towns—in varying forms, because they didn't have a copy of his rules. The rules were published in the school newspaper in 1892, approximately as Naismith originally set them down:

1. The ball may be thrown in any direction with one or both hands.
2. The ball may be batted in any direction with one or both hands (never with the fist).
3. A player cannot run with the ball. The player must throw it from the spot on which it is caught; allowance is to be made for a player who catches the ball when running at a good speed and who tries to stop.
4. The ball must be held in or between the hands; the arms or body must not be used for holding it.
5. No shouldering, holding, pushing, tripping, or striking, in any way, the person of an opponent shall be allowed; the first infringement of this rule by any person shall count as a foul, the second shall disqualify the player until the next goal is made; or, if there was

evident intent to injure the person, for the whole of the game, no substitute shall be allowed.

6. A foul is striking at the ball with the fist, violation of Rules 3, 4, and such as described in Rule 5.

7. If either side makes three consecutive fouls, it shall count as a goal for the opponents. (Consecutive means without the opponents in the meantime making a foul.)

8. A goal shall be made when the ball is thrown or batted from the ground into the basket and stays there, providing those defending the goal do not touch or disturb the goal. If the ball rests on the edge and the opponent moves the basket, it shall count as a goal.

9. When the ball goes out-of-bounds, it shall be thrown into the field and played by the person first touching it. In case of a dispute, the umpire shall throw it straight into the field. The thrower-in is allowed 5 sec. If it is held longer, it shall go to the opponent. If any side persists in delaying the game, the umpire shall call a foul on them.

10. The umpire shall be judge of the players and shall note the fouls and notify the referee when three consecutive fouls have been made. The umpire shall also have power to disqualify players according to Rule 5.

11. The referee shall be judge of the ball and shall decide when the ball is in play, in bounds, to which side it belongs, and shall keep the time. The referee shall also decide when a goal has been made, and keep account of the goals, with any other duties that are usually performed by a referee.

12. The time shall be two 15-min halves, with 5-min rest between.

13. The side making the most goals in that time shall be declared the winners. In case of a draw, the game may, by agreement of the captains, be continued until another goal is made.

It should be noted that Naismith's rules did not provide for the dribble, but players quickly realized that, under Rule 3, it would be possible to throw the ball to oneself by bouncing it off the floor, and Naismith quickly incorporated the dribble into his game. The rules also didn't specify how the ball was to be put into play. Naismith himself evidently wasn't quite sure about this at first. He thought of lining the teams up at opposite ends of the court, setting the ball in the middle, and letting them race for it, but visions of the ensuing mayhem gave him pause. Then he thought of lining the teams up, facing one another, at centercourt and tossing the ball in between them. It isn't known just what method he used in that first game, but he very soon came upon the idea of the center jump between two players. It wasn't written into the rules until 1897, however, and until then other ways of putting the ball into play were used in various areas. Rule 9, incidentally, led to much of the mayhem Naismith wanted to avoid. It provides that, if the ball goes out-of-bounds, the first player to touch it gets possession, which led to a lot of mad out-of-bounds scrambles. Oddly, that rule remained in effect until 1913, when the present out-of-bounds rule was adopted. The new game didn't get a name for some months, until a student suggested it be called Naismith ball; Naismith quickly countered with "basketball," and basketball it was.

Early Growth and Development. Because students from the Springfield school went to work for YMCAs all over the country, basketball spread quickly. And Naismith did some crusading for his sport. In 1892 he organized a team that went on an exhibition tour in the East. In the same year, he organized the first game between two YMCAs and the first game between women's teams. YMCA teams and leagues quickly sprang up, and sectional tournaments were held as early as 1893. In 1896, a YMCA tournament for the national championship was held, but most of the teams were from the New York City area.

The first intercollegiate game was played in Minnesota in 1895, but Yale led the way in spreading the sport among colleges. Yale and Pennsylvania played the first game with five players per side in 1897, and in 1900 Yale went on a tour of Western states. In the following year, the Eastern Intercollegiate League was formed by Columbia, Cornell, Harvard, Princeton, and Yale. A problem was developing. The Springfield YMCA was more or less in charge of the rules at first, but the sport was spreading so rapidly that rules changes couldn't keep up with its growth. In 1893, the YMCAs and the Amateur Athletic Union got together to agree on a set of rules, but in 1908 the National Collegiate Athletic Association developed its own rules. Most of the chaos was eliminated when the NCAA and the AAU formed a joint basketball rules committee in 1915. Although rules changes were made as experience proved them necessary, Naismith's game remained surprisingly well intact. Major changes in the early years were the addition of free throws in 1894, outlawing of the double dribble and the "air dribble" in 1898, and the five-foul elimination rule in 1908.

In 1923, the Joint Rules Committee decided that the player who was fouled should take the free throw—until then a team could designate any player to take the shot. A major improvement made in the same year was the removal of some violations from the "foul" category, to cut down on free throws. Such rules violations as the double dribble and running with the ball now merely meant loss of possession, without a free throw by the other team. One major change was in the basket. A mesh basket with a chain pull to release the ball was introduced in 1893, but the open-bottomed basket didn't arrive until 1906, and wasn't approved for all amateur play until 1912.

The First Pros. Ironically, before 1900, a number of YMCAs decided that Dr. Naismith's "noncontact" sport was decidedly too rough. All the YMCAs in Philadelphia dropped the sport from their programs, and Y's in other Eastern cities did the same. But the sport was already firmly entrenched. Converts to the new game, forced out of YMCAs, organized teams of their own, rented halls in which they could play, and then charged admission in order to pay the rent. Extra money they split up among themselves. This happened, according to one account, as early as 1893 in Herkimer, New York. However, it's generally considered that the first professional game was played in 1896 in Trenton, New Jersey. Proceeds were large enough to pay each Trenton player $15 after expenses, and the captain received $16.

In 1898, the professional National Basketball League was organized, and other leagues sprang up throughout the East during the first two decades of the century. Most such games were played on dance floors, closed in by fences of chicken wire to keep spectators off the court. Thus basketball players became known as "cagers"—a nickname that persists to this day, although the reason for it has long since disappeared.

As with most sports in their infancy, professional basketball was very loosely organized. A player might "belong" to several different teams in several different leagues and, given a better offer, would probably jump from one team to another overnight. Nevertheless, some legendary teams were built up. The Buffalo Germans, originally a YMCA team, won the first Olympic basketball demonstration tournament in 1904, and went professional in 1905, with Forrest C. "Phog" Allen as player-manager. In a 30-year period, beginning with their formation in 1895, they won 792 games and lost 86 against all comers. In 1931, they made a comeback for one exhibition; averaging 51 years of age, they scored their last victory. The New York Trojans, organized by Ed Wachter, won five championships in six years and then won 38 consecutive games on a barnstorming tour in 1908. Wachter, who later coached at Harvard, was credited with inventing the fast break.

The New York Celtics were organized in 1914. A new promoter reorganized them as the Original Celtics after World War I, and in 1919, they were generally recognized as the best pro team around. The Celtics emphasized team play and played an aggressive, switching one-on-one defense that was almost a zone. Celtic Dutch Dehnert "accidentally" invented pivot play. It was common at the time for a team to have a "standing guard" who remained at the defensive foul line at all times. Dehnert would stand with his back to the guard to receive a pass; then, when the guard tried to move around him to get at the ball, Dehnert would pivot in the other direction for a layup. Other players on this outstanding team were Joe Lapchick, one of the first big men and later a fine coach; Johnny Beckman, a great foul shooter (at a time when one player was designated to take all the team's free throws); and Nat Holman, who had begun his pro career with the New York Whirlwinds.

The Whirlwinds had been organized by boxing promoter Tex Rickard. In Holman and Barney Sedran they had two great little men. The Whirlwinds and Celtics met in what was supposed to be a three-game series in 1921. They split the first two games and the third was never played, because the crowd had been growing increasingly boisterous. In 1922, Celtic manager Jim Furey lured Holman and Chris Leonard, another star, away from the Whirlwinds and signed all his players to exclusive contracts. Although a viable league was still a long time off, Furey's move was a big step toward modern professional basketball.

College Basketball

The Early Era. Possibly because of a resurgence in college football after a number of rules changes in 1906, basketball about that time became a favorite sport at smaller colleges, particularly in the Midwest, which didn't have enough students or money to concentrate on football. One of the first outstanding college teams was Wabash College in Crawfordsville, Indiana, which had a 66-3 record during the 1908–1911 period. The sport was especially popular in two quite different kinds of places; in large, crowded cities, where it was easier to play basketball in a small playground than to try to find a football field, and in rural areas, where the people were too spread out to get enough of them together to make up two football teams. Thus, some of the outstanding teams in college basketball's early era came from such disparate schools as New York University and Westminster (Mis-

souri) College; the University of Chicago and Washington University, in St. Louis.

The first great college player was Christian Steinmetz of Wisconsin, who scored 50 points in one game in 1905—at a time when 9-8 was not an unusual final score. The University of Chicago, led by John Schommer (1909) and Harlan O. "Pat" Page (1910), compiled a 53-4 record from 1907 to 1909, coached by Joseph Raycroft. Other outstanding teams during the pretournament period were produced at Wisconsin, 1912–1916, by Walter E. Meanwell; at Pennsylvania, which compiled a 43-3 record during seasons ending in 1920 and 1921; at Kansas, which won 33 and lost 3 over a two-season period, 1922–1923, thanks to "Phog" Allen's coaching and the play of All-Americans Paul Endacott and Charles Black; and at Syracuse, where Vic Hanson led the Orangemen to a 19-1 record in 1926. Coaching at Pittsburgh, Dr. Clifford Carlson came up with the game's first "patterned" offense, the Figure 8; his 1927–1928 team was 21-0, and his 1929–1930 team was 23-2. Charles Hyatt was a two-year All-American for Carlson. A major three-team rivalry, which continues today, began in the late twenties in Indiana, among Purdue, Indiana University, and Notre Dame. Indiana produced a 1930 All-American in Branch McCracken, later a great coach there, but Purdue had two, Charles "Stretch" Miller and John Wooden, who was a three-year All-American under the coaching of Ward L. "Piggy" Lambert. Football overshadowed basketball at Notre Dame, but that didn't keep George Keogan from producing winning teams when he wasn't assisting Knute Rockne with the gridders. Although spectator interest was high in the local areas, and conference play began as early as 1902 (in the Eastern, later the Ivy, League), basketball was not a national-headline sport, in the way college football was, because there was virtually no intersectional play. Another problem was that few gyms could hold more than 1,000 fans, so no matter how fanatical they were, not many people could see any given game.

The Garden. In 1931, Ned Irish was a young New York sportswriter who, according to legend at least, had once torn his pants climbing through a window into a gym to cover a college basketball game. If the story is true, basketball owes a lot to the rip in his pants. Irish decided that college basketball deserved a better showcase than the gyms of the era. He was among a group of sportswriters who organized a college triple-header at Madison Square Garden in 1931 to benefit the New York Relief Fund. The show drew a full house that year and in repeats in 1932 and 1933.

In 1934, Irish became a basketball promoter. That season, he arranged eight Garden double-headers, which drew a total of nearly 100,000 people. The previous events there had involved New York area teams, but Irish booked teams from all over the country, and they were willing to come, for the exposure as well as the money. Suddenly, college basketball was attracting nationwide interest. In 1938, the Metropolitan Basketball Writers Association organized the first major postseason tournament, the National Invitational (NIT). Six schools competed. Temple, the Eastern Intercollegiate League champion, beat Colorado, which had tied for the Big Seven Conference Championship, in the finals. The NIT has been a major tournament ever since, although it is now overshadowed by the NCAA's own championship tournament.

Angelo "Hank" Luisetti, who invented—or at least popularized— the one-handed jump shot to start a basketball revolution, was a three-time All-American at Stanford and was twice named college player of the year, in 1937 and 1938. *(Basketball Hall of Fame.)*

The NCAA Tourney. The success of the NIT convinced NCAA leaders that they needed a tournament which would formally decide the country's college basketball champion. The first NCAA tournament, in 1939, began with Eastern and Western regionals, the respective champions meeting at Northwestern University. Oregon edged Ohio State, 46-43. For the first several years, entrants in the NCAA tournament were chosen rather haphazardly. For example, the NCAA champion in its second year, 1940, was Indiana, which had finished second in the Big Ten. However, Indiana had twice beaten conference champion Purdue. The NCAA was basically an invitational tournament, and conference champions sometimes refused bids. However, the NCAA has since organized its tournament as a true championship event, with major conference champions and strong independents competing in a series of games, starting with regional tournaments and moving through sectional and divisional events into the finals.

The Modern Era. It was not just the NIT that marked the 1937–1938 season as a kind of watershed in basketball. One revolution had arrived the year before, when Stanford, led by Hank Luisetti, came to the Garden to end Long Island University's 43-game winning streak.

Luisetti had developed remarkable accuracy with a one-handed jump shot, which stunned not only LIU's players but the New York spectators. Many coaches, brought up in the "use both hands to shoot" tradition, didn't like it; but other coaches and many young players did, and basketball has never been the same since.

The center jump after each basket was eliminated in 1937. This meant that, after a team scored, it could move quickly to the other end of the court to set up a defense, and the offensive team had to work on ways to penetrate the defense. Elimination of the center jump also led to higher scores. Another 1937 rules change required a team to bring the ball across the half-court line within 10 sec of gaining possession.

Long Island, after losing to Stanford, won 26 more in a row, including the 1939 NIT championship game. They repeated in 1941. They were coached by Clair Bee. The New York area had two other consistently strong teams, NYU, coached by Howard Cann, and CCNY.

World War II slowed the sport's growth, as travel was reduced and many athletes entered the armed services, but the two major tournaments continued. In 1942, Long Island lost in the first round of the NIT to surprising West Virginia, which went on to win the championship, while Stanford beat Dartmouth for the NCAA title. Jim Pollard, Stanford's star, missed the finals because of flu. In the meantime, a smaller school, Rhode Island State, had been winning a lot of games with what Coach Frank Keaney called "firehouse basketball." His players just ran and ran and ran, the ultimate in the fast break, and consistently averaged more than 70 points a game—high for the period—over a number of years. Stanley "Stutz" Modzelewski set a new four-year college scoring record by getting his 1,730th point in Rhode Island's final game in 1942.

NCAA champ, Wyoming, and NIT champ, St. John's, played a special Red Cross benefit game in 1943, Wyoming winning 52-47. Illinois' "Whiz Kids," led by Andy Philips, were another strong team, but stayed out of postseason play because some players entered the armed services before tournament time. As the war continued, colleges had younger and younger players.

Utah's "Cinderella Kids," of 1943–1944, averaged only 18½ years in age. They lost in the first round of the NIT, but got a special invitation to the NCAA and won the championship, 42-40, over Dartmouth. Their freshman guard, Arnie Ferrin, was named the tournament's Most Valuable Player. Elsewhere, two giants were emerging. 7-ft Bob Kurland of Oklahoma A&M and 6-9 George Mikan of DePaul were both adept at leaping into the air to knock opponents' shots away from the basket, so the NCAA in 1944 introduced the goal-tending rule: If a defensive player touches the ball while it is on the downward arc toward the basket, the shot counts as a field goal.

The two big men were quite different: Kurland played for Hank Iba, a defense-minded coach, and his main job was blocking shots and getting rebounds. (He was turned loose to score on occasions, though; he got 58 points in his last home game, in 1946.) Mikan was a solidly built specimen who could also play defense and get rebounds, but his forte was using his muscle to get close to the basket and score.

DePaul won the NIT in 1945, and Oklahoma A&M won the NCAA, then repeated in 1946 to become the first team to win two in a row. Adolph Rupp of Kentucky, who had had good teams before and was to have many more good teams later, coached his club to a 46-45 win over Rhode Island in the NIT finals in 1946.

The postwar years brought a real boom in basketball, as in most sports. Many athletes returned from the service to resume their college careers, and fans were eager to start enjoying themselves, free of the fears and the rationing of wartime. Holy Cross, which had to play all its games on the road, won the 1946 NCAA tournament, sparked by George Kaftan. They won their last 23 games, including tournament play. Kentucky again got to the finals of the NIT, but lost to Utah, 49-45.

But Kentucky's best—and worst—years were ahead. "Baron" Rupp produced a team known as the "the Fabulous Five" in 1947-1948. Led by 6-7 center Alex Groza (brother of football star Lou), Ralph Beard, and clutch player "Wah Wah" Jones, the Wildcats were 36-3—one of the losses was to the AAU champion Phillips 66 Oilers in the Olympic tryouts—and won the NCAA. All five Kentucky starters were named to the U.S. Olympic team. With much the same cast, Kentucky rolled to a second straight NCAA title in 1949, beating Oklahoma A&M 46-36 in the finals. However, they were upset in the NIT—a loss that was to have major repercussions later.

CCNY was the team of the year in 1950. With a lineup dominated by sophomores and coached by Nat Holman, they became the first team to win the NCAA and the NIT in the same year, beating Bradley in both final games. But Kentucky came back in 1950-1951, led by 7-ft Bill Spivey, to become the first school to win three NCAA titles.

The Scandal. Early in 1951, Junius Kellogg of Manhattan College told the New York District Attorney's office he had been offered $1,000 to "shave points" in a basketball game. (A point spread is used, instead of odds, to even up betting on basketball; if you bet on an 11-point favorite, you win only if the team wins by more than 11 points.)

Kellogg's revelation led to a major scandal, the biggest sports scandal since the "Black Sox" World Series of 1919. The ensuing investigation involved 32 players from seven colleges, including three of CCNY's stars and two of Kentucky's. (Apologists for the players, including Coach Rupp, said that at least they were only shaving points, not blowing games; but the Kentucky culprits had gone a little too far with their point shaving in the NIT, resulting in the upset loss to Loyola of Chicago.) Other schools involved were Bradley, Long Island University, New York University, and Toledo, along with Manhattan, where two of Kellogg's teammates were implicated. Some players were indicted but not convicted; however, all implicated were barred from playing professional basketball.

The scandal led to more problems for Kentucky. Beard and Groza revealed that there had been recruiting violations at the school, and the NCAA forced cancelation of Kentucky's 1952-1953 schedule. Rupp had three great players ready, Lou Tsioropoulos, Frank Ramsey, and Cliff Hagan, but they had to wait a year.

After the Scandal. Kentucky was rated tops in the country in 1952, but surprising Kansas, led by Clyde Lovellette, won the NCAA title. Lovellette, who had 33 points in the final game, set a new collegiate season scoring record. Meanwhile, Freshman Tom Gola led LaSalle to the NIT championship. Without Lovellette, Kansas made it to the NCAA finals again in 1953, but was beaten by Indiana and 6-10 sophomore center Don Schlundt, 69-68. LaSalle was succeeded by another Philadelphia area school, Seton Hall, as NIT champion.

Bigger and bigger players and higher and higher scores were a continuing trend throughout the fifties. Back in business, Kentucky had a 25-0 record in 1953-1954, but passed up tournament play because its postgraduate players, Tsioropoulos, Ramsey, and Hagan, were ineligible. Indiana was again strong, and LSU, led by Bob Pettit, had tied Kentucky for the Southeastern Conference title, but LaSalle won the NCAA crown, Gola scoring 114 points in the four games.

The next two seasons belonged to the defense-minded Dons of San Francisco. Their center, Bill Russell, inaugurated a new style of play (although it was, in a sense, a flashback to Kurland's days at Oklahoma A&M). Russell was a mediocre shot but a great rebounder and an intimidating defender. The Dons also had a great defensive guard and playmaker in K. C. Jones. They rolled to a 26-1 record and the NCAA title, with Russell named MVP. LaSalle came close again, but lost 77-63, in the final—they had averaged 89 points in three previous tournament games.

San Francisco went on to stretch its unbeaten streak to 55 games while winning a second straight NCAA championship in 1955-1956, although Jones was declared ineligible for postseason play.

The best one-season record ever, 32-0, was compiled by NCAA champion North Carolina in 1956-1957. The Tarheels, led by Lennie Rosenbluth, had to win two consecutive triple-overtime games to do it, beating Michigan State 74-70 in the semifinals and then standing off Kansas and sophomore star Wilt Chamberlain, 54-53, in the finals.

The 1957-1958 season brought a superfluity of fine teams and great players. At Cincinnati, Oscar Robertson became the first sophomore ever to win a national scoring championship. Wilt Chamberlain of Kansas and Elgin Baylor of Seattle both averaged more than 30 points a game, but finished behind Robinson's 35.1. But Adolph Rupp's Kentucky team—known as the "Fiddling Five," because Rupp felt they fiddled around too much, early in the game, before they started to play the way they should—won a fourth NCAA title, beating Seattle 84-72 in the final.

Robertson and West were still around the following year, and Kansas State, led by Bob Boozer, was No. 1 in both wire service polls at season's end, but another defense-minded team, California, won the NCAA, beating West Virginia 71-70 in the finals, while St. John's of New York won its third NIT title, the first team to do so.

Then the emphasis shifted to Ohio for three years. Ohio State, with sophomores Jerry Lucas and John Havlicek, beat California in the 1960 NCAA finals, 75-55, and Robertson, who won his third straight scoring title, led Cincinnati to victory in the consolation game. It looked as if Ohio State might reign for years. However, without Robinson, Cincinnati Coach Ed Jucker shifted the emphasis to team defense, and Ohio State's 32-game winning streak was ended in the 1961 NCAA finals, Cincinnati winning in overtime, 70-65.

Another, milder scandal shook college basketball in

1961. A number of freshmen were involved this time, having accepted money from gamblers before their varsity careers ever began. It didn't affect either Ohio State or Cincinnati, however, and again the two schools met in the NCAA finals. Great defense by guards Tom Thacker and Tony Yates and the defense and rebounding of Paul Hogue prevailed as Cincinnati won again, 71-59. The Bearcats had a chance to make it three in a row in 1963, but the nation's highest scoring team, Loyola of Chicago, beat them 60-58 in overtime in the NCAA finals.

Bruin Dynasty. Both Cincinnati and Ohio State, like other schools before them, had had great teams for three consecutive years. But the very format of an NCAA tournament—where a single defeat eliminates a team—made it seem virtually impossible for even a great team to win three NCAA titles in a row. More than three seemed absolutely impossible, since a college team can have the same lineup for only three years (now four: the NCAA has allowed freshmen to play for varsity teams since 1972).

But John Wooden, the former Purdue All-American, and his UCLA teams were to destroy any such theories. The UCLA basketball dynasty is considered by some the greatest dynasty in the history of sports, since Wooden coached nine NCAA champions in a 10-year period, including seven in a row, and often had to reshape a team completely after graduation losses during that span.

It began quietly enough in 1964. UCLA had a small team that year, led by guards Walt Hazzard and Gail Goodrich, but they methodically won 30 in a row, beating Duke 98-82 in the NCAA finals. Despite the streak, they were often unimpressive, but somehow they always managed to put a streak together in the late going. (Their first three victories in the tournament were by a total margin of only 15 points.)

Wooden emphasized team play—hitting the open player on offense, helping out on defense—and conditioning. His teams could keep running long after the opponents were worn out, and they used a full-court press from the opening tapoff to further wear down opponents and force them to commit errors.

With All-American Hazzard in the pros, UCLA made it two straight in 1965, Goodrich scoring 42 points in a 91-80 defeat of Michigan in the NCAA finals. The following season, UCLA was rebuilding. A lot of coaches felt this was the year to win the NCAA, since Wooden had a freshman named Lew Alcindor (Kareem Abdul-Jabbar) who seemed likely to establish a three-year dynasty. Duke and Kentucky were favored, but a surprising Texas Western team upset Kentucky, 72-65, in the title game. (It was the first time an all-black starting five appeared in the NCAA—and against an all-white Kentucky five.)

Alcindor did bring a three-year dynasty to UCLA. The 7-ft sophomore, a complete basketball player, was MVP in the 1967 tournament, capping a 30-0 season. The Bruins whipped Dayton, 79-64, in the finals.

What seemed like *the* big game in 1967–1968 came long before the NCAA. The largest crowd ever to see a basketball game in this country, 52,693, filled Houston's Astrodome to watch Alcindor face Elvin "Big E" Hayes of Houston. Alcindor had missed three games with a scratched eyeball and was below par. Houston won, 71-69, to end UCLA's winning streak at 47. The Bruins picked up right where they had left off, however. In an

NCAA semifinal game, Alcindor held Hayes to 10 points in an easy 101-69 win, and UCLA beat North Carolina 78-55 in the finals—the biggest margin of victory ever in a championship game.

Could they possibly win three in a row, though? Just one loss in the pressure-packed tournament would eliminate them. But UCLA made it look easy. After an 85-82 squeaker in the semifinals, against Drake, the Bruins bombed Purdue, 92-72, with Alcindor scoring 37 points. (Their overall record was 29-1, the only loss coming to Southern California in the last game of the regular season.)

So much for that dynasty, the experts thought. Kentucky was No. 1 in the polls at the end of the 1969–1970 season. The Wildcats lost, 106-100, to Jacksonville in the Mideast regionals, however. And UCLA beat Jacksonville, 80-69, in the NCAA championship. Wooden was happy with this team; with Alcindor gone, he could go back to coaching the team balance he always liked. Guard John Vallely, center Steve Patterson, and forwards Sidney Wicks and Curtis Rowe all hit in double figures in the final, while the UCLA defense held Jacksonville and 7'2" Artis Gilmore well below their average of 100.3 points a game.

Wicks, Rowe, and Patterson returned in 1970–1971, and the Bruins made it five in six years, beating Villanova, 68-62, in the final. UCLA lost one game that season, to Notre Dame. There were two major undefeated teams, Pennsylvania and Marquette, both with 26-0 records, but both were eliminated in regional tournaments.

The following season, UCLA again had a big, talented, sophomore center—Bill Walton. Though he suffered from painful knees and lacked some of Alcindor's finesse, some think Walton was an even more dominant figure than Alcindor, especially on defense and as a rebounder. In his first year with the varsity, UCLA made it 45 consecutive victories, 6 consecutive NCAA championships, and their average margin of victory was a record of 32.3 points.

The "Walton Gang" kept rolling in 1972–1973, beating Memphis State for their seventh straight NCAA title, and they extended their record winning streak to 88 games during the 1973–1974 season. But 1974 brought an end to both UCLA streaks.

Notre Dame had been the last team to beat UCLA, 89-82, way back in 1970. On January 19, 1974, they did it again, ending the Bruins' streak, in a nationally televised game. UCLA held a 17-point lead at one time in the first half, and led by 11 points with little more than 3 min to play. Then Notre Dame made five consecutive baskets to cut the UCLA lead to 1 point, and with 21 sec left, Dwight Clay made a shot from the corner for a 71-70 lead that stood up.

The UCLA streak of national championships was ended by North Carolina State, led by forward David Thompson, in the NCAA semifinal game. In the second overtime, UCLA took a 7-point lead with about 3 min left, but North Carolina State scored 13 points to only 3 for UCLA and won, 80-77. The Wolfpack then beat Marquette, 76-64, in the final.

In Wooden's final season, 1974–1975, UCLA came back to win yet another NCAA title, even though Bobby Knight's Indiana team was ranked first in the polls at the end of the regular season. Indiana was unbeaten until losing to Kentucky in the quarterfinal round of the NCAA tournament. Kentucky went all the way to the finals, losing 92–85 to UCLA.

Knight's Hoosiers, led by player of the year Scott May and burly, 6–10 center Kent Benson, won the 1976 tournament, beating Michigan. It was the first time two teams from the same conference (the Big 10) had met in the finals.

The Others. In a way, it's too bad UCLA has so dominated college basketball for the last decade, because during that period skills increased phenomenally. Even most of the giants demonstrated speed, agility, and shooting ability. Many of the outstanding college players of this era chose to enter the pros before finishing out their college career. For the reasons, *see* MAJOR LEAGUE BASKETBALL.

Bill Bradley of Princeton set an NCAA tournament record by scoring 58 points in the 1965 consolation game, leading his team to a 118-82 win over Wichita State. Then he turned down professional offers for a year to accept a Rhodes scholarship.

Cazzie Russell of Michigan was one of the losers, scoring 28 points against UCLA in the 1965 final, while Rick Barry averaged 37.4 points that season for Miami of Florida.

Pete Maravich of LSU and little Calvin Murphy of Niagara were among top scorers for three years. In 1967–1968, Maravich became the second sophomore to win the national scoring title, and set a record with a 43.8 average.

He repeated in 1968–1969 with 44.2, while Rick Mount of Purdue scored 28 in the losing battle against UCLA, and finished second in the season to Maravich.

Dan Issell starred at Kentucky and ended his college career prematurely to play in the pros. Another who turned pro early was Spencer Haywood of Detroit, a standout with the 1968 Olympic team.

In 1969–1970, big Bob Lanier starred for a strong St. Bonaventure team, but tore knee ligaments in an NCAA regional game. Maravich again led the major colleges in scoring with a 44.5 average, and Austin Carr of Notre Dame set an NCAA tournament single-game record with 61 points. Carr scored 38 points in UCLA's only defeat in 1970–1971, while Mississippi sophomore Johnny Neumann led the nation with a 40.1 average—and then joined the pros. Providence had fine teams that year, and for two more years, led by flashy guard Ernie DiGregorio and big Marvin Barnes.

Smaller Colleges. The first college basketball tournament was neither the NCAA nor the NIT, but a small-college tourney organized in 1937 by Dr. Naismith, then teaching at Kansas; Emil Liston, athletic director of Baker University, a small school in Kansas; and a number of Kansas City people who wanted a tournament to replace the AAU tourney, which had moved to Denver. Eight Midwestern conference champions were invited to that first tournament, won by Central Missouri State. The following year, it became the National Intercollegiate Basketball Championship tournament, and 32 teams were invited. In 1940, the National Association of Intercollegiate Basketball was organized to run the tournament. The group became the National Association of Intercollegiate Athletics (NAIA) in 1952, and now conducts national championship programs for smaller schools in 13 sports. The NCAA organized its own College Division tournament in 1957. Until 1973, the NCAA had two divisions in major sports, based not on school size but on the caliber of opposition. The NCAA has been reorganized into three divisions, each with its own tournament.

Major League Basketball

The Beginnings. George Preston Marshall, better known as the long-time owner of the Washington Redskins of the National Football League, made the first attempt to organize a genuine major league in basketball in 1926. The Original Celtics were forced to join this pioneer American Basketball League—it was the only way they could play against good teams—and they won championships in 1927 and 1928. Then they were broken up, three of their players going to the Cleveland Rosenblums, who won in 1929 and 1930. The Celtics eventually reorganized and went back on the road, but the ABL struggled along, changing shape practically every year as franchises folded or moved, and never really becoming major league because so many of its teams were in smaller cities.

The first pro dynasty was a club from the South Philadelphia Hebrew Association, the Philadelphia SPHAs, organized by Edward J. Gottlieb. The SPHAs dominated the Eastern League for several years and moved into the ABL in 1933. They won a total of eight championships.

Another outstanding pro team was a "barnstorming" group of blacks from Harlem, the New York Renaissance, whose owner owned a nightclub, the Renaissance Casino. In 22 seasons, the Rens won 2,318 games and lost

One of the first of the really big players, 6'9" George Mikan was college player of the year in 1944 and 1945 and then became an outstanding professional player, leading the Minneapolis Lakers to four NBA championships. *(Basketball Hall of Fame.)*

381. Two of the outstanding players were also stars in Negro baseball, Harold "Fat" Jenkins and Bill Yancey.

Pro basketball really became a major-league sport only after World War II; and then, oddly, because of pro hockey.

Although the ABL was still operating in 1946, there was a much more important professional league, the National Basketball League, which had been established in 1937. This league was actually a Midwestern operation, with teams in such disparate cities as Chicago, Detroit, Sheboygan, Wisconsin, and Anderson, Indiana. The NBL had some top players, though—including George Mikan, fresh out of DePaul, who had signed with the Chicago American Gears, an NBL team "sponsored" by the American Gear Company, for a $25,000 bonus.

In the meantime, a New York sportswriter, Max Kase of the *Journal American*, had decided the time was ripe for a real major basketball league, with teams in major cities. Ned Irish, busily promoting college games at the Garden, agreed; so did a number of hockey owners, who wanted another attraction to keep their arenas filled on nights when they didn't have hockey games.

The new Basketball Association of America was organized in June of 1946, essentially as an offshoot of the Arena Managers Association. The BAA was to have a playoff format similar to hockey's; the same financial setup as professional hockey, with the home team keeping all gate receipts; and its first commissioner was Maurice Podoloff, who had been commissioner of the American Hockey League. The original franchises were in Toronto, New York, Philadelphia, Washington, Detroit, Pittsburgh, Cleveland, and Chicago.

The BAA's first star was the previously unheard-of Joe Fulks of little Murray State College. A Marine veteran who became a pro basketball rookie at twenty-six, Fulks played for the Philadelphia Warriors and led the league in scoring with a 23.2 average that first season.

The NBL still had better players, though, including Mikan. But the owner of the Chicago Gears, and of Mikan's contract, decided to start his own professional league in 1947–1948. His league didn't last long. After it folded, rights to its players were distributed among NBL teams, and the Minneapolis Lakers got Mikan by picking his name out of a hat.

The BAA was in trouble that year. Cleveland, Detroit, Pittsburgh, and Toronto had given up, and only one franchise—the Baltimore Bullets, a minor-league team—was added. The BAA struggled along while the NBL did fairly well, thanks largely to Mikan's drawing power.

Podoloff realized the simplest way to strengthen his league would be to talk some of the NBL franchises into switching. He persuaded the owners of the Indianapolis and Fort Wayne teams to move, and Minneapolis and Rochester followed suit. In 1949, what was left of the NBL merged with the BAA to form an unwieldy 17-team league, the National Basketball Association. After the NBA operated with a three-division setup for one season, six teams dropped out and the league went to a two-division format.

The Minneapolis Lakers finished second in their division in 1948–1949, but won the championship playoff, sparked by Mikan, the league's leading scorer; forwards Vern Mikkelsen and Jim Pollard, and guards Arnie Ferrin and Slater Martin. It was the beginning of a dynasty that

kept on reigning through the merger and various vicissitudes of the new league.

In the first year of the merger, the Lakers were tied with Rochester for first place in the Central Division. They won that playoff, then whipped Chicago, Fort Wayne, and Anderson to get into the finals, where they beat Syracuse four games out of six.

In 1951, however, second-place Rochester beat the Lakers in the semifinals and then won the championship in a tough seven-game series with New York. The Rochester club was led by Arnie Risen and Bob Davies. Mikan, however, won his third consecutive scoring title.

Because of Mikan and other big men, for the 1951–1952 season the NBA widened the free-throw lane from 6 to 12 ft. (Since an offensive player can remain in the lane for only 3 sec, the rule had the effect of keeping them farther from the basket.)

It may have had a slight effect; Mikan finished second in scoring to Paul Arizin of Philadelphia, and the Lakers finished second in their division. But they beat first-place Rochester in the semifinals, and won the championship in another seven-game series against New York.

The Lakers rolled on for two more championships, in 1953 and 1954, but then Mikan retired to attend law school, and the title was up for grabs. The 1954–1955 season saw the introduction of two new rules, designed to speed up play. The 24-sec rule requires a team to get off a shot at the basket within 24 sec after taking possession of the ball. And teams were limited to six personal fouls per quarter, with a bonus free throw awarded for each foul after the sixth. This rule helped eliminate intentional fouling near the end of a period.

Neil Johnston of Philadelphia won the scoring title for the third straight year, and teammate Paul Arizin finished second; but Philadelphia finished last in its division, and the 1954–1955 champion was Syracuse, featuring center Dolph Schayes, guard Paul Seymour, and fine team play. It wasn't easy. The seven-game series with Fort Wayne went down to the final seconds of the final game, when George King made a free throw for a 92-91 win.

The Milwaukee Hawks—who moved to St. Louis the following season—appeared to be the team of the future. They had the Rookie of the Year in Bob Pettit of LSU, and another rookie, Frank Selvy from Furman, finished fifth in scoring, right behind Pettit.

In 1955–1956, although Pettit led the league in scoring and rebounding and was named Most Valuable Player, Philadelphia won the league title, led by Johnston and Arizin.

The Celtics. The Boston entry in the NBA had a proud basketball name that also endeared it to many of the Boston Irish. And after some bad years, they had become the top-scoring team in the league and had acquired a certain amount of respectability with two second-place division finishes in three years.

They had a fine center in "Easy Ed" Macauley and a pair of outstanding guards in Bob Cousy and Bill Sharman. Sharman was a tough defensive player who could also shoot—he still holds NBA records for highest free-throw percentage for career and season. Cousy was a flashy ball-handler who had been greeted with some skepticism after arriving in the pros from Holy Cross, because his behind-the-back dribbles and passes seemed like mere showboating to some.

In the summer of 1956, Auerbach traded Macauley and Cliff Hagen to St. Louis for the rights to Bill Russell, who had been the Hawks' first-round draft choice. All teams in the league had to approve the trade of a first-round choice at the time, but they went along with it because they believed Russell would accept a lucrative offer from the Harlem Globetrotters. Besides, he was going to play for the U.S. Olympic team, so he'd miss the first couple of months of the season.

Russell, having led the University of San Francisco to two consecutive NCAA championships, led the United States to an Olympic title and then joined the Celtics on December 22, 1956. He was an instant success. As he had at USF, he brought a new dimension to the game: defense. For the first time, big centers were having their shots blocked. (In one of his first starts. Russell held the great Neil Johnston scoreless for the first 38 min of play.) And a guard who tried to drive the lane against Russell ran the risk of having the ball knocked back into his face. Russell had not only height and great leaping ability, he had superb reflexes and quickness. He looked skinny, but he quickly proved he could stand up to the punishment dealt out near the basket. And his rebounding skills made the Celtics' fast break go.

In his first season, the Celtics won their first division title, and then won the championship playoff. In his second season, Russell's importance to the Celtics was underscored: He injured an ankle in the third game of the final series against the St. Louis Hawks, and Boston lost four out of six. After that, a healthy Russell led the Celtics to eight straight championships.

Solidification and Expansion. Throughout the early years, the NBA trend was to get out of the smaller cities and into the bigger ones. Anderson, Waterloo, Sheboygan, and Denver dropped out in 1950; so did two large cities, Chicago and St. Louis. In 1951, the Tri-Cities Blackhawks, formerly of the NBL, became the Milwaukee Hawks—in 1955, as we've seen, they moved to St. Louis.

Indianapolis dropped out after the 1952–1953 season, and the league was to remain relatively stable, with eight franchises, for some years. But shifts to large cities were still in order: Rochester moved to Cincinnati in 1957 and Fort Wayne to Detroit in 1957.

Pro basketball went to the West Coast before the 1960–1961 season, when the Minneapolis Lakers became the Los Angeles Lakers. And, in 1962, the Philadelphia Warriors moved to San Francisco. However, the sport failed in Chicago once again. The Chicago Packers, after two seasons, moved to Baltimore and became the Bullets in 1963–1964. At the same time, the Syracuse franchise went to Philadelphia.

Attendance was booming—it climbed past 2 million for the first time in 1963–1964—and television money was coming in as well. The league moved into Chicago for a third time, with a team called the Bulls, and this time it seemed to work—perhaps because the Bulls made the playoffs in their first season. That evened the two divisions at five teams apiece.

There was talk of expansion, and some planning for it. But the NBA's first major expansion came with something of a rush, because a new professional league, the American Basketball Association, had suddenly appeared. In a preemptive action, the NBA placed franchises in San Diego and Seattle before the 1967–1968 season. After that season, the NBA added two more cities, Phoenix and Milwaukee, and the much-traveled Hawks moved from St. Louis to Atlanta.

After operating with two 7-team divisions, the NBA expanded to 17 teams—the original number—in 1970, adding franchises in Buffalo, Cleveland, and Portland. In 1971, the Rockets, unable to make it in San Diego, moved to Houston, and the San Francisco Warriors decided to split their home games between Oakland and San Diego—so they became the Golden State Warriors.

Pretenders to the Throne. For three seasons, the division champions in the NBA were the same: Boston and St. Louis. In Bob Pettit, St. Louis had a genuinely great player. But the perils of the playoff system told in 1959: St. Louis lost in the semifinals to the Lakers, who were wiped out by the Celtics in a four-game final series. The Celtics beat St. Louis in a tough seven-game playoff in 1960, but it took them only five games to repeat in 1961.

Another good team had taken shape in the Celtics' own Eastern Division: the Philadelphia Warriors, paced by 7'1" Wilt Chamberlain, who led the league in scoring and rebounding as a rookie in 1959–1960, and became the first player to score more than 3,000 points in a season the following year.

With the addition of Elgin Baylor in 1958–1959 and Jerry West in 1960–1961, the Lakers, transplanted to Los Angeles, regained some of their former glory. They became the top team in the Western Division in 1961–1962. But the Celtics' balance and playoff experience continually frustrated both these challengers. Philadelphia and Los Angeles were both good enough to push the Celts to a seven-game series in 1961–1962—but the Celtics won the seventh game both times.

After the Warriors moved to San Francisco, and the Western Division, in 1962, Cincinnati offered the biggest challenge to the Celtics' domination of the East. The Royals had a fine running team, led by the great Oscar Robertson and Jack Twyman, with the rebounding of Jerry Lucas, but they had to settle for three consecutive second-place finishes and three consecutive defeats by Boston in semifinal play.

Philadelphia reentered the picture in 1965–1966. The transplanted Syracuse team traded for Wilt Chamberlain, and he, along with sharp-shooting guard Hal Greer and all-around standout Chet Walker, took first place in the Eastern Division that season—the first time anyone but the Celtics had won since 1956–1957.

However, the Celtics beat them easily in the playoffs, four games to one, and then met the Lakers, whose time seemed ripe, for the championship. Except for Russell, the Celtics had changed completely since the beginning of the dynasty. Cousy, Sharman, and Tom Heinsohn were gone. John Havlicek had arrived from Ohio State as the best "sixth man" in the league, and as a frequent starter. The Jones boys, defender K. C. and shooter Sam, were in the backcourt. And even this cast was getting old.

After Boston lost the first game, at home, "Red" Auerbach announced that he would retire after the playoffs. It seemed to fire Boston up. They won the next three in a row, two of them in Los Angeles. But the Lakers, getting 41 points from Baylor, won in Boston, and then won at home to even the series. The final game, in Boston, was a strange one. The Celtics led, 76-60, as the fourth period began, but they looked tired and ineffectual. A Sam Jones bucket in the last minute put the game out of reach—the Celtics hung on to win 95-93. That was too close. The aging Celtics, with Auerbach gone, seemed completely vulnerable now, despite their eighth straight championship. Bill Russell became their player-coach—the first black coach in the NBA.

Who's Got the Dynasty? Philadelphia again won the Eastern Division title in 1966–1967, with the greatest record compiled by an NBA team up to that time, 68 wins and 13 losses. It was an unusual year for Chamberlain—he averaged "only" 24.6 points, the lowest of his career, but he was getting the rebounds and assisting on baskets. Greer and Walker could do the scoring, with help from Billy Cunningham, coming off the bench, or long-shot specialist Wallie Jones.

In the semifinal confrontation against Boston, Chamberlain dominated, and Philadelphia won four games out of five. In the final game, Chamberlain got 36 rebounds to Russell's 21 and 29 points to Russell's 4. He also had 13 assists. The 76ers then beat the Warriors, four games to two, and there was talk of a new dynasty.

The 1967–1968 playoffs produced an incredible outcome. The old Celtics again finished second to Philadelphia in their division. And the 76ers won three of the first four games in the Eastern playoff. But the Celtics battled to win the next three in a row, two of them in Philadelphia—the first time a team had won the title after losing three of the first four playoff games.

It seemed little more than a last gasp by an aging team. As the 1968–1969 season began, a new dynasty was shaping up: Chamberlain had been traded to Los Angeles, joining West and Baylor. It seemed an unbeatable combination. Baltimore had the Rookie of the Year and Most Valuable Player, Wes Unseld of Louisville, and they finished first in the East; the Celtics were a tired fourth.

Nevertheless, when the playoffs were finished, the Celtics were once again the champions. The New York Knickerbockers eliminated Baltimore in the first round of the Eastern Division playoffs, while Boston beat Philadelphia in five games. The Knicks had an emergent team, and the homecourt advantage—but the Celtics won the first game, in New York, and the second, in Boston, then went on to eliminate the Knicks in six.

They met the Lakers in the finals—another of those Russell-Chamberlain confrontations, only Chamberlain now was counted on more for defense and rebounding than for scoring. Los Angeles won the first two games, at home, but the Celtics won the next two, in Boston. They traded homecourt victories again, and the final was in Los Angeles. The Celtics took over in the third quarter to go ahead by 15 points. Los Angeles whittled away in the fourth quarter. With the lead down to 7, Chamberlain injured a knee and went to the sidelines. Nevertheless, the Lakers cut the margin to 1 point, with about 3 min left. Both teams, tired and tight, got cold. But the Celtics got a lucky shot from Don Nelson with 80 sec left, the Lakers lost the ball and were forced to foul, and the final was Boston 108, Los Angeles, 106—the Celtics' eleventh title in 13 years.

Bill Russell retired, as player and coach, after that. And the question now became: Would the next dynasty belong to the Lakers or the Knickerbockers? Or might it be Milwaukee?

The Knicks had the same kind of team that had worked for the Celtics—five good players who blended together beautifully, and played exceptional team defense: Willis Reed at center, Dave Debusschere and Bill Bradley at forward, Walt Frazier and Dick Barnett at guard. Any one of them could get hot on any given night. They also had three good men on the bench, chief among them the high-scoring Cazzie Russell, who could break a game open all by himself.

They were the team of 1969–1970. The Lakers lost Chamberlain to a knee operation for most of the season, and finished second in the West; however, Wilt was back for the playoffs. The Milwaukee Bucks had won a coin toss for the rights to UCLA's Lew Alcindor, and he led them to a second-place finish in the East.

The Knicks had trouble with the Bullets in the first playoff round, but handled Milwaukee easily in the division finals. The Lakers, getting readjusted to Chamberlain's presence, beat Phoenix in seven games, then eliminated Atlanta in five.

The finals seemed to be decided when Willis Reed tore a thigh muscle in the fifth game. Despite his loss, however, the Knicks won to take a 3-2 edge. With Reed out, the Lakers evened the series at home, and the teams came back to New York. Full of medication, Reed played. He was not effective, but his presence was inspirational. The Knicks, led by Frazier's 36 points and 19 assists, played perfectly and won going away.

The NBA expanded to 17 teams and a four-division setup in its silver-anniversary season, but the biggest event was Milwaukee's acquisition of Oscar Robertson, who teamed with Lew Alcindor to lead a potent offense. The Bucks won 80 percent of their games, Alcindor led the league in scoring and was fourth in rebounds, and Robertson was third in assists.

The Baltimore Bullets surprised everyone by beating the Knicks in a four-game series for the Eastern Conference title, but the Bucks beat them easily in four straight games for the championship—and again there was talk about a new dynasty.

But, in 1971–1972, the Lakers reemerged, setting new records with 33 consecutive victories and a 69-13 record. Milwaukee rolled to another division title, Alcindor again leading in scoring and winning the MVP award, and Boston returned as a division champ.

However, the Celtics were eliminated in five games by the Knicks in the semifinal round, while Los Angeles beat Milwaukee, four games to two, and the Lakers won an easy five-game final over New York for the first championship since the team moved from Minneapolis.

The finalists were the same in 1972–1973, although the Knicks again finished second to Boston in their division. The Golden State Warriors knocked Milwaukee out of the playoffs in the first round, the Knicks dispatched the Celtics in a tough seven-game series in the Eastern Conference finals, and then, playing incredible defense, the Knicks beat the Lakers in a five-game championship series—holding the high-powered Lakers to 95 points or less in four of those games.

A new Celtics' team won its division for the third year in a row and finally also won the NBA championship in 1973–1974. John Havlicek, Don Nelson, and Tom "Satch" Sanders were the only players left from the previous Celtic champions. Dave Cowens, a fiery, red-haired, "short" (only 6-9) center inspired the team with hustle and determination under both baskets; "Jo Jo" White was an outside threat; and guard Don Chaney played exceptional defense, while Havlicek did everything well. The Celtics eliminated their old nemesis, the Knicks, in the Eastern playoffs, then surprised almost everyone by beating the Bucks in the championship finals, winning the seventh game in Milwaukee.

The Golden State Warriors were the surprise team of 1974–75. Coach Al Attles shuffled players in and out of the lineup constantly, using 10 or 11 of his 12 men in virtually every game. Rick Barry was the team's only genuine star, averaging 30.6 points a game and leading the league in steals and free throw percentage. But the Warriors beat the heavily favored Washington Bullets in four straight games in the NBA final. The Celtics came back to win their 13th NBA title the following season, beating the Phoenix Suns in a six-game playoff. The Suns had eliminated the Warriors in a seven-game semifinal playoff series.

The American Basketball Association. Abe Saperstein, the founder and owner of the Harlem Globetrotters, thought the time was ripe for a new professional basketball league in 1961. He organized the American Basketball League, with franchises in Cleveland, Pittsburgh, Chicago, Washington, Kansas City, Los Angeles, San Francisco, and Hawaii, and he served as commissioner.

The new league introduced a 3-point field goal, for a shot from 30 or more feet away from the basket, and had one really outstanding player—Connie Hawkins, who was banned from the NBA because of alleged involvement with gamblers while a college freshman.

One other unique feature of the ABL was a split season, with first-half champions playing second-half champions for division titles before going on to championship finals. In the 1961–1962 season, Cleveland won the Eastern title and beat Kansas City for the championship. The Los Angeles team disbanded before the season was over, and the Washington franchise moved to Long Island midway through the season.

Beset by financial difficulties, the league folded partway through its second season.

The time was riper in 1967, when the American Basketball Association was formed, picking up the ABL's 3-point field goal. There were 11 franchises in the original league, in Anaheim, Dallas, Denver, Houston, Indiana, Kentucky, Minnesota, New Jersey, New Orleans, Oakland, and Pittsburgh. George Mikan was the first commissioner.

The ABA's first great coup was the signing of NBA scoring leader Rick Barry for its Oakland team, and the new league outbid the NBA for some top collegians. Connie Hawkins also got into the major leagues again and led the ABA in scoring in its first season, with a 26.8-point average. (Barry had to sit out a year because courts ruled that the one-year option clause in his contract with San Francisco of the NBA was binding.)

Hawkins, the league's first MVP, led Pittsburgh to the ABA title in a seven-game playoff series against New Orleans.

In 1968–1969, Barry got to play in a realigned ABA. The Minnesota franchise had moved to Miami, the Pittsburgh franchise to Minnesota, the New Jersey franchise to Long Island, and the Anaheim franchise to Los Angeles. Barry led in scoring on point-per-game average—he missed much of the season with an injury—and Oakland won the

Bob Cousy of the Boston Celtics accelerates past Jerry West of the Los Angeles Lakers. Cousy and West are two of the all-time great pro guards. *(Public Broadcasting Service.)*

title from Indiana in five games, thanks to the fine play of Rookie of the Year Warren Armstrong and two overtime victories.

The following season really marked the ABA's arrival, despite the fact that Hawkins jumped to the NBA. Spencer Haywood, who had led the United States to victory in the 1968 Olympics and was due to be a junior at the University of Detroit, signed with Denver as a "hardship case." The NBA at the time would not sign players with college eligibility remaining, but the ABA decided to do so in certain cases. A fine NBA center, Zelmo Beaty, jumped to the ABA. And the young league gained a lot of respect by inducing four professional referees to jump, as well.

There were more franchise shifts, Houston moving to Carolina, Oakland to Washington, and Minnesota going back to Pittsburgh. Haywood led Denver to a rout in the Western Division and won the league's top honors: scoring leader, rebounding leader, Rookie of the Year, and Most Valuable Player. But the Los Angeles Stars won the Western playoffs, and Indiana beat the Stars in six games for the ABA title.

Before the 1970–1971 season began, there was talk of merger between the two leagues. Owners were afraid— probably with justification—that a merger would be nullified by the courts, as a violation of the antitrust laws, however, and congressional action was sought.

Spencer Haywood jumped to the NBA, but Beaty played for the first time after sitting out a year because of an injunction, and the ABA also landed three top college stars, Dan Issel, Charlie Scott, and Rick Mount. Issel led in scoring, and he and Scott shared Rookie of the Year honors.

There were more franchise shifts: Washington became Virginia, Los Angeles moved to Utah, and New Orleans moved to Memphis. In addition, regionalization continued as teams dropped names of cities for names of states, often playing their home games in two or three different locations. The Miami team, for example, was renamed the Floridians, the Dallas team became the Texans. Both second-place finishers, Kentucky and Utah, won their division playoffs, and Beaty and Willie Wise led Utah to a seven-game final victory over Kentucky.

Owners formally agreed on a merger in 1971, but the NBA Players Association opposed it on the grounds that it would lead to reduced player salaries, and congressional action still was not forthcoming. The three-year agreement expired in 1974 without a merger taking place.

The ABA signed three more outstanding undergraduates, Julius Erving of Massachusetts (Virginia), George McGinnis of Indiana (Indiana), and Johnny Neumann of Mississippi (Memphis). Top graduating seniors signed by the NBA included 7-2 Artis Gilmore of Jacksonville (Kentucky) and 7-ft Jim McDaniels of Western Kentucky (Carolina).

For the first time, the leagues engaged in exhibition play, Dallas losing the first interleague game by 3 points to NBA champion Milwaukee, but more court battles arose during the season as McDaniels signed with the NBA Seattle team, Charlie Scott signed with Phoenix, and Erving signed a contract with Atlanta, to begin in 1975. In the meantime, Billy Cunningham of the NBA Philadelphia 76ers was ordered by the courts to honor an ABA contract for 1972–1973—he had signed the contract with Carolina, then had attempted to back out of it.

New York, third in the Eastern Division, beat Kentucky and Virginia to get into the finals but lost to the Indiana Pacers for the championship. New York was led by Barry and Rookie John Roche, while guard Freddie Lewis was the Indiana star in the playoffs. The Pacers thus became the first team to win two ABA titles.

The Pacers made it three in 1973, although they finished second in their division. They beat division champion Utah in the semifinals and won a close, hard-fought seven-game series with Kentucky for the championship.

In the 1974 playoffs, however, the young New York Nets beat Utah in a five-game final, after Utah had eliminated the Pacers in the semifinal round. The Nets were led by Julius Erving, the league's most valuable player, rookie forward Larry Kenon, and second-year guard Brian Taylor.

The Kentucky Colonels, who had won more regular season games during the ABA's existence than any other team, finally won a championship in 1974–75. Artis Gilmore, Kentucky's 7-2 center, was the most valuable

player in the playoffs as the Colonels beat Memphis, St. Louis, and Indiana, in that order. In the fifth and final playoff game against Indiana, Gilmore scored 28 points and had 31 rebounds.

In the meantime, a number of ABA teams were having financial difficulties. The Baltimore Claws collapsed just before the 1975–76 season. The Memphis Sounds moved to Baltimore, briefly, but folded early in the season, as did the San Diego Sails. The ABA shrank to one seven-team division, and the Denver Nuggets were the class of the league, winning 60 of 84 regular season games. Nevertheless, the Nets won the championship playoff, beating Denver in six games.

Shortly after the season, the NBA and ABA agreed on a "merger," which was virtually an ABA surrender. Four ABA teams—the New York Nets, Denver Nuggets, Indiana Pacers and San Antonio Spurs—were admitted to the NBA. Players from the other three ABA teams were distributed to other teams in a special dispersal draft. The new, 22-team NBA retained its four-division format.

Amateur Basketball

The AAU. The Amateur Athletic Union first got involved with basketball in 1893, joining with the arbiters at Springfield to establish a uniform set of rules, and in 1915, the AAU and NCAA formed a Joint Basketball Rules Committee.

The AAU and YMCA cosponsored the first national basketball tournament, in 1897, with most of the entrants from the New York City area. For many years, teams that entered the AAU National tournament were primarily from YMCAs, local athletic clubs, or colleges.

In the 1920s, however, AAU basketball began to take a different shape. Industrial leagues were organized, with companies in hot basketball cities and towns organizing teams of employees, and such teams dominated the AAU tournament from 1926 on, with occasional intrusions by service teams.

Because professional basketball was a shaky proposition at best, many college stars chose AAU basketball instead. Companies would hire stars, often financing further education, in order to get them to play for their teams. Among them were outstanding players like Bob Kurland and Hank Luisetti.

With increasing attendance, television money, and the salary war between the NBA and ABA, however, professional basketball began to get all the stars, and AAU basketball declined. A few companies still sponsor teams, but they no longer have the impact or spectator interest that they had in the days before television and before the NBA became a genuine major league.

International Basketball and the Olympics. Because of the YMCA's international scope, basketball spread to other countries rather quickly. Its chief advantages, as in the United States, are that it can be played by teams of only two or three if other players aren't available, little equipment is needed, and it doesn't require much space.

As early as 1931, it had become quite popular in China; in that year, basketball attracted more than 70,000 fans in one 3-night period. By World War II, the sport had been introduced into more than 75 countries.

Largely through the efforts of "Phog" Allen, then coach

at the University of Kansas, basketball was added to the Olympic Games program in 1936, and Dr. Naismith himself was invited as an honored guest of the International Olympic Committee.

The United States won the first championship easily, beating Spain, Estonia, the Philippines, Mexico, and Canada. The championship game against Canada was played on an outdoor court during a driving rainstorm; the United States won, 19-8.

This country resumed its domination of the sport when the Olympics resumed after World War II, winning 62 consecutive games and 6 more Olympic titles. In the earlier Olympiads, the Americans could virtually win on superior height alone. Later, other countries came up with some giant players, but they couldn't match the finesse and team play of the United States entries.

The domination ended abruptly—and controversially—in 1972. After winning eight games, including a narrow victory over Brazil, the United States met a strong Russian team for the championship. The U.S.S.R. led most of the way, but the Americans came back to go ahead 50-49 with 3 sec to play. All the Russians could do was to throw an inbounds pass the length of the court, hoping that one of their tall players could grab it and score before time ran out.

The attempt failed, but the officials ruled that the clock had been wrong. It was reset, and the Russians tried again and failed again. However, the officials ruled once again that the play didn't count, and the Russians got a third chance. This time they scored the winning basket.

The 51-50 victory was bitterly disputed by the United States, and it didn't become official until after an emergency meeting of the International Basketball Federation. The angry American players refused to accept the silver medal symbolic of second place.

The very closeness of the game, however, served notice that the United States can no longer take for granted its superiority in basketball. Many Iron Curtain countries and many countries in South America have developed basketball skills rapidly, and international competition is becoming more evenly matched and more interesting.

One fact that somewhat hampers Americans in international competition is that the rules are different, requiring some adjustment. The foul lanes are fan-shaped, tapering from 19 ft wide at the baseline to 6 ft at the free throw line. There is a 30-sec time limit for taking a shot after gaining possession of the ball. Until the last 5 min of play, no free throws are awarded unless a player is fouled in the act of shooting, provided the shot doesn't go. The player then gets two free throws. For all other fouls, the only penalty is that the ball is awarded out-of-bounds to the team offended against.

During the last 5 min of the game, every foul is a two-shot foul.

American fans got a good opportunity to see the international rules in operation during the Russian national team's tour of the country in the summer of 1973. Most of the games were televised, and the Americans got some measure of revenge by beating the Russians in the series. Perhaps the most noticeable difference was the fact that officials geared to the international rules don't call many fouls during rebounding action, and sheer muscle and roughness under the boards counts for a lot. On the other

hand, they seem to call fouls much more closely when there is contact with the player who has possession of the ball.

In the 1976 Olympics, the United States capitalized on its innate advantages: greater depth and more overall speed. Coach Dean Smith of the University of North Carolina substituted five men at a time to keep players fresh and used a pressing team defense—something most other teams weren't used to. Russia was eliminated by Yugoslavia in the semifinals and the U.S. beat Yugoslavia easily—for the second time in the tournament—to win the gold medal.

Women's Basketball

Dr. Naismith felt from the beginning that basketball would be an ideal sport for women. As already noted, he organized the first women's game in Springfield in 1892 (and later married one of the players, Maude Sherman). By 1895, Wellesley College had 20 intramural basketball teams, and the sport was quickly incorporated into physical education programs at other women's schools.

Early in this century, however, the women's physical education movement made drastic changes in the women's version of the sport. "Girls' basketball" is a rather static, dull sport. The court is divided into three zones, and a player must remain in her zone throughout the game. Dribbling is limited to two or three bounces.

Despite that form of the sport, some women have always played essentially the men's version of basketball. Industrial leagues were organized for women's teams in the 1920s, and in 1926 the AAU inaugurated its national tournament for women's amateur teams.

The present rules of the National Association for Girls and Women in Sport are quite similar to the men's rules, and "girls' basketball" is declining, although it is still played in a number of junior high schools and high schools.

NAGWS rules call for 8-min quarters, but the experimental rules for 1974–1975 did bring the game even closer to the men's version, with two 20-min halves and the same general rules pertaining to team fouls and free throws. In 1972, the first national women's collegiate basketball tournament was held under the auspices of the Division for Girls' and Women's Sports of the American Association for Health, Physical Education, and Recreation.

A "barnstorming" professional women's team, the All-American Redheads, has played before several million people in gyms across the country—usually competing against, and beating, men's teams.

The Rules

Basketball is played by two teams of five players each on a rectangular court, generally 50 by 94 ft for college and professional teams, 50 by 84 ft for high school players. (These dimensions are called "ideal" in the rules; they are not definitely prescribed, and high school teams often have smaller courts.) The court is divided into halves by the half-court line. At the center of a court is the center jump circle, and at either end of the court, 4 ft from the end line, there is a basket, a rim 18 in in diameter and 10 ft above the floor, from which hangs a net of white cord 15 to 18 in long. Behind each basket is a backboard. For

Sam Jones of Boston hooks a shot while "Hot Rod" Hundley of Los Angeles leaps vainly during a 1962 NBA championship game. Boston won the title, four games to three. (*Public Broadcasting Service.*)

college and professional play, it is a glass rectangle 72 in wide by 48 in high; high schools may use a fan-shaped backboard 54 in wide. Beneath each basket a 12-ft lane (16 ft in professional play) is marked, ending at the free-throw line, which is 15 ft from the basket. The free-throw circle is inscribed around the line. The basketball is spherical, 29½ to 30 in in circumference and 20 to 22 oz in weight. When dropped from a height of 6 ft, a properly inflated ball will bounce to a height of 49–54 in.

Timing. A professional game consists of four 12-min quarters; a college game of two 20-min halves; a high school game of four 8-min quarters. The clock is started when the ball is tapped on the opening center jump. It stops when a foul is called, a violation occurs, a jump ball is signaled, or time-out is called.

An official may call a time-out because of an injury, in order to confer with scorers or timers, or because of a delay in getting a dead ball alive (if, for example, a ball goes out-of-bounds into a crowd, and there is delay in

getting it back—but the clock doesn't stop merely because the ball has gone out-of-bounds). A player can also call time-out for the team, if the player's team has possession of the ball or the ball is dead. Each team is allowed five-time-outs in a game (seven in professional basketball) and one time-out in an overtime period (two in professional basketball).

The clock starts again on a jump ball, when the ball is tapped by one of the players; on a missed free throw, when the ball is touched by a player; on a throw-in, when the ball is touched by a player on the court.

If the regulation game ends in a tie, there is an overtime period of 5 min in college and professional ball, 3 min in high school. If the score is still tied at the end of the overtime period, there is another overtime period, and so on, until time expires with one team ahead.

Scoring. A successful shot from the field (field goal) counts 2 points, a successful free throw 1 point. In the American Basketball Association, a successful shot from more than 30 ft away counted 3 points.

For a shot to be successful, the ball must enter the basket from above and either go through or remain in the netting. However, a field goal is also scored if a shot from the field is touched by a defensive player on its downward arc toward the basket, or while the ball is wholly or partly in the imaginary cylinder above the basket. Formally known as basket interference, this violation is better known as "goaltending," and the field goal is awarded to the player who attempted the shot. An offensive player may also commit basket interference; in a case of offensive goaltending, the shot is nullified, and the ball goes out-of-bounds to the other team.

Out-of-Bounds. The ball is out-of-bounds when it touches a player, the floor, or any object which is out-of-bounds. (The inside edge of the out-of-bounds line is the boundary; therefore, if a ball touches the line, it is out-of-bounds). If it goes over the rectangular backboard, it is out-of-bounds; however, this doesn't apply if the fan-shaped backboard is used. It is also out-of-bounds if it touches the supports or the back of the backboard, or any overhead equipment or supports in the gymnasium or arena.

The ball is presumed to have been caused to go out-of-bounds by the last player who touched it or was touched by it, and the ball is awarded to the other team. If a player touches the ball while that player is already out-of-bounds, the ball goes to the other team. (For example, if a player on Team A makes a poor pass, and a player from Team B catches the ball while the latter is out-of-bounds, the ball goes to Team A.)

A player who is in the air is in-bounds if that player was in-bounds before jumping; out-of-bounds if the player was out-of-bounds before jumping. When an out-of-bounds is called, an official hands the ball to a nearby player on the team that is to gain possession. This player has 5 sec to make a throw-in from the designated spot. The player must not leave the spot, nor can any part of the body be across the boundary line until the throw-in has been made. The throw-in is also used after a score, by the team scored against; in this case, the throw-in is made from behind the end line, and the player has the option of making a throw to a teammate who is also behind the end line. (This maneuver is most commonly used when the opposing team is using a full-court press.)

Violations. A violation is an infraction of the rules, not usually a foul, which results in loss of possession. After a violation, the ball is awarded to the opposing team for a throw-in.

The most common violations are the following:

Traveling. Also called "walking" or "steps"; in general, this is taking more than one step with the ball, without dribbling. In advancing the ball, a player must bounce it on the floor once for every two steps taken; the ball is controlled with the fingertips, not the palm, and the dribble must be continuous. Many traveling violations are caused by a player illegally moving the pivot foot. If both feet are on the floor when the ball is received, the player may move either foot. Once a foot is moved, however, the other foot becomes the pivot foot, and the player cannot take a step with it without dribbling. The player can pivot on the pivot foot but must not slide it along the floor.

Double dribble. Formally known as "discontinued dribble"; the dribble ends when the dribbler catches the ball, holds it, or touches it with both hands simultaneously. Once the dribbling has stopped, the player cannot dribble again until after another player touches the ball. (There is one exception: A player may stop dribbling, take a shot at the basket, and begin dribbling again after gaining the rebound.)

3-second violation. An offensive player cannot remain partly or wholly within the free-throw lane for more than 3 sec. The player's team must be in control of the ball for the whole period, however, and some allowance is made if, before the 3 sec has passed, the player dribbles toward the basket to try a shot. (The line marking the free-throw lane is considered part of the lane.)

10-second violation. Once a team gains possession of the ball in its own backcourt, it must advance the ball across the half-court line within 10 sec. Having crossed the half-court line, the ball must not return to the backcourt while the team is still in possession. If a player on Team A in the forecourt makes a poor pass, and the ball goes into the backcourt, it is a live ball. If a player from Team A touches it while it is in the backcourt, it is a violation. However, if Team B was responsible for the ball going into the backcourt, it is a free ball, and Team A can recover it.

Palming the ball. Also called "turning the ball over," this violation involves using the palm to control the ball when dribbling.

Kicking or striking the ball with the fist. Kicking the ball is a violation only when it is a deliberate act; accidentally striking the ball with the leg or foot is not a violation.

24-second violation. In professional basketball, a team is given 24 sec to attempt a shot after gaining control of the ball. The time is marked off on a special 24-sec clock installed near the basket the team is shooting at. The shot must hit the rim or the backboard if it doesn't go in the basket; if it merely brushes the net, or misses entirely, it is not considered to be a shot. After an attempted shot, if the offensive team gains the rebound, the clock starts again at 24 sec. If, within 10 sec or less on the shooting clock, the ball is awarded out-of-bounds to the offensive team, the clock is restarted at the 10-sec mark. Note that the ball must definitely change possession for the clock to be stopped; for example, if there is a loose ball, and a scramble, with the offensive team regaining possession, the clock continues to run.

30-second violation. In international basketball, a 30-sec shooting clock is used, and the provisions are generally the same. The 30-sec clock has also been used experimentally in college play, chiefly in the Big Eight and Southwest Conferences, which have used it for conference games and, when a nonconference visiting team agrees, for other home games.

Throw-in violations. It is a violation if the player making a throw-in leaves the designated spot, fails to pass it in within 5 sec, carries the ball onto the court, touches it in the court before it has touched another player, or makes a shot at the basket. The player must not allow any part of the body, or the ball, to project over the boundary line before a legal throw-in has been made. Other violations, relating to jump balls and free throws, are discussed in those sections.

Jump Balls. The jump ball, used to start play at the beginning of each period, is also used in other situations to determine which team controls the ball, most often in the case of a "held ball."

It is a held ball when two opponents are struggling for possession of the ball, and it would take undue roughness for either of them to gain control; when a player is so closely guarded as to be compelled to hold or dribble the ball for 5 sec and not be able to pass it to a teammate; or when a team controls the ball for more than 5 sec in an area screened off by teammates. A jump ball is also called if the ball goes out-of-bounds and the officials cannot determine which team was responsible.

The "closely guarded" provision involves a difficult bit of judgment by the official, and is subject to some special provisions. The player's opponent must be in a guarding stance, within 6 ft. When a player dribbles from the midcourt area into the forecourt, a new 5-sec count begins; and if the player begins to dribble in the forecourt, and then ends it and holds the ball, a new 5-sec count begins.

If a jump is called because of a held ball, the two opponents involved are the jumpers; in other cases, any player from either team may jump. The jump takes place in the nearest restraining circle—the center circle or one of the free-throw circles. Each jumper must have at least one foot touching the 2-ft jumping circle (imaginary at the free-throw circles), and all other players must remain outside the 6-ft restraining circle until the ball is tapped. The official throws the ball up between them, higher than they can jump, and they attempt to tap the ball on its way down.

It is a violation if a jumper touches the ball on its way up, catches the jump ball, taps it more than once, or leaves the 2-ft jumping circle before the ball has been tapped. The restrictions end when the ball touches one of the nonjumpers or the floor. It is also a violation if a nonjumper enters the restraining circle before the ball has been tapped.

Personal Fouls. Generally speaking, the basketball rules allow no personal contact. But, of course, a great deal of contact is allowed in basketball, particularly during rebounding action. Most personal fouls are not specifically spelled out in the rules—one of the most common fouls, "hacking," has an official signal but no official definition. ("Hacking" is striking the player who has the ball across the hands, wrists, or forearms.)

The most difficult judgment call arises when the player

with the ball runs into a defensive player. The offensive player is guilty of charging if the defensive player was entitled to that spot on the floor; the defensive player is charged with a foul if that player moved into the path of the opponent with the ball. A defensive player is entitled to stand in the dribbler's path, if the player got there far enough in advance for the dribbler to be able to avoid contact.

Professional rules, incidentally, allow "hand-checking"—a defensive player may keep a hand on an opponent, provided the hand doesn't keep the opponent from moving freely. Hand-checking is not allowed in college or high school play.

In efforts to reduce the number of free throws and so speed up the game, collegiate and professional basketball have both made a number of rules changes in recent years, setting up various foul categories. A foul by an offensive player results in loss of ball, not a free throw. A loose-ball foul—a personal foul committed while the ball belongs to neither team, usually during rebounding action—also results in the ball being awarded to the other team.

In college play, a team is "allowed" six fouls in each half. Starting with the seventh team foul, the other team is in a "one-and-one" situation, meaning that if a player makes the first free throw, that player is awarded a second one.

In professional play, a team is allowed four fouls per period. Starting with the fifth team foul, the other team is in a bonus situation; a bonus free throw is awarded for each foul, whether the player makes the first shot or not. (The player who is awarded two free throws is given three shots to make 2 points; that is, the player who makes the first two free throws doesn't get a third, but if the player misses one or both of the first two, the player is awarded a third shot.) One special note: An offensive foul counts as a personal foul, but not as a team foul.

The player who is fouled while in the act of shooting is awarded two free throws, if the shot is not successful, and one free throw if it is successful.

Two free throws are also awarded for an intentional foul—one judged by an official to have been premeditated—and for a flagrant foul, defined as a personal or technical foul of a violent or savage nature, or a noncontact foul involving vulgar or abusive contact. A player is disqualified from the game for a flagrant foul. A fifth personal foul is also a disqualification in college play, a sixth personal foul in professional play.

Technical Fouls. The term "technical foul" covers a multitude of basketball sins. By far the most common is vehement protesting of an official's call. Other technical fouls include the following: delaying the game, taking an excess time-out, grabbing the rim of either basket, failing to raise the hand after being called for a personal foul, having too many players on the court, inciting undesirable actions by the crowd, and others.

When a technical foul is called, the other team is awarded a free throw, to be taken by any player. In college play, that team then gets the ball out-of-bounds at midcourt. In pro play, the ball returns to the team that had possession when the foul occurred.

Three technical fouls disqualify a player or coach in college basketball, two in professional play.

Free Throws. A free throw, or foul shot, is just what the name implies—an unmolested shot at the basket awarded as the result of a foul. After giving the teams time to line up properly, the official gives the ball to the thrower, who has 10 sec to attempt the shot. The thrower must shoot from within the free-throw circle and from behind the line. Other players must remain outside the lane until the ball touches the ring or backboard. Along the lane, spaces are marked at intervals of 3 ft. Opponents of the thrower are entitled to the two spaces nearest the basket; the thrower's teammates are entitled to the next two spaces; and so on, alternately, through the four spaces. No one is required to occupy a space at the lane, but if a space is not occupied by a player from the team entitled to it, it must remain unoccupied.

If any of these provisions are violated by the shooter or a teammate, the shot cannot count, and the ball is awarded out-of-bounds to the other team, at the sideline. If there is a violation by the opposing team, it is ignored if the free throw is successful; the shooter gets another chance if it is not successful. If both teams commit a violation, the throw doesn't count, and there is a jump ball at center court.

Special Situations. There are two rare situations that should be mentioned: a double foul and a multiple foul. A double foul occurs when two opponents commit fouls against each other at approximately the same time. No free throw is awarded, and the ball is put in play by a jump at the center circle.

A multiple foul occurs when two or more players foul the same opponent at approximately the same time. Each offending player is charged with a personal foul, but there is only one penalty; a player who is fouled by two opponents while attempting an unsuccessful shot, for example, gets only two free throws.

A false double foul occurs when both teams commit fouls at about the same time, with different sets of players involved. In this case, the appropriate free throws are taken, and the ball is then put in play with a center jump.

A false multiple foul occurs when two or more members of the same team commit fouls against two or more members of the other team. Again, all appropriate foul shots are taken. (For example, Player A-1 fouls Player B-1 while B-1 is attempting an unsuccessful shot; at the same time, Player A-2 fouls Player B-2. B-1 is awarded two free throws, B-2 is awarded one free throw.)

Another special situation can arise in professional basketball: a defensive foul away from the ball. If a defensive player fouls an offensive player who is away from the ball and who, in the opinion of the official, is not involved in the play, the offensive player is awarded one free throw, and that player's team then gets the ball out-of-bounds at midcourt.

Principles of Play

Basically, a basketball team tries to score more points than its opponents—first, by getting the ball close to the basket as often as possible, for good percentage shots; second, by trying to keep the other team from getting close to the basket; third, by getting more rebounds than the other team (and thus more scoring opportunities); fourth, by making as few turnovers as possible; fifth, by trying to make the other team commit turnovers. A team may choose to emphasize just one of these basic principles or any combination of them. The choice will determine the team's basic style of play.

Offense. Most teams today use a variation of the fast

break as a basic offense. The fast break doesn't mean quite what it once did. In its original form, the main purpose of the fast break was to spring one player free for an easy layup. A fast breaking team is still happy to get that easy shot, but shooting skills have developed so much in the last 15 or 20 years that the fast break can succeed in other ways, too.

For example, it can get a player free for a shot from 18 to 20 ft away, a good percentage shot for almost any professional or top collegiate player. It can get a big player downcourt faster than the defender, so that a smaller player is forced to guard the larger—which is also likely to lead to a good percentage shot. Or it can simply get the ball into the forecourt and the offense operating so fast that the defense cannot get set up properly.

Although any coach loves to see two players fast-breaking against one opponent, or three of them fast-breaking against two opponents, a fast break can also be effective in three-on-three, four-on-four, or even five-on-five situations.

A fast break begins with the rebounder. Certain outstanding rebounders can go up, get the ball off the backboard, spin around in midair, and get a pass off before hitting the floor. Whether the rebounder can do this or not, the quick pass to get the ball moving downcourt is essential. A good fast break is built on quick sharp passes, not dribbling, since no dribbler can travel faster than a pass.

Breaking players should stay in definite lanes. One player will generally go right down the middle of the floor, straight at the basket, while another player will be 15 ft or so to the first one's left, a third (if there is a third) about 15 ft on the other side. The player coming down the middle stops at just about the free-throw line; if a teammate can't get a layup, the ball will come back to the original player for an easy shot.

If the players stay in their lanes, they will spread out the defense to keep routes open to the basket. If they outnumber the defenders, they work to make the defenders commit themselves; when they do, offensive players have to be open. If a defender stays near the basket instead of picking up one player, someone can draw up short for an easy shot.

The fast break can't work every time. When it doesn't result in a score, a team goes to a set offense, which can vary greatly with different types of personnel. Again, the principle is to get a player free for the shot, whether a short hook shot by a big center or a 25-ft set shot by a deadly accurate guard.

The simplest way to do this is with a screen. Offensive players get a teammate between themselves and the opponent who is supposed to be covering them. The center does most of the screening for the team, but any player can screen for any other player.

A pick is slightly different, although the two words are often used interchangeably. One offensive player is setting a screen for another; the other player moves in such a way that the defender has to run into the first player or go behind the player. The defender has been picked off; the offensive player is now behind a screen.

The defense has two ways of countering against a screen. The defender can try to fight past the screen or switch assignments. For example, Player A-1, who is guarded by B-1, sets a screen for A-2, who is guarded by B-2; as A-2 moves behind the screen, B-2 is picked off; B-

1 (usually) shouts "Switch!" and moves to cover A-2, leaving A-1 to be guarded by B-2. This may be momentarily effective, but it can also cause problems. Team B may now have a 6-ft guard covering a 7-ft center, who is almost certain to score on getting the ball.

The pick and roll is meant to take advantage of defensive switching. A player (usually but not always the center) sets a pick, a teammate gets the ball, and the player who set the pick now pivots and moves toward the basket. This maneuver is especially effective against a team that depends a great deal on its center to "clog up the middle" by intimidating any shooter who gets near the lane.

A player can also get free without help, with or without the ball. Coaches emphasize the importance of "moving without the ball," and good players move constantly, for two purposes: to keep their defenders out of the area where a play is being set up, and to try to get free for a shot. It should be noted that a player who doesn't have the ball can also use a pick to get clear of the opposing player and then take a pass and score.

Certain outstanding players will do a certain amount of free-lancing when they have the ball, working to shake the defender off. To be an effective free-lancer, a player needs at least two very good, and contrasting, shots. Jerry West of the Los Angeles Lakers, for example, had a deadly jump shot, and was also quick enough to drive for the basket. West might fake the jump shot to get his defender off balance, then drive past him; or dribble the ball once, faking a drive, then pull up to take the jump shot.

A team's center is called a pivot for two reasons: First, the center plays most of the time with back to the basket, so the pivot toward the basket is an essential move; second, the center is the pivot around which an offense often revolves. Many teams with a big center who is not a particularly good shot will take advantage of the center's size by "cutting off the pivot" or "weaving" around a center who has the ball. In essence, the center is being used as a semipermanent pick, with the teammates taking turns using the center until one of them gets free for a pass. Or the pivot might fake a pass or two, then take advantage of the confusion to make a move toward the basket.

The pivot who is positioned in the area of the free-throw line is playing a high post; when nearer the basket, a low post. The pivot who is quick and can shoot from outside is more likely to play a high post; it may also be an advantage if the pivot is smaller than the defensive opponent, since the high post will force the opponent to play away from the basket. The pivot who is big and a strong rebounder who prefers to shoot from near the basket is more likely to play a low post.

However, any center is likely to play both high post and low post at various times. Some teams will occasionally use a double post, with two pivots, one high and one low. This will get their big pivot near the basket, with another big player who can shoot from outside in the high-post position, and will leave outside areas of the court relatively open for the other three players to maneuver in.

Teams also occasionally use set plays, almost all of which call for a pick or a screen somewhere, but any set play involves some alternatives. A set play is generally used to get an offense organized when things haven't been going too well. Watch a team go a couple of minutes

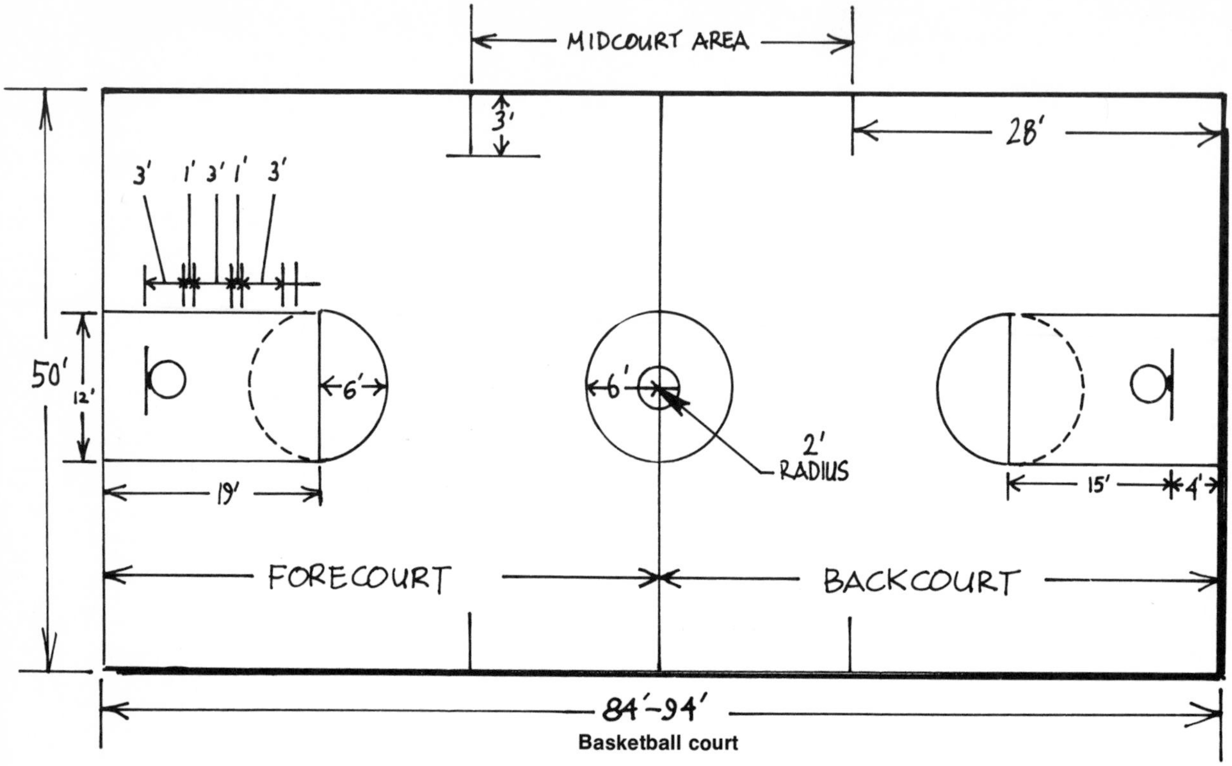

MIDCOURT AREA
3'
28'
3' 1' 3' 1' 3'
50'
12'
6'
6'
2'
RADIUS
19'
15'
4'
FORECOURT
BACKCOURT
84'-94'
Basketball court

A
B
2
3
1
Three-man fast break

1
2
2
1
2
2
Pick and roll

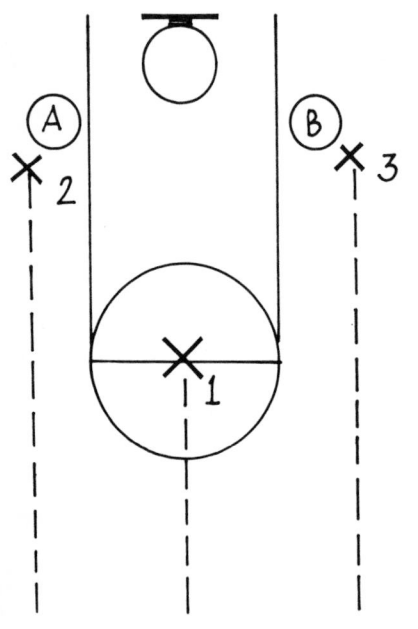

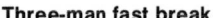

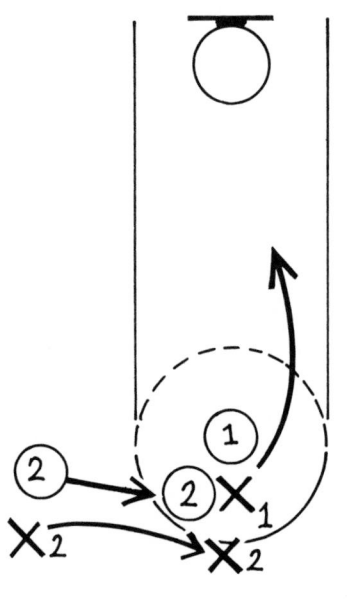

without a point, and you're likely to see them using a set play the next time they get the ball.

Every team uses set plays for throw-ins from under the enemy basket. The purpose here is simply to get a player free to receive the pass, although occasionally a throw-in will lead to an immediate basket.

Defense. Perhaps the most important job of a coach, particularly a professional coach, is deciding on the matchups—which of the players will guard which opponent. There are times when a forward will guard an opposing center or even an opposing guard, and on rarer occasions a guard will be asked to defend against a forward.

Several factors enter into the decision. Height is generally the most important, but also important are bulk, and quickness, and a little-noted factor—an important offensive player given a tough defensive assignment may become less effective on offense.

The matchups are important in a player-to-player defense, which a professional team must use (the zone defense is outlawed by professional rules). A player-to-player, in its simplest form, is just what it sounds like: Each player covers a specific opponent. A defensive player follows one basic rule: Stay between your player and the basket. (There is one major exception: A center is usually played to the side, and sometimes the defender stays between the center and the ball. There are two reasons: A center usually plays with back to the basket and so isn't ready to shoot immediately on receiving the ball; and keeping the ball away from the center may be virtually the only way of keeping the center from scoring.)

Shooting is so superior in professional basketball that the prospect of a bad matchup might make a coach change the starting lineup. If the coach has a 6-1 guard, for example, and the opposing team has two 6-5 guards, the coach may decide to start a taller guard in place of the regular one. Generally speaking, it is almost impossible for a much shorter player to keep a taller one from getting off a good shot.

The player-to-player defense has several different variations. An effective defense might start when a team is on the offense. If the opponent is an excellent fast-breaking team, for example, a coach might tell the guards to stay farther from the basket than usual on offense, so they'll be able to get back faster on defense.

The most important variation is the "collapsing" or "sagging" player-to-player, most commonly used against a team with a high-scoring center. Whenever the ball goes into the pivot, the guards will "sag" into the area to bother the center. If the center gets the ball near a basket, a forward will help a guard. Against an especially dangerous forward a team may also use a kind of "sagging" defense, only now it will be a double team; whenever the forward gets the ball, the defensive guard on that side will help out.

These are defenses tailored to meet the offensive threat; some defenses are tailored, instead, to capitalize on a special defensive strength. When the Boston Celtics had Bill Russell, for example, their defense "funneled everything into the middle," with the idea that Russell would take care of everything in that area, and virtually any team with an exceptional defensive center will play the same way. The other four players will play their opponents somewhat to the outside, but they'll let them move

Kareem Abdul-Jabbar, formerly Lew Alcindor, is visible at lower left as Boston's Paul Silas battles another Milwaukee Buck for a rebound. *(Boston Celtics.)*

rather freely into the foul circle area, and in the meantime they'll be dropping off, on the alert for an interception or a rebound.

The Press. The full-court press used to be considered an emergency measure, an attempt to get the ball when a team was behind late in the game, but some teams—notably UCLA—now use it regularly.

Normally, after scoring a basket or losing the ball on a rebound, a team will drop quickly into the backcourt to set up a defense. In the full-court press, however, the defense is applied immediately. If the other team is making the throw-in from the end line, one player will cover the other guard very closely, and if other offensive players come downcourt to help out, they will also be closely covered by their defenders.

The zone press can be especially effective. It has been for UCLA. In the zone press, players basically cover certain areas, and pick up anyone in the area. The player making the throw-in might not be harrassed as much as with the player-to-player press, but the people likely to get the pass are under even more pressure. Generally, two guards will play the zones nearest the base line, two forwards the areas behind them—still in the frontcourt area, although they'll follow a player across the half-court line if the player tries to break away—and the center will be a kind of safety player, ready to stop the offense if it breaks through and ready, too, to gamble on intercepting a long pass.

The purpose of the press, of course, is to pressure the other team into committing turnovers in its own backcourt. It is particularly effective for a well-conditioned team that has a strong bench, since it can wear out the offense rather rapidly.

Occasionally a team will use a half-court press, allowing the other team to advance the ball to the half-court line and then playing an aggressive player-to-player defense. (Normally, defensive players don't guard their opponents closely until the ball moves beyond the mid-court area.)

Somewhat similar to the press, but usually used in the forecourt area, is a ball defense, in which defensive players will constantly double-team the player with the ball. One will try to keep the offensive player from making a pass while the other will usually go directly for the ball in an attempt to steal it. This defense is normally used only if the defensive team is behind and has to get the ball.

Zone Defenses. Forbidden in professional basketball, the zone defense is part of the repertory of any high school or college team, and some of them use a zone almost exclusively. In a zone defense, each defensive player is responsible for an area rather than a specific player.

There are many different kinds of zone defenses, usually described by a set of numbers. In a 2-3 zone, for example, two players form a front line, each of them responsible for half of the area between the free-throw line and the half-court line, and the other three form a back line of defense, with one player in the lane and the other two covering the areas on either side of the lane. In a 1-2-2 defense, one player is out front as a "chaser"— the player will go after a guard with the ball, usually— two are stationed on either side of the free-throw line, and two more are on either side of the lane, near the end line.

The basic purpose of a zone defense is to keep the offense from penetrating the area near the basket. It is vulnerable to the long shot, but many coaches are happy to give up the long shot, which is less likely to score than a shot from closer in. Another advantage of the zone is that it often results in many interceptions when used against an impatient team; a player may appear to be wide open for a pass, but if the pass has to go through or across a zone, the defender responsible for that zone may well get in the way.

An offense has three ways of attacking a zone. A series of successful outside shots may force the defense out of the zone. If the offensive players spread out, they will force each defender to cover a wider area than possible, opening up seams between the zones. Quick offensive movement, of the ball and of players without the ball, can also cause problems for a zone, since the defenders have to keep readjusting to the location of the ball and to offensive players passing from one zone to another.

Rebounding. Height, leaping ability, good reflexes, and timing are all important to the good rebounder. Perhaps just as important, though not as often noted, is a player's ability to block out, or box out, an opponent. If two players have equal height and equal leaping ability, the player who is at the spot where the ball comes down is the one who will get the rebound. And a smaller player has a good chance of getting the rebound by getting between the ball and a bigger player.

Glossary

assist—A pass that directly results in a basket by a teammate.

backcourt—The half of the court nearest the basket being defended by a team.

backcourt player—A guard.

bank shot—A shot, usually taken from a severe angle, deliberately bounced off the backboard and into the basket.

base line—An end line.

basket hanging—Remaining in the forecourt when the other team is on offense, in the hope of getting a quick, easy basket.

blocking—Illegally impeding the progress of an opponent who does not have the ball.

bunny—An uncontested layup or other easy shot.

burn—A steal that results in an immediate score.

buzzer—The device that is sounded to mark the end of a period.

buzzer play—An offensive play used near the end of a period to get a score before time runs out.

charging—The offensive foul committed when the player with the ball runs into a defensive player.

charity line—The free-throw line.

charity toss or throw—A free throw.

chaser—In a zone defense, a player assigned to chase the player with the ball.

clear out—A pass downcourt by a player who has just taken a defensive rebound.

clear out one side—An offensive maneuver in which four players go to one side of the lane, leaving the fifth player a lot of room to operate in on the other side.

clear the ball—To move the ball out of the deep backcourt.

clear the boards—To get a rebound.

common foul—Any personal foul which is neither flagrant nor intentional.

cornerman—A forward.

cripple—An easy layup.

double team—Two defensive players guarding one offensive player.

drive—A move toward the basket by the dribbler in an attempt to score.

dunk—A shot in which a player leaps high and drops the ball into the basket from directly above (permitted only in professional play).

feed—To hand the ball to a teammate; or, to make a pass likely to result in a score.

force a shot—To take a poor percentage shot.

force out—When the player with the ball is so pressured by a defender that the player has no choice but to go out-of-bounds; the player's team retains possession of the ball with a throw-in.

foul out—To be disqualified for having committed five (in pro basketball, six) personal fouls.

free-lance—To make an attempt to get into scoring possession with no help from teammates.

freeze the ball—To retain possession of the ball with little or no attempt to score.

frontcourt—The half of the court which contains the basket being attacked by a team.

give a foul—To commit a deliberate foul; done by a team that has not reached its foul limit, giving up a possible point in order to gain possession of the ball and a chance for two points.

give and go—An offensive maneuver in which a player passes to a teammate and immediately cuts toward the basket in the hope of receiving a return pass.

gunner—A player who shoots a lot, with the implication that the shooting is excessive.

jumper—A jump shot.

key or keyhole—The area bounded by the free-throw lane and circle. (Before the lane was widened, the area looked like an old-fashioned keyhole.)

kill the clock—To stall near the end of a period in order to get the last shot.

mismatch—A situation in which an offensive player, because of a defensive switch, is covered by a much smaller (or larger but much slower) player. When the one with the ball is covered by a larger opponent, the player "looks for the mismatch." When a defensive player covers a larger opponent, the defensive player is "caught in the mismatch."

one-and-one—The bonus free-throw situation; a player makes one free throw, then gets another one.

one-on-one—A confrontation between a dribbler and a defender, in which the dribbler is doing everything to score—i.e., free-lancing. When a team clears out one side, it is to get a player one-on-one with a defender in order to free-lance.

outlet pass—Same as "clear out."

over the limit—Said of a team that has committed more than its limit of fouls.

penalty free throw—In professional play, the extra free throw awarded to a team when the opposing team is over the limit.

play loose—To guard an opponent from a distance.

play tight—To guard an opponent very closely.

point player—A player, usually a guard, who directs the team's attack; the playmaker. For example, the "1" in a 1–2–2 offense.

stuff—Similar to a "dunk," except that the player pushes the ball into the basket from above, instead of merely dropping it. Permitted only in professional play.

substitute free throw—The free throw awarded when a player misses a free throw but the opposing team has committed a free-throw violation.

swish—A shot that scores without touching the rim.

three-point play—When a player makes a shot, is fouled in the act of shooting, and makes the resulting free throw.

tip-in—When an offensive player, instead of pulling down a rebound, tips the ball into the basket.

trailer—On a fast break, a player who is slightly behind the other members of the team, in a position to get the ball for a short jump shot if a teammate can't get a layup.

turnover—Loss of possession without a shot; caused by an offensive foul, a violation, the ball going out-of-bounds, an interception, or a steal.

work the ball around—To pass the ball, quickly and continuously, in an attempt to find or create an opening in the defense.

National Basketball Association

First-Place Finishers

1947	East: Washington	49	11	.817
	West: Chicago	39	22	.639
1948	East: Philadelphia	27	21	.563
	West: St. Louis	29	19	.604

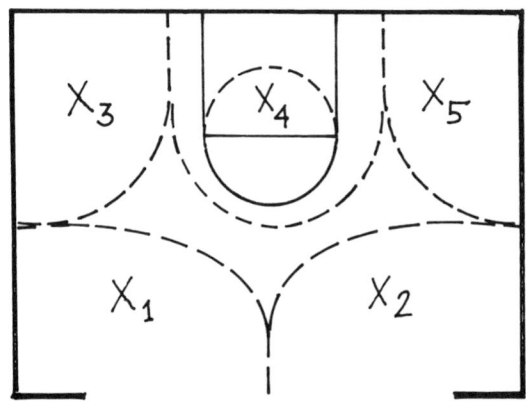

2-3 zone defense

1949	East: Washington	38	22	.633
	West: Rochester	45	15	.750
1950	East: Syracuse	51	13	.797
	Central: Minneapolis*	51	17	.750
	West: Indianapolis	39	25	.609
1951	East: Philadelphia	40	26	.606
	West: Minneapolis	44	24	.647
1952	East: Syracuse	40	26	.606
	West: Rochester	41	25	.621
1953	East: New York	47	23	.671
	West: Minneapolis	48	22	.686
1954	East: New York	44	28	.611
	West: Minneapolis	46	26	.639
1955	East: Syracuse	43	29	.597
	West: Ft. Wayne	43	29	.597
1956	East: Philadelphia	45	27	.625
	West: Ft. Wayne	37	35	.514
1957	East: Boston	44	28	.611
	West: St. Louis	34	38	.472
1958	East: Boston	49	23	.681
	West: St. Louis	41	31	.569
1959	East: Boston	52	20	.722
	West: St. Louis	49	23	.681
1960	East: Boston	59	16	.787
	West: St. Louis	46	29	.613
1961	East: Boston	57	22	.722
	West: St. Louis	51	28	.646
1962	East: Boston	60	20	.750
	West: Los Angeles	54	26	.675
1963	East: Boston	58	22	.725
	West: Los Angeles	53	27	.663
1964	East: Boston	59	21	.738
	West: San Francisco	48	32	.600
1965	East: Boston	62	18	.715
	West: Los Angeles	49	31	.613
1966	East: Philadelphia	55	25	.688
	West: Los Angeles	45	35	.563
1967	East: Philadelphia	68	13	.840
	West: San Francisco	44	37	.543
1968	East: Philadelphia	63	20	.756
	West: St. Louis	56	26	.683
1969	East: Baltimore	57	25	.695
	West: Los Angeles	55	27	.671
1970	East: New York	60	22	.732
	West: Atlanta	48	34	.585
1971	Atlantic: New York	52	30	.634
	Central: Baltimore	42	40	.512
	Midwest: Milwaukee	66	16	.805
	Pacific: Los Angeles	48	34	.585

*Won playoff for division championship.

1972	Atlantic: Boston	56	26	.683
	Central: Baltimore	38	44	.463
	Midwest: Milwaukee	63	19	.768
	Pacific: Los Angeles	69	13	.841
1973	Atlantic: Boston	68	14	.829
	Central: Baltimore	52	30	.634
	Midwest: Milwaukee	60	22	.732
	Pacific: Los Angeles	60	22	.732
1974	Atlantic: Boston	56	26	.683
	Central: Capital	46	35	.568
	Midwest: Milwaukee	59	23	.720
	Pacific: Los Angeles	47	35	.573
1975	Atlantic: Boston	60	22	.732
	Central: Washington	60	22	.732
	Midwest: Chicago	47	35	.573
	Pacific: Golden State	48	34	.585
1976	Atlantic: Boston	54	28	.659
	Central: Cleveland	49	32	.605
	Midwest: Milwaukee	38	44	.463
	Pacific: Golden State	59	23	.720

Playoff Winners

1947	Philadelphia 4, Chicago 1
1948	Baltimore 4, Philadelphia 2
1949	Minneapolis 4, Washington 2
1950	Minneapolis 4, Syracuse 2
1951	Rochester 4, New York 3
1952	Minneapolis 4, New York 3
1953	Minneapolis 4, New York 1
1954	Minneapolis 4, Syracuse 3
1955	Syracuse 4, Ft. Wayne 3
1956	Philadelphia 4, Ft. Wayne 1
1957	Boston 4, St. Louis 3
1958	St. Louis 4, Boston 2
1959	Boston 4, Minneapolis 0
1960	Boston 4, St. Louis 3
1961	Boston 4, St. Louis 1
1962	Boston 4, Los Angeles 3
1963	Boston 4, Los Angeles 2
1964	Boston 4, San Francisco 1
1965	Boston 4, Los Angeles 1
1966	Boston 4, Los Angeles 3
1967	Philadelphia 4, San Francisco 2
1968	Boston 4, Los Angeles 2
1969	Boston 4, Los Angeles 3
1970	New York 4, Los Angeles 3
1971	Milwaukee 4, Baltimore 0
1972	Los Angeles 4, New York 1
1973	New York 4, Los Angeles 1
1974	Boston 4, Milwaukee 3
1975	Golden State 4, Washington 0
1976	Boston 4, Phoenix 2

Scoring Leaders

(Based on per-game average)

1947	Joe Fulks, Philadelphia	23.1
1948	Joe Fulks, Philadelphia	22.1
1949	George Mikan, Minneapolis	28.3
1950	George Mikan, Minneapolis	27.4
1951	George Mikan, Minneapolis	28.4
1952	Paul Arizin, Philadelphia	25.4
1953	Neil Johnston, Philadelphia	22.3
1954	Neil Johnston, Philadelphia	24.4
1955	Neil Johnston, Philadelphia	22.7
1956	Bob Pettit, St. Louis	25.7
1957	Paul Arizin, Philadelphia	25.6
1958	George Yardley, Detroit	27.8
1959	Bob Pettit, St. Louis	29.2
1960	Wilt Chamberlain, Philadelphia	37.6
1961	Wilt Chamberlain, Philadelphia	38.4
1962	Wilt Chamberlain, Philadelphia	50.4
1963	Wilt Chamberlain, Philadelphia	44.8
1964	Wilt Chamberlain, Philadelphia	36.5

1965	Wilt Chamberlain, Philadelphia–San Francisco	34.7
1966	Wilt Chamberlain, Philadelphia	33.5
1967	Rick Barry, San Francisco	35.6
1968	Dave Bing, Detroit	27.1
1969	Elvin Hayes, San Diego	28.4
1970	Jerry West, Los Angeles	31.2
1971	Lew Alcindor (Kareem Abdul-Jabbar), Milwaukee	31.7
1972	Kareem Abdul-Jabbar, Milwaukee	34.8
1973	Nate Archibald, Kansas City–Omaha	34.0
1974	Bob McAdoo, Buffalo	30.6
1975	Bob McAdoo, Buffalo	34.5
1976	Bob McAdoo, Buffalo	31.1

Rookie of the Year

1953	Don Meineke, Ft. Wayne
1954	Ray Felix, Baltimore
1955	Bob Pettit, Milwaukee
1956	Maurice Stokes, Rochester
1957	Tom Heinsohn, Boston
1958	Woody Sauldsberry, Philadelphia
1959	Elgin Baylor, Minneapolis
1960	Wilt Chamberlain, Philadelphia
1961	Oscar Robertson, Cincinnati
1962	Walt Bellamy, Chicago
1963	Terry Dischinger, Chicago
1964	Jerry Lucas, Cincinnati
1965	Willis Reed, New York
1966	Rick Barry, San Francisco
1967	Dave Bing, Detroit
1968	Earl Monroe, Baltimore
1969	Westley Unseld, Baltimore
1970	Lew Alcindor (Kareem Abdul-Jabbar), Milwaukee
1971	Dave Cowens, Boston
	Geoff Petrie, Portland
1972	Sidney Wicks, Portland
1973	Bob McAdoo, Buffalo
1974	Ernie DiGregorio, Buffalo
1975	Keith Wilkes, Golden State
1976	Alvan Adams, Phoenix

Most Valuable Player

1956	Bob Pettit, St. Louis
1957	Bob Cousy, Boston
1958	Bill Russell, Boston
1959	Bob Pettit, St. Louis
1960	Wilt Chamberlain, Philadelphia
1961	Bill Russell, Boston
1962	Bill Russell, Boston
1963	Bill Russell, Boston
1964	Oscar Robertson, Cincinnati
1965	Bill Russell, Boston
1966	Wilt Chamberlain, Philadelphia
1967	Wilt Chamberlain, Philadelphia
1968	Wilt Chamberlain, Philadelphia
1969	Westley Unseld, Baltimore
1970	Willis Reed, New York
1971	Lew Alcindor (Kareem Abdul-Jabbar), Milwaukee
1972	Kareem Abdul-Jabbar, Milwaukee
1973	Dave Cowens, Boston
1974	Kareem Abdul-Jabbar, Milwaukee
1975	Bob McAdoo, Buffalo
1976	Kareem Abdul-Jabbar, Los Angeles

NBA Coach of the Year

1963	Harry Gallatin, St. Louis
1964	Alex Hannum, San Francisco
1965	"Red" Auerbach, Boston
1966	Dolph Schayes, Philadelphia
1967	Johnny Kerr, Chicago
1968	Richie Guerin, St. Louis
1969	Gene Shue, Baltimore

1970	"Red" Holzman, New York
1971	Dick Motta, Chicago
1972	Bill Sharman, Los Angeles
1973	Tom Heinsohn, Boston
1974	Ray Scott, Detroit
1975	Al Attles, Golden State
1976	Bill Fitch, Cleveland

American Basketball Association

First-Place Finishers

1968	East: Pittsburgh	54	24	.692
	West: New Orleans	48	30	.615
1969	East: Indiana	44	34	.564
	West: Oakland	60	18	.769
1970	East: Indiana	59	25	.702
	West: Denver	51	33	.607
1971	East: Virginia	55	29	.655
	West: Indiana	58	26	.690
1972	East: Kentucky	68	16	.810
	West: Utah	60	24	.714
1973	East: Carolina	57	27	.679
	West: Utah	56	218	.667
1974	East: New York	55	29	.655
	West: Utah	51	33	.607
1975	East: Kentucky	59	25	.694
	West: Denver	65	19	.774
1976	Denver	60	24	.720

Playoff Champions

1968	Pittsburgh 4, New Orleans 3
1969	Oakland 4, Indiana 1
1970	Indiana 4, Los Angeles 2
1971	Utah 4, Kentucky 3
1972	Indiana 4, New York 2
1973	Indiana 4, Kentucky 3
1974	New York 4, Utah 1
1975	Kentucky 4, Indiana 1
1976	New York 4, Denver 2

Scoring Leaders

1968	Connie Hawkins, Pittsburgh	26.8
1969	Rick Barry, Oakland	34.0
1970	Spencer Haywood, Denver	30.0
1971	Dan Issel, Kentucky	29.9
1972	Charlie Scott, Virginia	34.6
1973	Julius Erving, Virginia	31.9
1974	Julius Erving, New York	27.4
1975	George McGinnis, Indiana	29.8
1976	Julius Erving, New York	29.4

Rookie of the Year

1968	Mel Daniels, Minnesota
1969	Warren Armstrong, Oakland
1970	Spencer Haywood, Denver
1971	Dan Issel, Kentucky
	Charlie Scott, Virginia
1972	Artis Gilmore, Kentucky
1973	Brian Taylor, New York
1974	Sven Nater, San Antonio
1975	Marvin Barnes, St. Louis
1976	David Thompson, Denver

Most Valuable Player

1968	Connie Hawkins, Pittsburgh
1969	Mel Daniels, Indiana
1970	Spencer Haywood, Denver
1971	Mel Daniels, Indiana
1972	Artis Gilmore, Kentucky
1973	Billy Cunningham, Carolina
1974	Julius Erving, New York
1975	Julius Erving, New York
	George McGinnis, Indiana
1976	Julius Erving, New York

Coach of the Year

1968	Vince Cazetta, Pittsburgh
1969	Alex Hannum, Oakland
1970	Bill Sharman, Los Angeles
	Joe Belmont, Denver
1971	Al Bianchi, Virginia
1972	Tom Nissalke, Dallas
1973	Larry Brown, Carolina
1974	Joe Mullaney, Utah
	Babe McCarthy, Kentucky
1975	Larry Brown, Denver
1976	Larry Brown, Denver

College Basketball

NCAA Division I Tournaments

Year	Final Score	Most Valuable Player
1939	Oregon 46, Ohio State 43	No selection
1940	Indiana 60, Kansas 42	Marv Huffman, Indiana
1941	Wisconsin 39, Washington State 34	John Kotz, Wisconsin
1942	Stanford 53, Dartmouth 38	Howard Dallmar, Stanford
1943	Wyoming 46, Georgetown 34	Kenny Sailors, Wyoming
1944	Utah 42, Dartmouth 40	Arnie Ferrin, Utah
1945	Oklahoma A&M 49, New York University 45	Bob Kurland, Oklahoma A&M
1946	Oklahoma A&M 43, North Carolina 40	Bob Kurland, Oklahoma A&M
1947	Holy Cross 58, Oklahoma 47	George Kaftan, Holy Cross
1948	Kentucky 58, Baylor 42	Alex Groza, Kentucky
1949	Kentucky 46, Oklahoma A&M 36	Alex Groza, Kentucky
1950	CCNY 71, Bradley 68	Irwin Dambrot, CCNY
1951	Kentucky 68, Kansas State 58	Bill Spivey, Kentucky
1952	Kansas 80, St. John's 63	Clyde Lovellette, Kansas
1953	Indiana 69, Kansas 68	Bertram Born, Kansas
1954	LaSalle 92, Bradley 76	Tom Gola, LaSalle
1955	San Francisco 77, LaSalle 63	Bill Russell, USF
1956	San Francisco 83, Iowa 71	Hal Lear, Temple
1957	North Carolina 54, Kansas 53	Wilt Chamberlain, Kansas
1958	Kentucky 84, Seattle 72	Elgin Baylor, Seattle
1959	California 71, West Virginia 70	No selection
1960	Ohio State 75, California 55	Jerry Lucas, Ohio State
1961	Cincinnati 70, Ohio State 65	Jerry Lucas, Ohio State
1962	Cincinnati 71, Ohio State 59	Paul Hogue, Cincinnati
1963	Loyola (Ill.) 60, Cincinnati 58	Art Heyman, Duke

1964	UCLA 98, Duke 83	Walt Hazzard, UCLA
1965	UCLA 91, Michigan 80	Bill Bradley, Princeton
1966	Texas Western 72, Kentucky 65	Jerry Chambers, Utah
1967	UCLA 79, Dayton 64	Lew Alcindor (Kareem Abdul-Jabbar), UCLA
1968	UCLA 78, North Carolina 55	Lew Alcindor, UCLA
1969	UCLA 92, Purdue 72	Lew Alcindor, UCLA
1970	UCLA 80, Jacksonville 69	Sidney Wicks, UCLA
1971	UCLA 68, Villanova 62	Howard Porter, Villanova
1972	UCLA 81, Florida State 76	Bill Walton, UCLA
1973	UCLA 87, Memphis State 66	Bill Walton, UCLA
1974	North Carolina State 76, Marquette 64	David Thompson, No. Carolina St.
1975	UCLA 92, Kentucky 85	Richard Washington, UCLA
1976	Indiana 86, Michigan 68	Kent Benson, Indiana

Helms College Basketball Players of the Year
1924   Charles Black, Kansas
1925   Earl Mueller, Colorado College
1926   John Cobb, North Carolina
1927   Victor Hanson, Syracuse
1928   Victor Holt, Oklahoma
1929   John A. Thompson, Montana State
1930   John Hyatt, Pittsburgh
1931   Bart Carlton, E. Central Oklahoma
1932   John Wooden, Purdue
1933   Forrest Sale, Kentucky
1934   Wesley Bennet, Westminster (Pa.)
1935   Leroy Edwards, Kentucky
1936   John Moir, Notre Dame
1937   Angelo Luisetti, Stanford
1938   Angelo Luisetti, Stanford
1939   Chester Jaworski, Rhode Island
1940   George Glamack, North Carolina
1941   George Glamack, North Carolina
1942   Stan "Stutz" Modzelewski, Rhode Island
1943   George Senesky, St. Joseph's (Pa.)
1944   George Mikan, DePaul (Chicago)
1945   George Mikan, DePaul (Chicago)
1946   Robert Kurland, Oklahoma State
1947   Gerald Tucker, Oklahoma
1948   Ed Macauley, St. Louis
1949   Anthony Lavelli, Yale
1950   Paul Arizin, Villanova
1951   Richard Groat, Duke
1952   Clyde Lovellette, Kansas
1953   Robert Houbregs, Washington
1954   Tom Gola, LaSalle
1955   Bill Russell, San Francisco
1956   Bill Russell, San Francisco
1957   Leonard Rosenbluth, North Carolina
1958   Elgin Baylor, Seattle
1959   Oscar Robertson, Cincinnati
1960   Oscar Robertson, Cincinnati
1961   Jerry Lucas, Ohio State
1962   Paul Hogue, Cincinnati

Ernie DiGregorio, an All-American at Providence College in 1973, was NBA Rookie of the Year in 1974 with a promising young Buffalo Braves squad. (*Hank Seaman,* New Bedford Standard-Times)

1963   Arthur Heyman, Duke
1964   Walter Hazzard, UCLA
1965   Bill Bradley, Princeton; Gail Goodrich, UCLA
1966   Cazzie Russell, Michigan
1967   Lew Alcindor (Kareem Abdul-Jabbar), UCLA
1968   Lew Alcindor, UCLA
1969   Lew Alcindor, UCLA
1970   Pete Maravich, LSU; Sidney Wicks, UCLA
1971   Sidney Wicks, UCLA; Austin Carr, Notre Dame
1972   Bill Walton, UCLA
1973   Bill Walton, UCLA
1974   David Thompson, North Carolina State; Bill Walton, UCLA
1975   David Thompson, North Carolina State
1976   Scott May, Indiana

College Coach of the Year
(Selected by U.S. Basketball Writers Association)
1959   Ed Hickey, Marquette
1960   Pete Newell, California
1961   Fred Taylor, Ohio State
1962   Fred Taylor, Ohio State
1963   Ed Jucker, Cincinnati
1964   John Wooden, UCLA
1965   Bill van Breda Kolff, Princeton
1966   Adolph Rupp, Kentucky
1967   John Wooden, UCLA
1968   Guy Lewis, Houston
1969   John Wooden, UCLA
1970   John Wooden, UCLA
1971   Al McGuire, Marquette
1972   John Wooden, UCLA

1973 John Wooden, UCLA
1974 Al McGuire, Marquette
1975 Bobby Knight, Indiana
1976 Johnny Orr, Michigan

Naismith Memorial Basketball Hall of Fame

(Formally opened in 1968, Naismith Hall of Fame in Springfield, Massachusetts, was primarily a project of the National Association of Basketball Coaches. Inductees are chosen in six categories: Coach, Contributor, College Player, Pro Player, AAU Player, and Referee.)

Forrest C. "Phog" Allen—Coach; Allen succeeded Dr. Naismith as basketball coach at Kansas in 1908, and coached a total of 39 seasons; his teams won 771 games, were Helms national champions in 1922–1923 and NCAA champions in 1952. He was instrumental in founding the National Association of Basketball Coaches in 1927 and in having basketball adopted as an Olympic sport in 1936.

Arnold "Red" Auerbach—Coach; in 20 seasons of coaching pro basketball (Washington Caps 1946–1949; Tri-Cities 1950–1951; Boston Celtics 1951–1966), Auerbach produced 11 division champions and 9 NBA champions, including 8 in a row, 1959–1966, at Boston. His overall record was 939 wins and 485 losses in regular-season play.

Clair F. Bee—Contributor; as coach at Long Island University 1931–1952, Bee compiled a winning percentage of .950, with undefeated teams in 1936 and 1939 and NIT champions in 1939 and 1941. At one point, his teams won 43 straight. He coached the NBA Baltimore Bullets 1952–1954.

John F. Beckman—Pro player; one of the first great pro players, with the original Celtics, starting in 1919. Beckman was the greatest foul shooter of his era—and one player then took all his team's foul shots.

Bernhard "Benny" Borgmann—Pro player; only 5-8, Borgmann was a great set shooter who often scored half or more of his team's points. Between 1918 and 1942, he played more than 2,500 pro games with a number of teams, including the Paterson Crescents and New York Celtics. He coached pro basketball for seven seasons and later coached at St. Michael's and Muhlenberg College.

Ernest A. Blood—Coach; best known for his "Wonder Teams" at Passaic, New Jersey, High School, Blood also coached at the U.S. Military Academy and at Clarkson. His Passaic teams won 200 games and lost 1 in the 1915–1924 period, compiling a 159-game winning streak and winning seven state titles. At St. Benedicts's Prep, he won 421 games, 1925–1949, and had a 56-7 collegiate record.

Joseph Brennan—Pro player; starred for 17 seasons, 1919–1936, for Brooklyn Visitations, New York Whirlwinds, and Union City Reds. He also coached St. Francis College, Brooklyn, 1941–1948, compiling a 96-44 record.

Walter A. Brown—Contributor; President of the Boston Garden and Arena Corporation from 1937 until his death in 1964, Brown was a major force in organizing the NBA in 1946, and his team, the Celtics, dominated the league for more than a decade.

John W. Bunn—Contributor; winner of 10 varsity letters at Kansas (1921), Bunn coached at Stanford, Springfield College, and Colorado State. His 1937 Stanford team

won the Helms national title. He edited the *Basketball Guide* and was official rules interpreter, 1959–1967, and he wrote six books on the sport.

Howard G. Cann—Coach; Cann was chosen college player of the year in 1920, with an NYU team that won the AAU national title. He coached at NYU 1923–1958, compiling a 409-232 record; his 1935 team (19-1) won the Helms national championship.

Dr. H. Clifford Carlson—Coach; as coach at Pittsburgh, 1922–1953, Carlson developed the Figure 8, basketball's first patterned offense. His teams won 370 and lost 246; the 1928 (21-0) and 1930 (23-2) teams were named national champions.

Bernard L. Carnevale—Coach; after playing at NYU and in the pros, Carnevale coached at North Carolina, 1944–1946 and the U.S. Naval Academy, 1947–1966, compiling an overall 308-171 record.

Robert J. Cousy—Pro player; an All-American at Holy Cross in 1950, Cousy played for the Boston Celtics, 1950–1963, and was first team All-NBA 10 years in a row, scoring 16,960 career points and compiling 6,959 assists. He was named to the all-time NBA all-star team. He coached Boston College 1963–1969 and the Cincinnati Royals 1969–1973.

Robert E. Davies—Pro player; after captaining Seton Hall to 43 straight wins, Davies played 10 years of pro basketball, was named all-league seven times and Most Valuable Player three times. A great ball-handler, he led the league in assists for six straight years, and scored 7,771 pro points. Davies is credited with "inventing" the behind-the-back dribble.

Everett S. Dean—Coach; an All-American at Indiana, 1921, Dean coached at Carleton, 1921–1924, Indiana, 1924–1938, and Stanford, 1938–1955. His 1942 team won the NCAA and Helms championships; overall, he coached 398 victories.

Forrest S. "Red" DeBernardi—AAU player; an All-American at little Westminster (Missouri) College (1921), DeBernardi played in 11 AAU tournaments and was named to the all-tournament team seven times. In 1938 he was named to the first all-time All-American team.

Henry J. "Dutch" Dehnert—Pro player; though he never played in high school or college, Dehnert was already a pro star before joining the original Celtics in 1920, where he invented the pivot play. He played with the Cleveland Rosenblums championship teams in 1928, 1929, and 1930, coached the Detroit Eagles to world championships in 1940 and 1941 and the Sheboygan Indians to Western Division titles in 1945 and 1946.

Edgar A. Diddle—Coach; Diddle coached at Western Kentucky State, 1922–1964, compiling a 759-302 record; his teams won or shared 22 titles in three different conferences and went to the NCAA tournament three times, the NIT eight times.

Robert L. Douglas—Contributor; Douglas in 1922 organized the Renaissance Five, a barnstorming Black team that once won 88 consecutive games; in 1934, they won 128 games and in 1939 they won the world pro championship in a Chicago tournament.

Bruce Drake—Coach; at the University of Oklahoma, 1939–1955, Drake compiled a 200-181 record.

Paul Endacott—College player; called by "Phog" Allen "the greatest player I ever coached," Endacott starred at Kansas 1921–1923, leading his team to the Helms national championship in 1923, when he was chosen player of the year. He was named in 1951 to an all-time college team.

Harry Fisher—Contributor; at Columbia, Fisher set a record that stood for 48 years of scoring 13 field goals in a 1905 game. The first full-time coach at Columbia, he had a 101-39 record, 1905–1916, and compiled a 45-6 record at Army, 1922–1924. He was a member of the original college rules committee.

Harold "Bud" Foster—College player; a 1930 graduate of Wisconsin, where he was an All-American, he played professional basketball and then coached at Wisconsin, 1934–1959, winning Big Ten titles in 1935, 1941, and 1947 and the NCAA championship in 1941.

Max Friedman—Pro player; Friedman began his pro career in 1909 and played in every pro league through 1927, when he coached and played for the champion Cleveland Rosenblums.

Amory T. "Slats" Gill—Coach; an All-American at Oregon State in 1924, Gill coached there 1928–1964, compiling a 599-392 record and winning five Pacific Coast Conference titles.

Thomas Gola—College player; as a freshman at La Salle, Gola was co-winner of the Most Valuable Player award in the 1952 NIT, won by LaSalle. An exceptional clutch player, he was a consensus All-American three times. Gola also played 10 seasons of professional basketball.

Edward Gottlieb—Contributor; Gottlieb organized South Philadelphia Hebrew Association team in 1918; the SPHAs beat the Original Celtics and the Rens in 1926, then won a total of 11 championships in the Eastern and American Leagues during the 1930s. He helped organize the BAA in 1946, and his Philadelphia Warriors won the league's first title.

Robert F. "Ace" Gruenig—AAU player; a 6-8 center, Gruenig was an AAU All-Tournament choice 10 times between 1937 and 1948; he led the Denver Safeways to the 1937 championship and the Denver Legion to the 1942 title.

Dr. Luther H. Gulick—Contributor; it was Gulick who, as director of the Springfield Training School's physical education program, asked Dr. James H. Naismith to develop a new sport. Gulick was also active in the early development and growth of basketball.

Victor Hanson—College player; a three-year star and All-American at Syracuse (1925–1927), Hanson led his club to a 48-7 record, including the Helms national title in 1926; he was chosen player of the year in 1927.

George T. Hepbron—Referee; a friend of Naismith and a YMCA director, Hepbron refereed the first AAU tournament and helped compile the first *Basketball Guide,* in 1896. He was secretary of the Joint Rules Committee, 1915–1936.

Edward J. Hickox—Contributor; as coach at Springfield College, 1927–1943, Hickox had a 209-85 record and was 21-3 in one season at American International College, 1945–1946. He was a Rules Committee member for 18 years, and a driving force behind establishment of the Naismith Hall of Fame.

Paul D. "Tony" Hinkle—Contributor; after starring at the University of Chicago, Hinkle went to Butler College as athletic director and coach of three sports, winning more than 500 basketball games in his career. He also coached the Great Lakes Naval Training Station to the national service championship in 1943.

Howard A. Hobson—Coach; Hobson compiled 495 wins at Southern Oregon, 1932–1935; Oregon, 1935–1947; and Yale, 1947–1956; his 1939 Oregon team won the first NCAA tournament.

Nat Holman—Pro player; Holman played for three of the great early pro teams, Germantown, the New York Whirlwinds, and the Original Celtics. In 1933 he began a 20-year career coaching at City College of New York; his 1950 team won both the NCAA and NIT titles.

George H. Hoyt—Referee; Hoyt acted as a major promoter of basketball in New England during the early 1900s, conducting many clinics to explain the rules to players, coaches, and officials. He also coached several amateur teams.

Charles D. Hyatt—College player; an All-American at Pittsburgh, where he led the team to a 60-7 record in three years, Hyatt was player of the year in 1930. He was also an AAU All-American nine times.

Henry P. "Hank" Iba—Coach; Iba recorded nearly 800 victories at Oklahoma State 1934–1970; his teams won consecutive NCAA titles in 1945 and 1946. He coached the U.S. Olympic teams in 1964, 1968, and 1972.

Edward S. "Ned" Irish—Contributor; after a brief sportswriting career, Irish became basketball director of Madison Square Garden and immediately began promoting college double-headers, which turned collegiate basketball into a truly national sport and attracted widespread spectator interest. He also helped organize the NBA and the New York Knickerbockers in 1946.

R. William Jones—Contributor; Jones, a graduate of Springfield College, was cofounder of the International Amateur Basketball Federation in 1932 and was first secretary-general of the Federation.

Alvin F. "Doggy" Julian—Coach; Julian coached basketball at Albright College, 1927–1928; Muhlenberg, 1936–1954; Holy Cross, 1945–1948; and Dartmouth, 1950–1967. His 1947 Holy Cross team won the NCAA title, and he had an overall record of 486-341. He also coached the Boston Celtics, 1948–1950.

Frank W. Keaney—Coach; coaching at Rhode Island State (now the University of Rhode Island) from 1920 through 1948, Keaney compiled a 402-124 record, using "firehouse basketball," an extreme version of the fast break.

Matthew P. Kennedy—Referee; after graduating from college in 1928, Kennedy became a referee, officiating at high school, college, and pro games for 18 years. He was supervisor of NBA officials, 1946–1950, and then became referee for the Harlem Globetrotters for seven years.

George E. Keogan—Coach; after 24 seasons of coaching high schools and small colleges, Keogan went to Notre Dame in 1923, and remained until his death in 1943, compiling a 327-96 record. His 1927 (19-1) and 1936 (22-2) teams won Helms national titles.

Edward "Moose" Krause—College player; at Notre Dame, he was an All-American three years in a row, 1932–1934. He coached at Holy Cross, 1939–42, and at his alma mater, 1946–1951, compiling an 82-38 record.

Robert A. Kurland—College player; the first of the great 7-ft players, Kurland led the nation in scoring in 1946 and led his Oklahoma A&M team to consecutive NCAA titles in 1945 and 1946. He was an AAU All-American for six years and played on the U.S. Olympic teams in 1948 and 1952.

Ward L. "Piggy" Lambert—Coach; Lambert coached at Purdue from 1916 through 1946, compiling a 365-145 record and winning 11 Big Ten titles.

Joseph Lapchick—Pro player; in a 20-year pro career, Lapchick spent four seasons with the Original Celtics, 1923–1927, then reorganized the team, 1930–1936, before becoming an outstanding coach at St. John's University and with the New York Knicks. He had a 335-129 record at St. John's, winning four NIT titles, and was 300-222 with the Knicks.

Emil S. Liston—Contributor; as athletic director at Baker University in Kansas, Liston was one of the founders of the NAIA tournament.

Harry Litwack—Coach; at Temple, 1952–73, Litwack compiled 373 wins against 191 losses. His team won the 1969 NIT tournament.

Kenneth D. Loeffler—Coach; after five seasons in pro ball, Loeffler coached for a total of 22 years at Geneva, Yale, LaSalle, and Texas A&M, winning 310 games. His 1952 LaSalle team won the NIT and the 1954 team won the NCAA title. He also coached for three years in the NBA.

A. C. "Dutch" Lonborg—Coach; Northwestern University coach 1928–1950, after briefer stints at McPherson and Washburn Colleges.

Angelo "Hank" Luisetti—College player; the popularizer of the one-handed jump shot, Luisetti was an outstanding all-around player for Stanford. He was named player of the year in both 1937 and 1938.

Edward C. "Easy Ed" Macauley—College player; a three-time All-American at St. Louis, Macauley was named player of the year and NIT most valuable player in 1948. He scored more than 11,000 points in nine NBA seasons, and was named All-NBA five times.

Branch McCracken—College player; an All-American forward at Indiana in 1930, McCracken coached at the school 1937–1942 and 1945–1965, compiling a 364-174 record, after having been 93-41 at Ball State for seven seasons. His 1940 and 1953 teams won the NCAA title.

Jack McCracken—AAU player; after starring at Northwest Missouri State, McCracken played 10 years of AAU basketball, 1933–1943, and was named an AAU All-Star seven times.

Dr. Walter E. Meanwell—Coach; although he never played basketball, Meanwell was a successful coach at Wisconsin, 1911–17 and 1921–1934, and at Missouri, 1917–1920. His teams won or tied for 11 conference titles and won a total of 290 games.

George L. Mikan—College player; a three-year All-American at DePaul, Mikan was college player of the year in 1944 and 1945, then became a nine-time All-Pro with the Minneapolis Lakers of the NBA. He led the league in scoring three times and in rebounding twice.

William G. Mokray—Contributor; Mokray saw basketball at its best at Passaic High School during the "Wonder Team" era and at Rhode Island State during the "firehouse basketball" era. He was basketball director at Boston Garden for many years, has edited the *NBA Guide,* and has written the history of the sport for *Encyclopedia Britannica.*

Ralph Morgan—Contributor; a founding member of the Collegiate Rules Committee, Morgan served on the Committee through 1931; he was also a founder of the Eastern Intercollegiate Basketball League (now the Ivy League) and served as league secretary-treasurer for many years.

John Wooden, an All-American guard at Purdue in 1930, 1931, and 1932, coached UCLA to 10 NCAA basketball championships in a 12-year span. He is the only man elected to the Hall of Fame twice—as a player and as a coach. *(Basketball Hall of Fame.)*

Frank "Pop" Morgenweck—Contributor; Morgenweck began as manager of a National League team in 1901 and managed several championship pro teams through 1931.

Charles C. "Stretch" Murphy—College player; an All-American at Purdue, Murphy captained the undefeated 1930 team. He was named to the all-time All-American team in 1938.

James Naismith—Contributor; the inventor of basketball; for further information, see text.

John J. O'Brien—Contributor; O'Brien played pro basketball and officiated, but his chief contribution was as an organizer and administrator. He helped organize the Interstate Professional League in 1914, the Metropolitan Basketball League in 1921, and the American Basketball League in 1925. He served all three leagues as president.

Harold G. Olsen—Contributor; Olsen coached at Ripon (Wis.) College, 1919–1921; Ohio State, 1922–1946; and Northwestern, 1950; his Ohio State teams won five Big Ten titles. He also coached the professional Chicago Stags, 1946–1949, winning 95 and losing 63.

Harlan O. "Pat" Page—College player; Page played for outstanding teams at the University of Chicago; they won the AAU title in 1907, were undefeated in 1909, and Page was named Player of the Year in 1910. He later coached at Chicago, Butler, Idaho College, and Indiana.

Robert Pettit—Pro player; averaging 27.4 points a game in his career at LSU, Pettit became NBA Rookie of the Year in 1955, was named to the All-NBA team 11 times, and was Most Valuable Player in 1956 and 1959. He was named to the All-NBA 25-year team in 1971.

Andy Phillip—College player; an All-American at Illinois in 1943, Phillip then entered the service and returned to Illinois for another All-American year. He played 11 seasons in the NBA.

Maurice Podoloff—Contributor; though only about 5 ft tall and a hockey man, Podoloff became president of the Basketball Association of America when the pro league was formed in 1946; he was largely responsible for the merger with the National Basketball League to form the National Basketball Association, of which he served as commissioner from 1949 through 1963.

Henry V. Porter—Contributor; Porter became executive director of the National Federation of State High School Athletic Associations in 1928, and he helped pioneer the development of the molded basketball and the fan-shaped backboard. He also helped codify national rules; he was a member of the Rules Committee for 30 years and its secretary for 18 years.

Ernest C. Quigley—Referee; an official of collegiate and AAU basketball games for 40 years, Quigley was also a National League baseball umpire, working in five World Series, and a college football official.

William A. Reid—Contributor; Reid coached at Colgate for 10 years, 1919–1929, winning 151 games; he became athletic director in 1935.

Elmer Ripley—Contributor; Ripley coached at Georgetown, 1938–1943 and 1947–1949, compiling a 109-76 record, and at Army 1951–1953, where he was 19-17.

John S. Roosma—College player; after playing for the Passaic, New Jersey, "wonder teams," Roosma starred at Army, scoring 44 percent of his team's points while Army won 73 and lost 13; he won 10 letters in three sports.

Adolph F. Rupp—Coach; "The Baron" coached at Kentucky from 1930 through 1972, winning 874 games and losing 190, an .821 percentage. His teams won four NCAA tournaments, in 1948, 1949, 1951, and 1956, and the NIT title in 1946.

John D. "Honey" Russell—Pro player; Russell began his pro career while still in high school, in 1919, and played for 28 years, in more than 3,200 games, with the top teams of his era. He was a player-coach for 20 years. He later coached Seton Hall to 294 wins, including 44 straight, and to the 1953 NIT title, and he was the first coach of the Boston Celtics.

William Russell—Pro player; a two-time All-American at the University of San Francisco, Russell was most valuable player in the 1955 NCAA tourney. In 13 seasons with the Boston Celtics, 1956–1969, his team won 11 NBA championships and he was the league's most valuable player five times. He was a player-coach for two of those championship teams.

Leonard D. Sachs—Coach; Sachs combined college coaching at his alma mater, Loyola of Chicago, with pro football for several years. Between 1924 and 1942, his teams won 224 games and lost 129; they won 21 straight in 1939 and 31 straight, 1928–1930.

Lynn W. St. John—Contributor; a 1900 graduate of Ohio State, St. John coached basketball at Wooster, Ohio Wesleyan, and Ohio State, and was OSU athletic director, 1915–1947. For 25 years he was a member of the NCAA Rules Committee, for 18 years its chairman.

Abraham Saperstein—Contributor; Saperstein founded the Harlem Globetrotters in 1927, who traveled more than 6 million miles and visited more than 100 countries with their unique blend of basketball skills and clowning. Saperstein also founded the short-lived American Basketball League.

Arthur A. Schabinger—Contributor; Schabinger coached a total of 20 years at Ottaway (Kansas), Emporia State, and Creighton University, compiling an 80 percent winning record. He directed the first Olympic basketball tournament in 1936, was a long-time member of the Rules Committee, and founded the Official Sports Film Service in 1946.

Ernie Schmidt—College player; Schmidt played for three state high school champions and three college conference champions at Pittsburgh (Kansas) Teachers, where he scored an even 1,000 points, earning the nickname "One Grand."

John J. Schommer—College player; the first University of Chicago athlete to win 12 letters, Schommer led the Western Conference (Big Ten) in scoring three years in a row, 1907–1909; he was Helms player of the year in 1909, when he captained an undefeated team.

Barney Sedran—Pro player; though only 5-4, Sedran led City College of New York in scoring for three seasons and captained the team in his senior year, 1910–1911. He played for many pro teams during his 15-year career, leading the New York Whirlwinds in scoring for two seasons; his 31 points in one game was a long-time pro record.

William Sharman—Pro player; a four-time All-Star in 11 seasons with the Boston Celtics, 1950–1961, Sharman scored 12,665 points in 710 games, a 17.8 average, and had a fine .423 Field goal percentage. He also had a career free-shooting percentage of .883, and his .905 percentage in 1956–57 is the NBA single-season record. He played college basketball at the University of Southern California and has also been a successful professional coach.

Amos Alonzo Stagg—Contributor; the "Grand Old Man of Football," a friend of Naismith's at Springfield, introduced basketball to the University of Chicago and the Western Conference and coached seven conference champions. He also helped organize the national high school tournament in 1917.

Christian Steinmetz—College player; Steinmetz organized and starred for the first team at Wisconsin, averaging 25.7 points a game, a long-time record, in 1905; he was named the first Helms player of the year.

Charles H. "Chuck" Taylor—Contributor; in the interests of promoting basketball shoes, Taylor was also a tireless ambassador of basketball, conducting clinics all over the United States and in Europe, South America, and Africa. He began the Converse Yearbook of Basketball in 1922, and selected All-American teams for the publication for many years.

John A. "Cat" Thompson—College player; Thompson scored 1,539 points in three years at Montana State; he was player of the year in 1929, when his team won the Helms national title.

David Tobey—Referee; Tobey played pro ball and was a successful high school and college coach; he also refereed professional and college games from 1918 through 1946, and he wrote the first book on officiating in 1943.

Oswald Tower—Contributor; Tower had a powerful influence on the development of basketball as official rules interpreter from 1915 through 1959 and as editor of *Basketball Guide*. He refereed games for more than 35 years and was a member of the Rules Committee, 1910–1959.

Arthur L. Trester—Contributor; Trester in 1913 became secretary of the Indiana High School Athletic Association and turned it into a strong organization, whose state tournament has been the model for high school tournaments in many other states.

Robert Vandiver—A three-time All-Indiana High School selection, 1920–22, Vandiver is the only person elected to the Hall of Fame as a high school player.

Edward A. Wachter—Pro player; Wachter began playing pro basketball when it was still a brand-new sport, and he continued as a pro player until 1924, for a total of 1,800 games; he led four different leagues in scoring.

David H. Walsh—Referee; Walsh began officiating high school, college, and pro games in 1911; starting in 1914 he concentrated on the college game. He was long-time associate director of the Collegiate Officials Bureau.

W. R. Clifford Wells—Contributor; coaching at various Indiana high schools, Wells won 617 games for a .710 percentage, then moved to Tulane, 1945–1963. Overall, his teams won 885 and lost 418 in 47 seasons.

John R. Wooden—College player and coach; the only man honored twice by the Naismith Hall of Fame, Wooden was an All-American at Purdue and player of the year in 1932. He had a 47-14 record at Indiana State, 1946–1948, then went to UCLA to establish the greatest coaching record in collegiate history. Wooden's teams won 10 NCAA titles in 12 years, including seven straight. Through the 1973–1974 season, his record at UCLA was 640 wins, 157 losses.

Bibliography. Auerbach, "Red": *Basketball for the Player, the Fan and the Coach*, Pocket Books, New York, 1971; Hollander, Zander: *The Modern Encyclopedia of Basketball*, Four Winds Press, New York, 1973; Jares, Joe: *Basketball, the American Game*, Follett, Chicago, 1971; Koppett, Leonard: *Championship NBA*, Dial, New York, 1970; Mokray, William G.: *Ronald Encyclopedia of Basketball*, Ronald, New York, 1963; Weyand, Alexander M: *The Cavalcade of Basketball*, Macmillan, New York, 1960.

BELMONT STAKES—The third race in horse racing's "Triple Crown," the Belmont is also the oldest—first run in 1867—and longest, at 1½ mi. Now run at Belmont Park, it originated at Jerome Park and was later run at Morris Park. The race is named for August Belmont, Sr., cofounder of Jerome and Monmouth Parks and owner of the top money-winning stable in 1889 and 1890.

For further information and a list of winning horses, *see* HORSE RACING.

BETTING—*See* GAMBLING.

BIATHLON—An unusual, quasi-military competition combining cross-country skiing and rifle shooting, biathlon originated in the Scandinavian countries as a form of hunting and as military training. As a sport, it was originally called "military ski patrol."

In Olympic competition, the biathlon is run over a 20-km (approximately 12.2-mi) course. Four targets are located at stations between the fifth and eighteenth kilometer of the ski run. Shooting range is 150 m (about 164 yd). Competitors fire five shots from a prone position at the first and third targets, five shots from a standing position at the second and fourth targets. The prone target has a 12.5-cm center ring and a 25-cm ring. The standing target has a 35-cm center ring and a 45-cm outer ring. If a shot hits in the second ring, the competitor is penalized 1 min; if a shot hits outside the second ring, the competitor is penalized 2 min. Penalty minutes are added to a competitor's time to determine the place of finish. The rifle must not be larger than 8 mm in caliber; it must not be loaded until the competitor arrives at the firing station; and optical sights are not allowed.

Relay. The relay event, added to the world championships in 1965 and to the Olympics in 1968, uses a 7.5-km course, skied in turn by each of four team members. There are two sets of five breakable targets; a competitor fires up to eight rounds at each set of targets, first from a prone position and then from a standing position. Prone targets are 12.5 cm in diameter; standing targets are 30 cm. For each target that fails to break, the competitor must ski once around a penalty loop about 150 m in length. The first team to finish wins.

Biathlon in the United States. The first major biathlon competition in the United States was held in 1956. The sport in this country is under the supervision of the U.S. Modern Pentathlon and Biathlon Association (USMPBA), which is associated with the *Union Internationale de Pentathlon Moderne et Biathlon*.

The USMPBA works with the National Rifle Association, the U.S. Ski Association, and the U.S. Olympic Committee to develop the sport in this country. Since 1963, training clinics have been conducted in areas across the snow belt. Special events are conducted for juniors (under 21), who race over a 15-km course and have only three shooting bouts, and for small-bore biathlon, using small-bore rifles and a range of 50 m. The U.S. Army maintains a Biathlon Training Center at Ft. Richardson, in Anchorage, Alaska.

United States Champions

1965	Charles Kellogg
1966	William Spencer
1967	William Spencer
1968	John Ehrensbeck
1969	William Bowerman
1970	Peter Karns
1971	Cancelled
1972	Peter Karns
1973	Dennis Donahue
1974	John Morton (20-km)
	Dennis Donahue (sprint and overall)
1975	John Morton
1976	John Morton

BICYCLE RACING—*See* CYCLING.

BILLIARDS—There are two stories about the origin of billiards, and it's impossible to determine which is correct. One is that billiards is derived from lawn bowls, the other that it is derived from croquet. Whichever version is right, it's certain that all three sports are related.

Lawn bowls is the most ancient. In this sport, players roll balls across the grass, attempting to get as close as possible to a target ball. This ancient sport was popular in England as long ago as the fourteenth century.

Some enthusiasts either miniaturized the game, creating croquet, and then croquet moved indoors to become—after a long time—billiards or moved lawn bowls directly indoors to create a croquetlike form of billiards. The more likely story seems to be that these enthusiasts attempted to set up a lawn bowls game indoors. But lack of space changed the game considerably: Cones were used as targets for small balls, which were struck by a club instead of being rolled. To make the game more difficult, wire arches and hoops were added, and the ball had to be driven through them before hitting the cone.

The full-scale version of this game then moved back outdoors, becoming croquet, while a smaller-scale version was developed for indoor play, on a table, with another major rule change: The ball had to be pushed, not struck. So the heavy end of the club became the handle and the narrower end the striking surface. Eventually, the cones, arches, and hoops were done away with, and two pockets were put into the table, one at each end. Now two balls were used, and the object was to use one ball to knock the other into a pocket.

Whatever the exact origin, billiards went through a long gestation period in a number of countries before emerging as several different games. It's likely that much of the early development of the sport took place in France. The name *billiards* comes from the French for "stick." And it was a Frenchman, a Captain Mingaud, who did a great deal to modernize the game.

For a long time, the cue stick used was curved. A player, holding one end of the stick at about chest level, rested it on the side of the table for stability and then pushed the ball. This curved stick was replaced about 1698 by the tapered cue.

In the late eighteenth century, Captain Mingaud was a political prisoner in Paris, and he whiled away his time by playing billiards. He enjoyed the game so much that when it was time to be released from prison, he insisted on remaining so he could further perfect his techniques. In 1790, Mingaud discovered that he could aim more accurately if he used a file to round the cue tip, thus getting closer to achieving real point-to-point contact between stick and ball.

Mingaud left the prison and began staging trick-shot exhibitions throughout France, and billiards became a fad. In 1807 he began to glue a leather tip on his cue, giving him even better control of the cue ball. The most popular game at the time was known as "French billiards," and was a four-ball carom game.

The next step in developing modern techniques was taken by Jack Carr, a billiards instructor in England. He was annoyed at miscues caused by the leather tip becoming glossy after much use, and he discovered that applying chalk to the tip helped prevent miscues. Even more important, he discovered that he could control the path of the cue ball by hitting it off-center.

Carr was evidently a bit of a charlatan: He claimed to have developed a magical kind of "twisting chalk," which he sold at 10 shillings a box, along with a free lesson on how to use "side"—which we now call "English." However, his customers began to learn that ordinary chalk would do the job, and the word spread quickly.

On tours through Spain and France, Carr took on all comers and was generally considered the "world" champion.

Billiards in America. The Spaniards brought billiards to this continent in 1565, in what is now St. Augustine, Florida. Later, English settlers introduced the game into the Colonies. It was not particularly popular, but George Washington, Thomas Jefferson, and Alexander Hamilton were frequent players. Probably the Marquis de Lafayette had something to do with it—he was an enthusiast of French billiards.

The sport's literature mentions a Professor Lake—the "Professor" may well have been an honorary title—as an outstanding American billiards player about 1800, but not much is known about the development of the sport in this country in the first half of the nineteenth century. The first recorded match of any importance was between Michael Phelan and John Seereiter in 1855; Phelan won. The game, called "old style," was a four-ball carom version.

In 1858, an eight-day tournament was held in New York. Each of the eight contestants put up an entry fee of $250 in the winner-take-all tournament. Dudley Kavanagh won the $2,000 purse. On April 10, 1859, admission was charged to a match, for the first time, between Kavanagh and Michael Foley. Kavanagh again won. Just two days later, Phelan and Seereiter played at a Detroit billiard academy in a match "for the billiard championship of the United States." The academy owner put up $5,000, and each contestant put up $5,000 for a side bet. Phelan won. As far as official records are concerned, the first real American title contest took place in 1870, at four-ball carom. It was a tournament. John Deery and A. P. Rudolphe tied for the championship.

Skills were becoming so good by this time that simple billiards couldn't last much longer. Too many players knew how to "rail-nurse" the balls: They could cluster them together in a corner and, with the right English and a gentle touch, could simply keep scoring billiards and coming up with the same shot all over again. Simple billiards games were pretty well out after 1890, when Jacob Schaefer, Sr., ran 3,000 points in a single turn to beat J. F. B. McCleery, 3,004 to 15.

The balkline games were introduced to make billiards more interesting. (Details of the rules will be given below.) An 8-in balkline was introduced in 1883; 14.2 balkline entered in 1884, with George F. Slosson winning the first championship; 18.1 arrived in 1897 and 18.2 in 1902.

Equipment. As often happens in sports, once techniques began to improve, better equipment was also developed. Until about 1826, the table's playing surface was made of small panels of wood. Large panels had been tried previously, but they warped easily. In 1826, marble was tried as a base, but marble "sweats" in warm weather. Slate was introduced in 1827 and is still the standard base for good tables.

The early cushions were made of wood with a heavy padding of felt. India rubber was introduced in 1835 and vulcanized rubber in 1865. Vulcanized rubber is still generally used.

Billiards led directly to the invention of the first plastic, in 1868. Because of the high price of ivory, a $10,000 prize had been offered for a satisfactory substitute to be used in making billiard balls. John Wesley Hyatt mixed nitrocellulose and camphor and applied heat and pressure to produce celluloid. He won the prize, but celluloid became much better known for other uses. Billiard balls are now usually made of plastic, though cheaper ones are of painted wood.

Billiards tables vary in size, but they should be twice as long as wide. The championship pocket billiards table

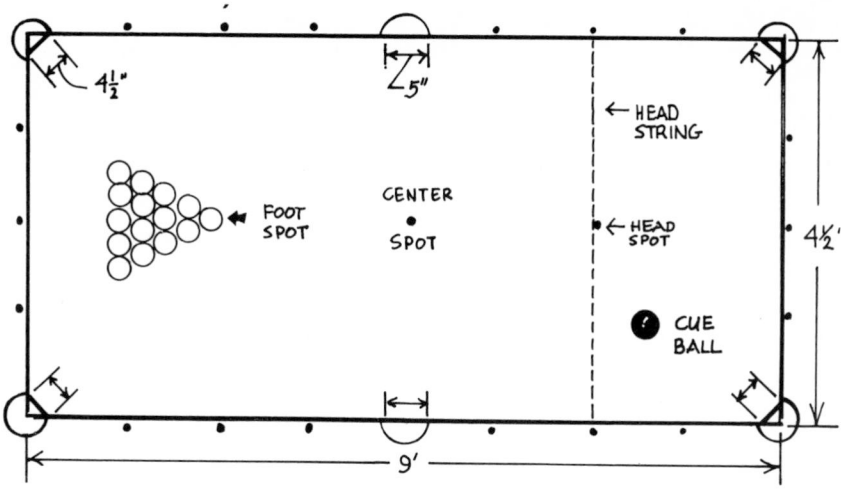

Regulation pocket billiards table

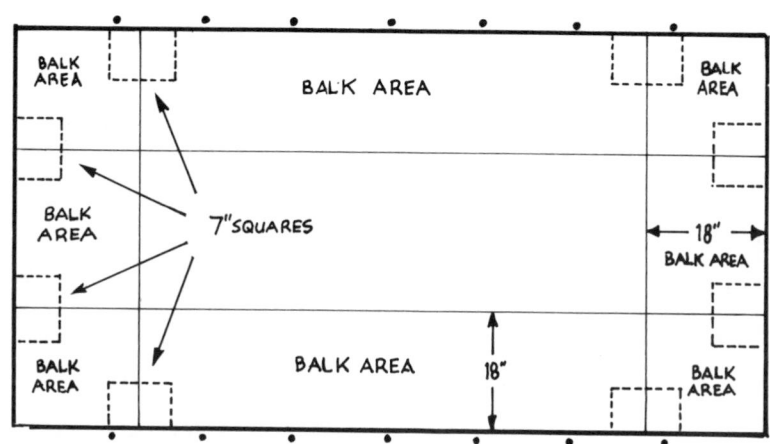

**Table markings for 18.1 and 18.2
balkine carom billiards; 7″ squares
marked by dotted lines are called "anchors."**

was 5 by 10 ft until 1950; it's now 4½ by 9. Tables for championship carom billiards are still 5 by 10, and snooker tables are 6 by 12. The corner pockets in a pocket billiards table are 4½ in wide, and the side pockets are 5 in wide. Cue sticks range from 53 to 57 in in length and from 12 to 22 oz in weight. They are tapered wooden sticks with leather tips, 11 to 15 mm in diameter. Pocket billiards balls, usually made of plastic, are 2¼ in in diameter. Carom billiards balls are still ivory, for championship play, and are 2²⁵⁄₆₄ in in diameter.

Rules in General. These rules generally apply to all billiards games: The shooter must have at least one foot on the floor when stroking the cue ball; must not disturb any of the balls in any way, except by stroking the cue ball; must keep on shooting, losing the turn on the first

miss. A foul is penalized by loss of turn and, usually, forfeiture of 1 point.

Pocket Billiards. In the United States, pocket billiards is usually called "pool," and the word "billiards," used alone, means one of the carom games, usually three-cushion. The basic object of pocket billiards is to knock object balls into pockets by action of the cue ball.

The championship game is called 14.1, or "straight" pool. The 15 object balls are racked in a pyramid, with its apex at the spot at one end of the table. The break shot must be made from behind an imaginary line through the spot at the other end.

On the opening break, a player must either pocket a called ball or send two or more object balls into a cushion. Failure to accomplish either of these goals means a penalty of 2 points; the opponent may then accept the balls just as they are or require the starting player to take another break shot.

Throughout the game, on each turn, a player must call a ball and the pocket it is intended for; failure to make the called ball in the called pocket results in loss of turn. The player is not penalized for failing to hit the designated object ball, provided that the cue ball hits a different object ball and that either the object ball or the cue ball then hits a cushion. If the player fails to accomplish one of these alternatives, it is a "table scratch," and calls for a penalty of 1 point; table scratches on three consecutive turns call for an additional penalty of 15 points, or a total penalty of 18 points, and the balls are reracked, with the penalized player making the break shot. It is a "scratch" if at any time the cue ball goes into a pocket. The penalty is 1 point and loss of turn; if the player pocketed a ball on the shot, the ball is brought back up and spotted.

A player who doesn't feel able to make a shot may call a "safe," or "safety shot." The cue ball must hit an object ball, and either the cue ball or the object ball must then hit the rail.

The game is called 14.1 because after 14 balls have been sunk, the fifteenth ball is left in place on the table, as is the cue ball, for the break shot on the next rack, with the player who sank the fourteenth ball continuing to play. A game between good players is often characterized by a succession of safe shots, because neither player wants to break the balls out until there is a shot that is easy to make.

Game is 150 points in major matches.

Eight ball is probably the most popular of the pool games. The balls are racked and broken as in 14.1, with the 8 ball in the middle of the rack. The first player to pocket a ball has a choice of shooting low balls (1–7) or high balls (9–15) for the rest of the game. After making all seven balls, a player shoots the 8 ball. The one who sinks the 8 ball wins. However, if a player pockets the 8 ball before sinking the other balls, that player loses.

The phrase "behind the 8 ball" is based on the fact that, in the game, it is a foul (sometimes even a scratch or an automatic loss) if the cue ball hits the 8 ball before hitting any other object ball.

There are many local variations in the rules. Generally, a player who sinks the 8 ball on the break wins the game. A player may or may not have to call the shots, depending on the caliber of the competition. Under some house or local rules, the 8 ball has to be made off one bank or more, or has to be sunk in the same pocket in which a player pocketed the seventh ball. (It's wise to find out about these rules before getting involved in a game.) The rules pertaining to scratches are the same as in 14.1—except that, on the very popular coin-operated pool tables, it is impossible to bring a ball back up after a scratch, so the player receives credit for it.

There are two versions of rotation pool. In this game, the balls are racked with the 1 ball at the front point of the triangle, the 2 ball and 3 ball at the back corners. The cue ball must first strike the lowest-numbered ball on the table; if it does, the player gets credit for all balls pocketed on the shot. If, however, the player fails to hit the lowest-numbered ball, any balls sunk are brought up and spotted. (In some versions of the game, this is treated as a scratch.) Generally a player gets credit on a rack for the

values of the balls sunk. Since the total value of the whole rack, 1 through 15, is 120 points, 61 points is game. In some versions, the player who sinks the most balls wins.

Line-up pool is very similar to 14.1, except for the reracking position. After a player finishes a turn, all the balls sunk are spotted on the "long string," a line running from the back cushion through the foot spot. Game is usually 50, 100, or 150 points.

There are many other versions of pocket billiards— Kelly pool, 9 ball, and 15 ball, for example—but the specific rules vary so much from place to place that general descriptions aren't of much value.

Snooker. Though essentially a pocket billiards game, snooker is quite different from those listed above. It has its own special table, and it's played with 22 balls, each $2\frac{1}{8}$ in in diameter. All pockets are 4 in in diameter. There are fifteen red object balls, a cue ball, and six colored object balls, numbered from 2 through 7.

The red object balls are racked as in pocket billiards, and the other object balls are placed on their own designated spots. The cue ball is put in play from within a semicircle behind the end string. A player must first make a red ball and then one of the numbered balls. The numbered balls are respotted until all the red balls have been sunk; then the numbered balls stay down. The player with the highest number of points after all balls are off the table is the winner. A foul in American snooker calls for a forfeiture of 7 points.

Carom Billiards. The carom billiards game are played on pocketless tables, and the object is to score "caroms" or "billiards" involving all the balls on the table. The most widely played version today is three-cushion, in which there are two object balls and one cue ball. The cue ball has to strike three rails before it strikes the second object ball. The first object ball may be struck first, or a player may hit one or more cushions with the cue ball before hitting the first object ball—but the cue ball must always hit three or more cushions before touching the second object ball. A point is scored for each successful shot. Game is usually 50 points.

There are similar one-cushion and two-cushion games, but they are obsolete. Straight-rail billiards is the one-cushion game. This is essentially the game rendered obsolete by experts with their "rail-nursing." To prevent rail-nursing, the balkline billiards games were invented. All versions have essentially the same rules. Balklines are drawn a certain distance from each cushion, and "anchors," 7-in squares, are drawn where the balklines meet the cushions. Except for the center rectangle, each rectangle formed by the balklines is a "balk area."

Each balkline game is identified by a number. In 18.2 balkline, the balklines are drawn 18 in from the cushions; and when two object balls are in the same balk area, the player is allowed to score only 2 points in that area. After scoring the second point, the player must drive one of the object balls out of the balk area. If it hits a cushion and returns to the same balk area, the player can continue.

In 14.1 balkline, the balklines are drawn 14 in from the cushion, and a player is allowed only 1 point when both balls are in the same balk area.

Other forms of the game are 14.2, 18.1, and 28.2.

Techniques. Two essentials to billiards skill are a good "bridge" and a smooth, level stroke. The bridge is formed by the left hand (for a right-handed player). The simplest way for a novice to form a bridge is to make a fist with the left hand and place it on the table, thumb up. The stick is then placed under the forefinger, which is looped around it, with the thumb acting as a support behind and underneath. The other three fingers are then spread out to form a tripod base. The right hand grips the butt of the cue, 3 or 4 in behind the stick's balancing point. The stick is actually cradled in the fingers of the right hand—the palm shouldn't touch the stick.

The player takes a stance with feet set fairly wide apart for a firm base and approximately at right angles to the direction of the shot. Knees are slightly bent. Leaning forward from the hips and keeping the weight evenly distributed on both feet, the player forms the bridge, with head directly over the cue so as to be able to sight down it.

On the backswing, the right hand should come back as far as it can; then it moves forward to stroke the cue ball. The follow-through should carry the cue tip 3 or 4 in beyond the point of impact. The key to a smooth stroke is that there should be very little shoulder action; the right arm should be close to the body and should move like a pendulum.

In pocket billiards, a player determines the point of aim by drawing an imaginary line from the center of the pocket through the center of the object ball. This line intersects the object ball at a point on the surface nearest the billiard player; it is that point which the cue ball should hit.

English and Banks. The key to good play is "shape"— the position in which a player leaves the cue ball after making a successful shot. A player may be an excellent shot, but unless the cue ball is left in good position for the next shot, it will be difficult to run many balls.

Good shape can often be achieved without English, through knowledge of the banks and control of the cue ball's speed. There are three important principles to remember: (1) If hit dead center, the cue ball, after hitting the object ball, will travel at a right angle to the path of the object ball. (2) If the cue ball hits the object ball almost straight on, it will lose a good deal of speed; if it hits at a sharper angle, it will lose less speed. (3) When the cue ball hits a rail, it behaves like light hitting a mirror—the angle of incidence equals the angle of reflection. That is, if the cue ball hits the rail at a 45-degree angle, it will come off the rail at a 45-degree angle in the other direction.

There are times when a player needs to use English in order to get a desired shape—or, more often, to avoid scratching. The novice trying to use English usually makes a number of mistakes—using too much English, which can often result in miscues. Or, in trying to use top or bottom English, the novice fails to keep the cue moving parallel to the table top. Side English—achieved by hitting the cue ball right or left of center—causes several complications. If right English is applied to the cue ball, it will make the cue ball curve slightly to the left, and it will apply left English to the object ball, making it curve slightly to the right. This is the reason why a player determined to get good shape through side English will frequently miss a shot.

Generally, if English is necessary to get good shape, top or bottom English will do the trick. Top English, or "follow," gives the cue ball a tendency to follow the object ball. Instead of traveling at a right angle to the path of the object ball, it will travel, say, at an 80-degree angle, or a 70-degree angle, depending on the amount of English used. Bottom English, or "draw," has the opposite effect—the cue ball will travel at a 100- or 110-degree angle to the path of the object ball.

With an absolutely straight shot, follow will cause the cue ball to follow the object ball toward the pocket. Draw will pull the cue ball straight back, traveling in the direction opposite to that of the object ball. A player who wants to stop the cue ball dead at the point of impact with a straight shot has to violate one of our basic principles: hit the cue ball dead center, but with *no* follow-through.

A beginning player will have to spend some time learning the banks and how a ball behaves traveling around the banks. Banks will vary from one table to another—on a much-used table, they will probably be dead, and bounces will not be true. On a very new table, they are apt to be very lively.

Organizations. Billiards in the United States is basically supervised by the Billiard Congress of America. Three-cushion billiards, which had declined severely in the 1950s, has been revived somewhat in recent years by the World Union of Billiards, which was organized in 1966. The WUB now conducts an annual world three-cushion championship. The Billiards Federation of the United States is affiliated with the WUB and conducts an annual three-cushion championship to select an American entrant for the world tournament.

World Pocket Billiard Champions

(The list that follows was developed through exhaustive research by Clement F. Trainer, of Philadelphia. It differs somewhat from the list maintained by the Billiard Congress of America. Frequently, two or more champions are listed for the same year. This is because, in the early days, a billiards champion was like a boxing champion, holding the title until beaten by a challenger. It was possible for the championship to change hands several times in a year. The player who did not successfully defend the title at least once during a year, or went the entire year without being challenged, was not listed as champion for that year. For example, Albert Frey held the title for part of 1884, but in his first defense that year lost it to J. L. Malone. Frey is not listed as champion in 1884; Malone is. From 1940 through 1953, the champion was chosen in several different ways: in league competition, in sanctioned tournament play, and in the old method of a challenge match. L = League; T = Tournament; M = Match; * indicates title won by forfeit.)

1878–80	Cyrille Dion
	Samuel F. Knight
	Alonzo Morris
	Gottlieb Wahlstrom
	Samuel F. Knight
1881	Gottlieb Wahlstrom
1882–83	Albert Frey
1884–85	J. L. Malone
1886	Albert Frey
1887	J. L. Malone*
	Alfredo DeOro
1888	Alfredo DeOro
	Albert Frey
	Frank Powers
1889	Albert Frey
	Alfredo DeOro

1890	Frank Powers
	H. Manning
1891	Frank Powers*
	Alfredo DeOro
1892–94	Alfredo DeOro
1895	William Clearwater
	Alfredo DeOro
1896	Frank Stewart
1897	Grant Eby
	Jerome Keogh
1898	William Clearwater
	Jerome Keogh
1899–1900	Alfredo DeOro
1901	Frank Sherman
	Alfredo DeOro
1902	William Clearwater
	Grant Eby
1903	Grant Eby
1904	Alfredo DeOro
1905	Jerome Keogh*
	Alfredo DeOro
	Thomas Hueston*
1906	John Horgan
	Jerome Keogh*
	Thomas Hueston
1907	Thomas Hueston
1908	Frank Sherman
	Alfredo DeOro
	Thomas Hueston
1909	Charles Weston
	John Kling
	Thomas Hueston
1910	Jerome Keogh
	Alfredo DeOro
1911	Alfredo DeOro
1912	Edward Ralph
	Alfredo DeOro
1913–15	Benjamin Allen
1916	Emmet Blankenship
1917–18	Frank Taberski
1919–24	Ralph Greenleaf
1925	Frank Taberski
1926	Ralph Greenleaf
1927	Erwin Rudolph
	Thomas Hueston
	Frank Taberski*
1928	Ralph Greenleaf
	Frank Taberski
1929	Ralph Greenleaf
1930	Erwin Rudolph
1931–32	Ralph Greenleaf
1933	Erwin Rudolph
1934	Andrew Ponzi
1935–36	James Caras
1937	Ralph Greenleaf
1938–39	James Caras
1940	Andrew Ponzi (L)
1941	Willie Mosconi (L)
	Erwin Rudolph (T)
1942	Irving Crane (M)
	Willie Mosconi (T)
1943	Andrew Ponzi (M)
1944–45	Willie Mosconi
1946	Irving Crane (T)
1947–48	Willie Mosconi
1949	James Caras
1950–54	Willie Mosconi
1955	Irving Crane
	Willie Mosconi
1956–57	Willie Mosconi

(There have been no geniune World Championship matches or tournaments since 1957.)

U.S. Open (Pocket Billiards)

Men

1966	Irving Crane
1967	James Caras
1968	Joe Balsis
1969	Luther Lassiter
1970	Steve Mizerak
1971	Steve Mizerak
1972	Steve Mizerak
1973	Steve Mizerak
1974	Joe Balsis
1975	Dallas West
1976	Tom Jennings

Women

1967	Dorothy Wise
1968	Dorothy Wise
1969	Dorothy Wise
1970	Dorothy Wise
1971	Dorothy Wise
1972	Jean Balukas
1973	Jean Balukas
1974	Jean Balukas
1975	Jean Balukas
1976	Jean Balukas

Billiard Congress of America Hall of Fame

Welker Cochran—Won world professional 18.2 balkline championships in 1927 and 1934, three-cushion championships in 1933, 1935, 1936, 1937, and 1944–1946.

Alfredo DeOro—A Spanish diplomat, DeOro won the world pocket billiards championship 16 times from 1887 through 1912, and was three-cushion champion 10 times from 1908 through 1919.

Ralph Greenleaf—Considered by many the greatest pocket billiards player of all time, Greenleaf won the world championship 12 times between 1919 and 1937 and was also a great trick-shot artist on the vaudeville circuit.

William F. Hoppe—Won his first world title in 1906, when he was eighteen, beating Maurice Vignaux for the 18.1 balkline championship. He also held the 18.2 championship in 1908, 1910–1920, 1922–1924, and 1927, and was three-cushion champion in 1936, 1940–1943, and 1947–1952. He holds most of the all-time three-cushion records.

John W. Hyatt—Hyatt founded the American plastics industry in 1868 by inventing a celluloid billiard ball, to win a $10,000 prize offered by a billiards firm for an ivory substitute.

Willie Mosconi—If Greenleaf wasn't the greatest pocket billiards player in history, Mosconi certainly was. He won 15 world championships between 1940 and 1957, and once had an incredible run of 526 balls in an exhibition.

Benjamin B. Nartzik—Owner of the National Billiard Chalk Company, Nartzik did a great deal to revive interest in billiards in the late 1950s.

Charles C. Peterson—A fine competitive player until injured seriously in an auto accident, Peterson became known as "the missionary of billiards" for his trick-shot exhibitions that stirred interest in the sport among servicemen and college students.

Herman J. Rambow—Rambow perfected the jointed cue, which can be broken into two pieces for easy carrying. His custom-made cues, "Rambow Specials," were world-famous for their perfect balance, and were used by most of the top players of this century.

Jake Schaefer, Sr.—"The Wizard" was responsible for the development of balkline billiards because he was virtually unbeatable at earlier versions of the game. He was 18.1 balkline champion in 1898, 1901–1902, and 1907.

Jake Schaefer, Jr.—Taking over where his father left off, young Jake was 18.1 champion in 1926, 1927, and 1938, and 18.2 champion in 1921, 1925, 1926, 1927, and 1929–1933.

Harold Worst—Worst was the youngest player to win the world three-cushion title when, at twenty-four, he won it in 1954. The sport went into eclipse after that year, but he was generally considered world three-cushion champion for long after 1954.

Bibliography. *Official Rules and Record Book,* Billiard Congress of America, Chicago, 1974.

BLACK ATHLETES—One of the sad ironies of American sports is that the first athletes from the United States to win any measure of international success were blacks, long before sports had assumed much importance in our society. Once sports did become important, blacks were more or less systematically barred from full recognition in almost every sport.

The first two great black athletes were boxers, who presented a study in contrasts. Tom Molineaux was a slave who allegedly was given his freedom because of his fighting ability—possibly for winning his master a large amount of money in a bout against a slave from another plantation. Bill Richmond, on the other hand, was a free native of Staten Island, New York, who became the servant of a British general during the Revolutionary War. Richmond won a series of matches against British soldiers, and then returned with the general, Lord Percy, to England in 1777 to become a professional boxer. He fought the British heavyweight champion, Tom Cribb, in 1805, but lost on a knockout. He continued fighting until he was 52 and never lost again. He also never got another match for the championship.

Molineaux, having been given his freedom, also set out for England, and in 1810, he fought Cribb for the title. He was knocked out in the thirty-third round and, in a rematch, had his jaw broken in the tenth round and suffered a knockout in the eleventh.

Most outstanding jockeys during the nineteenth century were also blacks, undoubtedly because the job was a kind of extension of their duties. Isaac Murphy was the first jockey to win three Kentucky Derbies, in 1884, 1890, and 1891. Oliver Lewis was the winning jockey in the first Kentucky Derby, in 1875. Jimmy Winkfield was the second jockey, after Murphy, to win consecutive Derbies, in 1901 and 1902.

In those early days, however, the jockey was not much noted by the average fan, and jockey fees were negligible, often running as low as $5 for a winning ride. One outstanding black jockey is known to us, from an 1884 book, only as the "celebrated Abe." When the Jockey Club was organized to license jockeys and a percentage scale of fees was set up around the turn of the century, the black jockey virtually disappeared from racing.

Boxing was somewhat kinder to the black, in some ways. As early as 1890, there was a black world champion, bantamweight George Dixon. Dixon went on to win the featherweight championship in 1891. Other early black champions were Joe Walcott, who became welterweight champion in 1901, and Joe Gans, who won the lightweight title in 1902.

The championship, however—the heavyweight title—was first won by a black, Jack Johnson, in 1908, and only after a long, determined pursuit of champion Tommy Burns. Johnson finally caught up with Burns in Sydney, Australia, and beat him in a fight that was stopped in the fourteenth round. The victory was a crushing defeat for many white persons, and the search for "the great white hope" began immediately. Finally, former champion James J. Jeffries agreed to come out of retirement to fight Johnson, but Johnson knocked him out in the fifteenth round of a 1910 fight.

After a hectic, harried reign (*see* BOXING for further details on Johnson's career), Johnson lost the title to Jess Willard in 1915. In the ensuing years, there were many legitimate black heavyweight contenders, but none could get a title fight. Among the fine black heavyweights before Joe Louis were Joe Jeannette, Sam McVey, and Sam Langford. Nevertheless, black champions did rise to the top in other weight divisions during the 1920s, among them Tiger Flowers, who became middleweight champion in 1926, and Panama Al Brown, who won the bantamweight title in 1929.

Finally, a black heavyweight emerged who simply had to be given a shot at the title. Joe Louis was just beating too many people too impressively to be ignored; and besides, the "Cinderella Man," James J. Braddock, wanted a good money fight before he retired, and he thought a fight with Louis would be a good draw. On June 22, 1937, Louis knocked out Braddock in the eighth round. Since then, there has been only one white heavyweight champion, Rocky Marciano.

Boxing has traditionally been a sport that offers upward mobility for the lower economic classes. Indeed, one can almost read the history of the progress of various ethnic groups by tracing the appearance and then gradual disappearance of distinctive ethnic names among boxing contenders. Once almost the sole province of the Irish, boxing gradually became the sport of various big city ghetto groups—the Italians, the Jews, the Poles, and, most recently, the Puerto Ricans. It is not surprising that it was in boxing that the American black first made his way in sports; and that, despite the problems of Jack Johnson and many others, this athletic door was much easier for the black to open than most other doors. In most other sports, it has been quite different, and although it is impossible to offer detailed sociological analyses of the problems involved in this or that sport, it might be possible to offer some hints.

Football

One of the mysteries of pro football is the sudden disappearance of the black player from team rosters between 1933 and 1946. There have always been a certain number of blacks from families wealthy enough to send their children to college, and some of these children were good football players. Several of them played professional football during the early years of the sport.

The first black All-American was John Henry Lewis, a Harvard center, named to the fourth All-American team, chosen by Casper Whitney in 1892 and reselected in 1893.

Arthur Ashe was the first black male to win the U.S. national singles title, in 1968, and the Wimbledon (All-England) singles, in 1975. (*U.S. Lawn Tennis Association.*)

Lewis later became line coach at Harvard, probably the first black assistant coach in the history of football. Other early black All-Americans were Fritz Pollard, Brown (1916); Paul Robeson, Rutgers (1917–1918), and Duke Slater, Iowa (1921). All three of them played pro football, with a handful of other blacks. (The first black in pro football was Hank McDonald, who played for the Rochester Jeffersons before the National Football League was organized.)

The disappearance of blacks from pro football has been explained by George Halas, among others, as caused by the Depression, which kept most blacks from going to college. That may be true; but one may also suggest that professional football was just beginning to win real spectator interest and nationwide attention during the 1930s—and perhaps owners felt that black players would hurt the sport's image. Whatever the truth, blacks did disappear from the sport until 1946. And when they returned, it was with surprisingly little notice. There was nothing like the controversy that swirled around Jackie Robinson's debut in major-league baseball.

Paul Brown, founder and long-time coach of the Cleveland Browns, has been given credit for many innovations in pro football, but he hasn't received much credit for reintroducing blacks into the game. Brown was one of the key figures in the establishment of the All-American Football Conference, the first real challenge to the NFL. Almost as soon as World War II ended, Brown began signing players for his franchise in the new league; among them were Bill Willis, a guard from Ohio State, and Marion Motley, a fullback from Nevada. Ironically, the old Cleveland franchise in the NFL, the Rams, moved

to Los Angeles in 1946. They decided to go after some local talent to bolster spectator appeal, and among the rookies they signed were two UCLA blacks, halfback Kenny Washington and end Woody Strode. And suddenly the NFL had become reintegrated.

Football and other sports have been greatly praised for helping blacks achieve higher status in our society, and they unquestionably deserve some credit. In recent years, however, many blacks have begun to criticize sports for racism and for exploitations of blacks. Both college and professional football, especially, have been criticized for racial stereotyping by position—allowing blacks to play the defensive line, the outside linebacker positions, the defensive backfield, and "speed" positions, such as running back and wide receiver, while allowing relatively few at such positions as quarterback, the offensive line, and middle linebacker. Another criticism has been that blacks have to be relatively a good deal better than their white counterparts to make a team; that a black is much less likely to win a second-string job than a white. And college football has been criticized for exploiting blacks by giving them scholarships to play football but then quite callously shunting them aside without helping them get degrees if they fail to make the grade on the field or if they suffer injuries.

An important factor in the increasing number of blacks in pro football has been the rise of the predominantly black football college. Fifteen years or so ago, few people had heard of such schools as Grambling, Morgan State, Florida A&M, or Tennessee A&I. Now the average pro football fan knows these schools because so many of their alumni are playing pro ball.

Baseball

There is no great mystery about the long absence of blacks from major-league baseball, because there is no doubt that, until 1947, team owners and general managers simply refused to sign them. There are different accounts of how this systematic discrimination began, however. As early as 1867, the National Association of Base Ball Players voted to exclude teams with black players. The NABBP was succeeded by the National Association of Professional Base Ball Players in 1871; this group had no formal ban against blacks, but there was a gentlemen's agreement among team managers to exclude them. However, some blacks did manage to play professional baseball side by side with whites during the 1880s. The first, apparently, was John W. "Bud" Fowler, who played on an otherwise all-white team in 1872. He played in the Northwestern League in 1884 and in the Western League in 1885.

The first black major-league player was Moses Fleetwood Walker. He played with Toledo in the Northwestern League in 1883, and when the club joined the major-league American Association in 1884, he went with it. Walker suffered an injury late in the season and was released, but his younger brother, Weldy, then joined the team. Other early black professionals were George W. Stovey, a pitcher, and Frank Grant, an infielder, both of whom played in the Eastern League in 1886. By 1887, there were as many as 20 blacks playing at various levels of professional baseball. That year, however, the International League decided not to approve any contracts with black players. By 1892, there were no black players in organized baseball.

By 1900, baseball was following the "separate" but supposedly "equal" path of many social institutions. There were five "colored" teams by that year. There were numerous attempts to organize black leagues—one of them, the International League of Independent Professional Base Ball Clubs, which lasted the full season of 1906, included two all-white teams and four all-black teams—but the first real success didn't arrive until 1920, when the National Negro Baseball League was formed by Andrew "Rube" Foster, manager of the Chicago American Giants. The league had eight teams. The NNL lasted through the 1931 season; the absence of Foster, who had become ill in 1927, and the economic hardships of the Depression killed it. In 1933, W. A. "Gus" Greenlee of Pittsburgh organized another Negro National League, which was to last until 1948 despite many internal difficulties—most of them similar to the difficulties experienced by the white major leagues until a single commissioner was appointed to run the game, although, so far as is known, there were no gambling scandals in the black league.

During the 1930s, many black players from the United States also played baseball in Mexico, Cuba, the Dominican Republic, and other Latin-American countries. They could not only get better pay in those countries, but they were treated as equals, not as second-class citizens.

However, Negro baseball in this country did relatively well during the 1940s. The Negro American League was formed in 1937, and from 1942 through 1948, the leagues held an annual Black World Series.

By the end of World War II, many blacks were growing tired of their "separate-but-equal" status—because, while "separate" meant "separate," "equal" did not mean "equal." One of them was sportswriter Wendell Smith, of the *Pittsburgh Courier*, the largest black weekly newspaper in the country. In 1939, Smith systematically interviewed white players and managers with National League teams when they visited Pittsburgh and discovered that about 75 percent of them were in favor of having black players in the major leagues. Wendell's columns favoring integration of major-league baseball struck a responsive chord with several white sportswriters in major cities.

In 1945, the major leagues were feeling some pressure. The Yankees' home opener against the Red Sox was picketed by blacks. Larry MacPhail of the Yankees and Branch Rickey of the Dodgers were appointed by organized baseball to study the problem. As early as 1942, Rickey had decided to integrate the Dodgers. He kept his plans secret, however, and announced that he was forming a new black league to explain his active scouting of black players. By August of that year, he had picked the player to break the color barrier: Jackie Robinson, a shortstop for the Kansas City Monarchs.

Interestingly, at UCLA Robinson had been a football teammate of Kenny Washington and Woody Strode, the first blacks to play in the NFL since 1931. After a long conference, during which Rickey told him he would have to have the guts, initially, not to fight back at Negro-baiters, Robinson agreed. In October, he signed a contract with the Montreal Royals, the Dodger farm club in the International League.

Robinson responded by leading the league in hitting and runs scored, and in 1947, he started the National League season at first base for the Dodgers. An incipient mutiny among some Southerners on the Dodgers was quelled by Rickey; at least two clubs threatened to strike if Robinson played against them, but they backed down; Robinson had to contend with some vicious bench-jockeying from opponents and hate letters from "fans." He hit .295, stole 29 bases, scored 125 runs, and was named the National League Rookie of the Year.

The door was open. In July of 1947, Larry Doby joined the Cleveland Indians as the first black in the American League. By 1957, there were 36 black players in the major leagues, and all but two teams were integrated. Another barrier was broken in 1971, when the legendary Satchel Paige was admitted to the Baseball Hall of Fame at Cooperstown, New York. Paige was not the first black admitted—Robinson and Roy Campanella had preceded him—but he was the first chosen primarily for his play in the black leagues, under a new policy. At first, the plans had been to enshrine these black players in a special wing of the building, but the Baseball Writers' Association insisted that they be admitted through the "front door." Since Paige's induction, the Hall of Fame's special Committee on Negro Baseball Leagues has also chosen Josh Gibson, Buck Leonard, Monte Irvin, and James "Cool Papa" Bell. The last barrier went down in 1974, after years of controversy over whether there would ever be a black manager in the majors. At the end of the season, the Cleveland Indians signed Frank Robinson as their manager for the 1975 season.

Why baseball's systematic banning of black players, even during years when they were admitted to professional football? Much of the answer must lie in baseball's origins in small rural towns in the farm areas of the Midwest and the South, where racial prejudice was rampant. And among baseball owners, there was an expressed belief in the inferiority of the black—as a baseball player, at least. This may have been a mere public relations ploy to justify discrimination, for whatever reasons. But some owners, and some players, were apparently convinced, before Jackie Robinson made his appearance, that black players just weren't good enough for the major leagues.

On the other side, Rickey and others who eventually signed black players were not acting from sheer altruism—although Rickey was, unquestionably, a humanitarian who disliked racial discrimination. Rickey was also in command of a team that had been good but was growing old, and he certainly realized that, by being the first team to tap the black talent pool, the Dodgers would gain in the standings. The Dodgers, with black players like Robinson, Campanella, Junior Gilliam, Don Newcombe, and relief pitcher Joe Black, won pennants in 1949, 1952–1953, and 1955–1956.

Since 1948, the National League has had 18 black Most Valuable Players, the American League 6; the National League has had 13 black Rookies of the Year, the American League 5. Blacks have won 24 batting championships, 23 home run championships, and 21 RBI championships in both leagues. And one of the greatest black milestones was reached in 1974, when Henry Aaron of the Atlanta Braves broke Babe Ruth's legendary record for most home runs in a career.

Basketball

Basketball is a kind of schizophrenic sport. Almost since the beginning, it has had its greatest popularity in two completely different settings: big-city ghettos, where there was not enough land for organized baseball and football games; and rural areas, where there was so much land that it was difficult to get enough players together for the sports that required bigger teams, and where small high schools and colleges found it much easier to assemble a basketball squad of a dozen players or so than to put together a football squad of 20 or 30 or more.

The prototypical basketball player, then, begins as a child of the ghetto, who learns basketball skills in pickup games at the local Y or on the local asphalt playground, or as a lonely country child spending leisure hours throwing the ball at a hoop set up just below the hayloft of a barn.

As with boxing, basketball can tell us something about the progress of ethnic groups. During the early years, many of the outstanding players were Jews and Italians from New York, Philadelphia, or Pittsburgh, and many of the outstanding basketball colleges were in the big cities. On the other hand, colleges like Purdue, Indiana, Wisconsin, and Kansas were also developing strong teams, built around—in those days—country boys.

Pro basketball was very slow to develop on an organized basis. But one of the first great teams—a team admitted en masse to the Basketball Hall of Fame in Springfield, Massachusetts—was formed in Harlem. The owner was also the owner of the Renaissance Casino in Harlem, and his team was called the Renaissance. They quickly became known as the Rens. They were barnstormers who, between 1922 and 1936, played all comers. During the 1932–1936 period, they won 473 games and lost only 49; in the 1933–1934 season, they won 127 and lost 7. Among the stars of the club were Clarence "Fat" Jenkins and Bill Yancey, both of whom were also outstanding baseball players in the Negro leagues.

A similar team was organized in Chicago in 1926 by a promoter named Abe Saperstein. He called them the Harlem Globetrotters—"Harlem" to indicate the players were all black, "Globetrotters" because Saperstein wanted to give the impression that the team did travel all over the world. Since 1926, they have, visiting more than 90 countries and playing before millions of spectators. In recent years, with the arrival of blacks in organized professional basketball, the Globetrotters have been often criticized for their show-boating tactics and for "Uncle Tomism." There is no question, though, that the team did at one time allow many black players to make a living from sport that was denied them elsewhere.

The National Basketball Association was not formally organized until 1949, with the merger of the young Basketball Association of America and the older National Basketball League. Black players entered the league in 1950, when Nat "Sweetwater" Clifton left the Globetrotters to join the New York Knicks and Chuck Cooper came out of Duquesne to play for the Boston Celtics. From there the progress has been steady. About 60 percent of the NBA players are black; the sport was the first to have a black professional coach, Bill Russell of the Celtics, and there are now five black coaches in the league. Wayne Embry of the Milwaukee Bucks is the first black general manager of a professional sports team, and the NBA has a black deputy commissioner, Simon Gourdine, who seems likely to become the first black commissioner in pro sports.

Track and Field

Track offered black athletes their first real chance at national prominence, for several reasons. First, in its essentials, track is a lonely sport, which requires individual dedication much more than experienced coaching, in most events. Second, it has always been, basically, an amateur sport, with little need to worry about the possibility of suffering at the box office through a white boycott of black athletes. Third, it is decentralized sport, without a ruling clique that could agree on and enforce a ban against the black athlete.

Blacks especially made their early marks in the speed events—sprints, high hurdles, long jump, and high jump. George C. Poage was the first black to compete in the Olympic Games, finishing second in the 400-m hurdles in 1904. Other early black track stars were William DeHart Hubbard, Olympic broad jump champion in 1924, and also a fine sprinter; Howard P. Drew, AAU 100-yd champion in 1912–1913, 220-yd champion in 1913; Edward O. Gourdin, who was Silver Medalist in the 1924 Olympic long jump; Eddie Tolan, who won the 100- and 200-m dashes in the 1932 Olympics; and Ralph Metcalfe, three times the AAU 100-yd and five times the 220-yd champion.

But one of the most fabled track and field athletes of all time was Jesse Owens, who performed incredible feats in the mid-thirties. On one memorable afternoon—May 25, 1935—Owens established five world records and equaled another. It was the NCAA outdoor track and field meet. The Ohio State youngster set records for the long jump, the 220-yd dash, and the 220-yd hurdles. His dash and hurdle times, clocked over 200 m, also set records at that distance. And he matched the world record of 9.4 sec in the 100-yd dash.

An even greater succession of moments was to come, in the 1936 Olympics, in Nazi Germany. The United States had 10 blacks on its track and field team for the games. Owens won both dashes and the long jump, tying the 100-m record, twice breaking the 200-m record, and establishing a long jump record that was to stand for 25 years. Two blacks, Cornelius Johnson and Dave Albritton, finished 1-2 in the high jump, and Johnson set an Olympic record. Archie Williams won the 400-m, John Woodruff the 800-m. And Owens and Metcalfe—who had finished second in the 100—won gold medals on the U.S. 400-m relay team, which also set a world record.

Since then, there have been so many black track and field stars that it would be impossible to mention all of them, or even touch on their accomplishments. One of the more interesting developments, though, has come in the longer-distance runs. Not very long ago, there were those who said that, while Negroes might be blessed with speed, they would never produce great runners at the longer distances. That myth was smashed in the 1968 Olympics, but not by United States representatives. African blacks did it. Kipchoge Keino of Kenya won the 1,500-m run, Mohammed Gammoudi of Tunisia won the 5,000-m, Naftali Temu of Kenya won the 10,000-m, Amos Biwott of Kenya won the 3,000-m steeplechase, and Mamo Wolde of Ethiopia won the marathon. (They were, of course, aided by the fact that they come from high-altitude countries and were more accustomed to the Mex-

Bill Russell, the first black to be elected to the National Basketball Hall of Fame, was a two-time All-American at the University of San Francisco, College Player of the Year in 1956, a five-time most valuable player in the NBA, and the first black coach in the NBA. (*Basketball Hall of Fame.*)

ico City atmosphere than the athletes from most other countries.)

There have not been many outstanding black distance runners for basically the same reasons that there have been practically no outstanding black swimmers: Such intensive training is demanded, with the assistance of a good coach, that this form of the sport requires an enormous amount of leisure time. And the relatively small rewards involved for such an investment of hard-to-get time has not made distance running a very attractive pastime for blacks.

The "Social" Sports

In many other sports, outstanding black athletes have been scarce, not because of discrimination within the sport itself but because the sport's social milieu has been discriminatory.

Tennis and golf, for example, for a long time were basically country club sports, and not many blacks belonged to country clubs. Black golfers did, for a time, have their own professional golf tour, but most of those golfers had learned their trade as caddies—as did many white golfers from poor families. The golf cart has virtually eliminated the caddie on most courses, and so golf may be the last white bastion among the sports, since there aren't many black country clubs.

Tennis courts have for a long time been available on public playgrounds, but the sport requires considerable

individual instruction to produce top players, and the instruction has not been easily available except to those who could pay for it. For many years, blacks were not allowed to play in U.S. Lawn Tennis Association tournaments, so they formed their own organization.

The two top black tennis players, Althea Gibson and Arthur Ashe, were both students of Dr. R. Walter Johnson, a Lynchburg, Virginia, physician who spent a great deal of time and money working with young black players. Dr. Johnson would bring promising youngsters into his home, treat them as his own children, and give them intensive training in tennis.

Miss Gibson was the first black woman to play in major tournaments, in 1950, and in 1957 and 1958 she won both the Wimbledon and U.S. National championships. Ashe was the first black to play for the U.S. Davis Cup team, in 1964. In 1968 he won the first U.S. Open tennis championship. After going several years without a major title, Ashe in 1975 became the first black to win the men's singles championship at Wimbledon. In that year, he also won the $50,000 first prize in the World Championship of Tennis tournament.

Other social sports are billiards, bowling, fencing, boating, swimming, and skating—all requiring a certain mix of leisure time, discretionary income, and access to special facilities. Blacks have only recently begun to appear in the upper echelons of the first three sports—notably Cicero Murphy in billiards, Al Pujol in professional bowling, and Uriah Jones and Tyrone Simmons in fencing. Blacks have yet to appear as champions or potential champions in the others.

Black Power

The Black Power movement of the late 1960s reached into sports in 1968, under the leadership of Harry Edwards, who had once been an outstanding track and field man at San Jose State. Edwards, a teacher of anthropology and sociology, called for black athletes to boycott the 1968 Olympic Games. He insisted that blacks should not compete for a country that didn't grant them equal rights. He also pointed to many examples of the exploitation of blacks in sports, and called for the return of the heavyweight championship to Cassius Clay (Muhammad Ali).

The black boycott did not come off—partly because the International Olympic Committee decided not to readmit South Africa to the Games, as had previously been planned. However, two of Edwards' followers, John Carlos and Tommie Smith, staged a Black Power demonstration on the victory podium in Mexico City. Smith had won the 200-m dash and Carlos had finished third. On the podium, Smith wore a black glove on his right hand, Carlos a black glove on his left hand, and when the national anthem was played, they raised their black-gloved fists in the Black Power salute and refused to look at the American flag. They were suspended from the team and expelled from the Olympic Village as a result of their demonstration.

A milder demonstration occurred after the 400-m run, in which American blacks finished 1–2–3. All three wore black berets on the podium, but took them off for the national anthem and the flag raising.

The 1972 Olympics brought another small demonstration. Vince Matthews and Wayne Collette, the first two finishers in the 400-m dash, appeared to show disrespect for the anthem and the flag while on the victory podium, and were barred from ever again competing in the Olympics, which prevented the United States from participating in the 1,600-m relay. Both athletes said later that they had intended no disrespect.

Black Athletes Hall of Fame

The Black Athletes Hall of Fame was the brainchild of Charlie Mays, a former Olympic high jumper. Established in early 1974, the hall doesn't yet have a permanent site. There were 29 members inducted in March of 1974, and 14 more in March of 1975.

Henry Aaron—Long almost overlooked despite an outstanding major-league career of more than 20 years, Aaron broke Babe Ruth's career home run record in 1974. He led the National League in hitting in 1956 and 1959; in home runs in 1957, 1963, 1966, and 1967; in RBIs in 1957, 1960, and 1963; and was most valuable player in 1957.

Muhammad Ali—Formerly Cassius Clay, Ali won the heavyweight championship in 1964. It was taken from him in 1967 after he refused to accept induction into the U.S. Army. In 1974, he won the title back with a knockout of George Foreman.

Henry Armstrong—The only man ever to hold three world championships simultaneously, Armstrong was featherweight champion 1937–1938, welterweight champion 1938–1940, and lightweight champion 1938–1939.

Hank Aaron broke Babe Ruth's "unbreakable" home run record by hitting the 715th of his career in 1974, and is certain to be elected to the Baseball Hall of Fame when he becomes eligible. (*Milwaukee Brewers.*)

Arthur Ashe—The first black to play Davis Cup tennis for the United States; U.S. Open and National singles champion 1968; Wimbledon singles champion 1975; WCT Champion 1975.

Elgin Baylor—An All-American basketball player at Seattle University in 1958, then a professional star for 14 seasons with the Minneapolis–Los Angeles Lakers. He averaged 27.4 points a game as a professional.

Jim Brown—The greatest rusher in National Football League history, Brown led the league in rushing eight times, gained 1,000 or more yd in a season seven times, gained 100 or more yd in 58 games, and had a record career total of 12,313 yd in nine seasons with the Cleveland Browns. He previously starred at Syracuse, where he was an All-American in 1956.

Roy Campanella—Also a member of the Baseball Hall of Fame, Campanella caught for the Brooklyn–Los Angeles Dodgers for 10 seasons before being paralyzed in an auto accident. He hit 242 home runs and drove in 856 runs. "Campy" was the National League's most valuable player in 1951, 1953, and 1955.

Roberto Clemente—A great all-around player for 18 seasons, Clemente was killed in a plane crash on December 31, 1972, while helping transport supplies to earthquake victims in Nicaragua. He had a lifetime batting average of .317, with 3,000 hits, 240 home runs, 1,305 RBIs. Writers elected him to the Baseball Hall of Fame in 1973, waiving the rule that a player isn't eligible until five years after his career ends.

Alice Coachman—She won the U.S. outdoor 50-m dash from 1943 through 1947; the 100-m dash in 1942, 1945, and 1946; the high jump from 1939 through 1948; the indoor 50-m dash in 1945 and 1946 and high jump in 1941, 1945, and 1946. She won the Olympic Gold Medal in the high jump in 1948.

Chuck Cooper—The first black to play in the National Basketball Association, Cooper starred at Duquesne, then played for the Boston Celtics 1950–1954, Milwaukee 1954–1955, and Fort Wayne 1955–1956.

Harrison Dillard—Winner of two Gold Medals in the Olympics, in the 100-m dash in 1948 and the 110-m hurdles in 1952, Dillard was the AAU high hurdle champion in 1946, 1947, and 1952, the low hurdle champion in 1946 and 1947, and the indoor 60-yd hurdle champion from 1947 through 1953 and in 1955.

Bob Douglas—Douglas organized the first all-black professional basketball team, the Harlem Renaissance Big Five, known as the Rens, in 1922. From 1932 through 1936, they won 473 and lost only 49. The entire team is in the Basketball Hall of Fame.

Joe Frazier—Olympic heavyweight champion in 1964, Frazier won the New York State title in 1968 and the world title in 1970. He lost the title to George Foreman in 1973.

Althea Gibson—The first black to play in a USLTA national tournament, in 1950, and U.S. National and Wimbledon singles champion in 1957 and 1958.

Josh Gibson—The "black Babe Ruth," Gibson was an outstanding catcher in the black major leagues from 1930 through 1946. He is credited with the longest home run ever hit in Yankee Stadium, a drive of an estimated 580 feet; he reportedly hit 278 home runs in one four-season period, and twice he hit over .400 for a season.

Edwin B. Henderson—Author of *The Negro in Sports* and

the first man to do intensive research into black sports history.

William DeHart Hubbard—Olympic broad jump champion in 1924, Hubbard was the AAU outdoor broad jump champion from 1922 through 1927 and triple jump champion in 1922 and 1923. Representing Michigan, he won the NCAA broad jump in 1923 and 1925, the 100-yd dash in 1925.

Monte Irvin—Irvin played 11 seasons in the black major leagues before joining the New York Giants as a thirty-year-old rookie in 1949. In seven seasons with the Giants and one with the Cubs, he hit .293; he led the National League in RBIs in 1951. Irvin is in the Baseball Hall of Fame.

Jack Johnson—The first black heavyweight champion, Johnson won the title in 1907 and held it until 1915. He was rated by Nat Fleischer of *Ring* magazine as the greatest fighter in history.

Rafer Johnson—AAU decathlon champion in 1956, 1958, and 1960, Johnson won the Olympic event in 1960 and the Pan-American event in 1955.

Morris Levitt—A scholar and historian, Levitt was a coauthor of *The Black Book*.

John Henry "Pop" Lloyd—Known as "the black Honus Wagner," Lloyd played primarily at shortstop in the Negro major leagues from 1906 through 1931. He was a big, powerful hitter, an exceptional fielder and a deceptively fast baserunner. Lloyd was a player-manager from 1918 through 1931.

Hank McDonald—The first black professional football player, McDonald was a left halfback for the Rochester, New York, Jeffersons before the National Football League was established.

Willie Mays—Considered by some the greatest baseball player of all time, and the only modern candidate for the title, Mays played for the New York–San Francisco Giants 1951–1971 and for the New York Mets 1972–1973. His 680 home runs is third behind Ruth and Aaron. Mays led the National League in home runs in 1955, 1962, 1964, and 1965 and was most valuable player in 1954 and 1965. He collected 3,283 hits, scored 2,062 runs, and stole more than 300 bases.

Ralph Metcalfe—Metcalfe was the AAU outdoor 100-m champion from 1932 through 1934; the 200-m champion from 1932 through 1936; and the indoor 60-m champion 1933, 1934, and 1936.

Jesse Owens—Best known for winning four Gold Medals and setting two world records in the 1936 Olympics, Owens turned in what might have been an even more memorable performance in the 1935 NCAA track meet, when he set five world records and tied another in a single afternoon.

Satchel Paige—A legend in his own time, Paige pitched in the Negro leagues for 25 years, then joined the Cleveland Indians as a forty-two-year-old rookie in 1948 to compile a 6-1 record and a 2.48 earned run average. He made his last major-league appearance in 1965, at the age of fifty-nine, to pitch three scoreless innings for the Kansas City Athletics. He is a member of the Baseball Hall of Fame.

Eulace Peacock—The AAU pentathlon champion from 1933 through 1935, in 1937, and from 1943 through 1945; Peacock also won the 100-m dash and the broad jump in 1935.

Pele—His real name is Edson Arantes do Nascimento; he is also known as the "Black Pearl," and he is the only soccer player ever to have scored more than 1,000 goals. At seventeen, he scored the winning goals in Brazil's 3-1 victory over Sweden in the 1958 World Cup finals. He also led Brazil to World Cup victories in 1962 and 1970.

Frederick "Fritz" Pollard—Also a member of the National Football Foundation Hall of Fame, Pollard was a star halfback with Brown University's 1916 Rose Bowl Team, and he was one of the first blacks to play in the National Football League, starting with the Akron Pros, in 1919.

Branch Rickey—By signing Jackie Robinson and then bringing him up to the Brooklyn Dodgers despite threatened strikes by a number of players, Rickey once and for all broke the color barrier in baseball.

"Sugar Ray" Robinson—Pound for pound, the greatest boxer ever, say most experts. He was world welterweight champion from 1946 to 1951 and world middleweight champion three times, 1951–1952, 1955–1957, and 1958–1960. Robinson, born Walker Smith, is also a member of the Boxing Hall of Fame.

Wilma Rudolph—Miss Rudolph won three Gold Medals in the 1960 Olympics, in the 100-m and 200-m dashes and as a member of the U.S. 400-m relay team. She was the AAU outdoor 100-m champion in 1959 and 1960, the 100-yd champion in 1961 and 1962, and the 200-m champion in 1960.

Bill Russell—The dominant figure in the Boston Celtics' basketball dynasty, Russell was the National Basketball Association's most valuable player in 1958, 1961–1963 and in 1965. As a player-coach, the first black coach in NBA history, he led the Celtics to the 1969 championship.

Abe Saperstein—Though little more than 5 ft tall, Saperstein loved basketball. He was turned down for a tryout at the University of Illinois, but he organized and managed his own team, the Harlem Globetrotters, who brought basketball to millions of spectators all over the world.

Gale Sayers—A two-year All-American halfback at Kansas, Sayers starred for the Chicago Bears from 1965 through 1971, gaining 4,956 yards and scoring 56 touchdowns. He led the National Football League in rushing in 1966 and 1969 and was its leading scorer in 1965, with a record 22 touchdowns.

Charlie Sifford—The first black to join the PGA tour, Sifford won his first tournament, the Long Beach Open, in 1957; his last tour victory, at the age of forty-six, was the 1969 Los Angeles Open.

Maurice Stokes—The National Basketball Association rookie of the year in 1956, Stokes was paralyzed in 1958 by an injury and was incapacitated until his death in 1970. In his brief career with the Rochester–Cincinnati Royals, he averaged 16.4 points a game and was one of the league's top rebounders.

Jack Twyman—Twyman was a fine player with the Rochester–Cincinnati Royals from 1955 through 1966, averaging 19.2 points a game, with a career high of 31.2 points a game in 1959–1960. But he is honored by the Black Athletes Hall of Fame because, after Maurice Stokes' injury, Twyman became his legal guardian. He worked to raise funds for Stokes' treatment, helped with his physical therapy, and offered him encouragement and friendship through his long hospitalization.

Willye White—Miss White was AAU outdoor long jump

champion in 1960, 1961, 1962, 1964–1966, 1969, 1970, and 1972 and indoor champion in 1962.

Joe Yancey—Yancey organized and coached the Pioneer Club of New York, a major power in track and field.

Claude "Buddy" Young—Also a member of the College and Professional Football Halls of Fame, Young was a halfback at Illinois in 1946, then played for the New York Yankees 1947–1949, the New York Yanks 1950–1951, the Dallas Texans 1952, and the Baltimore Colts 1953–1955.

BLACK SOX SCANDAL—In 1919, the Chicago White Sox were heavily favored to win the World Series from the Cincinnati Reds. But the Reds won, 5 games to 3. Gambling odds had dropped abruptly before the Series began, and during the Series rumors began to circulate that something fishy was going on.

What actually happened has never been fully explained. Evidence indicates that a gambler, Arnold Rothstein, using a former featherweight boxing champion, Abe Attell, as his go-between, had offered bribes to several White Sox to throw the Series. After the 1920 season, eight White Sox players were permanently banned from baseball as the result of an investigation. They were Ed Cicotte, Chick Gandil, Buck Weaver, "Shoeless Joe" Jackson, Swede Risberg, Happy Felsch, Lefty Williams, and Fred McMullin. However, seven of them, and a number of gamblers, were acquitted in a 1921 trial; charges against McMullin had been dropped even before the trial began.

For further information on the case and its aftermath, *see also* BASEBALL.

BOBSLEDDING—Now usually thought of as a European sport, bobsledding was actually invented by Americans, and for many years, American teams dominated international competition.

Sleds are ancient, so informal sled racing is probably also ancient. But bobsledding is a relatively recent derivation from tobogganing. The toboggan is a flat, runnerless sled which became very popular among American and English vacationers in the Alps about 1890. They delighted in traveling down slopes at breakneck speed; but, for some of them, the toboggan wasn't fast or dangerous enough, so they added runners to increase speed. This sled was a little too fast, and it was also difficult to hold on course because of its lightness. But in 1895, a Toboggan Club was formed at St. Moritz, Switzerland—most of the members were Americans—and a better sled was developed. It was heavier than the original model and easier to steer. It was christened the "bob-sleigh" because the riders worked together to increase speed on straightaways, leaning slowly back, then "bobbing" quickly into an upright position to give the sled forward impetus.

The first formal course, in the Alps, was known as the Cresta Run. The first organized race was held there on January 5, 1898. The rules called for five-passenger sleds, with two of the passengers to be women. As faster bobsleds were developed, the steep Cresta Run became too dangerous, and an artificial run was build at St. Moritz in 1904. The sport quickly caught on in various Alpine countries. The first European championships were held in 1914, a few months before World War I began.

In 1923, bobsleigh clubs in a number of countries organized the Fédération Internationale de Bobsleigh et Tobogganing (FIBT) to govern the sport and formulate international rules—a prerequisite to the inclusion of bobsledding in the first Winter Olympics in 1924. The FIBT held the first world championship in 1927.

There was no bobsled run in the United States at this time, but a number of Americans had learned the sport during trips to the Alps, and in 1927 some of them petitioned the U.S. Olympic Committee for permission to compete in the Olympics. The Amateur Athletic Union agreed to sanction bobsledding in this country, and American teams finished first and second in the 1928 Olympics. The 1932 Olympics were awarded to Lake Placid, New York, and German engineer Stanislaus Zentzytski supervised construction of a run at nearby Mount Van Hoevenberg. Two-passenger competition was introduced in 1932, and the five-passenger team was cut to four.

The two-passenger bobsled is distinctly an American development: It is essentially two small sleds, linked together. The front sled turns on a pivot and is steered by the driver, while the second passenger acts as brake. United States teams won both events in 1932, and won at least one of the Olympic events each year until 1952, when they finished second in both. Technical improvements had a lot to do with the United States' success. The United States introduced plated runners of fine-grade tool steel, held in wooden shoes and nearly V-shaped, in the 1936 Olympics. The FIBT banned these runners from further competition, largely because of damage done to the run.

A pair of brothers, Bill and Bob Linney, also came up with new ideas in bobsleds. They introduced a steel plank, linking the two halves of the sled; its flexibility greatly increased speed around turns. In 1939, they added push handles—U-shaped bars welded to the sides of the sled—to allow crew members to push a sled to a flying start before jumping on, just at or across the starting line. And in 1946, Bill Linney developed an all-steel sled with shock absorbers.

The modern bobsled is much improved in other ways as well. It is generally a blend of steel and aluminum, and its cowl, originally just a crude windshield to protect the driver from the airstream, is now carefully streamlined to reduce wind resistance.

Bobsledders are usually fairly heavy persons, because weight helps hold the sled down, making it more maneuverable. On a four-person sled, the two in the middle are there primarily as ballast, but they also need a great deal of practice to coordinate their movements with those of the driver (also known as the skipper) and the brake.

Competition. A bobsled race is essentially a series of races against the clock. The bobsleds go down a run one at a time and are electronically timed. In championship racing, each sled makes four runs, and its final time is simply the four times added together. If two sleds have exactly the same total, the winner is the sled that had the fastest heat. The reason for the number of runs is that sleds that start early go slower; as more and more sleds come down the run, a groove begins to appear, helping the sleds that come along later. In each heat, sleds start in a different order to help equalize times.

A championship race occasionally has to be called off after two heats, because of weather or the condition of the run. Even if all sleds have run three heats, totals for the first two heats only are used in determining the winner, because the starts can't be arranged fairly for a three-heat race.

See also LUGE.

AAU National Champions

Two-Person

1931	J. Hubert Stevens–Arthur Adams
1932	No competition
1933	J. Hubert Stevens–Don Deloria
1934	Ivan E. Brown–Alan M. Washbond
1935	J. Hubert and Paul Stevens
1936	Charles Storrin–Hubert Nye
1937	No competition
1938	Ivan E. Brown–Alan M. Washbond
1939	Ivan E. Brown–Alan M. Washbond
1940	Tuffield A. Latour–Paul Dupree
1941	Tuffield A. Latour–Paul Dupree
1942	Waightman "Bud" Washbond–Adrian Aubin
1943–45	No competition
1946	Tuffield A. Latour–Richard Morse
1947	Tuffield A. Latour–James Bickford
1948	Richard Surphlis–Henry Stearn
1949–50	No competition
1951	Larry McKillip–Henry Stearn
1952	Arthur Tyler–Edgar Seymour
1953	Arthur Tyler–Edgar Seymour
1954	Stan Benham–James Bickford
1955	Waightman "Bud" Washbond–Pat Martin
1956	Stan Benham–Pat Martin
1957	Stan Benham–Pat Martin
1958	No competition
1959	F. Latour–F. Morgan
1960	Eugenio Monti–Gary Sheffield
1961	William Dodge–Steven Phillips
1962	Larry McKillip–James Lamy
1963	Larry McKillip–James Lamy
1964	Larry McKillip–Charles Hoffer
1965	No competition
1966	Howard Clifton–James Crall
1967	Gary Sheffield–Howard Silver
1968	Gary Sheffield–Howard Silver
1969	Paul Lamey–Robert Huscher
1970	Paul Lamey–Robert Huscher
1971	Paul Lamey–Robert Huscher
1972–73	No competition
1974	Paul Lamey–Robert Huscher
1975	Jim Morgan–Jeff Beamish
1976	Paul Lamey–Robert Huscher

Four-Person (Driver in Parentheses)

1931	Saranac Lake Sports Association (Henry Homburger)
1932	Saranac Lake Sports Association (Henry Homburger)
1933	Lake Placid AC (Curtis Stevens)
1934	Lake Placid AC (Curtis Stevens)
1935	Lake Placid AC (Curtis Stevens)
1936	Keene Valley AC (Aubrey Wells)
1937	No competition
1938	Keene Valley AC (Aubrey Wells)
1939	Keene Valley AC (Aubrey Wells)
1940	Sno-Birds of Lake Placid (Katharin Dewey)
1941	Sno-Birds of Lake Placid (Francis Tyler)
1942	Saranac Lake BC (James Bickford)
1943–45	No competition
1946	Republic Miners BC (Bill Linney)
1947	Saranac Lake BC (James Bickford)
1948	Lake Placid BC (Stanley Benham)
1949–50	No competition
1951	Sno-Birds of Lake Placid (Stanley Benham)

The U.S. Air Force 1 four-man bobsled, driven by Jim Hickey, is about to enter a turn at the Mount Van Hoevenberg run near Lake Placid, New York. *(F. Kelly MacNeill.)*

1952	Saranac Lake BC (Robert Dupree)
1953	Sno-Birds of Lake Placid (Stanley Benham)
1954	Sno-Birds of Lake Placid (Stanley Benham)
1955	Saranac Lake BC (Monroe Flagg)
1956	Sno-Birds of Lake Placid (Stanley Benham)
1957	Sno-Birds of Lake Placid (Stanley Benham)
1958	Adirondack BC (Art Tyler)
1959	Au Sable BC (B. Snow)
1960	Saranac Lake BC (Joseph McKillip)
1961	Saranac Lake BC (Larry McKillip)
1962	Saranac Lake BC (Larry McKillip)
1963	Lake Placid BC (Bill Hickey)
1964	U.S. Air Force (Lester Fenner)
1965	No competition
1966	Lake Placid BC (Joseph McKillip)
1967	Lake Placid BC (Bill Hickey)
1968	U.S. Air Force (Lester Fenner)
1969	Cleveland BC (Fred Fortune)
1970	U.S. Navy (Paul Lamey)
1971	U.S. Air Force (Jim Hickey)
1972–73	No competition
1974	Lake Placid BC (Mike Hollrock)
1975	Lake Placid BC (Mike Hollrock)
1976	Hurricane BC (Wade Whitney)

BOCCIE—An Italian sport, derived from the Romans, similar to lawn bowls. It is played on a hard dirt court of variable size, usually about 10 by 60 ft, enclosed by wooden boards, 10 to 12 in high at the sides and 18 in high at either end. Teams are made up of one, two, or four players each. Each team has four balls, 4½ to 5 in in diameter; in addition, there is a "jack" ball, 2¾ in in diameter.

A player from one team tosses the jack toward the other end of the court, then rolls or tosses one of the other balls as close to the jack as possible. The opposing players then throw their balls in turn, until one of them is closer to the jack than the original player's first ball. The first team then takes its turn. Once a team has used all its balls, the other team bowls its remaining balls.

The balls must be thrown underhand, but they can be tossed or rolled, and they can be caromed off the side walls. It is permissible to move the jack with a bowl, or to knock an opponent's ball farther away from the jack. Scoring is as in horseshoes, except, of course, there are no ringers. A team gets one point for each ball closer to the jack than the opponents' closest ball. Game is 12 points, but a team must win by a margin of 2.

In the United States, the game is still played by Italian immigrants and some of their descendants.

BOWL GAMES—The first bowl game was played in 1902, as part of the Tournament of Roses, a Pasadena civic festival that needed publicity. Michigan beat Stanford 49-0. However, the Rose Bowl game wasn't repeated until 1916, when it became an annual event. Miami initiated the Orange Bowl in 1933, New Orleans the Sugar Bowl in 1935, and Dallas the Cotton Bowl in 1937. These are still the top football bowl contests. Basically, a bowl game is simply a postseason contest between college teams. However, the term "bowl" has been applied to other events, including basketball tournaments and professional football's championship game, the "Super Bowl."

See also FOOTBALL.

BOWLING (TENPIN)—The idea behind bowling is a fairly basic idea in sports, and undoubtedly many peoples through the ages have had one sort of game or another in which they threw rocks in an attempt to knock down standing objects. Polynesian Islanders still have such a sport, and implements for a game similar to what we call bowling have been found in an Egyptian tomb.

But our version of the sport evidently originated in a German religious ceremony fifteen or sixteen centuries ago. The original alley was a church aisle; the pin was a club called the "Heide," meaning "heathen"; and a religious man had to demonstrate the strength of his faith by

Steve Nagy, bowler of the Year in 1952 and 1955, is a member of the ABC Hall of Fame. *(Courtesy of American Bowling Congress.)*

rolling a stone down the aisle to knock down the heathen. If he hit it, his faith was proven; if he missed, he had to come back to church regularly to practice.

Even without religious significance, the sport became popular among German churchmen, who would put their pins together and take turns bowling at them. When the ceremony disappeared from the church, it became a secular pastime throughout Germany and spread into Spain, Austria, and the low countries. The number of pins varied from one place to another—perhaps even from one day to the next.

By 1325, bowling—and betting on the sport—were widespread enough that the amount to be bet on a bowling match was limited by law in both Berlin and Cologne. Bowling had become an important part of any feast or festival in a large area of Europe, although it seemed to find little favor at all in some countries, perhaps because they had their own kind of bowling, without pins. (See LAWN BOWLS.) By the early sixteenth century, nine had become a more or less standard number of pins, though the arrangement varied. Sometimes the pins were set up in three rows of three pins each, sometimes in a diamond arrangement.

It is not known exactly when bowling at pins arrived in this country. As early as 1623, the Dutch introduced lawn bowls in what is now New York City, and apparently bowling at pins arrived not much later. At least, a painting of about 1650 shows New Amsterdam Dutch bowling at ninepins.

Legend has it that ninepins was forbidden by law, because of gambling, and that the tenth pin was added to circumvent the law. There is no evidence that this is true. Tenpin bowling arrived in New York City apparently about 1820, and it was this sport, usually played indoors, that drew legislative bans in many states. These laws were aimed at all forms of bowling—evidently including even bowling on the green. The gambling problem, and the legislative actions, eventually led in 1875 to a meeting of representatives from nine bowling clubs of New York and Brooklyn. They established a standard set of rules, the foundation for bowling as we know it, and tried to curb gambling. This second purpose was apparently not accomplished. The American Amateur Bowling Union was organized in 1890 for the same purpose, but didn't last long.

The ABC. A large number of bowling enthusiasts met at Beethoven Hall in New York City on September 9, 1895, to form the American Bowling Congress, basically a federation of bowling clubs. These men hammered out rules, pertaining not only to how the sport should be played but also to how it should be policed to prevent excessive gambling and the resultant possibility of fixed matches.

The ABC held its first national tournament in 1901. It is still the major tournament, for all but the touring pros, in a sport that has more active participants in this country—about 10 million—than any other sport. The ABC tournament features competition among individuals, two-player teams (doubles), and five-player teams. The most prestigious title, though, is the all-events, based on a bowler's total scores in the other three competitions.

Because of the growth of professional bowling, the ABC in 1961 split the tournament into two divisions, Regular, for league bowlers from all over the country, and Classic, for tournament professionals.

The WIBC. Because of the rather unsavory reputation acquired by bowling alleys before the formation of the ABC, not many women entered the sport before the twentieth century. But the Women's International Bowling Congress was organized in 1916 and the first national WIBC tournament was held in the same year.

The WIBC is to women bowlers what the ABC is to men. It charters local associations which sanction league play for women, establishes rules and standards for the women's version of the sport, keeps records, etc. Membership is now about 4 million.

Other Organizations. On the college level, championship tournaments are conducted by the Association of College Unions (since 1959) and the National Association of Intercollegiate Athletics (since 1962). Many athletic conferences have intercollegiate team competition, and the sport on this level is growing rapidly, as more and more modern college union buildings with bowling alleys are erected.

Bowlers of high school age and younger are sanctioned through the American Junior Bowling Congress, an ABC affiliate with a membership of about 500,000.

Professional Bowling. The Professional Bowlers Association was organized in 1958, primarily to set up a tour of tournaments similar to the pro golf tour. The PBA tour now encompasses nearly 40 tournaments a year, with a total of more than $2 million in prize money. Its growth has been rapid: In 1960, the total prize money on the three-tournament tour was only $49,500; in 1975, Earl Anthony became the first bowler to win more than $100,000.

The Professional Women's Bowling Association has also established a tour, for women pros. As in other sports, women's prize money has grown rather slowly, largely because of the lack of television interest, but it has grown. In 1974, the largest first prize ever offered for a women's tournament, $12,500, was won by Loa Boxberger in the Brunswick Red Crown Open.

Types of Competition. In most tournaments, each bowler rolls a set number of games, and the bowler with the highest pinfall is the winner. In match-play tournaments, bowlers are paired off against one another, usually in three-game series, and the player with the highest pinfall advances, while the loser is eliminated. The finals may often involve more than three games.

Round-robin tournaments, often considered the highest form of competition, match bowlers against one another in pairs, but losers are not eliminated. Every bowler rolls against every other bowler, and a complicated point system is used to determine the winner. The most often used is the Peterson point system, which awards 1 point for each game won, 1 point for each 50 pins (or fraction thereof) scored, and ½ point for winning a three-game series in total pinfall. (Thus, a bowler can gain ½ point even if he loses two out of three games in a series.)

For spectator and television interest, most tournaments for touring pros use an unusual format: Bowlers roll a specified number of qualifying games. Then a specified number of the top qualifiers either roll more qualifying games or engage in match play until there are five finalists. These finalists are ranked by total pinfall. The fifth-place finalist plays the fourth-place finalist; the winner plays the third-place finalist, the winner of that match

Paul Vorisek rolled a 288 game for his team in the 1974 ABC tournament. Here he's getting his tenth consecutive strike in the game. *(Courtesy American Bowling Congress.)*

plays the second-place finalist, and, finally, the winner of that match plays the first-place finalist for the championship.

Major Tournaments. Despite the growth of professional bowling, the annual ABC tournament is still probably the sport's premier event, bringing together professional and league bowlers from all over the country. The WIBC tournament is the major event for women.

As in golf, match play has decreased drastically. The first match-game tournament was held in 1922, by Louis P. Peterson of Chicago (the man who conceived the Peterson point system). In 1933, the Bowling Proprietors Association of America (BPAA) took over sponsorship.

The All-Star Tournament, first sponsored by the *Chicago Tribune* in 1941, was taken over by the BPAA the following year to decide the nation's match-play champion—this tournament was also based on Peterson points.

By 1970, the numbers of bowlers entering the tournament had become too great to conduct all the necessary matches, and the BPAA switched to its "Open." The tournament now begins with 192 bowlers, of whom 96 are professionals and 96 are league bowlers chosen in sectional qualifying tournaments. They roll eight games a day for three days. The top 64 qualifiers then roll eight more games, and the field is reduced to 24. These 24 engage in match play until there are 5 finalists; then they

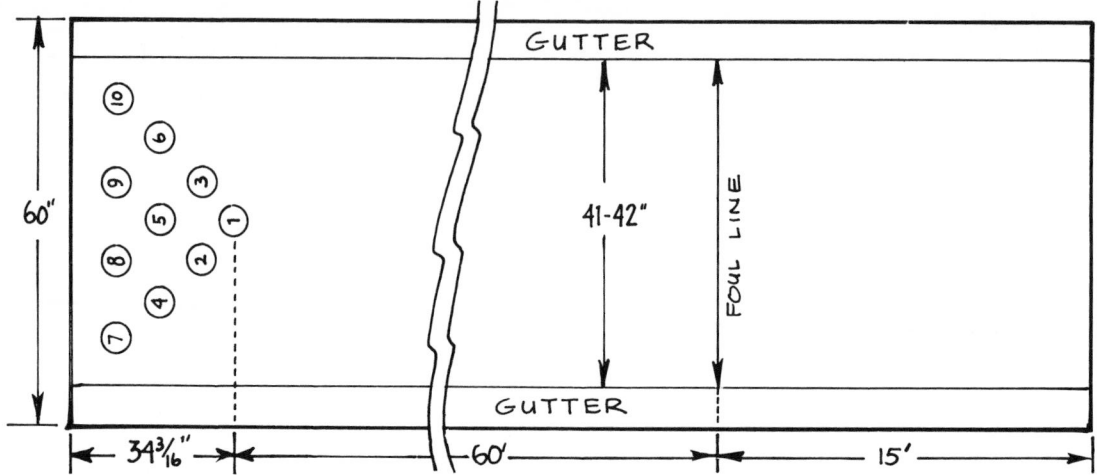

Bowling lane

follow the match-play format used in most professional tournaments.

Of the pro tournaments, the most important is the Firestone Tournament of Champions. The top 52–ranked bowlers compete in this event, which now offers a total of $129,500 in prize money.

The top pure match-play tournament for men is the ABC Masters; the women's counterpart is the WIBC Queens.

International Competition. Bowling has been offered as a demonstration at the Olympic Games, but has never been admitted to the program. However, in recent years bowling has spread rapidly to other countries. The Fédération Internationale des Quilleurs (FIQ), organized in 1952, is the worldwide governing body. It now has 50 member countries, and conducts its own "Olympics," a worldwide competition held every four years, for amateur bowlers only. The first world competition was held in Mexico in 1963, with the United States dominating, winning seven out of eight titles. However, other countries have been catching up rapidly.

Only the United States and Japan have professional bowlers; in other countries, all bowlers are eligible to take part in the worldwide amateur competition.

Method of Play

The playing surface is an alley, or lane, approximately 78 ft long and 41 to 42 in wide. On either side of the alley are gutters; if the ball goes off the edge of the alley, it will drop into the gutter and be carried past the pins. The approach is an area 15 ft long, ending at the foul line. The bowler, in making the approach, must not step over the line; 60 ft beyond it is the headpin. The pins are arranged in four rows, with one pin in the first row, two in the second, three in the third, and four in the fourth. They are numbered as shown in the diagram above; the pins themselves don't carry specific numbers, but the spots on which they are placed do.

The regulation pin is made of hard maple; it is 15 in high and has a diameter of 2¼ in at the base and a circumference of 15 in at its widest point. Weight must be between 2 lb 14 oz and 3 lb 10 oz. The regulation ball is of solid composition, has a circumference of no more than 27 in, and weighs 10 to 16 lb. A ball may have two or three finger holes; most bowlers use the three-holed ball, inserting the two middle fingers and the thumb into the holes.

Bowling in ordinary shoes isn't permitted, because it can damage the lanes. The peculiarities of the sport demand an unmatched pair of shoes. The right-handed bowler wears a left shoe with a relatively slippery sole, usually of hard leather or vinyl, and a right shoe with a rubber sole that will help "brake."

A game, or "string," is made up of 10 frames. Each frame represents one turn for the bowler, and in each turn the player is allowed to roll the ball twice. If the player knocks down all the pins with the first roll, it is a strike; if not, a second roll at the pins still standing is attempted. If all the pins are knocked down with two balls, it is a spare; if any pins are left standing, it is an "open frame."

If a bowler commits a foul, by stepping over the foul line during delivery, it counts as a shot, and any pins knocked down are respotted without counting. If pins are knocked down by a ball that has entered the gutter, or by a ball bouncing off the rear cushion, they do not count, and are respotted.

Scoring. In an open frame, a bowler simply gets credit for the number of pins knocked down. In the case of a spare, a slash mark is recorded in a small square in the upper right-hand corner of that frame on the score sheet, and no score is entered until the first ball of the next frame is rolled. Then credit is given for 10 plus the number of pins knocked down with that next ball. For example, a player rolls a spare in the first frame; with the first ball of the second frame, the player knocks down seven pins. The first frame, then, gets 17 points. If two of the remaining three pins get knocked down, 9 points are added, for a total of 26 in the second frame.

If a bowler gets a strike, it is recorded with an X in the small square, the score being 10 plus the total number of pins knocked down in the next two rolls. Thus, the bowler who rolls three strikes in a row in the first three frames gets credit for 30 points in the first frame.

Bowling's perfect score, a 300 game, represents 12

strikes in a row—a total of 120 pins knocked down. Why 12 strikes, instead of 10? Because, if a bowler gets a strike in the last frame, the score for that frame can't be recorded before rolling twice more. Similarly, if a bowler rolls a spare in the last frame, one more roll is required before the final score can be tallied.

Splits. A split occurs when the pins that are left after one roll are so widely spread out that it's difficult to knock them all down with the second throw. A split is usually identified by the numbers of the remaining pins; the most difficult of all is the 7-10, in which the two outside pins in the last row are standing.

Techniques

It would seem that the simplest way to knock down all the pins is to roll the ball right down the center of the alley, at the headpin. But a straight-on hit on the headpin is likely to result in a split. Instead, a bowler tries to hit the "pocket"—for a right-hander, between the 1 and 3 pins. A novice who throws a straight ball is usually taught to roll from the right-hand side of the alley toward this pocket. A better way of doing it, though, is to throw a hook—a ball that starts straight down the right side of the alley and then, at the last moment, breaks sharply to the left and into the pocket.

Another type of delivery, no longer commonly used, is the curve, which curves from the moment it leaves the hand until it strikes the pins. A right-hander's curve is delivered from the left of center; it curves toward the right gutter and then back into the pocket.

There are two advantages to the hook. Because it can be thrown straight down the alley, it will hit the pocket more consistently and a slight miss will not hurt the bowler as badly as a straight ball would. And the spin on the ball that makes it hook also gives the pins more action when it hits, resulting in a higher pinfall.

Grip. There are basically three types of grips. In the conventional grip, the bowler simply inserts the thumb and middle two fingers into the appropriate holes, with the second knuckle of each finger slightly above the surface, while the thumb is as far in as it can go. In the semifingertip-grip, the thumb is still all the way in. The fingers are not inserted quite as far, and the knuckles, instead of projecting straight above the hole, are slightly in back of the hole, closer to the thumb. In the fullfingertip-grip, the fingers are inserted to a point about halfway between the first and second knuckles.

The conventional grip is the easiest to master. The other two are more difficult, but the increased finger flexibility gives the bowler more control over the hook of the ball, making it easier to adjust to difficulties, including changing alley conditions.

The Approach. The purpose of the approach is to establish a rhythm and momentum that can be duplicated on each delivery of the ball. Approaches vary; a bowler may take three, four, or five steps, and may move rather rapidly or quite slowly. The most important thing is to be consistent.

The bowler begins by holding the ball in front of the body, somewhere between the knees and the chin, depending on how straight the person stands. If the bowler uses a deep crouch, the ball will be near the knees. Both hands are used to support the ball.

The beginning of the approach is the "push-away": The ball is pushed forward, away from the body, to begin a pendulum swing. For the four-step approach, the most common, the right foot makes the first step, and the ball is pushed out, down, and slightly to the right so that the bowler can walk past it. As the second step is taken, on the left foot, the ball goes into a downswing, and then into a backswing, which is completed with the third step. The ball is brought up behind the bowler, to shoulder level, or slightly below. The path taken by the ball on the backswing must also be the path it will take when it comes forward—the path that will send it on its proper path down the lane.

As the backswing is completed, the bowler begins the fourth step, a sliding step on the left foot—sometimes called the "timing step." The left foot comes forward, the toes pointing directly at the pins, and the bowler slides on the ball of the foot. The ball has come forward and should be even with the left foot when the slide begins. The right foot, directly behind the left, is dragging, acting as a brake.

Important things to bear in mind throughout the approach: The shoulders must always be parallel to the target, the steps must follow a straight line, and the feet should always be perpendicular to the foul line.

The Release. The whole point of the approach has been to establish a pendulum swing, backward and forward, that establishes a straight path and builds up momentum. The release of the ball must allow it to travel the straight path without losing any of the momentum. It must be done gently. The ball is neither dropped nor thrown; it is laid down on the lane. The thumb comes out first, then the fingers lift out, and the ball is on its way.

The Follow-through. After release, the arm and hand continue in their straight path. The hand should come up approximately to eye level, pointing down the lane at the target.

Type of Delivery. When a bowler rolls a straight ball, the thumb is pointed at the target. After the thumb comes out, just before release, the fingers, following behind, keep the ball on a straight line.

To throw a hook, the bowler has the thumb on the left side of the ball; if the front of the ball is considered "12 o'clock," the thumb is at 9, 10, or 11, depending on the bowler. When the fingers lift out, they impart a spin to the ball that makes it break into the pocket.

The curve is thrown much the same way as a hook, but it is thrown much more slowly. The speed of the ball keeps the hook from breaking until it is well down the lane; with less speed, the ball begins curving much sooner.

Picking Spares. Ideally, a bowler wants to get a strike in every frame. It doesn't happen often, however, and the difference between a spare and an open frame is often the difference between victory and defeat.

Establishing the proper angle is the most important part of converting the remaining pins into a spare. For most spares, a cross-lane angle offers the best percentage. The 2-4-7, for example, on the left side of the lane, is shot at from the right side. A spare on the right side that includes the head pin—the 1-3-6, for example—is treated just as if the bowler were trying for a strike with the first ball. Headpin spares on the left-hand side are treated the same way, except that the bowler begins slightly to the left of the normal starting point. The bowler wants to hit the head pin squarely instead of in the pocket.

Aside from the split, the most difficult spare is one in which one pin is directly behind another—the 2-8 and 3-7. Here, it is important to hit the front pin straight on, so that the ball will roll right back through the back pin. This is true of any leaves that include these pins.

Splits. A "fit-in" split is not really a split. It is a leave in which two pins are side by side. The ball must go directly between them. The "baby splits" are 2-7 and 3-10, which should be picked in the same way, with the ball taking both pins. Trying to slide the front pin into the back pin offers a poor percentage.

With wider splits, however, the only way to convert is to hit one pin thinly enough so that it will slide into the other. This is true of the 5-10, 4-9, 7-10, and similar splits. Unless a bowler desperately needs a spare, it may be better to go for one pin on such splits, rather than attempt to get the spare and miss both of them.

Spot Bowling. Any lane has "spots," triangular markings, pointing toward the pins, which can be used by the bowler as sighting marks. Many bowlers aim at the spots instead of at the pins. The exact point of aim will vary from bowler to bowler. In general, a person who throws a straight ball will line up with the second spot in from the right and will try to roll the ball over the right-hand side of the third spot in. A bowler who throws a hook will probably roll the bowl directly over the second spot from the right.

A spot bowler may find it much easier to pick up spares, since almost exactly the same delivery can be used, with different spots as aiming points. For the 2-4-7, for example, the hook is usually thrown over the third spot from the right.

Adjusting. No two lanes are exactly alike, although recent developments in lane finishes and treatments have eliminated some of the inconsistencies. The condition of the lane is very important to the hook bowler. If a lane is faster than usual, the hook will break too late; if it is slower than usual, the hook will break too soon.

Different bowlers have different ways of adjusting. Most top bowlers, however, will simply change their aiming spots to meet different conditions, but many of them will adjust by changing the speed of the ball.

See also CANDLEPIN BOWLING; DUCKPIN BOWLING.

Glossary

alley—Now in disrepute, largely replaced by "lane," at least among bowling proprietors and promoters. The playing surface, including the approach area, the bed, gutters, restraining borders, etc.

anchor man—The fifth bowler on a five-person team.

backup—A ball that curves or hooks in the wrong direction; toward the right gutter, for a right-hander.

bedposts—The 7-10 split.

bed—The portion of the lane from the foul line to the drop-off behind the pins.

blind—In team bowling, a score given for an absent bowler. Usually the player's average; sometimes, the average minus a certain penalty, or an arbitrary figure.

break—An open frame after a string of spares and strikes.

Brooklyn side—The wrong pocket; for a right-hander, the 1-2 pocket.

broom ball—A very active ball.

bucket—The 2-4-5-8 or 3-5-6-9 leaves.

chop—To knock down just one pin of a leave of two or more pins; commonly used when the pin chopped is the front pin in the 2-8 or 3-7.

Christmas tree—The 3-7-10 or 2-7-10 splits.

Cincinnati—The 8-10 split.

cross-over—A ball that hits the Brooklyn side.

dead ball—A ball with little or no action.

double—Two strikes in a row.

double pinochle—The 4-6-7-10.

double wood—A leave with one pin directly behind another—the 2-8, 3-9, 1-5.

Dutch 200—A 200 game with spares and strikes alternating throughout.

fenceposts—The 7-10 split.

fill—To get a spare.

foul—Crossing or touching the foul line.

foundation—A strike in the ninth frame.

Golden Gate—The 4-6-7-10 split.

gutter ball—A ball that lands in the gutter.

headpin—The 1 pin.

kingpin—The 5 pin.

leadoff person—The first bowler on a five-person team.

leave—The pins remaining after the first roll.

maples—The pins.

mark—A strike or spare.

miss—Failure to convert a spare which is not a split.

mixer—A ball with a lot of action.

mother-in-law—The 7 pin; so called probably because it can spoil a good game.

nose hit—Hitting the headpin dead-on.

railroad—A split.

scratch—A game in which actual scores count, with no handicap allowances.

tandem—Same as "double wood."

turkey—Three strikes in a row.

washout—The 1-2-10 or 1-2-4-10 leaves.

ABC Champions

(In 1961, all events were split into two divisions, Regular for league bowlers and Classic for professionals.)

All-Events

1901	Frank Brill	1736
1902	John Koster	1841
1903	Fred Strong	1896
1904	Martin Kern	1804
1905	Jack G. Reilly	1791
1906	J. T. Peacock	1794
1907	H. C. Ellis	1775
1908	Russell Crable	1924
1909	James Blouin	1885
1910	Thomas Haley	1961
1911	Jimmy Smith	1913
1912	Phil Sutton	1843
1913	Ed Hermann	1972
1914	William Miller	1897
1915	Matty E. Faetz	1876
1916	Frank Thoma	1919
1917	H. Miller	1945
1918	Harry Steers	1959
1919	Mort Lindsey	1933
1920	Jimmy Smith	1915
1921	Abe Schieman	1909
1922	Barney Spinella	1999
1923	William J. Knox	2019
1924	A. F. Weber	1975
1925	Clarence Long	1977
1926	Harry Gerloski	1981

1927	Barney Spinella	2014
1928	Phil Wolf	1937
1929	Otto Stein, Jr.	1974
1930	George Morrison	1985
1931	Mike Mauser	1966
1932	Hugh Stewart	1980
1933	Gil Zunker	2060
1934	Walt Reppenhagen	1972
1935	Ora Mayer	2022
1936	John Murphy	2006
1937	Max Stein	2070
1938	Donald Beatty	1978
1939	Joseph Wilman	2028
1940	Fred Fischer	2001
1941	Harold Kelly	2013
1942	Stanley Moskal	1973
1943–45	No competition	
1946	Joseph Wilman	2054
1947	Junie McMahon	1965
1948	Ned Day	1979
1949	John Small	1941
1950	Frank Santore	1981
1951	Tony Lindemann	2005
1952	Steve Nagy	2065
1953	Frank Santore	1994
1954	Brad Lewis	1985
1955	Fred Bujack	1993
1956	Bill Lillard	2018
1957	Jim Spalding	2088
1958	Al Faragalli	2043
1959	Ed Lubanski	2116
1960	Vince Lucci	1985

Regular All-Events

1961	Luke Karan	1960
1962	Billy Young	2015
1963	Wilford "Bus" Oswalt	2055
1964	Les Zikes	2001
1965	Tom Hathway	1922
1966	John Wilcox	2004
1967	Gary Lewis	2010
1968	Vince Mazzanti	1971
1969	Eddie Jackson	1988
1970	Mike Berlin	2004
1971	Al Cohn	2063
1972	Mac Lowry	2026
1973	Ron Woolet	2104
1974	Bob Hart	2087
1975	Bobby Meadows	2033
1976	Jim Lindquist	2071

Classic All-Events

1961	Bob Brayman	1963
1962	Jack Winters	2147
1963	Tom Hennessey	1998
1964	Billy Hardwick	2088
1965	Tom Hennessey	2049
1966	Les Schissler	2112
1967	Bob Strampe	2092
1968	Jim Stefanich	1983
1969	Larry Lichstein	2060
1970	Bob Strampe	2043
1971	Gary Dickinson	2000
1972	Teata Semiz	1994
1973	Jimmy Mack	1994
1974	Jim Godman	2184
1975	Bill Beach	1993
1976	Gary Fust	2050

Singles

1901	Frank Brill	648
1902	Fred Strong	649
1903	Dan A. Jones	683

1904	Martin Kern	647
1905	C. M. Anderson	651
1906	Frank Favour	669
1907	M. T. Levey	624
1908	Archie Wengler	699
1909	Larry Sutton	691
1910	Thomas Haley	705
1911	James Blouin	681
1912	Larry Sutton	679
1913	F. Peterson	693
1914	William Miller	675
1915	Wallace H. Pierce	711
1916	Sam Schliman	685
1917	Otto Kallusch	698
1918	C. J. Styles	702
1919	Harry Cavan	718
1920	Joe Shaw	713
1921	Fred Smith	702
1922	Walter Lundgren	729
1923	Carl A. Baumgartner	724
1924	Harry E. Smyers	749
1925	Al Green	706
1926	Ed Votel	731
1927	William Eggars	706
1928	Henry Summers	705
1929	Adolph Unke	728
1930	Larry Shotwell	774
1931	Walter Lachnowski	712
1932	Otto Nitschke	731
1933	Earl Hewitt	724
1934	Jerry Vidro	721
1935	Don Brokaw	733
1936	Charles Warren	735
1937	Eugene Gagliardi	749
1938	Knute Anderson	746
1939	James Danek	730
1940	Ray Brown	742
1941	Fred Ruff, Jr.	745
1942	John Stanley	756
1943–45	No competition	
1946	Leo Rollick	737
1947	Junie McMahon	740
1948	Lincoln Protich	721
1949	Bernard Rusche	716
1950	Everett Leins	757
1951	Lee Jouglard	775
1952	Al Sharkey	758
1953	Frank Santore	749
1954	Tony Sparando	723
1955	Eddie Gerzine	738
1956	George Wade	744
1957	Bob Allen	729
1958	Ed Shay	733
1959	Ed Lubanski	764
1960	Paul Kulbaga	726

Regular Singles

1961	Lyle Spooner	726
1962	Andy Renaldy	720
1963	Fred Delello	744
1964	Jim Stefanich	726
1965	Ken Roeth	700
1966	Don Chapman	761
1967	Frank Perry	723
1968	Wayne Kowalski	738
1969	Greg Campbell	751
1970	Jake Yoder	746
1971	Al Cohn	738
1972	Bill Pointer	739
1973	Ed Thompson	762
1974	Gene Krause	773
1975	Jim Setser	756
1976	Mike Putzer	758

Gene Krause won the ABC regular singles title in 1974 with a 773 series. Here he's finishing the series with his ninth consecutive strike. (*Courtesy of American Bowling Congress.*)

Classic Singles

1961	Earl Johnson	733
1962	Bob Poole	759
1963	Tom Hennessey	732
1964	Billy Hardwick	730
1965	Bob Kennicutt	697
1966	Les Schissler	760
1967	Lou Mandragona	736
1968	Dave Davis	741
1969	Nelson Burton, Jr.	732
1970	Glenn Allison	730
1971	Victor Iwlew	750
1972	Teata Semiz	754
1973	Nelson Burton, Jr.	724
1974	Ed Ditolla	747
1975	Les Zikes	710
1976	Jim Schroeder	750

ABC Masters Champions

1951	Lee Jouglard
1952	Willard Taylor
1953	Rudy Habetler
1954	Eugene Elkins
1955	Basil "Buzz" Fazio
1956	Dick Hoover
1957	Dick Hoover
1958	Tom Hennessey
1959	Ray Bluth
1960	Bill Golembiewski
1961	Don Carter
1962	Bill Golembiewski
1963	Harry Smith
1964	Billy Welu
1965	Billy Welu
1966	Bob Strampe
1967	Lou Scalia
1968	Pete Tountas

1969	Jim Chestney
1970	Don Glover
1971	Jim Godman
1972	Bill Beach
1973	Dave Soutar
1974	Paul Colwell
1975	Ed Ressler
1976	Nelson Burton, Jr.

WIBC Tournament Champions

All-Events

1916	A. J. Koster	1423
1917	No competition	
1918	Emma Jaeger	1552
1919	B. Husk	1580
1920	Mae Leibrich	1606
1921	Emma Jaeger	1557
1922	Hattie Abraham	1659
1923	Deane Fritz	1582
1924	Rose Steger	1647
1925	Grayce Hatch	1703
1926	Ermil Lackey	1641
1927	Grayce Hatch	1644
1928	Emma Jaeger	1713
1929	Emma Jaeger	1700
1930	Sally Twyford	1727
1931	Myrtle Schulte	1742
1932	Marie Warmbier	1807
1933	Sally Twyford	1765
1934	Esther Ryan	1763
1935	Marie Warmbier	1911
1936	Ella Mankie	1683
1937	Louise Stockdale	1761
1938	Dorothy Miller	1843
1939	Ruth Troy	1724
1940	Tess Small	1777
1941	Sally Twyford	1799
1942	Nina Burns	1888
1943–45	No competition	
1946	Catherine Fellmeth	1835
1947	Marge Dardeen	1826
1948	Virgie Hupfer	1850
1949	Cecelia Winandy	1840
1950	Marion Ladewig	1796
1951	LaVerne Carter	1788
1952	Virginia Turner	1854
1953	Doris Knechtges	1886
1954	Anne Johnson	1880
1955	Marion Ladewig	1890
1956	Doris Knechtges	1867
1957	Anita Cantaline	1859
1958	Mae Bolt	1828
1959	Pat McCormick	1927
1960	Judy Roberts	1836
1961	Evelyn Teal	1848
1962	Flossie Argent	1808
1963	Helen Shablis	1849
1964	Jean Havlish	1980
1965	Donna Zimmerman	1833
1966	Kate Helbig	1835
1967	Carol Miller	1862
1968	Janice Sue Reichley	1889
1969	Helen Duval	1927
1970	Dorothy Fothergill	1984
1971	Lorrie Koch	1840
1972	Mildred Martorella	1877
1973	Toni Calvery	1910
1974	Judy Cook Soutar	1924
1975	Virginia Park	1821
1976	Betty Morris	1866

Singles

1916	A. J. Koster	486
1917	No competition	
1918	Mrs. F. Steib	537
1919	Mrs. R. Littlefield	594
1920	Birdie Humphreys	559
1921	Emma Jaeger	579
1922	Emma Jaeger	603
1923	Emma Jaeger	594
1924	Alice Feeney	593
1925	Eliza Reich	622
1926	L. Weismann	579
1927	F. Ahrhart	577
1928	Anita Rump	622
1929	Agnes Higgins	637
1930	Anita Rump	613
1931	Myrtle Schulte	650
1932	Audrey McVay	668
1933	Sally Twyford	628
1934	Marie Clemensen	712
1935	Marie Warmbier	652
1936	Ella Mankie	612
1937	Ann Gottstine	647
1938	Rose Warner	622
1939	Helen Hengstler	626
1940	Sally Twyford	626
1941	Nancy Huff	662
1942	Tillie Taylor	659
1943–45	No competition	
1946	Val Mikiel	682
1947	Agnes Junker	650
1948	Shirlee Wernecke	696
1949	Clara Mataya	658
1950	Cleo McGovern	669
1951	Ida Simpson	639
1952	Lorene Craig	672
1953	Marge Baginski	637
1954	Helen Bassett	668
1955	Nellie Vella	695
1956	Lucille Noe	708
1957	Eleanor Towles	664
1958	Ruth Hertel	622
1959	Mae Bolt	664
1960	Marge McDaniels	649
1961	Elaine Newton	661
1962	Martha Hoffman	693
1963	Dorothy Wilkinson	653
1964	Jean Havlish	690
1965	Doris Rudell	659
1966	Gloria Bouvia	675
1967	Glorian Paeth	652
1968	Norma Parks	691
1969	Joan Bender	690
1970	Dorothy Fothergill	695
1971	Mary Scruggs	698
1972	D. D. Jacobson	737
1973	Bobbie Buffaloe	706
1974	Shirley Garms	702
1975	Barbara Leicht	689
1976	Bev Shank	686

Match-Play Champions

(The first formal match-game championship tournament was conducted by Louis P. Petersen in 1922; it was taken over by the BPAA in 1933. The *Chicago Tribune* sponsored the first All-Star tournament in 1941; it was taken over by the BPAA and merged with the older match-game tournament in 1943. In 1971, it became the BPAA Open.)

Petersen Tournament

1922	Jimmy Blouin
1923	Jimmy Blouin
1924	Jimmy Blouin
1925	Jimmy Blouin
1926	Frank Kartheiser
1927	Charles Daw
1928	Adolph Carlson
1929	Joe Scribner
	Joe Falcaro
1930	Joe Falcaro
1931	Joe Falcaro
1932	Joe Falcaro

BPAA Tournament

1933	Joe Miller
1934–35	Otto Stein
1935–36	Hank Marino
1936–37	Hank Marino
1938–42	Ned Day

All-Star Tournament

1941	John Crimmins
1942	Connie Schwoegler
1943	Ned Day
1944	Buddy Bomar
1945	Joe Wilman
1946	Andy Varipapa
1947	Andy Varipapa
1948	Connie Schwoegler
1949	Junie McMahon

Bowling is probably the most popular sport for women, in terms of total participation. This young woman is just one of an estimated 15 million who bowl more or less regularly. (*Hank Seaman, New Bedford Standard-Times.*)

1950	Dick Hoover
1951	Junie McMahon
1952	Don Carter
1953	No competition
1954	Don Carter
1955	Steve Nagy
1956	Don Carter
1957	No competition
1958	Don Carter
1959	Billy Welu
1960	Harry Smith
1961	Bill Tucker
1962	Dick Weber
1963	Dick Weber
1964	Bob Strampe
1965	Dick Weber
1966	Dick Weber
1967	Les Schissler
1968	Jim Stefanich
1969	Billy Hardwick
1970	Bobby Cooper

BPAA-PBA Open

1971	Mike Lemongello
1972	Don Johnson
1973	Mike McGrath
1974	Larry Laub
1975	Steve Neff
1976	Paul Moser

Women's All-Star

1949	Marion Ladewig
1950	Marion Ladewig
1951	Marion Ladewig
1952	Marion Ladewig
1953	No competition
1954	Marion Ladewig
1955	Sylvia Wene
1955	Anita Cantaline
1956	Marion Ladewig
1957	No competition
1958	Merle Matthews
1959	Marion Ladewig
1960	Sylvia Wene
1961	Phyllis Notaro
1962	Shirley Garms
1963	Marion Ladewig
1964	LaVerne Carter
1965	Ann Slattery
1966	Joy Abel
1967	Gloria Bouvia
1968	Dorothy Fothergill
1969	Dorothy Fothergill
1970	Mary Baker

Women's Open

1971	Paula Sperber
1972	Lorrie Koch
1973	Millie Martorella
1974	Pat Costello
1976	Paula Sperber
1976	Patty Costello

WIBC Queens Tournament

1961	Janet Harman
1962	Dorothy Wilkinson
1963	Irene Monterosso
1964	D. D. Jacobson
1965	Betty Kuczynski
1966	Judy Lee
1967	Millie Ignizio
1968	Phyllis Massey
1969	Ann Feigel
1970	Millie Martorella

1971	Millie Martorella
1972	Dorothy Fothergill
1973	Dorothy Fothergill
1974	Judy Cook Soutar
1975	Cindy Powell
1976	Pam Rutherford

Bowlers of the Year

Men

1942	Johnny Crimmins
1943	Ned Day
1944	Ned Day
1945	Buddy Bomar
1946	Joseph Wilman
1947	Buddy Bomar
1948	Andy Varipapa
1949	Connie Schwoegler
1950	Junie McMahon
1951	Lee Jouglard
1952	Steve Nagy
1953	Don Carter
1954	Don Carter
1955	Steve Nagy
1956	Bill Lillard
1957	Don Carter
1958	Don Carter
1959	Ed Lubanski
1960	Don Carter
1961	Dick Weber
1962	Don Carter
1963	Dick Weber
1964	Billy Hardwick
1965	Dick Weber
1966	Wayne Zahn
1967	Dave Davis
1968	Jim Stefanich
1969	Billy Hardwick
1970	Nelson Burton, Jr.
1971	Don Johnson
1972	Don Johnson
1973	Don McCune
1974	Earl Anthony
1975	Earl Anthony
1976	Earl Anthony

Women

1948	Val Mikiel
1949	Val Mikiel
1950	Marion Ladewig
1951	Marion Ladewig
1952	Marion Ladewig
1953	Marion Ladewig
1954	Marion Ladewig
1955	Sylvia Martin
1956	Anita Cantaline
1957	Marion Ladewig
1958	Marion Ladewig
1959	Marion Ladewig
1960	Sylvia Martin
1961	Shirley Garms
1962	Shirley Garms
1963	Marion Ladewig
1964	LaVerne Carter
1965	Betty Kuczynski
1966	Joy Abel
1967	Mildred Martorella
1968	Dorothy Fothergill
1969	Dorothy Fothergill
1970	Mary Baker
1971	Paula Sperber
1972	Patty Costello
1973	Judy Cook
1974	Judy Cook Soutar

1975 Judy Cook Soutar
1976 Patty Costello

All-Time All-American Teams

(Selected in 1970 by veteran bowling writers)

Pre-1950

Hank Marino, Jimmy Smith, Ned Day, Joe Wilman, Andy Varipapa.

Post-1950

Don Carter, Dick Weber, Billy Hardwick, Steve Nagy, Ed Lubankski.

ABC Hall of Fame

Bowlers

Frank Benkovic
James Blouin
Ray Bluth
Joseph Bodis
Herbert B. "Buddy" Bomar
Albert R. "Allie" Brandt
Eddie Brosius
Fred Bujack
William Bunetta
Nelson Burton, Sr.
Louis Campi
Adolph D. Carlson
Donald J. Carter
Martin Cassio
Graz Castellano
John Crimmins
Charley Daw
Edward P. "Ned" Day
Ebber D. "Ed" Easter
Alfred J. " Lindy" Faragalli
Basil "Buzz" Fazio
Russell H. Gersonde
Therman Gibson
Richard L. Hoover
Joseph G. Joseph
Frank C. "Midge" Kartheiser
Edward Kawolics
Joe Kissof
William Knox
John Koster
Edward H. Krems
Joseph F. Kristof
Paul A. Krumske
Herbert W. Lange
Hank Lauman
William T. Lillard
Mortimer J. Lindsey
Edward A. Lubanski
Enrico "Hank" Martino
John O. Martino
James "Junie" McMahon, Jr.
Walter "Skang" Mercurio
Steve J. Nagy
Joseph J. Norris
Charles O'Donnell
Claude "Pat" Patterson, Jr.
Conrad A. "Connie" Schwoegler
Louis A. Sielaff
William Sixty, Jr.
James Smith (Né Mellilo)
Tony "Ace" Sparando
Barney Spinella
Harry H. Steers
Otto Stein, Jr.
Frank "Sykes" Thoma
Andrew Varipapa
Walter G. Ward
Richard A. Weber

Joseph "Buck" Wilman
Phil Wolf
George Young
Gilbert Zunker

Meritorious Service

Harold Allen
E. H. Baumgarten
R. F. Bensinger
LeRoy Chase
C. O. Collier
Walt Ditzen
William Doehrman
Jack Hagerty
Cone Hermann
Peter Howley
A. L. Langtry
Sam Levine
Mort Luby, Sr.
Howard McCullough
Louis Petersen
Milton Raymer
Dennis J. Sweeney
Sam Weinstein
Fred Wolf

WIBC Hall of Fame

Stars of Yesteryear

Winifred Berger
Philena Bohlen
Catherine Burling
Emily Chapman
Doris Coburn
Catherine Fellmeth
Deane Fritz
Olga Gloor
Goldie Greenwald
Stella Hartrick
Grayce Hatch
Madalene "Bee" Hochstadter
Emma Jaeger
Merle Matthews
Floretta McCutcheon
Dorothy Miller
Jo Mraz
Connie Powers
Leona Robinson
Anita Rump
Addie Ruschmeyer
Esther Ryan
Myrtle Schulte
Violet Simon
Tess Small
Grace Smith
Louise Stockdale
Elvira Toepfer
Sally Twyford
Marie Warmbier

Superior Performance

Helen Duval
Shirley Garms
Joan Holm
Marion Ladewig
Sylvia Martin
Beverly Ortner
Judy Cook Soutar

Meritorious Service

Margaret Higley
Nora Kay
Jeannette Knepprath
Iolia Lasher
Bertha McBride

Emma Phaler
Gertrude Rishling
Berdie Speck
Pearl Switzer
Georgia E. Veach
Ann Wood

Bibliography. Fraley, Oscar: *The Complete Handbook of Bowling,* Prentice-Hall, Englewood Cliffs, N.J.; *Tournament Press Guide,* American Bowling Congress, Milwaukee, 1974 (annual).

BOWLING ON THE GREEN—*See* Lawn Bowls.

BOXING—It is easy enough to say that boxing is an ancient sport that originated the first time an angry caveman attacked a colleague with his bare hands, or to facetiously describe Cain and Abel as the first two boxers. But it should be noted that boxing is a fairly civilized sport, as different from primitive fighting as modern fencing is from a duel to the death. Boxing still contains an element of brutality, and it can cause injury and death, but it is a long way from primitive hand-to-hand combat, in which biting, kicking, kneeing, eye-gouging, and wrestling tactics are all acceptable.

When we limit the definition of boxing to a sporting fight between two individuals who can use only their fists, we can still find evidences of its antiquity, however. A Babylonian plaque of more than 4,000 years ago shows two men with raised fists facing one another, and similar scenes have been found in Sumeria and Crete. But, of course, it is impossible to be certain that these are boxing matches; such scenes might merely depict two men who are angry at each other.

Boxing was a rather late addition to the Olympic games of Greece, being added to the program only in 688 B.C., during the Twenty-third Olympiad. But the sport had apparently become pretty well developed among the Greeks by that time. In one type of boxing match, the combatants had to sit on stones facing one another, and no retreat was permitted. They simply hammered away until one of them was unconscious.

Greek boxers in the Olympics protected their hands with leather wrappings. After the Roman conquest, the sport became increasingly brutal. The Romans first used a wrapping of hard leather, called the *cestus.* Then they substituted something similar to brass knuckles, and finally they developed the *myrmex* or "limb piercer," a bronze, spurlike instrument that could inflict terrible punishment. So many deaths resulted that first the *myrmex* was abolished and then boxing was banned entirely, about 30 B.C. (The Romans did make some improvements in the sport. Perhaps because of its brutal nature, they felt that the ability to escape from an opponent should be important, but at the same time, they didn't want anyone to escape too far, so they invented the ring, originally a marked circle from which neither combatant could depart.)

The sport seems to have disappeared almost entirely for more than 1,500 years. There is, however, a newspaper reference to a boxing match in England in 1681, written in a matter-of-fact tone, as if every reader would know what boxing meant. The origin of the word, incidentally, has led to some fanciful conjecture. An often seen speculation is that it originally referred to a good fighter's ability to "box up" an opponent. However, the Middle English *box* meant a blow, or slap, from the Danish word *bask,* and

the English still use the word frequently, as in "boxing someone's ears."

Boxing was really resurrected by an Englishman named James Figg. Figg was an excellent fencer as well as a fighter, and he seems to have applied some of the principles of fencing to the sport. In 1719 Figg, already known as an expert boxer, opened his Academy of Boxing in London, patterned after the fencing academies of the time. He also offered to take on all comers, in boxing or fighting with cudgels, and he beat every challenger. He quickly became recognized as the champion of Great Britain, if not of the world, and he was still considered champion when he retired, undefeated, in 1730. Figg's success had led to the establishment of many other boxing academies in England, especially in London, and his reputation as a fencer had attracted a number of "gentlemen" to the sport, as amateurs who wanted to learn the art of self-defense and at the same time were ready to applaud the skill of professional fighters.

In Figg's academy, a boxing match was a fight to the finish, with no rest periods. The next great champion, Jack Broughton, called upon to referee a fight in 1743, established a new set of rules. He drew them up especially for the fight he was to referee, but they were quickly adopted for many other fights as well.

Broughton's rules allowed for a 3-ft square in the center of the ring; if a fighter was knocked down, the opponent had to stop fighting, and the downed boxer's helpers were given 30 sec to get their fighter into position on one side of the square, facing the opponent. The rules also specified that a boxer fallen to the knees would be considered down. Although Broughton's rules didn't put it this way, a fight was now divided into rounds, with a round ending when one contender was knocked down, and the next round beginning when both fighters were "up to scratch" and ready to resume.

Boxing, at least in this refined form, remained a British monopoly until about 1850. The United States did produce two outstanding fighters, but both had to go to England to win their reputations. And both of them were black. It seems that boxing—or at least fighting—was commonly practiced by slaves, with the urging and under the sponsorship of their owners, and it's quite likely there were many unsung black fighters during the early nineteenth century.

Bill Richmond, however, was not a slave. A native of Staten Island, he became a servant for a British General, Lord Percy, who was with British forces occupying New York. Percy often arranged fights between Richmond and British soldiers, and Richmond won them all. When Percy returned to England in 1777, he took Richmond with him and the "Black Terror," as he became known, knocked out his first opponent in 25 min—a very fast victory in that era. Richmond lost on a knockout to British champion Tom Cribb in 1805, but continued fighting until he was fifty-two and never lost again.

In the meantime, Tom Molineaux, a South Carolina slave, had won a great many fights, and was given his freedom in 1809—perhaps because of his fighting skill. Molineaux promptly went to England to make his living in the ring. He had two tremendous championship fights with Cribb. The first, in 1810, went 33 rounds, most of it in heavy rain. It seemed that either fighter might collapse of exhaustion at any moment when Cribb threw a knockout punch. In their second fight, in 1811, Molineaux's jaw was broken in the tenth round and he was knocked out in the eleventh.

By the middle of the nineteenth century, most towns and cities in England had outlawed boxing, and staging a fight was becoming more and more difficult. One British champion of the era, Bendigo (whose real name was William Thompson), was arrested and sentenced to jail 28 times before retiring to become an evangelist.

Because of the difficulties with the law, an increasing number of English boxers came to the United States to tour. The first of them was James "Deaf" Burke, the British champion, in 1835, but he couldn't find much competition in this country.

By about 1860, the United States had quite a few good boxers, and the sport had declined somewhat in England, where no champion was recognized between 1851 and 1855. In 1860, John C. Heenan, who claimed the American title, went to England and fought Tom Sayers for the championship. The fight ended with no decision in the forty-second round when spectators burst into the ring.

Another English champion, Jem Mace, came to the United States in 1870 and had several fights in this country, including two no-decisions with Joe Coburn, who was considered the American titlist. Mace retired in 1873 and taught boxing both in this country and in England. His successor, Joe Goss, also came to the United States to find matches. On May 31, 1880, Paddy Ryan knocked out Goss in 85 rounds at Colliers Station, West Virginia, and the championship for the first time belonged to an American.

The Marquis of Queensberry. All this fighting had been done under the old London Prize Ring Rules, a revised edition of Broughton's rules. Experiments were made early in the nineteenth century with the use of gloves, and it is sometimes considered that the Queensberry Rules marked the end of bare-knuckle fighting and the beginning of gloved fighting. That is not quite true—the Queensberry Rules did specify that gloves must be used, but in such a manner that it is obvious that gloves already existed and were sometimes being used. The real change made under the Queensberry Rules was the establishment of a definite time period for a round. The 3-min round, with 1 min of rest between rounds, is still standard, as is the 10-sec knockout count.

The rules were written, not by the Marquis of Queensberry, but by John Graham Chambers, a member of the Amateur Athletic Club. When the code was published in 1867, the Marquis' name appeared as patron and sponsor.

The Queensberry Rules weren't actually used until a London tournament in 1872, which was also the first time that definite divisions, with specific weight limits, were established. This was a real amateur tournament, with trophies awarded to the winners, and no bets or prize money allowed. Fights under Queensberry Rules were generally permitted by British police, even if not specifically allowed by law, and bare-knuckle fighting under the old London Prize Ring Rules was on its way to extinction.

John L. Sullivan. Paddy Ryan's reign didn't last long. He managed to avoid John L. Sullivan's challenge for a while, but Sullivan finally caught up with him and knocked him out in nine rounds in a championship fight in Mississippi City.

Sullivan was very shrewd as well as very strong. He realized first that it would be possible to capitalize on his championship through nonring appearances and, second, that bare-knuckle fighting was becoming obsolete and that boxing with gloves, under the Queensberry Rules, represented the sport's future. Sullivan fought all over the country, primarily in nonchampionship bouts, often taking on two or three opponents per appearance, sometimes using Queensberry Rules, sometimes the London Prize Ring Rules.

Shortly after the formal presentation of his championship belt in 1887, he sailed to England, sparred with Jack Ashton for the benefit of the Prince of Wales, and fought a 39-round draw with Charley Mitchell early in 1888. The last bare-knuckle championship fight took place in 1889, when Sullivan knocked out Jake Kilrain in 75 rounds. He spent 1890 touring in a stage production, *Honest Hearts and Willing Hands,* went on tour to Australia in 1891, and then returned to the United States to defend his title under the Queensberry Rules.

The opponent was Gentleman Jim Corbett. Sullivan was heavily favored, at odds of 3 and 4 to 1. But, on September 7, 1892, at New Orleans, Corbett won the championship with a knockout in the twenty-first round. Corbett's speed and boxing ability overcame Sullivan's great weight advantage—212 lb to 178. It was too big an "advantage," undoubtedly reflecting Sullivan's lack of conditioning.

Early Queensberry Champions. Corbett was managed by William A. Brady, a theatrical promoter who quickly put the champion on tour in a specially written show, "Gentleman Jack." Corbett also went on a tour of England, and in 1894, he fought Peter Courtney in Trenton, New Jersey, for motion picture cameras—the first time a boxing match was filmed. A championship match in Texas was arranged in 1895 between Corbett and Robert Fitzsimmons, but the Texas Legislature passed a law against boxing. Later in the year, Corbett announced his retirement, and appeared in a new show. Meanwhile, Fitzsimmons, who had won the middleweight title, was touring with a vaudeville company.

By 1897, Corbett was out of retirement, and the pair met at Carson, Nevada. Fitzsimmons, a spindly-legged 165-pounder, knocked out Corbett in the fourteenth round. Fitzsimmons was an unlikely looking champion, but he had developed a powerful upper body through working with his blacksmith father, and he was the first fighter to realize that body punching could win matches. Fitzsimmons's style was to aim most of his punches at this opponent's chest and abdomen. He knocked out Corbett with a paralyzing blow to the solar plexus.

That wasn't enough against the next champion, James J. Jeffries, a mammoth, solidly built, 225-pounder. Jeffries was not only big and powerful, he was fast, and Fitzsimmons was badly overmatched in their 1899 championship fight. Jeffries scored a knockout in the twelfth round. Jeffries never lost the title. By 1904, it was hard for him to find an opponent, and he decided to retire. He agreed to referee a fight between Marvin Hart and Jack Root and to give the title to the winner.

A Black Champion. By the turn of the century, there were already a lot of good black fighters around, and there had already been a black champion, George Dixon, who won the bantamweight title in 1890 and then moved up to the featherweight crown. But in the top division, no black had been able to get a title fight.

Hart won the watered-down title in the fight with Root, and Tommy Burns took the title from him in 1906. Burns had a challenger waiting—Jack "Little Arthur" Johnson, a black from Galveston, Texas, who had built up an impressive record of knockouts. Johnson didn't get the title fight until the day after Christmas, 1908, in Sydney. Police entered the ring and stopped the fight in the fourteenth round. Johnson was beating Burns badly, and was acclaimed as the new champion.

Johnson had a long reign, but it wasn't an easy one. Almost as soon as he won the title, the search began for a "great white hope" who could dethrone him. Finally, Jeffries agreed to come out of retirement. It was a mistake. He was overweight and out of condition. Johnson whipped the former champion, finally knocking him out in the fifteenth round. The victory made things worse. Race riots broke out after the fight. Johnson's second wife, a white woman, committed suicide, touching off a public furor. And the search for a white hope went on.

In 1912, Johnson appeared in a federal court in Chicago on charges of abduction and transporting a woman across a state line for immoral purposes. The woman in question, also white, had become his third wife. The prosecution produced, instead, another girlfriend who had traveled with Johnson; he was found guilty and sentenced to a year and a day in federal prison. Free on bail while awaiting an appeal, Johnson slipped out of the United States into Canada and then to Europe. He spent the next four years in exile, fighting in Paris, South America, and Cuba. In 1915, he met the "Pottawatomie Giant," Jess Willard, in a title bout in Havana. Willard, who fought at about 250 lb, knocked Johnson out in the twenty-sixth round. Johnson claimed later that he had thrown the fight; his claim has not been widely believed. Shortly afterward, he returned to the United States to serve his prison term.

Willard defended his title once in 1916 and didn't defend again until 1919. By then, he was obviously out of condition, partly because he didn't take his much smaller opponent very seriously. The small challenger was named Jack Dempsey. His brutal attack knocked Willard out in the third round.

The Golden Age. In the early part of the century, boxing was illegal in many states and only quasi-legal in others. In New York State, from 1900 until 1911, boxing was permitted only for members of private clubs, until a new law was passed permitting public fights but without decisions. A fight could be won only by a knockout. This law was repealed in 1917, when boxing became entirely illegal in the state.

The man basically responsible for the relegalization of the sport was William A. Gavin, an Englishman who came to the United States in 1919 with a plan to organize a private club where members could watch fights. His International Sporting Club was to be patterned after London's successful National Sporting Club. Gavin sold about $350,000 worth of memberships and then discovered that his plan was illegal.

His lobbying convinced Senate Speaker James J. Walker to sponsor legislation which would make boxing legal, under the control of a state commission. The law was actually too broad for Gavin's purposes. His private club was not yet built, and Frank Armstrong and Tex Rickard became promoters of fights at Madison Square Garden. The first fight under the new law was staged at the Garden on September 17, 1920. Suddenly, boxing was not only legal but actually sanctioned by a state government,

and New York was to be the center of the revitalized sport.

The success of boxing in New York, and the money in taxes and fees that rolled in, quickly persuaded other states to pass similar laws and organize state boxing commissions. The Golden Age of American sports was beginning, and Jack Dempsey was to be one of its brightest stars.

Dempsey and Tunney. Most of the Golden Age stars—Babe Ruth, Red Grange, Bobby Jones—were national heroes. Dempsey was not; at least, not at the beginning of his reign. For one thing, he had beaten a popular champion; for another, he was accused of having dodged the draft during World War I. Dempsey's manager, Jack "Doc" Kearns, and promoter Rickard realized that a villain could be a drawing card. People would be willing to buy tickets in the hope of seeing him take a beating. As hero-challenger, they selected Georges Carpentier of France, the light-heavyweight champion, after Dempsey had defended his title twice. Carpentier was good-looking and modest, and he had served in the French Army's aviation corps during the War.

Rickard hastily had a grandstand built at a place in New Jersey called Boyle's Thirty Acres, and he went to work ballyhooing the fight and selling tickets, with the goal of reaching the first million-dollar gate. The goal was far exceeded: More than $1.6 million worth of tickets were sold, and on July 2, 1921, more than 90,000 people watched Dempsey knock Carpentier out in the fourth round.

Dempsey spent all of 1922 fighting exhibitions. In 1923, the people of Shelby, Montana, decided to put their town on the map by hosting a championship fight, and they offered Kearns a guarantee of $300,000. He agreed. Dempsey's challenger was to be Tommy Gibbons, a tough 172-pounder who had never been knocked out. The people of Shelby wanted extra time to raise the second $100,000 payment, but Kearns insisted on getting his money on schedule, and he did get most of it. The gate receipts were disappointing. Kearns collected all that money, too—about $50,000, which still left him short of the $300,000 he had been guaranteed. The fight was not an artistic success, either. Dempsey won a 15-round decision but didn't look impressive. He and Kearns fled with the money immediately afterward. Shelby's banks closed, several of its businesses went broke, and it looked for a while as if the town might be wiped off the map.

Kearns, undaunted, wanted another million-dollar gate. He got it. Rickard matched Dempsey with the Argentine fighter, Luis Firpo, who outweighed the champion by 24 lb. The fight, which took place at the Polo Grounds on September 14, 1923, was one of the most dramatic ever. Dempsey was knocked down in the first round. He got up and knocked Firpo down. He knocked Firpo down six more times in the round. Then he rushed in to finish him off, but Firpo landed a terrific right that knocked Dempsey through the ropes and onto a sportswriter's typewriter. Dempsey barely got back into the ring without being counted out. In the second round, Dempsey knocked Firpo down three times. The third time, the big Argentinian stayed down, and Dempsey was suddenly a popular hero. He spent the next three years cashing in on his popularity, fighting exhibitions here and there, once taking on six opponents on one card and knocking out four of them.

Then came an unlikely challenger: the handsome, clean-living, poetry-reciting Gene Tunney, a clever boxer who had also demonstrated great courage in staying all 15 rounds while taking a merciless beating from Harry Greb. (It was Tunney's only defeat as a professional.) The fight, in Philadelphia, drew a gate of nearly $2 million. It was a fine contrast: the "Manassa Mauler" against a scientific boxer; the champion who had begun his career boxing in Western saloons, against the challenger who had chosen fighting as a way of amassing some money so he could meet the right people and live the good life. Dempsey was an 11 to 5 favorite. The crowd didn't take to a boxer who read Shakespeare and conversed with George Bernard Shaw. But Tunney thoroughly whipped Dempsey and won a 10-round decision, reflected in the battered face of the ex-champion.

Their rematch, at Chicago's Soldier Field, drew a gate of $2.6 million, which is still a record for live gate receipts. This fight, on September 22, 1927, has become famous for the "long count" controversy. Tunney was ahead on points in the seventh round, when Dempsey sent him down with a left hook to the jaw. The referee began counting, then realized that Dempsey hadn't gone to a neutral corner. By the time the count resumed, several seconds had elapsed. Tunney got up before the count reached 10 and proceeded to win his decision. Study of the fight film has shown that he was down for 16 sec.

Tunney defended his title just once, against New Zealander Tom Heeney, for a guarantee of $525,000. The fight was stopped in the eleventh round; Tunney was still the champion, and he announced his retirement.

Interregnum. The next nine years represented a not-very-golden-age for boxing—at least, not for the heavyweight division. The farcical happenings began with a fight between Max Schmeling and Jack Sharkey for Tunney's vacated title. Sharkey appeared to have command through the first three rounds. In the fourth, he threw a low, hard left. Schmeling fell. His manager, Joe Jacobs, rushed into the ring with seconds and carried him back to his corner. Jacobs spoke angrily to the referee. After some moments of indecision, the referee stopped the fight and declared Schmeling the new heavyweight champion of the world—on a foul.

There had to be a rematch. This time, Schmeling appeared to be in command all the way. Awaiting the decision, he smiled and waved at friends. Suddenly, Sharkey's right hand was being raised, and Schmeling's smile disappeared. He couldn't believe he had lost. A lot of other people didn't believe it either.

Then came Primo Carnera, a gentle giant from Italy, known as the "Ambling Alp." The 6-6, 260-lb Carnera had been discovered on exhibition in a traveling circus in Europe. Brought to the United States, he racked up a string of victories. Carnera himself didn't know it, but most of his victories had been paid for by the mob that had made him a puppet. In 1933, Carnera got the ultimate fight, against champion Sharkey. Carnera hit him with an uppercut in the sixth round and Sharkey was counted out. A cynical sportswriter remarked, "It's the first time I've seen a guy get hit by an uppercut and fall on his face." Carnera's awakening came, brutally, a year later. Max Baer knocked him down 11 times in as many rounds. The battered Carnera kept getting up, but the fight was finally stopped, and Baer was the fourth champion in four years.

Baer was a well-liked, amiable, sometimes deliberately clownish fighter who had a lot of talent but unfortunately didn't always use it. He was champion for one day less than a year. On June 13, 1934, he lost a 15-round decision to twenty-nine-year-old James J. Braddock, a 10 to 1 underdog who quickly became known as "the Cinderella Man." Braddock, near the end of an up-and-down career, wanted one big purse before retiring. He knew the best way to get that purse—by accepting the challenge of a tough, young, black heavyweight named Joe Louis.

The Brown Bomber. In the years before and after Jack Johnson, there had been some fine black heavyweights. At least two of them had tried hard to get title matches, without success. Probably Joe Louis Barrow—his full name—would have been given a shot eventually anyway. By the time he turned pro, in 1934, black fighters had gained a certain amount of public acceptance. John Henry Lewis and Henry Armstrong were soon to win titles in other weight divisions, and Tiger Flowers had been middleweight champion. But Braddock's willingness certainly speeded up Louis' timetable. The young "Brown Bomber" was a genuine contender, having won 34 of 35 professional fights, 29 of them by knockout. His only loss had been a twelfth-round knockout by former champion Max Schmeling; he had knocked out three former champions, Carnera, Baer, and Sharkey.

The fight took place on June 22, 1937. Braddock knocked Louis down in the first round, but the rest of the fight was all Louis. The game Braddock took a lot of punishment and kept coming, but Louis knocked him out in the eighth round.

Louis quickly became the most active heavyweight champion ever. After 12 title defenses in three years, Louis in 1941 faced and beat nine more challengers. Sportswriters scornfully referred to Louis's "Bum of the Month Club." But, in fact, Louis was taking on everyone who could be considered a real contender, along with some who couldn't. He avenged his only loss by knocking out Schmeling in the first round. After two 1942 defenses—one purse went to the Naval Relief Fund, the other to the Army Relief Fund—Louis entered the Army, where he boxed a whole series of exhibitions through 1944 and 1945. He returned to civilian life and his title in 1946, older and not nearly as sharp, but still good enough to defend the championship twice before boxing another long string of exhibitions. In 1949, Louis announced his retirement. He had held the world heavyweight championship for nearly 12 years and 25 defenses—both records for any weight division.

After Louis. The chief contenders for the title after Louis's retirement were Ezzard Charles and "Jersey Joe" Walcott, both rather venerable. Charles, twenty-eight, and Walcott, thirty-five, fought for the NBA version of the title in 1949, with Charles winning the decision. In 1951, he won another decision from Walcott, but later that year Walcott—now thirty-seven, at least—knocked out Charles to win the title. He defended against Charles in 1952 and then ran into the "Brockton Blockbuster."

Rocky Marciano of Brockton, Massachusetts, was a latecomer to professional boxing. He had his first pro fight when he was twenty-three, in 1947. He knocked out that opponent in the third round, and that set the style for his entire career. Considered one of the hardest hitters in history, Marciano reeled off KO after KO during the next three years, most of them in the early rounds. By 1951, he was beating some highly regarded heavyweights, including Joe Louis, who had returned from retirement to try to win back his title. Marciano knocked Louis out in the eighth round.

In the 1952 title fight, Marciano had trouble catching the wily Walcott, but he finally knocked him out in the thirteenth round. He defended his title six times—five times by knockout—before retiring in 1956, the only heavyweight champion ever to retire without suffering a professional defeat. Of his 49 fights, he won 43 by knockout.

A tournament was held to determine the next champion. The winner was twenty-one-year-old Floyd Patterson. The youngest champ, Patterson also became the only heavyweight ever to lose the title and win it back. He lost on a third-round knockout by Ingemar Johansson of Sweden in 1959, then knocked out Johansson less than a year later to regain the championship. In 1961, Patterson lost the title in ignominious fashion. Charles "Sonny" Liston knocked him out in the first round, and did it again in a rematch in 1962.

Liston had a powerful punch, a baleful glare, and a prison record that made him a controversial figure. When he defended his title for the second time, in 1964, a lot of people were hoping he would lose. The challenger was a fast-talking, fast-moving young man who had won a certain amount of popularity by beating an experienced Russian for the Olympic light-heavyweight championship in 1960. Those who rooted for him had no idea that he was going to become much more controversial than Liston had ever dreamed of being.

Clay-Ali. Cassius Clay fought Liston twice, and controversy swirled around both fights, a fitting start for his tempestuous reign. In the first fight, Clay wanted to quit after the fifth round, claiming that a foreign substance from Liston's gloves had rubbed off in his eyes. However, he gave Liston a thorough beating in the sixth round. When the bell rang for the seventh round, Liston remained in his corner, and Clay was the new champion. (Liston claimed an injured shoulder had forced him to quit.)

The rematch had an unlikely setting—a youth center in Lewiston, Maine—and an even unlikelier ending. Former champion Walcott was refereeing for the first time. In the first round, Clay suddenly decked Liston with a quick, hard right. The inexperienced Walcott failed to pick up the count from the ringside timekeeper, who couldn't get his attention. Liston got up and the fight resumed. But Walcott suddenly rushed between them, stopped the fight, and raised Clay's hand in victory. The timekeeper had informed him that Liston had been down for a count of 22.

Clay became the fightingest champion since Louis, defending the title eight times in a 16-month period. He also adopted the Muslim faith, changed his name to Muhammad Ali, and refused induction into the Army on religious grounds. As a result, he was banned from fighting in the United States and stripped of his title.

In 1970, after two years of inactivity, Clay announced his retirement. There were already two new champions— Jimmy Ellis, who had won an NBA elimination tournament, and Joe Frazier, who had won the New York version of the title. Frazier defended his version four times before meeting Ellis for the undisputed championship, just after Clay's announced retirement. Frazier knocked Ellis out in the fifth round.

The championship was disputed, however, by Clay-Ali's fans. After winning a court decision that upheld his right to refuse induction, Ali returned to the ring. He met Frazier on March 8, 1971. Again there was controversy, most of it about the fact that the fight was blacked out not only on TV but radio as well, and the promoters even attempted to keep the wire services from sending out round-by-round reports.

The two champions fought a grueling 15 rounds, Frazier winning a unanimous decision and, at last, general recognition as champion, although Ali and some followers disputed the decision. A rematch seemed inevitable, but negotiations dragged on. In 1973, Frazier was a heavy favorite in his defense against George Foreman, a big, solid-punching former Olympic titlist who was considered too inexperienced to win this one. But Foreman stunned the boxing world, not to mention Frazier, with an onslaught that had the champion on the canvas six times in two rounds before the fight was finally stopped. And Ali won back the championship he had never really lost by knocking out Foreman in a 1974 fight in Zaire, Africa.

Other Divisions. In the public eye, the history of boxing is to a great extent the history of the heavyweight division and its champions. But there have been great champions in other weight divisions who deserve attention. Information on those who are in the *Ring* magazine or Citizens Savings hall of fame will be found at the end of this entry.

Financial Structure. That $2.6 million gate for the second Dempsey-Tunney fight has never been surpassed. It was the greatest promotional job of a great promoter, Tex Rickard. But Rickard would undoubtedly be intrigued by the financial arrangements for the most recent heavyweight championship fights. Tunney got less than $1 million for his 1927 title fight. By contrast, Muhammad Ali and Joe Frazier received $2.5 million apiece for their 1971 fight, which had gate receipts of only $1,350,000. The difference, of course, is closed-circuit television. Up until about 1949, a bout had to make it on gate receipts alone. (Some movie and radio money was sometimes involved, but these amounts were negligible.)

A few fights were televised experimentally in the late thirties and early forties. In 1944 the Gillette Safety Razor Company signed an agreement with Madison Square Garden to sponsor weekly telecasts of fights. At the time, there were few privately owned sets in the country; the main outlets were veterans' hospitals throughout the country. As television sets proliferated, however, viewers and revenue increased.

The weekly shows came to an end in 1964. Madison Square Garden had made about $15 million in TV revenues in the 20-year period, and at the peak of popularity of televised fights, each fighter was getting about $4,000 a contest. That doesn't sound like much, but it should be borne in mind that these were, for the most part, non-championship fights.

Closed-circuit television began in 1951, when Joe Louis defended against Lee Savold. The fight was telecast to eight theaters in six cities. Promoters, of course, love closed-circuit TV—they can charge for ringside seats at locations all over the world. One of the first big closed-

Sugar Ray Robinson, right, considered by many experts the greatest fighter ever, pound for pound, knocked out Rocky Graziano in the third round of their middleweight title fight in April 1952. *(Public Broadcasting Service.)*

circuit fights was Sugar Ray Robinson's battle with Carmen Basilio for the middleweight title in 1958, which went to 174 outlets in 140 cities, grossing $1.4 million at the box offices.

Satellite communications opened a whole new treasure chest for fight promoters. The 1971 Ali-Frazier fight was telecast to more than 300 million people at closed-circuit TV sites in 46 countries. Total revenues were about $20 million—no other fight had ever grossed more than $5 million.

Closed-circuit telecasts have been criticized for turning boxing into a sport for the rich. But, except for the free-TV era—and, as noted, few title fights were on free TV—boxing has always been a sport for rich spectators. Ringside seats sold for $100 when Corbett fought Sullivan in 1892. The income tax structure has made it unwise for a heavyweight champion to defend his title more than once a year, and when two fighters and their entourages have to get all their money for a year or more from one fight, naturally they want a good purse. And promoters, offering enormous guarantees to the fighters, naturally want to pull in the most receipts possible. Closed-circuit television is the way—and will continue to be the way, for a long time to come.

The Rules

There is nothing very complicated about boxing. Two boxers wearing padded gloves (usually 8 oz for heavyweights, more for lighter fighters) fight in a ring, 18 to 20 ft², marked off by three or four 1-in ropes. They fight for a specified number of 3-min rounds, with 1-min rest periods between rounds.

A fighter is not allowed to hit an opponent below the belt, to butt or knee, to hit an opponent who is down or in the process of getting up, or to hit on the back of the neck (a "rabbit punch"). A foul is punished in various ways. If the opponent is disabled, the boxer who struck the blow loses by disqualification. A boxer may also be disqualified for repeated fouling. One foul usually brings a warning from the referee; if there are two or more fouls in the same round, the referee can award the round to the opponent.

Clinching—holding onto the opponent—is allowed, up to a point. But, if a clinch is so effective that neither fighter can throw a punch, the referee will order them to break. Each fighter must take one step backward from the clinch before a punch can be thrown; the referee will usually step between them to separate them and prevent fighting during the break.

When a fighter is knocked down, a timekeeper at ringside begins counting the seconds, and the referee ordinarily picks up the count from the timekeeper. Counting doesn't begin until the other fighter is in a neutral corner. The downed fighter is given 10 sec in which to stand up; the fighter who doesn't make it has been knocked out. It is no longer possible for a fighter to be "saved by the bell." If the bell marking the end of a round sounds while a fighter is down, the count continues, except at the end of the final round; when the fight is over, the count is ended, and a decision results.

It is also a knockout if a fighter cannot continue for any reason (unless injured by a foul). If in the referee's opinion one of the fighters has been injured or is so groggy that defense is no longer possible, the referee may stop the fight.

Minor rules and regulations may vary from state to state. Generally speaking, a fighter, when down, is required to take an 8 count; if the boxer gets up before the count reaches 8, the referee will continue counting and will allow the fight to resume only on reaching 8. This mandatory 8-count rule is often waived for title fights.

In some states, three knockdowns in a round constitute a knockout. The "technical knockout" is largely a convenient fiction. In popular language, a technical knockout occurs when a fight is stopped without a fighter actually having been knocked out. Actually, as far as official records are concerned, it is a knockout. If a fight is stopped between rounds, the knockout is considered to have taken place in the earlier round.

Some states do recognize a "technical win," "technical loss," and "technical draw," however. When a fighter is injured, it is a technical draw if less than one-third of the fight has been completed; if more than one-third has been completed, it is a technical win for the fighter who is ahead in the scoring and, of course, a technical loss for the opponent.

Scoring Systems. If there is no knockout, the outcome of a fight comes down to a decision. Usually two ringside judges and the referee participate. The simplest scoring system is round-by-round; after each round, the judge decides which fighter won that round, or scores it even. At the end of the fight, the winner is the fighter who has won the most rounds.

A supplementary point system is sometimes used if the fighters are even in rounds won. In this system, a judge gives a fighter 1 point for winning a close round, 2 points for winning a round handily, 3 points for winning a one-sided round, and 4 points for winning a one-sided round in which the opponent is knocked down twice or more. These points are totaled only if the round-by-round score results in a draw.

Most WBA states use the "5-point-must" system, meaning the winner of a round must get 5 points, while the opponent gets anywhere from 0 to 4 points. (If a round is even, each fighter gets 5 points.) At the end of the fight, the points are totaled; there is no round-by-round scoring breakdown under this system.

Other states use the 10-point-must system, which is similar. California uses a 5-point system in which the loser of a round gets no points and the winner gets anywhere from 1 to 5 points. An even round is scored 0 to 0.

Governing Bodies

Professional Championships. In the early days of boxing, a championship was an informal title. Any fighter became generally recognized as champion who consistently took on and beat all comers. Weight classes were similarly informal. During the eighteenth century, there were generally two divisions, heavyweight and lightweight, though there was no definite weight limit established for the lightweight division. Early in the nineteenth century, some fighters, in the 150-to-160-lb range, became known as middleweights.

Around the turn of the century, weight divisions began to proliferate. They were often created by fighters or their managers. Weight divisions and championships became formalized with the growth of state boxing and athletic commissions, who set definite weight limits for each class during the 1920s. Differences among states were generally ironed out through commission agreements. Most of the state commissions joined the National Boxing Association (now the World Boxing Association), which formally recognizes world champions. New York State is not a member of the WBA, and occasionally New York recognizes other champions. Other non-WBA states usually follow New York's lead.

The World Boxing Council is an organization of national boxing authorities, primarily from countries outside North America and Europe. The WBC and WBA usually recognize the same champions in the higher weight divisions, but they frequently differ in the lower divisions. The European Boxing Union recognizes European champions in all weight classes.

Weight limits for professional divisions are as follows: flyweight, 112 lb; bantamweight, 118 lb; featherweight, 126 lb; lightweight, 135 lb; welterweight, 147 lb; middleweight, 160 lb; light-heavyweight, 175 lb; heavyweight, over 175 lb.

Three other divisions are now recognized by various states and by the WBA or WBC. They are the junior lightweight (130 lb), junior welterweight (140 lb), and junior middleweight (154 lb). Although the divisions are based on weight, not age, their names are appropriate. A "junior" champion is usually a rather young fighter who is likely to grow out of the division within a few years, and these are not considered major titles, as the longer-established championships are.

Amateur Boxing. The Amateur Athletic Union started a boxing program in 1888, and still conducts national championships for amateurs. The sport has been on the Olympic Games program since 1920.

The amateur version of the sport places a premium on boxing ability as opposed to slugging. An amateur fight usually consists of only three 2-min rounds, so there's little chance for a knockout. Gloves are usually 8 oz for lighter boxers and 10 oz for heavier boxers, and protective helmets must be worn. Generally, an amateur boxer, especially in international competition, gets as much credit for avoiding a blow as for landing one, and the judges watch footwork, as well as fists, very carefully.

The best publicized amateur boxing in this country takes place in the annual Golden Gloves tournaments, inaugurated in 1926 by the *Chicago Tribune,* under the urging of sports editor Arch Ward, who later conceived the annual baseball and football all-star games. In 1927, the New York *Daily News* held the first tournament in that city. Fighters progress through regional and sectional tournaments to the national finals, which pit Western against Eastern champions.

National collegiate championships were conducted for many years by the NCAA, but the sport was dropped after 1960, largely because of the death of a University of Wisconsin boxer. Some colleges still have intramural boxing programs.

Championship Fights

The following list of championship fights covers boxing's modern era, beginning roughly in 1890. In general, NBA-WBA title lines are followed, but in some of the lower weight divisions, the WBC line is followed in recent years. The list includes only those fights in which a title actually changed hands, along with a few other fights involving a title that was in doubt.

Heavyweights

Feb. 7, 1882—John L. Sullivan KOed Paddy Ryan, 9th round.

Sept. 7, 1892—James J. Corbett KOed John L. Sullivan, 21st round.

Mar. 17, 1897—Bob Fitzsimmons KOed James J. Corbett, 14th round.

June 9, 1899—James J. Jeffries KOed Bob Fitzsimmons, 11th round.

(James J. Jeffries retired in 1905 and refereed the Hart-Root fight.)

July 3, 1905—Marvin Hart KOed Jack Root, 12th round.

Feb. 23, 1906—Tommy Burns decisioned Marvin Hart, 20 rounds.

Dec. 26, 1908—Jack Johnson KOed Tommy Burns, 14th round.

Ap. 5, 1915—Jess Willard KOed Jack Johnson, 26th round.

July 4, 1919—Jack Dempsey KOed Jess Willard, 3rd round.

Sept. 23, 1926—Gene Tunney outpointed Jack Dempsey, 10 rounds.

(Gene Tunney retired in 1928; title was vacant until 1930.)

June 12, 1930—Max Schmeling beat Jack Sharkey on a foul, 4th round.

June 21, 1932—Jack Sharkey decisioned Max Schmeling, 15 rounds.

Amateur competition in Golden Gloves tournaments still draws thousands of boxing fans across the country. This is welterweight action in a New England Golden Gloves tournament. (*Hank Seaman*, New Bedford Standard-Times.)

June 29, 1933—Primo Carnera KOed Jack Sharkey, 6th round.

June 14, 1934—Max Baer KOed Primo Carnera, 11th round.

June 13, 1935—Jim Braddock decisioned Max Baer, 15 rounds.

June 22, 1937—Joe Louis KOed Jim Braddock, 8th round. (Joe Louis announced retirement in 1949.)

June 22, 1949—Ezzard Charles decisioned "Jersey Joe" Walcott, 15 rounds, to win NBA title.

July 18, 1951—"Jersey Joe" Walcott KOed Ezzard Charles, 7th round.

Sept. 23, 1952—Rocky Marciano KOed "Jersey Joe" Walcott, 13th round.

(Rocky Marciano retired in 1956 and a tournament was held.)

Nov. 30, 1956—Floyd Patterson KOed Archie Moore, 5th round.

June 26, 1959—Ingemar Johansson KOed Floyd Patterson, 3rd round.

June 20, 1960—Floyd Patterson KOed Ingemar Johansson, 5th round.

Sept. 25, 1962—Sonny Liston KOed Floyd Patterson, 1st round.

Feb. 25, 1964—Cassius Clay (Muhammad Ali) KOed Sonny Liston, 7th round.

(Cassius Clay was stripped of his title after being indicted for refusing induction into the armed forces on religious grounds, and a tournament was held.)

Apr. 27, 1968—Jimmy Ellis decisioned Jerry Quarry, 15 rounds.

Feb. 16, 1970—Joe Frazier KOed Jimmy Ellis, 5th round.

Jan. 22, 1973—George Foreman KOed Joe Frazier, 2nd round.

Oct. 30, 1974—Muhammad Ali (Cassius Clay) KOed George Foreman, 8th round.

Light Heavyweights

This division was created in 1903 by Lou Houseman, the manager of Jack Root, who was too big to be a middleweight and too light to be a serious heavyweight contender.

Apr. 22, 1903—Jack Root decisioned Kid McCoy, 10 rounds.

July 4, 1903—George Gardner KOed Jack Root, 12th round.

Nov. 25, 1903—Bob Fitzsimmons decisioned George Gardner, 20 rounds.

Dec. 20, 1905—Philadelphia Jack O'Brien KOed Bob Fitzsimmons, 13th round.

(Nearly 11 years elapsed before the next title fight.)

Oct. 24, 1916—Battling Levinsky decisioned Jack Dillon, 12 rounds.

Oct. 12, 1920—Georges Carpentier KOed Battling Levinsky, 4th round.

Sept. 24, 1922—Battling Siki KOed Georges Carpentier, 6th round.

Mar. 17, 1923—Mike McTigue decisioned Battling Siki, 20 rounds.

May 30, 1925—Paul Berlenbach decisioned Mike McTigue, 15 rounds.

July 16, 1926—Jack Delaney decisioned Paul Berlenbach, 15 rounds.

(Jack Delaney became heavyweight; Mike McTigue claimed title.)

Oct. 7, 1927—Tommy Loughran decisioned Mike McTigue, 15 rounds.

(Tommy Loughran became a heavyweight and a tournament was held.)

Feb. 10, 1930—Jimmy Slattery decisioned Lou Scozza, 15 rounds.

June 25, 1930—Maxie Rosenbloom decisioned Jimmy Slattery, 15 rounds.

Nov. 16, 1934—Bob Olin decisioned Maxie Rosenbloom, 15 rounds.

Oct. 31, 1935—John Henry Lewis decisioned Bob Olin, 15 rounds.

(John Henry Lewis retired in 1939 and a tournament was held.)

Feb. 3, 1939—Melio Bettina KOed Tiger Jack Fox, 9th round.

July 13, 1939—Billy Conn decisioned Melio Bettina, 15 rounds.

(Billy Conn became a heavyweight and a tournament was held.)

Jan. 13, 1941—Anton Christoforidis decisioned Melio Bettina, 15 rounds.

May 22, 1941—Gus Lesnevich decisioned Anton Christoforidis, 15 rounds.

July 26, 1948—Freddie Mills decisioned Gus Lesnevich, 15 rounds.

Jan. 24, 1950—Joey Maxim KOed Freddie Mills, 10th round.

Dec. 17, 1952—Archie Moore decisioned Joey Maxim, 15 rounds.

(In 1960, Archie Moore's title was vacated.)

Feb. 7, 1960—Harold Johnson KOed Jesse Bowdry, 9th round.

June 1, 1963—Willie Pastrano decisioned Harold Johnson, 15 rounds.

Mar. 30, 1965—Jose Torres KOed Willie Pastrano, 9th round.

Dec. 16, 1966—Dick Tiger decisioned Jose Torres, 15 rounds.

May 24, 1968—Bob Foster KOed Dick Tiger, 4th round.

(Bob Foster retired in 1974.)

Dec. 7, 1974—Victor Galindez KOed Len Hutchins, 13th round.

Middleweights

Jan. 14, 1891—Bob Fitzsimmons KOed Jack "The Nonpareil" Dempsey, 13th round.

(Bob Fitzsimmons outgrew the division and entered heavyweight division.)

Feb. 25, 1898—Tommy Ryan decisioned George Green, 18 rounds.

(Tommy Ryan retired in 1907.)

Feb. 22, 1908—Stanley Ketchel KOed Mike "Twin" Sullivan, 1st round.

Sept. 7, 1908—Billy Papke KOed Stanley Ketchel, 12th round.

Nov. 26, 1908—Stanley Ketchel KOed Billy Papke, 11th round.

(Stanley Ketchel was killed and Billy Papke claimed the title.)

Mar. 5, 1913—Frank Klaus beat Billy Papke on a foul, 15th round.

Oct. 11, 1913—George Chip KOed Frank Klaus, 6th round.

Apr. 6, 1914—Al McCoy KOed George Chip, 1st round.

Nov. 14, 1917—Mike O'Dowd KOed Al McCoy, 6th round.

May 6, 1920—Johnny Wilson decisioned Mike O'Dowd, 12 rounds.

Aug. 31, 1923—Harry Greb decisioned Johnny Wilson, 15 rounds.

Feb. 26, 1926—Tiger Flowers decisioned Harry Greb, 15 rounds.

Dec. 3, 1926—Mickey Walker decisioned Tiger Flowers, 10 rounds.

(Mickey Walker relinquished the title in 1931 and there was no generally recognized champion for 10 years.)

Nov. 28, 1941—Tony Zale decisioned Georgie Abrams, 15 rounds.

July 16, 1947—Rocky Graziano KOed Tony Zale, 6th round.

June 10, 1948—Tony Zale KOed Rocky Graziano, 3rd round.

Sept. 21, 1948—Marcel Cerdan KOed Tony Zale, 12th round.

June 16, 1949—Jake LaMotta KOed Marcel Cerdan, 10th round.

Feb. 14, 1951—Sugar Ray Robinson KOed Jake LaMotta, 13th round.

July 10, 1951—Randy Turpin decisioned Sugar Ray Robinson, 15 rounds.

Sept. 12, 1951—Sugar Ray Robinson KOed Randy Turpin, 10th round.

(Sugar Ray Robinson announced his retirement in 1952; a tournament was held.)

Oct. 21, 1953—Bobo Olson decisioned Randy Turpin, 15 rounds.

Dec. 9, 1955—Sugar Ray Robinson (out of retirement) KOed Olson, 2nd round.

Jan. 2, 1957—Gene Fullmer decisioned Sugar Ray Robinson, 15 rounds.

May 1, 1957—Sugar Ray Robinson KOed Gene Fullmer, 5th round.

Sept. 23, 1957—Carmen Basilio decisioned Sugar Ray Robinson, 15 rounds.

Mar. 25, 1958—Sugar Ray Robinson decisioned Carmen Basilio, 15 rounds.

(Sugar Ray Robinson's title was vacated for nondefense in 1959.)

Oct. 23, 1962—Dick Tiger decisioned Gene Fullmer, 15 rounds.

Dec. 7, 1963—Joey Giardello decisioned Dick Tiger, 15 rounds.

Oct. 21, 1965—Dick Tiger decisioned Joey Giardello, 15 rounds.

Apr. 25, 1966—Emile Griffith decisioned Dick Tiger, 15 rounds.

Apr. 17, 1967—Nino Benvenuti decisioned Emile Griffith, 15 rounds.

Sept. 29, 1967—Emile Griffith decisioned Nino Benvenuti, 15 rounds.

March 4, 1968—Nino Benvenuti decisioned Emile Griffith, 15 rounds.

Nov. 7, 1970—Carlos Monzon KOed Nino Benvenuti, 12th round.

June 26, 1976—Carlos Monzon, WBA champion, decisioned Rodrigo Valdes, WBC champion, to unite the championships.

Welterweights

Dec. 14, 1892—"Mysterious" Billy Smith KOed Danny Needham, 14th round.

July 26, 1894—Tommy Ryan decisioned "Mysterious" Billy Smith, 20 rounds.

Mar. 2, 1896—Charles "Kid" McCoy KOed Tommy Ryan, 15th round.

(Charles "Kid" McCoy moved up in class; "Mysterious" Billy Smith claimed the title.)

Jan. 15, 1900—Jim Ferns beat Billy Smith on a foul, 21st round.

Oct. 16, 1900—Matty Matthews decisioned Jim Ferns, 15 rounds.

May 24, 1901—Jim Ferns KOed Matty Matthews, 10th round.

Dec. 18, 1901—Joe Walcott KOed Jim Ferns, 5th round.

Apr. 30, 1904—Dixie Kid beat Joe Walcott on a foul, 20th round.

(Dixie Kid outgrew class in 1905; Joe Walcott claimed title.)

Oct. 16, 1906—Honey Mellody decisioned Joe Walcott, 15 rounds.

Apr. 23, 1907—Mike "Twin" Sullivan decisioned Mellody, 20 rounds.

(Mike "Twin" Sullivan surrendered the title and there was no recognized champion for seven years.)

Aug. 31, 1915—Ted "Kid" Lewis decisioned Jack Britton, 12 rounds.

Apr. 24, 1916—Jack Britton decisioned Ted "Kid" Lewis, 20 rounds.

June 25, 1917—Ted "Kid" Lewis decisioned Jack Britton, 20 rounds.

Mar. 17, 1919—Jack Britton KOed Ted "Kid" Lewis, 9th round.

Nov. 1, 1922—Mickey Walker decisioned Jack Britton, 15 rounds.

May 20, 1926—Pete Latzo decisioned Mickey Walker, 10 rounds.

June 3, 1927—Joe Dundee decisioned Pete Latzo, 15 rounds.

July 25, 1929—Jackie Fields beat Joe Dundee on a foul, 2nd round.

May 9, 1930—Young Jack Thompson decisioned Jackie Fields, 15 rounds.

Sept. 5, 1930—Tommy Freeman decisioned Young Jack Thompson, 15 rounds.

Apr. 14, 1931—Young Jack Thompson KOed Tommy Freeman, 12th round.

Oct. 23, 1931—Lou Brouillard decisioned Young Jack Thompson, 15 rounds.

Jan. 28, 1932—Jackie Fields decisioned Lou Brouillard, 10 rounds.

Feb. 22, 1933—Young Corbett III decisioned Jackie Fields, 10 rounds.

May 29, 1933—Jimmy McLarnin KOed Young Corbett III, 1st round.

May 28, 1934—Barney Ross decisioned Jimmy McLarnin, 15 rounds.

Sept. 17, 1934—Jimmy McLarnin decisioned Barney Ross, 15 rounds.

May 28, 1935—Barney Ross decisioned Jimmy McLarnin, 15 rounds.

May 31, 1938—Henry Armstrong decisioned Barney Ross, 15 rounds.

Oct. 4, 1940—Fritzie Zivic decisioned Henry Armstrong, 15 rounds.

July 29, 1941—Freddie "Red" Cochrane decisioned Fritzie Zivic, 15 rounds.

Feb. 1, 1946—Marty Servo KOed "Red" Cochrane, 4th round.

(Marty Servo retired; the top two challengers fought for the title.)

Dec. 20, 1946—Sugar Ray Robinson decisioned Tommy Bell, 15 rounds.

(Sugar Ray Robinson resigned after winning middleweight title in 1951.)

May 18, 1951—Kid Gavilan decisioned Johnny Bratton, 15 rounds.

Oct. 20, 1954—Johnny Saxton decisioned Kid Gavilan, 15 rounds.

Apr. 1, 1955—Tony DeMarco KOed Johnny Saxton, 14th round.

June 10, 1955—Carmen Basilio KOed Tony DeMarco, 12th round.

Mar. 14, 1956—Johnny Saxton decisioned Carmen Basilio, 15 rounds.

Sept. 12, 1956—Carmen Basilio KOed Johnny Saxton, 9th round.

(Carmen Basilio resigned after winning middleweight title in 1957.)

June 6, 1958—Virgil Akins KOed Vince Martinez, 4th round.

Dec. 5, 1958—Don Jordan decisioned Virgil Akins, 15 rounds.

May 27, 1960—Benny "Kid" Paret decisioned Don Jordan, 15 rounds.

Apr. 1, 1961—Emile Griffith KOed Benny "Kid" Paret, 13th round.

Sept. 30, 1961—Benny "Kid" Paret decisioned Emile Griffith, 15 rounds.

Mar. 24, 1962—Emile Griffith KOed Benny "Kid" Paret, 12th round.

Mar. 21, 1963—Luis Rodriguez decisioned Emile Griffith, 15 rounds.

June 8, 1963—Emile Griffith decisioned Luis Rodriguez, 15 rounds.

(Emile Griffith resigned after winning middleweight title in 1966.)

Nov. 28, 1966—Curtis Cokes decisioned Jean Josselin, 15 rounds.

Apr. 18, 1969—Jose Napoles KOed Curtis Cokes, 13th round.

Dec. 9, 1970—Billy Backus KOed Jose Napoles, 4th round.

June 4, 1971—Jose Napoles KOed Billy Backus, 4th round.

(Jose Napoles' title was vacated for nondefense in 1975.)

June 27, 1975—Angel Espada decisioned Clyde Gray, 15 rounds.

July 17, 1976—Jose Cuevas KOed Angel Espada, 2nd round.

Lightweights

June 1, 1896—George "Kid" Lavigne KOed Dick Burge, 17th round.

July 3, 1899—Frank Erne decisioned George "Kid" Lavigne, 20 rounds.

May 12, 1902—Joe Gans KOed Frank Erne, 1st round.

July 4, 1908—Battling Nelson KOed Joe Gans, 17th round.

Feb. 22, 1910—Ad Wolgast KOed Battling Nelson, 40th round.

Nov. 28, 1912—Willie Ritchie beat Ad Wolgast on a foul, 16th round.

July 7, 1914—Freddy Welsh decisioned Willie Ritchie, 20 rounds.

May 28, 1917—Benny Leonard KOed Freddy Welsh, 9th round.

(Benny Leonard retired in 1925 and a tournament was held.)

July 13, 1925—Jimmy Goodrich KOed Stan Layza, 2nd round.

Dec. 7, 1925—Rocky Kansas decisioned Jimmy Goodrich, 15 rounds.

July 3, 1926—Sammy Mandell decisioned Rocky Kansas, 10 rounds.

July 17, 1930—Al Singer KOed Sammy Mandell, 1st round.

Nov. 14, 1930—Tony Canzoneri KOed Al Singer, 1st round.

June 23, 1933—Barney Ross decisioned Tony Canzoneri, 10 rounds.

(Barney Ross resigned in 1935 after winning welterweight title.)

May 10, 1935—Tony Canzoneri decisioned Lou Ambers, 15 rounds.

Sept. 3, 1936—Lou Ambers decisioned Tony Canzoneri, 15 rounds.

Aug. 17, 1938—Henry Armstrong decisioned Lou Ambers, 15 rounds.

Aug. 22, 1939—Lou Ambers decisioned Henry Armstrong, 15 rounds.

May 10, 1940—Lew Jenkins KOed Lou Ambers, 3rd round.

Dec. 19, 1941—Sammy Angott decisioned Lew Jenkins, 15 rounds.

Mar 8, 1944—Juan Zurita decisioned Sammy Angott, 15 rounds.

Apr. 18, 1945—Ike Williams KOed Juan Zurita, 2nd round.

May 25, 1951—James Carter KOed Ike Williams, 14th round.

May 14, 1952—Lauro Salas decisioned James Carter, 15 rounds.

Oct. 15, 1952—James Carter decisioned Lauro Salas, 15 rounds.

Mar. 5, 1954—Paddy DeMarco decisioned James Carter, 15 rounds.

Nov. 17, 1954—James Carter KOed Paddy DeMarco, 15th round.

June 29, 1955—Wallace "Bud" Smith decisioned James Carter, 15 rounds.

Aug. 24, 1956—Joe Brown decisioned Wallace "Bud" Smith, 15 rounds.

Apr. 21, 1962—Carlos Ortiz decisioned Joe Brown, 15 rounds.

Apri. 10, 1965—Ismael Laguna decisioned Carlos Ortiz, 15 rounds.

Nov. 13, 1965—Carlos Ortiz decisioned Ismael Laguna, 15 rounds.

June 29, 1968—Carlos "Teo" Cruz decisioned Carlos Ortiz, 15 rounds.

Feb. 18, 1969—Mando Ramos KOed Carlos "Teo" Cruz, 11th round.

Mar. 3, 1970—Ismael Laguna KOed Mando Ramos, 9th round.

Sept. 26, 1970—Ken Buchanan decisioned Ismael Laguna, 15 rounds.

June 26, 1972—Roberto Duran KOed Ken Buchanan, 13th round.

Featherweights

July 28, 1891—George Dixon KOed Abe Willis, 5th round.

Oct. 4, 1897—Solly Smith decisioned George Dixon, 20 rounds.

Sept. 26, 1898—Dave Sullivan KOed Solly Smith (injury), 5th round.

Nov. 11, 1898—George Dixon beat Dave Sullivan on a foul, 10th round.

Jan. 9, 1900—Terry McGovern KOed George Dixon, 8th round.

Nov. 28, 1901—Young Corbett KOed Terry McGovern, 2nd round.

(Young Corbett became a lightweight; Abe Attell claimed title.)

Feb. 1, 1904—Abe Attell KOed Harry Forbes, 4th round.

Feb. 22, 1912—Johnny Kilbane decisioned Abe Attell, 20 rounds.

June 2, 1923—Eugene Criqui KOed Johnny Kilbane, 6th round.

July 26, 1923—Johnny Dundee decisioned Eugene Criqui, 15 rounds.

(Johnny Dundee resigned; a tournament was held.)

Jan. 2, 1925—Louis "Kid" Kaplan KOed Danny Kramer, 9th round.

(Louis "Kid" Kaplan resigned in 1927—a tournament was held.)

Sept. 19, 1927—Benny Bass decisioned Red Chapman, 10 rounds.

Feb. 10, 1928—Tony Canzoneri decisioned Benny Bass, 15 rounds.

Sept. 28, 1928—Andre Routis decisioned Tony Canzoneri, 15 rounds.

Sept. 23, 1929—Battling Battalino decisioned Andre Routis, 15 rounds.

(Battling Battalino resigned in 1932; a tournament was held.)

May 26, 1932—Tommy Paul outpointed Johnny Pena, 15 rounds.

Jan. 13, 1933—Freddie Miller decisioned Tommy Paul, 10 rounds.

May 11, 1936—Petey Sarron decisioned Freddie Miller, 15 rounds.

Oct. 29, 1973—Henry Armstrong KOed Petey Sarron, 6th round.

(Henry Armstrong resigned in 1938.)

Apr. 18, 1939—Joey Archibald decisioned Leo Rodak, 15 rounds.

May 20, 1940—Harry Jeffra decisioned Joey Archibald, 15 rounds.

May 12, 1941—Joey Archibald decisioned Harry Jeffra, 15 rounds.

Sept. 11, 1941—Chalky Wright KOed Joey Archibald, 11th round.

Nov. 20, 1942—Willie Pep decisioned Chalky Wright, 15 rounds.

Oct. 29, 1948—Sandy Saddler KOed Willie Pep, 4th round.

Feb. 11, 1949—Willie Pep decisioned Sandy Saddler, 15 rounds.

Sept. 8, 1950—Sandy Saddler KOed Willie Pep, 8th round.

(Sandy Saddler retired in 1957; a tournament was held.)

June 24, 1957—Hogan "Kid" Bassey KOed Cherif Hamia, 10th round.

Mar. 18, 1959—Davey Moore KOed Hogan "Kid" Bassey, 13th round.

Mar. 21, 1963—Sugar Ramos KOed Davey Moore, 10th round.

Sept. 26, 1964—Vicente Saldivar KOed Sugar Ramos, 12th round.

(Vicente Saldivar retired in 1967.)

Jan. 23, 1969—Johnny Famechon decisioned Jose Legra, 15 rounds.

May 9, 1970—Vicente Saldivar returned and decisioned Johnny Famechon, 15 rounds.

Dec. 11, 1970—Kiniaki Shibata KOed Vincente Saldivar, 13th round.

May 19, 1972—Clemente Sanchez KOed Kiniaki Shibata, 3rd round.

(Clemente Sanchez retired in 1972 and the title fell into dispute.)

Sept. 7, 1974—Bobby Chacon KOed Alfredo Marcano, 9th round.

June 20, 1975—Ruben Olivares KOed Bobby Chacon, 2nd round.

Sept. 16, 1975—David Kotey decisioned Ruben Olivares, 15 rounds.

Nov. 6, 1976—Danny Lopez decisioned David Kotey, 15 rounds.

Bantamweights

Dec. 6, 1897—Jimmy Barry KOed Walter Croot, 20th round.

(Jimmy Barry retired in 1899.)

Sept. 12, 1899—Terry McGovern KOed Pedlar Palmer, 1st round.

(Terry McGovern became a featherweight in 1901.)

Feb. 27, 1903—Harry Forbes decisioned Andy Tokell, 10 rounds.

Aug. 13, 1903—Frankie Neil KOed Harry Forbes, 2nd round.

Oct. 17, 1904—Joe Bowker decisioned Frankie Neil, 20 rounds.

(Joe Bowker shortly resigned to become a featherweight.)

Oct. 20, 1905—Jimmy Walsh decisioned Digger Stanley, 15 rounds.

(Jimmy Walsh resigned in 1906; title was vacant for four years.)

Mar. 6, 1910—Johnny Coulon KOed Jim Kendrick, 19th round.

June 9, 1914—Kid Williams KOed Johnny Coulon, 3rd round.

Jan. 9, 1917—Pete "Kid" Herman decisioned Kid Williams, 20 rounds.

Dec. 22, 1920—Joe Lynch decisioned Pete "Kid" Herman, 15 rounds.

July 25, 1921—Pete "Kid" Herman decisioned Joe Lynch, 15 rounds.

Sept. 23, 1921—Johnny Buff decisioned Pete "Kid" Herman, 15 rounds.

July 10, 1922—Joe Lynch KOed Johnny Buff, 14th round.

Mar. 21, 1924—Abe Goldstein decisioned Joe Lynch, 15 rounds.

Dec. 19, 1924—Eddie "Cannonball" Martin decisioned Abe Goldstein, 15 rounds.

Mar. 20, 1925—Charlie Phil Rosenberg decisioned Eddie "Cannonball" Martin, 15 rounds.

(Charlie Phil Rosenberg's title was vacated for failure to make weight in 1927.)

June 24, 1927—Bud Taylor decisioned Tony Canzoneri, 10 rounds.

(Taylor vacated title in 1928 to move up in class.)

June 18, 1929—Panama Al Brown decisioned Vidal Gregorio, 15 rounds.

June 1, 1935—Baltazar Sangchilli decisioned Panama Al Brown, 15 rounds.

June 29, 1936—Tony Marino KOed Baltazar Sangchilli, 14th round.

Aug. 31, 1936—Sixto Escobar KOed Tony Marino, 13th round.

Sept. 23, 1937—Harry Jeffra decisioned Sixto Escobar, 15 rounds.

Feb. 20, 1938—Sixto Escobar decisioned Harry Jeffra, 15 round.

(Sixto Escobar, overweight, resigned in 1939.)

Sept. 24, 1940—Lou Salica decisioned Georgie Pace, 15 rounds.

Aug. 7, 1942—Manuel Ortiz decisoned Lou Salica, 12 rounds.

Jan. 6, 1947—Harold Dade decisioned Manuel Ortiz, 15 rounds.

Mar. 11, 1947—Manuel Ortiz decisioned Harold Dade, 15 rounds.

May 31, 1950—Vic Toweel decisioned Manuel Ortiz, 15 rounds.

Nov. 15, 1952—Jimmy Carruthers KOed Vic Toweel, 1st round.

(Jimmy Carruthers retired in 1954.)

Sept. 19, 1954—Robert Cohen decisioned Chamren Songkitrat, 15 rounds.

June 29, 1956—Mario D'Agata KOed Robert Cohen, 5th round.

Apr. 1, 1957—Alphonse Halimi decisioned Mario D'Agata, 15 rounds.

July 8, 1959—Joe Becerra KOed Alphonse Halimi, 8th round.

(Joe Becerra retired in 1960.)

Jan. 18, 1962—Joe Jofre KOed Johnny Caldwell, 10th round.

May 17, 1965—Fighting Harada decisioned Joe Jofre, 15 rounds.

Feb. 27, 1968—Lionel Rose decisioned Fighting Harada, 15 rounds.

Aug. 22, 1969—Ruben Olivares KOed Lionel Rose, 5th round.

Oct. 16, 1970—Chucho Castillo KOed Ruben Olivares, 14th round.

Apr. 3, 1971—Ruben Olivares decisioned Chucho Castillo, 15 rounds.

Mar. 19, 1972—Rafael Herrera KOed Ruben Olivares, 8th round.

July 30, 1972—Enrique Pinder decisioned Rafael Herrera, 15 rounds.

Jan. 20, 1973—Romeo Anaya KOed Enrique Pinder, 3rd round.

Nov. 3, 1973—Arnold Taylor KOed Romeo Anaya, 14th round.

July 3, 1974—Soo Hwan Hong decisioned Arnold Taylor, 15 rounds.

Mar. 15, 1975—Alfonso Zamora KOed Soo Hwan Hong, 4th round.

Flyweights

Dec. 18, 1916—Jimmy Wilde KOed Zulu Kid, 11th round.

June 18, 1923—Pancho Villa KOed Jimmy Wilde, 7th round.

(Pancho Villa died of blood poisoning in 1925; Frankie Genaro claimed title.)

Aug. 22, 1925—Fidel LaBarba decisioned Frankie Genaro, 10 rounds.

(Fidel LaBarba retired in 1927, and for 12 years the title was in considerable confusion; at times, there were three different "champions" recognized by various organizations. The championship line followed here is based on my own reasoning and is subject to some dispute.)

Mar. 2, 1929—Emile "Spider" Pladner KOed Frankie Genaro, 1st round.

Apr. 18, 1929—Frankie Genaro beat Emile "Spider" Pladner on a foul, 5th.

Dec. 26, 1930—Frankie Genaro and Midget Wolgast fought 15-round draw.

Oct. 27, 1931—Young Perez KOed Frankie Genaro, 2nd round.

Oct. 31, 1932—Jackie Brown KOed Young Perez, 13th round.

Sept. 8, 1935—Benny Lynch KOed Jackie Brown, 2nd round.

(Lynch resigned because he couldn't make the weight in 1938, and Peter Kane won wide recognition as champion.)

June 19, 1943—Jackie Paterson KOed Peter Kane, 1st round.

Mar. 23, 1948—Dinty Monaghan KOed Jackie Paterson, 7th round.

(Dinty Monaghan retired in 1950.)

Apr. 25, 1950—Terry Allen decisioned Honore Pratesi, 15 rounds.

Aug. 1, 1950—Dado Marino decisioned Terry Allen, 15 rounds.

May 19, 1952—Yoshio Shirai decisioned Dado Marino, 15 rounds.

Nov. 26, 1954—Pascual Perez decisioned Yoshio Shirai, 15 rounds.

Apr. 16, 1960—Pone Kingpetch decisioned Pascual Perez, 15 rounds.

Oct. 10, 1962—Fighting Harada KOed Pone Kingpetch, 11th round.

Jan. 12, 1963—Pone Kingpetch decisioned Fighting Harada, 15 rounds.

Sept. 18, 1963—Hiroyuki Ebihara KOed Pone Kingpetch, 1st round.

Jan. 23, 1964—Pone Kingpetch decisioned Hiroyuki Ebihara, 15 rounds.

Apr. 23, 1965—Salvatore Burruni decisioned Pone Kingpetch, 15 rounds.

June 14, 1966—Walter McGowan decisioned Salvatore Burruni, 15 rounds.

Dec. 30, 1966—Chartchai Chionoi KOed Walter McGowan, 9th round.

Feb. 23, 1969—Efren Torres KOed Chartchai Chionoi, 8th round.

Mar. 20, 1970—Chartchai Chionoi decisioned Efren Torres, 15 rounds.

Dec. 7, 1970—Erbito Salvarria KOed Chartchai Chionoi, 2nd round.

Feb. 9, 1973—Venice Borkorsor decisoned Erbito Salvarria, 15 rounds.

(Venice Borkosor outgrew division and title was vacated.)

Apr. 27, 1974—Chartchai Chionoi decisioned Fritz Chervet, 15 rounds.

Oct. 18, 1974—Susumu Hanagata KOed Chartchai Chionoi, 6th round.

Apr. 1, 1975—Erbito Salvarria decisioned Susumu Hanagata, 15 rounds.

Oct. 12, 1976—Alfonso Lopez KOed Erbito Salvarria, 15th round.

Fighter of the Year

(Chosen by *Ring* Magazine)

1928	Gene Tunney
1929	Tommy Loughran
1930	Max Schmeling
1931	Tommy Loughran
1932	Jack Sharkey
1933	No award
1934	Barney Ross
	Tony Canzoneri
1935	Barney Ross
1936	Joe Louis
1937	Henry Armstrong
1938	Joe Louis
1939	Joe Louis
1940	Billy Conn
1941	Joe Louis
1942	Sugar Ray Robinson
1943	Fred Apostoli
1944	Beau Jack
1945	Willie Pep
1946	Tony Zale
1947	Gus Lesnevich
1948	Ike Williams
1949	Ezzard Charles
1950	Ezzard Charles
1951	Sugar Ray Robinson
1952	Rocky Marciano
1953	Carl "Bobo" Olson
1954	Rocky Marciano
1955	Rocky Marciano
1956	Floyd Patterson
1957	Carmen Basilio
1958	Ingemar Johansson
1959	Ingemar Johansson
1960	Floyd Patterson
1961	Joe Brown
1962	Dick Tiger
1963	Cassius Clay (Muhammad Ali)
1964	Emile Griffith
1965	Dick Tiger
1966	No award
1967	Joe Frazier
1968	Nino Benvenuti
1969	Jose Napoles
1970	Joe Frazier
1971	Joe Frazier
1972	Cassius Clay (Muhammad Ali)
	Carlos Monzon
1973	George Foreman

1974 Muhammad Ali
1975 Muhammad Ali
1976 George Foreman

Halls of Fame

Halls of fame for boxing are maintained by *Ring* magazine and by Citizens Savings Hall. In the following list, R at the end of an entry indicates the *Ring* Hall of Fame, C the Citizens Savings Hall. In the record summaries, W indicates Wins, L indicates Losses, D indicates Draws or other no-decision fights, KO indicates Knockout. When a fighter fought under a ring name, his real name is given in parentheses.

"Young Barney" Aaron—Lightweight champion 1857–1858, 1867. Record: 4 W, 1 L, 1 D. R

Lou Ambers (Louis D'Ambrosio)—Lightweight champion 1936–1938, 1939–1940. Record: 88 W, 29 by KO; 8 L, 2 by KO; 6 D. C, R

Sammy Angott (Samuel Engotti)—Lightweight champion 1941–1942. Record: 94 W, 22 by KO; 23 L, 1 by KO; 8 D. R

Henry Armstrong (Henry Jackson)—The only fighter to hold three world titles simultaneously: featherweight 1937–1938, welterweight 1938–1940, lightweight 1938–1939. Record: 146 W, 97 by KO; 22 L, 2 by KO; 9 D. C,R

Abe Attell—Featherweight champion 1901–1912. Record: 91 W, 47 by KO; 10 L, 3 by KO; 67 D. C, R

Max Baer—Heavyweight champion 1934–1935. Record: 65 W, 50 by KO; 13 L, 3 by KO; 1 D. R

Carmen Basilio—Welterweight champion 1955–1957, middleweight champion 1957–1958. Record: 56 W, 27 by KO; 16 L, 2 by KO; 7 D. R

Paul Berlenbach—Light-heavyweight champion 1925–1926. Record: 37 W, 30 by KO; 7 L, 3 by KO; 5 D. C,R

James J. Braddock—Heavyweight champion 1935–1937. Record: 51 W, 26 by KO; 22 L, 2 by KO; 12 D. C, R

Jack Britton (William J. Breslin)—Welterweight champion 1915–1917, 1919–1922. Record: 99 W, 21 by KO; 28 L, 1 by KO; 198 D. C,R

Jack Broughton—Known as the "father of boxing," for drawing up the first formal rules for the sport; world champion 1729–1750. R

James "Deaf" Burke—Heavyweight champion 1833–1839; helped popularize boxing in the United States during a tour in 1836–1837. R

Tommy Burns (Noah Brusso)—Heavyweight champion 1906–1908. Record: 46 W, 36 by KO; 5 L, 1 by KO; 9 D. R

Tony Canzoneri—Featherweight champion 1928, lightweight champion 1930–1933, 1935–1936. Record: 138 W, 44 by KO; 29 L, 1 by KO; 14 D. C, R

Georges Carpentier—Light-heavyweight champion 1920–1922. Record: 85 W, 51 by KO; 15 L, 8 by KO; 6 D. R

Marcel Cerdan—Middleweight champion 1948–1949. Record: 109 W, 66 by KO; 4 L, 1 by KO; 0 D. R

Ezzard Charles—Heavyweight champion 1949–1951. Record: 96 W, 58 by KO; 25 L, 7 by KO; 0 D. R

Kid Chocolate (Eligio Sardinias)—Junior lightweight 1931–1933; fought for featherweight and lightweight titles. Record: 145 W, 64 by KO; 10 L, 2 by KO; 6 D. C, R

Joe Choynski—Never a champion, the 168-pounder usually fought heavyweights. Record: 50 W, 25 by KO; 14 L, 10 by KO; 15 D. R

Arthur Chambers—Lightweight champion 1872–1879. Record: 11 W, 9 by KO; 1 L, by KO; 2 D. C, R

Tom Chandler—Middleweight champion 1867. Record: 3 W, 2 by KO; 0 L; 1 D. R

William "Nobby" Clark—Never defeated in more than 30 fights, Clark never got a fight for the featherweight title. Born in England, he did all his fighting in the United States, 1860–1865. R

Sam Collyer (Walter Jamieson)—Lightweight champion 1866–1867, 1867–1868. Record: 9 W, 0 by KO; 5 L, 1 by KO; 1 D. R

Billy Conn—Light-heavyweight champion 1939–1940; Conn had two exciting fights with Joe Louis in bids for the heavyweight title. Record: 64 W, 14 by KO; 10 L, 2 by KO; 0 D. C, R

James J. Corbett—Heavyweight champion 1892–1897. Record: 20 W, 9 by KO; 5 L, 3 by KO; 8 D. C, R

Young Corbett II (William H. Rothwell)—Featherweight champion 1901–1902. Record: 53 W, 34 by KO; 14 L, 8 by KO; 37 D. R

Johnny Coulon—Bantamweight champion 1910–1914. Record: 56 W, 24 by KO; 4 L, 2 by KO; 36 D. C, R

Tom Cribb—Considered heavyweight champion 1805–1810. Record: 10 W, 1 L. R

Les Darcy—Australian welterweight and middleweight champion 1912–1916, Darcy failed in his only chance for a world title. Record: 35 W, 20 by KO; 4 L, 0 by KO; 0 D. R

Jack Delaney (Ovila Chapdelaine)—Light-heavyweight champion 1926–1927. Record: 70 W, 46 by KO; 10 L, 3 by KO; 6 D. C, R

Jack Dempsey (William H. Dempsey)—Heavyweight champion 1919–1926. Record: 60 W, 49 by KO; 7 L, 1 by KO; 15 D. C, R

Jack "The Nonpareil" Dempsey (John Kelly)—Middleweight champion 1884–1891. Record: 50 W, 8 by KO; 3 L, 2 by KO; 15 D. R

Jack Dillon (Ernest C. Price)—Light-heavyweight champion 1914–1916. Record: 91 W, 60 by KO; 6 L, 0 by KO; 143 D. C, R

Dixie Kid (Aaron L. Brown)—Claimed welterweight title 1900, recognized 1904. Record: 78 W, 63 by KO; 18 L, 3 by KO; 30 D. C

George Dixon—The first black champion in any division; bantamweight champion 1890, featherweight champion 1891–1897, 1898–1900. Record: 78 W, 30 by KO; 26 L, 4 by KO; 46 D. C, R

Dan Donnelly—An Irish fighter, Donnelly toured England with Jack Carter and fought many times before large crowds between 1815 and 1819. R

Professor Mike Donovan—Middleweight champion 1881–1884. Record: 24 W, 2 by KO; 2 L, 0 by KO; 7 D. R

Jem Driscoll—British featherweight champion 1906–1913. Record: 53 W, 27 by KO; 2 L, 1 by KO; 15 D. R

Johnny Dundee (Joseph Corrara)—Featherweight champion 1923–1924. Record: 113 W, 19 by KO; 31 L, 2 by KO; 177 D. C, R

Jackie Fields (Jacob Finkelstein)—Welterweight champion 1929–1930, 1932–1833. Record: 70 W, 28 by KO; 9 L, 1 by KO; 5 D. C

James Figg—Figg virtually invented modern boxing, as a fighter and instructor. He was considered *the* champion from 1720 to his retirement in 1729. R

Robert Fitzsimmons—Middleweight champion 1891–1894; heavyweight champion 1897–1899; light-heavyweight champion 1903–1905. Record: 28 W, 23 by KO; 7 L, 6 by KO; 6 D. C, R

Nat Fleischer—Founder and longtime editor of *Ring* magazine, Fleischer was accepted as the outstanding authority on boxing until his death in 1972. He covered, refereed, and acted as judge for thousands of fights all over the world. C

Theodore "Tiger" Flowers—Middleweight champion 1926. Record: 115 W, 49 by KO; 13 L, 8 by KO; 21 D. R

Joe Gans (Joseph Gaines)—Lightweight champion 1902–1906. Record: 121 wins, 55 by KO; 8 L, 5 by KO; 28 D. C, R

Kid Gavilan (Gerardo Gonzalez)—Welterweight champion 1952–1955. Record: 106 W, 27 by KO; 30 L, 0 by KO; 7 D. R

Frankie Genaro (Frank Di Gennara)—Flyweight champion 1928–1929, 1929–1931. Record: 83 W, 19 by KO; 22 L, 4 by KO; 24 D. C, R

Mike Gibbons—Claimed middleweight title 1910, but was never recognized. Record: 62 W, 38 by KO; 3 L, 0 by KO; 62 D. C, R

Tom Gibbons—A light-heavyweight, Gibbons lost a 15-round decision to Dempsey for the heavyweight title in 1923. Record: 57 W, 47 by KO; 4 L, 1 by KO; 45 D. C, R

Joe Goss—Though only 150 pounds, Goss fought many top heavyweights, including John L. Sullivan. R

Rocky Graziano (Rocco Barbella)—Middleweight champion 1947–1948. Record: 67 W, 52 by KO; 10 L, 3 by KO; 6 D. R

Edward H. "Harry" Greb—Middleweight champion 1923–1926. Record: 111 W, 46 by KO; 7 L, 2 by KO; 172 D. C, R

Young Griffo (Albert Griffiths)—A claimant to the featherweight title during the late nineteenth century. Record: 49 W, 5 by KO; 9 L, 3 by KO; 49 D. R

John Gully—Generally recognized as heavyweight champion 1805–1808. R

John C. Heenan—Claimed heavyweight championship in 1859; fought 42-round draw with British champion Tom Sayers in 1860. R

Pete Herman (Peter Gulotta)—Bantamweight champion 1917–1920, 1921. Record: 61 W, 19 by KO; 12 L, 1 by KO; 65 D. C, R

Leo Houck (Hauck)—Fought successfully in every division from flyweight to heavyweight, 1902–1926, but never won a title. Record: 158 W, 21 by KO; 9 L, 0 by KO; 45 D. R

Ace Hudkins—Twice fought for middleweight title. Record: 50 W, 18 by KO; 13 L, 1 by KO; 13 D. C

Jacob Hyer—First American to claim world title, in 1816. R

Tom Hyer—Jacob's son, Tom is considered the first real American champion. He knocked out the British fighter, Yankee Sullivan, in 1849. R

Beau Jack (Sidney Walker)—New York lightweight champion 1942–1943, 1943–1944. Record: 83 W, 40 by KO; 23 L, 3 by KO; 5 D. R

Gentleman John Jackson—Jackson beat all-time great Daniel Mendoza in 1795 and was considered a champion, but retired shortly afterward. R

Peter Jackson—Australian heavyweight champion 1886–1892. Record: 18 W, 12 by KO; 3 L, 3 by KO; 6 D. R

Joe Jeannette—Beat many top heavyweights of his day, 1904–1919, but never got a title fight because he was black. Record: 72 W, 56 by KO; 9 L, 1 by KO; 73 D. R

James J. Jeffries—Heavyweight champion 1899–1905. Record: 20 W, 16 by KO; 1 L, 1 by KO; 2 D. C, R

Jack Johnson—The first black heavyweight champion, 1908–1915. Record: 78 W, 44 by KO; 7 L, 5 by KO; 28 D. C, R

Louis "Kid" Kaplan—Featherweight champion 1925–1927. Record: 101 W, 17 by KO; 13 L, 3 by KO; 17 D. C

Stanley Ketchel (Stanislaus Kiecal)—Middleweight champion 1907–1908, 1908–1910. Record: 49 W, 46 by KO; 4 L, 2 by KO; 8 D. C, R

Johnny Kilbane—Featherweight champion 1912–1923. Record: 46 W, 22 by KO; 4 L, 2 by KO; 90 D. C, R

John J. "Jake" Kilrain—Kilrain and John L. Sullivan fought for heavyweight title in 1888, Sullivan winning on a 75-round KO. Record: 18 W, 3 by KO; 6 L, 3 by KO; 13 D. R

Frank Klaus—Middleweight champion 1913. Record: 69 W, 25 by KO; 4 L, 2 by KO; 36 D. C

Fidel LaBarba—Flyweight champion 1927–1931. Record: 72 W, 15 by KO: 15 L, 0 by KO; 10 D. C, R

Sam Langford—Another black with a long successful career, 1902–1924, who never got a title fight. Record: 137 W, 99 by KO; 23 L, 4 by KO; 92 D. C, R

George "Kid" Lavigne—Lightweight champion 1896–1899. Record: 35 W, 16 by KO; 5 L, 2 by KO; 15 D. C, R

Benny Leonard (Benjamin Leiner)—Lightweight champion 1917–1924. Record: 88 W, 68 by KO; 5 L, 4 by KO; 116 D. C, R

Gus Lesnevich—Light-heavyweight champion 1941–1948. Record: 57 W, 21 by KO; 14 L, 5 by KO; 5 D. R

Battling Levinsky (Barney Lebrowitz)—Light-heavyweight champion 1916–1920. Record: 66 W, 25 by KO; 19 L, 4 by KO; 187 D. C, R

Ted "Kid" Lewis (Gershon Mendeloff)—Welterweight champion 1915–1916, 1917–1919. Record: 155 W, 68 by KO; 24 L, 4 by KO; 74 D. C, R

Tommy Loughran—Light-heavyweight champion 1927–1929. Record: 96 W, 18 by KO; 23 L, 2 by KO; 53 D. C, R

Joe Louis (Joe L. Barrow)—Heavyweight champion 1937–1949. Record: 68 W, 54 by KO; 3 L, 2 by KO; 0 D. C, R

Joe Lynch—Bantamweight champion 1920–1921, 1922–1924. Record: 42 W, 29 by KO; 13 L, 0 by KO; 79 D. C

Jem Mace—Heavyweight champion 1861–1862, 1862–1890. R

Rocky Marciano (Rocco Marchegiano)—Heavyweight champion 1952–1956; the only champion ever to retire without a professional defeat. Record: 49 W, 43 by KO; 0 L, 0 D. C, R

Jack McAuliffe—American lightweight champion 1886–1896; he and Jem Carney of England both claimed the world title and fought a 74-round draw in 1887. Record: 41 W, 9 by KO; 0 L; 11 D. R

Charles "Kid" McCoy (Norman Selby)—Welterweight champion 1896–1899. Record: 81 W, 35 by KO; 6 L, 2 by KO; 18 D. C, R

Patrick "Packy" McFarland—Never got a title fight despite a fine record: 64 W, 47 by KO; 1 L, 1 by KO; 39 D. R

Terry McGovern—Bantamweight champion 1899, featherweight champion 1900–1901. Record: 59 W, 34 by KO; 4 L, 2 by KO; 14 D. C, R

Jimmy McLarnin—Welterweight champion 1933–1934,

1934–1935. Record: 63 W, 20 by KO; 11 L, 1 by KO; 39 D. C, R

Daniel Mendoza—Though only 160 lb, Mendoza was heavyweight champion 1791–1795. R

Charley Mitchell—Middleweight and heavyweight champion 1882–1883. Record: 13 W, 0 by KO; 3 L, 1 by KO; 11 D. R

Tom Molineaux—One of the first Americans to fight for the world championship, in 1810 and 1811. R

Archie Moore (Archibald Wright)—Light-heavyweight champion 1952–1962. Record: 193 W, 141 by KO; 26 L, 7 by KO; 9 D. C, R

Davey Moore—Featherweight champion 1959–1963; died of brain injuries received in fight in which he lost title. Record: 59 W, 30 by KO; 7 L, 2 by KO; 1 D. C

Owen Moran—Three times fought for featherweight title, 1908–1913, and all three times the champion retained his title on a draw. Record: 62 W, 25 by KO; 17 L, 2 by KO; 27 D. R

John Morrissey—American heavyweight champion 1858; later founded Saratoga race track. R

Battling Nelson (Oscar Nielson)—Lightweight champion 1908–1910. Record: 59 W, 38 by KO; 19 L, 2 by KO; 54 D. C, R

Philadelphia Jack O'Brien (Joseph F. Hagen)—Light-heavyweight champion 1905–1912. Record: 101 W, 36 by KO; 7 L, 4 by KO; 73 D. C, R

Manuel Ortiz—Bantamweight champion 1942–1947, 1947–1950. Record: 92 W, 45 by KO; 27 L, 1 by KO; 3 D. C

Billy Papke—Middleweight champion 1908, 1910–1911, 1912–1913. Record: 39 W, 29 by KO; 10 L, 1 by KO; 16 D. C, R

Willie Pep (William G. Papaleo)—Featherweight champion 1942–1948, 1949–1950. Record: 229 W, 65 by KO; 11 L, 6 by KO; 1 D. C, R

Billy Petrolle—Fought once for lightweight title, in 1932, but lost. Record: 89 W, 63 by KO; 21 L, 3 by KO; 48 D. R

Ned Price—On May 1, 1856, fought 160-round draw with Joe Coburn, most rounds ever in a bare-knuckled fight in the United States, but was better known as an early promoter and matchmaker in and around Boston. R

Bill Richmond—A free black, Richmond went to England in 1777 to box; in 1805, at the age of 42, he lost to heavyweight champion Tom Cribb. R

George L. "Tex" Rickard—The first of the great promoters, Rickard established the idea of guaranteeing fighters definite sums instead of a share of gate receipts, and staged most of the world's most important fights during the 1920s. C

Willie Ritchie (Gerhardt A. Steffen)—Lightweight champion 1912–1914. Record: 36 W, 8 by KO; 9 L, 1 by KO; 26 D. C, R

Sugar Ray Robinson (Walker Smith)—Welterweight champion 1946–1951; middleweight champion 1951–1952, 1955–1957, 1958–1960. Record: 175 W, 109 by KO; 9 L, 1 by KO; 7 D. C, R

Jack Root (Janos Ruthaly)—Root became the first light-heavyweight champion in 1903, but lost the title later that year. He spent most of his career fighting heavyweights. Record: 44 W, 24 by KO; 3 L, 3 by KO; 6 D. C, R

Maxie Rosenbloom—Light-heavyweight champion 1932–1934. Record: 210 W, 18 by KO; 35 L, 2 by KO; 44 D. C, R

Barney Ross (Barnet Rosofsky)—Lightweight champion 1933; welterweight champion 1934, 1935–1938. Record: 74 W, 24 by KO; 4 L, 0 by KO; 4 D. C, R

Paddy Ryan—American heavyweight champion 1880–1882; lost title to John L. Sullivan. R

Tommy Ryan (Joseph Youngs)—Welterweight champion 1894–1896; middleweight champion 1898–1907. Record: 86 W, 48 by KO; 3 L, 1 by KO; 21 D. C, R

Joe "Sandy" Saddler—Featherweight champion 1948–1949, 1950–1957. Record: 144 W, 103 by KO; 16 L, 1 by KO; 2 D. C, R

Everett L. Sanders—Member, California State Athletic Commission, 1939–1955; rewrote California boxing rules in 1940–1941 and most of his rules are still in use. C

Tom Sayers—Heavyweight champion 1855–1860; he and John C. Heenan of the United States fought one of the first international championship fights in 1860, a 42-round draw. R

Max Schmeling—Heavyweight champion 1930–1932. Record: 56 W, 39 by KO; 10 L, 5 by KO; 5 D. R

Thomas J. Sharkey—Lost to James Jeffries in 1899 in bid for heavyweight title. Record: 40 W, 37 by KO; 6 L, 2 by KO; 8 D. C, R

Jeff Smith (Jerome Jeffords)—Despite a long winning career (1910–1927), Smith never had a title fight. Record: 99 W, 46 by KO; 10 L, 1 by KO; 69 D. R

Mysterious Billy Smith—Welterweight champion 1892–1894, 1898–1900. Record: 30 W, 13 by KO; 18 L, 4 by KO; 34 D. C

Tom Spring (Thomas Winter)—Heavyweight champion 1821–1824. R

John L. Sullivan—Heavyweight champion 1882–1892; the last of the bare-knuckle champions and the first of the Queensbeery Rule champions. Record: 31 W, 16 by KO; 1 L, 1 by KO; 43 D. C, R

Charles "Bud" Taylor—Bantamweight champion 1927–1928. Record: 70 W, 35 by KO; 23 L, 4 by KO; 66 D. C, R

Lew Tendler—Successful at four different weights, Tendler lost fights for the lightweight (1923) and welterweight (1924) titles. Record: 59 W, 37 by KO; 11 L, 1 by KO; 98 D, C, R

William "Bendigo" Thompson—Heavyweight champion 1839, 1845. R

James J. "Gene" Tunney—Heavyweight champion 1926–1928. Record: 56 W, 41 by KO; 1 L, 0 by KO; 19 D. C, R

Pancho Villa (Francisco Guilledo)—Flyweight champion 1923–1925. Record: 71 W, 22 by KO; 5 L, 0 by KO; 27 D. C, R

Jersey Joe Walcott (Arnold R. Cream)—Heavyweight champion 1951–1952. Record: 49 W, 30 by KO; 17 L, 6 by KO; 1 D. R

Joe Walcott—Welterweight champion 1901–1904, 1906. Record: 81 W, 34 by KO; 24 L, 4 by KO; 45 D. C, R

Edward P. "Mickey" Walker—Welterweight champion 1922–1926; middleweight champion 1926–1931. Record: 93 W, 58 by KO; 18 L, 5 by KO; 37 D. C, R

Jem Ward—Heavyweight champion 1822–1831. R

Freddie Welsh (Frederick H. Thomas)—Lightweight champion 1914–1917. Record: 77 W, 24 by KO; 4 L, 1 by KO; 86 D. R

Jimmy Wilde—Flyweight champion 1916–1923. Record: 126 W, 77 by KO; 4 L, 3 by KO; 10 D. R

Kid Williams (Johnny Gutenko)—Bantamweight champion 1914–1917. Record: 107 W, 48 by KO; 17 L, 3 by KO; 86 D. C, R

Harry Wills—A black heavyweight, Wills spent most of his career fighting other black heavyweights without getting a title shot. Record: 62 W, 45 by KO; 8 L, 4 by KO; 32 D. R

Ad Wolgast (Adolph Wolgust)—Lightweight champion 1910–1912. Record: 60 W, 38 by KO; 12 L, 2 by KO; 63 D. R

Midget Wolgast (Joseph R. Loscalzo)—American flyweight champion 1930–1935; Wolgast fought for the world title in 1930, but the fight was a draw. Record: 96 W, 11 by KO; 35 L, 6 by KO; 16 D. C, R

Tony Zale (Anthony F. Zaleski)—Middleweight champion 1940–1947, 1948. Record: 70 W, 46 by KO; 16 L, 4 by KO; 2 D. R

Fritzie Zivic—Welterweight champion 1940–1941. Record: 155 W, 80 by KO; 65 L, 4 by KO; 10 D. R

Bibliography. Fleischer, Nat: *Fifty Years at Ringside,* Putman, New York, 1946; ———: *The Heavyweight Championship,* Fleet Publishing, New York, 1958; Liebling, A. J.: *The Sweet Science,* Grove, New York, 1963; Loubet, Nat, *et al.* (eds.): *The Ring Boxing Encyclopedia and Record Book,* Ring Book Shop, New York, 1973. (Revised annually.)

BROAD JUMP—Formally called the long jump; a field event in which athletes compete to see who can jump the farthest.

See TRACK AND FIELD.

C

CANADIAN FOOTBALL—While American football was evolving, Canada was developing its own special brand of the sport, from Rugby, and undoubtedly with some influence from the United States. McGill University in Montreal had a Rugby team as early as 1874, and McGill played two games with Harvard, one under Rugby rules, the other under Harvard's own football rules. Those games led directly to the development of American football and possibly had some influence on the development of the Canadian game as well.

Rugby has 15 players on a side; in 1920 Canadian football still had 14 players on a team, and the game was quite similar to Rugby. In 1912 Frank Shaughnessy, best known for developing the "Shaughnessy play-off" method for the International Baseball League when he was league president, became football coach at McGill. Shaughnessy brought American tactical ideas to the sport, and was also influential in two major 1921 rules changes, eliminating two players and adopting the pass from center and the football scrimmage to put the ball into play.

Canadian football remained a Rugbylike sport until 1931, when the forward pass was legalized. Another important influence on the development of the sport was the fact that American football was popular in the western provinces of Canada. The Western teams joined the Canadian Rugby Union in 1921 in order to challenge for the Grey Cup, awarded to the Canadian football champion, and that move helped bring about the rules changes.

The Grey Cup's history is rather like that of the Stanley Cup. Donated by Governor-General Earl Grey in 1909, the cup was intended primarily to encourage amateur and collegiate football. By 1936, however, competition for the cup was entirely professional, with three different leagues involved. The cup now goes to the champion of the professional Canadian Football League.

The CFL has a number of head coaches from the United States, and each of the nine teams in the league is allowed to have seven imported players on its roster. A number of American college stars, over the years, have chosen to play in Canada.

Rules. Despite the many influences of American football, Canadian football remains a unique sport, somewhat higher-scoring than the American version. There are 12 men on a side—the 12th, known as the flying wing, may be either a back or a lineman, but is usually a back on offense.

The field, which is larger than that used in the United States, measures 110 yd from goal line to goal line and 65 yd wide, and the end zones are 25 yd deep. Goal posts are on the goal line. Because of the extra width of the field and the fact that downfield blocking is not permitted more than 10 yd beyond the line of scrimmage, the lateral pass is an important feature of the game. Good punting is also important.

A team has only 3 downs in which to gain 10 yd for a first down. A touchdown counts 5 points, a conversion 2 points; the line of scrimmage for a conversion attempt is the 5-yd line. The field goal is 3 points. In addition, a team can score a point (called a "single") by punting the ball over the "dead ball" line that marks the back of the end zone. If the ball is kicked into the end zone, the receiving team must run it out, or lose a point—called a "rouge."

CANDLEPIN BOWLING—A form of bowling once quite popular in New England and Canada, candlepin bowling (or candlepins) has declined sharply in recent years as "big-pin" bowling has moved strongly into those areas.

In candlepin bowling the 10 pins are 15 in tall and slightly wider in the middle (2¼ in) than at the top or bottom (2 in). The ball is small enough to be held easily in one hand. The bowler gets three throws per frame, as in duckpin bowling. Knocking down all 10 pins on the first ball is a strike, knocking down all 10 pins with two balls is a spare, and strikes and spares are scored as in regular bowling. If the bowler knocks down all 10 pins with three balls, he simply gets credit for 10 points.

A unique feature of the sport is that "deadwood"—pins that fall down and stay on the lane—remain there throughout a bowler's turn, and hitting the deadwood to knock down other pins with it is part of the game.

See also BOWLING; DUCKPIN BOWLING.

CANOEING—The canoe was probably the second vehicle invented by man. Having seen logs floating downriver, some primitive ancestor of ours probably conceived the idea of lashing logs together to make a raft. And at some time after that, someone else thought of hollowing out a single log so that it could carry a person. Dugout canoes, which date at least to the Stone Age, are still used by certain primitive tribes. It is quite likely, also, that men began friendly canoe races centuries ago.

Canoes are still useful vehicles. The birchbark canoe of the American Indian was adopted by many French explorers and fur traders during the seventeenth century. Although generally considered a fragile craft, the birchbark canoe proved exceptionally durable. Its shallow draft can take it through white-water rapids that would demolish most vessels, and its exceptional lightness makes it easy to carry on portages past absolutely impassable rapids or on creeks from one body of water to another.

Two birchbark canoes carried Père Marquette and his party on their explorations from Lake Michigan to what is now Louisiana, via the Fox, Wisconsin, and Mississippi rivers. They returned by way of the Illinois River, and both canoes were still in good shape when they got back. Alexander MacKenzie, searching for the Northwest Passage, used a 28-ft birchbark canoe to travel from the Athabasca River in Canada to the Arctic Ocean.

Although the canoe was in frequent use in North America during the nineteenth century, it was an English lawyer who popularized canoeing as a recreational sport. John MacGregor, starting in 1849, went on a whole series of canoe cruises in Europe and the Holy Land, and he wrote a number of books about his experience. In 1865, MacGregor and other enthusiasts organized the Royal Canoe Club.

The British example led to the formation in 1871 of the New York Canoe Club, and by 1880 many similar organizations had sprung up along the East Coast. In that year the American Canoe Association was formed. William L. Alden, one of the founders of the New York Canoe Club, was the first commodore of the ACA.

The chief purposes of the ACA were to develop information about canoe construction, maintenance, paddling techniques, and the like, and to spur the recreational aspect of the sport, but various types of races also fell into the organization's purview.

After World War I, Waldemar Van B. Claussen of the ACA began correspondence with similar clubs in Europe, leading to the formation in 1924 of the Internationale Representationschaft des Kanusport (IRK). Through the IRK, which had 19 member nations, canoeing was accepted as a sport in the 1936 Olympics, with 9 racing events on the program. The IRK was reorganized as the International Canoe Federation (ICF) after World War II.

Types of Competition

There are basically two types of canoeing competition, canoe and kayak. A canoe is an open boat; a kayak has a partly enclosed deck, with openings for the paddlers' seats. A canoeist uses a single-bladed paddle, similar to a rowing oar; a kayak paddle has a blade on each end.

Races are conducted for one-, two-, and four-person

boats at various distances. There are also a number of different classifications, ranging from pleasure craft to vessels designed specifically for racing.

Flat-water races pit vessels against one another, with elimination heats conducted much as they are in rowing events.

White-water races, added to the Olympics in 1972, are time trials conducted through a short stretch of rapids. Ordinary white-water races are simply straight, down-river races. In white-water "slalom" events, the course is marked with a series of gates through which the canoe must pass. Competitors have to go through "reverse" gates backward. There are also some upstream gates; competitors must go past an upstream gate, then paddle against the current to go through before continuing the downstream journey.

The results of a white-water slalom are based on the number of seconds taken to negotiate the course, plus penalty points. Penalties are: 10 points for hitting one pole of a gate, 20 points for hitting both poles, and 50 points for missing a gate entirely. Penalty points are counted as elapsed time. If the canoeist negotiates the course in 90 sec, for example, but misses a gate, the total time recorded is 140 sec.

In addition to these rather short races, there are a number of annual marathon canoeing events. One of the best-known is the annual International White-water Race at Salida, Colorado, on a 23-mi downriver course. Established in 1948, this race draws competitors from all over the world.

Sailing. In its days as an explorer's vehicle, the canoe was often equipped with sails, and sailing competitions are still held. The standard decked sailing canoe is 17 ft, 9 in long and 33 in across the beam. Maximum sail area is 10 m² (about 107 ft²).

Canoe sailing is usually conducted in the United States under the auspices of the ACA, but it also falls under the jurisdiction of yachting associations. The decked sailing canoe, for example, is in the 10 Square Meter International Class established by the International Yacht Racing Union.

One of the first important international yachting trophies, the Seawanhaka International Challenge Cup, was actually established for races between sailing canoes in 1895. From these races evolved the type of racing sailboat known as the scow, which has a wide, rather flat-bottomed hull. However, when the boat is heeled to one side, during a race, the part of the boat actually traveling through the water is similar in shape to a canoe's hull.

Canoe Specifications. Modern canoes follow the general design of the birchbarks, and modern materials range from wood and canvas to aluminum and fiberglass. There are also many variations in design details, depending on the specific purpose of the canoe. In general, modern canoes are somewhat broader in the beam, for greater stability, than the primitive varieties, and many of them are equipped with thin keels, to protect the bottom and to help keep a straight course. Modern canoes are usually curved in, somewhat, above the waterline, also for greater stability.

Canoes built for racing range in length from 17 to 36 ft, in width from 20 to 29 in, and in weight from about 26 to about 66 lb. Aluminum is the favored material, because it is much lighter than fiberglass. Those used in Olympic

Gene and Henry Krawczyk of the New York AC form one of the top kayak doubles teams in the country. (*Courtesy of National Paddling Committee.*)

and other major forms of competition are built to rigid ICF specifications, usually of thin plywood.

The canoe used for both singles and tandem (C-1 and C-2) competition is 17 ft long, with a 29½-in beam. The canoe for four (C-4) is 20 ft long and has a 30-in beam.

The single-seat kayak (K-1) has a 17-ft length and 20-in beam; the K-2 is 21 ft long, with a 21½-in beam, and the K-4 is 36 ft long, with a 23½-in beam.

The canoe paddle is usually made of maple, and sometimes of ash or spruce. The paddle should be long enough to reach approximately to the canoeist's chin; the paddle used by the stern paddler in a two-person boat is somewhat longer. The parts of a paddle are the grip, or handle; the throat, where the paddle begins to broaden into the blade; and the blade itself.

The kayak is heavier than a canoe and sits lower in the water, but it's generally faster than the canoe. It is also more maneuverable and will go through white water that even a canoe couldn't navigate. If a canoe capsizes, getting it upright can be a real struggle; when a kayak capsizes, taking the rider underwater with it, he can right it rather quickly and simply by using an "Eskimo roll." The paddler, upside down, uses a stroke basically like the forward stroke. Since the water will be moving faster than the kayak, it will help provide lift when it hits the paddle blade.

The kayak paddle, usually about 9 ft long, is actually two short paddles held together by a metal connector. Each end has a "drop ring" about halfway between the end of the blade and the connector, which keeps water from running all the way down to the paddler's hands when the blade is out of the water. By adjusting the connector, a paddler can set the blades at an angle to one another. Some paddlers believe that "feathering" the blades—setting them at right angles—reduces air resistance.

Canoeing Techniques

In single-blade canoeing events, the canoeist stands on the floor of the vessel. The canoeist holds the paddle with one hand, grasping it firmly at the shaped grip; the other hand, near the throat, holds the paddle loosely, since the blade will usually have to be twisted during the stroke.

If there is just one paddler, that person paddles on the same side at all times, in flat water. This would ordinarily make the canoe turn in the opposite direction. To keep on a straight path, the paddler uses the J stroke: The blade is stroked backward, then allowed to drift backward slightly, and, as it is withdrawn from the water, it is given a slight twist away from the boat. The path of the paddle through the water gives the stroke its name.

In doubles events, the canoeists paddle on opposite sides. The bow paddler uses a straight stroke, just back to the hip; the stern paddler uses the J stroke.

There are a number of different kinds of strokes of importance to the recreational canoeist. Since flat-water races are run in a straight line, however, the forward stroke alone is important. And the most important elements are: using shoulder and body weight, rather than mere arm strength, for power, and keeping the blade at right angles to the canoe's course throughout the power stroke.

Kayak paddling seems more difficult, but is actually somewhat easier to master. The canoeist sits, instead of

Marcia Smoke was the first U.S. woman to win an Olympic medal in canoeing, a bronze in the 1964 singles kayak competition, and she has won many national kayak championships. (*Courtesy of National Paddling Committee.*)

kneeling, back firmly against the back rest, legs almost fully extended, and feet braced for leverage. The paddle is grasped with the thumbs down and on the inside; when the canoeist's arms are extended, the hands are just slightly farther apart than the shoulders. The canoeist extends the right blade forward and down, drawing out the arm fully while the left arm is bent at the elbow. The blade is dipped into the water, then propelled backward; most of the power should be furnished by pushing with the left arm, not by pulling with the right. When the left arm is fully extended, the process is reversed: The left blade is lowered into the water and propelled backward with a forward thrust of the right arm.

The connector between the two halves of the paddle should be thought of as a fulcrum that barely moves; unlike canoe paddling, kayak paddling is almost entirely done by arm action, and the body should not be twisted at all. Keeping the back firmly against the back rest at all times is very important; otherwise fatigue will quickly set in.

The stroke is exactly the same for singles as for doubles. The only difference is that the stern paddler should match the paddling rhythm employed to that of the bow paddler. Many paddlers use a cadence count at the beginning of a race, in order to establish the beat.

The white-water canoeist, above all, has to be able to read water, especially when the race is conducted through natural rapids. In running natural rapids, however, the recreational canoist will often use a pole rather than a paddle; in competitive events, poles are not permitted.

The basic stroke used to alter direction in a canoe is the draw: The paddle is inserted vertically in the water, parallel with the path of the boat and about 2 ft away from it, and the blade is then pulled straight toward the canoe until it is flat against the side. Done on the right side, this will make the bow turn sharply to the right, and vice versa.

In doubles the stern paddler does the same on that side of the boat. To turn in the opposite direction, the movement can simply be reversed (since paddlers usually paddle on the same side at all times): The paddle is inserted in the water very near the vessel and thrust outward.

The emergency draw is used to move the boat rapidly sideways without changing the course. Both paddlers draw in the same direction. To move the boat to the right, for example, the bow paddler pushes away from the boat from the right while the stern paddler pulls toward it on the left.

The draw stroke changes the course less acutely than the draw. The bow paddler sets the blade in the water at a 45-degree angle forward, then sweeps it back, in an outward arc. The stern paddler meanwhile also puts blade in water just behind the hips and at a 45-degree angle, and draws it forward. (If the bow paddler is paddling on the right, this maneuver results in a rather sharp left turn.)

For the jam, which will stop the canoe or slow it down greatly, each paddler simply thrusts the blade into the water, straight up and down and at right angles to the course, and holds it there, hooking the thumb over the gunwale.

Riding a kayak through white water doesn't involve as many kinds of strokes. The basic way of turning is to back-paddle on the side of the turn, since that also serves to slow the boat down somewhat.

In either kind of doubles racing, white-water canoeing requires exceptional teamwork. The partners must have practiced together so much that each knows almost exactly what the other will do in any given situation. Usually the bow paddler is responsible for a fairly steady

forward stroke, while the stern paddler is the one who steers the boat—that is, sets the general course. The bow paddler has to be alert for the minor obstacles which only that member of the team can see.

U.S. Flat-water Champions

(All men's races at 1,000 m until 1966; all women's races at 500 m until 1970)

Canoe Singles—Men

1930	William Gaehler	
1931	Charles Robinson	
1932	Harry Knight	
1933	Howard LaBrant	
1934	Eric Rodman	
1935	Eric Rodman	
1936	Stephen Lysak	
1937	Leo Hickey	
1938	Ernest Riedel	
1939	Howard Woodward	
1940	Theodore Blackman	
1941	Joe Ryan	
1942–45	No competition	
1946	Andrew Kulakowich	
1947	William Havens, Jr.	
1948	Andrew Macknowski	
1949	Andrew Kulakowich	
1950	Frank Havens	
1951	Frank Havens	
1952	Frank Havens	
1953	George Byers	
1954	Frank Havens	
1955	George Byers	
1956	Frank Havens	
1957	Frank Havens	
1958	Paul Donohue	
1959	Steven Hernek	
1960	Steven Hernek	
1961	Frank Havens	
1962	Roger Van de Meulebroecke	
1963	William Gates	
1964	Dennis Van Valkenburgh	
1965	Andy Weigand	
1966	Jim O'Rourke	(1,000 m and 10,000 m)
1967	Andy Weigand	(1,000 m)
	Jim O'Rourke	(10,000 m)
	Billy Gates	(1,000 m)
1968	Mike Ausley	(10,000 m)
1969	Andy Toro	(1,000 and 10,000 m)
1970	Andy Weigand	(1,000 and 10,000 m)
1971	Andy Weigand	(1,000 and 10,000 m)
1972	Roland Muhlen	(500 and 1,000 m)
	Ray Effinger	(10,000 m)
1973	Andy Toro	(500 m)
	Peter Ross	(1,000 m)
	Ray Effinger	(10,000 m)
1974	Roland Muhlen	(500 and 1,000 m)
	Andy Weigand	(10,000 m)
1975	Roland Muhlen	(500 and 1,000 m)
	Andy Weigand	(10,000 m)
1976	Andy Weigand	(500 and 10,000 m)
	Roland Muhlen	(1,000 m)

Kayak Singles—Men

1930	Ernest Riedel
1931	Ernest Riedel
1932	Ernest Riedel
1933	Gerald Mosher
1934	Adam Balko
1935	Ernest Riedel
1936	Harold Bruns
1937	Ernest Riedel
1938	Ernest Riedel
1939	William Havens, Jr.

The start of a singles canoe 500-m sprint during the Lincoln Park Boat Club regatta in 1973; note that racing canoists are much higher above the boat than the sports canoist. (*Courtesy of National Paddling Committee.*)

The Rusty Pelican Oaring Association has won many national titles; this is the association's four-man kayak team. *(Courtesy of National Paddling Committee.)*

1940	Ernest Riedel
1941	Ernest Riedel
1942–45	No competition
1946	Ernest Riedel
1947	Ernest Riedel
1948	Ernest Riedel
1949	Andrew Kulakowich
1950	Michael Budrock
1951	John J. Anderson
1952	Richard Moran
1953	Michael Budrock
1954	Bob Dermond
1955	John Pagkos
1956	Raymond Clark
1957	Dave Merwin
1958	Ken Wilson
1959	Joseph Rodela
1960	Paul Beecham
1961	Donald Dodge
1962	Charles Lundmark
1963	Bill Jewell
1964	Tony Ralphs
1965	John Van Dyke

1966	John Glair	(500 and 1,000 m)
1967	Pete Weigand	(500 m)
	John Van Dyke	(1,000 m)
	Kenneth Wilson	(10,000 m)
1968	John Pickett	(500, 1,000, and 10,000 m)
1969	Jack Brosius	(500 m)
	Pete Weigand	(1,000 m)
	Attila Libertini	(10,000 m)
1970	Henry Krawczyk	(500 and 1,000 m)
	Pete Weigand	(10,000 m)
1971	Henry Krawczyk	(500 m)
	Tony Ralphs	(1,000 and 10,000 m)
1972	John Van Cleave	(500 m)
	Pete Weigand	(1,000 m)
	Joe Beczak	(10,000 m)
1973	Phil Rogosheske	(500, 1,000, and 10,000 m)
1974	Steve Kelly	(500 and 1,000 m)
	Bill Leach	(10,000 m)
1975	Steve Kelly	(500 and 1,000 m)
	Bill Leach	(10,000 m)
1976	Steve Kelly	(500 and 1,000 m)
	Brent Turner	(10,000 m)

Kayak Singles—Women

1958	B. Budrock	
1959	Mary Ann Duchai	
1960	Glorianne Perrier	
1961	Glorianne Perrier	
1962	Francine Fox	
1963	Glorianne Perrier	
1964	Marcia Jones	
1965	Marcia Smoke	
	Sperry Jones	
1966	Marcia Smoke	
1967	Marcia Smoke	
1968	Marcia Smoke	
1969	Marcia Smoke	
1970	Marcia Smoke	
1971	Marcia Smoke	(500 and 5,000 m)
1972	Marcia Smoke	(500 m)
	Sperry Rademaker	(5,000 m)
1973	Marcia Smoke	(500 m)
	Sperry Rademaker	(5,000 m)
1974	Linda Murray	(500 m)
	Sperry Rademaker	(5,000 m)
1975	Linda Murray	(500 m)
1976	Ann Turner	(500 and 5,000 m)

CASTING—Fishing, for survival, began in primitive times, and casting became a technique of fishing nearly 2,000 years ago. As a sport in its own right, however, casting is a rather recent development. Like trapshooting and skeet, it evolved from a form of practice into a self-contained type of competition, and most of today's top tournament casters are casters first and fishermen second.

The most common kind of recreational angling, still fishing, is simple and pleasurable. But it is not a very efficient method, because the participant has to wait for the fish to come to the bait. By casting, the bait can be sent to where the fish are—or where, it is thought, they ought to be.

Artificial flies were used before the birth of Christ, in the form of feathers tied to hooks. The Roman poet Martial wrote of artificial flies some time between 10 B.C. and A.D. 20. It is assumed that the artificial flies were cast by anglers, but that is mere assumption: Artificial bait can be used for still fishing as well as live bait. (And live bait can be cast.) But casting was evidently widespread in the British Isles at least late in the fifteenth century, when the first crude reel was invented. And two seventeenth-century Englishmen, Thomas Barker, in 1651, and Izaak Walton, in 1653, wrote exhaustive treatises on angling which included descriptions of fly casting. Barker is now little known, but Walton is considered the secular patron saint of fishermen for his *The Compleat Angler.*

By the middle of the eighteenth century, fly-casting competitions were popular in many sections of Great Britain. Casting tournaments were held in the United States as early as 1871. They became truly nationwide in 1893, when the Chicago Fly-Casting Club staged the first national tournament during the Chicago World's Fair. The tournament took place on dry land—many tournaments still do—because it was too difficult to measure distance accurately over water.

In 1906, during the national tournament at Kalamazoo, Michigan, it was decided to form a national organization of casters. The National Association of Scientific Angling Clubs was formally established and the first tournament under its aegis was held in 1907. That body has since been reorganized as the National Association of Angling and Casting Clubs.

Steve Rajeff, the winner of many national titles, is shown casting during the ¼-oz-bait accuracy event at the 1974 championships. *(Courtesy of Paul Jones, American Casting Association.)*

Types of Casting

The two basic types of casting, fly casting and bait casting, are quite different from one another. An artificial fly is too light to pull line along behind it, so the line has to be cast first, to pull the fly along. A heavy line and a very long rod are used.

The "bait" in bait casting is an artificial lure, or plug, generally ⅜ or ⅝ oz in weight—heavy enough to be cast by its own weight. The line used is quite light and the rod is only 5 to 6½ ft long, compared with the 7 to 9 ft fly rod.

A more recent type, spin casting, or spinning, is a kind of compromise between the two. The rod is midway between the fly rod and the bait rod, and light lures—¼ to ⅜ oz—are used.

Surf casting is another rather recent development. The rod is extremely long—8½ to 10 ft—and very heavy, and the weight of the lures ranges up to about 4 oz.

Fresh-water and surf casting competitions are held separately. The specific categories have changed frequently. Generally speaking, competition involves casting for distance and for accuracy with various types of flies and baits. Championships are awarded in each category and for various combined events: fly accuracy and fly distance, bait accuracy and bait distance, overall accuracy, overall distance, and all-around. Women compete only in accuracy, with both baits and flies.

Rules. In accuracy events, targets are rings or disks, 10 to 30 in in diameter, placed at unknown, random distances from the caster. Minimum and maximum distances

are set, and they vary from one event to another. For example, in the ⅝-oz bait event, the nearest target must be 40 to 45 ft away and the farthest 45 to 50 ft away.

The caster is allowed to use only one hand on the rod, and casts must be made from within a box, generally 4 ft wide and open at the back. After stepping into the box, the caster must remain in it until all casts have been made. The rules usually specify two casts at each target. A perfect cast—one that lands within the ring or on the disk—scores 10 points. A point is subtracted from that total for each ft or fraction of a ft by which a cast misses the target, with a maximum of 10 demerit points per cast. The caster is allowed three false casts *(see below);* each false cast over three results in a point demerit.

In distance events, casts must usually be made single-handed, but there are sometimes special two-handed events. The caster is allowed no more than five and no fewer than three casts; scores are based on the average distance of the three most successful casts.

Techniques

Fly Casting. The right-handed caster stands with right foot forward, holding the rod in the right hand. The left hand holds the line out to the left side. About 20 to 25 ft of line should extend out into the water. The tip of the rod is now raised until only a few feet of line remain in the water, and the back cast begins, equivalent to the backswing in golf. The rod is brought to just behind vertical; a loop should appear in the line as it travels backward. When the loop disappears, the forward cast begins; the rod is whipped forward to somewhat above the horizontal, and the line travels out in front of the caster.

In a false cast the angler casts the line backward and

Steve Aleshi is casting in the dry fly accuracy event at the 1974 national championships. *(Courtesy of Paul Jones, American Casting Association.)*

forward without letting it hit the water. The purpose is to help in gauging distance, or to extend more line to get greater distance on the cast.

Bait Casting. The basic techniques are the same as those used in fly casting, except that the left hand doesn't have to hold any line. The weight of the bait itself will pull line from the reel. The back cast is stopped abruptly when the rod is just about vertical, and the forward cast begins after the plug's weight has bent the rod backward.

Surf Casting. The surf caster is allowed to use two hands. The caster stands square to the target, with feet well apart, left hand on the rod's rubber butt plate and right hand just below the reel. The back cast is made by pushing up on the butt with the left hand, using the right hand as a fulcrum. When the weight and the tip of the rod are almost touching the ground just behind, the caster begins the forward cast, pushing with the right hand and pulling with the left hand. The rod is stopped at just about the vertical.

National Freshwater Champions

All-Around—Men

1959	Marion Garber	1968	Zack Willson, Jr.
1960	Jon Tarantino	1969	Edward Lanser
1961	Jon Tarantino	1970	Zack Willson, Jr.
1962	Jon Tarantino	1971	Zack Willson, Jr.
	Terry Schneider	1972	Steve Rajeff
1963	Jon Tarantino	1973	Steve Rajeff
1964	Zack Willson, Jr.	1974	Steve Rajeff
1965	Casper Rigamer	1975	Steve Rajeff
1966	Zack Willson, Jr.	1976	Steve Rajeff
1967	Zack Willson, Jr.		

All-Accuracy—Women

1959	Mel Gavin	1968	Donna Monty
1960	Mel Gavin	1969	Cheryl Engle
1961	Mel Gavin	1970	Mollie Schneider
1962	Mollie Schneider	1971	Mollie Schneider
1963	Mel Gavin	1972	Ann Strobel
1964	Mel Gavin	1973	Mollie Schneider
1965	Dawn Holiday	1974	Ann Strobel
1966	Mel Gavin	1975	Pauline Cathcart
1967	Mel Gavin	1976	Mollie Schneider Light

Bibliography. American Association for Health, Physical Education and Recreation: *Casting and Angling,* Washington, D.C., 1958; National Association of Angling and Casting Clubs: *Manual for Tournament Fly and Bait Casting,* Nashville, Tenn., 1970 (annual).

CHARIOT AND CUTTER RACING—Although the name automatically makes one think of ancient Rome and *Ben Hur,* chariot racing in its modern form is actually a farm sport popular in areas of the Southwest and Midwest.

The chariot resembles a trash can with two small, bicycle-type wheels. The driver stands in it and is pulled by a two-horse team. Quarter horses are usually used. Most races are run on a ¼-mi straightaway. The cutter, for winter racing, is essentially a chariot with runners instead of wheels.

There are 28 associations that run regular races, in Colorado, Montana, Idaho, Utah, Washington, and Wyoming. The governing body is the World's Championship Cutter and Chariot Racing Association. Any club that has nine or more race meetings can send its four top teams to the world championship meet, held annually in March. The meet consists of a series of two-team races, with the winner of each race going on to further competition.

CITIZENS SAVINGS ATHLETIC FOUNDATION—In October, 1936, Paul Helms, Sr. founded the Helms Athletic Foundation, with W. R. "Bill' Schroeder, who became managing director. The purpose of the foundation was to support athletics in various ways. Trophies and other memorabilia were collected and in, 1948, put on display in the foundation's own building in Los Angeles. The following year, the foundation began organizing halls of fame for a number of sports, including college and professional football, track and field, and college and amateur basketball.

The Helms family supported the foundation and its growing number of enterprises until 1970, when the United Savings and Loan Association of California took over sponsorship; in 1973, United merged into Citizens Savings, and the foundation adopted its present name, the Citizens Savings Athletic Foundation.

One of the foundation's major projects is the World Trophy; every year, six athletes, one from each of the six continents, are named World Trophy winners and their names are engraved on the huge trophy in the athletic museum.

In addition, the foundation maintains halls of fame in the following fields: athletic trainers, auto racing, badminton, baseball, basketball, boxing, fencing, football, golf, gymnastics, handball, noteworthy contributors, rowing, soaring, swimming and diving, synchronized swimming, tennis, track and field, volleyball, weightlifting, winter sports, and wrestling.

The 7,500-volume sports library maintained at the foundation's headquarters is believed to be the largest of its kind in the world.

Members of the various Citizens Savings halls of fame are listed under the individual sports they represent.

Hall of Fame of Noteworthy Contributors

Avery Brundage—National Amateur Athletic Union (AAU) all-around champion 1914, 1916, 1918; World Trophy (North America) 1918; president, AAU, 1928–1936; president, U.S. Olympic Committee, 1929–1952; member, International Olympic Committee, 1936–1972, president 1952–1972.

Walter Camp—The "Father of American Football," coach and special football assistant at Yale and long-time All-American selector. *See also* FOOTBALL.

Dean Cromwell—Long-time track coach at the University of Southern California; his teams won 12 National Collegiate Athletic Association (NCAA) championships between 1926 and 1943, including 9 in a row.

Dwight F. Davis—Donor of the Davis Cup for international tennis competition.

Baron Pierre de Coubertin—Founder of the modern Olympic Games and enthusiastic promotor of recreation and physical education.

Daniel Ferris—Executive secretary, Amateur Athletic Union, 1927–1957.

William May Garland—A tireless promotor of sports, who was chiefly instrumental in having the 1932 Olympic Games awarded to Los Angeles.

John L. Griffith—Developed the U.S. Army's physical fitness program during World War I; instrumental in organizing the first National Collegiate Athletic Association (NCAA) track meet in 1921; commissioner of the Western Conference (Big Ten) 1922–1944.

W. R. "Bill" Schroeder, managing director, Citizens Savings Athletic Foundation, escorts guests through the Citizens Savings Hall sports museum. Here Schroeder comments on a section of the football displays. Shortly thereafter Schroeder placed the University of Minnesota football uniform worn by the late Bruce Smith, elected to the College Football Hall of Fame, in a display case.

Gustavus T. Kirby—President, U.S. Olympic Committee, 1924–1928; coinventor of the first timing camera device, 1931.

Douglas MacArthur—Onetime Army football player and president of the U.S. Olympic Committee.

Connie Mack—See BASEBALL: Hall of Fame.

James Naismith—Inventor of basketball, 1891. *See* BASKETBALL.

Knute K. Rockne—Notre Dame football coach, 1918–1930; his teams won 105 games, lost 21, and tied 5. *See also* FOOTBALL.

Theodore Roosevelt—A physical fitness devotee who, as President, urged vigorous exercise and the outdoor life; spurred the formation of the NCAA by his outspoken concern for the increasing number of football injuries and fatalities in 1905.

Grantland Rice—Recognized as one of the greatest of all sportswriters; from 1914 through 1953, he saw virtually every major sports event in the world. It is estimated that, in one year alone, he traveled 16,000 mi and wrote 1 million words about sports.

Albert G. Spalding—Great early baseball player and founder of the country's first major sports-equipment company. *See also* BASEBALL.

Amos Alonzo Stagg—The "Grand Old Man of Football," Stagg is also a member of the Naismith Memorial Basketball Hall of Fame and helped organize major track meets. *See also* BASKETBALL; FOOTBALL.

James E. Sullivan—One of the founders of the AAU, 1888; secretary 1888–1896, president 1906–1909, secretary-treasurer 1909–1914. The James E. Sullivan Memorial trophy is awarded annually by the AAU to the outstanding American amateur athlete of the year. *See also* SULLIVAN AWARD.

See WORLD TROPHY.

CLIFF DIVING—One of the newest of competitive sports, cliff diving originated among many coastal peoples. The divers of Mexico and the Caribbean islands, who often put on spectacular displays for tourists, have become fairly well known. The competitive version undoubtedly arose when American divers began leaping from cliffs.

The sport is confined almost entirely to the United States and Mexico—the only two countries that compete in the International Cliff Diving Championship. Each diver makes two dives—one from 65 ft, the other from 85 ft—into a narrow, shallow body of water. Dives are scored by judges on execution, as in ordinary diving competition.

See also DIVING.

CODEBALL—This actually comprises two different recreational sports invented by Dr. William E. Code of Chicago: codeball-in-the-court, played indoors, a form of handball employing the feet; and codeball-on-the-green, played outdoors and patterned on golf.

Both sports use a codeball, 12 oz in weight and with a 6-in diameter. The indoor game is played on a handball court, basically using the rules and scoring procedures of handball. The outdoor game is played on a course of approximately 10 acres; distances between holes measure 50 to 300 yd. There are 14 holes, or bowls, so called because the hole is actually a conical bowl, in diameter 18 in at the top and 41 in at the bottom. Players kick the ball from the tee to the green and then into the bowl.

Codeball became fairly popular in the 1930s and showed some growth as a recreation for wounded veterans after World War II. It was demonstrated to Olympians before the 1952 games, but has made little if any headway since then.

COLLEGE SPORTS—In most European countries, amateur sports of all kinds are controlled primarily by athletic clubs, some of which are devoted to single sports, others to a variety of sports.

In North America, however, and to a lesser extent in Great Britain, colleges and universities play a major role in many sports. One reason for the importance of sports in American colleges was that, during the early nineteenth century, students were virtually the only leisure class. During the latter part of the century, American colleges adopted to a certain extent the ancient Greek idea of training the body as well as the mind, and various sports programs were developed for this purpose. Rowing and gymnastics were especially important as part of the formal physical training program from about 1870 until 1900.

During the same period, other sports were usually extracurricular activities developed and guided by the students themselves. Football and basketball were, at the beginning, coachless, democratic activities; team captains, elected by the players, conducted practices, planned strategy, and acted as tactical leaders. There was even less organization in individual sports such as golf or tennis. Students who chose to enter the national tournaments in these sports did so on their own, not because they had performed well for the "team," since there were no tennis or golf teams. (The intercollegiate golf tournament was first held in 1897, the tennis tournament in 1883. The tennis team championship began only in 1946; the golf team championship, before 1939, was based solely on how individuals representing the school had finished, not on any kind of team competition.)

By the early twentieth century, the schools began to take over control of extracurricular athletic programs. To develop standards for these programs, and to prevent questionable practices, colleges also began to band together into conferences. As the name implies, a conference was originally a meeting, usually annual, of college representatives to set rules and standards, including ways of determining championships. Eventually a college conference became a sort of league. The largest of them, however, the Eastern College Athletic Conference (ECAC), remains very close to the original idea. Its members include many colleges that belong to other conferences or leagues.

The oldest existing conference is the Big Ten, organized as the Intercollegiate Conference of Faculty Representatives in 1896. There had been leagues and associations organized in specific sports before then, but the Big Ten, as it is now known, was the first group of colleges to form a "conference" to govern a whole range of sports.

In the original sense, the major "conference" today is the National Collegiate Athletic Association, which began as a conference of 13 colleges in 1905, to draw up new football rules. The NCAA, of course, is now the major governing body for intercollegiate athletics; its rules are binding on all member colleges and conferences, but its members (including conferences) are free to draw up more stringent regulations of their own. NCAA standards represent a minimum.

Through the years, however, more and more conferences have been organized primarily as leagues. The chief difference between the usual college conference and the professional sports league is that a conference operates in several different sports. A school that competes for the Southeastern Conference football championship, for example, also competes for the conference's basketball, baseball, golf, and other championships.

Major Conferences

Atlantic Coast—Clemson, Duke, Maryland, North Carolina, North Carolina State, Virginia, Wake Forest.

Big Eight—Colorado, Iowa State, Kansas, Kansas State, Missouri, Nebraska, Oklahoma, Oklahoma State.

Big Sky—Boise State, Gonzaga, Idaho, Idaho State, Montana, Montana State, Northern Arizona, Weber State.

Big Ten—Illinois, Indiana, Iowa, Michigan, Michigan State, Minnesota, Northwestern, Ohio State, Purdue, Wisconsin.

Ivy League—Brown, Columbia, Cornell, Dartmouth, Harvard, Pennsylvania, Princeton, Yale.

Mid-American—Bowling Green, Central Michigan, Eastern Michigan, Kent State, Miami (Ohio), Ohio University, Toledo, Western Michigan.

Missouri Valley—Bradley, Drake, Louisville, New Mexico State, North Texas State, Tulsa, West Texas State, Wichita State.

Ohio Valley—Austin Peay, Eastern Kentucky, Eastern Michigan, Middle Tennessee, Morehead, Murray, Tennessee Tech, Western Kentucky.

Pacific Coast—Fresno State, Fullerton State, Long Beach State, Pacific, San Diego State, San Jose State.

Pacific Eight—California, Oregon, Oregon State, Southern California, Stanford, UCLA, Washington, Washington State.

Southeastern—Alabama, Auburn, Florida, Georgia, Kentucky, Louisiana State, Mississippi, Mississippi State, Tennessee, Vanderbilt.

Southern—Appalachian, Citadel, Davidson, East Carolina, Furman, Richmond, Virginia Military, William and Mary.

Southland—Arkansas State, Lamar, Louisiana Tech, McNeese State, Texas-Arlington.

Southwest—Arkansas, Baylor, Houston, Rice, Southern Methodist, Texas, Texas A & M, Texas Christian, Texas Tech.

West Coast Athletic Conference—Loyola, Nevada-Las Vegas, Nevada-Reno, Pepperdine, St. Mary's, San Francisco, Santa Clara, Seattle.

Western Athletic Conference—Arizona, Arizona State, Brigham Young, Colorado State, New Mexico, Texas–El Paso, Utah, Wyoming.

Yankee—Boston University, Connecticut, Maine, Massachusetts, New Hampshire, Rhode Island, Vermont.

See also NAIA; NCAA.

COURSING—An ancient sport in which dogs chase a live animal, coursing long ago came to mean a competition between pairs of greyhounds. Although most important as the original version of modern dog racing, coursing is still practiced in some areas of the United States, chiefly the Southwest, and in England, Ireland, and Australia.

In the United States the sport is supervised by the National Coursing Association, which is also responsible for registering greyhounds, including racing animals. Headquartered in Abilene, Kansas, the NCA conducts national championships and maintains a Greyhound Hall of Fame.

Modern coursing takes place on a fenced-in field, 450 yd long and 150 yd wide. Caged hares are released through a chute at one end of the field, and they attempt to reach escape ports at the other end. One hare is released at a time; when it has gone 60 to 80 yd, a "slipper" releases a pair of greyhounds.

The dogs are graded by judges; the ability to "turn" the hare—make it change course away from its goal—is more important than catching and killing it. In major stakes competitions, there are usually 36 greyhounds, matched by pairs, tournament-style, until 2 dogs remain to compete in the final round for the championship.

See also Dog Racing.

COURT TENNIS—The direct ancestor of all our modern tennis games, court tennis was originally a kind of handball game, called *jeu de paume*—"game of the hand"—in thirteenth-century France. There were two versions of the game, for outdoors and indoors, and the indoor variety was played in the courtyards of medieval buildings. The best guess is that it originated in monastery courtyards, as a form of exercise for monks.

In 1230 the first court specifically for the sport was built in Poitiers, and during the fourteenth century a number of courts, called *tripots*, were set up throughout France, as the sport became very popular. It may have been the Western world's first really popular spectator sport. Gambling became such a problem that Charles V—himself a player—banned the sport in 1369. However, it has been estimated that the sport's professional guild in Paris alone still had 1,400 members 30 years after the ban. Despite its popularity, court tennis was also known as the sport of kings, both in France and in England, where it had been introduced by the late fourteenth century.

Court tennis didn't become a racket sport until about 1500, and it became remarkably popular in both France and England by 1600—there were about 1,800 courts in Paris by that year. Again, however, gambling scandals arose and by about 1750 the sport was played primarily by the upper classes.

Almost every feature of the medieval courtyard was incorporated into the sport, and it has been said that it takes months of study to understand the rules thoroughly. That fact and the expense of building a suitable court make court tennis today a sport played by very few people, in England, France, and the United States.

Although there is brief mention of a tennis court that existed in New York as early as 1763—and this was quite likely a court for fives, as a much simpler handball game is known—the sport was probably not introduced to the United States until 1876, two years after lawn tennis had arrived. Court tennis flourished briefly, at least among the wealthy, during the early part of this century, but there are now only a handful of courts in the United States.

Court and Equipment. The court is 110 ft by 38 ft, 8 in, with a concrete floor and concrete walls. Located 30 ft above the floor is a skylight. The court is divided into halves, the service side and the hazard side, by a net, which is 5 ft high at each end and 3 ft high in the middle.

The court in many ways resembles the medieval courtyard in which the sport was originally played. Along one long wall and both short walls runs the penthouse, a shed with a roof that slopes from a height of 10 ft, 7 in, to 7 ft, 1½ in; it is 7 ft in depth. The tambour, a sloping buttress, reduces the width of the court at the service end to 30 ft, 2 in. Set in a short wall above the tambour is the grille, a window 3 ft, 1 in square. The grille is one of several net-covered openings in the walls. The dedans, at the service end, is 21 ft, 8 in wide, and has a roof that slopes from 6 ft, 10 in to 3 ft, 3 in. Set in the penthouse are a number of openings called galleries.

The ball is 2¼ in in diameter and weighs about 2½ oz. It is made of strips of cloth wound tightly together, tied with twine, and covered with white melton cloth. The ball used in France is somewhat livelier than that used in England, and the American ball is somewhere between the two.

The racket is about 27 in long and weighs about 16 oz. Its head is rather pear-shaped, about 9 by 6 in, and is curved upward, to enable a player to put a good deal of "cut" on the ball. It is strung with heavy gut.

Method of Play. Scoring in court tennis is similar to scoring in lawn tennis. The chief difference is that, to win a set in a three-set match, a player needs to win eight games. However, in a five-set match, a player needs to win only six games to win a set, as in lawn tennis. Court tennis usually uses the "vantage" system, as in lawn tennis; that is, a player must have a two-game advantage over his adversary to win a set.

The method of play is quite different, however. The server always serves from the service side of the net, toward the hazard side, and the serve must hit the side penthouse and fall into the service area, which is marked by a service line, 21 ft, 1 in from the grille wall, and a pass line, 7 ft, 8 in from the main wall.

A player scores a point by hitting the ball into the grille, the dedans, or the winning gallery, or when the opponent hits the ball into the net or out of the court. The ball can be played off the walls, and a shot is out of court only if it strikes a wall above the play line, which is 18 ft above the floor at the sides and 23 ft above the floor at the ends of the court.

The really unique feature of court tennis is the chase, which puts the premium on skill as opposed to force. A player is supposed to return the ball before it bounces twice; failing that, however, the player doesn't lose the point. A chase results; the point is, in effect, postponed until one player has a score of 40 (as in lawn tennis' 15-30-40 scoring system) or until there are two chases to be played.

Suppose, for example, that Player A fails to return a shot which bounces for the second time 1 yd from the wall. The umpire calls, "Chase—1 yd." When it is time to play off the chase, the players change sides. Every shot that Player A makes during the play-off must be hit so that the ball will take its second bounce within 1 yd of the wall. If Player B sees that a shot by A isn't going to travel far enough, B can let it go and thereby wins the point. Player A can win a point in this play-off only through an error by B, or by making a shot into the dedans or the winning gallery.

The series of chase lines on the court help the referee make the decision as to how a chase should be played. Shots into a gallery other than the winning gallery also result in a chase, and specific chase lines are marked for gallery shots.

U.S. Amateur Champions

(A champion reigns until defeated by a qualified challenger. Listing a champion for a given year doesn't necessarily mean that a defense of the title was made during that year.)

1892	Richard D. Sears	1923	Jay Gould
1893	Fiske Warren	1924	Jay Gould
1894	B. Spalding de Garmendia	1925	Jay Gould
1895	B. Spalding de Garmendia	1926	C. Suydam Cutting
1896	Lawrence M. Stockton	1927	George Huband
1897	George R. Fearing, Jr.	1928	Hewitt Morgan
1898	Lawrence M. Stockton	1929	Hewitt Morgan
1899	Lawrence M. Stockton	1930	Lord Aberdare
1900	Eustace H. Miles	1931	William C. Wright
1901	Joshua Crane	1932	William C. Wright
1902	Joshua Crane	1933	James H. Van Alen
1903	Joshua Crane	1934	Ogden Phipps
1904	Joshua Crane	1935	Ogden Phipps
1905	Charles E. Sands	1936	Ogden Phipps
1906	Jay Gould	1937	Ogden Phipps
1907	Jay Gould	1940	James H. Van Alen
1908	Jay Gould	1941	Alastair B. Martin
1909	Jay Gould	1942–45	No competition
1910	Jay Gould	1946	Robert Grant III
1911	Jay Gould	1947	E. M. Beals, Jr.
1912	Jay Gould	1948	Ogden Phipps
1913	Jay Gould	1949	Ogden Phipps
1914	Jay Gould	1950	Alastair B. Martin
1915	Jay Gould	1951	Alastair B. Martin
1916	Jay Gould	1952	Alastair B. Martin
1917	Jay Gould	1953	Alastair B. Martin
1918–19	No competition	1954	Alastair B. Martin
1920	Jay Gould	1955	Alastair B. Martin
1921	Jay Gould	1956	Alastair B. Martin
1922	Jay Gould	1957	Northrup Knox

1958	Northrup Knox	1968	G. H. "Pete" Bostwick, Jr.
1959	Northrup Knox		
1960	Northrup Knox	1969	James C. Bostwick
1961	Northrup Knox	1970	James C. Bostwick
1962	Northrup Knox	1971	G. H. "Pete" Bostwick, Jr.
1963	Northrup Knox		
1964	James C. Bostwick	1972	James C. Bostwick
1965	James C. Bostwick	1973	Howard R. Angus
1966	G. H. "Pete" Bostwick, Jr.	1974	Gene Scott
		1975	Gene Scott
1967	James C. Bostwick	1976	Gene Scott

CRICKET—Because cricket is considered the traditional British sport, it has often been assumed that it is a very old one. A drawing of 1344, showing a pitcher and a batter, has been offered as evidence that cricket was played more than 600 years ago, and occasional mentions of "cricket" as a sport in the twelfth and thirteenth centuries have been adduced as proof that the game is even more ancient. It has been suggested that cricket sprang, centuries ago, from croquet or field hockey or even *kolf,* the Lowlands sport believed to have been an early form of golf. And some writers have offered cricket as the ancestor of baseball.

Actually, however, it appears that cricket is only a distant cousin of baseball, and a relatively recent offshoot of one or more of the sports that eventually became baseball. The 1344 drawing doesn't show any form of the wicket that makes cricket the unique game it is. And the name may have been used in the past to describe almost any type of sport played with a crooked stick—since the term derives from *cryce,* the Saxon word for crooked stick.

Stoolball, a sport played often by young girls during the fifteenth and sixteenth centuries and later, was probably the direct ancestor of cricket. In the original form of stoolball, a stool is set up as a target for one player, who attempts to hit it with a ball, while the other player protects the stool, using the hand as a bat. One point is scored for each time the ball is hit with the hand. When the "pitcher" hits the stool, the players change sides, and the eventual winner is the player who has hit the ball more often.

By the early eighteenth century, stoolball players were using a bat, and there were two or more stools in the game. By that time, cricket had already developed as a separate sport. The first recorded cricket match was played in 1728. Evidently the sport was objected to as disreputable by some people, since a British court in 1748 ruled that the game was legal, but added that betting on it was a bad thing.

The first written rules for the sport were drawn up by the London Cricket Club in 1744. At the time, a wicket consisted of just two stumps with a bail across the top, and the bowler, as the name implies, usually rolled the ball to the batsman. However, in midcentury, bowlers began delivering the ball on one bounce. In 1777 a third stump was introduced, so that the ball couldn't pass between stumps without knocking them down, and in 1817 provision was made for two bails instead of one.

Aside from the change to two bails and minor changes in dimensions, the rules of cricket have remained very much as they were in 1817. The size of the ball and bat have been standardized since 1774.

Field and Equipment. There are no standard dimensions for a cricket field, but the pitch—the area between the two wickets—is standardized at 22 yd long and 10 ft wide. The wicket is 28 in high and 9 in wide; the maximum length of the bails is 4⅜ in, and they must not extend more than ½ in above the steps.

The batsman's ground is marked by a popping crease—a line 8 ft, 8 in long and 4 ft in front of the wicket. A line extending 3 ft, 11½ in on either side of the stumps marks the bowling crease. At each end a white line runs back about 12 in at right angles to the crease.

A batsman must have the bat or part of his person behind the popping crease to prevent being "run out" or "stumped." Until recently the bowler was required to have the back foot behind and within the bowling crease when delivering the ball, but the rule was difficult to enforce because the bowler's momentum tended to drag the back foot beyond that point; the bowler is now required to have the front foot behind the popping crease on the bowler's end.

A field may be enclosed, but, if it is not, the teams

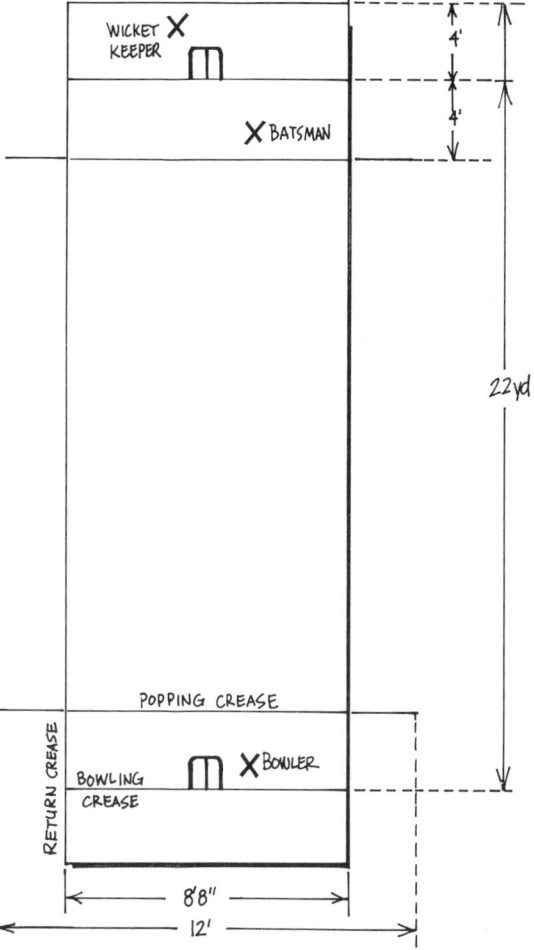

The pitch

agree upon boundaries before the game. Most commonly used cricket fields, whether enclosed or not, have traditional boundary markers.

The ball is similar to a baseball but slightly smaller—between $8\frac{13}{16}$ and 9 in, in circumference, and $5\frac{1}{2}$ to $5\frac{3}{4}$ oz in weight—and it has a thicker, harder leather cover, which is colored red.

The bat, which is made of willow, has a triangular cross section, with a flat surface, the longest side of the triangle, used as the batting side. A handle of tightly bound cane is wedged into a hole in the top. Overall length must not exceed 38 in, and the width must not exceed $4\frac{1}{2}$ in.

The batsmen and the wicketkeeper wear wide, heavy shin and knee pads, and the wicketkeeper wears two heavy leather gloves. No other players wear protective equipment of any kind. The customary "uniform" consists of white flannel trousers, white shoes or boots, white open-necked shirts, and caps similar to those worn in baseball.

Method of Play. A cricket match is played for a predetermined period of time, ranging from several hours to several days. (Recently, the one-day match has become relatively popular in England, since it is more adaptable to television.) There are 11 players on each team. The batting team has two batsmen on the field at a time, one at each wicket, and the opposing team has a bowler, a wicketkeeper, and nine other fielders who may take up any positions outside the pitch. The usual positions are shown in the diagram.

The bowler pitches in an attempt to hit the wicket and knock down the bails, to put the batsman out. The batsman defends the wicket with the bat, using it merely to deflect the ball from the wicket, or to hit the ball to any part of the field. There is no such thing as a foul ball in cricket. If the ball is hit far enough, the batsmen can try to score a run by exchanging positions before being put out; they may keep running back and forth between the wickets, scoring additional runs, for as long as they think it is safe.

If the ball, thrown by a fielder, hits the wicket when the batsman is "out of ground," he is "run out." If the batsman swings and misses, and is out of his ground, the wicketkeeper can break the wicket—the batsman is then "stumped."

If the ball is caught on the fly by a fielder, the batsman is "out, caught." The batsman who knocks the wicket down while trying to hit the ball or while running is "out, hit wicket"; if the batsman hits the ball twice, handles the ball, intentionally obstructs a fielder, or uses any part of the body to stop the ball, he is out.

The bowler, who usually throws overhand, must keep the delivery arm straight; if that arm is bent during delivery, it is "no ball," which counts as a run for the batting team. It is also "no ball" if the bowler is not in the prescribed area at the moment of delivery.

If the pitch is out of the reach of the batsman, it is a "wide," which also counts as a run. If the pitch gets past the wicketkeeper, the batsmen may run just as if it were a hit—this is called a "bye." If the ball strikes the batsman while the batsman is trying to hit it, and then eludes the wicketkeeper, it is a "leg bye" if any runs are scored. (This applies only if, in the judgment of the umpires, there was no deliberate attempt by the batsmen to get hit by the ball.)

A batsman, when out, is replaced by another. An "innings" (always plural in cricket) ends after there are 10 outs—since the man remaining doesn't have a partner. Since a man stays at bat until he is out, it is perfectly possible for the first batsman to remain at bat throughout an innings.

Four runs are automatically scored if the ball goes beyond the boundary; six runs if it is hit beyond the boundary on the fly. However, if the batsmen score more than four runs before the ball crosses the boundary, they are credited with the higher total.

The umpire calls an "over" after six balls, ordinarily; sometimes after eight balls, as in Australian cricket. When an over is called, the wicketkeeper moves to the other wicket and a new bowler begins bowling from the other end. The fielders will also, of course, change positions. Generally, a team uses the same two bowlers throughout a game but a "relief bowler" is sometimes substituted.

The usual regulation cricket match consists of two complete innings. However, play is much more flexible than in baseball. If the first team to bat still holds a lead after the second team has had its innings, it can compel the second team to "follow on"—to bat again, for another innings. And, if the second team cannot take the lead, the match is over. As in baseball, if the second team to bat is in the lead after the other team's second innings, there is no need to bat again.

Major matches are always two innings. However, in less important matches, where the time limit is a factor, a team captain may declare the team's innings to be over before the required 10 outs. Such a declaration will be made only if the captain feels the team has built up an unbeatable lead.

Cricket in the United States. Cricket was played in this country as early as 1709, and there was a major match in Savannah in 1741. During the Colonial period, there were two different kinds of cricket. One of them, the "London method," was based on the revised rules of 1744. Nothing much is known about the other, except that it was not London method; it may possibly have been a completely different game, played with crooked sticks. It was often called "wicket," which is the name of an older form of cricket still played in the north of England.

Modern cricket became quite popular in the Philadelphia area during the 1830s and 1840s when large numbers of mill workers emigrated from Nottingham and Yorkshire, and the first international matches were played between the United States and Canada. The first touring team from England came to this country in 1859, and in 1878 an Australian team played a draw with a Philadelphia team before traveling to England for a series of matches.

The Philadelphia Union Cricket Club was organized in 1832, and in 1843 the University of Pennsylvania organized a cricket team. The game also became popular in metropolitan New York during the 1890s. The Staten Island Cricket and Tennis Club, organized in 1873, is still in existence, and the club has been host to many international matches. Many other clubs were established in the New York area and in New Jersey.

It should also be noted that the man who organized and managed the first all-professional baseball team, George Wright, was a professional cricket player. Wright organized the Red Stockings in Cincinnati, where he was a cricket instructor at a club, and he is now a member of the Baseball Hall of Fame.

The greatest American cricket player was a Philadelphian, John Barton King, who led the English bowling averages in 1908 with an average of 11.01 wickets taken, a record until 1958. He also set a North American record for batsmen in 1906, scoring 344 runs not out (meaning that the other 10 batters on his team had all been retired, and the innings was over).

Cricket declined in this country from the 1920s until the 1950s, when a revival began. There are now more than 100 cricket clubs in the United States, under the jurisdiction of the U.S. Cricket Association, established in 1961, and annual matches with Canada are again being conducted.

International Cricket. Cricket is the national summer sport of Great Britain and is played in many countries of the British Commonwealth and in former colonies—among them Australia, New Zealand, the West Indies, India, Pakistan, and South Africa. It is also fairly popular in Holland and Denmark.

The most important international matches are the Test Matches, which are played among teams representing Commonwealth nations. The matches between Australia and England are the most widely watched, with the Australia–West Indies matches probably ranking second.

Cricket has achieved such status in England that two great players, John B. Hobbs and Donald G. Bradman, have been knighted for their contributions to it. The sport is perhaps more popular in Australia, however, where crowds of nearly 100,000 have watched Test Matches.

Other Cricket Terms. There have been many fanciful explanations of the term "hat trick" as used in ice hockey, but the simple fact is that it originated in cricket to describe the feat of taking three wickets with three consecutive rolls. When a bowler achieved the feat, his club presented him with a hat.

Another prized cricket feat is a "century," scoring 100 or more runs in a time at bat. (A batsman is credited only with those runs scored as the result of hitting; wides, no balls, and byes are not credited to him.)

Scores are kept for individuals as well as for teams, and cricket has built up an astonishing collection of statistics over the years. The basic statistic about a batsman is a simple statement of the number of runs scored, and the way in which he was finally retired, if he was—"97, stumped," for example, means that he scored 97 runs before being put out when the wicketkeeper knocked down the wicket while the batsman was out of ground. The phrase "not out," as already noted, means that the batsmen was not retired, but his 10 teammates were, bringing the innings to an end. (It may also mean that the captain of the team declared the innings was over.)

A team is said to have won by a certain number of runs and an innings if it scored more runs in one innings than the other team could score in two.

A bowler is credited with the number of wickets he takes, and with outs recorded by stumping, caught balls, and interference with the ball by the batsman. A fielder is credited with outs scored by catches.

CROQUET—The name for the sport has the same basic root as "cricket," only it is from the French. *Crochet*

means "crooked stick," and the original form of croquet was probably played with the same sort of stick used in ancient golf, field hockey, and the baseball-type games that led to cricket.

Croquet, however, has a strange, intriguing history. The game apparently descended from lawn bowls, by way of billiards. At some time in the fourteenth century, lawn bowls enthusiasts tried to find a way to play their game indoors, and they set up a bowling layout, first on large floors, later on tables, that used arches as obstacles between the ball and the target, originally a stake. Rolling the ball through the obstacles was too easy, so the use of a "mace" was introduced.

This indoor game eventually evolved into billiards. But, in the meantime, it moved back outdoors to become something quite different from lawn bowls.

The new sport became known as croquet in France and pall mall in England (from the Latin *palla mallens*, "ball and mallet"). It was not terribly popular in either country, though apparently it was more popular in France than in England. In any event, a Frenchman named Jean Jacques wrote the first book about the game in 1857, and four years later a book called *Routlege's Handbook of Croquet* was published in England, creating a new wave of popularity for the sport, this time under its French name.

As a fad, croquet spread rather quickly through the British Isles and arrived in the United States in the 1870s, becoming particularly popular in the Norwich, Connecticut, area. This burst of popularity lasted only 20 years or so, as lawn tennis became the new rage.

The National Croquet Association, formed in 1882 to govern the sport in the United States, found itself with not much to govern. However, at a meeting in Norwich in 1899, a group of enthusiasts decided the sport could be revived with some rules changes, and a new game was developed. The initial and final letters of "croquet" were chopped off; the result was "roque," a faster game that could be played in a smaller area and that called on some of the skills of billiards, particularly the ability to put "English" on the ball.

The American Roque League was organized in 1916 to govern this new sport. Roque, however, requires a somewhat more elaborate court than croquet, which can be played on any flat, grassy area, and a compromise sport, called American lawn croquet to distinguish it from the English version, was also developed. In 1950, the National Croquet Association was reorganized to govern the non-roque versions of the sport.

The American lawn version is the type of croquet commonly played by families in their yards. Roque is played primarily by roque enthusiasts at playgrounds where there are special courts, many of which were built in a cooperative effort by the National Recreation Association and the Works Progress Administration during the Depression.

The basic idea of the croquet-roque games is that a mallet is used to knock a ball around a course, through hoops in a predetermined sequence, and then hitting a final stake to win. All three versions use wooden or composition balls, $3^{1}/_{4}$ in in diameter.

Roque. The roque court is an octagonal area of hard-packed clay, 60 by 30 ft, marked by a concrete border. The actual playing area is marked by a line 28 in inside the border. The balls are of hard rubber or composition.

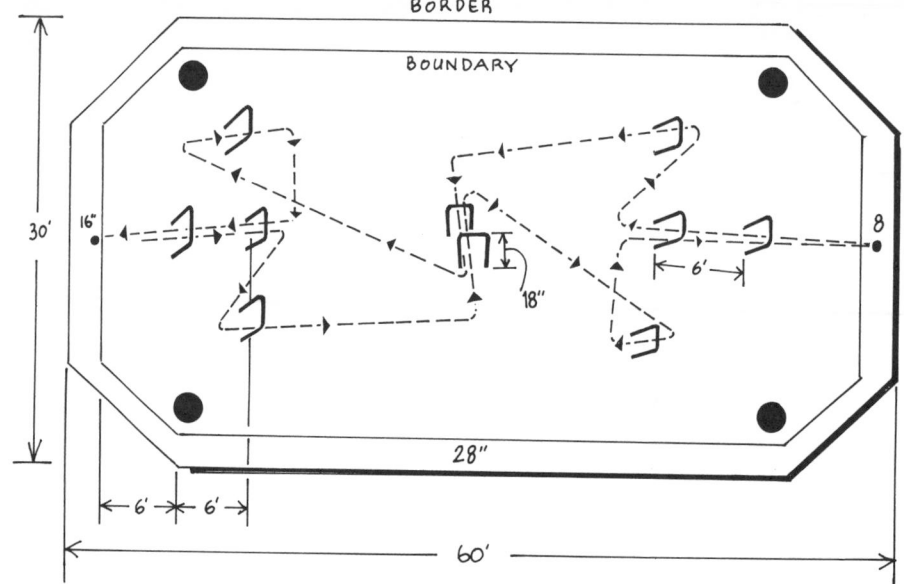

Roque court

The arches are wire hoops set in concrete or wood, with the legs just 3⅜ in apart. The roque mallet has a handle 15 in long. The head is about 6 in long and 1 in in diameter. One side is covered with plastic or aluminum, the other with rubber.

Roque is played by two opposing teams, of one or two players each. There are always four balls. In singles, with one player per team, each player plays two balls. The balls are placed in the four corners of the court, as shown in the diagram. Balls *belonging* to a single team are diagonally opposite each other.

The object of the game is to have one team get both its balls all the way around the court, scoring 16 points per ball by going through the 14 hoops and hitting the 2 stakes. Whenever a player goes through an arch or hits a stake, another shot is awarded, but going through the two arches at the center of the court entitles the player to only one shot. (If the ball goes through one of these arches without going through the other, no additional shot is awarded.)

When a player's ball hits one of the other three balls, it is a "roquet," provided the other ball was "live." A roquet gives the player two more turns. The first turn must be used to take a croquet: The player's own ball is placed in contact with the ball hit, then the player's own ball is struck so that both balls move. On the second turn the player's own ball is struck again singly, the usual procedure.

A player is allowed to roquet on a first turn of the game, or after the player has scored (by passing through an arch or hitting a stake) on any other turn. All three other balls are then live; once a player hits a ball, however, that ball is "dead" until the player scores again, on the same turn or on the next turn. If a player deliberately hits a dead ball, the player's turn ends, and the opponent can choose

to have the balls replaced, or to leave them where they are.

When a player makes the 15th point with one ball, that ball becomes a "rover," and cannot be staked out until the partner ball has also made its 15th point. To win the game, both partner balls must become rovers, and must be staked out by one player in the same stroke or consecutive strokes.

The intelligent use of bank shots off the concrete borders and of roquets is the key to the sport. A player can roquet the partner's ball, for example, croquet it through the proper arch, then stroke the player's own ball through an arch, and so on. It is possible for a player to score all 32 of the team's points on the first turn in this fashion.

American Lawn Croquet. This is a less formal sport which can be played on any fairly level lawn. The rules are generally the same as those of roque, but there are a number of possible local variations.

A player can win, in some versions, by simply completing the course and hitting the final stake. In other versions, when the final stake is hit, a player's ball becomes "poison," and that player can rove the course, "killing" the other players' balls—which eliminates them from the game—until the "poison" ball is the only one left.

Some versions allow a player three options after making a roquet: One is to croquet, as in roque, but in this case by putting a foot on the player's own ball, to keep it from moving, while sending the other ball "for a ride"; the player may place his or her own ball a mallethead away in any direction, from the ball that has been hit; or the player's own ball may be played from the spot where it has stopped. Sometimes two extra shots are awarded for a croquet.

Lawn croquet also admits as many as eight players, in singles or in partnerships of two, three, or four.

CROSS-COUNTRY—Often classified with track and field, cross-country running is really a separate sport, with a season of its own—although it is often a training sport for long-distance track runners, and most of its outstanding competitors have also been fine track performers.

Undoubtedly the first running races were cross-country, at some unknown date in the distant past. The first recorded, formally organized cross-country race was the "Crick Run," first held in 1837 at Rugby School, England. By 1876, England had a national cross-country championship race.

A cross-country race is run over natural terrain, sometimes including ditches, streams, and perhaps even fences. In this respect it is the ancestor of steeplechase running. Modern cross-country races aren't run over as rough terrain as were those of the past; but they are still run basically over trails and paths, rather than roads or tracks.

Cross-country was on the Olympic program in 1912, 1920, and 1924, but was then dropped because it was believed to be too strenuous for the summer. The sport generally takes place in the fall. (The much longer marathon, however, has remained on the Olympic program, for tradition's sake.)

There is no standardized distance, but cross-country is usually run at 4, 5, or 6 mi (3 mi for women). The race may begin on a regular track, but the major portion must be run over the countryside. The course is marked with flags, red to the left and white to the right, that can be seen at a distance of about 125 yd.

A cross-country team consists of five or more runners. The team score is obtained by adding up the places won by its top five finishers; the team with the lowest point total wins.

See also TRACK AND FIELD.

AAU Champions

Men	Min:Sec
1890 W. D. Day	47:41
1891 M. Kennedy	46:30⅘
1892 Edward C. Carter	43:54
1893–1896 No competition	
1897 George W. Orton	35:58
1898 George W. Orton	35:41⅖
1899–1900 No competition	
1901 Jerry Pierce	43:27⅓
1902 No competition	
1903 John Joyce	32:23⅘
1904 No competition	
1905 W. J. Hail	32:59⅘
1906 Frank Nebrich	34:29⅘
1907 F. G. Bellars	33:12
1908 F. G. Bellars	34:15⅗
1909 W. J. Kramer	37:17⅕
1910 F. G. Bellars	33:03
1911 W. J. Kramer	37:08
1912 W. J. Kramer	34:32
1913 Abel R. Kiviat	33:52
1914 Hannes Kolehmainen	33:36
1915 N. Giannakopoulos	32:46⅗
1916 Willi Kyronen	32:46
1917 James Henigan	33:58
1918 Max Bohland	33:00
1919 Fred Faller	32:26⅕
1920 Fred Faller	29:01

1921 R. E. Johnson	24:23⅘
1922 Willi Ritola	34:37
1923 Willi Ritola	31:56
1924 Fred Wachsmuth	31:35
1925 Willi Ritola	29:27
1926 Willi Ritola	30:00⅗
1927 Willi Ritola	29:27⅕
1928 Gus Moore	31:18
1929 Gus Moore	31:10
1930 William C. Zepp	29:43
1931 Clark S. Chamberlain	29:40⅘
1932 Joseph P. McCluskey	32:30
1933 R. A. Sears	32:51
1934 Donald Lash	32:17.2
1935 Donald Lash	32:42.6
1936 Donald Lash	32:27
1937 Donald Lash	32:57.4
1938 Donald Lash	33:33.8
1939 Donald Lash	32:26
1940 Donald Lash	30:25.8
1941 J. Gregory Rice	29:18.7
1942 Frank Dixon	32:52
1943 William Hulse	32:41
1944 James Rafferty	31:38
1945 Thomas Quinn	34:14
1946 Robert Black	32:46.4
1947 Curtis Stone	32:28.7
1948 Robert Black	30:02
1949 Fred Wilt	30:31
1950 Browning Ross	31:24
1951 William Ashenfelter	30:26
1952 Fred Wilt	32:31
1953 Fred Wilt	31:17.6
1954 Gordon McKenzie	29:27.5
1955 Horace Ashenfelter	31:39.1
1956 Horace Ashenfelter	30:08
1957 John Macy	31:12
1958 John Macy	29:47.8
1959 Al Lawrence	32:22.4
1960 Al Lawrence	31:20.8
1961 Bruce Kidd	32:02.0
1962 Peter McArdle	29:53.0
1963 Bruce Kidd	30:47.2
1964 Dave Ellis	30:49.5
1965 Ron Larrieu	31:11.8
1966 Ron Larrieu	31:23.0
1967 Ken Moore	30:08.8
1968 John Mason	30:34.2
1969 Jack Bachelor	30:49.8
1970 Frank Shorter	30:15.7
1971 Frank Shorter	29:19
1972 Frank Shorter	30:42
1973 Frank Shorter	29:52.5
1974 John Ngeno	29:59
1975 Greg Fredericks	28:57
1976 Rick Rojas	30:23.8

Women	
1966 Doris Brown	7:51.2
1967 Vicki Foltz	11:46.65
1968 Doris Brown	10:53
1969 Doris Brown	10:56.2
1970 Doris Brown	
1971 Doris Brown	
1972 Francie Larrieu	13:11
1973 Francie Larrieu	17:17
1974 Lynn Bjorklund	17:03
1975 Lynn Bjorklund	16:32.6
1976 Janice Merrill	16:37

CURLING—Both Holland and Scotland claim to have originated curling, as well as golf, and it is possible that both sports derived from an old Dutch game called *kolf,* in which a ball was hit over an icy surface with a pole as a target. It is also quite possible that curling is simply an icy version of lawn bowls.

There can be no doubt, however, that the Scots were responsible for the elevation of the game into a sport. It was played in Scotland as long ago as 1551 (a curling stone with that date on it has been found in Scotland), and the oldest club still in existence is the Dudingston Curling Society, which was organized in Edinburgh in 1795. The Amateur Curling Club of Scotland, formed in 1834, standardized rules throughout the country. In 1838 that group was merged into the Grand Caledonian Curling Club, still considered the sport's ruling body—it has been known as the Royal Caledonian Curling Club since Queen Victoria watched and enjoyed a curling contest in 1842.

The name comes from the fact that a good curler can use spin to make a curling stone curve, or curl, around another and into the position wanted—possibly evidence of a link with lawn bowling, in which the bias of the ball is used to control the amount of curve.

For a long time, irregularly shaped stones were used, but the smooth rounded stone was introduced to the sport about 1800 and is still used. For a time, Canadian players used iron weights instead of stones, but iron is no longer allowed.

Curling in North America. The sport evidently arrived in Canada in 1807 and in the United States about 1820. The early strongholds in the United States were in northern New York. The Utica Curling Club is one of the oldest and, through the years, has been one of the most successful in this country. Curling has become particularly popular along the Great Lakes, especially in those areas where there is a long winter season. Superior, Wisconsin and Minneapolis–St. Paul, Minnesota are now among the major strongholds of curling.

The Dominion Curling Association is the governing body in Canada; the United States has separate associations for men and women.

Rink and Equipment. The curling rink is a patch of ice, 138 by 14 ft, with identical targets marked by concentric

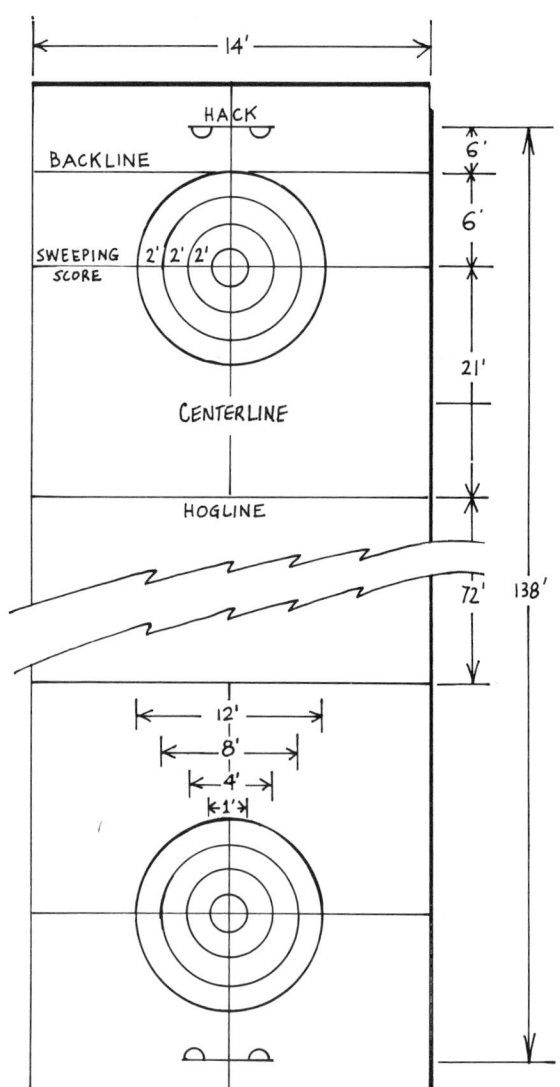

Curling rink

Bob Schley and Mrs. Mark Daliere sweep ahead of a teammate's stone during mixed competition at a Milwaukee curling rink. *(Courtesy of Mrs. C. F. Pollen.)*

circles at each end. (It should be noted that the word "rink" means both the playing area and a curling team.) At the center of the target, which is called the "house," is a "tee," which is simply an aiming point, a small circle of arbitrary size. Around the tee are circles with diameters of 4, 8, and 12 ft.

The tees are 38 yd apart. At each end is a "hack," a foothold projecting from the ice, which keeps the player from sliding down the rink behind the stone after its release by the player.

The ice is pebbled, rather than smooth. Pebbling is accomplished by sprinkling warm water on the prepared ice surface. The purpose is to give the stones something to grip so that their spin will make them curve; if the ice were perfectly smooth, it would be impossible to curl the stone.

The stone has maximum measurements of 36 in, in circumference, and 4½ in, in height. In Canada and the United States the weight has been standardized at 42½ lb. The stone has two soles, or sliding surfaces, one of which is rough, for very fast ice, and the other smooth, for slow ice. The gooseneck handle is detachable so that a player can use whichever sole is best for the ice conditions that prevail.

Method of Play. Curling is a team sport, with a team, or rink, made up of four players headed by a "skip." The skip, usually the fourth person to play, directs team members as to the kind of shot wanted, the path it should take, the amount of spin and force that should go into it, and so on.

Each player delivers two stones, alternately with an opponent. The delivery is similar to that used in bowling; the "sweeping score" represents the foul line. A player is assisted by teammates, who use their brooms to sweep ice dust, snow, and moisture from in front of the delivered stone, as it moves, to help guide it.

The basic purpose is to get a stone as close to the tee as possible. However, many types of strategic shots are also used, to knock an opponent's stone out of position, to guard a teammate's scoring stone, or to knock a teammate's stone into better position.

When all 16 stones have been thrown, an "end" has been completed. Only one team can score on each end—the team that has a stone lying nearest to the tee. The team gets 1 point for each stone that is nearer to the tee than any of the opposition's stones. In order to count, a stone must be at least partly within the house.

Play then continues from the other end. A game is usually made up of 10 complete ends; sometimes, however, the first team to get 21 points is the winner.

Glossary

big end—An end in which a team scores 4 or more points.

biter—A stone that barely touches the outside circle.

chip—To nick another stone.

counter—A stone that is closer to the tee than any of the opponent's stones.

draw—The amount of arc put on a stone when it is curled.

guard—A stone placed in front of another stone, to protect it.

hog—A stone that doesn't clear the hog line.

hog line—A line in front of the goal; a stone must cross it to be in play.

in-turn—A stone that turns clockwise as it slides.

in-wick—A shot in which the played stone hits the inside edge of another stone and then deflects toward the tee.

lead—The player who shoots first for a team.

out-turn—A stone that turns counterclockwise.

out-wick—A shot in which the played stone hits the outside edge of another stone, thus moving it toward the tee.

pat lid—A stone placed right in the center of the goal.

port—An opening between two stones big enough for another stone to slide through.

promotion—Hitting a stone and knocking it nearer the center of the goal.

runner—A rapidly thrown stone.

take-out—A shot that knocks another stone outside the rings.

weight—The speed of the stone; a "light weight" stone has not been thrown fast enough to reach the scoring circles.

wicke—Same as "chip."

CURTIS CUP—A golfing trophy donated by Margaret and Harriet Curtis of the United States for international competition among teams of amateur women. The United States and Great Britain compete for the cup in even-numbered years. For results, *see* GOLF.

CYCLING—If "bicycle" is taken in its literal sense, to mean a two-wheeled vehicle, it dates to at least 1690, when a Frenchman, the Comte de Sivrac, invented something similar to what we call a scooter. The rider mounted a "backbone" joining two wheels and propelled the vehicle by pushing backward on the pavement with his feet. De Sivrac called it a *celerifere*—literally, a "fast-goer."

(What appears to be a bicycle is shown in a stained-glass window in England, dated 1580. And there is other evidence that there were two-wheeled vehicles in existence before 1690, but de Sivrac's is the first that we definitely know about.)

Similar scooter-type vehicles were developed during the eighteenth century, and one sort, called the velocipede, became quite popular in Napoleonic France, in the form of a wooden horse—although many writers believe that this vehicle had four wheels.

A German nobleman, Baron Karl Drais von Sauerbronn of Mannheim, added a steerable front wheel and a padded seat in 1816, and with this vehicle the first kind of bicycle racing began. As with other nineteenth-century developments in transportation, bicycles were first raced against the clock, usually for long distances. The improved bicycle, in one early test, went 37 km (about 23 mi) in 2½ hr, an average of a little more than 9 mph.

The first great step toward the modern bicycle was taken by a young Scots blacksmith, Kirkpatrick Macmillan, in 1839. Macmillan's bicycle was propelled by a foot-operated crank, connected by rods to the rear wheel, and it was evidently quite efficient. On one occasion, Macmillan challenged the driver of a mail coach to a long-distance race and won quite easily—partly because the coach had to make a number of stops to drop off and pick up mail along the way.

Macmillan continually improved his bicycle for a number of years, but he was unfortunately dismissed as an eccentric even by his friends, and his work had little impact on the future of the bicycle. The vehicle that really began to popularize the bike was a distinct step backward from Macmillan's machine. This was the invention of Pierre and Ernest Michaux of France, who got their idea from the crank used to turn a grindstone. They attached similar cranks to either side of the front hub to produce a pedal-driven bicycle that won the public fancy.

The chief disadvantage of this bike was that it took one revolution of the pedals for each revolution of the wheel. In attempts to get more distance for each thrust of the pedals, the size of the front wheel was gradually

Riders are massed at the start of a national championship road race. (*Robert F. George*, Cyclenews.)

increased, until in some cases it had a diameter of more than 5 ft, while the diameter of the back wheel diminished to as little as 1 ft. The British called this bicycle the "Penny-farthing," not because of the price, but because the relative sizes of the wheels were comparable to the two coins.

The first real bicycle road races were held a day apart, on May 31, 1869, in France, and on June 1, in England. The French race covered 83 mi between Paris and Rouen, and was won by an Englishman, James Moore.

Two Englishmen brought the bicycle to its modern form. In 1870, James Starley, a foreman at the Coventry Sewing Machine Company, developed the Ariel bike, which had a gear that permitted the wheel to travel at twice the speed of the crank. Another Coventryman, H. J. Lawson, developed the chain drive in 1874. This "safety bicycle" quickly became popular; it was much more efficient and much more stable than any previous bike. Because of its hard rubber tires, it was often called "boneshaker," but this was remedied with the invention of the pneumatic tire by J. B. Dunlop in 1888.

Cycling in the United States. In 1877, Col. Albert A. Pope, a retired Union officer who manufactured carriages in Boston, decided to start marketing bicycles. He had one built at a cost of $313, and then ordered some more from a sewing machine company. The company couldn't meet the order, however, so Pope began his own manufacture of bicycles. By 1893 his firm was the largest bicycle manufacturer in the world, and the Pope "Columbia" was a household word in this country—and was pretty well known in other countries, as well.

Bicycling remained remarkably popular in the United States until the mass production of the automobile began, and it regained a good deal of its popularity during the depression of the 1930s. It has since had another revival chiefly because of the ecology movements and the energy shortage.

Racing. The National Cyclists Union was established in Great Britain as a federation of local clubs in 1878, and sponsored the first national championship races in the same year. The local clubs had already had set up many racing events of their own, and racing had undoubtedly also begun in the United States during the 1870s.

The first American champion was G. M. Hendrie, who won a challenge race in 1883 from W. G. Rowe. Undoubtedly the challenge came about because both men had already won other races. Hendrie, later known as a builder of automobiles and motorcycles, was from Springfield, Massachusetts, where a dirt harness-racing track was used for bicycle races during the 1880s and perhaps earlier.

By 1889, board tracks were being built for bicycle racers, and professional racing entered the picture. The move into an enclosed area made it easy to charge admission, and thus made it possible to award cash prizes to winners. Amateur racing was largely confined to road races, although amateurs did sometimes move to board tracks during the winter, primarily for training purposes.

Great Britain pretty much dominated bicycle racing, administratively and competitively, until 1900, when other European countries got together to organize the Union Cyclistes Internationale, which now governs the sport through the world.

The sport has had its ups and downs in the United States. This country made one unique contribution, the six-day race, originated at Madison Square Garden, New York, in 1891. Under the original rules, individual racers simply went around a track as many times as they could during a six-day period. The possibility of cyclists dying of exhaustion forced a change to two-man teams in 1899. The two cyclists are usually allowed to relieve one another whenever they want, but one member of the team must be on the track at all times. In order to sustain spectator interest, sprints are held at various periods during the day, with cash prizes going to the winner. Points gained in sprints are also used to break possible ties in the order of finish. The six-day race hit its peak of popularity in the late 1920s and early 1930s, but the popularity declined rapidly and Madison Square Garden dropped the race after a poor spectator turnout in 1939. There have been periodic attempts to revive six-day racing, but with little success.

Types of Competition. The original form of competition, the road race, is still a popular spectator sport in Europe. The Tour de France, established in 1903, is the world's most important race. This is a grueling event of between 2,500 and 3,000 mi, which usually takes about three weeks. One stretch is a gravel road that takes the cyclists over a 7,500-ft mountain.

The biggest such event in the United States is the 50-mi Tour of Somerville, New Jersey, held annually on Memorial Day.

The road race, and certain long-distance races held on tracks, are straightforward and easy enough to follow. Other cycling events can be puzzling to the observer, however. In a scratch sprint, competitors travel the specified distance one at a time, as fast as they can, racing against the clock, and the one with the fastest time is declared the winner. There are also tandem scratch sprints, in which two-person teams race bicycles built for two—and often figure in spectacular spills.

A match sprint is an entirely different kind of race, in which cunning tactics are more important than sheer speed. Although the race is generally about ¾ mi. in length, the sprinting takes place only during the last 200 or 300 yd. Until that point, the competitors move warily, the one in front setting a slow pace and keeping a constant watch on the opponent, perhaps moving the bike back and forth to block the opponent if the latter should attempt to pass, while the trailing competitor watches the leader for any sign of an attempt to break away. At some point when the end is in sight, one of the two will make a break. This generally occurs when the competitor making the move is near the top of the banked track at the turn, and takes the form of sudden acceleration, using the slope of the bank to provide additional speed. That is when the sprint actually begins, and the two pedal furiously from that point until they reach the finish line.

All this maneuvering may seem very peculiar to a person who has never tried pedaling a bike in such competition. Pace is extremely important in bicycle racing, because even an outstanding competitor can go flat-out for only a limited period. The bicycle sprinter who begins the sprint too early is just as certain to lose as the mile runner who begins a finishing kick too soon. But it is also important not to let the front runner get too far ahead—again, as in a running event of any distance.

Match sprint races usually match pairs of competitors, in an elimination tournament that ultimately ends with two finalists racing for the championship. If there are a large number of entrants, however, there may be three or four sprinters in the first several elimination heats. There is often a provision for *repechage,* giving defeated racers a second chance to advance in competition, as in a double-elimination tournament.

Pursuit races also look strange to the uninitiated. There are individual and team pursuits, the teams usually made up of four cyclists. In a pursuit race the competitors start at opposite sides of the track and attempt to catch and pass each other. The races used to continue until someone did, in fact, win by passing an opponent. Now they are generally run for set distances; the pursuit format eliminates the problem, common in the sprints, of opponents slowly jockeying for position. The usual distance for a pursuit race is 4,000 m, for individual men and teams, and 3,000 m for women.

Since a cyclist can benefit by being pulled along by the slip stream of a competitor immediately in front, the cyclists in a pursuit team take turns leading the pack, usually for a lap apiece. At the end of such a lap, the leader will ride up the bank to let teammates pass, and will then drop into the fourth spot: there the leader can rest for a while, pulled along by the three riders in front.

The one other type of bicycle race is easy enough to understand—a road race, generally covering a fairly long distance. (The individual road race in the Olympics is 165 km, or about 100 mi.) There is an unusual twist, though, in the team time trial, also a road race. This event involves teams of four persons, and they race much like pursuit teams, taking turns leading. The team time is the time it takes the third finisher to pedal the distance. Only three members of a team need finish for the team to win.

A track event popular in Europe but not often seen in the United States is the *demi-fond,* or motor-paced race. Each cyclist is led by a motorcycle; the motorcycle rider sits straight up, to provide as good a wind break as possible, and travels about 60 mph while the cyclist pedals furiously along behind.

Cyclo-Cross. A rather recent development as an organized competitive sport, cyclo-cross is essentially a cross-country race by bicycle. A cyclo-cross course is not really considered complete unless the cyclists have to carry their bikes over a body of water somewhere along the way. The course is not merely a road; it consists of trails over rough country that really tests endurance.

Equipment. For serious competition, cyclists use lightweight racing bikes with the high seats and turned-down handlebars that keep the rider leaning forward, back almost parallel to the ground.

For track races, the bikes weigh 18 to 21 lb and have a single, noncoaster gear that provides top acceleration. Road-racing bikes are more rugged and somewhat heavier—about 22 to 25 lb. The frames are built of seamless

In team pursuit racing, members take turns leading the way and acting as windbreak for the other cyclists on their team. This is a West German team. (*Robert F. George,* Cyclenews.)

alloy tubing to absorb the punishment of road racing, and they generally have the 10-speed *derailleur* gears, with two front sprockets and five rear sprockets, to enable the racer to choose a gear for any eventuality.

U.S. Amateur Champions

Sprint

1899	Frank L. Kramer	1932	Amos Hoffman
1900	Willie Fenn, Sr.	1933	Eddie Miller
1901	M. L. Hurley	1934	Robert Lipsett, Jr.
1902	M. L. Hurley	1935	Albert Sellinger
1903	M. L. Hurley	1936	Mickey Francoise
1904	M. L. Hurley	1937	Mickey Francoise
1905	Matt Downey	1938	Mickey Francoise
1906	C. Sherwood	1939	Howard Rupprecht
1907	W. Van den Dries	1940	Buster Logan
1908	Charley Stein	1941	Bob Stauffacher
1909	Percy Lawrence	1942–50	No competition
1910	Frank Blatz	1951	Dave Rhoades
1911	Frank Blatz	1952	Ronald Rhoades
1912	Donald McDougal	1953	Richard Gatto
1913	Donald McDougal	1954	Jack Disney
1914	Harry Kaiser	1955	Jack Disney
1915	Hans Ohrt	1956	Jack Disney
1916	John L. Staehle	1957	No competition
1917	John L. Staehle	1958	Jack Disney
1918	Gus Land	1959–64	No competition
1919	Charles Osterriter	1965	Jack Simes, 3rd
1920	Fred Taylor	1966	Jack Disney
1921	Robert Walthour, Jr.	1967	Jack Simes, 3rd
1922	Willie Grimm	1968	Jack Disney
1923	Willie Fenn, Jr.	1969	Tim Mountford
1924	Paul Croley	1970	Harry Cutting
1925	Charles Winter	1971	Gary Campbell
1926	William Coles	1972	Gary Campbell
1927	James Walthour, Jr.	1973	Roger Young
1928	Charles Ritter	1974	Steve Woznick
1929	Sergio Matteini	1975	Steve Woznick
1930	Dominick Tucillo	1976	Leigh Barczewski
1931	Arthur Rose		

Pursuit—Men

1965	Harry Cutting	1971	Mike Neel
1966	Dave Brink	1972	John Vande Velde
1967	Dave Brink	1973	Mike Neel
1968	Dave Brink	1974	Ralph Therrio
1969	John Vande Velde	1975	Ron Skarin
1970	John Vande Velde	1976	Leonard Nitz

10-Mile—Men

1965	William Kund	1971	Hans Nuerenberg
1966	Jim Rossi	1972	Bob Phillips
1967	Steven Maarinen	1973	Mike Neel
1968	Steven Maarinen	1974	Ralph Therrio
1969	Jack Simes, 3rd	1975	Leroy Gatto
1970	Bob Phillips	1976	Ron Skarin

Kilometer—Men

1971	Tim Zasadny	1974	Steve Woznick
1972	Steve Woznick	1975	Wayne Stetina
1973	Steve Woznick	1976	Bob Vehe

Team Pursuit—Men

1971	So. California	1974	So. California
1972	So. California	1975	So. California
1973	New Jersey	1976	So. California

Road

1921	Arthur Nieminsky	1952	Steve Hromjak
1922	Carl Hambacher	1953	Ronald Rhoads
1923	Charles Barclay	1954	Jack Disney
1924	Charles Winter	1955	Jack Disney
1925	Edward Merkner	1956	Jack Disney
1926	Edward Merkner	1957	Jack Disney
1927	James Walthour, Jr.	1958	Jack Disney
1928	R. J. Connor	1959	James Rossi
1929	Sergio Matteini	1960	James Rossi
1930	Robert Thomas	1961	James Rossi
1931–34	No competition	1962	James Rossi
1935	Cecil Hursey	1963	James Rossi
1936	Jackie Simes	1964	Jack Simes, 3rd
1937	Charles Bergna	1965	Michael Hiltner
1938	A. Jurca	1966	Bob Tetzlaff
1939	Martin Deras	1967	Bob Parsons
1940	Furman Kugler	1968	John Howard
1941	Marvin Thomson	1969	Alan De Fever
1942–44	No competition	1970	Mike Carnahan
1945	Ted Smith	1971	Steve Dayton
1946	Don Hester	1972	John Howard
1947	Ted Smith	1973	John Howard
1948	Ted Smith	1974	John Allis
1949	Jimmy Lauf	1975	John Howard
1950	Robert Pfarr	1976	Wayne Stetina
1951	Gus Gatto		

Women's Road

1937	Doris Kopsky	1958	Maxine Conover
1938	Dolores Amundsen	1959	Joanne Speckin
1939	Gladys R. Owens	1960	Edith Johnson
1940	Mildred Kugler	1961	Edith Johnson
1941	Jean Michels	1962	Nancy Burghart
1942–44	No competition	1963	Edith Johnson
1945	Mildred M. Dietz	1964	Nancy Burghart
1946	Mildred M. Dietz	1965	Nancy Burghart
1947	Doris Travani	1966	Audrey McElmury
1948	Doris Travani	1967	Nancy Burghart
1949	Doris Travani	1968	Nancy Burghart
1950	Doris Travani	1969	Donna Tobias
1951	Anna Piplak	1970	Audrey McElmury
1952	Jeanne Robinson	1971	Mary Jane Reoch
1953	Nancy Nieman	1972	Debby Bradley
1954	Nancy Nieman	1973	Eileen Brennan
1955	Jeanne Robinson	1974	Jane Robinson
1956	Nancy Nieman	1975	Linda Stein
1957	Nancy Nieman	1976	Connie Carpenter

Sprint—Women

1966	Edith Johnson	1972	Sue Novarra
1967	Nancy Burghart	1973	Sheila Young
1968	Nancy Burghart	1974	Sue Novarra
1969	No competition	1975	Sue Novarra
1970	Jeanne Kloska	1976	Sheila Young
1971	Sheila Young		

Pursuit—Women

1966	Audrey McElmury	1972	Clara Teyssier
1967	Nancy Burghart	1973	Mary Jane Reoch
1968	Nancy Burghart	1974	Mary Jane Reoch
1969	No competition	1975	Mary Jane Reoch
1970	Audrey McElmury	1976	Connie Carpenter
1971	Kathy Ecroth		

Bibliography. League of American Wheelmen: *Cycling Handbook*, 1947.

D

DARTS—One of England's oldest sports is one of the United States' newest crazes. Darts originated in England during the late Middle Ages—Anne Boleyn gave King Henry VIII a set of jewel-encrusted darts as a birthday gift. The sport was an offshoot of an indoor form of archery, which was England's national sport.

Archers first began practicing with short, light arrows, using butts—the tops of wine barrels—as targets. In small areas, however, they discovered they could use shorter arrows for throwing. In England there are more than 1 million darts players registered in leagues, and an estimated total of more than 8 million players. Darts is the great indoor sport in England, practiced largely in pubs.

The United States has had several versions of darts, including children's games in which suction cups or magnets are used instead of sharp points, but none of them has gained much popularity—although "dartball," in which the darters play baseball by throwing darts at a board that simulates a baseball diamond, was once a very popular indoor winter sport.

The recent craze in this country has been for the English game, which uses a circular target, having a diameter of 13½ in, divided into 20 sections. Around the outside of the board is a double ring, and halfway between the center and the circumference is a triple ring; they double and triple the value of the score. The darts have brass barrels and steel or tungsten points. The center of the board is mounted 5 ft, 8 in above the floor, and players throw from behind a line 8 ft away.

The U.S. Darting Association, organized in 1969, conducts a national open championship. There are now about 20,000 serious players in this country, and the USDA says the number is growing daily.

In serious competition, a game called "301" is usually played. A player starts with 301 points and has to whittle that total down to nothing. There are two catches: The player can't start counting until the thin double ring is hit with a shot, and must reach zero exactly with another double shot.

DASHES—Also called "sprints" in track, short foot races, ranging from 100 to 440 yd or their metric equivalents.

In harness racing, any race that consists of just one heat.

See HARNESS RACING; TRACK AND FIELD.

DAVIS CUP—An international team tennis trophy, originally for amateurs, donated by Dwight F. Davis in 1900. It was, until 1972, decided by a challenge tournament; that is, the country holding the cup didn't compete until the final round, after a series of tournaments throughout the world had selected one challenging team. Now the defending champion has to take part in elimination tournaments and doesn't automatically get the home-court advantage, and professional players are allowed to compete.

See TENNIS.

DECATHLON—A single competitive event, involving 10 different track and field events: the 100- and 440-yd dashes, the mile run, and the 110-yd high hurdles (or their metric equivalents); the shot put, discus throw, javelin throw, long jump, high jump, and pole vault. Events are staged over a two-day period, and points are scored by comparing an individual's performance in each event with a theoretical norm.

See TRACK AND FIELD.

DISCUS—A "flying saucer"-shaped object (about 8¾ in, measured in diameter, and 4 lb, 6⅔ oz in weight, for men) that is thrown with a scaling motion in a field event.

See TRACK AND FIELD.

DIVING—As a sport, diving is an offshoot of gymnastics. Formal gymnastics as physical training became popular in Germany and Sweden during the seventeenth century, and gymnasts took their exercises to the beach. From there it was a simple step to performing various exercises during a dive into the water.

Diving, however, didn't become a formal kind of competition until about 1880. Swimming had become a major competitive sport in England, and diving competition was added to many English swimming meets beginning in that year. "Fancy diving," as it was then called, was added to the Olympic program in 1904; high diving, from a tower, became an Olympic event in 1908.

Major impetus to diving in the United States came from Ernest Brandsten. An Olympic competitor for Sweden in 1908, Brandsten came to this country in 1912 as diving coach at Stanford University. He not only developed some great divers, he instituted methods of instruction that were adopted all over the country and that helped to make the United States a power in diving from 1920 on.

Types of Dives

Dives may be performed from either a springboard or a platform. The same kinds of dives are performed from either surface—except that occasionally a diver will make a dive from a handstand in platform competition.

The springboard is either 1 m or 3 m high; the distance is measured from the surface of the water to the bottom of the board. In major competition, the board is 16 ft long

Mike Finneran has won one NCAA and three AAU national diving titles. *(International Swimming Hall of Fame.)*

and 20 in wide, and is covered with a nonskid material. The board should overhang the edge of the pool by at least 5 ft, and the water should be 11 to 12 ft deep.

The platform is either 5 m or 10 m high. The nonskid runway should be at least 20 ft long and at least 10 ft wide, and the water should be at least 16 ft deep.

Categories. All dives are divided into six categories. They are:

Forward dives—The diver faces forward and dives forward.

Backward dives—The diver faces backward and dives in such a way that the body rotates away from the board.

Reverse dives—The diver faces forward but dives so that the body rotates back toward the board.

Inward dives—The diver faces backward but dives so the body rotates toward the board.

Twisting dives—The diver, from either starting position, twists the body in the air before reaching the water.

Handstand dives—These are performed from the platform only; the diver begins the dive from a motionless handstand on the edge of the platform.

The most dangerous are the inward and reverse dives, since the diver who doesn't spring out far enough might hit the board on the way down.

Positions. Dives are further classified as to the body positions used. There are three basic body positions:

Layout, in which the body is kept straight.

Pike, in which the body is bent at the waist, with the legs straight (the most familiar is the jackknife).

Tuck, in which the body is bent at the hips, and the knees are kept together and drawn into the chest.

There is also a so-called "free" position, for use in very complicated dives—in effect, the diver has a choice of which position to use, or can use a combination of positions.

Judging. Like gymnastics, diving is judged subjectively. Each judge rates each dive on its approach, take-off, elevation, execution, and entry. Then a score is given, ranging from 0 to 10. In major contests there are five or seven judges; the highest and lowest scores are thrown out, and the remaining scores are added. They are then multiplied by the degree of difficulty for the specific dive, to give the score for that dive.

Degree-of-difficulty ratings range from 1.0 for very simple dives to 2.9 for very difficult dives. If two dives get the same raw score from the judges, the more difficult dive will get a higher score.

Fundamental Approach. Judging begins when a diver stands in the starting position on the front end of the board. The contestant should hold the body straight, head erect, with heels together and arms straight and at the sides. The approach should be smooth and straight, and should consist of at least three steps before the hurdle.

Take-off. The hurdle, the jump to the end of the board, is the beginning of the take-off. Both feet should hit the end of the board simultaneously; the take-off should be made without hesitation and should be forceful.

Execution. In the passage through the air, the body should be definitely in the layout, the pike, or the tuck position (unless the dive involves somersaults combined with twists, in which case the free position may be used).

In the layout, the body should not bend at the knees or the hips; the back, however, will normally be arched. The arms should be straight, the feet together, and the toes pointed.

In the closed pike position, the legs and arms should be kept straight, and both hands should touch the toes simultaneously. The open pike position, used for some dives, involves a simple bending at the waist, to a 90-degree angle with the legs; the arms are extended overhead, at approximately a 45-degree angle from the shoulders, with the palms turned outward.

In the tuck, judges above all look for compactness: The diver should be rolled as tightly as possible into a ball, thighs touching chest, arms locked tightly around the legs, between shin and knee.

Entry. The entry should be vertical, or as nearly vertical as possible, with body and legs straight and toes pointed. Most entries are made headfirst, and the arms should be straight overhead, hands touching. In the rare dives with a feet-first entry, the arms should be kept straight and close to the sides.

Compulsory and Optional Dives. As in gymnastics and figure skating, diving competition is broken into two parts, compulsory and optional. The springboard diver is generally required to perform five compulsory dives, one from each of the five categories, and six optional dives. The platform diver must perform six compulsory and six optional dives.

See also SWIMMING.

AAU Outdoor Champions—Men

1-Meter Springboard

1964	Bernie Wrightson	1970	Jim Henry
1965	Bernie Wrightson	1971	Mike Brown
1966	Bernie Wrightson	1972	Don Dunfield
1967	Jim Henry	1973	Michael Finneran
1968	Jim Henry	1974	Tim Moore
1969	Jim Henry	1975	Tim Moore
		1976	Jim Kennedy

3-Meter Springboard

1921	Arthur W. Hartung	1949	David Browning
1922	Albert C. White	1950	Joe Marino
1923	Clarence Pinkston	1951	Robert Clotworthy
1924	Albert C. White	1952	David Browning
1925	Pete Desjardins	1953	Robert Clotworthy
1926	Pete Desjardins	1954	Joaquin Capilla
1927	Pete Desjardins	1955	Don Harper
1928	Mickey Riley Galitzen	1956	Robert Clotworthy
1929	Mickey Riley Galitzen	1957	Ron Smith
1930	Harold Smith	1958	Gary Tobian
1931	Harold Smith	1959	Don Harper
1932	No competition	1960	Sam Hall
1933	Richard Degener	1961	John Vogel
1934	Richard Degener	1962	Lou Vitucci
1935	Richard Degener	1963	Larry Andreasen
1936	Richard Degener	1964	Bernie Wrightson
1937	Al Patnik	1965	Bernie Wrightson
1938	Al Patnik	1966	Rick Gilbert
1939	Al Patnik	1967	Keith Russell
1940	Al Patnik	1968	Bernie Wrightson
1941	Earl Clark	1969	Jim Henry
1942	Sammy Lee	1970	Jim Henry
1943	Floyd Stauffer	1971	Jim Henry
1944	Norman Sper, Jr.	1972	Michael Finneran
1945	Norman Sper, Jr.	1973	Phil Boggs
1946	Bruce Harlan	1974	Keith Russell
1947	Bruce Harlan	1975	Phil Boggs
1948	Bruce Harlan	1976	Jim Kennedy

Platform

1909	George W. Gaidzik	1941	Earl Clark
1910	George W. Gaidzik	1942	Sammy Lee
1911	George W. Gaidzik	1943	Miller Anderson
1912	J. F. Dunn	1944	Norman Sper, Jr.
1913	No competition	1945	No competition
1914	C. Wolfield	1946	Sammy Lee, M.D.
1915	A. E. Downes	1947	Bruce Harlan
1916	A. E. Downes	1948	Bruce Harlan
1917	W. Williams	1949	Norman Sper, Jr.
1918	Clyde Swendsen	1950	John McCormick
1919	Fred Spongberg	1951	John McCormick
1920	Clarence Pinkston	1952	David Browning
1921	Clarence Pinkston	1953	Joaquin Capilla
1922	Clarence Pinkston	1954	Joaquin Capilla
1923	Clarence Pinkston	1955	Gary Tobian
1924	Clarence Pinkston	1956	Gary Tobian
1925	Pete Desjardins	1957	Gary Tobian
1926	Pete Desjardins	1958	Gary Tobian
1927	Pete Desjardins	1959	Gary Tobian
1928	Mickey Riley Galitzen	1960	Gary Tobian
1929	John Riley Galitzen	1961	Don Harper
1930	Farid Samaika	1962	Robert Webster
1931	Farid Samaika	1963	Tom Gompf
1932	No competition	1964	Bob Webster
1933	Frank Kurtz	1965	Bernie Wrightson
1934	Marshall Wayne	1966	Rick Gilbert
1935	Richard Degener	1967	Keith Russell
1936	Marshall Wayne	1968	Win Young
1937	Elbert Root	1969	Dick Rydze
1938	Elbert Root	1970	Dick Rydze
1939	Earl Clark	1971	Dick Rydze
1940	Earl Clark	1972	Rick Early

1973	Tim Moore	1975	Kent Vosler
1974	Keith Russell	1976	Kent Vosler

AAU Outdoor Champions—Women

1-Meter Springboard

1948	Zoe Ann Olsen	1959	Irene MacDonald
1949	Zoe Ann Olsen	1960–63	No competition
1950	Patricia Keller McCormick	1964	Patsy Willard
1951	Patricia Keller McCormick	1965	Joel Lenzi O'Connell
		1966	Joel Lenzi O'Connell
1952	No competition	1967	Micki King
1953	Patricia Keller McCormick	1968	Cynthia Potter
1954	Patricia Keller McCormick	1969	Cynthia Potter
		1970	Cynthia Potter
1955	Patricia Keller McCormick	1971	Cynthia Potter
		1972	Cynthia Potter
1956	Patricia Keller McCormick	1973	Cynthia Potter
		1974	Cynthia Potter
1957	Paula Jean Myers	1975	Cynthia Potter MacIngvale
1958	Paula Jean Myers	1976	Cynthia Potter MacIngvale

3-Meter Springboard

1921	Helen Meany	1952	No competition
1922	Helen Meany	1953	Patricia Keller McCormick
1923	Aileen Riggin	1954	Patricia Keller McCormick
1924	Aileen Riggin		
1925	Aileen Riggin	1955	Patricia Keller McCormick
1926	Helen Meany		
1927	Helen Meany	1956	Patricia Keller McCormick
1928	Lillian Fergus		
1929	Georgia Goleman	1957	Paula Jean Myers
1930	Georgia Coleman	1958	Paula Jean Myers
1931	Georgia Coleman	1959	Irene MacDonald
1932	Katherine Rawls	1960	Patsy Willard
1933	Katherine Rawls	1961	Joel Lenzi
1934	Katherine Rawls	1962	Barbara McAlister
1935	Mary Hoerger	1963	Jeanne Collier
1936	Claudia Eckert	1964	Barbara McAlister
1937	Marjorie Gestring	1965	Micki King
1938	Marjorie Gestring	1966	Sue Gossick
1939	Helen Crlenkovich	1967	Micki King
1940	Marjorie Gestring	1968	Jerrie Adair
1941	Helen Crlenkovich	1969	Micki King
1942	Ann Ross	1970	Micki King
1943	Ann Ross	1971	Cynthia Potter
1944	Ann Ross	1972	Cynthia Potter
1945	Helen Crlenkovich Morgan	1973	Carrie Irish
		1974	Christine Loock
1946	Zoe Ann Olsen	1975	Cynthia Potter MacIngvale
1947	Zoe Ann Olsen		
1948	Zoe Ann Olsen	1976	Cynthia Potter MacIngvale
1949	Zoe Ann Olsen		
1950	Patricia Keller McCormick		
1951	Patricia Keller McCormick		

Platform

1916	Evelyn Burnett	1928	Helen Meany
1917	Aileen Allen	1929	Georgia Coleman
1918	Josephine Bartlett	1930	Georgia Coleman
1919	Betty Grimes	1931	Georgia Coleman
1920	No competition	1932	No competition
1921	Helen Meany	1933	Dorothy Poynton
1922	Helen Meany	1934	Dorothy Poynton Hill
1923	Helen Meany	1935	Dorothy Poynton Hill
1924	No competition	1936	Ruth Jump
1925	Helen Meany	1937	Ruth Jump
1926	Esther Foley	1938	Ruth Jump
1927	No competition	1939	Marjorie Gestring

1940	Marjorie Gestring	1957	Paula Jean Myers
1941	Helen Crlenkovich	1958	Paula Jean Myers
1942	Margaret Reinholdt	1959	Paula Jean Myers Pope
1943	Jeanne Kessler	1960	Juno Irwin
1944	No competition	1961	Barbara McAlister
1945	Helen Crlenkovich Morgan	1962	Linda Cooper
1946	Victoria Manalo Draves	1963	Barbara McAlister Talmage
1947	Victoria Manalo Draves	1964	Patsy Willard
1948	Victoria Manalo Draves	1965	Lesley Bush
1949	Patricia Keller McCormick	1966	Shirley Teeples
1950	Patricia Keller McCormick	1967	Lesley Bush
1951	Patricia Keller McCormick	1968	Ann Peterson
1952	No competition	1969	Micki King
1953	Paula Jean Myers	1970	Cynthia Potter
1954	Patricia Keller McCormick	1971	Cynthia Potter
1955	Juno Irwin	1972	Janet Ely
1956	Patricia Keller McCormick	1973	Deborah Keplar
		1974	Terri York
		1975	Janet Ely
		1976	Barbara Weinstein

1943	Frank Dempsey	1960	Jozsef Gerlach
1944	Charles Batterman	1961	Ronald O'Brien
1945	Frank McGuigan	1962	Richard Gilbert
1946	Miller Anderson	1963	Richard Gilbert
1947	Miller Anderson	1964	Kenneth Sitzberger
1948	Miller Anderson	1965	Kenneth Sitzberger
1949	Bruce Harlan	1966	Bernie Wrightson
1950	Bruce Harlan	1967	Keith Russell
1951	David Browning	1968	Win Young
1952	David Browning	1969	Win Young
1953	Jerry Harrison	1970	Jim Henry
1954	David Browning	1971	Mike Finneran
1955	Jerry Harrison	1972	Phil Boggs
1956	Donald Harper	1973	Phil Boggs
1957	Glenn Whitten	1974	Phil Boggs
1958	Donald Harper	1975	Phil Boggs
1959	Jozsef Gerlach	1976	Tim Moore

Platform

1964	Tom Gompf	1971	Dick Rydze
1965	Chuck Knorr	1972	Dick Rydze
1966	Chuck Knorr	1973	Steve McFarland
1967	Keith Russell	1974	Steve McFarland
1968	Larry Andreason	1975	Tim Moore
1969	Dick Rydze	1976	Tim Moore
1970	Klaus DiBiasi		

AAU Indoor Champions—Men

1-Meter Springboard

1923	Leo Fracer	1950	Bruce Harlan
1924	Albert C. White	1951	David Browning
1925	Albert C. White	1952	David Browning
1926	Albert C. White	1953	Robert Clotworthy
1927	Farid Simaika	1954	David Browning
1928	Harold D. Smith	1955	Jerry Harrison
1929	Mickey Riley Galitzen	1956	Robert Clotworthy
1930	Harold D. Smith	1957	Donald Harper
1931	Mickey Riley Galitzen	1958	Gary Tobian
1932	Mickey Riley Galitzen	1959	Sam Hall
1933	Richard Degener	1960	Sam Hall
1934	Richard Degener	1961	Lou Vitucci
1935	Elbert A. Root	1962	Bob Webster
1936	Al Greene	1963	Richard Gilbert
1937	Al Patnik	1964	Ken Sitzberger
1938	Al Patnik	1965	Ken Sitzberger
1939	Al Patnik	1966	Chuck Knorr
1940	Al Patnik	1967	Luis Rivera
1941	Earl Clark	1968	Jim Henry
1942	James Cook	1969	Jim Henry
1943	Frank Dempsey	1970	Jim Henry
1944	Charles Batterman	1971	Craig Lincoln
1945	Ted Christakos	1972	Don Dunfield
1946	Miller Anderson	1973	Tim Moore
1947	Miller Anderson	1974	Steve MacFarland
1948	Miller Anderson	1975	Tim Moore
1949	Bruce Harlan	1976	Tim Moore

3-Meter Springboard

1909	F. Bornaman	1926	Albert C. White
1910	George Gaidzik	1927	Pete Desjardins
1911	F. Bornaman	1928	Pete Desjardins
1912	George Gaidzik	1929	Mickey Riley Galitzen
1913	Arthur McAleenan	1930	Mickey Riley Galitzen
1914	C. Wohlfield	1931	Mickey Riley Galitzen
1915	Arthur McAleenan	1932	Richard Degener
1916	Arthur McAleenan	1933	Richard Degener
1917	A. E. Downes	1934	Richard Degener
1918	Arthur W. Hartung	1935	Richard Degener
1919	Clyde Swendsen	1936	Richard Degener
1920	Clyde Swendsen	1937	Al Patnik
1921	Clarence Pinkston	1938	Al Patnik
1922	Albert C. White	1939	Al Patnik
1923	Albert C. White	1940	Al Patnik
1924	Albert C. White	1941	Earl Clark
1925	Albert C. White	1942	Miller Anderson

AAU Indoor Champions—Women

1-Meter Springboard

1923	Aileen Riggin	1953	Patricia Keller McCormick
1924	Elizabeth Becker	1954	Patricia Keller McCormick
1925	Helen Wainwright	1955	Patricia Keller McCormick
1926	Helen Meany	1956	Ann Cooper
1927	Helen Meany	1957	Paula Jean Myers
1928	Helen Meany	1958	Barbara Gilders
1929	Jane Fauntz	1959	Irene MacDonald
1930	Jane Fauntz	1960	Patsy Willard
1931	Georgia Coleman	1961	Joel Dina Lenzi
1932	Dorothy Poynton	1962	Patsy Willard
1933	Katherine Rawls	1963	Patsy Willard
1934	Katherine Rawls	1964	Barbara McAlister Talmage
1935	Dorothy Poynton Hill	1965	Joel Lenzi O'Connell
1936	Marian Mansfield	1966	Joel Lenzi O'Connell
1937	Arlite Smith	1967	Lesley Bush
1938	Arlite Smith	1968	Keala O'Sullivan
1939	Arlite Smith	1969	Cynthia Potter
1940	Mary Patricia Fairbrother	1970	Cynthia Potter
1941	Anne Ross	1971	Cynthia Potter
1942	Anne Ross	1972	Cynthia Potter
1943	Anne Ross	1973	Cynthia Potter
1944	Anne Ross	1974	Christine Loock
1945	Zoe Ann Olsen	1975	Jenni Chandler
1946	Zoe Ann Olsen	1976	Cynthia Potter MacIngvale
1947	Zoe Ann Olsen		
1948	Victoria Manalo Draves		
1949	Zoe Ann Olsen		
1950	Sara Wakefield		
1951	Patricia Keller McCormick		
1952	Patricia Keller McCormick		

3-Meter Springboard

1916	Aileen Allen	1925	Helen Meany
1917	Constance Myers	1926	Betty Pinkston
1918	Thelma Payne	1927	Helen Meany
1919	Thelma Payne	1928	Rose Roczek
1920	Thelma Payne	1929	Georgia Coleman
1921	Helen Wainwright	1930	Georgia Coleman
1922	Elizabeth Becker	1931	Georgia Coleman
1923	Elizabeth Becker	1932	Georgia Coleman
1924	Carol Fletcher	1933	Dorothy Poynton

1934	Dorothy Poynton	1955	Patricia Keller
1935	Claudia Eckert		McCormick
1936	Marjorie Gestring	1956	Barbara Gilders
1937	Marjorie Gestring	1957	Paula Jean Myers
1938	Marjorie Gestring	1958	Irene MacDonald
1939	Helen Crlenkovich	1959	Barbara Gilders
1940	Helen Crlenkovich	1960	Irene MacDonald
1941	Helen Crlenkovich	1961	Joel Dina Lenzi
1942	Helen Crlenkovich	1962	Joel Lenzi O'Connell
1943	Anne Ross	1963	Barbara McAlister
1944	Anne Ross	1964	Barbara McAlister
1945	Zoe Ann Olsen		Talmage
1946	Patsy Elsener	1965	Joel Lenzi O'Connell
1947	Patsy Elsener	1966	Sue Gossick
1948	Zoe Ann Olsen	1967	Sue Gossick
1949	Zoe Ann Olsen	1968	Lesley Bush
1950	Mary Frances	1969	Cynthia Potter
	Cunningham	1970	Cynthia Potter
1951	Patricia Keller	1971	Micki King
	McCormick	1972	Micki King
1952	Patricia Keller	1973	Cynthia Potter
	McCormick	1974	Janet Ely
1953	Paula Jean Myers	1975	Carrie Irish
1954	Patricia Keller	1976	Jenni Chandler
	McCormick		

Platform

1964	Barbara McAlister		
	Talmage	1971	Micki King
1965	Micki King	1972	Ulrika Knape
1966	Patsy Willard	1973	Debby Lipman
1967	Patty Simms	1974	Janet Ely
1968	Lesley Bush	1975	Carrie Irish
1969	Beverley Boys	1976	Melissa Briley

Citizens Savings Hall of Fame

Elizabeth Becker (Pinkston)—AAU Indoor 1-m 1924, 3-m 1922–1923; Olympic springboard 1924, platform 1928.

David "Skippy" Browning—University of Texas; NCAA 1-m 1951–1952, 3-m 1951–1952; AAU Outdoor 3-m 1949, 1952, platform 1952; Indoor 1-m 1951–1952, 1954, 3-m 1951–1952, 1954; Olympic springboard 1952.

Lesley Bush—AAU Outdoor platform 1965, 1967; AAU Indoor 1-m 1967, 3-m 1968, platform 1968; Olympic platform 1964.

Earl Clark—Ohio State; NCAA 1-m 1941, 3-m 1940–1941; AAU Outdoor 3-m 1941, platform 1939–1941; AAU Indoor 1-m 1941, 3-m 1941.

Robert Clotworthy—Ohio State; NCAA 3-m 1953; AAU Outdoor 3-m 1951, 1953, 1956; AAU Indoor 1-m 1953, 1956; Olympic springboard 1956.

Georgia Coleman—AAU Outdoor 3-m 1929–1931, platform 1929–1931; AAU Indoor 1-m 1931, 3-m 1929–1932; Olympic springboard 1932. Miss Coleman contracted polio in 1937 and learned to swim all over again before her death in 1940.

Richard Degener—Michigan; NCAA 3-m 1933–1934; AAU Outdoor 3-m 1933–1936, springboard 1935; AAU Indoor 1-m 1933–1934, 3-m 1932–1936; Olympic springboard 1936.

Peter Desjardins—AAU Outdoor 3-m 1925–1927, platform 1925–1927; AAU Indoor 3-m 1927–1928; Olympic platform and springboard 1928.

Victoria Manalo Draves—AAU Outdoor platform 1946–1948; AAU Indoor 1-m 1948; Olympic springboard and platform 1948.

George Gaidzik—AAU Outdoor platform 1909–1911; AAU Indoor 3-m 1910, 1912.

Mickey Riley Galitzen—Southern California; NCAA 3-m 1931–1932; AAU Outdoor 3-m 1928–1929, platform 1928–1929; AAU Indoor 1-m 1929, 1931–1932, 3-m 1929–1931; Olympic springboard 1932.

Marjorie Gestring—AAU Outdoor 3-m 1937–1938, 1940, platform 1939–1940; AAU Indoor 3-m 1936–1938; Olympic springboard 1936.

Sue Gossick—AAU Outdoor 3-m 1966; AAU Indoor 3-m 1966–1967; Olympic springboard 1968.

Bruce Harlan—Ohio State; NCAA 1-m 1948–1950, 3-m 1948–1950; AAU Outdoor 3-m 1946–1948, platform 1947–1948; AAU Indoor 1-m 1949–1950, 3-m 1949–1950; Olympic springboard 1948.

Juno Irwin—AAU Outdoor platform 1955, 1960.

Dr. Sammy Lee—AAU Outdoor platform 1942, 1946; Olympic platform 1948, 1952.

Patricia Keller McCormick—AAU Outdoor 1-m 1950–1951, 1953–1956, 3-m 1950–1951, 1953–1956, platform 1949–1951, 1954, 1956; AAU Indoor 1-m 1951–1955, 3-m 1951–1952, 1954–1955, Olympic springboard and platform, 1952, 1956.

Helen Meany—AAU Outdoor 3-m 1921–1922, 1926–1927, platform 1921–1923, 1925; AAU Indoor 1-m 1926–1928, 3-m 1925, 1927; Olympic springboard 1928.

Helen Crlenkovich Morgan—AAU Outdoor 3-m 1941, 1945, platform 1941, 1945; AAU Indoor 3-m 1939–1942.

Paula Jean Myers (Pope)—AAU Outdoor 1-m 1957–1958, 3-m 1957–1958, platform 1953, 1957–1959; AAU Indoor 1-m 1957, 3-m 1953, 1957.

Zoe Ann Olsen—AAU Outdoor 1-m 1948–1949, 3-m 1946–1949; AAU Indoor 1-m 1945–1947, 1949, 3-m 1945, 1948–1949.

Al Patnik—Ohio State; NCAA 1-m 1938–1940, 3-m 1938–1939; AAU Outdoor 3-m 1937–1940; AAU Indoor 1-m 1938–1940, 3-m 1937–1940.

Clarence Pinkston—AAU Outdoor 3-m 1923, platform 1920–1924; AAU Indoor 3-m 1921; Olympic platform 1920.

Thelma Payne (Sanborn)—AAU Indoor 3-m 1918–1920.

Dorothy Poynton (Hill)—AAU Outdoor platform 1933–1935; AAU Indoor 1-m 1932, 1935, 3-m 1933–1934; Olympic platform 1932, 1936.

Katherine Rawls—AAU Outdoor 3-m 1932–1934; AAU Indoor 1-m 1933–1934.

Aileen Allen Riggin—AAU Outdoor 3-m 1923–1925; AAU Indoor 1-m 1923, 3-m 1916; Olympic springboard 1920.

Anne Ross—AAU Outdoor 3-m 1942–1944; AAU Indoor 1941–1944, 3-m 1943–1944.

Kenneth Sitzberger—Indiana; NCAA 1-m 1965–1967, 3-m 1965, 1967; AAU Indoor 1-m 1964–1965, 3-m 1964–1965; Olympic springboard 1964.

Harold Smith—AAU Outdoor 3-m 1930–1931; AAU Indoor 1-m 1928, 1930; Olympic platform 1932.

Gary Tobian—AAU Outdoor 3-m 1958, platform 1955–1960; AAU Indoor 1-m 1958; Olympic springboard 1960.

Robert Webster—AAU Outdoor platform 1962, 1964; AAU Indoor 1-m 1962; Olympic platform 1960, 1964.

Albert C. White—AAU Outdoor 3-m 1922, 1924; AAU Indoor 1-m 1924–1926, 3-m 1922–1926; Olympic platform and springboard 1924.

Bernard Wrightson—Arizona State; NCAA 3-m 1966; AAU Outdoor 3-m 1964–1965, 1968, platform 1965; AAU Indoor 3-m 1966; Olympic springboard 1968.

DOG RACING—The ancestor of modern dog racing is an ancient sport called coursing. Essentially, any time a dog chases a game animal, it is coursing, and the sport in that form is probably thousands of years old. Scenes of what are apparently coursing races have been found on Egyptian tombstones dating back to 2500 B.C. and perhaps beyond, and a skeleton of a dog similar to a greyhound, found in England, is believed to date back about 3,500 years.

Coursing as a race between two greyhounds, chasing a hare or rabbit, is also ancient, probably also dating back to Egypt. In seventeenth-century England, it was the sport of kings and nobles. Up until about 1700, commoners were forbidden to own greyhounds, but the animals roamed freely around the grounds and palaces of many nobles. It was fashionable to install ornamental gates at the foot of staircases in great homes to keep the dogs from rambling through the upper stories.

The first standardized rules for coursing were laid down by the Duke of Norfolk in 1776, for the Swaffham Coursing Society. They specified that only two greyhounds were to course a single hare, and that the hare was to be given a head start of 240 yd, if the field was large enough. The 17th rule seems remarkably humane

WIN

PHOTO TRACKMASTER

Photofinish cameras are probably more important in greyhound racing than in any other racing event. *(Courtesy of Taunton Greyhound Association, Inc.)*

for the time; it awarded the hare as a prize to whoever rescued the animal from the dogs at the end of the contest.

Just a century later an artificial lure was used for the first time, in Hendon, England. According to a London *Times* account, the artificial hare rode on "an apparatus like a skate on wheels" along a single rail.

Coursing in the United States. Coursing, as a race between greyhound and antelopes, is briefly mentioned in a book, *Oregon and California in 1848*, but its origin in this country is generally dated 1878, when Maj. James H. "Hound Dog" Kelly and an assistant set a record with a four-greyhound team that ran down six out of a dozen antelopes. Kelly had been the orderly for Lt. Col. George Armstrong Custer, a long-time greyhound lover. Custer and his Seventh Cavalry were wiped out at the Little Big Horn in 1876, but Kelly had learned how to breed and train greyhounds while serving with Custer, and he carried on the tradition.

In the Midwest, where hares and rabbits were considered "varmints" because of their destruction of crops, coursing was a popular Sunday afternoon diversion. The American version, like the English version, matched two dogs chasing a live rabbit.

Coursing had one great drawback: A lot of people didn't relish the sight of a rabbit being torn to pieces by a pair of dogs, and the rabbit's scream, often compared to a child's scream, was horrifying to many.

In 1905, Owen Patrick Smith, then director of the Hot Springs, South Dakota, Chamber of Commerce, was asked to organize a coursing meet to attract visitors to the town. Though Smith knew little about the sport, he organized a successful meet. He felt the sport was cruel, but the attendance impressed him, and he decided to find a way to make coursing a more humane sport, with wider appeal. His goal was to organize a national greyhound-racing circuit similar to the flat and harness horse-racing circuits.

Smith quickly realized something that most intelligent greyhound fanciers had known for centuries: The greyhound's key sense is sight, not smell, and a hound will chase a rapidly moving object that looks somewhat like a rabbit, even if it doesn't smell like one. He conceived of an artificial lure to lead greyhounds around a track.

Oddly, most American greyhound owners didn't like the idea, many of them insisting that a greyhound wouldn't chase a scentless lure. Among them was George Sawyer, a wealthy greyhound owner who had many other interests—including a boxing arena in Oakland, California. Sawyer at first refused to go along with Smith's grandiose plans for greyhound racing. Smith persevered, organizing an Intermountain Coursing Association, which held a race meeting at Salt Lake City in 1907, then building a small circular track near Salt Lake City and introducing his artificial lure: a stuffed rabbit skin, pulled around the track behind a motorcycle. It worked—but many greyhound owners still didn't like the idea.

In 1910, Smith got some financial backing from Sawyer, and he patented an "inanimate hare conveyor," basically an overhead arm that carried a phony rabbit, trolley-style, over a single straight track. However, the device failed in a test when water seeped into the ditch that held the track and short-circuited the whole system.

It was nine years before Smith could test his invention

on a major scale. Sawyer and other Oakland businessmen financed the construction of a grandstand at Emeryville, California, using the lumber from Sawyer's dismantled boxing arena. The cost was estimated at $10,000, but it actually ran to $40,000. Attendance was disappointing. And Smith's new device, a small, four-wheeled, motorized cart that carried an artificial rabbit around a $\frac{3}{16}$-mi track, was cumbersome and unreliable. On several occasions it jumped the track, bringing the race to a halt.

Wagering and Success. Sawyer felt greyhound racing had a future, but he was convinced that, to attract spectators, it would have to allow wagering. Smith was personally opposed to gambling, but Sawyer won him over. The operation moved to Tulsa, Oklahoma, and betting was allowed, through bookmakers at the track. Sawyer and Smith formed the International Greyhound Racing Association to run the Tulsa track. The mechanism was still not perfect, but the Tulsa meeting was a success, and it marks the real beginning of greyhound racing in its modern form.

The first great racing greyhound, Mission Boy, set records for four different distances at Tulsa. Mission Boy won 28 of 30 races in his career, and is said to have been the first greyhound that would chase only a mechanical lure; real rabbits didn't interest him at all.

After five weeks in Tulsa, Smith and Sawyer brought the racing-meet idea to East St. Louis, Illinois, where night racing was introduced for the first time—because afternoon races were causing too much absenteeism in offices. A $100,000 track there went bankrupt, despite an average daily attendance of 2,000 during the 5-week meet.

Smith then moved on to Florida, where dog racing got the financial backing needed to make it a permanent success. The first Florida track was built in an area called Humbuggus, now Hialeah. It opened in 1922. Night racing, inaugurated in 1925, was the key to success: New owners, with fresh money, began arriving—and so did some less savory characters. Smith didn't stay around long at any site in those years; he was too busy helping to set up new tracks, at Erlanger, Kentucky, and New Orleans in 1925; then in Milwaukee, Butte, Montana, and East St. Louis again. The fastest growth, however, was in Florida. The Hialeah plant closed in 1926, but tracks opened in St. Petersburg in 1925, Miami (Biscayne Kennel Club) in 1926, Sanford-Orlando and Miami Beach in 1927, Miami (West Flagler Kennel Club) in 1930, and Tampa in 1932.

Greyhound racing also became remarkably popular in England, where it was introduced in 1926. Two years later there were 68 dog tracks operating or under construction in Great Britain.

Unfortunately, many dog tracks, especially those in Florida, acquired unsavory reputations in the late 1920s and early 1930s. Mobsters were involved with many of them, and many races were fixed. (Fixing a greyhound race is relatively easy—feeding seven of the eight starters a couple of extra pounds of meat before a race will virtually guarantee victory for the eighth dog.)

There were two major problems in those early years: Although Smith had pioneered a number of safeguards, he wasn't involved long enough with the tracks he helped set up to see that the safeguards were employed; and almost all betting had to be done through bookmakers, many of whom already had gangland links.

Pari-mutuel Betting and Security. In 1932 pari-mutuel betting was legalized in Florida, and brought with it many of the safeguards that today prevent the fixing of races.

Each dog is registered and identified with a tattooed number on the inside of each ear. In addition, an elaborate Bertillon identification system requires that each greyhound be represented by a card which includes information on age, racing weight, color, scars, toenails, and other identifying marks, along with data on its breeding. These measures make it almost impossible for one dog to be substituted for another without detection.

Once a greyhound is brought to a track for racing, it is confined in a lockout kennel, under the supervision of track personnel until after the races have been run. Random blood and urine specimens are taken to help prevent drugging or similar tampering.

Pari-mutuel betting on greyhounds and thoroughbreds was also legalized in Massachusetts in 1934, and two major tracks opened there in 1935. Greyhound racing and pari-mutuel betting is now legal in nine states.

The AGTOA. The supervisory body of the sport is the American Greyhound Track Operators Association, which was originally an organization of Florida track owners, established in 1947. It became a national body in 1960.

Registering of greyhounds is the responsibility of the National Coursing Association, headquartered at Abilene, Kansas. The association also conducts the national coursing championships, and supervises other coursing events—the ancient sport is still popular in many areas of the Southwest, where rabbits are considered undesirable vermin.

Near the NCA headquarters is the Greyhound Hall of Fame and Museum, a joint project of the AGTOA and the NCA.

Dogs and Training. The full-grown male greyhound is a tall, long-bodied dog that stands about 26 in at the shoulder and weighs 65 lb, on the average. Despite the name, the dog is most likely to be brindled or red in color, but greyhounds may also be many different shades of white, black, blue, or fawn. (The name is believed to be a corruption of "Greek hound," since the animal was evidently introduced into England by Cretans about five centuries before Christ.)

The whippet, also sometimes used for racing, was produced by breeding small greyhounds with terriers; the animal averages about 25 lb in weight.

Breeders do not usually race dogs. They train them for racing and then sell or lease them to a racing kennel when they are of racing age, about two years. The breeders do the early schooling because a dog's value is based on his performances on a training track.

A young greyhound lives in a large pen or field, in which he will have enough room to enable him to exercise. It is instinctive in the dog to chase moving objects, and trainers develop this trait as early as possible by dragging white objects as lures for the animals. The dogs are trained in groups, so they get used to the excitement and bustle of racing conditions.

Some trainers believe that a pup should go to coursing meets before training on a track. They feel that chasing live animals sharpens the instinct for pursuit, and the meets also get the animals accustomed to performing before crowds. Other trainers feel coursing is unnecessary, and that form of the sport is under severe fire from humane groups in many areas.

When he is about a year old, the greyhound is given his own kennel, where he is fed one large meal a day. He is given daily exercise in large fields. At 15 to 24 months, the dog begins official schooling. Schooling races are non-betting races conducted at tracks to get the animals accustomed to actual race conditions. Results are recorded, and the charts become part of each dog's performance record. During the racing season, a greyhound will usually race twice a week, and other exercise is unnecessary. When he is not racing, however, he is usually given daily workouts.

How Races Are Run. The greyhound starting gate is a set of boxes, with sliding panels which open upward or to the side upon the starting signal. They are usually operated electronically, by push button. The gate most commonly used was invented by Walter Knight, an aircraft engineer, in the early 1950s.

The most widely-used lure was invented in 1937 by R. H. Alldritt of Miami. The lure itself is made of spring steel, covered with white imitation sheepskin, and it has two large red "eyes," not to fool the dogs, but to give the spectators the illusion that the dogs are chasing a real rabbit.

The lure rides suspended from a trolleylike overhead arm; its speed is controlled by a rheostat enclosed in a glass case so that only one hand—the lure operator's—can be inserted. The lure begins from behind the dogs, at top speed, slows to coast past the starting gate, then speeds up when the boxes open. The operator keeps it about 40 ft ahead of the dogs—far enough so none will catch it, close enough so that none will lose sight of it. The lure speeds up in the backstretch, slows down again in the final stretch so that the dogs almost catch up to it, and then maintains a lead of about 20 ft to the finish line. After the finish the lure speeds up again and disappears into an enclosure just around the first turn. Meanwhile, two artificial rabbits appear in a closed-in glass box and bob up and down to attract the greyhounds and keep them in one place until they can be collected by their handlers.

Most greyhound races are run at ⁵⁄₁₆- or ³⁄₈-mi, but a few are run at ⁷⁄₁₆- or ½-mi. Most tracks are oval and of sand or dirt.

To help equalize competition, the United States has a grading system used by most tracks in scheduling races. Dogs are graded from A to E with the better dogs in the A class. When a dog wins, he moves up one class. If he finishes out of the money three consecutive times, he moves down a class.

Greyhounds are remarkably consistent performers. A greyhound will turn in the same time over a given distance night after night after night—if he is allowed to run alone. This consistency would make every dog race easily predictable—it is the "interference" that takes place when eight dogs are running that makes a race interesting.

If a dog consistently turns his head to try to fight off dogs attempting to pass him, he may be barred from racing. But, other than that, there is no such thing as a disqualification for a foul in dog racing. The bumping that takes place at the first turn usually does more to determine the outcome of a race than the sheer speed of the dogs.

Another factor that makes the races interesting is that every dog has his own preferred "groove" around the track. Some like to run on the far outside, some like to hug the rail, some stick to the rail on the straightaways and go very wide at the turns—and any racing dog sticks to his path, making no adjustments regardless of what gets in his way.

All this makes dog racing an exciting sport to watch. And, to the casual fan, one of its greatest attractions is that the usual card carries 12 races, with a race run every 17 min, so the whole program takes less time than 8 thoroughbred races.

Pari-mutuel Betting. The pari-mutuel betting system used at dog tracks is very similar to that used at horse and harness racing tracks. The breakdown of what happens to the "handle" is also just about the same. Approximately 83 percent is returned to winning bettors; the rest is split approximately in half between the state (for taxes) and the track (for operating expenses). From 2 to 5 percent of the handle goes to the racing kennels that own the greyhounds finishing in the money.

In Florida, revenue to the state from greyhound racing now surpasses revenue derived from Thoroughbred racing, harness racing, and jai alai combined.

See GAMBLING; HORSE RACING.

Glossary

(Many of the terms used in dog racing are borrowed from Thoroughbred and harness racing. The words and phrases in this list are primarily those peculiar to dog racing.)

alert—Used to describe a dog that breaks fast from the starting box.

baseball—To bet three or more numbers in every possible combination for a quiniela or daily double. "Baseball the 1-2-3," for example, signifies three separate bets, on the 1-2, 1-3, and 2-3 combinations. Also *box*.

bear out—To force another greyhound wide.

beat the box—To start faster than most other greyhounds.

Bertillon—The system used to identify a greyhound through body measurements, color, and the like; based on a system developed by Alphonse Bertillon to identify criminals before fingerprinting was used.

Big Q—A type of parlay in which a bettor holding a winning quiniela ticket on one race exchanges it for a quiniela ticket on the next race. Usually allowed only on the last two races of a program, if at all.

blanket—The identifying cover worn by a racing greyhound; it carries a color and a number identifying the post position: red for 1, blue for 2, white for 3, green for 4, black for 5, yellow for 6, green and white for 7, yellow and black for 8, purple and white for 9.

blanket finish—Equivalent to a photo finish, with two or more dogs so close that a blanket could cover them.

box—The starting enclosure; to bet three or more numbers in every possible combination for a quiniela or daily double (see *baseball*, above).

box-buster—An eager greyhound that hits against the front of the box before it opens.

buy the board—To buy every betting combination available in a quiniela or daily double.

chalk—The favorite.

chalk player—A bettor who wagers consistently on favorites.

chute—An extension of the straightaway from which greyhounds start in races which are longer than the distance around the track.

combination—A bet to win, place, and show on a single dog; a $6 combination on a dog involves a $2 bet to win, $2 bet to show, and $2 bet to place.

dropped muscle—A ruptured muscle in the inner loin or shoulder.

early foot—Early speed.

fighter—A dog that deliberately interferes with dogs that attempt to pass him.

fly the turn—To veer well out on a turn.

forty-niner—A six-race parlay; an attempt to pick the winners of six consecutive races (the fourth through the ninth), staking the accumulated winnings.

head chopped off—Said of a greyhound that was cut off by another, usually by a dog that cut into the rail ahead of him.

hot box—A race involving top-rated greyhounds; sometimes, any race in classification A; or, the feature race on a program.

inside lure—A lure that travels on the inside of the track.

jinny pit—The lockout kennels in which dogs are kept between their arrival at the track and the beginning of their race.

juvenile—A dog in his first year of racing; sometimes, a dog at his first race meeting, or a dog that has not won a race.

maiden—A dog that has never won a race, except for a match or private sweepstakes.

numbers player—A bettor who consistently wagers on certain numbers, no matter which greyhounds are wearing them.

oddsboard—The tote (totalizator) board.

outside lure—A lure that runs around the outer edge of the track.

pop the box—To start ahead of the other greyhounds; also, *beat the box*.

prop—To slow down or stop during a race.

quiniela (also *quiniella, quinela*)—A type of bet in which the bettor attempts to pick the first two greyhounds to finish in a given race, in whatever order.

refuse—To stay in the starting box after it opens.

router—A greyhound that shows a good finishing kick at distances longer than the usual 5/16 mi.

shuffled back—Said of a dog that loses considerable ground because of interference or crowding.

sprinter—A dog that usually runs in races of 5/16 mi or less.

stayer—A dog that has great stamina over distances.

straight bet—A bet to win.

strip—The racing surface.

twin double—A daily-double parlay on two consecutive races.

twin quin—Same as Big Q; a quiniela parlay, usually on the last two races of a program.

wheel—A betting system in which one greyhound is bought in all combinations with other dogs. "Wheel the 1," for example, represents a series of quiniela bets on the 1-2, 1-3, 1-4, 1-5, 1-6, 1-7, and 1-8 combinations in an eight-dog race.

wire—The finish line; also, to *baseball* or *box* three or more numbers.

Bibliography. *American Greyhound Racing Encyclopedia*, American Greyhound Track Operators Association, Miami, 1963; and *Supplement*, 1964.

DOGSLED RACING—*See* SLED DOG RACING.

DRAG RACING—This sport might be considered the poor man's version of the quest for the mile land-speed record. The cars use a standing start and fly just ¼ mi, reaching top speeds of up to 230 mph.

Drag racing seems to have originated in southern California during the 1930s, with youngsters racing stripped-down Model T's and Model A's. Much of the racing took place in the Mojave Desert. After World War II, the sport—still informal and usually illegal—got new impetus, because of the shortage of automobiles before car factories got geared up again. More and more young men started piecing their hot rods together from whatever parts they could find. In many areas the authorities decided that the racing couldn't be stamped out, but that it might be organized and controlled. Police often helped young men organize hot-rod clubs, and the first formal drag strips were unused airport runways.

Drag racing is essentially an acceleration competition. The runways of the late forties were usually not much more than a ½ mi long, so the standard race was set at ¼ mi, giving the drivers room in which to stop their vehicles after their runs.

The National Hot Rod Association was organized in 1951. It now conducts nearly 4,000 meets a year, attracting about 6 million paying spectators. Total purses are close to $3 million. The NHRA has an intricate setup, recognizing more than 100 classes of cars, and conducting seven national championship events a year—the Winternationals, Gatornationals, Springnationals, Summernationals, Nationals, World Finals, and Supernationals.

There are two major categories, professional and sports racing. The professional races are run from even starts, while races in the sports category are handicapped.

In the professional category there are only four classes:

Fuel Dragsters. Sometimes called a "slingshot" or "rail job," the dragster is a very specialized vehicle. The chassis is just two long rails that connect in front with two bicycle wheels and in back with two fat airplane-type tires. The engine, usually a supercharged Ford or Chrys-

Don "Big Daddy" Garlits, shown here in his fuel dragster, has been one of America's top drag racers for years. *(National Hot Rod Association.)*

A "funny car" looks like an ordinary car, but it's a plastic or fiberglass shell on a special chassis built for drag racing. (*National Hot Rod Association.*)

ler that turns out up to 1,500 hp, is mounted amidships, and the driver sits at the rear. The dragster is about 45 ft long, 3 ft wide, and 1 to 3 ft high, and weighs 1,200 to 1,500 lb. The fuel dragster burns a mixture of methanol and nitromethane.

Gas Dragsters. The gas dragster is essentially the same as the fuel dragster, except that it burns commercial gasoline. Its top speed is about 200 mph, compared with 225 to 230 for the fuel dragster.

Funny Cars. "Funny" was originally used in the sense of "illegal," as "queer" sometimes means "counterfeit." The funny car is a dragster with a fiberglass shell that makes it look like a fairly ordinary Detroit production car. The whole top can be opened, like a clamshell, to reveal the innards. This kind of car was illegal just a few years ago, but fans liked them so much that a special class was created for them. The funny cars use the methanol-nitromethane mixture and hit top speeds of about 200 mph.

Stock Cars. This class was added in 1970; it includes American production cars, no more than three years old. The car must use its original type of engine, but many modifications are allowed. However, the engine cannot be supercharged, cannot use more than two four-barrel carburetors, and must burn ordinary commercial gasoline. And there is a required ratio of 7 lb of weight for each cubic inch of engine displacement. The minimum weight is 2,700 lb; a 385-in³ engine displacement would be permitted for a car of that weight.

Sports Racing. This category also recognizes winners in four classes, but the classes contain some interesting mixtures, with the handicap system to help even things out. The four classes are: competition eliminator, for dragsters smaller than those used in the professional category, and for some special roadsters and coupes built especially for drag racing; modified eliminator, which includes about 30 classes, among them extensively modified coupes, roadsters, dragsters, and some "street" vehicles, all running on gasoline, with no superchargers; super-stock

eliminator, for late-model, high-performance production cars, with some modifications permitted; and stock eliminator, for less powerful, late-model stock production cars.

Just for Fun. The NHRA also sanctions amateur drag racing in two other classifications, which are not represented in the national championship events. The pure-stocks category is just what it sounds like; it is composed of ordinary stock production cars with very few modifications. And there is a Volkswagen category, including two stock classes and two modified classes. Both of these categories are highly popular in local and regional meets.

The Competition

A drag meet is conducted like a tournament, with competitors racing two at a time, the winner moving on to further competition while the loser is eliminated.

The drag strip is about ¾ mi long and about as wide as a four-lane highway. The competitors gun their engines and wait at the starting line, watching the "Christmas tree," a series of lights on a pole about 20 ft down the course. There is one set of lights for each competitor. Reading down from the top of the pole, there are two white lights, five amber lights, one green light, and one red light.

The first white light indicates "prestaged"—it tells the driver that the car wheels are getting close to the electric eye that monitors the starting line. The second, "staged," tells the driver that the car is right on the line; if it moves any farther forward before getting the green light, it will be disqualified. Once both competitors are staged, the starter pushes a button, and the amber lights begin flashing. Each remains on for ½ sec; after the fifth amber light flashes, the green light goes on and the driver can start. If the driver jumps the gun, the red light goes on instead, and disqualification results.

The winner is the driver who travels the ¼-mi distance in the shortest elapsed time (et). This is measured in thousandths of a second by a timing device triggered by the electric eye at the starting line and stopped by another electric eye, at the finish line. Terminal velocity—the car's speed at the finish line—is also determined electronically, to the nearest hundredth of an mph. This is done by electric eyes at either end of a 132-ft slice of the drag strip, starting 66 ft short of the finish line and ending 66 ft beyond it. Terminal velocity is just an interesting statistic; a car can have the higher terminal velocity and still lose.

Because of the many different classes of cars in each category, races in the sports category are handicapped. Handicaps are based on world speed records for the various classes. For example, assume the cars of the mythical Classes A and B are going to race. The world record for Class A is 12.31 sec; the world record for Class B is 13.97 sec. The Class B car gets a 1.66-sec head start. This is programmed into the computer that operates the Christmas tree, and Car B gets the green light 1.66 sec before Car A.

World Championship Series. The biggest event in drag racing is the NHRA's World Finals, the climax of the World Championship Series of drag racing. Each of NHRA's geographical divisions conducts five special meets a year, during the April-to-September season, and the top point getters from these 35 events compete in the World Finals in October.

See also AUTOMOBILE RACING.

DRESSAGE—*See* EQUESTRIAN SPORTS.

DRUGS IN SPORTS—The use of drugs to improve performance, and occasionally to lower performance, first emerged as a problem in horse racing, where urine tests have long been used to detect any tampering with animals. The most celebrated case arose in the 1968 Kentucky Derby, when Dancer's Image finished first but was disqualified after traces of butazolidine, a painkiller, were found in his urine. "Bute" is allowed in some states, but banned in others, including Kentucky.

The problem of drug abuse among human athletes didn't get much serious attention until the late 1960s, when the use and abuse of drugs throughout society was perceived as a growing problem. It was *Ball Four*, a lighthearted book by a former major-league pitcher, Jim Bouton, that first focused attention on the problem. Bouton said that a large number of baseball players "couldn't function" without taking amphetamines—so-called "pep pills." Shortly afterward, another book, by former pro football player Dave Meggyesy, charged that many pro football teams "dispense amphetamines and barbiturates like penny candy."

The problem had been attacked in Europe much earlier. In 1961 the Italian Soccer Federation carried out urinalysis on 36 soccer players chosen at random and discovered that 8 of them had been taking amphetamines. In 1970, at the World Cup Soccer championships, two players from each team were selected at random for urinalysis. Urinalysis is now also routinely used to prevent the use of drugs in cycling races in Europe.

In 1972 a U.S. Senate committee looked into the problem. Among former athletes testifying was Harold Connolly, Olympic hammer throw champion in 1956. Connolly said that he had been "a hooked athlete" for eight years and added, "I knew any number of athletes on the 1968 Olympic team who had so much scar tissue and so many puncture holes in their backsides that it was difficult to find a fresh spot to give them a new shot."

Connolly also brought up the problem of anabolic steroids, body-building drugs which had been used by many athletes to increase muscle weight. In 1973, Dr. Roger Bannister, who had been the first man to run a mile in under 4 min, announced that a research group had developed a test to detect the use of anabolic steroids, and he urged that international sports bodies adopt the principle of spot checks of athletes.

Although the principle is distasteful to many, especially in the United States, where required drug tests are seen by many as unconstitutional, it has won some acceptance. The National Collegiate Athletic Association (NCAA) in 1973–1974 asked athletes participating in championship events to participate in urinalysis tests. The purpose was to determine the extent of drug use, and no punitive action was to be taken against those whose results were positive. At about the same time, however, the Amateur Athletic Union (AAU) announced that it was opposed to drug screening of athletes.

The first major drug scandal in sports in the United States arose in professional football, when Houston Ridge, a former player, brought suit against the San Diego Chargers. Ridge charged that drug use had helped cause an injury that ended his career; he won a $260,000 settlement. Depositions in the case revealed a pattern of drug use among several National Football League teams.

One former player testified that members of the Chargers who did not take amphetamines were fined. As a result of the case, the Chargers' owner, general manager, and eight players were fined a total of $40,000 by NFL Commissioner Alvin "Pete" Rozelle, and there was some discussion about requiring drug tests of NFL players. The director of the Players' Association, however, opposed tests on the ground that they would constitute an invasion of privacy.

The situation is similar in other sports. While many experts feel the only way to control the problem is by requiring tests, the legal obstacles have not yet been overcome. There is some evidence that publicity has lessened the problem, but it still undoubtedly exists.

Ironically, most doctors insist that amphetamines, though they give an athlete the idea that he is performing better, actually tend to impair performance. And anabolic steroids, while they do increase muscle weight, may also lead to injuries to bones and joints that were never meant to bear such increased weight.

DUCKPIN BOWLING—At the turn of the century, before 10-pin bowling had reached anything like the popularity it enjoys today, there was a form of 5-pin bowling that was fairly popular along the East Coast of the United States. It employed a small ball, which made it especially popular among women.

The manager of a Baltimore bowling alley, Frank Van Sant, suggested to the co-owners that they try scaling down the 10-pin version of the sport. The co-owners happened to be John J. McGraw and Wilbert Robinson, both now members of the Baseball Hall of Fame. They agreed, and had a woodworker produce some small pins. When they tried the new sport, according to legend, one of them felt that the small pins scattering around the alley looked like a flock of frightened ducks, and the game was christened "duckpins."

That was in 1900. By 1903 duckpin bowling had become quite popular in Baltimore and Washington, D.C., and it began to spread into New England and other Eastern areas. To standardize rules of the sport, the National Duck Pin Bowling Congress was formed in 1927, patterned after the American Bowling Congress. By 1960 there were an estimated 3 million duckpin bowlers in the country, concentrated along the Eastern seaboard. However, the sport has lost some ground in recent years, as a number of duckpin alleys have gone out of business or converted to "big pins."

A variation is rubber-band duckpin bowling, which uses wooden pins encased in rubber; because of the increased action, rubber-band scores tend to be considerably higher than ordinary duckpin scores. The American Rubberband Duck Pin Bowling Congress, which was established in 1945, is affiliated with the NDPBC.

In duckpin bowling, a bowler gets three rolls per frame. Scoring is exactly like the scoring in 10-pin bowling except that, if all 10 pins are knocked down on three rolls, the bowler simply gets a score of 10 for that frame; it is not a mark. (For more scoring details, *see* BOWLING.) In the rubber-band version, the bowler gets only two balls per frame in some states, three balls in other states.

Duckpins are short and squat, $9\frac{3}{8}$ in high and $4\frac{3}{8}$ in maximum diameter. The ball, in diameter only about 5 in, doesn't have holes. The duckpin lane has the same dimensions as the 10-pin bowling lane.

National Tournament Champions
(* Indicates won roll-off to break tie)

Men's All-Events

1928	Howard Campbell	1,113
1929	Sam Benson	1,141
1930	Athol Miller	1,203
1931	Ray Barnes	1,179
1932	Charles Bauer	1,195
1933	Mike Bogino	1,279
1934	Joe Morelli	1,192
1935	John Waters	1,215
1936	William Dente	1,274
1937	William Tato	1,194
1938	W. S. McNew	1,226
1939	Nick Tronsky	1,240
1940	Nick Tronsky	1,283
1941	Nick Tronsky	1,198
1942	Jimmy Libertini	1,282
1943–45	No competition	
1946	Joe Radocy	1,250
1947	Frank Guethler	1,239
1948	Jack Kamerzel	1,231
1949	George Young	1,267
1950	Nova Hamilton	1,274
1951	Mike Litrenta	1,339
1952	Frank Hanley*	1,239
1953	Charles Kebart	1,306
1954	Frank D'Imperio	1,259
1955	Tom Fitzgerald	1,249
1956	August Recchia	1,200
1957	Pat Crescenzi	1,240
1958	Joseph Serapillia	1,227
1959	Bill Bursey	1,301
1960	James Chearno	1,292
1961	Fosco Fatorini	1,293
1962	James Jenkins	1,280
1963	Dave Volk	1,284
1964	James Wolfenberger	1,287
1965	Al Grandy	1,323
1966	William Glaeser	1,303
1967	Al Barnhart	1,335
1968	Lindsey Hammonds	1,324
1969	Sterling Fitz	1,333
1970	Paul Popowyck	1,319
1971	Don Meyd	1,336
1972	James Garton	1,292
1973	Keith Dashno	1,332
1974	Basil Boone	1,337
1975	Bob Wilson	1,310
1976	Mike Piersanti	1,426

Men's Singles

1928	Albert Fischer	403
1929	Howard Campbell*	430
1930	Jack Otto	432
1931	Jack Whalen	435
1932	William Arnold	428
1933	Howard Furlong	440
1934	Nick Tronsky	453
1935	John Bianchi	458
1936	Carl Frisk	445
1937	William E. Powell	439
1938	Astor Clarke*	448
1939	Nick Tronsky	447
1940	Eddie Johnson	482
1941	Julian Easterday	459
1942	Bill Krauss	456
1943–45	No competition	
1946	Charles Kebart	471
1947	Winny Guerke	445
1948	Mike Dziadik	446
1949	John Catino	480
1950	Hal Tucker	487
1951	Steve Witkowski*	457
1952	Frank Shanley	452
1953	Al Rush	457
1954	Vince Della	443
1955	Walter Surowiecki	445
1956	Al Burrell	430
1957	Pat Crescenzi	444
1958	Francis Toolin	456
1959	Hilmar Sperschneider	473
1960	Tony DellaRocco	485
1961	Robert Goss	463
1962	Frank Chiodi	450
1963	Earl Hartman	464
1964	Jesse Davis	465
1965	Norwood Heselbach	480
1966	Leon Stetson	458
1967	Charles Guess	502
1968	Andy Constantinople	489
1969	William Wall	485
1970	Travis Cook	473
1971	Joe Bitner	488
1972	Irwin Wagner	468
1973	Fred Bellivear	466
1974	Smith Green	489
1975	Jeffrey Ferrando	469
1976	Bob Atkins	501

Men's Doubles

1928	Ray Von Dreele–F. Smith	779
1929	Red Morgan–G. Friend	775
1930	J. Mulroe–Paul Harrison	780
1931	Eddie Espey–Paul Harrison	774
1932	C. Bild–E. Blakeney	801
1933	Mike Bogino–Clark Frisk	821
1934	Walter Megaw–J. Waters	789
1935	Charles Bauer–Wilmer Robey	831
1936	A. Christopher–Andy Friar*	831
1937	Astor Clarke–Bill Krauss	809
1938	R. Haines–A. Felter	918
1939	Hal Tucker–T. Keene	828
1940	T. Iannarone–G. Brown	843
1941	P. Motyl–Mike Dziadik	793
1942	Jimmy Libertini–R. Haines	884
1943–45	No competition	
1946	H. Roetzel–B. Powley	825
1947	Joe Radocy–A. Balducci	852
1948	D. Cost–F. Micalizzi	808
1949	J. Aler–George Young	891
1950	W. Stalcup–Cletus Pannell*	828
1951	Nick Tronsky–Harry Peters	911
1952	Mike Avon–Paul Jarman	929
1953	Carroll Hildebrand–Hal Tucker	841
1954	Dr. H. Carbaugh–C. Harshman	834
1955	T. Fitzgerald–G. Vetos	861
1956	August Recchia–C. Becker	777
1957	J. Mordarski–E. Wotton	836
1958	R. DeMatteis–M. Carboni	854
1959	V. Marsch–F. Hugelmeyer	850
1960	A. Rush–D. Little*	874
1961	W. Stalcup–P. Crescenzi	875
1962	R. Rhue–O. Wynne	871
1963	B. Gochenour–L. Tommey	844
1964	J. Wolfenberger–M. Alexander	882
1965	F. Caruso–J. Ferrando	901
1966	A. Onefrey–J. Mammone	854
1967	Joe Serapilia–Tony Fratini	919
1968	George Haugh–Robert Cleary	919
1969	Al Grandy–Jerry Rosen	885
1970	Tony Zagryn–Adolph Petro	867
1971	Ed Brown–Paul Sharpe	871
1972	Charles Creamer–W. M. Jenkins	915
1973	Larry Shepley–Tom Ramsberg	901
1974	Bob Burchard–Bob Devine	925
1975	George Teague–Bernie Ruzin Sr.	867
1976	Tony Adams–Mike Piersanti	923

Men's Team

1928	King Pins, Washington, D.C.	1,735
1929	Recreation Center, Baltimore, Md.	1,812
1930	Bethesda Bowling Alleys, Bethesda, Md.	1,805
1931	Sokol Rosebuds, Bridgeport, Conn.	1,762
1932	Silver Spring Bowling Alleys, Silver Spring, Md.	1,819
1933	Morgan Recreation, Hartford, Conn.	1,951
1934	Connecticut Yankees, Stratford, Conn.	1,943
1935	Northeast Temple, Washington, D.C.	1,956
1936	Blue Ribbons, Willimantic, Conn.	1,948
1937	Borders Friction Stop, Springfield, Vt.	1,995
1938	Holland Five, Bridgeport, Conn.	1,968
1939	Holland Five, Bridgeport, Conn.	1,933
1940	Blue Ribbons, Willimantic, Conn.	2,057
1941	Newfield Men, Bridgeport, Conn.	1,919
1942	Savoia-Franklin, Baltimore, Md.	2,044
1943–45	No competition	
1946	Casino Five, Meriden, Conn.	1,950
1947	Holland Five, Bridgeport, Conn.*	1,919
1948	Davidson's Recreation, Baltimore, Md.	1,978
1949	Kingsway, Fairfield, Conn.	1,929
1950	Valley Forge Beer, Washington, D.C.	1,951
1951	Forest Park, Baltimore, Md.	2,034
1952	Washington Club, Providence, R.I.	1,933
1953	Broadway Candy & Tobacco Co., Baltimore, Md.	2,031
1954	Patterson, Baltimore, Md.	1,976
1955	Guida's Dairy-Blue Ribbons, New Britain, Conn.	1,988
1956	Arrow 77, Baltimore, Md.	1,900
1957	Langley Sport Center, Washington, D.C.	1,894
1958	All-Stars, East Haven, Conn.	1,878
1959	Chevy Chase Chevrolet, Washington, D.C	2,081
1960	Pla-Mor Bowling Lanes, Arlington, Va.	2,009
1961	Airway Major, Warwick, R.I.	2,083
1962	W. Stalcup Furniture, Washington, D.C.	1,933
1963	Bregialo's Sausage, Stamford, Conn.	1,982
1964	Caithness Buick, Bethesda, Md.	2,044
1965	Bowl America, Baltimore, Md.	2,104
1966	Candee-Whitney, New Haven, Conn.	2,054
1967	LaPerle's Memorials, Plainfield, Conn.	2,064
1968	Valley Oilers, Portland, Conn.	2,085
1969	Snelling & Snelling, Baltimore, Md.	2,057
1970	Kahlua Hut, Washington, D.C.	2,054
1971	Auto Electric Service, Hagerstown, Md.	2,114
1972	Guida's Dairy, New Britain, Conn.	2,070
1973	Dudley Excavating, Washington, D.C.	2,063
1974	Marchone's Italian Deli, Washington, D.C.	2,091
1975	Fair Lanes Westview, Baltimore, Md.	2,008
1976	Conn Frozen Food, Hamden, Conn.	2,125

Women's All-Events

1928	Irene Mischou	973
1929	Marjorie Smith*	975
1930	Lorraine Gulli	1,051
1931	Pauline Ford	992
1932	Naomi Zimmerman	1,052
1933	Anne Griffin	1,081
1934	Lorraine Gulli	1,114
1935	Lorraine Gulli	1,065
1936	Lucille Young	1,169
1937	Ida Simmons	1,101
1938	Lorraine Gulli	1,130
1939	Ida Simmons	1,130
1940	Katherine Vick	1,161
1941	Drusilla Kellum	1,034
1942	Lucy Rose	1,126
1943–45	No competition	
1946	Lorraine Gulli*	1,087
1947	Lorraine Gulli	1,117
1948	Lillian Young	1,184
1949	Maxine Allen	1,231
1950	Doris Leigh	1,121
1951	Betty Covelly	1,151
1952	Anne Wissman	1,186

1953	Gladys Broska	1,153
1954	Mary Kuebler	1,139
1955	Elizabeth Barger	1,152
1956	Betty Mooney	1,137
1957	Elizabeth Barger	1,198
1958	Lee Myers	1,126
1959	Francis Wilson	1,190
1960	Ethel Dize	1,259
1961	Jessie Falls	1,210
1962	Cecilia Rohlfing	1,215
1963	Laura Morgan	1,207
1964	Dorothy Czajka	1,205
1965	Betty Powers	1,190
1966	Elizabeth Barger	1,207
1967	Jean Stewart	1,260
1968	Mary Ann Mitchell	1,202
1969	Minerva Weisenborn	1,248
1970	Jean Harris	1,214
1971	Peggy Nichols	1,236
1972	Cathy Sanders	1,203
1973	Nancy Brindle	1,214
1974	Phyllis Rapson	1,239
1975	Wilda Guerrette	1,209
1976	Susan Slattery	1,244

Women's Singles

1928	Arline Roberge	372
1929	Margaret Miltner	374
1930	Margaret Holliday	350
1931	Lotta Janowitz	351
1932	Helen Clements	358
1933	Lois Clopton	397
1934	Florence La Barr	375
1935	Lorraine Gulli	423
1936	Lucille Young	418
1937	Ida Simmons	416
1938	Mabelle Hering	375
1939	Mabelle Hering*	379
1940	Ruth Hampel	413
1941	Carolyn McGinn	398
1942	Edna Hughes	428
1943–45	No competition	
1946	Kitty Sheuchik	405
1947	Flo Reynolds	410
1948	Betty Bainbridge	426
1949	Doris Leigh	418
1950	Estelle Warrington	399
1951	Lorraine Gulli	431
1952	Elizabeth Lowry	430
1953	Gladys Broska	425
1954	Elaine Perlin	399
1955	Edith Christensen	420
1956	Betty Mooney	391
1957	Margie Yeatts	428
1958	Mary Simmons	396
1959	Dorothy Cridlin*	432
1960	Inez Rhine	458
1961	Jessie Falls	458
1962	Alva Brown	434
1963	Donna Moissonies	422
1964	Jean Morris	465
1965	Ruth King	428
1966	Cecilia Rohlfing	441
1967	Shirley McAneney	429
1968	Mary Ann Mitchell	467
1969	Gertha Wilson	438
1970	Pat Pirce, Lor LeBlanc	431
1971	Sue Marchone	460
1972	Barbara Brown	461
1973	Agnes Claughsey	435
1974	Lori Cabral	432
1975	Delina Rock	437
1976	Doris Short	467

Women's Doubles

1928	B. Foote–Arline Roberge	625
1929	M. Whalen–Marjorie Smith	688
1930	M. Hassell–M. Degnan	662
1931	Margaret Miltner–Elsie Fischer	676
1932	E. McCurdy–Polly Dozier	694
1933	Margaret Holliday–Lotta Janowitz	747
1934	Evelyn Ream–Billie Butler	701
1935	Olivia Schmidt–Helen Randlett	764
1936	M. Stapleton–Ida Simmons	784
1937	Phyllis Wills–Dorothy Lawson	738
1938	O. Schmidt–Helen Randlett	737
1939	A. D'Lugo–C. Kirk	743
1940	E. Andrus–Katherine Vick	778
1941	H. Staron–N. Urdan	695
1942	M. MacDonnell–A. D'Lugo	771
1943–45	No competition	
1946	G. Bohn–L. Krahl	711
1947	Ingomar Moen–Lorraine Gulli	727
1948	M. Anderson–Ruth Zentz	783
1949	R. Gould–Maxine Allen	797
1950	E. Branch–B. Smith	768
1951	A. Wissman–Naomi Wargo	748
1952	Ruby Hovanic–R. Martinelli	764
1953	Myrtle Liphard–Elizabeth Barger	752
1954	L. Rakowski–J. Johnson	787
1955	J. Dubiel–A. Plude	766
1956	L. Farmer–H. Lawrence	757
1957	R. Rainey–E. Klutz	760
1958	N. McNamara–A. Clark	758
1959	R. Freeman–A. Atkinson	774
1960	J. Robinson–E. Dize	825
1961	N. and D. Moissonnier	837
1962	F. Perkins–B. Boyer	793
1963	M. Fontana–M. Galloway	787
1964	M. Wierdak–H. Sudol	780
1965	P. Stroessner–B. Mooney	813
1966	H. Pappas–G. Wilson	811
1967	Laura Morgan–Jean Stewart	803
1968	Doris Short–Jean Stewart	780
1969	Mary Ann Mitchell–Cathy Dyak	803
1970	Nancy Skidmors–Martha Reed	872
1971	Betty Stevens–Allena Roberts	826
1972	Terry Vaccaro–Dorothy Czjaka	798
1973	Roland Ough–Miki Irish	799
1974	Nancy Gawor–Jean Stewart	844
1975	Dotti Warren–Norma Gallagher	806
1976	Lorraine Watts–Kathy Cahoon	810

Women's Team

1928	Commercials, Washington, D.C.	1,534
1929	King Pins, Washington, D.C.	1,572
1930	Recreation Girls, Baltimore, Md.	1,638
1931	John Blick Girls, Washington, D.C.	1,533
1932	Burk & Co. Girls, Norfolk, Va.	1,630
1933	Recreation Girls, Baltimore, Md.	1,671
1934	Lucky Strike Girls, Washington, D.C.	1,762
1935	Tivoli Girls, Baltimore, Md.	1,606
1936	Lucky Strike Girls, Washington, D.C.	1,762
1937	Charlotte, N.C., Bowling Center	1,635
1938	WICC Yankee Network, Bridgeport, Conn.	1,729
1939	Diamond Cab, Baltimore, Md.	1,688
1940	WICC Yankee Network, Bridgeport, Conn.	1,729
1941	Rendezvous Bowling Center, Washington, D.C.	1,651
1942	Eureka Maryland Assurance, Baltimore, Md.	1,785
1943–45	No competition	
1946	All States Life Ins. Co., Baltimore, Md.	1,755
1947	Dundalk Center, Baltimore, Md.	1,740
1948	Frank's Restaurant, Hartford, Conn.	1,731
1949	Aristocrat Dairy-Recreation, Baltimore, Md.	1,759
1950	Frederick Generator-Franklin, Baltimore, Md.	1,802
1951	Sena's Recreation, Waterbury, Conn.	1,843

1952	Newfield Girls, Bridgeport, Conn.	1,727
1953	Frederick Generator-Franklin, Baltimore, Md.	1,749
1954	Hyattsville, Washington, D.C.	1,740
1955	Brunswick Red Crowns-Pimlico, Baltimore, Md.	1,800
1956	New Essex, Baltimore, Md.	1,737
1957	Brunswick Red Crowns, Baltimore, Md.	1,803
1958	Fulford's, Washington, D.C.	1,738
1959	Carousel-Eastway, Baltimore, Md.	1,882
1960	Aristocrat Dairy, Baltimore	1,834
1961	Coppola Ford Girls, Bridgeport, Conn.	1,876
1962	Guilford Lanes, Baltimore, Md.	1,826
1963	Pin Path, Baltimore, Md.	1,862
1964	Brunswick-Pikeville, Baltimore, Md.	1,834
1965	Crestlanes Five, Lynchburg, Va.	1,840
1966	Phil-Mar Inn Major Girls, Baltimore, Md.	1,869
1967	Holiday Lanes, Manchester, Conn.	1,911
1968	Johnny's New & Used Cars, Baltimore, Md.	1,849
1969	Eudowood Gardens, Baltimore, Md.	1,871
1970	Johnny's New & Used Cars, Baltimore, Md.	1,843
1971	Overlea Catering, Baltimore, Md.	1,861
1972	Ports Sport Shop, Baltimore, Md.	1,902
1973	Parkville Majors, Baltimore, Md.	1,902
1974	Scallops, Washington, D.C.	1,899
1975	Eastwood Trophies, Baltimore, Md.	1,904
1976	Overlea Exxon, Baltimore, Md.	1,926

Mixed Doubles

1931	Elsie Fisher–Paul Harrison	699
1932	Lorraine Gulli–F. Moore	714
1933	R. Quinn–Howard Furlong	772
1934	M. Jenson–Wallie Pipp	780
1935	E. Ellis–A. Clarke	735
1936	F. Maroney–F. O'Brien	768
1937	D. Dudley–B. Gauer	777
1938	M. Akers–W. Robey	762
1939	C. Kirk–H. Parsons	789
1940	Lucille Young–Ja. Talbert	806
1941	Ida Simmons–A. Liebler	802
1942	Caroline Hiser–P. Wolfe	771
1943–45	No competition	
1946	E. Kidd–C. Kidd	774
1947	Blanche Wooton–Silly Stalcup	795
1948	H. Bourgery–T. Carpenter	793
1949	Audrey Atkinson–O. Ellis	791
1950	Elizabeth Barger–Bill Brozey	792
1951	Betty Covelly–H. Lanasa	807
1952	H. Ploss–Jack White	765
1953	Marion Hamilton–Larking Weedon	802
1954	F. Reynolds–H. Peters	794
1955	F. Kupec–G. Pelletier	792
1956	P. Heim–G. Young	809
1957	E. Cozza–J. Curran	804
1958	K. Foley–N. Chouniard	771
1959	A. Bufford–L. Kaye	810
1960	F. and J. Hudson	848
1961	G. Darchik–D. Riccio	831
1962	G. Darchik–O. Riccio	824
1963	P. Jones–F. Fattorini	842
1964	F. Dennis–M. Correnti	864
1965	B. Mooney–E. Hartman	830
1966	W. Guerrette–J. Fernando	852
1967	Selina Connor–Wally Lookingland	884
1968	Beverly Conner–Randy Tull	859
1969	Fran Haas–Dab Lepardo	867
1970	Jean Stewart–Adolph Petro	876
1971	Kathy Vail–Alan Kickox	843
1972	Mary Orme–Bob Marchone	830
1973	Patty and Robert Stroesner	866
1974	Anita Rothman–Bill Mueller	862
1975	Medora Kaltenbach–Wayne Krauss	890
1976	Debbie Nettleton–Dennis Pontes	955

DUNE BUGGY RACING—*See* OFF-ROAD RACING.

E

ÉPÉE—A fencing weapon with a tapered triangular blade, the modern equivalent of the original dueling sword.

See also FENCING.

EQUESTRIAN SPORTS—Modern equitation began to develop in sixteenth-century Europe, when the horse-riding skills developed for military purposes became of interest to the civilian aristocracy, and riding schools were organized in Austria, France, Italy, Sweden, and other countries to teach those skills.

By 1896, when the first modern Olympics were held, equitation had become a relatively important international sport though still largely dominated by cavalrymen. Jumping events were on the Olympic program in 1900. In 1912 there were five equestrian events, and equitation has remained on the program ever since.

The United States, represented by the U.S. Army Cavalry team, did well until shortly after World War II, when the team was disbanded. In 1949, International Equestrian Competitions, Inc., was organized to supervise the sport in this country; the name was changed to the U.S. Equestrian Team, Inc. in 1950. Through USET efforts, the United States has again done well in recent Olympics, despite the fact that there is little international-style competition in this country.

The Olympic equestrian sports are the three-day event, the Grand Prix de Dressage, and the Prize of Nations jumping event.

In the Grand Prix de Dressage, three competitors enter from each nation. The rider's own horse is trained by the rider from the time it arrives in the host nation. The competition is a 12-min drill in which horse and rider must perform a complicated series of maneuvers in a limited area; judges award points for each maneuver, and deduct points for errors and omissions, and for exceeding the time limit.

The three-day event begins with a similar, but less complicated, test of dressage, also 12 min in length. On the second day the horses run an endurance test over a cross-country course—a test rather similar to a sports-car rally in that each of the five segments must be ridden at a certain specified speed. If the time limit for one of them is exceeded, the rider is eliminated from the event. Bonus points are given for finishing the second and fourth segments in less than the allotted time, and penalty points are incurred by mistakes at obstacles.

The third day is devoted to jumping contests, simpler than grand-prix jumping, with penalty points allotted for various faults, and bonus points given for beating time limits. The three-day winner is determined by the lowest number of penalty points, after bonus points have been deducted from the total. In team competition, each nation is allowed to enter four riders, but only the top three scores count.

The grand-prix jumping contest is run over an obstacle course 1,000 m or less in length, with 13 or 14 obstacles. The speed is 400 m a minute; ¼ penalty point is given for each second over the time limit, and there are also penalty points for failure to clear an obstacle cleanly. However, bonus points are not given. Each horse and rider goes over the course twice, and penalty points for the two rounds are totaled; the rider with the fewest points is the winner. The teams are judged by totaling the penalty points for all three riders.

See also HORSE SHOWS; OLYMPICS (for Olympic champions).

Bibliography. Wynmalen, Henry: *Dressage, a Study of the Fine Points of Riding,* A. S. Barnes, New York, 1954.

F

FENCING—The sword is an ancient weapon, dating to at least 5,000 years ago, when blades were made of bronze because man didn't yet know how to work iron. Fencing as a craft or art, however, is much younger; ironically, it was the invention of firearms that led to the development of fencing techniques, because firearms made armor obsolete.

While men wore armor, swords were very heavy, almost axelike, and the sword was often used like a club on an opponent's helmet. When armor became obsolete, the sword gradually became lighter and lighter, and fencing became possible.

Fencing developed basically as a type of defense—indeed, the word is an abbreviation of "defence"—but it also has roots in the tradition of dueling to settle disputes. "Duel" is usually considered a corruption of the Latin phrase, *duorum bellum,* or "war of two," which was used in the Middle Ages. In that period a duel was sometimes used as a trial by combat, when a judicial issue couldn't be solved in any other way. It often involved more than two men; in a famous Scottish judicial combat of 1396, two clans sent 30 men apiece into the field to do battle before King Robert III. The issue was settled when only 10 members of the winning clan were still upright.

The duel was banned in most European countries about the middle of the sixteenth century, but it continued despite the ban. The challenge was often disguised behind an innocuous-sounding phrase such as "Will you walk in the fields with me?" It was common during the sixteenth century for each duelist to use two weapons, a long rapier in the right hand and a short dagger in the left. The dagger was usually used for the death blow. The rapier of that period was unwieldy, and swordplay was rough and tumble, depending more on strength of arm than on skill of hand and eye.

Although duels were usually affairs of the upper class, it was the middle class that first developed any real skills in fencing, because members of the middle class had rarely, if ever, worn armor, and they had had to learn some ways of defending themselves. Certain skills were studied by members of swording guilds, the earliest of which was the Marxbruders of Frankfurt, Germany, formed in 1383.

Guilds of all kinds protected their trade secrets jealously during the Middle Ages; for many years fencing was a secret art. This secrecy was not merely a result of the guilds. There was a certain supposed link, in many minds, between fencing skill and magic, and those who taught fencing were often afraid of being accused of witchcraft or necromancy. Even early writers on fencing were cautious about exposing too many secrets of the art, and there are often references in Italian to the *botta segreta* (secret thrust), which probably varied from place to place and from time to time.

Until about 1560 the emphasis was on cutting strokes, with the edge of the sword, since the heavy broadsword was the type commonly used. The first practical book on the sport, by Achille Marozzo, was published in Italy in 1536, and was devoted largely to methods of cutting the opponent with the edge of the sword.

Later in the sixteenth century, however, the thrusting rapier was developed, and the point of the sword became more important in attacking. The lunge—stepping forward with the right foot as the sword is thrust forward with the right arm—was developed during this period, but was guarded as a *botta segreta*. It was first referred to by Angelo Viggiani in a book published in 1575.

Fencing with rapiers developed rapidly in Italy, and became fashionable in Elizabethan London, where it was primarily an exercise in skill. The button-tipped sword used in such exercises was well enough known for Shakespeare to refer to it several times; Hamlet received his mortal wound in a duel in which he and Laertes were supposed to be using button-tipped rapiers.

Many of the common terms used in fencing are French because the sport's modern techniques were largely developed in France during the early seventeenth century. (Most of the terms, however, were first used in 1570 by Henri Saint-Didier.) During that period the rapier became lighter and the lunge became the basic method of attack. The French master Charles Besnard in 1653 laid down many of the principles of modern fencing. With heavier swords, the style had been to ward off a blow and attack with a single motion; the new, lighter blades, being much more maneuverable, made possible the modern method of first parrying and then attacking. Besnard and, a little later, La Tousche, another French master, described a number of modern parries.

During the late eighteenth century, the smallsword came into use. This was a blade only about 30 in long (the rapier was usually about 45 in long). One type, the colichemarde, invented about 1685, had a blade with a triangular cross section; the sides were slightly concave, reducing the weight without reducing the strength of the blade. The modern épée developed from the colichemarde.

Another development of the eighteenth century was the saber, a curved sword derived from the Eastern scimitar, which became a standard cavalry weapon while a close relative, the cutlass, was developed for naval use.

The cutlass was somewhat shorter than the saber, since it was meant for use in rather crowded quarters, during boarding operations. The saber used by the cavalry was only slightly curved, since it was meant to be used either for cutting or thrusting. The modern fencing saber is straight, but it still has one sharp edge, and is the only fencing weapon used for a cutting type of touch.

During the nineteenth century, although swords were still of some minor importance in warfare—and sometimes of major importance, still, to cavalrymen and sailors—fencing developed into a pure sport, practiced by men who would never use it in warfare. The weapons became lighter, and padded jackets and masks became standard equipment.

Basic Principles. The basic object of fencing is to touch your opponent without allowing the opponent to touch you. The sword, like a boxer's fists, is used both for defense and for offense. The fencer's "guard" position is a crouch, with the body in profile to the opponent, offering as little target area as possible. The knees are bent, the sword is held point out with the arm bent, and the hand is slightly above the waist.

There are four basic lines of attack, defined in relation to the position of the defender's sword hand: the high lines (above), the low lines (below), the inside (to the left), and the outside (to the right). For each line of attack, there are two kinds of parry: with the nails of the sword hand up and the thumb to the right, or the reverse. Thus there are eight basic parries.

The attack is almost always a lunge. A parry is a movement of the sword that closes the line of attack; it may be followed by a counterattack, or riposte. In foil and saber events, the attacker is said to have the right of way, and the defendant must parry before riposting. In the case of simultaneous touches, the point goes to the fencer who had the right of way. This is not true in the épée, in which each competitor gets a point if there is a double touch.

The fencer parries by meeting the weak part of the opponent's blade—the third nearest the tip—with the strong part of his or her own weapon—the third nearest the handle. The fencer can then riposte by making a small movement of the tip to get it into an open line; with a beat, a forcible movement which gets the opponent's weapon out of line; or with a disengagement, using pressure to force the opponent's weapon out of line and then sliding his or her own weapon along the opponent's blade to make the touch. Retreating and sidestepping are permissible, unless the fencer leaves the fencing strip, but parrying is preferred, since it makes a counterattack possible.

A fencer may also, of course, feint—feign an attack to try to create an opening—or may make a false attack, anticipating the opponent's parry so that the fencer can parry the riposte and score on a counter-riposte.

Foil and épée events are quite similar except that different target areas are involved. Saber fencing is based on the same general principles, but the fact that cuts as well as point thrusts are used makes for a much broader, more vigorous style of swordplay.

Basic Rules. The maximum overall length for foil and épée is 1,100 mm (43.407 in), and maximum blade length is 900 mm (35.433 in). Maximum for the saber is 1,050 mm (41.338 in) overall and 880 mm (34.646 in) for the blade.

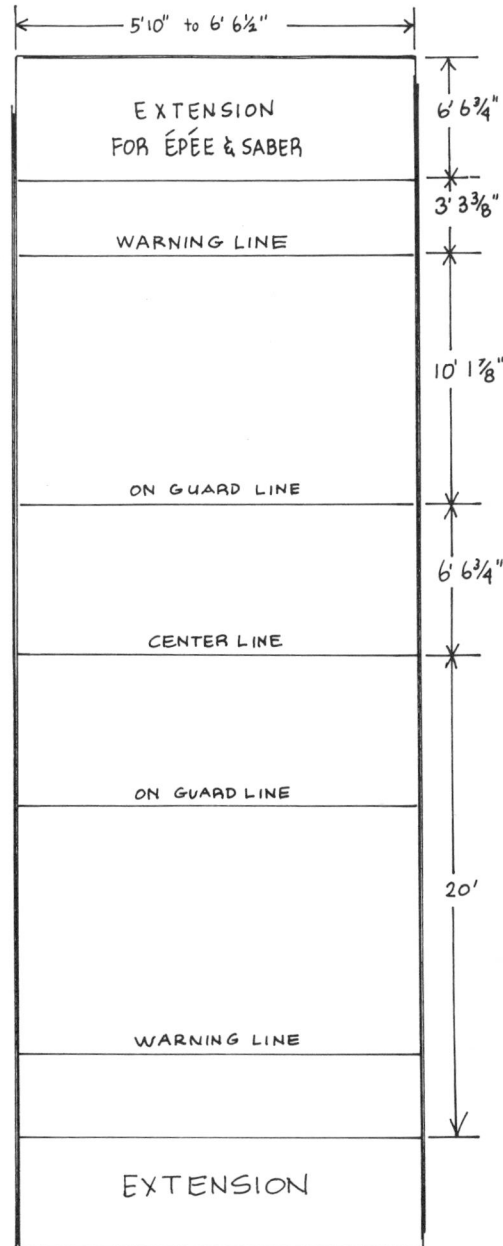

Fencing strip

Maximum weights are 500 g (17.637 oz) for foil and saber, 770 g (27.16 oz) for the épée.

The fencing strip is an area 40 ft long and 5 ft, 10 in to 6 ft, 6½ in wide. At each end is an extension of 6 ft, 6¾ in. Each fencer stands at an on-guard line, 6 ft, 6¾ in from the center line, until the director gives the order, "Fence." The shorter strip is used for foils; if a fencer retreats off the strip, it is scored as a touch. The extensions mark the end boundaries in épée and saber. If a fencer steps off the side of the strip, the penalty is a 1-m (3 ft, 3⅜ in) shortening of that competitor's end of the strip until the next touch.

Fencing officials are the director, who is in charge, and two or four judges. Foil and épée bouts are now almost always judged electronically; when a legal touch is made, a light goes on to signal the touch. The director is the only official in electrically scored bouts. The saber has not been electrified, since edge cuts are permitted, and judges must rule on touches. When a judge sees a touch, he raises his hand to inform the director, who halts play and awards the touch. The fencers then begin again at their on-guard lines.

The entire body is a valid target for the épée. In saber, any part of the body from the waist up, including head and arms, is a valid target. In foil, a touch can be scored only on the trunk, from the top of the collar to the groin lines in front and to the line across the tops of the hip bones in back. (For women, the hip-bone line is also the lower limit in the front of the body.) A hit scored outside the valid target area is a foul; there is no penalty, but the bout stops immediately and the fencers return to their on-guard lines to resume.

It is a "clinch" in fencing when the contestants are body to body or if, in the judgment of the director, they are so close to one another that they cannot fence properly. In épée, clinches are frequent and permissible. In foil and saber, however, the fencer who forces a clinch is given a warning the first time, and penalized a touch for a second such occurrence during the bout.

The first fencer to score five touches (four in women's foils) wins the bout.

Fencing is a team sport as well as an individual one. A team is composed of four fencers in each event; the teams engage in round-robin competition, a total of 16 bouts in each event. If each team wins eight bouts, the winner is the team that received the fewer touches.

Women compete only in foils.

Governing Bodies. The Amateur Athletic Union (AAU) had direct supervision of fencing in this country until 1894, when the Amateur Fencers League of America (AFLA) was formed. An AFLA affiliate, the Intercollegiate Fencing Association, and the National Collegiate Athletic Association (NCAA) both conduct collegiate tournaments. There is also a Women's Intercollegiate Fencing Association affiliated with the AFLA.

The international governing body is the Fédération Internationale d'Escrime, which conducts world championships annually. In Olympic years, the world champions are the Olympic champions.

United States Champions

Men's Foil

1892	W. Scott O'Connor	1903	F. Townsend
1893	William T. Heintz	1904	Charles G. Bothner
1894	Charles G. Bothner	1905	Charles G. Bothner
1895	A. V. Z. Post	1906	S. D. Breckinridge
1896	G. Kavanaugh	1907	C. Waldbott
1897	Charles G. Bothner	1908	W. L. Bowman
1898	No competition	1909	O. A. Dickinson
1899	G. Kavanaugh	1910	G. K. Bainbridge
1900	F. Townsend	1911	George H. Breed
1901	Charles T. Tatham	1912	Sherman Hall
1902	J. Brooks Parker	1913	P. J. Meyland

1914	S. D. Breckinridge	1946	Jose R. de Capriles
1915	O. A. Dickinson	1947	Dean Cetrulo
1916	A. E. Sauer	1948	Nathaniel Lubell
1917	Sherman Hall	1949	Daniel Bukantz
1918	No competition	1950	Silvio Giolito
1919	Sherman Hall	1951	Silvio Giolito
1920	Sherman Hall	1952	Daniel Bukantz
1921	F. W. Honeycutt	1953	Daniel Bukantz
1922	H. M. Raynor	1954	Joseph L. Levis
1923	R. Peroy	1955	Albert Axelrod
1924	Leo G. Nunes	1956	Sewall Shurtz
1925	George C. Calnan	1957	Daniel Bukantz
1926	George C. Calnan	1958	Albert Axelrod
1927	George C. Calnan	1959	Joseph Paletta
1928	George C. Calnan	1960	Albert Axelrod
1929	Joseph L. Levis	1961	Lawrence Anastasi
1930	George C. Calnan	1962	Edwin Richards
1931	George C. Calnan	1963	Edwin Richards
1932	Joseph L. Levis	1964	Herbert Cohen
1933	Joseph L. Levis	1965	Robert Russell
1934	Hugh V. Alessandroni	1966	Max Genter
1935	Joseph L. Levis	1967	Heizaburo Okawa
1936	Hugh V. Alessandroni	1968	Heizaburo Okawa
1937	Joseph L. Levis	1969	Carl Borack
1938	Dernell Every	1970	Albert Axelrod
1939	Norman Lewis	1971	Uriah Jones
1940	Dernell Every	1972	Bert Freeman
1941	Dean Cetrulo	1973	Ed Ballinger
1942	Warren A. Dow	1974	Heik Hambarzumian
1943	Warren A. Dow	1975	Ed Ballinger
1944	A. Snyder	1976	Ed Donofrio
1945	Dernell Every		

Men's Épée

1892	F. Barnard O'Connor	1930	M. Pasche
1893	Graeme M. Hammond	1931	Miguel A. de Capriles
1894	R. O. Haubold	1932	Leo G. Nunes
1895	Charles G. Bothner	1933	Gustave M. Heiss
1896	A. V. Z. Post	1934	Gustave M. Heiss
1897	Charles G. Bothner	1935	Thomas J. Sands
1898	No competition	1936	Gustave M. Heiss
1899	M. Diaz	1937	Thomas J. Sands
1900	W. D. Lyon	1938	José R. de Capriles
1901	Charles T. Tatham	1939	L. Tingley
1902	Charles T. Tatham	1940	F. Seibert
1903	Charles T. Tatham	1941	Gustave M. Heiss
1904	Charles G. Bothner	1942	Henrique Santos
1905	W. Scott O'Connor	1943	R. Driscoll
1906	W. Grebe	1944	Miguel A. de Capriles
1907	W. D. Lyon	1945	Max Gilman
1908	Paul Benzenberg	1946	A. Wolff
1909	A. de la Poer	1947	James Strauch
1910	A. de la Poer	1948	Norman Lewis
1911	George H. Breed	1949	Norman Lewis
1912	A. V. Z. Post	1950	Norman Lewis
1913	A. E. Sauer	1951	José R. de Capriles
1914	F. W. Allen	1952	Abelardo Menendez
1915	J. A. MacLaughlin	1953	Donald Thompson
1916	William H. Russell	1954	Sewall Shurtz
1917	Leo G. Nunes	1955	Abram Cohen
1918	No competition	1956	Abram Cohen
1919	William H. Russell	1957	Richard Berry
1920	R. W. Dutcher	1958	Richard Berry
1921	C. R. McPherson	1959	Henry Kolowrat
1922	Leo G. Nunes	1960	David Micahnik
1923	George C. Calnan	1961	Robert Beck
1924	Leo G. Nunes	1962	Gilbert Eisner
1925	William H. Russell	1963	Lawrence Anastasi
1926	Leo G. Nunes	1964	Paul Pesthy
1927	Harold Van Buskirk	1965	Joseph Elliott
1928	Leo G. Nunes	1966	Paul Pesthy
1929	F. S. Righeimer	1967	Paul Pesthy

1968	Paul Pesthy	1973	Scott Bozek
1969	Stephen Netburn	1974	Dan Cantillon
1970	Joseph Elliott	1975	Scott Bozek
1971	James Melcher	1976	George Masin
1972	James Melcher		

Men's Saber

1892	R. O. Haubold	1935	Norman C. Armitage
1893	Graeme M. Hammond	1936	Norman C. Armitage
1894	Graeme M. Hammond	1937	John R. Huffman
1895	Charles G. Bothner	1938	John R. Huffman
1896	Charles G. Bothner	1939	Norman C. Armitage
1897	Charles G. Bothner	1940	Norman C. Armitage
1898	No competition	1941	Norman C. Armitage
1899	G. Kavanaugh	1942	Norman C. Armitage
1900	J. L. Ervin	1943	Norman C. Armitage
1901	A. V. Z. Post	1944	Tibor Nyilas
1902	A. V. Z. Post	1945	Norman C. Armitage
1903	A. V. Z. Post	1946	Tibor Nyilas
1904	A. G. Anderson	1947	James Flynn
1905	K. B. Johnson	1948	Dean Cetrulo
1906	A. G. Anderson	1949	Umberto Martino
1907	A. G. Anderson	1950	Tibor Nyilas
1908	G. W. Postgate	1951	Tibor Nyilas
1909	A. E. Sauer	1952	Tibor Nyilas
1910	J. T. Shaw	1953	Tibor Nyilas
1911	A. G. Anderson	1954	George Worth
1912	C. A. Bill	1955	Richard Dyer
1913	A. G. Anderson	1956	Tibor Nyilas
1914	W. Von Blejenburgh	1957	Daniel Magay
1915	Sherman Hall	1958	Daniel Magay
1916	Sherman Hall	1959	Tomas Orley
1917	Arthur S. Lyon	1960	Eugene Hamori
1918	No Competition	1961	Daniel Magay
1919	Arthur S. Lyon	1962	Michael Dasaro
1920	Sherman Hall	1963	Eugene Hamori
1921	C. R. McPherson	1964	Attila Keresztes
1922	Leo G. Nunes	1965	Alex Orban
1923	L. M. Schoonmaker	1966	Al Morales
1924	L. E. Gignoux	1967	Al Morales
1925	Joseph Vince	1968	A. Jack Keane
1926	Leo G. Nunes	1969	Alex Orban
1927	Nickolas Muray	1970	Alex Orban
1928	Nickolas Muray	1971	Alex Orban
1929	Leo G. Nunes	1972	Alex Orban
1930	Norman C. Armitage	1973	Paul Apostol
1931	John R. Huffman	1974	Peter Westbrook
1932	John R. Huffman	1975	Peter Westbrook
1933	John R. Huffman	1976	Tom Losonczy
1934	Norman C. Armitage		

Women's Foil

1912	A. Baylis	1933	Dorothy Locke
1913	Mrs. W. H. Dewar	1934	Helene Mayer
1914	M. Stimson	1935	Helene Mayer
1915	Jessie Pyle	1936	Joanne de Tuscan
1916	Mrs. C. H. Voorhees	1937	Helen Mayer
1917	Florence Walton	1938	Helene Mayer
1918–19	No competition	1939	Helene Mayer
1920	Adeline Gehrig	1940	Helena Mroczkowska
1921	Adeline Gehrig	1941	Helene Mayer
1922	Adeline Gehrig	1942	Helene Mayer
1923	Adeline Gehrig	1943	Helena Mroczkowska
1924	Mrs. C. H. Hopper	1944	Madeline Dalton
1925	Florence Schoonmaker	1945	Maria Cerra
1926	Florence Schoonmaker	1946	Helene Mayer
1927	Stefanie Stern	1947	Helena Mroczkowska Dow
1928	Marion Lloyd		
1929	Florence Schoonmaker	1948	Helena Mroczkowska Dow
1930	Mrs. Harold Van Buskirk		
1931	Marion Lloyd	1949	Polly Craus
1932	Dorothy Locke	1950	Janice Lee York

1951	Janice Lee York	1964	Janice Lee York Romary
1952	Maxine Mitchell	1965	Janice Lee York Romary
1953	Paula Sweeney	1966	Janice Lee York Romary
1954	Maxine Mitchell	1967	Harriet King
1955	Maxine Mitchell	1968	Janice Lee York Romary
1956	Janice Lee York Romary	1969	Ruth White
1957	Janice Lee York Romary	1970	Harriet King
1958	Maxine Mitchell	1971	Harriet King
1959	Pilar Roldan	1972	Ruth White
1960	Janice Lee York Romary	1973	Tatanya Adamovich
1961	Janice Lee York Romary	1974	Gay Jacobsen
1962	Yoshi Takeueji	1975	Nikki Tomlinson
1963	Harriet King	1976	Anne O'Donnell

Citizens Savings Fencing Hall of Fame

Norman C. Armitage	John Huffman
George D. Calnan	Tracy Jaeckel
Hugo Castello	Edward F. Lucia
Julio M. Castello	Helena Mayer
José R. de Capriles	James Montague
Miguel de Capriles	James Murray
Lajos S. Csiszar	Leo G. Nunes
Irving DeKoff	W. Scott O'Connor
Andre Deladrier	J. Brooks B. Parker
Clovis F. J. Deladrier	Janice Lee York Romary
Maxwell Garret	J. Sanford Saltus
Ralph Goldstein	Georgio Santelli
Robert Grasson	Charles R. Schmitter
Sherman Hall	Stanley S. Sieja
Graeme M. Hammond	Maria Cerra Tishman
Alvar Hermanson	Marion Lloyd Vince

Bibliography. Vince, Joseph: *Fencing*, 2d ed., Ronald, New York, 1961.

FIELD ARCHERY—A type of archery competition meant to simulate hunting. Archers shoot at targets of various shapes and sizes from various distances.

See also ARCHERY.

FIELDBALL—This American version of team handball is played almost exclusively by women. The game, which combines elements of soccer and basketball, is played on a field 100 to 110 yd long and 60 to 70 yd wide by two teams of 11 players each. The goals are similar to those used in field hockey or soccer.

The ball is a soccer ball. It may be thrown or batted through the air, but may not be carried or kicked. The object is to score by throwing the ball into the goal. Most body contact is forbidden, unless it is accidental and minor.

The sport is primarily a girls' physical-education activity in the United States.

See also TEAM HANDBALL.

FIELD HANDBALL—*See* TEAM HANDBALL.

FIELD HOCKEY—Many historians believe that field hockey is among the most ancient of sports, tracing its origin to Persia and, perhaps, to Egypt, where it may have grown out of a religious ceremony. It has even been suggested that the original field-hockey game was the ancestor, not only of stick and ball games such as cricket, baseball, and golf, but of ball and goal games such as soccer and football.

Even the modern version of the sport is quite old. The name comes from the French *hoquet*, "shepherd's crook."

Various forms of the sport are called "hurley" or "hurling" in Ireland, "shinty" or "shinny" in Scotland, and "banty" or "bandy" in Wales. The sport was known simply as hockey until ice hockey became popular in North America; it is now called field hockey to distinguish it from ice hockey.

Hockey may have been played in England as early as 1175. The name *hokay* wasn't introduced until the early sixteenth century, however, so it may have been then that the French version of the game was introduced. It was popular enough in England by 1527 to be among several sports specifically forbidden by law.

The first English hockey club was formed in 1840, and in 1875 standardized rules were adopted at a meeting in London. The Wimbledon Hockey Club introduced new rules to speed up the sport in 1883, and three years later a national governing body, the Hockey Association, was formed. The English reintroduced the sport into India,

and that country and Pakistan are now among the outstanding field-hockey countries in the world.

Field hockey became a women's sport in 1887, with some rules changes. Ironically, in the United States it was considered primarily a women's sport for many years; American men had tried it earlier and found it too rough.

The real introduction of the sport to the United States occurred in 1901, when Constance M. K. Applebee of England gave a demonstration at Harvard Summer School. Miss Applebee, in this country to study, was astounded on learning that Americans apparently didn't know anything about field hockey; she used ice-hockey sticks and a baseball for her demonstration. Harriet I. Ballantine, director of physical education at Vassar College, saw the demonstration and invited Miss Applebee to teach the sport at Vassar. They located 24 field-hockey sticks which had been abandoned by a group of male collegians who decided the game was too rough; with those sticks and a cricket ball, Miss Applebee taught field hockey at Vassar. Later she taught the sport at other women's schools, and in 1922 she opened a summer field-hockey camp in the region of the Pocono Mountains of Pennsylvania.

In 1922 the United States Field Hockey Association was formed as the sport's national governing body. It still supervises the women's version of the sport.

Field hockey is not widely accepted as a men's sport in the United States. The first regularly scheduled games among men's teams were organized in 1926 by an association in the New York City area. The Germantown Cricket Club of Philadelphia played the Westchester Field Hockey Club of Rye, New York, in 1928 to mark the real beginning of serious competition, and the Field Hockey Association of America was formed in 1930 to supervise the men's sport nationally.

One reason for that move was the desire to have an American team in the 1932 Olympic Games, which were to be played in Los Angeles. Field hockey had been on the program earlier, and has been a permanent Olympic sport since 1928. The United States hasn't done well in Olympic competition; there is no real national field-hockey program for men, and the sport is played in only a few areas.

American women, on the other hand, have played many international matches. There is a national tournament, involving sectional all-star teams, and an All-American team is chosen annually. American women have played against touring teams of all-stars from other countries, and have gone on international tours. Twice the United States has been host to the conference of the International Federation of Women's Hockey Associations.

Field and Equipment. The hockey field is 90 to 100 yd long and 50–60 yd wide. At either end is a goal, 7 ft high and 12 ft wide. The striking circle is actually a white line, 4 yd long and 16 yd from the goal (15 yd for women), connected to the goal line by two quarter circles, each 15 yd in diameter and centered on a goalpost. The field is divided by a center line and by two 25-yd lines.

The ball has a circumference of 8¾ to 9¼ in, and weighs 5½–5¾ oz. It has a white leather cover. The stick is 36–40 in long, weighs 18–20 oz, and has a crook 5–7 in long. The crook is curved, and has one flat side and one rounded side.

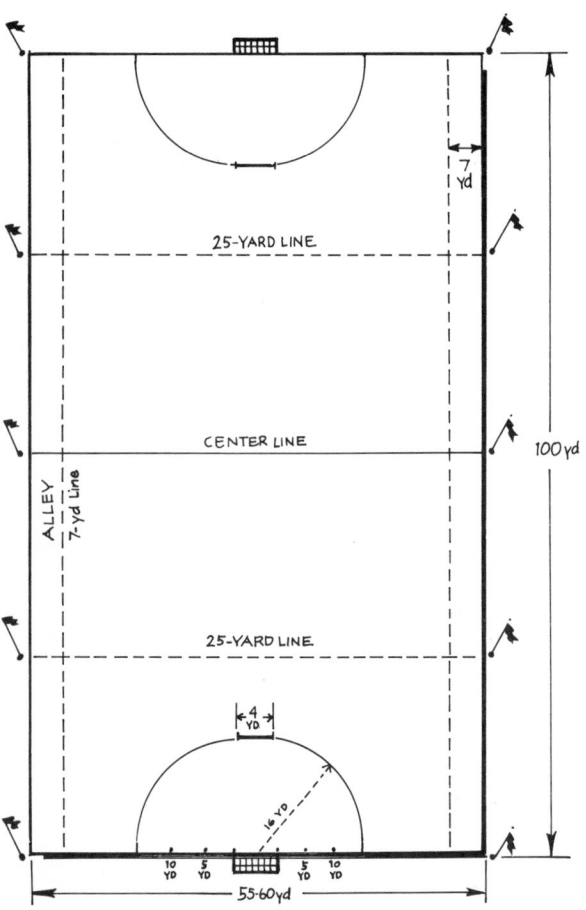

Men's field hockey field: Goals are 7 ft high and 12 ft wide. Women's field is similar, except that the striking circle is 15 yd from the goal line, the alley is 5 yd wide, and there is a small "bully circle" in the center of the field.

Method of Play. Each team is made up of 11 players: five forwards, three halfbacks, two fullbacks, and a goalkeeper. The forwards are considered attacking players, the others defending players, but there are no rules regulating the manner of play by position.

A game begins with a "bully" at the center circle. The ball is placed on the ground between two opposing players; each touches the opponent's stick and the ground, alternately, three times, and then attempts to get possession of the ball to pass it to a teammate. No other player can be within 5 yd of the center circle during a bully.

The bully is also used to put the ball in play after a goal or when the ball goes out of bounds across an end line.

The ball must be advanced with the stick, either by hitting or by rolling it along the ground as the player moves. A player is allowed to stop the ball with the hand, when the ball is in flight, but may not bat it forward. The goalkeeper only can use hand, stick, or body to stop the ball.

The object is to score goals by knocking the ball across the goal line, between the goal posts. A goal can be scored only from within the striking circle.

In major matches, there are halves of 35 min each (30 min for women), with a 5-min intermission. There are no time-outs or substitutions, except for injury. (In the United States, substitutions are permitted if both teams agree beforehand.)

When the ball rolls out of bounds at the sidelines, the team that last touched it loses possession, and a player from the other team puts the ball in play by rolling it in. It must cross the boundary within 1 yd of the point where it went out of bounds, and all other players must be behind the restraining line (7 yd from the sidelines in men's play, 5 yd in women's).

Rules are generally similar to those of soccer; a major difference is that obstruction—placing oneself between an opponent and the ball—is forbidden. Fouls include raising the stick above the shoulder when approaching or striking the ball; deliberately undercutting the ball to lift it into the air; hooking, holding, and other forms of interference with the stick; batting the ball with the hand or stopping it with the feet or body.

It is an offside if a player receives a pass on the attacking side of the center line with fewer than two (three in women's play) opponents between him and the goal line.

The usual penalty is a free hit for the opposition from the spot of the foul. If the defense deliberately hits the ball over the goal line, or commits a foul in the striking circle, the penalty is a "penalty corner" hit: The other team gets a free hit from a point on the goal line, at least 10 yd from a goal post. (In men's play, six defenders must remain behind the goal line until the ball is hit.)

If the offense accidentally knocks the ball over the goal line, a bully is played on the 25-yd line. If the defense accidentally knocks the ball over the goal line, the other team is given a corner hit: The ball is hit into play from the goal line or sideline within 3 yd (5 yd in women's play) of the corner flag; six defenders must be behind the goal line and other defenders must be beyond the center line (beyond the 25-yd line in women's play) until the ball has been touched by another player or has gone outside the striking circle, while all attackers must be outside the striking circle until the ball is hit.

For a deliberate foul in the striking circle, or a foul in the striking circle that prevents a goal from being scored, the offensive team is given a penalty shot in men's play, a penalty bully in women's play. A penalty shot is taken from a spot 8 yd in front of the goal; the attacker may take one step forward before hitting the ball, but may hit it only once. The goalie must stay on the goal line and must not move either foot until the ball has been hit. All other players must be behind the 25-yd line.

A penalty bully is taken by the offending player and any selected opponent at a spot 5 yd in front of the goal. All other players (including the defending goaltender) must be beyond the 25-yd line. If the defender knocks or deflects the ball over the goal line, inside the striking circle, the bully is taken again. If the ball goes outside the striking circle, it is dead and is put in play again with a bully at the center of the field.

FIELD TRIALS—A field trial is a competition among hunting dogs to test their performance under actual field conditions. The first field trial on record was held in England in 1681, with hounds following a trail scent 4 mi. There were probably field trials before then, and undoubtedly many field trials were held during the eighteenth century, but there is little record of them. The first major field trial of which a complete record exists was held in England in 1866; the first one in the United States was held at Memphis, Tennessee, in 1874.

In a field trial dogs are released in a field of 5 acres or more to seek out birds in cover. With younger dogs—those less than two years of ago—natural instincts are most important in field performance. With older dogs, however, training is also important, and the way a dog responds to his handler's commands and carries out taught maneuvers also enters into performance.

In early American trials, dogs were judged on a point system; out of 100 possible points, specific values were assigned to such features as keenness of nose, breakaway, running style, pointing, backing, and roading. This was soon replaced by the heat system, in which dogs were run in braces, with the best dog in each brace selected for competition in the next heat. This elimination-tournament kind of trial, however, consumed too much time.

The modern method of judging is known as the "spotting" system: The dogs are run in braces, but the judges follow each brace and choose the best dog out of the entire running. Sometimes, if two or more dogs appear to show equal ability in the first running, a second series is held to allow the judges to choose the winner.

Types of Trials. There are about 7,000 field trials held in the United States annually, and they fall into many different types. Trials are conducted for pointing dogs, retrievers, spaniels, hounds beagles, and sheep dogs. The most numerous are those for the pointing dogs, the pointer and setter. Pointing-dog trials are held on four different types of game birds, bobwhite quail, pheasant, prairie chicken, and ruffed grouse.

There are puppy stakes, for dogs born on or after January 1 immediately before the winter trial season; derby stakes, for dogs born on or after January 1 of the previous year; and all-age stakes.

Trials are further classified as amateur or open. Amateur events are open only to amateur handlers—those

Dogs are shown during breakaway at a championship field trial. *(Henry Reynolds Photo.)*

who train or handle only their own dogs. Open events are open to amateur and professional handlers.

Competitions are sanctioned by the American Field Trial Club, the Amateur Field Trial Club of America, the American Kennel Club, and by local clubs belonging to one or more of those organizations. The premier event in the United States is the National Field Trial Championship, held on the plantation of the late Hobart Ames in Grand Junction, Tennessee.

FIGURE SKATING—Ice skates of iron have been definitely dated to about the year 200, but it is certain that bone skates were used long before that, in the Scandinavian countries and quite likely in other countries of northern Europe. It is also possible that wooden skates were used before the first iron skate was invented. Because bone is itself slippery, skating on bone is difficult, since it is almost impossible to push off to get moving. Those early skaters probably used some kind of pole to propel themselves and to steer and brake.

A description of ice skaters enjoying themselves in London was published in 1180; even then a pole was used for propulsion, indicating that the skates were not bladed, but were wide runners. The bladed skate was first pictured in a 1498 Dutch woodcut.

The origin of the woodcut is appropriate, since it was

in the Netherlands that skating was most practiced and most fully developed during its early years. The Dutch canals were the country's major means of communication, and when ice made the canals impassable by boat, skates were used instead. By the late sixteenth century, Dutch skaters were quite proficient, and the iron-bladed skate was in wide use throughout the Netherlands.

Modern ice-skating apparently reached England only about 1660, after restoration of the monarchy, and it is possible that Charles II and his court brought the novelty from Holland. In his diary, Samuel Pepys recorded seeing skating for the first time on December 1, 1662.

The move to England was important. The Dutch were fine skaters, but their basic goal was speed. To the English, skating was a pastime, and English skaters sought ways to make it more interesting. The Dutch skate had a long straight runner; by about 1750 the English had developed the first figure skate, with a short, curved blade, permitting much greater maneuverability, and by 1770 the grooved skate had been invented.

In 1772 the first English book on ice skating was published. The author, Robert Jones, included a good deal of information on how to skate various figures. Within a few years, figure skating had become popular both in France and in Germany, and it seems possible that Jones's book may have had some influence.

It was in France, during the early nineteenth century, that the next major advances in figure skating took place, and the next major book was *The Real Skater,* by J. Garcin, a member of the *Gilet Rouges* (Red Vests), an outstanding group of French figure skaters. The book, significantly, was dedicated to a ballet dancer.

The first half of the century also saw two major technical innovations. An Englishman, Henry Boswell, in 1836 developed a new skate iron. The old iron curved up in front of the skating boot, and extended back only as far as the beginning of the heel. This required the skater to lean forward at all times, and made backward skating very difficult. Boswell, who later became a professional figure skater, cut off the front of the blade and extended the back of the blade all the way to the back of the heel. The new skate iron was soon in common use throughout Great Britain and elsewhere.

The skate, however, still consisted of an iron attached to a plate, which was in turn fastened to the boot by straps. E. V. Bushnell, of Philadelphia, invented the all-metal skate in 1848. Shortly afterward he realized that, with a metal iron and footplate, it would be easy to clamp the plate tightly to the boot, and straps were done away with. This enabled the skater to perform many more maneuvers, at faster speeds, without the danger of losing a skate or of having a skate become loose.

Skating in North America. It would seem logical that Dutch settlers brought skating to this continent, but there is no indication that they did. It appears that British soldiers introduced skating to the Colonies. It was especially popular among British officers stationed at Philadelphia, which was a major skating center about 1750 and well beyond—as evidenced by Bushnell's invention.

The first skating club in this country was the Skating Club of the City and County of Philadelphia, formed in 1849. The Schuylkill River was a popular skating area for club members and others. Transplanted Philadelphians helped spread the sport to other regions. The New York Skating Club was formed in 1863.

The Bushnell boot-skate, and other technological advancements, led to what was known as the American style of figure skating, which included many maneuvers—particularly those performed on one foot—that had previously been unheard of, including the sketching of intricate designs on the ice. At this point, figure skating, while popular in many countries, had no real nucleus or

Dorothy Hamill won the U.S. women's title in 1974 and 1976, and the Olympic and world championships in 1976. (*U.S. Figure Skating Association.*)

centering point. It was still a pastime, not a sport. The Americans, skating their marvelously intricate patterns, looked ungainly and ungraceful in the performance, and the American style was becoming something of a fad in other countries. But an American was to "invent" modern figure skating.

Jackson Haines. Haines was born about 1840, perhaps in Chicago, perhaps in Troy, New York. He wanted to enter the theater, and decided on ballet as his métier. But when he was about 18, he discovered skating, and he quickly realized that skating and ballet could be combined. Haines developed a new approach to skating: An appearance of grace and of beauty in the curve of the body and the posture of the limbs should be more important, he felt, than tracing intricate patterns on the ice.

In 1864, Haines went to Europe to exhibit his new skating style. He was well received in most countries, but his ideas genuinely took root in Vienna, where music, the waltz, and the romantic ballet were so important. The Viennese immediately saw the possibilities of dancing on ice. Among Haines's pupils in Vienna were Leopold Frey, who was to win the first International Skating Tournament, in 1882, and Diamantidi, who melded Haines' showmanship with a system of figures and with a certain amount of athleticism, in the form of spins and jumps.

Gordon McKellen was twice U.S. men's singles champion. *(U.S. Figure Skating Association.)*

(Haines himself had invented the sitting spin, which is still a common element of figure-skating performances.)

The International Style. Haines's style was scorned in England, where it was called "fancy skating"—not a compliment, as far as the English were concerned—and the English were meanwhile working on pure figure skating. They were not very interesting to watch. They emphasized the science, not the art of skating—the proper tracing of certain figures, combined with a stiffness of the body and the limbs. This scientific approach, however, advanced the sport. The English developed a thorough understanding of the principles of ice skating, and they also invented competition in figure skating, in a roundabout way.

It was in England, also, that pairs skating developed. It was originally called hand-in-hand skating, and the main reason was that, in the Victorian era, it was more than dangerous for a woman to fall; it was a disgrace for anyone to see her falling. By skating hand-in-hand with a partner, a woman could avoid possible disgrace.

In 1879 the National Skating Association of Great Britain was formed, primarily to control the sport of speed skating. But in 1881 the society also took over figure skating, and began offering badges for those who could pass examinations. There was opposition from some who feared, correctly, that this would turn skating into a sport and would ultimately lead to professionalism. But the prospects of winning badges—which were presented for three different levels of merit—had thousands of Englishmen carefully practicing the correct way of doing the prescribed figures.

The NSA was the first national skating organization to be formed, and one of its goals was to work toward international skating contests. Partly as a result of this English resolve, the International Skating Congress was held in 1892, and a governing body, the International Skating Union, was formed by Austria, Germany, Great Britain, Holland, Hungary, and Sweden.

The first ISU figure-skating championships were held in 1896. In 1898, England was host to the world championships. Many English skaters were still opposed to what they called the "Continental Style"—it was known elsewhere as the "International Style"—but the demonstration of artistic skating at the championships persuaded many English skaters that grace and style should be emphasized, after all.

U.S. Figure Skating. The National Amateur Skating Association of the United States was organized in 1886, and national championships were held before there was an official world championship event, but there was surprisingly little interest in figure skating in the country that had produced Jackson Haines. Competition here was based largely on the English method of compulsory figures which each skater had to trace.

Then Irving Brokaw visited Europe to study figure skating and, upon his return, he wrote a textbook on the sport. He also began traveling from one skating club to another along the East Coast to encourage the "International Style."

The first major breakthrough came in 1913, when the Skating Club of Boston hired a professional skater from Germany as an instructor. The following year the first United States championship of "fancy skating" was held, in New Haven, Connecticut.

At Brokaw's suggestion the New York Hippodrome in 1915 engaged an ice-ballet company from Berlin for a season. The Hippodrome also staged a series of amateur competitions in figure skating, and more than 3 million people attended the ballet or the competitions, each of them receiving a booklet on figure skating.

Theater on ice became an immediate hit from New York to Chicago. Despite World War I, figure skating in this country began to develop rapidly. In 1920 the United States for the first time sent a figure-skating team to the Winter Olympics (figure skating had been on the Olympic program as early as 1908). The Olympics—and one Olympic champion in particular—contributed greatly to the popularization of figure skating, in the United States and elsewhere during the 1920s and 1930s.

Sonja Henie. In 1924 an 11-year-old Norwegian girl entered the women's figure-skating event at the Winter Olympics. She finished last. But she returned to win Gold Medals in 1928, 1932, and 1936, in a string of 10 consecutive world championships. Then she became a professional and further popularized artistic skating in many American movies.

She was the first really international celebrity from the world of figure skating. And she also introduced an athletic approach to the sport that would have been unusual even for a male skater at the time. She was much younger—13 when she won her first world championship—than any outstanding figure skater before her, and she established figure skating as a sport for the young—at a time when it needed youthful vigor.

Sonja Henie had also studied ballet, and she brought to free skating an overall choreography that made one movement flow into another; previously, free skating had consisted of a series of stunts and figures with little relation to one another. Perhaps most important, she inspired young girls all over the world to try to emulate her. At the 1936 Olympics, Miss Henie was seriously challenged by a 15-year-old English girl, Cecilia Colledge. As a result, 200,000 people turned up at the rink in Garmisch-Partenkirchen, Germany, to watch the free skating—a crowd rarely equaled in the history of any sport.

The new youth and athleticism of the women skaters also served to influence pairs skating. No longer did the male skater have to hold himself back to keep from eclipsing his partner; now the partners could skate together on equal terms. Indeed, the women skaters now tended to overshadow the men, who didn't have the feminine charm, or the short skirts, of their female counterparts.

Dick Button. After World War II, a new American school appeared in figure skating and one of its greatest exponents, Dick Button, did for men what Sonja Henie had done for women.

The ground was laid by an Englishman, Freddie Tomlins, who was a speed skater as well as a figure skater. He used his speed in free skating, becoming the first person ever to perform a double Salchow, a leap with a 1¾-turn in midair. During World War II, Tomlins, with the Royal Air Force in Canada, gave exhibitions for war charities, and Canadians and Americans absorbed a lesson from his example.

Then there was a former Swiss ski jumper, Gustave Lussi, who became Button's teacher. Like Tomlins, Lussi emphasized athletic ability in skating. Under Lussi's tutelage, Button developed a new, vigorous, athletic style

Jim Millns and Colleen O'Connor won three consecutive national ice dancing championships. *(Bob McIntyre/U.S. Figure Skating Association.)*

that simply shattered previous conceptions of what men's figure skating should be. Like Sonja Henie, he was young—18 when he won his first Gold Medal.

Button showed that a male figure skater could be a virile, athletic performer. He did double jumps and spinning jumps, and performed his whole program with much skating speed. It was a kind of skating that couldn't be emulated, although others tried. Another American, Hayes Alan Jenkins, incorporated much of Button's athleticism into a program that also featured skating elegance and artistic expression.

In the meantime, Barbara Ann Scott of Canada tempered Sonja Henie's athletic brilliance with faultless precision and poise.

Every great figure skater is an individual—some are more athletic than others, some are flashier, some are more ballet-oriented, and some are more nearly perfect in technique. But any modern champion must present a program that incorporates all those elements, in whatever proportion.

Method of Competition. Major figure-skating events now include men's and women's singles, pairs, and ice dancing, which is a form of pairs skating quite different from figure skating.

The singles competition is made up of two parts, generally held on consecutive days. In school figures, each contestant must skate 41 prescribed patterns, which are divided into 8 tests. Each pattern is a two- or three-lobed eight; some are skated forward, some backward, some on the right foot, some on the left foot, and certain compulsory types of turns are required in some of them.

Skaters are judged quite specifically on their compulsory figures, which count toward 50 percent of the final score. In free skating, the skater must also incorporate certain figures into the routine, but in no prescribed order, and is free to use such spectacular moves as spins, jumps and dance steps. The program is skated to music and can last up to five minutes.

In championship pairs skating, male and female partners skate together, first in a 2½-min compulsory program and then in a 5-min free-skating program. Various kinds of lifts and spins make this a very exciting event for spectators.

Competitive skate dancing is a fairly recent development. Skate dancing itself dates to about 1885, but its acceptance as a sport has come very slowly. It was made part of the Olympic program in 1976, but previous attempts to get it on the program had been voted down on the grounds that ice dancing is not a sport. In championship competition, each couple has to skate four compulsory dances and one free dance of 3-min duration. Partners have to perform exactly the same steps and movements.

See also SPEED SKATING; WINTER OLYMPICS FOR OLYMPIC CHAMPIONS.

United States Champions

Men

1914	Norman N. Scott	1947	Richard T. Button
1915–17	No competition	1948	Richard T. Button
1918	Nathaniel W. Niles	1949	Richard T. Button
1919	No competition	1950	Richard T. Button
1920	Sherwin C. Badger	1951	Richard T. Button
1921	Sherwin C. Badger	1952	Richard T. Button
1922	Sherwin C. Badger	1953	Hayes Alan Jenkins
1923	Sherwin C. Badger	1954	Hayes Alan Jenkins
1924	Sherwin C. Badger	1955	Hayes Alan Jenkins
1925	Nathaniel W. Niles	1956	Hayes Alan Jenkins
1926	Chris I. Christenson	1957	David Jenkins
1927	Nathaniel W. Niles	1958	David Jenkins
1928	Roger Turner	1959	David Jenkins
1929	Roger Turner	1960	David Jenkins
1930	Roger Turner	1961	Bradley R. Lord
1931	Roger Turner	1962	Monty Hoyt
1932	Roger Turner	1963	Thomas Litz
1933	Roger Turner	1964	Scott Allen
1934	Roger Turner	1965	Gary Visconti
1935	Robin H. Lee	1966	Scott Allen
1936	Robin H. Lee	1967	Gary Visconti
1937	Robin H. Lee	1968	Tim Wood
1938	Robin H. Lee	1969	Tim Wood
1939	Robin H. Lee	1970	Tim Wood
1940	Eugene Turner	1971	John M. Petkovics
1941	Eugene Turner	1972	Ken Shelley
1942	Robert Specht	1973	Gordon McKellen
1943	Arthur R. Vaughn, Jr.	1974	Gordon McKellen
1944–45	No competition	1975	Gordon McKellen
1946	Richard T. Button	1976	Charlie Tickner

Women

1914	Theresa Weld	1926	Beatrix Loughran
1915–17	No competition	1927	Beatrix Loughran
1918	Mrs. R. S. Beresford	1928	Maribel Y. Vinson
1919	No competition	1929	Maribel Y. Vinson
1920	Theresa Weld	1930	Maribel Y. Vinson
1921	Theresa Weld Blanchard	1931	Maribel Y. Vinson
1922	Theresa Weld Blanchard	1932	Maribel Y. Vinson
1923	Theresa Weld Blanchard	1933	Maribel Y. Vinson
1924	Theresa Weld Blanchard	1934	Suzanne Davis
1925	Beatrix Loughran	1935	Maribel Y. Vinson

1936	Maribel Y. Vinson	1957	Carol Heiss
1937	Maribel Y. Vinson	1958	Carol Heiss
1938	Joan Tozzer	1959	Carol Heiss
1939	Joan Tozzer	1960	Carol Heiss
1940	Joan Tozzer	1961	Laurence R. Owen
1941	Jane Vaughn	1962	Barbara Roles Pursley
1942	Jane Vaughn Sullivan	1963	Lorraine Hanlor
1943	Gretchen Merrill	1964	Peggy Fleming
1944	Gretchen Merrill	1965	Peggy Fleming
1945	Gretchen Merrill	1966	Peggy Fleming
1946	Gretchen Merrill	1967	Peggy Fleming
1947	Gretchen Merrill	1968	Peggy Fleming
1948	Gretchen Merrill	1969	Janet Lynn
1949	Yvonne Sherman	1970	Janet Lynn
1950	Yvonne Sherman	1971	Janet Lynn
1951	Sonya Klopfer	1972	Janet Lynn
1952	Tenley Albright	1973	Janet Lynn
1953	Tenley Albright	1974	Dorothy Hamill
1954	Tenley Albright	1975	Dorothy Hamill
1955	Tenley Albright	1976	Dorothy Hamill
1956	Tenley Albright		

Pairs

1914	Jeanne Chevalier-Norman N. Scott
1915–17	No competition
1918	Theresa Weld-Nathaniel W. Niles
1919	No competition
1920	Theresa Weld-Nathaniel W. Niles
1921	Theresa Weld Blanchard-Nathaniel W. Niles
1922	Theresa Weld Blanchard-Nathaniel W. Niles
1923	Theresa Weld Blanchard-Nathaniel W. Niles
1924	Theresa Weld Blanchard-Nathaniel W. Niles
1925	Theresa Weld Blanchard-Nathaniel W. Niles
1926	Theresa Weld Blanchard-Nathaniel W. Niles
1927	Theresa Weld Blanchard-Nathaniel W. Niles
1928	Maribel Y. Vinson-Thornton Coolidge
1929	Maribel Y. Vinson-Thornton Coolidge
1930	Beatrix Loughran-Sherwin C. Badger
1931	Beatrix Loughran-Sherwin C. Badger
1932	Beatrix Loughran-Sherwin C. Badger
1933	Maribel Y. Vinson-George E. B. Hill
1934	Grace E. and James L. Madden
1935	Maribel Y. Vinson-George E. B. Hill
1936	Maribel Y. Vinson-George E. B. Hill
1937	Maribel Y. Vinson-George E. B. Hill
1938	Joan Tozzer-M. Bernard Fox
1939	Joan Tozzer-M. Bernard Fox
1940	Joan Tozzer-M. Bernard Fox
1941	Donna Atwood-Eugene Turner
1942	Doris Schubach-Walter Noffke
1943	Doris Schubach-Walter Noffke
1944	Doris Schubach-Walter Noffke
1945	Donna Jeanne Popisil-Jean Pierre Brunet
1946	Donna Jeanne Popisil-Jean Pierre Brunet
1947	Yvonne Sherman-Robert Swenning
1948	Karol and Peter Kennedy
1949	Karol and Peter Kennedy
1950	Karol and Peter Kennedy
1951	Karol and Peter Kennedy
1952	Karol and Peter Kennedy
1953	Carole Ann Ormaca-Robin Greiner
1954	Carole Ann Ormaca-Robin Greiner
1955	Carole Ann Ormaca-Robin Grenier
1956	Carole Ann Ormaca-Robin Greiner
1957	Nancy Rouillard-Ronald Ludington
1958	Nancy and Ronald Ludington
1959	Nancy and Ronald Ludington
1960	Nancy and Ronald Ludington
1961	Maribel Vinson Owen and Dudley S. Richards
1962	Dorothyann Nelson-Pieter Killen
1963	Judianne and Jerry Fothergill
1964	Judianne and Jerry Fothergill

1965 Vivian and Ronald Joseph
1966 Ronald and Cynthia Kauffman
1967 Ronald and Cynthia Kauffman
1968 Ronald and Cynthia Kauffman
1969 Ronald and Cynthia Kauffman
1970 Ken Shelley-Alicia Starbuck
1971 Ken Shelley-Jo Jo Starbuck
1972 Ken Shelley-Jo Jo Starbuck
1973 Mark and Melissa Militano
1974 Johnny Johns-Melissa Militano
1975 Johnny Johns-Melissa Militano
1976 Randy Gardner-Tai Babilonia

Ice Dancing

1960 Margie Ackles-Charles W. Phillips, Jr.
1961 Diane Sherbloom-Larry Pierce
1962 Yvonne Littlefield-Peter F. Betts
1963 Sally Schautz-Stanley Urban
1964 Darleen Streick-Charles Fetter, Jr.
1965 Kristin Fortune-Dennis Sveum
1966 Kristin Fortune-Dennis Sveum
1967 John Carroll-Lorna Dyer
1968 Judy Schwomeyer-James Sladky
1969 Judy Schwomeyer-James Sladky
1970 Judy Schwomeyer-James Sladky
1971 Judy Schwomeyer-James Sladky
1972 James Sladky-Judy Schwomeyer
1973 Mary Ann Campbell-Johnny Johns
1974 Colleen O'Connor-Jim Millns
1975 Colleen O'Connor-Jim Millns
1976 Colleen O'Connor Jim Millns

Bibliography. Brown, Nigel: *Ice Skating*, A. S. Barnes, New York, 1959; Owen, Maribel: *The Fun of Figure Skating*, Harper, New York, 1960.

FISHING—Strictly speaking, fishing is a recreation, not a competitive sport. However, there are a large number of fishing tournaments in which, during a specified period of time, fishermen compete for prizes awarded for the largest fish of a particular species, the greatest number of fish, greatest total weight of catch, and the like.

The world's largest such event is the Metropolitan Miami Fishing Tournament. Other important events are the New Orleans Big Game Fishing Club Invitational; the Hilton Head, South Carolina, Invitational; and the Hatteras Marlin Club Marlin Tournament.

Still Fishing. The most popular type of fishing is the simplest: In still fishing, the fisherman baits his hook, drops it into the water, and waits for fish to bite. Equipment normally includes a long pole, a line that is somewhat longer than the pole, a "floater" or "bobber" which can be adjusted to keep the hook at the desired depth, a sinker that takes the hook down, and the hook itself. In some cases the fisherman doesn't use a pole at all. Instead he uses a hand line or throw line—the latter is weighted heavily so the fisherman can throw it well out into the water.

Commonly used baits include worms and minnows in fresh water, and various types of worms, shrimp, bits of crab, squid, and other sea creatures for salt water. Artificial lures can also be used for still fishing.

Fly Casting. Artificial flies can be used for freshwater or saltwater fishing. The flies are made of feathers, thread, and other materials, tied directly on the hook. Rather heavy line is required, since the fly itself is too light to be cast by its own weight. Selection of the right line is very important. Size is determined either by diameter or weight; there are level, single-taper, double-taper, and forward-taper fly lines available in many sizes; and there are floating, sinking, and intermediate types of lines.

Sinking lines, usually made of Dacron, are used with wet flies, which must sink into the water. Floating lines are used with dry flies, which float on top of the water. Intermediate lines will normally sink, but can be made to float by applying a special dressing. Level lines have the same dimension throughout; tapered lines drop lightly onto the water, while forward-taper ("torpedo-head") lines allow for longer casts. Double-taper line is tapered at both ends so it can be reversed when one end becomes worn.

There are also many types and sizes of hooks available.

Once used only for catching trout, fly fishing is now used for any type of fish that will strike an artificial fly or other light lure. Saltwater fly fishing has become popular only in recent years. The equipment is similar to that used in freshwater fishing, but the fly line must be backed with a heavier line, since saltwater fish are generally larger than freshwater fish. The line must also be carefully cleaned and dressed after use, to get all the salt out of it.

Bait Casting. In bait casting, the fisherman uses relatively heavy artificial lures that can be cast by their own weight. Plugs are solid lures of wood or plastic, usually painted to look like small fish, mice, or frogs. When reeled in, they make lifelike movements. Spoons are metal lures, shaped like shoehorns, that make dodging movements when reeled in. Spinners are pieces of metal that spin around a wire axis when reeled in. In bait casting, light lines are used and the lures are cast out a fairly long distance and then reeled in. The depth of a sinking lure can be regulated by the speed of the retrieve; the faster it is reeled in, the higher it will ride in the water.

Spinning. A relatively recent innovation, spinning came to the United States in 1936. Rather light lures are used—⅛- to ½-oz for fresh water, 1 to 3 oz for salt water.

The spinning rod has a long cork handle and a reel that releases line automatically during the cast. The spool doesn't rotate, so the spincaster does not have to cope with backlashes. Spinning tackle can be used for almost any type of fishing that involves casting.

Surf Casting. As the name implies, surf casting involves casting into the surf near the shore. A relatively long rod and heavy tackle are used. In many cases the surf caster uses heavy spinning tackle. This is a popular method of fishing in many areas on the Atlantic and Pacific coasts.

Deep-Sea Fishing. The ultimate in sport fishing as far as many people are concerned, deep-sea fishing is done from a rather large boat in deep water, and there are several types of fishing and many kinds of tackle involved. In still fishing, the boat is anchored, and bait is thrown into the water to attract fish to the area. Then natural bait is used on the hooks. In drifting, the boat is not anchored, and the baited hooks are permitted to drift in the water with the boat. In trolling, the baited hooks are pulled along behind the boat, which travels at a speed of 5 or 6 mph.

Records. Records of the largest saltwater game fishes caught are kept by the International Game Fish Association. The magazine *Field and Stream* keeps track of freshwater fishing records.

See also CASTING.

Bibliography. Cone, Arthur L., Jr.: *Fishing Made Easy,* Macmillan, New York, 1968; Gabrielson, Ira N. and Francesa LaMonte (eds.): *The Fisherman's Encyclopedia,* Stackpole, Harrisburg, Pa., 1954.

FLAG FOOTBALL—A kind of touch football in which a defender has to pull a flag (or handkerchief or similar object) from the pocket of the player who has the ball, instead of merely touching the ball carrier.
See also TOUCH FOOTBALL.

FLIGHT ARCHERY—Archery competition in which only distance, not accuracy, counts.
See also ARCHERY.

FLYING RINGS—A gymnastics event in which competitors perform on a pair of rings slung freely from a bar.
See also GYMNASTICS.

FOIL—A fencing weapon with a flexible, rectangular blade.
See also FENCING.

FOOTBALL—In 1969, the National Collegiate Athletic Association (NCAA) proudly observed the centennial of college football, celebrating the famous Rutgers-Princeton game of November 6, 1869. But the game played that day was actually soccer—which is what "football' means in virtually every country but ours. The teams had goalies; scores were made only by kicking the ball between goalposts, as in soccer; players were not allowed to run with the ball or to throw it.

As a matter of fact, soccer might still be a major college sport in the United States, except that Harvard refused to play. When Yale, Princeton, Columbia, and Rutgers met in 1873 to organize the Intercollegiate Football Association, the rules they adopted were based on the London Football (soccer) Association rules. Harvard declined the invitation to attend because Harvard had its own kind of football: the Boston game, which was similar to Rugby, in that a player could hold the ball, and, if pursued, could run with it.

The Beginnings: 1874–1912

It would be more accurate to say that American football was born on May 14, 1874, when a Harvard team played a team from McGill University of Montreal. On that day they played the Boston game. The following day they played Rugby—which used an egg-shaped ball much closer in shape to the modern football than the spherical soccer ball. Harvard players enjoyed Rugby, too, and adopted it, with some modifications, as their version of football.

In 1875, Yale and Harvard agreed on a set of "Concessionary Rules" that combined some elements of Rugby with some elements of soccer, and the first Harvard-Yale "football" game was played, Harvard winning 4-1. That game persuaded Princeton to switch from soccer to the Rugby-style football, and in 1876 a new Intercollegiate Football Association was organized, with Harvard, Yale, Princeton, Rutgers, and Columbia joining.

Walter Camp was a freshman at Yale in that first year of the reorganized IFA, and he was a pretty fair player. But Camp was to make much more important contributions to the sport off the field. He felt, after four years of playing this American Rugby-soccer, that the game was too disorganized. In 1880, Camp proposed a rules change that really began the evolution of a new sport: Instead of the continuous play of Rugby and soccer, with teams continually switching back and forth from offense to defense, he suggested that a team should be given possession of the ball for a period of time, with play stopping when the ball was dead and resuming when the ball was put into play from scrimmage.

The idea was adopted. Two other major rules changes that year set the number of players at 11 per team and reduced the size of the field from the old dimensions, 140 by 70 yd, to 110 by 53 yd. With the new scrimmage, a team could keep possession of the ball for as long as it could run plays without fumbling or otherwise losing the ball. The center began play by kicking the ball backward to the quarterback, who could not run with it, but had to pass it off to a teammate. This enabled a team to run planned plays from set formations.

In 1881, Yale and Princeton played a strange game—each team thought that a tie would give it the IFA championship. As a result, Princeton held on to the ball without genuinely attempting to score for almost all of the first half, and Yale repeated the procedure during the entire second half. Despite planned plays and set formations,

Walter Camp, shown here as a member of the 1879 Yale team, was a major force in shaping modern American football. *(Courtesy of Yale University.)*

the game was a bore, and Camp realized that there had to be some kind of incentive to make the offensive team try to move the ball.

So, in 1882, another major step toward modern football was taken—a rule requiring a team to gain 5 yd, or lose 10, in three downs, to retain possession of the ball; that is, to continue functioning as the offensive team. This established a new kind of game, one that was to remain essentially unchanged for nearly a quarter of a century.

The Flying Wedge. Yale was usually the team to beat during the nineteenth century, and not many other teams could do it. The Elis won 41 games in a row between 1876 and 1887; they won 10 intercollegiate championships in an 18-year period, 1883–1900. One good reason was Camp, first as a player, then as coach—though his official title was "chief football advisor," since it was usually the team's captain who made game decisions on substitutions, tactics, and the like.

It was Princeton, however, that came up with the V trick, a tactic soon to develop into the feared flying wedge that, in a negative way, brought the next major innovation in football. During an 1884 game against Pennsylvania, the Princeton quarterback invented a play in which offensive players formed a V to protect the ballplayer. It resulted in an immediate touchdown. The next step, also taken by Princeton, was to have the players in the V lock arms to give the ball carrier even more protection. The V trick remained a popular play until 1892, when Harvard turned it into the flying wedge. At that time there was no kickoff; a team was simply given the ball at midfield to start the game or the second half. When Harvard was given the ball at the beginning of the second half, nine players formed a moving V and swept past the ball; the quarterback handed it to halfback Charlie Brewer, and he ran 30 yd, until tripping over one of his own players at the Yale 20-yd line.

Other variations were tried by other teams, for plays from scrimmage. A. A. Stagg in 1890 invented the ends-back formation, in which the ends lined up 5 yd behind the line of scrimmage, in order to develop momentum before making their blocks. George Woodruff at Penn invented the guards-back formation; Camp devised a tackles-back formation. Increasingly the emphasis was on brutal power plays, and the growing injury lists showed it. In 1896 the flying wedge was prohibited on kickoffs, and restrictions were placed on other "mass momentum" plays. But that was just a stopgap measure.

By 1900, collegiate football was a truly national sport. Eastern schools were still strong, but they were being challenged for national supremacy by the Western Conference (now the Big Ten). In 1902, Michigan's first "Point-a-Minute" team, coached by Fielding "Hurry Up" Yost, outscored its opposition, 501 to 0, and walloped Stanford, 49-0, in the first Rose Ball game—piling up 1,463 yd in 142 plays from scrimmage! The University of Chicago, under A. A. Stagg, also had fine teams shortly after the turn of the century.

However, the brutality of the sport was bringing protests from many quarters; 18 collegiate football players were killed in 1905, and President Theodore Roosevelt told college athletic leaders that they had better do something about their sport if they didn't want it banned. The result was the first step toward formation of the National Collegiate Athletic Association.

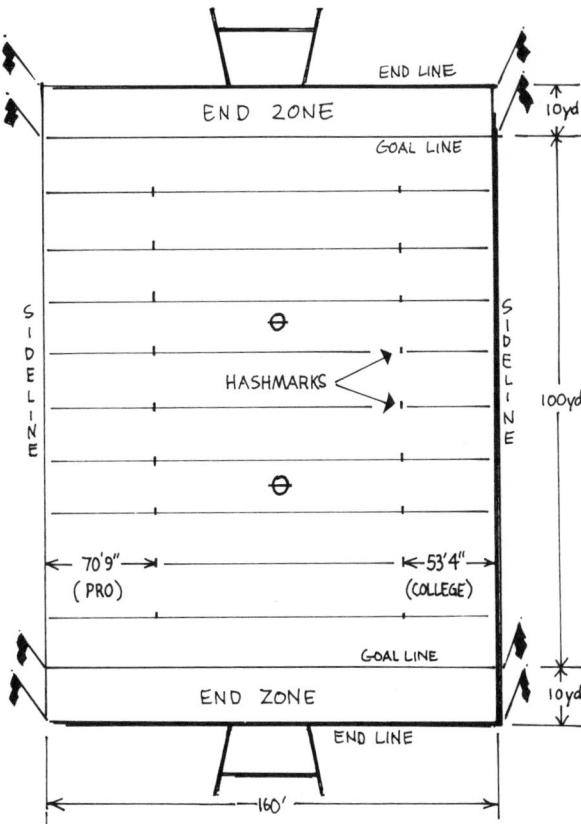

Football field: Goal posts are 18'4" apart, in professional football; 23'6" apart in college football.

The Forward Pass. Representatives of 62 colleges and universities met in New York on December 28, 1905 to form the Intercollegiate Athletic Association. The prime purpose, at that point, was to draw up a new set of football rules. Adopted at another meeting, on January 12, 1906, major rules changes created a neutral zone between the offensive and defensive lines; required the offense to have at least six men on the line of scrimmage when the ball was snapped; increased first-down yardage from 5 to 10; and made the forward pass legal for the first time.

Though they represented a step in the right direction, these changes weren't enough. Indeed, in the 1909 season, the death toll in college football was up to 33. More changes were made in 1910: Seven offensive players were required on the line of scrimmage, and interlocked interference, pushing or pulling the ball carrier, and the flying tackle were outlawed. Two years later, the offense was given a fourth down on which to try for first-down yardage, the length of the field was reduced from 110 to 100 yd, and the game was opened up by removing the 20-yd limit on the forward pass.

In addition, the scoring system, after a great deal of juggling through the years, was brought to its modern state in 1912. In 1875 a touchdown didn't count for any points at all—it simply allowed a team to have a free try for a goal. The following year, however, a touchdown became the equivalent of 1 point, with a goal worth 4 points. In 1883 the same system was used, but a team scoring four touchdowns would be given a victory over a team scoring a single goal. As time went on, a touchdown acquired more and more value. It became worth 2 points in 1883, 4 points in 1884, and 5 points in 1897, with the goal after touchdown (extra point) worth 1 and the field goal worth 5 points. In 1904 the value of the field goal was reduced to 4 points, and in 1909 it was cut to 3. Finally, in 1912, the value of a touchdown was raised to 6 points, and the scoring system has remained the same ever since (except for the possibility of a 2-point conversion, now allowed under high-school and college rules).

So, by 1912, the sport had become less rough, which was the purpose of most of the rules changes. Probably the most important rules, in that respect, were those requiring a minimum number of players on the line of scrimmage, and the prohibition of interlocked interference. But the sport had also, by then, evolved into an entirely new sport. The emphasis had shifted from scoring goals, by kicking, to scoring touchdowns, by crossing the opposition's goal line. And there were now two ways of doing that, from anywhere on the field: by running with the ball or by throwing it.

The forward pass is the unique feature of American football—the feature that sets it apart from Rugby, in the same way that allowing a player to run with the ball sets Rugby apart from soccer. Thus a purist could say, with some accuracy, that American football was really born in 1906, and came of age in 1912. Or, perhaps, in 1913.

Modern College Football

Changing Formations. Changing rules had brought changing strategy and tactics. One of the first offensive sets was the T formation. It was a way of preserving a form of the old, forbidden "mass momentum" play. The quarterback stood close to the center, to receive the kickback, then turned and lateraled to one of three backs (that is, tossed the ball laterally to one of them), while the other two, often helped by the quarterback, formed a moving vanguard of blockers.

When the center snap replaced the kickback, the quarterback could now take a direct handback from the center (who handed the ball, through his legs, to the quarterback). But it also became possible for the center to snap the ball accurately—to pass it backwards—to a back stationed 5 yd or more behind the center. So the single-wing formation evolved. The quarterback stayed where he had been, but the center moved over, and could now snap the ball to either of two deep backs (stationed relatively far behind the line of scrimmage). A wingback, close to the line of scrimmage, became a blocker, along with the quarterback; since seven players had to be on the line of scrimmage, backs close to the line replaced the old guards-back and tackles-back of previous offensive formations.

The single-wing was a power formation. Its basic play was the off-tackle smash, which massed blocking at the point of attack. Then came the end run, followed by the cutback, which looked like an end run, but was actually a delayed variation of the off-tackle play. When defenses

began to concentrate on the basic plays, the wingback reverse was introduced.

It turned out that the single-wing could also be used for pass plays. Until 1945, the passer had to be at least 5 yd behind the line of scrimmage, and the single-wing tailback was already at least that far back. To increase the passing threat, Glenn "Pop" Warner developed the double-wing formation, which could get four receivers into the secondary very quickly. Warner is also credited with inventing the backfield shift, in 1900. Shifts were common throughout the 1920s and 1930s—a team would line up in one formation and shift into another.

The single- and double-wing formations were dominant until the T came back in the 1940s. But one great football school usually preferred its own formation—the Notre Dame box formation, invented by Coach Jesse C. Harper to take advantage of the new rules and the unusual skills of two talented players.

Dorais to Rockne. Notre Dame was not known as a football power in 1913. And Harper's Notre Dame box formation didn't impress many other coaches. With a balanced line and split ends, it lacked the power of the single wing. The fullback was too deep to get to the line of scrimmage quickly and the wingback, outflanked by his own end, could not be an effective blocker. But Harper had a small team, and he felt he could use the formation for deception rather than power. He also thought it would make the pass an effective weapon. And, in a back and an end respectively named Charles E. "Gus" Dorais and Knute Rockne, he had the players who could use the weapon. The two of them spent the summer throwing a football around at a resort.

Little Notre Dame came up against powerhouse Army on November 1, 1913, and Dorais completed 13 of 17 passes for 243 yards as the Irish turned in a stunning upset, 35-13. When the Cadets finally began to cover Dorais' pass receivers, Notre Dame used running plays to advance the ball. It was a victory that not only launched Notre Dame as a football power; it also showed the potential of the forward pass, which until then had generally been used only in desperation.

The Golden Age. The forward pass in football, like the home run in baseball, also created new excitement and new fans. The United States in the 1920s was eagerly receptive to sports, anyway, but the dull games of the era before the forward pass would probably not have been welcomed by the new breed of American: the sports fan who would attend a game that promised to be exciting, even though having no particular rooting interest.

The fact that the sport could attract fans also interested more colleges in it. Following Notre Dame's example, other schools began to play intersectional games. The Southwestern Conference began play in 1915. Georgia Tech was the first major football power in the South, but other Southern schools quickly followed Tech's lead. Andy Smith left Penn in 1916 to turn California into a West Coast power, and in 1924 "Pop" Warner went to Stanford to install his double-wing attack.

The growth of collegiate football into a national sport is shown by the All-American teams. Once dominated by players from Eastern schools, with an occasional Midwesterner sprinkled in, the All-American teams began to include players from all over the country.

The time was ripe for superstars, and they arrived on

cue. Harold "Red" Grange, the "Galloping Ghost" of the University of Illinois, as a junior in 1924 handled the ball four times in the first 17 min against Michigan and scored all four times, on runs of 95, 67, 56, and 44 yd. Later he passed for a touchdown and scored yet another himself. Michigan gave up only 55 points that year; Grange scored 30 of them. On a muddy field, against previously unbeaten Penn, Grange in 1925 scored three touchdowns, gaining 363 yd in 36 carries, while leading Illinois to a 24-2 win.

Meanwhile, Notre Dame and Knute Rockne (now as coach) had the "Four Horsemen": Elmer Layden, Harry Stuldreher, Jim Crowley, and Don Miller. They were small, but Rockne's Notre Dame box, an adaptation of Harper's formation, emphasized backfield speed, and the Four Horsemen led Notre Dame to 29 victories in 31 games during their three-year career, including a 27-10 victory over Stanford in the 1925 Rose Bowl.

Stanford had a great All-American of its own: Ernie Nevers, a triple-threat fullback. Pop Warner, who coached him at Stanford, said Nevers was a greater player than the legendary Jim Thorpe—and Warner had coached Thorpe, too, at Carlisle Institute. Appearing in that Rose Bowl contest with both legs so heavily bandaged that the circulation was almost cut off, and receiving occasional shots of Novocain to deaden the pain, Nevers played the entire 60 min, gained 142 yd offensively, was a linebacker on defense and intercepted a pass, and averaged 42 yd per punt as a kicker.

During the 1920s Knute Rockne was one of the best-known and most admired men in the country, in any field. In 13 seasons he produced five unbeaten teams. When he was killed in a plane crash in 1931, an entire nation mourned.

More Passing. During the 1930s the forward pass became even more prominent in college football. The "razzle-dazzle" Southwestern Conference, particularly Southern Methodist University under Ray Morrison, had led the way. Morrison built his offense around the pass during the twenties, producing unbeaten teams in 1923 and 1926. Other colleges followed suit, especially schools that had small players who couldn't meet bigger players head-to-head to win supremacy on the ground.

Another series of rules changes, in 1934, also favored the use of the pass: The ball assumed its present size, which made it a good deal easier to throw. Previously, any pass thrown incomplete in the end zone had been considered a touchback, but now a team was allowed to throw one incomplete pass into the end zone on a series of downs, except on fourth down. And the former 5-yd penalty for the second incompletion in a series of downs was eliminated.

Single-wing tailbacks of the day still had to be triple-threats, but many of them were much better passers than they were runners or kickers. There was Harry Newman, for example, who led Michigan to an undefeated season in 1932, when Coach Harry Kipke used "a punt, a pass and a prayer" as his formula for winning. Alabama won the 1935 Rose Bowl over Stanford with passes from Millard "Dixie" Howell to Don Hutson. At Texas Christian, "Dutch" Myers installed a spread formation to get five receivers quickly into the secondary, and two great passers—first Sammy Baugh and then Davey O'Brien—made it work. O'Brien led the 1938 team to an undefeated

Harold "Red" Grange, the "Galloping Ghost," was a three-time All-American at Illinois, 1923–1925, and was also named to the first All-Pro team, in 1931. *(Pro Football Hall of Fame.)*

season and a Sugar Bowl win.

There were coaches and schools, though, that still believed in the single-wing's off-tackle power. Among them were Pittsburgh and Jock Sutherland, Tennessee and Gen. Robert R. Neyland, Minnesota and Bernie Bierman, Texas A & M and Homer Norton; and the Fordham teams that played Pittsburgh to three consecutive scoreless ties (1935–1937) on the strength of the "Seven Blocks of Granite" who formed their forward wall were in the same tradition.

The T Formation. The T had been one of football's first offensive formations. It had been used occasionally in the 1930s. The professional Chicago Bears had used it almost constantly. A man in motion had been tried, also occasionally, to keep defenses from ganging up on the middle. But the T hadn't worked very well for very long for anybody.

Then along came Clark Shaughnessy, one of the true coaching geniuses. He left the University of Chicago when that school gave up football, after the 1939 season, and arrived at Stanford, which had won one, lost seven, and tied one in 1939. Shaughnessy had been thinking about the T formation, and he decided it might suit the material available at Stanford. His squad didn't have a real triple-threat. Tailback Frankie Albert, who became Shaughnessy's T-formation quarterback, was a rather small, deft, left-handed passer. Norm Standlee was a powerful fullback. Hugh Gallarnau and Pete Kmetovic were both quick-starting halfbacks, Gallarnau big enough to power off tackle, and Kmetovic fast enough to be a threat either as an outside runner or as a potential pass receiver when he went in motion. (An outside runner's

Felix "Doc" Blanchard, an All-American fullback and Heisman Trophy winner at Army, scores a touchdown in the classic Army-Navy game of 1946. Army won, 21–18. *(Public Broadcasting Service.)*

path follows an essentially lateral course, around or near the extremities of an opposing team's line; the so-called inside runner pursues a more direct course into the section of an opposing line near its middle.)

Shaughnessy didn't invent the formation nor, as some writers have suggested, did he invent the man-in-motion off the T. What he did was to develop a philosophy of T-formation football, a system that would make the formation more flexible than any other coach had ever believed it could be. The key was a quarterback who could handle the ball and throw it well, and Albert was the perfect choice as the pioneer.

The T's first threat was a quick-opening "dive" to the halfback over tackle. Power blocking wasn't needed; offensive guard, tackle, and end could simply brush-block or screen-block defensive linemen for a second or so, enough time for the halfback to travel 5 yd, which would take him beyond the hole opened in the opposing line. The second threat was a fake to this halfback and a handoff to the fullback, hitting a different hole. The third threat was a fake to both backs, followed by a forward pass. There were many other possible plays, of course, and one halfback usually went in motion, pulling a defensive player to the outside and at the same time getting into a position from which to run a pass pattern.

The T formation quickly took on many other shapes. Lou Little of Columbia eliminated the man in motion and instead put a halfback on the wing; thus the "winged T." But Don Faurot of Missouri invented the variation that ruled much of college football for a long time—the split T. In a sense, Faurot carried Shaughnessy's ideas to their logical conclusion. If linemen were going to use brush-blocking, instead of trying to open holes in the opposing line through sheer power, the holes could be created by splitting the linemen, so their chief job would be to keep them open. Faurot then developed two simple, basic plays. The quarterback, instead of meeting the halfback halfway to the line of scrimmage, would slide along the line and give the halfback the ball just before the latter got to the hole. Or the quarterback would fake to the halfback and continue along the line to run the split-T option play.

The beauty of the option is that no block at all is required to get the key defender—end or outside linebacker—out of the play. If this defender goes after the trailing halfback, the quarterback cuts inside, keeps pos-

session of the ball, and runs. If the defender goes after the quarterback, the ball is pitched by the latter to the trailing halfback.

The split T was the formation of 1950s and some of the 1960s. So we have raced ahead of the story. Stanford went undefeated in 1940, then beat powerful Nebraska, 21-13, in the Rose Bowl. And Albert was an All-American that year and the next. But single-wing teams still flourished. Tailback Tom Harmon of Michigan won the Heisman Trophy in 1940, and tailback Bruce Smith of Minnesota won it in 1941. Frank Sinkwich of Georgia and Bill Dudley of Virginia were both All-American halfbacks in the triple-threat mold.

But the trend to the T was virtually irresistible. Frank Leahy installed it at Notre Dame, where quarterback Angelo Bertelli entered military service, to be replaced by an outstanding sophomore, Johnny Lujack. And Earl Blaik installed it at Army. But Army, with Glenn Davis and Doc Blanchard—"Mr. Outside" and "Mr. Inside," the "Touchdown Twins"—would have had a great offense using any formation. During their three years together, 1944–1946, the Cadets won 27 games and tied 1, without a loss. The tie came in 1946, a scoreless battle with Notre Dame. In 1947, Lujack led Notre Dame to the National championship; in 1948 it was Michigan; in 1949, Notre Dame again—and end Leon Hart became the second lineman in history to win the Heisman Trophy.

The 1950s. The 1948 season can be considered a pivotal one in college football. Free substitution had been approved by the College Football Rules Committee in 1941, but World War II made it hard for colleges to field a team complement of 11 men, without trying to field special platoons for offense and defense. The rule allowed free substitution only when the clock was stopped. In 1948, however, the clock was stopped every time the ball changed hands, and the way was paved for two-platoon football. The new arrangement did not take full effect for a time, however, because it meant training players for their specialties. By 1950 the great majority of football colleges were fielding two platoons. One was in action when the team had possession of the ball and was attempting to score; the other saw action when the opposing team had gained possession.

It was in 1948, Bud Wilkinson's second year of coaching the split T at Oklahoma, that the Sooners began a 31-game winning streak. After a loss to Kentucky in the 1951 Sugar Bowl, and a loss to Notre Dame in 1952, Oklahoma reeled off another unbeaten streak of 47 games. During an 11-

year period, 1948–1958, Oklahoma teams won 107 games, lost 7, and tied 3—including bowl contests.

The two-platoon system was eliminated, over the objections of most coaches, in 1953, but the split T remained the dominant offense and Oklahoma the dominant school through most of the decade. Jim Tatum produced strong teams at Maryland and Woody Hayes ruled at Ohio State with a running offense built aroung the split T. Two schools that didn't go to the split T, entirely, were Michigan State, where Biggie Munn used a multiple offense that included single-wing, double-wing, and spread formations, and UCLA, under Red Sanders, one of the last major colleges to use the single-wing exclusively.

Two major rules changes were made at the end of the decade. In 1958 the optional two-point conversion, to be scored by running or passing from the 3-yd line, was added. And in 1959 the goal posts were set farther apart: 23 ft, 14 in, as opposed to the former 18 ft, 6 in.

The 1960s and 1970s. More new formations and the restoration of the two-platoon system highlighted the 1960s in college football. The rules committee again legalized free substitution in 1965. The pure split T gave way to other kinds of option attacks: the "belly T," in which the quarterback puts the ball into the first back's belly and rides with that player momentarily before deciding whether to let the player have the ball or pull it back; the veer, developed by Bill Yeomans of Houston; and the wishbone, invented by a Texas high school coach and adopted by Darrell Royal at the University of Texas and then by other college coaches.

An earlier, and still popular formation, is the I, developed by Tom Nugent during the 1950s. In the I formation, the running backs line up, one behind the other, behind the quarterback. A variation is the "power I," in which a third back lines up alongside one front back in the I, for additional blocking power. Often a team will line up in the I and then shift into a variation of the T.

The wishbone is similar to the ordinary T, except that the fullback lines up much closer to the line of scrimmage than the halfbacks. This enables him to hit a hole, either as a runner or a blocker, very quickly, putting additional pressure on the defense. All four backs are running backs out of the wishbone, and the quarterback, if he fakes to the fullback, has the same options available to him as in the split T.

Paul "Bear" Bryant's Alabama teams won two national championships and shared another during the 1960s, with a fine succession of quarterbacks: Joe Namath, Steve Sloan, and Kenny Stabler. Notre Dame, under Ara Parseghian, again became a national power. Woody Hayes's Ohio State teams were consistent winners, and a Hayes disciple, Glenn "Bo" Schembechler, went to Michigan to produce teams that challenged Ohio State for the conference championship, and a trip to the Rose Bowl, year after year. In the Southwest, Darrell Royal produced powerhouses at Texas, first with the belly T and then with the wishbone, and Oklahoma switched to the wishbone and became a power once again. The Sooners, however, were often overshadowed in their own conference, the Big Eight, by a succession of outstanding Nebraska teams turned out by Bob Devaney. From 1963 through 1972 the Cornhuskers won three national titles and eight conference championships, and shared another.

The other major national power during the period was Southern California, coached by John McKay. The Trojans were national champions in 1962 and 1967 and went to the Rose Bowl five times in 11 years.

Professional Football

John Braillier has generally been singled out as the first professional football player; he received $10 in 1895 to play quarterback for the Latrobe, Pennsylvania, YMCA team in a game against a team from nearby Jeannette. However, the Pro Football Hall of Fame has evidence that W. W. "Pudge" Heffelfinger received $500 to play for the Duquesne Athletic Club in Pittsburgh during 1893, and it appears that there was actually a professional league that year. As far as can be determined, the league didn't complete a full season.

There were two fairly important professional games in 1902. In an indoor game at Madison Square Garden in New York, Syracuse professionals beat a Philadelphia team, 6-0. Another Philadelphia team, the Athletics, was organized by Connie Mack and named after his baseball team. Mack claimed the world championship after his Athletics beat a Pittsburgh team.

These, however, were eccentricities. The real beginnings of pro football as we know it lay in semiprofessional town teams, most of them concentrated in Ohio and western Pennsylvania. The pattern was rather simple: A local athletic club would organize a football team, then bolster its roster by hiring an outside player or two. The Morgan Athletic Club in Chicago had a well-organized team as early as 1898, and the St. Louis (formerly

George Halas, at right, founded, coached, and played for the Decatur Staleys in 1920. They became the Chicago Bears in 1922. In 40 years of coaching, Halas won 320 games and seven NFL championships. (*Pro Football Hall of Fame.*)

Chicago) Cardinals of the modern National Football League can trace their lineage to the Morgans.

But it was in Ohio towns like Massillon, Canton, Dayton, Columbus, and Youngstown that important rivalries were established—rivalries that were to lead to the hiring of more and more outsiders. Canton paid Michigan All-American Willie Heston $500 to play the 1905 season; he broke his leg in the first game, ending his career. (Heston had starred on the "point-a-minute" teams that went unbeaten in 56 consecutive games.) By 1915 a group of college stars were performing for various semipro teams in Ohio. Knute Rockne and Gus Dorais of Notre Dame played for a number of teams; most important, Jim Thorpe and his former Carlisle Institute teammate, Pete Calac, signed with the Canton Bulldogs.

Thorpe, of course, is one of the legendary athletes, and by 1915 he was already a legend. He had been an All-American at Carlisle, coached by "Pop" Warner. He had been acclaimed "the greatest athlete in the world" after winning both the pentathlon and the decathlon in the 1912 Olympics—and then he had been forced to return his medals when it was discovered that he had played semipro baseball one summer. He had, by 1915, played parts of three major-league baseball seasons, with the New York Giants, and he would play parts of three more seasons in the majors, finishing up with a .327 batting average in 62 games in 1919. Above all, Thorpe was a drawing card. Fans came out to see him. And that fact was an indication of the potential that lay buried in this new professional sport, which was to retain its town-team look for many more years.

By 1919, the professionalism was getting out of hand. Thorpe was firmly attached to the Canton team, but many college players would sign to play one game with one team, the next game with another. Joseph F. Carr, manager of the Columbus Panhandles, realized that this would hurt the sport by making it impossible for local fans to build up any sense of identification with their supposedly home-town teams. A second problem was that colleges were growing increasingly upset about professional teams that would hire a player still in college for a game or two.

Carr suggested that existing professional teams should form an alliance, agreeing not to tamper with one another's players and not to use any players who still had college eligibility. The alliance was organized rather informally in July of 1919. The original teams in the American Professional Football Association were Akron, Canton, Cleveland, Columbus, Dayton, Detroit, Hammond (Indiana), Massillon, Rochester (New York), Rock Island (Illinois), Toledo, and Wheeling (West Virginia). Membership cost $25 a team. There was no formal schedule and no official records of the 1919 season were kept, but Canton and Massillon played what was considered a championship game, and Thorpe's field goal won for Canton, 3-0.

In 1920, the association was reorganized. The admission price for member teams was now $100. Thorpe was elected president, primarily because of the publicity value of his name, and among new teams joining was the Staley A.C. of Decatur, Illinois, managed by George Halas, who also played end. Again, no formal records were kept, but the Akron Pros, who were not only unbeaten but unscored upon, were generally considered champions.

Another reorganization took place in 1921, with Carr elected to the presidency. One of the new franchises went to the Green Bay Packers, who had been organized in 1919 by Earl L. "Curly" Lambeau. Although official standings show the Staleys, ancestor of the National Football League team now in Chicago, as the 1921 champions, Buffalo players were given championship gold footballs after beating the Staleys, 7-6, in the last game of the season. The Staleys, however, beat Buffalo in a postseason game billed in Chicago as the championship contest, and the modern standings reflect that view.

Two important name changes were made in 1922: Halas renamed his team the Bears and, at his suggestion, the APFA became the National Football League (NFL). For the first time, scheduling was more formalized, and official standings were kept. The Canton Bulldogs, coached by Berlin Guy Chamberlin, an end from Nebraska, were clear-cut champions, with a 10-0-2 record, and they repeated in 1923 with an 11-0-1 record. There were 20 franchises that year; the number dropped to 18 in 1924, and the Canton Bulldogs moved to Cleveland—and won their third straight championship.

In 1925 came a major controversy about the championship. The Pottsville Maroons and the Chicago Cardinals played for the title, and Pottsville won, 21-7. The Maroons then played a postseason exhibition game against a collection of Notre Dame all-stars, in Philadelphia, bringing a protest from the Frankford Yellowjackets that their territorial rights had been violated. To punish Pottsville, President Carr told the Cardinals to play another game. They easily beat a Milwaukee team, which used some high school players. That victory gave the Cardinals a better record than Pottsville, and they were awarded the championship—despite the fact that Carr canceled the Milwaukee franchise because of the use of high school players, and suspended the team's "manager," Arthur Folz, for life. Strangely enough, Folz was on the Cardinals' roster, as a quarterback.

Red Grange. All of this went virtually unnoticed, except in Pottsville. The National Football League was making big headlines in a different, and much more positive, way. Immediately after playing his last college game at Illinois, "Red" Grange signed a contract with the Chicago Bears and joined them on a barnstorming tour in 1925. It was not a complete success; Grange was injured or tired and below par in a number of the 18 games, but the Bears drew 73,000 fans in New York, and exposed whole new sections of the country, including the South and the West Coast, to professional football.

Grange had not signed directly with the Bears. He had signed a personal-services contract with C. C. "Cash and Carry" Pyle, who in turn sold Grange's services to the Bears for the barnstorming tour. Pyle wanted an NFL franchise in New York City but the league wouldn't give him one—so he formed his own American Football League, with Grange as the headliner, playing for the New York Yankees.

Fortunately, the owner of the Duluth Eskimos of the NFL, Ole Haugsrud, had been a high school friend of another great All-American of 1925, Ernie Nevers of Stanford. Haugsrud signed Nevers and agreed that the Eskimos would be a road team, to give every other team in the league a chance to have a Nevers-augmented gate. In 1926 the Eskimos played 29 games, league and exhibition, in 117 days, and Nevers was in all but 27 min of the action. Virtually all the franchises suffered from the inter-league war—there were 31 of them in 1926, and only 12 remained in 1927—but Haugsrud and Nevers certainly helped save some of them.

The AFL folded after the 1926 season, so did 11 of the NFL's 22 teams, and Grange's New York Yankees joined the NFL in 1927. The New York Giants won their first championship that year. The league was down to 10 teams in 1928, as player-coach Jimmy Conzelman led the Providence Steamrollers to a title.

The First Packer Dynasty. Curly Lambeau had always liked the forward pass as a basic offensive weapon, perhaps because he had played at Notre Dame for one season, 1918, under the young Rockne. Forced by tonsilitis to go home to Green Bay before completing his freshman year, Lambeau had got a job instead of returning to college and then, after a year away from football, had formed his own team.

The Packers had built a solid nucleus of players, among them Red Dunn and Lavvie Dilweg, a fine passing combination from Marquette, and Verne Lewellen, an outstanding all-around back from Nebraska. But in 1929 Lambeau added three players who were to help give Green Bay three consecutive championships. They were tackle Cal Hubbard, guard Mike Michalske, and halfback Johnny Blood, whose real name was John V. McNally. All three are now in the Pro Football Hall of Fame.

Using a good passing attack and a strong defense, the Packers won the 1929 championship with a 12-0-1 record; they repeated in 1930 and 1931, with home-town boy Arnie Herber now doing much of the throwing and Blood doing much of the receiving—he scored 13 touchdowns in 1931, more than most teams scored.

In 1932 the Packers were 10-3-1, but lost the championship to a team with four fewer victories—the Chicago Bears, who won 6, lost 1, and tied 6. (Ties did not, at the time, count in the standings.) It was a pivotal year in several ways. The Bears played Portsmouth, which had a 6-1-4 record, for the championship, and the game had to be indoors at Chicago Stadium because of the weather. The field was only 90 yd long and the sidelines were very close to the stadium wall. The teams agreed to move the goalposts to the goal line, and to have the ball put in play 10 yd from the sidelines whenever it went out of bounds, or when the previous play ended closer than that to the sidelines. The Bears won, 9-0, scoring their only touchdown when Bronko Nagurski faked a plunge and threw a pass, bringing protests that he hadn't been 5 yd behind the line of scrimmage when he threw the ball—the rule at the time.

As a result of that championship game, the league voted to put the goalposts on the goal line, to put hashmarks on the field to mark the nearest spot to the sideline where a play could start, and to legalize a forward pass from any point behind the line of scrimmage. Owners also agreed to George Preston Marshall's suggestion that the league be split into two divisions to set up an annual championship play-off game. The Bears, with Nagurski throwing for two touchdowns, beat the Giants, 23-21, before 26,000 fans in that first play-off (1933), which netted each winning player $210.34.

Nagurski, another legend, could play tackle or fullback. He was a bruising runner, and the new forward-pass rule was made to order for him. When he started toward the line with the ball, defenders had to converge on him, and Nagurski could then throw it. In 1934 the Bears won all 13

regular-season games for another division championship, but that season Nagurski functioned primarily as a blocker, as rookie Beattie Feathers from Tennessee became the first NFL player ever to rush for more than 1,000 yd—to gain that yardage on running plays. However, the Giants beat the Bears, 30-13, in the famous "sneakers" game. Trailing 10-3 at halftime, the Giants wore basketball shoes on the icy Polo Grounds field during the second half and scored four touchdowns.

The first annual College All-Star game, between newly graduated collegiate players and the professional champions, was inaugurated in 1934. It was a 0-0 tie between the Bears and the All-Stars. The game demonstrated the growing public acceptance of the professional version of the sport. That first game also demonstrated that a professional champion could at least hold its own against a group of highly talented players—an idea which had been disputed by some college coaches, on the grounds that professional players must lack the spirit and determination of college players.

By this time, also, the National Football League had lost its town-team look—except that the Green Bay Packers were still around. Gradually the smaller towns had given up their franchises, to oblivion or to larger cities. The Frankford Yellowjackets had become the Philadelphia Eagles; the Portsmouth Spartans had become the Detroit Lions; the Duluth Eskimos had become first the Orange, New Jersey, Tornadoes, then the Boston Redskins, and, in 1936, they would become the Washington Redskins. Akron, Canton, Columbus, Massillon—those founding teams were all gone.

The Green Bay story is a long and complicated one. But a basic reason for the continued existence of the franchise was that Green Bay had fielded good teams at a very crucial time. And Lambeau's passing offense excited spectators. In 1935 the Packers added a rookie end, the "Alabama Antelope," Don Hutson; the Detroit Lions won the championship that year. In 1936, passer Cecil Isbell of Purdue arrived in Green Bay. With Isbell and Herber throwing to Hutson and Blood, and crushing fullback Clarke Hinkle keeping defenses honest with his plunges, Green Bay rolled to a 10-1-0 record and whipped the Redskins, 21-6 for the title. The following year the Redskins, now in Washington, had rookie Sammy Baugh, out of Texas Christian, throwing the ball. After the Bears led, 14-7, at halftime, Baugh threw touchdown passes of 55, 78, and 35 yd in the second half for a 28-21 championship win.

The new passing trend, and the divisional setup, spurred greater attendance. Crowds climbed 15 percent in 1938. The big-city Giants and the little-city Packers played for the title, the Giants winning, 23-17. In 1939, however, the Packers won their fifth championship in 11 seasons, 27-0, over New York.

The T Arrives. The Chicago Bears had used the T formation consistently through the years. They had had some fine seasons—but their success had been built more on outstanding defense than on scoring. They had experimented with the man-in-motion to make the formation more flexible, but it hadn't helped much, once defenses learned to send one of their own men in motion with the offensive back.

In 1940 the Bears won the Western Division title and met the Redskins for the championship. The Redskins had beaten the Bears, 7-3, during the regular season.

George Halas called on Clark Shaughnessy of Stanford for help. They studied films and noticed that the Redskins had consistently overshifted in the direction of the motion. Shaughnessy drew up some plays to take advantage of the overshift. On the second play from scrimmage, they sent a halfback in motion to the right and Quarterback Sid Luckman faked to his halfback. Fullback Bill Osmanski turned to the right, then cut back to the left and took the handoff. The play was meant to go off tackle, but the hole was plugged, and Osmanski cut outside. He went 73 yd for a touchdown. On their next series, the Bears marched 80 yd for a touchdown. By the end of the first quarter it was 21-0; at the half it was 28-0. As the Redskins tried desperation passes to get back into the game, the Bears continually intercepted. The game ended 73-0.

It was not so much a victory for the T formation as a victory for film scouting (this was one of the first times films had systematically been used), for an intelligent game plan designed to capitalize on opposition weaknesses, and for the combination of perfect execution and luck that comes to a team on a day when everything just seems to go right. But the one-sided victory, plus the success Shaughnessy had had at Standford, started professional as well as college coaches stampeding toward the T formation.

The "Monsters of the Midway" and their T-formation attack, now completely redesigned by Shaughnessy, again dominated in 1941. The Bears, 10-1-0, beat the Packers for a Western Division championship, 33-14, then whipped the Giants, 37-9, for their second straight title. The game was played just two weeks after Pearl Harbor Day; attendance was only 13,341.

World War II depleted rosters, but the NFL, and the Bears, rolled on. Chicago lost to Washington and Baugh, 14-6, in 1942, but won another title in 1943 by beating Washington, 41-21, with Luckman passing for five touchdowns. The schedule had been cut to 10 games, and Philadelphia and Pittsburgh had to merge to field a team. In 1944, Pittsburgh merged with the Chicago Cardinals, and the Packers, led by receiving and scoring leader Don Hutson, won another title, again beating the Giants, 14-7.

The war ended before the 1945 season began. A number of stars returned from service to rejoin their teams. But younger players were about to establish semi-dynasties in Philadelphia and Cleveland (although the Cleveland Rams would move to Los Angeles in 1946, making way for a different dynasty, in a different league). And the NFL was about to face the greatest threat to its supremacy since the short-lived Red Grange American Football League of 1926.

A young quarterback named Bob Waterfield outpassed Baugh to lead Cleveland to a 15-14 victory in the 1945 championship game. He threw for two touchdowns on a cold, windy, slippery day, but the margin of victory was a safety scored by the Rams when one of Baugh's passes hit his own goal post. And a young fullback named Steve Van Buren led the league in rushing and scoring as the Philadelphia Eagles finished just behind Washington in the Eastern Division.

Another League. The first postwar year was an important one for professional football in many ways. The All-American Football Conference was formed, with fran-

Bronko Nagurski, an All-American tackle at Minnesota in 1929, also played fullback. He gained more than 4,000 yards in nine seasons with the Chicago Bears and was All-Pro fullback three straight years, 1932–1934. *(Pro Football Hall of Fame.)*

chises in Buffalo, Brooklyn, Chicago, Cleveland, Los Angeles, Miami, New York, and San Francisco. The NFL's Cleveland Rams moved to Los Angeles, making the NFL a truly national league. And, for the first time since 1933, black players were signed; Kenny Washington and Woody Strode with the Rams, Marion Motley and Bill Willis with the Cleveland Browns of the new league.

The AAFC's biggest problem was that in four years of existence, the Browns won four titles, losing only 4 of 59 games. Attendance lagged in other cities. But Paul Brown, founder, owner, and coach of the Browns, had brought a new dimension to coaching. His methods of meticulous planning—careful design of pass patterns, thorough study of films, and complete overall attention to detail—were soon adopted by other coaches.

The NFL was largely dominated by the Eagles during the period. They lost to the Chicago Cardinals in the 1947 championship game, but won in 1948 and 1949. After the 1949 season the AAFC and NFC "merged"—actually, only three AAFC teams, Cleveland, Baltimore, and San Francisco, survived. Many felt that the Browns would be just another team against NFL competition, but they beat the Rams, 30-28, for the championship. The Rams, a high-scoring powerhouse with Bob Waterfield and Norm Van Brocklin passing to Elroy "Crazylegs" Hirsch and Tom Fears, avenged that loss in 1951, beating the Browns, 24-17.

Both Cleveland and Los Angeles represented a new trend in pro football: the "three-end" formation, although neither of them used it in the way it is used today. On occasion, the man in motion would become the third end; at other times, he would line up as a wingback. The Browns used a system of timed spot passing, with quarterback Otto Graham throwing to the spot where his receiver should end up, and Dante Lavelli, Mac Speedie, and Dub Jones were all outstanding receivers. Their most dangerous running play was a delayed trap to fullback Marion Motley—very similar to the modern draw play. The Rams, on the other hand, believed in the long pass, or "bomb," and all three of their receivers were exceptionally fast.

Within a few years, every team in pro football was

using three ends, as they still do. Defenses had to change. The old 5-3-3, with only three defensive backs, couldn't cope with three talented receivers, all being covered one-on-one. It gave way to the 4-3-4.

Another change brought by the 1950s was the two-platoon system. Free substitution went into effect in the NFL in 1949, and by 1952 virtually all professional players were offensive or defensive specialists.

The trend toward more passing and the conversion to the T formation also brought a new breed of hero, the quarterback. Bobby Layne passed the Detroit Lions to championships in 1952 and 1953, beating the Browns both times, but in 1954 the Browns whipped the Lions, 56-10, with Otto Graham scoring three touchdowns and passing for three others. Graham led the Browns to another championship in 1955, beating the Rams, 38-14, before retiring.

The outstanding teams to emerge in the late 1950s were the New York Giants and the Baltimore Colts, quarterbacked respectively by Charlie Conerly and John Unitas. The Giants overwhelmed the Bears, 47-7, in the 1956 championship game. In 1957 the Lions got revenge on the Browns, 59-14, with Tobin Rote filling in for the injured Layne to pass for four touchdowns and score one himself, but the next two years saw the Colts and the Giants battling for the title. The 1958 game has been called the most dramatic football game ever played. It was the first to go into overtime. The score was tied, 17-17, at the end of regulation time; the Giants received the kickoff at the beginning of the extra period, but had to punt. Unitas then took his team 80 yd in 13 plays, fullback Alan Ameche scoring the winning touchdown at 8 min, 51 sec of overtime. In a 1959 rematch, the Colts scored 24 points in the fourth quarter for a 31-16 victory.

The New AFL. In 1960 another American Football League—the fourth one—began operating. Few people gave it any chance to succeed against the long-established NFL. But the AFL had, for the most part, well-bankrolled owners who were willing to take losses for several years if necessary; chief among them were Lamar Hunt of the Dallas Texans (now the Kansas City Chiefs) and Barron Hilton of the Los Angeles Chargers (now the San Diego Chargers).

The new league struggled along until 1964; then NBC signed a five-year, $36-million contract with the AFL for television rights, and show-business entrepreneur Sonny Werblin took over the shaky New York Titans franchise, renamed the team the Jets, and signed Alabama quarterback Joe Namath for $442,000 in a head-on battle with the NFL Giants. Suddenly the AFL looked like a success. The final move came in 1966. Teams in both leagues had scrupulously avoided "raiding" teams in the other league until the New York Giants signed kicker Pete Gogolak of the AFL Buffalo Bills. New Commissioner Al Davis of the AFL retaliated by signing two prominent NFL quarterbacks to AFL contracts and talking to seven others about switching, for sizable amounts of money. Owners could see a costly, all-out war on the horizon. They decided on peace, instead. On June 8, 1966, a merger was announced, to become fully effective in 1970. A common draft and a postseason AFL-NFL championship game—quickly dubbed the Super Bowl—were initiated immediately.

During the AFL's six seasons of independent operation, the dominant teams were the Chargers and the Buffalo Bills. The Chargers won just one title, in 1963, whipping Boston, 51-10, for the championship, but they were also in the finals in 1960, 1961, 1964, and 1965. The Bills won championships in 1964 and 1965.

The NFL in the 1960s. This was the decade of Vince Lombardi and the Green Bay Packers in the NFL. Building a dynasty on strong defense, a strong running attack, and short passes by Bart Starr, the Packers lost to Philadelphia in the decisive game for the 1960 championship, then won five titles in the next seven years, in 1961–1962 and 1965–1967.

There were other fine teams during that period, but they couldn't seem to beat the Packers in the big games. Cleveland, led by the great running of fullback Jim Brown, shut out Baltimore, 27-0, for the 1964 title but lost to the Packers, 23-12, in 1965. Then the Dallas Cowboys challenged the dynasty and came close twice, but lost both times. In 1966 the Cowboys were within yards of tying with less than a minute left, but an end zone interception ended the threat and gave the Packers a 34-27 win. In 1967, Dallas was ahead of the Packers, 17-14, with 13 sec left, but Starr scored on a quarterback sneak for a 21-17 victory.

The Packers also won the first two Super Bowls, whipping Kansas City, 35-10, and then Oakland, 33-14. Those were the top AFL teams of the period. Oakland won the league title in 1967 and divisional titles in 1968, 1969, and 1970, while Kansas City won league titles in 1966 and 1969.

Sammy Baugh, an All-American at TCU in 1935 and 1936, was one of the game's greatest passers. He led the NFL in passing six times and in punting four times and was a six-time All-Pro in a 16-year career with the Washington Redskins. *(Pro Football Hall of Fame.)*

The Super Bowl. The Packers' convincing victories in the 1967 and 1968 Super Bowls led many to believe that the AFL was a long way from "parity," and the New York Jets were 21-point underdogs against Baltimore in the 1969 game. But Joe Namath completed 17 of 28 passes for 206 yd, and the Jets used ball control and solid defense to upset the NFL champions, 16-7. Then the Chiefs made it two in a row for the AFL by stunning the Minnesota Vikings, 23-7, in 1970.

With the merger of the following season, the NFL was realigned into two conferencss, American and National. Three NFL teams moved into the American Conference—Baltimore, Pittsburgh, and Cleveland. In Super Bowl V, two old NFL teams, Dallas and Baltimore, clashed. The game was called by some the "Stupor Bowl," by others the "Stumble Bowl." There were six fumbles, five by Baltimore, and six interceptions, three by each team. The Colts survived the battle of attrition, winning, 16-13, on a Jim O'Brien field goal with 5 sec left in the game.

The tremendously talented Cowboys were now thought of as the team that couldn't "win the big one." But they devastated Miami in the next Super Bowl, 24-3, rushing for 252 yd while holding the Dolphins to only 185 yd in total offense. The running of Duane Thomas and Walt Garrison and the passing of Roger Staubach (12 for 19) did the job.

The Dolphins, however, emerged as the team of the early 1970s. In 1972 they won all 14 regular-season games, two play-off games for the conference championship, and the Super Bowl—a total of 17 consecutive victories. They

Don Hutson, shown catching a touchdown pass despite close coverage by Milt Piepul of the Detroit Lions, was named an All-Time All-Pro in 1970. He played 11 seasons with the Green Bay Packers and was named an All-Pro end nine times, catching a total of 488 passes, 101 of them for touchdowns. (*Pro Football Hall of Fame.*)

beat the Washington Redskins, 14-7, in the big game. With an offense built on the powerful running of fullback Larry Csonka and halfback Jim Kiick, occasional outside runs by "Mercury" Morris, and accurate if infrequent passing by Bob Griese, the Dolphins kept on going in 1973. They did lose two games, but not the ones they had to win. In their three postseason games, including the Super Bowl, they scored 85 points to 33 for their opponents. Their Super Bowl victims were the Minnesota Vikings: the score was 24-7.

Then came the Pittsburgh Steelers, a team built around a powerful, mistake-creating defense led by defensive tackle "Mean Joe" Greene. The offense was led by the power running of Franco Harris. Pittsburgh won its first championship by beating Minnesota 16-6 in the 1975 Super Bowl and repeated with a 21-17 victory over Dallas in 1976.

Rules Changes. The 1972 season was referred to as the "Year of the Runner," as 10 men rushed for more than 1,000 yd. In 1973, O. J. Simpson of Buffalo became the first player in history to rush for more than 2,000 yd in a season, and four other players passed the 1,000-yd mark. One reason for the trend was the increasing use of zone defenses, which made it more difficult to complete long passes. The new conservatism, on the part of offense and defense alike, led many sportswriters and fans to complain about dull football.

As a result—and perhaps partly because of the new World Football League—the NFL owners voted a number of important rules changes for the 1974 season. The new rules had three broad purposes: to cut down on field goal attempts, to encourage longer kick runbacks and therefore better field position for the returning team, and to free the passing game somewhat.

The major changes were:

Goalposts were moved from goal line to end line, 10 yd back.

On a missed field-goal attempt from beyond the 20-yd line, the ball was returned to the original line of scrimmage.

Kickoffs were moved from 40-yd line to 35-yd line.

Members of punting teams, except for the two outside men, were no longer permitted to run downfield until the ball was kicked.

A wide receiver could not be cut down by a block below the knees; once a wide receiver was more than 3 yd beyond the line of scrimmage, he could be hit only once by a defender.

The penalty for offensive holding in the interior line area was reduced from 15 to 10 yd.

A wide receiver was not allowed to return to the line of scrimmage to block a defender below the waist, eliminating the dangerous "crackback" block on linebackers.

If a game was tied after regulation time (60 min), one sudden-death overtime period of 15 min would be played; that is, the first team to score would win the game. But if there was no scoring during the overtime period, the tie would stand.

World Football League. Late in 1973, Garry Davidson announced that a new league, the World Football League, was being organized. Davidson had been the man behind the American Basketball Association and the World Hockey Association, two newer leagues that had challenged existing big leagues. His WFL idea was somewhat different, though: The league would not really be involved in a head-on confrontation with the NFL. Davidson's plan was to begin a season in mid-July, well before the NFL, and to play games on Wednesdays and Thursdays, avoiding direct competition with the NFL. He also knew he needed television money, but by then all three networks were already involved with the NFL. The WFL did get coverage from Hughes Sports Network, but HSN had difficulty displacing prime-time major network shows in many cities.

The league began operations with 12 franchises: Birmingham, Chicago, Detroit, Florida, Hawaii, Houston, Jacksonville, Memphis, New York, Philadelphia, Portland, and Southern California. Attendance figures seemed good for the first couple of games, but it developed that many of the figures had been inflated by giving away tickets or by sheer overoptimism. Nevertheless, Davidson indicated that most WFL owners were well-bankrolled and willing to lose about $500,000 a year during the first three years.

The WFL early announced six rules changes to increase scoring; many of the changes were adopted in whole or in part by the NFL before the 1974 season, as outlined in the preceding section. The special WFL rules called for kickoffs from the 30-yd line, goal posts on the end line, returning the ball to the line of scrimmage on a missed field-goal attempt taken from beyond the 20-yd line, the 2-point optional conversion attempt by running or passing, a pass completion if the receiver had just one foot in bounds when catching the ball, and a fifth period in the case of a tie. The WFL overtime period didn't specify sudden death but, instead, a full 15 min of play, with kickoffs at the start and at the 7½-min mark.

Several NFL players jumped to the WFL in 1975—among them Kiick, Csonka and wide receiver Paul Warfield of the Dolphins—but that wasn't enough. On October 22 of that year, WFL owners voted to disband. Two of the teams applied for membership in the NFL, but the established league decided instead to expand into Tampa Bay, Fla., and Seattle, Wash. Several WFL players joined NFL teams for the 1976 season.

The Strike. While the new WFL was signing some NFL stars for future delivery, in 1975 or later, upon the expiration of contracts, the NFL faced another major problem: a strike by its Players Association. The issue involved in the 63 demands originally made by the players was not so much money as "freedom."

A key demand was the elimination of the option clause, which binds a player to his team for one year after his contract expires. A player has the right to "play out his option" by refusing to sign another contract and, meanwhile, playing, or sitting out, the option year. But, if he then signs with another NFL team, upon becoming a free agent, the "Rozelle rule" empowers NFL Commissioner Alvin J. "Pete" Rozelle to order that team to give compensation to the player's original team. The players contended that such an arrangement severely limited their freedom to move to other teams, once the option year was past.

Players also wanted the elimination of the reserve list and the waiver system, the easing of curfews and other disciplinary rules, and the right to negotiate individually not only for salaries but for expense money and other nonsalary items.

The strike forced cancellation of the College All-Star Game, and conglomerations of rookies and older free agents played in most of the exhibition games during the first three weeks of preseason activity. Then the players voted to return to camp for a three-week cooling-off period. The 1974 season was played with no real agreement being reached on the major issues.

Court decisions apparently decided, or helped to decide, some of the issues, however. The "Rozelle rule" was declared a violation of antitrust laws, and in 1976 the college player draft was ruled an unlawful restraint of trade by a federal court.

Football Rules

(This summary is based on the National Football League rule book. Where there is a major difference in college rules, it is noted in parentheses. Generally, high school rules are much closer to the NFL rules than to college.)

Field and Equipment. The football field is 120 yd long, 100 yd from goal line to goal line, and 160 ft wide. The hashmarks are 70 ft, 9 in (53 ft, 4 in) from either sideline. On each end line is a goalpost, with a crossbar 10 ft above the ground and uprights 18 ft, 6 in apart. (In college, the goalposts are 23 ft, 4 in apart.)

The ball is a prolate spheroid, 28 to 28½ in around its long circumference, 21¼ to 21½ in around its short circumference; it weighs 14 to 15 oz and is inflated to 12½ to 13½ lb pressure.

Kickoff and Free Kicks. Shortly before the game the referee flips a coin and the captain of the visiting team calls the flip. The winner of the toss may choose to kick off or to receive, or may choose the goal the winner's team will defend at the beginning of the first quarter. The other option is then given to the other captain.

The kickoff is made from a team's own 35-yd line (40-yd line in college). It must be a placekick or a drop kick, and a kicking tee of up to 3 in high may be used. Members of the kicking team must remain behind the line until the ball is kicked; members of the receiving team must remain behind a restraining line 10 yd away.

The ball is not in play until it goes 10 yd or has been touched by the receiving team. Once it is in play, it is a free ball, and may be recovered by either team; the kicking team, however, cannot advance it.

If the kickoff goes out of bounds (beyond a sideline) without being touched by a receiver and before it goes over the goal line, a 5-yd penalty is assessed, and the ball must be kicked again. (In college, the receiving team has the option of taking the ball at the spot where it went out of bounds.)

The kickoff is also used at the beginning of the second half, with the captain who lost the opening coin toss given the option; and it is used, as well, after a field goal and after an extra-point attempt, by the team that scored.

The kickoff is a special kind of free kick. For an ordinary free kick, the kicking team can use a punt, drop kick, or placement, but a kicking tee is not allowed. After a safety, the team scored upon puts the ball in play with a free kick from its own 20-yd line. A team can also use a free kick after a fair catch; and, in this situation, a field goal can be scored.

Progress of Play. After a team has gained possession of the ball, it has four downs in which to gain 10 yd; if it fails to gain the 10 yd, possession goes to the other team (except that a team can get a first down on a penalty without advancing the necessary distance).

Each play begins with a scrimmage. The offense must have seven or more players on the line of scrimmage when the ball is centered; players who are not on the line of scrimmage must be at least 1 yd behind it (except for the quarterback taking a hand-to-hand snap from the center). Once an offensive player has assumed a set position, the player may not move. One offensive back may be in motion at the time of the snap, but must be moving parallel to or away from the line of scrimmage.

Once the ball is marked for play by an official, a neutral zone is in effect. The neutral zone is the length of the football, and no player from either team, except the offensive center, may encroach on this zone until the ball is snapped.

Passing. The offensive team is allowed to make one forward pass on any play from scrimmage. Any number of lateral or backward passes is permitted. The passer must be behind the line of scrimmage when throwing the ball. Only ends and backs (eligible receivers) may catch a pass—the quarterback, having taken a hand-to-hand snap from center, is not an eligible receiver. Once the passed ball is touched by a defensive player, any offensive player may catch it. However, if the ball is touched by an offensive player, it cannot be caught legally by another offensive player until a defensive player touches it.

On a pass play, an ineligible receiver may cross the line of scrimmage on an initial charge, while blocking an opponent, but must not go farther downfield. Any eligible receiver, together with all 11 defensive players, is entitled to try to catch the ball. A player may not interfere with another player's effort to get to the ball or catch it; however, body contact is allowed if, in the official's judgment, it resulted from a legitimate attempt to catch the ball. The moment the ball touches a receiver, it is permissible for an opponent to tackle the receiver.

Until the 1974 season, a defender was allowed to cut down a potential pass receiver at the line of scrimmage, or to "bump" the receiver continually as the latter went downfield, as long as the ball was not in the air. Now, however, a wide receiver cannot be cut down with a block below the knees, and the defender is allowed to bump such a receiver only once after the receiver has gone 3 yd downfield.

Personal Fouls. Rules regarding use of the hands are different for the offensive and defensive teams. An offensive player, except for a ball carrier, cannot use hands and arms to obstruct an opponent. When blocking, an offensive player may extend the elbows to the side, but the hands must be cupped or closed, and they must not be extended in front of the body.

A defender may not tackle or hold an opponent, except the runner, but may use hands and arms to ward off a blocker, and to push or pull a blocker out of the way at or near the line of scrimmage. It is illegal to block an opponent from behind, or for a legal receiver, having gone 3 yd downfield, to come back toward the line of scrimmage and block an opponent below the waist.

Punts and Fair Catches. Once a punt has crossed the line of scrimmage, the ball belongs to the receiving team. A receiver has every right to the ball, and members of the kicking team must not interfere with that player's attempt to get to the ball or to catch it. Once the player touches the ball, contact may be made.

Once a member of the receiving team touches the ball, it is a free ball, and a member of the kicking team may recover it. If a member of the kicking team touches it first, the ball is dead at the spot. If such a player touches it before it hits the ground, however, a 15-yd penalty is assessed against the kicking team.

If the ball is fumbled by a receiver, a member of the kicking team may advance it. If it is muffed, the kickers may recover the ball but not advance it. (It is a muff when a player touches the ball without clearly gaining possession.)

A blocked kick which doesn't cross the line of scrimmage is a free ball, and either team may advance it. The kicking team must gain enough yardage on the advance to make a first down in order to retain possession, however. If a blocked kick crosses the line of scrimmage, it is considered a kicked ball, and the kicking team has no right to it.

A receiver can signify a "fair catch" by raising an arm overhead and waving it. The receiver doesn't have to catch the ball; if it hits the ground without being touched by that player, the fair catch is off and all kicked-ball rules apply. (In high school and college, the fair-catch signal binds all members of the receiving team, and the ball may not be returned by any receiver.) When a receiver has called for a fair catch, a member of the kicking team may not tackle or run into the receiver, who in turn may not advance the ball. The receiving team takes possession at the spot where the catch is made.

Touchbacks. The simplest explanation of a touchback is that it occurs any time a team moves the ball into the opposition's end zone without scoring a touchdown. It most commonly arises on punts, kickoffs, and missed field-goal attempts that go into the end zone; the receiving team takes possession at its own 20-yd line. In pro football, it is a touchback when, on fourth down from inside the 20-yd line, a team throws an incomplete pass into the end zone. In high school and college, however, the other team takes possession at the original line of scrimmage, not at the 20.

It is also a touchback if a player on Team A fumbles into Team B's end zone, and the ball goes out of bounds or across the end line, or if it is recovered by Team B.

Out of Bounds. The ball is out of bounds whenever it touches or crosses a sideline, or when it is in possession of a player who touches or crosses a sideline. The ball is dead at the spot, and usually belongs to the team that last touched it inbounds.

There are a couple of exceptions. When a punt or field-goal attempt goes out of bounds, the ball belongs to the receiving team at that point. If a punt is muffed by a receiver, touched by a member of the kicking team, and then goes out of bounds, the ball belongs to the kicking team only if it has advanced enough yardage to give that team a first down.

Timing. A game consists of 15-min quarters, with 2-min intermissions between the first and second and third and fourth quarters, and a 20-min intermission at halftime. The clock starts running when the ball is kicked on the opening kickoff (in high school and college, when a player on either team touches the ball in the field of play).

It is stopped when:

- The ball is out of bounds.
- A receiver makes a fair catch.
- A score is made, or there is a touchback.
- Action is completed for a play on which there was a foul.
- A pass is incomplete.
- A kicked ball is declared dead.
- The ball changes hands.
- The 2-min warning is given, signifying the amount of time remaining in the half or game.
- Time out is called.
- In college play, the clock stops after every first down.

In most cases, time resumes the next time the ball is snapped or otherwise put into play. During the last 2 min of a half, a special timing rule is in effect: On a kickoff, the clock doesn't start until a player touches the ball. Each team is allowed three time-outs per half (four per half in high school and college). The offense is allowed 30 sec (25 sec in college) to put the ball in play. The time starts when the ball is spotted and the referee signals the number of the next down.

Fumbles. A fumble may be recovered and advanced by a member of either team (in college, only a member of the offensive team may advance a fumble). An exception is a fumble inside the opposition's 10-yd line; the only offensive player who may advance the ball is the player who fumbled.

A lateral or backward pass that is not caught is a free ball; it may be recovered, but may not be advanced by the defense.

Scoring. A *touchdown,* worth 6 points, is scored when a team has possession of the ball in the opposition's end zone. The team is then given the chance to attempt a point after touchdown (also called "extra point" or "conversion"), worth 1 point. The ball is put in play at the opposition's 2-yd line and the team may (a) placekick or dropkick the ball between the goalposts and over the upright, or (b) pass or run the ball, on a single offensive play, into the end zone. (In high school and college, a 2-point conversion is an option. The ball is put in play on the opposition's 3-yd line. A successful kick scores 1 point but, if the team advances the ball into the end zone on a single offensive play, 2 points are scored.)

A *field goal,* worth 3 points, is scored when a team dropkicks or placekicks the ball between the opposition's goal posts and above the crossbar. A field goal may be attempted on any play from scrimmage and from any place on the field.

A *safety,* worth 2 points, is scored by the defense when the offensive team has possession of a dead ball in its own end zone, provided that the offensive team furnished the impetus that put the ball in the end zone. For example, if a player retreats into the end zone and is tackled there, it is a safety. However, if a player fields a punt in the end zone and doesn't attempt to advance the ball, or recovers an opponent's fumble in the end zone, it is a touchback, and the ball comes out to the 20-yd line, because the impetus was provided by the other team.

Penalties. On most fouls, the team offended against has a choice between accepting a penalty or declining a penalty and accepting the results of the play. If both teams commit a foul on the same play, the penalties offset each other and the play is nullified.

Generally speaking, yardage penalties are marked off from the original line of scrimmage. There are some obvious exceptions, as when the ball changes hands on a play. If Team A punts to Team B, and either team is guilty of a foul in the ensuing action, the penalty is enforced from the spot of the foul, except in cases where this would amount to an injustice. Assume, for example, that the punt returner receives the ball on the returner's own 30-yd line and runs it back to the 50-yd line, and Team A committed a personal foul on B's 30—the 15-yd penalty would bring the ball only to B's 45, a net loss of 5 yd for B. This penalty would be enforced from the 50-yd line, putting the ball on A's 35.

When the spot from which a foul should be enforced is in an end zone, it is enforced either from the goal line or, if a touchback is involved, from the 20-yd line. Contrary to popular belief, a score can result from a penalty, though it doesn't happen often. If, for example, a team is guilty of a clip in its own end zone, the penalty is a safety. A touchdown can be awarded if a palpably unfair act interferes with a play that would have resulted in a touchdown (when, for example, a player comes off the bench to tackle an opponent who has a clear field ahead).

In most cases, however, a team cannot score on a penalty. If the ball is on B's 5-yd line, and B is offside, the ordinary 5-yd penalty would result in a touchdown. Instead, the penalty is half the distance to the goal, 2½ yd.

Common fouls and their penalties are:

- Encroachment or offside—5 yd.
- Illegal motion or formation—5 yd.
- Illegal substitution—5 yd.
- Too many players on the field—5 yd.
- Accidentally running into the kicker—5 yd.
- Accidentally grabbing face mask of opponent—5 yd.
- Delay of game, taking more than 30 sec to start a play—5 yd.
- Too many time-outs.
- Forward pass accidentally touched by ineligible receiver—5 yd and loss of down.
- Defensive holding—5 yd and automatic first down.
- Illegal use of hands or arms by offense—10 yd.
- Clipping—15 yd from spot of foul.
- Fair-catch interference—15 yd.
- Offensive pass interference—15 yd.
- Batting, kicking, or punching a loose ball—15 yd (automatic first down if by defense).
- Ineligible receiver downfield—15 yd.
- Unnecessary roughness—15 yd (automatic first down if by defense).
- Unsportsmanlike conduct—15 yd (automatic first down if by defense).
- Forward pass intentionally touched by ineligible receiver—15 yd and loss of down.
- Intentional grounding (intentionally throwing an incomplete pass to avoid loss of yardage)—15 yd and loss of down.
- Roughing the passer or kicker—15 yd and automatic first down.
- Defensive pass interference—Ball advanced to spot of foul and automatic first down; when spot of foul is the end zone, ball is placed on 1-yd line.
- Piling on—15 yd and automatic first down.

Penalties for flagrant roughness and unsportmanlike conduct may also result in the guilty player's ejection from the game. If the officials rule that a player be thus put out, the ejection takes effect even if the penalty is declined.

Glossary

audible—A signal called at the line of scrimmage to change the play that was specified originally (in the huddle).

automatic—same as "audible."

balanced line—An offensive setup in which there are three players on either side of the center.

ball control—A style of play in which a team attempts to gain a few yards at a time, using many plays and a lot of time to move down the field, thus keeping possession of (controlling) the ball.

blitz—A defensive maneuver in which a linebacker or defensive back rushes the quarterback.

bomb—A long pass.

bootleg—A play in which the quarterback fakes to another back and keeps the ball himself; strictly speaking, he should hide the ball against his hip, but the term is now used to describe almost any running play by the quarterback.

bread-and-butter play—A basic offensive play on which a team depends for sure yardage.

buttonhook—A pass route on which a receiver goes downfield, then hooks back toward the passer; more commonly "hook"; *see also* "curl."

check off—When the quarterback calls an audible, or automatic, he is said to "check off" the play.

circle—A pass route on which a back swings out around the flank, then comes back toward the middle of the field.

coffin corner—The sideline area between a team's 10-yd line and goal line.

comeback—A pass route; either a hook (buttonhook) or curl.

conversion—Extra point after touchdown.

cornerback—Defensive halfback.

corner linebacker—An outside linebacker.

crossing pattern—A pass pattern in which the paths of two receivers cross.

cup—The "pocket" (see below).

curl—A pass route on which the receiver goes downfield, then circles backward to the passer.

delay—A running play in which the runner waits for a period of time before getting the ball; also a pass route in which the receiver appears to be a blocker before going on his route.

dive—A straight-ahead running play, usually by a halfback.

double-team—When two players block the same opponent, or defend against the same opponent.

down and in—A pass route on which a receiver goes downfield, then cuts toward the middle of the field.

down and out—A pass route on which a receiver goes downfield, then cuts toward a sideline.

draw play—A type of delayed play in which the quarterback drops back as if to pass, then gives the ball to a runner, or runs with it himself. So called because the intent is to draw defensive linemen into the backfield, then run past them.

eat the ball—What a passer does when he decides to be tackled for a loss instead of throwing a possible interception.

fill the gap—Usually said of a linebacker who sees a hole developing and moves into it.

flag—A penalty marker thrown by an official; also one of the markers at the intersections of goal line with sidelines.

flag pattern—A pass route on which a receiver goes downfield, then angles toward the flag.

flanker—A back who lines up outside his own end, usually near the line of scrimmage.

flare—A pass route on which a back starts toward a sideline, then turns upfield.

flat—The area outside the offensive end, near the line of scrimmage.

flood—A pass pattern that sends two or more receivers into the same defensive zone.

flow of the play—The direction in which a play is moving, or appears to be moving.

fly—A pass route on which a receiver simply tries to outrun his defender.

free ball—A ball that belongs to anyone who can recover it; a kickoff, for example, is a free ball once it has traveled 10 yd, but a punt is a free ball only if a receiver has touched it.

free safety—A safety who doesn't have to guard any specific receiver, and who is therefore free to roam around, depending on where he thinks the play is going.

front four—The defensive ends and tackles.

gap—The space between linemen.

gap defense—A defense, used in short-yardage and goal-line situations, in which the defenders line up in the gaps between offensive linemen.

keeper—A play in which the quarterback fakes to another back but keeps the ball and runs with it.

key—Anything that will tell a player what the other team is probably doing. If an offensive guard pulls, it is a key that the team is probably running in that direction. If a defensive player watches the offensive guard and moves with him, he is "keying on" the offensive guard, and the offensive guard is said to be his key. The quarterback may also use a certain defender as a key to tell him what kind of defense is being used.

line of scrimmage—An imaginary line, parallel to the goal lines, drawn through the spot at which the ball is placed between downs.

look-in pass—A quick pass to a receiver who is slanting toward the middle of the field, just across the line of scrimmage.

loop—A maneuver in which a defensive lineman, instead of charging straight ahead, moves behind a teammate and then charges.

loose ball—A ball that, at the moment, isn't clearly in possession of either team; any kick, pass, or fumble.

man-for-man—A pass defense in which each defensive back is responsible for a specific eligible receiver.

onside kick—A type of kickoff on which the kicking team is attempting to recover the free ball; usually kicked on the ground, just hard enough to travel 10 yd, at which point it is a free ball.

option—A play on which the quarterback or another back has a choice between running and passing.

option blocking—A blocking assignment on which a player has to decide which opponent should be blocked; *see* "zone blocking."

overshift—A type of defense that concentrates on the offense's strong side.

pass pattern—The pattern formed by the routes of individual receivers; sometimes used to mean "pass route."

FOOTBALL OFFENSIVE FORMATIONS

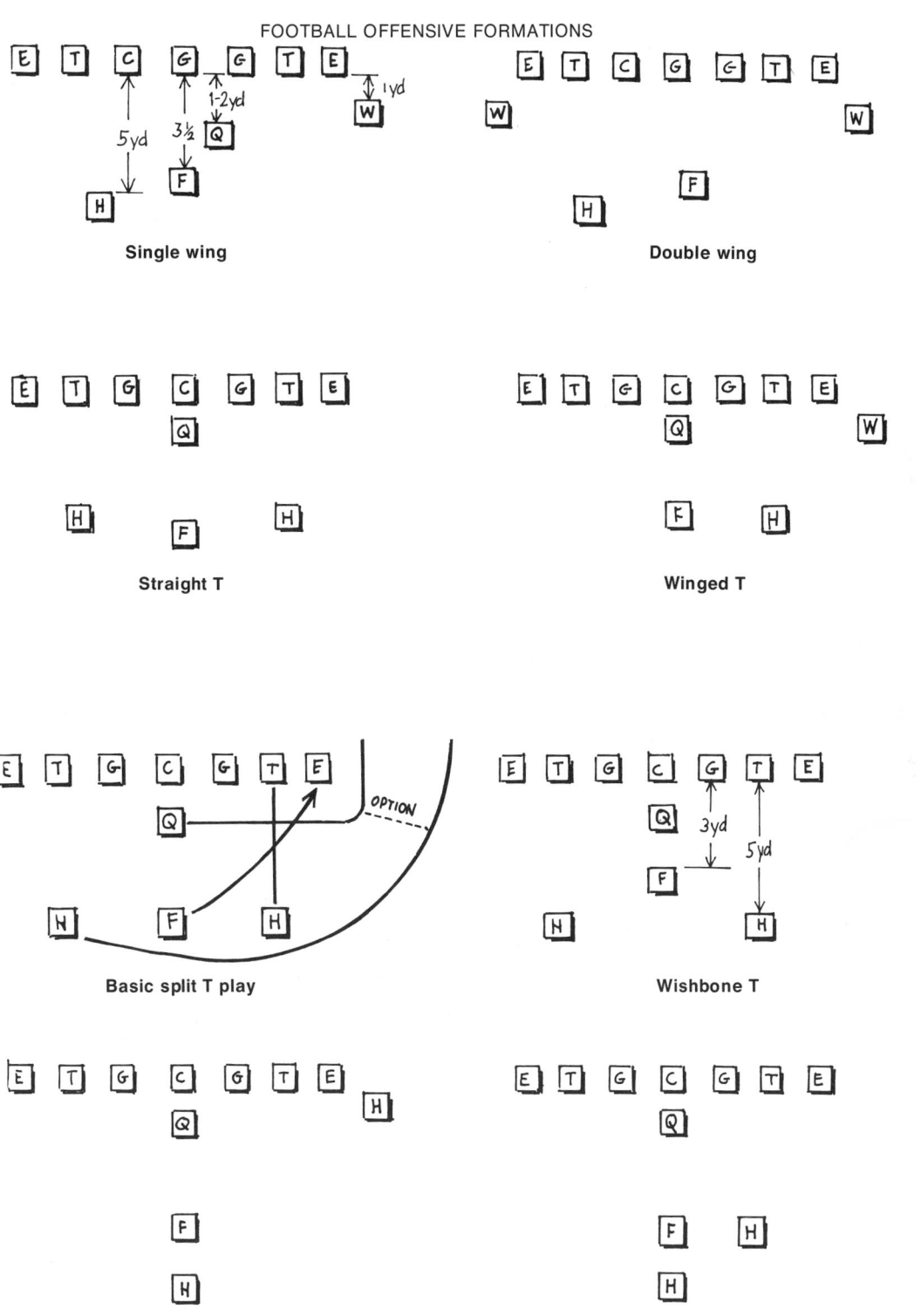

Single wing

Double wing

Straight T

Winged T

Basic split T play

OPTION

Wishbone T

I formation with wingback

Power I formation

(Cont.)

FOOTBALL OFFENSIVE FORMATIONS
(Cont.)

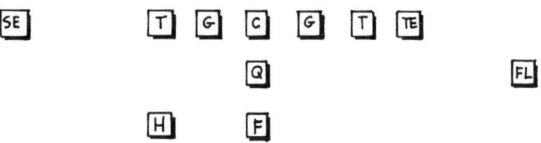

Pro set

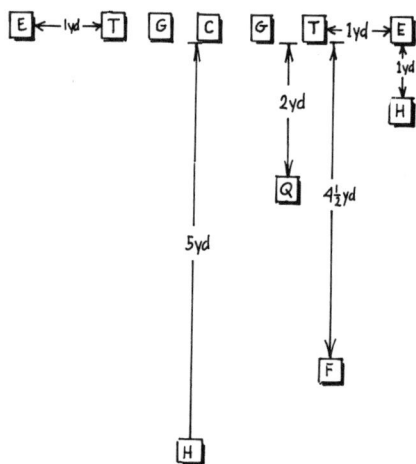

Notre Dame box

pass route—The path followed by one receiver on a pass play.

passing situation—A down on which the offensive team needs a good deal of yardage and is therefore likely to attempt a pass.

pitchout—A short pass, usually an underhanded lateral, to a back.

play-action pass—A pass preceded by a running fake.

pocket—The area from which a passer throws, protected in front and on both sides by teammates.

post—A pass route on which a receiver runs downfield, then angles toward the goalposts.

power sweep—An end run on which two or more linemen pull to block for the ball carrier.

prevent defense—A defense in which the backs and usually the linebackers drop back rapidly, willing to permit a short pass completion but not a long one.

primary receiver—Any pass pattern is designed to get one receiver in the clear against a specific defense; that player is the primary receiver.

pull—What an offensive lineman does upon stepping back, then running parallel to the line of scrimmage and behind it before turning upfield to block.

pursuit—Chasing a play, by the defense; when a defender makes a tackle a long way from the defender's original position, it is "good pursuit."

quick release—What a quarterback has when throwing the ball quickly after setting up (preparing to pass) in the pocket.

read—To use a key; to see quickly what the other team is doing. A quarterback who recognizes the defense he is facing and takes an action to defeat it is said to have read the defense.

red dog—*See* "blitz."

reverse—A running play that appears to be going in one direction and ends up going in the other.

rollout—A play on which the quarterback follows a semicircular path, away from and then toward the line of scrimmage, usually looking for a receiver; a rollout is often an option play.

safety blitz—A blitz by a safetyman.

safetyman—A defensive back (also called "safety") whose chief purpose is to prevent a long gain; or any defensive back who plays relatively deep. Most teams now use two safetymen.

safety valve—A receiver, usually a back and not the primary receiver, to whom the passer throws the ball only because the passer can't find another receiver.

scramble—An unplanned play on which the quarterback runs around behind the line of scrimmage, eluding defenders while trying to find a pass receiver.

screen pass—A pass play on which one or more offensive linemen block briefly and then slip to the outside to get in front of a pass receiver, usually a back.

secondary—The defensive backfield.

secondary receiver—The receiver for whom the quarterback looks when the primary receiver is covered (that is, closely pursued or guarded by a defensive player or players).

shoot the gap—What a linebacker does upon charging quickly through a hole between offensive linemen, or a spot vacated by an offensive lineman who has pulled.

sideline pass—A pass to a receiver who goes downfield, then cuts at a right angle toward the sideline.

slant—A running play on which the runner moves diagonally toward the line of scrimmage, or a pass route on which the receiver moves diagonally downfield.

slot—The area between the wide receiver and the nearest offensive lineman; a back who lines up in that area is "in the slot."

slot back—A back who lines up in the slot.

split end—An end who is "split" (removed) some distance from the nearest interior lineman.

sprint-out—A play on which the quarterback moves quickly toward the flank usually with an option to run or pass.

square-in—A route on which the pass receiver runs downfield, then cuts sharply toward the middle of the field.

square-out—A short sideline route.

strong safety—The safetyman opposite the offensive strong side.

strong side—In an unbalanced line, the side of the center where most of the linemen are stationed.

sudden-death—An overtime period in which the team

that scores first wins automatically. The act of scoring terminates play.

suicide squad—The players used on kickoffs and kickoff returns.

swing pass—A flare pass.

tailback—A back who is farther from the line of scrimmage than any other back; in the I formation, the back at the top of the I.

tight end—An end who lines up closer to the adjoining tackle than the split end.

tight safety—The strong safety.

trap—A play on which a defender is allowed to penetrate, then blocked from the side to create a hole in the area the defender vacated.

unbalanced line—A setup in which the offense has more linemen on one side of the center than on the other.

wingback—A back who lines up just outside an offensive end and near the line of scrimmage.

weak safety—A safetyman who lines up opposite the weak side of the offense; usually a free safety.

weak side—The side of the unbalanced line that has fewer linemen.

zig in—A route on which a receiver cuts or fakes to the outside, then angles toward the center of the field.

zig out—A route on which a receiver cuts or fakes inside, then angles toward a sideline.

zone blocking—A system in which an offensive player blocks anyone in a certain area, rather than a specific defender.

zone defense—A type of pass defense in which each defender is responsible for an area, not for a particular receiver.

Professional Champions

National Football League

Year	Team (Coach)	Record
1919	Canton Bulldogs (Jim Thorpe)	—
1920	Akron Pros (Elgie Tobin)	—
1921	Chicago Staleys (George Halas)	10-1-1
1922	Canton Bulldogs (Guy Chamberlin)	10-0-2
1923	Canton Bulldogs (Guy Chamberlin)	11-0-1
1924	Cleveland Indians (Guy Chamberlin)	7-1-1
1925	Chicago Cardinals (Norman Barry)	11-2-1
1926	Frankford Yellowjackets (Guy Chamberlin)	14-1-1
1927	New York Giants (Earl Potteiger)	11-1-1
1928	Providence Steamrollers (Jim Conzelman)	8-1-2
1929	Green Bay Packers (Curly Lambeau)	12-0-1
1930	Green Bay Packers (Curly Lambeau)	10-3-1
1931	Green Bay Packers (Curly Lambeau)	12-2-0
1932	Chicago Bears (Ralph Jones)	7-1-6
1933	East—New York Giants (Steve Owen)	11-3-0
	West—Chicago Bears (George Halas)	10-2-1
	Championship—Chicago 23, New York 21	
1934	East—New York Giants (Steve Owen)	8-5-0
	West—Chicago Bears (George Halas)	10-2-1
	Championship—New York 30, Chicago 13	
1935	East—New York Giants (Steve Owen)	9-3-0
	West—Detroit Lions ("Potsy" Clark)	7-3-2
	Championship—Detroit 26, New York 7	
1936	East—Boston Redskins (Ray Flaherty)	7-5-0
	West—Green Bay Packers (Curly Lambeau)	10-1-1
	Championship—Green Bay 21, Boston 6	
1937	East—Washington Redskins (Ray Flaherty)	8-3-0
	West—Chicago Bears (George Halas)	9-1-1
	Championship—Washington 28, Chicago 21	
1938	East—New York Giants (Steve Owen)	8-2-1
	West—Green Bay Packers (Curly Lambeau)	
	Championship—New York 23, Green Bay 17	
1939	East—New York Giants (Steve Owen)	9-1-1
	West—Green Bay Packers (Curly Lambeau)	9-2-0
	Championship—Green Bay 27, New York 0	
1940	East—Washington Redskins (Ray Flaherty)	9-2-0
	West—Chicago Bears (George Halas)	8-3-0
	Championship—Chicago 73, Washington 0	
1941	East—New York Giants (Steve Owen)	8-3-0
	West—Chicago Bears (George Halas)	8-3-0*
	(*Beat Green Bay Packers, 33-14, in division play-off)	
	Championship—Chicago 37, New York 9	
1942	East—Washington Redskins (Ray Flaherty)	10-1-0
	West—Chicago Bears (George Halas)	11-0-0
	Championship—Washington 14, Chicago 6	
1943	East—Washington Redskins (Dutch Bergman)	6-3-1*
	West—Chicago Bears (Luke Johnsos, Hunk Anderson)	10-1-0
	(*Beat New York Giants, 28-0, in division play-off)	
	Championship—Chicago 41, Washington 21	
1944	East—New York Giants (Steve Owen)	8-1-1
	West—Green Bay Packers (Curly Lambeau)	8-2-0
	Championship—Green Bay 14, New York 7	
1945	East—Washington Redskins (Dudley DeGroot)	8-2-0
	West—Cleveland Rams (Adam Walsh)	9-1-0
	Championship—Cleveland 15, Washington 14	
1946	East—New York Giants (Steve Owen)	7-3-1
	West—Chicago Bears (George Halas)	8-2-1
	Championship—Chicago 24, New York 14	
1947	East—Philadelphia (Greasy Neale)	8-4-0*
	West—Chicago Cardinals (Jim Conzelman)	9-3-0
	(*Beat Pittsburgh Steelers, 21-0, in division play-off)	
	Championship—Chicago 28, Philadelphia 21	
1948	East—Philadelphia Eagles (Greasy Neale)	9-2-1
	West—Chicago Cardinals (Jim Conzelman)	11-1-0
	Championship—Philadelphia 7, Chicago 0	
1949	East—Philadelphia Eagles (Greasy Neale)	11-1-0
	West—Los Angeles Rams (Clark Shaughnessy)	8-2-2
	Championship—Philadelphia 14, Los Angeles 0	

(NFL and All-American Football Conference merged; three AAFC teams joined the NFL, which was divided into American and National Conferences for the next three years, before reverting to Eastern and Western.)

1950	Am.—Cleveland Browns (Paul Brown)	10-2-0*
	Nat.—Los Angeles Rams (Joe Stydahar)	9-3-0**
	(*Beat New York Giants, 8-3, in conference play-off)	
	(**Beat Chicago Bears, 24-14, in conference play-off)	
	Championship—Cleveland 30, Los Angeles 28	
1951	Am.—Cleveland Browns (Paul Brown)	11-1-0
	Nat.—Los Angeles Rams (Joe Stydahar)	8-4-0
	Championship—Los Angeles 24, Cleveland 17	
1952	Am.—Cleveland Browns (Paul Brown)	8-4-0
	Nat.—Detroit Lions (Buddy Parker)	9-3-0*
	(*Beat Los Angeles Rams, 31-21, in conference play-off)	
	Championship—Detroit 17, Cleveland 7	
1953	East—Cleveland Browns (Paul Brown)	11-1-0
	West—Detroit Lions (Buddy Parker)	10-2-0
	Championship—Detroit 17, Cleveland 16	
1954	East—Cleveland Browns (Paul Brown)	9-3-0
	West—Detroit Lions (Buddy Parker)	9-2-1
	Championship—Cleveland 56, Detroit 10	
1955	East—Cleveland Browns (Paul Brown)	9-2-1
	West—Los Angeles Rams (Sid Gillman)	8-3-1
	Championship—Cleveland 38, Los Angeles 14	
1956	East—New York Giants (Jim Lee Howell)	8-3-1
	West—Chicago Bears (George Halas)	9-2-1
	Championship—New York 47, Chicago 7	

1957	East—Cleveland Browns (Paul Brown)	9-2-1
	West—Detroit Lions (George Wilson)	8-4-0*
	(*Beat San Francisco 49ers, 31-27, in conference play-off)	
	Championship—Detroit 59, Cleveland 14	
1958	East—New York Giants (Jim Lee Howell)	9-3-0*
	West—Baltimore Colts (Weeb Ewbank)	9-3-0
	(*Beat Cleveland Browns, 10-0, in conference play-off)	
	Championship—Baltimore 23, New York 17 (sudden death)	
1959	East—New York Giants (Jim Lee Howell)	10-2-0
	West—Baltimore Colts (Weeb Ewbank)	9-3-0
	Championship—Baltimore 31, New York 16	
1960	East—Philadelphia Eagles (Buck Shaw)	10-2-0
	West—Green Bay Packers (Vince Lombardi)	8-4-0
	Championship—Philadelphia 17, Green Bay 13	
1961	East—New York Giants (Allie Sherman)	10-3-1
	West—Green Bay Packers (Vince Lombardi)	11-3-0
	Championship—Green Bay 37, New York 0	
1962	East—New York Giants (Allie Sherman)	12-2-0
	West—Green Bay Packers (Vince Lombardi)	13-1-0
	Championship—Green Bay 16, New York 7	
1963	East—New York Giants (Allie Sherman)	11-3-0
	West—Chicago Bears (George Halas)	11-1-2
	Championship—Chicago 14, New York 10	
1964	East—Cleveland Browns (Blanton Collier)	10-3-1
	West—Baltimore Colts (Don Shula)	12-2-0
	Championship—Cleveland 27, Baltimore 0	
1965	East—Cleveland Browns (Blanton Collier)	11-3-0
	West—Green Bay Packers (Vince Lombardi)	10-3-1
	Championship—Green Bay 23, Cleveland 12	
1966	East—Dallas Cowboys (Tom Landry)	10-3-1
	West—Green Bay Packers (Vince Lombardi)	12-2-0
	Championship—Green Bay 34, Dallas 27	

(Between the 1966 and 1967 seasons, the NFL reorganized into four divisions, the Capitol and Century Divisions in the Eastern Conference and the Coastal and Central Divisions in the Western Conference, with a semifinal round of playoffs before the championship game.)

1967	Capitol—Dallas Cowboys (Tom Landry)	9-5-0
	Century—Cleveland Browns (Blanton Collier)	9-5-0
	Coastal—Los Angeles Rams (George Allen)	11-2-2
	Central—Green Bay Packers (Vince Lombardi)	9-4-1
	Dallas 52, Cleveland 14	
	Green Bay 28, Los Angeles 7	
	Championship—Green Bay 21, Dallas 17	
1968	Capitol—Dallas Cowboys (Tom Landry)	12-2-0
	Century—Cleveland Browns (Blanton Collier)	10-4-0
	Coastal—Baltimore Colts (Don Shula)	13-1-0
	Central—Minnesota Vikings (Bud Grant)	8-6-0
	Cleveland 31, Dallas 20	
	Baltimore 24, Minnesota 14	
	Championship—Baltimore 34, Cleveland 0	
1969	Capitol—Dallas Cowboys (Tom Landry)	11-2-1
	Century—Cleveland Browns (Blanton Collier)	10-3-1
	Coastal—Los Angeles Rams (George Allen)	11-3-0
	Central—Minnesota Vikings (Bud Grant)	12-2-0
	Cleveland 38, Dallas 14	
	Minnesota 23, Los Angeles 20	
	Championship—Minnesota 27, Cleveland 7	

(Between the 1969 and 1970 seasons, the NFL and American Football League merged, forming two conferences—American and National—with three divisions in each, and the playoff system was changed so that the second-place division team with the best record was also entitled to enter championship play. Two rounds of play-offs determine conference champions, and they meet in the "Super Bowl" for the NFL championship. Super Bowl results are listed separately below.)

1970	American Conference:	
	East—Baltimore Colts (Don McCafferty)	11-2-1
	Central—Cincinnati Bengals (Paul Brown)	8-6-0
	West—Oakland Raiders (John Madden)	8-4-2
	National Conference:	
	East—Dallas Cowboys (Tom Landry)	10-4-0
	Central—Minnesota Vikings (Bud Grant)	12-2-0
	West—San Francisco 49ers (Dick Nolan)	10-3-1
	Baltimore 17, Cincinnati 0	
	Oakland 21, Miami* 14	
	Dallas 5, Detroit* 0	
	San Francisco 17, Minnesota 14	
	(*Indicates second-place qualifier)	
	Conference Finals—Baltimore 27, Oakland 17;	
	Dallas 17, San Francisco 10	
1971	American Conference:	
	East—Miami Dolphins (Don Shula)	10-3-1
	Central—Cleveland Browns (Nick Skorich)	9-5-0
	West—Kansas City Chiefs (Hank Stram)	10-3-1
	National Conference:	
	East—Dallas Cowboys (Tom Landry)	11-3-0
	Central—Minnesota Vikings (Bud Grant)	11-3-0
	West—San Francisco 49ers (Dick Nolan)	9-5-0
	Miami 27, Kansas City 24**	
	Baltimore* 20, Cleveland 3	
	Dallas 20, Minnesota 12	
	San Francisco 24, Washington* 20	
	(*Indicates second-place qualifier)	
	(**Sudden death—two overtimes)	
	Conference Finals—Miami 21, Baltimore 0;	
	Dallas 14, San Francisco 3	
1972	American Conference:	
	East—Miami Dolphins (Don Shula)	14-0-0
	Central—Pittsburgh Steelers (Chuck Noll)	11-3-0
	West—Oakland Raiders (John Madden)	10-3-1
	National Conference:	
	East—Washington Redskins (George Allen)	11-3-0
	Central—Green Bay Packers (Dan Devine)	10-4-0
	West—San Francisco 49ers (Dick Nolan)	8-5-1
	Miami 20, Cleveland 14	
	Pittsburgh 13, Oakland* 7	
	Washington 16, Green Bay 3	
	Dallas* 30, San Francisco 28	
	(*Indicates second-place qualifier)	
	Conference Finals—Miami 21, Pittsburgh 17;	
	Washington 26, Dallas 3	
1973	American Conference:	
	East—Miami Dolphins (Don Shula)	12-2-0
	Central—Cincinnati Bengals (Paul Brown)	10-4-0
	West—Oakland Raiders (John Madden)	9-4-1
	National Conference:	
	East—Dallas Cowboys (Tom Landry)	10-4-0
	Central—Minnesota Vikings (Bud Grant)	12-2-0
	West—Los Angeles Rams (Chuck Knox)	12-2-0
	Dallas 27, Los Angeles 16	
	Minnesota 27, Washington* 10	
	Miami 34, Cincinnati 16	
	Oakland 33, Pittsburgh* 14	
	(*Indicates second-place qualifier)	
	Conference Finals—Miami 27, Oakland 10;	
	Minnesota 27, Dallas 10	
1974	American Conference:	
	East—Miami Dolphins (Don Shula)	11-3-0
	Central—Pittsburgh Steelers (Chuck Noll)	10-3-1
	West—Oakland Raiders (John Madden)	12-2-0
	National Conference:	
	East—St. Louis Cardinals (Don Coryell)	10-4-0
	Central—Minnesota Vikings (Bud Grant)	10-4-0
	West—Los Angeles Rams (Chuck Knox)	10-4-0
	Oakland 28, Miami 26	

Pittsburgh 32, Buffalo* 14
Minnesota 30, St. Louis 14
Los Angeles 19, Washington* 10
(*Indicates second-place qualifier)
Conference Finals—Pittsburgh 24, Oakland 13;
Minnesota 14, Los Angeles 10

1975	American Conference:	
	East—Baltimore Colts (Ted Marchibroda)	10-4-0
	Central—Pittsburgh Steelers (Chuck Noll)	12-2-0
	West—Oakland Raiders (John Madden)	11-3-0
	National Conference:	
	East—St. Louis Cardinals (Don Coryell)	11-3-0
	Central—Minnesota Vikings (Bud Grant)	12-2-0
	West—Los Angeles Rams (Chuck Knox)	12-2-0

Dallas* 17, Minnesota 14
Los Angeles 35, St. Louis 23
Pittsburgh 28, Baltimore 10
Oakland 31, Cincinnati* 28
(*Indicates second-place qualifier)
Conference Finals—Pittsburgh 16, Oakland 10
Dallas 37, Los Angeles 7

1976	American Conference:	
	East—Baltimore Colts (Ted Marchibroda)	11-3-0
	Central—Pittsburgh Steelers (Chuck Noll)	10-4-0
	West—Oakland Raiders (John Madden)	13-1-0
	National Conference:	
	East—Dallas Cowboys (Tom Landry)	11-3-0
	Central—Minnesota Vikings (Bud Grant)	11-2-1
	West—Los Angeles Rams (Chuck Knox)	10-3-1

Minnesota 35, Washington*
Los Angeles 14, Dallas 12
Oakland 24, New England* 21
Pittsburgh 40, Baltimore 14
(*Indicates second-place qualifier)
Conference Finals—Oakland 24, Pittsburgh 7;
Minnesota 24, Los Angeles 14

American Football League (1960-69)

1960	East—Houston Oilers (Lou Rymkus)	10-4-0
	West—Los Angeles Chargers (Sid Gillman)	10-4-0
	Championship—Houston 24, Los Angeles 16	
	East—Houston Oilers (Lou Rymkus, Wally Lemm)	10-3-1
	West—San Diego Chargers (Sid Gillman)	12-2-0
	Championship—Houston 10, San Diego 3	
1962	East—Houston Oilers (Pop Ivy)	11-3-0
	West—Dallas Texans (Hank Stram)	11-3-0
	Championship—Dallas 20, Houston 17 (sudden death)	
1963	East—Boston Patriots (Mike Holovak)	7-6-1*
	West—San Diego Chargers (Sid Gillman)	11-3-0
	(*Beat Buffalo, 26-8, in division play-off)	
	Championship—San Diego 51, Boston 10	
1964	East—Buffalo Bills (Lou Saban)	12-2-0
	West—San Diego Chargers (Sid Gillman)	8-5-1
	Championship—Buffalo 20, San Diego 7	
1965	East—Buffalo Bills (Lou Saban)	10-3-1
	West—San Diego Chargers (Sid Gillman)	9-2-3
	Championship—Buffalo 23, San Diego 0	
1966	East—Buffalo Bills (Lou Saban)	9-4-1
	West—Kansas City Chiefs (Hank Stram)	11-2-1
	Championship—Kansas City 31, Buffalo 7	
1967	East—Houston Oilers (Wally Lemm)	9-4-1
	West—Oakland Raiders (John Rauch)	13-1-0
	Championship—Oakland 40, Houston 7	
1968	East—New York Jets (Weeb Ewbank)	11-3-0
	West—Oakland Raiders (John Rauch)	12-2-0*
	(*Beat Kansas City Chiefs, 41-6, in division play-off)	
	Championship—New York 27, Oakland 23	
1969	East—New York Jets (Weeb Ewbank)	10-4-0
	West—Oakland Raiders (John Madden)	12-1-1

Kansas City* 13, New York 6
Championship—Kansas City 17, Oakland 7
(*Indicates second-place team in division)

Super Bowl Winners

(The Super Bowl, formally the AFC-NFC championship game, is played in January of the year following the season. Therefore, the winner of, for example, the 1967 Super Bowl was actually the 1966 professional football champion.)

1967	Green Bay Packers 35, Kansas City Chiefs 10
1968	Green Bay Packers 33, Oakland Raiders 14
1969	New York Jets 16, Baltimore Colts 7
1970	Kansas City Chiefs 23, Minnesota Vikings 7
1971	Baltimore Colts 16, Dallas Cowboys 13
1972	Dallas Cowboys 24, Miami Dolphins 3
1973	Miami Dolphins 14, Washington Redskins 7
1974	Miami Dolphins 24, Minnesota Vikings 7
1975	Pittsburgh Steelers 16, Minnesota Vikings 6
1976	Pittsburgh Steelers 21, Dallas Cowboys 17

Other Professional Leagues

American Football League (1926)

1926	Philadelphia Quakers (Bob Folwell)	7-2-0

American Football League (1936-37)

1936	Boston Shamrocks (George Kenneally)	8-3-0
1937	Los Angeles Bulldogs (Gus Henderson)	8-0-0

American Football League (1940-41)

1940	Columbus Bullies (Phil Bucklew)	8-1-1
1941	Columbus Bullies (Phil Bucklew)	5-1-2

All-American Football Conference (1946-49)

1946	West—Cleveland Browns (Paul Brown)	12-2-0
	East—New York Yankees (Ray Flaherty)	10-3-1
	Championship—Cleveland 14, New York 9	
1947	West—Cleveland Browns (Paul Brown)	12-1-1
	East—New York Yankees (Ray Flaherty)	11-2-1
	Championship—Cleveland 14, New York 3	
	West—Cleveland Browns (Paul Brown)	14-0-0
	East—Buffalo Bills (Lowell Dawson)	7-7-0*
	(*Beat Baltimore Colts, 28-18, for division championship)	
	Championship—Cleveland 49, Buffalo 7	
1949	First Place—Cleveland Browns (Paul Brown)	9-1-2
	Second Place—San Francisco 49ers (Buck Shaw)	9-3-0
	Championship—Cleveland 21, San Francisco 7	

Pro Football Statistical Leaders

(NFL leaders are listed 1932–69, AFL leaders 1960–69; thereafter the leader of each conference is listed for each year, with the NFC leader listed first.)

Passing

Year	Leader	Att.	Com.	Yd.	TD
1932	Arnie Herber, Green Bay	101	37	639	9
1933	Harry Newman, New York Giants	132	53	963	8
1934	Arnie Herber, Green Bay	115	42	799	8
1935	Ed Danowski, New York Giants	113	57	795	9
1936	Arnie Herber, Green Bay	173	77	1,239	9
1937	Sammy Baugh, Washington	171	81	1,127	7
1938	Ed Danowski, New York Giants	129	70	848	8
1939	Parker Hall, Cleveland Rams	208	106	1,227	9
1940	Sammy Baugh, Washington	177	111	1,367	12

1941	Cecil Isbell, Green Bay	207	117	1,479	15
1942	Cecil Isbell, Green Bay	268	146	2,021	24
1943	Sammy Baugh, Washington	239	133	1,754	23
1944	Frank Filchock, Washington	147	84	1,139	13
1945	Sammy Baugh, Washington	182	128	1,669	11
1946	Bob Waterfield, Los Angeles	251	227	1,747	18
1947	Sammy Baugh, Washington	354	210	2,938	25
1948	Tommy Thompson, Philadelphia	246	141	1,965	25
1949	Sammy Baugh, Washington	255	145	1,903	18
1950	Norm Van Brocklin, Los Angeles	233	127	2,061	13
1951	Bob Waterfield, Los Angeles	176	88	1,566	13
1952	Norm Van Brocklin, Los Angeles	205	113	1,736	14
1953	Otto Graham, Cleveland	258	167	2,722	11
1954	Norm Van Brocklin, Los Angeles	260	139	2,637	13
1955	Otto Graham, Cleveland	185	98	1,721	15
1956	Eddie Brown, Chicago Bears	168	96	1,667	11
1957	Tommy O'Connell, Cleveland	110	63	1,229	9
1958	Eddie LeBaron, Washington	145	79	1,365	11
1959	Charlie Conerly, New York Giants	194	113	1,706	14
1960	Milt Plum, Cleveland (NFL)	250	151	2,297	21
	Jack Kemp, Los Angeles (AFL)	406	211	3,018	20
1961	Milt Plum, Cleveland (NFL)	302	177	2,416	18
	George Blanda, Houston (AFL)	362	187	3,330	36
1962	Bart Starr, Green Bay (NFL)	285	178	2,438	12
	Len Dawson, Dallas (AFL)	310	189	2,759	29
1963	Y. A. Tittle, New York (NFL)	367	221	3,145	36
	Tobin Rote, San Diego (AFL)	286	170	2,510	20
1964	Bart Starr, Green Bay (NFL)	272	163	2,144	15
	Len Dawson, Kansas City (AFL)	354	199	2,879	30
1965	Rudy Bukich, Chicago (NFL)	312	176	2,641	20
	John Hadl, San Diego (AFL)	348	174	2,798	20
1966	Bart Starr, Green Bay (NFL)	251	156	2,257	14
	Len Dawson, Kansas City (AFL)	284	159	2,527	26
1967	C. A. "Sonny" Jurgensen, Washington (NFL)	508	288	3,747	31
	Daryle Lamonica, Oakland (AFL)	425	220	3,228	30
1968	Earl Morrall, Baltimore (NFL)	317	182	2,909	26
	Len Dawson, Kansas City (AFL)	224	131	2,109	17
1969	C. A. "Sonny" Jurgensen, Washington (NFL)	442	274	3,102	22
	Greg Cook, Cincinnati (AFL)	197	106	1,854	15
1970	John Brodie, San Francisco (NFC)	378	223	2,941	24
	Daryle Lamonica, Oakland (AFC)	363	179	2,516	22
1971	Roger Staubach, Dallas (NFC)	211	126	1,882	15
	Bob Griese, Miami (AFC)	263	145	2,089	19
1972	Norm Snead, New York Giants (NFC)	325	196	2,307	17
	Earl Morrall, Miami (AFC)	150	83	1,360	11
1973	Roger Staubach, Dallas (NFC)	286	179	2,428	23
	Ken Stabler, Oakland (AFC)	260	163	1,997	14
1974	C. A. "Sonny" Jurgensen, Washington (NFC)	167	107	1,185	11
	Ken Anderson, Cincinnati (AFC)	328	213	2,667	18
1975	Fran Tarkenton, Minnesota (NFC)	425	273	2,994	25
	Ken Anderson, Cincinnati (AFC)	377	228	3,169	21
1976	James Harris, Los Angeles (NFC)	158	91	1,460	8
	Ken Stabler, Oakland (AFC)	291	194	2,737	27

Rushing

Year	Leader	Att.	Yd.	Av.	TD
1932	Bob Campiglio, Stapleton	104	504	4.8	2
1933	Cliff Battles, Boston	146	737	5.0	4
1934	Beattie Feathers, Chicago Bears	101	1,004	9.9	9
1935	Doug Russell, Chicago Cardinals	140	499	3.6	0
1936	Alphonse Leemans, New York Giants	206	380	4.0	2
1937	Cliff Battles, Washington	216	874	4.0	6
1938	Byron White, Pittsburgh	152	567	3.7	4
1939	Bill Osmanski, Chicago Bears	121	699	5.8	7
1940	Byron White, Detroit	146	514	3.5	5
1941	Clarence Manders, Brooklyn	111	586	4.4	7
1942	Bill Dudley, Pittsburgh	164	696	4.3	6
1943	Bill Paschal, New York Giants	147	572	3.9	10
1944	Bill Paschal, New York Giants	196	737	3.8	9
1945	Steve Van Buren,				
1946	Bill Dudley, Pittsburgh	146	604	4.1	3
1947	Steve Van Buren, Philadelphia	217	1,008	4.6	13
1948	Steve Van Buren, Philadelphia	201	145	4.7	10
1949	Steve Van Buren, Philadelphia	263	1,146	4.4	11
1950	Marion Motley, Cleveland	140	810	5.8	3
1951	Eddie Price, New York Giants	271	971	3.6	7
	Philadelphia	143	832	5.8	15
1952	Dan Towler, Los Angeles	196	894	5.7	10
1953	Joe Perry, San Francisco	192	1,018	5.2	10
1954	Joe Perry, San Francisco	173	1,049	6.1	8
1955	Alan Ameche, Baltimore	213	961	4.5	9
1956	Rick Casares, Chicago Bears	234	1,126	4.8	12
1957	Jim Brown, Cleveland	202	942	4.7	9
1958	Jim Brown, Cleveland	257	1,527	5.9	17
1959	Jim Brown, Cleveland	290	1,329	4.6	14
1960	Jim Brown, Cleveland (NFL)	215	1,257	5.8	9
	Abner Haynes, Dallas (AFL)	156	875	5.6	9
1961	Jim Brown, Cleveland (NFL)	305	1,408	4.6	8
	Billy Cannon, Houston (AFL)	200	948	4.7	6
1962	Jim Taylor, Green Bay (NFL)	272	1,474	5.4	19
	Cookie Gilchrist, Buffalo (AFL)	214	1,096	5.1	13
1963	Jim Brown, Cleveland (NFL)	291	1,863	6.4	12

Year	Leader				
	Clem Daniels, Oakland (AFL)	215	1,099	5.1	3
1964	Jim Brown, Cleveland (NFL)	280	1,446	5.2	7
	Cookie Gilchrist, Buffalo (AFL)	230	981	4.3	6
1965	Jim Brown, Cleveland (NFL)	289	1,544	5.3	17
	Paul Lowe, San Diego (AFL)	222	1,121	5.5	7
1966	Gale Sayers, Chicago (NFL)	229	1,231	5.4	8
	Jim Nance, Boston (AFL)	299	1,458	4.9	11
1967	Leroy Kelly, Cleveland (NFL)	235	1,205	5.1	11
	Jim Nance, Boston (AFL)	269	1,216	4.5	7
1968	Leroy Kelly, Cleveland (NFL)	248	1,239	5.0	16
	Paul Robinson, Cincinnati (AFL)	238	1,023	4.3	8
1969	Gale Sayers, Chicago (NFL)	236	1,032	4.4	8
	Dick Post, San Diego (AFL)	182	873	4.7	6
1970	Larry Brown, Washington (NFC)	237	1,125	4.7	5
	Floyd Little, Denver (AFC)	209	901	4.3	3
1971	John Brockington, Green Bay (NFC)	216	1,105	5.1	4
	Floyd Little, Denver (AFC)	284	1,133	4.0	6
1972	Larry Brown, Washington (NFC)	285	1,216	4.3	8
	O. J. Simpson, Buffalo (AFC)	292	1,251	4.3	6
1973	John Brockington, Green Bay (NFC)	265	1,144	4.3	3
	O. J. Simpson, Buffalo (AFC)	332	2,003	6.0	12
1974	Lawrence McCutcheon, Los Angeles (NFC)	236	1,109	4.7	3
	Otis Armstrong, Denver (AFC)	263	1,407	5.3	9
1975	Jim Otis, St. Louis (NFC)	269	1,076	4.0	5
	O. J. Simpson, Buffalo (AFC)	329	1,817	5.5	16
1976	Walter Payton, Chicago (NFC)	311	1,390	4.5	13
	O. J. Simpson, Buffalo (AFC)	290	1,503	5.2	8

Scoring

Year	Leader	TD	PAT	FG	Pts.
1932	Earl "Dutch" Clark, Portsmouth	4	6	3	39
1933	Ken Strong, New York Giants	6	13	5	64
	Glenn Presnell, Portsmouth	6	10	6	64
1934	Jack Manders, Chicago Bears	3	31	10	79
1935	Earl "Dutch" Clark, Detroit	6	16	1	55
1936	Earl "Dutch" Clark, Detroit	7	19	4	73
1937	Jack Manders, Chicago Bears	5	15	8	69
1938	Clarke Hinkle, Green Bay	7	7	3	58
1939	Andy Farkas, Washington	11	2	0	68
1940	Don Hutson, Green Bay	7	15	0	57
1941	Don Hutson, Green Bay	12	20	1	95
1942	Don Hutson, Green Bay	17	33	1	138
1943	Don Hutson, Green Bay	12	36	3	117
1944	Don Hutson, Green Bay	9	31	0	85
1945	Steve Van Buren, Philadelphia	18	2	0	110
1946	Ted Fritsch, Green Bay	10	13	9	100
1947	Pat Harder, Chicago Cardinals	7	39	7	102
1948	Pat Harder, Chicago Cardinals	6	53	7	110
1949	Pat Harder, Chicago Cardinals	8	45	3	102
	Gene Roberts, New York Giants	17	0	0	102
1950	Doak Walker, Detroit	11	38	8	128
1951	Elroy Hirsch, Los Angeles	17	00	0	102
1952	Gordon Soltau, San Francisco	7	34	6	94
1953	Gordon Soltau, San Francisco	6	48	10	114
1954	Robert Walston, Philadelphia	11	36	4	114
1955	Doak Walker, Detroit	7	27	9	96
1956	Bobby Layne, Detroit	5	33	12	99
1957	Sam Baker, Washington	1	29	14	77
	Lou Groza, Cleveland	0	32	15	77
1958	Jim Brown, Cleveland	18	0	0	108
1959	Paul Hornung, Green Bay	7	31	7	94
1960	Paul Hornung, Green Bay (NFL)	15	41	15	176
	Gene Mingo, Denver (AFL)	6	33	18	123
1961	Paul Hornung, Green Bay (NFL)	10	41	15	146
	Gino Cappelletti, Boston (AFL)	2	35	22	147
1962	Jim Taylor, Green Bay (NFL)	19	0	0	114
	Gene Mingo, Denver (AFL)	4	32	27	137
1963	Don Chandler, New York (NFL)	0	52	18	106
	Gino Cappelletti, Boston (AFL)	2	35	22	113
1964	Lenny Moore, Baltimore (NFL)	20	00	0	120
	Gino Cappelletti, Boston (AFL)	7	36	25	155
1965	Gale Sayers, Chicago (NFL)	22	0	0	132
	Gino Cappelletti, Boston (AFL)	9	27	17	132
1966	Bruce Gossett, Los Angeles (NFL)	0	29	28	113
	Gino Cappelletti, Boston (AFL)	6	35	16	119
1967	Jim Bakken, St. Louis (NFL)	0	36	27	117
	George Blanda, Oakland (AFL)	0	56	20	116
1968	Leroy Kelly, Cleveland (NFL)	20	0	0	120
	Jim Turner, New York (AFL)	0	43	34	145
1969	Fred Cox, Minnesota (NFL)	0	43	26	121
	Jim Turner, New York (AFL)	0	33	32	129
1970	Fred Cox, Minnesota (NFC)	0	35	30	125
	Jan Stenerud, Kansas City (AFC)	0	26	30	116
1971	Curt Knight, Washington (NFC)	0	27	29	114
	Garo Ypremian, Miami (AFC)	0	33	28	117
1972	Chester Marcol, Green Bay (NFC)	0	29	33	128
	Bobby Howfield, New York Jets (AFC)	0	40	27	121
1973	David Ray, Los Angeles (NFC)	0	40	37	130
	Roy Gerela, Pittsburgh (AFC)	0	36	29	123
1974	Chester Marcol, Green Bay (NFC)	0	19	25	94
	Roy Gerela, Pittsburgh (AFC)	0	33	20	93
1975	Chuck Foreman, Minnesota (NFC)	23	0	0	132
	O. J. Simpson, Buffalo (AFC)	23	0	0	138
1976	Jim Bakken, St. Louis (NFC)	0	33	27	93
	Toni Linhart, Baltimore (AFC)	0	49	20	109

Pass Receiving

Year	Leader	Rec.	Yd.	Av.	TD
1932	Luke Johnsos, Chicago Bears	24	321	13.4	2
1933	John Kelly, Brooklyn	21	219	10.4	3
1934	Joe Carter, Philadelphia	16	237	14.8	4
1935	Tod Goodwin, New York	26	432	16.6	4
1936	Don Hutson, Green Bay	34	526	15.5	9
1937	Don Hutson, Green Bay	41	552	13.5	7
1938	Gaynell Tinsley, Chicago Cardinals	41	516	12.6	1
1939	Don Hutson, Green Bay	34	846	24.9	6
1940	Don Looney, Philadelphia	58	707	12.2	4
1941	Don Hutson, Green Bay	58	738	12.7	10
1942	Don Hutson, Green Bay	74	1,211	16.4	17
1943	Don Hutson, Green Bay	47	776	16.5	11
1944	Don Hutson, Green Bay	58	866	14.9	9
1945	Don Hutson, Green Bay	47	834	18.7	9
1946	Jim Benton, Los Angeles	63	981	15.6	6
1947	Jim Keane, Chicago Bears	64	910	14.2	10
1948	Tom Fears, Los Angeles	51	698	13.7	4
1949	Tom Fears, Los Angeles	77	1,013	13.2	9
1950	Tom Fears, Los Angeles	84	1,116	13.3	7
1951	Elroy Hirsch, Los Angeles	66	1,495	22.7	17
1952	Mac Speedie, Cleveland	62	911	14.7	5
1953	Pete Pihos, Philadelphia	63	1,049	16.7	10
1954	Pete Pihos, Philadelphia	60	872	14.5	10
	Billy Wilson, San Francisco	60	830	13.8	5
1955	Pete Pihos, Philadelphia	62	864	13.9	7
1956	Billy Wilson, San Francisco	60	889	14.8	5
1957	Billy Wilson, San Francisco	52	757	14.6	6
1958	Ray Berry, Baltimore	56	794	14.2	9
	Pete Retzlaff, Philadelphia	56	766	13.7	2
1959	Ray Berry, Philadelphia	66	959	14.5	14
1960	Ray Berry, Baltimore (NFL)	74	1,298	17.5	10
	Lionel Taylor, Denver (AFL)	92	1,235	13.4	12
1961	Jim Phillips, Los Angeles (NFL)	78	1,092	14.0	5
	Lionel Taylor, Denver (AFL)	100	1,176	11.8	4
1962	Bobby Mitchell, Washington (NFL)	72	1,384	19.2	11
	Lionel Taylor, Denver (AFL)	77	908	11.8	4
1963	Bobby Joe Conrad, St. Louis (NFL)	73	967	13.4	10
	Lionel Taylor, Denver (AFL)	78	1,101	14.1	10
1964	Johnny Morris, Chicago (NFL)	93	1,200	12.7	10
	Charley Hennigan, Houston (AFL)	101	1,546	15.3	8
1965	Dave Parks, San Francisco (NFL)	80	1,344	16.8	12
	Lionel Taylor, Denver (AFL)	85	1,131	13.3	6
1966	Charley Taylor Washington (NFL)	72	1,119	15.4	12
	Lance Alworth, San Diego (AFL)	73	1,383	18.9	13
1967	Charley Taylor, Washington (NFL)	70	990	14.1	9
	George Sauer, New York (AFL)	75	1,189	15.9	6
1968	Clifton McNeil, San Francisco (NFL)	71	994	14.0	7
	Lance Alworth, San Diego (AFL)	68	1,312	19.3	10
1969	Dan Abramowicz, New Orleans (NFL)	73	1,015	13.9	7
	Lance Alworth, San Diego (AFL)	64	1,003	15.7	4
1970	Dick Gordon, Chicago (NFC)	71	1,026	14.5	13
	Marlin Briscoe, Buffalo (AFC)	57	1,036	18.2	8
1971	Bob Tucker, New York (NFC)	59	791	13.4	4
	Fred Biletnikoff, Oakland (AFC)	61	929	15.2	9
1972	Harold Jackson, Philadelphia (NFC)	62	1,048	16.9	4
	Fred Biletnikoff, Oakland (AFC)	58	802	13.8	7
1973	Harold Carmichael, Philadelphia (NFC)	67	1,116	16.7	9
	Bill Willis, Houston (AFC)	57	371	6.5	1
1974	Charles Young, Philadelphia (NFC)	63	696	11.0	3
	Lydell Mitchell, Baltimore (AFC)	72	544	7.6	2
1975	Chuck Foreman, Minnesota (NFC)	73	691	9.5	9
	Reggie Rucker, Cleveland (AFC)	60	770	12.8	3
1976	Drew Pearson, Dallas (NFC)	58	806	13.9	6
	MacArthur Lane, Kansas City (AFC)	66	686	10.4	1

Pass Interceptions
(Not tabulated until 1941)

Year	Leader	No.	Yd
1941	Marshall Goldberg, Chicago Cardinals	7	54
	Arthur Jones, Pittsburgh	7	35
1942	Clyde "Bulldog" Turner, Chicago Bears	8	96
1943	Sammy Baugh, Washington	11	112
1944	Howard Livingston, New York Giants	9	172
1945	Roy Zimmerman, Philadelphia	7	90
1946	Bill Dudley, Pittsburgh	10	242
1947	Frank Reagan, New York Giants	10	203
	Frank Seno, Boston Yanks	10	100
1948	Dan Sandifer, Washington	13	258
1949	Bob Nussbaumer, Chicago Cardinals	12	157
1950	Orban "Spec" Sanders, New York		

	Yanks	13	199
1951	Otto Schnellbacher, New York Giants	11	194
1952	Dick Lane, Los Angeles	14	298
1953	Jack Christiansen, Detroit	12	238
1954	Dick Lane, Chicago Cardinals	10	181
1955	Will Sherman, Los Angeles	11	101
1956	Lindon Crow, Chicago Cardinals	11	170
1957	Milt Davis, Baltimore	10	219
	Jack Christiansen, Detroit	10	137
	Jack Butler, Pittsburgh	10	85
1958	Jim Patton, New York	11	183
1959	Dean Derby, Pittsburgh	7	127
	Milt Davis, Baltimore	7	119
	Don Shinnick, Baltimore	7	70
1960	Dave Baker, San Francisco (NFL)	10	96
	Jerry Norton, St. Louis (NFL)	10	96
	Austin Gonsoulin, Denver (AFL)	11	98
1961	Dick Lynch, New York (NFL)	9	60
	Billy Atkins, Buffalo (AFL)	10	158
1962	Willie Wood, Green Bay (NFL)	9	132
	Lee Riley, New York (AFL)	11	122
1963	Dick Lynch, New York (NFL)	9	251
	Roosevelt Taylor, Chicago (NFL)	9	172
	Fred Glick, Houston (AFL)	12	180
1964	Paul Krause, Washington (NFL)	12	140
	Dainard Paulson, New York (AFL)	12	157
1965	Bobby Boyd, Baltimore (NFL)	9	78
	W. K. Hicks, Houston (AFL)	9	156
1966	Larry Wilson, St. Louis (NFL)	10	180
	Johnny Robinson, Kansas City (AFL)	10	136
	Bobby Hunt, Kansas City (AFL)	10	113
1967	Lem Barney, Detroit (NFL)	10	232
	Dave Whitsell, New Orleans (NFL)	10	178
	Miller Farr, Houston (AFL)	10	264
	Tom Janik, Buffalo (AFL)	10	220
	Dick Westmoreland, Miami (AFL)	10	127
1968	Willie Williams, New York (NFL)	10	103
	Dave Grayson, Oakland (AFL)	10	195
1969	Mel Renfro, Dallas (NFL)	10	118
	Emmitt Thomas, Kansas City (AFL)	9	146
1970	Dick Le Bean, Detroit (NFC)	9	106
	John Robinson, Kansas City (AFL)	10	155
1971	Bill Bradley, Philadelphia (NFC)	11	248
	Ken Houston, Houston (AFC)	9	220
1972	Bill Bradley, Philadelphia (NFC)	9	73
	Mike Sensibaugh, Kansas City (AFC)	8	65
1973	Bobby Bryant, Minnesota (NFC)	7	105
	Dick Anderson, Miami (AFC)	8	163
	Mike Wagner, Pittsburgh (AFC)	8	134
1974	Ray Brown, Atlanta (NFC)	8	164
	Emmitt Thomas, Kansas City (AFC)	12	214
1975	Paul Krause, Minnesota (NFC)	10	201
	Mel Blount, Pittsburgh (AFC)	11	121
1976	Monte Jackson, Los Angeles (NFC)	10	173
	Ken Riley, Cincinnati (AFC)	9	141

NFL Most Valuable Players

Official League Selections
1938 Mel Hein, New York Giants, center
1939 Parker Hall, Cleveland Rams, halfback
1940 Clarence "Ace" Parker, Brooklyn Dodgers, halfback
1941 Don Hutson, Green Bay Packers, end
1942 Don Hutson, Green Bay Packers, end
1943 Sid Luckman, Chicago Bears, quarterback
1944 Frank Sinkwich, Detroit Lions, quarterback
1945 Bob Waterfield, Los Angeles Rams, quarterback
1946 Bill Dudley, Pittsburgh Steelers, halfback
      (Discontinued)

Jim Thorpe Trophy
1955 Harlon Hill, Chicago Bears, end
1956 Frank Gifford, New York Giants, halfback

1957 John Unitas, Baltimore Colts, quarterback
1958 Jim Brown, Cleveland Browns, fullback
1959 Charlie Conerly, New York Giants, quarterback
1960 Norm Van Brocklin, Philadelphia Eagles, quarterback
1961 Y. A. Tittle, New York Giants, quarterback
1962 Jim Taylor, Green Bay Packers, fullback
1963 Jim Brown, Cleveland Browns, fullback
      Y. A. Tittle, New York Giants, quarterback
1964 Lenny Moore, Baltimore Colts, halfback
1965 Jim Brown, Cleveland Browns, fullback
1966 Bryan Bart Starr, Green Bay Packers, quarterback
1967 John Unitas, Baltimore Colts, quarterback
1968 Earl Morrall, Baltimore Colts, quarterback
1969 Roman Gabriel, Los Angeles Rams, quarterback
1970 John Brodie, San Francisco 49ers, quarterback (NFC)
      George Blanda, Oakland Raiders, quarterback (AFC)
1971 Alan Page, Minnesota Vikings, defensive tackle (NFC)
      Bob Griese, Miami Dolphins, quarterback (AFC)
1972 Larry Brown, Washington Redskins, halfback (NFC)
      Earl Morrall, Miami Dolphins, quarterback (AFC)
1973 John Hadl, Los Angeles Rams, quarterback (NFC)
      O. J. Simpson, Buffalo Bills, running back (AFC)
1974 Chuck Foreman, Minnesota Vikings, running back (NFC)
      Ken Stabler, Oakland Raiders, quarterback (AFC)
1975 Fran Tarkenton, Minnesota Vikings, quarterback (NFC)
      O. J. Simpson, Buffalo Bills, running back (AFC)
1976 Chuck Foreman, Minnesota Vikings, running back (NFC)
      Bert Jones, Baltimore Colts, quarterback (AFC)

College Champions

Among major colleges, the national championship is mythical, based on polls conducted by various organizations, including both wire services, the Football Writers Association of America, and others. The Citizens Savings-Helms Athletic Foundation has also reconstructed a list of national champions, starting in 1889. The following list is based on the Helms choices; the Rissman Trophy winners from 1924 through 1930, when Notre Dame retired the trophy by winning it for a third time; the Knute Rockne Memorial Trophy, awarded by the Associated Press 1931-40; the AP, United Press, and FBWAA polls. Where one team won a majority of polls, that team is listed; where opinion was clearly split, two teams are listed. (Won-lost records include postseason games.)

Major Colleges

1889	Princeton (no coach)	10-0-0
1890	Harvard (G. A. Stewart, G. C. Adams)	11-0-0
1891	Yale (Walter C. Camp)	13-0-0
1892	Yale (Walter C. Camp)	13-0-0
1893	Princeton (no coach)	11-0-0
1894	Yale (William C. Rhodes)	16-0-0
1895	Pennsylvania (G. W. Woodruff)	14-0-0
1896	Princeton (no coach)	10-0-1
1897	Pennsylvania (G. W. Woodruff)	15-0-0
1898	Harvard (W. Cameron Forbes)	11-0-0
1899	Harvard (Benjamin H. Dibblee)	10-0-1
1900	Yale (Malcolm L. McBride)	12-0-0
1901	Michigan (Fielding H. Yost)	11-0-0
1902	Michigan (Fielding H. Yost)	11-0-0
1903	Princeton (Doc Hillebrand)	11-0-0
1904	Pennsylvania (Carl S. Williams)	12-0-0
1905	Chicago (A. A. Stagg)	10-0-0
1906	Princeton (William W. Roper)	9-0-1
1907	Yale (William F. Knox)	9-0-1
1908	Pennsylvania (Sol S. Metzger)	11-0-1
1909	Yale (Howard H. Jones)	10-0-0
1910	Harvard (Percy D. Haughton)	8-0-1
1911	Princeton (William W. Roper)	8-0-2
1912	Harvard (Percy D. Haughton)	9-0-0

1913	Harvard (Percy D. Haughton)	9-0-0
1914	Army (Charles D. Daly)	9-0-0
1915	Cornell (Albert H. Sharpe)	9-0-0
1916	Pittsburgh (Glenn S. Warner)	8-0-0
1917	Georgia Tech (John W. Heisman)	9-0-0
1918	Pittsburgh (Glenn S. Warner)	4-1-0
1919	Harvard (Robert T. Fisher)	9-0-1
1920	California (Andrew L. Smith)	9-0-0
1921	Cornell (Gilmour Dobie)	8-0-0
1922	Cornell (Gilmour Dobie)	8-0-0
1923	Illinois (Robert C. Zuppke)	8-0-0
1924	Notre Dame (Knute Rockne)	9-0-0
1925	Alabama (Wallace Wade)	10-0-0
	Dartmouth (Jess Hawley)	8-0-0
1926	Alabama (Wallace Wade)	9-0-1
	Dartmouth (Glenn S. Warner)	10-0-1
1927	Illinois (Robert C. Zuppke)	7-0-1
1928	Georgia Tech (William A. Alexander)	10-0-0
1929	Notre Dame (Knute Rockne)	9-0-0
1930	Notre Dame (Knute Rockne)	10-0-0
1931	So. California (Howard H. Jones)	10-1-0
1932	So. California (Howard H. Jones)	10-0-0
1933	Michigan (Harry G. Kipke)	7-0-1
1934	Minnesota (Bernard W. Bierman)	8-0-0
	Alabama (Frank Thomas)	10-0-0
1935	Minnesota (Bernard W. Bierman)	8-0-0
	Southern Methodist (Madison Bell)	12-1-0
1936	Minnesota (Bernard W. Bierman)	7-1-0
1937	Pittsburgh (John B. Sutherland)	9-0-1
1938	Texas Christian (Dutch Meyer)	11-0-0
	Tennessee (Robert R. Newland)	11-0-0
1939	Texas A&M (Homer H. Norton)	11-0-0
1940	Minnesota (Bernard W. Bierman)	8-0-0
1941	Minnesota (Bernard W. Bierman)	8-0-0
	Georgia (Wally Butts)	11-1-0
1942	Wisconsin (Harry Stuldreher)	8-1-1
	Ohio State (Paul E. Brown)	9-1-0
1943	Notre Dame (Frank Leahy)	9-1-0
1944	Army (Earl "Red" Blaik)	9-0-0
1945	Army (Earl "Red" Blaik)	9-0-0
1946	Army (Earl "Red" Blaik)	9-0-1
	Notre Dame (Frank Leahy)	8-0-1
1947	Notre Dame (Frank Leahy)	9-0-0
	Michigan (Benjamin G. Oosterbaan)	10-0-0
1948	Michigan (Benjamin G. Oosterbaan)	9-0-0
1949	Notre Dame (Frank Leahy)	10-0-0
1950	Oklahoma (Bud Wilkinson)	10-1-0
1951	Tennessee (Robert R. Neyland)	10-1-0
1952	Michigan State (Clarence L. Munn)	9-0-0
1953	Maryland (James M. Tatum)	10-1-0
	Notre Dame (Frank Leahy)	9-0-1
1954	UCLA (Henry R. "Red" Sanders)	9-0-0
	Ohio State (Woody Hayes)	10-0-0
1955	Oklahoma (Bud Wilkinson)	11-0-0
1956	Oklahoma (Bud Wilkinson)	10-0-0
1957	Auburn (Ralph "Shug" Jordan)	10-0-0
	Ohio State (Woody Hayes)	9-1-0
1958	Louisiana State (Paul Dietzel)	11-0-0
1959	Syracuse (Ben Schwartzwalder)	11-0-0
1960	Minnesota (Murray Warmath)	8-2-0
	Mississippi (John Vaught)	10-0-1
1961	Alabama ("Bear" Bryant)	11-0-0
1962	So. California (John McKay)	11-0-0
1963	Texas (Darrell Royal)	11-0-0
1964	Alabama ("Bear" Bryant)	10-1-0
1965	Alabama ("Bear" Bryant)	9-1-1
	Michigan State (Hugh "Duffy" Daugherty)	10-0-1
1966	Notre Dame (Ara Parseghian)	9-0-1
1967	So. California (John McKay)	10-1-0
1968	Ohio State (Woody Hayes)	10-0-0
1969	Texas (Darrell Royal)	10-0-0
1970	Texas (Darrell Royal)	10-1-0
	Nebraska (Bob Devaney)	10-0-1

1971	Nebraska (Bob Devaney)	12-0-0
1972	So. California (John McKay)	12-0-0
1973	Notre Dame (Ara Parseghian)	12-0-0
1974	Oklahoma (Barry Switzer)	11-0-0
	So. California (John McKay)	9-1-1
1975	Oklahoma (Barry Switzer)	11-1-0
1976	Pittsburgh (Johnny Majors)	12-0-0

Heisman Trophy Winners
(Outstanding College Player of the Year)

1935	Jay Berwanger, Chicago, halfback
1936	Larry Kelley, Yale, end
1937	Clint Frank, Yale, halfback
1938	Davey O'Brien, TCU, quarterback
1939	Nile Kinnick, Iowa, halfback
1940	Tom Harmon, Michigan, halfback
1941	Bruce Smith, Minnesota, halfback
1942	Frank Sinkwich, Georgia, halfback
1943	Angelo Bertelli, Notre Dame, quarterback
1944	Les Horvath, Ohio State, quarterback
1945	Felix "Doc" Blanchard, Army, fullback
1946	Glenn Davis, Army, halfback
1947	John Lujack, Notre Dame, quarterback
1948	Doak Walker, SMU, halfback
1949	Leon Hart, Notre Dame, end
1950	Vic Janowicz, Ohio State, halfback
1951	Dick Kazmaier, Princeton, halfback
1952	Billy Vessels, Oklahoma, halfback
1953	John Lattner, Notre Dame, halfback
1954	Alan Ameche, Wisconsin, fullback
1955	Howard "Hopalong" Cassady, Ohio State, halfback
1956	Paul Hornung, Notre Dame, quarterback
1957	John David Crow, Texas A&M, halfback
1958	Pete Dawkins, Army, halfback
1959	Billy Cannon, LSU, halfback
1960	Joe Bellino, Navy, halfback
1961	Ernie Davis, Syracuse, halfback
1962	Terry Baker, Oregon State, quarterback
1963	Roger Staubach, Navy, quarterback
1964	John Huarte, Notre Dame, quarterback
1965	Mike Garrett, So. California, halfback
1966	Steve Spurrier, Florida, quarterback
1967	Gary Beban, UCLA, quarterback
1968	O. J. Simpson, So. California, halfback
1969	Steve Owens, Oklahoma, fullback
1970	Jim Plunkett, Stanford, quarterback
1971	Pat Sullivan, Auburn, quarterback
1973	Johnny Rodgers, Nebraska, halfback
1973	John Cappelletti, Penn State, halfback
1974	Archie Griffin, Ohio State, halfback
1975	Archie Griffin, Ohio State, halfback
1976	Tony Dorsett, Pittsburgh, halfback

Outland Trophy
(Outstanding Interior Lineman of the Year)

1946	George Connor, Notre Dame, tackle
1947	Joe Steffy, Army, guard
1948	Bill Fischer, Notre Dame, guard
1949	Ed Bagdon, Michigan St., guard
1950	Bob Gain, Kentucky, tackle
1951	Jim Weatherall, Oklahoma, tackle
1952	Dick Modzelewski, Maryland, tackle
1953	J. D. Roberts, Oklahoma, guard
1954	Bill Brooks, Arkansas, guard
1955	Calvin Jones, Iowa, guard
1956	Jim Parker, Ohio St., guard
1957	Alex Karras, Iowa, tackle
1958	Zeke Smith, Auburn, guard
1959	Mike McGee, Duke, tackle
1960	Tom Brown, Minnesota, guard
1961	Merlin Olsen, Utah State, tackle
1962	Bobby Bell, Minnesota, tackle

1963 Scott Appleton, Texas, tackle
1964 Steve DeLong, Tennessee, tackle
1965 Tommy Nobis, Texas, guard
1966 Lloyd Phillips, Arkansas, tackle
1967 Ron Yary, So. California, tackle
1968 Bill Stanfill, Georgia, tackle
1969 Mike Reid, Penn State, defensive tackle
1970 Jim Stillwagon, Ohio State, linebacker
1971 Larry Jacobson, Nebraska, defensive tackle
1972 Rich Glover, Nebraska, middle guard
1973 John Hicks, Ohio State, tackle
1974 Randy White, Maryland, defensive tackle
1975 Leroy Selmon, Oklahoma, defensive end
1976 Ross Browner, Notre Dame, defensive end

NCAA Statistical Leaders
(Major Colleges)

(Since 1970, leadership has been based on per-game average, not raw statistics)

Passing

Year	Player, School	Att.	Com.	Pct.	Yd
1937	Davey O'Brien, TCU	234	94	.402	969
1938	Davey O'Brien, TCU	167	93	.557	1,457
1939	Kay Eakin, Arkansas	193	78	.404	962
1940	Bill Sewell, Washington St.	174	86	.494	1,023
1941	Bud Schwenk, Washington (Mo.)	234	114	.487	1,457
1942	Ray Evans, Kansas	200	101	.505	1,117
1943	Johnny Cook, Georgia	157	73	.465	1,007
1944	Paul Richards, Pittsburgh	178	84	.472	997
1945	Al Dekdebrun, Cornell	194	90	.464	1,227
1946	Travis Tidwell, Auburn	158	79	.500	943
1947	Charlie Conerly, Mississippi	233	133	.571	1,367
1948	Stan Heath, Nevada	222	126	.568	2,005
1949	Adrian Burk, Baylor	191	110	.576	1,428
1950	Don Heinrich, Washington	221	134	.606	1,846
1951	Don Klosterman, Loyola (Cal.)	315	159	.505	1,843
1952	Don Heinrich, Washington	270	137	.507	1,647
1953	Bob Garrett, Stanford	205	118	.576	1,637
1954	Paul Larson, California	195	125	.641	1,537
1955	George Welsh, Navy	150	94	.627	1,319
1956	John Brodie, Stanford	240	139	.579	1,633
1957	Ken Ford, Hardin-Simmons	205	115	.561	1,254
1958	Buddy Humphrey, Baylor	195	112	.574	1,316
1959	Dick Norman, Stanford	263	155	.578	1,963
1960	Harold Stephens, Hardin-Simmons	256	145	.566	1,254
1961	Chon Gallegos, San Jose St.	197	117	.594	1,480
1962	Don Trull, Baylor	229	125	.546	1,627
1963	Don Trull, Baylor	308	174	.565	2,157
1964	Jerry Rhome, Tulsa	326	224	.687	2,870
1965	Bill Anderson, Tulsa	509	296	.582	3,464
1966	John Eckman, Wichita St.	458	195	.426	2,339
1967	Terry Stone, New Mexico	336	160	.475	1,946
1968	Chuck Hixson, SMU	468	265	.566	3,103
1969	John Reaves, Florida	396	222	.561	2,896
1970	Sonny Sixkiller, Washington	362	186	.514	2,303
1971	Brian Sipe, San Diego St.	369	196	.531	2,532
1972	Don Strock, Virginia Tech	427	228	.534	3,243
1973	Jesse Freitas, San Diego St.	347	227	.654	2,993
1974	Steve Bartkowski, California	325	182	.566	2,580
1975	Craig Penrose, San Diego St.	349	198	.567	2,660
1976	Tom Kramer, Rice	501	269	.536	3,317

Rushing

Year	Player, School	Att.	Yd
1937	Byron "Whizzer" White, Colorado	181	1,121
1938	Len Eshmont, Fordham	132	831
1939	John Polanski, Wake Forest	137	882

When Ray Berry retired in 1968 after 13 seasons with the Baltimore Colts, he had caught 631 passes for 9,275 yards and 68 touchdowns, and had been named to three All-Pro teams. *(Pro Football Hall of Fame.)*

1940	Al Ghesquiere, Detroit	146	957
1941	Frank Sinkwich, Georgia	209	1,103
1942	Rudy Mobley, Hardin-Simmons	187	1,281
1943	Creighton Miller, Notre Dame	151	911
1944	Wayne Williams, Minnesota	136	911
1945	Bob Fenimore, Oklahoma St.	142	1,048
1946	Rudy Mobley, Hardin-Simmons	227	2,262
1947	Wilton Davis, Hardin-Simmons	193	1,173
1948	Fred Wendt, Texas-El Paso	184	1,570
1949	John Dottley, Mississippi	208	1,312
1950	Wilford White, Arizona St.	199	1,502
1951	Ollie Matson, San Francisco	245	1,566
1952	Howie Waugh, Tulsa	164	1,372
1953	J. C. Caroline, Illinois	194	1,256
1954	Art Luppino, Arizona	179	1,359
1955	Art Luppino, Arizona	209	1,313
1956	Jim Crawford, Wyoming	200	1,104
1957	Leon Burton, Arizona St.	117	1,126
1958	Dick Bass, Pacific	205	1,361
1959	Pervis Atkins, New Mexico St.	130	971
1960	Bob Gaiters, New Mexico St.	197	1,338
1961	Jim Pilot, New Mexico St.	191	1,278
1962	Jim Pilot, New Mexico St.	208	1,247
1963	Dave Casinelli, Memphis St.	219	1,016
1964	Brian Piccolo, Wake Forest	252	1,044
1965	Mike Garrett, So. California	267	1,440
1966	Ray McDonald, Idaho	259	1,329
1967	O. J. Simpson, So. California	266	1,415
1968	O. J. Simpson, So. California	355	1,709
1969	Steve Owens, Oklahoma	358	1,523
1970	Ed Marinaro, Cornell	285	1,425
1971	Ed Marinaro, Cornell	356	1,884
1972	Pete Van Valkenburg, Brigham Young	232	1,386
1973	Mark Kellar, No. Illinois	291	1,719
1974	Louis Giammona, Utah State	329	1,534
1975	Rickie Bell, So. California	357	1,875
1976	Tony Dorsett, Pittsburgh	338	1,948

Pass Receiving

Year	Player, School	Rec.	Yd	TD
1937	Jim Benton, Arkansas	47	754	NA*
1938	Sam Boyd, Baylor	32	537	NA
1939	Ken Kavanaugh, LSU	30	467	NA
1940	Eddie Bryant, Virginia	30	222	NA
1941	Harry Stanton, Arizona	50	820	NA
1942	Bill Rogers, Texas A&M	39	432	NA
1943	Neil Armstrong, Oklahoma St.	39	317	NA
1944	Reid Moseley, Georgia	32	506	NA
1945	Reid Moseley, Georgia	31	662	NA
1946	Neil Armstrong, Oklahoma St.	32	479	1
1947	Barney Poole, Mississippi	52	513	8
1948	John O'Quinn, Wake Forest	39	605	7
1949	Art Weiner, No. Carolina	52	762	7
1950	Gordon Cooper, Denver	46	569	8
1951	Dewey McConnell, Wyoming	47	725	9
1952	Ed Brown, Fordham	57	774	6
1953	John Carson, Georgia	45	663	4
1954	Jim Hanifan, California	44	569	7
1955	Hank Burnine, Missouri	44	594	2
1956	Art Powell, San José St.	40	583	5
1957	Stuart Vaughan, Utah	53	756	5
1958	Dave Hibbert, Arizona	61	606	4
1959	Chris Burford, Stanford	61	756	6
1960	Hugh Campbell, Washington St.	66	881	10
1961	Hugh Campbell, Washington St.	53	723	5
1962	Vern Burke, Oregon St.	69	1,007	10
1963	Larry Elkins, Baylor	70	873	8
1964	Howard Twilley, Tulsa	95	1,178	13
1965	Howard Twilley, Tulsa	134	1,779	16
1966	Glenn Meltzer, Wichita St.	91	1,115	4
1967	Bob Goodridge, Vanderbilt	79	1,114	6
1968	Ron Sellers, Florida St.	86	1,496	12
1969	Jerry Hendren, Idaho	95	1,452	12
1970	Mike Mikolayunas, Davidson	87	1,128	8
1971	Tom Reynolds, San Diego St.	67	1,070	7
1972	Tom Forzani, Utah St.	85	1,169	8
1973	Jay Miller, Brigham Young	100	1,181	8
1974	Dwight McDonald, San Diego St.	86	1,157	7
1975	Bob Farnham, Brown	56	701	2
1976	Billy Ryckman, Louisiana Tech.	77	1,382	10

(*Data not available)

Scoring

Year	Player, School	TD	XP	FG	Pts
1937	Byron "Whizzer" White, Colorado	16	23	1	122
1938	Parker Hall, Mississippi	11	7	0	73
1939	Tom Harmon, Michigan	14	15	1	102
1940	Tom Harmon, Michigan	16	18	1	117
1941	Bill Dudley, Virginia	18	23	1	134
1942	Bob Steuber, Missouri	18	13	0	121
1943	Steve Van Buren, LSU	14	14	0	98
1944	Glenn Davis, Army	20	0	0	120
1945	Felix "Doc" Blanchard, Army	19	1	0	115
1946	Gene Roberts, Chattanooga	18	9	0	117
1947	Lou Gambino, Maryland	16	0	0	96
1948	Fred Wendt, Texas-El Paso	20	32	0	152
1949	George Thomas, Oklahoma	19	3	0	117
1950	Bobby Reynolds, Nebraska	22	25	0	157
1951	Ollie Matson, San Francisco	21	0	0	126
1952	Jackie Parker, Mississippi St.	16	24	0	120
1953	Earl Lindley, Utah St.	13	3	0	81
1954	Art Luppino, Arizona	24	22	0	166
1955	Jim Swink, TCU	20	5	0	125
1956	Clendon Thomas, Oklahoma	18	0	0	108
1957	Leon Burton, Arizona St.	16	0	0	96
1958	Dick Bass, Pacific	18	8	0	116
1959	Pervis Atkins, New Mexico St.	17	5	0	107
1960	Bob Gaiters, New Mexico St.	23	7	0	145
1961	Jim Pilot, New Mexico St.	21	12	0	138
1962	Jerry Logan, W. Texas St.	13	32	0	110
1963	Cosmo Iacavazzi, Princeton	14	0	0	84
	Dave Casinelli, Memphis St.	14	0	0	84

1964	Brian Piccolo, Wake Forest	17	9	0	111
1965	Howard Twilley, Tulsa	16	21	0	127
1966	Ken Hebert, Houston	11	41	2	113
1967	Leroy Keyes, Purdue	19	0	0	114
1968	Jim O'Brien, Cincinnati	12	31	13	142
1969	Steve Owens, Oklahoma	23	0	0	138
1970	Brian Bream, Air Force	20	0	0	120*
	Gary Kosins, Dayton	18	0	0	108*
1971	Ed Marinaro, Cornell	24	4	0	152
1972	Harold Henson, Ohio St.	20	0	0	120
1973	Jim Jennings, Rutgers	21	2	0	130
1974	Bill Marek, Wisconsin	19	0	0	114
1975	Pete Johnson, Ohio St.	25	0	0	150
1976	Tony Dorsett, Pittsburgh	22	2	0	134

(*Bream played 10 games, Kosins 9 games; each averaged 12.0 points per game.)

Major Bowl Results

Cotton Bowl (Dallas)
1937 Texas Christian 16, Marquette 6
1938 Rice 28, Colorado 14
1939 St. Mary's (Calif.) 20, Texas Tech 13
1940 Clemson 6, Boston College 3
1941 Texas A&M 13, Fordham 12
1942 Alabama 29, Texas A&M 21
1943 Texas 14, Georgia Tech 7
1944 Texas 7, Randolph Field 7
1945 Oklahoma A&M 34, Texas Christian 0
1946 Texas 40, Missouri 27
1947 Louisiana State 0, Arkansas 0
1948 Penn State 13, Southern Methodist 13
1949 Southern Methodist 21, Oregon 13
1950 Rice 27, North Carolina 13
1951 Tennessee 20, Texas 14
1952 Kentucky 20, Texas Christian 7
1953 Texas 16, Tennessee 0
1954 Rice 28, Alabama 6
1955 Georgia Tech 14, Arkansas 6
1956 Mississippi 14, Texas Christian 13
1957 Texas Christian 28, Syracuse 27
1958 Navy 20, Rice 7
1959 Texas Christian 0, Air Force 0
1960 Syracuse 23, Texas 14
1961 Duke 7, Arkansas 6
1962 Texas 12, Mississippi 7
1963 Louisiana State 13, Texas 0
1964 Texas 28, Navy 6
1965 Arkansas 10, Nebraska 7
1966 Louisiana State 14, Arkansas 7
1967 Georgia 24, Southern Methodist 9
1968 Texas A&M 20, Alabama 16
1969 Texas 36, Tennessee 13
1970 Texas 21, Notre Dame 17
1971 Notre Dame 24, Texas 11
1972 Penn State 30, Texas 6
1973 Texas 17, Alabama 13
1974 Nebraska 19, Texas 3
1975 Penn State 41, Baylor 20
1976 Arkansas 31, Georgia 10

Gator Bowl (Jacksonville, Fla.)
1946 Wake Forest 26, South Carolina 14
1947 Oklahoma 34, No. Carolina State 13
1948 Maryland 20, Georgia 20
1949 Clemson 24, Missouri 23
1950 Maryland 20, Missouri 7
1951 Wyoming 20, Washington & Lee 7
1952 Miami (Fla.) 14, Clemson 0
1953 Florida 14, Tulsa 13
1954 Texas Tech 35, Auburn 13
1955 Auburn 33, Baylor 13
1956 Vanderbilt 25, Auburn 13
1957 Georgia Tech 21, Pittsburgh 14

1958   Tennessee 3, Texas A&M 0
1959   Mississippi 7, Florida 3
1960   Arkansas 14, Georgia Tech 7
1961   Florida 13, Baylor 12
1962   Penn State 30, Georgia Tech 15
1963   Florida 17, Penn State 7
1964   No. Carolina 35, Air Force 0
1965   Florida State 36, Oklahoma 19
1966   Georgia Tech 31, Texas Tech 21
1967   Tennessee 18, Syracuse 12
1968   Penn State 17, Florida State 17
1969   Missouri 35, Alabama 10
1969   (Dec.) Florida 14, Tennessee 13
1971   Auburn 35, Mississippi 28
1972   Georgia 7, North Carolina 3
1973   Auburn 24, Colorado 3
1973   (Dec.) Texas Tech 28, Tennessee 19
1975   Auburn 27, Texas 3
1976   Maryland 13, Florida 0

Orange Bowl (Miami)
1933   Miami 7, Manhattan 0
1934   Duquesne 33, Miami 7
1935   Bucknell 26, Miami 0
1936   Catholic U. 20, Mississippi 19
1937   Duquesne 13, Mississippi St. 12
1938   Auburn 6, Michigan State 0
1939   Tennessee 17, Oklahoma 0
1940   Georgia Tech 21, Missouri 7
1941   Mississippi State 14, Georgetown 7
1942   Georgia 40, Texas Christian 26
1943   Alabama 37, Boston College 21
1944   Louisiana State 19, Texas A&M 14
1945   Tulsa 26, Georgia Tech 12
1946   Miami 13, Holy Cross 6
1947   Rice 8, Tennessee 0
1948   Georgia Tech 20, Kansas 14
1949   Texas 41, Georgia 28
1950   Santa Clara 21, Kentucky 13
1951   Clemson 15, Miami 14
1952   Georgia Tech 17, Baylor 14
1953   Alabama 61, Syracuse 6
1954   Oklahoma 7, Maryland 0
1955   Duke 34, Nebraska 7
1956   Oklahoma 20, Maryland 6
1957   Colorado 27, Clemson 21
1958   Oklahoma 48, Duke 21
1959   Oklahoma 21, Syracuse 6
1960   Georgia 14, Missouri 0
1961   Missouri 21, Navy 14
1962   Louisiana State 25, Colorado 7
1963   Alabama 17, Oklahoma 0
1964   Nebraska 13, Auburn 7
1965   Texas 21, Alabama 17
1966   Alabama 39, Nebraska 28
1967   Florida 27, Georgia Tech 12
1968   Oklahoma 26, Tennessee 24
1969   Penn. State 15, Kansas 14
1970   Penn. State 10, Missouri 3
1971   Nebraska 17, Louisiana State 12
1972   Nebraska 38, Alabama 6
1973   Nebraska 40, Notre Dame 6
1974   Penn State 16, Louisiana State 9
1975   Notre Dame 13, Alabama 11
1976   Oklahoma 14, Michigan 6

Rose Bowl (Pasadena, Calif.)
1902   Michigan 49, Stanford 0
1916   Washington State 14, Brown 0
1917   Oregon 14, Pennsylvania 0
1918   Mare Island Marines 19, Camp Lewis Army 7
1919   Great Lakes Navy 17, Mare Island Marines 0
1920   Harvard 7, Oregon 6
1921   California 28, Ohio State 0

1922   Washington & Jefferson 0, California 0
1923   So. California 14, Penn State 3
1924   Navy 14, Washington 14
1925   Notre Dame 27, Stanford 10
1926   Alabama 20, Washington 19
1927   Alabama 7, Stanford 7
1928   Stanford 7, Pittsburgh 6
1929   Georgia Tech 8, California 7
1930   So. California 47, Pittsburgh 14
1931   Alabama 24, Washington State 0
1932   So. California 21, Tulane, 12
1933   So. California 35, Pittsburgh 0
1934   Columbia 7, Stanford 0
1935   Alabama 29, Stanford 13
1936   Stanford 7, Southern Methodist 0
1937   Pittsburgh 21, Washington 0
1938   California 13, Alabama 0
1939   So. California 7, Duke 3
1940   So. California 14, Tennessee 0
1941   Stanford 21, Nebraska 13
1942   Oregon State 20, Duke 16
1943   Georgia 9, UCLA 0
1944   So. California 29, Washington 0
1945   So. California 25, Tennessee 0
1946   Alabama 34, So. California 14
1947   Illinois 45, UCLA 14
1948   Michigan 49, So. California 0
1949   Northwestern 20, California 14
1950   Ohio State 17, California 14
1951   Michigan 14, California 6
1952   Illinois 40, Stanford 7
1953   So. California 7, Wisconsin 0
1954   Michigan State 28, UCLA 20
1955   Ohio State 20, So. California 7
1956   Michigan State 17, UCLA 14
1957   Iowa 35, Oregon State 19
1958   Ohio State 10, Oregon 7
1959   Iowa 38, California 12
1960   Washington 44, Wisconsin 8
1961   Washington 17, Minnesota 7
1962   Minnesota 21, UCLA 3
1963   So. California 42, Wisconsin 37
1964   Illinois 17, Washington 7
1965   Michigan 34, Oregon State 7
1966   UCLA 14, Michigan State 12
1967   Purdue 14, So. California 13
1968   So. California 14, Indiana 3
1969   Ohio State 27, So. California 16
1970   So. California 10, Michigan 3
1971   Stanford 27, Ohio State 17
1972   Stanford 13, Michigan 12
1973   So. California 42, Ohio State 17
1974   Ohio State 42, So. California 21
1975   So. California 18, Ohio State 17
1976   UCLA 23, Ohio State 10

Sugar Bowl (New Orleans)
1935   Tulane 20, Temple 14
1936   Texas Christian 3, Louisiana State 2
1937   Santa Clara 21, Louisiana State 14
1938   Santa Clara 6, Louisiana State 0
1939   Texas Christian 15, Carnegie Tech 7
1940   Texas A&M 14, Tulane 13
1941   Boston College 19, Tennessee 13
1942   Fordham 2, Missouri 0
1943   Tennessee 14, Tulsa 7
1944   Georgia Tech 20, Tulsa 18
1945   Duke 29, Alabama 26
1946   Oklahoma A&M 33, St. Mary's 13
1947   Georgia 20, North Carolina 10
1948   Texas 27, Alabama 7
1949   Oklahoma 14, North Carolina 6
1950   Oklahoma 35, Louisiana State 0
1951   Kentucky 13, Oklahoma 7

1952	Maryland 28, Tennessee 13
1953	Georgia Tech 24, Mississippi 7
1954	Georgia Tech 42, West Virginia 19
1955	Navy 21, Mississippi 0
1956	Georgia Tech 7, Pittsburgh 0
1957	Baylor 13, Tennessee 7
1958	Mississippi 39, Texas 7
1959	Louisiana State 7, Clemson 0
1960	Mississippi 21, Louisiana State 0
1961	Mississippi 14, Rice 6
1962	Alabama 10, Arkansas 3
1963	Mississippi 17, Arkansas 13
1964	Alabama 12, Mississippi 7
1965	Louisiana State 13, Syracuse 10
1966	Missouri 20, Florida 18
1967	Alabama 34, Nebraska 7
1968	Louisiana State 20, Wyoming 13
1969	Arkansas 16, Georgia 2
1970	Mississippi 27, Arkansas 22
1971	Tennessee 34, Air Force 13
1972	Oklahoma 40, Auburn 22
1973	Oklahoma 14, Penn State 0
1974	Notre Dame 24, Alabama 23
1975	Nebraska 13, Florida 10
1976	Alabama 13, Penn State 6

College Coach of the Year

(American Football Coaches Assn.)

1935	Lynn O. Waldorf, Northwestern
1936	Richard Harlow, Harvard
1937	E. E. "Hooks" Mylin, Lafayette
1938	William F. Kern, Carnegie Tech
1939	Dr. Edward N. Anderson, Iowa
1940	Clark Shaughnessy, Stanford
1941	Frank Leahy, Notre Dame
1942	William Alexander, Georgia Tech
1943	Amos Alonzo Stagg, Pacific
1944	Carroll Widdoes, Ohio State
1945	Alvin "Bo" McMillin, Indiana
1946	Earl H. "Red" Blaik, Army
1947	H. O. "Fritz" Crisler, Michigan
1948	Bennie Oosterbaan, Michigan
1949	Charles "Bud" Wilkinson, Oklahoma
1950	Charles Caldwell, Princeton
1951	Charles Taylor, Stanford
1952	Clarence L. "Biggie" Munn, Michigan State
1953	James Tatum, Maryland
1954	Henry "Red" Sanders, UCLA
1955	Hugh "Duffy" Daugherty, Michigan State
1956	Bowden Wyatt, Tennessee
1957	Wayne W. "Woody" Hayes, Ohio State
1958	Paul E. Dietzel, Louisiana State
1959	Ben Schwartzwalder, Syracuse
1960	Murray Warmath, Minnesota
1961	Paul "Bear" Bryant, Alabama
1962	John McKay, So. California
1963	Darrell Royal, Texas
1964	Ara Parseghian, Notre Dame; Frank Broyles, Arkansas
1965	Tommy Prothro, UCLA
1966	Tom Cahill, Army
1967	John Pont, Indiana
1968	Joe Paterno, Penn. State
1969	Bo Schembechler, Michigan
1970	Darrell Royal, Texas; Charles McClendon, Louisiana State
1971	Paul "Bear" Bryant, Alabama
1972	John McKay, So. California
1973	Paul "Bear" Bryant, Alabama
1974	Grant Teaff, Baylor
1975	Barry Switzer, Oklahoma
1976	Johnny Majors, Pittsburgh

All-Time All-Americans

(In 1969, the Football Writers Association of America chose two All-Time All-American teams, one for the first 50 years of collegiate football and the other for the second 50 years.)

1869–1918

Ends—Frank Hinkey, Yale, 1891–94; Huntington "Tack" Hardwick, Harvard, 1912–14

Tackles—Wilbur "Fats" Henry, Washington and Jefferson, 1916–19; Josh Cody, Vanderbilt, 1914–16, 1919

Guards—W. W. "Pudge" Heffelfinger, Yale, 1888–91; T. Truxton Hare, Pennsylvania, 1897–1900

Center—Adolf "Germany" Schulz, Michigan, 1904–05, 1907–08

Quarterback—Walter Eckersall, Chicago, 1903–06

Halfbacks—Jim Thorpe, Carlisle, 1907–08, 1911–12; Willie Heston, Michigan, 1901–04

Fullback—Elmer Oliphant, Purdue, 1911–13 and Army, 1914–17

1919–1969

Ends—Bennie Oosterbaan, Michigan, 1925–27; Don Hutson, Alabama, 1932–34

Tackles—Bronislaw "Bronko" Nagurski, Minnesota, 1927–29; Frank "Bruiser" Kinard, Mississippi, 1935–37

Guards—Jim Parker, Ohio State, 1954–56; Bob Suffridge, Tennessee, 1938–40

Center—Mel Hein, Washington State, 1928–30

Quarterback—Sammy Baugh, Texas Christian, 1934–36

Halfbacks—Jay Berwanger, Chicago 1933–35; Harold "Red" Grange, Illinois, 1923–25

Fullback—Ernie Nevers, Stanford, 1923–25

Football Halls of Fame

(Citizens Savings Hall maintains halls of fame for college football and major-league football; the National Football Foundation maintains a hall of fame for college football; the National Football League maintains the Professional Football Hall of Fame in Canton, Ohio. In the following lists, C denotes Citizens Savings, NFF denotes National Football Foundation, and NFL denotes the Pro Football Hall of Fame.)

Professional

Ben Agajanian—Place kicker: Pittsburgh Steelers, Philadelphia Eagles 1945; Los Angeles Dons 1947–48; New York Giants 1949, 1954–57; Los Angeles Rams 1953; Los Angeles Chargers 1960; Dallas Texans 1961; Green Bay Packers 1961; Oakland Raiders 1962; San Diego Chargers 1964. C

Frank Albert—Quarterback: San Francisco 49ers 1946–52. C

Lance Alworth—Wide receiver: San Diego Chargers 1962–70; Dallas Cowboys 1971–72. C

Jon Arnett—Halfback: Los Angeles Rams 1957–63; Chicago Bears 1964–66. C

Douglas Atkins—Defensive end; Cleveland Browns 1953–54; Chicago Bears 1955–66; New Orleans Saints 1967–69. C

Cliff Battles—Halfback-quarterback: Boston Braves 1932; Boston Redskins 1933–36; Washington Redskins 1937. C, NFL

Bruno Banducci—Guard: Philadelphia Eagles 1944–45; San Francisco 49ers 1946–54. C

The field goal has become a very important scoring weapon in professional football. Here Nick Mike-Meyer of the Atlanta falcons follows through on a successful kick. *(Atlanta Falcons.)*

Samuel Baugh—Quarterback: Washington Redskins 1937–52. C, NFL

Chuck Bednarik—Center-linebacker: Philadelphia Eagles 1949–62. C, NFL

James Benton—End: Cleveland Rams 1938–40, 1942, 1944–45; Chicago Bears 1943; Los Angeles Rams 1946–47. C

Raymond Berry—End: Baltimore Colts 1955–67.

Johnny Blood (McNally)—Halfback: Milwaukee Badgers 1925; Duluth Eskimos 1926–27; Pottsville Maroons 1928; Green Bay Packers 1929–33, 1935–36; Pittsburgh Pirates 1934, 1937–39. C, NFL

Raymond Bray—Guard: Chicago Bears 1939–42, 1946–51; Green Bay Packers 1952. C

Gene Brito—Defensive end: Washington Redskins 1951–53, 1955–58; Los Angeles Rams 1959–60. C

Bert Bell—NFL commissioner, 1946–59. C, NFL

Charles Bidwill—Chicago Cardinals' owner 1933–47. C, NFL

Jim Brown—Fullback: Cleveland Browns 1957–65. C, NFL

Paul Brown—Founder, coach of Cleveland Browns 1946–62; Cincinnati Bengals 1968–1975. C, NFL

Roosevelt Brown—Tackle: New York Giants 1953–65. NFL

Tony Canadeo—Halfback: Green Bay Packers 1941–44, 1946–52. C, NFL

Gino Cappelletti—End, placekicker: Boston Patriots 1960–68. C

Joe Carr—NFL president 1921–39. C, NFL

Berlin Guy Chamberlin—End, coach: Decatur Staleys 1920, Chicago Staleys 1921; Canton Bulldogs 1922–23; Cleveland Bulldogs 1924; Frankford Yellowjackets 1925–26; Chicago Cardinals 1927. NFL

Earl "Dutch" Clark—Quarterback: Portsmouth Spartans-Detroit Lions 1931–38. C, NFL

Jack Christiansen—Defensive back: Detroit Lions 1951–58. NFL

Charles Conerly—Quarterback: New York Giants 1948–61. C

George Connor—Tackle-linebacker: Chicago Bears 1948–55. NFL

James Conzelman—Halfback: Decatur Staleys 1920;

Rock Island Independents 1921–22; Milwaukee Badgers 1923–24; Detroit Panthers 1925–26; Providence Steamrollers 1927–29; player-coach 1922–29; coach, Chicago Cardinals 1940–42, 1946–48. C, NFL

Arthur Donovan—Defensive tackle: Baltimore Colts 1950, 1953–61; New York Yanks 1951; Dallas Texans 1952. C, NFL

John "Paddy" Driscoll—Halfback: Decatur Staleys 1919–20; Chicago Cardinals 1920–25; Chicago Bears 1926–29. C, NFL

Bill Dudley—Halfback: Pittsburgh Steelers 1942, 1945–46; Detroit Lions 1947–49; Washington Redskins 1950–51, 1953. C, NFL

A. G. "Turk" Edwards—Tackle: Boston Braves 1932; Boston Redskins 1933–36; Washington Redskins 1937–40. C, NFL.

Tom Fears—End: Los Angeles Rams 1948–56. C, NFL

Ray Flaherty—End: Los Angeles Wildcats 1926; New York Yankees 1927–28; New York Giants 1928–29, 1931–35. C, NFL

Len Ford—End: Los Angeles Rams 1948–49; Cleveland Browns 1950–57; Green Bay Packers 1958.

Daniel Fortmann—Guard: Chicago Bears 1936–43. C, NFL

Bill George—Linebacker: Chicago Bears 1952–65; Los Angeles Rams 1966. NFL

Frank Gifford—Halfback: New York Giants 1952–60, 1962–64. C

Otto Graham—Quarterback: Cleveland Browns 1946–55. C, NFL

Harold "Red" Grange—Halfback: Chicago Bears 1925, 1929–34; New York Yankees 1926–27. C, NFL

Forrest Gregg—Tackle: Green Bay Packers 1956, 1958–70; Dallas Cowboys 1971. C

Louis Groza—Tackle, place kicker: Cleveland Browns 1946–59; 1961–67. C, NFL

Joe Guyon—Halfback: Canton Bulldogs 1919–20; Cleveland Indians 1921; Orange Indians 1922–23; Rock Island Independents 1924; Kansas City Cowboys 1924–25; New York Giants 1927. NFL

George Halas—End: Hammond Pros 1919; Decatur Staleys 1920; Chicago Staleys-Bears 1921–29; coach: Decatur Staleys, 1920; Chicago Staleys-Bears 1920–29; 1933–42, 1946–55, 1958–68. C, NFL

Ed Healey—Tackle: Rock Island Independents 1920–22; Chicago Bears 1922–27. NFL

Melvin Hein—Center: New York Giants 1931–45. C, NFL

Wilbur "Fats" Henry—Tackle: Canton Bulldogs 1920–23, 1925–26; New York Giants 1927; Pottsville Maroons 1927–28. C, NFL

Arnold Herber—Halfback: Green Bay Packers 1930–40; New York Giants 1944–45. C, NFL

William Hewitt—End: Chicago Bears 1932–36; Philadelphia Eagles 1937–39; Philadelphia-Pittsburgh Steelers 1943. C, NFL

Clarke Hinkle—Fullback: Green Bay Packers 1932–41. C, NFL

Elroy "Crazylegs" Hirsch—Halfback-end: Chicago Rockets 1946–48; Los Angeles Rams 1949–57. C, NFL

Robert "Cal" Hubbard—Tackle: New York Giants 1927–28, 1936; Green Bay Packers 1929–33, 1935; Pittsburgh Pirates 1936. C, NFL

Lamar Hunt—Founder of Dallas Texans (now Kansas

City Chiefs); first president of American Football League. NFL

Art Hunter—Tackle-center: Green Bay Packers 1954; Cleveland Browns 1956–59; Los Angeles Rams 1960–64; Pittsburgh Steelers 1965. C

Don Hutson—End: Green Bay Packers 1935–45. C, NFL

Walter Kiesling—Guard: Duluth Eskimos 1926–27; Pottsville Maroons 1928; Chicago Cardinals 1929–33; Chicago Bears 1934; Green Bay Packers 1935–36; Pittsburgh Pirates 1937–38; coach: Pittsburgh 1939–42, 1954–56, Philadelphia-Pittsburgh 1943, Chicago Cardinals-Pittsburgh 1944. C, NFL

Frank "Bucko" Kilroy—Tackle: Philadelphia-Pittsburgh 1943, Philadelphia Eagles 1944–55. C

Frank "Bruiser" Kinard—Tackle: Brooklyn Dodgers 1938–44; New York Yankees 1946–47. NFL

Earl "Curly" Lambeau—Halfback: Green Bay Packers, 1921–29; founder and coach: Green Bay Packers 1921–49; coach: Chicago Cardinals 1950–51, Washington Redskins 1952–53. C, NFL

Dick "Night Train" Lane—Defensive back: Los Angeles Rams 1952–53; Chicago Cardinals 1954–59, Detroit Lions 1960–65. NFL

Dante Lavelli—End: Cleveland Browns 1946–56. NFL

Bobby Layne—Quarterback: Chicago Bears 1948; New York Bulldogs 1949; Detroit Lions 1950–58; Pittsburgh Steelers 1958–62. C, NFL

Eddie LeBaron—Quarterback: Washington Redskins 1952–53, 1955–59; Dallas Cowboys 1960–63. C

Alphonse "Tuffy" Leemans—Halfback: New York Giants 1936–43. C

Vince Lombardi—Coach: Green Bay Packers 1959–67; Washington Redskins 1969. C, NFL

Sid Luckman—Quarterback: Chicago Bears 1939–50. C, NFL

Roy "Link" Lyman—Tackle: Canton Bulldogs 1922–23, 1925; Cleveland Bulldogs, 1924; Frankford Yellowjackets 1925; Chicago Bears 1926–28, 1930–31, 1933–34. C, NFL

Jack Manders—Fullback, place kicker: Chicago Bears 1933–40. C

Gino Marchetti—Defensive end: Dallas Texans 1952; Baltimore Colts 1953–64, 1966. C, NFL

Jim Martin—End-linebacker-kicker: Cleveland Browns 1950; Detroit Lions 1951–61; Baltimore Colts 1963; Washington Redskins 1964. C

Ollie Matson—Halfback: Chicago Cardinals 1952, 1954–58; Los Angeles Rams 1959–62; Detroit Lions 1963; Philadelphia Eagles 1964–66. C, NFL

Timothy J. Mara—Founder: New York Giants. C, NFL

George McAfee—Halfback: Chicago Bears 1940–41, 1945–50. C, NFL

Hugh McElhenny—Halfback: San Francisco 49ers 1952–60; Minnesota Vikings 1961–62; New York Giants 1963; Detroit Lions 1964. C, NFL

George Preston Marshall—Founder: Boston-Washington Redskins. C, NFL

Marlin McKeever—End-linebacker: Los Angeles Rams 1961–66; Minnesota Vikings 1967; Washington Redskins 1968–70; Los Angeles Rams 1971–72. C

August "Mike" Michalske—Guard: New York Yankees 1926–28; Green Bay Packers 1929–35, 1937. NFL

Wayne Millner—End: Boston-Washington Redskins 1936–41, 1945. NFL

Dick Modzelewski—Defensive tackle: Washington Redskins 1953–54; Pittsburgh Steelers 1955; New York Giants 1956–63; Cleveland Browns 1964–66. C

Lennie Moore—Halfback-wide receiver: Baltimore Colts 1956–67. NFL

Marion Motley—Linebacker-fullback: Cleveland Browns 1946–53; Pittsburgh Steelers 1955. C, NFL

Ed Meador—Defensive back: Los Angeles Rams 1959–70. C

George Musso—Guard: Chicago Bears 1933–44. C

Earle "Greasy" Neale—Coach: Philadelphia Eagles, 1941–50. C, NFL

Bronko Nagurski—Tackle-fullback: Chicago Bears 1930–37, 1943. C, NFL

Al Nesser—Guard: Akron Pros 1919–26; Cleveland Bulldogs 1925; Cleveland Panthers 1926; New York Giants 1926–28; Cleveland Indians 1931. C

Ernie Nevers—Fullback: Duluth Eskimos 1926–27; Chicago Cardinals 1929–31. C, NFL

Ray Nitschke—Linebacker: Green Bay Packers 1958–73. C

Leo Nomellini—Tackle: San Francisco 49ers 1953–63. C, NFL

Steve Owen—Tackle: Kansas City Cowboys 1924–25; New York Giants 1926–31, 1933; coach: New York Giants, 1931–52. C, NFL

Raymond "Buddy" Parker—Coach: Detroit Lions 1951–56; Pittsburgh Steelers 1957–64. C

Clarence "Ace" Parker—Quarterback: Brooklyn Dodgers 1937–41; Boston Yanks 1945; New York Yankees 1945–46. NFL

Don Paul—Linebacker: Los Angeles Rams 1948–55. C

Jim Parker—Guard: Baltimore Colts 1957–67. NFL

Joe Perry—Fullback: San Francisco 49ers 1948–60, 1963; Baltimore Colts 1961–62. C, NFL

Pete Pihos—End: Philadelphia Eagles 1947–55. C, NFL

Hugh "Shorty" Ray—NFL technical advisor, supervisor of officials 1938–56. NFL

Dan Reeves—Founder: Cleveland-Los Angeles Rams. C, NFL

Ray Renfro—End: Cleveland Browns 1952–63. C

Les Richter—Linebacker: Los Angeles Rams 1954–62. C

Jim Ringo—Center: Green Bay Packers 1953–63; Philadelphia Eagles 1964–67. C

Andy Robustelli—Defensive end: Los Angeles Rams 1951–55; New York Giants 1956–64. C, NFL

Art Rooney—Founder: Pittsburgh Steelers. NFL

Kyle Rote—Halfback-end: New York Giants 1951–64. C

Tobin Rote—Quarterback: Green Bay Packers 1950–56; Detroit Lions 1957–59; San Diego Chargers 1963–64; Denver Broncos 1966. C

Robert St. Clair—Tackle: San Francisco 49ers 1953–63. C

Joseph Schmidt—Linebacker: Detroit Lions 1953–65. C, NFL

Victor Sears—Tackle: Philadelphia Eagles 1941–42, 1945–53; Philadelphia-Pittsburgh 1943. C

Lawrence T. "Buck" Shaw—Coach: San Francisco 49ers 1946–54; Philadelphia Eagles 1958–60. C

Carl Storck—Secretary-Treasurer of the NFL 1921–39, president 1939–41. NFL

Ernie Stautner—Defensive tackle: Pittsburgh Steelers 1950–63. C, NFL

Edward Sprinkle—End: Chicago Bears 1944–55. C

Bryan Bart Starr—Quarterback: Green Bay Packers 1956–71. C

Joseph Stydahar—Tackle: Chicago Bears 1936–42, 1945–46. C, NFL

Jim Taylor—Fullback: Green Bay Packers 1958–66; New Orleans Saints 1967. NFL

James Thorpe—Halfback: Canton Bulldogs, 1919–20, 1926; Cleveland Indians 1921; Oorang Indians 1922–23; Toledo Maroons 1923; Rock Island Independents 1924; New York Giants 1925. C, NFL

Ken Strong—Fullback: Staten Island Stapletons 1929–32; New York Giants 1933–35, 1939, 1944–47; New York Yanks 1936–37. C, NFL

Y. A. Tittle—Quarterback: Baltimore Colts 1948–50; San Francisco 49ers 1951–60; New York Giants 1961–64. C, NFL

George Trafton—Center: Chicago Bears 1920–32. C, NFL

Charlie Trippi—Halfback: Chicago Cardinals 1947–55. C, NFL

Emlen Tunnell—Defensive back: New York Giants 1948–58; Green Bay Packers 1959–61. C, NFL

Clyde "Bulldog" Turner—Center: Chicago Bears 1940–52. C, NFL

John Unitas—Quarterback: Baltimore Colts 1956–72; San Diego Chargers 1973. C

Norm Van Brocklin—Quarterback: Los Angeles Rams 1949–57; Philadelphia Eagles 1958–60. C, NFL

Steve Van Buren—Halfback: Philadelphia Eagles 1944–52. C, NFL

Doak Walker—Halfback: Detroit Lions 1950–55. C

Bob Waterfield—Quarterback: Cleveland-Los Angeles Rams 1945–52. C, NFL

Alex Webster—Halfback: New York Giants 1955–64. C

Fred Williams—Defensive tackle: Chicago Bears 1952–63; Washington Redskins 1964–65. C

Larry Wilson—Defensive back: St. Louis Cardinals 1960–72. C

Alex Wojciechowicz—Center: Detroit Lions 1938–46; Philadelphia Eagles 1946–50. C, NFL

Claude "Buddy" Young—Halfback: New York Yankees 1947–49; New York Yanks 1950–51; Dallas Texans 1952; Baltimore Colts 1953–55. C

Paul "Tank" Younger—Fullback: Los Angeles Rams 1949–57; Pittsburgh Steelers 1958. C

College Players

Alex Agase—Purdue-Illinois guard 1941–43. NFF

Harry Agganis—Boston U. quarterback 1949–52. NFF

Frankie Albert—Stanford quarterback 1939–41. C, NFF

Charles "Ki" Aldrich—Texas Christian center 1936–38. C, NFF

Malcolm Aldrich—Yale halfback 1919–21. NFF

Joseph Alexander—Syracuse guard 1918–20. C, NFF

Alan Ameche—Wisconsin fullback 1951–54. C, NFF

Knowlton "Snake" Ames—Princeton fullback 1887–89. NFF

Heartley "Hunk" Anderson—Notre Dame guard 1918–21. NFF

Clarence E. Bacon—Wesleyan quarterback 1909–12. NFF

Stanley N. Barnes—California end 1918–20. C, NFF

Charles Barrett—Cornell quarterback 1914–17. NFF

Bert Baston—Minnesota end 1914–16. C, NFF

Clifford Battles—W. Virginia Wesleyan halfback 1929–31. NFF

Samuel Baugh —Texas Christian quarterback 1934–36. C, NFF

James Bausch—Kansas halfback 1931–33. NFF

Gary Beban—UCLA quarterback 1965–67. C

Hubert Bechtol—Texas end 1944–46. C

John W. Beckett—Oregon tackle 1914–16. NFF

Charles Bednarik—Pennsylvania center 1946–48. NFF

Angelo Bertelli—Notre Dame quarterback 1941–43. C, NFF

John J. Berwanger—Chicago quarterback 1933–35. C, NFF

Larry Bettencourt—St. Mary's (Calif.) center 1925–27. C

Felix "Doc" Blanchard—Army fullback 1944–46. C, NFF

Edward Bock—Iowa State guard 1936–38. NFF

Lynn Bomar—Vanderbilt end 1921–23. C, NFF

Douglas Bomeisler—Yale end 1910–12. NFF

Albert Booth—Yale halfback 1929–31. NFF

Fred "Buzz" Borries—Navy halfback 1932–34. NFF

Victor Bottari—California fullback 1936–38. C

Benny Lee Boynton—Williams quarterback 1918–20. NFF

James Bradshaw—Nevada halfback 1919–21. C

Charles Brickley—Harvard quarterback 1911–14. C

George Brooke—Pennsylvania halfback 1893–95. NFF

Gordon F. Brown—Yale guard, 1897–1900. NFF

John H. "Babe" Brown—Navy guard 1910–13. C, NFF

John Mack Brown—Alabama halfback 1923–25. C, NFF

Paul Bunker—Army tackle-fullback, 1900–02. NFF

Dick Butkus—Illinois center-linebacker 1962–64. C

Bob Butler—Wisconsin tackle 1911–13. NFF

George "Bad News" Cafego—Tennessee halfback 1937–39. NFF

Christian K. Cagle—Army halfback 1926–29. C, NFF

John "Hurry" Cain—Alabama halfback 1930–32. C, NFF

David C. Campbell—Harvard end, 1899–1901. C, NFF

Billy Cannon—Lousiana State halfback 1957–59. NFF

Jack Cannon—Notre Dame center 1927–29. NFF

Frank Carideo—Notre Dame quarterback 1928–30.

Charles "Chuck" Carroll—Washington halfback 1927–

C. Hunter Carpenter—Virginia Polytechnic Institute halfback 1900–03, 1905. C, NFF

Charles "Chuck" Carroll—Washington halfback 1927–29. C, NFF

Edward L. Casey—Harvard halfback 1916–17, 1919. NFF

Howard "Hopalong" Cassady—Ohio State halfback 1952–55. C

Berlin Guy Chamberlin—Nebraska halfback 1913–15. C, NFF

Frank Christensen—Utah halfback 1930–32. C, NFF

Paul Christman—Missouri quarterback 1938–40. C, NFF

Earl "Dutch" Clark—Colorado quarterback 1926–28. C, NFF

Zora "Clev" Clevenger—Indiana halfback 1901–03. C

Josh Cody—Vanderbilt tackle 1915–17, 1919. C, NFF

Don Coleman—Michigan State tackle 1949–51. NFF

Charles A. Conerly—Mississippi halfback 1945–47. NFF

George Connor—Holy Cross-Notre Dame tackle 1942, 1946–47. C, NFF

William H. "Pa" Corbin—Yale center 1886–88. NFF

William Corbus—Stanford guard 1931–33. C, NFF

Hector W. Cowan—Princeton tackle 1887–89. C, NFF

Edwin H. "Ted" Coy—Yale fullback 1907–09. C, NFF

Fred Crawford—Duke tackle 1931–33. NFF
"Sleepy Jim" Crowley—Notre Dame halfback 1922–24. NFF
Slade D. Cutter—Navy Tackle 1932–34. NFF
Gerald Dalrymple—Tulane end 1929–31. C, NFF
John P. Dalton—Navy back 1908–11. NFF
Charles D. Daly—Harvard-Army quarterback 1898–1902. C, NFF
Averell Daniell—Pittsburgh tackle 1934–36. NFF
Tom Davies—Pittsburgh halfback 1918–21. C, NFF
Ernie Davis—Syracuse halfback 1959–61. C
Glenn Davis—Army halfback 1944–46. C, NFF
Peter Dawkins—Army halfback 1956–58. NFF
Paul R. "Shorty" DesJardien—Chicago center 1912–14. C, NFF
John R. DeWitt—Princeton guard 1901–03. C, NFF
Glenn Dobbs—Tulsa halfback 1940–42. C
Robert Lee Dodd—Tennessee quarterback 1928–30. C, NFF
John "Paddy" Driscoll—Northwestern halfback 1915–17. NFF
Nathan W. Dougherty—Tennessee guard 1907–09. NFF
Nick Drahos—Cornell tackle 1939–41. C
Morley Drury—So. California quarterback 1925–27. C, NFF
William M. Dudley—Virginia halfback 1939–41. C, NFF
Marshall Duffield—So. California quarterback 1928–30. C
Walter H. Eckersall—Chicago quarterback 1903–06. C, NFF
A. G. "Turk" Edwards—Washington State tackle 1928–30. C
Ray Eichenlaub—Notre Dame fullback 1911–13. NFF
Ray Evans—Kansas halfback 1940–42. NFF
Albert Exendine—Carlisle end 1904–07. NFF
Nello Falaschi—Santa Clara end 1934–36. C
Beattie Feathers—Tennessee halfback 1931–33. C, NFF
Robert Fenimore—Oklahoma State halfback 1942–44. C, NFF
John Ferraro—So. California tackle 1943–47. C, NFF
Wesley Fesler—Ohio State end 1928–30. C, NFF
William Fincher—George Tech end 1917–20. C, NFF
Hamilton Fish—Harvard tackle 1907–09. C, NFF
A. R. "Buck" Flowers—Georgia Tech halfback 1918–20. NFF
Clinton Frank—Yale halfback 1935–37. C, NFF
Raymond Frankowski—Washington halfback 1939–41. C
Rod Franz—California guard 1947–49. C
Benjamin Friedman—Michigan quarterback 1924–26. C, NFF
Edgar W. Garbisch—Army-Washington and Jefferson center-guard 1920–24. C, NFF
Mike Garrett—So. California halfback 1963–65. C
Charles Gelbert—Pennsylvania end 1894–96. NFF
Paul Giel—Minnesota halfback 1951–53. NFF
Frank Gifford—So. California halfback 1949–51. NFF
Walter Gilbert—Auburn center 1934–36. NFF
George Gipp—Notre Dame fullback 1917–20. C, NFF
Chet Gladchuk—Boston College center 1938–40. NFF
Marshall Goldberg—Pittsburgh halfback 1936–38. C, NFF
Otto Graham—Northwestern halfback 1941–43. C, NFF
Harold "Red" Grange—Illinois halfback 1923–25. C, NFF
Robert H. Grayson—Stanford fullback 1933–35. C, NFF

Merle Gulick—Toledo-Hobart quarterback. NFF
Edwin "Goat" Hale—Mississippi College halfback. NFF
Robert "Bones" Hamilton—Stanford halfback 1933–35. NFF
Victor Hanson—Syracuse end 1924–26. NFF
H. R. "Tack" Hardwick—Harvard end 1912–14. C, NFF
T. Truxton Hare—Pennsylvania guard 1897–1900. C, NFF
Charles W. "Chic" Harley—Ohio State fullback 1916, 1918–19. C, NFF
Thomas D. Harmon—Michigan halfback 1938–40. C, NFF
Howard Harpster—Carnegie Tech quarterback 1926–28. C, NFF
Edward J. Hart—Princeton tackle 1909–11. C, NFF
Leon Hart—Notre Dame end 1947–49. C, NFF
Homer H. Hazel—Rutgers fullback-end 1916, 1922–24. C, NFF
Ed Healey—Dartmouth tackle 1915–16. NFF
W. W. "Pudge" Heffelfinger—Yale guard 1888–91. C, NFF
Melvin J. Hein—Washington State center 1928–30. C, NFF
Ted Hendricks—Miami (Fla.) end-linebacker 1966–68. C
Wilbur "Fats" Henry—Washington and Jefferson tackle 1918–19. C, NFF
Clarence Herschberger—Chicago fullback 1896–98. NFF
Robert J. Herwig—Calfironia center 1935–37. C, NFF
Willie Heston—Michigan halfback 1901–04. C, NFF
Herman M. Hickman—Tennessee guard 1929–31. C, NFF
Dan "Tiger" Hill—Duke center 1936–38. NFF
A. R. T. "Doc" Hillebrand—Princeton tackle 1897–99. NFF
Frank A. Hinkey—Yale end 1891–94. C, NFF
Carl Hinkle—Vanderbilt center 1935–37. NFF
Clarke Hinkle—Bucknell fullback 1928–30. C
Elroy "Crazylegs" Hirsch—Wisconsin halfback 1941–43. NFF
James Hitchcock—Auburn halfback 1930–32. C, NFF
James J. Hogan—Yale tackle 1902–04. C, NFF
Jerome H. "Brud" Holland—Cornell end 1936–38. NFF
William M. Hollenback—Pennsylvania halfback 1904, 1906–08. C, NFF
E. J. Holub—Texas Tech center 1958–60. C
Edwin C. "Babe" Horrell—California center 1922–24. NFF
Leslie Horvath—Ohio State halfback 1942–44. C, NFF
Millard "Dixie" Howell—Alabama halfback 1932–34. NFF
Robert "Cal" Hubbard—Centenary-Geneva tackle 1922–24, 1926. NFF
John Houghton Hubbard—Amherst halfback 1903–05. NFF
Allison "Pooley" Hubert—Alabama fullback 1923–25. NFF
Weldon G. Humble—Rice guard 1940–42, 1946. NFF
Joel Hunt—Texas A&M halfback 1925–27. NFF
Ellery C. Huntington—Colgate quarterback 1911–13. NFF
Donald Hutson—Alabama end 1932–34. C, NFF
Jonas H. Ingram—Navy fullback 1904–06. NFF
Cecil F. Isbell—Purdue halfback 1935–37. NFF
Herbert Joesting—Minnesota fullback 1925–27. C, NFF
Jimmie Johnson—Carlisle quarterback 1900–02. NFF

Calvin Jones—Iowa guard 1953–55. C

Frank A. Juhan—University of the South center 1908–10. NFF

Charles "Choo Choo" Justice—North Carolina halfback 1947–49. C, NFF

Morton Kaer—So. California halfback 1924–26. C, NFF

Kenneth Kavanaugh—Louisiana State end 1937–39. C, NFF

Edgar L. Kaw—Cornell halfback 1920–22. C, NFF

Richard W. Kazmaier—Princeton halfback 1949–51. C. NFF

James S. Keck—Princeton tackle 1919–21. NFF

Lawrence M. Kelley—Yale end 1934–36. NFF

William "Wild Bill" Kelly—Montana quarterback 1924–26. NFF

Henry H. Ketcham—Yale center-guard 1911–13. NFF

John Reed Kilpatrick—Yale end 1908–10. NFF

John C. Kimbrough—Texas A&M halfback 1938–40. C, NFF

Frank "Bruiser" Kinard—Mississippi tackle 1935–37. C, NFF

Philip King—Princeton quarterback 1890–93. NFF

Nile Kinnick—Iowa fullback 1937–39. C, NFF

Harry G. Kipke—Michigan halfback 1921–23. C, NFF

John Kitzmiller—Oregon halfback 1928–30. NFF

Barton "Botchy" Koch—Baylor guard 1929–31. NFF

Mal Kutner—Texas end 1939–41. NFF

Ron Kramer—Michigan end 1954–56. C

John Lattner—Notre Dame halfback 1950–53. C

Elmer F. Layden—Notre Dame halfback 1922–24. C, NFF

Miles Layne—Dartmouth halfback 1924–26. NFF

Robert "Bobby" Layne—Texas quarterback 1945–47. NFF

Langdon "Biffy" Lea—Princeton tackle-end 1893–95. C, NFF

James Leech—Virginia Military Institute (VMI) halfback 1914, 1919–20. C, NFF

Darrell Lester—Texas Christian center 1933–35. C

Gordon C. Locke—Iowa fullback 1920–22. C, NFF

Donald Lourie—Princeton back 1919–21. Nff

Sid Luckman—Columbia quarterback 1936–38. C, NFF

John Lujack—Notre Dame quarterback 1944–47. C, NFF

Francis L. "Pug" Lund—Minnesota halfback 1932–34. C, NFF

Bart Macomber—Illinois halfback 1914–16. NFF

Edward W. Mahan—Harvard fullback 1913–15. C, NFF

"Memphis Bill" Mallory—Yale fullback 1921–23. NFF

Gerald C. Mann—Southern Methodist quarterback 1925–27. NFF

J. L. "Pete" Mauthe—Penn. State halfback 1910–12. NFF

Robert "Tiny" Maxwell—Swarthmore guard 1904–06. NFF

George A. McAfee—Duke halfback 1937–39. NFF

Thomas L. "Bum" McClung—Yale halfback 1888–91. NFF

William McColl—Stanford end 1949–51. Cn NFF

James B. McCormick—Princeton fullback 1905–07. NFF

Eugene T. McEver—Tennessee halfback 1927–29. NFF

John J. McEwan—Army center 1914–16. NFF

James Banks McFadden—Clemson halfback 1937–39. NFF

Lewis "Bud" McFadin—Texas guard 1948–50. C

John F. McGovern—Minnesota quarterback 1908–10. NFF

George W. "Tank" McLaren—Pittsburgh fullback 1916–18. NFF

Alvin "Bo" McMillin—Centre quarterback 1919–21. C, NFF

Frank McPhee—Princeton end 1950–52. C

Robert McWhorter—Georgia halfback 1911–13. C, NFF

E. Leroy Mercer—Pennsylvania fullback 1910–12. C, NFF

Louis Michaels—Kentucky tackle 1955–57. C

Abe Mickal—Louisiana State halfback 1932–34. NFF

Don Miller—Notre Dame back 1922–24. NFF

Edgar E. "Rip" Miller—Notre Dame tackle 1922–24. NFF

Eugene "Shorty" Miller—Penn. State back 1910–13. NFF

Wayne Millner—Notre Dame end 1933–35. C

John H. Minds—Pennsylvania fullback 1895–97. NFF

Cliff Montgomery—Columbia quarterback 1931–33. NFF

Donn Moomaw—UCLA linebacker 1950–52. C, NFF

Bill Morton—Dartmouth quarterback 1929–31. NFF

Harold "Brick" Muller—California end 1920–22. C, NFF

Clarence "Biggie" Munn—Minnesota guard 1929–31. C

Bronko Nagurski—Minnesota tackle 1927–29. C, NFF

Ernest A. Nevers—Stanford fullback 1923–25. C, NFF

Marshall "Ma" Newell—Harvard tackle 1890–93. C, NFF

Leo Nomellini—Minnesota tackle 1947–49. C

Andrew J. "Swede" Oberlander—Dartmouth halfback 1924–26. C, NFF

Robert David O'Brien—Texas Christian halfback 1937–39. C, NFF

Pat O'Dea—Wisconsin fullback 1897–99. C, NFF

John O'Hearn—Cornell end 1912–14. NFF

Elmer Oliphant—Purdue-Army halfback 1911–13, 1915–18. C, NFF

Merlin Olsen—Utah State tackle 1959–61. C

Benjamin G. Oosterbaan—Michigan end 1925–27. C, NFF

Charlie O'Rourke—Boston College quarterback 1938–40. NFF

Winchester D. Osgood—Cornell-Pennsylvania halfback 1890–94. NFF

William Osmanski—Holy Cross fullback 1936–38. NFF

Vito "Babe" Parilli—Kentucky quarterback 1948–50. C

Clarence "Ace" Parker—Duke halfback 1934–36. C, NFF

Jim Parker—Ohio State guard 1954–56. C, NFF

Vincent "Pat" Pazzetti—Wesleyan-Lehigh quarterback 1909–12. NFF

Endicott "Chub" Peabody—Harvard guard 1939–41. NFF

Robert Peck—Pittsburgh center 1914–16. C, NFF

Stanley B. Pennock—Harvard guard 1912–14. C, NFF

George R. Pfann—Cornell quarterback 1921–23. C, NFF

Henry D. Phillips—University of the South guard 1903–05. NFF

Peter L. Pihos—Indiana end-fullback 1941–43. NFF

Ernie Pinckert—So. California halfback 1929–31. C, NFF

John S. Pingel—Michigan State halfback 1936–38. NFF

Arthur Poe—Princeton end 1897–99. NFF

Frederick "Fritz" Pollard—Brown halfback 1914–16. C, NFF

Barney Poole—Mississippi-Army end 1942–48. C, NFF

Henry R. "Peter" Pund—Georgia Tech center 1926–28. NFF

Duane Purvis—Purdue halfback 1932–34. C

Rick Redman—Washington guard 1962–64. C

Claude Reeds—Oklahoma fullback 1910–13. NFF

William Reid—Harvard fullback 1896–98. NFF

Robert Reinhard—California tackle 1939–41. C

Robert "Horse" Reynolds—Stanford tackle 1932–34. C, NFF

Les Richter—California guard-linebacker 1949–51. C, NFF

Charles "Babe" Rinehart—Lafayette guard 1895–97. NFF

Ira E. "Rat" Rodgers—West Virginia fullback 1917–19. C, NFF

Edward L. Rogers—Carlisle-Minnesota end 1900–03. NFF

Aaron David Rosenberg—So. California guard 1931–33. C, NFF

Kyle Rote—Southern Methodist halfback 1948–50. NFF

Joseph Routt—Texas A&M guard 1937–39. NFF

George H. Sauer—Nebraska fullback 1931–33. NFF

George Savitsky—Pennsylvania tackle 1943–45. C

Gale Sayers—Kansas halfback 1962–64. C

Hunter Scarlett—Pennsylvania end 1906–08. NFF

Wear K. Schoonover—Arkansas end 1927–29. NFF

David N. Schreiner—Wisconsin end 1940–42. NFF

Adolf "Germany" Schulz—Michigan center 1906–08. C, NFF

Frank J. Schwab—Lafayette guard 1920–22. C, NFF

Marchy Schwartz—Notre Dame back 1929–31. NFF

Paul Schwegler—Washington tackle 1929–31. C, NFF

Gaius Shaver—So. California fullback 1929–31. C

Thomas L. Shevlin—Yale end 1902–04. C, NFF

Claude "Monk" Simons—Tulane halfback 1932–34. NFF

O. J. Simpson—So. California halfback 1966–68. C

Frederick W. Sington—Alabama tackle 1928–30. C

Frank Sinkwich—Georgia halfback 1940–42. C, NFF

Emil Sitko—Notre Dame halfback 1947–49. C

Fred F. "Duke" Slater—Iowa tackle 1919–21. C, NFF

Ernest Smith—So. California tackle 1930–32. C, NFF

Bruce Smith—Minnesota halfback 1939–41. C, NFF

Harry Smith—So. California guard 1937–39. C, NFF

Neil Snow—Michigan end 1898–1900. C, NFF

Clarence W. Spears—Dartmouth guard 1913–15. NFF

W. D. "Bill" Spears—Vanderbilt quarterback 1925–27. NFF

William Earl Sprackling—Brown quarterback 1909–11. NFF

Mortimer "Bud" Sprague—Texas-Army tackle 1923–28. C, NFF

Amos Alonzo Stagg—Yale end 1888–89. NFF

Wally Steffen—Chicago quarterback 1906–08 NFF

Herb Stein—Pittsburgh center 1918–21. NFF

Don Stephenson—Georgia Tech center 1955–57. C

Mal Stevens—Washburn-Yale back 1918–23, NFF

Vincent M. Stevenson—Pennsylvania quarterback 1903–05. NFF

Kenneth Strong—New York U. fullback 1926–28. C, NFF

Everett Strupper—Georgia Tech halfback 1915–17. C, NFF

Joe Stydahar—West Virginia tackle 1932–35. NFF

Robert L. Suffridge—Tennessee guard 1938–40. C, NFF

George Tallaferro—Indiana halfback 1946–48. C

Samuel B. Thorne—Yale halfback 1893–95. NFF

James Thorpe—Carlisle halfback 1908, 1911–12. C, NFF

Benjamin H. Ticknor—Harvard center 1928–30. C, NFF

John J. Tigert—Vanderbilt halfback-end 1901–03. NFF

Gaynell Tinsley—Lousiana State end 1934–36. C, NFF

Eric "The Red" Tipton—Duke back 1936–38. C, NFF

Ed "Brick" Travis—Tarkio-Missouri back 1918–20. NFF

Charles Trippi—Georgia halfback 1943–46. C, NFF

J. Edward Tryon—Colgate halfback 1923–25. C, NFF

Clyde "Bulldog" Turner—Hardin-Simmons center 1937–39. C, NFF

Joe Utay—Texas A&M back 1905–07. NFF

Norm Van Brocklin—Oregon quarterback 1946–48. NFF

Henderson Van Surdam—Wesleyan back 1903–05.

Billy Vessels—Oklahoma halfback 1950–52. NFF

Doak Walker—Southern Methodist halfback 1946–48. C, NFF

Adam Walsh—Notre Dame center 1922–24. NFF

Kenneth Washington—UCLA halfback 1937–39. C, NFF

Jim Weatherall—Oklahoma tackle 1948–50. C

George Webster—Michigan State back 1964–66. C

Harold H. Weekes—Columbia halfback 1899–1902. C, NFF

Ed Weir—Nebraska tackle 1923–25. C, NFF

John A. C. Weller—Princeton guard 1933–35. NFF

Percy Wendell—Harvard halfback 1910–12. NFF

D. Belford West—Colgate tackle 1916–19. C, NFF

Alexander "Babe" Weyand—Army tackle 1911–15. NFF

Charles "Buck" Wharton—Pennsylvania guard 1894–96. NFF

Arthur Wheeler—Princeton guard 1891–94. NFF

Byron "Whizzer" White—Colorado halfback 1935–37. C, NFF

Donald Whitmire—Alabama-Navy tackle 1941–44, C, NFF

Frank Wickhorst—Navy tackle 1924–26. NFF

Edwin Widseth—Minnesota tackle 1934–36. C, NFF

Richard Wildung—Minnesota tackle 1940–42. C, NFF

James A. "Froggy" Williams—Rice end 1940–42. NFF

Bobby Wilson—Southern Methodist back 1933–35. NFF

George Wilson—Washington halfback 1923–25. C, NFF

Harry Wilson—Penn. State-Army halfback 1922–26. NFF

Albert A. "Ox" Wistert—Michigan tackle 1940–42. C, NFF

Alvin Wistert—Michigan tackle 1947–49. C

Francis M. "Whitey" Wistert—Michigan tackle 1931–33. C, NFF

Alexander Wojciechowicz—Fordham center 1935–37. C, NFF

Andrew R. E. Wyant—Bucknell-Chicago guard 1890–93. NFF

Clinton Wyckoff—Cornell quarterback 1893–95. NFF

Bowden Wyatt—Tennessee end 1936–38. NFF

Ron Yary—So. California tackle 1965–67. C

Claude "Buddy" Young—Illinois halfback 1942–43, 1946. NFF

H. K. "Cy" Young—Washington and Lee halfback 1913–16. NFF

Gust Zarnas—Ohio State guard 1935–37. NFF

College Coaches

William A. Alexander—Georgia Tech 1920–44. C, NFF

Edward N. Anderson—Holy Cross 1933–38, 1950–60; Iowa 1939–42, 1946–49. C, NFF

Ike Armstrong—Utah, 1925–49. C, NFF

Charles Bachman—Northwestern 1919; Kansas State 1920–27; Florida 1928–32; Michigan State 1933–42, 1944–46. C

Harry Baujan—Dayton 1923–42, 1946. C

Madison "Matty" Bell—Haskell 1920–21; Carroll 1922; Texas Christian 1923–28; Texas A&M 1929–33; Southern Methodist 1935–41, 1945–49. C, NFF

Hugo F. Bezdek—Arkansas 1908–12; Oregon 1913–17; Penn State 1918–29. C, NFF

Dana X. Bible—Louisiana State 1916; Texas A&M 1917, 1919, 1928; Nebraska 1929–36; Texas 1937–45. C, NFF

Bernard W. Bierman—Mississippi A&M 1925–26; Tulane 1927–32; Minnesota 1932–41, 1945–50. C, NFF

Earl H. "Red" Blaik—Dartmouth 1934–40; Army 1941–58. C, NFF

J. Wallace Butts—Georgia 1939–59. C

Harry C. Byrd—Maryland 1913–34. C

Charles W. Caldwell, Jr.—Williams 1928–44; Princeton 1945–56. C, NFF

Walter Camp—Yale 1888–92; Stanford 1893–95. C, NFF

Leonard Casanova—Santa Clara 1946–49; Pittsburgh 1950; Oregon 1951–66. C

Frank W. Cavanaugh—Holy Cross 1903–05; Dartmouth 1911–16; Boston College 1919–26; Fordham 1927–32. C, NFF

Herbert O. "Fritz" Crisler—Minnesota 1930–31; Princeton 1932–37; Michigan 1938–47. C, NFF

Jack Curtice—W. Texas State 1940–41; Texas-El Paso 1946–49; Utah 1950–57; Stanford 1958–1961. C

Hugh "Duffy" Daugherty—Michigan State 1954–72. C

Dudley DeGroot—Santa Barbara State; Rochester; San Jose State 1932–39; West Virginia 1948–49; New Mexico 1950–52. C

A. S. "Jake" Gaither—Florida A&M 1945–70.

Howard H. Jones—Syracuse 1908; Yale 1909, 1913; Ohio State 1910; Iowa 1916–23; Duke 1924; So. California 1925–40. C, NFF

L. McC. "Biff" Jones—Army 1926–29; Louisiana State 1932–34; Oklahoma 1935–36; Nebraska 1937–42. C, NFF

Lloyd P. Jordan—Harvard 1950–56. C

Andrew Kerr—Stanford 1922–23; Washington and Jefferson 1926–28; Colgate 1929–46. C, NFF

Frank Kimbrough—Hardin-Simmons 1935–40; Baylor 1941–42, 1945–46; W. Texas St. 1947–57. C

Francis W. Leahy—Boston College 1939–40; Notre Dame 1941–43, 1946–53. C, NFF

George E. Little—Cincinnati 1914–16; Miami (O.) 1916–17, 1919–22; Wisconsin 1925–27. NFF

Louis L. Little—Villanova 1921–22; Georgetown 1924–29; Columbia 1930–56. C, NFF

Edward P. "Slip" Madigan—St. Mary's (Calif.) 1921–40; Iowa 1943–44. C

Daniel E. McGugin—Vanderbilt 1904–34. C, NFF

DeOrmond "Tuss" McLaughry—Westminster 1916–17, 1919–21; Amherst 1922–25; Brown 1926–40; Dartmouth 1941–42. C, NFF

Alvin N. "Bo" McMillin—Centenary 1922–24; Geneva 1925–27; Kansas State 1928–33; Indiana 1934–47. C

John F. "Chick" Meehan—Syracuse 1920–24; New York U. 1925–31; Manhattan College 1932–37. C

Leo R. "Dutch" Meyer—Texas Christian 1934–52. C, NFF

Bernie H. Moore—Louisiana State 1935–47. NFF

Charles Moran—Texas A&M 1909–14; Centre 1919–23; Bucknell 1924–26. C

J. Ray Morrison—Southern Methodist 1915–16, 1922–34; Vanderbilt 1935–39; Temple 1940–48; Austin 1949–52. C, NFF

Clarence "Biggie" Munn—Michigan State 1947–53. NFF

Francis J. Murray—Marquette 1922–36, 1946–49; Virginia 1937–45. C

William D. Murray—Delaware 1940–42, 1946–50; Duke 1951–65. C, NFF

Edward "Hooks" Mylin—Lebanon Valley 1923–33; Bucknell 1934–36; Lafayette 1937–42, 1946; New York U. 1947–49. C, NFF

A. Earle "Greasy" Neale—Muskingum, Marietta, Washington and Jefferson 1921; Virginia 1923–28; West Virginia 1931–33. NFF

Jess C. Neely—Clemson 1931–39; Rice 1940–1963. C

Robert R. Neyland—Tennessee 1926–34, 1936–40, 1946–52. C, NFF

Homer H. Norton—Centenary 1920–21; Texas A&M 1934–47. C, NFF

Jordan Olivar—Villanova 1943–48; Yale 1952–69. C

Frank J. "Buck" O'Neill—Colgate 1902; Syracuse 1906–07; Columbia 1920–22. NFF

Benjamin G. Owen—Oklahoma 1905–26. C, NFF

Donald Peden—Ohio U. 1924–42, 1945–46. C

James M. Phelan—Missouri 1920–21; Purdue 1922–29; Washington 1930–41. C

Edward N. Robinson—Nebraska 1896–97; Brown 1898–1901, 1904–07, 1910–25. C, NFF

Stanley Robinson—Mississippi State 1918–19; Mississippi Coll. 1920–22, 1928–41, 1946–54; Mercer 1923–25. C

Knute K. Rockne—Notre Dame 1918–31. C, NFF

Ernest L. "Dick" Romney—Utah State 1919–48. C, NFF

William W. Roper—Princeton 1906–08, 1910–11, 1919–30; Missouri 1909. C, NFF

Henry R. "Red" Sanders—Vanderbilt 1940–43, 1946–48; UCLA 1949–57. C

Francis A. Schmidt—Tulsa 1919–21; Arkansas 1922–28; Texas Christian 1929–33; Ohio State 1934–40; Idaho 1941–42. C

Clark D. Shaughnessy—Tulane 1915–20; Loyola of the South 1926–32; Chicago 1933–39; Stanford 1940–41; Maryland 1942, 1946; Pittsburgh 1943–45. C, NFF

Lawrence T. "Buck" Shaw—North Carolina State 1924; Nevada 1925–28; Santa Clara 1936–42; California 1945; Air Force Academy 1956–57. C, NFF

Andrew L. Smith—Pennsylvania 1909–12; Purdue 1913–15; California 1916–25. C, NFF

Carl G. Snavely—Bucknell 1927–33; No. Carolina 1934–35; Cornell 1936–44; Washington (Mo.) 1953–58. C, NFF

Oscar M. "Ossie" Solem—Luther 1920; Drake 1921–31; Iowa 1932–36; Syracuse 1937–45; Springfield 1946–57. C

William H. Spaulding—Minnesota 1922–24; UCLA 1925–38. C

Clarence W. Spears—Dartmouth 1917, 1920; West Virginia 1921–24; Minnesota 1925–29; Oregon 1930–31; Wisconsin 1932–35. C

Amos Alonzo Stagg—Chicago 1892–1933; Pacific 1934–46. C, NFF

Emmett R. "Abe" Stuber—Westminster (Mo.) 1929–31; Cape Girardeau 1932–46; Iowa State 1947–53. C

Harry Stuldreher—Villanova 1925–36; Wisconsin 1937–47. C

John B. "Jock" Sutherland—Lafayette 1919–23; Pitt 1924–38. C, NFF

James M. Tatum—No. Carolina 1942, 1956–58; Oklahoma 1946; Maryland 1947–55. C

Frank W. Thomas—Chattanooga 1925–28; Alabama 1931–46. C, NFF

John Vaught—Mississippi 1947–70, 1972. C

W. Wallace Wade—Alabama 1922–30; Duke 1931–41. C, NFF

Lynn O. "Pappy" Waldorf—Oklahoma State 1929–33; Kansas State 1934; Northwestern 1935–46; California 1947–56. C, NFF

Douglas "Peahead" Walker—Wake Forest 1937–50. C

Glenn S. "Pop" Warner—Georgia 1895–96; Cornell 1897–98; Carlisle 1899–1914; Pittsburgh 1915–24; Stanford 1925–32; Temple 1933–38. C, NFF

E. E. "Tad" Wieman—Secretary, Rules Committee; coach: Michigan 1927–28; Princeton 1938–42. NFF

John W. Wilce—Ohio State 1913–28. C, NFF

Charles "Bud" Wilkinson—Oklahoma 1947–63. C, NFF

Henry L. Williams—Minnesota 1900–21. C, NFF

Warren B. Woodson—Hardin-Simmons 1941–42, 1946–51; Arizona 1952–56; New Mexico State 1958–70. C

George W. Woodruff—Pennsylvania 1892–1900; Illinois 1903; Carlisle 1905. NFF

Fielding H. Yost—Michigan 1900–28. C, NFF

Bibliography. Baker, L. H.: *Football: Facts and Figures,* Farrar and Rinehart, New York, 1945; Claasen, Harold, and Steve Boda, Jr.: *Encyclopedia of Football,* Rev. ed., Ronald, New York, 1963; Danzig, Allison: *The History of American Football,* Prentice-Hall, Englewood Cliffs, N.J., 1956; *The NFL's Official Encyclopedic History of Professional Football,* Macmillan, New York, 1973; Treat, Roger: *The Official Encyclopedia of Football,* 7th rev ed., A. S. Barnes, New York, 1969; Zimmerman, Paul: *A Thinking Man's Guide to Pro Football,* Dutton, New York, 1970.

G

GAELIC FOOTBALL—The Irish say that their version of football is much older than the British version, but they are probably talking about hurling, not Gaelic football.

Gaelic football does apparently go back more than 400 years, but its early descriptions sound like the early descriptions of soccer, as played in England about the same time: Whole towns or parishes would compete against one another, starting at a point midway between goal lines—which were sometimes 10 mi apart, or more—and kicking opponents much more often than they kicked the ball.

Until 1884 the sport was a real free-for-all. Then the Gaelic Athletic Association was formed to standardize rules. As played now, there are 15 members on a team, and the field is 140 to 160 yd long and 84 to 100 yd wide. There is a goalpost, with a net, at each end of the field, 21 ft wide and 8 ft high. The ball can be advanced up the field by dribbling, kicking, or punching; 1 point is scored by kicking or punching the ball over the crossbar and 3 points by kicking or punching it into the net. The game has halves of 30 minutes each.

There are some Gaelic football teams around New York City, originally formed by Irish immigrants about the turn of the century.

See also FOOTBALL; HURLING; SOCCER.

GAMBLING—Betting on sports is probably almost as old as sports activity itself. And, even though most forms of gambling are outlawed in most states, gambling on sports flourishes in the United States. It is estimated that about $50 billion a year is bet on team sports alone, most of it illegally, since Nevada is the only state where such gambling is legal.

The fact that it does flourish had led to repeated proposals in many other states that it should be legalized, as a new source of tax revenue. The chief fruit of this movement so far has been the establishment of off-track betting (OTB) in New York State. OTB allows betting only on Thoroughbred and harness racing.

A National Gambling Commission was established by the federal government in the 1970s to study the whole problem of gambling and possible results of its legalization. The commission was charged with issuing a full report on its findings, including legislative proposals.

Parimutuel Betting

In parimutuel betting, all money bet goes into a pool and the amounts bet on each entry determine the payoff odds for that entry. First, a certain percentage of the pool—15 to 17 percent—is deducted and shared by the track and the state. Then the remaining money is split equally among those who hold winning tickets. If, for example, the amount bet on the race after the commission is deducted is $10,000, and there are 1,000 people who bet on the winning entry, each winning bettor would be paid $10. The payoff is expressed in terms of the amount paid on a $2 ticket. If, for example, a horse pays $2.20 to win, the holder of a $2 ticket collects that amount—in effect, the holder has bet $2 against 20 cents, thus giving 10-to-1 odds.

There are many different kinds of bets at most tracks, and each type of bet has its own pool. A place bet is a bet that an entry will at least place second. If someone bets on a horse to place, that person also collects if the horse wins. A show bet is a bet that the horse will place third or better.

Daily Double. This is a separate pool on two different races, often the first two. The bettor must pick the winner of each race to collect.

Twin Double. In this form of wagering, the bettor attempts to pick the winners of four races. A ticket for the first two races is purchased at the outset; if the buyer has picked the winners of those races, the ticket is turned in for another ticket, with the buyer's choices for the other two races.

Quinella. The bettor attempts to pick the horses that will finish first and second, but doesn't have to pick the order of finish.

Exacto (or Exacta or Perfecta). This is a variation of the quinella, but the bettor must pick the first two horses in the order of their finish.

Bookmaking

What most people fail to understand about illegal betting, with a bookmaker, or "bookie," is that the bettor doesn't bet against the bookie. Like the race track, the bookie depends on a commission for his profit. Many bookies know very little about the sports on which they book bets. What the bookie attempts to do is to set odds or point spreads that will bring in approximately equal amounts of money on each side. If it is found that too much money is coming in on one side, the bookie will then adjust the odds to make a bet on the other side somewhat more attractive.

If, for example, a football team is a 7-point favorite and large amounts of money are being bet on that team, the bookie will adjust the spread upward, to 8, 9, or 10 points or more. If large amounts of money are being bet on the other team, the bookie will lower the point spread. In any event, the odds or point spread are, in the long run, determined by the bettors themselves, not by the bookie.

In practice, the "line" is originally set in Las Vegas or Miami. First, an early line, or "soft line," is established; only a handful of professionals are allowed to bet this.

Their reaction to it determines whether the line changes when it becomes "official." Although individual bookies may adjust the line somewhat to allow for regional betting habits, they have another recourse when confronted with the possibility of a big loss: They can "lay off" some of the money by making a bet of their own, in effect, with a bigger bookie.

Although there have been many allegations that bookies are all underworld figures, and that gambling profits help support other illegal activities, such as prostitution and loan sharking, the fact seems to be that the small bookie is basically an independent operator, but organized crime handles much of the layoff money, more or less as a service to the bookies.

Baseball Odds. Bets on baseball are simple bets on a team to win; odds are usually determined by the identities of the starting pitchers. This is called a "money" or "price" line, since odds are used. If the line on a game between the Pirates and the Braves, for example, is "7-8 Pirates," it means a bettor has to put up $8 to make $5 if he bets on the Pirates; he puts up $5 to win $7 if he bets on the Braves. The difference between the odds is the bookie's commission, or "vigorish." Newspapers that carry charts of starting pitchers only carry the odds, in disguised form, as a number rating of each pitcher against the opposing team.

Point Spreads. In higher-scoring sports, simple odds cannot be used because, if a team was an overwhelming favorite, hardly anyone would bet on the other team, regardless of the odds, and it would be impossible to get a "balanced book." So, in football and basketball (and, oddly, in hockey), point spreads are used to equalize betting. If a bettor places a bet on a team that is favored by 10 points, the team must win by more than 10 points for the bettor to win the bet. (If the point spread results in a tie—in this case, if the team wins by exactly 10 points—the bettor simply gets back the money wagered.)

Because point spreads do shift on occasion, a bettor might at times bet on the same team twice, with two different point spreads—or even bet on two different teams in the same game. Suppose, for example, that Team A is favored by 3 points over Team B, and a person bets on Team A. Two days later, the spread has gone up to 5 points; the same bettor might now bet on Team B. The bettor is "playing a middle"—chances are the bettor will win one bet and lose the other, which means the bettor simply pays the bookie's commission. But if Team A wins by 4 points, the bettor wins both wagers—has "hit a middle," in short.

In point-spread betting, the bettor has to put up $11 to win $10. The extra dollar, collected from the loser, is the bookie's commission.

Legalized Gambling

At the beginning of 1975, 31 states permitted parimutuel betting on some or all of the following; Thoroughbred racing, harness racing, dog racing, jai alai. In addition, 13 states had legal, organized lotteries, and New York's OTB was handling close to $1 billion a year.

Betting on team sports was legal only in Nevada. But several states were seriously considering legalized gambling on team sports. In Nevada the state merely collects revenue from gambling, without getting involved in the technical details. The actual betting is done with licensed bookies, who pursue their business independently.

Many observers believe that other states should follow the same pattern, although legislators in those states don't necessarily agree.

A major argument against the government's trying to operate gambling is the fact that the bookies themselves are the most effective monitors of team sports. It is the bookies who stand to get hurt if a game is fixed and large amounts of money are bet at the last minute. The nationwide network of bookies has very sensitive antennae tuned in to possible fixes, and many people doubt that a government bookmaking system would be as effective.

Scandals

There have been several gambling and fix scandals in American sports through the years. During the nineteenth century and well into the twentieth, baseball was plagued by gambling. The worst scandal that ever occurred was the "Black Sox" case of 1919, when eight members of the Chicago White Sox apparently conspired to throw the World Series with the Cincinnati Reds. (*See also* BASEBALL; BLACK SOX SCANDAL.)

Professional football and basketball have been relatively free of such scandals, although two players on the New York Giants, Frank Filchock and Merle Hapes, were suspended in 1946 for not reporting an offered bribe before the championship play-off game of the National Football League. In 1963, Paul Hornung of the Green Bay Packers and Alex Karras of the Detroit Lions were suspended for a year for betting on games; both insisted that they had never bet against their own football teams.

Much more flagrant scandals struck college basketball. In 1951, investigation revealed that 86 college games had been fixed over a three-season period; 32 players at 7 colleges were involved. They were guilty of "point shaving"—deliberately holding down winning margins in order to help bettors beat the point spread. But in at least one case, a much-favored team went a little too far with point shaving and lost the game. The second scandal was milder, but still shocking, because it occurred just 10 years later. This time, most of the players involved were freshmen who had accepted "retainers" from gamblers, the assumption being that they would eventually start shaving points when they became varsity players.

Hockey has had just one scandal of this type, in 1948, when Bill Taylor of the Detroit Red Wings and Don Gallinger of the Boston Bruins were banned from the sport for life for betting with bookmakers.

Glossary

big nickel—$5,000.

big one—$1,000.

buck—$100.

circle game—A game on which a bookie will accept only relatively small bets, or only bets from special customers.

dime—$1,000.

dog—The underdog; or, a team that is a very poor bet.

edge—An advantage; usually information known only to a few.

feeler line—In football betting, the first line offered to the public, on the Monday before the game day; it is likely to change as bets come in.

goal spread—The point spread in hockey.

hanger—A game suspected of being fixed.

lay—To make a bet; to bet a favorite.

line—The odds or point spread.

make the spread—What a team does when it beats the point spread, whether it wins or loses; people who bet on the team win their bets.

middle—A situation in which a point spread has changed sufficiently for a bettor to be able to win bets on both teams.

money line—A line based on wagering odds, rather than on a point spread.

nickel—$500.

off the board—When the bets will not be accepted on a game, it is said to be off the board; this happens because one team is an overwhelming favorite, or because a fix is suspected.

opening line—Same as "feeler line."

over or under —A type of bet in which a figure is established and the bettor wagers that the total number of points in a selected game will be over or under that figure.

pick 'em—A game in which neither team is favored.

players—Bettors.

push—A tie caused by the point spread, as when a 3-point favorite wins by 3 points; the bettor gets back the money wagered.

short end—A bet on the underdog is a short-end bet.

small nickel—$50.

total-points bet—Same as "over or under" bet.

vigorish—The bookie's commision.

GLIDING—*See* SOARING.

GOLDEN GLOVES—Arch Ward, sports editor of the *Chicago Tribune,* in 1926 conceived the idea of an annual amateur boxing tournament for youngsters, and his newspaper agreed to sponsor it. The Golden Gloves tournament was adopted by the New York *Daily News* in that city in 1927, and other newspapers around the country soon began sponsoring tournaments in their own areas. National championships were first held in 1929, after a series of local, regional, and sectional qualifying tournaments.

GOLF—Many scholars feel that a Roman sport, *paganica,* is the direct ancestor of golf. The sport involved hitting a feather ball with a crooked stick—and that is all that is known about it. The presumption is that Roman soldiers brought *paganica* to Europe and the British Isles, and that it was fairly well established in those areas by the fourth century, when the Roman legions withdrew.

During the Middle Ages, a sport called *kolf* was played in the Low Countries. Usually played on a large patch of ice, *kolf* involved striking a ball with a crooked stick; the target was a pole set in the ice. Golf, croquet, curling, and a number of other sports may have been derived from *kolf*—or perhaps it was just a member of the same family of sports, and all were derived from *paganica* or some even more ancient game.

However, the Scots developed golf as we know it. By about 1500, Scotsmen were using clubs whittled from tree branches to knock feather-stuffed leather balls into holes, and this pastime was popular enough to be banned in 1457, since it was considered to be keeping men from their all-important archery practice. The ban was never really enforced, though; evidently a love of golf was already too widespread.

The first match of which we have a definite record was a remarkably democratic affair. The Prince of Wales, paired with an Edinburgh cobbler, played and beat two English noblemen in 1682 for a sizable bet. With his share of the winnings, the cobbler built himself a house which stood until 1961.

In 1744 the Honourable Company of Edinburgh Golfers was organized; in 1754 the St. Andrews Society of Golfers, which has since become the Royal and Ancient Golf Club of St. Andrews, was organized. The rules drawn up by the St. Andrews group form the nucleus of modern golf rules. Among other things, those rules specified: that a golfer must use the same ball from tee to green; that stones and similar impediments must not be removed from around the ball, except on the green; that a golfer is entitled to remove a ball in play from water and drop it behind the hazard, with a one-stroke penalty; that the player whose ball lies farthest from the hole must play first.

The St. Andrews course originally had 12 holes; at the time, the number of holes varied from course to course. In 1764 the club cut down its course to 10 holes. Going out, a golfer played holes 2 through 10; coming in, the golfer played holes 9 through 1, for a total of 18 holes per round. That soon became the standard.

The sport really began to spread beyond Scotland in the mid-nineteenth century. At just about the same time—in 1848, to be exact—the feather-stuffed ball was replaced by the gutta-percha ball, made of a rubberlike resin from certain Malaysian trees.

Originally a golfer used just one club, for driving, putting, and all strokes in between. Specialized clubs began to come into play during the sixteenth century; by the early nineteenth century there were many kinds of special clubs available.

In the second half of the nineteenth century, as sports began to become a more important part of life for many people, golf really began to come into its own. The first British Open was played in 1860, the first British Amateur in 1885. Golf was also one of the first sports in which women competed. Britain's Ladies Golf Union held its first championship in 1894.

Golf Arrives in the United States. There are references to golf having been played in this country as early as 1786, in Charleston, South Carolina. The real beginning of golf in the United States, however, came less than a century ago, in 1888. By then, there were five golf clubs in Canada and the sport had been played sporadically in Chicago; Sarasota, Florida; Burlington, Iowa; Oakhurst, West Virginia; and possibly other places.

On February 22, 1888, Scots-born John Reid of Yonkers, New York, laid out a three-hole course in his cow pasture and invited some neighbors to try the sport with him. On November 19 of that year, St. Andrew's Golf Club of Yonkers was formed. By 1894 the club had headquarters in nearby Grey Oaks, where an informal national championship was held; a year later, there were 75 golf clubs in the country, and five of them formed the Amateur Golf Association of the U.S., now the U.S. Golf Association (USGA).

Other groups involved early in golf in the United States included the Tuxedo, New York, Club; a club in Newport, Rhode Island; the Country Club of Brookline, Massachusetts; and Shinnecock Hills of Long Island, New York. The first USGA championships were held at Newport in 1895. The amateur championship was match play, the open championship medal play.

Golf spread rapidly in this country during the early years of the twentieth century, and many professionals from England and Scotland came to the United States to teach the sport. They also won most of the U.S. Opens. But in 1913 a young Massachusetts amateur golfer suddenly made the sport nationwide news, and was responsible for thousands of Americans becoming golfers, almost literally overnight. Francis Ouimet was then 20 years old. He had learned the sport as a caddie. In the 1913 U.S. Open, he tied two of the top British professionals, Harry Vardon and Ted Ray, at 304; then he shot a 72 to Vardon's 77 and Ray's 78 to win the 18-hole play-off.

Walter Hagen won many tournaments, but his greatest accomplishment was winning four consecutive PGA championships when that tournament was decided by match play. (U.S. Golf Association.)

By the 1920s, the United States was taking over international leadership in the sport. In 1922, Walter Hagen became the first native-born American to win the British Open, and American golfers were to keep winning it until 1933. By 1930 there were nearly 6,000 golf courses in the United States, out of approximately 9,000 in the entire world. Spectators were charged admission fees at most major tournaments.

Prosperity and the availability of land on which to build courses were major factors in this country's growing dominance of the sport. It was largely United States industry, too, that made the major technological advances in equipment. Perhaps most important, though, was the establishment of the pro tour. Like other major sports in this country, golf went professional in the 1920s and became a really major professional sport before football and long before basketball.

Nevertheless, one of the great American golfers—one of the greatest golfers the world has ever seen—remained an amateur to the end of his life. He was Robert Tyre "Bobby" Jones, Jr., who retired from major competition when he was only 28, after having won four U.S. Opens, three British Opens, five U.S. Amateurs, and one British Amateur. His retirement came in 1930, a year in which he won all four major tournaments—the two amateurs and the two opens.

Professional Golf

The early professionals were not highly regarded—just as most professionals in other sports were not highly regarded. The English, especially, looked down on professional athletes. Their professional golfers were, in a sense, servants who existed primarily to teach the game to gentlemen. That was undoubtedly part of the reason why so many British pros did come to the United States early in the century.

Professionals, of course, were allowed to compete for money. At first the money usually came from bets placed on them by gentlemen backers; the golfers also often made side bets among themselves.

In 1916, Rodman Wanamaker, of a famous mercantile family, called a meeting of United States golf professionals and offered to donate some prize money for their own tournament. As a result the Professional Golfers Association (PGA) was formed. Its first tournament—the first PGA championship—was held that year. Wanamaker donated a total prize of $2,580. The winner of the tournament, Long Jim Barnes, received $500.

At about the same time, other professional tournaments were organized in Florida, although the prizes given were usually negligible. The professional tour began, in a sense, in 1922, with tournaments in resort areas, sponsored by wealthy golf enthusiasts—often with real-estate promotion in the backs of their minds. In 1922 some Texans got together a purse of $5,000, and the Texas Open began.

Oddly, it was during the Depression that the tour really got going. The PGA in 1936 hired a promoter, Fred Corcoran, as tournament director. By 1946 Corcoran had built the tour to a total of 30 tournaments with total prizes of about $750,000.

The early pros deserve a lot of credit for the establishment of the tour. They had proved that professional golfers could attract crowds, and sizable fees, for putting on exhibitions. Chief among them was the colorful Walter

Hagen, the first professional to earn more than $1 million. Hagen was the personification of the professional golfer—always at his best at the crucial moments, always possessing some psychological edge over his opponent. He was incredibly successful at match play—head-to-head against one other golfer. He won four consecutive PGA tournaments, when that tournament was at match play. Another great early pro, Gene Sarazen, once wrote, "All the professional golfers who have a chance to go after the big money today should say a silent thanks to Walter Hagen each time they stretch a check between their fingers."

Women's professional golf didn't really start until 1946, when the Women's Professional Golfers' Association was formed. Corcoran tried to assist the group; when he failed, he organized the rival Ladies' Professional Golf Association (LPGA), which now rules this aspect of the sport. Under Corcoran's leadership—and with help from two important sponsors, clothing manufacturer Alvin Handmacher and publisher Helen Lengfield—the beginning of a women's tour was organized in 1949, with total prizes of about $30,000.

Mildred "Babe" Didriksen Zaharias was one of the early drawing cards. Her name was known because of her Olympic exploits, and she played well to crowds.

The first Women's Open was held in 1946 under WPGA auspices; the tournament has been conducted by the USGA since 1953. The LPGA championship—the women's equivalent of the PGA championship—was inaugurated in 1955.

In the Money. The men's professional golf tour had grown phenomenally by 1946, but the average total purse per tournament was then little more than $12,000; the average is now about $150,000.

There are several reasons for the growth. George S. May was one of them. May inaugurated a major tournament in 1946, the World Championship of Golf. In that first year it had a $10,000, winner-take-all purse. In 1952 it offered a total purse of $75,000, with a first prize of $25,000—at a time when that was more than the total purse of most tournaments. In 1954 it became the first $100,000 tournament, and first prize was $50,000.

Then television arrived, and did a lot to boost the monetary awards even higher. Corporate sponsors began to appear, realizing that their companies would get nationwide television publicity for a major tournament; and, of course, the TV money also helped.

As golfers became national and international celebrities, sponsors got the benefit of another interesting device: the pro-amateur, usually played before the formal tournament. In a "pro-am," amateur golfers pay to become the temporary partners of touring pros. For various reasons, corporate sponsorship of major men's tournaments has declined somewhat since those early television years. Many of the major tournaments today are sponsored by civic or charitable groups.

Women's pro golf, on the other hand, has picked up some important corporate sponsors in recent years. As in other sports, the money paid to women has lagged, but sponsorship by such companies as Sears, Sealy, and Colgate-Palmolive has helped to bring it closer to par. While Johnny Miller set a record by earning $353,030 in 1974, JoAnne Carner came close to the $100,000 mark—which had first been reached by a male pro, Arnold Palmer, in 1963. So the women are still behind—and probably always will be, because sponsors feel the men can attract larger crowds, both live and on TV—but they have made rapid gains.

Outstanding Pros. The first star of the professional tour was Byron Nelson. In 1945 he won 18 tournaments and finished in the top four 10 other times. He also won 11 tournaments in a row.

Then came Ben Hogan and Sam Snead, a study in contrasts. Hogan, known to the Scots as "the wee ice man" and to many sportswriters as the "mechanical man," was a dour, methodical player who excelled with the irons. Snead, on the other hand, was a gregarious player with a near-perfect swing who sometimes had difficulty on the greens. Other top touring professionals during the late 1940s and the 1950s were Jimmy Demaret, Lloyd Mangrum, Dr. Cary Middlecoff (a dentist), Jack Burke, Jr., and E. J. "Dutch" Harrison.

The golfer who has been credited with ushering in the sport's golden era is Arnold Palmer. Palmer hit his peak at just the right time, for his own sake and for golf's. National television was just becoming important to the tour when Palmer began winning championships in inimitable style. As often as not, Palmer trailed with five or six holes to play in a tournament and then started one of his famous charges, cutting strokes off his opponent's lead with virtually every hole and finally emerging as the winner.

Palmer was quickly challenged by Jack Nicklaus, fresh out of Ohio State and the amateur ranks in 1962. As an amateur in 1960, Nicklaus finished second to Palmer in the U.S. Open—the first amateur to finish that high since John G. Goodman had won the title in 1933. In 1962, Nicklaus was a 22-year-old rookie professional; playing on Palmer's home course, Oakmont, Pennsylvania, Nicklaus tied Palmer for the title and then beat him, 71-74, in an 18-hole play-off.

During the early 1960s, South African Gary Player formed a golfing triumvirate, the so-called Big Three, with Palmer and Nicklaus. By the late years of that decade, Palmer had faded somewhat, and a previously unknown Mexican-American, Lee Trevino, suddenly emerged to replace him among the Big Three.

Although Nicklaus, Trevino, and Player were still going strong in the early 1970s, a new kind of tour had begun to form, loaded with strong young players, and at times it seemed that there was a new hero every week. With the tour paying enormous amounts of money to winners, and with more and more colleges offering full scholarships to outstanding golfers to give them a strong education in the competitive realities of the sport, it seems likely that this pattern will continue for years to come.

(For further information on outstanding amateur and professional golfers, see the Hall of Fame section at the end of this entry.)

Organizations

Golf's major ruling bodies in the United States have already been mentioned. The USGA has overall responsibility for amateur play and for play involving amateurs—including the men's and women's opens. The PGA has overall supervision of male professionals, the LPGA of women professionals.

The USGA. Basically, the USGA is actually an organization of golf clubs—including clubs of golfers who use public courses as well as clubs that have their own courses. A member club must be made up of individual dues-paying members who elect officers. Associate memberships are open to courses not controlled by a club—meaning most public courses.

Besides conducting the U.S. Open and U.S. Amateur championships, the USGA represents this country in international amateur play, which has grown to remarkable size. It is the United States representative on the World Amateur Golf Council, which conducts the World Amateur Team Championship and the Women's World Team Championship. The USGA is also responsible for organizing this country's teams in Walker Cup and Curtis Cup play.

The PGA. Although the touring pros are easily the most visible members of the PGA, they represent only a small percentage of that group's membership. Members also include those who have served for at least five years as head professionals and assistant pros at recognized golf courses. Only the head pros are full-fledged members; others, including touring pros, can be members, but they don't have voting rights.

This situation led to a number of disputes with touring pros, as a result of which the PGA set up the Tournament Players Division (TPD), which has basic control over the professional tour. The first TPD commissioner was Joe Dey, who had been executive director of the USGA for 34 years. He became commissioner in 1969.

The Tour. Its very monetary success has brought a number of problems to the pro golf tour. The basic problem is that it has attracted so many golfers, and only a limited number can play in a tournament.

To play in any tour tournament, a golfer first has to attend the PGA Approved Tournament Players qualifying school, where he must earn a card that gets him into the tournaments. Even then, however, he has to qualify for each tournament. The usual tournament is played from Thursday through Sunday, and is automatically open only to 60 golfers—those who have earned the right to play without qualifying, through a point system based on their performances the year before. Other spots in the tournament are filled through a qualifying round on the Monday before the tournament. As many as 150 golfers might play to fill just 15 or 20 vacancies.

As a result, several "mini-tours" sprang up in 1972 and 1973. The first, of the National Tournament Golf Association in Tampa, Florida, was organized in 1972. It signed up 102 players, who paid $7,000 each to enter; they played a series of 20 tournaments, each with a $20,000 purse. By 1973 there were eight such mini-tours. They began to die out in 1974, however; the problem was that the prize money came almost entirely from the golfers' own entry fees and, as the losers dropped out for lack of money, there weren't enough others to replace them.

The TPD made several changes in 1974 to alleviate the problems of the younger players and to deal with complaints from many tour sponsors. Certain major tournaments were called "designated" tournaments, and all 60 top pros were required to play in them. (Sponsors had been upset by the lack of "name" golfers in a number of tournaments.) Second, substantial steps were taken toward setting up a true "satellite" tour for younger, less experienced golfers.

The LPGA. Organization of the LPGA is similar to that of the PGA, except that there are not nearly as many women pros outside the tour and, because the women's tour is not nearly as big in terms of number of players, number of tournaments, and amount of prize money, the LPGA has not yet had to cope with problems of mini-tours or complaining sponsors. The organization exercises much more direct control over its tour than the PGA, which has left that task almost entirely up to its Tournament Players Division.

Major Tournaments

By and large, the importance of a tournament is measured by its prize money. There are several tournaments, however, that transcend that kind of measurement.

British Open. The oldest of all tournaments, the British Open pays relatively small prizes, but the prestige of a victory in the event attracts top golfers from all over the world. From 1927 through 1962, it was essentially a 108-hole tournament, since all golfers had to play 36 qualifying holes before beginning the 72-hole tournament. In 1963, however, a number of exemptions were established, so that many golfers now don't have to qualify. Only 120 players are admitted to the field.

U.S. Open. This was also, at one time, a more strenuous event than it is today; until 1965, the final 36 holes were played in one day. The Open has earned its name: It is open to all professionals and to all amateurs with a handicap of two strokes or less.

Among those exempt from qualifying are the winners of the last five Opens, the 15 lowest scorers in the previous Open, the tour's 15 leading money winners, and some others who have won major championships in the preceding year. All others compete in a series of qualifying rounds, on the local, regional, and sectional levels. There are 150 starters; the field is cut to the 60 lowest scorers (and ties) after the first 36 holes.

U.S. Women's Open. This event and the LPGA championship are the only major women's tournaments played over 72 holes; others are played over 54 holes. The tournament is open to all professionals and to amateurs with handicaps of five strokes or less. After 36 holes, the field is cut to the 40 low scorers (and ties).

PGA Championship. At one time the only major match-play tournament, the PGA became a medal-play tourney in 1957. It is open only to professionals, including the low 25 scorers (and ties) in the PGA Club Professionals' Championship. The field, of about 144, is cut to the low 70 scorers and ties after the first 36 holes.

LPGA Championship. This also was once match play—in its inaugural year, 1955—but it has been a medal-play tournament since 1956. It is open only to professionals, and is played at 72 holes.

USGA National Amateur. Begun in 1895 with 32 entries, the U.S. Amateur was a match-play tournament until 1965, when it was changed to 72-hole stroke play. However, it went back to match play in 1973. The tournament is open to amateurs with handicaps of three strokes or less. Most of the 150 players must qualify through 36-hole sectional qualifying rounds.

USGA Women's Amateur. This was a stroke-play tournament in its first year, 1895, but has been a match-play tournament since 1896. Entries are open to women amateurs with handicaps of five strokes or less. There are 150 entrants, who compete in two 18-hole medal-play rounds; the 32 low scorers qualify for match play.

The Masters. This is strictly an invitational tournament, held annually at the Augusta National Golf Club. The invitation list is based on rather strict rules as to who is eligible in any given year; some foreign golfers are issued special invitations, based on their play in international events.

The Grand Slam. When Bobby Jones scored his "grand slam," the Masters tournament had not yet begun and Jones, being an amateur, was not eligible for the PGA championship. The four events in his 1930 grand slam were the U.S. Amateur, U.S. Open, British Amateur, and British Open. As professionals have come to the fore, however, the two amateur tournaments have lost much of their importance. The modern grand slam is composed of four tournaments open to professionals: the U.S. and British Opens, the PGA championship, and the Masters.

International Golf

Golf is now played in an untold number of countries; it is thriving in at least 60 of them, and it has boomed in the Orient, particularly in Japan. The British brought the sport to colonies in the nineteenth century, establishing courses in Australia, India, Hong Kong, and South Africa, among others. The United States, and international television of major events, have done the rest.

The United States leads the world with an estimated 12 million more-or-less "serious" golfers; Japan has about 3 million; Australia has an estimated 500,000, out of a total population of only about 10 million. The first major international competitions took place between teams of golfers from Great Britain and the United States, but events involving many other countries are now also becoming important.

Walker Cup. This trophy was donated by George H. Walker, former USGA president, in 1922 for competition between British and American amateurs. Play is now biennial, in odd-numbered years. Each team is made up of eight players and two alternates. Competition consists of eight foursome matches and 16 individual matches. In the formal scoring, a team gets a point for each match won; if a match is tied after 18 holes, neither team gets a point.

Curtis Cup. The women's counterpart to the Walker Cup was donated by Harriot and Margaret Curtis, both former U.S. Amateur champions, in 1932. Each team consists of six golfers and two alternates. Teams play six 18-hole foursomes and twelve 18-hole singles. Half points are awarded for drawn matches. Curtis Cup competition is biennial, in even-numbered years.

Ryder Cup. In 1927, Samuel Ryder of Great Britain donated a trophy for competition between British and U.S. professionals. The U.S. team is chosen through a complicated point system based on finishes in major PGA tour events. The competition involves foursome matches, singles matches, and four-ball matches. It is held in odd-numbered years.

World Cup. Originally called the Canada Cup, this trophy was originated in 1953 by John Jay Hopkins of Canada for competition among two-man teams of professionals from various countries. There were 7 countries in the first tournament; now there are more than 40. United States representatives are usually the winners of the Open and the PGA. The World Cup, as it has been known since 1967, now goes to the low-scoring team in a 72-hole tournament. The lowest individual scorer since 1954 has won the International Trophy.

Bobby Jones never played as a professional, but won 13 major tournaments, including the 1930 grand slam—the U.S. Open, British Open, U.S. Amateur, and British Amateur. In the nine-year period, 1922 through 1930, he won four U.S. Opens, finished second three times, and tied for second once. *(U.S. Golf Association.)*

World Amateur Team Championship. The World Amateur Golf Council sponsors this event, for teams of three or four players. There are four 18-hole rounds; the three lowest scores each day from each team count toward the championship. Originated in 1958, this championship is played biennially.

A similar event for women has been conducted since 1964. Women's teams have two or three players, and only the two lowest scores count in each day's play.

Equipment

Probably no other sport—with the possible exception of pole vaulting—has changed and improved so much through the years as the direct result of improvements in equipment. Progress is still going on, but golf's supervisory bodies now take long, hard looks at any major equipment change that alter scores too substantially.

The Ball. As already mentioned, the old feather-stuffed ball was succeeded by the gutta-percha ball in 1848. The "guttie" cost less, was more durable, and rolled more truly on the greens than the old feather ball. The surface of the ball was covered with indentations to promote proper flight.

A Cleveland golfer, Coburn Haskell, invented the rubber ball in 1898 with help from Bertram G. Work of the B. F. Goodrich Company. The first versions were made of rubber thread, wound tightly on a solid rubber core, then covered with gutta-percha. This ball carried well—about 25 yd farther than the "guttie"—but it was difficult to control on the greens.

The rubber ball was, and still is, the subject of much experimentation. In 1932 the USGA standardized the ball's weight at no more than 1.62 oz and its diameter at no less than 1.68 in. The British rules specify a minimum diameter of 1.62 in. There have been moves in recent years to try to get the two countries to agree on a single standard.

Because the standards for measurement are minimums, the British ball cannot be used in American tournaments, since it is smaller than the minimum, but the American ball can be used in Great Britain. In international play involving both countries, such as the Ryder Cup, players can use either ball.

Many types of centers are used in golf balls. The best balls usually have liquid centers, but some contain a small solid core inside a rubber core. The covers are made of vulcanized rubber, painted white; most balls have 336 dimples, which make the ball carry farther and also keep it truer in flight.

A more recent development is the one-piece ball, molded from a plasticlike material. A variation is the two-piece ball, with a core of this material covered by adhesive or threaded rubber.

Clubs. The feather ball was relatively soft, and the clubs used during that period were rather slender, and made of softer woods. When the gutta-percha ball was introduced, harder woods were substituted, and heads were made larger. Iron clubs also increased. Clubs of the period were hand-made.

When the rubber ball arrived, even harder woods were needed. Wooden heads were usually made of persimmon or laminated woods. As more and more people became golfers, hand-crafting gave way to machine manufacture.

In 1911 the steel-shafted club was introduced, but it wasn't totally satisfactory until 1924, when a method was developed of making a seamless shaft of high-carbon steel. In the early 1950s the fiberglass shaft—made of fiberglass fibers running lengthwise around a central spiral of fiberglass—was introduced. Then came aluminum and, most recently, the controversial, and highly expensive, graphite shaft.

There are three basic categories of clubs: drivers, irons, and putters. The first two categories are numbered; the higher the number, the higher the loft of the club. While there are eight different woods, the 7 and 8 woods are rarely used. There are nine numbered and some special, nonnumbered irons. The clubs also have common names, many of which go back at least two centuries.

The most common clubs, and their names, are: 1 wood, driver; 2 wood, brassie; 3 wood, spoon; 4 wood, cleek or short spoon; 5 wood, baffy; 1 iron, driving iron; 2 iron, midiron; 3 iron, mid mashie; 4 iron, mashie iron; 5 iron, mashie; 6 iron, spade mashie; 7 iron, mashie niblick; 8 iron, pitching niblick; 9 iron, niblick.

Among the special irons are the pitching wedge, used for high shots from very close to the green; the chipping iron, similar to a 4 iron but with a shorter shaft, used for pitch-and-run shots; and the sand wedge, which has a heavy flange to keep the head from digging deeply into the sand.

The putt is the most important single type of shot in golf, and as a result there has been a great deal of experimentation with putters. What they all have in common is a straight, or almost straight, striking surface.

Techniques

Countless numbers of books have been written on how to play golf, and the average golfer, apparently, has not benefited much from any of them. It would be presumptuous, therefore, to try to offer help in this short space; this section will be devoted only to the simplest essentials of the sport.

The Grip. The best players usually use the Vardon, or overlapping, grip. The left hand is placed on the club first; then the right hand is placed with part of the palm covering the left thumb, the little finger overlapping the first finger of the left hand. The V formed by the thumbs should point approximately toward the chin or slightly to the right.

Players with smaller hands often use the interlocking grip, which is similar, except that the little finger of the right hand is thrust between the middle and forefingers of the left hand and is wrapped around the forefinger.

The full-finger grip is essentially the same as the grip usually used on a baseball bat.

The Stance. In the basic golf stance, weight should be distributed about evenly between the two legs; the toes should be pointed slightly outward, the knees should be turned slightly inward, and both toes should be touching an imaginary line parallel to the desired line of flight.

The stance must be varied somewhat for different shots, however. As the distance of the shot decreases, the feet are brought closer together (actually the left foot is left in the same place, and the right foot is brought closer to it), the right foot moves somewhat across the line, toward the ball, and the right toe begins to turn inward. The right shoulder whould be slightly below the left, and the left hip should be turned slightly away from the ball.

Footwork. At the start of the backswing, the weight shifts to the ball of the right foot, the left knee bends inward, and the left foot rolls slightly, the heel barely rising from the ground. When the downswing is about to begin, the left heel must be set to accommodate the shift in weight as the swing takes place.

The Swing. Although a good golf swing is made up of many important parts, at its best it is a single, continuous, fluid motion. First comes the waggle: The club is moved back and forth a few times behind the ball, in a kind of miniature swing that is a rehearsal for the real thing. At the end of the waggle, the club head is rested on the ground behind the ball, and simultaneously comes the forward press, a slight forward movement of the right knee, hip, and shoulder to the left, which also moves the hands slightly forward, without moving the club head.

The forward press immediately recoils into the backswing. The hips turn from left to right, the shoulders turn with them, and the club is brought back and up. The left arm must remain straight all the way through the swing. The club should be kept low to the ground at the beginning of the backswing, with no hand action; as the arms follow the swing of the rest of the body, the wrists will begin to cock automatically, bringing the club up. The length of the backswing varies from golfer to golfer and from shot to shot. Hitting off the tee, the minimum backswing ends when the left arm is parallel to the ground. The backswing should never continue beyond the point where the club shaft is parallel to the ground.

After a slight pause at the top, the downswing begins with a shift of weight to the left side and a counterclockwise rotation of the left hip. The body, which coiled to initiate the backswing, is now uncoiling to initiate the downswing. The shoulders follow the hips, bringing the club back down. The wrists should be kept cocked for as long as possible; ideally, they uncock only when the hands are above the hitting area, 6-8 in behind the ball. Uncocking the wrists at this point brings the club head into and through the ball with top speed and power. At impact, the arms should be straight, the wrists completely uncocked.

After impact, the entire body keeps turning. The head, which to this point has been kept down, should also begin to turn with the shoulders to allow an easy, free follow-through. The hands continue up beyond the shoulders, the head turns toward the target area, and the weight is now almost entirely on the left foot.

Fairway Woods. Using a wood for a fairway shot is similar to using a wood on a tee shot. The major difference, of course, is that the ball is not teed up, so the golfer should hit slightly down on the ball, and the club should hit just below the surface of the turf immediately after impact. The ball, which is played off the left heel for a tee shot, should be slightly closer to the right foot.

Irons. The hardest thing for the average player to realize when playing an iron shot is that the loft of the club will get the ball into the air. Any iron shot should be hit sharply, and the golfer must hit down on the ball, taking a divot beyond it.

As the distance of the shot decreases, the number of the iron increases (a 1 iron is for the longest shots, a 9 iron for the shortest); and, as the number of the iron increases, the golfer chokes up more on the club, the backswing and follow-through become shorter, and the ball is played closer to the right foot.

A 5-iron shot should be played just about from the middle of the stance, a chip shot from just off the right instep. Because the golfer is choking up on the club, it is also necessary to get closer to the ball for shorter shots.

Chips and Pitches. A pitch shot is a short, high-trajectory shot used when the golfer is 20-25 yd from the green or when there are obstacles to be cleared en route to the green. A club with a good deal of loft is used, to get the ball into the air. The stance is opened, there is slightly more weight on the left foot, the waist is bent as if the golfer were beginning to sit down; the key to the shot is that the hands and arms do most of the work. The club must be brought down on the ball with a smooth swing, to get it into the air and to impart the backspin that will stop the ball when it hits the green.

The chip shot, sometimes called the pitch-and-run, is used when the ball is about 20-25 yd from the green with no intervening obstacles. The ball is hit low and is expected to run toward the hole after it lands on the green. A good chip shot takes some experience, because many of the factors involved in putting—the speed of the green, the grain of the grass, among them—come into play in determining just how far the ball will run after it lands.

The stance is somewhat open, the feet are only about 10 in apart, and the weight is well on the left foot. A middle iron is usually used, and the golfer has to choke up on it and use an easy swing to keep from hitting the ball too far. As in a pitch shot, the hands and arms must do most of the work.

Sand Shots. The biggest problem with shots from the sand trap is psychological. The shot is similar to a chip shot, except that the ball is played close to the left heel. At address, the club should be opened—turned toward the right of the target—and the club should hit behind the ball, so the club-head impact is actually transferred to the sand, and then to the ball. If the ball is really buried, the club head should be slightly closed, and it should hit even farther behind the ball, so it can truly get into the sand and take the ball out.

Water Shots. The shot from shallow water is similar to the shot from sand. But for the average golfer, the best way to play the shot is to take the drop and the one-stroke penalty.

Putting. Tee shots are important; long irons are important; short irons and trouble shots are important. But, day in and day out, the good putter has an edge. As a result, the club design and the method of putting are subjects of remarkable amounts of experimentation.

There are some basics, though. The stance should be comfortable, and should permit good balance. The feet are generally close together. The ball is just off the left heel. The arms and hands have to make the stroke; the rest of the body exists just to get out of the way, making the stroke comfortable. The golfer must hit through the ball, resisting the temptation to poke at it without follow-through.

All of this doesn't take into account the line the putt must take, and the speed with which it must be hit. Putting requires a touch, which requires practice. The golfer must know how fast or how slow the green is, the direction of the grain, the type of grass, and other factors that determine how the ball will roll on its way to the hole.

The Rules

Clubs and the Ball. The shaft of the club must be straight, from the top to no more than 5 in above the sole, and should be generally circular in cross section. A grip may be attached to the upper end of the shaft; it may have flat sides, but must not be channeled, furrowed, or molded to fit the hands.

The ball, in the United States, must weigh no more than 1.620 oz; the diameter must be not less than 1.680 in. A player must carry no more than 14 clubs.

Match and Stroke Medal Play. In match play, each hole is essentially a separate contest. The player or team with the lowest score wins the hole. If they have the same score, the hole is said to be "halved." When one player or team has a lead that cannot be overcome in the holes remaining, the match is over, and the rest of the holes are not played. If, for example, after 15 holes one player has a 4-hole lead, that contestant cannot lose, since only 3 holes remain; the player has won by 4 holes, with 3 to play—or, in abbreviated form, "4 and 3." If all 18 holes are played, the winner wins either by one or by two holes—"1 up" or "2 up."

Stroke play takes place at a specified number of holes—72 holes in major men's tournaments—and the winner is the player who has used the fewest strokes for the round. Stroke play is commonly called medal play because, when match play was common, the winner received a trophy, while a separate prize, usually a medal, was awarded to the player who shot the best qualifying round.

Teeing Off. The order of play at the first tee is determined by flipping a coin or through some other chance method. Partners play alternately. After the first hole, the player or team that has won the previous hole tees off first at the next hole; when a hole is halved, the player or team with the honor of teeing off first retains the honor.

The ball must be teed up within a specified area, the teeing ground, but the golfer may stand outside the area to hit the ball. If the ball is hit from outside the teeing ground, in match play, an opponent may require the golfer to replay the shot, without penalty. In stroke play, the golfer must replay the ball, and the initial, illegal, stroke is counted. In match play, if partners play out of order, they lose the hole. In stroke play, their side is penalized two strokes; the ball played illegally is replaced and played again, in proper order.

Order of play as outlined above applies only to teeing off. Once all golfers have teed off and their balls are in play, the ball farthest from the hole is played first.

Playing the Lie. A basic rule of golf is that the ball must be played as it lies; it cannot be moved or touched. The player can't improve position or line of play by bending or breaking anything that is fixed or growing, by pressing down loose soil, or the like. However, loose impediments may be removed, unless both the impediments and the ball are lying in or touching a hazard. The penalty for breaking these rules is loss of hole in match play, and two strokes in stroke play.

Lifting, Dropping, and Placing. There are certain areas from which a player is allowed to move the ball in some way without penalty. Among these are casual water—puddles and the like, not part of a water hazard—animal holes, areas of ground being repaired, and areas in which there are obstructions between his ball and the hole.

Obstructions are man-made objects that are not meant to be hazards. A common example is a tower erected for television cameras. If the obstruction is movable, it may be removed. If it is immovable, and if it is touching the ball or interfering with the player's stance, swing, or backswing, the ball may be lifted and dropped within two club-lengths of its original position. If on the putting green, the ball may be placed in the nearest spot that affords relief. The same is true of a ball touching casual water, an animal hole, or ground under repair.

In a hazard, the player must drop the ball as near as possible to the original spot, in the hazard; or the ball may be dropped outside the hazard, but the player then incurs a one-stroke penalty. If, after dropping, the golfer still hasn't received relief, the ball may be dropped again. If it is impossible to drop the ball so the golfer will gain relief, the ball may be placed.

At no time may the ball be dropped or placed so that it ends up closer to the hole than it was originally.

Identifying and Cleaning. There are times when it is necessary for a golfer to lift a ball to make sure it is the

From 1940 through 1960, Ben Hogan won four U.S. Opens and never finished out of the top 10; he won two Masters, was runner-up four times, and never finished worse than seventh from 1941 through 1956. He won the British Open in 1953, the only year he played in it, and he also won two PGA Championships. *(U.S. Golf Association.)*

golfer's own. This may be done, except in a hazard, provided the player places the ball back in the same spot. In a hazard, the ball must be played; if it turns out to be an opponent's, the golfer then plays the proper ball, and the opponent gets the benefit of the other shot, without penalty.

The golfer may clean the ball for purposes of identification. Cleaning is also permitted after lifting it from an unplayable lie, from casual water, an animal hole, ground under repair, and the like, for relief from an obstruction.

Lost, Unplayable, and Provisional Balls. If a ball is lost or goes out of bounds, the golfer plays the next shot as close as possible to the spot from which the previous shot was made, adding a penalty stroke to the score.

If the player decides that the prevailing lie is unplayable, the ball may be dropped within two club-lengths of the spot or anywhere behind the spot. A one-stroke penalty is assessed in that event.

If a player believes a shot has gone out of bounds, or thinks that the ball might be lost, another shot may be played from the same spot. This is called a "provisional ball." If the player then cannot find the original ball, or discovers that it is out of bounds, the provisional ball continues in play. Once again a one-stroke penalty is prescribed.

Hazards. If the ball is in a hazard, the golfer may do absolutely nothing to improve the lie; the player may not touch the club to the ground in the hazard, move loose impediments within the hazard, or do anything to check the condition of the hazard. When the ball is in a water hazard, it may be dropped at any distance behind the hazard, at the cost of a one-stroke penalty.

Putting. Some special rules apply on the putting green. A player must not touch the line of the putt. Loose impediments may be moved—picked up or brushed aside—but nothing on the green may be pressed down. The ball may be lifted and cleaned.

If a player feels that a ball lying nearer the hole may be in the way, the player may require that opponent to lift the ball, in match play; in stroke play, the player may give the opponent the option of lifting or playing first.

If one player's putt, or a shot from less than 20 yd away from the flag, strikes another player's ball, the first player is penalized two strokes, in stroke play, and the second player's ball is replaced. In match play, there is no penalty; the player whose ball was struck may re-place it, or play it as it lies.

Handicap. A handicap is a figure that, when subtracted from a player's average score, would give the player a par score. If, for example, a player averages 76 strokes per round on a course rated at 72, the player's handicap is four.

Handicaps are based on the average of a certain minimum number of rounds, and on the ratings of the course on which the rounds were played. The rating of a course is not the same as its par; it is based on special distance formulas worked out by the USGA. A par-72 course may be rated as a 68, or as a 76, depending on the distances of its individual holes and on certain special conditions, such as prevailing winds, unusual ground slopes, and narrow fairways.

In stroke play, the player's handicap is deducted from the score for a round to give the net score. In match play, the player is entitled to deduct a stroke from the score only on certain holes. A 1-handicap player can use the stroke only on the longest hole on the front nine. A 5-handicap player is given a stroke on the three longest holes on the front nine, and the two longest on the back nine.

The Courses

One striking feature of golf, as opposed to most other sports, is that the playing fields vary so much. A good golf course has a character of its own, and each good course presents certain unique challenges to the golfer.

There are two basic approaches to course design: the "penal" approach, in which the course is designed to penalize the poor shot, and the "strategic" approach, in which the intent is to reward the good shot.

"Penal" courses are characterized by an abundance of traps and, usually, by very small greens. "Strategic" courses, on the other hand, have fewer traps and larger greens. On such a course the golfer must figure out what the best landing area is for each shot, and then must hit that landing area. Often, on a strategic course, a golfer has a problem if the ball travels too far, even if it is hit straight. Such a course will penalize the gambling shot that doesn't come off, rather than the merely errant shot.

There are thousands of golf courses in the world; among those in the United States that are considered truly outstanding are Merion Golf Club's East Course, Ardmore, Pennsylvania; Pinehurst, North Carolina, Country Club; Augusta, Georgia, National Golf Club (home of the Masters); Pebble Beach Golf Links, Monterey, California; Oakland Hills Country Club, Brimingham, Michigan;

Arnold Palmer, golf's first millionaire, helped establish golf as a popular TV spectator sport. His dramatic "charges" to victory on national TV began in 1960, when he birdied the last two holes to win the Masters by a stroke and shot a final-round 65 to win the U.S. Open. He also won a U.S. Amateur, two British Opens, and three other Masters. *(U.S. Golf Association.)*

Olympic Country Club's Lakeside Course, San Francisco; Winged Foot Golf Club, Mamaroneck, New York; Oakmont, Pennsylvania, Country Club; Baltusrol Golf Club, Springfield, New Jersey; Shinnecock Hills Golf Club, Southampton, New York; and The Country Club, Brookline, Massachusetts.

Glossary

ace—A hole in one.

approach—A shot played to the green.

apron—The grass area bordering the green; also called "fringe."

away—Said of the ball or player farthest from the hole; the player who is away shoots first.

back nine—The second nine holes on an 18-hole course; also "back side."

beach—A sand hazard.

best ball—A type of match in which the lower score turned in on each hole by a team member is the score that counts for the team on that hole; scores are totaled at the end of the round.

birdie—A score of one stroke below par on a hole.

bite—Backspin that makes the ball stop when it hits the green.

blast—A shot out of sand that takes large quantities of sand out of the trap.

blind hole—A hole on which the green cannot be seen by a golfer attempting an approach shot.

bogey—A score of one stroke over par on a hole.

bunker—A hazard of bare ground, usually covered with sand.

caddie—Someone who carries a golfer's clubs and may also offer advice; from the French *cadet*.

can—To make a putt.

casual water—Temporary water that is not a hazard or part of a hazard.

chip-and-run—A shot from off the green in which the ball is lofted very little and allowed to roll toward the cup.

chip—A short approach shot with little loft.

collar—The edge of a sand hazard.

cup—The hole.

cut shot—A high shot that stops as soon as it hits the green.

divot—A piece of turf removed by the club during a shot.

dogleg—A bend in the fairway.

dormie—Said of a player or team with a lead equal to the number of holes remaining in the match; a player 3-up with 3 to play is dormie.

double bogey—A score two strokes above par on a hole.

double eagle—A score two strokes below par on a hole.

draw—To hit the ball with a deliberate, controlled hook.

duck hook—A severe hook in which the ball travels low and not very far.

duffer—A poor golfer.

dunk—To hit a water hazard.

eagle—A score of two strokes below par on a hole.

explode—Same as "blast."

fade—To hit the ball with a slight, controlled slice.

flat swing—A type of swing in which the club, during the backswing, is kept quite close to the ground.

fore—A cried warning that a ball has been, or is about to be, struck.

fore caddie—A person stationed down the fairway to mark the position of balls after they have been driven.

fringe—Same as "apron."

front nine—The first nine holes of an 18-hole course; also "front side."

gimme—An easy putt, often conceded.

go to school—To learn something from the path taken by a previous player's putt along approximately the same line.

green—The entire golf course; but usually used to mean the putting surface.

gross—A player's actual score before the handicap is deducted.

hacker—Same as "duffer."

handicap allowance—In some kinds of play, a golfer is allowed to use only a percentage of his handicap; that is the handicap allowance.

heel—The part of the club head nearest the shaft.

hole high—A ball that is even with the hole, on one side or the other.

hole in one—A hole made with a single stroke.

hole out—To put the ball in the hole.

hook—A shot that curves sharply to the left of the intended line of flight.

hosel—The part of the club head, on an iron, into which the shaft fits.

in—A player "coming in" is playing the back nine.

lag—A long putt by means of which the golfer is simply trying to get close to the hole.

links—A golf course; originally a course on the seaside.

lip—The rim of the hole.

lob—A very high shot hit a short distance to the green.

make the cut—In most professional tournaments, the field is cut to the 60 or 70 low scorers after two 18-hole rounds; a golfer still in the field has "made the cut."

medalist—The player with the lowest qualifying score.

Mulligan—In informal play, a second shot allowed a golfer off the first tee, without penalty. Also "Shapiro."

Nassau—A type of competition in which a point is awarded for winning the front nine, another point for winning the second nine, and a third point for winning the entire 18-hole round.

net—A player's score after the player's handicap or allowance is subtracted from the gross score.

out—A player on the front nine is "going out."

overclubbing—Using a club that will hit the ball too far.

pitch—A short shot to the green, hit with a good deal of loft and a lot of backspin.

pitch-and-run—A lower shot to the green, in which the ball is meant to roll toward the cup.

plugged lie—A lie in which the ball is buried in sand.

pull—To hit the ball to the left of target without any appreciable curve in flight.

punch—A low shot, usually hit into the wind.

push—To hit the ball to the right of target with little appreciable curve in flight.

rabbit—A touring pro who must qualify on Mondays.

rough—Areas where a golfer should not hit the ball, though not out of bounds; usually applied to areas of relatively long grass on either side of the fairway.

rub of the green—The luck of the game, something to be accepted; in the official rules of golf, the expression means a lucky or unlucky break for which there is no official penalty or remedy, as when a ball hits a spectator.

run-up—An approach shot, usually from the apron of the green, in which the ball is hit along the ground; a putter is often used for the stroke.

Scotch foursome—A type of match in which two partners play one ball and take turns hitting it.

scratch golfer—A golfer who has no handicap.

shank—The part of the hosel nearest the face of the club; or, to hit the ball with the shank of the club, resulting in a wildly erratic shot.

sky—To hit well underneath the ball, sending it high into the air.

slice—A shot that curves far to the right of the intended line of flight.

snake—A long, curving putt.

sole—The bottom of the club head; to sole the club is to put this part of the club on the ground while addressing the ball.

sole plate—A metal plate that protects the sole of a wooden club.

square—Even, as in "the match is square after 12 holes."

stymie—Originally, a situation in which an opponent's ball is in the line of a player's putt; the player putting was said to be stymied. Now the term usually means a situation in which a player is behind a tree.

sudden death—A form of play-off in which the first player to win a hole wins the match.

sweet spot—The spot on the club face that should hit the ball square for the best possible shot.

Texas wedge—The putter, when used for a shot from off the green.

toe—The part of the club head farthest from the point where the head joins the shaft.

turn—To move from the front nine to the back nine; a player teeing off on the 10th hole is "making the turn."

underclubbing—Using a club that will not give the distance needed on a shot; when a player uses a 9-iron for a 7-iron shot, he has "underclubbed himself."

waggle—A preliminary movement of the club back and forth behind the ball, usually leading up to the backswing.

water hole—A hole on which a dangerous water hazard must be negotiated.

winter rules—Local rules that allow golfers to improve their lies because of adverse weather conditions.

yips—Extreme nervousness while putting, often resulting in involuntary muscle actions that will cause a bad miss even on a short putt.

Leading Money Winners

Men

1934	Paul Runyan	$ 6,767
1935	Johnny Revolta	9,543
1936	Horton Smith	7,682
1937	Harry Cooper	14,138
1938	Sam Snead	19,543
1939	Henry Picard	10,303
1940	Ben Hogan	10,655
1941	Ben Hogan	18,358
1942	Ben Hogan	13,143
1943	Not available	
1944	Byron Nelson	37,967
1945	Byron Nelson	63,335
1946	Ben Hogan	42,556
1947	Jimmy Demaret	27,936
1948	Ben Hogan	32,112
1949	Sam Snead	31,593
1950	Sam Snead	35,758
1951	Lloyd Mangrum	26,088
1952	Julius Boros	37,032
1953	Lew Worsham	34,002
1954	Bob Toski	65,819
1955	Julius Boros	63,121
1956	Ted Kroll	72,835
1957	Dick Mayer	65,835
1958	Arnold Palmer	42,607
1959	Art Wall, Jr.	53,167
1960	Arnold Palmer	75,262
1961	Gary Player	64,450
1962	Arnold Palmer	81,448
1963	Arnold Palmer	128,230
1964	Jack Nicklaus	113,284
1965	Jack Nicklaus	140,752
1966	Billy Casper, Jr.	121,944
1967	Jack Nicklaus	188,988
1968	Billy Casper, Jr.	205,168
1969	Frank Beard	175,224
1970	Lee Trevino	157,037
1971	Jack Nicklaus	244,490
1972	Jack Nicklaus	320,942
1973	Jack Nicklaus	308,362
1974	Johnny Miller	353,030
1975	Jack Nicklaus	298,149
1976	Jack Nicklaus	266,438

Women

1948	Mildred D. Zaharias	$ 3,400
1949	Mildred D. Zaharias	4,650
1950	Mildred D. Zaharias	14,800
1951	Betsy Rawls	15,087
1952	Louise Suggs	14,505
1953	Patty Berg	19,816
1954	Patty Berg	16,011
1955	Marlene Hagge	16,497
1956	Patty Berg	20,235
1957	Bev Hanson	16,272
1958	Betsy Rawls	12,639
1959	Louise Suggs	26,774
1960	Mickey Wright	16,892
1961	Mickey Wright	22,236
1962	Mickey Wright	21,641
1963	Mickey Wright	31,269
1964	Mickey Wright	29,800
1965	Kathy Whitworth	28,658
1966	Kathy Whitworth	33,517
1967	Kathy Whitworth	32,937
1968	Kathy Whitworth	48,379
1969	Carol Mann	49,152
1970	Kathy Whitworth	30,235
1971	Kathy Whitworth	41,181
1972	Kathy Whitworth	65,063
1973	Kathy Whitworth	82,854
1974	JoAnne Carner	89,872
1975	Sandra Palmer	76,374
1976	Judy Rankin	150,734

Award Winners

Radix and Vardon Trophy

(The Radix Trophy was awarded 1934–1942 and 1945–1946 to the male professional with the best total score in certain specified tournaments on the PGA tour. It was succeeded by the Vardon Trophy, which, since 1947 has been awarded to the player compiling the lowest strokes-per-round average in major tour events.)

1934	Ky Laffoon	
1935	Paul Runyan	
1936	Ralph Guldahl	
1937	Harry Cooper	
1938	Sam Snead	
1939	Byron Nelson	
1940	Ben Hogan	
1941	Ben Hogan	
1942	Ben Hogan	
1943-44	No award	
1945	Byron Nelson	
1946	Ben Hogan	
1947	Jimmy Demaret	69.90
1948	Ben Hogan	69.30
1949	Sam Snead	69.37
1950	Sam Snead	69.23
1951	Lloyd Mangrum	70.05
1952	Jack Burke, Jr.	70.54
1953	Lloyd Mangrum	70.22
1954	Dutch Harrison	70.41
1955	Sam Snead	69.86
1956	Cary Middlecoff	70.35
1957	Dow Finsterwald	70.30
1958	Bob Rosburg	70.11
1959	Art Wall, Jr.	70.35
1960	Billy Casper, Jr.	69.95
1961	Arnold Palmer	69.85
1962	Arnold Palmer	70.27
1963	Billy Casper, Jr.	70.58
1964	Arnold Palmer	70.01
1965	Billy Casper, Jr.	70.58
1966	Billy Casper, Jr.	70.27
1967	Arnold Palmer	70.18
1968	Billy Casper, Jr.	69.82
1969	Dave Hill	70.34
1970	Lee Trevino	70.64
1971	Lee Trevino	70.30
1972	Lee Trevino	70.89
1973	Bruce Crampton	70.60

1974	Lee Trevino	70.50
1975	Bruce Crampton	70.50
1976	Don January	70.56

Vare Trophy

(Lowest strokes-per-round average among women professionals)

1953	Patty Berg	75.00
1954	Mildred Zaharias	75.48
1955	Patty Berg	75.47
1956	Patty Berg	54.57
1957	Louise Suggs	74.64
1958	Bev Hanson	74.92
1959	Betsy Rawls	74.03
1960	Mickey Wright	73.25
1961	Mickey Wright	73.55
1962	Mickey Wright	73.67
1963	Mickey Wright	72.81
1964	Mickey Wright	72.46
1965	Kathy Whitworth	72.61
1966	Kathy Whitworth	72.60
1967	Kathy Whitworth	72.74
1968	Carol Mann	72.04
1969	Kathy Whitworth	72.38
1970	Kathy Whitworth	72.26
1971	Kathy Whitworth	72.88
1972	Kathy Whitworth	72.38
1973	Judy Rankin	73.08
1974	JoAnne Carner	72.87
1975	JoAnne Carner	72.40
1976	Judy Rankin	72.25

PGA Player of the Year

1948	Ben Hogan	1963	Julius Boros
1949	Sam Snead	1964	Ken Venturi
1950	Ben Hogan	1965	Dave Marr
1951	Ben Hogan	1966	Billy Casper, Jr.
1952	Julius Boros	1967	Jack Nicklaus
1953	Ben Hogan	1968	No Award
1954	Ed Furgol	1969	Orville Moody
1955	Doug Ford	1970	Dave Hill
1956	Jack Burke, Jr.	1971	Lee Trevino
1957	Dick Mayer	1972	Jack Nicklaus
1958	Dow Finsterwald	1973	Tom Weiskopf
1959	Art Wall, Jr.	1974	Johnny Miller
1960	Arnold Palmer	1975	Jack Nicklaus
1961	Jerry Barber	1976	Ray Floyd
1962	Arnold Palmer		

LPGA Player of the Year

1966	Kathy Whitworth	1972	Kathy Whitworth
1967	Kathy Whitworth	1973	Kathy Whitworth
1968	Kathy Whitworth	1974	JoAnne Carner
1969	Kathy Whitworth	1975	Sandra Palmer
1970	Sandra Haynie	1976	Judy Rankin
1971	Kathy Whitworth		

Major Tournament Champions—Men

U.S. Open (*denotes amateur)

1895	Horace Rawlins	173
1896	James Foulis	152
1897	Joe Lloyd	162
1898	Fred Herd	328
1899	Willie Smith	315
1900	Harry Vardon	313
1901	Willie Anderson	331
	Alex Smith	331
	(Anderson won play-off, 85-86)	
1902	Lawrence Auchterlonie	307
1903	Willie Anderson	307
	David Brown	307
	(Anderson won play-off, 82-84)	

1904	Willie Anderson	303
1905	Willie Anderson	314
1906	Alex Smith	295
1907	Alex Ross	302
1908	Fred McLeod	322
	Willie Smith	322
	(McLeod won play-off, 77-83)	
1909	George Sargent	290
1910	Alex Smith	298
	John J. McDermott	298
	Macdonald Smith	298
	(A. Smith won play-off, 71-75-77)	
1911	John J. McDermott	307
	Michael J. Brady	307
	George O. Simpson	307
	(McDermott won play-off, 80-82-85)	
1912	John J. McDermott	294
1913	Francis Ouimet*	304
	Harry Vardon	304
	Edward Ray	304
	(Ouimet won play-off, 72-77-78)	
1914	Walter Hagen	290
1915	Jerome D. Travers*	297
1916	Charles Evans, Jr.*	286
1917–18	No tournament	
1919	Walter Hagen	301
	Michael J. Brady	301
	(Hagen won play-off, 77-78)	
1920	Edward Ray	295
1921	James M. Barnes	289
1922	Gene Sarazen	288
1923	Robert T. Jones, Jr.*	296
	Robert A. Cruickshank	296
	(Jones won play-off, 76-78)	
1924	Cyril Walker	297
1925	William Macfarlane	291
	Robert T. Jones, Jr.*	291
	(Macfarlane won play-off, 147-148)	
1926	Robert T. Jones, Jr.*	293
1927	Tommy Armour	301
	Harry Cooper	301
	(Armour won play-off, 76-69)	
1928	Johnny Farrell	294
	Robert T. Jones, Jr.*	294
	(Farrell won play-off, 143-144)	
1929	Robert T. Jones, Jr.*	294
	Al Espinosa	294
	(Jones won play-off, 141-164)	
1930	Robert T. Jones, Jr.*	287
1931	Billy Burke	292
	George Von Elm	292
	(First 36-hole play-off was tied, 149-149; Burke won second, 148-149)	
1932	Gene Sarazen	286
1933	John G. Goodman*	287
1934	Olin Dutra	293
1935	Sam Parks, Jr.	299
1936	Tony Manero	282
1937	Ralph Guldahl	281
1938	Ralph Guldahl	284
1939	Byron Nelson	284
	Craig Wood	284
	Denny Shute	284
	(Nelson and Wood tied in first play-off, 68-68 to 76 for Shute; Nelson won second, 70-73)	
1940	Lawson Little, Jr.	287
	Gene Sarazen	287
	(Little won play-off, 70-73)	
1941	Craig Wood	284
1942–45	No Tournament	

1946	Lloyd Mangrum	284
	Byron Nelson	284
	Victor Ghezzi	284
	(All three shot 72 in first play-off; Mangrum won second, 72-73-73)	
1947	Lew Worsham	282
	Sam Snead	282
	(Worsham won play-off, 69-70)	
1948	Ben Hogan	276
1949	Cary Middlecoff	286
1950	Ben Hogan	287
	Lloyd Mangrum	287
	George Fazio	287
	(Hogan won play-off, 69-73-75)	
1951	Ben Hogan	287
1952	Julius Boros	281
1953	Ben Hogan	283
1954	Ed Furgol	284
1955	Jack Fleck	287
	Ben Hogan	287
	(Fleck won play-off, 69-72)	
1956	Cary Middlecoff	281
1957	Dick Mayer	282
	Cary Middlecoff	282
	(Mayer won play-off, 72-79)	
1958	Tommy Bolt	283
1959	Billy Casper, Jr.	282
1960	Arnold Palmer	280
1961	Gene Littler	281
1962	Jack Nicklaus	283
	Arnold Palmer	283
	(Nicklaus won play-off, 71-74)	
1963	Julius Boros	293
	Jacky Cupit	293
	Arnold Palmer	293
	(Boros won play-off, 70-73-76)	
1964	Ken Venturi	278
1965	Gary Player	282
	Kel Nagle	282
	(Player won play-off, 71-74)	
1966	Bill Casper, Jr.	278
	Arnold Palmer	278
	(Casper won play-off, 69-73)	
1967	Jack Nicklaus	275
1968	Lee Trevino	275
1969	Orville Moody	281
1970	Tony Jacklin	281
1971	Lee Trevino	280
	Jack Nicklaus	280
	(Trevino won play-off, 68-71)	
1972	Jack Nicklaus	290
1973	Johnny Miller	279
1974	Hale Irwin	287
1975	Lou Graham	287
	John Mahaffey	287
	(Graham won playoff, 71-73)	
1976	Jerry Pate	277

PGA Championship
(Match play 1916–1957; medal play 1958–present)

1916	James M. Barnes
1918	James M. Barnes
1920	Jock Hutchison
1921	Walter Hagen
1922	Gene Sarazen
1923	Gene Sarazen
1924	Walter Hagen
1925	Walter Hagen
1926	Walter Hagen
1927	Walter Hagen
1928	Leo Diegel

1929	Leo Diegel	
1930	Tommy Armour	
1931	Tom Creavy	
1932	Olin Dutra	
1933	Gene Sarazen	
1934	Paul Runyan	
1935	John Revolta	
1936	Denny Shute	
1937	Denny Shute	
1938	Paul Runyan	
1939	Henry Picard	
1940	Byron Nelson	
1941	Victor Ghezzi	
1942	Sam Snead	
1943	No tournament	
1944	Bob Hamilton	
1945	Byron Nelson	
1946	Ben Hogan	
1947	Jim Ferrier	
1948	Ben Hogan	
1949	Sam Snead	
1950	Chandler Harper	
1951	Sam Snead	
1952	Jim Turnesa	
1953	Walter Burkemo	
1954	Chick Harbert	
1955	Doug Ford	
1956	Jack Burke, Jr.	
1957	Lionel Hebert	
1958	Dow Finsterwald	276
1959	Bob Rosburg	277
1960	Jay Hebert	281
1961	Jerry Barber	277
	Don January	277
	(Barber won play-off, 67-68)	
1962	Gary Player	278
1963	Jack Nicklaus	279
1964	Bob Nichols	271
1965	Dave Marr	280
1966	Al Geiberger	280
1967	Don January	281
	Don Massengale	281
	(January won play-off, 69-71)	
1968	Julius Boros	281
1969	Ray Floyd	276
1970	Dave Stockton	279
1971	Jack Nicklaus	281
1972	Gary Player	281
1973	Jack Nicklaus	277
1974	Lee Trevino	276
1975	Jack Nicklaus	276
1976	Dave Stockton	281

Masters

1934	Horton Smith	284
1935	Gene Sarazen	282
	Craig Wood	282
	(Sarazen won play-off, 144-149)	
1936	Horton Smith	285
1937	Byron Nelson	283
1938	Henry Picard	285
1939	Ralph Guldahl	279
1940	Jimmy Demaret	280
1941	Craig Wood	280
1942	Byron Nelson	280
	Ben Hogan	280
	(Nelson won play-off, 69-70)	
1943–45	No tournament	
1946	Herman Keiser	282
1947	Jimmy Demaret	381
1948	Claude Harmon	279
1949	Sam Snead	282

1950	Jimmy Demaret	283
1951	Ben Hogan	380
1952	Sam Snead	286
1953	Ben Hogan	274
1954	Sam Snead	289
	Ben Hogan	289
	(Snead won play-off, 70-71)	
1955	Cary Middlecoff	279
1956	Jack Burke, Jr.	289
1957	Doug Ford	283
1958	Arnold Palmer	284
1959	Art Wall, Jr.	284
1960	Arnold Palmer	282
1961	Gary Player	280
1962	Arnold Palmer	280
	Gary Player	280
	Dow Finsterwald	280
	(Palmer won play-off, 68-71-77)	
1963	Jack Nicklaus	286
1964	Arnold Palmer	276
1965	Jack Nicklaus	271
1966	Jack Nicklaus	288
	Tommy Jacobs	288
	Gay Brewer, Jr.	288
	(Nicklaus won play-off, 70-72-78)	
1967	Gay Brewer, Jr.	280
1968	Bob Goalby	277
1969	George Archer	281
1970	Billy Casper	279
	Gene Littler	279
	(Casper won play-off, 69-74)	
1971	Charles Coody	279
1972	Jack Nicklaus	286
1973	Tommy Aaron	283
1974	Gary Player	278
1975	Jack Nicklaus	276
1976	Ray Floyd	271

British Open (* denotes won play-off)

1860	Willie Park, Sr.	174
1861	Tom Morris, Sr.	163
1862	Tom Morris, Sr.	163
1863	Willie Park, Sr.	168
1864	Tom Morris, Sr.	167
1865	Andrew Strath	162
1866	Willie Park, Sr.	169
1867	Tom Morris, Sr.	170
1868	Tom Morris, Jr.	170
1869	Tom Morris, Jr.	157
1870	Tom Morris, Sr.	149
1871	No tournament	
1872	Tom Morris, Jr.	166
1873	Tom Kidd	179
1874	Mungo Park	159
1875	Willie Park, Sr.	166
1876	Robert Martin	176
1877	Jamie Anderson	160
1878	Jamie Anderson	157
1879	Jamie Anderson	170
1880	Robert Ferguson	162
1881	Robert Ferguson	170
1882	Robert Ferguson	171
1883	Willie Fernie*	159
1884	Jack Simpson	160
1885	Robert Martin	171
1886	David Brown	157
1887	Willie Park, Jr.	161
1888	Jack Burns	171
1889	Willie Park, Jr.	155
1890	John Ball	164
1891	Hugh Kirkaldy	166
1892	Harold H. Hilton	305

1893	William Auchterlonie	322
1894	John H. Taylor	326
1895	John H. Taylor	322
1896	Harry Vardon*	316
1897	Harold H. Hilton	314
1898	Harry Vardon	307
1899	Harry Vardon	310
1900	John H. Taylor	309
1901	James Braid	309
1902	Alexander Herd	307
1903	Harry Vardon	300
1904	Jack White	296
1905	James Braid	318
1906	James Braid	300
1907	Arnaud Massy	312
1908	James Braid	291
1909	John H. Taylor	295
1910	James Braid	299
1911	Harry Vardon*	303
1912	Edward Ray	295
1913	John H. Taylor	304
1914	Harry Vardon	306
1915–19	No tournament	
1920	George Duncan	303
1921	Jock Hutchison*	296
1922	Walter Hagen	300
1923	Arthur Havers	295
1924	Walter Hagen	301
1925	James Barnes	300
1926	Robert T. Jones, Jr.	291
1927	Robert T. Jones, Jr.	285
1928	Walter Hagen	292
1929	Walter Hagen	292
1930	Robert T. Jones, Jr.	291
1931	Tommy Armour	296
1932	Gene Sarazen	283
1933	Denny Shute*	292
1934	T. Henry Cotton	283
1935	Alfred Perry	283
1936	Alfred Padgham	287
1937	T. Henry Cotton	290
1938	R. A. Whitcombe	295
1939	Richard Burton	290
1940–45	No tournament	
1946	Sam Snead	290
1947	Fred Daly	293
1948	T. Henry Cotton	284
1949	Bobby Locke*	283
1950	Bobby Locke	279
1951	Max Faulkner	285
1952	Bobby Locke	287
1953	Ben Hogan	282
1954	Peter W. Thomson	283
1955	Peter W. Thomson	281
1956	Peter W. Thomson	286
1957	Bobby Locke	279
1958	Peter W. Thomson*	278
1959	Gary Player	284
1960	Kel Nagle	278
1961	Arnold Palmer	284
1962	Arnold Palmer	276
1963	Robert J. Charles*	277
1964	Tony Lema	279
1965	Peter W. Thomson	285
1966	Jack Nicklaus	282
1967	Roberto De Vicenzo	278
1968	Gary Player	289
1969	Tony Jacklin	280
1970	Jack Nicklaus*	283
1971	Lee Trevino	278
1972	Lee Trevino	278
1973	Tom Weiskopf	276

1974	Gary Player	282
1975	Tom Watson*	279
1976	Johnny Miller	279

U.S. Women's Open
(Match play, 1946; medal play, 1947–present)

1946	Patty Berg	
1947	Betty Jameson	295
1948	Mildred D. Zaharias	300
1949	Louise Suggs	291
1950	Mildred D. Zaharias	291
1951	Betsy Rawls	293
1952	Louise Suggs	284
1953	Betsy Rawls	302
	Jackie Pung	302
	(Rawls won play-off, 71-77)	
1954	Mildred D. Zaharias	291
1955	Fay Crocker	299
1956	Kathy Cornelius	302
	Barbara McIntire	302
	(Cornelius won play-off, 75-82)	
1957	Betsy Rawls	299
1958	Mickey Wright	290
1959	Mickey Wright	287
1960	Betsy Rawls	292
1961	Mickey Wright	293
1962	Murie Lindstrom	301
1963	Mary Mills	289
1964	Mickey Wright	290
	Ruth Jessen	290
	(Wright won play-off, 70-72)	
1965	Carol Mann	290
1966	Sandra Spuzich	297
1967	Catherine Lacoste	294
1968	Susie Maxwell Berning	289
1969	Donna Caponi	294
1970	Donna Caponi	287
1971	JoAnne Carner	288
1972	Susie Maxwell Berning	299
1973	Susie Maxwell Berning	290
1974	Sandra Haynie	295
1975	Sandra Palmer	295
1976	JoAnne Carner	292
	Sandra Palmer	292
	(Carner won playoff, 76-78)	

Ladies' PGA Championship
(Match-play final between two low scorers in 1955; medal play 1956–present)

1955	Beverly Hanson	
1956	Marlene Hagge	291
	Patty Berg	291
	(Hagge won sudden-death play-off)	
1957	Louise Suggs	285
1958	Mickey Wright	288
1959	Betsy Rawls	288
1960	Mickey Wright	292
1961	Mickey Wright	287
1962	Judy Kimball	282
1963	Mickey Wright	294
1964	Mary Mills	278
1965	Sandra Haynie	279
1966	Gloria Ehret	282
1967	Kathy Whitworth	284
1968	Sandra Post	294
	Kathy Whitworth	294
	(Post won sudden-death play-off)	
1969	Betsy Rawls	293
1970	Shirley Englehorn	285
	Kathy Whitworth	285
	(Englehorn won play-off, 74-78)	

1971	Kathy Whitworth	278
1972	Kathy Ahern	293
1973	Mary Mills	288
1974	Sandra Haynie	288
1975	Kathy Whitworth	288
1976	Betty Burfeindt	287

International Team Matches

Walker Cup

1922	U.S. 8, Great Britain 4
1923	U.S. 6½, Great Britain 4½
1924	U.S. 9, Great Britain 3
1925	U.S. 6½, Great Britain 4½
1928	U.S. 11, Great Britain 1
1930	U.S. 10, Great Britain 2
1932	U.S. 9½, Great Britain 2½
1934	U.S. 9½, Great Britain 2½
1936	U.S. 10½, Great Britain 1½
1938	Great Britain 7½, U.S. 4½
1947	U.S. 8, Great Britain 4
1949	U.S. 10, Great Britain 2
1951	U.S. 7½, Great Britain 4½
1953	U.S. 9, Great Britain 3
1955	U.S. 10, Great Britain 2
1957	U.S. 8½, Great Britain 3½
1959	U.S. 9, Great Britain 3
1961	U.S. 11, Great Britain 1
1963	U.S. 14, Great Britain 10
1965	U.S. 12, Great Britain 12
1967	U.S. 15, Great Britain 9
1969	U.S. 13, Great Britain 11
1971	Great Britain 13, U.S. 11
1973	U.S. 14, Great Britain 10
1975	U.S. 15½, Great Britain 8½

Curtis Cup

1932	U.S. 5½, British Isles 3½
1934	U.S. 6½, British Isles 2½
1936	U.S. 4½, British Isles 4½
1938	U.S. 5½, British Isles 3½
1948	U.S. 6½, British Isles 2½
1950	U.S. 7½, British Isles ½
1952	British Isles 5, U.S. 4
1954	U.S. 6, British Isles 3
1956	British Isles 5, U.S. 4
1958	British Isles 4½, U.S. 4½
1960	U.S. 6½, British Isles 2½
1962	U.S. 8, British Isles 1
1964	U.S. 10½, British Isles 7½
1966	U.S. 13, British Isles 5
1968	U.S. 10½, British Isles 7½
1970	U.S. 11½, British Isles 6½
1972	U.S. 10, British Isles 8
1974	U.S. 13, British Isles 5
1976	U.S. 11½, British Isles 6½

Ryder Cup

1927	U.S. 9½, Great Britain 2½
1929	Great Britain 7, U.S. 5
1931	U.S. 9, Great Britain 3
1933	Great Britain 6½, U.S. 5½
1935	U.S. 9, Great Britain 3
1937	U.S. 8, Great Britain 4
1947	U.S. 11, Great Britain 1
1949	U.S. 7, Great Britain 5
1951	U.S. 9½, Great Britain 2½
1953	U.S. 6½, Great Britain 5½
1955	U.S. 8, Great Britain 4
1957	Great Britain 7½, U.S. 4½
1959	U.S. 8½, Great Britain 3½
1961	U.S. 14½, Great Britain 9½
1963	U.S. 23, Great Britain 9

1965	U.S. 19½, Great Britain 12½
1967	U.S. 23½, Great Britain 8½
1969	U.S. 16, Great Britain 16
1971	U.S. 18½, Great Britain 13½
1973	U.S. 19, Great Britain 13
1975	U.S. 21, Great Britain 11

World Cup (Team) and International Trophy (Individual)

1953	Argentina
	Antonio Cerda, Argentina
1954	Australia
	Stan Leonard, Canada
1955	United States
	Ed Furgol, U.S.
1956	United States
	Ben Hogan, U.S.
1957	Japan
	Torakichi Nakamura, Japan
1958	Ireland
	Angel Miguel, Spain
1959	Australia
	Stan Leonard, Canada
1960	United States
	Flory Van Donck, Belgium
1961	United States
	Sam Snead, U.S.
1962	United States
	Roberto De Vicenzo, Argentina
1963	United States
	Jack Nicklaus, U.S.
1964	United States
	Jack Nicklaus, U.S.
1965	South Africa
	Gary Player, South Africa
1966	United States
	George Knudson, Canada
1967	United States
	Arnold Palmer, U.S.
1968	Canada
	Al Balding, Canada
1969	United States
	Lee Trevino, U.S.
1970	Australia
	Roberto De Vincenzo, Argentina
1971	United States
	Jack Nicklaus, U.S.
1972	Taiwan
	Hsieh Min-nan, Taiwan
1973	United States
	Johnny Miller, U.S.
1974	South Africa
	Bobby Cole, South Africa
1975	United States
	Johnny Miller, U.S.

Halls of Fame

(Halls of fame for golf are maintained by the Citizens Savings Hall, by the Professional Golfers Association, and by the Ladies' Professional Golfers' Association. In addition there is a privately supported World Golf Hall of Fame, which opened in 1974 at Pinehurst, North Carolina. In the following list, C stands for Citizens Savings Hall, P for PGA, L for LPGA, and W for World.)

Willie Anderson—Won the U.S. Open in 1901, 1903, 1904, and 1905; finished among the top five seven other times. (C, W)

Tommy Armour—Won the 1927 U.S. and Canadian Opens, the 1930 PGA championship, and the 1931 Masters. (C)

Jerry Barber—Won the 1961 PGA championship. (C)

"Long Jim" Barnes—Won the first PGA championship, 1916, and the second, 1919; won the U.S. Open in 1921, the British Open in 1925. (C)

Patty Berg—Won the U.S. Amateur in 1938, the U.S. Women's Open in 1946, the Vare Trophy in 1953, 1955, and 1956; was top money winner among women pros in 1954, 1955, and 1957. (C, L, W)

Julius Boros—Won the U.S. Open 1952 and 1963, PGA championship in 1948; top money winner 1952, 1955; player of the year 1952. (C,P)

Michael J. Brady—Lost play-offs for the U.S. Open in 1911 and 1919. (P)

Billy Burke—Won the 1931 U.S. Open in two 36-hole play-offs with George Von Elm. (C, P)

Jack Burke, Jr.—Won the PGA championship and Masters in 1956; Vardon Trophy, 1952; Golfer of the Year, 1956. (C)

Dorothy Campbell (Mrs. Hurd)—Won the U.S. Amateur 1925, 1928, 1929, 1930, 1935. (C, L, W)

Glenna Collett (Mrs. Vare)—Won the U.S. Amateur 1922, 1925, 1928, 1929, 1930, 1935. (C, L,W)

Harry Cooper—Lost play-off in the 1927 U.S. Open, was runner-up in Open and Masters in 1936. (C, P)

Bobby Cruickshank—Lost play-off in the 1923 U.S. Open, was runner-up in 1932. (P)

Margaret Curtis—Won the U.S. Amateur 1907, 1911, 1912; medalist 1901, 1902, 1905, 1907, 1909, 1912. (C, L)

Jimmy Demaret—The first to win three Masters, 1940, 1947, and 1950; won Vardon Trophy, 1947; top money winner, 1947. (C, P)

Joe Dey—Executive director of the USGA, 1934–69, Dey then became the first commissioner of the PGA's Tournament Player Division, 1969–75. He was also a Founder of the World Golf Council in 1958. (W)

Leo Diegel—Won the PGA championship in 1928 and 1929; runner-up in 1927. (C, P)

Ed Dudley—Won more than 20 tournaments but never a major one; active in PGA during its formative years and later. (P)

Olin Dutra—Won the PGA in 1932, the U.S. Open in 1934; shot a 61 at the age of 60. (C, P)

H. Chandler Egan—Won the U.S. Amateur 1904, 1905, runner-up in 1909; medalist 1904; NCAA champion, fall of 1902. (C)

Charles "Chick" Evans, Jr.—Won the U.S. Amateur and Open in 1916; won the U.S. Amateur in 1920, runner-up in 1912, 1927. (C, P, W)

Johnny Farrell—Won the U.S. Open 1928; runner-up in British Open and PGA in 1929. (C, P)

Doug Ford—Won the 1955 PGA and the 1957 Masters; player of the year in 1955. (C)

Robert A. Gardner—The youngest U.S. amateur champion in 1909, when he was 19; also won in 1915 and was runner-up in 1916 and 1921; runner-up in the British Amateur in 1920. (C)

Victor Ghezzi—Won the 1941 PGA; lost play-off for the 1946 U.S. Open. (C, P)

Ralph Guldahl—Won the U.S. Open in 1937 and 1938, the Masters in 1939. (C, P)

JoAnne Gunderson (Mrs. Carner)—Won the U.S. Amateur in 1957, 1960, 1962, 1966, and 1968, runner-up in 1956, 1964; top money winner in 1974 with nearly $90,000. (C)

Walter Hagen—Won the PGA championship in 1921, 1924, 1925, 1926, and 1927, the British Open in 1922, 1924, 1928, and 1929, the U.S. Open in 1914 and 1919. (C, P, W)

Melvin R. "Chick" Harbert—Won the PGA in 1954, runner-up in 1947 and 1952. (P)

Chandler Harper—Won the PGA in 1950; set record of 259 in the 1954 Texas Open with consecutive 63s on the last three rounds. (P)

E. J. "Dutch" Harrison—Won the Vardon Trophy in 1954; won 29 championships, but no major ones. (P)

Ben Hogan—Won the U.S. Open in 1948, 1950, 1951, and 1953, the Masters in 1951 and 1952, the PGA in 1946 and 1948, and the British Open in 1953, the only time he played in it. Between 1940 and 1960, he finished among the top 10 in every U.S. Open; from 1941 through 1956, he was never lower than seventh in the Masters and finished second four times. (C, P, W)

Beatrix Hoyt—Won the U.S. Amateur in 1896, when she was 16, the youngest winner ever; also won in 1897, 1898, and was medalist in 1896, 1897, 1898, 1899, 1900. (C, L)

Jock Hutchison, Jr.—Won the PGA in 1920, was runner-up in 1916; won the British Open in 1921; runner-up in the U.S. Open in 1916 and 1920. (C, P)

Betty Jameson—Won the U.S. Amateur in 1939 and 1940, the Open in 1947, becoming the first woman to score lower than 300 in a 72-hole tournament. (C, L)

Robert T. Jones, Jr.—Won the Grand Slam—the U.S. and British Opens and U.S. and British Amateurs—in 1930; also won the U.S. Open in 1923, 1926, and 1929, the Brintish Open 1926 and 1927, and the U.S. Amateur in 1924, 1925, 1927, and 1928, for a total of 13 major championships. (C, P, W)

W. Lawson Little—Won the U.S. and British Amateurs both in 1934 and in 1935; won the U.S. Open in 1940; once won 31 consecutive matches. (C, P)

Lloyd Mangrum—Won the U.S. Open in 1946, lost a play-off in 1950; won the Vardon Trophy in 1951 and 1953; top money winner in 1951. (C, P)

John McDermott—Won the U.S. Open in 1911 and 1912; lost a play-off in 1910. (C, P)

Frederick McLeod—Won the U.S. Open in 1908; runner-up in the 1919 PGA. (P)

Cary Middlecoff—Won the U.S. Open in 1949 and 1956, the Masters in 1955; lost a play-off for the Open in 1957, runner-up in the 1959 Masters; won the Vardon Trophy in 1956. (C,P)

Tom Morris, Jr.—Though he died at 25, won four consecutive British Opens, the first in 1868, when he was 18. He also won in 1869, 1870, and 1872. (There was no tournament in 1871.) (W)

Byron Nelson—Won the Masters in 1937, 1942, the U.S. Open in 1939, the PGA in 1940, 1942, and 1945; set a record by winning 18 tournaments and 11 in a row, in 1945; won the Vardon Trophy in 1939 and 1945. (C, P, W)

Jack Nicklaus—Won the U.S. Amateur in 1959 and 1961, the U.S. Open in 1962, 1967, and 1972, the Masters in 1963, 1965, 1966, and 1972, the PGA in 1963, 1971, and 1973, the British Open in 1966 and 1970; top money winner in 1964, 1965, 1967, 1971, 1972, and 1973. (W)

Francis Ouimet—Won the U.S. Open in 1913, as an amateur; won the U.S. Amateur in 1914 and 1931. (C, P, W)

Arnold Palmer—Won the U.S. Open in 1960, the Masters in 1958, 1960, 1962, and 1964, the British Open in 1961 and 1962, the U.S. Amateur in 1954; won the Vardon

Trophy in 1961, 1962, 1964, and 1967; top money winner in 1958, 1960, 1962, 1963; player of the year in 1960 and 1962. (W)

Henry Picard—Won the 1936 Masters and the 1939 PGA. (C, P)

Gary Player—Won the British Open in 1959 and 1968, the U.S. Open in 1965, the Masters in 1961 and 1974, the PGA in 1962 and 1972. (W)

Betsy Rawls—Won the U.S. Women's Open in 1952, 1953, 1957, and 1960, the LPGA championship in 1959 and 1969; won the Vare Trophy in 1959; top money winner in 1952 and 1959; had total winnings of nearly $250,-000. (C, L)

Johnny Revolta—Won the PGA in 1935; top money winner in 1935. (C, P)

Paul Runyan—Won the PGA in 1934 and 1938; won the Vardon Trophy in 1935; top money winner in 1934. (C, P)

Gene Sarazen (Saraceni)—Won the U.S. Open in 1922 and 1932, the PGA in 1922, 1923 and 1933, the Masters in 1935, and the British Open in 1932. (C, P, W)

Denny Shute—Won the British Open in 1933, the PGA in 1936 and 1937. (C, P)

Alex Smith—Won the U.S. Open in 1906 and 1910; runner-up in 1898, 1901, and 1905. (C, P)

Horton Smith—Won the Masters in 1934 and 1936. (C, P)

Macdonald Smith—Alex's brother won many tournaments, but never a major one; 12 times he was within three strokes of the winner in the U.S. or British Open; in 1910 he lost a play-off for the U.S. Open. (C, P)

Sam Snead—Won the PGA in 1942, 1949, and 1951, the Masters in 1949, 1952, and 1954, and the British Open in 1946; won the Vardon Trophy in 1938, 1949, 1950, and 1955; top money winner in 1938, 1949, and 1950. (C, P, W)

Alexa Stirling (Mrs. Fraser)—Won the U.S. Amateur in 1916, 1919, and 1920, runner-up in 1921, 1923, and 1925; medalist in 1919, 1923, and 1925. (C, L)

Frank Stranahan—Won the British Amateur in 1952; runner-up in U.S. Amateur in 1950. (C)

Louise Suggs—Won the U.S. Amateur in 1947, the British Amateur in 1948, the U.S. Women's Open in 1949 and 1952, and the LPGA in 1957; won the Vare Trophy in 1957; top money winner in 1953 and 1960. (C, L)

Jess W. Sweetser—Won the U.S. Amateur in 1922; runner-up in 1923; NCAA Champion in 1920; won the British Amateur in 1926. (C)

John H. Taylor—Won the British Open five times, in 1894, 1895, 1900, 1909 and 1913. He also finished 2nd five times. (W)

Jerome Travers—Won the U.S. Open in 1915, as an amateur; won the U.S. Amateur in 1907, 1908, 1912, and 1913. (C, P)

Walter Travis—Won the U.S. Amateur in 1900, 1901, and 1903, the British Amateur in 1904. (C, P)

Willie Turnesa—Won the U.S. Amateur in 1938 and 1948, the British Amateur in 1947. (C)

Virginia Van Wie—Won the U.S. Amateur in 1932, 1933, 1934; runner-up in 1928, 1930. (C, L)

Harry Vardon—Won the British Open in 1896, 1898, 1899, 1903, 1911, and 1914, the U.S. Open in 1900. (W)

E. Harvie Ward, Jr.—Won the U.S. Amateur in 1955 and 1956, the British Amateur in 1952. (C)

Marvin "Bud" Ward—Won the U.S. Amateur in 1939 and 1941. (C)

Joyce Wethered (Lady Heathcoat-Amory)—Won the British Ladies' Amateur in 1922, 1924, 1925, and 1929. (L, W)

Jack Nicklaus won the Ohio Open at 16 and the U.S. Amateur at 19; he then won the U.S. Open at 22, in his first full year as a professional. By the end of 1975, he had broken Bobby Jones' record by winning 16 major tournaments. *(U.S. Golf Association.)*

Kathy Whitworth—Winner of the Ladies' PGA in 1967, 1971 and 1975, Whitworth has been top money-winner among women eight times, winner of the Vare Trophy seven times, and LPGA player of the year seven times. (L)

Craig Wood—Won the U.S. Open and the Masters in 1941. (C, P)

Lew Worsham—Won the U.S. Open in 1947. (C)

Mickey Wright—Won the U.S. Women's Open in 1958, 1959, 1961, and 1964, the LPGA championship in 1958, 1960, 1961, and 1963; won the Vare Trophy in 1960, 1961, 1962, 1963, and 1964; top money winner in 1961, 1962, 1963, 1964. (L)

Mildred "Babe" Didriksen Zaharias—Won the U.S. Amateur in 1946 and the British Women's Amateur in 1947, the U.S. Women's Open in 1948, 1950, and 1954; won the Vare Trophy in 1954; top money winner in 1948, 1949, 1950, and 1951. (L, W)

Bibliography. Grimsley, Will: *Golf: Its History, People and Events*, Prentice-Hall, Englewood Cliffs, N. J., 1966; McCormack, Mark: *The Wonderful World of Professional Golf*, Atheneum, New York, 1973; Price, Charles: *The World of Golf*, Random House, New York, 1962; Scharff, Robert et al. (eds.): *Golf Magazine's Encyclopedia of Golf*, Harper and Row, New York, 1970; Wind, Herbert Warren (ed.): *The Complete Golfer*, Simon and Schuster, New York, 1954; ———: *Herbert Warren Wind's Golf Book*, Simon and Schuster, New York, 1971.

GRAND PRIX RACING—In the broad sense, automobile road racing; strictly, a small circuit of Formula One auto races that count toward the World Drivers' championship. The name comes from the French *Grand Prix* ("great prize"), the first major road race in Europe.

See also AUTOMOBILE RACING.

GRAND SLAM—Originally the term meant taking all 13 tricks in contract bridge, and it then came into use in baseball to describe a home run with the bases loaded, which scores four runs. As an extension, it is also used to describe other athletic feats associated with four. The grand slam in tennis includes the Australian, British, French, and United States national championships. Golf's grand slam used to consist of the U.S. Open and Amateur and the British Open and Amateur, but the two amateur tournaments have been replaced by the PGA championship and the Masters Tournament.

GYMNASTICS—Originally any kind of physical training designed to promote physical fitness and to train the body for other sports, gymnastics as a competitive sport is less than a century old.

The word comes from the Greek *gymnos*, meaning "nude," because in ancient Greece athletes exercised and competed in the nude. The ancient Greek gymnasium was a public school and an area for training athletes. Greek gymnasia included running tracks, arenas, and baths, as well as indoor rooms for classes and for light exercises, and the term "gymnastics" embraced many of the track and field sports.

Early Greek physicians prescribed gymnastics, and the Greeks realized, more fully than any other people for centuries, that the body's abilities could actually be improved through exercise. The gymnasium was particularly important in Sparta, where the state required periods of prescribed exercises for young men and women.

The Romans, although they built some large gymnasia and had some regard for gymnastics as helpful preparation for soldiers, didn't place a high importance on sports. With the Middle Ages, gymnastics and the gymnasia virtually became extinct.

The Germans revived gymnastics in the late eighteenth century. Gyms were built in Germany in 1774 and 1784, and in 1811 a *Turnplatz*, or school for gymnastics, was opened in Berlin. The Germans generally used the word "gymnasium" to mean a secondary school; the sport was called "turning."

At that point, gymnastics was still basically a kind of physical education and training for other sports, but much of the equipment used for those purposes was similar to the equipment used today in gymnastic competition. During the nineteenth century, gymnastics spread through central Europe, and the International Gymnastics Federation was formed in 1881.

The sport came to this country with immigrants at least as early as 1848. German immigrants especially began to form *Turnverein*—gymnastics clubs—in various cities, and in 1871 the YMCA began offering gymnastic programs. Besides the various kinds of apparatus used in modern gymnastic events, the sport included exercising with light weights, such as Indian clubs and dumbbells.

About 1880, gymnastics competition began. In some

An unidentified performer is shown on the balance beam, used in women's competition. *(Courtesy of Nissen Co.)*

cases, there could be a quantitative measure to judge performances—chinning oneself a given number of times, for example—but in most gymnastic events (and in all the modern events) judging was necessary, as in such other sports as figure skating and diving.

The Amateur Athletic Union in 1897 took over supervision of the sport in the United States, and some established athletic clubs then began to get involved. The sport began on an organized basis in colleges in the 1930s, and in 1938 the National Collegiate Athletic Association conducted its first national championships.

Gymnastics was on the first modern Olympic program in 1896 and, after an on-again, off-again period, became a permanent part of the program in 1924. The AAU added women's competition in 1931. An Olympic program for women's teams began in 1928, but there were no individual Olympic events for women until 1952.

Types of Competition. Men and women both take part in floor exercises and vaulting. Women alone compete on the balance beam and the uneven parallel bars. Men alone compete on the parallel bars, the horizontal bar, flying rings, and side horse. (Men vault on the long horse, women on the side horse.)

Every gymnastics event involves judging. The number of judges varies from 3 to as many as 13. Each judge rates each performance on a scale ranging up to 10 points for perfection. The judges' scores are totaled to determine a competitor's final score.

Every event includes two parts: compulsory exercises, in which a competitor must perform a prescribed routine demonstrating basic skills, and free exercises, in which is performed a routine of the competitor's own choosing. (It should be noted that a specific event, the floor exercise, is also sometimes called "free" exercise.)

Every meet also has an all-around champion, the gym-nast who has compiled the highest point total in all events.

Specific Events. Floor exercises are balletlike routines of tumbling and gymnastic maneuvers, performed to music on a mat (Olympic size is 12 by 12 m). The time limit is 2 min. Contestants are penalized for touching outside the boundary; to get a good score, the gymnast must do some performing very near the boundary, to demonstrate good planning and balance.

The horse was originally used for training cavalrymen to mount a horse quickly. It is a leather-covered cylinder, a rough facsimile of a horse's body, 1,600 to 1,630 mm (about 63 in) long, 1,100 mm (about 43 in) high, and 350 mm (about 15 in) at its widest point.

As a side horse, or pommeled horse, it is fitted with two raised handles, or pommels, and the gymnast works from the side, performing a variety of exercises in which the hands, on the pommels, support the gymnast's weight.

When the pommels are removed, the apparatus is called a long horse, and in competition it is used solely for vaulting. The gymnast vaults over the horse, along its length. A variety of vaults can be performed.

The horizontal bar is a solid steel bar with a diameter of $1\frac{1}{8}$ in, suspended 96 to 99 in above the mat. The gymnast performs a variety of swings while hanging from the bar.

The parallel bars are two round wooden bars at least 11 ft, 6 in long and 16 to 22 in apart, supported about $5\frac{1}{2}$ ft above the mat. They are used for such exercises as swinging, vaulting, and handstands.

There are two types of ring apparatus, flying rings and still rings. The flying rings have gradually taken over the competitive field, and still-ring events are now rarely held. The wooden rings, with an outside diameter of about 9 in, are suspended about 94 in above the mat and about 18 in apart.

The balance beam is a wooden beam just 4 in wide, a little more than 16 ft long, and about 4 ft above the mat. Women gymnasts perform many moves on the balance beam, including cartwheels, flips, jumps, and splits.

Uneven parallel bars, used in women's competition, are two wooden bars, one $90\frac{1}{2}$ in, the other 59 in above the floor. They are 94.5 in long and about 20 in apart.

For a time, tumbling and rebound tumbling (trampolining) events were often included in gymnastics competition. But they have become, in combination, a separate sporting event.

See also TRAMPOLINE AND TUMBLING.

National Champions: Men

All-Around

1897	Earl Linderman	1913	Franz Kanis
1898	O. Steffen	1914	Franz Kanis
1899	O. Steffen	1915	Franz Kanis
1900	O. Steffen	1916	Peter Hol
1901	John F. Bissinger	1917	B. Jorgensen
1902	E. C. Brendlin	1918	Joseph Oszy
1903	John F. Bissinger	1919	Peter Hol
1904	Anton Heida	1920	Joseph Oszy
1905-06	No competition	1921	Curtis Rottman
1907	Fred Steffens	1922	Frank Kriz
1908	Fred Steffens	1923	Curtis Rottman
1909	Frank Jirasek	1924	Frank Kriz
1910	Frank Jirasek	1925	Alfred Jochim
1911	Paul Krimmel	1926	Alfred Jochim
1912	Paul Krimmel	1927	Alfred Jochim

1928	Alfred Jochim	1953	Robert Stout
1929	Alfred Jochim	1954	Charles Simms
1930	Alfred Jochim	1955	Karl Schwenzfeier
1931	Frank Haubold		John Miles
1932	Frank Haubold	1956	John Beckner
1933	Alfred Jochim	1957	John Beckner
1934	Frank Cumiskey	1958	John Beckner
1935	Frederick H. Meyer	1959	John Beckner
1936	Frank Cumiskey	1960	Fred Orlofsky
1937	George Wheeler	1961	Nobuyuki Aihara
1938	George Wheeler	1962	Donald Tonry
1939	George Wheeler	1963	Makoto Sakamoto
1940	George Wheeler	1964	Makoto Sakamoto
1941	George Wheeler	1965	Makoto Sakamoto
1942	Arthur E. Pitt	1966	Makoto Sakamoto
1943	Arthur E. Pitt	1967	Yoshi Hayasaki
1944	Arthur E. Pitt	1968	Makoto Sakamoto
1945	Frank Cumiskey	1969	Mauno Nissinen
1946	Frank Cumiskey	1970	Yoshuaki Juke
1947	Frank Cumiskey	1971	Yoshi Takei
1948	Edward Scrobe	1972	Makoto Sakamoto
1949	William Roetzheim	1973	Yoshi Takei
1950	William Roetzheim	1974	Yoshi Hayasaki
1951	William Roetzheim	1975	Mike Carter
1952	Robert Stout	1976	Koji Saito

National AAU Champions: Women

All-Around

1931	Roberta C. Ranck	1939	Margaret Weissmann
1932	No competition	1940	No competition
1933	Consetta Caruccio	1941	Mrs. Pearl Perkins Nightingale
1934	Consetta Caruccio	1942	No competition
1935	Thera Steppich	1943	Mrs. Pearl Perkins Nightingale
1936	Jennie Caputo	1944	Helm McKee
1937	Pearl Perkins	1945	Clara M. Schroth
1938	Helm McKee	1946	Clara M. Schroth

Parallel bars used by men are the same height, unlike those used in women's competition. *(Courtesy of Nissen Co.)*

The horizontal bar is a piece of apparatus used only in men's competition. *(Courtesy of Nissen Co.)*

1947	Helen Schifano	1962	Dale McClements
1948	Helen Schifano	1963	Muriel Davis Grossfeld
1949	Clara M. Schroth	1964	Marie Walther
1950	Clara M. Schroth	1965	Doris Fuchs Brause
1951	Clara M. Schroth	1966	Linda Metheny
1952	Mrs. Clara Schroth Lomady	1967	Carolyn Hacker
1953	Ruth Grulkowski	1968	Linda Metheny
1954	Ruth Grulkowski	1969	Joyce Tanac
1955	Ernestine Russell	1970	Linda Metheny
1956	Sandra Ruddick	1971	Linda Metheny
1957	Muriel Davis	1972	Linda Metheny
1958	Ernestine Russell	1973	Joan Moore Rice
1959	Ernestine Russell	1974	Joan Moore Rice
1960	Gail Sontgerath	1975	Roxanne Pierce
1961	Kazuki Kadowaki	1976	Roxanne Pierce

Citizens Savings Gymnastics Hall of Fame

Raymond Bass—Gymnast (Olympic Gold Medal, 1932)
Alfred Bergmann—Coach.
Dallas Bixler—Gymnast (Olympic Gold Medal, 1932).
Marshall Brown—Coach.
Frank Cumiskey—Gymnast (21 national titles; Olympic Gold Medal, 1932).
William Denton—Gymnast.
Vincent D'Autorio—Gymnast and contributor.
Hubert Dunn—Coach and contributor.
E. A. Eklund—Contributor.
Paul E. Fina—Gymnast (AAU title) and contributor.
Harold Frey—Gymnast, coach, and contributor.
Joseph Giallombardo—Gymnast (7 NCAA and 2 AAU titles) and coach.
Charles W. Graves—Coach.

Lester Griffin—Coach.

George Gulack—Gymnast (2 AAU titles, Olympic Gold Medal, 1932).

Frank Haubold—Gymnast (5 AAU titles, Olympic Gold Medal, 1932).

Gustav Heineman—Coach.

Daniel Hoffer—Coach.

Eric Hughes—Coach and contributor.

Alfred Jochim—Gymnast (35 AAU titles, Olympic Gold Medal, 1932).

Bruno Johnke—Coach.

Leslie L. Judd—Coach.

Gus Kern—Contributor.

Rene J. Kern—Coach.

Paul Krempel—Gymnast (9 AAU titles).

Frank Kriz—Gymnast (6 AAU titles, Olympic Gold Medal, 1924).

Walter J. Lienert—Coach and contributor.

Abe Lober—Contributor.

Newt Loken—Coach.

John Mais—Gymnast.

Tom Maloney—Coach.

Louis H. Mang—Coach.

William Matthei—Contributor.

Bill Meade—Coach and contributor.

Frederick Meyer—Gymnast (4 AAU titles, Olympic Gold Medal, 1932).

Roy E. Moore—Coach.

Harry G. Nelson—Coach.

Meta Neumann (Elste)—Gymnast (2 AAU titles).

George P. Nissen—Contributor (inventor of modern trampoline).

A. Carl Patterson—Contributor and coach.

Chester M. Phillips—Gymnast (2 AAU titles) and coach.

Adolph Picker—Contributor.

Ralph A. Piper—Coach.

Arthur Pitt—Gymnast (14 AAU titles).

Charles Pond—Coach.

Emil Preiss—Coach.

Ben Price—Coach.

Hartley Price—Coach.

Tony Rossi—Contributor.

Curtis Rottman—Gymnast (13 AAU titles).

James Rozanas—Coach.

Helen Schifano (Sjursen)—Gymnast (8 AAU titles) and contributor.

Henry Schiget—Coach.

A young gymnast is shown working out on the pommel of a side horse. (*Hank Seaman,* New Bedford Standard-Times.)

Henry Schroeder—Contributor.

Clara Schroth (Lomady)—Gymnast (39 AAU titles).

Henry Smidl—Coach.

Ted Steeves—Contributor.

George Szypula—Gymnast (4 AAU titles), coach, and contributor.

Paul Uram—Coach and contributor.

John Van Aalten—Coach.

Charles Vavra—Coach.

Herbert Vogel—Coach and contributor.

Erwin Volze—Coach.

Erna Wactel—Coach and contributor.

Lyle Welser—Coach.

Gene Wettstone—Coach.

George Wheeler—Gymnast (25 AAU titles).

Herman Witzig—Gymnast (1 AAU title).

Rowland Wolfe—Gymnast (1 AAU title; Olympic Gold Medal in 1932).

Max Younger—Coach.

Fred Zitta—Coach.

Leopold Zwarg—Coach.

Bibliography *AAU Official Handbook 1973–1974,* Amateur Athletic Union, Indianapolis, 1973; Price, Hartley D. et al.: *Gymnastics and Tumbling,* 3rd ed., Arco, New York, 1973.

H

HALLS OF FAME—The hall-of-fame idea in American sports began in 1939, baseball's "centennial" year, when the Baseball Hall of Fame was established at Coopers-town, New York. A couple other sports halls of fame were established in the next 10 years, but they existed only on paper. After World War II, the Helms Athletic Foundation, which had been organized in 1936, began recognizing athletes, coaches, and contributors in a number of sports. The foundation, now known as Citizens Savings, has 22 halls of fame for sports ranging from auto racing to wrestling.

Since about 1960 there has been a proliferation of sports halls of fame. One of the most interesting is the Professional Football Hall of Fame in Canton, Ohio, opened in 1963 with financial support from the National Football League. Another major display is the Basketball Hall of Fame in Springfield, Massachusetts. A College Football Hall of Fame, begun as a project in 1949 by the National Football Foundation, is still something of a paper organization: Long-dreamed-of plans for building on the Rutgers campus, site of the first "football" game, fell through and the foundation moved to headquarters in New York City, where it maintains a library and a collection of memorabilia, without the hall-of-fame displays that had been envisioned.

There are many other sports halls of fame in various categories. Some of them are little more than lists of names. Others, like the Automobile Racing Hall of Fame at the Indianapolis Motor Speedway and the Racing Hall of Fame at Saratoga Springs, New York, benefit from financial subsidies from interested organizations. Still others are more or less private concerns that exist largely on income derived from visitors. Many states also maintain their own sports halls of fame, sometimes as part of a larger hall of fame honoring people from many other fields.

Major sports halls of fame that have, or plan to build, their own quarters are listed below.

Auto Racing. Indianapolis Motor Speedway Museum; National Association of Stock Car Racing Hall of Fame, Darlington, South Carolina, Speedway.

Baseball. National Baseball Hall of Fame, Cooperstown, New York.

Basketball. Naismith Memorial Basketball Hall of Fame, Springfield, Massachusetts.

Bowling. National Bowling Hall of Fame and Museum, Greendale, Wisconsin.

Canadian Football. Canadian Football Hall of Fame, Hamilton, Ontario.

Figure Skating. U.S. Figure Skating Association Museum, Boston.

Fishing. World Sportfishing Hall of Fame, Fort Lauderdale, Florida.

Football. National Football Foundation Hall of Fame, 17 East 80th Street, New York City.

Harness Racing. Hall of Fame of the Trotter, Goshen, New York.

Hockey. Hockey Hall of Fame, Toronto; United States Hockey Hall of Fame, Eveleth, Minnesota.

Horse Racing. National Museum of Racing, Saratoga Springs, New York.

Lacrosse. Lacrosse Hall of Fame Foundation, Baltimore.

Skiing. National Ski Hall of Fame, Ishpeming, Michigan.

Soaring. National Soaring Museum, Elmira, New York.

Softball. National Softball Hall of Fame, Oklahoma City.

Swimming. International Swimming Hall of Fame, Fort Lauderdale, Florida.

Tennis. National Lawn Tennis Hall of Fame and Museum, Newport, Rhode Island.

Track and Field. U.S. Track and Field Hall of Fame, Angola, Indiana; National Track and Field Hall of Fame, Charleston, West Virginia.

For membership of specific halls of fame, *see* relevant sports; *see also* CITIZENS SAVINGS ATHLETIC FOUNDATION.

HAMMER THROW—A field event in which an athlete throws a stylized hammer, actually a weight on the end of a chain, for distance.

See also TRACK AND FIELD.

HANDBALL—The game that we know as handball almost certainly evolved directly from a sport invented in Ireland about A.D. 1000. The Irish played the game on a hard clay floor, with one stone wall, and they used a hard, leather-covered ball. Their game originally allowed kicking the ball, as well as striking it with the hand. There is an English version known as "fives" (after the five fingers of the hand), but that sport apparently evolved separately, from court tennis. The fives court still retains some of the features of the medieval tennis court. During the eighteenth century, handball was a very popular sport in Ireland. The rules and system of scoring have not changed much in the last 200 years, though they weren't formally codified until the 1880s.

Fives was apparently played in the United States as early as 1763, but handball as we know it was not introduced until Phil Casey emigrated from Ireland in 1872. Casey and others tried playing handball against brick walls, but the uneven surfaces were unsatisfactory. About

Paul Haber, considered the best handball player of all time, is shown in action during three-wall competition at Columbus, Ohio. (Courtesy of U.S. Handball Association.)

1883, Casey built a handball court in New York City. The sport quickly became popular; Casey built other courts and his students helped to spread it to other cities. Casey formally became United States champion in 1887, when he beat Bernard McQuade, another Irish immigrant. Then he challenged John Lawler, the Irish champion, for a $1,000 side bet. There were to be 10 games in Cork, Ireland, and 11 in New York; the first to win 11 games would claim the world title—and the money. Lawler won 6 of the 10 games in Ireland, but Casey won 7 in a row in New York. He beat all challengers until his retirement in 1900.

Meanwhile the Amateur Athletic Union adopted the sport, conducting its first tournament in 1897. Informal play began on bathing beaches, where a tennis ball was used, and players bounced it off just one wall. By 1914 one-wall courts were available on many beaches in the New York City area, and in gymnasiums. The YMCA also

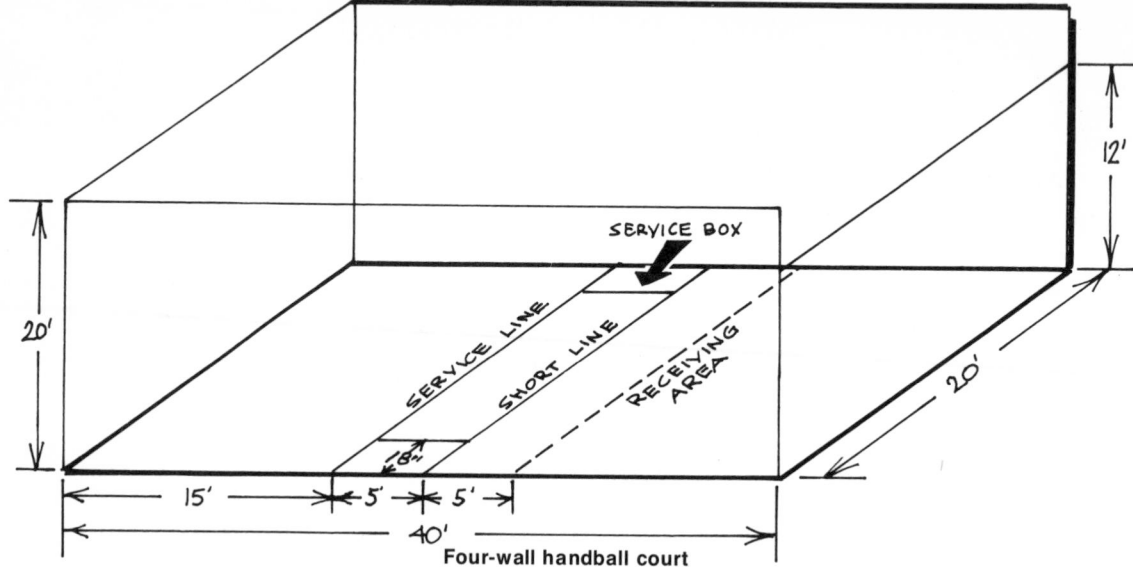

Four-wall handball court

took interest in handball, and courts were included in many of its buildings constructed in the early part of the century.

The one-wall version of the sport was responsible for the soft ball now used almost exclusively in the United States. The modern rubber ball, however, is considerably harder than a tennis ball, though not as hard as the handball still used in the Irish version.

The AAU conducted its first national four-wall championship tournament in 1919, and its first one-wall championship in 1924. Between 1924 and 1938, competition was conducted in both softball and hardball versions, but the hardball competition was discontinued after 1938.

In 1951 the Amateur Handball Union was formed as a players' organization. The group accepted the jurisdiction of the AAU in 1952 and the name was changed to the U.S. Handball Association.

The YMCA conducted its own national tournament from 1925 through 1958, but now is cosponsor of the AAU tournament. The USHA still holds its own tournaments. In 1952 the USHA and AAU tournaments were merged, and in 1958 all three groups combined for one major national tournament. In 1961, however, the USHA split with the AAU in order to allow professionals in other sports to compete as amateurs in handball.

There was surprisingly little standardization of courts until the USHA began campaigning for it—one of the basic reasons for the group's organization.

Rules of Play

Four-Wall Game. The four-wall court is 40 ft long and 20 ft wide, and there is a front wall 20 ft high. The back wall is only 12 ft high. A "short line" crosses the court 20 ft from the front wall; 5 ft in front of this is the service line. An 18-in strip on either side of the court, between these two lines, is called the service box. There is a vertical line on each side wall marking the receiving zone, 5 ft behind the short line.

The ball is made of black rubber; it weighs 2.3 oz and has a 1⅞-in diameter. Players usually wear gloves.

The server drops the ball to the floor, between the short and service lines, and as it bounces up, strikes it so that it hits the front wall and lands on the floor behind the short line. (The ball can strike a side wall, before hitting the floor.) The receiver must stand in the receiving zone until the server strikes the ball. Only the serving side can score a point. After a legal serve, the sides take turns hitting the ball; it can hit any wall, and the ceiling, in any order, provided that it hits the front wall before it hits the floor. Play continues until one side fails to make a proper return. Game is 21 points.

In four-wall doubles, the server's partner must stand in one of the service boxes; the partner's back must be against the side wall, until the serve has struck the floor.

One-Wall Game. The one-wall court is 34 ft long and 20 ft wide, and the one wall is 16 ft high. There is, of course, no ceiling. The short line is 16 ft from the front wall; the service line is a simple, 6-in mark 9 ft behind the short line. The rules are identical to those of the four-wall game except that there is only one wall to bounce the ball from.

Three-Wall Game. There are two versions of three-wall handball. The most common is played on a court without a back wall, and the rules are identical to those of the four-wall sport, except that a ball which carries over the back line on the fly is out, and results in either loss of point or loss of service. The other, played primarily in Greater New York, uses a court similar to that for jai alai, with a front wall, a back wall, and only one side wall.

Hinders. In all forms of the sport, a player has an obligation to let the opponent play the ball. If the player gets in the opponent's way, or if the ball strikes the player, it is a "hinder," if the obstruction or the being struck is judged accidental: The ball is dead and the point must be replayed. If it is an avoidable hinder, the penalty is loss of point or loss of service.

National Handball Club. In 1973–1974, a professional handball tour was organized, with the assistance of the USHA. Called the National Handball Club, Inc., the tour featured eight outstanding players, "the super eight," and nine substitute players who filled in during tournaments when any of the top eight weren't available. Fred Lewis was the tour's leading money winner in its first year of operation.

USHA Champions

Four-Wall Singles

1951	Walter Plekan	1964	Jim Jacobs
1952	Victor Hershkowitz	1965	Jim Jacobs
1953	Bob Brady	1966	Paul Haber
1954	Victor Hershkowitz	1967	Paul Haber
1955	Jimmy Jacobs	1968	Simon Singer
1956	Jimmy Jacobs	1969	Paul Haber
1957	Jimmy Jacobs	1970	Paul Haber
1958	John Sloan	1971	Paul Haber
1959	John Sloan	1972	Fred Lewis
1960	Jimmy Jacobs	1973	Terry Muck
1961	John Sloan	1974	Fred Lewis
1962	Oscar Obert	1975	Jay Bilyeu
1963	Oscar Obert	1976	Vern Roberts, Jr.

AAU Champions

One-Wall Singles

1959	Oscar Obert	1968	Steve Sandler
1960	Oscar Obert	1969	Steve Sandler
1961	Oscar Obert	1970	Steve Sandler
1962	Ken Davidoff	1971	Steve Sandler
1963	Oscar Obert	1972	Wally Ulbrich
1964	Oscar Obert	1973	Steve Sandler
1965	Oscar Obert	1974	Al Torres
1966	Steve Sandler	1975	Ruby Obert
1967	Steve Sandler	1976	Ruben Gonzolez

Citizens Savings Hall of Fame

Players

Sam Atcheson—YMCA four-wall singles champion 1921–1933, 1935–1937, doubles 1930–1932, 1935–1936; AAU four-wall singles 1933–1934, doubles 1945.

Al Banuet—AAU four-wall singles champion 1929, 1931, doubles 1929–1931.

Robert Brady—USHA four-wall singles 1953, three-wall doubles 1958; AAU four-wall singles 1957, doubles 1951.

Frank Coyle—USHA four-wall doubles 1951–1952; three-wall doubles 1952; AAU four-wall singles 1944, doubles 1938–1939, 1941, 1946, 1950, 1952.

Victor Hershkowitz—USHA four-wall singles 1952, 1954, doubles 1961; three-wall singles 1950–1958, doubles 1956; AAU four-wall singles 1949, 1952; one-wall singles 1947–1948, 1950, 1952–1953, 1957, doubles 1942, 1948, 1956; YMCA four-wall singles 1953, 1957.

Jim Jacobs—USHA four-wall singles 1955–1957, 1960, 1964–1965, doubles 1960, 1962–1963, 1965, 1967–1968; three-wall singles 1959–1961; AAU four-wall singles 1956, 1960.

Maynard Laswell—AAU four-wall singles 1924, 1926, doubles 1922, 1932.

Gus Lewis—AAU four-wall singles 1947–1948; YMCA four-wall singles 1946, 1954.

Oscar Obert—USHA four-wall singles 1962–1963; three-wall singles 1962–1963, doubles 1957, 1959–1960, 1963, 1965, 1967; AAU four-wall singles 1961, 1963–1964, doubles 1961–1964, 1968; three-wall singles 1958–1959, 1964, doubles 1955, 1957–1961, 1963–1964.

Joseph Platak—AAU four-wall singles 1935–1941, 1943, 1945, doubles 1937, 1944.

Kenneth Schneider—USHA four-wall doubles 1954–1956; AAU four-wall singles 1950; YMCA four-wall singles 1952.

Angelo Trulio—AAU four-wall singles 1946.

Shown during one-wall doubles semifinal in 1973 AAU tournament are, from left, Artie Reyer, Joel Wisotsky, Lou Russo, and Wally Ulbrich. Reyer and Ulbrich won. (*George Granofsky, AAU National Handball Committee.*)

Contributors

George Brotemarkle	*George E. Lee*
Robert Davidson	*Charles J. O'Connell*
Frank Garbutt	*Albert Schaufelberger*
Hyman Goldstein	*Joseph Shane*
Robert Kendler	*Les Shumate*

Bibliography. M and, C. L.: *Handball Fundamentals,* Merrill, Columbus, O., 1968; Nelson, Richard C. and Harlan S. Berger: *Handball,* Prentice-Hall, Englewood Cliffs, N.J., 1971.

HANDICAP—The term is believed to come from "hand in cap," a type of lottery in which numbers are put into a hat and one of them is drawn out to determine the winner. In a handicap, everyone theoretically has an equal chance to win. More generally, a handicap is a penalty imposed on a superior athlete to bring that contestant down to the level of an inferior one.

In formal competition, the concept began in horse racing. Horses are handicapped by being assigned weights to carry; the better the horse, based on past performance, the heavier the weight. A perfectly handicapped race would end with every horse crossing the finish line at the same time.

Among other sports, the handicap is most commonly used in amateur golf and bowling. The golfer is rated by a complicated method meant to determine an average score. A golfer with a handicap of 7, for example, is expected to average 79 strokes on a par-72 course, so the handicap should make that contestant a par golfer when subtracted from the contestant's actual score. In bowling a handicap is usually determined on a match-by-match basis, by subtracting the inferior team's average score from the superior team's average. This difference is then added onto the inferior team's actual score at the end of a game.

"Handicapping" has also come to mean rating horses in an attempt to pick a winner, or, in general, rating teams or performers in other sports, usually for gambling purposes.

HANG GLIDING—Sometimes known as "sky surfing," hang gliding is probably the newest of competitive sports. It began in the late 1960s as a participation sport, although its roots lay in the original form of sky surfing, in which water-skiers used kites to get into the air. Hang gliding was actually born, however, when it was discovered that the "Rogallo wing" can be used instead of a kite, and that it isn't necessary to get up to high speeds to use one.

The Rogallo wing was developed as a kind of parachute to get rockets and their landing capsules to earth safely. Then it was adapted as a kite; finally it went through another transformation for human use. As a hang glider, the wing consists of a central keel of aluminum tubing connected in front to two aluminum tubes which are the leading edges of a fabric wing, usually of Dacron. This wing is actually a nonrigid kite; its shape, and therefore the flight of the glider, are controlled by six flying wires. Beneath the wing frame a plastic seat is suspended on lines. The average size of the glider is about 18 ft of wing span—measured across the leading edge—and it weighs about 35 lb. Use of the Rogallo wing also spurred hang gliding by means of more conventional, rigid-wing craft, essentially large kites with suspended seats.

The sport became very popular in southern California; the Southern California Hang Gliding Association, formed in 1971, quickly gained 4,000 members, and in 1973 it became the U.S. Hang Gliding Association and conducted the first national championships.

Competitors are judged not on sheer distance but on such subjective points as overall form, proper execution of turns, accuracy and poise in landing, and soaring ability.

HARLEM GLOBETROTTERS—In 1926, Abe Saperstein, a five-footer who had played basketball in high school but hadn't even been allowed to try out for the University of Illinois squad, organized his own basketball team—a team of blacks who met all challengers at the Savoy Ballroom in Chicago. A year later the ballroom became a skating rink, and the team had to go on the road.

In a burst of genius, Saperstein named his athletes the "Harlem Globetrotters," to give the illusion that they had been around. The name was prophetic: After struggling through the Depression, the Globetrotters became world-famous, and they have played before millions of spectators in more than 90 countries.

Originally a serious team, the Globetrotters were so good that few of their games were contests, so they went to a showboating, comedy style of play to keep crowds interested. It worked. By the late 1940s the Globetrotters were actually several teams, because one team couldn't possibly fulfill all the bookings that were offered. Some early stars, notably Goose Tatum and Marques Haynes, left to form their own teams, and professional basketball began to take most of the best black players, but the Globetrotters continue to entertain crowds all over the United States and still, occasionally, in other countries.

HARNESS RACING—In a sense, chariot racing may be called an ancestor of modern harness racing. But only in a sense, because what makes harness racing unique is not the vehicle, but the gait of the horses. The Standardbred horses used in harness racing can run for distances of 1 mi or more, at top speed, in what is basically an artificial gait, either a trot or a pace, while most horses, asked for speed, will naturally break into a gallop.

Pacing was originally desired as a smooth gait for a saddle horse. In pacing, both feet on one side move forward at the same time. In order to maintain that gait, the horse must keep its feet very close to the ground, resulting in a minimum amount of shock to a rider. Trotting, on the other hand, was originally a gait for harness horses. In trotting, the right front and left rear feet move forward together, followed by the left front and right rear; this diagonal action keeps a carriage from swaying from side to side.

Most horses can be taught to trot or pace, but Standardbreds adopt one gait or the other automatically, virtually from birth. At what point in the past the gaits may have been bred into them is not known. But the Elgin Marbles, sculpted about 430 B.C., show soldiers mounted on trotters and pacers, as well as on galloping horses; the pace was the gait used by horses of the Roman legions; and the Great Seal of England shows an armored knight mounted on a pacing horse.

Colonial New England was important in the development of trotting and pacing horses. By 1650 the Narragansett Pacer, developed in Rhode Island, was known throughout the world as a fast, graceful animal, and the horses were traded all over the British Empire. Most of them could trot or pace; others were pure trotters.

As an organized event, harness racing evidently dates to at least 1747—in that year, Maryland passed a law prohibiting pacing races. In 1748, New Jersey passed a law limiting trotting and pacing races to certain days of the year. As horse-drawn vehicles became popular, in the late seventeenth century and early eighteenth, trotters became more important, and horsemen searched for stallions whose foals would be natural trotters. The English horse Messenger was imported in 1788. He was not a trotter, nor were any of his sons; but his sons' get were natural trotters, and virtually all of today's harness horses can trace their lineage to Messenger.

The first recorded public race took place in 1818, when a gray gelding named Boston Blue won a $1,000 bet for his owner by trotting 1 mi in less than 3 min, under saddle. In 1825 the New York Trotting Club was organized, and a track was built on Long Island. The first real race of record (one that matched competitors) was held in 1829 at the Hunting Park Track in Philadelphia. Two of Messenger's grandsons, Top Gallant and Whalebone, raced under saddle in 4-mi heats; the first horse to win three heats was to be declared the champion. Top Gallant won three heats; a fourth was a dead heat.

The same track was the site of the first trotting sweepstakes, in 1831, with an eight-horse field. Dread was the overall winner, taking two 3-mi heats; Top Gallant won one and Collector the other. However, the horses in this race were again under saddle. The origin of the sulky, the two-wheeled vehicle that carries the driver in harness racing, cannot be pinpointed, and it is not always clear from accounts of early races whether the horses were under saddle or pulling sulkies. There is even some doubt about the origin of "sulky." One explanation is that the vehicle is meant to carry just one passenger, and he is presumed to be sulky if he wants to ride alone. But it should be noted that one meaning of the word during the nineteenth century was "lazy."

In any event, the original high-wheeled sulky appeared

in the late 1830s or early 1840s. It wasn't universally accepted; the driver was so high above the ground that a fall could be very serious, and trotters were still often raced under saddle. They made better time pulling sulkies, however, and that fact led to the growth of sulky racing until it became virtually universal shortly after the Civil War.

During the 1830s and 1840s, races were usually run in 3- or 4-mi heats. Another popular type of race was the one-horse, one-hour event. In 1833 the owner of Paul Pry bet that his horse could do 18 mi in an hour, and the horse accomplished it in 59 min and 54 sec, under saddle. Another early record was set by Dutchman, a gelding, who did 3 mi in 7:32½ in 1839—a record that stood until 1872.

As the sport developed, the trotter was highly prized, but the pacer, considered basically a saddle horse, declined in popularity after the sulky came into general use. In the Northeast, trotters were raced, while pacers were generally shipped to the South, where there was more use for saddle horses.

In 1849 a mare named Flora Temple began racing, and a trotter named Hambletonian was foaled. Flora Temple, in one of her first races, established a new mile record, 2:27, and 10 years later, when she was 14, she lowered it to 2:19¾. That figure remained the record for eight years. Hambletonian, on the other hand, was not much of a racer. But he sired great racers, and others of his sons also turned out to be great sires. In 24 years at stud, Hambletonian sired 1,335 horses and earned more than $300,000 for his owner in stud fees. Although he never won a race himself, one of harness racing's triple-crown events is named for him. One of Hambletonian's sons, Dexter, set a new mile record of 2:18½, under saddle, in 1867 and a little later set a new mile record of 2:17¼ under harness.

The Standardbred. In 1867 the first volume of the *American Stud Book,* in which Thoroughbred horses are registered and their pedigrees recorded, was published by John H. Wallace. With support from men interested in harness horses and their breeding, Wallace in 1871 began publication of the *Trotting Register.* The first standard adopted was performance. Trotters to be listed would be those that could trot a mile in 2:30 or faster, or that had produced progeny that could meet that standard. Some horsemen objected, contending that few horses could trot at that speed. However, the rule went into effect, and the registered horses were called Standardbreds. Today the registration is based largely on blood lines, but the standard is the ability to run a mile in 2:20 or better for two-year-olds, 2:15 or better for other ages.

Return of the Pacer. Pacers, as noted, had been largely exiled to the South. There were many of them in Tennessee, where E. F. "Pop" Geers was one of the first men to try them at sulky racing. He discovered that a pacer was a good match for a trotter. He brought a stable of pacers North to demonstrate their ability, and they soon became as popular as the trotters.

In 1891 the "bicycle" sulky was introduced. It was both safer and faster than the old high-wheeler. Its construction was patterned after that of the bicycle: tubular steel for strength and light weight, 42-in wheels that were essentially bicycle wheels with pneumatic tires, and ball bearings to reduce friction between wheel and axle. The seat was now quite close to the ground.

The new vehicle quickly led to some new records. In 1891, Sunol had set the record at 2:08¼. Early in 1892 Nancy Hanks, pulling a "bike," turned in a time of 2:07¼ and in September of that year she set another record at 2:04. Then the pacers took over. Star Pointer, a pacer, was the first harness horse to break two minutes, pacing a mile in 1:59¼ in 1897. By 1905 the great Dan Patch, also a pacer, had lowered the mark to 1:55¼. That was the record until 1938.

Governing Organizations. Harness racing grew rapidly, along with state and county fairs, during the 1860s, but suffered from a lack of standardized rules and racing conditions. In 1870 a group of horsemen met at Providence, Rhode Island, to form the National Association for the Promotion of the American Trotting Turf, renamed the National Trotting Association in 1878. Most of its members were in the East, although its jurisdiction also extended to some areas in the South and on the Pacific Coast.

In 1887 the American Trotting Association was formed in the Midwest, and in the 1920s the United Trotting Association was organized by track operators in Ohio. Although it was better to have three governing bodies than none at all, conditions were rather chaotic. A driver or owner could be suspended by one group, but could continue to race at events sanctioned by another group, and the existence of three sets of rules was not in the best interests of the sport.

Under the leadership of E. Roland Harriman, representatives of the three groups met in Columbus, Ohio, in 1938 to form the United States Trotting Association, which has overall supervision of the sport at all tracks in the United States and in the Maritime Provinces of Canada. The USTA sanctions race meetings, issues licenses to track officials and to owners and drivers, sets standards for registration of horses and investigation of their pedigrees, establishes rules for the conduct of the sport and punishes violations, and in general works to advance public interest in the sport.

A pacer can often be distinguished by "hobbles" linking legs on the same side, to keep him in proper stride. Driver Francis Mahoney is leaving the paddock and moving toward the track. (*Courtesy of John Adams, Foxboro Raceway.*)

This pacer is getting a brisk workout under the guidance of Mark Lancaster. *(Courtesy of John Adams, Foxboro Raceway.)*

The *Trotting Register,* taken over by the National Association of Trotting Horse Breeders in 1879, later became the property of a special group, the American Trotting Register Association. That group folded in 1923, however, and for two years the all-important business of registration was neglected. The Trotting Horse Club of America, organized in 1925, bought out the ATRA and turned over the registration duties to the USTA when that group was formed. The club still exists as an association of horsemen that sponsors a number of annual racing events.

Rapid Growth. Harness racing's modern, prosperous era began in 1938, since the USTA brought order out of chaos. Two other important developments were the growth of night harness racing and the invention of the starting gate.

Night racing was tried as early as 1900 in Boston, but it was a flop, mainly because the lights just weren't good enough. Another unsuccessful attempt took place in 1928 in Toledo. In 1940, however, Roosevelt Raceway opened in Westbury, Long Island, New York, with a 27-night meeting that drew 75,000 spectators. In 1950, a second major New York track, Yonkers Raceway, opened and also offered night racing. The night races, with parimutuel betting, draw many spectators who would not otherwise be harness-racing fans. However, the sport is still also a mainstay at more than 400 county-fair tracks, most of which have afternoon racing without betting.

The modern starting gate was first used at Roosevelt Raceway. Until 1940, a race began with a running start and, if the horses weren't properly lined up when they reached the starting line, they would be called back for a new start. It sometimes took as many as 15 attempts to get a race under way. There was no hope of drawing any but the most rabid fans with such a system. In 1937, Steve Phillips, an Ohio starter, built a starting gate with two steel arms mounted on a pickup truck. Roosevelt officials subsidized development of the invention and used it first in 1946.

Equipment. The driver must wear a protective helmet of approved design, with a chin strap. Distinguishing colors

must also be worn. If a whip is carried by the driver, it must not exceed 4 ft, 8 in, and excessive use of the whip is forbidden.

Trotters usually wear level shoes in front and swedge shoes—which are creased for greater traction—in back. The shoes weigh about 8 oz each. Trotters also often wear toe weights of 2 to 4 oz each on each hoof; they tend to make the horse's stride longer. Pacers usually wear flat or half-round shoes in front, and a combination shoe, half round inside and half swedge outside, in back. Their shoes weigh about 5 oz each. Some pacers wear hobbles (or hopples), leather strips that link legs on the same side to help the horse maintain its gait.

Rules of the Race. Post positions are usually chosen by lot for a race or a first heat; in subsequent heats, the horses take the post positions corresponding to their finish in the first heat (the winning horse in the number-one pole position, and so on). Horses enter the starting gate about ¼ mi from the starting line, and they are led to the starting line at a constantly increasing speed. Once the starter gives the word "go," the race is under way; he can sound a recall only before he has given the "go" signal.

Because the drivers ride in rather frail vehicles that, in effect, make the horse a good deal wider than a horse under saddle, harness drivers are expected to exercise much more caution than Thoroughbred jockeys. Drivers are forbidden to make any move that would force another horse to shorten stride; to swerve in or out; to pull up quickly; to hook wheels with another sulky; or to impede the progress of another horse in any way. Once a sulky has reached the home stretch, it must remain in the lane chosen by the driver. It is also forbidden to help another horse either by letting it pass easily or by slowing down to leave an opening for it.

If a horse breaks its gait, it must be taken to the outside as soon as possible, without interfering with the horses behind, and must remain outside until it has resumed its proper gait.

If any of these rules are broken, the horse may be placed in the standings behind any horse it interfered with. If the violation prevented another horse from finishing, the offending horse may be disqualified and the driver fined or suspended.

Major Races. Harness racing has two "triple crowns," one for pacers and one for trotters. The three races in the triple crown of trotting are the Hambletonian, in DuQuoin, Illinois, in August; the Yonkers Futurity, at Yonkers (New York) Raceway in September; and the Kentucky Futurity, at Lexington in October. The triple crown for pacing comprises the William H. Cane Futurity at Yonkers in August; the Little Brown Jug, at Delaware, Ohio, in September; and the Messenger Stake, at Roosevelt (New York) Raceway in November. All the triple-crown races are for three-year olds.

Because of the need to run many races on a program, most racing at parimutuel tracks consists of just one heat per race. Such a race is called a "dash." Most of the classic races, however, consist of three heats. In most two-out-of-three races, a horse must win two heats to win the race. If no horse succeeds in that, the first-place finishers usually run a fourth heat to determine the winner.

In the results listed below, the fastest time doesn't always belong to the horse that won the race, since another horse may have won a heat in a faster time. When that occurred, the horse running the fastest heat is named in a footnote. In both the trotting and pacing categories, the triple-crown races are listed.

Major Trots

Yonkers Futurity

(1¹⁄₁₆-mi dash before 1963; now 1 mi)

1955	Scott Frost	Joe O'Brien, driver	2:12
1956	Add Hanover	John F. Simpson, Sr.	2:12⅘
1957	Hoot Song	Ralph N. Baldwin	2:16⅕
1958	Spunky Hanover	Howard R. Camper	2:13⅗
1959	John A. Hanover	Stanley F. Dancer	2:11
1960	Duke of Decatur	Delvin Miller	2:13⅗
1961	Duke Rodney	Eddie T. Wheeler	2:10⅗
1962	A. C.'s Viking	Sanders Russell	2:10⅘
1963	Speedy Scot	Ralph N. Baldwin	2:03⅗
1964	Ayres	John F. Simpson	2:01⅗
1965	Noble Victory	Stanley F. Dancer	2:02
1966	Polaris	George Sholty	2:06
1967	Pomp	Harry Pownall, Sr.	2:04⅘
1968	Nevele Pride	Stanley F. Dancer	2:03⅗
1969	Lindy's Pride	Howard Beissinger	2:03
1970	Victory Star	Vernon Dancer	2:03⅘
1971	Quick Pride	Stanley F. Dancer	2:02
1972	Super Bowl	Stanley F. Dancer	2:02
1973	Tamerlane	Charlie Clark	2:04⅘
1974	Spitfire Hanover	Delvin Miller	2:05⅖
1975	Surefire Hanover	Stanley F. Dancer	2:03
1976	Steve Lobell	William R. Haughton	2:01⅘

Hambletonian

(1-mi heats)

1926	Guy McKinney	Nat Ray, driver	2:04¾
1927	Iosola's Worth	Marvin Childs	2:03¾
1928	Spencer	W. H. Lessee	2:02½
1929	Walter Dear	Walter R. Cox	2:02¾
1930	Hanover's Bertha	Thomas S. Berry	2:03
1931	Calumet Butler	R. D. McMahon	2:03¼
1932	The Marchioness	William F. Caton	2:01¼ (a)
1933	Mary Reynolds	Ben F. White	2:03¾
1934	Lord Jim	H. M. Parshall	2:02¾
1935	Greyhound	Seth F. Palin	2:02¼
1936	Rosalind	Ben F. White	2:01¾
1937	Shirley Hanover	Henry Thomas	2:01½
1938	McLin Hanover	Henry Thomas	2:02¼
1939	Peter Astra	H. M. Parshall	2:04¼
1940	Spencer Scott	Fred Egan	2:02
1941	Bill Gallon	Lee Smith	2:05
1942	The Ambassador	Ben F. White	2:04
1943	Volo Song	Ben F. White	2:02½
1944	Yankee Maid	Henry Thomas	2:04
1945	Titan Hanover	Harry Pownall, Sr.	2:04
1946	Chestertown	Thomas S. Berry	2:02½
1947	Hoot Mon	Seth F. Palin	2:00
1948	Demon Hanover	Harrison R. Hoyt	2:02
1949	Miss Tilly	Fred Egan	2:01⅖
1950	Lusty Song	Delvin Miller	2:02
1951	Mainliner	Guy Crippen	2:02⅗
1952	Sharp Note	Bion Shively	2:02⅗
1953	Helicopter	Harry M. Harvey	2:01⅗ (b)
1954	Newport Dream	Adelbert Cameron	2:02⅘
1955	Scott Frost	Joe O'Brien	2:00⅗
1956	The Intruder	Ned F. Bower	2:01⅖
1957	Hickory Smoke	John F. Simpson, Sr.	2:00⅕
1958	Emily's Pride	Flave T. Nipe	1:59⅘
1959	Diller Hanover	Frank Ervin	2:01⅕
1960	Blaze Hanover	Joe O'Brien	1:59⅗ (c)
1961	Harlan Dean	James W. Arthur	1:58⅖
1962	A. C.'s Viking	Sanders Russell	1:59⅗
1963	Speedy Scot	Ralph N. Baldwin	1:57⅗ (d)
1964	Ayres	John F. Simpson, Jr.	1:56⅘
1965	Egyptian Candor	Adelbert Cameron	2:03⅗ (e)
1966	Kerry Way	Frank Ervin	1:58⅘
1967	Speedy Streak	Adelbert Cameron	2:00
1968	Nevele Pride	Stanley F. Dancer	1:59⅖
1969	Lindy's Pride	Howard Beissinger	1:57⅗
1970	Timothy T.	John F. Simpson, Jr.	1:58⅖ (f)
1971	Speedy Crown	Howard Beissinger	1:57⅖
1972	Super Bowl	Stanley F. Dancer	1:56⅖*
1973	Flirth	Ralph Baldwin	1:57⅖
1974	Christopher T.	William R. Haughton	1:58⅗
1975	Bonefish	Stanley F. Dancer	1:59(g)
1976	Steve Lobell	William R. Haughton	1:56⅖*

Harness racing, unlike thoroughbred racing, uses a mobile starting gate so that horses get into their proper strides gradually before the start. *(Courtesy of John Adams, Foxboro Raceway.)*

*Record for race. a—by Hollywood Dennis. b—by Morse Hanover. c—by Quick Song and Hoot Frost. d—by Florlis. e—by Armbro Flight. f—by Formal Notice. g—by Yankee Bambino.

Kentucky Futurity

1893	Oro Wilkes	J. A. Goldsmith, driver	2:14½
1894	Beuzetta	Guss Macey	2:14½
1895	Oakland Baron	W. W. Milam	2:16¼
1896	Rose Croix	M. E. McHenry	2:14
1897	Thorn	Orrin A. Hickok	2:13¼
1898	Peter the Great	P. V. Johnson	2:12½
1899	Boralma	Guss Macey	2:11½
1900	Fereno	Ed Benyon	2:10¾
1901	Peter Sterling	J. B. Chandler	2:11½
1902	Nella Jay	F. D. McKey	2:14¼
1903	Sadie Mac	A. McDonald	2:13¾
1904	Grace Bond	W. J. Andrews	2:19¼
1905	Miss Adbell	A. McDonald	2:09¾
1906	Siliko	M. E. McHenry, W. H. McCarthy	2:11¼
1907	General Watts	M. Bowerman	2:11
1908	The Harvester	E. F. Geers	2:08¾
1909	Baroness Virginia	T. W. Murphy	2:07¼
1910	Grace	Mc. McDevitt	2:08
1911	Peter Thompson	J. L. Serrill	2:07½
1912	Manrico B.	W. G. Durfee	2:07¼
1913	Etawah	E. F. Geers	2:05¾

1914	Peter Volo	T. W. Murphy	2:03½
1915	Mary Putney	R. D. McMahon	2:05½
1916	Volga	Ben F. White	2:04½
1917	The Real Lady	T. W. Murphy	2:03½
1918	Nella Dillon	J. L. Serrill	2:05¼
1919	Periscope	J. L. Dodge	2:04½
1920	Arion Guy	Harry Stokes	2:04¾
1921	Rose Scott	T. W. Murphy	2:03½
1922	Lee Worthy	Ben F. White	2:03¾
1923	Ethelinda	Walter R. Cox	2:03½
1924	Mr. McElwyn	Ben F. White	2:02
1925	Aileen Guy	Ben F. White	2:03¾
1926	Guy McKinney	Nat Ray	2:06¾
1927	Iosola's Worthy	Marvin Childs	2:05¼
1928	Spencer	W. H. Leese	2:05
1929	Walter Dear	Walter R. Cox	2:02¾
1930	Hanover's Bertha	Thomas S. Berry	2:00
1931	Protector	William F. Caton	1:59¼
1932	The Marchioness	William F. Caton	2:02
1933	Meda	Ben F. White	2:03¼
1934	Princess Peg	Seth F. Palin	2:00¾
1935	Lawrence Hanover	Henry Thomas	2:00¾
1936	Rosalind	Ben F. White	2:03
1937	Twilight Song	Ben F. White	2:01¼
1938	McLin Hanover	Henry Thomas	2:00¾
1939	Peter Astra	H. M. Parshall	2:02½
1940	Spencer Scott	Fred Egan	2:02
1941	Bill Gallon	Lee Smith	2:02¼
1942–45	No race		
1946	Victory Song	Seth F. Palin	2:00½
1947	Hoot Mon	Seth F. Palin	2:04⅕
1948	Egan Hanover	Ralph N. Baldwin	2:03⅖
1949	Bangaway	Ralph N. Baldwin	2:05⅖
1950	Star's Pride	Harry Pownall, Sr.	2:02
1951	Ford Hanover	John F. Simpson, Sr.	2:01⅖
1952	Sharp Note	Bion Shively	2:00
1953	Kimberly Kid	Thomas S. Berry	2:00⅗
1954	Harlan	Delvin Miller	2:01
1955	Scott Frost	Joe O'Brien	2:00⅗
1956	Nimble Colby	Ralph N. Baldwin	2:02
1957	Cassin Hanover	Fred Egan	2:02⅕
1958	Emily's Pride	Flave T. Nipe	1:59⅕ (a)
1959	Diller Hanover	Ralph N. Baldwin	2:02
1960	Elaine Rodney	Clint T. Hodgins	1:58⅗
1961	Duke Rodney	Eddie T. Wheeler	1:58⅕ (b)
1962	Safe Mission	Joe O'Brien	1:59⅕
1963	Speedy Scot	Ralph N. Baldwin	1:57⅕
1964	Ayres	John F. Simpson, Sr.	1:58⅕
1965	Armbro Flight	Joe O'Brien	1:59⅗
1966	Governor Armbro	Joe O'Brien	2:00⅖
1967	Speed Model	Arthur L. Hult	1:59⅗ (c)
1968	Nevele Pride	Stanley F. Dancer	1:57*
1969	Lindy's Pride	Howard Beissinger	1:59
1970	Timothy T.	John F. Simpson, Jr.	1:59⅘
1971	Savoir	James Arthur	1:58⅕
1972	Super Bowl	Stanley F. Dancer	1:59
1973	Arnie Almahurst	Joe O'Brien	1:59⅕ (d)
1974	Waymaker	John F Simpson, Jr.	1:59⅘
1975	Noble Rogue	J. Arthur, B. Herman	2:02³ ₅
1976	Quick Pay	Peter Haughton	1:59

*Record for race. a—by Senator Frost. b—by Caleb. c—by Rocket Speed. d—by Knightly Way.

Major Paces

William H. Cane Futurity

(1¹⁄₁₆-mi dash until 1963; now 1-mi)

1955	Quick Chief	William R. Haughton, driver	2:11⅕
1956	Noble Adios	John F. Simpson	2:09⅖
1957	Torpid	John F. Simpson	2:09⅕
1958	Raider Frost	Hugh A. Bell	2:08⅕
1959	Adios Butler	Clint Hodgins	2:09
1960	Countess Adios	Delvin Miller	2:08
1961	Cold Front	Clint Hodgins	2:08⅗
1962	Ranger Knight	Clint Hodgins	2:13⅕
1963	Meadow Skipper	Earle Avery	1:58⅘
1964	Race Time	George Sholty	2:01⅘
1965	Bret Hanover	Frank Ervin	2:01
1966	Romeo Hanover	William Myer	1:59⅘
1967	Meadow Paige	William R. Haughton	2:03
1968	Rum Customer	William R. Haughton	1:59⅘
1969	Kat Byrd	Eldon Harner	2:02⅖
1970	Most Happy Fella	Stanley F. Dancer	1:58⅗
1971	Albatross	Stanley F. Dancer	2:00
1972	Hilarious Way	John Simpson, Jr.	2:02⅖
1973	Smog	Vernon Dancer	1:58⅘
1974	Boyden Hanover	Billy Herman	
1975	Nero	Joe O'Brien	1:58⅘
1976	Keystone Ore	Stanley F. Dancer	1:57⅕ *

*Record for race.

Messenger Stake

(1-mi heats)

1956	Belle Acton	William R. Haughton, driver	2:01⅖
1957	Meadow Lands	Delvin Miller	2:04⅘ (a)
1958	O'Brien Hanover	James W. Jordan	2:01⅘
1959	Adios Butler	Clint Hodgins	2:00⅕
1960	Countess Adios	Delvin Miller	2:02⅕
1961	Adios Don	Howard R. Camper	2:02⅘
1962	Thor Hanover	John F. Simpson, Sr.	2:01⅕
1963	Overtrick	John Patterson, Sr.	2:00⅘
1964	Race Time	Ralph N. Baldwin	2:01⅖
1965	Bret Hanover	Frank Ervin	2:02
1966	Romeo Hanover	George Sholty	2:01
1967	Romulus Hanover	William R. Haughton	1:59⅕*
1968	Rum Customer	William R. Haughton	2:01⅘
1969	Bye Bye Sam	Stanley F. Dancer	2:02⅗
1970	Most Happy Fella	Stanley F. Dancer	2:02⅗
1971	Albatross	Stanley F. Dancer	2:00⅖
1972	Silent Majority	William R. Haughton	2:01⅘
1973	Valiant Bret	Lucien Fontaine	2:020⅗
1974	Armbro Omaha	William R. Haughton	1:59⅗
1975	Bret's Champ	William R. Haughton	1:59¼*
1976	Windshield Wiper	William R. Houghton	2:00

*Record for race. a—by Adios Express.

Little Brown Jug

(1-mi heats)

1946	Ensign Hanover	Wayne Smart, driver	2:02¾ (a)
1947	Forbes Chief	Adelbert Cameron	2:05
1948	Knight Dream	Franklin Safford	2:07⅕
1949	Good Time	Frank Ervin	2:03⅖
1950	Dudley Hanover	Delvin Miller	2:02⅗
1951	Tar Heel	Adelbert Cameron	2:00
1952	Meadow Rice	Wayne Smart	2:01⅗
1953	Keystoner	Frank Ervin	2:02⅗ (b)
1954	Adios Harry	Morris MacDonald	2:02⅖ (c)
1955	Quick Chief	William R. Haughton	2:00 (d)
1956	Noble Adios	John F. Simpson, Sr.	2:00⅘
1957	Torpid	John F. Simpson, Sr.	2:00⅘
1958	Shadow Wave	Joe O'Brien	2:01
1959	Adios Butler	Clint Hodgins	1:59⅖
1960	Bullet Hanover	John F. Simpson, Sr.	1:58⅗ (e)
1961	Henry T. Adios	Stanley F. Dancer	1:58⅘
1962	Lehigh Hanover	Stanley F. Dancer	1:58⅘
1963	Overtrick	John Patterson, Sr.	1:57⅕
1964	Vicar Hanover	William R. Haughton	2:00⅘ (f)
1965	Bret Hanover	Frank Ervin	1:57
1966	Romeo Hanover	George Sholty	1:59⅗
1967	Best of All	James K. Hackett	1:59 (g)
1968	Rum Customer	William R. Haughton	1:59⅗

1969	Laverne Hanover	William R. Haughton	2:00⅖
1970	Most Happy Fella	Stanley F. Dancer	1:57⅕
1971	Nansemond	Herve Filion	1:57⅖
1972	Strike Out	Keith Waples	1:56⅗*
1973	Melvin's Woe	Joe O'Brien	1:57⅗
1974	Armbro Omaha	William R. Haughton	1:57
1975	Seatrain	Ben Webster	1:59⅘
1976	Keystone Ore	Stanley F. Dancer	1:56⅘ (h)

*Record for race. a—by Royal Chief. b—by Newport Chief. c—by Phantom Lady. d—by Dottie's Pick. e—by Bullet Hanover and Muncy Hanover. f—by Combat Time. g—by Nardin's Byrd. h—by Armbro Ranger.

Harness Horse of the Year

1947	Victory Song
1948	Rodney
1949	Good Time
1950	Proximity
1951	Pronto Don
1952	Good Time
1953	Hi-Lo's Forbes
1954	Stenographer
1955	Scott Frost
1956	Scott Frost
1957	Torpid
1958	Emily's Pride
1959	Bye Bye Byrd
1960	Adios Butler
1961	Adios Butler
1962	Su Mac Lad
1963	Speedy Scot
1964	Bret Hanover
1965	Bret Hanover
1966	Bret Hanover
1967	Nevele Pride
1968	Nevele Pride
1969	Nevele Pride
1970	Fresh Yankee
1971	Albatross
1972	Albatross
1973	Sir Dalrae
1974	Delmonica Hanover
1975	Savoir
1976	Keystone Ore

Leading Drivers

In Money Won

1948	Ralph N. Baldwin	$ 153,222
1949	Clint Hodgins	184,108
1950	Delvin Miller	306,813
1951	John F. Simpson, Sr.	333,136
1952	William R. Haughton	311,728
1953	William R. Haughton	374,527
1954	William R. Haughton	415,777
1955	William R. Haughton	599,445
1956	William R. Haughton	572,945
1957	William R. Haughton	586,950
1958	William R. Haughton	816,659
1959	William R. Haughton	711,435
1960	Delvin Miller	567,282
1961	Stanley F. Dancer	654,723
1962	Stanley F. Dancer	760,343
1963	William R. Haughton	790,086
1964	Stanley F. Dancer	1,051,538
1965	William R. Haughton	889,943
1966	Stanley F. Dancer	1,218,403
1967	William R. Haughton	1,305,773
1968	William R. Haughton	1,654,172
1969	Del Insko	1,635,463
1970	Herve Filion	1,647,837
1971	Herve Filion	1,915,945
1972	Herve Filion	2,473,265
1973	Herve Filion	2,233,302
1974	Herve Filion	3,459,438
1975	Carmine Abbatiello	2,118,871
1976	Herve Filion	2,240,000

In Heats Won

1948	Larry Burright	129
1949	Clint Hodgins	128
1950	John F. Simpson, Sr.	111
1951	John F. Simpson, Sr.	118
1952	Levi Harner	129
1953	William R. Haughton	116
1954	William R. Haughton	153
1955	William R. Haughton	168
1956	William R. Haughton	167
1957	William R. Haughton	156
1958	William R. Haughton	176
1959	William Gilmour	165
1960	Del Insko	156
1961	Bob Farrington	201
1962	Bob Farrington	203
1963	Donald Busse	201
1964	Bob Farrington	312
1965	Bob Farrington	310
1966	Bob Farrington	283
1967	Bob Farrington	277
1968	Herve Filion	407
1969	Herve Filion	394
1970	Herve Filion	486
1971	Herve Filion	543
1972	Herve Filion	605
1973	Herve Filion	445
1974	Herve Filion	634
1975	Daryl Busse	300
1976	Herve Filion	445

Hall of Fame of the Trotter

The Hall of Fame of the Trotter was established in 1961 in Goshen, New York, former home of the Hambletonian.

W. J. Andrew
Charles Backman
W. W. Bair
E. J. Baker
Ralph N. Baldwin
Howard Beissinger
Tom Berry
C. K. G. Billings
I. O. Blake
Octave Blake
Robert Bonner
Adelbert Cameron
Sol Camp
William H. Cane
William Caton
Walter Cox
A. B. Coxe
Jack Curry
Stanley F. Dancer
H. K. Devereux
John L. Dickerson
William Dickerson
Budd Doble
John L. Dodge
James Dunnigan, Sr.
Dr. Ogden Edwards, Jr.
Fred Egan
Frank Ervin
Herve Filion
Harry Fleming
Vic Fleming
Stoughton Fletcher
J. Malcolm Forbes
Thomas Gahagan
William Gahagan
Edward F. Geers
Elbridge T. Gerry
Irvin Gleasson
John H. Goldsmith
C. J. Hamlin
Lamon V. Harkness
E. Roland Harriman
E. H. Harriman
William R. Haughton
John Hervey
Orrin Hickok
Clint Hodgins
Frank C. Jones
Henry Knight
George Morton Levy
David Look
W. H. McCarthy
David McClarey
Mary McCune
Michael McDevitt
Lon McDonald
Andrew McDowell
Myron McHenry
Richard McMahon
Leo McNamara
Guss Macey
John E. Madden

Charles Marvin	Millard Sanders
Walter J. Michael	Lawrence B. Sheppard
Delvin Miller	Bion Shively
Thomas W. Murphy	John Simpson, Sr.
Joseph C. O'Brien	T. Wayne Smart
Septimus Palin	John Splan
H. M. Parshall	George Starr
C. W. Phellis	Charles Tanner
Steven G. Phillips	Henry Thomas
Harry E. Pownall	Edward Tipton
W. N. Reynolds	Fred Van Lennep
Sanders Russell	John Wallas
William Rysdyk	Benjamin White
Monroe Salisbury	C. W. Williams
Joseph Serrill	Hiram Woodruff

Bibliography. Pines, Phillip A.: *Complete Book of Harness Racing,* Grosset and Dunlap, New York, 1967; Wrensch, Frank Albert: *Harness Horse Racing in the United States,* Van Nostrand, New York, 1951.

HEISMAN TROPHY—An award donated by the Downtown Athletic Club of New York and given to the best player in college football each year, selected by vote of sportswriters and broadcasters. Established in 1935, the trophy is named for John W. Heisman, long-time football coach at Georgia Tech and later athletic director of the Downtown AC.

See also FOOTBALL.

HELMS ATHLETIC FOUNDATION—*See* CITIZENS SAVINGS ATHLETIC FOUNDATION; WORLD TROPHY.

HICKOK BELT—Formally the S. Rae Hickok Professional Athlete of the Year Award, the belt was conceived in 1949 by Alan and Ray Hickok of the Hickok Belt Company and given in memory of their father. The first award was made in 1950. The belt is studded with jewels and is valued at $15,000. The "professional athlete of the year" is chosen by vote of sportswriters and sportscasters throughout the nation.

Winners

1950	Phil Rizzuto, baseball
1951	Allie Reynolds, baseball
1952	Rocky Marciano, boxing
1953	Ben Hogan, golf
1954	Willie Mays, baseball
1955	Otto Graham, football
1956	Mickey Mantle, baseball
1957	Carmen Basilio, boxing
1958	Bob Turley, baseball
1959	Ingemar Johansson, boxing
1960	Arnold Palmer, golf
1961	Roger Maris, baseball
1962	Maury Wills, baseball
1963	Sandy Koufax, baseball
1964	Jim Brown, football
1965	Sandy Koufax, baseball
1966	Frank Robinson, baseball
1967	Carl Yastrzemski, baseball
1968	Joe Namath, football
1969	Tom Seaver, baseball
1970	Brooks Robinson, baseball
1971	Lee Trevino, golf
1972	Steve Carlton, baseball
1973	O. J. Simpson, football
1974	Muhammad Ali, boxing
1975	Pete Rose, baseball
1976	Ken Stabler, football

HOCKEY—Some sort of ice hockey was played by the Royal Canadian Rifles, an army unit, at Kingston, Ontario, in 1855, according to research done by the Canadian Amateur Hockey Association. (As a result of that research, the association's hall of fame is now located in Kingston.) Ice hockey in some form is probably much older than that. It is logical to assume that it derived from field hockey, but it is possible that it developed in some way from *kolf,* that ancient Dutch sport which is also a likely ancestor of golf. *Kolf* was played on ice with crooked sticks and a ball, the object being to hit a stake with the ball.

Little is known about hockey's history before 1855, however—or, for that matter, between 1855 and 1875, when McGill University students became enthusiastic about the sport. The McGill students adapted some of the rules from Rugby. At first they used a hard rubber ball, but one of the students—unfortunately, his name isn't known—made a major contribution to the sport by slicing pieces off the top and bottom of a ball to produce a flat-surfaced disk. McGill students also added the net—previously the object had been simply to knock the disk, or puck, across a goal line—and began to experiment with player limits. The sport quickly spread beyond the university into Montreal, the rest of Quebec Province, and then into Ontario. By about 1890 there were also teams on Canada's west coast.

The first league was established in Kingston in 1885, and in 1893 the Stanley Cup was presented for the first time to the Canadian champion.

Hockey in the United States. Apparently hockey was being played at St. Paul's School in Concord, New Hampshire, as early as 1882. In 1885 a 17-year-old student at the school, Malcolm K. Gordon, wrote the first set of United States hockey rules. This may indicate that the sport had been imported only as a general idea without many specifics. Evidently it didn't spread far beyond St. Paul's, because most histories say that the sport first arrived in this country in 1893, at two colleges. In that year a Canadian student organized a team at Johns Hopkins University and invited a team from Quebec to play a game in Baltimore. At about the same time, two Yale tennis players, Malcolm G. Chace and Arthur E. Foote, who had discovered the sport while playing in a tennis tournament in Canada, introduced it at Yale.

The Amateur Hockey League was organized in New York in 1896, and in January, 1897 the Baltimore Hockey League appeared. Within a short time ice hockey had become a popular sport in New England and elsewhere in the East, as well as in areas of the United States near the Canadian border. The first United States professional team was organized in Houghton, Michigan, in 1903. That club, the Portage Lakers, won 24 of 26 games in its first season.

By 1915 there were two United States teams in the Pacific Coast League of Canada, a professional league. One of them, the Seattle Metropolitans, won the league title in 1917 and went on to become the first United States team to win the Stanley Cup. In 1924 Boston became the first United States city to be represented in the sport's major league, the National Hockey League. However, the league has always been dominated by Canadian players.

Amateur hockey in the United States reached a peak between 1910 and 1930, then began to lag somewhat—although northern Minnesota and areas of upstate New

York and New England have always been hockey hotbeds. The establishment of indoor skating rinks throughout the country, however, is bringing a resurgence in the sport among youngsters. The Amateur Hockey Association was formed in 1937 and conducts national tournaments in several age divisions, but there has been no national champion named since 1953.

The Stanley Cup. In 1893, Frederick Arthur, Lord Stanley of Preston, was about to retire as governor-general of Canada. His "going-away gift" to hockey was a trophy that he bought for $48.67. He presented it to the Montreal Amateur Athletic Association team, which had won the Amateur Hockey Association championship, with directions that it was to be a challenge trophy.

From 1894 through 1909, two trustees were in charge of the cup, and the team that held it was expected to defend it against all challenges. The trustees actually sorted out the challenges, however, to decide which teams were actually qualified, and they had to arrange play-off sites and formats. In 1910 the National Hockey Association, a professional group, took charge of the cup after convincing the trustees that professional hockey had become so strong that there were no major amateur teams left.

From 1910 through 1917, the NHA and the Pacific Coast Hockey Association champions played an annual match for the trophy. When Portland entered the Pacific Coast circuit in 1914, the trustees ruled that the cup was symbolic of world professional supremacy, allowing a United States team to challenge.

The NHA became the National Hockey League in 1917–1918, and from then through 1926, the NHL and Pacific Coast Hockey League played annually for the championship. Since 1926–1927 the cup has gone automatically to the NHL's postseason play-off series.

Professional Hockey

The first professional hockey league was formed in the United States. There was a strong four-team league in Michigan's Upper Peninsula in 1902–1903, and the following season a number of Canadian stars were lured across the border to play in that league. John L. "Doc" Gibson, captain of the Portage Lakers, spearheaded formation of the International Hockey League, which included Pittsburgh, three Upper Michigan teams, including the Portage Lakers, and two Canadian teams, Sault Ste. Marie and Ontario. The league operated through 1907. The main reason for its dissolution was that many of the league's players returned to Canada when the Eastern Canada Amateur Hockey Association ruled in 1907 that professionals could play in the league, as long as each team made public a list of the players who were being paid.

In the fall of 1909, Ambrose O'Brien, owner of the Renfrew, Ontario, Millionaires, applied to join the Eastern Canada league, but was turned down. He decided to form his own league; he financed three other teams, including the Montreal Canadiens, persuaded the Montreal Wanderers to leave the Eastern Canada league, and formed the National Hockey Association, which began play in January of 1910. The Ottawa Senators and Montreal Shamrocks quickly decided to join the NHA, and the Eastern Canada league folded.

By then, so many of the best Canadian players had become professionals that the Stanley Cup was taken over by the NHA. The association was disbanded in 1917 and

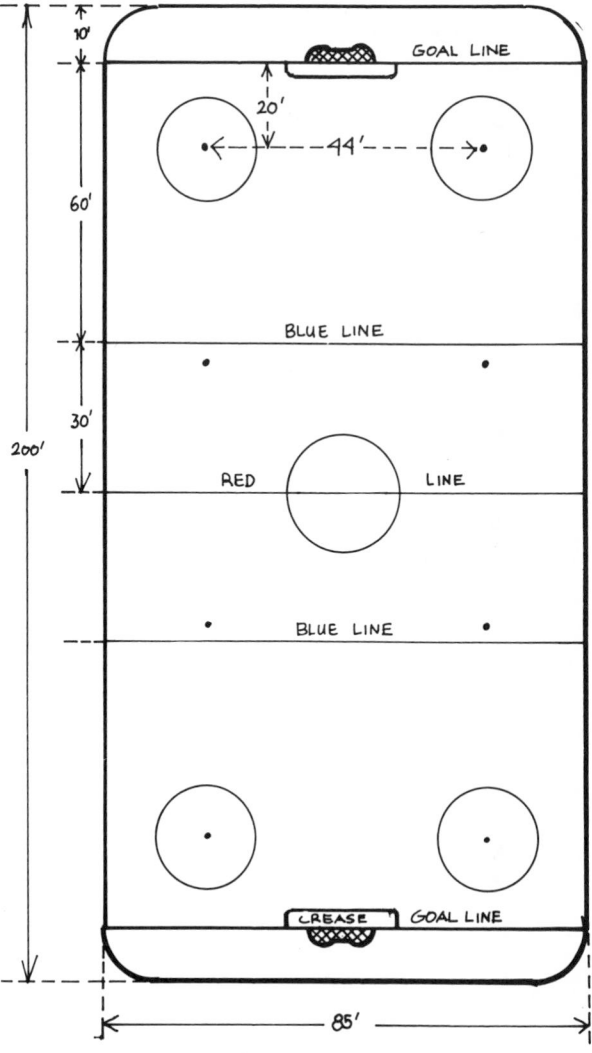

Hockey rink

replaced by the National Hockey League. The original members of the NHL were the Canadiens and Wanderers, the Toronto Arenas, Quebec, and Ottawa, but Quebec didn't operate its franchise until 1919. The first season began on December 19, 1917, and consisted of a 22-game schedule. The following season, the Wanderers had to drop out when their arena burned down, leaving just three teams.

Professionalism brought to hockey, as it has to other sports, a certain experimental spirit. "Tampering" with the sport, as some would put it, began almost as soon as the AHA was organized: In 1910, the game was changed from two 30-min periods to three 20-min periods; in 1911 the NHA cut teams from seven to six players (other leagues didn't follow suit until later); in 1918 the NHL added the blue lines, dividing the rink into three areas, and permitted forward passing in the center zone. Previously the only legal way to move the puck forward had been by carrying it on the stick.

Hobey Baker was a legendary hockey player at Princeton and with the St. Nicholas Arena team. In 1914, his first year with St. Nick's, he scored 8 goals in his first two games, and he assisted on all 5 goals in a 5–1 win over the Canadian champions from Ontario. A World War I pilot, he was killed in a plane crash shortly after that war ended. *(U.S. Hockey Hall of Fame.)*

During the next dozen years, the league experimented almost constantly with the passing rules, first allowing goaltenders only to pass the puck forward in the defending zone, then legalizing the forward pass in the defending and center zones, and then the forward pass into the attacking zone, if the player receiving the pass was in the center zone when the pass was made. In 1929–1930, forward passing was allowed within any of the three zones; finally, in 1930–1931, forward passing across blue lines was also permitted. The final major step toward modern professional hockey came in 1943–1944, when the red line was added at center ice.

During those years, the makeup of the league also changed frequently. Quebec finally operated its franchise in 1919–1920, but dropped out the following season, and Hamilton joined. In 1924 the Boston Bruins and the Montreal Maroons joined the league. The Hamilton franchise became the New York Americans in 1925, and Pittsburgh also joined, giving the United States three entries. Expansion from 7 to 10 teams came in 1926 with the addition of the New York Rangers, Chicago Black Hawks, and Detroit Cougars, and the league was split into American and Canadian Divisions. This was the first season in which the league play-off champion automatically became the

Stanley Cup winner. By 1938 the league was down to seven teams again; in 1941 the New York Americans became the Brooklyn Americans and in 1942 they dropped out of the league entirely. This left six teams: Boston Bruins, Chicago Black Hawks, Detroit Red Wings (formerly the Cougars), Montreal Canadiens, New York Rangers, and Toronto Maple Leafs, and that was the way it remained until expansion came in 1967.

"Pre-Modern" Teams and Stars. Most of the outstanding teams of the AHA era no longer exist; among them were the Montreal Wanderers, who had twice won the Stanley Cup during the amateur era. The Wanderers won the first Stanley Cup involving a play-off between the AHA and Pacific Coast champions. The Quebec Bulldogs were the only AHA team to win the Stanley Cup twice consecutively; the Vancouver Millionaires and the Seattle Metropolitans were the only Pacific Coast teams to win the cup.

In the early years of the NHL, the dominant team was the Ottawa Senators, who won the Stanley Cup four times in the course of eight seasons. Hockey's answer to the New York Yankees, the Montreal Canadiens, won their first Stanley Cup in 1916. They won their first NHL Stanley Cup in 1924. The Canadiens in their early years were largely a French-speaking team; among the stars of their first two cup champions was Georges Vezina, the legendary goaltender who played for them from 1911 until he collapsed in a 1926 game, and died a short time later of tuberculosis. Other outstanding early Canadiens were Howie Morenz, Newsy Lalonde, and Joe Malone. In an 18-game season in 1917–1918, Malone scored 44 goals. The Canadiens won back-to-back cups in 1930 and 1931, led by Morenz, who centered a small, fast line that included Aurel Joliat and Billy Boucher.

The NHL play-off system, which began in 1927, made it difficult for any team to establish a dynasty through the 1930s. And the league had fairly good balance during those years. The Rangers won in 1928, even though they lost their regular goalie. Lester Patrick, their 45-year-old coach, played goal for the first time in his life in a 2-1 overtime victory as the Rangers beat the Montreal Maroons in that year. Frank Boucher starred as a goal scorer and as a stick handler who controlled the puck for long periods, keeping the pressure off Patrick and Joe Miller, who was in goal for the final game of the five-game series.

The Bruins won in 1929. Their hero was defenseman Eddie Shore, "the Babe Ruth of hockey." Shore was the first of the "rushing defensemen," always willing to skate the length of the ice if necessary, at a time when defensemen usually stayed near their own blue lines. Shore was a rough, brawling player who collected more than 900 stitches during a career of nearly 20 years. Other Bruin stars were goaltender "Tiny" Thompson and the "Dynamite Line" of Cooney Weiland, Dutch Gainor, and Dit Clapper.

The Toronto Maple Leafs won their first Stanley Cup in 1932 and they, too, had a legendary defenseman, "King" Clancy, who had been acquired for an enormous price—$35,000 plus two players—from Ottawa. En route to the cup, the Leafs won one of the most dramatic games in hockey history. The fifth game of the best-of-five semifinal series against the Bruins was won, 1-0, in the sixth overtime period. The game finally ended about 2 A.M.

After the Rangers won in 1933, the Black Hawks got

outstanding goaltending from Charlie Gardiner to win in 1934. Gardiner recorded two shutouts and gave up a total of just 12 goals in the eight play-off games. In June of that year he died of a cerebral hemorrhage.

Meanwhile the Detroit Red Wings were assembling one of the first real dynasties. Between 1934 and 1937 they finished first three times and won the Stanley Cup twice; they were the first team ever to win both the Prince of Wales Trophy (for finishing first) and the Stanley Cup in consecutive years, in 1936 and 1937. Their top stars were Larry Aurie, Syd Howe, and goalie Normie Smith.

The 1938 series produced a stunning upset by the Black Hawks, who had in Bill Stewart the only U.S.-born coach since the league began. They had won only 14 games during the regular season, finishing third, and their regular goalie, Mike Karakas, couldn't play in the first two games of the cup series. An unknown minor leaguer, Alf Moore, won the first game, 3-1. Karakas was back for the last two games and the Hawks beat Toronto, three out of four.

The Bruins supplanted the Red Wings as the power team of the NHL at this point. They were the first team to finish in first place three straight times, and they won the cup in 1939 and 1941. The Bruins had one of the great goalies, Frank "Zero" Brimsek, and the "Kraut Line"— Milt Schmidt, Bob Bauer, and Woody Dumart. In 1940 the Bruins were eliminated in the semifinal, and New York met Toronto for the Stanley Cup in a remarkable series. The Rangers won four out of six—all four of their victories were overtime games.

Toronto figured in another remarkable final series in 1942. The Maple Leafs lost the first three games to Detroit, but then came back to win four in a row and the Stanley Cup—the only team ever to accomplish that.

Modern Teams and Players. The NHL dates its "modern" era to the 1943–1944 season, the first in which the red line was used. It was also the first season of the six-team format that was to remain unchanged until 1967–1968.

Detroit, led by Sid Abel and Carl Liscombe, won the

Prince of Wales Trophy and the Stanley Cup in 1943, but then Montreal and Toronto took over. The Canadiens finished first four consecutive times, 1944–1947, winning the Stanley Cup in 1944 and 1946, but Toronto became the first team to win three consecutive cups, in 1947, 1948, and 1949. They also won in 1945 and 1951.

The Canadiens had six-time Vezina Trophy winner, Bill Durnan, in goal during those years, and their scoring was led by the "Punch Line" of Maurice "Rocket" Richard, Toe Blake, and Elmer Lach. Toronto also had a great goalie, Turk Broda, called by some the best play-off goalie of all time. Howie Meeker, the rookie of the year, led their "Kid Line" in 1947, and in the 1947–1948 season Max Bentley came to the team from Chicago and again was named the league's most valuable player.

Detroit came back with another dynasty shortly after the war, winning the Prince of Wales Trophy eight times and the Stanley Cup four times between 1949 and 1957. Like any dynastic hockey club, the Red Wings had an outstanding goaltender, Terry Sawchuk, who was known for his brilliant play-off performances. But they also had an aging Sid Abel in 1950, a young Gordie Howe, and Ted Lindsay, who was voted the most valuable player that year. Howe missed the play-offs with a serious injury, but the Red Wings won anyway. In 1952, they were unbeatable, winning eight straight games and the cup, with Sawchuk turning in four shutouts. Howe was by now the league's outstanding player, on a line with Lindsay and Alex Delvecchio, and Detroit also had the league's top defenseman, Red Kelly.

The Red Wings repeated as cup champions in 1954 and 1955. But, despite their streak of first-place finishes, they had a lot of trouble with the Canadiens, who always seemed to be at a peak in the play-offs. Detroit won the Prince of Wales Trophy in 1953 and 1956, but both times the Canadiens won the Stanley Cup. The 1956 cup victory was the first of an unprecedented five in a row. The Canadiens had struck a balance between French-Canadian players, of whom they had a virtual monopoly, and English-speaking players. Their goalie was the great Jacques Plante, known for his willingness to roam out of the crease to pick up the puck, even occasionally starting rushes. The team leader was "Rocket" Richard. Other stars were Bernie "Boom-Boom" Geoffrion, the awesome Jean Beliveau, little Dickie Moore, and an outstanding pair of defensemen, Doug Harvey and Tom Johnson.

Montreal's streak was ended in 1961 by the Chicago Black Hawks. They had the "Golden Jet," Bobby Hull; Stan Mikita, a tough, clever center; Pierre Pilote, one of the league's top defensemen, and Glenn Hall, a fine goalie. In the next eight years, Toronto and Montreal each won the Stanley Cup four times. The Maple Leafs did it three times in a row, 1962–1964, and again in 1967. They finished first only once in that period. Manager "Punch" Imlach had acquired Red Kelly and moved him from defense to center. He'd also brought up some good young players from the farm system, including Frank Mahovlich, Dave Keon, and defenseman Carl Brewer.

Expansion. For 25 years, from 1942–1943 through 1966–1967, the NHL had been composed of the same six teams. Other sports had shifted franchises and expanded, but major-league hockey had stood pat, despite some pressures to add new teams. Undoubtedly one reason was that the league's earlier attempts at expansion, in the late

Walter A. Brown coached the first U.S. team to win the world amateur hockey championship, in 1933, and was the president of the Boston Bruins and owner of the Boston Garden and Arena Corp. from 1937 until his death in 1964. (*U.S. Hockey Hall of Fame.*)

1920s and early 1930s, had been nearly disastrous, while the six-team format, with four teams involved in the play-offs, kept spectator interest high for most of the season.

During the 1960s, however, the situation changed. Even poor teams were drawing good crowds, because a lot of people were discovering hockey and wanted to watch it wherever they could. Television had helped build interest, and the money from television gave the league assurance of financial stability.

Increased interest in the sport also increased expansion pressures from cities that wanted major-league hockey. When the NHL did decide to expand, it did it in a big way, adding six more teams and creating a whole new division. The new teams were all in the United States: Los Angeles, Minneapolis–St. Paul, Philadelphia, Pittsburgh, Oakland (later California), and St. Louis.

Expansion was a remarkable success, despite complaints from hard-line fans about watered-down hockey. The new division was criticized by some as a "minor league," but several teams had good blends of youngsters and older players drafted from the established teams. The St. Louis Blues became the first Western Division champions. They lost the Stanley Cup play-off in four straight games to Montreal, but each game was decided by just one goal, and two of them went into overtime.

Subsequent expansions didn't seem quite so successful. Vancouver and Buffalo were added to the Eastern Division in 1970–1971, with Chicago moving into the Western Division and easily winning that division's championship. In 1972–1973, the New York Islanders joined the East and Atlanta was added to the West. After a good start, Atlanta tailed off badly, and the inept Islanders won just 12 games and tied just 6 in a 78-game schedule.

However, "parity" of a sort seemed to arrive in 1973–1974, when the Philadelphia Flyers became the first expansion team to win the Stanley Cup, beating two long-established teams, the New York Rangers in the semifinals and the Boston Bruins in the final series. Having accepted expansion reluctantly, the NHL's governors couldn't seem to stop once they had started. For the 1974–1975 season, two more teams were added, in Kansas City and Washington, and the league went to a much-criticized four-division format, with three teams from each division to qualify for the play-offs. Thus, 18 teams now play an 80-game schedule to eliminate just six teams from play-off spots. And the two newest franchises seemed utterly overmatched; between them, they won just 23 of their first 160 games.

Not Quite a Dynasty. The emergent team of the 1970s seemed to be the Boston Bruins. They had the sport's youngest superstar, Bobby Orr, who scored as no other defenseman had ever scored. The league's perennial scoring leader, in goals and total points, was Phil Esposito, acquired with linemate Kenny Hodge in a trade with the Black Hawks. In 1970 the Bruins won their first Stanley Cup since 1941, and seemed on their way to building a real dynasty. They won 12 out of 14 play-off games. However, after roaring to a first-place finish in 1970–1971, the Bruins were eliminated by third-place Montreal in the opening series, and the Canadiens went on to win the cup again, bolstered by goalie Ken Dryden, who had played only six regular-season games.

The Bruins again finished first and won the Stanley

Cup in 1972, but in 1973 the Canadiens were back. Dryden again starred in goal, Guy LaPointe anchored a strong defense, and Frank Mahovlich, Jacques LeMaire, and Yvan Cournoyer did the scoring.

Then came the surprising Flyers, who combined skill and intimidating play to get their way. Center Bobby Clarke had been named the league's most valuable player in 1972–1973 and Rick MacLeish was an outstanding scorer. The style of play, though, was often set by the "Broad Street Bullies," Dave "Hammer" Schultz, Bob "Mad Dog" Kelly, and defenseman André "Moose" Dupont. Their top defenseman, Barry Ashbee, missed the finals against Boston with an eye injury that eventually forced his retirement, but the Flyers cut down on the roughhouse and concentrated on playing skillful hockey to beat the Bruins in six games. Goalie Bernie Parent was named the outstanding player of the play-offs.

The Flyers won again in 1975 with relative ease, becoming the first team to win the Stanley Cup two consecutive years since 1968–1969, and again there was talk of a dynasty. But the resurgent Canadiens, led by Guy Lafleur, beat the Flyers in four games in the 1976 final series. Lafleur led the league in goals and in scoring and was named most valuable player.

World Hockey Association. There were scoffers when the

Frank "Mr. Zero" Brimsek was one of the few U.S.-born players to become a genuine star in the NHL. In 10 seasons as a goalie, 9 with the Boston Bruins, he had 40 shutouts and a 2.73 goals-against average. *(U.S. Hockey Hall of Fame.)*

formation of a new major hockey league was announced in 1972. Spearheaded by Garry Davidson, who had been instrumental in establishing the American Basketball Association, the World Hockey Association began play with teams in Alberta, Chicago, Cleveland, Houston, Los Angeles, Minnesota, New England, New York, Ottawa, Philadelphia, Quebec, and Winnipeg.

The WHA attracted many established NHL players, chief among them Bobby Hull, Chicago's superstar. Others were Bernie Parent, Larry Pleau, and Brad Selwood. Despite difficulties, the inaugural season was surprisingly successful, with New England beating Hull's Winnipeg Jets in the play-off finals. In 1973 the WHA's Houston Aeros pulled off a major coup by signing Gordie Howe's teen-age sons, Mark and Matt, and luring their father out of retirement to return to hockey at age 43. After a slow start, Gordie began to play like the Howe of old and was named the league's most valuable player; Mark was voted rookie of the year, and the Aeros won the second WHA championship.

At 47, Howe became president of the Aeros but continued to play, leading the team in scoring as they repeated as champions in the 1975 playoffs. In 1976, Bobby Hull teamed with two young Swedish players, Anders Hedberg and Ulf Nilsson, to give Winnipeg the league's highest scoring line, and the Jets dethroned the Aeros in the playoff finals.

A kind of truce between the NHL and WHA came in 1974, when the leagues reached an out-of-court settlement in a $50-million suit brought by the WHA, charging the older league with restraint of trade and monopoly practices. The NHL agreed to pay the WHA an indemnity of $1.75 million. The leagues agreed to honor each other's player contracts, the NHL agreed to make its arenas available for WHA play, and arrangements were also made for a series of interleague exhibition games beginning in 1975.

But the continued battle for unsigned players, and a court ruling that made players free agents after having played out their option years, caused financial problems for a number of franchises in both leagues. Before the 1976–1977 season, the WHA shrank from 14 teams to 12. The Denver Spurs and Minnesota Fighting Saints folded. The Cleveland Crusaders moved to Minnesota and became the new Fighting Saints, and the Toronto Toros became the Birmingham Bulls.

At the same time, the NHL's California Seals became the Cleveland Barons and the Kansas City Scouts moved to Denver to become the Colorado Rockies.

The Russians. Canada has long considered hockey its sport. Although the NHL is now dominated by the United States, in terms of franchise locations, most professional players are still Canadians. As in so many other sports, however, the Soviet Union has emerged as a major international power. From 1963 through 1974, the Russians won every world and Olympic hockey championship but one.

In 1972, Hockey Canada, a government-backed corporation, and the Hockey Federation of the Soviet Union agreed on an eight-game series between Canadian and Russian teams—the Canadian pros of the NHL against the government-subsidized ''amateurs'' of the Soviet Union. The result was shattering to Canadian egos, even though Team Canada won four games, lost three, and tied one. The Russians won the first game, 7-3, and won two and tied one of the four games in Canada. The Canadians had a fine resurgence in Russia, however, winning the last three games, all by one goal, to emerge on top. A second series was played in 1974, this time with WHA all-stars against the Russians, who won four, tied three, and lost only one.

In 1976, the Canada Cup series was inaugurated, patterned after soccer's World Cup. Six countries—Canada, Czechoslovakia, Finland, Sweden, Russia and the United States—entered the round-robin tournament. Canada beat Czechoslovakia in two straight games in the best-of-three final series for the championship.

Rules

The Rink. Most major hockey rinks are 200 ft long and 85 ft wide, but the rules specify a length of 165–250 ft and a width of 60–110 ft. Corners are rounded with an arc 18–25 ft in diameter. The rink is surrounded by a board wall at least 3 ft high, usually topped with unbreakable glass or plastic to protect spectators.

At each end of the rink is a goal line, 10–15 ft from the backboards. The goal line passes across the mouth of a goal cage, 4 ft high, 6 ft wide, and 2–3 ft deep. In front of the goal is a crease, a rectangle 8 ft wide and 4 ft deep. (In international play, the crease is a segment of a circle.)

There is a blue line 60 ft from each goal line, and halfway between the blue lines is a red line. The blue lines divide the rink into attacking, defending, and neutral zones. One team's attacking zone, of course, is the other team's defending zone. There are also five face-off circles marked on the rink, each 10 ft in radius, with a 12-in circle in the center. One face-off circle is at center ice. Each of the others is 15 ft from a goal line and midway between the side boards and the nearest goalpost.

Equipment. The hockey puck is a vulcanized rubber disk having a diameter of 3 in and a thickness of 1 in. Its weight is 156–170 g (about 6 oz). Skates must be of an approved hockey design; speed skates and figure skates are not allowed. All players except goalies must wear skate heel guards.

The stick used by all players except the goalie must have a handle no longer than 4 ft, 5 in, with a blade no larger than 1 ft, 2½ in long and 3 in wide. The goalie's stick may have a blade up to 3½ in wide, and the lower 2 ft of the handle may be the same width.

All players usually wear shoulder pads, elbow pads, shin pads, and gloves; many of them wear helmets (helmets must be worn in junior play and college). The goalie also wears a chest protector, leg guards (no more than 10 in wide) and a face mask.

Timing and Scoring. A game consists of three periods of 20 min each, with 10-min breaks in between. The object is to score goals by putting the puck into the opposition's net. The puck must legally and completely cross the goal line, between the goalposts and underneath the crossbar. The puck is normally shot in directly from a player's stick, but it is also a legal goal if the puck deflects off the stick, person, or skates of an attacker, provided it was not deliberately kicked, thrown, or otherwise directed into the goal, except with the stick; if the puck is put into the goal by a defender; if an attacker kicks the puck and it is deflected into the goal by a defender other than the goalkeeper.

Progress of Play. The game begins with a face-off between the opposing centers at center ice. Each of the two players faces the goal the player's team is attacking; each must be within the face-off circle but outside the smaller circle in the center; the stick of each must be full-blade on the ice, clear of where the puck will drop; and each must not touch the puck until it touches the ice. The official is the only other person allowed in the circle until the puck has hit the ice; he drops the puck between the two players, who try to get possession of it or pass it to a teammate.

From this point on, play is continuous and the teams attempt to advance the puck and to score goals. Play stops when a goal is scored; when there is a violation or when a foul is committed by the attacking team; when the puck leaves the playing surface or is lodged in the goal netting; or when the referee is unable to see the puck in a melee. Play is always resumed with a face-off, usually at the face-off circle nearest the spot where the puck went out of play, the spot where the puck was last played, or the spot where it was located when play was stopped. After a goal, the face-off is held at center ice.

Players and Substitutions. A team may have only six players on the ice at one time, including one goaltender. The player designated as goaltender has some special privileges: The goalie alone can handle the puck, and is protected in certain ways while in the goal crease. On the other hand, the goalie can never cross the red line. For attacking purposes, a team may sometimes replace a goaltender with another player, but that player doesn't have the same privileges. (Of course, if the goalie is replaced by a substitute goalie, the latter does have those privileges.)

Substitutions may be made at any time, but the player being replaced must be off the ice before his replacement is on the ice.

Offsides. There are two types of offsides in hockey. An attacking player may not precede the puck into the attacking zone. If the player enters the attacking zone before the puck does, an offside is called; a face-off is held in the neutral zone.

A two-line offside results from a pass made from within the defending zone, across the blue line and the red line. A face-off is held near the spot from which the pass originated.

A player is offside when both the player's skates are completely beyond the relevant line. But note that, for a player to be offside, the puck must also cross the line. If a player is in the attacking zone, and stops a pass before the puck crosses the blue line, the player is not offside; but the player must go back into the neutral zone before bringing the puck into the passing zone.

Icing. This term refers to the act of a player who shoots the puck from behind the red line to the opponent's goal line, unless the puck goes into the goal. However, it is not icing if any intervening player touches the puck, or if, in the judgment of the official, a member of the defending team other than the goalie could have played the puck before it crossed the goal line. (Under United States college rules, the puck must pass across both blue lines, as well as the goal line, for icing to be called.) After an icing violation, a face-off is held in the offending team's defending zone. A team that is shorthanded because of a penalty may ice the puck legally.

Fouls. In general, fouls involve some kind of illegal contact with an opponent, and they are usually penalized by banishing the offender to a penalty box, with no substitution allowed, for a specified period, usually 2 min.

The following are among the most common fouls:

- Interference—A player may not deliberately impede the progress of an opponent who does not have possession of the puck. (It is legal, however, to make contact with a player who has just passed or shot the puck.) Another type of interference is impeding the movement of the goalkeeper while the goalkeeper, but not the puck, is in the goal crease.
- High-sticking—It is illegal to carry the stick above shoulder height; a minor penalty may be imposed. If the puck is hit with a high stick, a face-off is held; if a goal is scored off a high stick, it is disallowed.
- Kneeing and elbowing—A major penalty may be imposed in flagrant cases, or if injury is caused:
- Charging—This is the act of hitting a player after taking more than two normal skating strides or steps. A major penalty is imposed if it is done from behind or if the victim is the goalie while in the crease.
- Tripping—This may involve the stick, knee, foot, arm, hand, or elbow; the opponent must fall to the ice for a foul to be called.
- Cross-checking—By this is meant checking an opponent with the stick held across the body and off the ice, in both hands.
- Spearing—This consists of poking an opponent with the point of the stick.
- Butt-ending—Poking an opponent with the butt end of the stick is a foul.
- Slashing—Striking an opponent with the stick is also a foul.
- Hooking—Impeding the progress of an opponent by hooking the opponent with the stick blade is a form of illegal contact.
- Board-checking—It is permissible to check an opponent into the boards, but not if it is done violently.
- Clipping—This is falling and sliding into a puck carrier's path so that the player in question loses possession of the puck.
- Roughing—Such a foul usually stems from a fairly mild fight.
- Handling the puck—No player other than a goalkeeper may close the hand on the puck.
- Falling on the puck—No player other than the goalie may deliberately fall on the puck, or gather it into the body. The goalie may not do it when the puck is behind the goal line and the goalie is entirely out of the crease.

Penalties. When a foul is called on the team in possession of the puck, play stops immediately. If the foul is called on the defending team, it is signaled, but play is not stopped, and imposition of the penalty is delayed until the team to be penalized gains possession. If the other team scores a goal before play is stopped, the penalty is not imposed if it is a minor one (see below).

A team can never be shorthanded by more than two players. A player penalized while two teammates are already in the penalty box must go to the bench, but doesn't start serving the penalty time until one of the teammates is out of the penalty box.

A minor penalty ends when the other team scores a goal. If two players are in the penalty box when the other team scores a goal, the one with the least time remaining to be served may leave the box.

A minor penalty, imposed for most fouls, is 2 min in duration. A bench minor is a 2-min penalty imposed on a team for such violations as having too many men on the ice or delaying the game. It is also a bench minor when the goalkeeper leaves the crease to enter a fight. The penalty is served by any player designated by the coach.

A major penalty is 5 min; it is imposed for a flagrant

rules violation, usually extreme roughness, or when a foul results in injury to an opponent. A player serving a major penalty must serve the full 5 min, even if the other team scores. A second major penalty in the game is 15 min in duration, but a substitute may replace the penalized player after 5 min of this period of penalty time.

A misconduct penalty is imposed for misconduct toward officials: for example, using obscene, profane, or abusive language; persistent disputing of rulings; and banging the stick on the ice to show disrespect. The player is penalized 10 min, but the player's team is not: A substitute may enter the game.

A match penalty results in the player's being banished for the rest of the game. Such a penalty is usually called when a player continues to use abusive language in speaking to an official, or when the player strikes an official. It is, in effect, a suspension; the league office will investigate the case and may punish the player further by continuing the suspension through one or more future games, or by fining the player.

A game misconduct also results in permanent banishment from the game. The second misconduct penalty to a player is automatically a game misconduct. The third player in a fight between two others is given a game misconduct; so is a player who leaves the bench to take part in a fight.

A penalty shot is awarded when a player with a clear breakaway and in possession of the puck is interfered with. The interference may take the form of being fouled from behind, or having a stick or some other object thrown at the player in question. A penalty shot is also awarded if any defender besides the goalie falls on the puck deliberately, or picks up the puck while it is in the crease. On a penalty shot the puck is placed at the center face-off circle. All players but the goalie and the player taking the shot must remain behind the penalty line. The player taking the shot collects the puck and skates forward, toward the goalie, who must remain in the crease until the puck crosses the blue line. The attacking player must advance steadily toward the goal; the player may move at an angle, but may not stop or turn away. One shot on the goal is permitted; the player cannot score on the rebound.

The goaltender cannot be sent to the penalty box for a minor, major, or misconduct penalty. If the goalie commits a foul calling for such a penalty, the penalty is served by a teammate who was on the ice at the time. If the goaltender is given a game or match misconduct, however, the goalie does leave the game and is replaced by another goaltender.

Officials. On-ice officials are the referee, who has overall charge of the game, and two linesmen. The referee calls fouls and imposes penalties, rules on goals, and makes other major decisions. The linesmen are stationed at the blue lines, and their primary jobs are to rule on offsides and icing. They also help break up fights and they may tell the referee of rules infractions that the referee did not see, but they can never call penalties on their own initiative.

Behind each goal is a goal judge, who pushes a button that turns on a red light whenever that official sees the puck enter the cage. The goal judge cannot award a goal, however; the referee is the final arbiter here, too, and may rule that a goal was scored even if the goal judge didn't

Maurice "Rocket" Richard, in 18 seasons with the Montreal Canadiens, scored 544 goals; he was All-Star right wing eight times and led the NHL in goals five times. *(Montreal Canadiens.)*

turn on the red light, or may disallow apparent goals either for rules violations or because the referee believes the goal judge was wrong in signaling that the puck entered the cage.

Other minor officials are the game timekeeper, the penalty timekeeper, and the official scorer, who rules on goals and assists.

Strategy and Tactics

Hockey is essentially a positional battle. Amidst all the checking, all the skating up and down ice, and all the stick handling, each team is working for positional advantage. If a player momentarily has a lapse and is in the wrong position, it will probably result in a good scoring chance for the other team.

Offense. Offense begins the moment a team gains possession of the puck. Some teams like to have a defenseman bring the puck at least part of the way up the ice; others want a defenseman to pass the puck to a center or wing and let one of those players bring it up. The center and two wings together make up the principal offensive unit, or forward line. Any team uses certain "break-out" plays—based on proper positioning. As an example: The left defenseman gets the puck behind the net. The other defenseman takes a position in front of the net, slightly to the left. The left wing comes about halfway into the zone, near the boards. The right wing waits until sure his team has control of the puck, then begins to make a break up the ice along the right boards. The center takes a station inside the blue line, approximately in front of the goal.

The player with the puck now has several options. One is to bring the puck up, retaining possession, in which case the center should move across the blue line, ready for a pass. The first player can pass the puck to the left wing, then break up ice, ready for a return pass, and the wing can either pass the puck to the center or back to the defenseman. Or the first player can make a quick pass to the center and begin following the play.

Once a team is across the red line, there are basically two philosophies of attacking. The "Montreal" method is to keep control of the puck, "headmanning" it—passing it to a player skating ahead. The idea is to get a forward carrying the puck into the attacking zone at top speed. If it is a wing, that player should angle for the net, since an opposing defenseman will be attempting to force him to the boards or into the corner. The center will probably be swinging behind the wing for a drop pass.

If the center carries the puck in, the path pursued will usually be a swerve in one direction or the other rather than a direct line toward the goal. If the center swerves to the right, the right wing should slow down and drop behind, ready for a drop pass, while the left wing angles toward the net.

The Toronto method—sometimes called "play-off hockey"—is to throw the puck into the offensive zone from center ice and then rush in and try to get possession of it. The idea here is to keep constant pressure on the defense, to try to outfight them for the puck and eventually to force an error that will lead to a goal. Usually it will be a wing going in to try to collect the puck, while the center is stationed behind the wing and the other wing moves in front of the net.

Forwards are taught to stay in their lanes when breaking down the ice. But, whenever a player is out of position, it is up to teammates to adjust. For example, if a defenseman gets into a corner of the offensive zone in an attempt to get the puck, one of the forwards—probably the wing who would ordinarily be in that corner—will have to drop back to cover for the defenseman.

Defense. A team goes on defense the moment possession of the puck is lost. It begins with forechecking in the defensive zone. While the defensemen should drop back immediately, at least one forward, usually the center, will go in deep, trying to get the puck back. Sometimes a team will also send in a wing to help the center forecheck. Ordinarily, though, both wings are expected to drop back rather quickly to help the defense by back-checking.

Hockey teams use an alignment similar to a zone defense (in football), but the zones are lanes. Defensemen are primarily responsible for protecting the area in front of the net. They want to force attackers away from the goal, toward the boards or into the corners. When the puck is forced to one side of the rink, deep in the zone, the defenseman on that side may go after it, and the other defenseman then plays in front of the net on that side.

There are some one-on-one responsibilities, however, especially among the forwards. The center usually has basic defensive responsibility for the opposing center. A wing, when back-checking, should stay in the wing lane (side area), which usually means covering the opposing wing at least through the center-ice area.

Goaltending. An outstanding goaltender can make a great team out of a good team. Reflexes and courage can't be taught but, again, position play is very important. The goalie's basic move is to cut down the angle on certain shots by moving away from the net. Such movement gives the offensive player less area to shoot at. By keeping the leg pads together, the goaltender covers the other most vulnerable area. The goalie should follow the puck, moving from side to side as necessary to keep it centered in the goalie's pads, facing squarely at all times.

A goaltender should attempt to catch the puck whenever possible, even if a shot can be stopped in another way (with stick or pads); catching prevents rebounds, which may result in goals. But, whenever possible, the goaltender's body should be behind the glove to stop the puck if it should deflect off the catching hand.

When the puck is behind the net, the goalie has to be very quick to move with it, to one side or another, and must get the heel of the skate and the back of the leg against the goalpost on the side to which the puck moves. This is to lessen the danger of the puck's being shot off the goalie's leg into the net, or jammed in past the post.

Power Plays. When a team has a one-player advantage, because an opposition player is in the penalty box, it goes into a special, patterned kind of offense. Two good, hard shooters are stationed at the points, just inside the blue line. The wings play near the boards, about even with the face-off circles, and the center moves around in the center of the offensive zone. Setting up a shot usually involves passing the puck around the perimeter, hoping to get a defensive player to make a move that will provide an opening for an attacking player.

Passing will not always produce the desired goal. Moving with the puck toward the goal, or from the wing toward the center area, will eventually force a defensive commitment. If the player at the point sees a clear lane for a good shot, the shot will be taken. Even if the puck doesn't go in the opposition cage, the attacking team still will have a three-to-two chance to get the puck after the save by the opposition goalie.

Penalty Killing. There are usually two forwards and two defensemen on the ice when a team is a player short, following a penalty. They play an extreme zone, a box formation. Their job is to keep the puck out of the danger area in front of their net; for the most part they should let the opponents pass the puck around the perimeter, being very careful not to overcommit themselves. If the puck goes into a corner, a defenseman should not go after it unless it is almost certain that the defenseman can get it. If the puck is behind the net, the defenseman should be even more careful about committing himself.

One of the forwards of the penalty-killing unit is usually a very aggressive forechecker, who attacks the puck carrier in the latter's end of the rink, trying to disconcert the puck carrier and waste time. Some teams believe in sending two very aggressive forecheckers into the attacker's area to try to disrupt the power play before it can get set up.

Checking. Although usually associated with body checks, checking is any maneuver that slows or stops the puck carrier or separates that player from the puck.

In the body check, the shoulder of the defensive player

is used; the puck carrier's chest is the target. Body checking is most effective when a player has just received the puck or has just passed it. In the first instance, the player is preoccupied and more easily separated from the puck; in the second, the player may be trying to work a "give-and-go," and the check will destroy the plans.

A hip check is more often used on a puck carrier who is traveling at high speed. The defender bends low and, just as the puck carrier is going by, turns quickly, getting the hip into the rusher's path; the intent is to spin the carrier off the puck.

The poke check is most often seen just across the blue line in the defending zone. The defender suddenly takes a step forward and makes a quick, one-handed poke with the stick at the puck or the blade of an opponent's stick.

The sweep check is based on a similar idea, but used when attacking the puck carrier from the side. The defender cuts in front of the puck carrier and seems to overskate the latter, then lowers the stick to the ice, holding it in one hand and sweeping it across the path of the puck. This can be most effective when employed by a forechecking forward in the attacking zone.

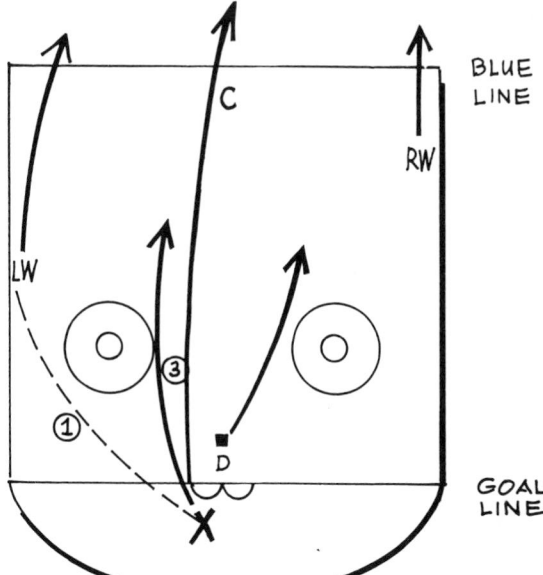

Breakout play. In this position, the defensive player has three options: (1) Pass to the left wing off the boards; (2) Pass directly out to the center; (3) Bring the puck up ice, ready to head-man it to a forward.

Glossary

A—When worn on a player's shirt, the letter stands for "alternate captain." The player may act as captain in discussing issues with an official when the team captain is not on the ice.

assist—When a goal is scored, one or two players who made passes to set up the goal may be given assists.

attacking zone—The zone in which the goal being attacked is located.

back-check—To check in the defensive zone.

backhand—A shot taken from the "wrong side"; for a right-handed player, a shot taken from the left side of the body.

blind pass—A pass made without looking.

breakaway—When the puck carrier has just one defender, the goalie, to beat, this term describes the situation.

break out—To get the puck out of the defending zone.

center—To pass the puck from a wing (side area) to the area in front of the net.

center ice—The center zone; sometimes used to mean the area in the immediate vicinity of the center face-off circle or the red line.

center zone—The area between the blue lines.

clear—To move the puck away from the net being defended, usually toward the sideboards or into the corner.

cover up—To fall on the puck; legal only when the goalie does it.

defensive zone—The zone in which the goal being defended is located.

deke—To fake (from "decoy").

dig—To fight for the puck in the corner.

dive—To approach the puck carrier head-on, which makes it much easier for the carrier to keep the puck from the defender or even to get around the defender.

draw—On a face-off, to get the puck back to a teammate.

drop pass—A pass by means of which the puck is simply left behind for a trailing teammate to pick up.

feed—An assist.

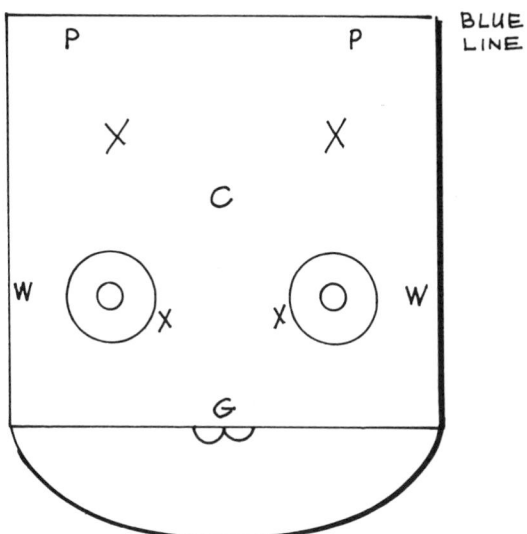

Power play vs. penalty killers

finish off a play—To score.

flip—A pass or shot in which the puck is lifted slightly from the ice.

forecheck—To check in the attacking zone.

freeze—To pin the puck against the boards or the goal net.

hat trick—Three goals by a player in one game.

hole—The slot.

on the fly—Changing on the fly is putting fresh players on the ice when play is still going on.

point—A position just inside the attacking zone; also, a player who takes up this position.

rag—To control the puck through clever stick handling, usually to consume time while a penalty is being served or near the end of the game.

save—A stop by the goalie that prevents a score.

telegraph—To look right at a teammate before passing to the teammate; to give any clear indication to opponents of what you are about to do.

trailer—A player who lags behind a puck-carrying teammate.

Stanley Cup Champions

(Amateur Years)

Year	Team	Coach
1893	Montreal AAA	——
1894	Montreal AAA	——
1895	Montreal Victorias	Mike Grant*
1896	(Feb.) Winnipeg Victorias	——
1896	(Dec.) Montreal Victorias	Mike Grant*
1897	Montreal Victorias	Mike Grant*
1898	Montreal Victorias	F. Richardson
1899	(March) Montreal Shamrocks	——
1899	(Feb.) Montreal Victorias	G. Drinkwater*
1900	Montreal Shamrocks	H. J. Trihey*
1901	Winnipeg Victorias	——
1902	Montreal AAA	——
1903	Ottawa Silver Seven	A. T. Smith
1904	Ottawa Silver Seven	A. T. Smith
1905	Ottawa Silver Seven	A. T. Smith
1906	Montreal Wanderers	——
1907	(March) Montreal Wanderers	Cecil Blachford
1907	(Jan.) Kenora Thistles	Tommy Phillips*
1908	Montreal Wanderers	Cecil Blachford
1909	Ottawa Senators	Bruce Stuart*
1910	Montreal Wanderers	——

(AHA-PCHA Years)

1911	Ottawa Senators	Pud Glass*
1912	Quebec Bulldogs	C. Nolan
1913	Quebec Bulldogs**	——
1914	Toronto Blueshirts	Scotty Davidson*
1915	Vancouver Millionaires	Frank Patrick
1916	Montreal Canadiens	George Kennedy
1917	Seattle Metropolitans	Pete Muldoon

Blanks indicate that there was no coach as such, or that coach's name is unknown.
*Indicates coach was captain.
**Victoria beat Quebec in challenge series, but was not officially recognized.

(NHL-PCL Years)

1918	Toronto Arenas	Dick Carroll
1919	Montreal-Seattle series canceled after five games (flu epidemic)	
1920	Ottawa Senators	Pete Green
1921	Ottawa Senators	Pete Green
1922	Toronto St. Pats	Eddie Powers
1923	Ottawa Senators	Pete Green
1924	Montreal Canadiens	Leo Dandurand
1925	Victoria Cougars	Lester Patrick
1926	Montreal Maroons	Eddie Gerard

(NHL Years)

1927	Ottawa Senators	Dave Gill
1928	New York Rangers	Lester Patrick
1929	Boston Bruins	Cy Denneny
1930	Montreal Canadiens	Cecil Hart
1931	Montreal Canadiens	Cecil Hart
1932	Toronto Maple Leafs	Dick Irvin
1933	New York Rangers	Lester Patrick
1934	Chicago Black Hawks	Tommy Gorman
1935	Montreal Maroons	Tommy Gorman
1936	Detroit Red Wings	Jack Adams
1937	Detroit Red Wings	Jack Adams
1938	Chicago Black Hawks	Bill Stewart
1939	Boston Bruins	Art Ross
1940	New York Rangers	Frank Boucher
1941	Boston Bruins	Cooney Weiland
1942	Toronto Maple Leafs	Hap Day
1943	Detroit Red Wings	Jack Adams
1944	Montreal Canadiens	Dick Irvin
1945	Toronto Maple Leafs	Hap Day
1946	Montreal Canadiens	Dick Irvin
1947	Toronto Maple Leafs	Hap Day
1948	Toronto Maple Leafs	Hap Day
1949	Toronto Maple Leafs	Hap Day
1950	Detroit Red Wings	Tommy Ivan
1951	Toronto Maple Leafs	Joe Primeau
1952	Detroit Red Wings	Tommy Ivan
1953	Montreal Canadiens	Dick Irvin
1954	Detroit Red Wings	Tommy Ivan
1955	Detroit Red Wings	Jimmy Skinner
1956	Montreal Canadiens	Toe Blake
1957	Montreal Canadiens	Toe Blake
1958	Montreal Canadiens	Toe Blake
1959	Montreal Canadiens	Toe Blake
1960	Montreal Canadiens	Toe Blake
1961	Chicago Black Hawks	Rudy Pilous
1962	Toronto Maple Leafs	Punch Imlach
1963	Toronto Maple Leafs	Punch Imlach
1964	Toronto Maple Leafs	Punch Imlach
1965	Montreal Canadiens	Toe Blake
1966	Montreal Canadiens	Toe Blake
1967	Toronto Maple Leafs	Punch Imlach
1968	Montreal Canadiens	Toe Blake
1969	Montreal Canadiens	Claude Ruel
1970	Boston Bruins	Harry Sinden
1971	Montreal Canadiens	Al MacNeil
1972	Boston Bruins	Tom Johnson
1973	Montreal Canadiens	Scotty Bowman
1974	Philadelphia Flyers	Fred Shero
1975	Philadelphia Flyers	Fred Shero
1976	Montreal Canadiens	Scotty Bowman

NHL Outstanding Players

Most Goals

1927	Bill Cook, New York Rangers	33
1928	Howie Morenz, Montreal Canadiens	33
1929	"Ace" Bailey, Toronto	22
1930	Cooney Weiland, Boston	43
1931	Charlie Conacher, Toronto	31
1932	Charlie Conacher, Toronto	34
1933	Bill Cook, New York Rangers	28
1934	Charlie Conacher, Toronto	32
1935	Charlie Conacher, Toronto	36
1936	Bill Thomas, Toronto	23
	Charlie Conacher, Toronto	23

1937	Larry Aurie, Detroit	23
	Nels Stewart, Boston-New York Americans	23
1938	Gordon Drillon, Toronto	26
1939	Roy Conacher, Boston	26
1940	Bryan Hextall, New York Rangers	24
1941	Bryan Hextall, New York Rangers	26
1942	Lynn Patrick, New York Rangers	32
1943	Doug Bentley, Chicago	33
1944	Doug Bentley, Chicago	38
1945	Maurice Richard, Montreal Canadiens	50
1946	Gaye Stewart, Toronto	37
1947	Maurice Richard, Montreal Canadiens	45
1948	Ted Lindsay, Detroit	33
1949	Sid Abel, Detroit	28
1950	Maurice Richard, Montreal Canadiens	43
1951	Gordie Howe, Detroit	43
1952	Gordie Howe, Detroit	47
1953	Gordie Howe, Detroit	49
1954	Maurice Richard, Montreal Canadiens	37
1955	Maurice Richard, Montreal Canadiens	38
	Bernie Geoffrion, Montreal Canadiens	38
1956	Jean Beliveau, Montreal Canadiens	47
1957	Gordie Howe, Detroit	44
1958	Dickie Moore, Montreal Canadiens	36
1959	Jean Beliveau, Montreal Canadiens	45
1960	Bobby Hull, Chicago	39
	Bronco Horvath, Boston	39
1961	Bernie Geoffrion, Montreal Canadiens	50
1962	Bobby Hull, Chicago	50
1963	Gordie Howe, Detroit	38
1964	Bobby Hull, Chicago	43
1965	Norm Ullman, Detroit	42
1966	Bobby Hull, Chicago	54
1967	Bobby Hull, Chicago	52
1968	Bobby Hull, Chicago	44
1969	Bobby Hull, Chicago	58
1970	Phil Esposito, Boston	43
1971	Phil Esposito, Boston	76
1972	Phil Esposito, Boston	66
1973	Phil Esposito, Boston	55
1974	Phil Esposito, Boston	68
1975	Phil Esposito, Boston	61
1976	Guy LaFleur, Montreal Canadiens	56

Most Points

		Goals	Assists	Pts.
1927	Bill Cook, New York Rangers	33	4	37
1928	Howie Morenz, Montreal Canadiens	33	18	51
1929	Ace Bailey, Toronto	22	10	32
1930	Cooney Weiland, Boston	43	30	73
1931	Howie Morenz, Montreal Canadiens	28	23	51
1932	Harvey Jackson, Toronto	28	25	53
1933	Bill Cook, New York Rangers	28	22	50
1934	Charlie Conacher, Toronto	32	20	52
1935	Charlie Conacher, Toronto	36	21	57
1936	Dave Schriner, New York Americans	19	26	45
1937	Dave Schriner, New York Americans	21	25	46
1938	Gordon Drillon, Toronto	26	26	52
1939	Toe Blake, Montreal Canadiens	24	23	47
1940	Milt Schmidt, Boston	22	30	52
1941	Bill Cowley, Boston	17	45	62
1942	Bryan Hextall, New York Rangers	24	32	56
1943	Doug Bentley, Chicago	33	40	73
1944	Herbie Cain, Boston	36	46	82
1945	Elmer Lach, Montreal Canadiens	26	54	80
1946	Max Bentley, Chicago	31	30	61
1947	Max Bentley, Chicago	29	43	72
1948	Elmer Lach, Montreal Canadiens	30	31	61
1949	Roy Conacher, Chicago	26	42	68
1950	Ted Lindsay, Detroit	23	55	78
1951	Gordie Howe, Detroit	43	43	86
1952	Gordie Howe, Detroit	47	39	86
1953	Gordie Howe, Detroit	49	46	95
1954	Gordie Howe, Detroit	33	48	81

1955	Bernie Geoffrion, Montreal Canadiens	38	37	75
1956	Jean Beliveau, Montreal Canadiens	47	41	88
1957	Gordie Howe, Detroit	44	45	89
1958	Dickie Moore, Montreal Canadiens	36	48	84
1959	Dickie Moore, Montreal Canadiens	41	55	96
1960	Bobby Hull, Chicago	39	42	81
1961	Bernie Geoffrion, Montreal Canadiens	50	45	95
1962	Bobby Hull, Chicago	50	34	84
1963	Gordie Howe, Detroit	38	48	86
1964	Stan Mikita, Chicago	39	50	89
1965	Stan Mikita, Chicago	28	59	87
1966	Bobby Hull, Chicago	54	43	97
1967	Stan Mikita, Chicago	35	62	97
1968	Stan Mikita, Chicago	40	47	87
1969	Phil Esposito, Boston	49	77	126
1970	Bobby Orr, Boston	33	87	120
1971	Phil Esposito, Boston	76	76	152
1972	Phil Esposito, Boston	66	67	133
1973	Phil Esposito, Boston	55	75	130
1974	Phil Esposito, Boston	68	77	145
1975	Bobby Orr, Boston	46	89	135
1976	Guy LaFleur, Montreal Canadiens	56	69	125

NHL Honored Players

Most Valuable Player

1924	Frank Nighbor, Ottawa
1925	Billy Burch, Hamilton
1926	Nels Stewart, Montreal Maroons
1927	Herb Gardiner, Montreal Canadiens
1928	Howie Morenz, Montreal Canadiens
1929	Roy Worters, New York Americans
1930	Nels Stewart, Montreal Maroons
1931	Howie Morenz, Montreal Canadiens
1932	Howie Morenz, Montreal Canadiens
1933	Eddie Shore, Boston
1934	Aurel Joliat, Montreal Canadiens
1935	Eddie Shore, Boston
1936	Eddie Shore, Boston
1937	"Babe" Siebert, Montreal Canadiens
1938	Eddie Shore, Boston
1939	"Toe" Blake, Montreal Canadiens
1940	Ebbie Goodfellow, Detroit
1941	Bill Cowley, Boston
1942	Tommy Anderson, New York Americans
1943	Bill Cowley, Boston
1944	"Babe" Pratt, Toronto
1945	Elmer Lach, Montreal Canadiens
1946	Max Bentley, Chicago
1947	Maurice Richard, Montreal Canadiens
1948	"Buddy" O'Connor, New York Rangers
1949	Sid Abel, Detroit
1950	Chuck Rayner, New York Rangers
1951	Milt Schmidt, Boston
1952	Gordie Howe, Detroit
1953	Gordie Howe, Detroit
1954	Al Rollins, Chicago
1955	Ted Kennedy, Toronto
1956	Jean Beliveau, Montreal Canadiens
1957	Gordie Howe, Detroit
1958	Gordie Howe, Detroit
1959	Andy Bathgate, New York Rangers
1960	Gordie Howe, Detroit
1961	Bernie Geoffrion, Montreal Canadiens
1962	Jacques Plante, Montreal Canadiens
1963	Gordie Howe, Detroit
1964	Jean Beliveau, Montreal Canadiens
1965	Bobby Hull, Chicago
1966	Bobby Hull, Chicago
1967	Stan Mikita, Chicago
1968	Stan Mikita, Chicago
1969	Phil Esposito, Boston
1970	Bobby Orr, Boston

1971   Bobby Orr, Boston
1972   Bobby Orr, Boston
1973   Bobby Clarke, Philadelphia
1974   Phil Esposito, Boston
1975   Bobby Clarke, Philadelphia
1976   Bobby Clarke, Philadelphia

Rookie of the Year
1933   Carl Voss, Detroit
1934   Russ Blinco, Montreal Maroons
1935   Dave Schriner, New York Americans
1936   Mike Karakas, Chicago
1937   Syl Apps, Toronto
1938   Cully Dahlstrom, Chicago
1939   Frank Brimsek, Boston
1940   Kilby Macdonald, New York Rangers
1941   Johnny Quilty, Montreal Canadiens
1942   Grant Warwick, New York Rangers
1943   Gaye Stewart, Toronto
1944   Gus Bodnar, Toronto
1945   Frank McCool, Toronto
1946   Edgar Laprade, New York Rangers
1947   Howie Meeker Toronto
1948   Jimmy McFadden, Detroit
1949   Pentti Lund, New York Rangers
1950   Jack Gelineau, Boston
1951   Terry Sawchuk, Detroit
1952   Bernie Geoffrion, Montreal Canadiens
1953   Lorne Worsley, New York Rangers
1954   Camille Henry, New York Rangers
1955   Eddie Litzenberger, Chicago
1956   Glenn Hall, Detroit
1957   Larry Regan, Boston
1958   Frank Mahovlich, Toronto
1959   Ralph Backstrom, Montreal Canadiens
1960   Bill "Red" Hay, Chicago
1961   Dave Keon, Toronto
1962   Bobby Rousseau, Montreal Canadiens
1963   Kent Douglas, Toronto
1964   Jacques Laperriere, Montreal Canadiens
1965   Roger Crozier, Detroit
1966   Brit Selby, Toronto
1967   Bobby Orr, Boston
1968   Derek Sanderson, Boston
1969   Danny Grant, Minnesota
1970   Tony Esposito, Chicago
1971   Gilbert Perreault, Buffalo
1972   Ken Dryden, Montreal Canadiens
1973   Steve Vickers, New York Rangers
1974   Denis Potvin, New York Islanders
1975   Eric Vail, Atlanta
1976   Bryan Trottier, New York Islanders

Vezina Trophy
(Best goalkeeper)
1927   George Hainsworth, Montreal Canadiens
1928   George Hainsworth, Montreal Canadiens
1929   George Hainsworth, Montreal Canadiens
1930   C. "Tiny" Thompson, Boston
1931   Roy Worters, New York Americans
1932   Charlie Gardiner, Chicago
1933   C. "Tiny" Thompson, Boston
1934   Charlie Gardiner, Chicago
1935   Loren Chabot, Chicago
1936   C. "Tiny" Thompson, Boston
1937   Normie Smith, Detroit
1938   C. "Tiny" Thompson, Boston
1939   Frank Brimsek, Boston
1940   Dave Kerr, New York Rangers
1941   W. "Turk" Broda, Toronto
1942   Frank Brimsek, Boston
1943   Johnny Mowers, Detroit
1944   Bill Durnan, Montreal Canadiens

1945   Bill Durnan, Montreal Canadiens
1946   Bill Durnan, Montreal Canadiens
1947   Bill Durnan, Montreal Canadiens
1948   W. "Turk" Broda, Toronto
1949   Bill Durnan, Montreal Canadiens
1950   Bill Durnan, Montreal Canadiens
1951   Al Rollins, Toronto
1952   Terry Sawchuk, Detroit
1953   Terry Sawchuk, Detroit
1954   Harry Lumley, Toronto
1955   Terry Sawchuk, Detroit
1956   Jacques Plante, Montreal Canadiens
1957   Jacques Plante, Montreal Canadiens
1958   Jacques Plante, Montreal Canadiens
1959   Jacques Plante, Montreal Canadiens
1960   Jacques Plante, Montreal Canadiens
1961   Johnny Bower, Toronto
1962   Jacques Plante, Montreal Canadiens
1963   Glenn Hall, Chicago
1964   Charlie Hodge, Montreal Canadiens
1965   Terry Sawchuk-Johnny Bower, Toronto
1966   "Gump" Worsley-Charlie Hodge, Montreal Canadiens
1967   Glenn Hall-Denis DeJordy, Chicago
1968   "Gump" Worsley-Rogatien Vachon, Montreal Canadiens
1969   Glenn Hall-Jacques Plante, St. Louis
1970   Tony Esposito, Chicago
1971   Ed Giacomin-Gilles Villemure, New York Rangers
1972   Tony Esposito-Gary Smith, Chicago
1973   Ken Dryden, Montreal Canadiens
1974   Bernie Parent, Philadelphia
1975   Bernie Parent, Philadelphia
1976   Ken Dryden, Montreal Canadiens

Norris Trophy
(Best defenseman)
1954   Red Kelly, Detroit
1955   Doug Harvey, Montreal Canadiens
1956   Doug Harvey, Montreal Canadiens
1957   Doug Harvey, Montreal Canadiens
1958   Doug Harvey, Montreal Canadiens
1959   Tom Johnson, Montreal Canadiens
1960   Doug Harvey, Montreal Canadiens
1961   Doug Harvey, Montreal Canadiens
1962   Doug Harvey, Montreal Canadiens
1963   Pierre Pilote, Chicago
1964   Pierre Pilote, Chicago
1965   Pierre Pilote, Chicago
1966   Jacques Laperriere, Montreal Canadiens
1967   Harry Howell, New York Rangers
1968   Bobby Orr, Boston
1969   Bobby Orr, Boston
1970   Bobby Orr, Boston
1971   Bobby Orr, Boston
1972   Bobby Orr, Boston
1973   Bobby Orr, Boston
1974   Bobby Orr, Boston
1975   Bobby Orr, Boston
1976   Denis Potvin, New York Islanders

Conn Smythe Trophy
(Most Valuable Player in "entire play-offs")
1965   Jean Beliveau, Montreal Canadiens
1966   Roger Crozier, Detroit
1967   Dave Keon, Toronto
1968   Glenn Hall, St. Louis
1969   Serge Savard, Montreal Canadiens
1970   Bobby Orr, Boston
1971   Ken Dryden, Montreal Canadiens
1972   Bobby Orr, Boston
1973   Yvan Cournoyer, Montreal Canadiens
1974   Bernie Parent, Philadelphia
1975   Bernie Parent, Philadelphia
1976   Reggie Leach, Philadelphia

Bill Masterton Trophy
(NHL player "who best exemplifies the qualities of perseverance, sportsmanship, and dedication to hockey")
1968 Claude Provost, Montreal Canadiens
1969 Ted Hampson, Oakland
1970 Pit Martin, Chicago
1971 Jean Ratelle, New York Rangers
1972 Bobby Clarke, Philadelphia
1973 Lowell MacDonald, Pittsburgh
1974 Henri Richard, Montreal Canadiens
1975 Don Luce, Buffalo
1976 Rod Gilbert, New York Rangers

Lady Byng Trophy
(For sportsmanship)
1925 Frank Nighbor, Ottawa
1926 Frank Nighbor, Ottawa
1927 Billy Burch, New York Americans
1928 Frank Boucher, New York Rangers
1929 Frank Boucher, New York Rangers
1930 Frank Boucher, New York Rangers
1931 Frank Boucher, New York Rangers
1932 Joe Primeau, Toronto
1933 Frank Boucher, New York Rangers
1934 Frank Boucher, New York Rangers
1935 Frank Boucher, New York Rangers
1936 "Doc" Romnes, Chicago
1937 Marty Barry, Detroit
1938 Gordon Drillon, Toronto
1939 Clint Smith, New York Rangers
1940 Bobby Bauer, Boston
1941 Bobby Bauer, Boston
1942 Syl Apps, Toronto
1943 Max Bentley, Chicago
1944 Clint Smith, Chicago
1945 Billy Mosienko, Chicago
1946 "Toe" Blake, Montreal Canadiens
1947 Bobby Bauer, Boston
1948 "Buddy" O'Connor, New York Rangers
1949 Bill Quackenbush, Detroit
1950 Edgar Laprade, New York Rangers
1951 Red Kelly, Detroit
1952 Sid Smith, Toronto
1953 Red Kelly, Detroit
1954 Red Kelly, Detroit
1955 Sid Smith, Toronto
1956 Earl Reibel, Detroit
1957 Andy Hebenton, New York Rangers
1958 Camille Henry, New York Rangers
1959 Alex Delvecchio, Detroit
1960 Don McKenney, Boston
1961 Red Kelly, Toronto
1962 Dave Keon, Toronto
1963 Dave Keon, Toronto
1964 Ken Wharram, Chicago
1965 Bobby Hull, Chicago
1966 Alex Delvecchio, Detroit
1967 Stan Mikita, Chicago
1968 Stan Mikita, Chicago
1969 Alex Delvecchio, Detroit
1970 Phil Goyette, St. Louis
1971 Johnny Bucyk, Boston
1972 Jean Ratelle, New York Rangers
1973 Gil Perreault, Buffalo
1974 Johnny Bucyk, Boston
1975 Marcel Dionne, Detroit
1976 Jean Ratelle, Boston

World Hockey Association

Play-off Champion
1973 New England Whalers
1974 Houston Aeros
1975 Houston Aeros
1976 Winnipeg Jets

Most Goals
1973 Danny Lawson, Philadelphia   61
1974 Mike Walton, Minnesota   57
1975 Bobby Hull, Winnipeg   77
1976 Marc Tardif, Quebec   71

Most Points
1973 André Lacroix, Philadelphia   50   72 124
1974 Mike Walton, Minnesota   57   60 117
1975 Andre Lacroix, Philadelphia   41 106 147
1976 Marc Tardif, Quebec   71   77 148

Most Valuable Player
1973 Bobby Hull, Winnipeg
1974 Gordie Howe, Houston
1975 Bobby Hull, Winnipeg
1976 Marc Tardif, Quebec

Rookie of the Year
1973 Terry Caffery, New England
1974 Mark Howe, Houston
1975 Anders Hedberg, Winnipeg
1976 Mark Napier, Toronto

Defenseman of the Year
1973 Jean-Claude Tremblay, Quebec
1974 Pat Stapleton, Chicago
1975 Jean-Claude Tremblay, Quebec
1976 Paul Shmyr, Cleveland

Outstanding Goalie
1973 Gerry Cheevers, Cleveland
1974 Don MacLeod, Houston
1975 Ron Grahame, Houston
1976 Michel Dion, Indianapolis

Paul Deneau Award (Sportsmanship)
1973 Ted Hampson, Minnesota
1974 Ralph Backstrom, Chicago
1975 Mike Rogers, Edmonton
1976 Vaclav Nedomansky, Toronto

Hockey Hall of Fame

(Opened in 1961, the Hockey Hall of Fame was financed by the National Hockey League and built on land provided by the City of Toronto, on the Canadian National Exhibition grounds.)

Players
Sidney Abel
John J. "Jack" Adams
Sylvanus "Syl" Apps
George Armstrong
Irving "Ace" Bailey
Donald H. "Dan" Bain
Hobart "Hobey" Baker
Martin J. Barry
Jean Beliveau
Clinton S. Benedict
Douglas W. Bentley
Maxwell H. L. Bentley
Hector "Toe" Blake
Richard R. Boon
Emile J. "Butch" Bouchard
Frank Boucher
Johnny Bower
Harry L. "Punch" Broadbent
Francis C. "Zero" Brimsek
Walter E. "Turk" Broda
William Bruch
Frank Buckland
Harold H. Cameron
Francis M. "King" Clancy

The amazing Gordie Howe retired in 1971, after 25 seasons with the Detroit Red Wings. Then, at the age of 45, he joined the Houston Aeros of the World Hockey Association, and was named that league's most valuable player in 1974; his son Mark was named rookie of the year. *(Houston Aeros.)*

Aubrey "Dit" Clapper
Sprague Cleghorn
Neil MacN. Colville
Charles W. Conacher
Alex Connell
William O. Cook
Art Coulter
William M. Cowley
Samuel R. "Rusty" Crawford
John P. "Jack" Darragh
Allan M. "Scotty" Davidson
Clarence H. "Hap" Day
Cyril Denneny
Gordon Drillon
Charles G. Drinkwater
Thomas Dunderdale
William R. Durnan
Mervyn A. "Red" Dutton
Cecil H. "Babe" Dye
Arthur F. Farrell
Frank Foyston
Frank Fredrickson
William A. Gadsby
Charles R. Gardiner
Herbert M. Gardiner
James H. Gardner
Bernard "Boom Boom" Geoffrion
Eddie Gerard
Dr. John L. Gibson
Hamilton "Billy" Gilmour
Frank X. "Moose" Goheen

Ebenezer R. Goodfellow
Michael Grant
Wilfred "Shorty" Green
Silas S. Griffis
George Hainsworth
Glenn Hall
Joseph H. Hall
Douglas Harvey
George Hay
William M. "Riley" Hern
Bryan H. Hextall
Harold "Hap" Holmes
Charles T. "Tom" Hooper
George R. "Red" Horner
Gordon Howe
Sydney H. Howe
John B. "Bouse" Hutton
Harry M. Hyland
James D. "Dick" Irvin
Harvey "Busher" Jackson
William M. Jennings
Ernest "Moose" Johnson
Ivan "Ching" Johnson
Thomas C. Johnson
Aurel Joliat
Gordon "Duke" Keats
Leonard P. "Red" Kelly
Theodore S. "Teeder" Kennedy
Elmer J. Lach
Edouard C. "Newsy" Lalonde
Jean B. "Jack" Laviolette
Hugh Lehman
Percy LeSueur
Robert B. T. "Ted" Lindsay
Duncan "Mickey" MacKay
Joseph Malone
Sylvio Mantha
John "Jack" Marshall
Fred G. "Steamer" Maxwell
Frank McGee
William G. McGimsie
George McNamara
Richard "Dickie" Moore
Patrick J. "Paddy" Moran
Howie Morenz
William Mosienko
Frank Nighbor
Edward R. "Reg" Noble
Harry Oliver
Lester Patrick
Tommy Phillips
Pierre Pilote
Didier "Pit" Pitre
Walter "Babe" Pratt
A. Joseph Primeau
Harvey Pulford
Bill Quackenbush
Frank Rankin
Kenneth J. Reardon
J. H. Maurice "Rocket" Richard
George T. Richardson
Dr. Gordon Roberts
Arthur H. Ross
Philip D. Ross
Blair Russell
Ernest Russell
J. D. "Jack" Ruttan
Fred Scanlan
Milton C. Schmidt
David "Sweeney" Schriner
Earl W. Seibert
Oliver L. Seibert

Edward W. Shore
Albert C. "Babe" Siebert
Harold "Bullet Joe" Simpson
Alfred E. Smith
Reginald "Hooley" Smith
Russell "Barney" Stanley
John S. "Black Jack" Steward
Nelson Stewart
Bruce Stuart
Hod Stuart
Frederick "Cyclone" Taylor
Cecil R. "Tiny" Thompson
Col. Harry J. Trihey
Georges Vezina
John P. "Jack" Walker
Martin Walsh
Harry E. Watson
Ralph "Cooney" Weiland
Harry Westwick
Fred Whitcroft
Gordon Wilson
William W. Wirtz
Roy Worters

Referees
William L. Chadwick
Chaucer Elliott
Robert Hewitson
Fred "Mickey" Ion
Michael J. Rodden
J. Cooper Smeaton
Roy "Red" Storey
Carl Voss

Builders
Charles Adams
Weston W. Adams
Frank Ahearn
Sir Montague Allan
George Brown
Walter Brown
Frank Calder
Angus D. Campbell
Clarence S. Campbell
Joseph V. "Leo" Dandurand
Francis P. Dilio
George S. Dudley
James A. Dunn
Thomas P. Gorman
Charles Hay
James C. Hendy
Foster Hewitt
William A. Hewitt
Fred J. Hume
Thomas Ivan
John Reed Kilpatrick
George A. Leader
Robert LeBel
Thomas F. Lockhart
Paul Loicq
Maj. Frederic McLaughlin
Francis Nelson
Bruce A. Norris
James Norris, Sr.
James D. Norris
William M. Northey
John A. O'Brien
Frank Patrick
Allan W. Pickard
Sen. Donat Raymond
John R. Robertson
Claude C. Robinson
Frank J. Selke

Frank D. Smith
Conn Smythe
Lord Stanley of Preston
Capt. James T. Sutherland
Lloyd Turner
Fred C. Waghorne
Arthur M. Wirtz

U.S. Hockey Hall of Fame

(Located at Eveleth, Minnesota, which has produced many outstanding hockey players, the U.S. Hockey Hall of Fame was dedicated in 1973 and 25 charter members were enshrined. The second enshrinement ceremony was held in 1974. An asterisk indicates the person is also in the Hockey Hall of Fame in Toronto.)

Players

Clarence "Taffy" Abel—Defenseman: New York Rangers, Chicago Black Hawks, 1926–1934.

*Hobart "Hobey" Baker—Forward: Princeton 1911–1914, St. Nicholas Club 1915–1917.

*Francis C. "Zero" Brimsek—Goaltender: Boston Bruins 1938–1943, Chicago Black Hawks 1945–1950.

Raymond C. Chaisson—Forward: Boston College, 1939–1940; scored 62 goals in 32 games as a junior and senior.

John P. Chase—Forward: Harvard 1924–1928, U.S. Olympic team 1932; coached at Harvard 1941–1950.

Carl S. "Cully" Dahlstrom—Forward: Chicago Black Hawks 1937–1945.

Victor DesJardins—Forward: Chicago Black Hawks 1930–1931, New York Rangers 1931–1932.

Doug Everett—Forward: Dartmouth 1922–1926, U.S. Olympic team 1932.

John B. Garrison—Forward-defenseman: Harvard 1928–1932, U.S. Olympic team 1932, 1936; U.S. world amateur champion team 1933.

*Francis F. X. "Moose" Goheen—Defenseman: St. Paul A.C. 1915, 1917–1932; U.S. Olympic team 1920.

Virgil Johnson—Defenseman: Chicago Black Hawks 1937–1938, 1943–1944.

Michael G. Karakas—Goaltender: Chicago Black Hawks 1935–1940, Montreal Canadiens 1940, 1944–1946.

Myles G. Lane—Defenseman: Dartmouth 1924–1928,

With the proliferation of indoor rinks, more and more American youngsters are playing hockey. This is action in a Massachusetts high school game. (*Hank Seaman,* New Bedford Standard-Times.)

New York Rangers 1928–1929, Boston Bruins 1929–1930, 1933–1934. Also a member of the National Football Foundation Hall of Fame.

Sam L. LoPresti—Goaltender: Chicago Black Hawks 1940–1942. Once made 80 saves in a game against the Boston Bruins.

John P. Mariucci—Defenseman: Chicago Black Hawks 1940–1942, 1945–1948. Coached at University of Minnesota 1953–1965.

William C. Moe—Defenseman: New York Rangers 1944–1945.

George Owen, Jr.—Defenseman: Boston Bruins 1928–1933.

Winthrop "Ding" Palmer—Forward: Yale 1928–1930, U.S. Olympic team 1932, U.S. world amateur champion team 1933.

Clifford "Fido" Purpur—Forward: St. Louis Eagles 1934–1935, Chicago Black Hawks 1942–1944, Detroit Red Wings 1944–1945. Coached University of North Dakota 1949–1956.

Elwyn "Doc" Romnes—Forward: Chicago Black Hawks 1931–1939, Toronto 1939, New York Americans 1940. Coached Michigan Tech 1940–1945, University of Minnesota 1947–1952.

Frank "Coddy" Winters—Forward-defenseman: Cleveland amateur teams 1908–1925.

Coaches

Malcolm K. Gordon—St. Paul's School, Concord, N. H., 1888–1917.

Victor Heyliger—Illinois 1938–1943; Michigan 1948–1956, Air Force Academy through 1974.

Edward J. Jeremiah—Dartmouth 1937–1943, 1945–1967.

John "Snooks" Kelly—Boston College 1933–1942, 1946–1974.

Clifford R. Thompson—Eveleth, Minn., High School 1920–1958; won 534, lost 26, tied 9; 11 alumni played in the National Hockey League.

Alfred "Ralph" Winsor—Harvard 1902–1917; coached 1932 Olympic team.

Administrators

George V. Brown—Managed Boston Athletic Association team 1910–1937, Boston Arena 1918–1937.

Walter A. Brown—Coached the only U.S. team to win the world amateur championship, 1933; operated Boston Garden and Boston Bruins 1933–1964.

J. L. "Doc" Gibson—Captained first U.S. professional team, the Portage, Michigan, Lakers; was instrumental in organizing the first pro league.

Thomas F. Lockhart—Founder, Amateur Hockey Association of the United States, 1937; president 1937–1972.

William Thayer Tutt—As president of the Broadmoor Hotel in Colorado Springs, sponsored the first NCAA Hockey tournament in 1948, and sponsorship continued through 1957; member, International Ice Hockey Federation 1959–1973.

Lyle Z. Wright—Minneapolis Arena 1924–1963.

Referee

William L. Chadwick—Linesman-referee: National Hockey League, 1939–1955; developed most modern hand signals.

Bibliography. Beddoes, Richard, Stan Fischler, and Ira Gitler: *Hockey!*, Macmillan, New York, 1971; Farrington, S. Kip, Jr.: *Skates, Sticks and Men*, David McKay, New York, 1972; Roxborough, Henry: *The Stanley Cup Story*, 3rd ed., Follett, Chicago, 1968.

HOP, STEP, AND JUMP—A field event, now formally known as the triple jump, although the older name is more descriptive.

See also TRACK AND FIELD.

HORSE RACING—Any form of racing is almost as old as the vehicle involved. We can therefore assume, even without any definite evidence, that horse racing dates almost to the time when man first rode on a horse. Or, rather, to the time when two men had horses to ride.

It is believed that the horse was first domesticated in Greece nearly 4,000 years ago. By the Olympic Games of 664 B.C., the horse was involved in competitive racing, pulling a chariot. In the Olympics of 624 B.C., horses were raced under saddle.

The modern form of the sport, however, can be traced to England in 1377. And it was England that developed the Thoroughbred, the horse bred for racing, not for work. Modern Thoroughbreds are all descended from three stallions, of Arabian, Turkish, or Syrian descent: Byerly's Turk, which was put into stud in Ireland in 1689; Darley's Arabian, brought to England in 1704; and Godolphin's Arabian or Barb (for Barbary), which arrived in England in 1724.

Racing for prizes began in England in 1512, but its first real acceptance came in 1702, when Queen Anne herself gave royal sanction to the sport. In 1703 she originated the custom of donating a valuable silver plate to the winner of a major race at Doncaster and in 1714 she "invented" the sweepstakes, by requiring owners to pay a 10-guinea entry fee, with the winner to collect all of the money.

By 1751 there was so much racing in England that the *Racing Calendar* began publishing, and the Jockey Club was organized in 1752 to supervise the sport. In 1791 the club began publication of the *Stud Book* for the registration of Thoroughbreds.

Racing in America

Both New York and Virginia have been credited with originating horse racing in the Colonies. New York seems to win, in terms of time. In 1665, Richard Nicolls, the royal governor of New York, announced plans to begin a series of races at what is now Hempstead, Long Island, near where Belmont Park and Aqueduct are located. It is definitely known that a race was held there in 1668, and that Nicolls' successor, Frank Lovelace, held at least one race in 1669.

The first known race in Virginia was held in 1674. But there were five race tracks in Virginia by 1680, and Virginia and Maryland were the early centers of horse breeding in the Colonies. The first Thoroughbred sire of record to arrive here was Bulle Rock, imported from England to Virginia about 1730.

Although racing spread into other parts of the country, tracks, as we think of them, did not. Many of the early settlers of Kentucky were from Virginia, and they brought horses with them. Informal races were held on town streets in many places, including Lexington, Kentucky. To put an end to the practice, a race track was built just outside Lexington in 1797. Even at the tracks, most races of the late eighteenth and early nineteenth centuries were rather informal affairs, often match races brought about by challenges from one horse owner to another.

One of the most celebrated of the match races was held in 1823, as a result of a challenge from the South to the North. A horse called American Eclipse was hailed in New York as the fastest in the United States. The challenge came from William R. Johnson of Virginia, who declared that he headed a syndicate of Southern horsemen who planned to pick a Southern champion. The race, three heats of 4 mi each, took place at Union Race Course on Long Island, for a side bet of $10,000. The Southern horse was Sir Henry. The race, it is said, drew 60,000 spectators. The Southerners knew Sir Henry couldn't beat American Eclipse. Not in a three-heat race, anyway. They bet most of their money on Sir Henry to win the first heat, and they got odds from eager takers. Sir Henry did win the first heat, because he went all-out, while American Eclipse's jockey wisely decided to conserve his horse's strength. American Eclipse easily won the next two heats, but the Southerners had won more than enough money on the first heat to pay off the side bet and still go home wealthy.

The Civil War. There were several other North-South challenge races between 1823 and 1845. A much more serious sectional confrontation, the Civil War, along with the Indian wars, helped promote the breeding of Thoroughbreds. Cavalrymen wanted the fastest possible horses, and most American horses of the mid-nineteenth century were crossbreeds of one sort or another. The Civil War alerted military leaders to the problem, and the steady importation of Thoroughbreds from England began during the war.

It was also during the Civil War that the first really major racing plant was established in the United States. John C. Morrissey, who had once claimed the world heavyweight championship, built a race track in Saratoga, New York, in 1864. He chose Saratoga because of the large number of wealthy people who visited the health resort during the summer. At his Saratoga track, Morrissey staged the first major series of stakes races. After the Civil War, horse racing—like many other sports—began to boom, and other entrepreneurs followed Morrissey's example. In 1870, Pimlico was opened in Baltimore, and a New Orleans Fair Grounds course opened in 1873.

By that time, Lexington was already in the center of the country's major Thoroughbred breeding area, as it is today. Churchill Downs opened in 1875 and inaugurated a race called the Kentucky Derby. (The Preakness Stakes had begun two years earlier at Pimlico.) Other major tracks sprang up in the 1880s. Jerome Park had opened in New York City in 1866, staging the first Belmont Stakes in 1867. When it was closed, it was replaced by Morris Park in 1889; the Belmont Stakes also moved.

Although there was a serious decline early in this century, when a nationwide reform movement stopped gambling, and with it major racing, in every state but Maryland and Kentucky for a period of time, Thoroughbred racing bounced back during the 1920s. The Depression hurt the sport, but again it came back strongly, after World War II.

There are now more than 100 race tracks in the United States, about 40 of them 1 mi or more in length. Between them, Thoroughbred and harness racing attract more than 70 million spectators annually, handle more than $6 million in parimutuel bets, and pay about $500 million in revenue to the states in which they operate.

The Horses

The Thoroughbred is a horse registered in the appropriate stud book of the horse's country. In the United States the American Stud Book is maintained by the Jockey Club. To be eligible for registration, a horse must be traceable, through horses already in the stud book, to one of the three foundation sires. Actually, however, all modern Thoroughbreds are traceable to three later stallions: Eclipse, foaled in 1764, the great-great-grandson of Darley's Arabian; Matchem, foaled in 1748, the grandson of Godolphin's Arabian; and Herod, a great-great-grandson of Byerly's Turk, foaled in 1758. About 80 percent of today's Thoroughbreds are traceable to Eclipse.

The Thoroughbred averages a little over 16 hands (64 in) in height and about 1,500 lb in weight. For racing purposes, a horse's birthday is the January 1 following the actual date of birth. Thus, a horse foaled late in the year usually cannot compete on the race tracks because, in early, formative years, the horse is too much younger than other horses of the same "age," which were actually foaled nearly a year earlier.

Nomenclature. Strictly speaking, a horse is a male Thoroughbred of five years or older. Until he is five, he is called a colt. The female is a filly until she is five, when she becomes a mare.

A stallion is a male horse at stud; his offspring are called his get, collectively. He is known as the sire of each of his get. (Strictly, he is not officially a sire until one of his get has won a race.)

A mare that has produced a foal is a broodmare; she is the dam. Her offspring are called her produce and, once one of them has won, she is called a producer. The female side of a pedigree is the family; the male side is the line.

Breeding. Although many scientific attempts at breeding have been made, it is nowhere near being an exact science. A mare may be valuable even if she's a poor racer, because of the blood lines she carries. A male, on the other hand, is not particularly valuable at stud unless he has proven he can run; if he has, his stud fees may approach the astronomical.

Generally the owner of the mare owns the foal. The owner of the stallion is paid a stud fee for his horse's service to the mare, and usually guarantees that a foal will be produced. In many cases, the same person or farm owns both the dam and the sire; a breeding farm is built up for the express purpose of mating stallions and mares in various combinations.

It is estimated that there are around 1,500 breeding farms in the United States. About 40 percent of all horses that are raced are bred within 20 mi of Lexington, Kentucky, where the famous bluegrass and the less famous limestone in soil and water (and also in the bluegrass) help to build strong Thoroughbreds.

Great Racers. There are 68 horses in the Racing Hall of Fame; they are listed at the end of this entry. Among those that have achieved superstardom by gaining fame among the general public are Man o' War, Gallant Fox, Seabiscuit, Citation, and Secretariat.

Man o' War is a true sports legend. One of the bits of

The immortal Man o' War, raced only as a two- and three-year-old, won 20 of 21 starts. His only defeat was by the appropriately named Upset at Saratoga in 1919. *(Courtesy of National Museum of Racing.)*

trivia about him is that he never won the "Triple Crown"—as a matter of fact, he didn't even run in the Kentucky Derby, but he did win the other two Triple Crown races, the Preakness and the Belmont Stakes, in 1920. Raced only as a two- and three-year-old, Man o' War raced 21 times and won 20. His only loss was to a horse appropriately named Upset, in the Sanford Memorial Stakes in 1919. He won just under a quarter-million dollars—a pheonomenal figure for the period. When he won the Belmont, he collected just $7,950; that race today is worth more than $100,000 to the winner.

Gallant Fox was the second horse to win the Triple Crown, in 1930 (the first was Sir Barton, in 1919). He won a total of $328,165, which was, for a time, the career record.

Seabiscuit was an unusual horse. Rarely raced as a three-year-old, he was horse of the year in 1938, aged five, and handicap horse of the year in 1937 and 1938. He raced through his seventh year, 1940, and retired as the leading money-winner of all time, with $437,730—most of it won carrying heavy weights in handicap events.

Citation won the Triple Crown in 1948—the last horse to do it until Secretariat came along. He raced through his sixth year, winning 32 of 45 starts—19 of 20 as a three-year-old—and finishing out of the money only once. He was the first horse to win more than $1 million.

Secretariat had a truly sensational year in 1973, as a three-year-old, before being retired to stud. He not only became the first horse in a quarter-century to win the Triple Crown, he set records in two of the three events and might have had a record in the third, but for faulty timing procedures. He won the third race in the crown, the Belmont, by an astonishing 31 lengths.

The People

There are basically four persons connected with every racing horse: the breeder, owner, trainer, and jockey. The breeder may sometimes be the owner, and on rare occa-

sions an owner may be the trainer; but, as in other sports, specialization has become the rule.

The trainer is perhaps most important in developing a winning race horse. The breeder tries to produce winners, but fails more often than not. The owner, or would-be owner, tries to judge yearlings by blood and older horses by workouts. But the trainer, by setting up the right training regimen and picking races properly, can make a money winner out of a rather ordinary Thoroughbred.

Today the breeder and owner is likely to be a farm or stable, even though there may be primarily one person behind it. A large stable usually has a private trainer with general responsibility for all the horses. He works for an annual salary plus a percentage of purses won. An owner who has just a few horses may hire a "public" trainer, who handles horses for several different owners, working on a per-day rate of $15–$20 and a percentage of winnings. The rate doesn't include special expenses.

Training. The trainer's first job is seeing that his horse is physically fit. That involves proper feeding, shoeing, and watching for signs of injury or illness. At one time trainers virtually had to be veterinarians; today they call on veterinarians when needed, but a trainer still has to have personal knowledge and intuition of horses and their possible physical problems.

The second part of the job is to get the horse ready for a race, whatever the race is. The training should vary from horse to horse, if the trainer is a good one. There is a difficult kind of compromise to make: A horse needs just the right amount of work to be ready. Too much work and the horse will be worn out before the race ends. Not enough work and the animal won't be in top form. The exact nature of the compromise depends on the horse itself, the length of the race, the distance the horse will have to travel simply to get to the track, and the field the horse faces.

Jockeys. Many horseplayers bet on the jockey rather than the horse. It makes some sense. A good jockey, like a good trainer, needs to know something about horses. And, most trainers agree, if a jockey really likes a horse, the rider is likely to get a better performance out of the mount.

In an ordinary race the jockey is hired by the trainer or owner to ride the horse. The jockey is told what kind of horse it is and what kind of race should be run. A speed horse should probably be taken to the front and kept there, if possible, while a slow starter with a strong finish should be kept back and out of trouble until it's time to make a stretch run. With a top horse in a major race, the jockey has probably been aboard the animal many times before. The rider knows the horse and what it can do. Jockey and trainer will go over the field they face and decide where the trouble may lie. They will plan the basic strategy of the race.

But it's the jockey who must do the job. The jockey has to know horses in general and this horse in particular, and has to cope quickly with whatever situations arise. If instructed to hold the horse back, and it's a terribly slow pace, should the jockey get out front to set the right pace? If horses are bunched in front, should the rider take the horse outside and try to go around them, or wait for an opening?

There are those who think a jockey should not be called

an athlete. But a jockey has to make those split-second decisions; has to remain cool under pressure; and has to be able to ride a horse, high in the stirrups, and control the horse with either hand while using the riding crop with the other. Athletic skills are unquestionably required.

Races and Tracks

Everybody wants a good horse race. Track managements make money by running good races. A bettor likes to see the horse selected at least come close, if victory isn't possible. Owners and trainers want to enter their horses in races they have a chance to win. And jockeys get more money for winning.

The racing secretary's job is to make good races by setting conditions for each race. The secretary issues a condition book, which explains the conditions that must be met for a horse to be entered in a track's races during a period of 7 to 10 days. If the racing secretary discovers that a race isn't getting enough entries, the conditions can be changed.

Variations are almost limitless, but the major categories of races are explained in the paragraphs that follow.

Stakes. In a stakes, a corruption of "sweepstakes," the owner of each horse must put up some money. It might be nothing more than an entry fee, but in most cases it includes a nominating fee paid well in advance, an entry fee when the horse is actually entered, and a starting fee if the horse actually goes to the post. If an owner nominates a horse but doesn't enter it, the nominating fee still goes into the total purse.

In the original sweepstakes, the winner got all the money. Today there is always added money, which is divided among the winner and the next three finishers; sometimes horses that finish farther back also get a share. But most of the money goes to the winner, and that's why a stakes is a race for top-class horses. The owners have to be willing to put up a considerable amount of money to get their horses in the race, and they have to have a certain amount of confidence that they can win some money.

Handicaps. In a handicap race the racing secretary evaluates the horses and assigns each horse a weight which must be carried. (The difference between the jockey's weight and the assigned weight is made up by putting lead weights into the saddle.) Theoretically, if a racing secretary did this job perfectly, and horses ran true to form, a handicap race would end in a dead heat among all the entries. Some stakes races are also handicaps.

Allowance. An allowance race is similar to a handicap, but the weights are based on definite conditions, such as the amount of money or the number of races won by a horse during a certain period of time.

Claiming. The claiming race may have been the most important "invention" in horse racing. With a minimum amount of effort, it gets horses of approximately equal class into a race. The owner has to put a price on the horse entered; if the owner feels the horse is worth $10,000, the animal is entered in a $10,000 claiming race. Any owner who has started a horse during the same race meeting can claim a horse in such a race, paying for it in cash immediately after the race.

If the owner entered the same horse in a $15,000 claiming race, the horse would probably not be claimed for that price, but it would almost certainly not win, running against a better field. If the owner entered the horse in a $5,000 claiming race, the horse would probably win, but would almost certainly be claimed.

In some claiming races, there is a range of $1,000 or $2,000 in the claiming price, and horses entered at the lower prices are given a weight allowance.

Maiden. A maiden race is for horses that have never won.

Futurity. Most of the futurities are fairly important races. They are for two-year-olds which must be entered as foals, two years in advance. An owner who enters a horse in a futurity has high expectations, because of the blood lines, that the horse will be a good one.

Produce. This is similar to a futurity, except that the horses are entered before they are even foaled. The owner enters the produce of a specific pair of parents.

Invitational. This is just what it sounds like: a race that specific horses are invited to enter, and no horse can enter without an invitation.

Races are measured in furlongs; one furlong is an eighth of a mile. Six furlongs is the most common racing distance; two-year-olds usually race at shorter distances than that, and there are a number of races at 1 mi or 1⅛ mi (9 furlongs). The Kentucky Derby is run at 1¼ mi, the Preakness at 1³⁄₁₆ and the Belmont at 1½ mi.

The Track. All racetracks are ovals, but there are many variations among them. Dirt racing is most common in the United States; the track is usually a combination of sand and loam, which drains well and is relatively easy on the horses. The condition of a track is important to bettors, since some horses run better on wet or muddy surfaces than others.

The standard words used to describe track conditions don't always mean quite what they seem to, in terms of the effect on horses. A "fast" track is dry and even. Immediately after a heavy rain, it is "sloppy," meaning there are surface puddles, but the base is still firm, allowing speed. Then it becomes "muddy," as the water sinks in; this is the slowest type of track. After the water has sunk in farther and the top has begun to dry, it is "slow." As it dries out more, it becomes "good," which is not quite as good as "fast."

At most large tracks, there is a course for turf or steeplechase racing on the grass infield inside the dirt track. Neither type of race is common in the United States, but in England almost all races are run on turf, and major steeplechases are much more popular than they are in this country.

Major Races. The American "Triple Crown" consists of three races: the Kentucky Derby, at Churchill Downs in Louisville; the Preakness Stakes, at Pimlico in Baltimore; and the Belmont Stakes, now run at Belmont Park in Belmont, New York. All three are stakes races for three-year-olds, and all three offer a winner's purse of more than $100,000. (In 1974 the winner's purse for the Kentucky Derby was $274,000.)

Just as important to the prestige of the races is their long tradition—the youngest, the Kentucky Derby, dates from 1875—and the tradition of the tracks. Churchill Downs in particular is a tradition-laden track in the country's greatest horse-breeding area. Pimlico is operated by the Maryland Jockey Club, the oldest organization of its kind in the country. Belmont, though not as old as the other two, carries on a long tradition of New York racing, as the direct successor of Jerome and Morris parks. The Belmont is the oldest of the Triple Crown races, having first been run at Jerome Park in 1867.

Winners of these three races are listed in the tabular material of this entry.

Parimutuel Betting

While there are people who simply love horses and racing, there is no question that the sport owes much of its popularity to parimutuel betting. Although it originated in France in 1865, parimutuel betting wasn't really successful in the United States until early in the twentieth century. Bookmaking originated in England, and English bookmakers arrived in the United States in the 1870s, operating right at the tracks. By shopping around, a bettor could often find the odds sought, since the bookmakers competed with one another.

Churchill Downs tried parimutuel machines, side by side with bookmaking, from 1878 until 1889, when the system was dropped because of complaints from the bookies. In 1908, Louisville outlawed bookmaking, and the parimutuel machines were revived. As other areas began to make bookmaking illegal, parimutuel betting was adopted at more and more tracks. By 1940, bookmaking was illegal virtually everywhere but parimutuel betting had been legalized in many states.

How It Works. In parimutuel betting, all bets on horses to win a given race go into a pool. A percentage is deducted for tax revenues to the state and operating revenue to the track, and the rest of the pool is then divided up among the winning bettors. It is also possible to bet on a horse to finish second or better—a "place" bet—or to finish third or better—a "show" bet. Each race has separate place and show pools. In addition, there are many kinds of combination bets available at some racetracks, each with its own pool.

See also GAMBLING.

Totalizators. The totalizator is an electric or electronic calculator that keeps constant track of the amount of money in each betting pool and the current odds, as information is fed into it from the cashiers who are selling tickets. When the starter presses the button that opens the starting gates, the totalizator is locked, the cashiers can no longer sell tickets on that race, and the final payoffs are computed.

Because the figures on the "tote board" change as new money comes in, a bettor may not get the odds expected. A horse might seem to be 3-to-1 when a wager is made, but if a great deal more money is bet on that horse before the start of the race, the odds may be driven much lower.

Organizations

The Jockey Club. The original Jockey Club was organized in London in 1752 as a small group of horsemen who drew up a set of rules to govern the sport. It still rules racing in Great Britain. The United States counterpart was incorporated in 1894. It adopted the rules of racing as laid down by the British group. State racing commissions have since taken over most rules-making functions within their states, but the Jockey Club is still an important body. The club maintains a registration bureau and the American Stud Book, and is also responsible for registering owners' distinctive colors.

The TRA. In 1942, management personnel from racetracks throughout the United States and Canada formed the Thoroughbred Racing Associations, which now has 54 members. In 1947 the group adopted a strict code of standards under which all member tracks operate.

The TRA acts as a trade association. One of its major functions is maintenance of the Thoroughbred Racing Protective Bureau (TRPB), established in 1945. The TRPB maintains its own investigative case files, fingerprints of persons involved with racing and of those considered undesirable, and lip-tattoo identification records of more than 150,000 Thoroughbreds. The lip-tattoo system was adopted to prevent the practice of substituting a "ringer" for a horse entered in a race.

Racing Commissions. Each state that has racing has its own racing commission, which is given basic responsibility for establishing and enforcing regulations governing racing in that state. (Actually, much of the enforcement responsibility is usually delegated to the individual tracks.)

Three stewards conduct the racing program—usually one appointed by the racing commission and two appointed by the track. They watch the race closely for fouling and other misconduct, and they must rule on any protests, assisted by patrol judges and movie patrol cameras. Saliva and urine samples from every winning horse are tested, and the stewards may arbitrarily select any other horse for sampling. (In some states the first three finishers in any stakes race are tested.)

See also STEEPLECHASE.

Glossary

also ran—A horse that finished worse than third "also ran" in racing summaries and is commonly known as an "also ran," as is a horse that consistently finishes out of the money.

back stretch—The straightaway farthest from the grandstand.

barrier—The starting gate.

blanket finish—When several horses finish in a close group—close enough to be covered by a blanket.

blow out—A fast, short workout, usually a day or two before a race.

breakage—An extra amount of money that goes to the state and the track; in most states, the payoff on a $2 bet is calculated to the lowest multiple of 10 cents, and the extra pennies are the breakage.

breeze—A short workout at less than top speeds.

bug boy—An apprentice jockey, so called because an asterisk ("bug") appears next to the jockey's name in the program, indicating that the rider in question gets a special weight allowance, usually 5 lb.

chalk—The favorite.

chute—A straight extension of a stretch from which horses start in races of certain distances to eliminate a turn.

clubhouse turn—The first turn past the grandstand.

colors—Each owner has distinctive colors, which must be worn by the jockey riding the owner's horse.

coupled—When two or more horses with the same owner or trainer run in the same race, they are coupled as an entry. A bet on one is a bet on all horses in the entry.

dead heat—A tie at the finish.

dwelt—A notation in racing summaries meaning that a horse was slow getting out of the starting gate.

eighth pole—A pole ⅛ mi from the finish.

entry—*See* "coupled."

extended—Said of a horse running at top speed under pressure from the jockey.

field—The group of starters in a race.

field horse—When there are many entries in a race, a group of horses considered least likely to win may be grouped together as a betting unit. A bettor who "plays the field" wins if any of the horses wins.

fractional time—A clocking taken at a point before the race ends.

Garrison finish—A burst of speed that carries a horse to victory right at the finish line; named for Edward "Snapper" Garrison, an outstanding jockey around the turn of the century.

gelding—A castrated male horse.

hand—A unit of height, now standardized at 4 in.

handicapper—Someone who assigns the weights to be carried in a handicap race; by extension, someone who tries to pick winners by analyzing past performances.

handily—A horse running easily is said to be running handily; "won easily" is the equivalent of "won handily."

home stretch—The straightaway leading to the finish.

in the money—Among the first three finishers in a race.

irons—The stirrups.

juvenile—A two-year-old.

minus pool—When there is very heavy betting on one horse, there may not be enough to pay bettors the required minimum (usually $2.20 on a $2 bet) after money is deducted for the state and the track. This is a minus pool, and the track has to add money to the pool to pay winning bettors.

morning line—Estimated odds posted before betting begins.

odds-on—Odds of less than even money; a horse that pays less than $4 on a $2 bet is odds-on.

overweight—In every race, each horse is assigned a certain overall weight. If a jockey and the jockey's equipment weigh more than the assigned weight, the rider is overweight. Usually no more than 5 lb of overweight is allowed.

plater—A horse that runs in claiming races.

post—The starting point.

post position—The horse's position in the starting gate, numbered from the inside of the track outward. Post positions are chosen by lot.

post time—The time at which all horses must be at the post and ready to start.

purse—Technically, a race in which owners don't contribute money to the prize; usually, the total amount of money to be split among the top finishers.

route—A race of more than 1⅛ mi.

router—A horse that runs well at long distances.

scratch—To withdraw a horse from a race.

set down—Suspended; said of a jockey.

sex allowance—In most races, except handicaps, mares and fillies get a weight allowance, usually 3 or 5 lb.

short—Said of a horse that finishes badly after a good start.

silks—The jockey's jacket and cap; the colors.

sophomore—A three-year-old.

stayer—Same as "router."

stick—The jockey's whip.

stud—A stallion used for breeding.

tack—Saddle and other riding equipment.

under wraps—Under restraint from a jockey or rider; usually used to describe a workout.

walkover—A race in which only one horse is entered.

weight-for-age—A type of race in which horses carry weights assigned arbitrarily according to age.

Results of Triple Crown Races

Kentucky Derby

(3-yr-olds—Churchill Downs—1¼ mi)

1875	Aristides	Lewis (jockey)	2:37¾
1876	Vagrant	Swim	2:38¼
1877	Baden Baden	Walker	2:38
1878	Day Star	Carter	2:37¼
1879	Lord Murphy	Schauer	2:37
1880	Fonso	G. Lewis	2:37½
1881	Hindoo	James McLaughlin	2:40
1882	Apollo	Hurd	2:40¼
1883	Leonatus	W. Donohue	2:43
1884	Buchanan	Isaac Murphy	2:40¼
1885	Joe Cotton	Henderson	2:37¼
1886	Ben Ali	P. Duffy	2:36½
1887	Montrose	I. Lewis	2:39¼
1888	MacBeth II	Covington	2:38¼
1889	Spokane	Kiley	2:34½
1890	Riley	Isaac Murphy	2:45
1891	Kingman	Isaac Murphy	2:52½
1892	Arra	A. Clayton	2:41½
1893	Lookout	Kunze	2:39¼
1894	Chant	Goodale	2:41
1895	Halma	Perkins	2:37½
1896	Ben Brush	Simms	2:07¾
1897	Typhoon II	F. Garner	2:12½
1898	Plaudit	Simms	2:09
1899	Manuel	Taral	2:12
1900	Lieutenant Gibson	Boland	2:06¼
1901	His Eminence	Jimmy Winkfield	2:07¾
1902	Alan-a-Dale	Jimmy Winkfield	2:08¾
1903	Judge Himes	H. Booker	2:09
1904	Elwood	Prior	2:08½
1905	Agile	J. Martin	2:10¾
1906	Sir Huon	R. Troxler	2:08⅘
1907	Pink Star	Minder	2:12⅗
1908	Stone Street	A. Pickens	2:15⅕
1909	Wintergreen	V. Powers	2:08⅕
1910	Donau	Herbert	2:06⅖
1911	Meridian	G. Archibald	2:05
1912	Worth	Carroll Schilling	2:09⅖
1913	Donerail	Roscoe Goose	2:04⅘
1914	Old Rosebud	J. McCabe	2:03⅖
1915	Regret	Joseph Notter	2:05⅖
1916	George Smith	John Loftus	2:04
1917	Omar Khayyam	C. Borel	2:04⅗
1918	Exterminator	William Knapp	2:10⅘
1919	Sir Barton	John Loftus	2:09⅘
1920	Paul Jones	T. Rice	2:09
1921	Behave Yourself	C. Thompson	2:04⅕
1922	Morvich	Albert Johnson	2:04⅗
1923	Zev	Earl Sande	2:05⅖
1924	Black Gold	J. D. Mooney	2:05⅕
1925	Flying Ebony	Earl Sande	2:07⅗
1926	Bubbling Over	Albert Johnson	2:03⅘
1927	Whiskery	Linus McAtee	2:06
1928	Raleigh Count	Chick Lang	2:10⅖
1929	Clyde Van Dusen	Linus McAtee	2:10⅘
1930	Gallant Fox	Earl Sande	2:07⅗
1931	Twenty Grand	Charles Kurtsinger	2:01⅘
1932	Burgoo King	E. James	2:05⅕
1933	Brokers Tip	Donald Meade	2:06⅘
1934	Cavalcade	Mack Garner	2:04
1935	Omaha	W. Saunders	2:05

1936	Bold Venture	I. Hanford	2:03⅗
1937	War Admiral	Charles Kurtsinger	2:03⅕
1938	Lawrin	Eddie Arcaro	2:04⅘
1939	Johnstown	Jimmy Stout	2:03⅖
1940	Gallahadion	C. Bierman	2:05
1941	Whirlaway	Eddie Arcaro	2:01⅖
1942	Shut Out	W. D. Wright	2:04⅖
1943	Count Fleet	John Longden	2:04
1944	Pensive	Conn McCreary	2:04⅕
1945	Hoop, Jr.	Eddie Arcaro	2:07
1946	Assault	W. Mehrtens	2:06⅗
1947	Jet Pilot	Eric Guerin	2:06⅘
1948	Citation	Eddie Arcaro	2:05⅖
1949	Ponder	Steve Brooks	2:04⅕
1950	Middleground	W. Boland	2:01⅗
1951	County Turf	Conn McCreary	2:02⅗
1952	Hill Gail	Eddie Arcaro	2:01⅗
1953	Dark Star	H. Moreno	2:02
1954	Determine	R. York	2:03
1955	Swaps	Willie Shoemaker	2:01⅘
1956	Needles	D. Erb	2:03⅖
1957	Iron Liege	William Hartack	2:02⅕
1958	Tim Tam	I. Valenzuela	2:05
1959	Tomy Lee	Willie Shoemaker	2:02⅕
1960	Venetian Way	William Hartack	2:02⅖
1961	Carry Back	Johnny Sellers	2:04
1962	Decidedly	William Hartack	2:00⅖
1963	Chateaugay	Braulio Baeza	2:01⅘
1964	Northern Dancer	William Hartack	2:00
1965	Lucky Debonair	Willie Shoemaker	2:01⅕
1966	Kauai King	Don Brumfield	2:02
1967	Proud Clarion	Robert Ussery	2:00⅗
1968	*Dancer's Image	Robert Ussery	2:02⅕
1969	Majestic Prince	William Hartack	2:01⅘
1970	Dust Commander	Mike Manganello	2:03⅖
1971	Canonero II	Gustavo Avila	2:03⅕
1972	Riva Ridge	Ron Turcotte	2:01⅘
1973	Secretariat	Ron Turcotte	1:59⅖**
1974	Cannonade	Angel Cordero, Jr.	2:04
1975	Foolish Pleasure	Jacinto Vasquez	2:02
1976	Bold Forbes	Angel Cordero, Jr.	2:01⅗

*Though recorded as winner, Dancer's Image was disqualified; Forward Pass, ridden by I. Valenzuela, was second and was awarded first-place money. **Record for race.

Preakness Stakes

(3-yr-olds—Plimlico Race Course—1 3/16 mi since 1925)

1873	Survivor	G. Barbee (jockey)	2:43
1874	Culpepper	M. Donohue	2:56⅕
1875	Tom Ochiltree	L. Hughes	2:43½
1876	Shirley	G. Barbee	2:44¾
1877	Cloverbrook	C. Holloway	2:45½
1878	Duke of Magenta	C. Holloway	2:41¾
1879	Harold	L. Hughes	2:40½
1880	Grenada	L. Hughes	2:40½
1881	Saunterer	W. Costello	2:40½
1882	Vanguard	W. Costello	2:40½
1883	Jacobus	G. Barbee	2:42½
1884	Knight of Ellerslie	S. H. Fisher	2:39½
1885	Tecumseh	John McLaughlin	2:49
1886	The Bard	S. H. Fisher	2:45
1887	Dunbine	W. Donoghue	2:39½
1888	Refund	F. Littlefield	2:49
1889	Buddhist	H. Anderson	2:17½
1890–93	No race		
1894	Assignee	Fred Taral	1:49¼
1895	Belmar	Fred Taral	1:50½
1896	Margrave	Henry Griffin	1:51
1897	Paul Kauvar	Thorpe	1:51¼
1898	Sly Fox	W. Simms	1:49¾
1899	Half Time	R. Clawson	1:47
1900	Hindus	H. Spencer	1:48⅖
1901	The Parader	Landry	1:47⅕
1902	Old England	L. Jackson	1:45⅘
1903	Flocarline	W. Gannon	1:44⅘
1904	Bryn Mawr	Eugene Hildebrand	1:44⅕
1905	Cairngorm	W. Davis	1:45⅘
1906	Whimsical	Walter Miller	1:45
1907	Don Enrique	G. Mountain	1:45⅖
1908	Royal Tourist	E. Dugan	1:46⅖
1909	Effendi	W. Doyle	1:39⅘
1910	Layminster	R. Estep	1:40⅗
1911	Watervale	E. Dugan	1:51
1912	Colonel Halloway	Nash Turner	1:56⅗
1913	Buskin	J. Butwell	1:53⅖
1914	Holiday	A. Schuttinger	1:53⅘
1915	Rhine Maiden	D. Hoffman	1:58
1916	Damrosch	Linus McAtee	1:54⅘
1917	Kalitan	E. Haynes	1:54⅗
1918*	War Cloud	John Loftus	1:53⅗
	Jack Hare Jr.	C. Peak	1:53⅖
1919	Sir Barton	John Loftus	1:53
1920	Man o' War	Clarence Kummer	1:51⅗
1921	Broomspun	Frank Coltiletti	1:54⅕
1922	Pillory	L. Morris	1:51⅗
1923	Vigil	B. Marinelli	1:53⅕
1924	Nellie Morse	J. Merimee	1:57⅕
1925	Coventry	Clarence Kummer	1:59
1926	Display	John Maiben	1:59⅘
1927	Bostonian	A. Abel	2:01⅗
1928	Victorian	Raymond Workman	2:00⅕
1929	Dr. Freeland	L. Schaefer	2:01⅗
1930	Gallant Fox	Earl Sande	2:00⅗
1931	Mate	G. Ellis	1:59
1932	Burgoo King	E. James	1:59⅘
1933	Head Play	Charles Kurtsinger	2:02
1934	High Quest	R. Jones	1:58⅕
1935	Omaha	W. Saunders	1:58⅖
1936	Bold Venture	George Woolf	1:59
1937	War Admiral	Charles Kurtsinger	1:58⅖
1938	Dauber	Maurice Peters	1:59⅘
1939	Challedon	G. Seabo	1:59⅘
1940	Bimelech	F. A. Smith	1:58⅗
1941	Whirlaway	Eddie Arcaro	1:58⅘
1942	Alsab	Basil James	1:57
1943	Count Fleet	John Longden	1:57⅖
1944	Pensive	Conn McCreary	1:59⅕
1945	Polynesian	W. D. Wright	1:58⅘
1946	Assault	W. Mehrtens	2:01⅖
1947	Faultless	Doug Dodson	1:59
1948	Citation	Eddie Arcaro	2:02⅗
1949	Capot	Ted Atkinson	1:56
1950	Hill Prince	Eddie Arcaro	1:59⅕
1951	Bold	Eddie Arcaro	1:56⅖
1952	Blue Man	Conn McCreary	1:57⅖
1953	Native Dancer	Eric Guerin	1:57⅘
1954	Hasty Road	Eddie Arcaro	1:57⅖
1955	Nashua	William Hartack	1:54⅗
1956	Fabius	Eddie Arcaro	1:58⅖
1957	Bold Ruler	I. Valenzuela	1:56⅕
1958	Tim Tam	John Adams	1:57⅕
1959	Royal Orbit	W. Harmatz	1:57
1960	Bally Ache	Robert Ussery	1:57⅗
1961	Carry Back	John Sellers	1:57⅗
1962	Greek Money	John Rotz	1:56⅕
1963	Candy Spots	Willie Shoemaker	1:56⅕
1964	Northern Dancer	William Hartack	1:56⅘
1965	Tom Rolfe	Ron Turcotte	1:56⅕
1966	Kauai King	Don Brumfield	1:55⅖
1967	Damascus	Willie Shoemaker	1:55⅗
1968	Forward Pass	I. Valenzuela	1:56⅘
1969	Majestic Prince	William Hartack	1:55⅗

1970	Personality	Eddie Belmonte	1:56⅕
1971	Canonero II	Gustavo Avila	1:54**
1972	Bee Bee Bee	E. Nelson	1:55⅖
1973	Secretariat	Ron Turcotte	1:54⅖
1974	Little Current	Miguel Rivera	1:54⅗
1975	Master Derby	Darrell McHargue	1:56
1976	Elocutionist	John Lively	1:55

*Raced in two divisions in 1918. **Record for race at 1 3/16 mi.

Belmont Stakes

(3-yr-olds—Belmont Park—1½ mi since 1926)

1867	Ruthless	J. Gilpatrick (jockey)	3:05
1868	General Duke	R. Swim	3:02
1869	Fenian	C. Miller	3:04¼
1870	Kingfisher	W. Dick	2:59½
1871	Harry Bassett	Walter Miller	2:56
1872	Joe Daniels	J. Rowe	2:58¼
1873	Springbok	J. Rowe	3:01¾
1874	Saxon	G. Barbee	2:39½
1875	Calvin	R. Swim	2:42¼
1876	Algerine	W. Donohue	2:40½
1877	Cloverbrook	C. Holloway	2:46
1878	Duke of Magenta	L. Hughes	2:43½
1879	Spendthrift	Evans	2:48¾
1880	Grenada	L. Hughes	2:47
1881	Saunterer	T. Costello	2:47
1882	Forester	James McLaughlin	2:43
1883	George Kinney	James McLaughlin	2:42½
1884	Panique	James McLaughlin	2:42
1885	Tyrant	P. Duffy	2:43
1886	Inspector B	James McLaughlin	2:41
1887	Hanover	James McLaughlin	2:43½
1888	Sir Dixon	James McLaughlin	2:40¼
1889	Eric	W. Hayward	2:47
1890	Burlington	S. Barnes	2:07¾
1891	Foxford	Edward Garrison	2:08¾
1892	Patron	W. Hayward	2:17
1893	Comanche	W. Simms	1:53¼
1894	Henry of Navarre	W. Simms	1:56½
1895	Belmar	Fred Taral	2:11½
1896	Hastings	Henry Griffin	2:24½
1897	Scottish Chieftain	J. Seherrer	2:23¼
1898	Bowling Brook	F. Littlefield	2:32
1899	Jean Beraud	R. Clawson	2:23
1900	Ildrim	Nash Turner	2:21½
1901	Commando	H. Spencer	2:21
1902	Masterman	J. Bullman	2:22½
1903	Africander	J. Bullman	2:23⅕
1904	Delhi	G. Odom	2:06⅗
1905	Tanya	Eugene Hildebrand	2:08
1906	Burgomaster	L. Lyne	2:20
1907	Peter Pan	G. Mountain	Not available
1908	Colin	Joseph Notter	Not available
1909	Joe Madden	E. Dugan	2:21⅗
1910	Sweep	J. Butwell	2:22
119–12	No race		
1913	Prince Eugene	R. Troxler	2:18
1914	Luke McLuke	M. Buxton	2:20
1915	The Finn	G. Byrne	2:18⅖
1916	Friar Rock	E. Haynes	2:22
1917	Hourless	J. Butwell	2:17⅘
1918	Johren	Frank Robinson	2:20⅖
1919	Sir Barton	John Loftus	2:17⅖
1920	Man o' War	Clarence Kummer	2:14⅕
1921	Grey Lag	Earl Sande	2:16⅘
1922	Pillory	C. H. Miller	2:18⅘
1923	Zev	Earl Sande	2:19
1924	Mad Play	Earl Sande	2:18⅘
1925	American Flag	Albert Johnson	2:16⅘

Citation won the Triple Crown—Kentucky Derby, Preakness Stakes, and Belmont Stakes—in 1948, and was the last horse to do it until Secretariat in 1973. *(Courtesy of National Museum of Racing.)*

1926	Crusader	Albert Johnson	2:32⅕
1927	Chance Shot	Earl Sande	2:32⅖
1928	Vito	Clarence Kummer	2:33⅕
1929	Blue Larkspur	Mack Garner	2:32⅘
1930	Gallant Fox	Earl Sande	2:31⅗
1931	Twenty Grand	Charles Kurtsinger	2:29⅗
1932	Faireno	T. Malley	2:32⅘
1933	Hurryoff	Mack Garner	2:32⅗
1934	Peace Chance	W. D. Wright	2:29⅕
1935	Omaha	W. Saunders	2:30⅗
1936	Granville	Jimmy Stout	2:30
1937	War Admiral	Charles Kurtsinger	2:28⅗
1938	Pasteurized	Jimmy Stout	2:29⅖
1939	Johnstown	Jimmy Stout	2:29⅗
1940	Bimelech	F. A. Smith	2:29⅗
1941	Whirlaway	Eddie Arcaro	2:31
1942	Shut Out	Eddie Arcaro	2:29⅕
1943	Count Fleet	John Longden	2:28⅕
1944	Bounding Home	G. L. Smith	2:32⅕
1945	Pavot	Eddie Arcaro	2:30⅕
1946	Assault	W. Mehrtens	2:30⅘
1947	Phalanx	R. Donoso	2:29⅖
1948	Citation	Eddie Arcaro	2:28⅕
1949	Capot	Ted Atkinson	2:30⅕
1950	Middleground	W. Boland	2: 28⅗
1951	Counterpoint	D. Gorman	2:29
1952	One Count	Eddie Arcaro	2:30⅕
1953	Native Dancer	Eric Guerin	2:28⅗
1954	High Gun	Eric Guerin	2:30⅘
1955	Nashua	Eddie Arcaro	2:29
1956	Needles	D. Erb	2:29⅘
1957	Gallant Man	Willie Shoemaker	2:26⅗
1958	Cavan	P. Anderson	2:30⅕
1959	Sword Dancer	Willie Shoemaker	2:28⅖
1960	Celtic Ash	William Hartack	2:29⅗
1961	Sherluck	Braulio Baeza	2:29⅕
1962	Jaipur	Willie Shoemaker	2:28⅘
1963	Chateaugay	Braulio Baeza	2:30⅕
1964	Quadrangle	Manuel Ycaza	2:28⅖
1965	Hail to All	John Sellers	2:28⅖
1966	Amberoid	W. Boland	2:29⅗

1967	Damascus	Willie Shoemaker	2:28⅘
1968	Stage Door Johnny	H. Gustines	2:27⅕
1969	Arts and Letters	Braulio Baeza	2:28⅘
1970	High Echelon	John Rotz	2:34
1971	Pass Catcher	Walter Blum	2:30⅖
1972	Riva Ridge	Ron Turcotte	2:28
1973	Secretariat	Ron Turcotte	2:24*
1974	Little Current	Miguel Rivera	2:29⅕
1975	Avatar	Bill Shoemaker	2:28²/₅
1976	Bold Forbes	Angel Cordero, Jr.	2:29

*Record for race at 1½-mi distance.

Top Money-Winning Horses

1910	Novelty	$ 72,630
1911	Worth	16,645
1912	Star Charter	14,655
1913	Old Rosebud	18,957
1914	Roamer	29,105
1915	Sorrow	20,195
1916	Campfire	49,735
1917	Sun Briar	59,505
1918	Eternal	56,137
1919	Sir Barton	88,250
1920	Man o' War	166,140
1921	Morvich	115,234
1922	Pillory	95,654
1923	Zev	272,008
1924	Master Charlie	95,525
1925	Pompey	121,630
1926	Crusader	166,033
1927	Anita Peabody	111,095
1928	High Strung	153,590
1929	Blue Larkspur	153,450
1930	Gallant Fox	308,275
1931	Top Flight	219,000
1932	Gusto	145,940
1933	Singing Wood	88,050
1934	Cavalcade	111,235
1935	Omaha	142,255
1936	Granville	110,295
1937	Seabiscuit	168,580
1938	Stagehand	189,710
1939	Challedon	174,535
1940	Bimelech	110,005
1941	Whirlaway	272,386
1942	Shut Out	238,972
1943	Count Fleet	174,055
1944	Pavot	179,040
1945	Busher	273,735
1946	Assault	424,195
1947	Armed	376,325
1948	Citation	709,470
1949	Ponder	321,825
1950	Noor	346,940
1951	Counterpoint	250,525
1952	Crafty Admiral	277,225
1953	Native Dancer	513,425
1954	Determine	327,700
1955	Nashua	752,550
1956	Needles	440,850
1957	Round Table	600,258
1958	Round Table	662,780
1959	Sword Dancer	537,004
1960	Bally Ache	455,045
1961	Carry Back	656,349
1962	Never Bend	402,969
1963	Candy Spots	604,481
1964	Gun Bow	58,100
1965	Buckpasser	568,096
1966	Buckpasser	669,078
1967	Damascus	817,941

1968	Forward Pass	546,674
1969	Arts and Letters	555,604
1970	Personality	444,049
1971	Riva Ridge	503,263
1972	Droll Role	471,633
1973	Secretariat	860,404
1974	Chris Evert	551,063
1975	Foolish Pleasure	716,278
1976	Forego	491,701

Horse of the Year

1936	Granville
1937	War Admiral
1938	Seabiscuit
1939	Challedon
1940	Challedon
1941	Whirlaway
1942	Whirlaway
1943	Count Fleet
1944	Twilight Tear
1945	Busher
1946	Assault
1947	Armed
1948	Citation
1949	Capot
1950	Hill Prince
1951	Counterpoint
1952	One Count
1953	Tom Fool
1954	Native Dancer
1955	Nashua
1956	Swaps
1957	Bold Ruler
1958	Round Table
1959	Sword Dancer
1960	Kelso
1961	Kelso
1962	Kelso
1963	Kelso
1964	Kelso
1965	Roman Brother
1966	Buckpasser
1967	Damascus
1968	Dr. Fager
1969	Arts and Letters
1970	Fort Marcy
1971	Ack Ack
1972	Secretariat
1973	Secretariat
1974	Forego
1975	Forego
1976	Forego

Leading Trainers

(In Winners Saddled)

1907	James Rowe	70
1908	Andrew J. Joyner	71
1909	H. Guy Bedwell	122
1910	F. Ernest	105
1911	W. B. Carson	72
1912	H. Guy Bedwell	84
1913	H. Guy Bedwell	87
1914	H. Guy Bedwell	84
1915	H. Guy Bedwell	97
1916	H. Guy Bedwell	123
1917	H. Guy Bedwell	66
1918	K. Spence	58
1919	K. Spence	96
1920	K. Spence	74
	S. A. Clopton	74
1921	Samuel C. Hildreth	85

1922	Henry McDaniel	78
	J. A. Parsons	78
1923	C. B. Irwin	147
1924	J. A. Parsons	93
1925	J. J. Duggan	70
1926	W. Perkins	82
1927	Samuel C. Hildreth	72
1928	J. F. Schorr	65
	J. Reed	65
1929	L. Gentry	74
1930	C. B. Irwin	92
1931	J. D. Mikel	72
1932	George Alexandra	76
1933	Hirsch Jacobs	116
1934	Hirsch Jacobs	127
1935	Hirsch Jacobs	114
1936	Hirsch Jacobs	177
1937	Hirsch Jacobs	134
1938	Hirsch Jacobs	109
1939	Hirsch Jacobs	106
1940	Dave Womeldorff	108
1941	Hirsch Jacobs	123
1942	Hirsch Jacobs	133
1943	Hirsch Jacobs	128
1944	Hirsch Jacobs	117
1945	Stanley Lipiec	127
1946	Willie Molter	122
1947	Willie Molter	155
1948	Willie Molter	184
1949	Willie Molter	129
	W. H. Bishop	129
1950	R. H. McDaniel	156
1951	R. H. McDaniel	164
1952	R. H. McDaniel	168
1953	R. H. McDaniel	211
1954	R. H. McDaniel	206
1955	F. H. Merrill, Jr.	154
1956	V. R. Wright	177
1957	V. R. Wright	192
1958	F. H. Merrill, Jr.	171
1959	V. R. Wright	172
1960	F. H. Merrill, Jr.	143
1961	V. R. Wright	178
1962	W. H. Bishop	162
1963	Howard Jacobson	140
1964	Howard Jacobson	169
1965	Howard Jacobson	200
1966	Louis Cavalaris, Jr.	175
1967	Everett Hammond	200
1968	Jack Van Berg	256
1969	Jack Van Berg	239
1970	Jack Van Berg	282
1971	Dale Baird	245
1972	Jack Van Berg	286
1973	Dale Baird	305
1974	Jack Van Berg	329
1975	Dick Dutrow	352
1976	Jack Von Berg	494

Leading Jockeys

(In Winning Mounts)

1900	C. Mitchell	195
1901	Winnie O'Connor	253
1902	J. Ranch	276
1903	G. C. Fuller	229
1904	Eugene Hildebrand	297
1905	Dave Nicol	221
1906	Walter Miller	388
1907	Walter Miller	334
1908	V. Powers	324
1909	V. Powers	173
1910	G. Garner	200
1911	T. Koerner	162
1912	P. Hill	168
1913	M. Buxton	146
1914	John McTaggart	157
1915	Mack Garner	151
1916	Frank Robinson	178
1917	Willie Crump	151
1918	Frank Robinson	185
1919	C. Robinson	190
1920	James Butwell	152
1921	Chick Lang	135
1922	Mark Fator	188
1923	Ivan Parke	174
1924	Ivan Parke	205
1925	A. Mortensen	187
1926	R. Jones	190
1927	L. Hardy	207
1928	J. Inzelone	150
1929	M. Knight	149
1930	H. R. Riley	177
1931	H. Roble	173
1932	John Gilbert	212
1933	Jackie Westrope	301
1934	Maurice Peters	227
1935	C. Stevenson	206
1936	Basil James	245
1937	John Adams	260
1938	John Longdon	236
1939	Donald Meade	255
1940	Earl Dew	287
1941	Donald Meade	210
1942	John Adams	245
1943	John Adams	228
1944	Theodore Atkinson	287
1945	Job D. Jessop	299
1946	Theodore Atkinson	233
1947	John Longden	316
1948	John Longden	319
1949	Gordon Glisson	270
1950	Joe Culmone	388
	Willie Shoemaker	388
1951	Charles Burr	310
1952	Anthony DeSpirito	390
1953	Willie Shoemaker	485
1954	Willie Shoemaker	380
1955	William Hartack	417
1956	William Hartack	347
1957	William Hartack	341
1958	Willie Shoemaker	300
1959	Willie Shoemaker	347
1960	William Hartack	307
1961	Johnny Sellers	328
1962	R. Ferraro	352
1963	Walter Blum	360
1964	Walter Blum	324
1965	Jesse Davidson	319
1966	Avelino Gomez	318
1967	Jorge Velasquez	438
1968	Angel Cordero	345
1969	Larry Snyder	352
1970	Sandy Hawley	452
1971	Laffit Pincay, Jr.	380
1972	Sandy Hawley	367
1973	Sandy Hawley	515
1974	Chris McCarron	546
1975	Chris McCarron	468
1976	Sandy Hawley	413

Racing Hall of Fame

The National Museum of Racing was chartered in New York State in 1950. Since 1955 it has been located in its own building near Saratoga Racetrack; in that year, the Racing Hall of Fame was established as part of the museum, to honor outstanding horses, jockeys, and trainers.

Horses

American Eclipse	Imp
Armed	Jay Trump
Artful	Jolly Roger
Assault	Kelso
Battleship	Kingston
Beldame	Lexington
Ben Brush	Longfellow
Blue Larkspur	Luke Blackburn
Bold Ruler	Man o' War
Boston	Miss Woodford
Broomstick	Nashua
Buckpasser	Native Dancer
Busher	Neji
Bushranger	Old Rosebud
Cicada	Omaha
Citation	Panzareta
Colin	Peter Pan
Commando	Regret
Count Fleet	Round Table
Damascus	Roseben
Dark Mirage	Salvator
Discovery	Sarazen
Dr. Fager	Seabiscuit
Domino	Secretariat
Elkridge	Sir Archy
Equipoise	Sir Barton
Exterminator	Swaps
Fair Play	Sysonby
Gallant Fox	Tom Fool
Gallorette	Top Flight
Good and Plenty	Twenty Grand
Grey Lag	Twilight Tear
Hanover	War Admiral
Hindoo	Whirlaway

Jockeys

F. "Dooley" Adams	Rigan McKinney
John Adams	James McLaughlin
Edward Arcaro	Conn McCreary
Theodore Atkinson	Walter Miller
Carroll K. Bassett	Isaac Murphy
George H. Bostwick	Ralph Neves
Steve Brooks	Joseph Notter
Samuel Boulmetis	Winnie O'Connor
Frank Coltiletti	George Odom
Robert "Specs" Crawford	Frank O'Neill
Lavelle "Buddy" Ensor	Gil Patrick
Laverne Fator	Samuel Purdy
Andrew "Mack" Garner	John Reiff
Edward "Snapper" Garrison	Earl Sande
Henry Griffin	Carroll Schilling
Eric Guerin	William Shoemaker
William Hartack	Todhunter "Tod" Sloan
Albert Johnson	A. P. "Paddy" Smithwick
William "Willie" Knapp	Jimmy Stout
Clarence Kummer	Fred Taral
Charles Kurtsinger	Bayard Tuckerman
John Loftus	Nash Turner
John Longden	George Woolf
Danny Maher	Raymond Workman
Linus "Pony" McAtee	

Trainers

H. Guy Bedwell
Preston M. Burch
W. P. Burch
Fred Burlew

J. D. "Dolly" Byers
Frank Childs
William Duke
Louis Feustal
James "Sunny Jim" Fitzsimmons
John M. Gaver
Thomas J. Healey
Samuel C. Hildreth
Maximilian Hirsch
Thomas Hitchcock, Sr.
Hollie Hughes
John Hyland
Hirsch A. Jacobs
Ben A. Jones
Horace A. "Jimmy" Jones
Andrew Jackson Joyner
J. Howard Lewis
Henry McDaniel
William Molter, Jr.
Winbert "Bert" Mulholland
John Nerud
John Rogers
John W. Rogers
James Rowe, Sr.
D. Michael Smithwick
H. J. "Derby Dick" Thompson
M. H. "Jack" Van Berg
Robert W. Walden
Charles Whittingham

Bibliography. Hedges, David and Fred Mayer: *Horses and Courses*, Viking, New York, 1972; Palmer, Joe H.: *This Was Racing*, A. S. Barnes, New York, 1953; Thoroughbred Racing Associations: *Directory and Record Book*, Hyde Park, N.Y. (annual).

HORSESHOE PITCHING—Conquering Roman soldiers, imitating the Greek discus throwers, used to bend horseshoes shut and compete at throwing them for distance. Eventually they decided it was pointless to go through all the effort of bending the horseshoes shut and, at some point in history, accuracy in throwing at a stake was substituted for distance.

For centuries this sport was popular primarily among soldiers and the nobles of many countries—two classes who found it easy to obtain used horseshoes for tossing. Sometime in the fifteenth or sixteenth century, the English developed quoits, using specially made iron rings in a kind of adult version of ring-toss. Quoits was a very popular game in England for more than 300 yr; but, because it required special equipment, while horseshoes were fairly easy to obtain, horseshoe pitching remained the sport of the soldiers. British soldiers introduced it into the American Colonies, and during the Revolutionary War it was a popular pastime among soldiers on both sides.

During the nineteenth century in the United States, quoits was popular in the East, but horseshoe pitching reigned in the Midwest, where there were more horses. During this period either game was a friendly pastime, and there was no serious standardization of rules. That began to change, however, with the formation of the first United States horseshoe-pitching club in Meadville, Pennsylvania, in 1899. In 1909 a tournament was held in Bronson, Kansas, and for the first time rules were formalized. The distance between stakes was set at 38½ ft; stakes were only 2 in above the ground; a ringer counted 5 points, a leaner 3, and a near shoe 1 point. There were no specifications for the horseshoes used, however.

The Grand League of American Horseshoe Pitchers was organized in 1914. The first national rules provided for a stake 8 in high, and the maximum weight of the horseshoe was set at 35 oz. The organization became the National Horseshoe Pitchers of the United States in 1921, and the National Horseshoe Pitchers Association of America in 1925, when the height of the stake was increased to 12 in and the value of a ringer was reduced to 3 points.

The modern era of horseshoe pitching began in 1920, when George May of Akron, Ohio, decided to take a scientific approach in an attempt to get ringers. Previously a player simply tried to get close to the stake, and a ringer was something like a hole-in-one in golf. May discovered that, like an expert knife thrower, he could control the number of revolutions the horseshoe took en route to the stake, and he astounded competitors and spectators alike at the national tournament in 1920 by averaging more than one ringer in every two throws.

That changed the whole character of horseshoe pitching, which, it might be said, turned from a game into a sport with May's accomplishment. Although horseshoes is still an enjoyable, back-yard kind of game for thousands of people, the pitchers who compete in major tournaments are in a class by themselves.

In the meantime, quoits is still with us. The rubber quoit has replaced the metal quoit, for greater safety. This sport is particularly popular in eastern Pennsylvania and New Jersey.

Rules. The official horseshoe, now made especially for competition, has a maximum length of 7½ in and width of 7 in; the maximum weight is 2½ lb. Each tip of the shoe is rolled down to form a heel calk, and there is a similar toe calk on the bottom of the closed end. The calks must not extend more than ¾ in; the distance between the heel calks must not exceed 3½ in. The official court is 50 ft long and 10 ft wide. The stakes are 40 ft apart (30 ft for women) and of 1-in diameter and project 12 in above the ground. They also lean forward 3 in, away from the perpendicular, toward the pitcher. Each stake is set in a 6-ft-square area of potter's clay, which is 6 in deep; the stake projects through the clay an additional 7 in into the ground beneath. This area is surrounded by a wooden frame, 1 in high. On either side is an 18-in strip covered with wood or concrete.

Each pitcher has two shoes, and throws both shoes in succession. A ringer (3 points) is scored if the shoe encircles the stake so that both heel calks can be touched with a measuring stick, provided that the measuring stick does not touch the stake. If each player has a ringer, they nullify each other and no points are scored; if one player has two ringers while the opponent has only one, the first player gets 3 points. A player also gets 1 point for each shoe that is closer to the stake than either of the opponent's shoes. (In formal competition a shoe must be within 6 in of the stake to score.)

In singles competition, both players pitch from one end, score, and then pitch from the other end. In doubles, partners are at opposite stakes and they take turns pitching; thus, each player always pitches in the same direction and against the same opponent throughout a match. After a player has scored in an inning, that player pitches second in the next inning. (In doubles, the team that scores pitches second in the next inning.) After a scoreless

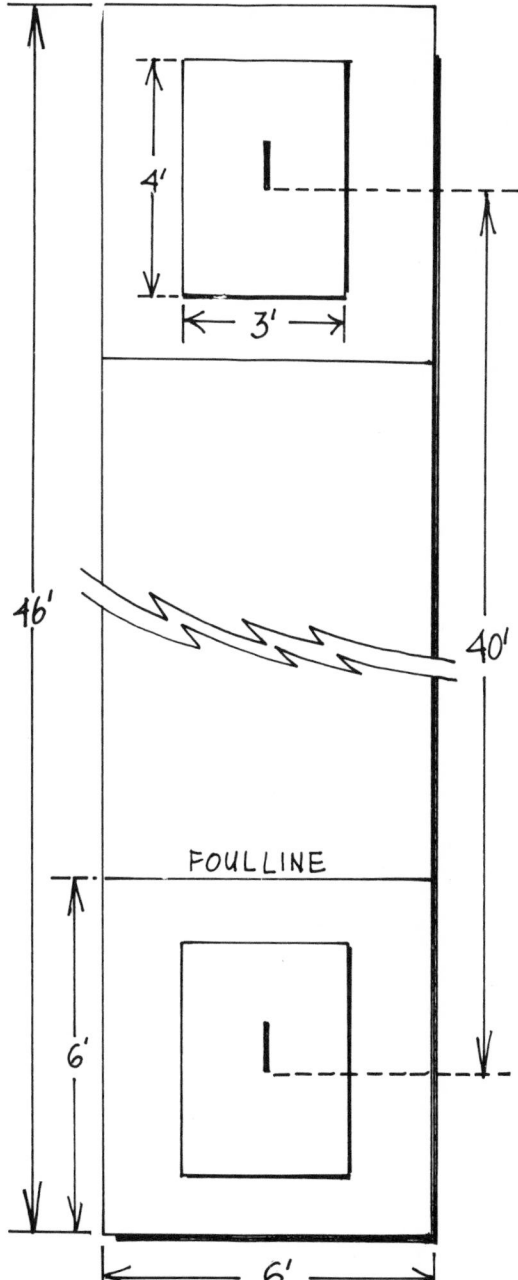

Men's court; women's court is 30' × 6'.

inning, the player (or team) who pitched last in that inning pitches first in the next inning.

In major matches, the first player to score 50 points wins the game. In less formal competition, 21 points is usually game. A match consists of 11 games in official tournaments, and of as many as 35 games in national or world championship tournaments.

HORSE SHOWS—The modern horse show is derived from two quite different kinds of exhibitions: demonstrations of *haute école*, which developed during the early seventeenth century, and horse fairs, in which, beginning in the Middle Ages, horses were exhibited by their owners to potential buyers.

The oldest show in the United States is believed to be the Upperville, Virginia, Horse and Colt Show, which originated in 1853 as an exhibit of colts sired by the stallion Scrivington. The country's major event is the National Horse Show, first held in 1883 in Gilmore's Gardens in New York City. Originally a rather simple event, this show has evolved into a 10-day demonstration of various kinds of skills by horses in 10 different divisions.

Many other shows are held across the country, but most of them are limited to just a few divisions. In general, hunter and jumper classes are most popular in the East; saddle, walking, and draft horses in the Midwest; and stock-horse classes in the West.

The governing body is the American Horse Shows Association (AHSA), founded in 1917.

Classifications

The 10 general divisions established by the AHSA are: hunter and jumper, saddle, light harness, heavy harness, polo, stock, walking, draft, military and police, and equitation. All horses are further separated into two major classifications, breeding and performance. Breeding horses are not ridden during a show; they are simply led into a ring by a handler and judged on general appearance, conformation, and way of moving. In performance classes, the horses display their skills while under saddle or harness, and may be judged solely on performance or on a combination of performance and conformation. In all divisions, if a horse shows any indication of unsoundness—made evident by difficulty in breathing—it is disqualified.

Hunters and Jumpers. There are two broad divisions, conformation and working, within the hunter division, and there are many classes and events. Conformation hunters are usually Thoroughbreds, judged 60 percent on conformation and 40 percent on performance. Working hunters are judged on performance alone. Hunters are further divided into four classes, based on size, and into another group of classes based on age and experience. An additional class is judged entirely on the appearance of its appointments, including the red coats of the riders.

Jumpers are judged entirely on performance, specifically on the ability to get over a series of obstacles meant to simulate the obstacles encountered in fox hunting. Form doesn't count; penalty points are deducted for various faults, including the slight touch of an obstacle.

A specialized class is military jumping, held under the rules of the Fédération Equestre Internationale (FIE). For further information on this class, *see* EQUESTRIAN SPORTS.

Saddle Horses. Most horses in this division belong to a special breed, the American Saddle Horse. There are two major subdivisions. Three-gaited horses must demonstrate the walk, trot, and canter. Five-gaited horses must also demonstrate the slow gait and the rack, a four-beat gait in which the feet hit the ground individually in a definite rhythmic pattern. There are also classes for saddle horses in harness.

Light Harness Horses. Most horses in this division are Standardbred, that is, the same breed that pace or trot in harness racing. They pull light carriages of the kind used for road journeys, and are called on to demonstrate a walk, a faster road gait, and speed at trotting or pacing.

Heavy Harness Horses. The usual breed is the English hackney, which pulls heavier carriages such as those used, in England, for park riding. Appointments, including the dress of footman and coachman, are carefully specified, and an overall impression of elegance is required.

Polo Ponies. Horses in this division are classified by weight-carrying ability. Lightweight horses carry up to 165 lb, middleweight up to 185 lb, and heavyweight more than 185 lbs. Ponies must perform a figure eight, execute a sudden stop at the end of a gallop, and show the ability to back up straight.

Stock Horses. These are essentially the work horses of the Western cowboy, separated into two classes by weight, under and over 1,100 lb. The horses have to demonstrate skills required in range riding, including work with a lasso.

Walking Horses. The original Tennessee walking horse was developed for carrying a rider, at a fast walk, over a Southern plantation during hot weather. Horses in shows must demonstrate a flat-footed walk, running walk, and slow canter.

Draft Horses. These are workhorses for the farm, divided into heavy and light divisions. The light draft horse ranges in height from 15 hands, 2 in, to 16 hands, 1 in, and in weight from 1,500 to 1,800 lb. The heavy draft horse ranges from 15 hands, 3 in, to 17 hands, and from 1,800 to 2,100 lb. They are shown individually in breeding classes and they perform in harness in two-, four-, and six-horse teams.

Military and Police. There are several different subdivisions and classes. The horses must show a variety of skills required in military or police work.

Equitation. In this division the rider is judged, rather than the horse, although the rider's training of the horse may also be a factor. In AHSA competition, in the saddle horse seat subdivision, there are 14 requirements for testing, listed in order of difficulty, from picking up the reins to trotting and cantering without stirrups. For younger contestants, there are fewer requirements.

Subdivisions are: Saddle horse seat, which may be astride or sidesaddle; jumping seat, which has eight requirements, including jumping with a strange horse supplied by the committee; and stock, or Western, saddle, in which the rider must show the horse performing range-riding maneuvers.

See also EQUESTRIAN SPORTS for types of international competition.

HUNTING—Once a necessity for many peoples, hunting is now primarily a sport, in advanced civilizations, and is necessary for survival only among a few primitive tribes. Hunting really began with the invention of weapons during the late stages of the Ice Age. Bones of large animals and drawings found in Paleolithic caves in France and Spain indicate that man was hunting animals with spears in late Paleolithic times, about 35,000 years ago. Hunting began to lose its importance for survival about 10,000 years ago, when men and women were learning how to farm and how to domesticate animals.

Like fishing, hunting is not basically a competitive sport and therefore will be treated rather briefly here.

There are several ways of classifying hunting: by weapon used (high-powered rifle, small-bore rifle, shotgun, handgun, bow and arrow); by the general or specific type of animal being hunted (big game, small game, varmint, upland game birds, waterfowl); or by the specific method of finding game (still hunting, in which the hunter hides and waits for the game, and stalking, in which the hunter actively seeks out the game).

Rifles and Cartridges. The hunter has available a wide variety of rifles and cartridges. (For detailed information, *see also* SHOOTING.) Exact choice of the gun and cartridge desired will depend on the hunter's personal preference, the type of game being sought, and the type of terrain in which the hunting takes place.

For bigger game, a heavier cartridge or greater muzzle velocity or both are desired, to ensure adequate killing power, since the worst sin a hunter can commit is to hit an animal without killing it. Woodland hunting also requires a cartridge with relatively high stopping power, since it may be difficult to place the bullet precisely where desired. The rifle should be suited to fast handling, fast sighting, and fast reloading. Slide, lever, or auto-loading actions are usually used.

In plains hunting, accuracy, flat trajectory, and power at high ranges are required. Speed is secondary, since the hunter will usually have a relatively long time in which to aim a weapon. A bolt-action rifle is often used. The mountain rifle should be similar to that used in the plains, but it must be lighter, since the hunter must carry it in the course of climbing.

Small-bore Rifles. The development of the relatively high-powered .22-caliber rifle using centerfire cartridges, together with the decline of big game in many areas, has brought a new form of hunting sport, varmint shooting with the small-bore rifles. Once a means of getting rid of undesirable small animals, varminting is now often practiced as a sport. The small-bore rifle is frequently equipped with a shooting scope, and some small animals may be shot from ranges of as great as 400 yd.

Handguns. A .22-caliber handgun may also be used for some kinds of varmint shooting. Real experts may use heavier handguns on larger game, including deer and occasionally elk or antelope. As with the bow, stalking is a major part of the job, since a handgun's range is limited.

Shotguns. The most common hunting use of the shotgun is for game birds, but such a weapon is also sometimes used for small game and for deer. In some areas, hunting deer with a rifle is forbidden because of the proximity of civilization, and a shotgun must be used.

Like rifles, shotguns are described by the type of action: slide or pump, bolt, single-shot, and auto-loading. The double shotgun, with side-by-side barrels, was long standard equipment, since it allows two quick shots and a choice of chokes. There is a trigger for each barrel. One disadvantage of the gun is that there is a different sighting point for each barrel. The over-under, with one barrel on top of the other, also offers choice of chokes, and there is but one sighting plane. Slide, bolt, and auto-loading shotguns were once the choice of many serious hunters, because they could carry up to five shells. Most now carry only three shells, because federal laws on waterfowl shooting call for that limitation.

The choke of a weapon is the constriction in the bore at the barrel, which forces the shot to go through a relatively small opening before beginning to scatter. Full choke, the narrowest, should put 70 percent of its pellets into a 30-in circle at a range of 40 yd. Improved-modified choke is 65 percent; modified, 60 percent; quarter choke, 50 percent; improved cylinder 45 percent; and cylinder, 35 percent.

There are six gauges of shotgun—the gauge is comparable to the caliber in a rifle. The gauges, and diameter in inches, are: 10 gauge, .775; 12 gauge, .730; 16 gauge, .670; 20 gauge, .615; 28 gauge, .550; and 410 bore, .410 in. The 12 and 20 gauges are most popular for hunting.

The type of load (amount of powder), size of shot, and type of choke all depend on the sort of game being hunted. For larger creatures to be shot at relatively short range, the load is heavy, the shot large, and the choke full. As the game gets smaller, faster moving, or more likely to be shot at a greater range, shot size decreases and the choke also decreases (that is, the constriction becomes larger).

Sights. The type of sight used will also vary with the type of game and kind of terrain. The open sight has a bead in front and a U- or V-shaped notch in back. This type is accurate at relatively short range. The peep sight also has a bead in front with a round aperture in back. It is more accurate at longer ranges.

The telescopic sight is most accurate of all, but it requires more time for aiming. One of its greatest virtues is that it can be used for spotting and identifying game, as well as for aiming the rifle. Different types of aiming points are available. The crosshair reticle is most commonly used; a post or dotted crosshair may be preferable in shooting at running game or at relatively close range.

Bow and Arrow. The hunting bow also varies somewhat with the type of game being sought, but not nearly as much as the rifle. The bow ranges in length from about 62 to about 66 in, the arrow from 27 to 29 in. The "weight" of the bow ranges from about 40 to about 50 lb for men, but is somewhat higher in bows used against large, dangerous species such as the grizzly bear. (The weight is the amount of force required to pull the string back to full draw.) Women usually use a bow of about 35 lb. A hunting bow generally has a contoured grip and a sight window. Some have telescopic sights.

In most states, a broadhead arrow must be used for big-game hunting. The broadhead ranges in width from 7/8 to 1 in, and should be about three times as long. It has two or three blades, and may be barbed. Cutting edges should be razor sharp.

Bow hunting is considered by many the most ethical form of the sport, since the hunter must get very close to the game, generally within 50 yd. It is, however, criticized by many humane and conservation groups, because an arrow causes death by bleeding, not by shock or sheer impact, and if an animal is not well hit it may suffer for a long time.

Tracking and Stalking. The hunter first needs to know something about an animal's habits and the type of terrain it likes. Such knowledge includes when and where the animal feeds, what types of trails it tends to follow, and what its breeding habits are. Armed with this knowledge, the hunter looks for spoor, including excreta and tracks. The hunter should be able to identify and, if necessary, to follow such trails—which means not merely following footprints, which may disappear, but telltale signs of passage such as bent grass, broken twigs, and clawmarks on trees.

Game is best spotted from above, not only because a high vantage point allows a greater range of vision, but also because most animals are less likely to look for enemies from above. The hunter may use a spotting scope or telescopic sight in the search for game.

Actual stalking of the game is more important to a bow hunter than to the rifle hunter. The latter is usually better off finding a trail and then traveling parallel to it; such a procedure will afford the hunter a better target than approaching the animal directly from the rear. The bow hunter must move very slowly, utilizing cover and moving into the wind so that the scent of the pursuer won't be carried toward the animal. The closer the hunter gets to the game, the more slowly must the hunter move—a fact that demands remarkable patience.

Trophies. Outstanding hunters often go in search of a record or a trophy. Records are periodically published in Rowland Ward's *World Records of Big Game.* In the United States, the Boone and Crockett Club recognizes trophy animals exceeding certain standards. Most hollow-horned species—mountain sheep, antelope, goats, and the like—are rated by the length of the outside curve of the horns from tip to base, by the widest spread, by the spread at the tip, and by the circumference of the base. Deer are also measured by the number of antler points; moose by the length and breadth of the antlers. Bears and feline animals are measured by length and width of the flat skin without stretching, and by the size and weight of the skull after cleaning.

The Pope and Young Club ranks the top trophies taken by bow and arrow.

Big Game. Types of big game most commonly hunted in North America are antelope, bears, caribou, deer, elk, moose, and mountain sheep and goats. The white-tailed deer is the most popular big-game animal. The mule deer is found in a rather limited area of mountainous terrain with heavy winter snows. The black-tailed deer is found in an even smaller range of country, from the middle of California to lower Alaska.

Most American elk are found in the Rocky Mountains. They're often stalked on horseback, and must usually be spotted with binoculars or scope sights at long range. The elk is a difficult animal to kill, since the range may be as much as 400 yd. There are three species of North American moose. They all like heavily wooded areas with a lot of water, cold weather, and large amounts of winter snow. Most moose hunting is done in Canada or Alaska; hunting the animal is illegal in most of the United States. In most cases, moose are hunted by well-outfitted parties led by professional guides.

The caribou is most often found above the timberline in mountainous, semibarren areas. Airplanes are usually used to get the hunter within range, and horses are then used for stalking. Getting within rifle range may be difficult, since the areas have relatively little cover. Shooting range is usually 200–400 yd.

The pronghorn antelope, one of the most prized of North American trophies, likes desert country with foothills or small mountains within easy range. It is most common in Wyoming, but is also found in other Western states. The animal has excellent vision and good hearing. It must usually be shot at a range of 300–400 yd; for its size, it is very difficult to kill.

There are four important North American bear species, the black, the brown, the grizzly, and the polar. Most of them are dangerous; the danger is compounded when such an animal is trapped or wounded. The black bear is found in a wide area of woodland throughout Canada, Alaska, and much of the United States. It is likely to be shot at relatively close range. The brown bear is found primarily in Alaska. Its dens are well up in coastal mountain areas but, during the summer, the animals move into valleys to catch salmon that are moving upstream. They're easily spotted and tracked, but they have a keen sense of smell, so the hunter must be careful to stay upwind. A powerful cartridge must be used, and it takes a very well placed shot to kill a brown bear or a grizzly.

The grizzly, so called because of silver-tipped hairs along the spine, is sparsely distributed over a wide area of remote country, including Wyoming, much of British Columbia, and Alaska. The animal likes high ground and searches for food over a wide area, as much as 20 mi in radius. It is the most ferocious of the bears. Polar bears are most commonly found on the ice pack of the Arctic Ocean, from Alaska east and north to Greenland. They can be reached by hunters only during February and March, when the ice cover has extended farther south. A commercial outfitter is needed, and hunters travel either by plane or by dogsled. Again, powerful rifle and cartridges must be used.

There are also four major species of wild sheep: the Dall, the Stone, the Rocky Mountain bighorn, and the desert bighorn. Most of them live in nearly inaccessible areas, well up in the mountains, even above the timberline (10,000 ft) in the Rockies. They have exceptional vision and are very difficult to stalk because they can cover terrain that is impassable for human beings. The shot may have to be made at very long range or at relatively short range; a fairly high-powered, but short-barreled, rifle with a sling should be carried.

Varmints. The word is a corruption of "vermin," and most varmints are considered pests in some areas, though they may not be pests in other areas. As mentioned, they are usually shot with a .22-caliber rifle, but handguns and shotguns are occasionally used. In bow hunting, a blunt arrow or a "flu-flu"—which has very large feathers, preventing it from traveling far—is usually used for small animals. Among animals classed as varmints are badgers, crows, foxes, ground squirrels, jackrabbits, magpies, porcupines, rabbits, skunks, wolverines, and woodchucks.

Bow and arrow are frequently used for ground squirrels and woodchucks. Handguns might be employed for almost any type of varmint. The shotgun is often used for hunting cottontail or snowshoe rabbits, foxes, crows, and magpies.

Hunting foxes is a rather special form of the sport. Dogs, either singly or in packs, are usually used. The most efficient method is to station hunters at several strategic areas and then turn dogs loose in an area where the foxes can be pretty well contained. The dogs will flush the foxes from cover and chase them into areas where the hunters, using shotguns, can get open shots.

Predators. Like varmints, predators were originally hunted because man judged them as undesirable—primarily because they may kill the big-game animals which he himself wants to hunt or because they prey on domesticated animals that are worth money, such as sheep.

Some predators have been hunted so heavily that they

are in danger of extinction. The red wolf is found only in North America. The gray wolf is also found in Northern Europe and Siberia; it has been driven out of the Continental United States into Alaska and Canada, where it often hunts moose and caribou.

The coyote rarely kills a large animal but scavenges those already dead. It does kill rodents and other small varmints. Like the fox, it is an exceptionally wily animal, difficult to stalk and kill, and hunting the coyote is considered good sport. The animal is often hunted with a shotgun from a snowplane or snowmobile; it may also be coursed with hounds. Sniping rifles are used in some areas to kill coyotes that live near farms.

Cats. Among the large North American cats are the cougar (also known as panther or mountain lion), the bobcat, and the lynx. Hunting cougar is also now a sport, rather than a means of getting rid of a predator. The animal often preys on deer and on domestic animals. A cougar hunts at night, on its own, and is usually tracked and treed by dogs before the hunter even sees it. Then the animal is dispatched with a rifle or handgun.

The bobcat and lynx usually feed on rodents but, when food is short in the winter, they may attack deer. They are similar animals, but the lynx averages about 40 lbs in weight and is now found only in Canada; the bobcat averages about 20 lbs and is much more widely distributed through North America. Bobcats also are often hunted by dogs, but they aren't often treed. When trapped, they'll try to fight off the dogs.

Waterfowl. The hunting of migratory waterfowl—ducks, geese, brant, and shore birds—is largely controlled by the federal government. The Duck Stamp Law of 1934 requires that every hunter over 16 must purchase a federal stamp in order to shoot migratory waterfowl. Money from the sale of stamps is used for conservation purposes.

There are many different species of duck, and they're found in many different areas. Among the major species are the green-winged teal, the blue-winged, or summer, teal, the bufflehead, the goldeneye, the ring-necked, the scaup, the ruddy duck, the wood duck, the mallard, the pintail, the canvasback, the merganser, and the redhead. Ducks are often shot from a blind, where the hunter can hide until the birds come into range. Decoys of many kinds are also often used to lure the ducks near. In some areas, stalking and jumpshooting may be effective, especially where the ducks may be found on small bodies of water. The hunter, either knowing or guessing where the birds may be, gets as close to them as possible without being seen, then startles them into the air and shoots at them.

Geese are larger than ducks—averaging about 8–10 lb—and more commonly feed on land than ducks. They're more difficult to approach, since they usually land in areas that give them good visibility in all directions. Blinds and decoys may also be used in hunting geese. Stalking and jumpshooting is much more difficult than with ducks, and geese usually have to be shot at longer range.

Brant are about midway in size between the goose and the duck, and they like offshore islands and eelgrass. Again, decoys and blinds are usually used.

The shore birds include the coots, the rails, the snipes, and the gallinules. They don't migrate nearly as far as ducks or geese, and they're rather small. They are usually stalked by hunters.

Ducks, geese, and brant are often hunted with a 12-gauge gun at full choke. For close-in duck shooting, over decoys, a 20-gauge may be used. A 10-gauge is sometimes used in hunting geese, where the range is likely to be greater. The 20-gauge is more commonly used for shore birds.

Upland Game Birds. There are many, many species of upland birds. In most cases the hunter either stalks birds with the help of a dog, or two hunters work together. Most of the birds feed in or near specific kinds of cover, and many species will freeze into immobility when approached, trusting to the cover to protect them. A dog will find and flush the birds, giving the hunter a shot. The hunter must know not only what kinds of cover to search, but how a bird acts when it is flushed, and how it flies. Among the species most commonly hunted are quail, pheasant, grouse, partridge, doves, and wild turkeys.

Quail live in groups of 15 to 30 and even more. They are usually hunted by several hunters working with a sizable group of dogs. Pointers and setters are most commonly used to locate the birds, and a hunter then goes in to flush the entire covey. For some species, however, flushing dogs must be used. The quail flies quite rapidly, and a 12-gauge gun with modified or improved-cylinder choke is most often used, frequently in double-barrel or over-under configurations.

The ring-necked pheasant was imported from China in 1881. It lives in the northern half of the United States, often in cultivated fields. It can be hunted with dogs, by a group of hunters, or by a single hunter. The pheasant is considered remarkably good sport because it is so unpredictable. In general, it rises very rapidly when it takes off, but a bird will often double back on its own flight path. A pheasant will often try to escape by running for long distances before taking off. The recommended gun is a 12-gauge, full-choked; a pump or automatic gun is best, but some hunters use the double-barrel.

There are several varieties of grouse; the most popular is the ruffed, which lives in thickets or underbrush, always near water. A dog usually isn't necessary, since the bird flushes rather easily. It almost always heads for timber immediately, so the hunter must get off a quick shot. The shotgun most often used for grouse is a 12-gauge with modified or improved-cylinder choke. A repeat-action gun isn't necessary, because a hunter will almost never get the opportunity to take more than two shots at the same bird.

The Hungarian partridge lives in rather open areas of prairie. Use of a dog is virtually necessary in hunting this bird successfully. The "Hun" will run from a dog; when flushed, it flies to an open field, alert and ready to run or fly again. Modified choke on a 12- or 20-gauge is best.

The Chukar partridge, recently imported from Asia, is similar in some respects; it lives in semiarid areas of the West. Again, dogs are almost a must; the bird tends to try to run away from danger before it will flush. A peculiarity is that one bird is often posted as a guard for a covey, and this bird will flush before the others. Experienced hunters will hold their fire until the rest of the birds take off. They don't fly in a straight line, which makes them difficult targets. The best gun is a 12-gauge repeater with modified choke.

The mourning dove has become a very popular game

bird in recent years; it is found all over the Continental United States, usually in small flocks near their food in fairly open country. In the evening the birds fly for water. A hunter has to locate a suitable area and then search. The hunter may often work alone; the birds flush rather easily, and can often be seen even before they flush. They fly rapidly and erratically.

The white-wing dove lives in arid areas and also travels to water daily. Since its habitat doesn't have many watering areas, a hunter will often get into a natural blind near water and wait for the birds to come along. The white-wing also is fast and erratic in flight.

Once almost extinct, the wild turkey is now found in a considerable area. It is a difficult bird to hunt; it has keen vision and keen hearing. Hunters may work from a blind and/or use an artificial call. Alone among the upland game birds, the wild turkey is sometimes hunted with a rifle.

See also SHOOTING; SKEET; TRAPSHOOTING.

Bibliography. Ormond, Clyde: *The Complete Book of Hunting,* 2d ed., Outdoor Life-Harper and Row, New York, 1972; Stringfellow, Robert (ed.): *The Standard Book of Hunting and Shooting,* Hawthorn, New York, 1950.

HURDLES—A type of race in which the competitors have to jump over barriers placed at regular intervals.

See also TRACK AND FIELD.

HURLING—This Irish sport is very similar to Gaelic football, except that the ball used has a circumference of about 10 in and weighs $3\frac{1}{2}$ to 4 oz, and the players use 3-ft-long sticks, somewhat like field-hockey sticks, to advance it. The player cannot pick up the ball with the hand. The field and the scoring rules are identical to those of Gaelic football. Hurling is played by some teams in the New York City area, and American teams have occasionally played games with visiting teams from Ireland.

See also GAELIC FOOTBALL.

ICAAAA (INTERCOLLEGIATE ASSOCIATION OF AMATEUR ATHLETES OF AMERICA)—Commonly known as the IC4A, this was the first major association to conduct collegiate athletic events in the United States. The IC4A was organized in 1876 to supervise running events that had been held since 1873, in conjunction with the Saratoga Rowing Regatta. In 1876 the IC4A conducted a full-scale track meet; in 1880 there was also a bicycle race and a tug of war on the program.

Since the National Collegiate Athletic Association (NCAA) has been organized, the IC4A meet has lost its former status as the major intercollegiate track meet, but it is still an important one, particularly for Eastern schools.

ICEBOATING—There have been suggestions that iceboating may date back as far as 2000 B.C., when boats were said to have run on skates made of large animal bones. Exhibits in a Stockholm museum suggest such a possibility. Nevertheless, the first iceboats of which we have definite knowledge were small "boxes," mounted on skates and carrying sails, that traveled on Holland's frozen canals early in the eighteenth century. It is likely that Dutch settlers also sailed similar boats on the Hudson River. According to an established record, a man named Oliver Booth sailed such a craft on the Hudson near Poughkeepsie, New York, in 1790, and the sport soon became popular around Red Bank and Long Branch, New Jersey.

Like many other sports, iceboating spread rapidly after the Civil War. The first club was formed in Poughkeepsie in 1865, and within a short time the Hudson River Ice Yacht Club and the New Hamburgh Ice Yacht Club were founded. The Hudson club was the most important in the early days of iceboating. By 1900 there were more than 50 yachts. The fastest were *Icicle,* owned by John E. Roosevelt, and *Jack Frost,* owned by Archibald Rogers. The major trophy during that period was the Ice Yacht Challenge Pennant of America, won by *Jack Frost* five times and by *Icicle* four times. Competition for the pennant, from 1883 to 1902, was open to all North American clubs, but the Hudson River Club never lost it.

American iceboats had originally been based on European designs, but in 1870 the so-called Hudson River Boat was developed. It had a T-shaped hull and three runners, with jib and mainsail rigging. These were stern-steering boats. A runner was mounted at each end of the crossbar, for stability, but the main runner ran to the end of the backbone, where it was pivoted and connected to a tiller. By turning the runner to the right, the helmsman could turn the boat left, and vice versa.

Big boats with large sail areas could reach great speeds. In 1907 the *Clarel,* sailed by Elisha Price, is said to have reached 144 mph at Long Branch. A major drawback was that, at high speeds, the steering runner would sometimes be lifted from the ice, sending the boat into an uncontrollable and dangerous spin.

Racing on the Hudson River began to decline in 1902, when icebreakers were used to keep the river open for commercial navigation. At the same time, however, the sport began to grow rapidly in the northern Midwest and in southern Ontario.

New Developments. Until about 1930, iceboats, like water yachts of the time, were big and expensive. Iceboating was a sport for the wealthy. In 1931 the Joys brothers of Milwaukee built the first front-steering iceboat, and another pioneer, Starke Meyer, quickly adopted the new design. A steering runner in the front of the boat could not be lifted off the ice, and the new boat was spinproof. However, Meyer suffered serious injuries when his boat reared up on two runners and spilled him at high speeds.

Meyer decided to experiment with smaller sails and discovered that, with a sail of just 75 ft², he could travel with safety in high winds that would be very dangerous for larger boats. Meyer's two discoveries—the stability of the bow-steering boat and the feasibility of small sails— brought the iceboat within reach of thousands of people who could not have afforded one of the bigger craft. Iceboating boomed, particularly on the lakes of Wisconsin and Michigan.

By about 1940 the basic design of the modern iceboat had been completely worked out. Harry Nye of Chicago developed the modern sail, which is a good deal different from the yacht sail, because it faces much higher air speeds. The most popular iceboat model has long been the "Skeeter." Originally the designation for any bow-steering iceboat, "Skeeter" now means a craft of a specific class—a single-seat boat with 75 ft² or less of sail area. Another popular class is the Yankee, a two-seat boat, permitting both cameraderie and instruction.

Another popular design was developed in 1937 in the *Detroit News* Craftsman Shop and was named the DN. This 12-ft boat has an 8-ft runner plank and carries 60 ft² of sail. In 1953 the International DN Ice Yacht Racing Association was formed, and it conducts its own regatta. The first world DN championship, the Ford Cup, was held in 1973 at Gull Lake, Michigan, and was won by a Russian skipper, Ain Vilde.

Associations and Major Races. Three major associations control iceboat racing in the United States. Two of them are regional—the Eastern Ice Yachting Association and

An iceboat flies on just two of its three runners over a frozen lake in upstate New York. *(Lockley Manufacturing Company.)*

the Northwestern Ice Yachting Association—and the third is the International Skeeter Association (ISA).

Each association conducts an annual championship regatta. The ISA has conducted its annual championships since 1942. The Northwestern Association was formed in 1912, the Eastern Association in 1937. Both recognize five classes of boats, based entirely on square feet of sail area. Classifications are: Class A, 350 and more; Class B, 200; Class C, 175; Class D, 125; and Class E, 75.

Although Class E is by far the most numerous, competition for two major trophies has helped keep alive interest in racing in the higher classifications. The Hearst Cup, donated in 1904 by William Randolph Hearst, and the Stuart Cup, put up originally in 1903, are both for Class A boats.

Competition for the Ice Yacht Challenge Pennant of America was reopened in 1951. The original pennant is on display at the Roosevelt Memorial Library in Hyde Park, New York; a nylon replica was made in 1951 and put in competition at an open invitation regatta. It was won by the Fox Lake, Illinois, Ice Yacht Club.

Racing Rules and Techniques. There are many similarities between iceboating and sailboating, both in rules and techniques. As in yachting, sheer speed is not enough to win a race. The tactics employed in getting around the course are of vital importance. One major difference is that the iceboater cannot rely on water signs as a guide to judging wind direction. A telltale ribbon in the rigging helps somewhat, but experience is very important, since the iceboat skipper must develop a good sense of the wind. The iceboat is also much more sensitive to the tiller than a sailboat but, because of its higher speed, it needs a great deal more room in which to turn.

Iceboat races are usually conducted on a windward-leeward course; triangular courses are rarely used. When crosswind conditions prevail on a course, a figure-8 circuit may be used. At the outset, the boats line up abreast along the starting line, 30 to 40 ft apart, their starting positions having been drawn by lot. The first tack is predetermined, and the boats start at about a 45-degree angle into the wind, with skippers (and crew, if any) pushing the boats until they're going fast enough for the wind to take over.

Iceboating rules vary somewhat from association to association and from club to club; essentially, they follow yacht racing rules in regard to right-of-way, establishing overlaps, and the like.

See also YACHTING.

Bibliography. Smith, S. Calhoun: *Ice Boating,* Van Nostrand, New York, 1962.

ICE HOCKEY—*See* HOCKEY.

ICE SKATING—*See* FIGURE SKATING; SPEED SKATING.

J

JAI ALAI—It is generally believed that jai alai (pronounced "hi-lie," with accent on the first syllable) originated in the Basque region of Spain, although some scholars believe the game was first played by the Mayas or Aztecs in Central America, and then brought back to Spain by the conquistadors. Whatever the origin, it was the Basques who developed the sport; they still dominate it. The Basques originally called it "pelota" (ball), the name by which it is still known in the rest of Spain; but the game was so closely associated with festive events that it became known as jai alai, which means "merry festival" in the Basque language.

Jai alai is one of several sports that have claimed the title of "the world's fastest sport"; the claim rests on the fact that the ball in jai alai travels at speeds of up to 150 mph—faster than anything in sport except a powered racing vehicle.

The game spread from Spain to Egypt, France, and other European countries, and to Mexico and Cuba. It was introduced into the United States during the 1904 World's Fair in St. Louis. It was briefly popular in Chicago, when gambling on the sport was legal, but when the gambling was prohibited the sport died. It moved to New Orleans, again was forced out of business by a change in the gambling laws, and finally arrived in Miami in 1924. In 1933 Florida legalized parimutuel betting on horse racing, dog racing, and jai alai, and the sport has flourished there ever since, primarily in the Miami area.

In its essentials, jai alai resembles handball. However, the players wear long, narrow, curved wicker baskets (cestas) on their playing hands, enabling them to propel the ball with terrific speed.

The ball has a diameter of about 2 in and is very hard; it is made of virgin de-para rubber from Brazil, is hand wound, and covered first with a layer of linen thread and then with two layers of goat skin. Traveling at top speed, the ball can kill a player if it hits him.

The *cancha* (court) is 176 ft long, 50 ft wide, and 40 ft high. There are three walls: a front wall *(frontis)*, a back wall *(rebote),* and one side wall, to the left of the players. On their right is the spectators' gallery, protected by steel netting. The front wall is made of granite; the rear and side walls of Gunite, a pressure-applied cement; and the floor of specially hardened concrete, 12 in thick.

The walls are marked with 17 lines. The server must stand behind the eleventh line; the server bounces the ball and throws it off the front wall so that it lands on the floor between the fourth and seventh lines. The other lines are merely guides to help players judge the distance and angle of the shot.

There are three forms of the sport: singles, doubles, and a special elimination system devised for parimutuel betting. In the elimination game, there are eight players on the floor; when one loses a point, that player is replaced.

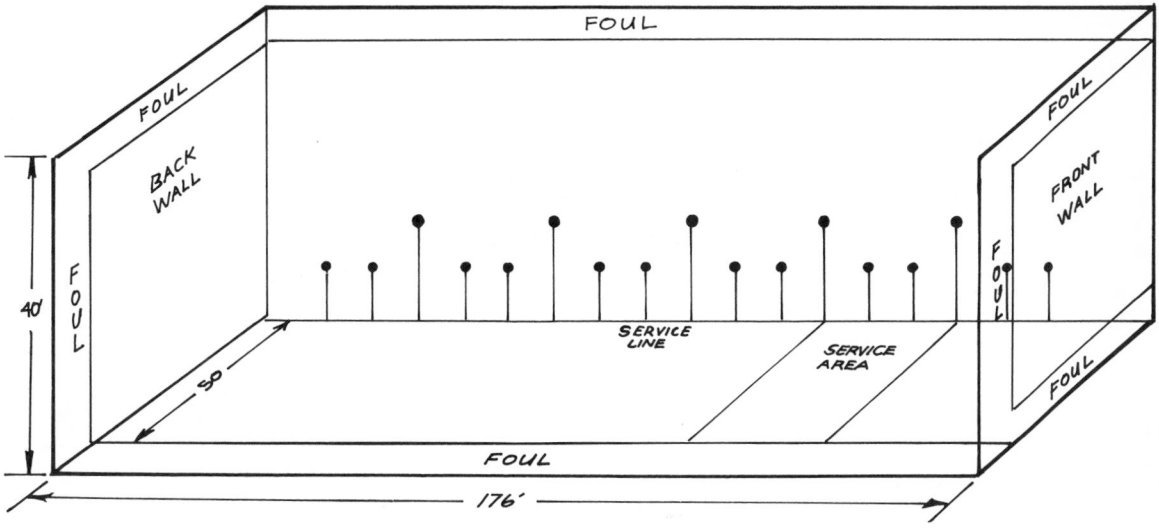

Jai alai court

The speed of jai alai is indicated by the blurring of this player's *cesta* as he returns a shot. *(Dan Forer, World Jai-Alai, Inc.)*

Winners stay on the court. A player who has made 3 points has qualified for the finals, and he leaves until two others have also qualified. Then the three qualifiers play off to determine win, place, and show positions for the betting.

A point is scored when another player's shot goes out of bounds, either by hitting the wire screen or by hitting one of the penalty areas marked on the walls; or when the ball hits the floor twice without being returned. The ball can be played off the back wall, side wall, or floor, but it must hit the front wall before it hits the floor a second time. As in tennis, the server gets two chances to make a good serve.

Jai alai has shown substantial growth as an amateur sport in the United States in recent years. United States amateur championships have been decided in competitions held since 1966, and two young American players, Joey Cornblit and Randy Lazenby, were playing professionally at the Miami Jai-Alai Fronton in the mid-1970s.

JAVELIN—A pointed, spear-shaped shaft thrown for distance in a field event; not less than 8.53 ft in length and 1.765 lb in weight.

See also TRACK AND FIELD.

JUDO—In ancient China, unarmed Tibetan monks developed ways of defending themselves from armed attackers. Their techniques laid the foundation for modern karate, judo, and other Oriental systems of defense. The Japanese borrowed certain techniques of defense from the Chinese and developed their system called "jujitsu," both as a way of self-defense for commoners, who were forbidden to carry weapons, and as a type of combat exercise for samurai warriors.

After the Japanese feudal regime broke down in the late sixteenth century, various forms of self-defense, under the general name of jujitsu, were taught, but there was no standardization. In 1882, Jigoro Kano, a young Japanese who had made a thorough study of jujitsu, evolved his own system, called "ju-do," meaning "gentle way." He taught it at an academy, the Kodokan. Although judo

techniques could be used in fighting, Kano emphasized that they were a way of training both the body and the mind. His students learned not only physical techniques but mental alertness, perseverance, and a respect for others.

One of the Kodokan instructors visited the United States in 1902 and gave a number of demonstrations and lessons. Among his pupils was President Theodore Roosevelt. Professor Kano himself came to this country in 1932 and organized several local judo associations. They were made up largely of Japanese-Americans, but membership was not restricted.

During World War II the U.S. armed services, particularly the Marine Corps, taught certain judo techniques, including some of the old jujitsu procedures which can disable or kill. This led to a certain public awareness of the word, if not of the techniques or the discipline involved in judo.

By 1953 there were enough associations taking part in the sport for the Amateur Athletic Union to take over nationwide supervision. The first national championships were held in 1953; in 1954 the Amateur Judo Association of the United States (now the U.S. Judo Federation) was organized as the sport's technical administrator. The National Collegiate Judo Association conducted its first national championships in 1962.

Rules. Judo is a form of combat involving various types of holds, throws, and falls. Through most of the action, both competitors are on their feet. The contest area is a square ranging from 27 to 30 ft on a side; it is usually bordered by Oriental mats called *tatami*. In minor tournaments, 24-by-24 contest areas are employed; for junior competition the measurements are 20 by 20.

The white, loose-fitting costume is called a *judogi*. The *uwagi* (jacket) is long enough to cover the buttocks and is tied at the waist with a judo belt *(obi)*; the sleeves must extend at least halfway down the forearm. The trousers must reach at least halfway down the calves of the legs. For identification, one contestant wears a red sash, the other a white sash.

In *katame-waza*—mat techniques—the match ends immediately if the opponent gives up. The match also ends if a hold is applied that cannot be broken within 30 sec. *(Nobua Hayashi, Tulane University.)*

A referee and two judges officiate in an important match. The referee has overall responsibility for the conduct of a match. If a judge disagrees with a referee's judgment call, the judge may stand up to get the referee's attention. After discussion the referee may adopt the judge's decision or reject it. The referee's judgment is final. However, if both judges agree on the point at issue, in opposition to the referee, the referee must defer to them.

A contest lasts a predetermined time, from 3 to 20 min. If there is no clear winner, there may be an overtime period. Overtime ranges from 2 min, for a 3-min match, to 7 min for a 20-min match.

The match begins with opponents about 12 ft apart, the referee between them. After bowing to one another, each takes a step forward and waits for the referee's command to begin: "Hajime." The winner is the first contestant to score an *ippon* (full point). There are many ways of doing this, including the combination of two *waza-ari*. A *waza-ari*, generally called a half-point, is actually somewhat closer to being a full point.

An *ippon* is scored when a contestant throws the opponent so that the latter lands with appreciable force on the back or side. Landing on the stomach or on the hands and knees may be ruled a *waza-ari*. An *ippon* is also scored when a contestant gives up; either contestant can surrender by saying "maitta" or by tapping the body, the opponent's body, or the mat twice with hand or foot. This generally happens because a contestant is being choked or is unable to escape from a hold (usually an elbow hold) that could break a joint. An *ippon* is also scored when a contestant, using skill and approved techniques, lifts the opponent, face up, to shoulder height.

Victory also results when a contestant keeps the opponent with back to the mat and under control for 30 sec, or when a joint-endangering hold is maintained for the same period. In either case, the aggressor is given a *waza-ari* after 20 sec of such action. A *waza-ari* may also be awarded for various rules violations by an opponent. Any two *waza-ari* make an *ippon*.

All of the action is supposed to take place within the combat area. However, if a contestant makes a proper throw and the opponent lands outside the combat area, an *ippon* can be scored, provided the thrower remains within the combat area. If one contestant has a hold on the other, and they go out of the area, or are about to go out, the referee orders them to stay as they are, has the clock stopped, moves them into the center of the area, and then starts the match and the clock again. Thus, a contestant cannot break a hold by forcing the action outside the prescribed area.

If a hold or a pin has begun when time runs out, the contest continues until the hold is broken, or until the prescribed time for an *ippon* has elapsed, in which case the *ippon* is scored. If a throw has begun before time runs out, it counts as a *waza-ari* or *ippon* even if time elapses before the thrown contestant lands.

Violations. Certain types of techniques are forbidden. Joint-endangering holds may be used only if a match involves two contestants of black-belt rank. Striking an opponent with hand or fist is not permitted. Some basic wrestling techniques are forbidden. A judo competitor cannot, for example, force an opponent to the mat in an attempt to pin the opponent; such an attempt must involve judo skill—an approved drag-down or throw.

A contestant is applying *nage-waza*—throwing technique—to his opponent. If the opponent lands on his back or side with force and with control, it ends the match. (*Nobuo Hayashi, Tulane University.*)

A contestant may not avoid contact deliberately, or adopt purely defensive techniques, such as holding an opponent at arm's length or deliberately stepping out of the contest area. It is also illegal to trip or tackle; to use a foot, hand, or forearm on an opponent's face; to use a leg-scissors hold; to use any hold that might injure the neck or vertebrae; or to use the open fingers in choking.

If a contestant is about to commit a violation, the referee can give the transgressor a warning—a *shido*. For minor violations, the first penalty is called *chui*; the second, called *keikoku*, is the equivalent of a *waza-ari*. A major violation calls for a *keikoku* as the first penalty and *hansoku-make*, or disqualification, on the second. Flagrant violations, unsporting conduct, and similar offenses result in immediate *hansoku-make*.

Since a *waza-ari* and a *keikoku* are approximately equivalent, one of each adds up to an *ippon*. A *chui* and a *keikoku* add up to disqualification.

Decisions. If neither combatant can score an *ippon* before the time has elapsed, a decision is necessary. Both judges and the referee take part, as in boxing. In the event of a tie, the referee's decision holds. (A tie, of course, can come about only if at least one judge votes for a draw.) If just one of the contestants has a *waza-ari*, that contestant is normally the winner. But there are other minor points that enter into the reaching of decisions, as the accompanying glossary indicates.

Tournaments. A tournament may be conducted as a straight elimination, with the winner of a contest moving on to the next round and the loser dropping out. Major tournaments, however, including the Olympic tournaments, are conducted under a "bad point" system. A contestant who wins a match with an *ippon* or two *waza-ari* is given no penalty points; the opponent is given 3 penalty points. A winner by decision gets 1 penalty point, the loser 2 penalty points. A contestant is eliminated from such a tournament upon accumulating 5 penalty points.

When only three contestants are left in a division, their penalty points are wiped out and they have another round robin, after which the contestant with the fewest penalty points is the winner. If two contestants are tied in penalty points, the one who defeated the other in their match is the winner. If all three are tied, the contestant with the lowest number of penalty points in the entire tournament wins. If this still produces a three-way tie, the championship goes to the lightest contestant; the next lightest is placed second, and the heaviest gets third place.

Classifications. In order to prevent injury during judo contests, participants are ranked both by age and by skill. White belt indicates a novice; green belt a junior, 12 years and under; purple belt an intermediate, 13–16 years; brown belt is awarded for advanced skills, usually to those 17 or older; and the black belt is for experts. The black-belt classification has 10 degrees. An active competitor may rise as high as the seventh degree. Eighth-, ninth-, and tenth-degree black belts are given only to those who have also devoted time to officiating, teaching, promoting, and making other contributive efforts after retiring from competition.

The classification system is under the jurisdiction of the U.S. Judo Federation, and it is based on the amount of instruction and the degree of skill shown in competition.

Weight Divisions. Theoretically, judo is a type of combat in which a weight difference means little. In practice, this doesn't always hold true. The AAU originally conducted competition in just four weight divisions, but it now has six divisions. At most tournaments, after the winners have been chosen in each weight division, they take part in a tournament to decide the overall winner.

Judo for Women. Women compete, not in combat, but in *kata*, essentially floor exercises in which judo techniques are demonstrated without actual contact with an opponent (although each contestant works with a partner). The contestants are judged on the basis of timing, correctness of movements, coordination, posture, and grace. In local competitions there is usually just one judge. In major competitions there are at least three judges, and their scores are averaged.

Certain prescribed techniques must be followed in a definite sequence, and each contestant is given a separate score of from 0 to 3 points for each technique. Additional points are awarded for overall quality of the routine.

Glossary

aka—Red; used to signify a contestant in a red sash.

atemi-waza—Striking techniques, most of which are forbidden in judo.

awase-waza—A combination of two *waza-ari;* equivalent to an *ippon.*

chui—Penalty for minor rules violation.

dojo—Judo club.

fusen-sho—Winner by forfeit.

hajime—Start.

hansoku—Penalty for three minor rules violations, two major violations, or one flagrant or unsportsmanlike violation; the approximate equivalent of an *ippon.*

hansoku-gachi—Win through rules violations by opponent.

hansoku-make—Disqualification.

hantei—Decision.

hiki-wake—Draw.

ippon—One point; sufficient for victory.

jikan—Time out; a verbal signal by the referee.

jogai—Referee's verbal signal that one or both contestants are outside the combat area.

judogi—The prescribed costume for contestants.

judoka—A judo practitioner.

kansetsu-waza—Joint-holding techniques.

katama-waza—Mat techniques, including choking, pinning, and joint holds.

keikoku—Penalty for two minor rules violations, or one major violation; approximately equivalent to a *waza-ari.*

kiken-gachi—Win because of an injury to an opponent.

kinga—Small advantages in combat; these form the basis for officials' decisions.

ma-te—Stop; a verbal command.

mattai—I surrender.

nage-waza—Throwing techniques.

obi—Judo belt.

osaekama-takete—Hold broken; a verbal signal to the timekeeper to stop timing the hold.

shido—Minor violation; warning from the referee that a contestant is about to commit or has committed a technical violation. A second *shido* brings the penalty of a *chui.*

shime-waza—Choking techniques.

shiro—White; the contestant with the white sash.

shodan—A first-degree black belt.

sono-mama—"Remain as you are"; a command used by the referee when contestants are near the edge of the combat area. They hold their positions while the referee moves them to the center of the area.

sogo-gachi—Win by combination of a *waza-ari* and a rules violation by the opponent.

sore-made—Verbal signal that time has expired.

uwagi—The judo jacket.

waza-ari—Usually considered a half-point; actually, a near-*ippon.* However, two *waza-ari* constitute an *ippon.*

waza-ari-ni-chikai-waza—A near *waza-ari.*

yudansha—Black belt holder.

yusei-gachi—Winner by superiority; the decision when one contestant has a *waza-ari* or the equivalent and the opponent does not, or when the referee and judges choose a winner by decision.

zoris—Judo slippers.

AAU National Champions

130 Pounds
1953	George Hata
1954	Asao Sakaki
1955	Ben Takahashi
1956	Sumikichi Nozaki
1957	Masatoshi Kumamoto
1958	Sumikichi Nozaki
1959	Sumikichi Nozaki

139 Pounds
1968	Yuzo Koga
1969	Shiro Oishi
1970	Larry Fukuhara
1971	Rodney Parr
1972	Brian Yakata
1973	David Pruzansky
1974	James Martin
1975	Keith Nakasone
1976	George Cozzi

140 Pounds
1960	Sumikichi Nozaki
1961	Sumikichi Nozaki

1962 Shintaro Yoshida
1963 No competition
1964 Yuzo Koga
1965 Yuzo Koga
1966 Yuzo Koga

150 Pounds
1953 Charles Nakashima
1954 Kenji Yamada
1955 Kenji Yamada
1956 Art Emi
1957 Takao Oishi
1958 Otto Chonko
1959–1962 No competition
1963 Toshiyuki Seino
1964 Renzo Shibata
1965 Toshio Seino

154 Pounds
1968 Tadashi Hiraoka
1969 Tadashi Hiraoka
1970 Paul Maruyama
1971 Patrick Burris
1972 Patrick Burris
1973 Patrick Burris
1974 Patrick Burris
1975 Paul Maruyama
1976 Patrick Burris

160 Pounds
1960 Toshiyuki Seino
1961 Toshiyuki Seino
1962 Kazuo Shinohara
1963–1964 No competition
1965 Hayward Nishioka
1966 Paul Maruyana
1967 Nario Arima

165 Pounds
1964 Jim Bregman

176 Pounds
1968 Masayuki Yamashita
1969 Masayuki Yamashita
1970 Hayward Nishioki
1971 Irwin Cohen
1972 Irwin Cohen
1973 Bill Sanford
1974 Irwin Cohen
1975 Steve Cohen
1976 Teimoc Johnston-Ono

180 Pounds
1953 Moon Kikuchi
1954 Vince Tamura
1955 John Osako
1956 Vince Tamura
1957 Shuzo Kato
1958 John Osako
1959 Vince Tamura
1960 Haruo Imamara
1961 Haruo Imamara
1962 Haruo Imamara
1963 Kazuo Shinohara
1964 Harry Kimura
1965 G. Tomoda
1966 Hayward Nishioki
1967 Tasuhiko Nagatoshi

205 Pounds
1964 Kinjiro Emura
1965 Makoto Ombayashi
1966 Motohiko Eguchi
1967 Larry Nelson
1968 Mitsutoshi Watanabe
1969 Toshi Ichinoe

1970 Rodney Haas
1971 Douglas Nelson
1972 Doug Graham
1973 Roy Sukimoto
1974 Steven Cohen
1975 Tommy Martin
1976 Irwin Cohen

Heavyweight
1953 Lyle Hunt
1954 Gene Lebell
1955 Gene Lebell
1956 John Osako
1957 George Harris
1958 George Harris
1959 Rudy Williams
1960 George Harris
1961 George Harris
1962 Ben Campbell
1963 Makoto Obayashi
1964 Gotaro Uemara
1965 Allen Coage
1966 Allen Coage
1967 Howard Fish
1968 Allen Coage
1969 Allen Coage
1970 Allen Coage
1971 Arthur Canario
1972 Doug Nelson
1973 Dean Sedgwick
1974 Jack Anderson
1975 Allen Coage
1976 Dean Sedgwick

Open
1968 Takenori Itoh
1969 Taizo Naguchi
1970 Kensuki Kobayashi
1971 Roy Sukimoto
1972 Johnny Watts
1973 Lee Person
1974 James R. Wooley
1975 D. Davis
1976 James R. Wooley

JUNIOR LEGION BASEBALL—Since 1926 the American Legion has sponsored a nationwide program of junior baseball for players up to 17 years. District champions meet in a play-off series to determine a national champion.

JUNIOR OLYMPICS—In its essence, the Amateur Athletic Union's Junior Olympics program is a nationwide program involving competition in 14 sports for youngsters aged 6 to 18, culminating in national championship meets and tournaments. Competition begins at the local level, and winners move up through regional competition to qualify for the national championship program. Inaugurated in 1949 with the permission of the U.S. Olympic Committee, the program has as a secondary goal the early training of athletes who may eventually represent the United States in the Olympics.

The AAU says the basic objective is to encourage systematic exercise and to offer the physical, mental, and social benefits of athletics to a wide cross section of young people.

Individual national championship events are held in some sports. There is also an annual multi-sport national championship event that includes competition in diving, gymnastics, judo, swimming, track and field, and trampoline.

K

As a noncontact sport, karate is considered a good way of teaching physical and mental discipline to youngsters. (*Hank Seaman*, New Bedford Standard-Times.)

KARATE—Like judo, karate developed among unarmed peasants in the Orient over a period of hundreds of years. It became a discipline on the island of Okinawa during the seventeenth century and became popular in Japan, probably because of its disciplinary similarities to judo, about 1920. (*Karate* is the Japanese word for "open hand.")

If judo is considered the Oriental version of wrestling, karate is the Oriental version of boxing. There is no grappling; the sport emphasizes the use of the hands and arms, and the feet and legs, for defense and attack. Blows are delivered with the hands, elbows, and forearms, with the heel, the ball of the foot, and the knee. The exhibitions in which boards and bricks are shattered by blows are merely demonstrations of the exercises used to toughen the hands and feet in preparation for their use in karate.

Like judo, karate in its true form is more than just a sport or a method of defense. Ideally, it is a whole way of life, involving mental preparation and discipline, self-control, courtesy displayed through ritualistic routines and gestures, and even a prescribed costume.

Men usually compete in a form of karate called *kumite,* which consists of sparring exhibitions in which blows are stopped just short of contact. Rules are very similar to those of judo: A "killing" blow is an *ippon,* or full point, which wins immediately. If neither contestant scores an *ippon,* the referee and judges render a decision. A match usually lasts 3 min, but the time may range from 2 to 5 min.

Women usually compete in a form called *kata,* in which each contestant demonstrates a predetermined series of movements and blows against a series of opponents. Performance is scored by a panel of judges, as in gymnastics.

Although karate has become rather popular as a participant sport in recent years, it has suffered somewhat in the public eye because there are several different styles, each represented by different schools and organizations, and there has been little overall supervision in the United States.

See also JUDO.

KARTING—The first go-kart was built in 1956 by two Californians, Art Ingels and Lou Borelli. Within a short time, racing was being conducted on specially built tracks. During the 1960s the sport became relatively popular in England and in some European countries.

A kart is a rear-engine vehicle with a chassis of tubular steel. The driver sits far forward, just a few inches above the racing surface. There are two general classes, for racing purposes. The 100-cm³ class has engines of that size and only one gear; the 250-cm³ class has a gearbox. In some races there are further subdivisions, based on the total cost of the kart, to promote competition.

The sport was something of a fad during the mid-1960s, when many public tracks were opened, where people could rent karts. Many of those tracks eventually went out of business as the fad died, but karting continues to be a serious sport among a hard core of drivers, particularly in California.

L

LACROSSE—If you don't mind making money on a sure thing, try betting that some friend of yours can't name the national sport of Canada. Chances are the friend will say ice hockey; but the Canadian parliament has officially named lacrosse the national sport.

Lacrosse is one of the few surviving sports that is actually native to North America (although some anthropologists believe that field hockey is so ancient that it was brought to the Americas by the original settlers, and that it is the direct ancestor of lacrosse). The prevailing modern opinion specifies a different origin. When early French voyagers sailed down the St. Lawrence River, they saw Iroquois Indians playing a warlike game in which crooked sticks with rawhide bags attached were used for carrying and throwing a ball. The Indians called the game *baggataway*. The French saw a resemblance betwen the game and their own form of field hockey, *jeu de la crosse* (game of the stick), so they also called the Indian game by that name.

In the Indian version, baggataway was played between members of opposing tribes—possibly, at times, as a substitute for warfare. The rival medicine men served as referees and as goal markers. When a medicine man moved, so did the goal. The sport among the Indians was very violent; as many as a thousand players were on a side, and the early part of the game was usually devoted to disabling as many of the opposition as possible. The first team to cross the rival's goal line won, as in very early versions of soccer.

In 1834 two Indian teams played an exhibition at a Montreal race course. It was probably the first time the game had been played in an enclosure, and special rules had to be developed. That might be considered the beginning of modern lacrosse.

It is possible that whites played the game as early as 1839, but the first definite record of white participation is dated 1844. In that year, at a meeting of the Olympic Club, an athletic organization in Montreal, an Indian team beat a white team. Games between Indians and whites also were played in 1848 and 1851. In 1856 the Montreal Lacrosse Club was formed, and two teams made up of club members played a match in 1857. A second lacrosse club, the Hochelaga, was formed in 1858, and a third, the Beaver Club, in 1859.

The first standardized rules were developed by the Montreal club, under the leadership of Dr. George W. Beers, in 1867. A hard rubber ball replaced the Indian ball, of hair stuffed into deerskin; the stick was made larger, and the number of players was set at 12 per team. In the same year, lacrosse was formally named Canada's national sport, and the National Lacrosse Association was organized.

Lacrosse in the United States. Lacrosse crossed the Canadian border into upstate New York rather early, and became especially popular in areas where ice hockey was also popular, either because of the similarities between the sports or because those areas had large populations of Canadian immigrants or students. Baltimore, which was an early ice-hockey center, is still the lacrosse capital of the United States, and a number of the colleges where lacrosse is a fairly important sport are also outstanding ice-hockey schools—Cornell, Harvard, New Hampshire, Princeton, and Rensselaer Polytech, for example.

A United States tournament was held as early as 1877, and the U.S. Amateur Lacrosse Association was organized in 1879. New York University established the first college team, in 1877, and by 1882 the Intercollegiate Lacrosse Association (USILA) was formed. In 1884 a United States team toured Europe to demonstrate the sport.

The USILA began naming a national college champion in 1881. The practice continued until the first NCAA national lacrosse tournament, in 1971. The USILA in 1934 inaugurated its U.S. Open tournament, which is basically for lacrosse clubs throughout the country.

Lacrosse for Women. Probably because of its similarity to field hockey, lacrosse was adopted as a women's sport about 1910 in England, where field hockey was very popular among women. It was being taught at Sargent College in Boston and Sweet Briar College in Virginia as early as 1912, but received its major impetus among American women at Constance Applebee's field-hockey camp in the Pocono Mountains. At the camp's 1931 session, the U.S. Women's Lacrosse Association was formed.

The first national tournament was held in 1934, and the first All-American women's team was named in the same year. Through the years, a number of women have been named All-American in both field hockey and lacrosse.

Rules

Field and Equipment. The lacrosse field is 110 yd long and 60 to 70 yd wide. The goals, 80 yd apart, are nets with mouths 6 ft high and 6 ft wide. The center of each goal mouth is the center of a circle with a 9-ft radius—the goal crease. The field is divided into halves by the offside line, at the center of which is the facing circle with a 10-ft radius. Near each end of the field there is a line, 6 ft long, that is 20 yd from the goal; the *goal area* is the area between this line and the nearest end line. On each side of the field there is a line, 20 yd long, that is 20 yd from the center of the field and parallel with the sideline; the area between one of these lines and the nearest sideline is called the *wing area.*

The lacrosse ball is made of hard sponge rubber; it is 5

Franz Wittlesberger (27) of Johns Hopkins goes against Maryland defender Steve Adams in NCAA lacrosse championship game. *(Jeff Wagner, Intercollegiate Lacrosse Association.)*

to 5¼ oz in weight and has a circumference of at least 7¾ in. When dropped from a height of 72 in onto a hardwood floor, it should bounce at least 45 in and no more than 49 in.

The stick, or crosse, must be no more than 6 ft and no less than 3 ft long, no more than 12 in and no less than 7 in wide across the face (the area of meshwork making up the stick's head). The handle is made of bent hickory. The head (net or face) is made of leather, cord, or gut, bounded on either side by a wall; on a right-handed stick, the right wall is of wood, the left wall usually of gut, though both walls may be of wood. Generally, the closer a player is stationed to the team's own goal, the larger is the stick used by the player. The goalkeeper, of course, uses the largest stick of all, usually near maximum size.

Progress of Play. There are 10 players on each team (the figure was reduced in 1933 from 12). Three are defensemen (point, cover point, and first defense, in old terminology); three are midfielders (second defense, center, and center attack); three are attackers (first attack, out home, and in home). The three attackers must always be on the side of the center line nearest the opposition goal; the three defensemen and the goalkeeper must always be on the side of the center line nearest their own goal.

When the game begins, there must be one midfielder in each wing area; an attacker in the attack goal area; and a defenseman and the goalie in the defense goal area. The game begins with a face-off: The centers place the backs of their stick nets together in the facing circle; the referee puts the ball between the two nets, touching both of them, and blows a whistle to start play. The centers then struggle to get possession of the ball. (A face-off is also used to resume play at the beginning of each succeeding quarter and after a goal.)

The object of the game is to score goals by getting the ball into the other team's goal. The ball may be carried, thrown, or batted with the stick, or kicked; it may never be touched by hand, except by a goalkeeper attempting to prevent the other team from scoring.

A game is made up of four 15-min quarters, with 1-min intermissions between the first and second and third and fourth periods, and a 10-min intermission at halftime. If a game is tied at the end of the regulation 60 min, two 5-min overtime periods are played. If the score is still tied, at that point, the game is declared a tie.

Fouls and Penalties. A player is not allowed to interfere with an opponent's progress unless the opponent has the ball, is about to catch the ball, or is within 5 yd of a loose ball.

If an attack player crosses midfield into the defensive zone, or if a defenseman or goalie crosses midfield into the attack zone, it is an offside.

There are two types of fouls, technical and personal. Technical fouls include illegal interference, offside, entering the opposition's crease, and touching the ball with the hand. The penalty is loss of ball (a free throw for the other team) or banishment of the offending player from the game, without a substitute, for 30 sec. Personal fouls include tripping, pushing, slashing, and unnecessary roughness. The penalty is banishment for 1 to 3 min, depending on the severity of the foul.

A player who has been banished for a technical foul can return to the game when the other team scores a goal, regardless of the fact that time may remain on the penalty. A player must serve the entire time for a personal foul, however. A disqualification foul, involving flagrantly unsporting conduct or unnecessary roughness, results in the player's being ejected from the game; a substitute can replace the departed player 5 min after the ejection.

Out of Bounds. If the ball goes out of bounds, the team that last touched it loses possession, with one exception: If the ball goes over the end line as the result of a shot on goal, it is awarded to the player nearest it when it went out. In either case the ball is put in play with a free throw from the spot where the ball went out or, if the spot is within 20 yd of the crease, from the 20-yd line. If players from opposing teams are equidistant from the ball when it goes over the end line, they face off at the 20-yd line. On a free throw, all other players must be at least 5 yd from the player making the throw.

Women's Rules. The women's version of lacrosse is played on a field without specific boundaries, with goals 90 to 110 yd apart. The referee decides when the ball is out of bounds, usually on the basis of certain natural boundaries agreed upon beforehand.

There are 12 players on a team; a game is made up of two 25-min periods with a 10-min intermission and there is no provision for overtime.

The face-off is replaced by a draw. The two centers stand with sticks held about hip-high, and the ball is placed between the sticks. At an order from the referee, the two players draw their sticks up and away, attempting to bring the ball away and thus gain possession of it.

Body contact is forbidden, unless purely incidental, and the referee may call a foul for any action considered dangerous. The penalty is "free position." When the whistle blows, signaling a foul, all players must stop where they are, and the fouled player is given the ball and told where she may stand. Any player within 5 yd of her must move farther away. The fouled player may then pass, run, or shoot.

Box Lacrosse. In 1932 an attempt was made to establish professional lacrosse as a spectator sport, but it failed. A year later, another attempt was made, with a new, indoor, version of the sport, called box lacrosse. That, too, failed, but "boxla" has since been revived by the North American Lacrosse Association, a league of eight teams, made up primarily of North American Indians. Established in 1969, the league plays two games a week, May through September.

Boxla is very similar to hockey, and is usually played in hockey rinks. Teams have six players apiece; the sticks are shorter and the goals are smaller. Because of the smaller area and the fact that there is no out-of-bounds area, the game is exceptionally fast.

National Champions

U.S. Open

1934	Mt. Washington Lacrosse Club
1935	Mt. Washington Lacrosse Club
1936	Mt. Washington Lacrosse Club
1937	Baltimore Athletic Club
1938	Mt. Washington Lacrosse Club
1939	Mt. Washington Lacrosse Club
1940	Mt. Washington Lacrosse Club
1941	Johns Hopkins University
1942	Mt. Washington Lacrosse Club
1943–45	No competition
1946	Mt. Washington Lacrosse Club
1947	Mt. Washington Lacrosse Club
1948	Mt. Washington Lacrosse Club
1949	Mt. Washington Lacrosse Club
1950	Mt. Washington Lacrosse Club
1951	Baltimore Lacrosse Club
1952	Mt. Washington Lacrosse Club
1953	Mt. Washington Lacrosse Club
1954	Mt. Washington Lacrosse Club
	U.S. Naval Academy
1955	Mt. Washington Lacrosse Club
	University of Maryland
1956	University of Maryland
1957	Johns Hopkins University
	Mt. Washington Lacrosse Club
1958	U.S. Military Academy
1959	Mt. Washington Lacrosse Club
1960	Mt. Washington Lacrosse Club
1961	Baltimore Lacrosse Club
1962	Mt. Washington Lacrosse Club
1963	Baltimore University Club
1964	Mt. Washington Lacrosse Club
1965	Baltimore University Club
1966	Mt. Washington Lacrosse Club
1967	Mt. Washington Lacrosse Club
1968	Long Island Athletic Club
1969	Long Island Athletic Club
1970	Long Island Athletic Club
1971	Long Island Athletic Club
1972	Carling Lacrosse Club, Baltimore
1973	Long Island Athletic Club
1974	Long Island Athletic Club
1975	Mt. Washington Lacrosse Club
1976	Mt. Washington Lacrosse Club

Intercollegiate

(Chosen by USILA until 1971)

1881	Harvard		Harvard
1882	Harvard		Swarthmore
1883	Yale	1906	Cornell
1884	Princeton		Johns Hopkins
1885	Princeton	1907	Cornell
1886-1901	No records		Johns Hopkins
1902	Johns Hopkins	1908	Harvard
1903-04	No records		Johns Hopkins
1905	Columbia	1909	Columbia
	Cornell		Harvard

	Johns Hopkins		Maryland
1910	Harvard		Navy
	Swarthmore		Rutgers
1911	Harvard	1929	Navy
	Johns Hopkins		Union
1912	Harvard	1930	St. John's (Baltimore)
1913	Harvard	1931	St. John's (Baltimore)
	Johns Hopkins	1932-35	No champion
1914	Cornell	1936	Maryland
	Lehigh	1937	Maryland
1915	Harvard		Princeton
	Johns Hopkins	1938	Navy
1916	Cornell	1939	Maryland
	Lehigh	1940	Maryland
1917	Lehigh	1941	Johns Hopkins
	Stevens Tech	1942	Princeton
1918	No champion	1943	Navy
1919	Johns Hopkins	1944	Army
	Stevens Tech	1945	Army
1920	Lehigh		Navy
	Syracuse	1946	Navy
1921	Lehigh	1947	Johns Hopkins
1922	Syracuse	1948	Johns Hopkins
1923	Johns Hopkins	1949	Johns Hopkins
1924	Syracuse		Navy
1925	Syracuse	1950	Johns Hopkins
1926	Johns Hopkins	1951	Army
1927	Johns Hopkins		Princeton
1928	Johns Hopkins	1952	Rensselaer Polytech

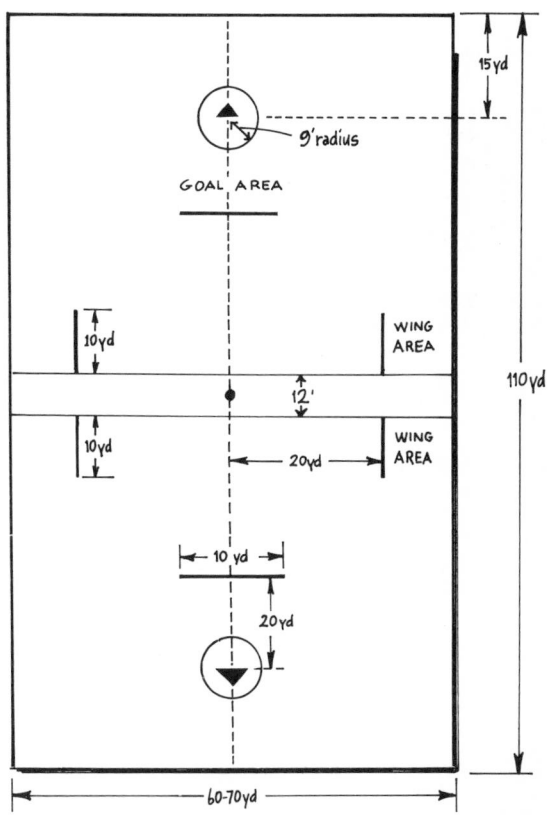

Men's Lacrosse field

Cortland State attackman Jud Smith circles the Baltimore-Maryland County cage in NCAA College Division tournament action. *(Cortland State College.)*

	Virginia	1967	Johns Hopkins
1953	Princeton		Maryland
1954	Army		Navy
1955	Maryland	1968	Johns Hopkins
1956	Maryland	1969	Army
1957	Johns Hopkins		Johns Hopkins
1958	Army	1970	Johns Hopkins
1959	Army		Navy
	Johns Hopkins		Virginia
	Maryland		
1960	Navy		**NCAA Division 1**
1961	Army	1971	Cornell
	Navy	1972	Virginia
1962	Navy	1973	Maryland
1963	Navy	1974	Johns Hopkins
1964	Navy	1975	Maryland
1965	Navy	1976	Cornell
1966	Navy		

Bibliography. Morrill, William K.: *Lacrosse,* Ronald, New York, 1952.

LAND SAILING—Similar to ice boating, land sailing is conducted primarily on dry lakes in California, with sailboats on wheels. It is not yet a formally organized competitive sport but, by 1975, there were an estimated 500 land sailors, and formal organization seemed likely in the near future.

LAWN BOWLS—"Bowling on the green," or "bowls," may be the oldest of the ball games. It is the ancestor of such other ball-and-target games as croquet and billiards, and possibly golf, and some scholars believe that many bat-and-ball games, including field hockey and modern baseball, may also have their original source in bowls, or rather in an ancient variation of it.

In any event, lawn bowls was played in ancient Egypt, Greece, and Rome, principally by members of the nobility. As early as the tenth century, the sport was fairly popular in northern Europe; possibly it was brought there by Roman soldiers, though it may have developed independently, since in its essence the game requires nothing more than fairly smooth stones, one of which can be used as a target. By the twelfth century, bowls was popular in England. The first club was formed in Southampton in 1299, and in 1511 it was banned by King Henry VIII because, he said, "the alleys are operated in conjuction with saloons, or dissolute places."

The sport was introduced into North America by Dutch settlers in New Amsterdam about 1690, but English and Scottish settlers were really responsible for its establishment in what eventually was to be the United States. There was a bowling green in Boston before 1714, and in 1732 one was established in New York City. Perhaps because of its British associations, the sport almost disappeared in this country after the Revolutionary War. During the nineteenth century, Scotland virtually took over the sport. The Scots worked out standardized rules during the 1840s, and those rules have changed very little since.

The sport was brought back to the United States in 1876 by Christian Schepflin, who returned from a trip to Scotland and laid out a bowling green at his home in Dunellen, New Jersey. His neighbors quickly became fellow enthusiasts and the sport spread rather quickly through New Jersey and into the Philadelphia area. Also adding impetus to its growth during the early twentieth century was the influx of textile workers from England and Scotland into southern New England. In 1915, the American Lawn Bowling Association was organized to govern the sport. Lawn bowls in the United States peaked in the 1930s, when the Work Projects Administration (WPA), furthering the public playground program, installed bowling greens in a number of municipal parks. The sport has declined a good deal since those years, but still has its pockets of popularity.

Rules. The standard bowling green is a 120-ft square, divided into six "rinks," each 20 by 120 ft. As the name implies, the surface is similar to a golf green (turf) in most cases; in some areas it is marl, a sand-clay mixture. The bowler must have one foot on a rubber mat, 14 by 24 in, when delivering the ball.

The target ball, or "jack," is a white ball, about 10 oz in weight, with a 2½-in diameter, or thereabouts. Each bowler has two "bowls" (balls) in diameter between 4½ and 5½ in and weighing no more than 3½ lb. The balls are usually made of lignum vitae, a very hard, heavy wood. They are not perfectly round; they bulge slightly on one side, enough to make the ball curve about 4 ft in that direction over a distance of 100 ft. This bulge is called the "bias."

The first contestant to bowl first rolls the jack ball; if it doesn't go at least 75 ft, or if it goes out of the rink boundaries, the other team rolls it. The jack then becomes the target for all the bowlers. Having rolled the jack, the first bowler (called the lead) rolls the other two balls in the possession of each contestant. Then the other team's lead rolls two balls, and so on until all balls have been rolled. It is permissible to knock an opponent's ball out of place. If the jack is knocked out of bounds, a player of the other team rolls it, while balls that have already been rolled remain in place.

In its purest form the game is played by two teams of four contestants each. The "skip," or team leader, usually bowls fourth. When not actually bowling, the skip stands at the far end of the rink and directs the team's play. Lawn bowls can also be a game between teams of two or between single players. In any event, each player gets only two balls per "end."

Once all the balls have been rolled, thus completing the

end, scoring is similar to the scoring in horseshoes or curling: A team gets 1 point for each of its balls that is closer to the jack than any of the opponent's balls. A team that scores in one end rolls first in the next end. Generally 21 ends constitute a game, though any number of ends may be agreed upon beforehand. In singles play, a game usually continues until one player has 21 points.

LAWN TENNIS—*See* TENNIS.

LITTLE LEAGUE BASEBALL—The first Little League was organized in Williamsport, Pennsylvania, in 1939 by Carl E. Stotz. Despite World War II, the idea spread rapidly through Pennsylvania; by 1958 it had spread across the United States and to many other lands.

Players are 8 to 12 years of age; younger players often get experience in a "minor league" before moving up to the "big leagues." The games are played on a scaled-down diamond, 60 ft square, with a pitching distance of 44 ft.

Since 1947 a Little League World Series has been held annually in Williamsport. It briefly became a true World Series; in the six-year period, 1969–1974, the championship was won five times by the Nationalist Chinese teams. As a result, Little League directors in 1974 decided to limit the "World Series" to teams from North America. However, that action was rescinded in 1976.

LONG HORSE—A piece of gymnastics apparatus originally used to train cavalrymen in the techniques of jumping on, off, and even over horses; now used by male competitors in performing various gymnastic exercises.

See also GYMNASTICS.

LONG JUMP—Formerly the broad jump on American track and field programs, and still called the broad jump by most people; a field event in which competitors jump for distance.

See also TRACK AND FIELD.

LUGE—Tobogganing is an active participation sport, but as a competitive sport it was replaced long ago by its descendant, bobsledding. Another young descendant, luge, was developed in the early twentieth century.

"Luge" is the French word for sled. As a sport, it is similar to tobogganing—but the luger half-sits and half-lies on the back, with head toward the back of the sled; the tobogganist lies on the stomach, head at the front of the sled.

The first European luge championships were held in 1914, but the sport had little potential until the flexible sled was developed in the 1930s. Since then, the sport has boomed in Europe, primarily because bobsleds need specially built runs, while a luge, like an ordinary sled, can be used on any mountain road. In 1955 the sport got its own administrative body, the Fédération Internationale de Luge de Course (FIL); previously, it had been under the control of the international bobsledding and tobogganing organization. The sport was to be added to the 1960 Winter Olympics, but a suitable Olympic-style run couldn't be built at Squaw Valley. Since 1964 it has been a regular sport on the Olympic program.

The Luge. The sled used in luging should be tailored to the rider for serious competition. It is about 18 in wide in

In luge, a racer lies on his back and guides a frail sled down an icy run at speeds of up to 90 mph. (*F. Kelly MacNeill.*)

back, about 13 in wide in front, and about 51 in long. It is made, essentially, of two steel runners mounted on two rails, with a canvas seat slung between them. The seat is about 22 by 16 in and about 6 in above the ground—higher if it is to be used on natural terrain. Maximum total weight of the sled for international competition is 20 kg (about 44 lb).

The Course. In international competition the luge course is about 1,000 to 1,200 m long for men's singles, about 200 m less for women's singles and men's doubles. It has an average drop of 10 to 11 percent; major courses have many turns, including hairpins.

Techniques. Although some lugers believe in sitting almost upright, the best competitors use a more efficient aerodynamic position, lying back as far as possible with the head up, the legs outside the runners, and the toes pointed straight up. The driver holds onto reins with one hand and grips the edge of the sled with the other. Steering is accomplished by pushing with the lower part of the leg on the runner on the side away from the direction of the turn, while lifting the other runner with the foot. Pulling on the rein on that side helps with the lifting; shifting body weight in the direction of the turn also helps.

In doubles, the driver is the contestant at the back of the sled. The rider in front is there primarily for ballast, to help through turns by shifting body weight.

AAU National Champions

Men's Singles

1972	Terry O'Brien
1973	Richard Genovese
1974	Terry O'Brien
1975	Richard Genovese
1976	James Murray

Women's Singles

1972	Kathleen Homstad
1973	Kathleen Homstad
1974	Kathleen Homstad
1975	Helena Thayer
1976	Kathleen Homstad

M

MARATHON—Although often considered a track and field event, the marathon, like cross-country running, is really a sport in and of itself. It is one of the most important races on the Olympic program; yet it was not an event in the ancient Greek Olympic games, even though it derives from a stirring event in Greek history.

In 490 B.C. the Athenian army defeated Darius' Persian army at the battle of Marathon, and Miltiades, the leader of the Athenian forces, called on a famous runner, Pheiddippides, to bring news of the victory to Athens. Pheiddippides ran the entire distance, gave the good news to the elders who were gathered in the marketplace, and then died of exhaustion.

When the first modern Olympics were held in Athens, in 1896, the marathon was an important feature of the program. It was run over approximately the same route followed by Pheiddippides, a distance of about 40 km (26 mi, 385 yd). There were 25 starters; appropriately, a Greek shepherd, Spiridon Loues, was the winner.

Although a number of marathons are staged in the United States, including an annual AAU event for the national championship, by far the best known is the Boston Marathon, run every Patriot's Day (originally April 12; now the third monday in April) from Hopkinton, Massachusetts, to Boston.

AAU Champions

1925	Charles L. Mellor	2:33:00⅗
1926	Clarence DeMar	2:45:05⅕
1927	Clarence DeMar	2:40:22⅕
1928	Clarence DeMar	2:37:07⅘
1929	John C. Miles	2:33:08⅘
1930	Karl Koski	2:25:21⅕
1931	William A. Agee	2:32:38
1932	Clyde D. Martak	2:58:18
1933	Dave Komonen	2:53:43
1934	Dave Komonen	2:43:26.6
1935	Frank "Pat" Dengis	2:53:53
1936	William T. McMahon	2:38:14⅕
1937	Mel Porter	2:44:22
1938	Frank "Pat" Dengis	2:39:38.2
1939	Frank "Pat" Dengis	2:33:45.2
1940	Gerard Cote	2:34:06
1941	Joseph Smith	2:36:06.8
1942	Fred A. McGlone	2:37:54
1943	Sgt. Gerard Cote	2:38:35.3
1944	Charles Robbins	2:40:48.6
1945	Charles Robbins	2:37:14
1946	Gerard Cote	2:47:53.6
1947	Ted Vogel	2:40:11
1948	John A. Kelley	2:48:32.3
1949	Victor Dyrgall	2:38:48.9
1950	John A. Kelley	2:45:55.3
1951	Jesse Van Zant	2:37:12.5
1952	Victor Dyrgall	2:38:24.4
1953	Karl Gosta Leandersson	2:48:12.5
1954	Ted Corbitt	2:46:13.9
1955	Nick Costes	2:31:12.4
1956	John J. Kelley	2:24:52.2
1957	John J. Kelley	2:24:55.2
1958	John J. Kelley	2:21:00.4
1959	John J. Kelley	2:21:54.4
1960	John J. Kelley	2:24:18.5
1961	John J. Kelley	2:26:53.4
1962	John J. Kelley	2:27:39.0
1963	John J. Kelley	2:25:17.6
1964	Leonard Edelen	2:24:25.6
1965	Gar Williams	2:33:50.6
1966	Norman Higgins	2:22:50.0
1967	Ron Dews	2:40:07
1968	George Young	2:30:48
1969	Tom Heinonen	2:24:11
1970	Bob Fitts	2:24:11
1971	Ken Moore	2:16:49
1972	Edmund Norris	2:24:42.8
1973	Doug Schmenk	2:15:45.0
1974	Ron Wayne	2:18:52
1975	Gary Tuttle	2:17:27
1976	Gary Tuttle	2:15:15

MIDGET RACING—*See* AUTOMOBILE RACING.

MINOR-LEAGUE BASEBALL—As soon as the first true major league, the National, was organized in 1876, there were minor-league teams, in a sense—all those professional teams not in the National League. There were as many as 50 such teams in 1877, and many of them wanted either to join the National League or to form a rival association. To forestall competition, the league organized its own group of 13 teams, the League Alliance; the minor and major teams agreed to honor one another's contracts under this agreement. The alliance was abolished in 1883.

In the meantime the first true minor league had been formed, the International Association of Professional Base Ball Players, which also included 13 clubs at the beginning of the 1877 season; 10 other teams joined during the season. It became the National Association in 1879, when its Canadian members dropped out, and it was defunct after the 1880 season.

Other early minor leagues were the Northwestern, which lasted just for the 1879 season, and the Eastern Championship Association, which also lasted one season in 1881. The Northwestern League, however, was reorganized in 1883. Later that year, the National League, the rival American Association, and the Northwestern League signed the first National Agreement, which formed the structure of Organized Baseball. Under the agreement, leagues agreed to honor one another's contracts and to uphold one another's suspensions and expulsions, and an arbitration committee was formed to settle all disputes and complaints that arose under the agreement.

Other minor leagues quickly sprang up as baseball gained popularity. In 1888, minor leagues included the International, the Western, the Central, the California, the New England, the Southern, the Texas, and the Tri-State. Many of them suffered from player raids during the Players' League war of 1890; that war led to a new National Agreement, involving just one minor league, the Western, which included several cities that had once been in the now-defunct Northwestern League. Other minor leagues were permitted to join, but didn't get the contract protection offered to the Western League.

In 1892, yet another National Agreement was drawn up. This gave the minor leagues the right to reserve their players for a season, but it also gave the major leagues the right to draft minor leaguers at the end of each season. The minors were divided into two classes, A and B, and Class A teams were given the right to draft Class B players.

About this time the farm system began to take shape: Major league teams would often assign a player to a minor team ("farm") to gain experience, while keeping him under contract.

Hit hard again by the American League–National League war, when both major leagues began raiding their rosters, the minor leagues in 1901 formed their own organization, the National Association of Professional Baseball Leagues, and drew up their own National Agreement. When the two major leagues made peace, before the 1903 season, the NAPBL became a third party to yet another National Agreement.

Farm Systems. At the end of the 1900 season there were eight minor leagues. By 1912 there were 48. However, the war with the Federal League and World War I hurt the minors badly; nine leagues started the 1918 season and only one of them played the full schedule. The minor leagues, it was obvious, were terribly dependent on the major leagues. Money paid by major leagues for players could mean the difference between going bankrupt and continuing operations; just as important, the minor leagues needed to be sure that the majors would honor their contracts.

In 1919 the minors withdrew from the National Agreement, dissatisfied with drafting procedures and prices. Not until 1921 were they formally brought back into Organized Baseball. By that time there were five classes of minor leagues: AA, A, B, C, and D (in descending order, according to caliber of play). A key to the new agreement was that any minor league could exempt itself from the draft if it also agreed not to draft players from any other leagues. For the stronger, higher-class leagues, this was very important, because they could now get more money when their players were sold to the major leagues.

There was still considerable stress and strain, but Branch Rickey, an executive of the St. Louis Cardinals, was already changing the whole nature of the major-minor relationship. In 1919 Rickey began buying partial or complete control of various minor-league teams, distributed through all the classifications. This enabled St. Louis to sign a young player, start him in Class D and move him up the chain until, if he had the talent, he arrived in the major leagues well seasoned. It worked so well for the Cardinals, who also made additional revenue by selling off surplus players, that other teams began to follow suit. Most minor-league teams were happy with major-league ownership, since it helped stabilize the franchise by assuring a steady flow of players to the team; and, of course, the major-league team would absorb any deficit.

As the farm system developed, not all farm teams were owned in whole or part by major-league teams; working agreements also came into being, under which a major-league team would agree to assign players to a certain minor team on the condition that they remain the property of the major-league team.

Minor-league baseball reached its peak in 1949, when there were 59 leagues. There were now six classifications, ranging from AAA to D. In 1951 the Pacific Coast League won an "Open" classification, which seemed a step toward major-league status. However, during the 1950s the minor leagues declined drastically. Television hurt, as fans in minor-league cities decided they would rather watch major-league games on television than go to the local park. Franchise moves and expansion also gradually encroached on many areas that had been of foremost importance to the top minors.

There are now 14 minor leagues ranging in classification from AAA to A, and three rookie leagues, in which only first-year professionals can play. Although virtually any player needs minor-league experience before he can reach the majors, college baseball has in many respects replaced the lower minor leagues as a training ground for future stars.

See also BASEBALL.

MODERN PENTATHLON—Like the biathlon, the modern pentathlon grew out of military training and, in a sense, is the modern replacement for the pentathlon of the ancient Olympics, which was designed by the Spartans as an overall test of military skills. That ancient pentathlon included spear (javelin) throwing, sprinting, the discus throw, wrestling, and broad jumping. The modern pentathlon was designed specifically for the Olympic Games of 1912, to attract military participation from all over the world. It is now somewhat outdated, but it is still a grueling test of athletic skills.

A five-day event, the modern pentathlon begins with a 1,000-m cross-country ride on horseback, over 20 obstacles, against time. The rider is given a strange horse and has just 20 minutes before the ride begins to get acquainted with the animal. On the second day all competitors take part in a round-robin schedule of épée fencing, with just one touch per bout. On the third day they take part in pistol shooting, four five-shot series at a standing silhouette target from a distance of 25 m. The fourth event is a 300-m freestyle swim, against time, and the last event is a 4,000-m cross-country run, also against time.

Scoring is based on an arbitrary point system established by the international governing body, the Union Internationale Pentathlon Moderne et Biathlon (UIPMB). The following are the established standards: riding, 2 min, 10 sec; fencing, 70 percent winning percentage; shooting, 194 of a possible 200; swimming, 3 min, 52 sec; running, 14 min, 15 sec. A competitor is given 1,000 points for equaling the standard, and points are added or deducted for falling short of or exceeding the standard.

In the United States. An American has never won a world or Olympic title in modern pentathlon, but several have come close. Between 1912 and World War II, virtually all competitors came from military services. In 1959, however, it was decided that competitors should be drawn from a broader spectrum of athletes, and a national organization was formed to recruit civilians for modern pentathlon.

The Army is still active in the sport, maintaining a training center at Fort Sam Houston, Texas, where military and civilian athletes can train and receive expert coaching. The sport is under the general supervision of the U.S. Modern Pentathlon and Biathlon Association.

MOTOCROSS—Cross-country motorcycle racing developed as a competitive event in France in the late 1940s and was formally organized in 1952. It was rather slow in spreading to the United States, but was sanctioned by the American Motorcycle Association in 1969. The AMA has developed rules for the conduct of the sport in this country, and now also conducts motocross races, including national championship events and two major series of races involving both European and American competitors.

See also MOTORCYCLE RACING.

MOTORBOAT RACING—*See* POWERBOAT RACING.

MOTORCYCLE RACING—The first internal-combustion gasoline engine, built by Gottlieb Daimler in 1885, was tested on a bicycle, and so, in a sense, the motorcycle predates the modern automobile. However, automobile

Pierre Karsmakers is used to being thoroughly splattered with mud, as one of the United States' top motocross racers. (AMA News *Photo by Rusty Rae.*)

racing had already gained some popularity before the first genuine motorcycle was invented, about 1900. And, as with automobiles, the first real motorcycle races were generally long-range, endurance events that gave manufacturers a chance to showcase their vehicles.

The motorcycle has long been popular as a utilitarian vehicle in Europe, because of its low cost, size, and low consumption of gasoline. As a result, the sport of motorcycle racing developed earlier in Europe than in the United States, and also followed a somewhat different pattern. Europe's motorcycle racing, like its automobile racing, was developed on public roads, closed off temporarily for racing purposes. The use of the motorcycle in World War I to carry dispatches across rough terrain, and the resultant development of effective suspension systems, also spurred the growth of a unique kind of race, the motocross (cross-country), in Europe.

Racing in the United States. An early organization, the Federation of American Motorcyclists (FAM), established Class A racing for professionals in 1906. There had been earlier racing in this country, on a rather informal basis. George Hendrie of Springfield, Massachusetts, who built the first American motorcycle, the "Indian," in 1902, set an endurance record in that year by traveling 250 mi in 16½ hr. Hendrie had been an early bicycle racer, often competing on dirt harness-racing tracks around Springfield, and he began racing motorcycles on the same tracks to publicize the vehicle. That set the pattern for the sport in this country; because of the prevalence of dirt tracks at county fairgrounds and the increasing ban on racing on public roads, the sport in the United States quickly became track-oriented.

The FAM, however, got involved in an internal disagreement over whether professional racing was a good idea, and the sport almost died after World War I. In 1924 the American Motorcycle Association was established to promote the sport. Following the pattern of American automobile racing, the orientation toward tracks rather than roads continued under AMA auspices. Although "road racing" is important in the AMA scheme of things, this country's "road races" are actually conducted over long paved tracks.

Racing motorcyclist leans hard to the inside as he comes around a turn. (AMA News *Photo by Rusty Rae.*)

The first major United States road race was conducted in 1937 on the Daytona, Florida, beach, where automobile time trials for world speed records had long been conducted. In the first 200-mi Daytona race, the motorcyclists simply raced up and down a 2½-mi stretch of beach. The Daytona "road race" today is conducted on the fast track of the Daytona International Speedway.

The United States also had a form of racing in the 1930s somewhat similar to the European road races—"Tourist Trophy" racing, in which motorcyclists compete on tracks designed to simulate some of the conditions experienced in true road racing. TT races are sometimes called steeplechasses because the tracks incorporate jumps where the motorcycles have to fly through the air for as much as 20 ft.

The European and American forms of the sport remained almost entirely separate until the late 1960s when a Swedish motorcycle firm, Husqvarna ("Husky"), sponsored some motocross races in the United States, importing European drivers for the purpose. This form of the sport caught on quickly, and the AMA now sponsors two major motocross series a year, with Europeans competing against Amercian riders.

American Amateur Racing. Motorcycle racing in the United States is rather similar to sports-car racing in that it is a sport for amateurs as well as professionals, and races are conducted in many classes, enabling even novices on low-powered bikes to compete. Motocross has become particularly popular among amateurs.

The AMA estimates that about 8,000 motorcycle-racing events are conducted each year in the United States, and only 1,000 of these are for professionals. More than 90,000 amateur riders compete in one or more events each year.

Types of Competition

Hill Climbs. Hill climbing is an indigenous American version of motorcycling. The first known hill climb was conducted near Boston in 1904, and the Pike's Peak Hill Climb, for autos and motorcycles, began in 1916. Although not as important a part of the national racing scene as it was in the 1920s and 1930s, the motorcycle hill climb is still with us.

Generally the climb takes place over a relatively small part of the hill, a nearly vertical face of up to 500 ft in height. The cyclist gets about 20 ft for a head start. Each rider usually gets two attempts, and the best attempt is the one that counts. Those who make it to the top are scored on time. Those who don't get over the top are scored on the basis of how high they actually did get.

Flat-Track. Racing on oval dirt tracks, ½ mi or 1 mi in length, is called flat-track racing. This is the "keep turning left" style of racing, an exciting form of the sport known for the long "rooster tails" of dirt thrown up by bikes as they go around corners. The motorcycles have engines of up to 750-cm³ displacement, and the riders use a three-point-stance method of riding; the left foot, equipped with a steel sole, is used as a kind of third wheel to help the rider maintain balance, going through the turns.

Short-Track. This form of the sport, on tracks of less than a ½ mi in length, is primarily for specialists. It is flat-track racing, but the bikes are limited to 360-cm³ displacement, and the races tend to be much rougher than the longer flat-track races. The bikes are much more closely bunched, and there's usually a good deal of banging around, much of it intentional, in the course of a race.

Tourist-Trophy (TT). The dirt tracks used for TT racing have right- and left-hand turns, as well as the steeplechase-style jumps. The bikes are similar to those used in flat-track racing, but the rider can't use the usual three-point style, and many mechanical items are specially designed for TT racing—especially the brakes.

Road Racing. This category is the motorcycle version of Grand Prix track racing. Much of it is conducted on speedway-type courses also used for automobiles, with right and left turns and long straightaways that permit speeds of up to 180 mph. The road-racing cyclist sits back and races, inside a streamlined shell that cuts wind resistance; the foot pedals are near the rear wheel, and the handlebars are miniscule and low slung. The machines range from 350- to 750-cm³ displacement.

Indoor Tracks. The ultimate in short-track racing, indoor competition in basketball and hockey arenas has gained a good deal of popularity in recent years, and the AMA now conducts a special indoor championship series. This is similar to short-track racing, except that the rider's left sole is now covered with a kind of carpeting that will slide easily along polished floors.

Speedway. Popular in Europe, speedway racing has also shown a good deal of growth in this country in a relatively short time. This is flat-track racing with a type of bike built only for racing—it looks more like a racing

World motocross champion Heiki Mikkola grooves through heavy going during a race in the United States. (AMA News *Photo by Rusty Rae.*)

bicycle than like any other type of motorcycle. The vehicle has skinny wheels, practically no seat, and a minimum amount of weight, and can be ridden sideways almost all the way around a short track. The 500-cm^3 engines burn a special mixture of racing fuel.

Motocross. The form of the sport that has drawn the most attention in the 1970s is, as already noted, a relatively recent import from Europe. A true motocross is run over natural terrain, complete with holes, gullies, and uphill and downhill stretches that offer a severe test of bike and rider. There are three classes of bikes, 125-, 250-, and 500-cm^3, and a race consists of two or three heats, called "motos."

Major Series

The American Motorcycle Association's premier championship is the Grand National, established in 1954. The emphasis is on versatility. The Grand National series includes five different types of competition, with 150 points awarded to the winner in each event, 120 to the second-place finisher, and so on, down to 1 point for twentieth place. Other major competitions include:

Inter-AMA Motocross. Also known as the summer series, the Inter-AMA series of motocross races is conducted during July, when European riders are free to compete in the United States. The series is now conducted for 125- and 250-cm^3 motorcycles. The same point system used for Grand National racing is used in the Inter-AMA.

Trans-AMA Motocross. Conducted in the fall, after the European Grand Prix motorcycle season is over, the Trans-AMA series is for 500-cm^3 motocross riders.

National Championship Motocross. In addition to the two international motocross series, the AMA names national champions in 125-, 250- and 500-cm^3 classes, based on a series of selected races. Some of the races are also part of the Inter-AMA and Trans-AMA series, while some are for American riders only. Riders are allowed to compete in one class only.

Grand National Champions

(Winner of 50-mi race at Springfield, Ill., 1946-1953; since 1954, determined by a point system based on selected races).

1946	Chet Dykgraff
1947	Jimmy Chann
1948	Jimmy Chann
1949	Jimmy Chann
1950	Larry Headrick
1951	Bobby Hill
1952	Bobby Hill
1953	Bill Tuman
1954	Joe Leonard
1955	Brad Andres
1956	Joe Leonard
1957	Joe Leonard
1958	Carroll Resweber
1959	Carroll Resweber
1960	Carroll Resweber
1961	Carroll Resweber
1962	Bart Markel
1963	Dick Mann
1964	Roger Reiman
1965	Bart Markel
1966	Bart Markel
1967	Gary Nixon
1968	Gary Nixon
1969	Mert Lawwill
1970	Gene Romero
1971	Dick Mann
1972	Mark Brelsford
1973	Ken Roberts
1974	Ken Roberts
1975	Gary Scott
1976	Jay Springsteen

Bibliography. *AMA Competition Yearbook,* American Motorcycle Association, Westerville, Ohio (annual).

N

NATIONAL ASSOCIATION FOR INTERCOLLEGIATE ATHLETICS (NAIA)

In 1937 a group of college administrators in the Midwest decided to organize a basketball tournament. For that purpose they formed the National Association of Intercollegiate Basketball, and the tournament was held in Kansas City, Missouri. During the next couple of years, members of the organization began to realize there was a need for a body that could promote the cause of athletic programs among smaller colleges. And so, in 1940, the NAIB became the National Association for Intercollegiate Athletics, or NAIA.

The NAIA functions somewhat like the NCAA, except that its members are all small to medium-sized colleges (although any four-year college or university can be admitted to membership). The chief function is to organize and promote local, district, and national tournament events in 16 sports—although the NAIA also sets standards controlling the financing of athletic programs, the granting of financial aid to athletes, and related matters. "The basic premise," according to the NAIA, "is that the athletic program must be a part of the general education process in the institution and not a membership apart."

In addition the organization awards an annual scholarship to an outstanding student-athlete, maintains halls of fame in a number of sports, and represents its member institutions on the U.S. Olympic Committee and in the Amateur Athletic Union.

There are now nearly 600 colleges and universities and 46 conferences that belong to the NAIA, which is governed by an executive committee elected by the membership. The NAIA is organized into 32 districts, each of which is administered by its own committee and chairman, elected from within the district.

NAIA Hall of Fame
General Contributors

(For those who have made significant contributions to athletics in general)

Ernest Anderson, Augsburg College (Minnesota)
Dr. Jack Bell, East Texas State
Dr. M. C. Cunningham, Fort Hays State (Kansas)
Frank Casey, Simpson College (Iowa)
A. O. Duer, NAIA executive secretary 1949–1975
Charles Cramer, Cramer Chemical Company
Frank Cramer, Cramer Chemical Company
Al Garten, Eastern New Mexico
Dr. Eldon Graber, Bluffton College (Ohio)
Dr. Jesse Hawthorne, East Texas State
Dr. Herbert Hearsey, Western Washington
Paul H. Helms, Sr., founder of Helms Athletic Foundation
George W. Hine, Jr., Howard Payne College (Texas)
Dr. Francis Hoover, Appalachian State

Dr. John D. Lawther, Westminster College (Pennsylvania)
Dr. L. D. Ligon, Midwestern University (Texas)
Ernest Mehl, *Kansas City Star*
Perry Mitchell, Central Washington State
Dr. Roswell D. Merrick, Springfield College (Massachusetts)
C. E. McBride, *Kansas City Star*
Lee Prather, Northwestern State of Louisiana
William R. Schroeder, United Savings-Helms Athletic Foundation
Dr. Harry Scott, Columbia University
John Strahl, Greenville College (Illinois)
Wilmont Toalson, Fort Hays State (Kansas)
W. L. Zorn, Wisconsin State, Eau Claire

NATIONAL COLLEGIATE ATHLETIC ASSOCIATION (NCAA)

President Theodore Roosevelt became concerned in 1905 about the future of football. There were public complaints about the roughness of the sport. Deaths and serious injuries had led some state legislatures to consider abolishing it. Roosevelt wanted to save football, but he realized rules changes would be necessary, so he called two White House conferences of college athletic leaders to talk about reforming the sport.

Representatives of 13 colleges met in December, 1905 to consider some rules changes. Later that month, 62 colleges and universities met in New York City to establish a new football rules committee. At the same time they made plans to form a national body to draw up standards for a variety of intercollegiate sports. The Intercollegiate Athletic Association was formally organized on March 31, 1906. The name was changed to the National Collegiate Athletic Association in 1910.

In its early years, the NCAA was primarily a rules-making body for various intercollegiate sports. The group did draw up eligibility rules, but they were merely proposed rules to be followed by schools and conferences. No enforcement machinery was established at first. In 1921 the NCAA sponsored its first national championship event, the National Collegiate Track and Field Championships. That year the NCAA also took over responsibility for the national Collegiate Tennis Tournament, which had been established in 1883.

The first big step in the evolution of the NCAA toward its present form was taken in 1939, when the constitution was rewritten to include definite standards that were to be requirements for membership; at the same time provisions were made for expelling members that didn't meet those standards. The new constitution was ratified in 1941.

The postwar years brought a new set of problems. The so-called Sanity Code was difficult to administer, television was beginning to become an important factor in sports, and postseason events, especially football bowl games, were proliferating, leading to potential and actual abuses of NCAA policies and standards.

New principles were adopted in 1948, but by 1951 it was apparent that a new kind of organization, with full-time leadership, would be necessary. The 1951 convention knocked some standards out of the constitution, in order that the standards could be set up separately in bylaws, which could be more easily changed to meet new conditions, and Walter Byers, who had been a part-time executive assistant, became the first full-time executive director. National headquarters was established in Kansas City, Missouri, the following year.

Tougher enforcement policies were adopted in 1953, when a 17-member council was set up to direct general policies between conventions. The council was given the power to take a number of disciplinary steps against members who violated rules and regulations, and was also empowered to order all members to refrain from competition with unsanctioned institutions.

Present Organization. The NCAA today has nearly 800 member institutions, conferences, and organizations. The governing body is the annual convention, at which each member is entitled to one vote on issues that arise. An 18-member council, elected by the convention, directs policy. The council is made up of eight district vice-presidents, eight vice-presidents at large, a secretary-treasurer, and a president.

An executive committee of 10 members transacts business and administers the association's events. The council president and secretary-treasurer and one representative from each of the eight districts form the executive committee. Policy is developed by committees which channel reports and recommendations to the convention, by way of the council or executive committee.

Divisions. At a special convention in 1973 the NCAA voted to reorganize into three divisions, representing, in general, three different levels of competition. Each member college can choose the division in which it wishes to be placed. A Division II or III school is allowed to compete for Division I championships in one sport, other than football or basketball.

Each division may adopt its own bylaws by unanimous vote. However, proposed division bylaws may be vetoed by a two-thirds majority vote of all delegates voting at a convention. Each division is entitled to representation on the council, the executive committee, and many of the standing committees.

Championships. The NCAA now conducts annual competition leading to championships in 39 sports—17 in Division I, 12 in Division II, and 10 in Division III. If a championship is not offered in a school's division, the school is eligible to compete in the next higher division. A Division III school may compete for a Division I championship if that sport doesn't have a championship event in Divisions II or III. The following national championship competitions are now sponsored by the NCAA:

Division I—Baseball, basketball, cross-country, fencing, golf, gymnastics, hockey, lacrosse, skiing, soccer, swimming, tennis, indoor track, outdoor track, volleyball, water polo, wrestling.

Division II—Baseball, basketball, cross-country, football, golf, gymnastics, lacrosse, soccer, swimming, tennis, outdoor track, wrestling.

Division III—Baseball, basketball, cross-country, football, golf, soccer, swimming, tennis, outdoor track, wrestling.

Functions. The chief function of the NCAA is to act as a rules-making body for intercollegiate athletics. This involves not only playing rules for specific sports but rules relating to eligibility of athletes and to amateur standing. A second major function is to conduct championship events and to maintain and preserve athletic records.

The NCAA also offers athletic insurance programs to member institutions, including group-travel and medical insurance covering student-athletes and loss-of-revenue insurance to prevent serious financial losses when games must be canceled for various reasons.

Aside from the periodic national championship events, the NCAA is most noted by the public when taking disciplinary action against members for violating its rules pertaining to recruiting, financial aid, and eligibility. The association has a standing committee on infractions and an investigative staff to look into possible violations. After a preliminary investigation, the institution is notified of the possible violation, and may appear before the committee to offer a defense. The committee on infractions may make a finding and impose a penalty. The institution is entitled to an appeal to the NCAA council, which can accept the committee's findings and penalty, alter either or both, or make its own findings and impose its own penalty, if warranted.

If found guilty of an infraction, an institution may merely be warned, or may be placed on probation, with or without sanctions. Probation without sanctions is imposed for a relatively minor violation. If further infractions occur during the probation period, heavier penalties are imposed. Probation periods range from one year to indefinite. In the case of indefinite probation, a minimum period may be specified.

Sanctions may involve banning a school's team, or all of its teams, from postseason and championship competition, or banning the institution from appearances on any NCAA-regulated television shows. A school may also be limited in the number of grants-in-aid it can award to scholar-athletes in the sport or sports in which violations occurred.

The most extreme penalty would be expulsion from the association. However, that penalty has never been imposed.

Recruiting and Eligibility. Specific standards vary from sport to sport and from one division to another, and they are frequently changed. It can be said, in general, that the NCAA sets certain minimum admissions standards for student-athletes; limits the number of grants-in-aid (scholarships) that can be given annually in a given sport; limits the monetary value of grants-in-aid awarded; attempts to prevent overzealous recruiting and "under-the-table" forms of financial aid; and sets certain standards of amateurism, since student-athletes are expected to be amateurs.

In 1973, for example, the NCAA adopted new standards for football players at Division I institutions. To be given a grant-in-aid, a student must have maintained a 2.0 grade average (the equivalent of a C) in high school. No more than 30 grants-in-aid may be given to students in a class. A student-athlete may not be offered more than a scholarship for room, board, tuition, and books and equipment, plus $15 a month expense money.

In attempting to recruit an athlete, a college may pay for just one visit to the campus, to last no more than 48 hours, and during that time the athlete must live in a dormitory or similar living quarters, and must be given meals comparable to those given the undergraduate students. Recruiters may visit a boy any number of times off campus, but they can't pay for his transportation to any meeting place or spend any money on entertainment or food for him off campus.

Amateurism and International Sports. Because the NCAA is involved in setting standards of amateurism for the student-athletes under its jurisdiction, it has also become increasingly involved in international sports, and this involvement has led, during the last 12 or 15 years, to a power struggle with the Amateur Athletic Union.

In most countries, there is either one strong central organization that controls amateur sport or a number of individual-sport organizations that are responsible for standards of amateurism within their sports. Amateur sports in the United States, however, have been built on two foundations: athletic clubs, under the general supervision of the Amateur Athletic Union (AAU), and colleges, under the supervision of the NCAA. For many years, the two major organizations cooperated closely. As the NCAA grew in stature and built up its own administrative structure, however, friction developed, and the friction has generally peaked at times when Olympic representatives are being selected.

Complicating the situation is the fact that the AAU doesn't actually have direct control over many sports; most of them are controlled by their own governing bodies, which have generally in turn been allied members of the AAU. Many of these one-sport associations are federations of local, state, and regional clubs.

During the 1960s, the NCAA began to resent the control exercised by the AAU over collegiate athletics, and began its own federation movement. These new federations, often set up in opposition to similar groups that belong to the AAU, are alliances of clubs and organizations similar to the AAU sports organizations, which are usually called associations instead of federations. The most successful of the federations are those in gymnastics, wrestling, and basketball. The U.S. Track and Field Federation has become an important organization, conducting its own national championship track meet annually, and the gymnastics and wrestling federations have won major victories by being accepted as the official sanctioning bodies by the International Olympic Committe.

See also AMATEUR ATHLETIC UNION; AMATEURISM.

NEGRO ATHLETES —*See* BLACK ATHLETES.

O

OFF-ROAD RACING—While off-road racing is generally taken to mean desert racing involving dune buggies and similar vehicles, there are two other versions of the sport: swamp-buggy racing, primarily in the Florida Everglades, and all-terrain-vehicle racing, for vehicles rather similar to dune buggies but intended primarily for traveling through muddy terrain.

Off-road racing apparently developed in the 1920s, with the original dune buggies, Model T's equipped with belts in back. These vehicles were developed originally for running rum from shore drops across sandy terrain to highways. After World War II the sport took another form, as surplus Army jeeps became available to civilians. Then in the early 1960s Bruce Meyers of Newport Beach, California, developed the prototype of the modern dune buggy by putting a new fiberglass body on a wrecked Volkswagen.

Record runs on the Baja peninsula of Mexico began in 1962. Motorcycles turned in the fastest times. The first formal race, the Mexico 1,000, was held in 1967. A shorter version over some of the same terrain, the Baja 500, was inaugurated in 1969; a third major race, the Mint 400, held near Las Vegas, started in 1968.

This form of the sport is controlled by the National Off-the-Road Racing Association (NORRA), founded in 1968. The NORRA sanctions the three major races, which are held for seven classes of vehicles, including motorcycles, production cars, and modified vehicles. Some of the "pro-duction" classes, however, are for cars produced in kit form, with only 50 complete kits or 10 complete cars produced in a 12-month period necessary for inclusion.

Dune buggies also race on closed-circuit sand tracks. The most common type of buggy has a wheelbase of 78 to 84 in, Volkswagen floor pans with fiberglass panels, and molded plastic seats, and is powered by a 1,200-cm³ VW, Corvair, or Porsche engine. Giant, low-pressured rear tires enable the buggy to travel over virtually any kind of terrain.

Swamp-buggy racing is a less formal kind of competition. The buggies, developed originally for travel through the shallow, vegetation-filled waters of the Everglades, were first used for formal racing in 1949. The major race is the "Mile o' Mud," held annually near Naples, Florida.

The all-terrain vehicle (ATV), developed about the same time as the dune buggy, is essentially an uncovered metal box with six large, soft tires, inflated to a pressure of only about 2 lb. There are also some experimental three-wheeled models. At one time a fad in several upper Midwestern states, the vehicle has run into a good deal of opposition from conservationist groups and is now banned from many areas. A national championship race, begun in 1970, is held annually in Monroe, Michigan.

See also SNOWMOBILING.

OLYMPIC GAMES—The first recorded Olympics took place in 776 B.C. in a stadium built to honor the god Zeus. The stadium was beside a temple dedicated to Zeus, in a section of Peloponnesus called Olympia. There was one event, a foot race of about 200 yd; it was won by Coroebus.

It is certain, however, that the Olympic Games originated before that year. Among the ancient Greeks, athletic contests were customarily held in honor of a god or dead hero. Homer's *Iliad* describes games held at the funeral of Patroclus, and it is possible that, in later years, such games were held periodically to honor all those who had died during the period. In the fifth century B.C., Pindar wrote that Heracles (Hercules) originated the games to celebrate his victory over King Augeas and the city-state of Elis. There are other legends, including one that Zeus himself established the games after defeating Cronus for the sovereignty of heaven.

The original Olympics were a midsummer festival, held every fourth year. The Greeks dated their chronology in four-year periods, called Olympiads; the Olympics, which celebrated the beginning of a new Olympiad, included religious rites and competition in oratory, music, poetry, and other arts, as well as in sports.

Originally the city-state of Pisa controlled the games,

This type of six-wheeled all-terrain vehicle now runs in formal races, particularly in the upper Midwest. *(Courtesy of All-Terrain Vehicle Association.)*

but another city-state, Elis, had taken over by 572 B.C. When powerful Sparta formed an alliance with Elis, the games took on new importance. Elis controlled the religious aspects of the Olympics and Sparta enforced the sacred truce that allowed athletes to come from any part of Greece or the Greek colonies to compete, without fear even when states of war existed among various city-states.

Each competitor had to swear that he was a freeborn Greek who had committed no sacrilege to the gods. A pig would be sacrificed to Zeus and a black ram to Pelops at the opening ceremonies, and an olive grove in the area was sacred territory. An Olympic victor was given a crown of olive and a palm branch as trophies, and was expected to give a victory banquet for friends and relatives. There were also special compensations, however: Each winner was exempted from taxes for an Olympiad, he was often honored with a statue in his home town, and, in Athens, he was allowed to live free in the Pyrtaneum, a public hall set aside for distinguished citizens.

The single foot race the length of the stadium was the only Olympic event until the fifteenth Olympiad, when a long-distance foot race, the *dolichos*, was added: a race at varying distances ranging from a little less than 1 mi to 5,040 yd. Wrestling and the pentathlon, which comprised broad jumping, spear throwing, discus throwing, wrestling, and racing, were added for the eighteenth games. Gradually other events were added, including Greek boxing, chariot racing, horseback racing, the pancratium (a combination of boxing and wrestling), and a foot race in armor. Special events for boys were introduced in 632 B.C. and for heralds and trumpeters in 416 B.C.

The Olympic Games lasted even after the Greek states lost their independence to Rome. However, under Roman influence, the games lost their religious character and became something akin to the Roman circus. Professionalism crept in as athletes began to seek prizes and money for their victories; aliens were allowed to compete, which would have been a sacrilege in the old days. The games were finally abolished by Emperor Theodosius I, A.D. 394, after more than a thousand years of existence. The temple was destroyed early in the fifth century and then rebuilt as a fort; in 426, Theodosius II had the protective walls razed, and during the sixth century an earthquake devastated what was left, and the Alphaeus River covered the plain.

The Modern Olympics

In 1887 the 25-year-old Baron Pierre de Coubertin of France saw university students in England taking part in sports, and he was impressed with the idea that athletics could be part of an educational program. He later traveled to the United States to study athletic programs, and in 1889 he organized the Congress of Physical Education in Paris. The baron soon began to develop an even more ambitious plan. The ancient Olympic Games had provided an opportunity for athletes from all over Greece to meet in friendly competition during a period of enforced truce; certainly, Coubertin reasoned, a revival of the idea could help lead to new international friendship and understanding through competition on the playing field.

During his travels throughout the world to study systems of physical education, Coubertin talked about his idea for modern Olympics, and the idea was generally received with enthusiasm. In 1892, plans were formally announced for the first modern Olympic Games, to be held in 1896—in Greece, of course. George Averoff of Alexandria donated a million drachmas to build a stadium in Athens, and athletes from all over the world were invited.

Only eight countries were actually represented in those first modern games: Denmark, England, France, Germany, Greece, Hungary, Switzerland, and the United States. Competition included track and field events, the marathon, a 100-m swimming race, gymnastics, cycling, lawn tennis, and target shooting. Nations didn't organize formal teams. The United States was represented primarily by a contingent from the Boston Athletic Association. The first man to win an Olympic gold medal was James B. Connolly, who won the triple jump; Connolly, whose request for a leave of absence from Harvard University had been turned down, simply left school to compete and never returned, except as a lecturer, after he had become a well-known writer.

The second modern Olympics, in 1900, were held in Paris, and were overshadowed by the Universal Exposition being held at the same time. Many athletes didn't even realize they were taking part in the Olympics until they received their medals, and the program mentioned the exposition but not the Olympic Games! The United States, however, was well represented by 55 athletes, many of whom had competed in the English track and field championships before moving on to Paris.

It was in 1900 that the first of the many controversies that have often marked the modern Olympics erupted: The French had planned to hold opening ceremonies on a Sunday, but most United States athletes refused to take part on Sunday and so the games were opened on Saturday, July 14—Bastille Day, a major French holiday. However, competition was held on Sunday and many of the best American athletes didn't compete. But Alvin Kraenzlein of Princeton did, and won the first of his four gold medals.

There were no swimming events on the 1900 program; lawn tennis was also dropped, and gymnastics was cut back to a single event, for the all-around championship. No new sports were added, although the track and field program was expanded.

In 1904, however, the games were held in St. Louis, again in conjunction with a major fair, the Louisiana Purchase Exposition, and a remarkably ambitious program was undertaken. There was a full schedule of swimming events, along with springboard diving and water polo; boxing, wrestling, weightlifting, rowing, and fencing were all added, and a full gymnastics program was restored along with lawn tennis. Only cycling and target shooting were dropped. The turnout, both of athletes and spectators, was rather disappointing, however. England and France sent no athletes. Australia, Canada, Cuba, Germany, Greece, Hungary, Ireland, and South Africa were represented. The United States' previous dependence on college athletes disappeared; instead, athletic clubs from all over the country sent representatives, and at times the track and field meet looked like a dual competition between the New York A.C. and the Chicago A.A.

It was decided to stage another Olympics just two years later, the tenth anniversary of the first modern games, and again Athens was the site. For the first time the

United States sent an official national team, with expenses paid by donations from across the country. Again the program was expanded: Cycling and target shooting were restored and archery and soccer were added. Boxing was dropped.

The 1908 games, originally scheduled for Rome, were held in London instead, and the British did a typically excellent job of organization. Nevertheless there was controversy. The Finns were told they would have to carry a Russian flag in the parade of athletes, and instead they carried no flag at all. Irish athletes were ordered to compete under the flag of Great Britain. The American team, and others, protested all sorts of official decisions. The 400-m race ended in confusion and controversy, with officials on the track and a claim of interference lodged against the apparent winner, J. C. Carpenter of the United States. When the race was ordered rerun, all three American runners withdrew and a lone Englishman was left to run the race all by himself. Dorando Pietri of Italy, leading in the marathon, collapsed, was helped across the line by officials, and then was disqualified for having received assistance, and the gold medal was awarded to the second finisher, John J. Hayes of the United States.

Despite all the problems, however, more athletes from more countries competed in more events than ever before, and attendance was good despite rain that fell almost constantly during the two weeks of competition. Yachting was on the program for the first time; racquets and polo were also added. Lacrosse, which had been on the St. Louis program, was an Olympic event for the second, and last, time.

After all the London bickering, many people were wondering whether the idea of modern Olympics was such a good one, after all. But the 1912 games, in Stockholm, were successful in every way—ironically so, since World War I was only two years away. For the first time, American newspapers were really interested: The Olympic Games were front-page news across the country. Twenty-six countries sent athletes. The games were now truly worldwide, since Asia was represented by three athletes from Japan. Electric timing was used for the first time. Women, who had previously competed only in figure skating and gymnastics, competed in two swimming events. New to the program were equestrian events and the modern pentathlon.

Above all, the 1912 Olympics belonged to the great American Indian athlete, Jim Thorpe. After winning both the pentathlon and the decathlon with remarkable ease, Thorpe was told by the King of Sweden, "You are the greatest athlete in the world," and Czar Nicholas of Russia sent him a silver model of a Viking ship for his performance. Unfortunately it was discovered later that Thorpe had once played professional baseball, and his trophies were taken away from him as a result.

There were two other major developments at the 1912 games: The Finns and Swedes both produced some fine distance runners. Chief among them was Hannes Kollehmainen of Finland, who won the 10,000-m run with a 45-sec lead over his nearest rival. Kollehmainen also won gold medals in the 5,000-m run and the cross-country race. The Finns were coached by Hannes' brother, who had visited the United States to study athletic training methods, and the Swedes had developed rapidly under the coaching of Ernie Hjertberg, a Swedish native who

had become an outstanding athlete in the United States before returning to his native country. The United States had won 13 of a possible 28 gold medals in track and field, and other countries decided that they, too, should study and copy American training techniques. Many of them hired American coaches to prepare them for the 1916 Olympics.

Berlin was to be the site. In 1913, to prepare, an international group met in Berlin and formed the International Amateur Athletic Federation to supervise amateur athletics around the world, primarily to set up standards of eligibility and to approve world records.

Between Wars

World War I broke out in August, 1914, however and the 1916 games were canceled. The Olympic movement resumed immediately after the war, and Antwerp, Belgium, was selected as the site for the 1920 games. Belgium had been devastated by war, but a stadium was built. Germany and Austria, losers of the war, were not invited. The games were held on a somewhat smaller scale than before the war, in terms of the number of countries and athletes taking part. Nevertheless, the program was expanded. Boxing was restored, after having been off the program since 1904, and it has been an Olympic event ever since. Wrestling was also put back on the program; for the first time, weightlifting events were offered in a variety of weight classes. Three new team sports, field hockey, ice hockey, and Rugby, were added and polo was again on the program, for the second time in the history of the games. At the 1908 games the English had offered three figure-skating events. The Belgians also restored those events to the program; their popularity, along with the addition of ice hockey, eventually led to the establishment of the Winter Olympics.

From an American point of view, the 1920 Olympics were a failure. In the strongest American suit, track and field, Finland won as many gold medals as the United States—eight. And the first of many clashes between United States athletes and their own Olympic officials had taken place. Accommodations on one of the ships, and accommodations in Belgium, were miserable. One athlete was thrown off the team for not staying in the abandoned schoolhouse which was the barracks for the athletes, and nearly 200 athletes signed a petition threatening to withdraw from competition if they weren't treated better. However, a compromise was worked out and no athletes actually withdrew.

The 1924 Olympics, in Paris, were a much greater success in every way. Nearly 1,500 athletes from 45 nations took part in the track and field events alone. The United States sent a squad of 320, including officials, on one ship, and athletes from the U.S Navy came on their own ship. But Paavo Nurmi, the Flying Finn, got a lot of the headlines, picking up and going beyond where Hannes Kollehmainen had left off in 1920. Nurmi won the 1,500- and 5,000-m runs in a two-hour period. He also won a gold medal in the 10,000-m cross-country run and finished first in the 3,000-m team race, won by Finland. (That race, however, was not included in official Olympic records.)

The Winter Olympics also began in 1924 (see separate entry), but there was one more great step to be taken. It came in 1928, in Amsterdam: Women athletes were admitted on a major scale. They had their own track and field program, their swimming program was greatly expanded, and women competed in team gymnastics (but not in individual events). Tennis, in which women had previously competed, was dropped from the program, largely because of the pre-eminence of Davis Cup competition. There were more than 4,000 athletes from 44 countries in the 1928 games, and attendance was outstanding. On opening day, the stadium was filled with 40,000 fans, and 75,000 more wanted to get in—just to see opening festivities, since no competition was scheduled for the day.

A year of worldwide economic depression, 1932 should have been a very bad year for the Olympic Games. The number of nations taking part was down to 39, and the number of athletes was almost halved. Nevertheless, a contribution of $1 million from the state of California and a $1.5 million bond issue from the city of Los Angeles resulted in the finest setting yet for the games, including a stadium that could seat 105,000, a rowing course with seats for 17,000, an auditorium that could seat 10,000, and a swimming stadium with room for 12,000 spectators. In addition, a 250-acre Olympic Village had been built outside Los Angeles to house and feed the athletes and officials.

The outstanding facilities and the fine weather led to an incredible array of new Olympic and world records. Virtually the only real problem arose when the 3,000-m steeplechase was allowed to go an extra lap. More than a half-million dollars was raised in attendance at the track and field events alone, and the future looked very bright for the Olympics.

In 1936, however, the atmosphere was gloomy. Berlin was the setting, and Adolph Hitler's Nazi Party was in charge. World war was on the horizon; several countries were torn by civil war and revolution. The economic depression had not yet ended. The Spanish squad had to return home before the games started, because of civil war. Brazil sent two teams, each representing a different political faction, and neither was allowed to compete. Despite all the gloom, there were more than 5,000 athletes from 53 nations in Berlin for the games. And the Berlin preparations exceeded even those of Los Angeles; Germany had invested about $30 million in its Olympic arenas and fields. In addition, the program was expanded to nearly its present size, with the additions of basketball and canoeing.

There was controversy in this country over whether the United States should even send a team to the "Nazi Olympics," in a country whose official policy now was discrimination against Jews, blacks, and other "non-Aryans." The issue was decided by a very close vote in the Amateur Athletic Union. On the American track and field team were 10 Negroes—contemptuously called "the Black Auxiliary" by German newspapers. One of them was Jesse Owens. But, before Owens competed in a final event, another black, Cornelius Johnson, won the high jump with an Olympic record leap of 6 ft, 7¹⁵⁄₁₆ in. Hitler, who had congratulated the first two winners, suddenly left his box—it looked as if it might rain, his aides explained.

The following day, Hitler was careful not to congratulate any winners. On that day Owens won the 100-m dash, tying the Olympic record. Later he also won the

Jim Thorpe, later a pro football star and major league baseball player, was proclaimed "the greatest athlete in the world" by the King of Sweden in 1912, after winning the Olympic decathlon and pentathlon. Later, his medals were taken from him because he had once played semiprofessional baseball. *(Pro Football Hall of Fame.)*

200-m, in world-record time, and set another Olympic record in the broad jump. Then he anchored the 400-m relay team to a world record, winning his fourth gold medal of the games. Despite everything, the 1936 Olympics was the most successful ever, in athletic performance (16 Olympic records were set in track and field), in participation, and in attendance.

Ironically, the 1940 Olympics were to be held in Tokyo. They would have been the first games held outside Europe and North America. But World War II forced their cancellation and the cancellation of the 1944 games as well.

After World War II

The end of the war, and the beginning of the Atomic Age, brought with it new hope for international understanding—a hope born of the war's anguish and the desperate realization that future wars would bring unprecedented holocaust and terror. The United Nations was put together; the International Olympic Committee decided it was imperative to begin a new Olympiad in 1948. The 1944 games had been assigned to London, and London was awarded the first postwar games—a rather questionable prize for a country undergoing an austerity program and a severe housing shortage. The British, ever

Eleanor Holm Jarrett, a swimming gold medal winner in 1932, was removed from the 1936 team by U.S. Olympic Committee Chairman Avery Brundage for drinking champagne on the team's ship, en route to Germany. *(International Swimming Hall of Fame.)*

intent on ceremony, borrowed one feature of the 1936 games that is still part of the Olympic tradition: A torch bearer lighted the Olympic torch at Olympia and began a 2,000-mi relay effort to bring the torch to London. Six thousand athletes represented 59 countries, and Britons turned out to watch, 82,000 of them filling Wembley stadium for the opening ceremonies.

Among the 1948 stars were Emil Zatopek, a Czech who won the 10,000-m run and the marathon and came within a whisker of winning the 5,000-m event as well; Bob Mathias, the 17-year-old American who won the grueling decathlon in 12 hr of miserable rain; and Fanny Blankers-Koen of Holland, who became the first woman to win three gold medals, in the 100-m, 200-m, and the 80-m hurdles.

The 1948 games also brought the chill of the Cold War into athletics. Some Czech and Hungarian athletes refused to go home after the games. And the 1952 games were held in Helsinki, Finland—behind the Iron Curtain. For the first time since the 1917 revolution the Soviet Union was represented. The official Olympic view is that the games are meant to be nothing more than competition among individuals, except in the team sports on the program—and some Olympic officials even deplore the idea of team sports, as tending toward nationalism. With the entry of Communist Russia into the Olympics, a new element was added. The 1952 games were to represent some kind of showdown between East and West, between capitalism and communism, between the United States and the Soviet Union.

The Cold War notwithstanding, the 1952 games set a

new record, with 5,780 athletes representing 67 countries. And the Finns turned out as enthusiastically as the British had. Despite rain, 70,000 cheered as Paavo Nurmi himself carried the Olympic torch to the top of the stadium to light the Olympic fire.

There were individual heroes. Emil Zatopek won the 10,000-m run again, breaking his own record by 42 sec! Then he also set records in the 5,000-m run and the marathon, and his wife, Dana Ingrova Zatopek, won a gold medal in the javelin. Bob Mathias, now 21, was again the decathlon champion. Lindy Remigino of Manhattan College astounded everyone, including himself, by winning the 100-m dash. Horace Ashenfelter, a converted miler from the United States, also surprised everyone by not only winning the 3,000-m steeplechase but also shattering the record by nearly 13 sec.

But what dominated the attention of the press, both in Europe and in the United States, was the unofficial contest between the United States and Russia for the "team championship." It was confused by the fact that there was no formal scoring system; the United States used one, the Russians another. According to the American figures, the United States won, 614-553½. According to the Russian figures, it was a tie, 494-494.

Despite the distasteful ramifications of the Cold War approach to the Olympics, the 1952 games did serve to focus American interest on some previously neglected sports. The United States was strong in track and field, swimming, and weightlifting, but improvement was needed in other areas. And improvement began in some of them.

The 1956 games were held in Melbourne, Australia. Because the seasons are reversed in the Southern Hemisphere, the games were staged in November and December instead of July or August. A record number of countries, 74, submitted entries. They didn't all make it, though. The short-lived Hungarian revolution of November produced rumors that Hungary would withdraw; however, her athletes did show up. And some of them refused to go back. But Spain, Switzerland, and the Netherlands withdrew in protest. Red China, angered when a Nationalist Chinese flag was displayed in the Olympic village, also pulled out. So did Egypt, Lebanon, and Iraq, protesting the action of Britain and France in taking over the Suez Canal after an Israeli attack on Egypt. So only 67 countries actually competed.

The weather again was bad a good part of the time—the season was actually spring, not summer—but every day Australians filled the stadium to its capacity, 103,000, and every day Olympic records were broken. Once more individual heroes tended to be overshadowed. Attention centered on the competition between the United States and the Soviet Union. Outstanding track performances were turned in by Bobby Morrow, who won every one of his heats of the 100-m dash, including the final, turned in an Olympic record time in the 200, and was also on the winning 400-m relay team; Glenn Davis, who won the 400-m hurdles, an event virtually unknown in the United States, except in Olympic years; Paul Anderson, who became known as the "strongest man in the world" for his victory in the heavyweight weightlifting competition; and Vladimir Kuts of Russia, who won the 5,000- and 10,000-m runs.

But those and other performances meant something, to

many people, only for the points they added to their country's team figures. The Soviet Union won, 722-593, even by the American scoring system. One reason was the fact that other nations, especially the host Australians, won many medals that American swimmers had usually won in previous Olympics.

In 1960 the Olympics went to Rome, to be greeted by sumptuous surroundings, including steps of marble in the main stadium. There was a record number of athletes—5,902—and a record number of participating nations, 84. Again it was a disappointing contest for the United States—not so much because American athletes were declining as because other nations were improving. For the first time since 1928, both short sprints went to other nations. The quick-starting Armin Hary of Germany won the 100-m dash in an Olympic record time, and Livio Berruti of the host country equaled the world record in the 200-m event.

For the first time since 1912, a country other than the United States won the 400-m relay, Hary anchoring a German victory in the event when the American team was disqualified for an illegal pass. In men's track and field, the United States won only 8 of a possible 24 gold medals. American women, however, did better than they ever had in the past, and slim, attractive Wilma Rudolph won three gold medals, in the 100-m dash, the 200-m, and the 400-m relay. Rafer Johnson kept the decathlon championship in the United States, setting an Olympic record.

As before, the Russians piled up points in gymnastics and weightlifting, and they showed new strength in target shooting and equestrian events. But small countries, too, had intermittent success. The marathon was won by an Ethiopian, while a Moroccan finished second. Pakistan won the field-hockey championship with a literally bloody victory over India. Peter Snell, in the 800-m run, and Murray Halberg, in the 5,000-m, won gold medals for New Zealand.

The 1940 games had been scheduled for Tokyo. In 1964, Tokyo finally was host—and spent an estimated $2 billion getting ready. The Japanese not only put up new buildings to handle the Olympics, they redesigned their highway system to cope with the expected traffic.

There were some interesting developments in 1964. One was that newspapermen finally agreed with the International Olympic Committee that those unofficial team point standings should be dropped: Newspapers reported specifically only on total medals won, country by country. Another was that, partly because of extensive television coverage and partly because of American heroes like Don Schollander, swimming stole much of the public thunder from the track and field events. Schollander was the first genuine American Olympic hero who was not a track-and-field competitor. He won the 100- and 400-m freestyle events in world-record times and also swam on two winning relay teams, for a total of four gold medals. But another major hero was Billy Mills, who won only one gold medal. It came in the 10,000-m run, which had never before been won by an American. Mills broke the Olympic record, running 50 sec faster than he ever had before.

There were other heroes. Bob Hayes nailed down his claim to the title, "world's fastest human," in the 100-m dash. Al Oerter, despite torn rib cartilages, won the dis-

cus event for the third straight time. Peter Snell of New Zealand repeated in the 800-m run and also won the 1,500-m run. Bob Schul of the United States became the first American to win the 5,000-m run. Abebe Bikila of Ethiopia easily won the marathon, for the second consecutive time. And a young butcher named Joe Frazier, of the United States, won a gold medal in the heavyweight boxing finals.

When Mexico City was awarded the 1968 Olympic Games, there were many anguished protests—not out of dislike of the country or its people, but because of the altitude. As Japan had, Mexico built a new highway system. And a subway system. And a magnificent stadium and an awesome sports palace.

There were problems with the 1968 games. But most of them had to do, one way or another, with the black-white problem. First a militant organization of black athletes in the United States called for blacks to boycott the games. Then the IOC voted to reinstate South Africa. African nations immediately announced they would boycott, and the Soviet Union said it might stay away, too. The call for American black athletes to boycott grew louder. Finally the IOC backed down, and relative quiet prevailed for a time. But just a month before the games were to open, student riots burst out at the University of Mexico. And new international tensions arose when Russia ruthlessly put down a Czech uprising, just as the Hungarian rebellion had been crushed shortly before the 1956 games. The riots were squelched—after 49 students were killed. The international tensions didn't lead to any angry withdrawals or boycotts. The games went on and, despite the tensions and the altitude, were considered by many the most successful ever. Nearly 8,000 athletes from 112 nations took part.

The United States returned to something like its old pre-eminence in track and field in 1968, winning 11 gold medals. Even more noticeable were the Russian slippages, and the gains of other countries. Kenya won three gold medals in men's track and field, matching the Russians. An Ethiopian again won the marathon, and a Tunisian won the 5,000-m run. (It should be noted that Kenya and Tunisia are both high-altitude countries.) The Russian women didn't win a single event.

Television spotlighted many American heroes. Al Oerter won his fourth consecutive discus title. Jim Hines not only won the 100-m dash, he became the first man ever to run it in less than 10 sec. For the first time the Olympic pole vault went over 17 ft, and nine men broke that barrier, Bob Seagren of the United States winning at 17-8½.

Television also spotlighted the controversial "black power" gestures of Tommie Smith, gold medal winner in the 200-m run, and John Carlos, who won the Bronze Medal. While the National Anthem was being played as they stood on the podium with their new medals, they raised black-gloved fists. The two men were suspended and expelled from the Olympic Village, and the remaining athletes, of whatever color, began debating the whole issue among themselves. But the games went on.

The most astounding performance—one of the most astounding in athletic history—came from Bob Beamon. Going into the Olympics, the world record for the long jump was 27 ft, 4¾ in. No one had yet come near jumping 28 ft, and some thought that that distance might be an insurmountable barrier. Beamon jumped an incredible 29-2½, breaking the old record by nearly 2 ft, in an event in which the world record had been inching upward only gradually for nearly 40 years.

Other heroes: Bill Toomey, winner of the decathlon; Kip Keino of Kenya, who turned in the second fastest 1,500 m in history, despite the altitude; Dick Fosbury of the United States, who set an Olympic high-jump mark with his twisting, backward "Fosbury Flop," delighting millions of TV viewers; and Debbie Meyer, who won three gold medals in swimming. The United States was also remarkably strong in boxing, winning 7 medals in the 11 events. The heavyweight winner was 19-year-old George Foreman, who staged his own counter-demonstration by waving an American flag during the victory ceremonies.

The whole idea of the Olympic Games was seriously questioned during and after the 1972 edition in Munich. Terror struck, in the shape of an Arab extremist group that broke into the Israeli team's quarters in the Olympic Village on September 5, killing two Israelis and taking nine others hostage. The eight terrorists wanted to fly their hostages to Cairo; they got as far as a military airport near Munich, where German police closed in. All the Israeli hostages were killed; so were five of the terrorists and a policeman. There was a question about whether the games should go on; it was decided they should, after a 24-hr suspension and a memorial service. But the Munich tragedy led many to suggest that the games have become too big, and that separate world-championship events for various sports should be held in scattered locations.

Even without the terrible tragedy of Munich, the value of the games might have been questioned in 1972. The Olympics, after all, were meant to promote international good will through friendly competition; the 1972 games, above all previous ones, demonstrated that the nationalistic pride involved in the Olympics can serve to promote international dissension, disagreement, and controversy. Shortly before the games were to open, a number of African nations threatened to boycott if white-ruled Rhodesia was allowed to compete. So Rhodesia was thrown out.

Politics also entered a bicycle road race, in the form of seven members of the Irish Republican Army who slipped into the massed start; one of them caused a 15-bike accident. And two black American athletes, Vince Matthews and Wayne Collett, winners of the gold and silver medals respectively in the 400-m dash, were barred from further Olympic competition for allegedly showing disrespect for the American flag during the victory ceremony. Their ouster, ironically, prevented the United States from fielding a 1,600-m relay team.

While electronic timing systems were clocking swimmers to within a thousandth of a second, there were many complaints of nationalism in the judging of those sports where subjectivity rules. Many Americans watching on television agreed with commentators and coaches that Iron Curtain judges had caused the defeats of several American boxers, and there were complaints from many countries about the judging in gymnastics and diving.

The greatest controversy, as far as the United States was concerned, came in basketball. The Americans, having won all of their 63 previous games in Olympic competition, starting in 1936, led Russia 50-49 with 3 sec to play

in the championship game. Twice the Russians threw the ball the length of the court without scoring; twice officials ruled that the scoreboard clock had been wrong and should be reset. On the third try, the Russians scored the winning basket. The United States lost an appeal and then refused to accept the silver medal.

There was more: Top pole vaulters Bob Seagren of the United States and Kjell Isaksson of Sweden weren't allowed to use their fiberglass poles, and an East German won the event; Rick DeMont had a gold medal taken away when it was discovered he'd taken a drug for his asthmatic condition before winning the 400-m freestyle; and two leading American sprinters missed their qualifying heats because their coach had given them the wrong starting time. (The last two incidents were blamed solely on the U.S. Olympic Committee and its officials, and did not involve international controversy.)

Despite all the problems, there were bright spots. Mark Spitz won an incredible seven gold medals in swimming, surpassing the record of five set by an Italian fencer, Nedo Nadi, in 1920. And tiny Russian gymnast Olga Korbut won the hearts of the world with gold medal performances in the free exercise and the balance beam and a silver medal in the horizontal bars. Spectators booed the judges failure to give her the third gold medal.

For the United States, men's swimming was the high point; this country won 9 of the 17 events and took 26 of a possible 51 medals. Track and field was a major disappointment, however: A Russian, Valery Borzov, won both the 100- and 200-m sprints, and American men won only five gold medals—despite Frank Shorter's surprising victory in the marathon, which marked the first time an American had won the event since 1908. American women didn't win a single track and field event and won only two medals, both bronze. The United States was also completely shut out in rowing, in weightlifting, and in gymnastics, where at least a couple of medals had been expected. All in all, 1972 was not a happy Olympic year for the United States; it was an even unhappier one for the world at large.

In 1973 the International Olympic Committee, to combat "gigantism," voted to drop 10 events from the Olympic program: one each from walking, cycling, and shooting; all four canoe slalom races; the 200-yd swimming medley relays; and the 400-m freestyle swim.

A year later, a federal law established a commission to study the question of whether the United States should continue to participate in the Olympics. The commission was also given the job of recommending new methods of selecting American representatives and of studying possible reorganization of the U.S. Olympic Committee.

The 1976 Olympics were staged in Montreal, and again extracurricular problems threatened at times to overshadow the athletics. The IOC intermittently inspected Montreal's preparations, and intermittently threatened to move the games elsewhere if construction didn't proceed more rapidly. Montreal did get ready on time, but some of the facilities weren't really completed.

Because a New Zealand Rugby team had toured South Africa, a number of black African countries wanted New Zealand to be banned from the games. When the IOC refused, 22 African countries and sympathizers withdrew, taking with them some of the world's outstanding track and field performers—among them John Akki-Bua of

Uganda, who held the world record in the 400-m hurdles, and Filbert Bayi of Tanzania, world record holder in the 1500-m run.

Virtually on the eve of the Olympics, the Canadian government announced that it would not admit competitors from "Nationalist China" unless they marched under the Taiwanese, rather than the Chinese, banner in opening ceremonies. The IOC threatened to cancel the games; the United States threatened to withdraw if the games did go on. But Canada held firm, and the games went on.

Olga Korbut was replaced, in the hearts of many fans, by 14-year-old Nadia Comaneci of Rumania, who not only won three gold medals, but recorded the first perfect (10.0) score in the history of Olympic gymnastics. She had four other perfect scores, and Nelli Kim of the Soviet Union scored a perfect 10.0, winning a gold medal in the vault.

Swimming was also highlighted. The East German women won 11 of 13 events, and Olympic records were set in all 13. U.S. men won 12 of 13 events, and 12 Olympic records were set. The big American star was John Naber, a tall, mustachioed, personable young man who won both backstroke events in world record time. The U.S. women came through with a surprising win in the 400-m freestyle relay.

The track and field medals were distributed rather evenly once again. Alberto Juantorena of Cuba scored an unprecedented double in the 400- and 800-m runs, and Lasse Viren of Finland again won the 5,000- and 10,000-meter runs. Representatives of 14 different countries won the 23 gold medals in the men's events. East Germany dominated women's track and field, winning nine of 14 events.

See also WINTER OLYMPICS.

Olympic Champions

Archery

Men
1972 John C. Williams, U.S.
1976 Darrell O. Pace, U.S.

Women
1972 Doreen Wilber, U.S.
1976 Luann Ryon, U.S.

Basketball

Men

1904 United States
1936 United States
1948 United States
1952 United States
1956 United States
1960 United States
1964 United States
1968 United States
1972 USSR
1976 United States

Women
1976 USSR

Boxing

Light Flyweight
1968 Francisco Rodriquez, Venezuela

1972 Gyoergy Geda, Hungary
1976 Jorge Hernandez, Cuba

Flyweight
1904 George V. Finnegan, U.S. (105 lb)
1920 Frank De Genero, U.S.
1924 Fidel La Barba, U.S.
1928 Anton Kocsis, Hungary
1932 Stephen Enekes, Hungary
1936 Willi Kaiser, Germany
1948 Pascuel Perez, Argentina
1952 Nate Brooks, U.S.
1956 Terence Spinks, Great Britain
1960 Guyle Torok, Hungary
1964 Fernando Atzori, Italy
1968 Ricardo Delgardo, Mexico
1972 Ghergy Kostadinov, Bulgaria
1976 Leo Randolph, U.S.

Bantamweight
1904 O. L. Kirk, U.S. (115 lb)
1908 A. Thomas, Great Britain
1920 Clarence Walker, South America
1924 W. H. Smith, South Africa
1928 Vittorio Tamagnini, Italy
1932 Horace Gwynne, Canada
1936 Ulderico Sergo, Italy
1948 Tibor Csik, Hungary
1952 Pentti Hamalainen, Finland
1956 Wolfgang Behrendt, Germany
1960 Oleg Grigoryev, USSR
1964 Takao Sakurai, Japan
1968 Valery Sokolov, USSR
1972 Orlando Martinez, Cuba
1976 Yong Jo Gu, North Korea

Featherweight
1904 O. L. Kirk, U.S.
1908 R. K. Gunn, Great Britain
1920 Paul Fritsch, France
1924 John Fields, U.S.
1928 L. Van Klavaren, Holland
1932 Carmelo A. Robledo, Argentina
1936 Oscar Casanova, Argentina
1948 Ernesto Formenti, Italy
1952 Jan Zachara, Czechoslovakia
1956 Vladimir Safronov, USSR
1960 Francesco Musso, Italy
1964 Stanislav Stepashkin, USSR
1968 Antonio Roldan, Mexico
1972 Boris Kousnetsov, USSR
1976 Angel Herrera, Cuba

Lightweight
1904 H. J. Spanger, U.S.
1908 F. Spanger, Great Britain
1920 Samuel Mosberg, U.S.
1924 Harold Nielsen, Denmark
1928 Carlo Orlandi, Italy
1932 Lawrence Stevens, South Africa
1936 Imre Harangi, Hungary
1948 Gerry Dreyer, South Africa
1952 Aureliano Bolognesi, Italy
1956 Richard McTaggart, Great Britain
1960 Kazmirierz Pazdzior, Poland
1964 Jozef Grudsien, Poland
1968 Ronnie Harris, U.S.
1972 Jan Szczepanski, Poland
1976 Howard Davis, U.S.

Light Welterweight
1952 Charles Adkins, U.S.
1956 Vladimir Enguibarian, USSR

1960   Bohumil Nomececk, Czechoslovakia
1964   Jerzy Kulej, Poland
1968   Jerzy Kulej, Poland
1972   Ray Seales, U.S.
1976   Ray Leonard, U.S.

Welterweight
1904   Al Young, U.S.
1920   T. Schneider, Canada
1924   Jean S. Delarge, Belgium
1928   Edward Morgan, New Zealand
1932   Edward Flynn, U.S.
1936   Sten Suvio, Finland
1948   Julius Torma, Czechoslovakia
1952   Zygmunt Chychia, Poland
1956   Nekolae Linca, Rumania
1960   Giovanni Benvenuti, Italy
1964   Marian Kasprzyk, Poland
1968   Manfred Wolke, East Germany
1972   Emilio Correa, Cuba
1976   Jochen Bachfeld, East Germany

Light Middleweight
1952   Laszlo Papp, Hungary
1956   Laszlo Papp, Hungary
1960   Wilbert McClure, U.S.
1964   Boris Lagutin, USSR
1968   Boris Lagutin, USSR
1972   Dieter Kottysch, West Germany
1976   Jerzy Rybicki, Poland

Middleweight
1904   Charles Mayer, U.S.
1920   Harry W. Mallin, Great Britain
1924   Harry W. Mallin, Great Britain
1928   Piero Toscani, Italy
1932   Carmen Barth, U.S.
1936   Jean Despeaux, France
1948   Laszlo Papp, Hungary
1952   Floyd Patterson, U.S.
1964   Valery Popechenko, USSR
1968   Chris Finnegan, Great Britain
1972   Viatcheslav Lemeches, USSR
1976   Mike Spinks, U.S.

Light Heavyweight
1920   Edward P. F. Eagan, U.S.
1924   Harry J. Mitchell, Great Britain
1928   Victoria Avendano, Argentina
1932   David E. Carstens, South Africa
1936   Rogert Michelot, France
1948   George Hunter, South Africa
1952   Norvel Lee, U.S.
1956   Jim Boyd, U.S.
1960   Cassius Clay, U.S.
1964   Cosimo Pinto, Italy
1968   Dan Pozdniak, USSR
1972   Mate Paulov, Yugoslavia
1976   Leon Spinks, U.S.

Heavyweight
1904   Sam Berger, U.S.
1920   R. Rawson, Great Britain
1924   Otto Von Porat, Norway
1928   Jurido Rodriguez, Argentina
1932   Santiago A. Lovell, Argentina
1936   Herbert Runge, Germany
1948   Rafael Iglesias, Argentina
1952   Edward Sanders, U.S.
1956   Pete Rademacher, U.S.
1960   Francesco de Piccoli, Italy
1964   Joe Frazier, U.S.
1968   George Foreman, U.S.
1972   Teofilo Stevenson, Cuba
1976   Teofilo Stevenson, Cuba

Canoeing

Men's Kayak Singles—500 Meters
1976   Vasile Diba, Rumania

Men's Kayak Singles—1,000 Meters
1936   Gregor Hradetzky, Austria
1948   Gert Fredriksson, Sweden
1952   Gert Fredriksson, Sweden
1956   Gert Fredriksson, Sweden
1960   Erik Hansen, Denmark
1964   Rolf Peterson, Sweden
1968   Mihaly Hesz, Hungary
1972   Aleksandr Shaparenko, USSR
1976   Rudiger Helm, East Germany

Men's Canadian Singles—500 Meters
1976   Aleksandr Rogov, USSR

Men's Canadian Singles—1,000 Meters
1936   Francis Amyot, Canada
1948   Josef Holecek, Czechoslovakia
1952   Josef Holecek, Czechoslovakia
1956   Leon Rottman, Rumania
1960   Janos Parti, Hungary
1964   Jurgen Eschert, Germany
1968   Tibor Tatai, Hungary
1972   Ivan Patzaichin, Rumania
1976   Matija Ljubek, Yugoslavia

Men's Kayak Pairs—500 Meters
1976   East Germany (Joachim Mattern, Berndt Olbricht)

Men's Kayak Pairs—1,000 Meters
1936   Austria (Adolf Kainz, Alphonse Dorfner)
1948   Sweden (Hans Berglund, Lenart Klingstroem)
1952   Finland (Kurt Wires, Yrio Hietanen)
1956   Germany (Michel Scheuer, Meinrad Miltenberger)
1960   Sweden (Gert Fredriksson, Sven Sjodelius)
1964   Sweden (Sven Sjodelius, Gunnar Utterberg)
1968   USSR (Aleksandr Shaperenko, Vladimir Morozov)
1972   USSR (Nikolai Gorbachev, Vicktor Kratassuk)
1976   USSR (Sergei Nagorny, Vladimir Romanovsky)

Men's Canadian Pairs—500 Meters
1976   USSR (Sergei Petrenko, Aleksander Vinogradov)

Men's Canadian Pairs—1,000 Meters
1936   Czechoslovakia (Vladimir Syrovatka, Felix Brzak)
1948   Czechoslovakia (Jan Brzak, Bohumil Kudrna)
1952   Denmark (Bent Rasch, Finn Haunstoft)
1956   Rumania (Alex Dumitru, Simion Ismailciuc)
1960   USSR (Leonid Geyshter, Sergei Marerenko)
1964   USSR (Andrei Khimich, Stepan Oschepov)
1968   Rumania (Ivan Patzaichin, Sergei Covaliov)
1972   USSR (Vladas Chessyunas, Yuri Lobanoc)
1976   USSR (Sergei Petrenko, Aleksander Vinogradov)

Men's Kayak Fours
1964   USSR
1968   Norway
1972   USSR
1976   USSR

Women's Kayak Singles
1948   K. Hoff, Denmark
1952   Sylvia Saimo, Finland
1956   Elisaveta Dementieva, USSR
1960   Antonina Seredina, USSR
1964   Ludmilla Khedosiuk, USSR
1968   Ludmilla Pinaeva, USSR
1972   Yulia Ryabchinskaya, USSR
1976   Carola Zirzow, East Germany

Women's Kayak Pairs
1960 USSR (Maria Shubina, Antonina Seredina)
1964 Germany (Roswitha Esser, AnneMarie Zimmerman)
1968 West Germany (Roswitha Esser, AnneMarie Zimmerman)
1972 USSR (Ludmilla Pinaeva, E. Katerina Kuryshka)
1976 USSR (Nina Gopova, Galina Kreft)

Cycling

Road Race—Individual
1896 Konstantinidis, Greece
1906 Vast and Bardonneau, France (T = tie)
1912 Rudolph Lewis, South Africa
1920 Harry Stenquist, Sweden
1924 Armand Blanchonnet, France
1928 Henry Hansen, Denmark
1932 Attilio Pavesi, Italy
1936 Robert Charpentier, France
1948 Jose Bayaert, France
1952 Andrae Noyelle, Belgium
1956 Ercole Baldini, Italy
1960 Viktor Kapitonov, USSR
1964 Mario Zanin, Italy
1968 Pier Franco Vianelli, Italy
1972 Hennie Kuiper, Holland
1976 Bernt Johansson, Sweden

Road Race—Team
1912 Sweden
1920 France
1924 France
1928 Denmark
1932 Italy
1936 France
1948 Belgium
1952 Belgium
1956 France
1960 Italy
1964 Netherlands
1968 Netherlands
1972 USSR
1976 USSR

1,000-Meter Scratch Sprint
1896 Paul Masson, France (2,000 m)
1900 George Tallendier, France
1906 Francesco Verri, Italy
1908 Void—time limit exceeded
1920 Maurice Peeters, Holland
1924 Lucien Michard, France
1928 Robert Beaufrand, France
1932 Jacobus van Edmond, Holland
1936 Toni Merkens, Germany
1948 Mario Ghella, Italy (920 m)
1952 Enzo Sacchi, Italy
1956 Michel Rousseau, France
1960 Sante Gaiordoni, Italy
1964 Giovanni Pettenella, Italy
1968 Daniel Morelon, France
1972 Daniel Morelon, France
1976 Anton Tkac, Czechoslovakia

Pursuit—Individual
1964 Jiri Daller, Czechoslovakia
1968 Daniel Rebillard, France
1972 Knut Knudsen, Norway
1976 Gregor Braun, West Germany

Pursuit—Team
1908 Great Britain
1920 Italy
1924 Italy
1928 Italy
1932 Italy
1936 France

Two Olympic swimming stars meet: Mark Spitz, left, set a record by winning seven gold medals in 1972. Johnny Weissmuller won a total of five gold medals in 1924 and 1928. *(International Swimming Hall of Fame.)*

1948 France
1952 Italy
1956 Italy
1960 Italy
1964 Germany
1968 Denmark
1972 West Germany
1976 West Germany

1,000-Meter Time Trial
1928 Willy Falck-Hansen, Denmark
1932 Edgar L. Gray, Australia
1936 Arie van Vliet, Holland
1948 Jacques Dupont, France
1952 Russell Mockridge, Australia
1956 Leonardo Faggin, Italy
1960 Sante Gaiordoni, Italy
1964 Patrick Sercu, Belgium
1968 Pierre Trentin, France
1972 Niels Fredborg, Denmark
1976 Klaus-Jurgen Grunke, East Germany

Equestrian

3-Day Event—Individual
1912 Lt. Axel Nordlander, Sweden
1920 Lt. Helmer De Moerner, Sweden
1924 Adolph D. C. Van Der Voort Van Zijp, Holland
1928 Lt. Ferdinand Pahud de Mortanges, Holland
1932 Lt. Ferdinand Pahud de Mortanges, Holland
1936 Ludwig Stubbendorf, Germany
1948 Capt. Bernard Chevallier, France
1952 Hans von Blixen-Finecke, Sweden
1956 Petrus Kastenman, Sweden
1960 Lawrence Morgan, Australia
1964 Mauro Checcoli, Italy
1968 Jean Guyon, France
1972 Richard Meade, Great Britain
1976 Tad Coffin, U.S.

3-Day Event—Team
1912 Sweden
1920 Sweden

Russian gymnast Olga Korbut excited crowds, and enormous television audiences, with her spectacular 1972 Olympic performance. She won three gold medals and one silver medal. *(Nissen Company.)*

1924   Holland
1928   Holland
1932   United States
1936   Germany
1948   United States
1952   Sweden
1956   Great Britain
1960   Australia
1964   Italy
1968   Great Britain
1972   Great Britain
1976   United States

Dressage—Individual
1912   Capt. Carl Bonde, Sweden
1920   Capt. Janne Lundblad, Sweden
1924   Ernst von Linder, Sweden
1928   Carl F. von Langen, Germany
1932   Francois Lesage, France
1936   Heinz Pollay, Germany
1948   Capt. Hans Moser, Switzerland
1952   Henri St. Cyr, Sweden
1956   Henri St. Cyr, Sweden

1960   Sergei Filatov, USSR
1964   Henri Chammartin, Switzerland
1968   Ivan Kizimov, USSR
1972   Liselott Lisenhoff, West Germany
1976   Christine Stueckelberger, Switzerland

Dressage —Team
1928   Germany
1932   France
1936   Germany
1948   Sweden
1952   Sweden
1956   Sweden
1964   Germany
1968   West Germany
1972   USSR
1976   West Germany

Jumping—Individual
1912   Capt. J. Cariou, France
1920   Lt. Tommaso Lequio, Italy
1924   Lt. Alphons Gemuseus, Switzerland
1928   F. Ventura, Czechoslovakia
1932   Takeichi Hishi, Japan
1936   Kurt Hasse, Germany
1948   Humberto Cores, Mexico
1952   Pierre d'Oriola, France
1956   Hans Winkler, Germany
1960   Raimondo D'Inzeo, Italy
1964   Jonquieres d'Oriola, France
1968   Bill Steinkraus, U.S.
1972   Graziano Mancinelli, Italy
1976   Alwin Sehockemoehle, West Germany

Jumping—Team
1912   Sweden
1920   Sweden
1924   Sweden
1928   Spain
1932   All teams disqualified
1936   Germany
1948   Mexico
1952   Great Britain
1956   Germany
1960   Germany
1964   Germany
1968   Canada
1972   West Germany
1976   France

Fencing

Men's Foils
1896   E. Gravelotte, France
1900   C. Coste, France
1904   Ramon Foust, Cuba
1906   Dillon Cavanagh, France
1912   Nedo Nadi, Italy
1920   Nedo Nadi, Italy
1924   Roger Ducret, France
1928   Ludien Gaudin, France
1932   Gustavo Marzi, Italy
1936   Giulio Gaudini, Italy
1948   Jean Buhan, France
1952   Christian d'Oriola, France
1956   Christian d'Oriola, France
1960   Viktor Zhanovich, USSR
1964   Egon Franke, Poland
1968   Ion Drimba, Rumania
1972   Witold Woyda, Poland
1976   Fabio Dal Zotto, Italy

Men's Team Foils
1904   Cuba
1920   Italy

1924	France
1928	Italy
1932	France
1936	Italy
1948	France
1952	France
1956	Italy
1960	USSR
1964	USSR
1968	France
1972	Poland
1976	West Germany

Men's Epée

1900	Ramon Fonst, Cuba
1904	Ramon Fonst, Cuba
1906	Comte G. de la Falaise, France
1908	Gaston Alibard, France
1912	Paul Anspach, Belgium
1920	Armand Massard, France
1924	Charles Delporte, Belgium
1928	Ludien Gaudin, France
1932	Giancarlo Cornaggia-Medici, Italy
1936	Franco Riccardi, Italy
1948	Luigi Cantone, France
1952	Eduardo Mangiarotti, Italy
1956	Carlo Pavesti, Italy
1960	Giuseppe Delfino, Italy
1964	Grigory Kriss, USSR
1968	Gyozo Kulcsar, Hungary
1972	Csaba Fenyvesi, Hungary
1976	Alexander Pusch, West Germany

Men's Team Epée

1906	Germany
1908	France
1912	Belgium
1920	Italy
1924	France
1928	Italy
1932	France
1936	Italy
1948	France
1952	Italy
1956	Italy
1960	Italy
1964	Hungary
1968	Hungary
1972	Hungary
1976	Sweden

Men's Saber

1900	Comte G. de la Falaise, France
1904	Jean Georgiadis, Greece
1904	Manuel De Diaz, Cuba
1906	Jean Georgiadis, Greece
1908	Jeno Fuchs, Hungary
1912	Jeno Fuchs, Hungary
1920	Nedo Nadi, Italy
1924	Alexandre Posta, Hungary
1928	Odon Tereztyanszky, Hungary
1932	Gyorgy Piller, Hungary
1936	Endre Kabos, Hungary
1948	Aladar Gervich, Hungary
1952	Paul Kovacs, Hungary
1956	Rudolf Karpati, Hungary
1960	Rudolf Karpati, Hungary
1964	Tibor Pezsa, Hungary
1968	Jerzy Pawlowski, Poland
1972	Viktor Sidiak, USSR
1976	Viktor Krovopouskov, USSR

Men's Team Saber

1906	Germany

1908	Hungary
1912	Hungary
1920	Italy
1924	Italy
1928	Hungary
1932	Hungary
1936	Hungary
1948	Hungary
1952	Hungary
1956	Hungary
1960	Hungary
1964	USSR
1968	USSR
1972	Italy
1976	USSR

Women's Foils

1924	Ellen O. Osiier, Denmark
1928	Helene Mayer, Germany
1932	Ellen Preis, Austria
1936	Ilone Schacherer-Elek, Hungary
1948	Ilona Schacherer-Elek, Hungary
1952	Irene Camber, Italy
1956	Gillian Sheen, Great Britain
1960	Adelheid Schmid, Germany
1964	Ildiko Ujlaki, Hungary
1968	Elene Novikova, USSR
1972	Antonella Rogno Lonzi, Italy
1976	Ildiko Shwarczenberger, Hungary

Women's Team Foils

1960	USSR
1964	Hungary
1968	USSR
1972	USSR
1976	USSR

Field Hockey

1908	Great Britain
1912	Great Britain
1920	Great Britain
1928	British India
1932	British India
1936	British India
1948	India
1952	India
1956	India
1960	Pakistan
1964	India
1968	Pakistan
1972	West Germany
1976	New Zealand

Gymnastics

Men's All-Around

1900	G. Sandras, France
1904	Anton Heida, U.S.
	Julius Lenhardt, U.S.
1906	Payssee, France
1908	Alberto Braglia, Italy
1912	Alberto Braglia, Italy
1920	Giorgio Zampori, Italy
1924	Leon Stukel, Yugoslavia
1928	George Miez, Switzerland
1932	Romeo Neri, Italy
1936	Karl Schwarzmann, Germany
1948	Veikko Huhtanen, Finland
1952	Viktor Tchoukarine, USSR
1956	Viktor Tchoukarine, USSR
1960	Boris Shakhlin, USSR
1964	Yukio Endo, Japan
1968	Sawao Kato, Japan
1972	Sawao Kato, Japan

1976   Nikolai Andrianov, USSR

Long Horse (Vault)
1896   Karl Schumann, Germany
1904   Anton Heida, U.S.
       George Eyser, U.S.
1924   Frank Kriz, U.S.
1928   Eagen Mack, Switzerland
1932   Savino Guglielmetti, Italy
1936   Karl Schwarzmann, Germany
1948   Paavo Aaltonen, Finland
1952   Viktor Tchoukarine, USSR
1956   Helmuth Bantz, Germany
       Valentine Mouratov, USSR
1960   Takashi Ono, Japan
       Boris Shakhlin, USSR
1964   Haruhiro Yamashita, Japan
1968   Mikhail Voronin, USSR
1972   Klaus Koesti, East Germany
1976   Nikolai Andrianov, USSR

Side Horse (Pommeled)
1896   Louis Zutter, Switzerland
1904   Anton Heida, U.S.
1924   Josef Wilheim, Switzerland
1928   Hermann Hanggi, Switzerland
1932   Istvan Pelle, Hungary
1936   Konrad Frey, Germany
1948   Paavo Altonen, Finland
       Veikko Huhtanen, Finland
       Heikki Savolainen, Finland
1952   Viktor Tchoukarine, USSR
1956   Boris Shakhlin, USSR
1960   Boris Shakhlin, USSR
       Eugen Ekman, Finland
1964   Miroslav Cerar, Yugoslavia
1968   Miroslav Cerar, Yugoslavia
1972   Viktor Klimenko, USSR
1976   Zoltan Magyar, Hungary

Parallel Bars
1896   Alfred Flatow, Germany
1904   George Eyser, U.S.
1924   August Guttinger, Switzerland
1928   Ladislav Vacha, Czechoslovakia
1932   Romeo Neri, Italy
1936   Konrad Frey, Germany
1948   Michael Reusch, Switzerland
1952   Hans Engster, Switzerland
1956   Viktor Tchoukarine, USSR
1960   Boris Shakhlin, USSR
1964   Yukio Endo, Japan
1968   Akinori Nakayama, Japan
1972   Sawao Kato, Japan
1976   Sawao Kato, Japan

Flying Rings
1896   Jean Mitropoulos, Greece
1904   Herman T. Glass, U.S.
1924   Franco Martino, Italy
1928   Leon Stukelj, Yugoslavia
1932   George Gulack, U.S.
1936   Alois Hudec, Czechoslovakia
1948   Karl Frei, Switzerland
1952   Grant Chaguinian, USSR
1956   Albert Azarian, USSR
1960   Albert Azarian, USSR
1964   Takuji Hayata, Japan
1968   Akinori Nakayama, Japan
1972   Akinori Nakayama, Japan
1976   Nikolai Andrianov, USSR

Horizontal Bar
1896   Herman Weingaertner, Germany
1904   Anton Heida, U.S.

       Edward A. Hennig, U.S.
1924   Leon Stukelj, Yugoslavia
1928   George Miez, Switzerland
1932   Dallas Bixler, U.S.
1936   Aleksanteri Saarvala, Finland
1948   Josef Stalder, Switzerland
1952   Jack Gunthard, Switzerland
1956   Takashi Ono, Japan
1960   Takashi Ono, Japan
1964   Boris Shakhlin, USSR
1968   Mikhail Voronin, USSR
       Akinori Nakayama, Japan
1972   Mitsuo Tsukahara, Japan
1976   Mitsuo Tsukahara, Japan

Men's Floor Exercises
1936   George Miez, Switzerland
1948   V. A. Huhtanen, Finland
1952   Karl Thoresson, Sweden
1956   Valentine Mouratov, USSR
1960   Nobuyuki Aihara, Japan
1964   Franco Menichelli, Italy
1968   Sawao Kato, Japan
1972   Nikolai Andrianov, USSR
1976   Nikolai Andrianov, USSR

Men's Team
1896   Germany
1904   United States
1906   Germany
       Norway
1908   Sweden
1912   Italy
1920   Italy
1924   Italy
1928   Switzerland
1932   Italy
1936 . Germany
1948   Finland
1952   USSR
1956   USSR
1960   Japan
1964   Japan
1968   Japan
1972   Japan
1976   Japan

Women's All-Around
1952   Maria Gorokhovskaya, USSR
1956   Larisa Latyina, USSR
1960   Larisa Latyina, USSR
1964   Vera Caslavska, Czechoslovakia
1968   Vera Caslavska, Czechoslovakia
1972   Ludmila Tourischeva, USSR
1976   Nadia Comaneci, Rumania

Women's Floor Exercises
1952   Agnes Keleti, Hungary
1956   Agnes Keleti, Hungary
       Larisa Latyina, USSR
1960   Larisa Latyina, USSR
1964   Larisa Latyina, USSR
1968   Vera Caslavska, Czechoslovakia
       Larisa Petrik, USSR
1972   Olga Korbut, USSR
1976   Nelli Kim, USSR

Balance Beam
1952   Nina Botcharova, USSR
1956   Agnes Keleti, Hungary
1960   Eva Bosakova, Czechoslovakia
1964   Vera Caslavska, Czechoslovakia
1968   Natalia Kutchinskaya, USSR
1972   Olga Korbut, USSR
1976   Nadia Comaneci, Rumania

Parallel Bars
1952 Margit Korondi, Hungary
1956 Agnes Keleti, Hungary
1960 Polina Astakhova, USSR
1964 Polina Astakhova, USSR
1968 Vera Caslavska, Czechoslovakia
1972 Karin Janz, East Germany
1976 Nadia Comaneci, Rumania

Vault
1952 Ekaterina Kalinthouk, USSR
1956 Larisa Latyina, USSR
1960 Margarita Nikolaeva, USSR
1964 Vera Caslavska, Czechoslovakia
1968 Vera Caslavska, Czechoslovakia
1972 Karin Janz, East Germany
1976 Nelli Kim, USSR

Women's Team
1928 Holland
1936 Germany
1948 Czechoslovakia
1952 USSR
1956 USSR
1960 USSR
1964 USSR
1968 USSR
1972 USSR
1976 USSR

Judo

Lightweight
1964 Takehide Nakatani, Japan
1972 Takao Kawaguchi, Japan
1976 Hector Rodriguez, Cuba

Welterweight
1972 Toyokazu Nomura, Japan
1976 Vladimir Nevzorov, USSR

Middleweight
1964 Isao Okano, Japan
1972 Shinobu Sekine, Japan
1976 Isamu Sonada, Japan

Light Heavyweight
1972 Shota Chochoshvili, USSR
1976 Kazuhiro Ninomiya, Japan

Heavyweight
1964 Isao Inokuma, Japan
1972 Willem Ruska, Holland
1976 Sergei Novikov, USSR

Open
1964 Anton Geesink, Holland
1972 Willem Ruska, Holland
1976 Haruki Uemura, Japan

Modern Pentathlon

Individual
1912 Gustaf Lilliehook, Sweden
1920 Gustaf Dyrssen, Sweden
1924 O. Lindman, Sweden
1928 Sven A. Thofelt, Sweden
1932 Johan G. Oxenstierna, Sweden
1936 Gotthard Handrick, Germany
1948 Capt. William Grut, Sweden
1952 Lars Hall, Sweden
1956 Lars Hall, Sweden
1960 Ferenc Nemeth, Hungary
1964 Ferenc Torok, Hungary
1968 Bjoern Ferm, Sweden
1972 Andras Balczo, Hungary

1976 Janusz Pyciak-Peciak, Poland

Team
1952 Hungary
1956 USSR
1960 Hungary
1964 USSR
1968 Hungary
1972 USSR
1976 Great Britain

Rowing—Men

Single Sculls
1900 H. Barrelet, France
1904 Frank B. Greer, U.S.
1908 Harry T. Blackstaff, Great Britain
1912 William D. Kinnear, Great Britain
1920 John B. Kelly, U.S.
1924 Jack Beresford, Jr., Great Britain
1928 H. Robert Pearce, Australia
1932 H. Robert Pearce, Australia
1936 Gustav Schaefer, Germany
1948 Mervyn Wood, Australia
1952 Yuri Chukalov, USSR
1956 Vyacheslav Ivanov, USSR
1960 Vyacheslav Ivanov, USSR
1964 Vyacheslav Ivanov, USSR
1968 Henri Wiense, Holland
1972 Yuri Malishev, USSR
1976 Pecti Karppinen, Finland

Double Sculls
1904 U.S. (William Varley-John Mulcahy)
1908 Great Britain (J. R. K. Fenning-F. L. Thomson)
1920 U.S. (John B. Kelly-Paul V. Costello)
1924 U.S. (John B. Kelly-Paul V. Costello)
1928 U.S. (Paul V. Costello-Charles J. McIlvaine)
1932 U.S. (Kenneth Myers-Garrett Gilmore)
1936 Great Britain (Jack Beresford-Leslie Southwood)
1948 Great Britain (B. H. Bushnell-Richard D. Burnell)
1952 Argentina (Tranquilo Cappozzo-Eduardo Guerrero)
1956 USSR (Alexander Berkoutov-Yuri Tiukalov)
1960 Czechoslovakia (I. Kozak-Pavel Schmidt)
1964 USSR (Oleg Tiurin-Boris Dubrovsky)
1968 USSR (Anetaly Sass-Alexander Timoshinin)
1972 USSR (Alexander Timoshinin-Gennedi Korshakov)
1976 Norway (Frank and Alf Hansen)

Pairs with Coxswain
1900 Holland
1906 Italy (1600 m)
     Italy (1000 m)
1924 Switzerland
1928 Switzerland
1932 United States
1936 Germany
1948 Denmark
1952 France
1956 United States
1960 Germany
1964 United States
1968 Italy
1972 East Germany
1976 East Germany

Pairs without Coxswain
1904 United States
1908 Great Britain
1920 Italy
1924 Holland
1928 Germany
1932 Great Britain
1936 Germany
1948 Great Britain

1952	United States
1956	United States
1960	USSR
1964	Canada
1968	East Germany
1972	East Germany
1976	East Germany

Fours with Coxswain

1900	Germany
1906	Italy
1912	Germany
1920	Switzerland
1924	Switzerland
1928	Italy
1932	Germany
1936	Germany
1948	United States
1952	Czechoslovakia
1956	Italy
1960	Germany
1964	Germany
1968	New Zealand
1972	West Germany
1976	USSR

Fours without Coxswain

1904	United States
1908	Great Britain
1924	Great Britain
1928	Great Britain
1932	Great Britain
1936	Germany
1948	Italy
1952	Yugoslavia
1956	Canada
1960	United States
1964	Denmark
1968	East Germany
1972	East Germany
1976	East Germany

Quadruple Sculls

1976	East Germany

Eight-Oared

1900	United States (Vesper)
1904	United States (Vesper)
1908	Great Britain (Leander)
1912	Great Britain (Leander)
1920	United States (Navy)
1924	United States (Yale)
1928	United States (California)
1932	United States (California)
1936	United States (Washington)
1948	United States (California)
1952	United States (Navy)
1956	United States (Yale)
1960	Germany (Kiel-Ratzeburg)
1964	United States (Vesper)
1968	West Germany
1972	New Zealand
1976	East Germany

Rowing—Women

Single Sculls

1976	Christine Scheiblich, East Germany

Double Sculls

1976	Bulgaria (Svetla Otsetova-Zdravka Yordanova)

Pairs without Coxswain

1976	Bulgaria

Fours with Coxswain

1976	East Germany

Quadruple Sculls

1976	East Germany

Eight-Oared

1976	East Germany

Shooting

Small-Bore Rifle, Prone

1912	Frederick Hird, U.S.
1928	Bertil Ronnmark, Sweden
1936	Willy Rogeberg, Norway
1948	Arthur Cook, U.S.
1952	Yosef Sarbu, Rumania
1956	Gerald Ouelette, Canada
1960	Peter Kohnke, Germany
1964	Lasio Hammerl, Hungary
1968	Jan Kurka, Czechoslovakia
1972	Ho Jun Li, North Korea
1976	Karlheinz Smieszek, West Germany

Small-Bore Rifle, 3 Positions

1952	Erling Kongshaug, Norway
1956	Anatoli Bogdanov, USSR
1960	Viktor Shamburkin, USSR
1964	Lones Wigger, U.S.
1968	Bernd Klinger, West Germany
1972	John Writer, U.S.
1976	Lanny Bassham, U.S.

Free Pistol—50 Meters

1896	Sumner Paine, U.S. (30 m)
1900	Roedern, Switzerland
1906	Georges Orphanidis, Greece
1912	Alfred P. Lane, U.S.
1920	Karl Frederick, U.S.
1936	Torsten Ullman, Sweden
1948	E. Vasquez Cam, Peru
1952	Heulet Benner, U.S.
1956	Pentti Linnosvuo, Finland
1960	Alexei Gustchin, USSR
1964	Vaino Markkanen, Finland
1968	Grigory Kosykh, USSR
1972	Ragnar Skanaker, Sweden
1976	Uwe Potteck, East Germany

Rapid-Fire Pistol

1936	Cornelius Von Oyen, Germany
1948	Karoly Takacs, Hungary
1952	Karoly Takacs, Hungary
1956	Stefan Petresca, Rumania
1960	Bill McMillan, U.S.
1964	Pentti Linnosvuo, Finland
1968	Jozef Zapedski, Poland
1972	Jozef Zapedski, Poland
1976	Norbert Klaar, East Germany

Moving Target

1972	Lakov Zhelezniak, USSR
1976	Aleksandr Gazov, USSR

Trap

1900	R. de Barbarin, France
1906	Gerald Merlin, Great Britain (single-shot)
	Sidney Merlin, Great Britain (double-shot)
1908	W. H. Ewing, Canada
1912	James R. Graham, U.S.
1920	Mark Arie, U.S.
1924	Jules Halasy, Hungary
1952	George Genereux, Canada
1956	Galliano Rossini, Italy
1960	Ion Dumitrescu, Rumania
1964	Ennio Mattarelli, Italy
1968	John Braithwaite, Great Britain
1972	Angelo Scalzone, Italy
1976	Don Haldeman, U.S.

Skeet

1968   Yevgeny Petrov, USSR
1972   Konrad Wirnhier, West Germany
1976   Josef Panacek, Czechoslovakia

Soccer

1900   Great Britain
1904   Canada
1906   Denmark
1908   Great Britain
1912   Great Britain
1920   Belgium
1924   Uruguay
1928   Uruguay
1936   Italy
1948   Sweden
1952   Hungary
1956   USSR
1960   Yugoslavia
1964   Hungary
1968   Hungary
1972   Poland
1976   East Germany

Swimming and Diving—Men

(R denotes Olympic record)

100-Meter Freestyle

1896	Alfred Hajos, Hungary	1:22.2
1904*	Zoltan de Holomay, Hungary	1:02.8
1906	Charles M. Daniels, U.S.	1:13.0
1908	Charles M. Daniels, U.S.	1:05.8
1912	Duke P. Kahanamoku, U.S.	1:03.4
1920	Duke P. Kahanamoku, U.S.	1:01.4
1924	John Weissmuller, U.S.	59.0
1928	John Weissmuller, U.S.	58.6
1932	Yasuji Miyazaki, Japan	58.2
1936	Ferenc Czik, Hungary	57.6
1948	Walter Ris, U.S.	57.3
1952	Clarke Scholes, U.S.	57.4
1956	Jon Henricks, Australia	55.4
1960	John Devitt, Australia	55.2
1964	Don Schollander, U.S.	53.4
1968	Mike Wenden, Australia	52.2
1972	Mark Spitz, U.S.	51.22
1976	Jim Montgomery, U.S.	49.99R

*100 yd

200-Meter Freestyle

1900	Frederick Lane, Australia	2:25.2
1904*	Charles M. Daniels, U.S.	2:44.2
1968	Mike Wenden, Australia	1:55.2
1972	Mark Spitz, U.S.	1:52.78
1976	Bruce Furniss, U.S.	1:50.29R

*200 yd

400-Meter Freestyle

1904*	Charles M. Daniels, U.S.	6:16.2
1906	O. Sheff, Australia	6:23.8
1908	Henry Taylor, Great Britain	5:36.8
1912	George R. Hodgson, Canada	5:24.4
1920	Norman Ross, U.S.	5:26.8
1924	John Weissmuller, U.S.	5:04.2
1928	Albert Zorilla, Argentina	5:01.6
1932	Clarence Crabbe, U.S.	4:48.4
1936	Jack Medica, U.S.	4:44.5
1948	Bill Smith, U.S.	4:41.0
1952	Jean Boiteux, France	4:30.7
1956	Murray Rose, Australia	4:27.3
1960	Murray Rose, Australia	4:18.3
1964	Don Schollander, U.S.	4:12.2

1968	Mike Burton, U.S.	4:09.0
1972	Bradford Cooper, Australia	4:00.27
1976	Brian Goodell, U.S.	3:51.93R

*440 yd

1,500-Meter Freestyle

1904*	Emil Rausch, Germany	27:18.2
1906**	Henry Taylor, Great Britain	
1908	Henry Taylor, Great Britain	
1912	George R. Hodgson, Canada	
1920	Norman Ross, U.S.	22:23.2
1924	Andrew M. Charlton, Australia	20:06.6
1928	Arne Borg, Sweden	19:51.8
1932	Kusuo Kitamura, Japan	19:51.6
1936	Norboru Terada, Japan	19:13.2
1948	Jimmy McLane, U.S.	19:18.5
1952	Ford Konno, U.S.	18:30.0
1956	Murray Rose, Australia	17:58.9
1960	John Konrads, Australia	17:19.6
1964	Bob Windle, Australia	17:01.7
1968	Mike Burton, U.S.	16:38.9
1972	Mike Burton, U.S.	15:52.58
1976	Brian Goodell, U.S.	15:02.4R

*1 mi
**1,600 m

100-Meter Backstroke

1904*	Walter Brock, Germany	1:16.8
1908	Arno Bieberstein, Germany	1:24.6
1912	Harry Hebner, U.S.	1:21.2
1920	Warren Kealoha, U.S.	1:15.2
1924	Warren Kealoha, U.S.	1:13.2
1928	George Kojac, U.S.	1:08.2
1932	Masaji Kiyokawa, Japan	1:08.6
1936	Adolph Kiefer, U.S.	1:05.9
1948	Allen Stack, U.S.	1:06.4
1952	Yoshinobu Oyakawa, U.S.	1:05.4
1956	Dave Thiele, Australia	1:02.2
1960	Dave Thiele, Australia	1:01.9
1968	Roland Matthes, East Germany	58.7
1972	Roland Matthes, East Germany	56.58
1976	John Naber, U.S.	55.49R

*100 yd

200-Meter Backstroke

1900	Ernst Hoppenberg, Germany	2:47.0
1964	Jed Graef, U.S.	2:10.3
1968	Roland Matthes, East Germany	2:09.6
1972	Roland Matthes, East Germany	2:02.82
1976	John Naber, U.S.	1:59.19R

100-Meter Breast Stroke

1968	Don McKenzie, U.S.	1:07.7
1972	Nobutaka Taguchi, Japan	1:04.94
1976	John Hencken, U.S.	1:03.11R

200-Meter Breast Stroke

1908	Frederick Holman, Great Britain	3:09.2
1912	Walter Bathe, Germany	3:01.8
1920	Haken Malmroth, Sweden	3:04.4
1924	Robert D. Skelton, U.S.	2:56.6
1928	Yoshiyuki Tsuruta, Japan	2:48.8
1932	Yoshiyuki Tsuruta, Japan	2:45.4
1936	Tetsuo Hamuro, Japan	2:42.5
1948	Joe Verdeur, U.S.	2:39.3
1952	John Davies, Australia	2:34.4
1956	Masaru Furukawa, Japan	2:34.7
1960	Bill Mulliken, U.S.	2:37.4
1964	Ian O'Brien, Australia	2:27.8
1968	Felipe Munoz, Mexico	2:28.7

| 1972 | John Hencken, U.S. | 2:21.55 |
| 1976 | David Wilkie, Great Britain | 2:15.11R |

100-Meter Butterfly

1968	Doug Russel, U.S.	55.9
1972	Mark Spitz, U.S.	54.27
1976	Matt Vogel, U.S.	54.35R

200-Meter Butterfly

1956	Bill Yorzyk, U.S.	2:19.3
1960	Mike Troy, U.S.	2:12.8
1964	Kevin Berry, Australia	2:06.6
1968	Carl Robie, U.S.	2:08.7
1972	Mark Spitz, U.S.	2:00.70
1976	Mike Bruner, U.S.	1:59.23R

400-Meter Individual Medley

1964	Dick Roth, U.S.	4:45.4
1968	Charles Hickcox, U.S.	4:48.4
1972	Gunnar Larsson, Sweden	4:31.98
1976	Rod Strachan, U.S.	4:23.68R

800-Meter Freestyle Relay

1908	Great Britain	10:55.6
1912	Australia	10:11.6
1920	United States	10:04.4
1924	United States	9:59.4
1928	United States	9:36.2
1932	Japan	8:58.4
1936	Japan	8:51.4
1948	United States	8:46.0
1952	United States	8:31.1
1956	Australia	8:23.6
1960	United States	8:10.2
1964	United States	7:52.1
1968	United States	7:52.3
1972	United States	7:38.78
1976	United States	7:23.22R

400-Meter Medley Relay

1960	United States	4:05.4
1964	United States	3:58.4
1968	United States	3:54.9
1972	United States	3:48.16
1976	United States	3:42.22R

Springboard Diving

1904	Dr. G. E. Sheldon, U.S.
1906	Gottlob Walz, Germany
1908	Albert Zurner, Germany
1912	Paul Gunther, Germany
1920	Louis E. Kuehn, U.S.
1924	Albert C. White, U.S.
1928	Pete Desjardins, U.S.
1932	Michael Galitzen, U.S.
1936	Dick Degener, U.S.
1948	Bruce Harlan, U.S.
1952	David Browning, U.S.
1956	Bob Clotworthy, U.S.
1960	Gary Tobian, U.S.
1964	Ken Sitzberger, U.S.
1968	Bernie Wrightson, U.S.
1972	Vladimir Vasin, USSR
1976	Phil Boggs, U.S.

Platform Diving

1928	Pete Desjardins, U.S.
1932	Harold Smith, U.S.
1936	Marshall Wayne, U.S.
1948	Dr. Sammy Lee, U.S.
1952	Dr. Sammy Lee, U.S.
1956	Joaquin Capilla, Mexico
1960	Bob Webster, U.S.
1964	Bob Webster, U.S.

| 1968 | Klaus DiBiasi, Italy |
| 1972 | Klaus DiBiasi, Italy |

Swimming and Diving—Women

(R denotes Olympic record)

100-Meter Freestyle

1912	Fanny Durack, Australia	1:22.2
1920	Ethelda Bleibtrey, U.S.	1:13.6
1924	Ethel Lackie, U.S.	1:12.4
1928	Albina Osipowich, U.S.	1:11.0
1932	Helene Madison, U.S.	1:06.8
1936	Rika Mastenbroek, Holland	1:05.9
1948	Greta Andersen, Denmark	1:06.3
1952	Katalin Szoke, Hungary	1:06.8
1956	Dawn Fraser, Australia	1:02.0
1960	Dawn Fraser, Australia	1:01.2
1964	Dawn Fraser, Australia	59.5
1968	Jan Henne, U.S.	1:00.0
1972	Sandra Neilson, U.S.	58.6
1976	Kornelia Ender, East Germany	55:65R

200-Meter Freestyle

1968	Debbie Meyer, U.S.	2:10.5
1972	Shane Gould, Australia	2:03.6
1976	Kornelia Ender, East Germany	1:59.26R

400-Meter Freestyle

1924	Martha Norelius, U.S.	5:45.4
1928	Martha Norelius, U.S.	5:42.8
1932	Helene Madison, U.S.	5:28.5
1936	Rika Mastenbroek, Holland	5:26.4
1948	Ann Curtis, U.S.	5:17.8
1952	Valeria Gyenge, Hungary	5:12.1
1956	Lorraine Crapp, Australia	4:56.6
1960	Chris von Saltza, U.S.	4:50.6
1964	Ginny Duenkel, U.S.	4:43.3
1968	Debbie Meyer, U.S.	4:31.8
1972	Shane Gould, Australia	4:19.0
1976	Petra Thumer, East Germany	4:09.89R

800-Meter Freestyle

1968	Debbie Meyer, U.S.	9:24.0
1972	Keena Rothhammer, U.S.	8:53.7
1976	Petra Thumer, East Germany	8:37.14R

100-Meter Backstroke

1924	Sybil Bauer, U.S.	1:23.2
1928	Marie Braun, Holland	1:22.0
1932	Eleanor Holm, U.S.	1:19.4
1936	Dina Senff, Holland	1:18.9
1948	Karen Harup, Denmark	1:14.4
1952	Joan Harrison, South Africa	1:14.3
1956	Judy Grinham, Great Britain	1:12.9
1960	Lynn Burke, U.S.	1:09.3
1964	Cathy Ferguson, U.S.	1:07.7
1968	Kaye Hall, U.S.	1:06.2
1972	Melissa Belote, U.S.	1:05.8
1976	Ulrike Richter, East Germany	1:01.83R

200-Meter Backstroke

1968	Pokey Watson, U. S.	2:24.3
1972	Melissa Belote, U.S.	2:19.2
1976	Ulrike Richter, East Germany	2:13.43R

100-Meter Breast Stroke

1968	Djurdjica Bjedov, Yugoslavia	1:15.8
1972	Cathie Carr, U.S.	1:13.6
1976	Hannelore Anke, East Germany	1:11.16R

200-Meter Breast Stroke

| 1924 | Lucy Morton, Great Britain | 3:33.2 |
| 1928 | Hilde Schrader, Germany | 3:12.6 |

1932	Clare Dennis, Australia	3:11.7
1936	Hideko Maehata, Japan	3:03.6
1948	Nel van Vliet, Holland	2:57.2
1952	Eva Szekely, Hungary	2:51.7
1956	Ursula Happe, Germany	2:53.1
1960	Anita Lonsbrough, Great Britain	2:49.5
1964	Galina Prosumenschikova, USSR	2:46.4
1968	Sharon Wichman, U.S.	2:44.4
1972	Beverley Whitfield, Australia	2:41.71
1976	Marina Koshevaia, USSR	2:33.35R

100-Meter Butterfly

1956	Shelley Mann, U.S.	1:11.0
1960	Carolyn Schuler, U.S.	1:09.5
1964	Sharon Stouder, U.S.	1:04.7
1968	Lynn McClements, Australia	1:05.5
1972	Mayumi Aoki, Japan	1:03.3
1976	Kornelia Ender, East Germany	1:03.13R

200-Meter Butterfly

1968	Ada Kok, Holland	2:24.7
1972	Karen Moe, U.S.	2:15.6
1976	Andrea Pollack, East Germany	2:11.41R

400-Meter Individual Medley

1964	Donna de Varona, U.S.	5:18.7
1968	Claudia Kolb, U.S.	5:08.5
1972	Gail Neall, Australia	5:03.0
1976	Ulrike Tauber, East Germany	4:42.71R

400-Meter Freestyle Relay

1912	Great Britain	5:52.8
1920	United States	5:11.6
1924	United States	4:58.8
1928	United States	4:47.6
1932	United States	4:38.0
1936	Holland	4:36.0
1948	United States	4:29.2
1952	Hungary	4:24.4
1956	Australia	4:17.1
1960	United States	4:08.9
1964	United States	4:03.8
1968	United States	4:02.5
1972	United States	3:55.2
1976	United States	3:44.82R

400-Meter Medley Relay

1960	United States	4:41.1
1964	United States	4:33.9
1968	United States	4:28.3
1972	United States	4:20.7
1976	East Germany	4:07.95R

Springboard Diving

1920	Aileen Riggin, U.S.
1924	Elizabeth Becker, U.S.
1928	Helen Meany, U.S.
1932	Georgia Coleman, U.S.
1936	Marjorie Gestring, U.S.
1948	Victoria Manalo Draves, U.S.
1952	Patricia McCormick, U.S.
1956	Patricia McCormick, U.S.
1960	Ingrid Kramer, Germany
1964	Ingrid Kramer Engel, Germany
1968	Sue Gossick, U.S.
1972	Micki King, U.S.
1976	Jenni Chandler, U.S.

Platform Diving

1912	Greta Johansson, Sweden
1920	Stefani Fryland Clausen, Denmark
1924	Caroline Smith, U.S.
1928	Elizabeth B. Pinkston, U.S.
1932	Dorothy Poynton, U.S.

1936	Dorothy Poynton Hill, U.S.
1948	Victoria Manalo Draves, U.S.
1952	Patricia McCormick, U.S.
1956	Patricia McCormick, U.S.
1960	Ingrid Kramer, Germany
1964	Lesley Bush, U.S.
1968	Milena Duchkova, Czechoslovakia
1972	Ulrika Knape, Sweden
1976	Elena Vaytsekhovskaia, USSR

Team Handball

Men

| 1972 | Yugoslavia |
| 1976 | USSR |

Women

| 1976 | USSR |

Track and Field—Men

(* Indicates wind-aided)
(R denotes Olympic record)

100-Meter Dash

1896	Thomas E. Burke, U.S.	12.0
1900	Francis W. Jarvis, U.S.	10.8
1094	Archie Hahn, U.S.	11.0
1906	Archie Hahn, U.S.	11.2
1908	Reginald Walker, South Africa	10.8
1912	Ralph Craig, U.S.	10.8
1920	Charles Paddock, U.S.	10.8
1924	Harold Abrahams, Great Britain	10.6
1928	Percy Williams, Canada	10.8
1932	Eddie Tolan, U.S.	10.3
1936	Jesse Owens, U.S.	10.3*
1948	Harrison Dillard, U.S.	10.3
1952	Lindy Remigino, U.S.	10.4
1956	Bobby Morrow, U.S.	10.5
1960	Armin Hary, Germany	10.2
1964	Robert Hayes, U.S.	10.0
1968	James Hines, U.S.	9.9R
1972	Valery Borzov, Russia	10.1
1976	Hasely Crawford, Trinidad-Tobago	10.06

200-Meter Dash

1900	J. W. B. Tewksbury, U.S.	22.2
1904	Archie Hahn, U.S.	21.6
1908	Robert Kerr, Canada	22.6
1912	Ralph Craig, U.S.	21.7
1920	Allan Woodring, U.S.	22.0
1924	Jackson V. Scholz, U.S.	21.6
1928	Percy Williams, Canada	21.8
1932	Eddie Tolan, U.S.	21.2
1936	Jesse Owens, U.S.	20.7
1948	Melvin Patton, U.S.	21.1
1952	Andrew W. Stanfield, U.S.	20.7
1956	Bobby Morrow, U.S.	20.6
1960	Livio Berruti, Italy	20.5
1964	Henry Carr, U.S.	20.3
1968	Tommie Smith, U.S.	19.8R
1972	Valery Borzov, USSR	20.0
1976	Donald Quarrie, Jamaica	20.23

400-Meter Dash

1896	Thomas E. Burke, U.S.	54.2
1900	Maxwell W. Long, U.S.	49.4
1904	Harry Hillman, U.S.	49.2
1906	Paul Pilgrim, U.S.	53.2
1908	Wyndham Halswelle, Great Britain	50.0**
1912	Charles D. Reidpath, U.S.	48.2
1920	Bevil G. D. Rudd, South Africa	49.6
1924	Eric H. Liddel, Great Britain	47.6

1928	Ray Barbuti, U.S.	47.8
1932	William A. Carr, U.S.	46.2
1936	Archie Williams, U.S.	46.5
1948	Arthur Wint, Jamaica	46.2
1952	George Rhoden, Jamaica	45.9
1956	Charles L. Jenkins, U.S.	46.7
1960	Otis Davis, U.S.	44.9
1964	Michael D. Larrabee, U.S.	45.1
1968	Lee Evans, U.S.	43.8R
1972	Vincent Matthews, U.S.	44.7
1976	Alberto Juantorena, Cuba	44.26

**Walkover

800-Meter Run

1896	Edwin H. Flack, Australia	2:11.0
1900	Alfred E. Tysoe, Great Britain	2:01.4
1904	James D. Lightbody, U.S.	1:56.0
1906	Paul Pilgrim, U.S.	2:01.2
1908	Melvin W. Sheppard, U.S.	1:52.8
1912	James E. Meredith, U.S.	1:51.9
1920	Albert G. Hill, Great Britain	1:53.4
1924	Douglas G. A. Lowe, Great Britain	1:52.4
1928	Doublas G. A. Lowe, Great Britain	1:51.8
1932	Thomas Hampson, Great Britain	1:49.8
1936	John Woodruff, U.S.	1:52.9
1948	Malvin Whitfield, U.S.	1:49.2
1952	Malvin Whitfield, U.S.	1:49.2
1956	Thomas W. Courtney, U.S.	1:47.7
1960	Peter Snell, New Zealand	1:46.3
1964	Peter Snell, New Zealand	1:45.1
1968	Ralph Doubell, Australia	1:44.3
1972	David Wottle, U.S.	1:45.9
1976	Alberto Juantorena, Cuba	1:43.50R

1,500-Meter Run

1896	Edwin H. Flack, Great Britain	4:33.2
1900	Charles Bennett, Great Britain	4:06.2
1904	James D. Lightbody, U.S.	4:05.4
1906	James D. Lightbody, U.S.	4:12
1908	Melvin W. Sheppard, U.S.	4:03.4
1912	Arnold N. S. Jackson, Great Britain	3:56.8
1920	Albert G. Hill, Great Britain	4:01.8
1924	Paavo Nurmi, Finland	3:53.6
1928	Harry E. Larva, Finland	3:53.2
1932	Luigi Beccali, Italy	3:51.2
1936	Jack E. Lovelock, New Zealand	3:47.8
1948	Henry Eriksson, Sweden	3:49.8
1952	Joseph Barthel, Luxembourg	3:45.2
1956	Ronald Delany, Ireland	3:41.2
1960	Herbert Elliott, Australia	3:35.6
1964	Peter Snell, New Zealand	3:38.1
1968	Kipchoge Keino, Kenya	3:34.9R
1972	Pekka Vasala, Finland	3:36.3
1976	John Walker, New Zealand	3:39.17

5,000-Meter Run

1912	Hannes Kolehmainen, Finland	14:36.6
1920	Joseph Guillemot, France	14:55.6
1924	Paavo Nurmi, Finland	14:31.2
1928	Willi Ritola, Finland	14:38.0
1932	Lauri Lehtinen, Finland	14:30.0
1936	Gunnar Hockert, Finland	14:22.2
1948	Gaston Reiff, Belgium	14:17.6
1952	Emil Zatopek, Czechoslovakia	14:06.6
1956	Vladimir Kuts, USSR	13:39.6
1960	Murray Halberg, New Zealand	13:43.4
1964	Robert K. Schul, U.S.	13:48.8
1968	Mohamed Gammoudi, Tunisia	14:05.0
1972	Lasse Viren, Finland	13:26.4
1976	Lasse Viren, Finland	13:24.76R

10,000-Meter Run

1912	Hannes Kolehmainen, Finland	31:20.8
1920	Paavo Nurmi, Finland	31:45.8
1924	Willi Ritola, Finland	30:23.2
1928	Paavo Nurmi, Finland	30:18.8
1932	Janusz Kusocinski, Poland	30:11.4
1936	Ilmari Salminen, Finland	30:15.4
1948	Emil Zatopek, Czechoslovakia	29:59.6
1952	Emil Zatopek, Czechoslovakia	29:17.0
1956	Vladimir Kuts, USSR	28:45.6
1960	Peter Bolotnikov, USSR	28:32.2
1964	William Mills, U.S.	28:24.4
1968	Naftali Temu, Kenya	29:27.4
1972	Lasse Viren, Finland	27:38.4R
1976	Lasse Viren, Finland	27:40.38

Marathon

1896	Spyros Loues, Greece	2:58:50.0
1900	Michael Theato, France	2:59:45.0
1904	Thomas J. Hicks, U.S.	3:28:53.0
1906	W. J. Sherring, Canada	2:51:23.6
1908	John J. Hayes, U.S.	2:55:18.4
1912	Kenneth McArthur, S. Africa	2:36:54.8
1920	Hannes Kolehmainen, Finland	2:32:53.8
1920	Hannes Kolehmainen, Finland	2:32:53.8
1924	Albin Stenroos, Finland	2:41:22.6
1928	A. B. El Ouafi, France	2:32:57.0
1932	Juan Zabala, Argentina	2:31:36.0
1936	Kitei Son, Japan	2:29:19.2
1948	Delfo Cabrera, Argentina	2:34:51.6
1952	Emil Zatopek, Czechoslovakia	2:23:03.2
1956	Alain Mimoun, France	2:25:00.0
1960	Abebe Bikila, Ethiopia	2:15:16.2
1964	Abebe Bikila, Ethiopia	2:12:11.2
1968	Mamo Wolde, Ethiopia	2:20:26.4
1972	Frank Shorter, U.S.	2:12:19.8
1976	Waldemar Gerpinski, East Germany	2:09.55R

110-Meter Hurdles

1896	Thomas P. Curtis, U.S.	17.6
1900	Alvin E. Kraenzlein, U.S.	15.4
1904	Frederick W. Schule, U.S.	16.0
1906	R. G. Leavitt, U.S.	16.2
1908	Forrest Smithson, U.S.	15.0
1912	Frederick W. Kelley, U.S.	15.1
1920	Earl J. Thompson, Canada	14.8
1924	Daniel C. Kinsey, U.S.	15.0
1928	Sydney Atkinson, S. Africa	14.8
1932	George Saling, U.S.	14.6
1936	Forrest Towns, U.S.	14.2
1948	William Porter, U.S.	13.9
1952	Harrison Dillard, U.S.	13.7
1956	Lee Calhoun, U.S.	13.5
1960	Lee Calhoun, U.S.	13.8
1964	Hayes W. Jones, U.S.	13.6
1968	Willie Davenport, U.S.	13.3
1972	Rod Milburn, U.S.	13.2R
1976	Guy Drut, France	13:30

400-Meter Hurdles

1900	J. W. B. Tewksbury, U.S.	57.6
1904	Harry Hillman, U.S.	53.0
1908	Charles J. Bacon, U.S.	55.0
1920	Frank F. Loomis, U.S.	54.0
1924	F. Morgan Taylor, U.S.	52.6
1928	Lord David Burghley, Great Britain	53.4
1932	Robert Tisdall, Ireland	51.8
1936	Glenn Hardin, U.S.	52.4
1948	Roy Cochran, U.S.	51.1
1952	Charles Moore, U.S.	50.8
1956	Glenn A. Davis, U.S.	50.1
1960	Glenn A. Davis, U.S.	49.3
1964	Warren "Rex" Cawley, U.S.	49.6
1968	David Hemery, Great Britain	48.1
1972	John Akki-Bua, Uganda	47.8
1976	Edwin Moses, U.S.	47.64R

3,000-Meter Steeplechase

1920	Percy Hodge, Great Britain	10:00.4
1924	Willi Ritola, Finland	9:33.6
1928	Toivo A. Loukola, Finland	9:21.8
1932	Volmari Iso-Hollo, Finland	10:33.4*
1936	Volmari Iso-Hollo, Finland	9:03.8
1948	Thore Sjostrand, Sweden	9:04.6
1952	Horace Ashenfelter, U.S.	8:45.4
1956	Chris Brasher, Great Britain	8:41.2
1960	Zdzislaw Krzyszkowiak, Poland	8:34.2
1964	Gaston Roelants, Belgium	8:30.8
1968	Amos Biwott, Kenya	8:51.0
1972	Kipchoge Keino, Kenya	8:23.6
1976	Anders Garderud, Sweden	8:08.02R

20-Kilometer Walk

1956	Leonid Spirine, USSR	1:31:27.4
1960	Vladimir Golubnichy, USSR	1:34:07.2
1964	Kenneth Matthews, Great Britain	1:29:34.0
1968	Vladimir Golubnichy, USSR	1:33:58.4
1972	Peter Frenkel, East Germany	1:26:42.4
1976	Daniel Bautista, Mexico	1:24:40.6R

400-Meter Relay

1912	Great Britain	42.4
1920	United States	42.2
1924	United States	41.0
1928	United States	41.0
1932	United States	40.0
1936	United States	40.0
1948	United States	40.3
1952	United States	40.1
1956	United States	39.5
1960	Germany	39.5
1964	United States	39.0
1968	United States	38.2
1972	United States	38.19R
1976	United States	38.33

1,600-Meter Relay

1908	United States	3:29.4
1912	United States	3:16.6
1920	Great Britain	3:22.2
1924	United States	3:16.0
1928	United States	3:14.2
1932	United States	3:08.2
1936	Great Britain	3:09.0
1948	United States	3:10.4
1952	Jamaica	3:03.9
1956	United States	3:04.8
1960	United States	3:02.2
1964	United States	3:00.7
1968	United States	2:56.1
1972	Kenya	2:59.8
1976	United States	2:58.65R

Pole Vault

1896	William K. Hoyt, U.S.	10-9¾
1900	Irving K. Baxter, U.S.	10-9.9
1904	Charles E. Dvorak, U.S.	11-6
1908	Albert C. Gilbert, U.S.	12-2
	Edward T. Cook Jr., U.S.	
1912	Harry S. Babcock, U.S.	12-11½
1920	Frank K. Foss, U.S.	12-5⁹⁄₁₆
1924	Lee S. Barnes, U.S.	12-11½
1928	Sabin W. Carr, U.S.	13-9¾
1932	William Miller, U.S.	14-1⅞
1936	Earle Meadows, U.S.	14-3¼
1948	O. Guinn Smith, U.S.	14-1¼
1952	Robert Richards, U.S.	14-11¼
1956	Robert Richards, U.S.	14-11½
1960	Donald Bragg, U.S.	15-5⅛
1964	Fred M. Hansen, U.S.	16-8¾
1968	Robert Seagren, U.S.	17-8½
1972	Wolfgang Nordwig, East Germany	18-½R
1976	Tadeusz Slusarski, Poland	18-½R

High Jump

1896	Ellery Clark, U.S.	5-11¼
1900	Irving K. Baxter, U.S.	6-2⅘
1904	Samuel Jones, U.S.	5-11
1906	Con Leahy, Ireland	5-9⅞
1908	Harry Porter, U.S.	6-3
1912	Alma W. Richards	6-4
1920	Richmond Landon, U.S.	6-4¼
1924	Harold Osborn, U.S.	6-5¹⁵⁄₁₆
1928	Robert W. King, U.S.	6-4⅜
1932	Duncan McNaughton, Canada	6-5⅝
1936	Cornelius Johnson, U.S.	6-7¹⁵⁄₁₆
1948	John Winter, Australia	6-6
1952	Walter Davis, U.S.	6-8¼
1956	Charles E. Dumas, U.S.	6-11¼
1960	Robert Shavlakadze, USSR	7-1
1964	Valery Brumel, USSR	7-1¾
1968	Richard Fosbury, U.S.	7-4¼
1972	Juri Tarmak, USSR	7-3¾
1976	Jacek Wszola, Poland	7-4½R

Long Jump

1896	Ellery Clark, U.S.	20-10
1900	Alvin Kraenzlein, U.S.	23-6⅞
1904	Myer Prinstein, U.S.	24-1
1906	Myer Prinstein, U.S.	23-7½
1908	Francis Irons, U.S.	24-6½
1912	Albert Gutterson, U.S.	24-11¼
1920	William Pettersson, Sweden	23-5½
1924	DeHart Hubbard, U.S.	24-5⅛
1928	Edward Hamm, U.S.	25-4¾
1932	Edward Gordon, U.S.	25-¾
1936	Jesse Owens, U.S.	26-5⅜
1948	Willie Steel, U.S.	25-8
1952	Jerome Biffle, U.S.	24-10
1956	Gregory C. Bell, U.S.	25-8¼
1960	Ralph H. Boston, U.S.	26-7¾
1964	Lynn Davies, Great Britain	26-5¾
1968	Robert Beamon, U.S.	29-2¼R
1972	Randy Williams, U.S.	27-½
1976	Arnie Robinson, U.S.	27-4¾

Triple Jump

1896	James B. Connolly, U.S.	45-0
1900	Myer Prinstein, U.S.	47-4¼
1904	Myer Prinstein, U.S.	47-0
1906	Patrick O'Connor, Ireland	46-2
1908	Timothy Ahearne, Great Britain	48-11¼
1912	Gustaf Lindblom, Sweden	48-5⅛
1920	Vilhu Tuulos, Finland	47-6⅞
1924	Archibald Winter, Australia	50-11⅛
1928	Mikio Oda, Japan	49-10¹³⁄₁₆
1932	Chuhei Nambu, Japan	51-7
1936	Naoto Tajima, Japan	52-5⅞
1948	Arne Ahman, Sweden	50-6¼
1952	Adhemar Ferreirada Silva, Brazil	53-2½
1956	Adhemar Ferreirada Silva, Brazil	53-7½
1960	Jozef Schmidt, Poland	55-1¾
1964	Jozef Schmidt, Poland	55-3¼
1968	Viktor Saneyev, USSR	57¾R
1972	Viktor Saneyev, USSR	56-11
1976	Viktor Saneyev, USSR	56-8¾

16-Pound Shot Put

1896	Robert Garrett, U.S.	36-9¾
1900	Richard Sheldon, U.S.	46-3⅛
1904	Ralph Rose, U.S.	48-7
1906	Matthew J. Sheridan, U.S.	40-4⅘
1908	Ralph Rose, U.S.	46-7½
1912	Patrick McDonald, U.S.	50-4
1920	Ville Porhola, Finland	48-7⅛

1924	Clarence Houser, U.S.	49-2½
1928	John Kuck, U.S.	52-13/16
1932	Leo Sexton, U.S.	52-63/16
1936	Hans Woellke, Germany	52-1¾
1948	Wilbur Thompson, U.S.	56-2
1952	Parry O'Brien, U.S.	57-1½
1956	Parry O'Brien, U.S.	60-11
1960	William Nieder, U.S.	64-6¾
1964	Dallas C. Long, U.S.	66-8¼
1968	J. Randel Matson, U.S.	67-4¾
1972	Wladyslaw Komar, Poland	69-6R
1976	Udo Beyer, East Germany	69-¾

Discus Throw

1896	Robert Garrett, U.S.	95-7½
1900	Rudolf Bauer, Hungary	118-2.9
1904	Martin Sheridan, U.S.	128-10½
1906	Martin Sheridan, U.S.	136-⅔
1908	Martin Sheridan, U.S.	134-2
1912	Armas Taipale, Finland	145-9/16
1920	Elmer Niklander, Finland	146-7
1924	Clarence Houser, U.S.	151-5¼
1928	Clarence Houser, U.S.	155-2⅘
1932	John Anderson, U.S.	162-4⅞
1936	Kenneth Carpenter, U.S.	165-7½
1948	Adolfo Consolini, Italy	173-2
1952	Sim Iness, U.S.	180-6½
1956	Alfred A. Oerter, U.S.	184-10½
1960	Alfred A. Oerter, U.S.	194-2
1964	Alfred A. Oerter, U.S.	200-1½
1968	Alfred A. Oerter, U.S.	212-6½R
1972	Ludvik Danek, Czechoslovakia	211-3½
1976	Mac Wilkins, U.S.	221-5R

16-Pound Hammer Throw

1900	John Flanagan, U.S.	167-4
1904	John Flanagan, U.S.	168-1
1908	John Flanagan, U.S.	170-4½
1912	Matthew McGrath, U.S.	179-7⅛
1920	Patrick Ryan, U.S.	173-5⅝
1924	Frederick Tootell, U.S.	174-10¼
1928	Patrick O'Callaghan, Ireland	168-7½
1932	Patrick O'Callaghan, Ireland	176-11⅛
1936	Karl Hein, Germany	185-4¼
1948	Imre Nemeth, Hungary	183-11½
1952	Jozef Csermak, Hungary	197-11¾
1956	Harold V. Connolly, U.S.	207-3½
1960	Vasiliy Rudenkov, USSR	220-1⅝
1964	Romuald Klim, USSR	228-9½
1968	Gyula Zsivotzky, Hungary	240-8
1972	Anatoli Bondarchuk, USSR	247-8½
1976	Yuri Syedekh, USSR	254-3.9R

Javelin Throw

1906	Erik Lemming, Sweden	175-6
1908	Erik Lemming, Sweden	179-10½
1912	Erik Lemming, Sweden	198-11¼
1920	Jonni Myrra, Finland	215-9¾
1924	Jonni Myrra, Finland	206-6¾
1928	Erik Lundquist, Sweden	218-6⅛
1932	Matti Jarvinen, Finland	238-7
1936	Gerhard Stock, Germany	235-85/16
1948	Tapio Rautavaara, Finland	228-10½
1952	Cyrus Young, U.S.	281-2¼
1956	Egil Danielson, Norway	281-2¼
1960	Viktor Tsibulenko, USSR	277-8⅜
1964	Pauli Nevala, Finland	271-2¼
1968	Janis Lusis, USSR	295-7¼
1972	Klaus Wolferman, West Germany	296-10
1976	Miklos Nemeth, Hungary	310-4R

Decathlon

(Point system was revised in 1936 and 1964)

1912	Hugo Wieslander, Sweden	7724.49
1920	Helge Lovland, Norway	6804.35
1924	Harold Osborn, U.S.	7710.77
1928	Paavo Yrjola, Finland	8053.29
1932	James Bausch, U.S.	8462.23
1936	Glenn Morris, U.S.	7900.00
1948	Robert Mathias, U.S.	7139.00
1952	Robert Mathias, U.S.	7887.00
1956	Milton G. Campbell, U.S.	7937.00
1960	Rafer Johnson, U.S.	8392.00
1964	Willi Holdorf, Germany	7887.00
1968	William Toomey, U.S.	8193.00
1972	Nikolai Avilov, Russia	8454.00
1976	Bruce Jenner, U.S.	8618.00R

Track and Field—Women

(R denotes Olympic record)

100-Meter Dash

1928	Elizabeth Robinson, U.S.	12.2
1932	Stella Walasiewicz, Poland	11.9
1936	Helen Stephens, U.S.	11.5
1948	Fanny Blankers-Koen, Holland	11.9
1952	Marjorie Jackson, Australia	11.5
1956	Betty Cuthbert, Australia	11.5
1960	Wilma Rudolph, U.S.	11.0R
1964	Wyomia Tyus, U.S.	11.4
1968	Wyomia Tyus, U.S.	11.0R
1972	Renate Stecher, East Germany	11.1
1976	Annegret Richter, West Germany	11.01

200-Meter Dash

1948	Fanny Blankers-Koen, Holland	24.4
1952	Marjorie Jackson, Australia	23.7
1956	Betty Cuthbert, Australia	23.4
1960	Wilma Rudolph, U.S.	24.0
1964	Edith McGuire, U.S.	23.0
1968	Irina Szewinska, Poland	22.5
1972	Renate Stecher, East Germany	22.4R
1976	Baerbel Eckert, East Germany	22.37R

400-Meter Run

1964	Betty Cuthbert, Australia	52.0
1968	Colette Besson, France	52.0
1972	Monika Zehrt, East Germany	51.1
1976	Irina Szewinska, Poland	49.29R

800-Meter Run

1928	Linda Radke, Germany	2:16.8
1960	Ludmila Shevcova, USSR	2:04.3
1964	Ann Packer, Great Britain	2:01.1
1968	Madeline Manning, U.S.	2:00.9
1972	Hildegrad Falck, West Germany	1:58.6
1976	Tatyana Kazankina, USSR	1:54.94R

1,500-Meter Run

1972	Ludmila Bragina, Russia	4:01.4R
1976	Tatyana Kazankina, USSR	4:05.48

400-Meter Relay

1928	Canada	48.4
1932	United States	47.0
1936	United States	46.9
1948	Holland	47.5
1952	United States	45.9
1956	Australia	44.5
1960	United States	44.5
1964	Poland	43.6
1968	United States	42.8
1972	West Germany	42.8
1976	East Germany	42.55R

1,600-Meter Relay

1972	East Germany	3:23.3
1976	East Germany	3:19.23R

80-Meter Hurdles

1932	Mildred Didrikson, U.S.	11.7
1936	Trebisonda Villa, Italy	11.7
1948	Fanny Blankers-Koen, Holland	11.2
1952	Shirley Strickland de la Hunty, Australia	10.9
1956	Shirley Strickland de la Hunty, Australia	10.7
1960	Irina Press, Russia	10.8
1964	Karin Balzer, Germany	10.5
1968	Maureen Caird, Australia	10.3R

100-Meter Hurdles

| 1972 | Annelie Ehrhardt, East Germany | 12.6 |
| 1976 | Johanna Schaller, East Germany | 12.77 |

High Jump

1928	Ethel Catherwood, Canada	5-3
1932	Jean Shiley, U.S.	5-5¼
1936	Ebolya Csak, Hungary	5-3
1948	Alice Coachman, U.S.	5-6⅛
1952	Ester Brand, S. Africa	5-5¾
1956	Mildred McDaniel, U.S.	5-9¼
1960	Yolanda Balas, Rumania	6-¾
1964	Yolanda Balas, Rumania	6-2¾
1968	Miloslava Rezkova, Czechoslovakia	5-11¾
1972	Ulrike Mayforth, West Germany	6-2¾
1976	Rosemarie Ackermann, East Germany	6-3.9R

Long Jump

1948	Olga Gyarmati, Hungary	18-8¼
1952	Yvette Williams, New Zealand	20-5.66
1956	Elizbieta Krzesinska, Poland	20-9¾
1960	Vera Krepinka, USSR	20-10⅞
1964	Mary Rand, Great Britain	22-2¼
1968	Viorica Viscopoleanu, Rumania	22-4½R
1972	Heidemarie Rosenthal, West Germany	22-3
1976	Angela Voigt, East Germany	22½

Discus Throw

1928	Helena Konopacka, Poland	129-11⅞
1932	Lilian Copeland, U.S.	133-2
1936	Gisela Maurmayer, Germany	156-3³⁄₁₆
1948	Micheline Ostermeyer, France	137-6½
1952	Nina Romaschkova, USSR	168-8½
1956	Olga Fikotova, Czechoslovakia	176-1½
1960	Nina Ponomareva, USSR	180-8¼
1964	Tamara Press, USSR	187-10¾
1968	Lia Manoliu, Rumania	191-2½
1972	Faina Melnik, USSR	218-7
1976	Evelyn Schlaak, East Germany	226-4½

Javelin Throw

1932	Mildred Didrikson, U.S.	143-4
1936	Tilly Fleischer, Germany	148-2¾
1948	Herma Baume, Austria	149-6
1952	Dana Zatopek, Czechoslovakia	165-7.05
1956	Inessa Iaounzem, USSR	176-8
1960	Elvira Ozolina, USSR	183-8
1964	Mihaela Penes, Rumania	198-7½
1968	Angela Nemeth, Hungary	198-½
1972	Ruth Fuchs, East Germany	209-7
1976	Ruth Fuchs, East Germany	216-4R

Shot Put

1948	Micheline Ostermeyer, France	45-1½
1952	Galina Zybina, USSR	50-2.58
1956	Tamara Tychkevitch, USSR	54-5
1960	Tamara Press, USSR	56-9⅞
1964	Tamara Press, USSR	59-6½
1968	Margitta Gummell, East Germany	64-4
1972	Nadezh Chizhova, USSR	69-0
1976	Ivanka Khristova, Bulgaria	69-7R

Pentathlon

1964	Irina Press, Russia	5,246
1968	Igrid Becker, West Germany	5,098
1972	Mary Peters, Great Britain	4,801
1976	Sigrun Siegl, East Germany	4,745

Volleyball—Men

1964	USSR
1968	USSR
1972	Japan
1976	Poland

Volleyball—Women

1964	Japan
1968	USSR
1972	USSR
1976	Japan

Water Polo

1900	Great Britain
1904	United States
1908	Great Britain
1912	Great Britain
1920	Great Britain
1924	France
1928	Germany
1932	Hungary
1936	Hungary
1948	Italy
1952	Hungary
1956	Hungary
1960	Italy
1964	Hungary
1968	Yugoslavia
1972	USSR
1976	Hungary

Weightlifting

Flyweight

| 1972 | Zygmunt Smalcerz, Poland | 744 |
| 1976 | Aleksandr Voronin, USSR | 533.5 |

Bantamweight

1948	Joe N. DePietro, U.S.	677.915
1952	Ivan Ododov, USSR	694.45
1956	Charles Vinci, U.S.	753.5
1960	Charles Vinci, U.S.	760.5
1964	Aleksei Vakhonin, USSR	786.5
1968	Mohammed Nasiri, Iran	809.75
1972	Imre Foeldi, Hungary	823.23
1976	Norair Nurikian, Bulgaria	588.5

Featherweight

1920	L. de Haes, Belgium	485
1924	Paolo Gabetti, Italy	887.35
1928	Franz Andrysek, Austria	633.822
1932	Raymond Suvigny, France	733.822
1936	Anthony Terlazzo, U.S.	688.937
1948	Mahmoud S. J. Fayad, Egypt	733.02
1952	Rafael Chimishkyan, USSR	744.05
1956	Isaac Berger, U.S.	776.5
1960	Yevgeni Minaev, USSR	821
1964	Yoshinobu Miyake, Japan	874.5
1968	Yoshinobu Miyake, Japan	865
1972	Norair Nourikian, Bulgaria	887.35
1976	Nikolai Kolesnikov, USSR	627

Lightweight

1920	Alfred Neyland, Estonia	567.68
1924	Edmond Decottignies, France	970.02
1928	Kurt Helbig, Germany	710.98
	Hans Hass, Austria	
1932	Rene Duverger, France	716.495
1936	Mohammed A. Mesbah, Egypt	755.085
	Robert Fein, Austria	
1948	Ibraim Shams, Egypt	793.656
1952	Tommy Kono, U.S.	777.12

1956	Igor Rybak, USSR	837.5
1960	Viktor Bushuev, USSR	876
1964	Waldemar Baszanowski, Poland	951.5
1968	Waldemar Baszanowski, Poland	964.5
1972	Mukharbi Kirzhinov, USSR	1104.11
1976	Zbigniew Kaezmarek, Poland	677.75

Middleweight

1920	B. Gance, France	540.012
1924	Carlo Galimberti, Italy	1085.725
1928	Francois Roger, France	738.54
1932	Rudolf Ismayr, Germany	760.507
1936	Khadr El Touni, Egypt	854.28
1948	Frank I. Spellman, U.S.	859.794
1952	Peter George, U.S.	881
1956	Fedor Bogdanovskii, USSR	925.75
1964	Hans Zdrazila, Czechoslovakia	979
1968	Viktor Kurentsov, USSR	1046.75
1972	Yordan Bikov, Bulgaria	1069
1976	Yordan Mitkov, Bulgaria	737

Light Heavyweight

1920	E. Cadine, France	639.334
1924	Charles Rigoulot, France	1107.811
1928	Saied Nosseir, Egypt	782.63
1932	Louis Hostin, France	804.679
1936	Louis Hostin, France	821.213
1948	Stanley A. Stanczyk, U.S.	920.42
1952	Trofim Lomakin, USSR	919
1956	Tommy Kono, U.S.	986.24
1960	Ireneusz Palinski, Poland	975.5
1964	Rudolf Plukfelder, USSR	1045
1968	Boris Selitsky, USSR	1068.75
1972	Leif Jenssen, Norway	1118
1976	Valeri Shary, USSR	803

Middle Heavyweight

1952	Norbert Schemansky, U.S.	981
1956	Arkadi Vorobiev, USSR	1019.25
1960	Arkadi Vorobiev, USSR	1039.5
1964	Vladimir Golovanov, USSR	1072.5
1968	Kaarlo Kangasniemi, Finland	1140.5
1972	Andon Nikolov, Bulgaria	1157
1976	David Rigert, USSR	841.5

Heavyweight

1920	Filippe Bottini, Italy	595.24
1924	Giuseppe Tonani, Italy	1140.879
1928	Josef Strassberger, Germany	821.213
1932	Jaroslaw Skobla, Czechoslovakia	837.748
1936	Josef Manger, Germany	903.886
1948	John Davis, U.S.	997.581
1952	John Davis, U.S.	1012
1956	Paul Anderson, U.S.	1102
1960	Yuri Vlasov, USSR	1182.5
1964	Leonid Zabotinsky, USSR	1259.5
1968	Leonid Zabotinsky, USSR	1261
1972	Van Talts, USSR	1297
1976	Valentin Khristov, Bulgaria	880

Super Heavyweight

1972	Vassili Alexeev, USSR	1,411
1976	Vassili Alexeev, USSR	968

Wrestling—Freestyle

Paperweight

1972	Roman Dmitriev, USSR	
1976	Khassan Issaev, Bulgaria	

Flyweight

1904	Robert Curry, U.S.	
1948	Lennart Vitala, Finland	
1952	Hassen Cemici, Turkey	
1956	Mirian Tsalkalmanidze, USSR	

1960	Ahmet Bilek, Turkey	
1964	Yoshikatsu Yoshida, Japan	
1968	Shigeo Nakata, Japan	
1972	Kiyomi Kato, Japan	
1976	Yuji Takata, Japan	

Bantamweight

1904	George N. Mehnert, U.S.	
1908	George N. Mehnert, U.S.	
1924	Kustaa Pihalajamaki, Finland	
1928	Kaarle Makinen, Finland	
1932	Robert E. Pearce, U.S.	
1936	Odon Zombory, Hungary	
1948	Nassuh Akkan, Turkey	
1952	Shohachi Ishii, Japan	
1956	Mustafa Kagistanii, Turkey	
1960	Terry McCann, U.S.	
1964	Yojuru Uetaje, Japan	
1968	Yojuru Uetaje, Japan	
1972	Hideaki Yanagida, Japan	
1976	Vladimir Umin, USSR	

Featherweight

1896	Karl Schumann, Germany	
1904	Isaac Niflot, U.S.	
1908	George S. Dole, U.S.	
1920	Charles E. Ackerly, U.S.	
1924	Robin Reed, U.S.	
1928	Allie Morrison, U.S.	
1932	Herman Pihlajamaki, Finland	
1936	Kustaa Pihlajamaki, Finland	
1948	Gazanfer Bilge, Turkey	
1952	Bayram Sit, Turkey	
1956	Shoze Sasabara, Japan	
1960	Mustafa Dagistanli, Turkey	
1964	Osamu Watanabe, Japan	
1968	Masaaki Kanedo, Japan	
1972	Zagalav Abdulbekov, USSR	
1976	Jung-Mo Jang, South Korea	

Lightweight

1904	Benjamin J. Bradshaw, U.S.	
1908	G. de Relwyskow, Great Britain	
1920	Kalle Antilla, Finland	
1924	Russell Vis, U.S.	
1928	Osvald Kapp, Estonia	
1932	Charles Pacome, France	
1936	Karoly Karpati, Hungary	
1948	Celal Atik, Turkey	
1952	Olle Anderberg, Sweden	
1956	Emamli Habibi, Iran	
1960	Shelby Wilson, U.S.	
1964	Enio Dimov, Bulgaria	
1968	Abdollah Movahed, Iran	
1972	Dan Gable, U.S.	
1976	Pavel Pinigin, USSR	

Welterweight

1904	Otto F. Roehm, U.S.	
1924	Herman Gehri, Switzerland	
1928	Arve J. Haavisto, Finland	
1932	Jack F. Van Bebber, U.S.	
1936	Frank Lewis, U.S.	
1948	Yasar Dogu, Turkey	
1952	William Smith, U.S.	
1956	Mistro Ikeda, Japan	
1960	Doug Blubaugh, U.S.	
1964	Ismall Ogan, Turkey	
1968	Mahmud Ataly, Turkey	
1972	Wayne Wells, U.S.	
1976	Date Jiichiso, Japan	

Middleweight

1904	Charles Erickson, U.S.	

1908 Stanley V. Bacon, Great Britain
1920 Eino Leino, Finland
1924 Fritz Haggmann, Switzerland
1928 Ernst Kyburg, Switzerland
1932 Ivar Johansson, Sweden
1936 Emile Poilve, France
1948 Glenn Brand, U.S.
1952 David Gimakuridze, USSR
1956 Nikola Nikolov, Bulgaria
1960 Hasan Gungor, Turkey
1964 Prodan Garjev, Bulgaria
1968 Boris Gurevich, USSR
1972 Levan Tediahsvili, USSR
1976 John Peterson, U.S.

Light Heavyweight
1920 Anders Larsson, Sweden
1924 John Spellman, U.S.
1928 Thure S. Sjostedt, Sweden
1932 Peter J. Mehringer, U.S.
1936 Knut Fridell, Sweden
1948 Henry Wittenberg, U.S.
1952 Wiking Palm, Sweden
1956 Gholam Takhti, Iran
1960 Ismet Atli, Turkey
1964 Aleksandr Medved, USSR
1968 Ahmet Ayuk, Turkey
1972 Ben Peterson, U.S.
1976 Levan Tediashvili, USSR

Heavyweight
1904 B. Hansen, U.S.
1908 G. C. O'Kelly, Great Britain
1920 Robert Roth, Switzerland
1924 Harry Steele, U.S.
1928 Johan C. Richthoff, Sweden
1932 Johan C. Richthoff, Sweden
1936 Kristjan Palusalu, Estonia
1948 George Bobis, Hungary
1952 Arsen Mekokishvili, USSR
1956 Hamid Kaplan, Turkey
1960 Wilfried Dietrich, Germany
1964 Aleksandr Ivanitsky, USSR
1968 Aleksandr Medved, USSR
1972 Ivan Yarygin, USSR
1976 Ivan Yarygin, USSR

Super Heavyweight
1972 Aleksandr Medved, USSR
1976 Soslan Andiev, USSR

Wrestling—Greco-Roman

Paperweight
1972 Georghe Berceanu, Rumania
1976 Aleksandr Schumakov, USSR

Flyweight
1948 Pietro Lombardi, Italy
1952 Boris Gourevitch, USSR
1956 Nicolai Soloviev, USSR
1960 Dumitru Pirvulescu, Rumania
1964 Tsutomu Hanahara, Japan
1968 Peter Kirov, Bulgaria
1972 Peter Kirov, Bulgaria
1976 Vitaly Koustantinov, USSR

Bantamweight
1924 Edward Putsep, Estonia
1928 K. Leucht, Germany
1932 Jakob Brendel, Germany
1936 Martin Lorincz, Hungary
1948 Kurt A. Peterson, Sweden
1952 Imre Hodos, Hungary

1956 Konstintin Vyropaev, USSR
1960 Oleg Karavaev, USSR
1964 Masamitsu Ichiguchi, Japan
1968 Jaros Varga, Hungary
1972 Rustem Kazakov, USSR
1976 Pertti Ukkola, Finland

Featherweight
1912 Kalle Koskelo, Finland
1920 Eriman, Finland
1924 Kalle Antilla, Finland
1928 Voldemar Wali, Estonia
1932 Giovanni Gozzi, Italy
1936 Yasar Erkan, Turkey
1948 Mohammed Octav, Turkey
1952 Jakov Punkine, USSR
1956 Rauno Makinen, Finland
1960 Muzahir Sille, Turkey
1964 Imre Polyak, Hungary
1968 Roman Rurua, USSR
1972 Gheorghi Markov, Bulgaria
1976 Kazimier Lipien, Poland

Lightweight
1906 Watzl, Austria
1908 E. Porro, Italy
1912 Emil Vare, Finland
1920 Emil Vare, Finland
1924 Oskari Friman, Finland
1928 Lajos Keresztes, Hungary
1932 Erik Malmberg, Sweden
1936 Lauri Koskela, Finland
1948 Karl Freij, Sweden
1952 Chasame Safine, USSR
1956 Kyosti Lehtonen, Finland
1960 Avtandil Kordize, USSR
1964 Kazim Ayvas, Turkey
1968 Muneji Munemura, Japan
1972 Shamil Khisamutdinov, USSR
1976 Suran Nalbandy, USSR

Welterweight
1920 Ivar Johansson, Sweden
1932 Ivar Johansson, Sweden
1936 Rodolf Svedberg, Sweden

Janis Lusis of the U.S.S.R. shows the form that won him a gold medal, and a world javelin record, in the 1972 Olympics. *(William J. Wallace, Duke University.)*

1948   Gosta Andersson, Sweden
1952   Miklos Szilvaski, Hungary
1956   Mithat Bayrak, Turkey
1960   Mithat Bayrak, Turkey
1964   Anatoly Kolesov, USSR
1968   Rudolph Vesper, East Germany
1972   Vitezslav Macha, Czechoslovakia
1976   Anatoly Bykov, USSR

Middleweight
1906   Weckman, Finland
1908   Fritjof M. Martenson, Sweden
1912   Claes E. Johansson, Sweden
1920   Carl Westergren, Sweden
1924   Edward Westerlund, Finland
1928   Vaino Kokkinen, Finland
1932   Vaino Kokkinen, Finland
1936   Ivar Johansson, Sweden
1948   Axel Gronberg, Sweden
1952   Axel Gronberg, Sweden
1956   Vulvi Kartozia, USSR
1960   Dimitrio Dobrev, Bulgaria
1964   Branislav Simie, Yugoslavia
1968   Lothar Metz, East Germany
1972   Csaba Hegedus, Hungary
1976   Momir Petkovic, Yugoslovia

Light Heavyweight
1908   Verner Weckman, Finland
1912   Anders O. Ahlgren, Sweden; Ivar Bohling, Finland
1924   Carl Westergren, Sweden
1928   Ibrahim Moustafa, Egypt
1932   Rudolph Svensson, Sweden
1936   Axel Cadier, Sweden
1948   Karl Nilsson, Sweden
1952   Kolpo Grondahl, Finland
1956   Valentine Nikolaev, USSR
1960   Teufik Kis, Turkey
1964   Bogan Alexandrov, Bulgaria
1968   Boyan Radev, Bulgaria
1972   Valeri Rezantsev, USSR
1976   Valeri Rezantsev, USSR

Heavyweight
1906   J. Jensen, Denmark
1908   Richard Wersz, Hungary
1912   Yrio Soarela, Finland
1920   Adolf Lindfors, Sweden
1924   Henri Deglane, France
1928   J. Rudolph Svensson, Sweden
1932   Carl Westergren, Sweden
1936   Kristjan Palusalu, Estonia
1948   Armet Kirecci, Turkey
1952   Ionganes Kotkas, USSR
1956   Anatoli Parfenov, USSR
1960   Ivan Bogdan, USSR
1964   Istvan Kozma, Hungary
1968   Istvan Kozma, Hungary
1972   Nicolae Martinescu, Rumania
1976   Nikolai Bolboshin, USSR

Super Heavyweight
1972   Anatoly Roshin, USSR
1976   Aleksandr Kolchinsky, USSR

Yachting

Flying Dutchman Class
1960   Peder Lunde, Jr., Norway
1964   Helmae Pederson, New Zealand
1968   Rodney Pattison, Great Britain
1972   Rodney Pattison and Christopher Davies, Great Britain
1976   Joerg Diesch, West Germany

Finn Class
1952   Paul Elvstrom, Denmark
1956   Paul Elvstrom, Denmark
1960   Paul Elvstrom, Denmark
1964   Willi Kuhweide, Germany
1968   Valentin Mankin, USSR
1972   Serge Maury, France
1976   Jocken Schumann, East Germany

Star Class
1932   Gilbert Gary, U.S.
1936   Dr. Peter Bischoff, Germany
1948   Hilary Smart, U.S.
1952   Agostino Straulino, Italy
1956   Herbert Williams, U.S.
1960   Timir Pinegin, USSR
1964   Durward Knowles, Bahamas
1968   Lowell North, U.S.
1972   David Forbes, Australia

Tempest Class
1972   Valentin Mankin, Russia
1976   John Albrechtson, Sweden

Dragon Class
1948   Thor Thorvaldsen, Norway
1952   Thor Thorvaldsen, Norway
1956   Folke Bohlin, Sweden
1960   Prince Constantine, Greece
1964   Ole Bernsten, Denmark
1968   George Friedricks, U.S.
1972   John Cuneo, Australia

Soling Class
1972   Harry "Buddy" Melges, U.S.
1976   Paul Jensen, Denmark

Tornado Class
1976   Reg White, Great Britain

470 Class
1976   Frank Huebner, West Germany

Bibliography. Kieran, John and Arthur Daley: *The Story of the Olympic Games,* Lippincott, New York, 1969.

OPEN COMPETITION—The term "open" in general means that an event is open to all competitors. In most cases it means that both amateurs and professionals are allowed to compete. The term was first used in connection with the British Open golf tournament, inaugurated in 1860; it then actually meant that the tournament was open to any citizen of Great Britain. The term really acquired its modern meaning in 1885, when the British Amateur golf tournament began. In 1895 the United States Golf Association confirmed this new meaning when that organization held its first two tournaments in Newport, Rhode Island—the first U.S. Amateur and the first U.S. Open.

At times, especially in connection with national championship events, "open" means that foreign citizens are also allowed to compete. In badminton, skiing, and other sports, a closed national championship event is open only to citizens of that nation. Sometimes, closed and open championship events are held in conjunction with each other.

ORIENTEERING—A major sport in the Scandinavian countries, orienteering was invented in 1918 by Ernest Killander of Sweden. The annual national competition in

Sweden draws about 10,000 men, women, and children, who compete in 25 different classes.

The sport combines distance running with compass skills: It consists of a cross-country race through a forest, with specific points to be found through use of a compass and a contour map. The competitors start at intervals of one or two minutes, first copying control points from a master board onto the contour map. The course is usually about 5 or 6 mi in length, and includes 4 to 12 points to be located. The points must be found in sequence; at each one there's a specially coded punch which the competitor uses to mark a card, to prove that he found the point.

OUTLAND TROPHY—Named for John Outland, an All-American guard at the University of Pennsylvania in 1897 and 1898, this trophy is given annually to the outstanding interior lineman in college football, as chosen by the Football Writers Association of America.

See also FOOTBALL.

P

PADDLEBALL—Like racquetball, paddleball is a racket sport played on a handball court. It was invented in 1930 by Earl Riskey, a physical-education teacher at the University of Michigan, who soaked a tennis ball in gasoline and stripped the felt from it to get the ball he wanted. The racket was adopted from paddle tennis.

The sport can be played on any handball court. The server bounces the ball and serves it off the front wall and beyond the short line. Only the server can score points; game is 21. The rules are essentially those of handball.

Paddleball grew slowly at first, but a National Paddleball Association was formed in 1952, and national championship play began in 1961.

National Four-Wall Champions

Singles

1962	Paul Nelson
1963	Bill Schultz
1964	Paul Nelson
1965	Mobey Benedict
1966	Bud Muehleisen
1967	Paul Lawrence
1968	Bud Muehleisen
1969	Charles Brumfield
1970	Charles Brumfield
1971	Steve Keeley
1972	Dan McLaughlin
1973	Steve Keeley
1974	Steve Keeley
1975	Howard Solomon
1976	Steve Keeley

Doubles

1962	Maurice Rubin-John Banchieu
1963	Dick and Bob McNamara
1964	Dick and Bob McNamara
1965	Harold Kronenberg-Galen Johnson
1966	Harold Kronenberg-Galen Johnson
1967	Harold Kronenberg-Galen Johnson
1968	Bud Muehleisen-Charles Brumfield
1969	Bud Muehleisen-Charles Brumfield
1970	Bob and Bernie McNamara
1971	Paul Lawrence-Craig Finger
1972	Dan Alder-Evans Wright
1973	Dan Alder-Evans Wright
1974	Steve Keeley-Leonard Baldari
1975	Howard Solomon-Robert Schwartz
1976	Steve Keeley-Andy Homa

Women's Singles

1974	Kathy Williams
1975	Donna Valeri
1976	Pat Krise

Women's Doubles

1974	Kathy Williams-Teri Davis
1975	Teri Davis-Peggy Boyce
1976	Elyse Jacob-Grace Louwsma

Mixed matches are fairly common in paddleball; this action is at the University of Michigan. (*Courtesy of U.S. Paddleball Association.*)

PADDLE TENNIS—Possibly inspired by deck tennis, then a popular shipboard game, the Rev. Frank P. Beal invented paddle tennis in 1898. It was originally intended as an introduction to tennis for children. Beal cut the dimensions of the tennis court in half (to 39 by 18 ft, thus reducing the area to one-quarter that of the tennis court), and substituted a sponge rubber ball for the tennis ball and a wooden paddle for the tennis racket.

At the time, Beal lived in Albion, Michigan. In 1921 he became a minister in the Greenwich Village section of New York City and introduced the sport to the metropolitan area. A city-wide tournament was held in 1922, and in the following year the American Paddle Tennis Association was formed. The name was changed to the U.S. Paddle Tennis Association in 1926.

Just two years later the sport of platform tennis was invented, and in 1934 platform tennis enthusiasts formed their own organization, unfortunately adopting the name "American Paddle Tennis Association." The two sports have been confused by many persons ever since.

As paddle tennis became increasingly popular among adults, there was a move to increase the size of the courts, led by Murray Geller of Brooklyn, who is still official rules interpreter for the paddle tennis group. In 1937 the court was enlarged to 44 by 20 ft for adults, although the smaller court was retained for children's play. Other changes

Paddle tennis is played on a half-sized tennis court with a punctured tennis ball and large paddles. (*U.S. Paddle Tennis Association.*)

followed, largely through Geller's efforts to make the sport even more acceptable to adults. The sponge rubber ball was discarded and replaced by a punctured tennis ball. The overhead serve was banned; the court was lengthened by the addition of a "lob area," 3 ft deep, at either end; finally, in 1963 the distinction between the children's sport and the adult sport was done away with.

Today, adults and children alike play on a 50-by-20 court, which is used for singles and doubles. The court is marked into four service areas, each 22 ft long by 10 ft wide, with a baseline 3 ft behind the service line. The net is 31 in high and stretched taut between two posts, each 18 in from the sidelines. The rules call for at least 15 ft of space behind each baseline and at least 10 ft of space on each side of the court. If there is less than 11 ft of back space, a special "lob area" rule goes into effect. Service lines then become the baselines, and the baselines become lob lines, marking a 20-by-3 lob area. A shot landing in this area must be a lob—that is, it must have reached a height of at least 10 ft above the court surface; otherwise it is out.

The paddle striking surface must be made of wood, but metal is allowed on the edging, throat, and grip. Maximum dimensions are 17½ in long and 8½ in wide. The surface may be perforated or solid, but virtually all players use a perforated racket, since it allows them to put more spin on the ball when desired.

In general, the rules of paddle tennis are the same as the rules of lawn tennis, with these exceptions:

- Service must be struck at a point no higher than 31 in above the court surface.
- Only one service is allowed; if it is a fault, the server loses the point.
- The server may toss the ball up, or bounce it once behind the baseline, before striking it. Once one method or the other is employed, it must be used for the entire set.
- In singles, the server must let the return of service bounce before returning it. (This, of course, prevents the server from rushing to net as soon as the serve has been made.)

See also PLATFORM TENNIS.

PAN-AMERICAN GAMES—In 1940 the Argentine Olympic Committee called a meeting of American countries to discuss holding their own version of the Olympics, and 16 countries agreed to a series of games to begin in 1942.

World War II prevented that, but the Pan-American Games did begin in 1951 in Buenos Aires, Argentina, and have been held every four years since then.

The games are patterned after the Olympic Games—the Pan-American Games oath, for example, is the Olympic oath, and the national Olympic committees are in charge of selecting their nation's teams. But the proximity to the Olympics has hurt the Pan-American Games in at least a couple of respects. They don't get anything like the publicity accorded the Olympics, and many outstanding competitors, particularly those from the United States, often choose to pass up the Pan-American Games in order to continue their training schedules for the Olympics.

United States domination of most of the sports has also hurt the games somewhat, to the point where Avery Brundage, then president of the International Olympic Committee, suggested in 1971 that "second string" athletes should represent the United States in Pan-American competition. That suggestion brought protests, not only from within the United States, but from South American countries as well, and there is no question that the competition against outstanding athletes from the Western Hemisphere can help many Central American and South American athletes develop their talents and techniques for other forms of major international competition.

Boxing

Light Flyweight
1971 Rafael Carbonell, Cuba
1975 Jorge Hernandez, Cuba

Flyweight
1951 Alberto Barenghi, Argentina
1955 Hilario Correa, Mexico
1959 Miguel Botta, Argentina
1963 Floreal Garcia Larrossa, Brazil
1967 Francisco Rodriguez, Venezuela
1971 Francisco Rodriguez, Venezuela
1975 Ramon Duvalon, Cuba

Bantamweight
1951 Ricardo Gonzales, Argentina
1955 Salvador Jesus Enriquez, Venezuela
1959 Waldo Claudiano, Brazil
1963 Abel Almaraz, Argentina
1967 Juvencio M. Gonzalez, Mexico
1971 Pedro Flores, Mexico
1975 Orlando Martinez, Cuba

Featherweight
1951 Francisco Nunez, Argentina
1955 Oswaldo Canete Insfran, Argentina
1959 Carlos Aro, Argentina
1963 Rosemiro dos Santos, Brazil
1967 Miguel Garcia, Argentina
1971 Juan Garcia, Mexico
1975 David Armstrong, U.S.

Lightweight
1951 Oscar Galareo, Argentina
1955 Miguel Angel Pendola, Argentina
1959 Abel Laudonio, Argentina
1963 Roberto Caminero, Cuba
1967 Enrico Blanco, Cuba
1971 Luis Davila, Puerto Rico
1975 Chris Clarke, Canada

Light Welterweight
1955 J. Carlos Rivero Fernandez, Argentina
1959 Vincent J. Shomo, U.S.

1963　Adolfo Moreyra, Argentina
1967　James R. Wallington, U.S.
1971　Enrique Reguiferos, Cuba
1975　Ray Leonard, U.S.

Welterweight
1951　Oscar Pita, Argentina
1955　Joseph Dorando, U.S.
1959　Alfred Cornejo, Chile
1963　Misael Vilugron, Chile
1967　Andres Modina Casanola, Cuba
1971　Emilio Correa, Cuba
1975　Clinton Jackson, U.S.

Light Middleweight
1955　Paul Wright, U.S.
1959　Wilbert McClure, U.S.
1963　Elcio Neves, Brazil
1967　Rolando Garbey, Cuba
1971　Rolando Garbey, Cuba
1975　Rolando Garbey, Cuba

Middleweight
1951　Ubaldo Pereyra, Argentina
1955　Orville E. Pitts, U.S.
1959　Abrao de Souza, Brazil
1963　Luiz Cezar, Brazil
1967　Jorge Victor Ahumada, Argentina
1971　Faustino Quinales, Venezuela
1975　Alejandro Montoya, Cuba

Light Heavyweight
1951　Reinaldo Ansaloni, Argentina
1955　Luis Ignacio, Brazil
1959　Amos Johnson, U.S.
1963　Fred Lewis, U.S.
1967　Arthur G. Redden, U.S.
1971　Raymond Russell, U.S.
1975　Orestes Pedrozo, Cuba

Heavyweight
1951　Jorge Vertone, Argentina
1955　Alecsi Pablo Mitef Ochoa, Argentina
1959　Allen Hudson, U.S.
1963　Lee W. Carr, U.S.
1967　Forest Ward, U.S.
1971　Duane Bobick, U.S.
1975　Teofilo Stevenson, Cuba

Cycling

1,000-Meter Sprint
1951　Antonio Gimenez, Argentina
1955　Cenobio Ruiz, Mexico
1959　Juan Canto, Argentina
1963　Roger Gibbon, Trinidad-Tobago
1967　Roger Gibbon, Trinidad-Tobago
1971　Leslie King, Trinidad-Tobago
1975　Steve Wosnick, U.S.

1,000-Meter Time Trials
1951　Clodomior Cortoni, Argentina
1955　Antonio DiMicheli, Venezuela
1959　Anezio Argentao, Brazil
1963　Carlos Vasquez, Argentina
1967　Roger Gibbon, Trinidad-Tobago
1971　Jocelyn Lovell, Canada
1975　Jocelyn Lovell, Canada

Road Race
1951　Oscar Muleiro, Argentina
1955　Ramon Hoyos, Colombia
1959　Ricardo Senn, Argentina
1963　Gregorio Carrizales, Venezuela
1967　Marcel Roy, Canada

1971　John Howard, U.S.
1975　Aido Arencibra, Cuba

4,000-Meter Pursuit
1951　Jorge Vallmitjana, Argentina
1955–63　No competition
1967　Martin Rodriguez, Colombia
1971　Martin Rodriguez, Colombia
1975　Balbino Jaramilio, Colombia

4,000-Meter Team Pursuit
1951　Argentina
1955　Argentina
1959　United States
1963　Uruguay
1967　Argentina
1971　Colombia
1975　United States

Team Road Race
1971　Cuba
1975　Mexico

40-Lap Miss and Out
1951　Ezequiel Ramirez, Chile

150-Lap Point Race
1951　Oscar Giacche, Argentina

10-Mile Scratch Race
1967　Carlos Alvarez, Argentina

Equestrian Events

Individual Dressage
1951　Jose Larrain Cuevas, Chile
1955　Hector Clavel, Chile
1959　Patricia Galvin, U.S.
1963　Patricia Galvin, U.S.
1967　Kyra G. Downton, U.S.
1971　Christilo Hanson, Canada
1975　Christilo Hanson Boylen, Canada

Individual 3-Day Event
1951　Julio C. Sagasta, Argentina
1955　Walter Staley, U.S.
1959　Michael O. Page, U.S.
1963　Michael O. Page, U.S.
1967　J. Michael Plumb, U.S.
1971　Manuel Mendevil, Mexico
1975　Tad Coffin, U.S.

Individual Jumping
1951　Capt. Alberto Larraguibel, Chile
1955　Lt. Roberto Vinals, Mexico
1959　No competition
1963　Mary Mairs, U.S.
1967　James Day, Canada
1971　Elisa D. Perez, Mexico
1975　Fernando Senderas, Mexico

Team Dressage
1951　Chile
1955　No competition
1959　Chile
1963　No competition
1967　Chile
1971　Canada
1975　United States

Team 3-Day Event
1951　Argentina
1955　Mexico
1959　Canada
1963　United States
1967　United States

1971 Canada
1975 United States

Team Jumping
1951 Chile
1955 Mexico
1959 United States
1963 United States
1967 Brazil
1971 Canada
1975 United States

Fencing

Foil
1951 Feliz Galimi, Argentina
1955 Harold Goldsmith, U.S.
1959 Harold Goldsmith, U.S.
1963 Guillermo Saucedo, Argentina
1967 Guillermo Saucedo, Argentina
1971 Eduardo John, Cuba
1975 Martin Lang, U.S.

Saber
1951 Tibor Nyilas, U.S.
1955 Antonio Haro Oliva, Mexico
1959 Allen Kwartler, U.S.
1963 Michael A. Dassaro, U.S.
1967 Anthony Keane, U.S.
1971 Alex Orban, U.S.
1975 Manuel Luis Ortiz, Cuba

Épée
1951 Antonio Villamil, Argentina
1955 Raul Martinez, Argentina
1959 Roland Wommack, U.S.
1963 Frank D. Anger, U.S.
1967 Arthur Telles, Brazil
1971 Steve Netburn, U.S.
1975 O. A. Vergara, Argentina

Team Foil
1951 United States
1955 Argentina
1959 United States
1963 United States
1967 Argentina
1971 United States
1975 Cuba

Team Saber
1951 United States
1955 United States
1959 United States
1963 United States
1967 United States
1971 Cuba
1975 Cuba

Team Épée
1951 Argentina
1955 Argentina
1959 United States
1963 United States
1967 United States
1971 United States
1975 Cuba

Women's Foil
1951 Elsa Irigoyen, Argentina
1955 Maxine Mitchell, U.S.
1959 Pilar Roldan, Mexico
1963 Mireya Rodrigues, Cuba
1971 Margarita Rodriguez, Cuba
1975 Margarita Rodriguez, Cuba

Women's Team Foil
1963 United States
1967 United States
1971 United States
1975 Cuba

Gymnastics—Men

All-Around
1951 William Rotzheim, U.S.
1955 John Beckner, U.S.
1959 John Beckner, U.S.
1963 Wilhelm Weiler, Canada
1967 Fred Roethlisberger, U.S.
1971 Jorge Rodriguez, Cuba
1975 Jorge Cuervo, Cuba

Pommeled Horse
1951 Rafael Lecuona, Cuba
1955 John Beckner, U.S.
1959 Gregor Weiss, U.S.
1963 Garland D. O'Quinn, U.S.
1967 Mark S. Cohn, U.S.
1971 Jorge Rodriguez, Cuba
1975 R. Leon, Cuba

Horizontal Bar
1951 William Rotzheim, U.S.
1955 Abraham I. Grossfeld, U.S.
1959 Abraham I. Grossfeld, U.S.
1963 Abraham I. Grossfeld, U.S.
1967 Fred Roethlisberger, U.S.
1971 Jorge Rodriguez, Cuba
1975 Jorge Cuervo, Cuba

Floor Exercise
1951 Juan Caviglia, Argentina
1955 John Beckner, U.S.
1959 Abraham I. Grossfeld, U.S.
1963 Wilhelm Weiler, Canada
1967 Hector Ramirez, Cuba
1971 John Crosby, U.S.
1975 Peter Kormann, U.S.

Rings
1951 Angel Aguiar, Cuba
1955 John Beckner, U.S.
1959 Jamile A. Ashmore, U.S.; Abraham I. Grossfeld, U.S.
1963 Jamile A. Ashmore, U.S.
1967 Armando Valles, Mexico
1971 John Crosby, U.S.
1975 Jorge Cuervo, Cuba; R. Leon, Cuba

Parallel Bars
1951 Pedro Lonchibucco, Argentina
1955 John Beckner, U.S.
1959 John Beckner, U.S.
1963 Donald R. Tonry, U.S.
1967 Fred Roethlisberger, U.S.; Richard G. Loyd, U.S.
1971 John Elias, U.S.
1975 R. Leon, Cuba

Long Horse Vault
1951 Angel Aguiar, Cuba
1955 Joseph Kotys, U.S.
1959 John Beckner, U.S.
1963 Wilhelm Weiler, Canada
1967 Jorge Rodriguez, Cuba
1971 Jorge Cuervo, Cuba
1975 Jorge Cuervo, Cuba

Team All-Around
1951 Argentina
1955 United States
1959 United States

1963   United States
1967   United States
1971   Cuba
1975   United States

Gymnastics—Women

All-Around
1959   Ernestine Russell, Canada
1963   Doris Fuchs, U.S.
1967   Linda Jo Metheny, U.S.
1971   Roxanne Pierce, U.S.
1975   Ann Carr, U.S.

Side Horse Vault
1959   Ernestine Russell, Canada
1963   Dale McClements, U.S.
1967   Linda Jo Metheny, U.S.
1971   Roxanne Pierce, U.S.
1975   Colleen Casey, U.S.

Balance Beam
1959   Ernestine Russell, Canada
1963   Doris Fuchs, U.S.
1967   Linda Jo Metheny, U.S.
1971   Kim Chase, U.S.
1975   Ann Carr, U.S.

Free Exercise
1959   Theresa Montefusco, U.S.
1963   Avis Tieber, U.S.
1967   Linda Jo Metheny, U.S.
1971   Linda Jo Metheny, U.S.
1975   Ann Carr, U.S.

Uneven Parallel Bars
1959   Ernestine Russel, Canada
1963   Doris Fuchs, U.S.
1967   Susan McDonnell, Canada
1971   Roxanne Pierce, U.S.
1975   Ann Carr, U.S.; Roxanne Pierce, U.S.

Team
1959   United States
1963   United States
1967   United States
1971   United States
1975   United States

Judo

Semi-Lightweight
1975   Brad Farrow, Canada

Lightweight
1975   Wayne Erdman, Canada

Middleweight
1975   Rainer Fischer, Canada

Light Heavyweight
1975   Ricardo de Oliveria Campos, Brazil

Heavyweight
1975   Allen Coage, U.S.

Open
1975   Jose Ibanez, Cuba

Rowing

Eights
1951   Argentina
1955   United States
1959   United States

1963   Canada
1967   United States
1971   Argentina
1975   United States

Fours with Coxswain
1951   Argentina
1955   Argentina
1959   United States
1963   Argentina
1967   United States
1971   Argentina
1975   Canada

Fours without Coxswain
1951   Argentina
1955   Argentina
1959   United States
1963   United States
1967   United States
1971   Brazil
1975   United States

Pairs with Coxswain
1951   Argentina
1955   Argentina
1959   United States
1963   Uruguay
1967   United States
1971   Argentina
1975   United States

Pairs without Coxswain
1951   Argentina
1955   Argentina
1959   United.States
1963   Uruguay
1967   United States
1971   Argentina
1975   Brazil

Single Sculls
1951   Roberto A. Alfieri, Argentina
1955   John B. Kelly, Jr., U.S.
1959   Harry Parker, U.S.
1963   Seymour L. Cromwell, U.S.
1967   Alberto Demiddi, Argentina
1971   Alberto Demiddi, Argentina
1975   Ricardo Ibarra, Argentina

Double Sculls
1951   Mario F. J. Guerci-Adolfo Yedro, Argentina
1955   Walter Hoover, Jr.,-James Gardiner, U.S.
1959   John B. Kelly, Jr.-William Knecht, U.S.
1963   Robert C. Lea-William J. Knecht, U.S.
1967   James Dietz-James Storm, U.S.
1971   Gilbertó Gebhardt-Mario Da Costro Filho, Brazil
1975   Gilberto Gebhardt-Mario Da Castro Filho, Brazil

Shooting

Rapid-Fire Pistol
1951   Huelet Benner, U.S.
1955   Huelet Benner, U.S. (white target); E. S. Valiente, Argentina (black target)
1959   David Cartes, U.S.
1963   Cecil L. Wallis, U.S.
1967   William McMillan, U.S.
1971   Victor Castellanos, Guatemala
1975   Melvin Makin, U.S.

Center-Fire Pistol
1959   Aubrey Smith, U.S.
1963   Thomas D. Smith, III, U.S.
1967   Francis Higginson, U.S.

1971   Francis Higginson, U.S.
1975   Marvin Black, U.S.

Free Pistol
1951   Edwin Vazquez Cam, Peru
1955   Huelet Benner, U.S.
1959   Nelson Lincoln, U.S.
1963   Franklin C. Green, U.S.
1967   S/Sgt. Hershel Anderson, U.S.
1971   Bertino de Sousa, Brazil
1975   Hershel Anderson, U.S.

Air Pistol
1975   Hershel Anderson, U.S.

Small-Bore Rifle, 3 Positions
1955   Arthur Jackson, U.S.
1959   Daniel Puckel, U.S.
1963   Gary L. Anderson, U.S.
1967   Margaret L. Thompson, U.S.
1971   John Writer, U.S.
1975   Margaret Murdock, U.S.

Skeet (Individual)
1951   Pablo Grossi, Argentina
1955   Kenneth Pendergras, U.S.
1959   Gilbert Navarro, Chile
1963   Kenneth Sedlecky, U.S.
1967   Allan Morrison, U.S.
1971   Robert Schuehle, U.S.
1975   Ahos Tisoni, Brazil

Trap (Individual)
1975   Dan Carlisle, U.S.

Air Rifle (Individual)
1975   Elegario Vasquez Rana, Mexico

Team Rapid-Fire Pistol
1951   Argentina
1955   U.S. (white target); U.S. (black target)
1959   No competition
1963   United States
1967   United States
1971   Cuba
1975   United States

Team Center-Fire Pistol
1959   United States
1963   United States
1967   United States
1971   United States
1975   United States

Team Free Pistol
1951   Mexico
1955   United States
1959   United States
1963   United States
1967   United States
1971   United States
1975   United States

Team Air Pistol
1975   United States

Team Small-Bore Rifle, Prone
1959   Canada
1963   United States
1971   United States
1975   United States

Team Small-Bore Rifle, 3 Positions
1959   United States
1963   United States
1967   United States

1971   United States
1975   United States

Team Skeet
1951   Argentina
1955   No competition
1959   United States
1963   United States
1967   United States
1971   United States
1975   Cuba

Team Service Rifle, 3 Positions
1951   Argentina
1955   Chile

Team Service Rifle, Standing
1951   Argentina

Team Free Rifle, 300 Meters
1951   Argentina
1955   United States

Team .22 Free Rifle
1951   Argentina
1955   United States

Team .22 Free Rifle, 3 Positions
1951   Argentina

English Match
1959   Arthur Cook, U.S.
1971   Victor Auer, U.S.
1975   David Ross, U.S.

Team English Match
1971   United States
1975   United States

Team Air Rifle
1975   United States

Swimming and Diving—Men

100-Meter Freestyle
1951	Dick Cleveland, U.S.	58.8
1955	Clarke Scholes, U.S.	57.7
1959	Felix Jeff Farrell, U.S.	56.3
1963	Stephen E. Clark, U.S.	54.7
1967	Donald Havens, U.S.	53.97
1971	Frank Heckl, U.S.	52.80
1975	Richard Abbott, U.S.	51.96

200-Meter Freestyle
1967	Don Schollander, U.S.	1:56:06
1971	Frank Heckl, U.S.	1:56.36
1975	Jorge Delgado, Ecuador	1:55.45

400-Meter Freestyle
1951	Tetsuo Okamoto, Brazil	4:52.4
1955	James McLane, U.S.	4:51.3
1959	George Breen, U.S.	4:31.4
1963	Roy A. Saari, U.S.	4:19.3
1967	Greg Charlton, U.S.	4:10.23
1971	James McConica, U.S.	4:08.97
1975	Doug Northway, U.S.	4:00.51

1,500-Meter Freestyle
1951	Tetsuo Okamoto, Brazil	19:23.3
1955	James McLane, U.S.	20:04.0
1959	Alan Somers, U.S.	17:53.2
1963	Roy A. Saari, U.S.	17:26.2
1967	Mike Burton, U.S.	16:44.40
1971	Pat Miles, U.S.	16:32.03
1975	Bobby Hackett, U.S.	15:53.10

100-Meter Backstroke

1951	Allen Stack, U.S.	1:08.0
1955	Frank E. McKinney, U.S.	1:07.1
1959	Frank E. McKinney, U.S.	1:03.6
1963	Edward C. Bartsch, U.S.	1:01.5
1967	Charles Hickox, U.S.	1:01.19
1971	Melvin Nash, U.S.	59.84
		58.31

200-Meter Backstroke

1967	Ralph Hutton, Canada	2:12.55
1971	Charlie Campbell, U.S.	2:07.09
1975	Dan Harrigan, U.S.	2:08.69

100-Meter Breaststroke

1967	José Fiolo, Brazil	1:07.52
1971	Mark Chatfield, U.S.	1:06.75
		1:06.28

200-Meter Breaststroke

1951	Hector Dominguez Nimo, Argentina	2:43.8
1955	Hector Dominguez Nimo, Argentina	2:46.9
1959	William Mulliken, U.S.	2:43.1
1963	Chester A. Jastremski, U.S.	2:35.4
1967	José Fiolo, Brazil	2:30.42
1971	Rick Colella, U.S.	2:27.12
1975	Rich Colella, U.S.	2:26.00

100-Meter Butterfly

1967	Mark Spitz, U.S.	56.20
1971	Frank Heckl, U.S.	56.92
1975	Michael Currington, U.S.	56.09

200-Meter Butterfly

1955	Eulalio Rios, Mexico	2:39.8
1959	J. David Gillanders, U.S.	2:18.0
1963	Carl J. Robie, U.S.	2:11.3
1967	Mark Spitz, U.S.	2:06.42
1971	George Delgado, Ecuador	2:06.41
1975	Greg Jagenburg, U.S.	2:03.48

200-Meter Individual Medley

1967	Doug Russell, U.S.	2:13.22
1971	Steve Furniss, U.S.	2:10.82
1975	Steve Furniss, U.S.	2:09.77

400-Meter Individual Medley

1967	William Utley, U.S.	4:48.12
1971	Steve Furniss, U.S.	4:42.69
1975	Steve Furniss, U.S.	4:40.38

400-Meter Freestyle Relay

1959	United States	4:14.9
1963	United States	4:05.6
1967	United States	3:34.08
1971	United States	3:32.15
1975	United States	3:27.67

800-Meter Freestyle Relay

1951	United States	9:06.0
1955	United States	9:00.0
1959	United States	8:22.7
1963	United States	8:16.9
1967	United States	8:00.46
1971	United States	7:45.82
1975	United States	7:50.96

400-Meter Medley Relay

1955	United States	4:29.1
1967	United States	3:59.31
1971	United States	3:56.08
1975	United States	3:53.81

Springboard Diving

1951	Joaquin Capilla, Mexico	
1955	Joaquin Capilla, Mexico	
1959	Gary Tobian, U.S.	

1963	Thomas Dinsley, Canada	
1967	Bernard Wrightson, U.S.	
1971	Mike Finneran, U.S.	
1975	Tim Moore, U.S.	

Platform Diving

1951	Joaquin Capilla, Mexico	
1955	Joaquin Capilla, Mexico	
1959	Alvaro Gaxiola, Mexico	
1963	Robert D. Webster, U.S.	
1967	Wynn Young, U.S.	
1971	Rick Early, U.S.	
1975	Carlos Giron, Mexico	

300-Meter Medley Relay

1951	U.S. (Stack, Stassforth, Cleveland)	3:16.9

Swimming and Diving—Women

100-Meter Freestyle

1951	Sharon Geary, U.S.	1:08.4
1955	Helen Stewart, Canada	1:07.7
1959	Chris von Saltza, U.S.	1:03.8
1963	Terri Stickles, U.S.	1:02.8
1967	Erika Bricker, U.S.	1:00.89
1971	Sandy Neilson, U.S.	1:00.60
1975	Kim Peyton, U.S.	58.24

200-Meter Freestyle

1951	Ana Maria Schultz, Argentina	2:32.4
1955	Wanda Lee Werner, U.S.	2:32.5
1959	Chris von Saltza, U.S.	2:18.5
1963	Robyn Johnson, U.S.	2:17.5
1967	Pamela Kruse, U.S.	2:11.91
1971	Kim Peyton, U.S.	2:09.62
1975	Kim Peyton, U.S.	2:04.57

400-Meter Freestyle

1951	Ana Maria Schultz, Argentina	5:26.7
1955	Beth Whittall, Canada	5:32.4
1959	Chris von Saltza, U.S.	4:55.9
1963	Sharon Finneran, U.S.	4:52.7
1967	Deborah Meyer, U.S.	4:32.64
1971	Ann Simmons, U.S.	4:26.19
1975	Kathy Heddy, U.S.	4:23.00

800-Meter Freestyle

1967	Deborah Meyer, U.S.	9:22.86
1971	Cathy Calhoun, U.S.	9:15.19
1975	Wendy Weinberg, U.S.	9:05.47

100-Meter Backstroke

1951	Maureen O'Brien, U.S.	1:18.5
1955	Leonore Fisher, Canada	1:16.7
1959	Carin Cone, U.S.	1:12.2
1963	Nina Harmar, U.S.	1:11.5
1967	Elaine Tanner, Canada	1:07.32
1971	Donna Marie Gurr, Canada	1:07.18
1975	Lynn Chenard, Canada	1:06.59

200-Meter Backstroke

1967	Elaine Tanner, Canada	2:24.55
1971	Donna Marie Gurr, Canada	2:24.73
1975	Donna Wennerstrom, U.S.	2:19.93

100-Meter Breaststroke

1967	Cathy Ball, U.S.	1:14.80
1971	Sylvia Dockerill, Canada	1:18.63
1975	Lauri Siering, U.S.	1:15.17

200-Meter Breaststroke

1951	Dorotea Turnbull, Argentina	3:08.4
1955	Mary Lou Elsenius, U.S.	3:08.4
1959	Ann K. Warner, U.S.	2:56.8
1963	Alice Driscoll, U.S.	2:56.2
1967	Cathy Ball, U.S.	2:42.18

| 1971 | Lynn Colella, U.S. | 2:50.03 |
| 1975 | Lauri Siering, U.S. | 2:42.35 |

100-Meter Butterfly
1955	Beth Whittall, Canada	1:16.2
1959	Becky Collins, U.S.	1:09.5
1963	Kathleen Ellis, U.S.	1:07.6
1967	Eleanor Daniel, U.S.	1:05.24
1971	Deena Deardurff, U.S.	1:06.22
1975	Camille Wright, U.S.	1:02.71

200-Meter Butterfly
1967	Claudia Kolb, U.S.	2:25.49
1971	Lynn Colella, U.S.	2:23.11
1975	Camille Wright, U.S.	2:18.57

200-Meter Individual Medley
1967	Claudia Kolb, U.S.	2:26.06
1971	Leslie Cliff, Canada	2:30.03
1975	Kathy Heddy, U.S.	2:22.22

400-Meter Individual Medley
1967	Claudia Kolb, U.S.	5:09.68
1971	Leslie Cliff, Canada	5:13.31
1975	Kathy Heddy, U.S.	5:06.05

400-Meter Freestyle Relay
1951	United States	4:37.1
1955	United States	4:31.8
1959	United States	4:17.5
1963	United States	4:15.7
1967	United States	4:04.57
1971	United States	4:04.20
1975	United States	3:53.31

400-Meter Medley Relay
1955	United States	5:11.6
1959	United States	4:44.6
1963	United States	4:49.1
1967	United States	4:30.0
1971	Canada	4:35.50
1975	United States	4:22.34

300-Meter Medley Relay
| 1951 | United States | 3:49.3 |

Springboard Diving
1951	Mary Frances Cunningham, U.S.
1955	Pat K. McCormick, U.S.
1959	Paula Jean Pope, U.S.
1963	Barbara McAlister, U.S.
1967	Sue Gossick, U.S.
1971	Elizabeth Carruthers, Canada
1975	Jenni Chandler, U.S.

Platform Diving
1951	Pat K. McCormick, U.S.
1955	Pat K. McCormick, U.S.
1959	Paula Jean Pope, U.S.
1963	Linda Cooper, U.S.
1967	Lesley Bush, U.S.
1971	Nancy Robertson, Canada
1975	Janet Nutter, Canada

Synchronized Swimming
Solo
1955	Beulah Gundling, U.S.
1963	Roberta Armstrong, U.S.
1971	Heidi O'Rourke, U.S.
1975	Gail Johnson Buzonas, U.S.

Duet
1955	Connie Todoroff-Ellen Richard, U.S.
1963	Barbara Burke-Joanne Schaack, U.S.
1971	Heidi O'Rourke-Joan Lang, U.S.
1975	Robin Curren-Amanda Norrish, U.S.

Team
1955	United States
1963	United States
1971	United States
1975	United States

Track and Field—Men

100-Meter Dash
1951	Rafael Fortun Chacon, Cuba	10.6
1955	J. Rodney Richard, U.S.	10.3
1959	Ray Norton, U.S.	10.3
1963	Enrique Figuerola, Cuba	10.3
1967	Henry Jerome, Canada	10.2
1971	Don Quarrie, Jamaica	10.24
1975	Silvio Leonard, Cuba	10.15

200-Meter Dash
1951	Rafael Fortun Chacon, Cuba	21.3
1955	J. Rodney Richard, U.S.	20.7
1959	Ray Norton, U.S.	20.6
1963	Rafael Sandrea, Venezuela	21.2
1967	John Carlos, U.S.	20.5
1971	Don Quarrie, Jamaica	19.81
1975	James Gilkes, Guyana	20.43

400-Meter Dash
1951	Malvin Whitfield, U.S.	47.8
1955	Louis Jones, U.S.	45.4
1959	George Kerr, West Indies	46.1
1963	James A. Johnson, U.S.	46.7
1967	Lee Evans, U.S.	44.9
1971	John Smith, U.S.	44.55
1975	Ronald Ray, U.S.	44.45

800-Meter Run
1951	Malvin Whitfield, U.S.	1:53.2
1955	Arnold Sowell, U.S.	1:49.7
1959	Thomas Murphy, U.S.	1:49.4
1963	Don Bertoia, Canada	1:48.3
1967	Wade Bell, U.S.	1:49.2
1971	Ken Swenson, U.S.	1:48.0
1975	Luis Medina, Cuba	1:47.98

1,500-Meter Run
1951	Browning Ross, U.S.	4:00.4
1955	Juan D. Miranda, Argentina	3:53.2
1959	Dyrol Burleson, U.S.	3:49.1
1963	James E. Grelle, U.S.	3:43.5
1967	Tom Von Ruden, U.S.	3:43.3
1971	Marty Liquori, U.S.	3:42.05
1975	Tony Waldrop, U.S.	3:45.09

5,000-Meter Run
1951	Ricardo Bralo, Argentina	14:57.2
1955	Osualdo Suarez, Argentina	15:30.6
1959	William Dellinger, U.S.	14:28.4
1963	Osualdo Suarez, Argentina	14:25.7
1967	Van Nelson, U.S.	13:47.4
1971	Steve Prefontaine, U.S.	13.52.5
1975	Domingo Tibaduiza, Columbia	14:02.00

10,000-Meter Run
1951	Curtis Stone, U.S.	31:08.6
1955	Osualdo Suarez, Argentina	32:42.6
1959	Osualdo Suarez, Argentina	30:17.2
1963	Peter J. McArdle, U.S.	29:52.1
1967	Van Nelson, U.S.	29:17.4
1971	Frank Shorter, U.S.	28:50.8
1975	Luis Hernandez, Mexico	29:19.28

Marathon
| 1951 | Delfo Cabrera, Argentina | 2:35:00.2 |
| 1955 | Doroteo Flores, Guatemala | 2:59:09.2 |

1959	John J. Kelley, U.S.	2:27:54.2
1963	Fidel Negrete Gamboa, Mexico	2:27:56.6
1967	Andrew Boychuk, Canada	2:23:02.4
1971	Frank Shorter, U.S.	2:22:47
1975	Rigoberto Mendoza, Cuba	2:25:02.81

110-Meter High Hurdles

1951	Dick Attlesey, U.S.	14.0
1955	Jack Davis, U.S.	14.3
1959	Hayes Jones, U.S.	13.6
1963	H. Blaine Lindgren, U.S.	13.8
1967	Earl McCulloch, U.S.	13.4
1971	Rod Milburn, U.S.	13.4
1975	Alejandro Casanas, Cuba	13.44

400-Meter Hurdles

1951	Jaime Aparicio, Colombia	53.4
1955	Josh Culbreath, U.S.	51.5
1959	Josh Culbreath, U.S.	51.2
1963	Juan Pablo Dryska, Argentina	50.2
1967	Ron Whitney, U.S.	50.7
1971	Ralph Mann, U.S.	49.1
1975	James King, U.S.	49.80

3,000-Meter Steeplechase

1951	Curtis Stone, U.S.	9:32.0
1955	Guillermo Sola, Chile	9:46.8
1959	Philip Coleman, U.S.	8:56.4
1963	Jeffrey Fishback, U.S.	9:07.9
1967	Chris McCubbins, U.S.	8:38.2
1971	Mike Manley, U.S.	8:42.2
1975	Mike Manley, U.S.	9:04.29

400-Meter Relay

1951	United States	41.0
1955	United States	40.7
1959	United States	40.4
1963	United States	40.4
1967	United States	39.0
1971	Jamaica	39.2
1975	United States	38.31

1,600-Meter Relay

1951	United States	3:09.9
1955	United States	3:07.2
1959	West Indies	3:05.3
1963	United States	3:09.6
1967	United States	3:02.0
1971	United States	3:00.6
1975	United States	3:00.76

20,000-Meter Walk

1963	Alex Oakley, Canada	1:42:43.2
1967	Ron Laird, U.S.	1:33:05.2
1971	Goetz Klopfer, U.S.	1:37:37.0
1975	Daniel Bautista, Mexico	1:33:05.87

50,000-Meter Walk

1951	Sixto Ibanez, Argentina	5:06:06.8
1955-63	No competition	
1967	Larry Young, U.S.	4:26:20.8
1971	Larry Young, U.S.	4:38:33.0

High Jump

1951	Virgil Severns, U.S.	6-4¾
1955	Ernie Shelton, U.S.	6-7⅛
1959	Charles Dumas, U.S.	6-10½
1963	Gene C. Johnson, U.S.	6-11
1967	Ed Caruthers, U.S.	7-2¼
1971	Pat Matzdorf, U.S.	6-10¾
1975	Tom Woods, U.S.	7-4⅝

Long Jump

1951	Gaylord Bryan, U.S.	23-7
1955	Roselyn Range, U.S.	26-4⅛

1959	Irvin Roberson, U.S.	26-2
1963	Ralph Boston, U.S.	26-7¼
1967	Ralph Boston, U.S.	27-2½
1971	Arnie Robinson, U.S.	26-3¼
1975	Joao Oliveira, Brazil	26-10½

Triple Jump

1951	Adhemar Ferreira da Silva, Brazil	50-0
1955	Adhemar Ferreira da Silva, Brazil	54-4
1959	Adhemar Ferreira da Silva, Brazil	52-2
1963	William Sharpe, U.S.	49-8¼
1967	Charles Craig, U.S.	54-3¼
1971	Pedro Perez, Cuba	57-1
1975	Joao Oliveira, Brazil	58-8¼

Pole Vault

1951	Bob Richards, U.S.	14-9½
1955	Bob Richards, U.S.	14-9½
1959	Donald Bragg, U.S.	15-2½
1963	David E. Tork, U.S.	16-¾
1967	Bob Seagren, U.S.	16-1
1971	Jan Johnson, U.S.	17-4⅗
1975	Earl Bell, U.S.	17-8

Shot Put

1951	James Fuchs, U.S.	56-7⅛
1955	Parry O'Brien, U.S.	57-8½
1959	Parry O'Brien, U.S.	62-½
1963	David Davis, U.S.	60-9
1967	Randy Matson, U.S.	65-1
1971	Al Feuerbach, U.S.	64-10
1975	Bruce Pirnie, Canada	63-3

Discus Throw

1951	James Fuchs, U.S.	160-4
1955	Fortune Gordien, U.S.	174-2½
1959	Alfred Oerter, U.S.	190-8
1963	Bob Humphreys, U.S.	189-8
1967	Gary Carlsen, U.S.	188-8
1971	Dick Drescher, U.S.	204-2
1975	John Powell, U.S.	204-7

Javelin Throw

1951	Ricardo Heber, Argentina	223-4⅜
1955	Franklin Held, U.S.	228-11
1959	Buster Quist, U.S.	231-3
1963	Daniel Studney, U.S.	248-0
1967	Frank Covelli, U.S.	234-8
1971	Gary Feldmann, U.S.	267-5
1975	Sam Colson, U.S.	275-0

Hammer Throw

1951	Emilio Ortiz, Argentina	157-7⅜
1955	Robert Backus, U.S.	180-1¾
1959	Albert Hall, U.S.	195-11
1963	Albert Hall, U.S.	205-10
1967	Tom Gage, U.S.	214-4
1971	Albert Hall, U.S.	216-0
1975	Larry Hart, U.S.	218-4

Decathlon

1951	Hernan Figueroa Bueg, Chile	6,615 pts.
1955	Rafer Johnson, U.S.	6,994 pts.
1959	David Edstrom, U.S.	7,254 pts.
1963	John D. Martin, U.S.	7,335 pts.
1967	Bill Toomey, U.S.	8,044 pts.
1971	Rick Wanamaker, U.S.	7,648 pts.
1975	Bruce Jenner, U.S.	8,045 pts.

Track and Field—Women

60-Meter Dash

1955	Bertha Diaz, Cuba	7.5
1959	Isabelle Daniels, U.S.	7.4

100-Meter Dash

1951	Julia Sanchez Deze, Peru	12.2
1955	Barbara Jones, U.S.	11.5
1959	Lucinda Williams, U.S.	12.1
1963	Edith McGuire, U.S.	11.5
1967	Barbara Ferrell, U.S.	11.5
1971	Iris Davis, U.S.	11.2
1975	Pamela Jiles, U.S.	11.38

200-Meter Dash

1951	Jean Patton, U.S.	25.3
1955	No competition	
1959	Lucinda Williams, U.S.	24.2
1963	Vivian Brown, U.S.	23.9
1967	Wyomia Tyus, U.S.	23.7
1971	Stephanie Berto, Canada	23.5
1975	Chandra Cheeseborough, U.S.	22.77

400-Meter Dash

1971	Marilyn Neufville, Jamaica	52.3
1975	Joyce Yakubowich, Canada	51.62

800-Meter Run

1963	Abigail Hoffman, Canada	2:10.2
1967	Madeline Manning, U.S.	2:02.3
1971	Abigail Hoffman, Canada	2:05.49
1975	Kathleen Weston, U.S.	2:04.93

1,500-Meter Run

1975	Jan Merrill, U.S.	4:18.32

80-Meter Hurdles

1951	Eliana Gaeto Lazo, Chile	11.9
1955	Eliana Gaeto Lazo, Chile	11.7
1959	Bertha Diaz, Cuba	11.2
1963	JoAnn Terry, U.S.	11.3
1967	Cherri Sherrard, U.S.	10.8

100-Meter Hurdles

1971	Pat Van Wolvelaere Johnson, U.S.	13.1
1975	Edith Noeding, Peru	13.56

400-Meter Relay

1951	United States	48.8
1955	United States	47.0
1959	United States	46.4
1963	United States	45.6
1967	Cuba	44.6
1971	United States	44.5
1975	United States	42.90

1,600-Meter Relay

1971	United States	3:32.4
1975	Canada	3:30.36

High Jump

1951	Jacinta Dandtford, Ecuador	4-9½
1955	Mildred McDaniel, U.S.	5-6⁵⁄₁₆
1959	Ann Flynn, U.S.	5-3¼
1963	Eleanor Montgomery, U.S.	5-6
1967	Eleanor Montgomery, U.S.	5-10
1971	Debbi Brill, Canada	6-0¾
1975	Joni Huntley, U.s.	6-2½

Long Jump

1951	Beatriz Kretchmer, Chile	17-9⅜
1955	No competition	
1959	Annie Smith, U.S.	18-9¾
1963	Willye White, U.S.	20-2
1967	Irene Martinez Tartabull, Cuba	20-9
1971	Brenda Elser, Canada	21-1¼
1975	Ana Alexander, Cuba	21-9

Shot Put

1951	Ingeborg Mello de Preiss, Argentina	40-10⅛
1955	No competition	
1959	Earlene Brown, U.S.	48-2
1963	Nancy McCredie, Canada	50-3
1967	Nancy McCredie, Canada	49-9¾
1971	Lynn Graham, U.S.	51-8
1975	Maria Sarria, Cuba	59-1¾

Discus Throw

1951	Ingeborg Mello de Preiss, Argentina	126-5¾
1955	Ingeborg M. de P. Pfuller, Argentina	141-8⅜
1959	Earlene Brown, U.S.	161-9
1963	Nancy McCredie, Canada	164-7
1967	Carol Moseke, U.S.	161-7
1971	Carmen Romero, Cuba	187-7
1975	Carmen Romero, Cuba	197-4

Javelin Throw

1951	Hortensia Lopez Garcia, Mexico	129-4½
1955	Karen E. Anderson, U.S.	161-3
1959	Marlene Ahrens, Chile	148-10
1963	Marlene Ahrens, Chile	163-9
1967	Barbara Friedrich, U.S.	174-9
1971	Tomasa Nunez, Cuba	177-2
1975	Sherry Calvert, U.S.	179.5

Pentathlon

1967	Pat Winslow, U.S.	4,860 pts.
1971	Debbie Van Kiekebelt, Canada	4,290 pts.
1975	Diane Jones, Canada	4,673 pts.

Weightlifting

Bantamweight

1951	Joe De Pietro, U.S.	622¼
1955	Charles Vinci, U.S.	661.39
1959	Charles Vinci, U.S.	717.00
1963	Dias Martins, British Guiana	693.00
1967	Fernando Baez, Puerto Rico	735.50
1971	Rolando Chang, Cuba	753.5
1975	Carlos Lastre, Cuba	522.5

Flyweight

1971	Juan Romero, Colombia	660.00
1975	F. Casamayer, Cuba	495

Featherweight

1951	Rodney Wilkes, Trinidad	716
1955	Carlos Chavez, Panama	733.03
1959	Isaac Berger, U.S.	782.50
1963	Isaac Berger, U.S.	797.50
1967	Walter Imahara, U.S.	777.00
1971	Manuel Mateos, Mexico	770
1975	Rolando Chana, Cuba	561

Lightweight

1951	Joe Pitman, U.S.	760
1955	Joe Pitman, U.S.	782.64
1959	Juan Torres, Cuba	766.50
1963	Anthony Garcy, U.S.	836.00
1967	Pastor Rodriguez, Cuba	848.00
1971	Pastor Rodriguez, Cuba	863.5
1975	Roberto Urrutia, Cuba	660

Middleweight

1951	Pete George, U.S.	837¼
1955	Pete George, U.S.	892.86
1959	Tommy Kono, U.S.	894.25
1963	Joseph R. Puleo, U.S.	880.00
1967	Russell Knipp, U.S.	948.00
1971	Russell Knipp, U.S.	990
1975	Ignacio Guanche, Cuba	665.5

Light Heavyweight

1951	Stanley Stanczyk, U.S.	892.12
1955	Tommy Kono, U.S.	964.51

1959	James George, U.S.	887.00
1963	Tommy Kono, U.S.	957.00
1967	Joseph Puleo, U.S.	992.00
1971	Mike Karchut, U.S.	1,042
1975	Lee James, U.S.	693

Middle Heavyweight

1955	Dave Sheppard, U.S.	876.33
1959	Clyde Emrich, U.S.	953.50
1963	William F. March, U.S.	1012.00
1967	Phil Grippaldi, U.S.	1047.00
1971	Phil Grippaldi, U.S.	1,089
1975	Phil Grippaldi, U.S.	753.5

Heavyweight

1951	John L. Davis, U.S.	1,062½
1955	Norbert Schemansky, U.S.	1,041.68
1959	David Ashman, U.S.	1047.00
1963	Sid Henry, U.S.	1023.00
1967	Joseph Dube, U.S.	1163.00
1971	Gary Deal, U.S.	1,171
1975	Russell Prior, Canada	803

Super Heavyweight

1971	Ken Patera, U.S.	1,310
1975	Gerardo Fernandez, Cuba	836

Wrestling—Freestyle

Paperweight
1971 Sergio Gonzalez, U.S.
1975 Jorge Frias, Mexico

Flyweight
1951 Robert H. Peery, U.S.
1955 Manuel V. Andrade, Venezuela
1959 J. Richard Wilson, U.S.
1963 Andrew Fitch, U.S.
1967 Richard Sofman, U.S.
1971 Miguel Tachin, Cuba
1975 Eloy Abreu, Cuba

Bantamweight
1951 Richard J. Lemeyre, U.S.
1955 Jack Blubaugh, U.S.
1959 David Auble, U.S.
1963 William G. Riddle, U.S.
1967 Richard Sanders, U.S.
1971 Don Behm, U.S.
1975 Jorge Ramos, Cuba

Featherweight
1951 Omar Blebel Torranzzini, Argentina
1955 Omar Blebel Torranzzini, Argentina
1959 Louis Giani, U.S.
1963 Ronald Finley, U.S.
1967 Michael Young, U.S.
1971 Dave Pruzansky, U.S.
1975 Egan Beiler, Canada

Lightweight
1951 Newton E. Copple, U.S.
1955 Jay T. Evans, U.S.
1959 James Burke, U.S.
1963 Gregory Ruth, U.S.
1967 Gerald Bell, U.S.
1971 Dan Gable, U.S.
1975 Lloyd Keaser, U.S.

Welterweight
1951 Melvin A. Northrup, U.S.
1955 Alberto Longarela, Argentina
1959 Douglas Blubaugh, U.S.
1963 Dennis Fitzgerald, U.S.
1967 Patrick Kelly, U.S.

1971 Francisco Lebequer, Cuba
1975 Francisco Lebequer, Cuba

Middleweight
1951 Leon Gemuth Hejtt, Argentina
1955 Leon Gemuth Hejt, Argentina
1959 James Ferguson, U.S.
1963 James Ferguson, U.S.
1967 Wayne Baughman, U.S.
1971 Lupe Lara, Cuba
1975 Gregory Hicks, U.S.

Light Heavyweight
1951 Ulises Martorella, Argentina
1955 Alfred E. Paulekas, U.S.
1959 Frank Rosenmayr, U.S.
1963 John Barden, U.S.
1967 Harry Houska, U.S.
1971 Dom Carollo, U.S.
1975 Ben Peterson, U.S.

Heavyweight
1951 Adolfo Ramirez, Argentina
1955 William Kerslake, U.S.
1959 Dale Lewis, U.S.
1963 Joe James, U.S.
1967 Larry Kristoff, U.S.
1971 Russell Hellickson, U.S.
1975 Russell Hellickson, U.S.

Super Heavyweight
1971 Jeffrey Smith, U.S.
1975 Michael McCready, U.S.

Wrestling—Greco-Roman

Paperweight
1975 Silvano Valdez, Cuba

Flyweight
1975 Bruce Thompson, U.S.

Bantamweight
1975 Daniel Mello, U.S.

Featherweight
1975 H. Stupp, Canada

Lightweight
1975 Patrick Marcy, U.S.

Welterweight
1975 Idalberto Barban, Cuba

Middleweight
1975 Dan Chandler, U.S.

Light Heavyweight
1975 Willie Williams, U.S.

Heavyweight
1975 Brad Rheingans, U.S.

Super Heavyweight
1975 William Van Worth, U.S.

Yachting

Snipe
1951 Jorge V. Castex, Argentina
1955 No competition
1959 Antonio Moraes, Brazil
1963 Reinald Conrad, Brazil
1967 N. Piccole, Brazil
1971 Pedro Reinhard, Brazil
1975 Jeff Lenhart, U.S.

Star

1951	R. Bueno, Brazil
1955	No competition
1959	Durwood Knowles, Bahamas
1963	Richard Stearns, U.S.
1967	No competition
1971	No competition
1975	No competition

Flying Dutchman

1951	No competition
1955	No competition
1959	Harry Sindle, U.S.
1963	Joaquin Roderbourg, Brazil
1967	Harry C. Melges, Jr., U.S.
1971	No competition
1975	Reinaldo Conrad, Brazil

Finn

1959	Kenneth Alburg, Bahamas
1963	H. Domschke, Brazil
1967	Joerg Bruder, Brazil
1971	Joerg Bruder, Brazil
1975	Bill Allen, U.S.

Lightning

1959	E. Schmidt, Brazil
1963	Thomas G. Allen, U.S.
1967	Bruce Goldsmith, U.S.
1971	Mario Buckup, Brazil
1975	Bruce Goldsmith, U.S.

Team Sports

Baseball

1951	Cuba
1955	Dominican Republic
1959	Venezuela
1963	Cuba
1967	United States
1971	Cuba
1975	Cuba

Basketball—Men

1951	United States
1955	United States
1959	United States
1963	United States
1967	United States
1971	Brazil
1975	United States

Basketball—Women

1955	United States
1959	United States
1963	United States
1967	Brazil
1971	Brazil
1975	United States

Field Hockey

1967	Argentina
1971	Argentina
1975	Argentina

Soccer

1951	Argentina
1955	Argentina
1959	Argentina
1963	Brazil
1967	Mexico
1971	Argentina
1975	Brazil, Mexico (TIE)

Volleyball—Men

1955	United States
1959	United States
1963	Brazil
1967	United States
1971	Cuba
1975	Cuba

Volleyball—Women

1955	Mexico
1959	Brazil
1963	Brazil
1967	United States
1971	Cuba
1975	Cuba

Water Polo

1951	Argentina
1955	Argentina
1959	United States
1963	Brazil
1967	United States
1971	United States
1975	Mexico

PARACHUTING—*See* SKY DIVING.

PARALLEL BARS—Gymnastics apparatus of two different types. Male competitors work on two bars of the same height, which are side by side. Women work on uneven parallel bars.
See also GYMNASTICS.

PARIMUTUEL—A type of betting, used when there are several possible outcomes of a competition, in which all money goes into a pool and the net amount is divided up among the winning bettors.
See also GAMBLING; HORSE RACING.

PENTATHLON—An athletic event composed of five different tests of skill. In track and field, the event consists of the 100-m (or 100-yd) hurdles, 200-m (or 200-yd) dash, shot put, high jump, and long jump. The modern pentathlon is meant to simulate the skills needed by a military courier of around the turn of the century: fencing, pistol shooting, horseback riding, swimming, and cross-country running.
See MODERN PENTATHLON; TRACK AND FIELD.

PIGEON RACING—The racing pigeon is a breed of homing pigeon, the type of bird that has been trained to return to its home loft. How the homing pigeon does this is still something of a scientific mystery, although it is known that the bird navigates by the sun. Homing pigeons were once used as messengers but, when the electric telegraph came into extensive use, the trained birds became obsolete for that purpose and were converted to racing instead.

Pigeon racing developed in Belgium, but has also become popular in the United States, France, and Great Britain. Most owners breed and train their own racing birds. Training begins at about one month of age, and it takes about three years before a bird is ready for major competition.

Birds are taken to the race start to have serial number bands placed on their legs, and then are released. When the bird arrives at its home loft, the owner removes the band from the leg and registers the time of arrival on a locked time recorder. The bird that has recorded the fastest average speed wins the race.

PING PONG—*See* TABLE TENNIS.

PISTOL SHOOTING—*See* SHOOTING.

PLATFORM TENNIS—Two tennis enthusiasts from Scarsdale, New York, developed platform tennis in 1928 as a winter sport for tennis players. Their basic inspiration was paddle tennis, which, at the time, was primarily a game for children.

Fessenden S. Blanchard and James K. Cogswell built an elevated wooden platform behind Cogswell's house, marked on it an undersized tennis court (44 by 20 ft) and put screening around it. The idea was that a platform could be more easily shoveled clear of snow than a flat stretch of ground, and that the screening would keep the ball from landing in the snow.

Unfortunately the platform began to warp, and the screening often interfered with play, even though they used a heavy sponge rubber ball instead of a tennis ball. So, when they built a second court in 1931, they covered it to keep the snow off entirely, and they decided to allow a player to play the ball off the screens.

The sport has now far outstripped ordinary paddle tennis in popularity in most parts of the United States. At first played primarily in Greater New York as off-season training for lawn tennis, platform tennis began to grow rapidly in the 1960s, and by the mid-1970s there were an estimated 150,000 players across the country.

Platform tennis in general follows the rules of lawn tennis, except that the server must get his first serve in the designated service area, and the ball is played off the screens. The usual game is doubles, since it is virtually impossible for a single player to cover the court, and the sport is characterized by long rallies, of up to 25 or 30 shots.

The sport is under the jurisdiction of the U.S. Platform Tennis Association, founded in 1934. National championships are now held only for doubles play.

PLAYER ASSOCIATIONS—Although the "unionization" of professional athletes seems to most fans a very recent phenomenon, it actually began a long time ago, at least in baseball. The first professional league was the National Association of Professional Base Ball Players, which lasted from 1871 through 1875. As the name implies it was, in many ways, an association of players. Its first president was a player, James Ferguson, and several of the teams were cooperatives—the players splitting up the gate receipts rather than taking salaries.

When the National League was established as a monopolistic association of owners, the player found much of his individual bargaining power slipping away. The reserve clause was introduced, forcing a player to remain with one team for as long as that team wanted him; at various times, owners imposed arbitrary salary limitations; and a blacklist was established.

In 1885 the Brotherhood of Professional Base Ball Players was established and John Montgomery Ward, a former player who later became a lawyer, was elected president. Ward attacked the standard player's contract as an unfair device which bound the player without binding the team, and condemned the reserve clause. By 1887 the brotherhood had about 90 members, and negotiators asked that the Salary Limitation Rule be abolished. The request was denied, and there was talk of a strike. There was no strike, but in 1890 the brotherhood formed its own league, the Players' National League of Base Ball Clubs. Most of the top players in baseball jumped to the new league, but the financial backing wasn't sufficient, and it lasted just one year.

After the collapse of the Players' League, the owners seemed to be in a stronger position than ever. In 1900, just as the National League was facing a challenge from the newly formed American League, the players once again organized, this time in the Protective Association of Professional Baseball Players. They discussed affiliating with the American Federation of Labor, but decided against it. The new association won some concessions, primarily because of the American League threat. Once the two major leagues ended their war, however, the Protective Association faded away.

In 1910 major-league baseball players made yet another attempt to organize. David Fultz, a lawyer who had once played in the majors and who often advised players on their contracts, became president of the Base Ball Players' Fraternity, which had a membership of more than 1,200 by 1914, when the Federal League challenged the baseball establishment. Unlike the earlier player organizations, the fraternity lived on after the interleague war ended with the dissolution of the Federal League. One of its major goals was to improve conditions in the minor leagues; to achieve that goal, the fraternity threatened a general strike in 1917. But most major-league players decided against striking to help minor-league players, and the fraternity, too, faded away.

One last abortive attempt to organize a "union" came in 1922, with the formation of the National Baseball Players Association of the United States. That organization died before the year ended, because the owners by and large ignored it.

Modern Associations. After World War II, there were movements to organize players in several professional sports. There were several reasons: the influx of money into sports because of general prosperity; the fact that postwar players were, on the whole, better educated and more sophisticated than players of the past; and the fact that a young man faced a much wider choice of alternate career opportunities during the period.

There was also the fact that the business aspect of sport became increasingly more complex; players felt the need for professional assistance in dealing with standard player contracts, and many owners even agreed that the need existed. In general, players' associations at first rather resembled company unions, but the word "union" was always carefully avoided.

Another major goal of players' associations in the early postwar years was to win pension benefits for their members. The goal was ultimately achieved in all four major professional team sports—baseball, basketball, football, and hockey.

Though not generally regarded as unions, players' associations perform many unionlike functions and, indeed, have become more militantly unionlike as television has added more money to sports revenues. The merger of the American and National Basketball Associations—which the players understandably felt would undermine their bargaining positions— was long stalled by suits brought by the players' associations directly involved.

Routinely, each association acts as a collective-bargaining unit with owners when provisions for the standard players' contract come up for renewal. These contracts spell out minimum salaries, maximum allowable pay cuts, provisions for expense money, punishment of players by fine or suspension, and even for some details of scheduling procedures.

Public opinion unquestionably limits the players' associations in some respects, however. The professional athlete has a dual role: He is simultaneously a public hero and a person engaged in an occupation. As a hero, he has no right to strike, in the eyes of many fans; as a career man, he is overpaid—from the average fan's standpoint.

Two associations that have gone on strike have come face to face with this problem. In 1972 the Major League Baseball Players Association went on strike to win higher pension benefits; 86 scheduled games were canceled before settlement was reached, and attendance suffered, not only from the cancellation of those games, but also from an apparent "backlash" on the part of fans.

In 1974, professional football players struck during the training season, primarily because of "freedom issues." Their chief complaint was directed against the "Rozelle rule," named for Commissioner "Pete" Rozelle, which requires a team that signs a player who has played out his option with another team to compensate that other team. Attendance for exhibition games, in which few veterans played, dropped severely. The players declared a truce and reported to training camp on August 11, and began the season without a new contract. Public reaction was largely against the players' position.

Those two bad experiences, in two different sports, make players' association strikes much less likely in coming years. However, the associations have shown every sign of increasing court action to win new rights and privileges.

PLAY-OFF—A play-off is a contest or series of contests held to determine a champion when two or more players or teams seem to have a right to the championship. Its simplest form is golf's sudden-death play-off when a tournament ends in a tie.

In team sports, pro football has a simple one-game play-off to determine its champion, while baseball's World Series is a seven-game series, with the first team to win four games recognized as world champion. Both those sports have adopted more complex pre-championship play-off systems as they have expanded, however.

When major-league baseball expanded to 24 teams in 1969, each league was reorganized into two divisions, and the division champions in each league meet in a five-game pennant play-off to decide which team wins the league title and the right to play in the World Series.

Professional football has two conferences of three divisions each. The three division champions and the second-place team with the best record in each conference take part in a two-round series of games to determine a conference champion; the conference champions then meet in the Super Bowl to determine the league champion.

Basketball and hockey use even more complex systems, based originally on a plan devised by Frank Shaughnessy, when he was president of baseball's International League, to keep fan interest from lagging when pennant races did. The Shaughnessy play-off system, devised in 1932, allows the top four teams in the final standings to enter the play-offs. In the original Shaughnessy system, the first- and third-place teams met in one semifinal round, the second- and fourth-place teams in the other. A better form of the system pits the first- and fourth-place teams and the second- and third-place teams against one another in the semifinal rounds. On the principle of "seeding," such an arrangement makes it more likely that the first-place team will get into the finals.

Another play-off system used in the past in minor-league baseball split the season into halves, with a post-season play-off between the first-half champion and the second-half champion.

See also Seeding; Tournaments.

POCKET BILLIARDS—*See* Billiards.

POLE VAULT—A field event in which contestants, using a long pole, attempt to vault over a high bar.
See Track and Field.

POLO—When field hockey developed from religious exercises in the Near East, the Persians, who were outstanding and enthusiastic horsemen, apparently gave it a new twist. By about A.D. 230, they were playing the game on horseback. Evidently that form of the sport then traveled to Tibet, China, and finally India, by about 600. The first European polo players were British tea planters in Assam, about 1850. In 1869 the British 10th Hussars played a game at the Hurlingham Hunt Club, near London, having read an account of how it was played in an Indian newspaper.

The game was called *pulu* in India, and many writers say that it was so named for the willow root from which the ball and sticks were made. *Pulu,* however, is also the Tibetan word for "ball," related to the Latin *pila,* and is quite possible that the willow root derived its name from the use that was made of it. In any event, the British turned *pulu* into "polo" and organized their own version of the game. Rules were standardized in 1873 by the Hurlingham Club, which is still the national governing body for the sport in England.

Polo was brought to the United States in 1875 by James Gordon Bennett, the sports-minded newspaper publisher, who brought a large supply of mallets and balls from England. Bennett also bought a carload of cow ponies from Texas and sold them to interested friends for $20 apiece. During the winter they practiced the new sport at Dickel's Riding Academy in New York, and in the spring of 1876 they began outdoor play at Jerome Park Racetrack. The game quickly spread to Long Island and then along much of the Atlantic seaboard. Indoor play, apparently unknown to the British, was developed in the United States during this early period.

In 1875 there were eight players to a side. This was quickly reduced to five and, in 1881, to four, the present number. An important development in the growth of polo was the establishment, in 1888, of an official handicapping system by H. L. Herbert, the first chairman of the U.S. Polo Association. Herbert's system, still in use with a few modifications, ranks players from 0, for a beginner, to 10, for an outstanding player. In 12-goal play, the rankings of the four players on the team must add up to not more than 12. If such a team had, for example, an outstanding, 10-goal player and a 2-goal player, the other two players would have to be beginners with 0 rankings.

International Play. In 1886 a British team was invited to the United States to play a best two-out-of-three series for the International Polo Challenge Cup. The matches were played at Newport, Rhode Island, and the British won handily, 10-4 and 14-2. In 1902 the United States won the first match of the series but the British won the next two. In the third challenge for the cup, in 1909, the United States not only won but changed the whole style of play.

The captain of the team was Harry Payne Whitney; his teammates were Lawrence and Monty Waterbury and Devereux Milburn. They came to be known as the "Big Four." Until this combination was assembled under Whitney's leadership, polo was basically a short-passing game that involved a lot of haphazard play in the middle of the field. Whitney and his teammates developed the equivalent of basketball's fast break, emphasizing "headmanning" the ball long distances to players traveling at top speed.

The Americans won the cup, 9-5 and 8-2. There have been 10 cup series since 1909, and the United States has won nine of them. World War II ended play until 1961, when the United States again successfully defended, but there has been no cup competition since then.

In 1928 the United States and Argentina played a series for the Copa de Las Americas (Cup of the Americas). This was to be held every four years, but was also ended by World War II after Argentina had won the cup in 1936. The great cost of shipping horses virtually eliminated international play during 1950s and early 1960s. A Copa de Las Americas match was held in 1950, but the series then lapsed until 1966. Play between the United States and Britain resumed in 1971, with Coronation Cup competition, which pits one top American team against one top British team.

The Horses. Until 1919, polo ponies were really ponies, since they were limited in height to 14.2 hands. The long-hitting game, however, required larger horses with more stamina, and there is now no size limitation. Most polo "ponies" today are actually full-sized thoroughbred horses. Others have been produced by mating thoroughbreds with range mustangs.

Training a horse for polo is a long, difficult task. After early training to the saddle, training for polo begins. The horse is first accustomed to the swinging of mallets near its head, then is trained to perform the near-acrobatic moves required in polo: sudden stops, turns, and acceleration to top speed in the shortest possible distance. Finally the horse is trained to accept the inevitable collisions—first ridden into deliberate collisions with much weaker animals, to build up confidence, and then gradually into collisions with stronger and older horses. By the time training is completed, the horse is five years old, and may have a polo career of 10 years or more.

The Field. The outdoor polo field is 300 yd long and 160 yd wide, and is surrounded by a safety zone, which is bordered by a wooden wall no more than 11 in high. The goals are each marked by a pair of posts 8 yd apart and at least 10 ft high. The posts are made of light, flexible materials that will give or break in collision.

At each end of the field a 30-yd line and a 60-yd line are marked, and an X marks a spot 40 yd from the goal and directly in front of it. At the center of the field is a mark in the shape of a T, the base of which is a segment of the midfield line.

Equipment. The ball has a 3¼-in diameter and weighs 4¼ to 4¾ oz. It is usually made of willow root, ash, or bamboo, but some plastics are also now used. The mallets, 48 to 54 in long, have cane handles and narrow wooden heads, 8½ to 9½ in long, set at a slight angle. Total weight is about 1 lb. The ball is struck with the side of the head, not the face.

Each player must wear a polo helmet or cap with a chin strap. Players usually wear boots and kneepads, which must be free of buckles or studs. Sharp spurs are not allowed.

The Teams. Each team is made up of four players, numbered 1 through 4. They are not restricted in their play in any way, but the No. 4 player functions more or less as a goalkeeper, while the No. 1 is usually the chief attacker. The No. 2 player usually starts offensive action by gaining the ball in the team's own end or by taking a pass from the No. 4 player and then starting upfield. The No. 3 player has to work hard on both offense and defense, trying to break up opponents' plays before they threaten to score, and also taking part in offensive passing combinations. Substitutes are allowed only when a player must be replaced because of injury or illness.

Timing and Scoring. A game consists of six, or less often of eight periods (chukkers) of 7 min each, with 3-min intermissions between chukkers and a 5-min intermission at halftime. Teams change ends at halftime. After 7 min of play in a period, a bell rings, and the period ends the next time the ball hits a board or goes out of play. A second bell rings 30 sec after the first, and the period then ends immediately if it is not already terminated.

Goals are scored by striking the ball between the goalposts at any height; the goalposts should be considered as extending indefinitely upward.

Fouls. The rules of polo are relatively simple and are designed primarily to protect the ponies and their riders from serious injury. Most important are the right-of-way rules:

■ The last player to hit the ball has the right of way over any opponent, so long as the player is following the line of the ball.

■ In general, the player following the ball on its exact line, or at the smallest angle to it, with the ball on the player's offside (the right), has the right of way. When the ball has stopped dead, its line is the line it was following before it stopped. If a player attempts to hit a dead ball and misses, its line is the direction in which that player was riding.

■ Two players approaching the ball from opposite directions, with the ball on their offsides, both have the right of way; but the player who actually gets the ball then assumes the right of way.

■ It is a foul to cross another player's right of way, if the crossing makes that player slow down or change direction.

Other fouls involve improper use of the stick. A player may not reach in front of or under an opponent's pony to hit the ball, and may not hit the ball into the legs of an opponent's pony; and, in general, the stick may not be used in a dangerous manner or held so that it will interfere with another player or pony.

It is proper for a player to use the stick to hook an opponent's stick only if both player and ball are on the same side of the opponent's pony, or in a direct line behind it. Hooking is permitted only when the opponent is about to strike the ball. An opponent's stick, however, must never be hooked above shoulder height.

Penalties. The officials have a good deal of leeway in how they award penalty hits. They try to choose a punishment that fits the nature of the offense. The most severe penalty is a penalty goal; the umpire awards a goal to a team because the official feels a goal would have been scored if a foul hadn't been committed.

Other fouls are punished by penalty hits from various locations:

■ From a spot 30 yd from the opponents' goal and directly in front of it. The penalized team must have all of its players behind the goal line until the ball is hit, and no member of the team may be behind the goal or ride out between the goalposts. Players on the team awarded the free hit must stay behind the ball until it is hit.
■ From the 40-yd spot; the same rules apply.
■ From a spot on the 60-yd line immediately in front of the goal. Players of the penalized team must remain 30 yd from the ball until it is hit. Players of the team taking the penalty hit may be placed anywhere.
■ From the spot where the foul occurred. The ball must be at least 4 yd from the sidelines; members of the team being penalized must remain 30 yd from the ball until it is hit, and members of the team awarded the hit may be placed anywhere.

The team that was fouled always has the option of taking the penalty hit from the spot where the penalty occurred; in that case, defenders must remain 30 yd from the ball until it is hit, but members of the offensive team must be no closer to the goal line than the ball is.

If the losing team is awarded a penalty with less than 20 sec to play in the game, the game ends only after 20 sec have elapsed or when a goal is scored.

Progress of Play. The game begins with the opposing sides lined up on opposite sides of the T mark at midfield, all facing the same sideline. The umpire faces them, at the head of the T, and rolls the ball between them from a distance of at least 5 yd. Players must not move until the umpire has released the ball; once it leaves the official's hand, they try to gain possession.

Play is continuous, stopping only when a goal is scored, a foul is called, or the ball goes out of play. After a goal, the teams change ends, unless it is a penalty goal.

Out of Play. When the ball goes over a sideline, the umpire rolls it in from the spot of crossing, with the two teams lined up as they did to begin the game, one team on each side of the umpire and all facing him.

If the attacking team hits the ball over the backline, the defending team puts it in play with a free hit from the spot, and all opponents must remain at least 30 yd away until the ball is hit. If the defending team hits it over the backline, the other team is awarded a penalty hit from the 60-yd line, opposite the point where the ball went out.

Officials. There are two mounted umpires; each has general responsibility for one half of the field. There is a third official, the referee, who stands at about the midway point, outside the field; his ruling is final if the umpires disagree. Behind each goal there are two goal judges, one

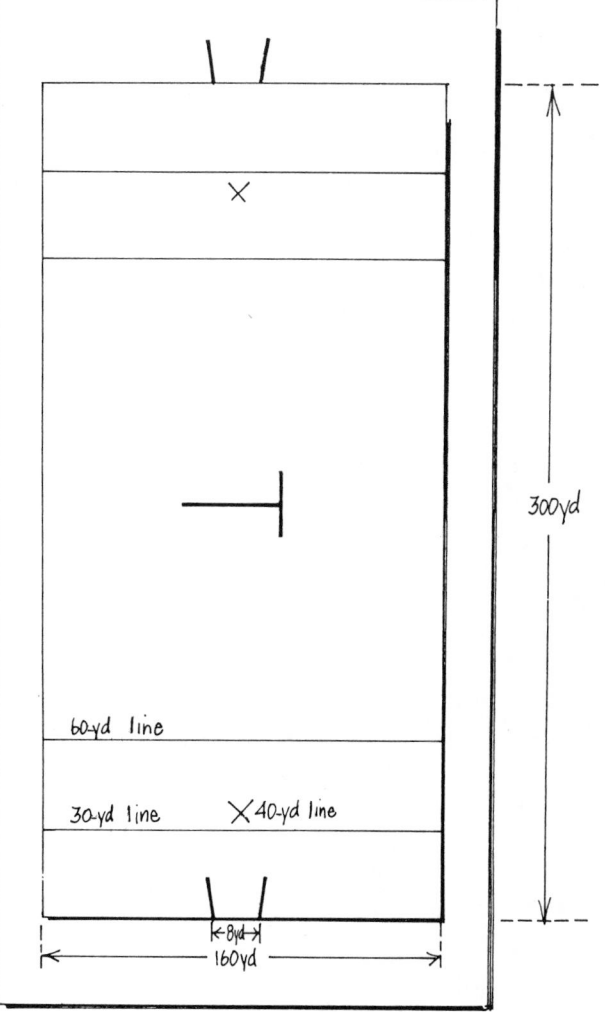

Polo ground

behind each goal post; they signal with flags when a goal has been scored. The goal judges may also be consulted by the umpires on incidents that occurred near the goal.

Indoor Polo. Indoors, polo is played on a field 100 yd long and 50 yd wide, surrounded by wooden boards 4–4½ ft high. The ball, of inflatable leather, has a 4½-in diameter and weighs at least 6 oz. There are only three players on a team. In general, the rules of outdoor polo are followed.

Bicycle Polo. Because of the great expense of good polo ponies, bicycle polo has gained a lot of ground in recent years. Developed in England in 1897, the sport was slow catching on in the United States, but the U.S. Bicycle Polo Association was organized in 1970.

Played on a field 110 ft long and 80 ft wide, with goals 12 ft wide, bike polo is similar to the horsy form of the sport, except that no contact is allowed, and a player is allowed to hit the ball only three times in a row.

U.S. Champions

Open

1904 Wanderers 4½, Freebooters 3
1905–09 No competition
1910 Ranelagh 7¾, Point Judith Perroquets 3¾
1911 No competition
1912 Cooperstown 9, Bryn Mawr 5¾
1913 Cooperstown 7, Point Judith 2¼
1914 Meadow Brook Magpies 11,
       Point Judith-Narragansett 8¾
1915 No competition
1916 Meadow Brook 8, Coronado 3
1917–18 No competition
1919 Meadow Brook 5, Cooperstown 4
1920 Meadow Brook 12, Cooperstown 3
1921 Great Neck 8, Rockaway 6
1922 Argentine 14, Meadow Brook 7
1923 Meadow Brook 12, British Army 9
1924 Midwick 6, Wanderers 5
1925 Orange County 11, Meadow Brook 9
1926 Hurricanes 7, Argentine 6
1927 Sands Point 11, Army-in-India 7
1928 Meadow Brook 8, U.S. Army 5
1929 Hurricanes 11, Sands Point 7
1930 Hurricanes 6, Templeton 5
1931 Santa Paula 11, Hurricanes 8
1932 Templeton 16, Greentree 3
1933 Aurora 14, Greentree 11
1934 Templeton 10, Aurora 7
1935 Greentree 7, Aurora 6
1936 Greentree 11, Templeton 10
1937 Old Westbury 11, Greentree 6
1938 Old Westbury 16, Greentree 7
1939 Bostwick Field 8, Greentree 7
1940 Aknusti 5, Great Neck 4
1941 Gulf Stream 10, Aknusti 6
1942–45 No competition
1946 Mexico 11, Los Amigos 9
1947 Old Westbury 10, Mexico 7
1948 Hurricanes 7, Great Neck 6
1949 Hurricanes 10, El Trebol 4
1950 Bostwick Field 7, California 5
1951 Milwaukee 6, Meadow Brook 2
1952 Beverly Hills 9, San Francisco 6
1953 Meadow Brook 7, Chicago 5
1954 Detroit C.C.C. 10, Brandywine 5
1955 Detroit C.C.C. 9, Brandywine 8
1956 Brandywine 11, Aurora 10
1957 Detroit C.C.C. 13, Aiken 3
1958 Dallas Circle F 7, Solocup 5
1959 Dallas Circle F 8, Aurora 7
1960 Oak Brook C.C.C. 8, Royal Palm 5
1961 Milwaukee 13, Beaver Ridge Farm 9
1962 Santa Barbara 8, Royal Palm 7
1963 Tulsa 7, Oakland Crescents 6
1964 Concar Oak Brook 10, Solo Cup Crescents 9
1965 Oak Brook-Santa Barbara 11, Bunn Tyco-Chicago 5
1966 Tulsa 10, Fountain Grove 5
1967 Bunn Tyco-Oak Brook 8, Milwaukee 2
1968 Midland, Texas 9, Milwaukee 0
1969 Tulsa Green Hills 11, Milwaukee 10
1970 Tulsa Green Hills 9, Oak Brook 5
1971 Oak Brook 8, Green Hill Farms 7
1972 Milwaukee 9, Tulsa 5
1973 Oak Brook 9, Willow Bend 4
1974 Milwaukee 7, Houston 6
1975 Milwaukee 16, Tulsa-Dallas 6
1976 Willow Bend 10, Tulsa 5

POOL—*See* BILLIARDS.

POWERBOAT RACING—Gottlieb Daimler, who is credited with inventing the motorcycle when he attached his new internal-combustion engine to a bicycle in 1885, also invented the motorboat, two years later. Daimler, however, didn't follow up on the invention; neither did anyone else until about 1900.

The early history of powerboating is surprisingly obscure. There were, reportedly, a few powerboats in the United States before the turn of the century, but little is known about them, except that their engines burned naphtha. About 1900 the English began to develop efficient boat engines. American engineers quickly followed the British lead, and in 1903 Sir Alfred Harmsworth donated a trophy for international competition. In the same year the Columbia, New York, Yacht Club called a meeting of all yacht clubs interested in powerboat racing. Twenty clubs attended the organizational meeting of what became the American Power Boat Association.

Most early races were patterned after sailing races, in that complicated formulas based on hull size, displacement, horsepower ratings, and other factors were used to calculate handicaps—an indication that most powerboats of the era were custom made, like most sail yachts of the era. This type of racing continued into the 1920s, when several factors—the increased mass production of many models, the development of engine reduction gear, and the planing hull—made it obsolete.

The APBA's first major race, for the Challenge Cup, was held on the Hudson River in June 1904. It was so popular that a second Challenge Cup race was held in September. The trophy soon became known as the Gold Cup.

Powerboat racing became truly international in 1922, with the organization of the Union for International Motorboating (UIM), headquartered in Belgium. The UIM now has affiliates in about 40 countries. The APBA is the United States affiliate. The UIM doesn't conduct races per se, but acts as a sanctioning body for certain international competitions and for world speed records.

Types of Competition

Like most kinds of racing involving motor vehicles, powerboat racing has a wide variety of classifications to

Dr. Robert Magoon won three consecutive U.S. offshore championships, two of them in this 36-foot Cigarette, Aeromarine III.
(Courtesy of Kiekhafer Aeromarine Motors, Inc.)

help equalize competition at many different levels. The APBA has nine major racing divisions, most of which have a number of subclassifications.

Unlimited Hydroplanes. These are the most glamorous of the racing boats. A hydroplane is a craft that skims over the surface of the water rather than riding through it. Obviously, this type of boat can travel at high speeds because of decreased resistance. Most hydroplanes are built with a three-point suspension system, with two planing surfaces in the bow, separated by an air tunnel, and one planing surface in the center of the stern.

The umlimiteds, as the name implies, can use inboard engines of any type or size, with or without superchargers. The boat must be propelled through the water by a propeller or screw. For safety reasons, the boats must be at least 28 ft in length and 4,500 lb in weight.

Most unlimited races are at three heats of 15 mi each—five laps of a 3-mi course, most often. The Gold Cup is now contested at four heats. Points are awarded for each heat: 400 for first place, 300 for second place, 225 for third, down to 1 point for 20th. The high point-winner in all heats wins the race.

Other major unlimited races are the President's Cup, at Washington, D.C.; the Kentucky Governor's Cup, at Owensboro, Kentucky; the Indiana Governor's Cup, at Madison, Indiana; and the Gar Wood Memorial, at Detroit.

Offshore Racing. An important development in recent years has been the growth of offshore ocean racing. The major races are conducted from point to point over large areas of open water. One of the most important is the 184-mi Miami-Nassau race, an international event.

The boats used in major offshore races are powered by inboard engines. One of the most successful designs is the Cigarette hull, named for a famous rum-running boat. Designed by Don Aronow, the Cigarette is appropriately named: 36 ft long, it has a beam of only 9 ft, 4 in. It has deep V bottoms on either side, and weighs about 7,700 lb. A 32-ft Cigarette hull is also available.

Class I boats are 28 to 45 ft long. There are three other international offshore classes, for boats 20–28 ft in length, for boats of more than 14 ft in length, and for standard production boats of more than 12 ft in length. Offshore races for the two smaller classes are usually conducted over a closed course, no more than 8 mi in length and no more than 2 mi offshore.

Outboards. The outboard class is subdivided into a class for boats with special racing engines, which usually burn racing fuels instead of gasoline; a class for boats with modified engines; and a class for boats with stock engines. Engine sizes are classified, from the 7½-in midget up to unlimited. And there are separate races for hydroplanes and for flat-hulled boats. Unlimited-performance outboard hydroplanes can reach straightaway speeds of 125 mph and more.

Each outboard race is limited to 12 boats; they race for one or more heats of about 5 mi each.

Put into production by Ole Evinrude of Milwaukee in 1909, the outboard began a tremendous boom in motorboating. The APBA first drew up rules for outboard racing in 1924. In terms of participation, this is easily the largest form of the sport.

Outboard Pleasure Craft. This division is organized into

Dr. Carlo Bonomi of Italy won two consecutive world offshore championships in Dry Martini. (*Courtesy of Kiekhafer Aeromarine Motors, Inc.*)

three groups: family outboard, sports, and unlimited. The unlimited boats may use up to three engines. The other groups are divided into classes based on boat length and engine size.

Stock Outboard. The main subdivisions here are runabouts (with flat-bottomed hulls) and hydroplanes. There are junior classes for children as young as nine.

Inboard. The main inboard subdivisions are also runabouts and hydroplanes. Runabouts are further separated into those that have racing engines and those that have service engines, which must be manufactured by boat builders as standard models. The hydroplanes are separated into classes ranging from 44-in³ engines up to 7-li engines.

Drag Racing. There are four main subclasses in powerboat drag racing: inboard and outboard runabouts and inboard and outboard hydroplanes. There are many classes based on number and types of engines and type of fuel used. Like similar auto races, powerboat drag races are conducted over a ¼-mi course, with two boats competing in each race, the winner moving on to another race, while the loser is eliminated from competition.

Special Events. This division is for a mixed bag of boats and races that don't fit into any other division. Among the special events are single-boat time trials, endurance and marathon races, and some offshore races for boats not specified in the offshore division.

Predicted Log. A very special form of the sport, predicted-log racing is similar to sports-car rallying. It is a test of navigational skill, not of speed. Before the race, the skipper predicts the amount of time it will take to cover a course. Then, without using any timekeeping device or any electronic instruments, the skipper navigates the course. The skipper who comes closest to matching the prerace prediction is the winner. Courses are usually set in offshore waters; boats used are usually cabin cruisers with inboard engines.

Gold Cup Winners

(Note: In the driver or owner column, the person listed is the owner unless otherwise indicated; * indicates driver, ** indicates driver-owner.)

Year	Boat	Driver or Owner	Speed
1904	Standard	C. C. Riotte**	23.6
1904	Vingt-et-Un II	W. Sharpe Kilmer**	25.3
1905	Chip	Jonathan Wainwright**	15.9
1906	Chip II	Jonathan Wainwright**	20.6
1907	Chip II	Jonathan Wainwright**	20.8
1908	Dixie II	E. J. Schroeder	30.9
1909	Dixie II	E. J. Schroeder	32.9
1910	Dixie III	F. K. Burnham	33.6
1911	Mit II	J. H. Hayden	36.1
1912	P.D.Q. II	Alfred G. Miles	44.5
1913	Ankle Deep	C. S. Mankowski	50.49
1914	Baby Speed Demon II	J. S. Blackton*	48.5
1915	Miss Detroit	Miss Detroit PBA	49.7
1916	Miss Minneapolis	Miss Minneapolis PBA	36.8
1917	Miss Detroit II	Garfield A. Wood**	56.5
1918	Miss Detroit III	Garfield A. Wood*	52.1
1919	Miss Detroit III	Garfield A. Wood**	56.3
1920	Miss America	Garfield A. Wood**	70.0
1921	Miss America	Garfield A. Wood**	56.5
1922	Packard-Chris-Craft	J. G. Vincent	40.6
1923	Packard-Chris-Craft	J. G. Vincent	44.4
1924	Baby Bootlegger	Caleb Bragg	46.4
1925	Baby Bootlegger	Caleb Bragg	48.4
1926	Greenwich Folly	George H. Townsend**	49.22
1927	Greenwich Folly	George H. Townsend**	50.99
1928	No competition		
1929	Imp	R. F. Hoyt	50.489
1930	Hotsy Totsy	V. Kliesrath	56.05
1931	Hotsy Totsy	V. Kliesrath-R. Hoyt	54.92
1932	Delphine IV	Horace E. Dodge	59.21
1933	El Lagarto	George C. Reis**	60.866
1934	El Lagarto	George C. Reis**	58.06
1935	El Lagarto	George C. Reis**	57.582
1936	Impshi	Kaye Don*	47.12
1937	Notre Dame	Herbert Mendelsohn**	68.645
1938	Alagi	Count Theo Rossi**	66.08
1939	My Sin	Zalmon G. Simmons, Jr.**	67.05
1940	Hotsy Totsy III	Sidney Allen	51.316
1941	My Sin	Zalmon G. Simmons, Jr.**	52.509
1942–1945	No competition		
1946	Tempo VI	Guy Lombardo**	70.878
1947	Miss Pepsi V	Daniel Foster*	57.02
1948	Miss Great Lakes	Daniel Foster*	52.89
1949	My Sweetie	William Cantrell*	78.645
1950	Slo-Mo-Shun IV	Ted Jones*	80.892
1951	Slo-Mo-Shun V	Lou Fageol*	91.766
1952	Slo-Mo-Shun IV	R. Stanley Dollar, Jr.*	84.355
1953	Slo-Mo-Shun IV	Fageol-Taggart*	95.628
1954	Slo-Mo-Shun V	Lou Fageol*	99.784
1955	Gale V	Lee Schoenith*	100.954
1956	Miss Thriftway	Bill Muncey*	100.906
1957	Miss Thriftway	Bill Muncey*	109.828
1958	Hawaii Kai	Jack Regas*	108.734
1959	Maverick	Bill Stead*	106.278
1960	No competition		
1961	Miss Century 21	Bill Muncey*	102.399
1962	Miss Century 21	Bill Muncey*	101.446
1963	Miss Bardahl	Ron Musson*	114.650
1964	Miss Bardahl	Ron Musson*	108.104
1965	Miss Bardahl	Ron Musson*	110.655
1966	Tahoe Miss	Mira Slovak*	97.861
1967	Miss Bardahl	Bill Schumacher*	104.691
1968	Miss Bardahl	Bill Schumacher*	——
1969	Miss Budweiser	Bill Sterett*	103.587
1970	Miss Budweiser	Dean Chenoweth*	101.848
1971	Miss Madison	Jim McCormick*	101.522
1972	Atlas Van Lines	Bill Muncey*	103.547
1973	Miss Budweiser	Dean Chenoweth*	105.354
1974	Pride of Pay 'n Pak	George Henley*	112.056
1975	Pride of Pay 'n Pak	George Henley*	113.350
1976	Miss U.S.	Dave Irwin*	108.021

Bibliography. *APBA Rule Book,* American Power Boat Association, St. Claire Shores, Mich. (annual).

POWER LIFTS—In weightlifting, a series of lifts that are meant to emphasize explosive strength and selective building of certain muscles in the body to develop attractive physiques.

See WEIGHTLIFTING.

Q

QUARTER-HORSE RACING—The richest horse race in the world is not the Kentucky Derby or any of the other major stakes races. It is not even a race for Throughbreds. It is the little-known All-American Futurity, run every Labor Day since 1959 at Ruidoso Downs, New Mexico—the third race in the "triple crown" of quarter-horse racing. In 1974 the All-American Futurity carried a total purse of more than $1 million, divided among a final and three consolation races. The final was worth $766,000, with $330,000 going to the winner.

The ancestors of the quarter horses were the first horses raced in this country. Those early horses, raced in Colonial times, were bred from Spanish-Indian stallions and English mares. The result, a close relative of the Thoroughbred, was a rather small but tough horse that could travel very fast for short distances. The name is said to have come from the fact that the horse's best distance is ¼ mi.

The quarter horse was supplanted in most major races by the Thoroughbred, but it moved to the West to become a favorite stock horse with cowboys, because of its intelligence and agility. In the West, as formerly in the East, the horse's great acceleration and speed over short distances led to many match races, and quarter-horse racing also began to win new popularity at county fairs in the Southwest. There are about 100 quarter-horse tracks in the United States now, and the sport has begun to move back into some Eastern areas.

The three races of the "triple crown" are the Kansas Futurity, the Rainbow Futurity, and the All-American; all are for two-year-olds. No horse has won all three.

Quarter horses usually race over 400 or 440 yd. The All-American Futurity draws well over 100 entries, who run in a series of elimination time trials until the 10 fastest horses have been selected for the final.

All-American Futurity Winners

1959	Galobar	Clifford Lambert	20.5
1960	Tonto Bars Hank	Curtis Perner	20.2
1961	Pokey Bar	Kenneth Chapman	20.1
1962	Hustling Man	Clifton Detiege	20.3
1963	Goetta	Charles Smith	20.40
1964	Decketta	Boyd Morris	20.30
1965	Savannah Jr.	Jack Wallace	20.30
1966	Go Dick Go	Buddy Nesmith	20.27
1967	Laico Bird	Bobby Harmon	20.11
1968	Three Oh's	Jerry Nicodemus	20.06
1969	Easy Jet	Willie Lovell	20.46
1970	Rocket Wrangler	Jerry Nicodemus	20.09
1971	Mr. Kid Charge	Johnny Cox	19.65
1972	Possumjet	Pete Herrera	20.04
1973	Timeto Thinkrich	John Watson	21.58
1974	Easy Date	Don Knight	21.60
1975	Bugs Alive in '75	Jerry Burgess	21.98
1976	Real Wind	Gary Sumpter	21.70

QUOITS—*See* HORSESHOE PITCHING.

R

RACQUETBALL—Developed in the early 1950s, racquetball is essentially handball played with racquets. The ball is somewhat larger (2¼ in, measured in diameter) and lighter (1.40 oz) than the ball used in handball. The racquet has a maximum head length of 11 in, maximum handle length of 7 in, and maximum width of 7 in. The total of the width and the overall length must not exceed 27 in. The racquet must be attached by a thong to the player's wrist.

At one time, racquetball was banned from many handball courts because handball players objected to the usurpation of their playing areas, and their rules, by a racquet sport. But the International Racquetball Association, formed in 1969, is an affiliate of the U.S. Handball Association, and racquetball has gained more acceptance by handball players in recent years. There are now an estimated 500,000 racquetball players in the United States.

Rules. The racquetball court is a handball court, 40 ft long, 20 ft wide and 20 ft high, with a back wall at least 12 ft high. The server may serve from any place between the short and service lines, but neither foot may extend beyond either line. The ball must be bounced first, and it must hit the front wall and then the floor, behind the short line, before it touches either side wall.

In doubles, the server's partner must remain in a service box, with back to the side wall and both feet on the floor, until the served ball passes the short line. As in handball, there are also one-wall and three-wall versions of the sport.

See also HANDBALL.

National Champions

Open Singles

1969	Bud Muehleisen
1970	Craig Finger
1971	Bill Schmidtke
1972	Charles Brumfield
1973	Charles Brumfield
1974	Bill Schmidtke
1975	Charles Brumfield
1976	Charles Brumfield

Women's Singles

1970	Fran Cohen
1971	Jan Pasternak
1972	Jan Pasternak
1973	Peggy Steding
1974	Peggy Steding
1975	Peggy Steding
1976	Peggy Steding

RACQUETS—It would seem that racquets must be fairly closely related to court tennis and/or handball, but there's no evidence to prove it. It has been suggested that racquets began on tennis courts in the sixteenth century, but the sport can be traced no further back than the early nineteenth century, when it was played in English jails and taverns on one-wall courts. Ironically, during the latter part of the century the sport, greatly changed, became popular among the upper-class and the wealthy, while it became virtually unknown in the debtors' prison, which had produced most of the early champions.

Racquets was adopted as an outdoor sport first at Harrow School, about 1822, and then at Eton. But bad weather too often prevented play, so the students decided to cover their courts, and more than one wall was required. In the 1840s a very expensive court was built at Woolwich, and in 1853 the Prince's Club built an even more elaborate court at even greater cost.

Racquets spread to the United States as early as 1850, when the Broadway Racquet Club in New York built the first American court. The sport continued to expand in this country, with more courts built in New York, Boston, Philadelphia, Chicago, Detroit, St. Louis, Cleveland, and Pittsburgh. But about 1920 interest suddenly declined.

The Racquet and Tennis Club of New York is the sport's major organization in this country, and racquets is also played by a few people in Boston and Philadelphia. As with court tennis, the chief problem of the sport is the tremendous cost of building the special courts.

The Rules. Racquets is played on a court 60 by 30 ft, with front and side walls 30 ft high and a back wall 15 ft high. Walls and floor are made of concrete. Spectators sit in a balcony above the back wall.

The front wall is marked with a service line, 9 ft, 7½ in above the floor. A 27-in-high wooden board, the "telltale," runs along the length of the front wall. The floor is marked with a short line, 24 ft from the back wall. A line from the short line to the back wall marks two service courts; the service boxes are small rectangles in front of the short line and adjoining the side walls.

The ball has a diameter of 1 in. It is made of tightly wound strips of cloth bound with twine and covered with kid. The racket, 30 in long and 8 to 10 oz in weight, has a long slender handle and a circular head, 7 to 8 in in diameter, strung tightly with gut.

The server must stand with at least one foot entirely in a service box. The serve must hit above the service line on the front wall and strike the floor in the service court on the other side. If the first serve is a fault, the server gets a second chance; if the second serve is a fault, the player loses the service. If he or she wants to, the receiver may return a faulty first serve, and the ball then continues in play.

Points are won on services and shots that cannot be returned, and lost on shots that strike the telltale; a shot can hit any wall, but it must touch the front wall, above the telltale, before it strikes the floor. Only the server ("hand in") can score a point. If the server loses an exchange, the server becomes "hand out"—that is, loses service.

Game is 15 points. However, when the score is 13-all, the player receiving service has the option of setting the game at 3 or 5 additional points. When it is tied at 14-all, the receiver may set the game at 3 points. Generally, a match is two games out of three or three games out of five. Major championship matches, however, are often four games out of seven.

U.S. Champions

Amateur

1890	B. Spalding de Garmendia
1891	B. Spalding de Garmendia
1892	J. S. Tooker
1893	B. Spalding de Garmendia
1894	B. Spalding de Garmendia
1895	J. S. Tooker
1896	B. Spalding de Garmendia
1897	B. Spalding de Garmendia
1898	F. F. Rolland
1899	Quincy A. Shaw, Jr.
1900	Eustace H. Miles
1901	Quincy A. Shaw, Jr.
1902	Clarence H. Mackay
1903	Payne Whitney
1904	George H. Brooke
1905	Lawrence Waterbury
1906	Percy D. Haughton
1907	Reginald Fincke
1908	Quincy A. Shaw, Jr.
1909	Harold F. McCormick
1910	Quincy A. Shaw, Jr.
1911	Reginald Fincke
1912	Reginald Fincke
1913	Lawrence Waterbury
1914	Lawrence Waterbury
1915	Clarence C. Pell
1916	Stanley G. Mortimer
1917	Clarence C. Pell
1918–19	No competition
1920	Clarence C. Pell
1921	Clarence C. Pell
1922	Clarence C. Pell
1923	Stanley G. Mortimer
1924	Clarence C. Pell
1925	Clarence C. Pell
1926	Stanley G. Mortimer
1927	Clarence C. Pell
1928	Clarence C. Pell
1929	Huntingdon D. Sheldon
1930	Stanley G. Mortimer
1931	Clarence C. Pell
1932	Clarence C. Pell
1933	Clarence C. Pell
1934	E. M. Edwards
1935	Huntingdon D. Sheldon
1936	E. M. Edwards
1937	Robert Grant III
1938	Robert Grant III
1939	Robert Grant III
1940	Warren Ingersoll III
1941	Robert Grant III
1942–45	No competition
1946	Robert Grant III
1947	J. Richards Leonard

Charley Brumfield, right, beat Steve Serot in this 1974 match during the national racquetball tournament. But he lost in his bid to win the tournament for the third straight time. (*Courtesy of International Racquetball Association.*)

1948	Robert Grant III
1949	Robert Grant III
1950	Robert Grant III
1951	Robert Grant, III
1952	Stanley W. Pearson, Jr.
1953	Robert Grant, III
1954	Geoffrey W. T. Atkins
1955	Geoffrey W. T. Atkins
1956	Geoffrey W. T. Atkins
1957	Charles Pearson
1958	Clarence C. Pell, Jr.
1959	Geoffrey W. T. Atkins
1960	Geoffrey W. T. Atkins
1961	David Norman
1962	David Norman
1963	David Norman
1964	P. B. Read
1965	Stephen Cox
1966	David Norman
1967	David Norman
1968	Geoffrey W. T. Atkins
1969	Geoffrey W. T. Atkins
1970	Geoffrey W. T. Atkins
1971	William Surtees
1972	William Surtees
1973	Howard Angus
1974	William Surtees
1975	William Surtees
1976	William Surtees

Open

1971	William Surtees
1972	William Surtees
1973	William Surtees
1974	William Surtees
1975	William Surtees
1976	William Surtees

RALLY—A type of auto racing in which navigational and driving skills, not speed, determine the winner.
See also AUTOMOBILE RACING.

RELAY—A type of team race; in most relays, each member of a team races the same distance. In a medley relay, different members run different distances or, in swimming, use different techniques. Roller skating has a unique type of relay in which one team member can take over any time his partner is growing tired.

See also ROLLER SKATING; SWIMMING; TRACK AND FIELD.

RIFLE SHOOTING—*See* HUNTING; SHOOTING.

ROAD RACING—*See* AUTOMOBILE RACING.

RODEO—Hard-working cowboys, after driving cattle to market in the years after the Civil War, relaxed by staging raucous entertainments which included impromptu competition in shooting, roping, riding, bronco busting, and other skills. One of the cow towns, Prescott, Arizona, decided in 1888 to formalize the competition a bit. The citizens of Prescott built a grandstand and sold tickets to the first real rodeo, and winning cowboys were given silver belt buckles as prizes. Within a short time, other towns began to stage their own rodeos (the Spanish word means "cattle market").

The rodeo at first was the range's equivalent of the harvest festivals held in farming communities. Gradually the competitive events became more and more formalized; the rodeo became a well-defined, standardized kind of meet; and the rodeo cowboy became, in most instances, a professional who did all of his roping and riding in competition for money. In 1945 the Rodeo Cowboys Association was formed as an organization of contestants. The association gradually took over more and more responsibilities until it became, as it is today, the chief supervising and sanctioning body for professional rodeo competition in the United States and Canada.

The RCA has about 3,000 licensed rodeo cowboys, and there are more than 500 sanctioned rodeos staged annually. Many of them are relatively minor, "home-town" events; but there are also many major rodeos, offering a total of more than $4 million in prize money each year. A full-time professional rodeo cowboy may compete in as many as 100 meets a year, traveling 150,000 mi in the process. Professional rodeos are staged in 42 states and they draw more than 12 million paying spectators a year.

The high point of the year is the National Finals Rodeo, a nine-day-long contest held in December in Oklahoma City, which has a total purse of more than $100,000. Only the top 15 money winners in each of eight events are eligible to compete for the world championships in the specific events. The all-around championship is awarded to the year's top money winner, provided he has placed in two or more events.

Competitive Events

A modern rodeo has many of the trappings of a circus. The setting is usually a large, outdoor arena, with spectators on three sides and, on the fourth side, a row of chutes from which animals and contestants enter. The show opens with a grand entry. While a brass band plays suitable music, the contestants, judges, and officials ride into the arena in Western outfits.

Also making the grand entry are the clowns. They add humor to the program, but they also have important jobs to perform: One of the clown's chief tasks is to entertain the crowd with high jinks at the same time that he is luring bulls or bucking horses away from a downed cowboy.

There are five major competitive events: bareback riding, bull riding, saddle-bronc riding, calf roping, and steer wrestling. Two other competitive events often seen are steer roping and team roping. In Canada, steer decorating is a sanctioned event. And, for the girls, there is the barrel race. A couple of humorous events may also be on the program: wild-cow milking and the wild-horse race.

Riding Events. Subjective judging is involved in all of the rodeo's riding events. The rider must stay aboard the mount a specified period of time—usually 8 or 10 sec—to get the maximum number of points. Judging takes into account the quality of the animal as well as the quality of the ride; a cowboy unlucky enough to draw a rather docile bronco, for example, cannot get a very good score.

In the bronc-riding contests, the rider must not touch horse, surcingle, or saddle with the free hand and, in the saddle contest, the feet must remain in the stirrups. A foul results in disqualification.

Calf Roping. A calf enters the arena from a chute and, after it crosses the scoreline, the mounted cowboy bursts from an adjacent chute. He has to rope the calf, dismount, throw the calf down, and tie its feet together. His cow pony is an important part of the performance; the pony must keep the rope taut by facing the calf and backing away as necessary to take up slack.

Steer Wrestling. Also known as "bulldogging," in this event a hazer rides alongside a steer to keep it on a straight course while the competitor approaches from the other side. He jumps from his horse, grabs the steer by its horns, and then tries to bring it to a stop and force it to the ground as rapidly as possible by twisting its neck. As in calf roping, the fastest time determines the winner.

Steer and Team Roping. Steer roping is an individual event, against time, in which the cowboy ropes and

Wes Hertzog rides Arizona Slim during bareback bronc competition in an Idaho rodeo. (*James Fain,* Rodeo Sports News.)

Ed Roth battles to stay aboard Two Ton Tony during rodeo competition at Puyallup, Washington. (*Gustafson Rodeo Photography,* Rodeo Sports News.)

1935	Everett Bowman	1957	Jim Shoulders
1936	John Bowman	1958	Jim Shoulders
1937	Everett Bowman	1959	Jim Shoulders
1938	Burel Mulkey	1960	Harry Tompkins
1939	Paul Carney	1961	Benny Reynolds
1940	Fritz Truan	1962	Tom Nesmith
1941	Homer Pettigrew	1963	Dean Oliver
1942	Gerald Roberts	1964	Dean Oliver
1943	Louis Brooks	1965	Dean Oliver
1944	Louis Brooks	1966	Larry Mahan
1945–1946	No award	1967	Larry Mahan
1947	Todd Whatley	1968	Larry Mahan
1948	Gerald Roberts	1969	Larry Mahan
1949	Jim Shoulders	1970	Larry Mahan
1950	Bill Linderman	1971	Phil Lyne
1951	Casey Tibbs	1972	Phil Lyne
1952	Harry Tompkins	1973	Larry Mahan
1953	Bill Linderman	1974	Tom Ferguson
1954	Buck Rutherford	1975	Tom Ferguson
1955	Casey Tibbs		Leo Camarillo
1956	Jim Shoulders	1976	Tom Ferguson

ROLLER DERBY—Early in 1935, Leo Seltzer read a magazine article that said 93 percent of the American people had done some roller skating at one time or another. Seltzer had been a promoter of walking marathons, and the article gave him an idea: Surely a roller-skating marathon would attract a lot of spectators.

Seltzer decided to call his marathon the Roller Derby; he copyrighted the name and presented the first such event in the Chicago Coliseum on August 13, 1935. At that time the derby was similar to six-day bicycle races but with a promotional gimmick added. Although all the skating took place in the Coliseum, it was billed as a transcontinental race. Working in pairs, skaters were to complete 57,000 laps, or about 4,000 mi, and lights on a huge map of the United States showed approximately where they were in their "cross-country" progress. There were 20,000 spectators on hand for the first race. Each team consisted of a man and a woman, and the rules required that one of them be on the track at all times.

The derby continued in that format for a few years, with shorter races, but the skaters began to develop some new wrinkles, among them the practice of blocking opponents who were trying to pass. When columnist Damon Runyon attended a derby in Miami in 1938, he told Seltzer he liked the contact part of the sport, and suggested that it be emphasized. Seltzer agreed, and also came up with the idea of pitting a "home team" against a "visiting team." The personnel never changed but, if a show was playing in Kansas City, one team would be called "Kansas City," the other "Chicago," to give the home-town fans some rooting interest. (In the East, the visiting team was usually called "New York.")

The Roller Derby limped along in that format through World War II. Its greatest period of success began on November 29, 1948, when the Columbia Broadcasting System telecast part of the derby while it was running in New York. The television exposure created thousands of instant fans, and the Roller Derby suddenly became the hottest show in town.

For the 1949–1950 season, Seltzer adopted a league format, with teams representing New York, Brooklyn, New Jersey, Philadelphia, Washington-Baltimore, and Chicago. However, the TV exposure quickly became overexposure; network telecasts ended and crowds dwindled. By 1958 the Roller Derby was confined to a number

---

throws a steer, with the aid of his horse. Then he dismounts, ties three of the steer's legs, and remounts. In team roping, two cowboys work together. One ropes the steer's head, the other ropes the steer's hind legs.

Humorous Events. In wild-cow milking, two cowboys work as a team to catch a wild cow. One holds the animal while the other tries to squeeze a few drops of milk into a bottle, then runs with the bottle to the finish line.

In wild-horse racing, a number of bucking broncos are released from chutes. Cowboy contestants, each with two assistants, attempt to saddle the horses and ride them to the other end of the arena.

Girls' Rodeo. Until very recently, women competed in just one regular rodeo event, barrel racing. Now, however, they compete in up to seven events and there is a national all-around championship. The highlight of the season is the National All-Girl Rodeo. Women's events are bareback riding, bull riding, calf roping, goat tying, ribbon roping, steer undecorating, and team roping.

National Champions

(Named by Rodeo Association of America, 1929–1944; top money-winners, 1945–1958; National Finals Rodeo Champions, 1959–present.)

All-Around

1929	Earl Thode	1932	Donald Nesbitt
1930	Clay Carr	1933	Clay Carr
1931	John Schneider	1934	Leonard Ward

of arenas in the San Francisco Bay area. The Bay Bombers, still the derby's best-known team, were the heroes, and teams representing other regions were generally the villains.

Jerry Seltzer took over the operation from his father and quickly moved to get back on television. He took a unique approach—first kinescoping, later taping the competition, and making it available to stations free of charge. The Roller Derby, unlike any other sport, uses its television time strictly for promotional purposes, not for revenue. And, as TV exposure has increased under the new arrangement, so has live attendance.

The Roller Derby is now split into two segments: league play, in the Bay area, and the annual tour, on which teams compete in arenas from coast to coast. Another unique aspect of the operation is that there are no individual franchise owners. A single corporation controls the entire derby and all its teams, and rosters can be juggled almost at will to keep the sport competitive.

In its early years the competition was less than completely honest. Fights were usually staged, and the outcomes of matches were often prearranged. But the Roller Derby has evidently become a more honest form of competition in the last decade or so. It probably ranks somewhere between professional wrestling and the Harlem Globetrotters' style of basketball as a serious competitive sport. It is at its most serious and most honest during the annual play-offs, when the skaters are competing for extra prize money and for the prestige of the championship.

Rules. From the original concept of a roller-skating marathon race between large numbers of man-woman teams, the Roller Derby has evolved into a quite different sport. Two teams, each of which has a men's squad and a women's squad, compete for points on an oval wooden track, usually 90 ft in length, 50 ft in width, and about 310 ft in circumference.

The squad is made up of five skaters. Two of them, who wear striped helmets, are designated "jammers." Two others are "blockers." The fifth, who wears a black helmet, is a pivot who usually acts as a blocker but can become a jammer. Only the jammers and the pivot can score points. Their object is to break away from the pack of skaters in the course of an offensive maneuver called a "jam," race around the track, and pass opponents. One point is scored each time a jammer passes an opponent. The blockers, as their name implies, try to keep the other team's jammers from breaking out. When a jam begins, the jammers are given just 60 sec to score. When the 60-sec span has elapsed, the jam ends. If a jammer feels scoring will be impossible within the allotted time, he or she can call off the jam by slowing down and signaling by putting hands on hips. A match consists of eight 12-min periods, and the male and female squads compete in alternate periods.

As in hockey, penalties are called for various roughing violations, and the violators are sent to a penalty box for 2 min for minor penalties, 5 min for major penalties. There are two referees who work a match from opposite sides of the track infield, walking in a clockwise direction to watch for violations. Also as in hockey, skaters can often get away with quite a bit of mayhem, either because the referees can't see everything happening at a given moment or because they have decided to display a certain amount of leniency.

ROLLER HOCKEY and ROLLER POLO—In areas where ice hockey is popular, various forms of street hockey have sprung up, to be played when ice is not available. As with most such sports, the rules may vary greatly from one area to another.

The United States of America Confederation of Amateur Roller Skating conducts national championships in two kinds of roller hockey, one played with a puck and the other with a ball. In many areas the sport is called roller polo when a ball is used. For a time during the 1930s, roller polo was a popular spectator sport on the semiprofessional and professional levels in the Northeast.

With increased interest in ice hockey in many parts of the United States, the various forms of street hockey are again becoming popular, often in roller rinks rather than in the street, and the National Hockey League has tried to help revive the sport with financial backing. The sport has long been fairly popular in several European countries, and a world championship tournament is played annually.

Rules. Roller hockey is similar in many ways to ice hockey. The rink is approximately 80 by 50 ft, divided into halves by a center line. At either end is a rectangle, 40½ ft by 18 ft, the penalty area; at each corner is a penalty-area spot. Goal cages are 5 ft, 1 in wide; 3 ft, 5½ in high; and 3 ft deep. In front of each goal cage is a line, 1½ ft from the cage, marking the crease, which is 5 ft, 1 in wide. At the center of the rink is a face-off circle, 1½ ft in diameter.

Each player has a wooden stick no more than 3 ft, 9 in long from the handle to the end of the blade, and no more than 2 in wide. It is curved like a field hockey stick. Maximum weight is 18 oz. The ball has a 9-in circumference and weighs 5½ oz.

Each team has five players, including the goalkeeper. The game begins at the center circle with a strike-off, which is similar to a hockey face-off. Players may advance the ball only by hitting it with the stick below shoulder height. The ball must not be hit more than 5 ft in the air. The goalkeeper may play the ball with any part of his body while within the crease. A goal can be scored only from the attacking half of the center line, unless the ball (or puck) touches a defensive player before entering the goal.

It is a foul to advance the ball illegally, to charge an opponent, to obstruct an opponent deliberately, to hold or use the stick against an opponent, and to kick, trip, or fight. An indirect free hit is the mildest punishment for a foul. This is a hit taken from one of the penalty-area spots by a player of the team that was fouled. Opponents must remain 9 ft away until the ball is struck. The player taking the free hit may not play the ball again until another player has touched it, and a goal cannot be scored directly (that is, on the indirect free hit itself). A direct free hit, taken from any of the penalty spots, is awarded for more serious offenses. All players except the one given the hit and the goalkeeper must be at least 15 ft behind the ball until it is hit. A goal can be scored directly.

A penalty shot is awarded for serious fouls inside the penalty area. It is taken from the penalty spot directly in front of the goal and 18 ft away from it. All players, except the one awarded the hit and the rival goalkeeper, must be on the other side of the center line. The player taking the shot may hit the ball only once unless it hits the goalkeeper. For flagrant fouls, a player may be ejected for 5 min, or for the rest of the game, without being replaced. For a second serious foul, the player is expelled permanently.

A game consists of two 20-min periods in international play. In other cases, a period ranges from 10 to 20 min. If the score is tied at the end of regulation play, 10-min sudden-death overtime periods are played until a team scores.

ROLLER SKATING—The roller skate is believed to have been invented by an unknown Hollander in the eighteenth century; undoubtedly the inventor felt an urge to skate in warm weather as well as cold, and attached wooden spool-like wheels to ice skates. The idea spread through Holland during the early part of that century.

Joseph Merlin, a Belgian, made a pair of roller skates about 1760 and shortly afterward J. Garcin, an accomplished ice skater, invented a skate on rollers and opened a gymnasium in Paris where skaters could practice their skills the year around. Garcin's project was not a success. The skates, which had just two rollers, front and back, were difficult to control, and his gymnasium went out of business.

The true forerunner of the modern roller skate was the invention of a New York man, J. L. Plimpton, who did away with the roller idea and designed a skate with four small wooden wheels, in 1863. This skate was greatly improved about 1875, when the metal-wheeled skate with roller bearings was developed. This new skate was durable; the bearings permitted greater speed and allowed a skater to coast for considerable distances once some speed had been attained; and the fact that there were four wheels, one on each corner, permitted skaters to practice the same kind of control that they could achieve on ice skates.

Roller skating was, for a time, a craze in Europe and England as well as North America. Its history has been one of sharp ups and downs. After peaking in 1885, it virtually disappeared, was revived near the turn of the century, declined sharply again about 1910, and then was revived once more in the 1930s. It is estimated that there are now about 4,000 roller rinks in the United States, and that nearly 20 million people take part in the sport in this country. It is also popular in Australia, Belgium, Canada, England, France, Ireland, Italy, Germany, New Zealand, and Spain.

Roller skating both influenced and was influenced by ice skating between 1875 and the 1930s. Like ice skating, as a sport it is split into two sharply different competitive categories, figures and speed.

The Roller Skating Rink Operators Association (RSROA), formed in 1937, established the first rules for amateur competition, first in speed skating and then, in 1939, in figure competition. A rival group, the U.S. Amateur Roller Skating Association, was formed in 1939 to conduct its own figure-skating championships, and speed championships were added in 1942. A merger took place late in 1972. The supervisory body for the sport now is the United States of America Confederation of Amateur Roller Skating (USAC), a member of the Fédération Internationale de Roller Skating (FIRS). USAC is, in turn, made up of three divisions: the Artistic Skating Union (ASU), the Speed Skating Union (SSU), and the Hockey

Many moves in the figure version of roller skating are similar to those seen in ice figure skating—this "sitz-spin," for example. (*Hank Seaman,* New Bedford Standard-Times.)

Skating Union (HSU), which controls the sport of roller hockey. (*See* preceding entry.)

Types of Competition

Speed. This form is straightforward enough. Races are run counterclockwise around an oval board track, usually of hardwood coated with plastic, and about 250 yd in circumference. The lead skater has the right of way. If there is a collision, the overtaking skater is responsible, unless judges are convinced the lead skater was guilty of deliberate obstruction. The penalty is immediate disqualification.

Relay racing on roller skates is rather unusual. One member of the team skates as long as he or she wants, until touched by another member of the team, who then takes over. However, there can be no replacement during the last two laps of the race.

Artistic skating comprises a variety of events:

Figures. In roller skating, unlike ice skating, the figures to be traced are done on circles marked on the rink surface, in figure-8 fashion. In American competition, only compulsory figures are used, and these are divided into groups. One group is specified for a preliminary round, upon completion of which the number of competitors is usually cut to eight; then another group of figures is specified for the final round. With a large number of entrants, there may be more than two rounds, each with its own group of compulsory figures.

In international-style competition, compulsories are used in the preliminaries, the field is cut to eight, and they skate freestyle in the finals. The compulsory and free-skating scores of the finalists are added to determine the winners. In contrast to compulsory figures, free skating consists of a routine of the competitor's own choice.

Dance. In dance events, a man and a woman skate together and must execute all movements in unison and in coordination with music. Dances are divided into two groups. In American dance, one group is drawn for the elimination round and the other group is danced in the finals. In international style, compulsory dances are used for the elimination round and free dance in the finals.

Singles, Pairs, and Fours. These are purely free-skating events, with no compulsory figures required.

Speed Skating Union Champions
(Includes former RSROA champions)

Men

1937	Lloyd Christopher
1938	George Moore
1939	No competition
1940	George Moore
1941	William Hay
1942	Anthony Merilli
1943	Frank Wander
1944	Anthony Merilli
1945	No competition
1946	Harold Wyant
1947	Harold Wyant
1948	Orville Godfrey, Jr.
1949	James Hibak
1950	Roland Grina
1951	Harold Slack
1952	Earl Knight
1953	William Kinney
1954	Richard Waltz
1955	Earl Wilmot
1956	Earl Wilmot
1957	Charles Wahlig
1958	Richard Edwards
1959	Gerald Gohs
1960	George Grudza
1961	Eddie Perales
1962	Eddie Perales
1963	Eddie Perales
1964	George Grudza
1965	Ted Attebury
1966	Ted Rendfrey
1967	John Drewry
1968	Malcolm Williamson
1969	Michael Layport
1970	Pat Bergin
1971	Pat Bergin
1972	Pat Bergin
1973	Danny Butler
1974	Chris Snyder
1975	Tim Small
1976	Tim Small

Women

1938	Vivian Bell
1939	No competition
1940	Verna Picton
1941	June Prater
1942	Dorothy V. Law
	Betty Jane Ross
1943	Jeannette Kiloren
1944	Ruth Jones
1945	No competition
1946	Mary Lou Dauer
1947	Betty Hosek
1948	Mary Lou Dauer
1949	Rita Conseiler
1950	Evalyn Olsen
1951	Betty Jane Hager
	Margaret O'Connell
1952	Evalyn Olsen
1953	Marie Orlando
1954	Evalyn Olsen
1955	Evalyn Olsen
1956	Noreen Knapp
1957	Noreen Knapp
1958	Suzanne Richardson
1959	Mary Merrell
1960	Mary Merrell
1961	Mary Merrell
1962	Linda Durbin
1963	Linda Jo Kurk
1964	Mary Merrell
1965	Janet Ford
1966	Mary Merrell
1967	Mary Merrell
1968	Sharon Van Lue
1969	Jan Irvin
1970	Jan Irvin
1971	Shelly Comella
1972	Jan Irvin
1973	Linda Brooks
1974	Robin Wilcock
1975	Marcia Yager
1976	Marcia Yager

Artistic Skating Union Champions
(Includes former RSROA champions)

American Dance

1939	Virginia Mount-Lloyd Young
1940	Mary Louise Durkin-Gordon Finnegan
1941	Gladys Koehler-George Werner
1942	Irene and Jack Boyer
1943	Norma Jeanne Wescher-Leo Carsner
1944	Ruth Crause-James Costigan
1945	No competition
1946	Ruth Crause-James Costigan
1947	Clifford Schattenkerk-Bettie Jennings
1948	Clifford Schattenkerk-Bettie Jennings
1949	Clifford Schattenkerk-Bettie Jennings
1950	Robert and Joan LaBriola
1951	Robert and Joan LaBriola
1952	Robert and Joan LaBriola
1953	Robert and Joan LaBriola
1954	Gary Castro-Marilyn Roberts
1955	Gary Castro-Marilyn Roberts
1956	Gary Castro-Marilyn Roberts
1957	Charles Wahlig-Miriam Centaro
1958	Charles Wahlig-Claire Farrell
1959	Charles Wahlig-Claire Farrell
1960	Linda Jo Baker-Jack Greer
1961	Linda Jo Baker-Jack Greer
1962	Adolph Wacker-Linda Mottice
1963	Adolph Wacker-Linda Mottice
1964	Adolph Wacker-Linda Mottice
1965	Adolph Wacker-Linda Mottice
1966	Adolph Wacker-Linda Mottice
1967	Adolph Wacker-Linda Mottice
1968	Adolph Wacker-Linda Mottice
1969	Marc Parker-Vicki Freeman
1970	Sanja Pulitz-Dick Manns
1971	Bob and Elayne Leonard
1972	Joseph Gaudy-Marie Spoleti
1973	Joseph and Marie Gaudy
1974	John LaBriola-Debra Coyne
1975	John LaBriola-Debra Coyne
1976	John LaBriola-Debra Coyne

American Free Dance

1964	David Tassinari-Patricia Fogarty
1965	David Tassinari-Patricia Fogarty
1966	David Tassinari-Patricia Fogarty
1967	Curtis Blau-Sylvia Haffke
1968	John and Chris Gustafson

1969	Mike Crickmore-Linda Gyenese
1970	Mike Crickmore-Linda Gyenese
1971	Phillip Scalmato-Jane Puracchia
1972	Dana Marshall-Janis Ford
1973	Kerry Cavazzi-Rosanne Franzone
1974	Richard Veliko-Karen Darling
1975	Edward Nilson-Fleurette Arsenault
1976	Mark Howard-Cindy Smith

International Dance

1972	Thomas Straker-Bonnie Lambert
1973	James Stephens-Jane Puracchio
1974	James Stephens-Jane Puracchio
1975	Kerry Cavazzi-Jane Puracchio
1976	Kerry Cavazzi-Jane Paracchio

American Figures—Men
(Included free skating until 1949)

1939	Walter Stokosa
1940	Walter Stokosa
1941	Robert Ryan
1942	Kenneth Chase
1943	Jack Seifert
1944	Arthur Russell
1945	No competition
1946	Ted Shufflebarger
1947	J. W. Norcross, Jr.
1948	J. W. Norcross, Jr.
1949	Ted Rosdahl
1950	J. W. Norcross, Jr.
1951	Ted Rosdahl
1952	Ted Rosdahl
1953	William Pate, Jr.
1954	William Pate, Jr.
1955	John Matejec
1956	Ronald Jelise
1957	Ronald Jelise
1958	Darrell Glenn
1959	Darrell Glenn
1960	Tom Gregory
1961	Philip Sukel
1962	Philip Sukel
1963	Joe Bark
1964	Joe Bark
1965	Joe Bark
1966	Keith Runnels
1967	Richard Gustafson
1968	Richard Gustafson
1969	Richard Gustafson
1970	Gary Lintz
1971	Ronald Milton
1972	William Boyd
1973	William Boyd
1974	Keith King
1975	Kim Rouse
1976	William Combs

American Figures—Women
(Included free skating until 1949)

1939	Jane Peace Holcombe
1940	Margot Allred
1941	Melva Block
1942	Melva Block
1943	Shirley Snyder
1944	Dorothy Law
1945	No competition
1946	Margaret Williams McMillan
1947	Margaret Wallace
1948	Nancy Lee Parker
1949	Nancy Lee Parker
1950	Nancy Lee Parker
1951	Laurene Anselmy

1952	Nancy Kromis
1953	Laurene Anselmy
1954	Laurene Anselmy
1955	Carol Halle
1956	Joan Brown
1957	Lynne Mathewson
1958	Christie Benda
1959	Paulette Stewart
1960	Christie Benda
1961	Linda Jo Baker
1962	Linda Jo Baker
1963	Linda Jo Baker
1964	Linda Mottice
1965	Linda Mottice
1966	Carol Langlois
1967	Carol Langlois
1968	Carol Langlois
1969	Margaret Lucas
1970	Margaret Lucas
1971	Susie Johnson
1972	Debbie Palm
1973	Debbie Palm
1974	Debbie Palm
1975	Kathleen O'Brien
1976	Donna Kiker

American Singles—Men

1949	Ted Rosdahl
1950	J. W. Norcross, Jr.
1951	Alvin Hurwitz
1952	Skipper Oakes
1953	Arthur Kerwin
1954	Arthur Kerwin
1955	Edgar Watrous
1956	Edgar Watrous
1957	James Mohler

A young man demonstrates his form in artistic roller skating. (*Hank Seaman*, New Bedford Standard-Times.)

1958	Ricky Mullican
1959	James Mohler
1960	Rob Wollard
1961	William Madigan
1962	John Renz
1963	John Renz
1964	John Renz
1965	Michael Jacques
1966	Michael Jacques
1967	Michael Jacques
1968	Michael Jacques
1969	Michael Jacques
1970	Michael Jacques
1971	Michael Jacques
1972	Michael Jacques
1973	Mark Revere
1974	Darryl Bayles
1975	Michael Glatz
1976	Paul Jones

American Singles—Women

1949	Nancy Lee Parker
1950	Nancy Lee Parker
1951	Laurene Anselmy
1952	Laurene Anselmy
1953	Laurene Anselmy
1954	Laurene Anselmy
1955	Susan Cowan
1956	Susan Cowan
1957	Carolyn Sliger
1958	Carolyn Sliger
1959	Sylvia Haffke
1960	Carolyn Sliger
1961	Beverly Bowers
1962	Beverly Bowers
1963	Sylvia Haffke
1964	Sylvia Haffke
1965	Sylvia Haffke
1966	Linda Hawthorne
1967	Mary Sue Wilcox
1968	Darlene Barile
1969	Mary Sue Wilcox
1970	Kathy Miller
1971	April Allen
1972	April Allen
1973	Natalie Dunn
1974	Natalie Dunn
1975	Moana Brigham
1976	Lisa Bergin

Bibliography. Martin, Bob: *Roller Skating,* A. S. Barnes, New York, 1944.

ROQUE—*See* Croquet.

ROWING—The oar is a development from the canoe paddle, but it is not known just when the oar—in effect, a fixed paddle—was developed. The rulers of ancient Egypt often traveled in slave-powered galleys, and there are accounts of galleys racing against one another for fun. As far as we are concerned, however, rowing as a competitive sport got its start in England during the sixteenth century.

The Thames River was a vital waterway, plied by boats small and large, and there were so many accidents caused by inexperienced boatsmen that Henry VIII (1509–1547) imposed a rule that an oarsman must serve an apprenticeship to get a license. By the end of the century, there were nearly 4,000 licensed boatmen operating on the Thames. The fact that they officially belonged to an elite group must have spurred a good deal of informal competition among them. Distances varied, ranging from ½ mi up, but after a time the 4¼-mi stretch from Putney to Mortlake became a popular course.

In 1715 an English comedian, Thomas Doggett, died; his will provided for a prize for an annual 4¼-mi race from London Bridge to Chelsea. This race, known as Doggett's Coat and Badge, is still held annually and is one of the oldest continuing competitions in all of sports. Early in the eighteenth century, English college students adopted the sport, and the first annual Oxford-Cambridge boat race was held on the Putney-Mortlake course in 1829. It became an annual event in 1856.

Competitive rowing had arrived in the United States by 1811. In that year a crowd of 60,000 turned out along the Hudson River to watch an American crew in a boat called *American Star* defeat the gig of a British ship, *Hussar,* for a $1,000 bet. The Hudson River was an early center of rowing competition in the United States, along with the Schuylkill in Philadelphia and the Charles in Boston and Cambridge. New York's Castle Garden Boat Club was organized in 1834 and the Detroit Boat Club held its first race in 1839. The most important of the early rowing clubs, however, was the "Schuylkill Navy," actually a federation of several clubs, organized in 1858.

The first major regatta was staged by the Schuylkill Navy in 1872. It touched off a furor because it was for amateurs only, and the race committee set down very strict rules. (*See* Amateurism.) But it was successful enough to spur the formation of the National Association of Amateur Oarsmen (NAAO), which took over the regatta in 1873 and has held it annually ever since, except for lapses during the World Wars. As a popular sport, rowing reached its peak before the turn of the century. Sculling races between individuals were particularly popular. Today the sport's chief popularity is on the collegiate level, particularly in regattas and dual races involving eight-oared shells.

Collegiate Rowing. Yale students began "rowing" in 1843, but their craft was actually a canoe. The sport arrived at Harvard in 1845. The first intercollegiate competition in any sport was the first Harvard-Yale boat race, on Lake Winnepesaukee, New Hampshire, August 3, 1852.

In 1871 five colleges—Amherst, Bowdoin, Brown, Harvard, and Massachusetts Agricultural (now the University of Massachusetts)—formed the Rowing Association of American Colleges (RAAC). Yale joined in 1873, but in 1876 Harvard and Yale both withdrew to take part in their own, eight-oared dual competition. (RAAC races had been for six-oared shells.) The RAAC collapsed, and there was little intercollegiate competition in the sport until 1895, when the Intercollegiate Rowing Association was formed to stage a regatta. Reorganized in 1899, the IRA expanded the regatta to include junior varsity and freshman competition in eight-oared shells.

Cornell was almost unbeatable in the early years, but Navy, Washington, and California became powerful rowing schools during the 1930s. In 1951, Wisconsin became the first Midwestern school to win the varsity race; in recent years, Cornell has shown a resurgence and Pennsylvania has also won a number of races.

The IRA regatta was usually at 4 mi until 1947, when the distance was cut to 3 mi. Since 1968 it has been raced at the Olympic distance, 2,000 m (about 1¼ mi).

There are many important trophies in college rowing,

most of them for triangular or dual competition. One of the oldest is the Childs Cup, first presented in 1879 to the winner in competition among Columbia, Pennsylvania, and Princeton. The Carnegie Cup, first presented in 1921, is for competition among Cornell, Princeton, and Yale. The Adams Cup since 1933 has gone to the winner of a Harvard-Navy-Pennsylvania regatta. Other major races include the Eastern and Western Sprints and the Pacific Coast regatta.

Improving Equipment. Ordinary rowboats were used in early races but, as racing became more popular, a new type of boat began to evolve. The first major development was the design of a four-oared scull by George Steers in 1838. Steers, who later designed the yacht *America*, of America's Cup fame, built a long, sleek shell with outriggers. Known as the "whirlwind," the shell drew only 4 in of water—making it practically a hydroplane—and weighed only 140 lb, though the length was 30 ft.

The six-oared shell, patterned after Steers' design, was the most popular collegiate racing boat until 1876. Eight-oared shells had been sent over from England in 1872, and, as already noted, in 1876 both Harvard and Yale withdrew from the RAAC in order to compete in eight-oared racing.

Other major developments were the design of the keel-less shell, by Matt Taylor in 1856, and the invention of the sliding seat, which has been credited to two men. Whichever of them deserves the honor, it was an important invention because, until the sliding seat came along, oarsmen had to sit in a layer of heavy grease to avoid getting blisters. The sliding seat may have been invented by John C. Babcock of New York, the first president of the NAAO, in 1870. Most accounts, however, credit Walter Brown with the invention, in 1872.

Types of Competition. The first important distinction to make is between rowing and sculling. Sculling is what most people think of as rowing: An oar (or scull) is held in each hand, so one person can propel a boat with two oars. In rowing, each competitor has just one oar, held with both hands.

In single sculls, one person propels the boat with two oars. The shell is 26 ft long and weighs about 30 lb. Each scull is about 9 ft, 10 in long, and weighs about 5 lb. Double sculls is a very difficult event because it calls for almost perfect synchronization between two persons, each of whom pulls two oars. The length of the shell is about 34 ft.

Pair oars without coxswain also demands exceptional teamwork, since one member is pulling an oar on the right while the other pulls an oar on the left. The two oars must operate as they would in single sculls, where only one person is rowing. The shell is about 34 ft long and weighs about 65 lb, and the oars are similar to those used in single sculls.

Pair oars with coxswain calls for great strength on the part of the oarsmen, but less teamwork, since the coxswain directs them. The oarsmen also have to pull the dead weight of the coxswain through the water, which makes sheer strength more important. The shell is about 35 ft long and weighs about 85 lb; the coxswain must weigh at least 110 lb and, like a jockey, is usually very close to the minimum weight.

The four oars without coxswain is another event calling for near-perfect timing, here among four team members. The one who rows in the bow steers by manipulating a small rudder with a line connected to the right shoe. The shell is 39 ft long, 19 in wide, 8 in deep, and 130 lb in weight.

The four oars with coxswain is a strength event, particularly popular among small rowing clubs because it offers a scaled-down version of crew racing without all the expense and training involved in the eight-oared event. The four-oared shell is about 42 ft long and weighs about 160 lb.

Easily the most popular kind of rowing, from the spectator point of view, is the eight-oared shell with coxswain. The shell is about 61 ft long, 10 in deep, 24 in in the beam, and 270 to 300 lb in weight.

The oarsmen are usually tall, heavy, and strong. The coxswain is a vitally important part of the crew, who not only keeps the members rowing together but is really the boat's skipper, responsible for deciding on proper tactics. The coxswain is rather like a jockey who enters a race with a general notion of overall strategy but may have to make tactical adjustments according to the demands of given situations. Attempting to outpsych competing crews may also be part of the cox's job. At a crucial moment in the race, the cox's cry "We're gaining on them!" or "We're holding them off!" may serve to deflate the members of the other crew at the same time that it inspires teammates.

Heats and Repechages. A full-scale regatta is rather similar to a double-elimination tournament. Heats are held in various events, and the winning boat in each heat advances in competition. However, once a boat is defeated, it is not automatically eliminated. It enters a *repechage* (idiomatic French for "second chance") heat against other early-round losers, and a *repechage* winner also advances. In the Olympics there are three preliminary heats and three *repechage* heats, and all six winners move directly into the finals.

All Olympic rowing contests are held over a 2,000-m course. In club and collegiate competition in the United States, distances range from ¼ mi for some single-sculls events to 4 mi for some eight-oared events. All event categories listed above are included in the Olympics. An eighth category not seen in the Olympics is the quadruple sculls, for four competitors and eight oars.

IRA Regatta Winners

(Note: The distance for this Intercollegiate Rowing Association event was 4 mi, 1895 through 1941, unless otherwise noted; 3 mi from 1947 through 1967; 2,000 m since 1968. * indicates 3 mi; ** 2 mi; *** 2,000 m.)

1895	Columbia	21:25
1896	Cornell	19:59
1897	Cornell	20:34
	Cornell	20:47.8
1898	Pennsylvania	15:51.5*
1899	Pennsylvania	20:04
1900	Pennsylvania	19:44.6
1901	Cornell	18:53.2
1902	Cornell	19:05.6
1903	Cornell	18:57
1904	Syracuse	20:22.6
1905	Cornell	20:29
1906	Cornell	19:36.8
1907	Cornell	20:02.4
1908	Syracuse	19:24.2
1909	Cornell	19:02
1910	Cornell	20:42.2
1911	Cornell	20:10.8

1912	Cornell	19:31.4
1913	Syracuse	19:28.6
1914	Columbia	19:37.8
1915	Cornell	19:36.6
1916	Syracuse	20:15.4
1917-19	No competition	
1920	Syracuse	11:02.6**
1921	Navy	14:07*
1922	Navy	13:33.6*
1923	Washington	14:03.2*
1924	Washington	15:02*
1925	Navy	19:24.8
1926	Washington	19:28.6
1927	Columbia	20:57
1928	California	18:35.8
1929	Columbia	22:58
1930	Cornell	21:42
1931	Navy	18:54.2
1932	California	19:55
1933	No competition	
1934	California	19:44
1935	California	18:52
1936	Washington	19:09.6
1937	Washington	18:33.6
1938	Navy	18:19
1939	California	18:12.6
1940	Washington	22:42
1941	Washington	18:53.3
1942-46	No competition	
1947	Navy	13:59.2
1948	Washington	14:06.4
1949	California	14:42.6
1950	Washington	8:07.5**
1951	Wisconsin	7:50.5**
1952	Navy	15:08.1
1953	Navy	15:29.6
1954	Navy	16:04.4
1955	Cornell	15:49.9
1956	Cornell	16:22.4
1957	Cornell	15:26.6
1958	Cornell	17:12.1
1959	Wisconsin	18:01.7
1960	California	15:57.0
1961	California	16:49.2
1962	Cornell	17:02.9
1963	Cornell	17:24.0
1964	California	6:31.1***
1965	Navy	16:51.3
1966	Wisconsin	16:03.4
1967	Pennsylvania	16:13.9
1968	Pennsylvania	6:15.6
1969	Pennsylvania	6:30.4
1970	Washington	6:39.3
1971	Cornell	6:06
1972	Pennsylvania	6:22.6
1973	Wisconsin	6:21
1974	Wisconsin	6:33
1975	Wisconsin	6:08.2
1976	California	6:31.0

NAAO Champions

Quarter-mile Single Sculls

1891	Joseph Bergin
1892–1908	No competition
1909	Fred Fuessel
1910	William Mehrhof
1911	E. B. Butler
1912	E. B. Butler
1913	R. Dibble
1914	E. B. Butler
1915	Walter M. Hoover

1916	T. J. Rooney
1917-18	No competition
1919	John B. Kelly
1920	John B. Kelly
1921	Walter M. Hoover
1922	Louis Zoha
1923	W. E. Garrett Gilmore
1924	A. E. Fitzpatrick
1925	A. E. Fitzpatrick
1926	Walter M. Hoover
1927	Joseph Wright, Jr.
1928	W. E. Garrett Gilmore
1929	E. J. McGreal
1930	A. E. Fitzpatrick
1931	E. J. McGreal
1932	W. E. Garrett Gilmore
1933	A. E. Fitzpatrick
1934	Georg von Opel
1935	Erwin Konrad
1936	Erwin Konrad
1937	Frank Silvio
1938	Joseph Hutton
1939	Frank Silvio
1940	Frank Silvio
1941	Arthur Gallagher
1942	Howard McCreesh
1943	Arthur Gallagher
1944-45	No competition
1946	John J. Kieffer
1947	John J. Kieffer
1948	John S. Trinsey
1949	John J. Kieffer
1950	John B. Kelly, Jr.
1951	Harold Finigan
1952	Larry Kelly
1953	Larry Kelly
1954	Eugene Loveless
1955	William Knecht
1956	William Knecht
1957	Walter M. Hoover, Jr.
1958	Robert Huston
1959	Paul Yeager
1960	William Knecht
1961	Seymour Cromwell
1962	Seymour Cromwell
1963	Seymour Cromwell
1964	Seymour Cromwell
1965	Donald Spero
1966	Jim Dietz
1967	John Van Blom
1968	Jim Dietz
1969	Jim Dietz
1970	Jim Dietz
1971	John Van Blom
1972	John Van Blom
1973	Jim Dietz
1974	Jim Dietz
1975	Jim Dietz
1976	Jim Dietz

Single Sculls

(Association 1½-mi winners 1873–1898; championship 1¼-mi winners since 1899)

1873	Charles Meyers
1874	F. E. Yates
1875	Charles E. Courtney
1876	F. E. Yates
1877	George W. Lee
1878	George W. Lee
1879	F. J. Mumford
1880	F. J. Mumford
1881	F. E. Holmes

1882	F. E. Holmes
1883	Joseph Laing
1884	Joseph Laing
1885	Daniel J. Murphy
1886	Martin F. Monahan
1887	J. F. Corbett
1888	C. G. Psotta
1889	D. Donahue
1890	William Caffrey
1891	William Caffrey
1892	John J. Ryan
1893	John J. Ryan
1894	Ferdinand Koenig
1895	J. J. Whitehead
1896	W. D. McDowell
1897	Joseph Maguire
1898	Edward Hanlan Ten Eyck
1899	Edward Hanlan Ten Eyck
1900	John Rumohr
1901	Edward Hanlan Ten Eyck
1902	C. S. Titus
1903	Frank B. Greer
1904	Frank B. Greer
1905	Frank B. Greer
1906	C. S. Titus
1907	Harry S. Bennett
1908	Frank B. Greer
1909	John W. O'Neil
1910	William Mehrhof
1911	E. B. Butler
1912	E. B. Butler
1913	R. Dibble
1914	R. Dibble
1915	R. Dibble
1916	T. J. Rooney
1917-18	No competition
1919	John B. Kelly
1920	John B. Kelly
1921	Walter M. Hoover
1922	Paul V. Costello
1923	Edward McGuire
1924	W. E. Garrett Gilmore
1925	Walter M. Hoover
1926	Walter M. Hoover
1927	Joseph Wright, Jr.
1928	G. Chester Turner
1929	Kenneth Myers
1930	William G. Miller
1931	William G. Miller
1932	William G. Miller
1933	William G. Miller
1934	Winthrop Rutherford, Jr.
1935	C. A. Campbell
1936	Daniel H. Barrow, Jr.
1937	Joseph W. Burk
1938	Joseph W. Burk
1939	Joseph W. Burk
1940	Joseph W. Burk
1941	Theodore A. DuBois
1942	Joseph Angyal
1943	Arthur Gallagher
1944-45	No competition
1946	John B. Kelly, Jr.
1947	Theodore A. DuBois
1948	John B. Kelly, Jr.
1949	Joseph Angyal
1950	John B. Kelly, Jr.
1951	Robert Williams
1952	John B. Kelly, Jr.
1953	John B. Kelly, Jr.
1954	John B. Kelly, Jr.
1955	John B. Kelly, Jr.
1956	John B. Kelly, Jr.
1957	Thomas McDonough
1958	Paul Ignas
1959	Harry Parker
1960	Harry Parker
1961	Seymour Cromwell
1962	Seymour Cromwell
1963	Donald Spero
1964	Donald Spero
1965	William Maher
1966	Donald Spero
1967	William Maher
1968	Thomas McKibbon
1969	William Maher
1970	Jim Dietz
1971	Jim Dietz
1972	Jim Dietz
1973	Jim Dietz
1974	Sean Drea
1975	Sean Drea
1976	Sean Drea

Citizens Savings Rowing Hall of Fame

(Maintained by Citizens Savings Athletic Foundation, this hall of fame was established in 1956. It honors a variety of inductees, from single scullers to entire crews.)

Pioneer Oarsmen (1857–1871)
Ellis Ward
Gilbert Ward
Joshua Ward
W. Henry Ward

Single Sculls
Joseph W. Burk
Frank B. Greer
John B. Kelly, Sr.
John B. Kelly, Jr.
Donald M. Spero
Edward Hanlan Ten Eyck

Double Sculls
Bernard P. Costello, Jr.
Paul V. Costello
James T. Fiffer
James Gardiner
W. E. Gilmore
Duvall Hecht
Charles McIlvaine
John B. Kelly, Sr.
John Mulcahy
Kenneth Myers
Edward Hanlan Ten Eyck
William M. Varley

Single and Double Sculls
Kenneth F. Burns

Coxswains
Donald F. Blessing
Clifford Goes
Donald Grant
Cornelius S. Seabring

Crew—Strokes
Darcy Curwen—Harvard 1941–43
Peter D. Donlon—California 1926–28
D. T. Eddy—Navy 1925–26
Elwood Foote—Cornell 1904–06
John Gardiner—Pennsylvania 1899–1901
Theodore Garhart—Washington 1940–42
Francis L. Higgson—Harvard 1898–1900
Clyde King—Navy 1920–22

John Leh—Princeton 1919–21
Edward N. Packard—Syracuse 1904–06
Edward G. Stevens—Navy 1952–54
R. W. "Si" Weed—Cornell 1907–09

Crew—Oarsmen
Raymond Andresen—California 1934–35
John Collyer—Cornell 1915–17
Horace E. Davenport—Columbia 1927–29
Wayne Frye—Navy 1952–54
Howard T. Kingsbury, Jr.—Washington 1924–26
Charles Lueder—Cornell 1901–03
Arthur J. Osman—Syracuse 1914–16
Rudolph Rauch—Princeton 1911–13
Howard W. Robbins—Syracuse 1912–14
R. H. Sanford—Washington 1924–26
Frank B. Shakespeare—Navy 1942–44
Fred Spuhn—Washington 1922–24
Alexander Strong—Harvard 1910–12
Frank Strong—Harvard 1947–49
Richard Walles—Yale 1956–58

Coaches
Thomas D. Bolles—Washington 1928–36, Harvard 1937–51
Russell S. Callow—Washington 1923–27, Pennsylvania 1928–50, Navy 1951–56
Hiram B. Conibear—Washington 1906–17
Charles E. Courtney—Cornell 1885–1920
Carroll F. Ebright—California 1924–59
Richard A. Glendon—Navy 1903–22, 1929–31; Columbia 1926–28
Richard J. Glendon—Navy 1923–25, Columbia 1929–33
Edwin O. Leader—Washington 1919–22, Yale 1923–42
Harry Parker—Harvard 1963–74
James A. Rathschmidt—Princeton 1936–50, Yale 1951
Allen P. Rosenberg—St. Joseph's 1958–62, Vesper 1963–66
Norman Sonju—Cornell, Wisconsin 1947–56
J. Duncan Spaeth—Princeton
James A. Ten Eyck—Syracuse 1903–38
Alvin M. Ulbrickson—Washington 1928–56
Henry Emerson Vail—Harvard, Wisconsin 1911–28
Charles S. Walsh—Navy 1923–44

Crews
Columbia 1878
Vesper Boat Club 1900
Harvard 1914
Navy 1920
Yale 1924
California 1928
Pennsylvania Barge Club 1928
Columbia 1929
California 1932
Washington 1936
California 1948
Navy 1953
Navy 1954
Yale 1956
Cornell 1957
Lake Washington Rowing Club 1960
Vesper 1964
Stanford Crew Association 1964
Potomac Boat Club 1968

Patrons
Richard Bronson
U. T. Bradley
Asa Bushnell
Allison Danzig
Clifford Goes
Edwin Harbach
Robert F. Herrick
Horace W. McCurdy
George Pocock

Albridge C. Smith III
James D. Taylor
Ben Wallis
Dean Witter

RUGBY—On the campus of Rugby College in England there is a monument that reads: "This stone commemorates the exploit of William Webb Ellis, who, with a fine disregard for the rules of football, as played in his time, first took the ball in his arms and ran with it, thus originating the distinctive feature of the Rugby game."

The invention of the sport we call Rugby was that simple. It happened in 1823, during an intramural soccer game. According to one account, Ellis was frustrated by his failure at an attempt to kick the ball, so he picked it up and ran with it—a flagrant violation of the rules of soccer. It occurred to other students that Ellis just might have something there, and games of soccer in which running with the ball was legal became frequent at Rugby. The new sport soon became known as "Rugby's game," and in 1839 students at Cambridge University also began playing it.

By 1841 there were enough colleges active in the sport so that representatives from them got together to draw up a standard set of rules. In 1871 the English Rugby Union, an association of 17 clubs, was formed and a new, modernized code was drawn up. The Scottish Rugby Union was organized in 1873, the Irish Rugby Union in 1874, and the Welsh Rugby Union in 1881. All these groups represented amateur clubs. During the 1890s, it became common for players to be compensated for time spent away from their jobs while playing Rugby, particularly in the northern part of England. The English Rugby Union in 1893 voted against that practice, and 21 teams thereupon withdrew to form the Northern Rugby Union, which permitted the pay for broken time, though it was opposed to sheer professionalism.

The northern group became the Rugby Football League in 1922, and the two games have become rather different through the years. The amateur version, called Union

Falling player is about to throw a lateral pass to a teammate—a common sight in Rugby. (*Courtesy of Huey Photo Systems.*)

Football without pads—Rugby often seems to fit that description. *(Courtesy of Huey Photo Systems.)*

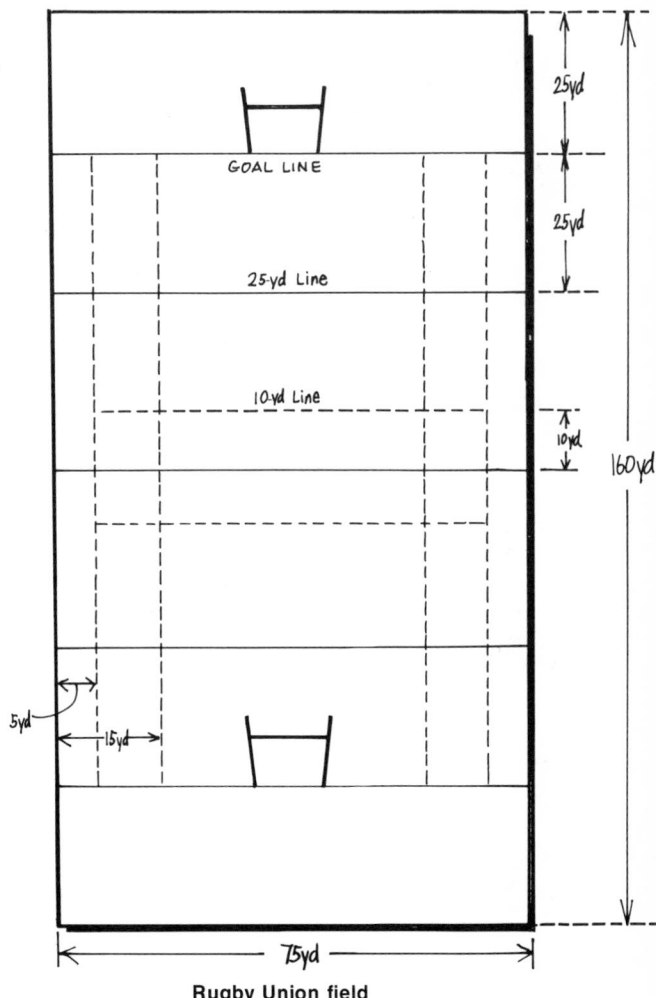

Rugby Union field

Rugby, has 15 players on a team, while League Rugby has 13 players. There are a number of rules differences, as well.

Rugby in North America. Rugby was being played at McGill University in Montreal at least as early as 1874. In the spring of that year, a team from McGill visited Harvard, which had rejected the type of football played by other American colleges at the time (essentially soccer) in favor of its own kind of football, known as the "Boston game." The teams played two games, one under Harvard's rules and the other under McGill's Rugby rules. The Harvard players enjoyed Rugby and, as a result, it helped to shape American football.

As a sport in its own right, however, Rugby has never been very popular in the United States. It did gain some impetus in 1905 and 1906, when football was being denounced as too violent. Several Pacific Coast colleges, including Stanford, dropped football and adopted Rugby instead. On the college level, Rugby is now generally played as a club sport, not a varsity sport. Various noncollege clubs also play Rugby. The major governing body is the Eastern Rugby Union of America, Inc., which awards the Clinton Blume Trophy annually to the team considered best in the country.

Field and Equipment. Rugby is played on a field with maximum dimensions of 160 yd long by 75 yd wide. The distance between the goal lines is 110 yd, and each end zone is 25 yd deep. On each goal line is a set of goalposts, similar to those used in American football. They are 18½ ft apart, and the crossbar is 10 ft above the ground.

The ball is oval-shaped, but it is much fatter than a football. It is 11–11¼ in long, 30–31 in measured in circumference, and 13½–15 lb in weight. It is inflated and covered with leather. The uniform consists of a jersey, shorts, and boots with leather studs on the bottom. Protective equipment is not worn.

Timing and Scoring. A match consists of 40-min halves, with an intermission of no more than 5 mins. The object is to score more points than the other team. A team can score by grounding the ball in the opponent's end zone (in-goal area), a feat known as a "try" rather than as a touchdown and worth 4 points in Union, 3 points in League; by place-kicking a goal after try (2 points); by making a free (penalty) kick for a goal (3 points in Union, 2 points in League); and by drop-kicking the ball for a goal during play (3 points in Union, 1 point in League). In

terms of American football, the try corresponds to a touchdown, the goal after try to an extra point, and the kicked goal to a field goal.

In order to score a try, a player must touch the ball down to the ground after crossing the opposition's goal line; this is the origin of the word "touchdown," but football no longer requires that the ball be touched down.

Progress of Play. Like soccer, Rugby is essentially a continuous-action sport. The game begins with a kickoff from the midfield line; all members of the kicking team must be behind the line and all members of the receiving team behind their 10-yd line until the ball is kicked. The ball must travel beyond the opponents' 10-yd line, after which any player may kick or dribble the ball with the feet, run with the ball, or pass it to a teammate.

There is no forward pass in Rugby for the simple reason that no member of the ball carrier's team may be in front of the ball carrier. For the same reason, there is no downfield blocking. Thus play consists largely of a series of lateral passes from one player to another; the typical Rugby pass is made underhanded, with both hands.

In Rugby, the ball is often punted on the run, especially when a team is trying to get the ball out of dangerous territory, or when protecting a lead. *(Courtesy of Huey Photo Systems.)*

When a player is tackled, the player must immediately release the ball, and it can then be picked up or kicked by any player from either team.

Players may not charge each other except with their shoulders, and a player not carrying the ball is not allowed to obstruct or charge an opponent who doesn't have possession of the ball. There are also rules against striking, tripping, and holding. The usual penalty is a free kick from the point where the infraction occurred.

After a score, the ball is again put in play by a kickoff, by the team that scored.

Scrummages and Line-outs. Play is stopped only after a score, when a penalty is called, or when the ball goes out of bounds.

If play has been stopped for a minor penalty, the ball is put in play again through a "scrummage" at the point where play was stopped. In a scrummage, at least three forwards from each team line up facing one another and then form a tunnel by leaning against one another's shoulders. Other forwards mass behind their teammates, usually forming a 3-2-3 arrangement, the players in back putting their arms around the waists of those in front of them. (The rules allow a maximum of only three players in the front row; occasionally a team will use a 2-3-2 arrangement, with the eighth forward acting as an extra back.)

A member of the team offended against, usually a player called the scrum half, now rolls the ball into the tunnel. The player must roll it midway between the two lines, not favoring the player's own teammates. Each pack of forwards pushes against the opposition and the forwards attempt to "heel" or kick the ball backward to their backs, who remain behind the scrummage line until the ball emerges.

When the ball goes out of bounds, a line-out is used to put it back in play at the spot where the ball left the playing area. The forwards line up next to one another, parallel to the goal lines, and the ball is then thrown in over their heads. They jump for the ball, attempting to get possession or to bat it to a teammate.

Players and Officials. Each team consists of 15 players, eight forwards (roughly corresponding to linemen) and seven backs (two halfbacks, four threequarter backs, and a fullback). No substitutions are permitted; if a player is injured or ejected from the game, the team must play shorthanded.

A referee and two touch judges are the officials. The referee is basically responsible for enforcing all rules and for keeping time. There is a touch judge on each sideline (called touchline in Rugby); this official's only responsibility is to signal, with a flag, when the ball or a player crosses the touchline (goes out of bounds).

RYDER CUP—An "informal" Ryder Cup golf match was played in 1926 between American and British professionals, the British winning overwhelmingly. Officially, the series dates from 1927, when the cup donated by Samuel Ryder of England was awarded to the winning United States team. The series is held in odd-numbered years, alternating between the two countries.

See also GOLF.

S

SABER—One of the three weapons used in fencing, the only one whose edge as well as point can be used for touches.

See also FENCING.

SAILING—*See* YACHTING.

SCULLING—*See* ROWING.

SEEDING—Tournament pairings are usually arranged so that the best players or teams will not play one another in early rounds. This is done by "seeding." To take an oversimplified example, assume that there are four players entered in a tennis tournament. Player A is considered the best—he or she is the first seed, or top seed. Player B is considered the second-best (the second seed). Player A is put in the top bracket, Player B in the bottom bracket so that, if they do play, it will be in the finals. If there are 64 entries in a tournament, there might be as many as 16 seeded entries, and no seeded entry would play another seeded entry until the third round of the tournament, when only 16 of the competitors remain.

See also TOURNAMENTS.

SHOOTING—In a sense, target shooting with firearms is probably just about as old as the firearms themselves. Soldiers have always been required to practice their marksmanship. But as a genuinely competitive sport, target shooting is fairly modern, simply because weapons were not accurate enough for consistent shooting until a little more than a century ago.

There are basically three kinds of target shooting: with rifle, with pistol, and with shotgun. (For shotgun target sports, *see* SKEET; TRAPSHOOTING.)

Portable guns were originally developed about the middle of the fourteenth century. The design was that of a small cannon: a short, heavy barrel on a wooden stock. A lighted fuse was applied to a touchhole at the top of the barrel to fire the weapon.

The next step was the matchlock, invented late in the fifteenth century. This was the first weapon that permitted any real accuracy of aim, since it could be steadied with both hands while it was fired. The slow-burning fuse, or match, was fitted into a serpentine—a curved lever on a pivot. When the trigger was pulled, the lever would dip the match into the touchhole. This was improved early in the sixteenth century by adding a sear and a mainspring—the first cocking device. The sear is a catch that holds the serpentine in a cocked position, counteracting the force of the compressed mainspring. When the trigger is pulled, it draws the sear back, allowing the mainspring to plunge the lighted match into the pan.

The wheel lock was invented, or at least designed, at about the same time as the matchlock. Drawings of the device were done by Leonardo da Vinci about 1483–1485. This firing device is similar to a cigarette lighter: A sear fitting into a perforation in the wheel holds it against the force of the mainspring. A hammer containing flint is cocked so that the flint rests on top of the pan cover. When the trigger is pulled, the sear is released, the mainspring makes the wheel spin, the pan cover opens, the flint contacts the wheel, and the resultant sparks ignite the powder.

The wheel lock was not considered as reliable as the matchlock, and didn't replace it. But it did make possible the first useful pistol, since a wheel lock weapon needed no lighted fuse and could be tucked away, out of sight and ready for immediate action. Invention of the pistol is credited to Caminello Vitello of Pistoia, Italy, about 1540. The pistol became an important cavalry weapon late in that century, since a horseman could hold the reins in one hand and the weapon in the other.

For nearly 500 years after the invention of firearms, improvements centered almost entirely on the firing device. The next major improvement was the flintlock, believed to have been invented by Marin le Bourgeoys of Lisieux, France, about 1600. This did away with both lighted fuse and wheel. A piece of flint, held in the jaws of the hammer, strikes against a hinged piece of steel (the battery or frizzen), sending a spark into the powder. The flintlock quickly became the most widely used firing device, and from 1700 until about 1825 most firearms were flintlocks.

Oddly, the first major improvements in accuracy were made for hunting, not for military purposes. The true rifle was developed in Germany sometime before the eighteenth century (the word is from the German *rifeln*, "to groove.") A musket or shotgun barrel is smooth; a rifle barrel has spiral grooves which impart a spinning motion to the projectile, giving it a flatter trajectory and greater accuracy.

The first truly accurate firearm was the Kentucky rifle, basically a hunting weapon. It was actually developed by Pennsylvania gunsmiths, patterned after a German rifle. The Kentucky rifle was a long, slender weapon of rather small caliber for the time (.44 to .46). The fact that it used smaller balls meant that a rifleman could stay in the field much longer with a given weight of ammunition. One of the biggest factors in the weapon's accuracy was the method of loading. The ball was somewhat smaller than the bore. The rifleman would wrap it in a greased piece of buckskin or linen before ramming it home. This wrapping acted as a lubricant, helped to clean the bore, and also made the ball fit snugly, resulting in high velocity and long range. Even a good shot, using a musket of the time, could just about hit a barn door at 100 yd; a good Kentucky rifleman could kill a man at 200 yd. Stories of experts who could make five consecutive shots touching a silver dollar at 100 yd are accepted as true.

The Percussion Cap. The final basic step in developing the modern firing device was the discovery by Alexander Forsyth, a Scots clergyman, that detonating powder (fulminate of mercury) could be used to fire a charge of powder. Forsyth's discovery, in the early nineteenth century, allowed instantaneous discharge, which improved accuracy. It also ultimately led to the breech-loading weapon as a feasible replacement for the muzzle-loader.

Joshua Shaw of Philadelphia developed the percussion cap about 1816 by filling a copper cap with a small amount of detonating powder. This cap could be slipped over a small, pierced nipple that led to the powder compartment. The cap, in turn, led to the development of the self-contained cartridge, first made of heavy paper and then, in 1847, of metal. The cartridge, which contained percussion cap, powder, and projectile in one package, led to the breech-loading gun (although a breechloader had been invented as early as 1537). The breechloader greatly increased accuracy and firepower. Increased accuracy in muzzle-loaders had already been achieved through use of the Minié ball, a conical, "sugar-loaf" bullet developed by Capt. C. E. Minié of the French army about 1840.

First Target Guns. The many developments that helped produce accurate firearms also made genuine competitive target shooting a possibility, and during the 1840s the first pure target guns were produced. They were rather short weapons, with very heavy barrels (up to 30 lb) for stability. Many of them were equipped with telescopic sights. Because of their weight, these target rifles were usually rested on benches or logs and fired at an aiming point at a known distance. The object of competition was usually to produce the smallest grouping of a predetermined number of rounds. Matches for side bets of $500 to $1,000 were not unusual.

One of the top marksmen of the period was Hiram Berdan, a mechanical engineer who was considered the New York State champion. When the Civil War broke out, Berdan became a colonel in the Union army and formed two regiments of 1,800 sharpshooters. Many of the sharpshooters carried their own weapons. Berdan himself, using his private target gun during exhibitions for his troops, often placed five shots in a 10-in circle at a range of 600 yd.

On April 5, 1862, at Yorktown, Berdan's sharpshooters silenced Confederate cannon by picking off the gun crews, one by one, at a distance of a quarter-mi. As the war went on, other troops learned to shoot reasonably well, and the importance of accurate marksmanship was gradually recognized by military leaders who had been steeped in principles of strategy and tactics that dated from an earlier era.

The Franco-Prussian War, which began in 1870, was also persuasive. The French army, considered the best in Europe, used muzzle-loading muskets; the Prussians, using much more accurate breech-loading rifles with self-contained cartridges, beat back the attempted French invasion and, within six months, captured Paris.

National Rifle Association. In 1859 the National Rifle Association of Great Britain had been formed to supervise competitive shooting in that country. One of its primary purposes was to bolster Britain's military strength by developing a trained and ready assortment of marksmen. The NRAGB constructed an elaborate rifle range at Wimbledon in 1860, with targets ranging up to 1,000 yd from the firing lines.

In the United States the *Army and Navy Journal* called for a similar organization with similar purposes, and the result was the incorporation of the National Rifle Association on November 17, 1871. The first president was Maj. Gen. Ambrose E. Burnside. On April 25, 1873 the NRA opened its impressive Creedmoor range on Long Island. The association's first annual matches were held on October 8 of that year.

United States vs. Ireland. The Irish shooting team won Great Britain's coveted Elcho Shield in 1873, and the Irish almost immediately issued a challenge to any American team for a match to take place in the United States. The Amateur Rifle Club, an affiliate of the NRA, accepted the challenge. And two arms companies, Remington and Sharps, produced special long-range rifles for the Americans to use. The match, with six men to a team, took place on September 26, 1874 at Creedmoor. With some incredible last-round shooting by Col. John Bodine, who hit three bull's-eyes on his final three shots, the United States won, 934-931.

The following year, the United States handily won a return match, in Ireland, 968-929. By now, American marksmen were national heroes, and target shooting quickly became a national sport; shooting clubs and state rifle associations formed rapidly, often as NRA affiliates.

Small-bore Shooting. The NRA's prime interest at first was in target shooting with long-range rifles. But target shooting with small-bore rifles—in the .22- to .38-caliber range—had long been a popular sport in the American Midwest. Brought to the country about 1850 by immigrants from Germany and Switzerland, the *schuetzen* match had evolved to the point where the weapons were specially made target rifles, fired from the standing position at ranges of up to 200 yd. The first shooting club in the United States was a North American *schuetzenbund* formed in 1865. By the turn of the century, this club had more than 130,000 members, and was active in promoting shooting events at indoor galleries. By that time the usual small-bore weapon was a .22-caliber rifle.

The NRA became involved in small-bore shooting in 1908, when it created classes for college and schoolboy marksmen. In 1909 the association accepted a challenge from the Miniature Rifle Association of Great Britain to take part in an international small-bore match, with the teams to compete on identical ranges in their own countries, comparing results by telegraph.

Small-bore shooting became increasingly more important, nationally and internationally, because it was much easier to find an indoor gallery than an outdoor, long-distance range. And during the Depression, the .22-caliber ammunition was by far the cheapest available, so small-bore shooting increased while other forms of shooting were declining.

World War II also disrupted high-power rifle shooting, because ammunition was impossible to get. The NRA tournament was not held in 1942–1945, but it resumed in 1946, with small-bore shooting. High-power rifles didn't return to the competition until 1951. High-power shooting has made something of a comeback since then, but the small-bore rifle is still by far the most popular weapon among target shooters today.

Pistol Shooting. Except for some use by the cavalry, the pistol was a relatively unimportant weapon until Samuel Colt (1814–1862) produced the first practical revolver. There was an exception, in France, where a rifled dueling pistol was produced early in the nineteenth century. Pistol shooting at indoor galleries became especially popular in Paris.

In the United States, it was the Wild West show of the post-Civil War period that helped to popularize the pistol. Colt's "Frontier" or "Peacemaker" revolver had been important in the West, since it could be easily fired by a man on horseback, and shooting exhibitions such as those staged by "Buffalo Bill" Cody popularized its use. Another popularizer was Ira Paine, an expert shot with pistol, rifle, or shotgun. Paine specialized in demonstrations of handgun skill, and during the 1880s he brought the sport to the East Coast, where it had been virtually unknown.

The U.S. Revolver Association was formed in 1900 to supervise the sport. Its first national matches were held in that year, and in 1901 the USRA held its second annual matches in conjunction with the NRA annual matches. In 1906 the NRA held its own pistol championships for the first time.

International Competition. Dual and triangular international meets of the type popular during the late nineteenth century have virtually disappeared. However, target shooting has been established as a major international sport through the International Shooting Union (ISU), which conducts world championships.

Shooting was an event at the first modern Olympic Games, in 1896, but United States shooters didn't enter the Olympics until 1908, under the sponsorship of the NRA and USRA. The NRA is the organization that officially represents the United States in the ISU and, through the U.S. Olympic Committee, in the International Olympic Committee.

Types of Competition

A major shooting match offers competition in a wide variety of classes, based on the experience of the shooter as well as on the type of weapon and type of shooting called for. International rules don't allow telescopic sights in small-bore shooting, but they are allowed in most American competitions.

Small-bore Rifle. The target rifle used in small-bore competition is made especially for the purpose, and special weapons are made for various types of this competition: prone, position, and "free," the last-named for international shooting.

In NRA prone competition, each competitor fires 40 shots, at 50 yd, 50 m, or 100 yd. There is a time limit of 1 min per shot.

Three- or four-position shooting, generally known as "position" shooting, involves the same number of shots (usually 40) from the prone, standing, and kneeling positions and sometimes from the sitting position. There is a time limit of 1 min per shot from the prone position, 1½ min per shot from the other positions.

International small-bore rules provide for a 60-shot prone match and a 120-shot three-position match. A six-hour period is allowed for the course—only 20 shots an hour, or 3 min per shot. The main reason for the long time allowance is that the only restrictions on the rifle are that

it must not weigh more than 8 kg (17.6 lb) and it must have metallic (nontelescopic) sights. On these "free rifles," almost everything is adjustable, for the most efficient possible shooting from each of the positions, and extra time is allowed so the competitor can make all the necessary adjustments.

Small-bore targets vary in size, according to the range at which they are to be used. The NRA 50-yd target has an X-ring with a diameter of .39 in, and a 10-ring of .89 in. The 100-yd target has a 1-in X-ring and a 2-in 10-ring. If two shooters are tied at the end of a match, the one with the most X hits wins. Perfect scores are not unusual, and the X hits usually have to be used to break ties. The ISU 50-m target has a .039-in X-ring and a .488-in 10-ring.

Big-bore Rifle. At one time high-power rifles were as big as .50-caliber, but "big-bore" now simply means more than .25-caliber, and virtually all big-bore weapons used in target shooting are only .30 caliber.

There are classes for four kinds of rifles: service rifle, match rifle, bullgun (or long-range, with no limit as to caliber or trigger weight), and international "free rifle." The service rifle is currently the M-14. The match rifle must be of a military caliber, either the 30/06 of the former service rifle, the M-1, or the 7.62-mm (.308 caliber) of the M-14. The match rifle must have a 3-lb trigger pull, the service rifle a 4½-lb.

Ranges are from 200 to 1,000 yd; the most common are 300-yd and 300-m. All international shooting is at the 300-m range. The target has a 1.968-in X-ring and a 3.937-in 10-ring.

The most important course of fire used in United States competition is the National Match Course, which consists of 10 shots standing, and 10 shots rapid-fire, standing to sitting, at 200 yd; 10 shots rapid-fire, standing to prone, at 300 yd; and 20 shots slow-fire, prone, at 600 yd. The targets have a V-ring instead of an X-ring and a black bull's-eye which counts 5 points instead of 10. The short-range A target, for 200 or 300 yd, has a 4-in V-ring and a 12-in bull's-eye. The long-range B target has a 12-in V-ring and a 20-in bull's-eye. The C target, for 1,000 yd, has a 20-in V-ring and 36-in bull's-eye.

Benchrest Shooting. This unusual type of shooting, based on the match-rifle techniques used between 1840 and 1880, has shown some growth in recent years and is governed by the National Benchrest Shooter's Association.

There are very few restrictions on the rifles used. Barrels must be at least 18 in long, and firing mechanisms must be manually operated. There are four classes. Bench rifles have no other restrictions. Heavy-varmint rifles must weigh no more than 13½ lb, light-varmint rifles no more than 10½ lb. The sporter rifle has the same limitations as the light-varmint rifle and must be larger than .22-caliber.

Because the use of the benchrest eliminates the physical skills necessary in prone and position shooting, consistency of ammunition is of vital importance, and most benchrest shooters manufacture their own cartridges.

Most shooting is at 100 or 200 yd. Although the targets have bull's-eyes and rings, scoring is not based on them. The object is to fire five or ten shots in the smallest possible group somewhere within the target border. Target sizes are 3½ by 4¾ in at 100 yd, 7 by 7 at 200 yd, and 17 by 17 at 300 m.

Pistol Shooting. The NRA rules for pistol target shooting

conform to ISU rules, for the most part. There are separate classifications for the .45-caliber service pistol, any .45-caliber semiautomatic pistol, any center-fire pistol or revolver, and the .22-caliber pistol or revolver.

NRA courses of fire and target sizes are:

- 50-ft slow-fire—.9-in 10-ring.
- 50-ft timed or rapid-fire—1.8-in 10-ring.
- 20-yd slow-fire—1.12-in 10-ring.
- 20-yd timed or rapid-fire—2.25-in 10-ring.
- 25-yd slow-fire—1.70-in 10-ring.
- 25-yd timed or rapid-fire—1.70-in 10-ring.
- 50-yd slow-fire—1.70-in X-ring, 3.39 in 10-ring.
- 50-m international—1.97-in 10-ring.

There is also an international rapid-fire target, with a stylized human shape marked with oblong scoring rings. Used at 25 m, it is 63 by 17¾ in, with a head 8¾ by 5⅞ in. The 10-ring is 5⅞ by 4 in.

Exact times allotted for the various courses vary somewhat. Generally speaking, in slow-fire the competitor is given 1 min for each shot, in rapid-fire 2 sec per shot, and in timed-fire 4 sec per shot.

The international slow-fire course, at 50 m, allows 20 min for each series of 10 shots, for a total of 60 shots in 2 hr. The rapid-fire course, at 25 m, consists of 60 shots, broken into groups of 20, with 8, 6, and 4 sec, respectively, for each shot in a group.

The shooter's stance is specified strictly in this type of shooting. The gun must be held in one hand only.

Combat Courses. Formal shooting has been criticized as having little practical purpose, and the combat courses of fire are considered by many to be much better tests of real skill. In combat courses the target represents a man or the vital areas of a man's body. The standard combat target is 30 by 18 in, with a 10-in X-ring. Silhouette targets are also often used.

There are many kinds of combat courses, including one developed for FBI training, which involves shooting a total of 50 rounds from a number of different positions at ranges of 60, 50, 25, and 7 yd. The course simulates a gradual advance on an enemy, with the shooter using barricades for cover at two points.

One of the most highly considered combat courses is the Mexican Defense Course, which involves six strings of six shots each, with 5 sec per string. Six silhouette targets are lined up, side by side. Each string begins with the shooter, pistol holstered, walking away from the targets. The shooter begins at an 8-m firing line; when one foot touches the ground beyond the 10-m firing line, a whistle sounds and the clock starts. The shooter must bring the other foot across the line, pivot, draw, and fire. On the first string, six shots are fired at one target. On the second, one shot is fired at each target. On the third, the shooter advances while firing six shots at one target; the first shot must come from beyond the 10-m line, the second when at least one foot is inside the 10-m line, and the sixth when both feet are inside the 8-m line. On the fourth string, the shooter fires one shot at each target, advancing in the same way.

There are also a number of "man-to-man" combat courses, in which contestants compete against each other in pairs, elimination-style. The oldest and best-known is the FBI's walk-and-draw duel. This contest uses two targets, usually 12-in circles. The two contestants stand side by side, facing the targets at a range of 25 yd, with holstered weapons. On command, they begin walking toward the targets. At any time before they reach the 5-yd mark, the judge may order them to fire, at which point they draw and begin shooting until a target is hit. The first shooter to hit a specified target wins; electronic timers are usually used, and hits within .05 sec of one another are considered ties. A contestant must achieve two or three clear wins over an opponent to win a match. If both contestants empty their weapons without a hit, they reload and continue firing.

Techniques of Shooting

The Rifle. There are three basic components to rifle shooting: sighting properly, holding the rifle steady, and squeezing the trigger without disturbing the aim.

There are several types of iron sights, but they all have the same basic principle: A bead (or post) on the front sight covers the aiming point, and this bead is then aligned correctly with the back sight, either centered in an aperture or "balanced" on a post. The preferred combination for target shooting has aperture (or "peep") sights in both front and back, and the shooter aims by centering the front aperture in the rear peep circle.

Telescopic sights are the best target sights, not only because the shooter gets an enlarged view of the target, but because only one sign—usually crosshairs, but sometimes a dot or a post—must be aligned.

The first step in proper aim is sighting in the rifle. The sights must be adjusted for the specific shooter, the type of cartridge, and the range. Further sighting in must be done for specific wind conditions found at the site of competition. (In virtually every competition, a shooter is

Jack Sicola won the 1974 National high-power rifle championship at Camp Perry, Ohio. (*NRA Photo by Steve Hines.*)

allowed a certain number of sighting-in shots before firing competitive rounds.)

There are basically five competitive shooting positions, and in each position the shooter must get the steadiest possible support for the weapon while aiming and firing.

The prone position is the steadiest. The shooter lies on the stomach, with body at an angle of 30 to 45 degrees to the line of aim. The legs are well spread, with the insides of both feet flat on the ground. The left elbow is directly beneath the rifle, the right elbow braced solidly on the ground.

The next steadiest position is sitting. The shooter faces about 45 degrees from the line of aim and leans forward, toward the target, with the left elbow directly underneath the rifle. The flat part of the arm, just above the elbow, is steadied on the flat part of the shin just below the left knee. The right forearm, just below the elbow, is rested on the right thigh, just above the knee. Some shooters stretch their legs out, somewhat, digging their heels in for balance; others like to cross their legs lightly at the ankles.

The kneeling position at first glance looks quite similar to the sitting position. The major difference is that the right knee must be touching the ground, so there is absolutely no support for the right elbow, which must be allowed to sag to the most comfortable possible position. The left leg is extended to the limit of comfort, with the foot flat on the ground; the buttock rests on the inside surface of the right foot.

The standing, or "offhand," position is the most difficult of all. The shooter stands at right angles to the target, with feet comfortably apart for good balance. The upper right arm should be horizontal, the elbow level with the top of the shoulder. There are two variations: In the Army standing position, there is no support for the left elbow; in the NRA standing position, the left elbow rests on the hip, and the left forearm is in a vertical position between the hip and the rifle. The heel of the palm is just ahead of the trigger guard.

The fifth position is strictly for target shooters and is used primarily in international free-rifle competition. It is a variation of the NRA standing position. The difference is that the free rifle is equipped with a palm rest that projects 3 to 4 in from the bottom of the rifle. The left elbow is on the hip, but the forearm is bent forward at an angle of 30 to 45 degrees and the palm rest is cushioned in the hand, offering vertical support for the rifle.

Perhaps the most neglected fundamental of shooting among beginners is the trigger squeeze. Most experts say that the trigger should be squeezed so smoothly and steadily that the shooter doesn't know exactly when it will fire. This will prevent flinching—tightening up in anticipation of the shot, or suddenly yanking at the trigger to make the gun fire, thus disturbing the aim. Other experts, however, say that a good shooter must know exactly when the rifle will fire, especially in the more difficult shooting positions, because if the aim is wavering slightly, the shooter can gain control and release the shot only at the exact instant when on target. In any event, the trigger squeeze should be very smooth and controlled, and the trigger should be cushioned at the pad of muscle between the first and second joints of the index finger, not at the tip of the finger.

The Pistol. In most competitive shooting, the pistol must be held with one hand only, and an offhand position is used. It is used only in competitive shooting. The shooter stands at an angle of 30–45 degrees to the left of the target and extends the right arm, unsupported, straight at the target. However, the two-handed grip should be used any time it is permitted. The pistol should be held high in the hand, with the thumb pointing forward above the trigger guard, the heel of the hand directly behind the weapon. The pad between the first and second joints of the index finger should be directly in the center of the trigger curve.

Additional support is given by the left hand (in the case of a right-handed shooter). This hand is placed alongside the pistol, with the fingers together and pointing toward the target, the thumb up. The fingers are now placed overlapping those of the gun hand, with the index finger right under the trigger guard. The left thumb is used to support the right thumb.

It should be noted that the main purpose of the supporting hand is to control the recoil of the piece, not to support the gun arm. A slight variation of the grip, used for slower, deliberate fire, brings the left thumb down so the tip touches the lower part of the trigger guard. Using this grip, some shooters keep the right arm fully extended, while others have it bent at the elbow, at varying angles, to bring the gun sights closer to the eye. Some of them also keep the head upright and bring the pistol to the center of the body, while others keep the pistol to the right and cock their heads to sight down the barrel.

Most of the fundamentals of shooting—sighting in, using sights, and squeezing the trigger—apply to pistols as well as rifles. There are some differences in stance, however. Most combat shooters use the Weaver stance, developed by Jack Weaver. The shooter faces the target directly, with the left foot slightly advanced and left shoulder slightly forward. The right arm is almost straight, the left arm bent somewhat. When shooting at moving targets or at changing targets (as in the Mexican Defense Course), the shooter pivots the entire body from the waist, without moving arms and shoulders separately.

For long-range shooting (100 yd or so), the preferred stance is kneeling, which is much steadier for a pistol shooter than for a rifleman. It is similar to a rifleman's kneeling position, but the left foot is directly under the left knee. The flat part of the elbow rests just above the knee, and the right arm is extended straight out from the shoulder.

The prone position is also very steady, but is used only in freestyle competition. The shooter lies flat on the stomach, legs spread and chin tucked in toward the chest to permit proper sighting. The pistol gets primary support from the left hand, and the little finger rests on the ground. Both arms are fully extended.

The sitting position is not much used in pistol shooting. The shooter faces the target squarely, feet rather close together and knees slightly spread, and leans forward, arms fully extended, so the elbows are just beyond the knees. The upper arms are supported by the insides of the knees.

The Anatomy of Firearms

The rifle consists of four basic parts: the stock, essentially a handle; the barrel, the tube through which the bullet is fired; the action, or moving parts that fire the cartridge; and the receiver, the metal chassis that contains the action and connects the barrel to the stock.

The Stock. Usually made of wood, the stock generally extends nearly half the length of the barrel. The rear end of the stock, which is placed against the shooter's shoulder, is the butt, usually protected by a butt plate. The comb is the part of the stock where the shooter's cheek rests. The small of the stock is a narrow area where the shooter's trigger hand grips the rifle. The other hand grips the fore-end. The upper sling swivel, near the front of the stock, and the lower sling swivel, near the butt, hold the sling in place.

The Barrel. The hole through the barrel is called the bore. It is rifled, and the rifling is made up of lands, or ridges, and grooves, which are only a few thousandths of an inch deep. The bore is measured from land to land and, in the United States, is commonly measured in hundredths of an inch to express the rifle's caliber. Thus a .22-caliber rifle measures .22 in from land to land across the bore. The muzzle is the front end of the barrel and the breech is the rear opening, where the cartridge is loaded. The chamber is an enlarged portion of the bore, at the rear, where the cartridge is placed for firing.

The Action. Basically, the action consists of a trigger which, when pulled, releases a series of levers that make up the sear. When the sear is released, the mainspring pushes the firing pin forward to strike the cartridge in the chamber, firing it through the barrel. The magazine carries additional cartridges, which are pushed into the chamber by another spring.

There are many types of rifles, usually described by the type of action. The lever-action rifle is operated by a lever which is an extension of the trigger guard. When the lever is pulled down, the breech block slides back, ejecting the fired cartridge. When it is pushed up again, a new cartridge is loaded into the chamber, the breech block slides back in place, and the gun is cocked.

The falling-block action is similar, but the breech block drops vertically instead of being pulled back. The falling-block rifle is a single-shot gun, so there is no magazine.

Pump-action guns are operated by pulling and pushing the sliding fore-end to eject the old cartridge and to load a new one into the chamber.

Semiautomatic rifles use some of the power generated by one shot to prepare the rifle for the next, by loading and cocking. In high-power rifles, gas pressure pushes a piston which operates the action; in small-bore rifles, the recoil does the work.

The bolt-action rifle is probably the most familiar. A bolt handle is lifted to unlock the bolt, and is then pulled to the rear, ejecting the old cartridge, opening the action, and reloading the weapon from the magazine. The bolt is pushed forward to compress the mainspring, and the handle is then pushed down to lock it again.

The Pistol. A pistol has the same four basic parts as the rifle; in the pistol, however, they are largely all one piece. (Strictly speaking, a pistol is a handgun that will fire and reload every time the trigger is pulled; a revolver, which requires a separate pull of the trigger to reload, is not a pistol. In this section, however, I use "pistol" to mean any handgun, for convenience.)

In the so-called automatic pistol (actually a semiautomatic), the weapon's recoil ejects the used cartridge, and a new cartridge is pushed into the chamber by a spring.

The gun's butt holds the magazine, which is loaded by inserting a clip of cartridges through the base.

A revolver uses a revolving cylinder, usually with five or six chambers. When a cartridge is fired, the empty cartridge remains in its chamber and is carried away when the cylinder revolves to bring the next chamber and its cartridge into line with the firing pin.

There are two types of revolvers, single-action and double-action, and the terms are often used improperly. A single-action revolver is one that can be cocked in only one way, usually by depressing the hammer with the thumb. There are also revolvers that can be cocked only by pulling the trigger; they are single-action but are often mistakenly called double-action. A true double-action revolver can be cocked in either of two ways, by depressing the hammer or by pulling the trigger.

Most "automatic" pistols must be cocked for the first shot, after which they cock themselves until the magazine is empty. The usual method of cocking an automatic is to pull back a slide at the top of the barrel, or to depress the hammer.

Target pistols are, for the most part, highly specialized weapons. Most of them are .22-caliber semiautomatics, chambered for the .22 Long Rifle cartridge for accuracy. For very fast target shooting—as in the Olympic rapid-fire course—the pistol is chambered for the .22 short, since that cartridge results in much less recoil. The "free pistol" used in international competition is a single-shot weapon, since time is not an important factor; it also takes the .22 Long Rifle cartridge.

Cartridges. The importance of a shooter's ammunition is sometimes overlooked. The proper cartridge is especially important to the target shooter, since even minute variations can detract from the pinpoint accuracy demanded.

The cartridge case is a cylinder of brass or copper which contains the primer, the powder charge, and the bullet. The primer is the detonating explosive which, when struck by the firing pin, flashes a hot flame into the powder charge. The modern charge is of smokeless powder, which can be ignited only by a spark or a flame. When ignited by the primer, it burns rapidly, generating hot gas that expands, building up thousands of pounds of pressure per square inch and propelling the bullet through the bore of the weapon.

There are two basic types of cartridges. The rimfire cartridge is relatively easy to manufacture and is therefore inexpensive. The primer is contained in a little gutter around the rim of the cartridge case. Since the firing pin must crush the case to ignite the primer, the case has to be of very soft brass, which can't resist very high pressures. Rimfire cartridges, therefore, are manufactured only for relatively low-powered weapons.

The center-fire cartridge has the primer in a small brass cup, which is inserted into a pocket in the center of the case's head. The rest of the case can be made very strong, so center-fire cartridges are used for higher-powered weapons. This distinction is rather important in target shooting, since there is a separate category for center-fire pistols, which are usually .38- or .45-caliber. The .22-caliber target pistols used for most competition take rimfire cartridges.

The problem of which cartridge is best for which purpose causes some debate even among experts, and a number of mathematical problems are involved. For example, the type of powder used depends on the size of the cartridge and the length of the muzzle; ideally the powder should finish burning just as the bullet leaves the muzzle. If it burns out sooner, the bullet is losing velocity even before it leaves the gun. If it burns out later, it is sheer waste.

In target shooting, the problem is somewhat simpler. The target shooter knows the exact range from which the shooting is being done, and doesn't have to worry much about the drop of the bullet in flight, as long as it's consistent from one cartridge to the next. This factor can be allowed for when the sights are adjusted. Usually the shooter wants the lowest possible charge of powder, for less recoil, especially in rapid-fire courses.

In types of competition where time doesn't matter much, a shooter will use a somewhat more powerful charge. Most likely, hand-loading of ammunition will be the course followed to get the consistency desired. In general, as the range increases, the shooter will want a heavier bullet and higher velocities—not just to get the bullet to the target, as might be supposed, but because such a combination will be less affected by the wind, "heavy" air, and other factors that become more important as the range increases.

Glossary

aggregate match—A competition based on totaled scores from certain matches.

backing card—A blank card, placed a specified distance behind the target card. Comparison of bullet holes in the two cards will show judges from which firing point a crossfire came.

bull—The bull's-eye.

bullgun—A target rifle with a heavy barrel, so called because it is meant to hit bull's-eyes, not to kill bulls.

clip—A metal holder for cartridges that slips into a magazine for fast reloading.

course of fire—A specific number of shots from certain ranges, positions, and so on, making up a match.

crossfire—A shot that hits someone else's target.

dry shooting—Practice shooting with an unloaded weapon, training a shooter to grip, aim, and squeeze the trigger properly.

ejector—The mechanism that throws an empty shell or cartridge from the gun.

extractor—The part of a gun's action that removes the empty cartridge or shell from the chamber.

flyer—A shot that is widely separated from an otherwise close grouping.

fouling shots—Preliminary shots taken to foul and warm the barrel.

group—A closely spaced series of shots; or, a series of shots fired at a single point of aim, with the same sight adjustment, so they should be closely grouped.

hull—An empty cartridge case.

loading block—A container for a predetermined number of cartridges, enabling a shooter to know how many shots he or she has fired in a match; usually a wooden block with holes drilled in it to hold the cartridges.

nipper—A shot that just touches a scoring ring; the highest ring touched is the ring that counts.

muzzle velocity—The speed of the bullet at the moment it leaves the gun's muzzle.

Margaret Murdock, one of the best women competitors ever produced in the United States, has won many national titles. (*NRA Photo by Steve Hines.*)

offhand—Loosely, a standing position; sometimes used to mean the Army or NRA standing position, but more often the official international standing position.

piece—A rifle, pistol, or shotgun.

pinwheel—A shot that hits the exact center of the bull's-eye.

plinking—Informal shooting in which the shooter aims at whatever targets are available: tin cans, stumps, and the like.

re-entry match—A match that a shooter can enter more than once; a certain number of the competitor's best targets will count for the prize.

round—A cartridge or a shot; in a 10-round match, the shooter fires 10 cartridges.

sighting shots—Shots fired at a special target, before competition, to allow a shooter to adjust the sights.

small-bore—Small caliber; in organized competition, a weapon that fires a .22-caliber rimfire cartridge.

spotting scope—A small telescope used by a shooter to see where shots are hitting the target.

stage—A single range or position in a match fired at more than one range or from more than one position; in the National Match Course, for example, the 10 shots of slow fire at 50 yd constitute one stage.

string—A series of shots fired by one shooter in one session; or a group of shots forming part of a stage.

trajectory—The path of the bullet.

trigger weight—The amount of force, in pounds, required to pull the trigger back to the firing point; tested by pointing the weapon into the air and attaching a weight to the trigger.

X-ring—A small circle in the center of the target's highest-scoring ring, used to determined the winner if the score is tied. If two shooters have perfect scores, for example, the one with the most hits in the X-ring wins.

See also HUNTING; SKEET; TRAPSHOOTING.

U.S. Shooting Champions

Men's High-Power Rifle

1904	George Sayer	1937	James G. Frazer
1905	James Durward, Jr.	1938	J. M. Holland
1906	T. H. Dillon	1939	Coats Brown
1907	Willis A. Lee	1940	William J. Coffman
1908	A. D. Rothrock	1941–50	No competition
1909	H. O. Roesch	1951	Thomas R. Barnes
1910	Scott Clark	1952	Walter R. Walsh
1911	Charles M. King	1953	Don Smith
1912	No competition	1954	Clifford Tryon
1913	E. W. Sweeting	1955	Lloyd G. Crow, Jr.
1914	No competition	1956	Lloyd G. Crow, Jr.
1915	J. S. Stewart	1957	Ammon E. Bell
1916	W. H. Spencer	1958	Middleton W. Tompkins
1917	No competition	1959	Ammon E. Bell
1918	H. J. Mueller	1960	Kenneth C. Erickson
1919	T. B. Crawley	1961	Jay G. Harris
1920	H. Whitaker	1962	Earl H. Burton
1921	Otho Wiggs	1963	Middleton W. Tompkins
1922	Otto Bentz	1964	Middleton W. Tompkins
1923	L. V. Jones	1965	J. A. Clerke
1924	W. W. Ashurst	1966	E. J. Shook
1925	Charles Hakala	1967	Middleton W. Tompkins
1926	No competition	1968	Middleton W. Tompkins
1927	R. M. Cutts	1969	Theodore Fasy
1928	Carl J. Cagle	1970	Ronald G. Troyer
1929	J. B. Jensen	1971	Ronald G. Troyer
1930	S. Bartlotti	1972	Martin Edmondson
1931	Emerald F. "Tod" Sloan	1973	Ronald G. Troyer
1932–34	No competition	1974	Jack P. Sicola
1935	C. N. Harris	1975	Gary Anderson
1936	Waldo A. Phinney	1976	Gary Anderson

Women's High-Power Rifle

1969	Marina A. Geipel
1970	Pauline S. Tubb
1971	Pauline S. Tubb
1972	Betty Swarthout
1973	Pauline S. Tubb
1974	Betty Swarthout
1975	Betty Swarthout
1976	Jamie M. Trombley

Men's Small-bore Rifle

(Note: Since 1968 there have been separate championships for prone and for position shooting.)

1919	Grosvenor L. Wotkyns
1920	William H. Richard
1921	M. D. Snyder
1922	J. F. Hauck
1923	Ralph H. McGarity
1924	Francis W. Parker
1925	Thomas J. Imler
1926	No competition
1927	Ralph H. McGarity
1928	V. Z. Canfield
1929	Eric Johnson
1930	Vere F. Hamer
1931	Fred Kuhn
1932	Bradford Wiles
1933	T. P. Samsoe
1934	E. L. Lord
1935	T. P. Samsoe

1936	William B. Woodring
1937	William B. Woodring
1938	William B. Woodring
1939	Vere F. Hamer
1940	Dave Carlson
1941	Ransford Triggs
1942–45	No competition
1946	G. Wayne Moore
1947	G. Wayne Moore
1948	Arthur Cook
1949	Robert McMains
1950	No competition
1951	Mason E. Kline
1952	Robert Perkins
1953	John J. Crowley
1954	Alonzo B. Wood
1955	Viola E. Pollum
1956	J. Kenneth Johnson
1957	John Moschkau
1958	Robert K. Moore
1959	John R. Foster
1960	Alan M. Dapp
1961	Tommy G. Pool
1962	Tommy G. Pool
1963	Lones W. Wigger, Jr.
1964	Presley W. Kendall
1965	Lones W. Wigger, Jr.
1966	Lones W. Wigger, Jr.
1967	Bruce A. Meredith
1968	Donald Adams (prone)
	Lones W. Wigger, Jr. (position)
1969	Thomas Whitaker (prone)
	Lones W. Wigger, Jr. (position)
1970	David Ross III (prone)
	John H. Writer (position)
1971	John Conley (prone)
	Lones W. Wigger, Jr. (position)
1972	Presley W. Kendall (prone)
	David I. Boyd III (position)
1973	Lones W. Wigger, Jr. (both)
1974	Presley W. Kendall (prone)
	Lones W. Wigger, Jr. (position)
1975	Lones W. Wigger, Jr. (prone)
	Robert Gustin, Jr. (position)
1976	David Weaver (prone)
	Lones W. Wigger, Jr. (position)

Women's Small-bore Rifle

1941	Susan Colege
1942–45	No competition
1946	Adelaide McCord
1947	Adelaide McCord
1948	No competition
1949	Adelaide McCord
1950	No competition
1951	Elinor Bell
1952	Betty Ingleright
1953	Viola E. Pollum
1954	Elinor Bell
1955	Viola E. Pollum
1956	Viola E. Pollum
1957	Mrs. Bertie Moore
1958	Janet S. Friddell
1959	Jilann O. Brunett
1960	Jilann O. Brunett
1961	Jilann O. Brunett
1962	Jean Linton
1963	Lenore Lemanski
1964	Jilann O. Brunett
1965	Marianne M. Jensen
1966	Inez Sargent
1967	Inez Sargent
1968	Marianne M. Jensen (prone)

Margaret Thompson (position)
1969   Margaret Murdock (both)
1970   Marianne M. Vittito (prone)
        Tricia Foster (position)
1971   Tricia Foster (prone)
        Mary M. Keys (position)
1972   Margaret Murdock (prone)
        Mary M. Keys (position)
1973   Lisa S. Helbing (prone)
        Janet S. Hays (position)
1974   Lisa S. Helbing (prone)
        Gloria K. Parmentier (position)
1975   Schuyler Helbing (prone)
        Sherri Lewellen (position)
1976   Mary Stidworthy (prone)
        Sherri Lewellen (position)

Men's Pistol
1906   John A. Dietz
1907   Willis A. Lee
1908–15 No competition
1916   G. E. Cook
1917–18 No competition
1919   A. P. Lane
1920–35 No competition
1936   J. Engbrecht
1937   Charles Askins, Jr.
1938   Al Hemming
1939   Emmett E. Jones
1940   Harry Reeves
1941   Harry Reeves
1942–45 No competition
1946   Harry Reeves
1947   Huelet Benner
1948   Harry Reeves
1949   Huelet Benner
1950   No competition
1951   Huelet Benner
1952   William T. Toney, Jr.
1953   Harry Reeves
1954   Harry Reeves
1955   Huelet Benner
1956   Huelet Benner
1957   William W. McMillan, Jr.
1958   James E. Clark
1959   Huelet Benner
1960   William B. Blankenship, Jr.
1961   William B. Blankenship, Jr.
1962   William B. Blankenship, Jr.
1963   William B. Blankenship, Jr.
1964   William B. Blankenship, Jr.
1965   Donald L. Hamilton
1966   R. D. Thompson
1967   William B. Blankenship, Jr.
1968   Franklin C. Green
1969   Donald L. Hamilton
1970   Francis Higginson
1971   John A. Smith
1972   Bonnie D. Harmon
1973   Hershel Anderson
1974   Hershel Anderson
1975   Bonnie D. Harmon
1976   Bonnie D. Harmon

Women's Pistol

1941	Mildred McCarthy	1953	Margaret Culbertson
1942–45	No competition	1954	Lucille Chambliss
1946	Alice Mathews	1955	Gertrude E. Backstrom
1947	Rosalind Noble	1956	Gertrude E. Backstrom
1948	No competition	1957	Gertrude E. Backstrom
1949	Alice Mathews	1958	Gertrude E. Backstrom
1950	No competition	1959	Irma Tesch
1951	Gloria Jacobs Norton	1960	Lucille Chambliss
1952	Maria Hulseman	1961	Lucille Chambliss

1962	Gail N. Liberty	1970	Sallie L. E. Carroll
1963	Sallie L. E. Carroll	1971	Barbara J. Hile
1964	Sallie L. E. Carroll	1972	Barbara J. Hile
1965	Sallie L. E. Carroll	1973	Barbara J. Hile
1966	Sallie L. E. Carroll	1974	Barbara J. Hile
1967–68	No competition	1975	Barbara J. Hile
1969	Trude Schlernitzauer	1976	Ruby Fox

Bibliography. O'Connor, Jack et al.: *Complete Book of Shooting,* Outdoor Life Series, Harper and Row, New York, 1965; National Rifle Association: *Americans and Their Guns,* Stackpole, Harrisburg, Pa., 1967.

SHOT-PUT—A field event in which a 16-lb metal ball is thrown for distance; the "put" is the specified method of throwing, with an overhand pushing motion.
See also TRACK AND FIELD.

SHUFFLEBOARD—One of the many sports and games whose exact origin is very uncertain, shuffleboard has been traced by some writers to ancient Persia and by others to medieval England. It is certain that Shakespeare refers to "shovel board" and to "shove groat," a similar game in which groats—coins—were used as the markers. It is reasonable to assume that the game, approximately as we know it, descended at least from Shakespeare's time, but it seems to have dropped out of sight some time during the nineteenth century, to be revived as a shipboard game in the late 1870s. It then came ashore, in England, Australia, and the United States.

In 1913 shuffleboard arrived in Daytona, Florida, and quickly became popular in that general area. A number of shuffleboard courts were built in Florida parks and playgrounds, and in 1924 the first shuffleboard club was organized in St. Petersburg. By 1929 there was an American national governing body, the National Shuffleboard Association, which standardized the rules and held the first national tournament in 1931. Women competed in a national tournament for the first time in 1932.

During the Depression, many new playgrounds were built as WPA projects and increased the game's popularity, since they often included shuffleboard courts. After World War II the basic game, usually played outdoors or in a sizable indoor area, was adapted for indoor play on a surface of polished wood, with metal "pucks" propelled by hand.

It has been estimated that about 4 million people in the United States play shuffleboard with some regularity, but an accurate figure is difficult to arrive at, because much play is informal, on indoor courts in church basements, recreation halls, and the like, and has no connection with any official body.

Rules. The shuffleboard court is 52 ft long and 6 ft wide, but the actual playing surface is only 39 ft long. There is a 12-ft neutral zone in the middle of the playing area, marked by a pair of "dead lines." At each end of the playing area is a scoring triangle; the point is 3 ft from the nearer dead line, the base 13½ ft from it. Each triangle is broken up into five scoring areas: a front triangle worth 10 points, two quadrilaterals worth 8 points each, two quadrilaterals worth 7 points each, and a wide rear area marked "10 off."

Each player has four disks, or pucks. The disk has a 6-in diameter and a thickness of 1 in, and weighs 11½ to 15 oz. The cue (the stick used to propel the disk) is 6 ft, 3 in long,

Mary Luhn, who won the first National Masters tournament in 1960, is shown delivering a puck, while opponent Bess Henderson, left, looks on. (*St. Petersburg, Fla., Shuffleboard Club.*)

and has a tip shaped like a half moon, into which a disk is fitted for shooting.

Shuffleboard can be played by two persons or by two rival teams of two players each. In singles, the player with red shoots first, from the right side of the "10-off" section. That player slides a disk toward the other end of the court, attempting to score a 10. The opponent then shoots a black disk from the other side of the court, and they continue alternating until all eight disks have been shot. It is permissible to knock an opponent's disk off the court or into a different scoring area, and to move or protect one's own disks by the same procedure. However, a disk that falls short of the farther dead line is removed from play immediately. After one "end" is completed (eight disks shot by two players from the same end of the court), scores are totaled. A disk scores only if it lies entirely within a scoring area, touching no boundary lines. Players then move to the opposite end to complete the round by repeating the described routine. Game may be 50, 75, or 100 points, as prearranged by the players. A disk lying within the 10-off area results in the loss of 10 points for the owner.

In doubles, play proceeds as in horseshoes: Two opponents play against one another from one end of the court, and the other two play against one another from the other end, throughout the game.

SIDE HORSE—Now formally known as the pommel horse, a piece of gymnastics apparatus made by attaching two pommels (handles) to the long horse.

See also GYMNASTICS.

SIX-MAN FOOTBALL—Invented in 1934 by Stephen T. Epler, a Nebraska high school coach, six-man football was originally a tackle version of the game, but can also be played as touch football. It is played on a field 100 yd long by 40 yd wide, with the goal lines 80 yd apart. Each team

has a center, two ends, a quarterback, a halfback, and a fullback. A team must gain 15 yd in four downs to retain possession; the ball must be thrown, either forward or backward, before it can cross the line of scrimmage. All players are eligible to receive a pass. A touchdown counts 6 points; a conversion 2 points by kick, 1 point by run or pass; and a field goal 4 points.

The game is played at many small high schools, especially in rural areas of the Midwest. There is also an eight-man version of the sport, in which each team has two additional linemen; they and the center are ineligible to receive a forward pass.

See also FOOTBALL.

SKATE SAILING—An outgrowth of iceboating, skate sailing was quite popular for a time in areas such as Red Bank and Long Branch, New Jersey, both iceboating centers, during the 1920s and 1930s, but has since declined. National championships, inaugurated by the Skate Sailing Association of America in 1922, were last held in 1952, after a 10-yr hiatus.

The sail, which is actually a hand-held kite, is 50 to 60 ft^2 in area, stretched tight and flat over two wooden or aluminum spars, and the skates used are similar to speed skates. Races are usually conducted over a triangular course of about 1 mi in length.

SKATING —*See* FIGURE SKATING; ROLLER SKATING; SPEED SKATING.

SKEET—While trapshooting was developed more or less as a replacement for hunting, skeet evolved primarily as a practice sport to improve shooting in the field; and though skeet is an end in itself for many shooters, it still retains much of that primary quality. Skeet and trapshooting are the principal competitive sports employing the shotgun.

Unlike most sports, skeet can be pinned down to a specific place and a specific person. The person was Charles E. Davies; the place, Andover, Massachusetts. Davies, a retired businessman, operated a kennel at Andover and was also an avid upland game hunter. When he missed a shot, he would go home to practice the same shot, with the help of his son and a portable trap, a device for throwing clay targets into the air. Young Davies would set up the trap to duplicate, as closely as possible, the range and angle of flight of the bird which his father had failed to hit while hunting.

Eventually they decided to work out a method by which the trap could remain stationary, and the shooter could change his position in order to get a variety of angles, similar to those found in actual hunting. Their first plan resulted in a sport known as "shooting around the clock," on a range built in 1915. The original range had 12 shooting stations, on a circle with a radius of 25 yd. The trap was located at the twelve-o'clock position, and it threw targets toward the six-o'clock position. In 1923 the radius was reduced to 20 yd.

Then fate intervened, in the form of a neighbor who built some hen houses within range of the shooting circle. The circle had to be reduced to a semicircle, with all six positions aiming away from the hen houses. A friend, Bill Foster, suggested that two traps be used, to double the number of directions and angles possible, and he also suggested raising one of the trap houses in order to simulate the flight of a game bird going slightly down. Foster was also an outdoors writer. He publicized the new sport in national magazines, and in 1926 he started a contest with a $100 prize for the best name. The winner was Mrs. Gertrude Hurlbutt of Dayton, Montana, who suggested the name "skeet"—from the Old Norse word for "shoot." Thus "skeet shooting" literally means "shoot shooting." Within a year, skeet had caught on all over the country.

The National Skeet Shooting Association (NSSA) was organized in 1927 to govern the sport. The organization, with headquarters in San Antonio, is now supported by more than 18,000 registered skeet shooters.

The Skeet Field. The range is still a large arc of a circle, marked by two curved lines, with radii of 21 and 23 yd. On this arc there are seven shooting stands, or stations, each 3 ft square, placed at regular intervals. Targets are released from two trap houses, called "high" and "low." The first stand is at the far left—the twelve-o'clock position—between the "high house" and the center of the imaginary circle. The seventh stand is at the far right, as is the "low house." There is also an eighth stand, in the center of the field, directly between the two trap houses.

At each station the shooter gets two or four targets. Starting at the first station, he or she fires one shot at a target sprung from the left (high house) trap and then at one from the right. This first shot is an almost directly overhead one from station 1. (Targets are released from the high house at a height of 10 ft, from the low house at a height of 3½ ft. The elevation of the trap in the high house provides generally high, flat-flying targets with a trajectory that is nearly horizontal; targets from the low house are thrown on a rising trajectory.) The procedure is repeated at each station—one shot at a target from each trap, sprung consecutively. Returning to stations 1, 2, 6, and 7, the shooter then fires twice at targets thrown simultaneously from the two traps, seeking to hit both targets. This adds up to 24 shots, but a round actually

consists of 25 shots. The extra one is called "optional," but there is usually no option involved. The first time a shooter misses, a second shot at that missed target is required. If the shooter breaks the first 24 targets on consecutive shots, the additional shot is taken from station 8, at a low-house target.

Rules involving "slow" or "quick" pulls, jammed weapons, and the like are identical to those of trapshooting.

Classifications. There is no provision for handicapping, as there is in trapshooting. Skeet shoots are conducted in a number of different classifications, with shooters sorted according to ability and experience. A shooter's classification is based on a record of having shot 300 targets in registered events during the present year or the previous year. If a shooter can't meet that requirement, he or she may compete as a nonclassified shooter, ineligible to win prizes, or the shooter may compete in Class AA, with the very best shooters.

The NSSA Universal Classification system:

CLASS	12-GAUGE	20-GAUGE	28-GAUGE	.410-GAUGE
		Men		
AA	97.5% and up	96% and up	95% and up	92% and up
A	95–97.49%	92.5–95.99%	91–94.99%	86.5–91.99%
B	93–94.99%	90–92.49%	86–90.99%	78.5–86.49%
C	90–92.99%	85–89.99%	Under 85%	Under 78.5%
D	86–89.99%	Under 85%	None	None
E	Under 86%	None	None	None
		Women		
A	94% and up	92% and up	90% and up	82.5% and up
B	90–93.99%	85–91.99%	84–89.99%	73–82.49%
C	85–89.99%	Under 85%	Under 84%	Under 73%
D	Under 85%	None	None	None
		Junior		
A	96% and up	92% and up	90% and up	82.5% and up
B	90–95.99%	Under 92%	Under 90%	Under 82.5%
C	Under 90%	None	None	None

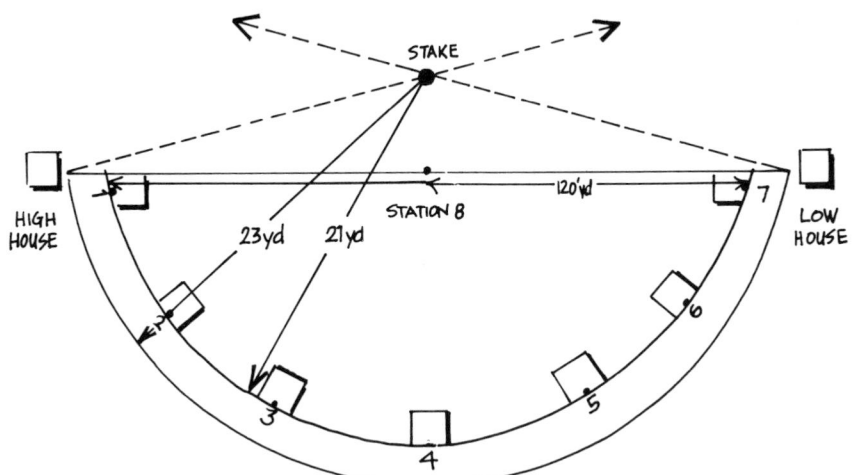

Skeet range: Dotted lines indicate paths of target. Stake indicates center of imaginary circle.

International Skeet. In the United States, skeet has been changed over the years to the point where many hunters feel it is not nearly as good training for the field as it might be. "International" skeet is very much the same as the sport that was originally worked out in the 1920s, and is excellent training for the upland game hunter.

The two major differences are, first, that the international shooter must have the butt of the gun touching the pelvic ridge when calling for the target; and second, that the target may come immediately when it is called for or the shooter may have to wait as much as 3 sec for the target's release. In addition, the target used in international skeet travels somewhat faster—it is propelled about 71 yd, not the 55 to 60 yd specified by the NSSA.

Because the National Rifle Association is responsible for selecting American teams for international competition, it sponsors the U.S. International Skeet Championships. In order to give the international version wider exposure, in 1973 the NRA held a series of 15 zonal championships to select competitors for the national championship tournament.

The NSSA also has a major international skeet competition, and there is a national intercollegiate trap and skeet tournament which features the international version of each of these American sports.

Equipment. A skeet gun can be used in the field, with some modifications, and a field gun can be used for skeet. But the serious competitive skeet shooter uses one gun just for skeet.

There is some difference of opinion over just what qualities make a good skeet gun. Generally speaking, however, it should have somewhat more weight at the front end than a field gun. A field gun is meant to be light in front, for quickness, since a game bird often makes a sudden change of direction and the hunter must be able to follow it with the gun. A skeet shooter, however, is tracking a target that moves in a predictable path, and if the front of the gun is too light, it may swing too rapidly, thus overleading the target.

Automatic shotguns are the most popular for skeet, since they have much less recoil than other types, and a skeet match is a test of endurance as well as of shooting skill. Because the range in skeet is usually about 30 yd, a tight choke is not desirable. Many skeet shooters remove all choke to get a wide pattern, and special skeet-bored guns have very little choke.

The serious skeet shooter probably competes in all four gun classes, and the differences in weight can be bothersome. A special end cap weight is available to make the lighter guns balance about the same as the heavier guns. Also available is a four-in-one gun—a gauge in which slip-in aluminum barrels can be used to create the other sizes. If a shooter uses four different guns, he or she will probably develop personal techniques of weighting to make them all feel and respond as nearly alike as possible.

Technique. The two methods of establishing lead described in the entry for trapshooting are also used in skeet. There are two major differences in technique, however: In skeet, the shooter knows at what angle the target will be traveling, and consequently doesn't have to spend any time figuring that out; and, because the target is closer, it appears to be moving faster, and requires more lead.

An experienced shooter knows at just about what point the target should be broken, and so can face toward that spot. The shooter aims the gun at a point in front of the trap house, just below the expected line of flight of the target. Then the shooter calls for the target, picks it up, establishes the lead and—if all goes well—breaks it.

Doubles shooting is similar to doubles shooting in trap. The important thing is that the shooter should first break the target going away (the outgoing one)—the high-house target at stations 1 and 2, the low-house target at stations 6 and 7—because it will get out of range if an attempt is made to shoot the incoming target first.

See also HUNTING; SHOOTING; TRAPSHOOTING.

NSSA All-Around Champions

(550 total shots except in 1946)

Men

1935	Henry Joy	517
1936	William Clayton	530
1937	Donald Sperry	537
1938	Jack Lindsey	540
1939	Robert Parker	534
1940	Felix Hawkins	544
1941	Alex Kerr	543
1942	Dick Shaughnessy	543
1943–45	No competition	
1946	Gerald Batten	347 × 350
1947	Alex Kerr	543
1948	Grant Ilseng	543
1949	Herman Ehler	544
1950	Alex Kerr	544
1951	Francis Ellis	543
1952	Louis Gordon	540
1953	Alex Kerr	541
1954	Salvador Roig	535
1955	Robert Rath	540
1956	Titus Harris, Jr.	542
1957	Alex Kerr	539
1958	Ken Sedlecky	540
1959	Barney Hartman	545
1960	William Hay Rogers	546
1961	Peter Candy	546
1962	Barney Hartman	546
1963	Marvin Hambrick	544
1964	William Sesnon III	548
1965	James Bellows	544
1966	Steve Hanzel	547
1967	James Bellows	546
1968	James Bellows	547
1969	Bob Shuley	546
1970	Tony Rosetti	544
1971	Robert Paxton	548
1972	Tony Rosetti	548
1973	Paul Laporte	547
1974	Noel Waters	548
1975	Robert Paxton	549
1976	Charles Parks	550

Women

1939	Jean Smythe	488
1940	Patricia Laursen	519
1941	Jean Smythe	527
1942	Harriet Sayre	516
1943–45	No competition	
1946	Mrs. John LaFore	326 × 350
1947	Nancy Childs	518
1948	Ann Martin Hecker	530
1949	Janice Jenkins Mason	522
1950	Ann Martin Hecker	530
1951	Ann Martin Hecker	535
1952	Nancy Burrus	513

1953	Mrs. Max Thomas	525
1954	Mrs. Leon Mandel	522
1955	Mrs. Alphonso Ragland, Jr.	522
1956	Mrs. Leon Mandel	526
1957	Thelma Anguish	507
1958	Betty Myers	523
1959	Katharine Dinning	528
1960	Katharine Dinning	527
1961	Mrs. Max Thomas	535
1962	Kathleen McGinn	535
1963	Kathleen McGinn	536
1964	Mrs. James R. Coulter	535
1965	Evelyn Jones	542
1966	Clarine Menzel	541
1967	Valerie Johnson	527
1968	Mrs. Philip D. Armour, Jr.	533
1969	Margaret Burdett	530
1970	Karla Roberts	535
1971	Karla Roberts	536
1972	Claudia Butler	542
1973	Karla Roberts	545
1974	Karla Roberts	542
1975	Jackie Ramsey	540
1976	Valerie Johnson	539

Bibliography. Nichols, Bob: *Skeet and How to Shoot It*, Putnam, New York, 1939.

SKIING—The first skis were evidently large animal bones strapped to the feet with leather thongs, and perhaps used 5,000 years ago. The Norwegian word "ski" essentially means "snowshoe," and it is possible that skis were originally used like snowshoes, to facilitate walking by distributing a person's weight over a wider area to keep the wearer from sinking into the snow.

In any event, although skiing is ancient, it was until recently used mainly as a method of crossing large areas of snow-covered country. In 1200, King Svarre of Norway equipped his military scouts with skis, and during the sixteenth century all Swedish troops were provided with skis or snowshoes. In 1721 the Norwegian army added a company of skiers; each member used a single pole both to push himself along and to control speed when going down slopes. But the major early developments occurred in a farming area, near Telemark, in Norway, where wooden skis were first introduced, and where ski racing began as a friendly sport in the early nineteenth century.

In the late 1830s, Sondre Norheim of Telemark invented the first formalized technique of turning on skis, as a method of stopping after a jump. Though now obsolete, the Telemark turn is still known to skiers. Shortly afterward the Hemmestveit brothers of Christiania (now Oslo) developed a different method of turning, still known as the "Christie." By the 1870s many Norwegian towns had periodic ski festivals featuring cross-country skiing and jumping—the traditional Nordic events of modern ski competition.

Emigrants from Norway, especially miners, began to spread the sport to other countries during the nineteenth century. The Kiandra, Australia, Ski Club was organized in 1851 by Norwegians, and shortly afterward Norwegian miners who had joined the gold rush were introducing skiing and ski racing to the California Sierras. (Races by "ski runners" in Onion Valley, California, in 1853 have been documented—but the phrase may mean foot races by men wearing "skis," or snowshoes.) By the 1880s more Norwegian immigrants were bringing the sport to Maine,

The downhill skier adopts the "egg" position to lower wind resistance as much as possible. (*F. Kelly MacNeill.*)

Michigan, New Hampshire, Minnesota, Wisconsin, Canada, and other parts of North America.

Alpine Skiing. Areas that now have some of the finest skiing in the world weren't suited for the sport—or, rather, the sport wasn't suited for them—until around the turn of the century. Skiing techniques and, to a certain extent, the equipment in use weren't easily adapted to traveling down steep slopes. The difficulty of turning to avoid small obstacles was one problem; stopping (which basically involves turning) at high speeds was even more of a problem.

An Austrian, Mathias Zardsky, began studying those problems in the 1890s. Zardsky, the first man to write a book on skiing technique and the first to become a full-time ski instructor, developed what was known as the Lilienfeld technique. Zardsky advocated a low crouch and keeping one ski at an acute angle to the fall line as means of keeping speeds low and making turning simpler. He also used a long pole for balance. Zardsky challenged a Norwegian champion to a downhill race and was soundly beaten. So he reworked his technique, advocated the use of two poles and shorter skis, and developed the "snowplow," still a basic method of turning or stopping for beginners, in which the tips of the skis are brought together and the tails spread wide apart to form a V.

The Zardsky method was much refined and popularized by Hannes Schneider of Steuben in the Arlberg section of Austria. Schneider, who became a ski teacher in 1907, developed many new methods which in aggregate came to be known as the Arlberg technique. Schneider's teachings were based largely on the principle of rotating the body in the direction of the turn, and the Arlberg technique virtually ruled skiing for nearly a half-century. Schneider was not only a pioneer in technique but a fine teacher and a great missionary of his own ideas. From his school, instructors traveled all over the world during the 1920s and 1930s.

One of his students, an Englishman named Arnold Lunn, was so enthusiastic about Schneider's methods that he developed a new kind of race to make use of them: He laid out the first slalom course in 1921. The Arlberg-Kandahar race (named for the region and for trophy donor Lord Roberts of Kandahar) was an enormous success and is still a prestigious event. Lunn also wrote a description of the race, and the type quickly became popular.

("Slalom," like "ski," is a Norwegian term; originally it meant a downhill race. Zardsky invented the single-pole slalom, in which a series of poles is set up along a downhill course, and racers have to make a turn around each pole. The slalom as invented by Lunn is described in detail later in this entry; essentially, it uses a series of two-pole "gates" through which skiers have to navigate while racing downhill.)

Skiing in North America. Ski clubs and competition originally grew up in areas in North America with large concentrations of Scandinavians. The Nansen Ski Club, the first in the United States, was organized in Berlin, New Hampshire, in 1882; the first formal jumping competition was held in Red Wing, Minnesota, in 1887; and the National Ski Association was formed in Ishpeming, Michigan, in 1904.

Ski clubs sprang up rapidly in eastern Canada around the turn of the century, and a trip to the Montreal Ski Club stirred a number of Dartmouth students to form the Dartmouth Outing Club in 1909. Dartmouth beat McGill University of Montreal in 1913 in the first intercollegiate competition. For a long time Dartmouth led in the introduction of new ideas and techniques in the United States; for example, in 1923, just two years after the world's first slalom race, Prof. Charles Proctor of Dartmouth laid out the first slalom course in the country. The proximity of the college probably had something to do with the establishment of the first full-scale skiing school in the country, at Franconia, New Hampshire, where Katherine Peckett in 1929 assembled a staff of European instructors.

The real boost for skiing in this country, however, came in 1932, when the third Winter Olympics were held in Lake Placid, New York, which had been a major winter resort since 1904. About $1 million was spent, during the depth of the Depression, getting the area ready for the Olympics, and all winter sports benefited from the publicity. The introduction of Alpine skiing, new techniques, and experienced instructors—many of them former pupils of Hannes Schneider—quickly followed, and stirred remarkable enthusiasm for the sport.

As more mountainous areas added ski slopes, attention turned to the problem of getting up the hill. A rope tow, driven by a motorcycle engine, was developed by the Swiss Gerhard Mueller in 1932; the first rope tow in the United States was installed at Woodstock, Vermont, in 1934, and the idea quickly spread across the country. In 1936, Fred Pabst of Wisconsin invented the J-bar for transporting a skier up a slope. Meanwhile the chair lift was developed for the most ambitious project of all—the development of Sun Valley, Idaho, as a ski resort. Union Pacific Railroad developed the site at a cost of more than $3 million, and its engineers hit on the idea of suspending a series of tandem chairs from a cable to give skiers a quick, comfortable ride up.

Another major area that opened to skiing in the mid-1930s was the Berkshire Hills region of Massachusetts. Thunderbolt Trail at Mount Greylock in the Berkshires and Taft Trail at Franconia were the first trails developed specifically for Alpine racing in this country. When the Eastern Downhill Championships were held at Mount Greylock in 1938, more than 6,000 spectators turned out.

In 1939, Hannes Schneider left his native Austria, which had been taken over by Nazi Germany, and arrived in North Conway, New Hampshire, to set up a ski school. Schneider's influence had already affected American skiing; his presence, and the flow of skiers and instructors from his school, were to have even more impact after World War II.

The first modern downhill races in the United States were run in the early 1930s: the Silver Skis at Mount Rainier, Washington, and the Inferno, at Mount Washington, New Hampshire. In 1940, promoters at Mount Lincoln, California, discovered that a downhill race had been held in California in 1854, with a silver-studded belt awarded to the winner, and so the Silver Belt downhill race was established—still a major event on the U.S. ski calendar.

World War II brought a lull, of course, but after the war many American servicemen discovered the pleasures of skiing in Central Europe and returned to the United States as confirmed enthusiasts. Postwar prosperity and the increase of leisure time have also contributed to the growing popularity of the sport in this country.

Types of Competition

Alpine. The Alpine skiing events, as the name implies, were developed on rather steep slopes. The three major events—downhill, slalom, and giant slalom—all emphasize maneuverability at relatively high speeds. The fastest event is the downhill, in which speeds may exceed 80 mph; the slalom, on the other hand, emphasizes maneuverability, and speeds are seldom much higher than 25 mph.

The original downhill races used the "geschmozzle" start: All the skiers would line up, side by side, at the top of a hill and race to a finish line. It was exciting—and dangerous. Almost all modern downhill races are strictly against time, with skiers racing individually. The course for world and Olympic championships has a drop of from 800 to 1,000 m for men, 500 to 700 m for women. (The "drop" is the vertical distance between the highest and lowest points.)

Although speed is of the essence, a course is also designed to test a skier's reactions and maneuverability, since the competitor must go over or avoid various natu-

This is a giant slalom course at Lake Placid, New York, site of the 1932 Winter Olympics and selected again for the 1980 Games. (*F. Kelly MacNeill.*)

ral obstacles: gullies, ditches, bumps, and the like. The course is also marked by "obligatory gates," sets of flagsticks 8 m or more apart, through which the skier must pass or be disqualified.

The slalom course is made up of a series of gates, each marked by a pair of poles, 1.8 m high and 3.2 to 4 m apart, through which the skier must pass. Both feet must pass between the poles; if a gate is missed, the skier must climb back and go through it properly or be disqualified. A slalom race generally consists of separate runs over two courses by each competitor; results are determined by the combined times. Courses are set just two hours before race time, and a competitor is allowed to examine the course only while on the way to the top of the hill for the run.

Setting a slalom course is an art in itself. By placing the gates, the setter should try to make the course a challenge without making it unfair. Certain combinations of gates are set up to demand special techniques from the skiers. A gate with an opening directly across the fall line (the hill slope, or line of descent) is "open"; if the opening is parallel to the fall line, the gate is said to be "closed" or "blind." Two successive blind gates constitute a "hairpin," three of them a "flush." An "H," as the name implies, consists of two blind gates sandwiching an open gate.

In world-championship competition, there are 55 to 75 gates for men, 40 to 60 for women; drops are 180 to 220 m for men, 120 to 180 for women, and one-fourth of the course must have a gradient of 30 degrees or more.

As racing continues, the slalom becomes more difficult because of the ruts and marking left by earlier skiers. Consequently, skiers are organized into seeds of 15 each, with the 15 top-seeded skiers racing first. They draw lots for the order of start. In the second run, they reverse that order; the skier who started fifteenth on the first run starts first on the second run.

The giant slalom, a newer event, is similar to the slalom but emphasizes cross-hill skills. There are 30 or more gates, 4 to 8 m wide, set up so that the skier has to spend a good part of the time skiing across or even slightly up the hill. The drop is 400 to 600 m for men, 300 to 450 m for women in world championships.

The Alpine Combined is a "paper race," based on the results of one slalom, one downhill, and one giant slalom.

Nordic. Although skiing in the United States originally emphasized the Nordic events, Alpine skiing took over nearly 50 years ago, and Nordic skiing is not particularly prominent in this country now, although it has been making something of a comeback.

Ski jumping, in the Nordic category, is one of the most exciting sporting events to watch. Jumping results are based on a combination of distance and style. Style is now judged only in flight and on landing. There are five judges, and each judge gives a skier 20 points before the run; points are then subtracted for various faults. Generally a small fault or a more serious fault that is quickly corrected draws a penalty of from ½ to 2 points; a serious fault that is not corrected draws a penalty of 2 to 4 points.

Among in-flight faults are bending the knees, hips, or back; having poor body position; and carrying the skiis too high, too low, too wide, unsteadily, or crossed. The most serious errors on landing are touching the snow or the skis with one or both hands. Touching with one hand calls for a penalty of 2 to 4 points; touching with both

hands, if the jumper rises quickly, 8 points; touching with both hands and not rising again, or falling, calls for a 10-point penalty. Minor landing faults include keeping the body too stiff, too far back, or too bent; unsteadiness; not using the Telemark position; and preparing for landing prematurely.

The highest and lowest scores are thrown out, and the three in-between scores are totaled. Thus a perfect jump would gain a total of 60 style points—20 points from each of the three judges whose scores count.

In major meets, each competitor is given three jumps. The first is an optional trial which is not scored. The points scored for the two required jumps are totaled to determine final standings.

Each hill is given a certain rating, and that rating, plus 10 percent, is a 60-point jump. On a hill rated at 70 m, for example, a jump of 77 m would be worth 60 points. Jumps falling short of the specified rating plus 10 percent are graded by substracting from 60, on the basis of a "points-per-meter" table that depends on the hill rating. The table:

Hill Rating	Points per Meter
Under 40 m	2.0
40.5–60 m	1.8
60.5–70 m	1.6
75.5–90 m	1.4
90 m and up	1.0

In world-championship competition, two jumping hills are used, one a "normal" hill, rated at about 70 m, the other a "big" hill, rated at 80 to 90 m. Ratings are based on the distance between takeoff and the hill's so-called critical point, which is the approximate halfway point of the straight section on which skiers normally land. Beyond the critical point, landing becomes more and more difficult.

"Ski flying," incidentally, is not a separate sport. It is ski jumping on very big hills, rated up to 120 m.

The second Nordic event, cross-country skiing, is simply racing on skis over open country, at distances ranging from 5 to 50 km (approximately 3 to 30 mi). Men usually race a relay of 40 m, with four skiers; the women's relay is usually 15 m with three skiers.

The race should be run over fairly ordinary ground, approximately one-third level, one-third uphill, and one-third downhill. Maximum ranges of height are 100 m on a 5-km course, 150 m on a women's 10-km, 200 m on a men's 10-km, and 250 m on a course 15-km or longer.

Cross-country skiers don't race head-to-head; they start one at a time, at intervals of 30 to 60 sec, and race against the clock.

The Nordic Combined competition is based on the contestants' finish in the 15-km cross-country race and the "normal" hill jumping. In some cases there are special Nordic Combined titles using results of the longer cross-country races, and these are specially identified. There might be, for example, a 15-km Nordic Combined and a 30-km Nordic Combined title at the same meet.

Equipment

Skis. To a great extent, the history of skiing is the history of ski development. The modern ski is carefully designed and built for its special purpose, and different types of skis are used for different purposes.

Basically, a ski still looks like a long board, 6 to 8 ft in length and 3 to 4 in wide, tapered and turned up at the forward tips. Modern skis are made of laminated wood (often ash and hickory), fiberglass, plastic, metal, or a combination of materials. A ski is arched upward (cambered) slightly at the center, to equalize distribution of weight over the total surface, and it also has a certain side camber so the edges can be used to bite into the snow on turns. A groove down the center of the ski helps to keep the ski on a straight path. Bottoms are usually of plastic, which slides over snow better than other materials.

For downhill racing, skis are built for straight speed: long, wide, and heavy, with little side camber. Slalom skis are short, light, and narrow and have more side camber, for better maneuverability. Jumping skis are long, wide, and heavy, and they usually have three center grooves. Cross-country skis are very light and narrow and don't have metal edges.

Boots and Bindings. Because they are the skier's link with the skis, and the means by which the skier controls the skis, boots and bindings are very important. Plastic boots have become quite popular because of their rigidity and durability. Boots are also made of plastic and leather laminate. Another recent development is the molded boot, which may be a single piece of synthetic or other material or two pieces hinged at the ankle for greater mobility. Leather boots are not as common as they were in the 1960s, but many skiers still prefer them. The leather boot is, in fact, two boots: a soft, comfortable inner boot fitted into a stiff outer shell that supports the ankle.

The type of skiing to be done also determines the type of boot. A downhill racer wants an exceptionally stiff boot, perhaps of the one-piece molded type. A slalom skier usually wears the double boot, with a steel shank in the sole. A cross-country racer uses a very light, flexible boot cut below the ankle, and a jumper uses a specially made lightweight boot with a lot of flex at the ankle, which permits the contestant to get the proper forward lean.

The bindings are the link between boot and ski, and are now almost always release bindings, which will automatically release the skier's feet in a fall, so the ski itself cannot cause injury. There are a number of different mechanisms in use, and many of them are still undergoing design improvements. The most convenient is a step-in boot-lock mechanism that grips the boot when the skier steps into the ski; the skier doesn't have to bend down to put skis on, and the toe and heel mechanisms work together as a unit, both in locking and in releasing.

It is extremely important that bindings be properly adjusted for the individual skier, and that the adjustment be checked frequently. Placement of the release on the ski must be accurate. The toe of the boot will be just behind the center of the ski for beginners and possibly for slalom racers; an advanced skier's will be about $\frac{1}{2}$ in farther back, and a downhill skier's about 1 in farther back.

A cross-country ski racer needs to be able to lift the heel off the ski, and consequently uses just a special toe clamp.

Poles and Other Equipment. Although the pole is a much simpler item of equipment, there's a wide variety on the market. The best ones are made of aluminum alloy, high-grade steel, or wound fiberglass bound in epoxy resin. A recent development is a pole with a top half of aluminum and a lower half of steel. Good poles have points of very hard steel or, in a few cases, titanium.

The snow baskets can also be made in a number of ways. The better ones are of high-quality rubber molded around an aluminum tube; cheap ones are often simply molded plastic. Pole grips may be made of neoprene (synthetic rubber), vinyl chloride, or polyethylene plastic.

A downhill or slalom racer wants the lightest, strongest poles obtainable. A cross-country racer will probably use old-fashioned, treated bamboo poles with snow baskets of rattan and metal tips set at an angle. However, aluminum poles have been specially developed for cross-country racing as well.

A rule of thumb in pole selection is that a person who is 5 ft, 8 in tall should use poles of 48 to 50 in long. For every additional 2 in of height, the pole should be 1 in longer. A cross-country skier, however, uses poles about 6 in longer than the rule would indicate.

Other items of equipment needed by the skier are safety straps, which keep the skis from traveling too far when they release in a fall; sunglasses or goggles, to protect the eyes against wind and against the glare of sun on snow; and wax, which is applied to ski bottoms to keep them from sticking to the snow. Modern plastic soles, however, need little or no waxing.

Competitive Techniques

Downhill. The downhill skier's technique is basically one of feel for snow and quick reaction, based on experience. The basic position is relatively simple: the tuck, or "egg," position, with the back parallel to the ground, the head up, feet 6 to 12 in apart, and knees about the same distance apart, to prevent accidental edging. The position should permit total relaxation. The skier's body will sometimes be raised somewhat from that position to permit better balance when the terrain is rough.

Study of the course is also important. The skier will normally practice on a course, a section or two at a time, to gain complete familiarity with each section and the problems it offers, gradually working up to top speed and to the point where all sections can be linked. What experience brings, above all, is the intuitive feel of the need to make tiny shifts of weight that will keep the skis flat, for top speed.

Downhill races are often won by hundredths or even thousandths of a second, so the start is very important. The starting technique in all three Alpine events is essentially the same. The racer must keep both feet (not both skis) behind the starting line until the command "go." In the waiting position the skier sits back on the hips, weight on the balls of the feet, poles held out in front with the knuckles on top. As the "go" signal nears, the racer springs up, driving the poles into the snow, almost vertically, to catapult forward and down the slope just as the starting signal is sounded. One or more additional pole pushes may be used after the line is crossed, as a means of increasing speed.

Slalom. The slalom racer gets no chance to practice the course. The only opportunity to study it comes on the way up for the run, and from such study a mental picture of what the course looks like and what its running requires must be made. The essentials of a good slalom run are that the skier wants to travel as close as possible to a straight line between gates, and wants to stay as close as possible to the fall line all the way down. Acceleration after coming out of a turn is very important, since a racer

In ski jumping, the tips are raised so the skis act as airfoils.
(F. Kelly MacNeill.)

normally has to slow down somewhat to get through a gate properly.

A slalom racer gains acceleration in either of two ways. In one method, upon coming out of a turn, the racer bends the knees and drops into a "sitting" position—down-unweighting—and simultaneously thrusts the feet forward to gain speed, now that the ski edges have been unset.

Step acceleration is an alternative method, especially just before or just after passing through a blind gate. This consists of a simple step uphill in order to gain height. The skier, with body weight on the downhill ski, steps slightly uphill with the other ski, then shifts weight to the uphill ski and steps up with the downhill ski. A similar maneuver, the step turn, is used both to gain height between gates and to get the skier in a straighter line toward the next gate. In a step turn, the skier steps uphill only with the tip of the uphill ski. Then all weight is shifted to that ski, bringing the unweighted downhill ski alongside it. Step turns enable a racer to run virtually on a straight line between the inside poles of successive gates, using the step to get far inside the pole for safety's sake.

Giant Slalom. The giant slalom emphasizes the traverse—skiing across a hill—and the racer wants to combine the fastest possible traverses with the quickest, sharpest turns. The skis will be edged hard on the traverse to avoid sideslipping, and the racer will step uphill when approaching a gate in order to gain height and extra space going through. Then a sharp turn through the gate will be carved.

Cross-Country. The basic cross-country technique, the diagonal stride, is something like a cross between skating and walking. It is like skating in that the skier is pushing with one leg and gliding with the other; like walking in that, while pushing with one leg, the skier employs the opposite arm as an aid in propelling the body forward.

It works like this: The skier has almost all weight on the pushing leg. That leg is thrust back in a kicking movement, which brings the heel well up off the ski and the ski off the snow; at the same time, the pole on the other side has been thrust into the snow at a point even with the thrusting foot, and is used for pushing. As the weight moves to the gliding ski, which is about to become the pushing ski, the other pole comes forward and is planted for a push. The basic thrust, however, comes from the kick of the ski, not the push of the pole.

In double-poling, used when the course is slightly downhill, the skis remain flat on the snow. The skier plants both poles in the snow, with elbows somewhat flexed and the poles set slightly back of the hands, then leans forward, gradually bending the knees and pushing down and back on the poles. The push should continue until the arms are well in back of the knees; then the poles are disengaged from the snow and the skier straightens up again while gliding.

A variation is the double-pole stride, in which the skier also pushes with one foot, as in the diagonal stride, while using both poles for thrust. Of course the skis alternate between pushing and gliding.

The cross-country skier uses a step turn somewhat different from that employed in the slaloms. For a left turn, for example, the skier lifts the left ski, turns it to the left, steps on it, and then steps the right ski alongside it.

Jumping. Ski jumping can be broken into four parts: the inrun, takeoff, flight, and landing. The inrun position is similar to the "egg" position used by the downhill racer; however, the tail may be somewhat higher, and many jumpers actually tuck their chests against their knees in a kind of rolled-up position. Weight is kept slightly back.

A good takeoff requires perfect timing. Approaching the lip of the takeoff run, the jumper rolls body weight forward onto the balls of the feet and begins to straighten up with a powerful leg push. The purpose is twofold: to get the ski tips up and to get the jumper into the best aerodynamic flight position as quickly as possible. The snap that completes the jumping motion should come just an instant late, after the jumper reaches the lip, since the ski tips will naturally drop after leaving the lip, and the snap should bring them back up.

In the flight position the jumper leans far forward, from the ankles, head almost touching ski tips. Most jumpers keep their hands in the fish position, flat at the sides like fins. Some, however, extend the hands straight overhead, with the arms straight. Once in the proper position, the jumper wants to hold it all the way to the landing point. Ski tips should be up, so wind pressure on the bottoms keeps the jumper in the air longer.

The position is broken only as the tails of the skis are about to hit the snow. The jumper straightens up, bringing the arms up, and still holding the tips up slightly. Upon hitting the snow, the jumper pushes one ski ahead of the other, sits back, and rolls the hips down, under, and then forward to absorb the shock. Weight should settle forward and the skis should be close together. Now the jumper is a skier again, and rides the rest of the hill, stopping with a snowplow or a turn.

Major Competitive Events

The Federation of International Skiing (FIS) official world championships were held annually before World War II, but are now held only in even-numbered, non-Olympic years. The most important international Alpine ski competition, however, is now the World Cup, a season-long competition which began in 1967. A series of races each season count toward World Cup points, and the best three finishes of each racer in each of the three Alpine races are counted in the standings. First place is worth 25 points, second place 20, and third place 15, with a lesser number of points awarded for lower finishes. To emphasize all-around skills, in the 1974–1975 season, points for placing among the top 10 in the Alpine Combined at three major meets were added to the system.

The United States and Canadian national championships also rank high in international competition, since they're the only national events that are open to citizens of other countries.

Nordic skiing has no equivalent of the World Cup. The oldest major event in skiing, the Holmenkollen, which became international in 1909, emphasizes the Nordic events, and Holmenkollen winners are considered world Nordic champions in odd-numbered years—those years in which there are no World championships or Winter Olympics. The Holmenkollen is held near Oslo, Norway. Alpine events were added to the program in 1936.

The single most important Alpine meet is the Arlberg-Kandahar, established in 1928. An "A-K" championship is considered as good as a world title, in odd-numbered years.

Professional Racing. Professional ski racing is a relatively recent development, once almost exclusively American, since European "amateurs" can, allegedly, earn up to $100,000 a year and, so far, professional skiers in the United States can't come close to that figure.

The professional ski tour was established in 1969–1970 and got an important boost in the 1971–1972 season, when Benson & Hedges assumed sponsorship, and women's races were added to the schedule. Many spectators consider pro racing more exciting than amateur racing, largely because results are based not on runs against time but on head-on-head dual races in which losers are eliminated and winners advance to the next bracket, tournament-style.

In the first season there were only three races, with total prize money of $8,500, but the amount has increased to more than $300,000 for a 12-race series.

Freestyle Skiing. A few years ago, they were called "hot doggers," not an entirely complimentary term; now they are called freestyle skiers and they have meets of their own at which they display acrobatics on skis. The first freestyle meet was held in 1971; in 1973 the International Freestyle Skiers Association was formed, with about 500 members. A group of women skiers in the same year organized the World Hot Dog Ski Association. In freestyle skiing, competitors are judged on their skill in performing acrobatics and other stunts on skis.

Glossary

Arlberg strap—A safety strap that keeps the ski from "running away" after the bindings release.

banking—Leaning the entire body toward the center of the turn.

base—Packed snow beneath the surface.

basket—The circular attachment on a ski pole that keeps it from going too deep into the snow.

bear trap—A type of binding that will not release.

boiler plate—Hard frozen surface.

bunny hill—An easy slope for beginners.

chatter—Vibration of the ski.

check—Any method of slowing down.

control gate—A set of two flags between which the racer must pass; usually used specifically to describe the gates on a downhill course.

corn—A honeycombed snow surface caused by alternate thawing and freezing.

double stem—The snowplow. (*See* p. 387, "Alpine Skiing.")

flat ski—A ski kept flat on the snow, without any setting of the edges, for top speed.

flush—A series of three closed slalom gates.

forebody—The part of the ski in front of the boot.

forerunner—A noncompetitor who tests a course before a race to make sure it is acceptable.

hairpin—Two consecutive closed slalom gates.

pole plant—A jab of a ski pole into the snow on the inside of a turn, to act as a pivot.

powder—Light, dry flakes of snow.

pre-jump—A jump made before reaching the crest of a bump, in order to clear it safely.

racing edges—Soft steel edges, which can be easily sharpened, used by racers.

schuss—To ski straight down the fall line at the highest possible speed.

skimeister—The winner of a four-way competition involving downhill, slalom, cross-country, and jumping.

tail—The part of the ski behind the boot.

waist—The narrowest part of the ski.

World Cup Winners

Men

1967	Jean-Claude Killy, France
1968	Jean-Claude Killy, France
1969	Karl Schranz, Austria
1970	Karl Schranz, Austria
1971	Gustavo Thoeni, Italy
1972	Gustavo Thoeni, Italy
1973	Gustavo Thoeni, Italy
1974	Piero Gros, Italy
1975	Gustavo Thoeni, Italy
1976	Ingemar Stenmark, Sweden

Women

1967	Nancy Greene, Canada
1968	Nancy Greene, Canada
1969	Gertrude Gabl, Austria
1970	Michele Jacot, France
1971	Annamarie Proell, Austria
1972	Annamarie Proell, Austria
1973	Annamarie Proell, Austria
1974	Annamarie Moser-Proell, Austria
1975	Annamarie Moser-Proell, Austria
1976	Rosi Mittermaier, West Germany

U.S. Alpine Champions—Men

(In various years, there have been closed and open championships conducted, closed for U.S. citizens only, open for citizens of any country. In those years, C indicates closed, O indicates open, and * indicates winner of both.)

Downhill

1933	Henry Woods
1934	J. J. Duncan, Jr.
1935	Hannes Schroll
1936	No competition
1937	Dick Durrance
1938	Ulrich Beutter*
1939	Dick Durrance (C)
	Toni Matt (O)
1940	Dick Durrance*
1941	William Redline (C)
	Toni Matt (O)
1942	Barney McLean (C)
	Martin Fopp (O)

1943–45 No competition
1946 Steve Knowlton
1947 Karl Molitor
1948 Jack Reddish*
1949 George Macomber (C)
      Yves Latreille (O)
1950 Jim Griffith*
1951 Jack Nagel (C)
      Ernie McCulloch (O)
1952 Dick Buek (C)
      Ernie McCulloch (O)
1953 Ralph Miller*
1954 Dick Buek
1955 Chiharu Igaya
1956 William Woods
1957 Bud Werner
1958 William Smith
1959 Bud Werner
1960 Oddvar Ronnestad
1961 No competition
1962 Dave Gorsuch
1963 William Marolt
1964 Ni Orsi
1965 Loris Werner
1966 Peter Rohr
1967 Dennis McCoy
1968 Scott Henderson
1969 Spider Sabich
1970 Rod Taylor
1971 Bob Cochran
1972 Steve Lathrop
1973 Bob Cochran
1974 No competition
1975 Andy Mill
1976 Greg Jones

Slalom

1935 Hannes Schroll
1936 No competition
1937 Dick Durrance*
1938 Ed Meservey*
1939 Dick Durrance (C)
      Friedl Pfeifer (O)
1940 Dick Durrance (C)
      Friedl Pfeifer (O)
1941 Bill Redlin (C)
      Dick Durrance (O)
1942 Barney McLean (C)
      Sigi Engl (O)
1943–45 No competition
1946 Dick Novitz
1947 Karl Molitor
1948 Jack Reddish*
1949 George Macomber*
1950 Jack Reddish*
1951 Guttorm Berge (C)
      Jack Nagel (O)
1952 Jack Reddish*
1953 Ralph Miller (C)
      Stein Eriksen (O)
1954 Chiharu Igaya
1955 Ralph Miller
1956 Tom Corcoran
1957 Tom Corcoran
1958 Charles Ferries
1959 Bud Werner
1960 Jim Heuga
1961 Rod Hebron
1962 Bill Barrier
1963 Charles Ferries
1964 Bill Marolt
1965 Rod Hebron

1966 Guy Perillat
1967 Jim Heuga
1968 Rick Chaffee
1969 Bob Cochran
1970 Bob Cochran
1971 Otto Tschudi
1972 Terry Palmer
1973 Masayoshi Kashiwaga
1974 Cary Adgate
1975 Steve Mahre
1976 Cary Adgate

Giant Slalom

1949 Dave Lawrence*
1950 Hans Senger
1951 Ernie McCulloch
1952 Gale Spence
1953 William Tibbits
1954 Darrell Robison
1955 Ralph Miller (amateur)
      Jack Nagel (O)
      Martin Strolz (foreign)
1956 Tom Corcoran (C)
      Christian Pravda (O)
1957 Toni Sailer
1958 Stanley Harwood
1959 Bud Werner
1960 Chiharu Igaya
1961 Gordon Eaton
1962 Jim Gaddis
1963 Bud Werner
1964 Billy Kidd
1965 Bill Marolt
1966 Jean-Claude Killy
1967 Dumenc Giovanoli
1968 Rich Chaffee
1969 Hank Hashiwa
1970 Tyler Palmer
1971 Bob Cochran
1972 Jim Hunter
1973 Dave Currier
1974 Bob Cochran
1975 Phil Mahre
1976 Geoff Bruce

Alpine Combined

1935 Hannes Schroll
1936 No competition
1937 Dick Durrance*
1938 Ulrich Beutter*
1939 Dick Durrance*
1940 Dick Durrance*
1941 William Redlin (C)
      Toni Matt (O)
1942 Barney McLean (C)
      Alf Engen (O)
1943–45 No competition
1946 Barney McLean
1947 Karl Molitor
1948 Jack Reddish*
1949 George Macomber
1950 Jack Reddish (C)
      Ernie McCulloch (O)
1951 Jack Nagel (C)
      Ernie McCulloch (O)
1952 Jack Reddish
1953 Ralph Miller
1954 Chiharu Igaya
1955 Chiharu Igaya
1956 William Woods
1957 Tom Corcoran
1958 Gary Vaughn (downhill and slalom)
      Frank Brown (all three events)
1959 Bud Werner

1960	Oddvar Ronnestad
1961	Rod Hebron
1962	Dave Gorsuch
1963	Bud Werner
1964	Gordon Eaton
1965	Peter Duncan
1966	Guy Perillat
1967	Dumenc Giovanoli
1968	Scott Henderson
1969	No competition
1970	William McKay
1971	Bob Cochran
1972	Bob Cochran
1973	Dave Currier
1974	No competition
1975	Greg Jones
1976	Cary Adgate

U.S. Alpine Champions—Women

Downhill

1938	Marian McKean
1939	Elizabeth Woolsey*
1940	Grace Carter Lindley*
1941	Nancy Reynolds (C)
	Gretchen Fraser (O)
1942	Shirley McDonald (C)
	Clarita Heath (O)
1943–45	No competition
1946	Paula Kann
1947	Rhoda Wurtele
1948	Jannette Burr*
1949	Andrea Mead*
1950	Jannette Burr*
1951	Katy Rodolph
1952	Andrea Mead Lawrence
1953	Katy Rodolph
1954	Nancy Banks
1955	Andrea Mead Lawrence
1956	Katherine Cox
1957	Linda Meyers
1958	Beverly Anderson
1959	Beverly Anderson
1960	Nancy Greene
1961	No competition
1962	Sharon Pecjak
1963	Jean Saubert
1964	Jean Saubert
1965	Nancy Greene
1966	Madeleine Wuilloud
1967	Nancy Greene
1968	Ann Black
1969	Ann Black
1970	Ann Black
1971	Cheryl Bechdolt
1972	Stephanie Forrest
1973	Cindy Nelson
1974	No competition
1975	Gail Blackburne
1976	Susie Patterson

Slalom

1938	Grace Carter Lindley
1939	Doris Friedrich (C)
	Erna Steuri (O)
1940	Nancy Reynolds*
1941	Marilyn Shaw*
1942	Gretchen Fraser*
1943–45	No competition
1946	Rhoda Wurtele
1947	Olivia Ausoni
1948	Ann Winn
1949	Andrea Mead

1950	Norma Godden (C)
	Georgette T. Miller (O)
1951	Katy Rodolph
1952	Andrea Mead Lawrence
1953	Katy Rodolph
1954	Jill Kinmont
1955	Andrea Mead Lawrence
1956	Sally Deaver
1957	Sally Deaver
1958	Beverly Anderson
1959	Linda Meyers
1960	Anne Heggtveit
	Nancy Holland (tie)
1961	Linda Meyers
1962	Linda Meyers
1963	Sandra Shellworth
1964	Jean Saubert
1965	Nancy Greene
1966	Marielle Goitschel
1967	Penny McCoy
1968	Judy Nagel
1969	No competition
1970	Patty Boydstun
1971	Barbara Cochran
1972	Marilyn Cochran
1973	Lindy Cochran
1974	Susie Patterson
1975	Cindy Nelson
1976	Cindy Nelson

Giant Slalom

1952	Rhoda Wurtele Gillies
1953	Andrea Mead Lawrence
1954	Dorothy Modenese
1955	Jannette Burr Bray
1956	Sally Deaver
1957	Noni Foley
1958	Beverly Anderson
1959	Beverly Anderson
1960	Anne Heggtveit
1961	Nancy Holland
1962	Tammy Dix
1963	Jean Saubert
1964	Jean Saubert
1965	Nancy Greene
1966	Florence Steurer
1967	Sandra Shellworth
1968	Marilyn Cochran
1969	Barbara Cochran
1970	Susan Corrock
1971	Laurie Kreiner
1972	Sandy Poulsen
1973	Debi Handley
1974	Marilyn Cochran
1975	Becky Dorsey
1976	Linda Cochran

Alpine Combined

1938	Marian McKean
1939	Elizabeth Woolsey (C)
	Erna Steuri (O)
1940	Marilyn Shaw*
1941	Nancy Reynolds (C)
	Gretchen Fraser (O)
1942	Shirley McDonald (C)
	Clarita Heath (O)
1943–45	No competition
1946	Rhona Wurtele
1947	Rhona Wurtele
1948	Suzy Harris
1949	Andrea Mead
1950	Lois Woodworth*
1951	Katy Rodolph

1952	Andrea Mead Lawrence
1953	Katy Rodolph (C)
	Sally Neidlinger (O)
1954	Nancy Banks
1955	Andrea Mead Lawrence
1956	Katherine Cox
1957	Madi S. Miller
1958	Beverly Anderson
1959	Linda Meyers
1960	Elizabeth Greene
1961	Nancy Holland
1962	Linda Meyers
1963	Starr Walton
1964	Jean Saubert
1965	Nancy Greene
1966	Florence Steurer
1967	Karen Budge
1968	Judy Nagel
1969	No competition
1970	Rosi Fortna
1971	Judy Crawford
1972	Judy Crawford
1973	Susie Corrock
1974	No competition
1975	Becky Dorsey
1976	Viki Fleckenstein

U.S. Nordic Champions—Men

Cross-Country

1907	Asario Autio
1908–09	No records
1910	T. W. Glesne
1911	P. Blegberg
1912	Julius Blegen
1913	Einar Lund
1914–15	No records
1916	Sigurd Overbye
1917–22	No competition
1923	Sigurd Overbye
1924	Robert Reid
1925	Martin Fredboe
1926	Sigurd Overbye
1927	Johan Satre
1928	Magnus Satre
1929	Magnus Satre
1930	Magnus Satre
1931	No records
1932	Hjalmar Hvam
1933	Magnus Satre
1934	D. Monson
1935	Ottar Satre
1936	Carl Sundqvist
1937	Warren Chivers
1938	Dave Bradley
1939	George Gustavson
1940	Peter Fosseide
1941	George Gustavson
1942	Howard Chivers
1943–46	No competition
1947	Wendell Broomhall
1948	Trygve L. Nielsen
1949	Hans Holaas
1950	Olavi Alakulpi (18 km)
	Theodore Farwell (30 km)
1951	Theodore Farwell
1952	Silas Dunklee (18 km)
	Richard Hale (30 km)
1953	Tauno Pulkkinen (18 km)
	Sheldon Varney (30 km)
1954	Tauno Pulkkinen (18 km)
	Ray Roy (30 km)

1955	Tauno Pulkkinen (18 km)
	Arne Borgness (30 km)
1956	Norman Oakvik
1957	Sven Johansson (18 km)
	Oddvar Ask (30 km)
1958	Leo Massa (18 km)
	Wayne Fleming (18 km—tie)
	Leslie Fono (30 km)
1959	Clarence Servold (15 km)
	Leo Massa (30 km)
1960	Clarence Servold (15 km)
	Richard Taylor (30 km)
1961	No competition
1962	Mike Gallagher (15 km)
	Raimo Ahti (30 km)
1963	Donald MacLeod (15 km)
	Ed Williams (30 km)
1964	Peter Lahdenpera (15 km)
	Ed Dermers (30 km)
1965	David Rikert (15 km)
	Bill Spencer (30 km)
1966	Mike Gallagher (15 km)
	Mike Elliott (30 km)
1967	Mike Gallagher (15 and 30 km)
1968	Mike Gallagher (15 and 30 km)
1969	Clark Matis (15 and 30 km)
1970	Mike Gallagher (15 and 30 km)
1971	Mike Elliott (15 km)
	Mike Gallagher (30 km)
	Bob Gray (50 km)
1972	Mike Elliott (15 and 30 km)
	Bob Gray (50 km)
1973	Tim Caldwell (15 km)
	Bob Gray (30 km)
	Joe McNulty (50 km)
1974	Larry Martin (15 km)
	Mike Devecka (30 km)
	Ron Yeager (50 km)
1975	Bill Koch (15 km)
	Tim Caldwell (30 and 50 km)
1976	Devin Sweigert (15 and 30 km)
	Stan Dunklee (50 km)

Jumping

1904	Conrad Thompson
1905	Ole Westgaard
1906	Ole Fiering
1907	Olaf Jonnum
1908	John Evenson
1909	John Evenson
1910	Anders Haugen
1911	Francis Kempe
1912	Lars Haugen
1913	Ragnar Omtvedt
1914	Ragnar Omtvedt
1915	Lars Haugen
1916	Henry Hall
1917	Ragnar Omtvedt
1918	Lars Haugen
1919	No competition
1920	Anders Haugen
1921	Carl Howelson
1922	Lars Haugen
1923	Anders Haugen
1924	Lars Haugen
1925	Alfred Ohrn
1926	Anders Haugen
1927	Lars Haugen
1928	Lars Haugen
1929	Strand Mikkelsen
1930	Caspar Oimoen
1931	Caspar Oimoen
1932	Anton Lekang

Cross-country skiing, a grueling sport, is also gaining much popularity in the United States, partly as the result of Bill Koch's silver medal performance in the 1976 Winter Olympics. (*F. Kelly MacNeill.*)

1933 Roy Mikkelsen
1934 Caspar Oimoen
1935 Roy Mikkelsen
1936 George Kotlarek
1937 Sigmund Ruud
1938 Sig Ulland (C)
      Birger Ruud (O)
1939 Reidar Andersen
1940 Alf Engen
1941 Torger Tokle
1942 Ola Aanjesen
1943–45 No competition
1946 Alf Engen (O)
      Arthur Devlin (C)
1947 Arnholdt Kongsgaard
1948 Arne Ulland
1949 Petter Hugsted
1950 Olavi Kuronen
1951 Arthur Tokle
1952 Clarence Hill (C)
      Merrill Barber (O)
1953 Arthur Tokle
1954 Roy Sherwood
1955 Rudi Maki
1956 Keith Zuehlke
1957 Ansten Samuelstuen
1958 Billy Olson
1959 W. P. Erickson
1960 James Brennan
1961 Ansten Samuelstuen
1962 Ansten Samuelstuen
1963 Gene Kotlarek
1964 John Balfanz
1965 David Hicks
1966 Gene Kotlarek
1967 Gene Kotlarek
1968 Jay Martin
1969 Adrian Watt
1970 Bill Bakke

1971 Jerry Martin
1972 Greg Swor
1973 Jerry Martin
1974 Ron Steele
1975 Jerry Martin
1976 Jim Denney

Nordic Combined
1932 Hjalmar Hvam
1933 Magnus Satre
1934–36 No competition
1937 Warren Chivers
1938 Dave Bradley
1939 Alf Engen
1940 Peter Fosseide
1941 Alf Engen
1942 Howard Chivers
1943–46 No competition
1947 Ralph Townsend
1948 Robert Wright
1949 Ralph Townsend
1950 Robert Arsenault
1951 Ted Farwell, Jr.
1952 Corey Engen
1953 No competition
1954 Norman Oakvik
1955 No competition
1956 Per Staavi
1957 Bill Purcell
1958 Alfred Vincellette
1959 Alfred Vincellette
1960 Alfred Vincellette
1961–62 No competition
1963 John Bower
1964 Jim Balfanz
1965 David Rikert
1966 John Bower
1967 John Bower
1968 John Bower
1969 Jim Miller
1970 Jim Miller
1971 Robert Kendall
1972 Mike Devecka
1973 Teyck Weed
1974 Bruce Cunningham
1975 Mike Devecka
1976 No competition

U.S. Cross-Country Champions—Women

1971 Sharon Firth (5 km)
      Martha Rockwell (10 km)
1972 Martha Rockwell (5 and 10 km)
1973 Martha Rockwell (5 and 10 km)
1974 Martha Rockwell (5, 10, and 15 km)
1975 Martha Rockwell (5, 10, and 20 km)
1976 Jana Hlavaty (5, 10, and 20 km)

Professional Skiing

Skier of the Year
1965 Ernst Hinterseer
1966 Hias Leitner
1967 Ernst Hinterseer
1968 Hias Leitner
1969 Adrien Duvillard
1970 William Kidd

Tour Champion
1971 Spider Sabich
1972 Spider Sabich
1973 Jean-Claude Killy
1974 Hugo Nindl
1975 Hank Kashiwa
1976 Henri Duvillard

National Ski Hall of Fame

(Established in 1954, the National Ski Hall of Fame is located in Ishpeming, Michigan, where the National Ski Association, now the U.S. Ski Association, was organized in 1904.)

Reidar Andersen—A Norwegian, Andersen won the U.S. and Canadian jumping championships in 1939.

Asario Autio—The first U.S. cross-country champion (1907).

Hermod Bakke—Ski jumper for more than 45 years and Leavonworth tournament chairman 1932–1969.

Magnus Bakke—Long-time coach of jumping and cross-country; with his brother, promoted the 90-m jumping hill in Leavonworth, Washington.

Arthur J. "Red" Barth—National Ski Association president in 1949.

LeMoine Batson—Olympic jumper in 1924 and 1936.

Paul Bietila—Rated the country's top ski jumper, Bietila was killed during a practice jump at the 1939 national championships.

Walter Bietila—Olympic jumper in 1936 and 1948.

Julius Blegen—U.S. cross-country champion in 1912; Olympic coach 1932.

Edward Blood—Olympic skier in 1932 and 1936.

John Bower—Won the Holmenkollen cross-country and combined championships in 1968.

Burton H. Boyum—Former curator of the National Ski Hall of Fame.

Harold C. "Doc" Bradley—Pioneer of skiing in Wisconsin, Idaho, Colorado, and California.

Alexander Bright—Olympic skier in 1936.

Clarita Heath Bright—Member of the first U.S. women's Olympic ski team in 1936.

Fred Bruun—Cofounder and first president of the Central Ski Judges' Association.

Richard Buek—U.S. downhill champion in 1952 and 1954; killed in a plane crash at 28.

John P. Carleton—Olympic skier in 1924; top college skier at Dartmouth College and Oxford University 1918–1925.

Hannah Locke Carter—Member of four national ski teams, 1936–1939; named to the 1940 Olympic team.

Howard Chivers—U.S. Nordic Combined champion in 1942; named to 1940 Olympic team.

John J. Clair, Jr.—Founder of the Long Island Ski Club and long-time official.

Nancy Reynolds Cooke—U.S. slalom champion in 1940, downhill and Alpine Combined champion in 1941; named to 1940 Olympic team.

Arthur Devlin—U.S. jumping champion in 1946; a member of the 1948, 1952, and 1956 Olympic teams.

Godfrey Dewey—A leader in the successful effort to bring the 1932 Winter Olympics to Lake Placid, New York.

Charles M. "Minnie" Dole—Founder of the National Ski Patrol System.

Henry P. Douglas—Founder and first president of the Canadian Amateur Ski Association (1921).

Richard Durrance—A member of the 1936 Olympic team and a top Alpine racer during the 1930s.

William T. Eldred—Founder of the *Empire State News*, which, after mergers with other magazines, became *Ski*, a national publication.

Frank Elkins—Ski editor of the *Long Island Press* for 18 years.

Dr. Raymond S. Elmer—President of the National Ski Association 1930–1931.

John Elvrum—Former holder of the American ski jumping record, at 240 ft.

Alf Engen—National jumping champion in 1940 and long-time holder of the distance record.

Corey Engen—Nordic combined champion in 1952; captain of the 1948 Olympic Nordic team.

Sverre Engen—Jumper, Alpine racer, instructor, writer, resort operator, and producer of ski movies.

Sigi Engl—Winner of the national slalom in 1942; operator of the Sun Valley, Idaho, Ski School.

E. O. "Buck" Erickson—Publicity director of the Pine Mountain jumping tournament in Upper Michigan since 1938.

James E. Flaa—First chairman of the Ski Hall of Fame committee.

Luggi Foeger—International competitor; ski teacher, ski-area manager and developer.

Donald Fraser—Long-time competitor and member of the 1936 Olympic team.

Gretchen Fraser—The first American to win medals in Olympic skiing, a gold medal in the slalom and silver medal in the Alpine Combined in 1948.

Sverre Fredheim—A member of the 1936 and 1948 Olympic teams; named to the 1940 Olympic team.

Nathaniel Goodrich—Editor of the *American* and *Eastern Ski Manuals* during the 1930s.

Nancy Greene—A Canadian skier who won an Olympic gold medal and the World Cup in 1968; won several U.S. championships and the 1967–1968 World Cups.

James Griffith—U.S. downhill champion in 1950; was killed in 1951 during Olympic training.

Harold Grinden—A founder of the National Ski Hall of Fame; National Ski Association president 1928–1929.

Thor C. Groswold, Sr.—A native of Norway, Groswold came to the United States in 1923 and was long active as a competitor, official, and manufacturer.

Henry Hall—National jumping champion in 1916 and the first American to establish world distance records, of 203 ft in 1917 and 225 ft in 1921.

Alf Halvorson—A founder of the U.S. Eastern Amateur and the Canadian Amateur Ski Associations.

Selden J. Hannah—Won several national Nordic and Alpine championships.

W. Averell Harriman—Founder of Sun Valley as a ski resort and of the Harriman Cup ski-racing tournament.

Fred Harris—National Ski Association treasurer 1929–1931; built first ski jump at Hanover, New Hampshire.

Lars Haugen—National jumping champion 1912, 1915, 1918, 1922, 1924, 1927–28; member of the 1924 and 1928 Olympic teams.

Ole Hegge—Member of the Norwegian Olympic team in 1928 and 1932; later a U.S. citizen and competitor.

Erling Heistad—An early organizer of interscholastic ski competition in New England.

James R. Hendrickson—A member of the 1936 Olympic team; killed during a 1948 jumping tournament.

Harry Wade Hicks—An organizer of the 1932 Winter Olympics; promoter of cross-country skiing.

Clarence M. "Coy" Hill—Veteran ski jumper; set a world record during the 1952 European ski flying meet.

Cortlandt T. Hill—A major force behind expansion of

the National Ski Association into the U.S. Ski Association.

Carl Holmstrom—Ski jumper, member of the 1932 and 1936 Olympic teams.

Aksel Holter—Secretary of the National Ski Association 1904–1909 and editor of the *American Ski Annual*.

John Hostvedt—National and international official; cofounder of the Hall of Fame.

Carl Howelsen—A champion in Norway and pioneer of skiing in Colorado; national jumping champion in 1921.

Sally Neidlinger Hudson—National Alpine Combined champion in 1953; member of the 1952 and 1956 Olympic teams.

Hjalmar Hvam—Won three titles, cross-country, Class B jumping, and Nordic combined, in the 1932 U.S. championships.

Chiharu "Chick" Igaya—Winner of six NCAA titles, representing Dartmouth, and a member of Japanese Olympic teams in 1952, 1956, and 1960.

Fred Iselin—A competitor in Switzerland and the United States; long-time teacher in Colorado.

Janette Burr Johnson—U.S. downhill champion in 1948 and 1950; member of the 1952 Olympic team.

Alice Damrosch Wolfe Kiare—Organized the first U.S. women's ski team, for the 1935 World Championships and the 1936 Olympics.

Jill Kinmont—National slalom champion in 1954; paralyzed in a 1955 skiing accident.

Arthur Knudsen—Outstanding fund raiser and official.

George Kotlarek—National jumping champion in 1936.

Felix Koziol—Developer of ski areas in Utah and Wyoming.

Dr. Hans Kraus—Used medical knowledge to contribute to the safety of the sport.

Sigrid Stromstad Laming—The first U.S. women's champion, in the 1932 cross-country.

Roger Langley—National Ski Association president 1936–1948 and executive secretary 1948–1954.

Andrea Mead Lawrence—Winner of gold medals in the slalom and giant slalom in the 1952 Olympics.

David Lawrence—First U.S. giant slalom champion, in 1949.

Col. George E. Leach—Managed the first Olympic ski team in 1924; represented the United States when the Federation of International Skiing was organized.

Harry Lien—Native of Norway; member of the 1924 Olympic team as a jumper.

Dr. Amos R. Little, Jr.—Manager of Olympic teams and official.

Earle B. Little—Director of competition for the 1959 North American jumping championships; secretary of competition for the 1960 Winter Olympics.

Sir Arnold Lunn—Set the first modern slalom course in 1922; drafted first world rules for downhill and slalom racing.

Ole Mangseth—Jumper; National Ski Association treasurer 1925–1928.

George Macomber—U.S. Alpine Combined champion in 1949, member of the 1948 and 1952 Olympic teams.

Toni Matt—U.S. downhill champion in 1939 and 1941, Alpine Combined champion in 1941.

Lawrence Maurin—Jumper and official; first American style judge in international events.

Helen McAlpin—A native of the United States who com-

peted for Britain, but then captained the first U.S. women's ski teams in 1935–1936.

Dave McCoy—Coach and developer of women racers; developer of Mammoth Mountain, California, ski area.

John McCrillis—Wrote the first American book on skiing; produced the first American instructional films.

Ernie McCulloch—Canadian; won the U.S. downhill and giant slalom, North American championships, and Harriman Cup in 1950.

Ron MacKenzie—Major figure in a 20-year battle to get a major ski development in New York State; coach-manager of U.S. Nordic teams.

Grace Carter Lindley McKnight—First U.S. slalom champion, in 1938.

Malcolm McLane—Captained Dartmouth team in 1949; Rhodes Scholar and international competitor.

Robert "Barney" McLean—Jumper and racer; captain of 1948 Olympic team.

L. B. "Barney" McNab—First president of Mount Hood Ski Patrol, 1937–1938; adviser to National Ski Patrol.

Fred H. McNeil—First president of Pacific Northwest Ski Association, 1930.

Allison Merrill—Director of Dartmouth College outdoor recreation program.

Roy Mikkelsen—U.S. jumping champion in 1933 and 1935; member of the 1932 and 1936 Olympic teams.

Strand Mikkelsen—U.S. jumping champion in 1929.

Rolf Monsen—A Canadian star in 1922–1923, Monsen became a U.S. citizen and competed on this country's Olympic teams in 1928, 1932, and 1936.

John P. Morgan—Helped design and build the first chair lift in the world, at Sun Valley.

Richard Movitz—U.S. slalom champion in 1946; member of the 1948 Olympic team.

J. Stanley Mullin—Long-time champion of amateur skiing.

Dorothy Hoyt Nebel—Named to the 1940 Olympic team; ski racing coach and ski teacher.

Nels Nelsen—Canadian who set a jumping record of 240 ft in 1925.

George A. Newett—Cofounder of the National Ski Association in 1904.

Sondre Norheim—Introduced behind-the-heel bindings and skis with side and bottom cambers.

Casper Oimoen—U.S. jumping champion in 1930–1931 and 1934; member of the 1936 Olympic team.

Willis S. Olson—Won jumping championships in every class; three-time NCAA champion; member of 1952 and 1956 Olympic teams.

Ragnar Omtvedt—U.S. jumping champion in 1913, 1914, and 1917; member of the 1924 Olympic team.

Fred Pabst—Ski jumper; financed creation of ski area conglomerate in eastern Canada, New England, and Wisconsin in 1930s.

Roland Palmedo—Organized ski teacher certification and founder of the Amateur Ski Club of New York.

Guttorm Paulsen—Native of Norway; won U.S. Class B jumping championship in 1929; judge during 1952 Olympics.

Ernest O. Pederson—Star at University of New Hampshire; won U.S.-Canada all-around championships in 1927, 1928, and 1930.

Paul J. Perrault—In 1949, "Jumping Joe" beat two world jumping champions and twice broke the North

American distance record; a member of the 1952 Olympic team.

Eugene Petersen—Secretary of the National Ski Association 1918–1921.

Charles A. Proctor—Set the first slalom course in North America.

Charles N. Proctor—Star with Dartmouth Outing Club; member of 1928 Olympic team.

Jack Reddish—U.S. downhill champion in 1948, slalom champion in 1948, 1950, and 1952; member of the 1948 and 1952 Olympic teams.

Wendell T. Robie—First president of the California Ski Association; organizer of Auburn, California, Ski Club.

Birger Ruud—U.S. jumping champion in 1938; won both downhill and special ski jump in 1936 Olympics.

Sigmund Ruud—U.S. jumping champion in 1937.

Magnus Satre—U.S. cross-country champion 1928–1930 and 1933; member of the 1928 Olympic team.

Ottar Satre—National cross-country champion in 1935; member of the 1936 Olympic team.

Willy Schaeffler—Long-time coach at University of Denver; won 13 NCAA team championships in 17 years.

Hannes Schneider—Developer of the Arlberg technique; great popularizer of skiing in the United States.

Otto Schniebs—Coach at Dartmouth College and St. Lawrence University.

Hannes Schroll—U.S. slalom champion in 1935.

Lloyd Severud—Coach of U.S. jumping teams.

Albert E. Sigal—President of the U.S. Ski Association 1954–1955.

Herman "Jack Rabbit" Smith-Johannsen—Helped cut North America's best-known ski touring trail, the Maple Leaf in the Laurentiens, and others in Vermont.

Harald Sorensen—Ski jumper; won 1971 Russell Wilder Memorial Award for work in interesting youth in skiing.

Siegfried Steinwall—Native of Sweden; coached at Dartmouth 1927–1928; founder of Swedish Ski Club of New York.

Marthinius Strand—Founder and first president of the Intermountain Ski Association, 1938–1944.

Erling Strom—Early competitor in Norway and the United States; established a school in Lake Placid, New York; in 1932 was a member of the first skiing party to reach the top of Mount McKinley.

Edward F. Taylor—Alpine competitor and second director of the National Ski Patrol System.

Hans "Peppi" Teichner—Alpine competitor; developer of recreational skiing in lower Michigan.

Carl Tellefsen—First president of the National Ski Association of America.

Lowell Thomas—Radio commentator and author who has done much to promote skiing.

Conrad Thompson—First U.S. jumping champion in 1904.

John A. "Snowshoe" Thompson—From 1856 to 1876, carried mail between California and what is now Nevada, skiing on "Norwegian snowshoes" during the winter.

Arthur Tokle—U.S. jumping champion in 1951 and 1953; member of the 1952 Olympic team; coach of U.S. jumping teams 1960–1968.

Torger Tokle—U.S. jumping champion in 1941; killed in action in 1945 with the 10th Mountain Troops.

Birger Torrisen—Member of the 1936 Olympic team; coach of many junior champions.

Paula Kann Valar—U.S. downhill champion in 1946; member of 1948 Olympic team.

George H. Watson—Deeded surface rights to vast mining claims to the federal government for winter sports.

Wallace "Buddy" Werner—Member of the 1956 and 1964 Olympic teams; was killed in a Swiss avalanche in 1964.

John Wictorin—First president of the Swedish Ski Club of New York.

Marian McKean Wigglesworth—First U.S. women's downhill champion, in 1938.

Henry S. Woods—First U.S. downhill champion, in 1933.

Betty Woolsey—Won U.S. downhill and Alpine Combined in 1939; member of the first U.S. women's ski teams, in 1935 and 1936.

Gordon Wren—First American to jump over 300 ft.

Rhoda Wurtele—U.S. downhill champion in 1947, slalom champion in 1946, and gaint slalom champion in 1952.

Rhona Wurtele—U.S. Alpine Combined champion in 1946 and 1947.

Katy Rodolph Wyatt—U.S. women's downhill slalom, and Alpine Combined champion in 1951 and 1953.

Bibliography. Bowen, Ezra: *The Book of American Skiing,* Lippincott, New York, 1963; Jerome, John *et al.: The Sports Illustrated Book of Skiing,* rev. ed., Lippincott, New York, 1971; Scharff, Robert *et al.* (eds.): *Ski Magazine's Encyclopedia of Skiing,* Harper and Row, New York, 1970.

SKIN DIVING—Diving deep beneath the sea has long been a dream of the human race. It may well be as old as the dream of flying. Many artists and writers, starting at least with Aristotle, have described possible means of allowing a person to breathe underwater. Pliny the Elder (A.D. 23–79) described a simple underwater breathing apparatus, a long tube secured above water by a float, that was used by sponge divers. Leonardo da Vinci "invented" a modern diving suit, complete with a webbed glove.

Skin diving in the purest sense, however, requires just one piece of equipment, a pair of goggles which will allow the diver to look around beneath the water's surface. Goggles were evidently first used by the Polynesians, at some unknown time in the past. The first goggles were probably polished pieces of transparent tortoise shell employed by Polynesian pearl divers. Divers in the South Seas also used improvised flippers of reed. During the 1920s the Japanese developed the single-lens mask, commonly known as a faceplate. Originally the fitted frame was of bamboo, carved to conform to the diver's face so as to keep water from seeping in. In 1938 the Japanese made another step forward with the rubber-framed mask. Some of these masks were shipped to the United States.

"The father of modern skin diving," Jacques-Yves Cousteau, and Emil Gagnan in 1943 invented the aqualung, the first self-contained underwater breathing apparatus (SCUBA). This allowed a diver to descend to greater depths and to stay down for longer periods of time, since a supply of oxygen was carried in a tank on the diver's back.

The term "skin diving," incidentally, is somewhat misleading. A more accurate term is "free diving," which encompasses any kind of diving in which the diver is not dependent on surface apparatus for air. The modern skin diver is often covered from head to toe with a wet suit, a tight-fitting suit of foam rubber into which a small amount of water is admitted. This water, quickly warmed by the body, helps keep the diver warm, and the air cells in the foam rubber act as insulation against surrounding cold water. Wearing a wet suit, with a tight-fitting hood around the face, a mask, fins, and a weight belt to offset the body's natural buoyancy, a diver can now descend in waters of below 40°F.

The diver not using SCUBA equipment may use a snorkel, an S- or J-shaped tube of plastic or rubber with a mouthpiece. The S-shaped device has a ball valve in the upper hook, meant to keep water from entering when the diver submerges. The J-shaped snorkel is cleared of water by the diver simply by blowing through it, when the diver surfaces for more air.

The wet suit has largely replaced the dry suit, which is a rubber suit sealed around the neck, wrists, or ankles to keep water out. Woolen or cotton clothing must be worn underneath to keep the diver warm. Once the suit begins to leak, the diver has to surface and either repair it or end diving for the day—unless the water is warm enough for real skin diving.

The weight belt should be fitted with a safety release so the diver can get out of it when the need to ascend quickly arises. For further safety, a diver may wear an inflatable life jacket, which can be quickly filled with carbon dioxide from a small, built-in cartridge.

A knife of stainless steel is virtually standard equipment—not so much for protection as for use as a handy underwater tool. Other pieces of equipment which are sometimes useful include a depth gauge, an underwater flashlight, and a special camera, either provided originally with underwater housing or fitted into a transparent plastic box to adapt it for use underwater.

Diving Hazards and Safety. In areas where there is much boating, a skin diver uses a diving flag, having a red field with a diagonal white stripe, to warn boats that there is a diver in the area. In some states it is against the law for a boat to come within 200 yd of a diving flag.

The first rule is that a diver should never go out alone. Diving clubs have adopted the "buddy system," under which two divers form a team and go diving together most or all of the time. The buddies get to know and trust each other thoroughly by constantly diving together.

There are several hand signals conventionally used by divers. Forming a circle with the thumb and forefinger and extending the other three fingers straight up is both a question—"Is everything O.K.?"—and the correct answer—"Everything's O.K." Running the index finger across the throat is a signal that the diver is exhausted or that there is danger in the area. A SCUBA diver who is out of air points to the mouth and then runs a finger across the throat.

The SCUBA diver faces some dangers that don't confront the ordinary skin diver. After a deep dive, the SCUBA diver must come back to the surface slowly—more slowly than the bubbles that rise from the regulator on the diver's air tank. Rising too rapidly could cause an air embolism, a blockage of circulation in the heart or brain caused by dissolved air entering the blood stream as external pressure lessens.

Surfacing too rapidly can also cause caisson disease, better known as "the bends." Water pressure at great depths causes the blood stream to absorb nitrogen from the inhaled air. The nitrogen must be gradually emitted from the system on the way up. If it isn't, the gas will come out of solution as the pressure decreases and will form bubbles that cause severe pain in the joints and that can also induce unconsciousness and death. The diver must undergo decompression, stopping every so often, on the way up, to allow the nitrogen to leave the system through respiration.

At depths of 150 ft and more, the dissolved nitrogen can also cause nitrogen narcosis, a kind of intoxication known as the "rapture of the deeps." The affected diver gets an illusion of tremendous well-being and power which, in the absence of awareness of the danger involved, can lead to foolhardy acts.

Basic Techniques. Before donning any other equipment, a novice skin diver learns to swim while wearing fins (flippers). The breaststroke, with a slow, easy flutter kick, is the recommended method. Once accustomed to the fins, whose extended fronts provide added thrust to the kick, the diver begins to get used to the mask. The mask is first rinsed out; then a small amount of saliva is rubbed over the lens to keep it from fogging up, and the mask is rinsed out again before being put on. Inhaling through the nose, the diver determines if the mask is tight enough; if it is, suction will be felt; if air leaks around the edges, tightening is needed.

The skin diver should learn snorkeling techniques before trying SCUBA diving. Snorkel diving is based on "hyperventilation:" The diver takes an extra-deep breath and holds it as the descent is made. The purpose is not only to build up a sizable air supply but to fill the chest with air pressure that will counterbalance the increasing water pressure as the diver goes down. In descending, the diver should also exhale occasionally into the mask to help equalize the pressure in the ears with the pressure outside.

Before diving, the novice will swim around on the surface for a while, getting used to breathing through the snorkel. Then he or she takes a first dive and learns, upon coming back to the surface, to drive the water out of the tube by snorting through the mouthpiece. The snorkel allows the diver to swim around near the surface, face down, keeping an eye out for whatever is being sought. Then, when that particular object is sighted, the diver takes a deep breath, as described, and uses the surface dive to descend. The surface dive is performed by jack-knifing, bringing the feet almost straight down and the snorkel below water, then kicking the legs back and up, breaking the surface with the feet, and stroking with both arms to swim downward. Only after a great deal of snorkeling experience should the participant take up SCUBA diving.

Competition. Skin diving is basically a participation sport. A number of sports have been adapted for relatively informal underwater play, however, and some special competitive sports have also been developed. The most important competitive version is spearfishing—which can, of course, also be purely participatory. Polynesian natives did spearfishing underwater, but the sport came to the United States from the Mediterranean, where it was discovered during the 1930s by an American, Guy Gilpatric.

There are three types of weapons used in spearfishing.

The sea gig, or trident, is about 40 to 50 in long and has three or five prongs. The sea spear is about 50 to 70 in long and has an arrow-type head. The sea lance, which usually measures about 90 in, may be as much as 12 ft long. All three can be used for spearing fish by hand.

A sling and an underwater "gun" may also be employed for fishing. The Hawaiian sling is simply a wooden tube with an elastic loop at one end. The spear is drawn through the tube and then pulled back, with the loop; when it is released from that position, the spear is propelled through the water. The "gun" is the underwater equivalent of the crossbow. It has a pistol grip and trigger mechanism and a long barrel. The spear is inserted into the barrel and gripped by one or more rubber strands. The strands are pulled tight to cock the gun. Then, when the trigger is pulled, the spear is released. The spear has several different kinds of removable heads, depending on the type of fish being hunted. Another type of gun uses compressed air or carbon-dioxide cartridges as the propelling force.

Bibliography. Sullivan, George: *The Complete Book of Skin and SCUBA Diving,* Coward-McCann, New York, 1969.

SKYDIVING

SKYDIVING—Sometimes known as sport or target parachuting, skydiving had its origin during the 1920s in special exhibitions at air shows. As a sport, it really came into its own after the Korean conflict, which trained a large number of young men as paratroopers. In 1957 the Parachute Club of America was formed as the national governing body of the sport, and in 1958 Jacques André Istel opened the nation's first sport jumping center at Orange, Massachusetts.

International competition had begun in 1951 with a five-country meet in Yugoslavia. The United States wasn't represented in the international championships until 1954. In 1960, Richard Fortenberry of the U.S. Army was the world overall champion, and since then the United States has done well in international competition. American women first competed internationally in 1960.

International meets generally include three individual events and one or two team events. Two of the individual

On-target landing is made by Bob Johns during national competition at Tahlequah, Oklahoma. (Parachutist *Photo by Jerry Irwin.*)

events are for accuracy, from altitudes of 1,000 and 1,500 m.

In the 1,000-m accuracy jump, a chutist begins with 200 points, and points are then deducted from that score for various penalties. A competitor is permitted to delay up to 10 sec in opening the chute, but loses 50 points if the delay (the period of free fall) exceeds that maximum. The chutist attempts to hit the center of a target 100 m (328 ft) in diameter; 2 points are deducted for each meter by which the center is missed. The 1,500-m event is similar, but the jumper must delay opening the parachute for at least 15 and no more than 21 sec; a penalty of 50 points is imposed for opening it too soon or too late. The target is the same. In both accuracy events, a jumper gets four attempts and only the three best jumps are scored. In team competition, four-man (or three-woman) squads compete, and the two best jumps of each team member are scored.

The third individual event is judged for style as the chutist performs a prescribed series of maneuvers during free fall. A competitor jumps from 2,000 m, on signal from the ground; after leaving the plane, the jumper gets another ground signal specifying which of three possible series of aerial maneuvers must be performed. The contestant is given 20 sec to perform the series, which includes 360-degree turns and back loops. If the series takes less than the prescribed time, the jumper (again starting with 200 points) gets 5 bonus points for each second under the limit; but each second over 20, consumed in the execution, results in the loss of 10 points. Other points are deducted by judges on the ground for various flaws in style and for errors. The jumper is also scored on the landing.

There were about 150 skydiving clubs in the United States in the late 1970s, with a total membership of more than 5,000.

Ten skydivers join hands to form a friendly circle in mid-air. (Parachutist *Photo by Jerry Irwin.*)

U.S. Overall Champions

Men

1969	Jim Lowe
1970	Clayton Schoelpple
1971	Clayton Schoelpple
1972	Roy Johnson
1973	Chuck Collingwood
1974	Jack Brake
1975	Jimmy Davis
1976	Jack Brake

Women

1969	Martha Huddleston
1970	Martha Huddleston
1971	Susie Neuman
1972	Susan Rademaekers
1973	Gloria Porter
1974	Debby Schmidt
1975	Debby Schmidt
1976	Cheryl Stearns

SLED DOG RACING—Although there was sled dog racing of a sort in northern European countries as early as the eighteenth century, the North American version of the sport is considerably more recent. In Europe, just one, two, or three dogs pull a sled similar to a toboggan. Most major North American races call for a minimum of seven dogs.

Sled dog racing, North American style, probably began with friendly challenges from one driver to another during the late nineteenth century. The first formal race was the All-Alaskan Sweepstakes, a 408-mi event from Nome to Candle, Alaska, and back to Nome in 1908. For some years the sport was pretty much confined to Alaska. In 1925, however, a diphtheria epidemic struck Nome, and the only way to get serum to the city was by dogsleds. Relay teams brought the serum 674 mi to save hundreds of lives, and the sled dogs and their drivers got international publicity.

Sled dog races began to spring up in other areas of North America, especially in eastern and western Canada and in northern New England. However, every region had its own set of rules, and most of the races were purely local. A major step toward developing uniform rules was the formation of the International Sled Dog Racing Association in 1966. This led, in turn, to the establishment of a number of races that attract sled dog teams from throughout North America—among them the "East Meets West" race at the St. Paul, Minnesota, Winter Carnival and the All-American Championship at Ely, Minnesota.

The best-known of the classic races is the World Championship Derby, held annually in Laconia, New Hampshire. The Laconia Sled Dog Club was organized in 1931 and sponsored the first World Championship Derby in 1936. The club was inactive from 1938 until 1956, when it was reorganized, and the race was resumed in the latter year. The derby is run in three 18-mi heats on three consecutive days, and the team with the best total time for the three heats is the winner. Until 1973, there were three 20-mi heats.

The Dogs. Most sled dogs are Siberian or Alaskan huskies, but other breeds are sometimes raced, including the Irish setter, the Doberman, and the Walker hound. The husky is better equipped for cold weather than the other breeds and stands a much better chance of winning the northernmost races. The setter's paws are troubled by

heavy snow, the Doberman has too short a coat to cope with extreme cold, and the Walker is basically a sprinter that lacks endurance.

Sled dog training begins when a puppy is a few weeks old. Early training focuses on teaching the puppy to know its master and to respond to the master's commands. When about eight months old, the dog is hitched with a team of veteran dogs to a wheeled vehicle to get used to the idea of pulling. Only after it has received considerable training of this kind is the dog actually hitched to a sled.

There are three very important dogs in each team. The lead dog, which usually runs alone at the head of the team, shows the way and gives direction to the entire team. The point dogs, which generally run in tandem behind the lead dog, are strong animals and willing to follow. The lead dog alone could not always control the direction of the team; the point dogs help keep the entire team on the right trail.

Rules. Although rules vary somewhat from race to race and area to area, there are some basics. The rules outlined here are based on those of the Laconia World Championship Derby.

There is no upper limit on the number of dogs, but the judge may order the size of a team reduced if he feels the driver can't handle the team properly. At least seven dogs must start the race. Dogs may be dropped from the team, but substitutes are not allowed; once a dog has been dropped, it may not rejoin the team. Where heats are involved, all dogs that start a heat must finish it. Whips up to 3 ft in length are allowed, but the dogs must never be struck. The whip is used for signaling only.

Races are based solely on time; teams usually start at 2-min intervals and race against time. A team is timed from the moment when the front part of the sled crosses the starting line to the moment the first dog reaches the finish line. When one team comes within 20 ft of another, the overtaking team has the right of way; its driver should call "trail" as a signal. The leading team must then make way for the following team or, if requested, must come to a complete stop to allow the following team to pass, unless the following team is repassing. The rule doesn't apply within ½ mi of the start or finish line.

A course is marked with red flags to indicate a turn, and with green flags on a straightaway. Red flags or markers on the right side mean there is a right turn ahead. Green flags just beyond an intersection or around a turn tell the driver to go straight ahead. If a team leaves the trail, it must go back and re-enter the trail at the point where it left before continuing along the course.

SNOWMOBILING—In 1922, Joseph-Armand Bombardier of the Province of Quebec put together a strange vehicle with two skis in front and two motorized tracks in back. Six years later, Carl Eliason of Wisconsin devised a similar contraption by fitting small skis to the front of a toboggan and attaching tracks powered by an outboard engine. In 1932, Eliason had a vehicle capable of doing 40 mph over snow. In 1936, Bombardier began marketing some of his vehicles, now powered by an 85-hp V-8, but there were no big sales. In 1958 he developed the prototype of the "Ski-Doo," the first well-known snowmobile make. The vehicle found its first real market among game wardens in the north. In 1959, 225 vehicles were sold.

Then snowmobiling really took off. During the late

1960s snowmobiles were selling at the rate of about 300,-000 a year in the United States and Canada. The primary reason was recreational. With a snowmobile a person can explore frozen, remote areas with little physical exertion.

Naturally, racing came next. In 1956 the U.S. Snowmobile Association (USSA) was organized at a meeting in Rhinelander, Wisconsin, and the group established the first racing rules and regulations with assistance from the U.S. Ski Association. Rhinelander was the site of the first World Series of Snowmobiling. By 1973 professional racing was so well established, with manufacturers paying drivers and equipping them with factory snowmobiles, that the Sno-Pro racing circuit was organized by the USSA.

Types of Races. Snowmobiles can be used for long-distance cross-country races, track races, or drag races. Cross-country races are based on elapsed time (time taken in covering the course) with the vehicles starting separately at regular intervals. The longest is the Midnight Sun 600, held through wild Alaskan country. In track racing, a number of trial heats are held to cut the field to six to eight racers, who compete head to head on an enclosed oval. The "Indy 500" of the sport is a 500-lap race on a 1-mi oval at Sault Ste. Marie, Michigan.

The Sno-Pro circuit, the most exciting form of snowmobiling, offers track racing in which factory vehicles travel up to 90 mph. Races are conducted at 11 major tracks in the United States and Canada. Racing is also conducted in many classes, including stock and modified, with separate classes for vehicles with similar horsepower ratings.

Rules. There is nothing very complicated about snowmobile racing. The driver must wear a safety helmet with a face shield, safety glasses or goggles, and boots that come above the ankle, and must have both feet on the machine at the start (to prevent the driver's pushing off). Just prior to a race the starter gives a warning signal and the snowmobilers then have a warm-up period. Then a flag is raised and the "go" signal is given. For a false start the snowmobiler is penalized one length. A second false start results in disqualification.

Bibliography. Tuite, James J.: *Snowmobiles and Snowmobiling,* Cowles, New York, 1969.

SOARING—The first heavier-than-air flights were made in gliders. Most of the aircraft pioneers, including the Wright brothers, tested their airplane designs in powerless flight before using engines. Between world wars, moreover, the glider was often used to give novice pilots inexpensive flight training. Today, a glider is basically a sport craft, and the sport of flying a glider is known as soaring.

There are two modern types of gliders. Those in the utility category are used for training, exhibitions, and some sport flight. They are of rather rugged construction, for safety's sake, and their wings are designed to give the craft glide-path slopes of between 1 in 8 and 1 in 12. (A glide-path slope of 1 in 8 means that the craft descends 1 ft for each 8 ft of forward flight.) The more advanced gliders, known as "sailplanes," reach glide-path slopes of 1 in 20 to 1 in 40. They are characterized by long, slender wings; smooth, streamlined fuselages; and clean, simple tail assemblies.

Glider controls are similar to those used in small airplanes, but the control surfaces are primarily in the tail, not in the wings. The rudder is usually operated by pedals, with a universally hinged control stick or steering wheel to control elevator and aileron action.

Most sailplanes are equipped with a single landing wheel just about under the center of gravity; some of them have landing skids, with rubber springs, instead. Wing tips are usually reinforced for protection during landing. Many utility gliders, however, are equipped with standard two-wheel landing gears.

Launching. There are several ways of launching a glider. A power winch or an automobile may be used to give the glider sufficient speed to get into the air. The best method, however, is to tow the glider behind a powered plane until an altitude of about 2,000 ft is reached, the glider pilot staying directly behind the towplane, but slightly above it, to avoid turbulence created by the propellers. When sufficient altitude has been achieved, the pilot can release the glider's end of the line to set the craft free.

Soaring Methods. "Soaring" actually means gaining altitude without using power. The basic method of soaring is "thermaling"—finding and using rising currents of warm air to lift the glider. The presence of thermals is often indicated by cumuli, the puffy white clouds that everyone knows by sight, if not by name. Thermals sometimes rise as rapidly as 2,000 ft a minute and can be ridden to great heights by gliders.

The easiest method of soaring is called slope soaring. When moving air hits a ridge, it is forced up, and a glider can also use this rising air for lift. A glider can soar for great distances along a ridge, or headed away from a ridge, but great care must be taken not to go over the ridge, since there may be severe downdrafts on the other side.

A third common method is wave soaring. Vertical "waves" of wind are often found on the lee side of mountain ranges (the side opposite prevailing winds), and are frequently signaled by the presence of lens-shaped clouds in the atmosphere. A glider pilot who is going to try wave soaring should have a supply of oxygen because the wave can carry the craft to great heights (the world record for altitude in a glider is 46,267 ft).

A glider is equipped with several standard aircraft instruments, including altimeter, air-speed indicator, turn-and-bank indicator, and compass, but the most important instrument for soaring is the variometer, a very sensitive rate-of-climb indicator. The variometer will indicate that the craft is moving upward or downward even when the movement is too small to be noticed by the pilot. This enables the pilot to detect thermals or downdrafts more quickly.

Training. Civil Aeronautics Administration regulations allow a student to get a permit to begin instruction at 14 years of age and a pilot's license at 16. There are two types of training. One type is similar to that used in training pilots: A two-seated glider carries both the instructor and the student, and the instructor gives "on-the-job" training and eventually checks out the student and allows the student to try solo flight. Other instructors start the student in a single-seated glider from the beginning. At first the student only taxis while being towed behind a car, learning to keep the craft's wings level. The next stage of training consists of very short flights. Then the aspiring pilot learns to control the glider while in tow behind a plane, and subsequently to release from the plane and glide back onto the runway.

Having mastered a training glider, the pilot is now ready for solo flight in a higher-performance glider, a sailplane. Throughout this type of training, the pilot is always alone in the glider, an arrangement that many instructors believe is conducive to increasing the student's self-confidence.

Competition. Organized in 1932, the Soaring Society of America, Inc. conducts national contests. The society also awards a number of achievement badges, on a graduated scale, ranging up to its Diamond Award: for a flight at a distance of 500 km (312 mi), for a flight to a predetermined goal at least 300 km (192 mi) in length, and for an altitude gain of at least 5,000 m (16,000 ft) above the release point.

Major competitions include a series of events based on speed on a triangular course, altitude, accuracy in returning to the starting point, and straightaway distance. Points are awarded for the pilot's finish in each category, and the point total for all events determines the overall champion.

U.S. Open Champions

1947	Richard J. Comey
1948	Paul B. MacCready, Jr.
1949	Paul B. MacCready, Jr.
1950	Richard H. Johnson
1951	Richard H. Johnson
1952	Richard H. Johnson
1953	Paul B. MacCready, Jr.
1954	Richard H. Johnson
1955	Kempes Trager
1956	Lyle A. Maxey
1957	Stanley W. Smith
1958	Richard E. Schreder
1959	Richard H. Johnson
1960	Richard E. Schreder
1961	A. J. Smith
1962	John D. Ryan
1963	Richard H. Johnson
1964	Richard H. Johnson
1965	Dean Svec
1966	Richard E. Schreder
1967	A. J. Smith
1968	Ben Greene
1969	George B. Moffat, Jr.
1970	Ross Briegler
1971	A. J. Smith
1972	Ray Gimmey
1973	George B. Moffat, Jr.
1974	George B. Moffat, Jr.
1975	George B. Moffat, Jr.
1976	Joe Emons

Bibliography. Wolters, Richard A.: *The Art and Techniques of Soaring,* McGraw-Hill, New York, 1971.

SOCCER—The most popular sport in the world, soccer is apparently also one of the most ancient. In more than 80 countries it is "football" (the game meant when the general term "football" is used, that is), and it is the direct ancestor of American football, Canadian football, Rugby, and several other sports.

Soccer can be traced directly to eleventh-century England, but its antecedents may well be much older than that. In many pagan religious ceremonies, perhaps as

A defender is about to attempt a "tackle," while the dribbler prepares to take elusive action. (*Hank Seaman,* New Bedford Standard-Times.)

long as 4,000 years ago, the head of a puppet representing the god of darkness was the ball in a kind of field-hockey contest. Evidently somewhere along the line, ball games became Christianized and were associated with Easter ceremonies—and sometimes, instead of using sticks, the combatants used their hands and feet to batter the ball.

Early football games in England were associated with religious ceremonies, and especially with Shrove Tuesday (the day before Ash Wednesday). Some writers have traced football games to A.D. 217 in Derby, England, and it is pretty well established that by 1175 London schoolboys were playing football every year on Shrove Tuesday. The game was banned by rulers several times, along with other sports which distracted people from the practice of archery. The first such ban was by proclamation of Edward II in 1314. However, the sport was apparently already quite popular; the very fact that it was proscribed at frequent intervals indicates that the bans weren't accomplishing much.

In 1603, when James I became king, people were urged to play football—a sign that firearms were rapidly replacing the bow and arrow in warfare. And football flourished throughout the British Isles. Every region, perhaps even every town, had its own set of rules, but one feature remained remarkably constant—the hands and arms could not be used to advance the ball. Rugby was "invented" when that rule was broken by William Webb Ellis of Rugby College, who picked up the ball and ran with it during an 1823 match.

As Rugby gained popularity, there was an increasing confusion about which sport was meant by "football." In 1863 the London Football Association was formed and voted to stick to the old style of play. That form of football became known as "association football," abbreviated "assoc football." Eventually the abbreviation gave way to "soccer football," or "soccer."

The sport was introduced by the British to India and South America during the nineteenth century, and it also spread rapidly across Europe. It is now played in more than 80 countries, under the overall supervision of the Federation Internationale de Football Association. There are professional leagues in Britain, Continental Europe, and South America.

The major international trophy is the World Cup, formally the Jules Rimet Trophy, awarded each four years. In World Cup play, each player represents his home country, regardless of where he normally plays, and there are 16 teams in the final tournament. After round-robin play, the field is cut to eight, then to four, and finally to two finalists. The 1974 World Cup competition, in West Germany, was watched by a television audience estimated at 80 million.

Soccer in North America

It is believed that soccer was played at Harvard and Yale as early as 1820. If so, it was apparently used primarily to haze freshmen, and it disappeared after 1830 because of the excessive roughness. The well-known "first intercollegiate football game" between Princeton and Rutgers on November 6, 1869 was actually soccer, and until 1875 soccer was played by several Eastern colleges. Harvard, which had developed its own kind of football, based on Rugby, didn't play soccer, and in 1875 other collegiate teams agreed to play something more like Harvard's version of football, which eventually developed into modern American football.

Soccer was reintroduced to the United States during the 1870s by Scotch, Irish, and English immigrants, especially in major textile cities. Among the early centers of the sport's popularity were Philadelphia, New York, areas of New Jersey, and Fall River, Massachusetts. In 1884 the American Football Association was organized, and in 1887 the New England Association Football League was formed.

St. Louis was also one of the early centers, and is now the most important soccer-playing area in the United States. The St. Louis Football Association was formed in about 1885, and in 1890 St. Louis had the first known team composed entirely of native-born Americans—the Kensingtons, who won the St. Louis championship without giving up a goal.

There was a Montreal Football Club as early as 1866, and the Dominion Football Association was formed in 1873; it is still the ruling body of the sport in Canada.

Soccer has never approached the popularity of American football in the United States. It has had its avid followers throughout this century, however, and has experienced a certain upsurge in recent years.

The United States Soccer Football Association (USSFA), the ruling body of the sport in this country, was organized in 1913, through a merger of the American Football Association, which controlled the professional leagues, and the American Amateur Football Association.

The two major trophies in this country are the National Challenge Cup, originally offered for amateur teams in 1913, but now open to amateurs and professionals, and the National Amateur Challenge Cup, instituted in 1923 for amateur teams.

The sport in the United States has also grown considerably on the collegiate level. The Intercollegiate Association Football League was formed by five Eastern schools in 1905. In 1925 it became the Intercollegiate Soccer Football Association of America—no longer a league but an administrative body for the sport. The NCAA and NAIA both inaugurated national championship tournaments in 1959. There are now about 600 college soccer teams in the United States. St. Louis University is recognized as the collegiate power, with 10 NCAA championships in 15 tournaments, conducted up to the mid-1970s.

Professional Soccer. While there had been professional soccer in the United States as early as 1910, those players and teams were really semiprofessional. Soccer as a professional sport in the modern sense didn't begin until 1966, when two North American leagues were formed with a total of 22 teams. Results were nearly disastrous; the two leagues merged into the North American Soccer League (NASL), with 17 teams, in 1967. That number dropped abruptly to five in the following season.

The NASL's first several years of existence were not particularly successful. The league then adopted, for the 1968–1969 season, a new format designed to build up spectator interest. For the first half of the season, foreign teams were invited to represent the United States clubs; the Wolverhampton Wolves, representing Kansas City, won the International Cup with a 6–2 record. In the second half of the season, the five cities fielded their own clubs; again, however, almost all the players were from other countries, and the few Americans were mostly foreign-born.

Since then, the NASL has embarked on a policy of encouraging American amateur soccer, in order to develop home-grown professional talent. The league has given financial support to the USSFA development program, which has raised United States soccer to a respectable level, and has also used a quota system. In 1972–1973, each team had to have at least three American players on its roster; that number was increased to four in 1973–1974, and the league expects its rosters to be made up entirely of American players by 1983.

The Southern Division champion in 1971–1972, St. Louis, had seven Americans on its squad. And the 1972–1973 season represented something of a breakthrough, when the rookie of the year was for the first time an American, Kyle Rote, Jr., son of a onetime star of professional football (New York Giants); the coach of the year was an American, Al Miller, just up from the college ranks; and the goalie of the year was another young American player, Bob Rigby.

The NASL has also gradually but continually expanded. In 1973–1974, the league added four West Coast franchises, bringing its total to 15 teams, and expanded to 20 teams for the 1974–1975 season. The major goal of the NASL now is to get television exposure, to gain new fans and financial security.

Until 1974 the NASL used an unusual scoring method in determining its standings: A team was given 6 points for a win, 3 points for a tie, and 1 point for each goal scored, up to a maximum of 3 per game. In 1974 the league adopted a method of breaking ties and, with it, another wrinkle in determining point totals.

If a game is tied at the end of regulation play, it is decided by a series of penalty kicks (described in the next section of this entry). Each team selects five players to attempt one penalty kick each from the 12-yd spot. If the tie still stands at the end of a round of penalty kicks, each team must select five different players for penalty kicks, and this time the round ends in sudden death; that is, if the first player from Team A misses his kick, while the first player from Team B makes a successful kick, play ends at that point with Team B the winner. When a team wins such a tie-breaker under the new system of scoring, it receives 3 points in the standings for the victory, not 6. And bonus points are given only for the first 3 goals scored in regulation play.

Rules

Although soccer can be played on a field ranging from 100 to 130 yd in length and 50 to 100 yd in width—the length always greater than the width—the usual playing field is 110 by 80. The field is divided into halves by a halfway line, parallel to the end lines. The midpoint of the halfway line is also the center of a center circle, 10 yd in radius. At each end of the field, in front of the goals, are goal areas, each 20 yd wide by 6 yd deep; these are surrounded by penalty areas, each 44 yd wide and 18 yd deep. Four corner areas, each a quarter-circle with a 1-yd radius, are at each of the field's four corners.

Each goal consists of two goalposts, 8 ft high and 8 yd apart, connected by a crossbar; a goal net is suspended from the crossbar, attached to the backs of the goalposts and anchored to the ground behind the goal line.

The ball, a little smaller than a basketball, has a circumference of 27 to 28 in. Its weight at the beginning of the game is 14 to 18 oz, and the inflation pressure is 12 to 13 lb. The cover is leather or rubber.

The usual soccer uniform consists of a shirt, shorts, knee socks—usually worn over shinguards—and soccer shoes, which have small round studs on sole and heel, or sneakers.

There are 11 players on each team. The goalkeeper is the only player permitted to lay hands on the ball, within the penalty area; no other player may touch the ball with the hands except in making an inbounds throw. The goalkeeper's handling of the ball is limited, moreover. It is restricted to the goalkeeper's own penalty area; the goalkeeper may not take more than four steps while holding the ball, and must get rid of it within a reasonable time. Taking more than four steps or delaying in getting rid of the ball is penalized by an indirect free kick. Handling the ball outside the penalty area calls for a direct free kick—the same penalty assessed when any other player handles the ball at any point on the field when the ball is in play. The object of the game is to get the ball into the opponent's goal, thereby scoring one point, by moving it with feet, legs, and head—or, on occasion, with other parts of the body except the hands.

There are no special rules for players in positions other than goaltender, and soccer formations can vary from team to team or from time to time. The most common modern formation, however, is the 4-2-4, in which there are four defenders, or backs; two linemen, or midfielders; and four strikers, or forwards. The 4-3-3 formation, which puts great emphasis on defense (the first number refers to the number of backs, the third number to the number of strikers), is also commonly used.

Progress of Play. A soccer game consists of two 45-min periods, with a 10-min rest period between them. (American college teams play four 22-min quarters). Play begins with a kickoff from the center circle, after a coin flip to determine which team kicks. (In soccer the kicking team will usually retain possession of the ball.) Members of the receiving team must stay 10 yd from the center (halfway) line until the ball is kicked; the kick must travel the length of the ball's circumference (27–28 in) to be in play, and the kicker isn't allowed to make contact with the ball a second time until another player has touched it.

Play in soccer is continuous; it stops only when a goal is scored, a foul is called, or the ball goes out of bounds. A goal is followed by a kickoff by the team that was scored upon. If the ball goes out of bounds across a sideline, it is put in play by a throw-in by a member of the team not responsible for putting the ball out of bounds. Some part of both feet of that player must be on the ground, outside the sideline, and both hands must be used to make the throw, which must be made from behind and over the head. If an illegal throw is made, the opposing team is awarded a throw-in from the same spot.

If the ball goes out of bounds across a goal line (without going into the goal), and is last touched by an offensive player, the defense puts it in play with a goal kick. The goal kick, usually but not always made by the goalkeeper, is made from the goal area and directed upfield. If last touched by a defensive player, the ball is put in play by the offense with a corner kick. For such a kick, the ball is placed in the corner area nearest the spot where the ball left the field.

Fouls. The major fouls in soccer are: handling the ball; holding, pushing, or striking an opponent; charging an opponent violently or dangerously, or charging from behind; and tripping, kicking, or jumping at an opponent.

Incidental body contact is permitted, but the only form of deliberate body contact allowed is shoulder charging. In playing the ball, a participant may move an opponent away from the ball by shoulder-to-shoulder contact, from the side. Charging from behind or making contact with other parts of the body is not permitted, and the purpose of legal charging is only to move the opponent away from the ball, not to knock the opponent down.

When committed within a team's own penalty area, a major foul is penalized by a penalty kick for the opposition. The ball is placed on the penalty spot, 12 yd from the goal line, and a player is given a direct shot at the goal, with only the goalkeeper to beat. All other players must be outside the penalty area, and the goalkeeper, once in position for the play, may not move the feet until the ball is kicked.

Major fouls committed elsewhere on the field are penalized by a direct free kick (an unhindered kick of the ball when stationary) from the point where the foul occurred. Defending players must be at least 10 yd from the ball when it is kicked. A player can attempt to score a goal directly on the free kick.

There are a number of minor offenses which are penalized by an indirect free kick. Here the kicker cannot score a goal directly; instead, the player passes the ball to a teammate. These minor offenses include excessive arguing with the referee, deliberate obstruction of an opponent, and illegal substitution.

The most complicated of the minor fouls is the offside

violation. A player in the act of receiving a pass is offside if these conditions prevail at the moment the ball is passed: the player is ahead of the ball, there are fewer than two opponents between the player and the goal line, and the player is in the opponent's half of the field (the half defended by the opponents). Note that all three of these conditions must exist for the player to be offside, and that what matters is where the player was when the pass play began, not where the player was when the pass was received.

Techniques

Kicking. One kind of soccer-style kick has become familiar to pro football fans, because so many field-goal kickers have come from soccer fields in recent years. However, there are many different kinds of kicks used in soccer. The field-goal kickers use the instep kick: The toes of the kicking foot are turned slightly outward, and the ball is hit by the instep, the curved part of the inside of the foot just in front of the ankle.

There are two variations: the lofted kick, commonly used for goal kicks to get the ball far downfield, and the low drive, a scoring kick. For the lofted kick, the kicker approaches the ball at a slight angle, takes a full back-swing, hits the ball just below the center, and seemingly kicks right through the ball. At follow-through, the kicker is leaning back, and the kicking toe is pointing in the direction of the ball's flight. For a low drive, the kicker plants one foot alongside the ball and with the other hits the ball directly in the center, again "kicking through the ball." One of the major differences is that, with the lofted kick, the kicker is leaning backward; with the low drive, the kicker is leaning slightly forward at the moment of impact.

The inside-of-the-foot kick (instep kick) is used for medium and long passes. It is similar to the low drive, but the kicking foot is turned outward even farther, virtually at a right angle to the line of flight, and the follow-through is short, only about 1 ft. The ball is hit right in the center with the upper part of the instep; the foot must be about 2 in off the ground to make contact in the proper spot.

The chip is usually used for a short pass, when an opponent is in the way, and is similar to the golf shot. The player kicks down through the ball, scooping it up with the instep and sliding the foot under it to impart backspin. The leg swings almost entirely from the knee, and there is a slow upward follow-through. The ball should rise quickly, to a height of about 10 ft, and then drop rather rapidly. The chip shot is frequently seen near the goal, and often results in a score by a teammate.

The outside of the foot can be used for short passing kicks when a player is traveling at top speed. As the foot approaches the ball in a running stride, the player turns the toes inward and kicks, sidewise, through the center of the ball.

Another deceptive type of pass is the back-heel. The player strides over the ball with the foot and then kicks it backward with the heel, while taking a quick hop on the other foot. A more difficult backward pass, made while dribbling the ball, is performed by crossing over with the nondribbling foot and swinging it backward to pass the ball back at an angle.

Dribbling. In soccer, dribbling is any method of keeping the ball under control while running. The front part of the foot is usually used to make solid contact with the center of the ball. The ball should be kicked just far enough and fast enough so that it is in position for another nudge when the kicker arrives on the next stride.

The dribbler can fake out an opponent by suddenly stopping the dribble (accomplished by putting the foot squarely on top of the ball), by suddenly pulling the ball back with the foot in order to cut around the defender, or by kicking the ball through the defender's legs and then breaking around the defender to pick up the ball on the other side—that is, to regain possession and resume dribbling.

If getting past an opponent seems impossible, and there is no teammate to whom to pass, the player in possession of the ball will screen it. Screening is similar to guarding a basketball while dribbling; the player, dribbling with the right foot, turns the left side of the body to the defender, keeping the body between the defender and the ball. From that position, the soccer player can do many of the things a basketball player might do from a similar position: break around the defender in one direction or the other, fake in one direction and break around the defender in the other, or pass the ball back to a teammate.

Tackling. This technique in soccer is completely different from tackling in American football. It is, in effect, the act of stealing the ball from an opponent, and must of course be done with the feet. Usually a tackle consists of blocking the ball, while it is being dribbled by an opponent, and then getting control of it to begin a dribble or to

This player has stopped the ball with his left foot and is about to give it a long ride. (*Hank Seaman*, New Bedford Standard-Times.)

Soccer often requires real acrobatics from its players; this player has just made a mid-air kick toward the opponent's goal, and his teammate is following the ball. (*Hank Seaman,* New Bedford Standard-Times.)

make a pass. At times, however, tackling consists of kicking the ball directly away from an opponent.

The sliding tackle in soccer is usually a desperation move to stop an opponent who is breaking away. The defender, running usually at a right angle to the dribbler's path, or even coming from slightly behind, moves in to kick the ball away. As the defender goes through the kicking motion, the other leg is permitted to buckle at the knee; the defender rolls to that side to hit the ground in a position similar to that of a sliding baseball player. If the sliding player misses the ball and trips the opponent, the defender has committed a foul. However, if the latter succeeds in kicking the ball away, the opponent is responsible for avoiding body contact in the action that follows.

The sliding block tackle is a similar device, except that the defender is trying to get possession of the ball rather than trying to kick it away. A player attempting such a tackle has to start a bit sooner than would be necessary for the ordinary sliding tackle, but much the same sequence of moves prevails: sliding, rolling slightly toward the opponent, and raising the top leg to get it on top of the ball. That leg is hooked back toward the body so that, when the player stands up again, the leg is just about in front and ready for the player's next move.

Trapping. A trap is a method of getting a flying ball under control and on the ground so it can be dribbled or kicked. When trapping a ball with the foot, the player catches it just as it hits the ground. The foot must give somewhat, to smother the bounce: If the player jabs at the ball instead of keeping the ankle relaxed, the result will be that the ball is kicked away.

When the ball is high in the air, the player uses a chest trap; if the ball is dropping, the player leans back to let the ball hit the chest at just about a right angle, and then leans over farther back on impact to keep the ball from bouncing far. It should bounce just a few inches and then drop straight down. If the ball is rising or coming in a straight line, the player leans forward, again to get the ball to strike the chest at a right angle, and cushions the impact.

When the ball arrives at medium height, the thigh trap is called for. The player brings the leg up, knee bent, so the ball will hit the soft inner thigh; at the moment of impact, the thigh is lowered slightly to keep the ball from bouncing away.

Heading. Perhaps soccer's most spectacular play is a goal scored on a header—a shot made with the head. Heading accurately requires a great deal of practice. The player should use the middle of the forehead, and must attack the ball instead of merely letting it bounce off the head. The body weight should be supported by the toes, and the knees should be flexed, so that the body's thrust is behind the head as it strikes the ball. Generally the player has to leap to head the ball properly. The jump must come a bit early, so that the player is at maximum height just before the ball arrives, the legs kicked up behind, the back arched slightly backward. As the ball arrives, the player jackknifes the body forward, striking the ball with the forehead and sending it straight forward and slightly downward with maximum speed and power.

Volleying. The good soccer player can't merely play the ball when it comes on the ground, or invariably take the time to trap it before playing it. Probably half or more of soccer kicks are directed at a ball that is considerably above ground level. Volley kicks (those made before the ball hits the ground) use the same techniques as ground kicks, but timing is exceptionally important. Moreover, some balls are at heights that make unusual techniques necessary.

On balls somewhat above knee level, the player must lean away from the kicking leg and then swing it almost horizontally, using a quick, sharp snap of the lower leg. One of the most difficult soccer kicks is the overhead volley; the ball arrives at shoulder height or above, and the player kicks it backward, over the head. To accomplish this, the player must leap off the ground, the kicking foot higher than the other foot and bent at the knee at about a right angle, the toe pointed toward the ground; then, as the player kicks up at the ball, the foot and ankle form a right angle that directs the ball backward. The player must fall backward, arms spread, with palms down, to cushion the landing.

Goalkeeping. Although there is a much larger net to protect, the soccer goalkeeper has a good deal in common with the goalie in ice hockey. One of the essentials is that, whenever possible, the soccer goalie get secure possession of the ball to prevent a score on a rebound.

Proper positioning is also vital, as in hockey. The basic position is in the center of the goal, about 1 yd in front of the goal line, but the goalie moves back and forth, as the ball does, and must also be ready, on occasion, to go out to get possession of the ball when it is some 8 yd from the goal, or even farther. The general rule is that, if a goalie has a reasonably sure opportunity to get to a loose ball (a ball in play) before an opponent can, the goalie should move out and get possession.

When an opponent comes in on a breakaway, the goalie moves out to cut down the angle: The farther out the goalie is, the less open goalmouth the opponent has to shoot at. If the goalie cannot get hold of the ball in stopping a shot, an alternative move is to make the save by punching the ball away from the goal area, with two clenched fists, if possible. On a high shot, the goalie's safest move is often simply to deflect the ball over the crossbar.

The goalie can also play an offensive role by starting the team's attack after getting possession of the ball. This is often accomplished by passing the ball to a nearby teammate, if there is no opponent in the immediate area. More often the goalie will do it with a long pass to an open teammate, which will start the offense and, at the same time, get the ball out of the danger area.

The goalie's pass resembles a baseball pitcher's throw more than a football pass. The goalie's hand is behind and slightly underneath the ball; the ball should be released at approximately head height, and is usually thrown hard and low to avoid interception. The goalie will not usually try to lob the ball over the head of an intervening opponent. If there is no open teammate to pass to, the goalie will punt the ball, very much as in American football, to get it far downfield.

North American Soccer League Champions

(The NASL has used several different play-off systems. In 1968 the league was split into two conferences, with two divisions in each. Division champions played for the conference championships, and the conference champions then met in a two-game play-off, with total goals in the two games determining the league champion. In 1969 no play-offs were held. In 1970 there were two divisions, and the division champions met in a two-game play-off, based on aggregate score. In 1971 the second-place finisher in one division met the first-place finisher in the other in a best-of-three series, and the winners of these two series met in a three-game series for the championship. In 1972 the same system was used, but each round of the play-offs consisted of just one game. In 1973 there were three divisions, and the second-place team with the best record among second-place finishers qualified for the semifinals, along with the three division champions. After a semifinal round of one-game play-offs, the two winners met in a single championship game. In 1974 there were four divisions. The four division champions and the two second-place teams with the best records in their class entered a quarterfinal play-off; the two teams with the best overall season records drew byes in the first round. Each play-off series consisted of just one game.)

Regular Season Champions

(Figures represent victories, losses, and ties respectively.)

1968	Atlantic—Atlanta	18	7	6
	Lakes—Cleveland	14	7	11
	Gulf—Kansas City	16	11	5
	Pacific—San Diego	18	8	6
1969	Kansas City	10	2	4
1970	North—Rochester	9	9	6
	South—Washington	14	6	4
1971	North—Rochester	13	5	6
	South—Atlanta	12	7	5
1972	North—New York	7	3	4
	South—St. Louis	7	4	3
1973	East—Philadelphia	9	2	8
	North—Toronto	6	4	9
	South—Dallas	11	4	4

Although most intentional body contact is prohibited, the accidental and incidental contact makes soccer a rough sport at times. These two players have collided in pursuit of the ball. (*Hank Seaman*, New Bedford Standard-Times.)

(In 1974, the NASL adopted the penalty-kick tie-breaker; figures in the third column represent the number of games a team won in tie-breaker periods. Tie-breaker losses are recorded in the loss column.)

1974	North—Boston	10	9	1
	East—Miami	9	5	6
	Central—Dallas	9	8	3
	West—Los Angeles	11	7	2

(In 1975, the NASL began to list won-lost records only, with tie-breaking wins and losses recorded along with regulation-time wins and losses.)

1975	North—Boston	13	9
	East—Tampa Bay	16	6
	Central—St. Louis	13	9
	West—Portland	16	6
1976	North—Chicago	15	9
	East—Tampa Bay	18	6
	South—San Jose	14	10
	West—Minnesota	15	9

Play-off Champions

1968	Atlanta 3-0, San Diego 0-0
1969	No play-off—Kansas City champion
1970	Rochester 3-1, Washington 0-3
1971	Dallas 1-4-2, Atlanta 2-1-0
1972	New York 2, St. Louis 1
1973	Philadelphia 2, Dallas 0
1974	Los Angeles 4, Miami 3
1975	Tampa Bay 2, Portland 0
1976	Toronto 3, Minnesota 2

Top Scorers

Year	Player, Team	G	A	Pts.
1967	Yanko Daucik, Toronto	20	8	48
1968	John Kowalik, Chicago	30	9	69
1969	Kaiser Motaung, Atlanta	16	4	36
1970	Kirk Apostolidis, Dallas	16	3	35
	Carlos Metidieri, Rochester	14	7	35
1971	Carlos Metidieri, Rochester	19	8	46
1972	Randy Horton, New York	9	4	22

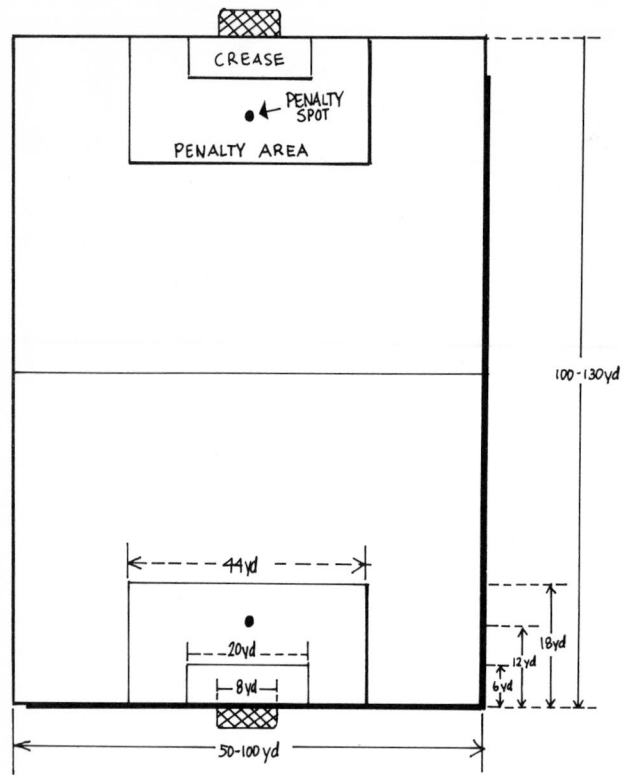

CREASE

PENALTY SPOT

PENALTY AREA

100-130yd

|← - - - - 44yd - - - - →|

|← -20yd - - →|

|← 8yd →|

18yd

12yd

6yd

|← - - - - 50-100 yd - - - - →|

Soccer field, or pitch

1973	Kyle Rote, Jr., Dallas	10	10	30
1974	Paul Child, San Jose	15	6	36
1975	Steve David, Miami	23	6	52
1976	Giorgio Chinaglia, New York	19	11	49

Top Goalies

Year	Player, Team	GA	Av.
1967	Mirko Stojanovic, Oakland	29	1.00
1968	Ataulfo Sanchez, San Diego	19	0.93
1969	Manfred Kammerer, Atlanta	15	1.07
1970	Lincoln Phillips, Washington	21	0.95
1971	Mirko Stojanovic, Dallas	11	0.79
1972	Ken Cooper, Dallas	12	0.86
1973	Bob Rigby, Philadelphia	8	0.62
1974	Barry Watling, Seattle	16	0.80
1975	Shep Messing, Boston	20	0.93
1976	Tony Chursky, Seattle	20	0.91

Most Valuable Player

1967   Ruben Navarro, Philadelphia
1968   John Kowalik, Chicago
1969   Cirilio Fernandez, Kansas City
1970   Carlos Metidieri, Rochester
1971   Carlos Metidieri, Rochester
1972   Randy Horton, New York
1973   Warren Archibald, Miami
1974   Peter Silvester, Baltimore
1975   Steve David, Miami
1976   Pele, New York

Rookie of the Year

1967   Willie Roy, Chicago
1968   Kaiser Motaung, Atlanta

1969   Siegfried Stritzl, Baltimore
1970   Jim Leeker, St. Louis
1971   Randy Horton, New York
1972   Mike Winter, St. Louis
1973   Kyle Rote, Jr., Dallas
1974   Doug McMillan, Los Angeles
1975   Chris Baker, Philadelphia
1976   Steve Pecher, Dallas

World Cup Winners

1930   Uruguay
1934   Italy
1938   Italy
1950   Uruguay
1954   West Germany
1958   Brazil
1962   Brazil
1966   England
1970   Brazil
1974   West Germany

Bibliography. Domini, Enzo: *The Book of Soccer*, Van Nostrand-Reinhold, New York, 1972; Glanville, Brian: *Soccer: A History of the Game, Its Players and Its Strategy*, Crown, New York, 1968; Woosnam, Phil with Paul Gardner: *Sports Illustrated Soccer*, Lippincott, Philadelphia, 1972.

SOFTBALL—There is a small amount of controversy about the origin of softball, but most authorities agree that a Minneapolis firefighter, Lewis Rober, made the first oversized baseball for an indoor game in 1895. His sport was originally called kittenball. Because it was to be played indoors, the baseball diamond was reduced to about two-thirds of its usual size and the ball was made larger and softer so it couldn't be hit as far. At first, the pitcher was allowed to throw overhand, but the shorter distance to home plate from the rubber gave the pitcher such an advantage over batters that, within a few years the rule was changed to require underhand pitching.

As indoor sport, the game moved out of the firehouses into Minneapolis and St. Paul in 1900, and in 1913 kittenball—as it had become known—was introduced to Minneapolis playgrounds. It soon spread to Canada, where it became remarkably popular in many areas within a short time.

In most areas of the United States, softball was basically an indoor sport until 1930. Then two Chicago men, Leo H. Fischer and M. J. Pauley, began organizing outdoor tournaments in Chicago. A "national" tournament was arranged by Fischer and Pauley as part of the Century of Progress World's Fair in 1933, and the sport was renamed "softball" for the occasion. It was discovered that, like basketball in its early years, the sport had spread faster than the semiofficial rules as drawn up in Minneapolis. There were 20 teams entered in the Chicago tournament, with 20 different sets of rules. As a result, the Amateur Softball Association (ASA) was organized, and rules were fairly well standardized.

Softball is now played in nearly 40 countries, mostly in the Americas, and in other countries where baseball has been introduced—including Japan, China, New Zealand, and Australia. The first world championship was a women's tournament in Australia in 1965. The first team world-championship tournament was held in Mexico

City in 1966. The women's tournament was repeated in 1970 and 1974. The men's tournament was repeated in 1968 and 1972.

Modern Game. At its highest level, softball is still dominated by pitching, despite the underhand delivery. Top softball pitchers can throw the ball at about 100 mph—almost as fast as the fastest baseball pitcher—and, at the softball pitching distance, such a speed is overpowering. No-hitters are frequent.

A prime example of the dominance of pitching in the game is Eddie "the King" Feigner. Since 1945, Feigner has traveled throughout the country to take on all challenging teams, with only three players to support him. In about 5,000 games, Feigner has pitched 750 no-hitters, including more than 200 perfect games—an average of nearly one no-hitter for every six games pitched. He has struck out about 90,000 hitters, an average of 18 per game (and there are only 21 outs in the regulation seven-inning softball game).

As a result of such domination by pitchers, two other forms of softball have been developed. The slow-pitch game is for hitters. The pitcher is required to deliver the ball with a 3-ft arc, and home runs are common, as are batting averages of above .500. This version of the game has grown rapidly, to the point where many purists think that "real" softball is on its way to extinction. Another slow-pitch game is played with a 16-in ball that is even less lively than the ordinary 12-in softball. This version of the game is particularly popular around Chicago.

There are now an estimated 25 million men, women, and youngsters in the United States who play softball, and an estimated total of 33 million in 47 countries, worldwide. The International Softball Federation has 39 member countries. The ASA holds six national championship tournaments: fast-pitch, industrial slow-pitch, and open slow-pitch in men's and women's divisions.

Rules. Softball rules are similar to baseball rules, with a few major exceptions. The base paths are only 60 ft in length (90 ft in baseball), and the pitcher is only 46 ft from home plate (as opposed to 60 ft, 6 in). As already noted, the pitcher has to throw underhand. Base runners may not leave their bases until the ball leaves the pitcher's hand. The regulation game is 7 innings.

The ball must weigh 6 to 6¾ oz and must have a circumference 11⅞ to 12⅛ in. It is filled with yarn-wrapped kapok and covered with smooth-seam leather. (Molded rubber covers are sometimes used.)

Women sometimes play on a diamond with 45-ft base paths; the pitching distance is 38 ft for women. Players in the ASA junior program, aged nine to twelve, use a diamond with 45-ft base paths and a pitching distance of 35 ft.

The bat must be 34 in or less in length and no more than 2⅛ in in diameter at its thickest part.

U.S. Champions

Year	Men's Team
1933	J. J. Gills, Chicago
1934	Ka-Nash-A's, Kenosha, Wis.
1935	Crimson Coaches, Toledo, Ohio
1936	Kodak Park, Rochester, N.Y.
1937	Briggs Manufacturing, Detroit
1938	Pohlers, Cincinnati, Ohio
1939	Carr's, Covington, Ky.
1940	Kodak Park, Rochester, N.Y.

Softball photos often resemble baseball photos, but this shot shows two of the distinctive elements of softball: The larger ball and the smaller bat. (*Hank Seaman*, New Bedford Standard-Times.)

1941	Bendix Brakes, South Bend, Ind.
1942	Deep Rock Oilers, Tulsa, Okla.
1943	Hammer Field, Fresno, Calif.
1944	Hammer Field, Fresno, Calif.
1945	Zollner's Pistons, Fort Wayne, Ind.
1946	Zollner's Pistons, Fort Wayne, Ind.
1947	Zollner's Pistons, Fort Wayne, Ind.
1948	Briggs Beautyware, Detroit
1949	Tip-Top Clothiers, Toronto, Can.
1950	Clearwater, Fla., Bombers
1951	Dow Chemical, Midland, Mich.
1952	Briggs Beautyware, Detroit
1953	Briggs Beautyware, Detroit
1954	Clearwater, Fla., Bombers
1955	Raybestos, Stratford, Conn.
1956	Clearwater, Fla., Bombers
1957	Clearwater, Fla., Bombers
1958	Raybestos, Stratford, Conn.
1959	Sealmasters, Aurora, Ill.
1960	Clearwater, Fla., Bombers
1961	Sealmasters, Aurora, Ill.
1962	Clearwater, Fla., Bombers
1963	Clearwater, Fla., Bombers
1964	Burch Gage & Tool, Detroit
1965	Sealmasters, Aurora, Ill.
1966	Clearwater, Fla., Bombers
1967	Sealmasters, Aurora, Ill.
1968	Clearwater, Fla., Bombers
1969	Raybestos, Stratford, Conn.
1970	Raybestos, Stratford, Conn.
1971	Welty Wag, Cedar Rapids, Iowa
1972	Raybestos, Stratford, Conn.

1973   Clearwater, Fla., Bombers
1974   Santa Rosa, Calif.
1975   Reading, Pa.
1976   Raybestos, Stratford, Conn.

Year	Women's Team
1933	Great Northerns, Chicago
1934	Hart Motors, Chicago
1935	Bloomer Girls, Cleveland
1936	National Manufacturing, Cleveland
1937	National Manufacturing, Cleveland
1938	J. J. Kreig's, Alameda, Calif.
1939	J. J. Kreig's, Alameda, Calif.
1940	Arizona Ramblers, Phoenix
1941	Higgins Midgets, Tulsa, Okla.
1942	Jax Maids, New Orleans, La.
1943	Jax Maids, New Orleans, La.
1944	Lind & Pomeroy, Portland, Oreg.
1945	Jax Maids, New Orleans, La.
1946	Jax Maids, New Orleans, La.
1947	Jax Maids, New Orleans, La.
1948	Arizona Ramblers, Phoenix
1949	Arizona Ramblers, Phoenix
1950	Orange, Calif., Lionettes
1951	Orange, Calif., Lionettes
1952	Orange, Calif., Lionettes
1953	Betsy Ross Rockets, Fresno, Calif.
1954	Leach Motor Rockets, Fresno, Calif.
1955	Orange, Calif., Lionettes
1956	Orange, Calif., Lionettes
1957	Hacienda Rockets, Fresno, Calif.
1958	Raybestos Brakettes, Stratford, Conn.
1959	Raybestos Brakettes, Stratford, Conn.
1960	Raybestos Brakettes, Stratford, Conn.
1961	Gold Sox, Whittier, Calif.
1962	Orange, Calif., Lionettes
1963	Raybestos Brakettes, Stratford, Conn.
1964	Lind Florists, Portland, Oreg.
1965	Orange, Calif., Lionettes
1966	Raybestos Brakettes, Stratford, Conn.
1967	Raybestos Brakettes, Stratford, Conn.
1968	Raybestos Brakettes, Stratford, Conn.
1969	Orange, Calif., Lionettes
1970	Orange, Calif., Lionettes
1971	Raybestos Brakettes, Stratford, Conn.
1972	Raybestos Brakettes, Stratford, Conn.
1973	Raybestos Brakettes, Stratford, Conn.
1974	Raybestos Brakettes, Stratford, Conn.
1975	Raybestos Brakettes, Stratford, Conn.
1976	Raybestos Brakettes, Stratford, Conn.

Amateur Softball Association Hall of Fame

(The ASA Hall of Fame was established in 1957 and since 1973 has been housed in the association's modern headquarters building in Oklahoma City.)

John Baker, Westport Conn., pitcher—Baker had a lifetime 780–120 record, with 58 no-hitters and more than 10,000 strikeouts. In 1938 he pitched four consecutive no-hitters.

Virginia Busick, Fresno, Calif., pitcher—In 227 innings in the Pacific Coast Softball League, Busick gave up only 87 hits and only 10 earned runs, and had 189 strikeouts. She led the Fresno Rockets to the 1957 national championship.

Estelle Caito, Phoenix, Ariz., second base—Caito played for the Orange Lionettes when they won three national championships, in 1955, 1956, and 1962, and she was an All-American in 1956, 1957, and 1960.

Tom Castle, Rochester, N.Y., first base—A .340 career hitter with the Rochester Kodaks, Castle played for the club when it won the 1936 and 1940 national championships.

Jim Chambers, Oshkosh, Wis., pitcher—Chambers struck out 43 men in one national tournament game in 1946 and had 117 strikeouts during the tournament. In his career he had 209 no-hitters and 4,380 strikeouts.

Jeanne Contel, Fresno, Calif., third base—With the Fresno Rockets, Contel played in 11 national tournaments in a 14-year span and was an All-American in 1953, 1955, 1957, and 1963.

Ben Crain, Omaha, Nebr., pitcher—Crain pitched nearly 1,000 games in a career that stretched from 1932 through 1949. He won 85 percent of his starts, hit .375, and averaged 20 home runs a year. He had more than 100 no-hitters.

Jerry Curtis, Clearwater, Fla., outfielder—Curtis played for seven national champion teams and was a four-time All-American. He was a Southern Region All-Star at four positions: pitcher, utility, second base, and outfield.

Margaret Dobson, Portland, Ore., third base—Dobson hit .615 in the 1950 national tournament, a record. She played in nine national tournaments overall and was an All-American in 1949 and 1950.

Sam Elliott, Decatur, Ga., pitcher—Elliott's first game was a no-hitter. In 21 seasons he won 1,046 games and lost only 84, with 107 no-hitters, 26 perfect games, and 13,936 strikeouts.

Robert Forbes, Clearwater, Fla., outfielder—Forbes was the youngest player, at 14, ever to play for the Clearwater Bombers. In 1956, when they won their third national championship, he led all tournament hitters with a .471 average. He was an All-American in 1951, 1953, and 1956.

Harold "Shifty" Gears, Rochester, N.Y., pitcher—Gears won 45 consecutive games in the 1928 season; during his career, he won 866 games and lost only 115; he had 373 shutouts, 61 no-hitters, and 13,244 strikeouts. He pitched for national champions in 1936 and 1940.

Warren "Fireball" Gerber, Cleveland pitcher—Gerber had a career total of more than 500 victories, including 50 no-hitters, and he averaged 15 strikeouts a game. He had four perfect games and, in 1945, pitched three consecutive no-hitters.

Betty Evans Grayson, Portland, Ore., pitcher—Grayson won 465 games and lost only 99 and once pitched 115 consecutive scoreless innings, in 1945. She had 51 no-hitters, three of them perfect games.

Carolyn Thome Hart, Pekin, Ill., outfielder—Hart had a lifetime .301 average and was four times an All-American.

Leroy Hess, Aurora, Ill., catcher—Hess was player-manager of the Stephens-Adamson Sealmasters when they won national championships in 1959 and 1961. He was an All-American in 1957, 1959, and 1961.

John Hunter, Clearwater, Fla., pitcher—Three times Hunter was named most valuable player in the national tournament, in 1951, 1953 and 1955. In his career, shortened by hip trouble, he won 275 and lost 19 and averaged just under two strikeouts per inning.

Hugh Johnston, Orlando, Fla., first base—Johnston was a National Softball League all-star from 1946 through 1953. He had a lifetime batting average of .295.

Bernie Kampschmidt, Fort Wayne, Ind., catcher—Kampschmidt caught for the Fort Wayne team that won national championships in 1945–1947; he had also played for the 1938 national champions. He was a player-man-

A runner is called out at home in a close play during the national championship tournament. *(Courtesy of Amateur Softball Association.)*

ager in 1946 and 1947. During his 15-year career, he played in more than 2,500 games.

Clyde "Dizzy" Kirkendall, Findlay, Ohio, pitcher—Kirkendall had a lifetime record of 1,144 wins and 52 losses, including 167 no-hit games—eight of them in national tournament play. He pitched for the national champions in 1935, 1938, 1945, 1946, and 1947.

Nina Korgan, New Orleans, La., pitcher—Korgan pitched for six national championship teams. In the 1941 tournament, she pitched four consecutive shutouts, including a perfect game; in one game she struck out 20 of 21 hitters.

Ronald Kronewitter, Mishawaka, Ind., pitcher—Kronewitter started playing in 1928. In one three-year period, he had a 53–5 record, including 16 no-hitters.

Al Linde, Midland, Mich., pitcher-outfielder—Linde was named an All-American as an outfielder and as a pitcher. He had more than 200 no-hitters during his career, and he hit .393 in the 1951 national tournament and .357 in the 1953 tournament.

B. E. "Gene" Martin—The only nonplayer in the Hall of Fame, Martin was one of the founders of the ASA, and was long-time executive secretary-treasurer of the organization.

Amy Peralta May, Tempe, Ariz., pitcher—May pitched for Phoenix Rambler teams that won national championships in 1940, 1948, and 1949. She won 35 national tournament games and was a six-time All-American. She totaled more than 300 shutouts and 50 no-hitters.

Gloria May, Fresno, Calif., first base—In 27 years of play, May took part in 15 national tournaments, was a three-time All-American, and played for the national champions in 1953, 1954 and 1957.

Clarence Miller, Memphis, Tenn., pitcher—An All-American in 1948, 1952, and 1954, he was most valuable player in the 1948 national tournament, during which he had a 6-2 record, 47 consecutive scoreless innings, a no-hitter, and 101 strikeouts.

James Ramage, Fort Wayne, Ind., shortstop—Ramage

played for the national champions in 1939, 1945, 1946, and 1947; he had a lifetime batting average of .293.

Myron Reinhardt, Alexandria, Ky., outfielder—Reinhardt was the first slow-pitch player elected; he played fast-pitch softball through 1950, then switched to slow-pitch and played on five national championship teams. He was National Tournament most valuable player in 1963.

Kay Rich, Fresno, Calif., outfielder infielder—Rich played in 12 national tournaments, was a three-time All-American and most valuable player in 1956, and played on three national champions. In nine years in the Pacific Coast Softball League, she had a .312 batting average.

Don Ropp, Aurora, Ill., third base—In 912 games with the Sealmasters, Ropp hit .325, with 131 home runs. He was an All-American in 1956 and 1963 and a member of the national champions in 1959, 1961, and 1965.

Ruth Sears, Santa Ana, Calif., third base—Sears played on four national championship teams and was a four-time All-American. She had a lifetime batting average of .425 in major competition and once hit .585 for a season.

Bob Sprentall, Clearwater, Fla., outfielder—An All-American in 1955, 1956, 1957, and 1960, Sprentall played for five national champion teams.

John Spring, Aurora, Ill., pitcher—At 19, Spring pitched a no-hitter in his first national tournament appearance. An eight-time All-American, he won 41 and lost 12 games in national tournament competition and had a 483-62 record during his career.

Roy Stephenson, Muttontown, N.Y., pitcher—Stephenson was an All-American in 1948, 1950, 1951, 1958, and 1959. He was 23-16 in national tournaments.

Mickey Stratton, Stratford, Conn., catcher—Stratton led the Stratford, Conn., Raybestos Brakettes to four national women's championships and was a five-time All-American. She had a .314 lifetime average.

Bertha Tickey, Stratford, Conn., pitcher—Tickey won 757 games and lost 88 in a 23-year career. She was an All-American 18 times and most valuable player in the national tournament 8 times, and played for 11 national champions. She had 162 no-hitters and, in her last pitching appearance, in 1968, she threw a 13-inning perfect game.

Richard Tomlinson, Clearwater, Fla., shortstop—A .345 career hitter, Tomlinson played for five national champions and was an All-American in 1959, 1960, 1961, and 1963; he batted .389 in the 1959 national tournament.

Bill West, Fort Wayne, Ind., pitcher—West once won 32 consecutive games in major competition; he was a member of the Zollner Piston team that won the national championship in 1946 and 1947; during those two seasons, he had a 60-6 record.

M. Marie Wadlow, Peoria, Ill., pitcher—One of the first two women named to the Hall of Fame, in 1957, Wadlow starred with the Caterpillar Diesellettes.

Nolan Whitlock, Rossville, Ga., shortstop—The All-American shortstop four consecutive years, 1954–1957, Whitlock played for national champion teams in 1954, 1956, and 1957.

Ray Wickersham, Palatine, Ill., outfielder—A lifetime .290 hitter, Wickersham had 67 home runs and 159 runs batted in in 617 games in major competition; he was an All-American in 1957, 1962, 1963, 1964, and 1965.

Dot Wilkinson, Phoenix, Ariz., catcher—A 19-time All-

American, Wilkinson had a .300 batting average in 33 years; she caught for national championship teams in 1940, 1948, and 1949.

Frankie Williams, Detroit, second base—Williams hit over .400 in three seasons and was an All-American in 1957, 1958, and 1962. In 10 seasons with the Raybestos Cardinals, his lowest average was .330.

Billy Wojie, New Haven, Conn., third base—A .286 lifetime hitter, Wojie was an All-American in 1955, 1959, and 1961. His grand-slam home run off Hall-of-Famer John Hunter won the 1956 championship for the Raybestos Cardinals.

John Ziegler, Miami, Fla., outfielder—Ziegler played in 10 national tournaments, and was an All-American in 1952 and 1960.

SPECIAL OLYMPICS—The Special Olympics games, conducted on local, state, regional, national, and international levels, are meant to give retarded children and adults a chance to participate in sports. Competition is open to persons of age 8 and older; generally, the IQ must be 80 or below, and youngsters who take part in regular school athletic programs are not eligible.

The competitive program includes track and field, basketball, bowling, diving, floor hockey, gymnastics, ice skating, swimming, and volleyball. In some cases, rules are modified somewhat to suit the abilities of the athletes.

All competitors must take part in a yearlong physical-fitness training program in order to participate in the Special Olympics at any level.

SPEEDBALL—This strange hybrid, combining elements of soccer, basketball, and football, was invented in 1921 by Elmer D. Mitchell of the University of Michigan. The field is basically an American football field, with end zones 100 yd apart and goalposts at each end of the field 120 yd apart. The game resembles soccer in that a ball on the ground must be kicked; it must not be touched by the hands. However, if the ball is kicked into the air, it may be caught by any player, who may then throw, punt, or drop-kick it.

The ball is a soccer ball, but the game is sometimes played on a smaller field with a basketball.

There are 11 players on each team, including a goalkeeper. The game starts with one team kicking off from its 40-yd line. The ball must reach the other team's 40-yd line before it is in play. Play is continuous, stopping only when the ball goes out of bounds or across an end line, when there is a score, or when a team or an official calls time out.

Although a player may not touch a ground ball with the hands, it is permissible to kick the ball into the air and then catch it. When catching an aerial ball, a player is allowed one overhead dribble.

Scoring in the men's game is somewhat different from that of the women's game. Methods of scoring are:

- Field goal—The ball must be legally kicked between the goalposts and *under* the crossbar; 3 points for men, 1 for women.
- Dropkick—The ball must be legally caught and drop-kicked over the crossbar; 2 points for men, 3 for women.
- Touchdown—A player catches a legal forward pass in the end zone; 1 point for men, 2 for women.
- Penalty kick—When a penalty kick goes into the goal, it produces 1 point.

- End kick—The ball must be legally kicked from within the end zone across the end line, outside the goal; 1 point for men. Women don't score on end kicks; men score only if both teams agree beforehand.

Fouls. It is a foul to kick, trip, push, hold, block, or be unnecessarily rough with an opponent. It is a violation if a player carries the ball; touches a ground ball with hands or arms; double dribbles; infringes on a kickoff, free kick, penalty kick, or tipoff; or kicks an aerial ball without first catching it.

Free Kicks. A free kick is awarded when a personal foul or a violation is committed by a player outside the player's end zone. It is awarded from the spot of the foul or from the spot where the ball was when the foul was committed, whichever is closer to the offending team's goal.

On a free kick, all opponents must be at least 10 yd away until the ball is kicked. The kicker may use a punt, dropkick, or place kick, and may kick the ball in any direction. Once it is kicked, the ball may not be played again by the kicker until it is touched by another player.

Penalty Kicks. There are two types of penalty kicks: with follow-up and without follow-up. On a kick with follow-up, if the kicker fails to score, the ball remains in play and the kicker's teammates may continue attempting to score. If there is no follow-up, the ball is dead.

The kick is taken from a spot directly in front of the goal and 10 yd away from it. One defender may be in the goal, and must stand on the end line until the ball is kicked. All other defenders must be behind the end line, and the kicker's teammates must be behind the ball.

When a foul is committed in the end zone, the fouled player is given two penalty kicks, one without a follow-up and the second with follow-up. For a violation in the end zone, one penalty kick, with follow-up, is awarded. For a technical foul (illegal substitution, delay of game, for example), one penalty kick without follow-up is awarded.

Out of Bounds. When the ball goes out of bounds over a sideline, the team that last touched it loses possession. The other team puts the ball into play from the spot with any type of kick or a pass. Opponents must be at least 5 yd away until the ball crosses the sideline. A goal cannot be scored directly.

If the defending team causes the ball to go over the end line, the attacking team puts it into play; the ball must leave the end zone before a score can be made.

Tipoffs. A tipoff is similar to a jump ball in basketball. It is used when two players simultaneously have possession of the ball, when opposing players commit simultaneous fouls, or when there is doubt about which team was responsible for the ball going out of bounds.

Duration. A game is made up of four 10-min quarters, with rest periods of 2 min after the first and third quarters and of 15 min at halftime. If the score is tied at the end of regulation time, overtime periods of 5 min each are played until one team wins.

In men's play, the ball is put into play at the beginning of each period with a kick or a pass from the sidelines at the point where the ball was in play at the end of the previous quarter, by the team that had possession. In women's play, each quarter begins with a kickoff by the team that last had possession.

SPEED SKATING—Although figure skating now gets much more attention, speed skating is a much older sport. It is probably nearly as old as the skate itself (for the early history of ice skating, see FIGURE SKATING). By the sixteenth century, speed-skating contests were well organized in Holland and, by the middle of the nineteenth century, the sport was a Dutch national craze. Even small villages held frequent contests, with prize money. A meet often included backward races, pair races, and obstacle races.

The first step toward international competition was taken in 1879, when the National Skating Association of Great Britain was formed, to promote speed skating in that country and to work for the establishment of international contests as well. In 1892, six countries attended an International Skating Congress in Holland and the first world speed-skating championships were held the following year, in Amsterdam.

The International Skating Union (ISU), organized in 1896, now conducts the world championships. Men race at distances of 500, 1,500, 5,000, and 10,000 m. An all-around champion is chosen through a point system, allotting a point a second for the 500 time, a third of a point per second for the 1,500, a tenth of a point for the 5,000, and a twentieth of a point for the 10,000.

Women race 500, 1,000, 1,500, and 3,000 m. Women's world championships were inaugurated in 1936.

Speed Skating in the United States. As in other countries, skating races in the United States were originally held outdoors, often as "touring" events over long distances. With the boom in indoor rinks during the 1920s, Holland and the Scandinavian countries built some rinks primarily for speed skating, with regulation Olympic 400-m tracks.

In the United States, however, indoor rinks are built primarily for pleasure skating, and while they can be used to train figure skaters, they are not easily adapted to speed skating—at least, not for skaters who want to compete on the international level. Many American skaters have had to learn on short indoor rinks, with 12 or 16 laps to the mile, where the skater is almost constantly turning. Only a handful of Olympic skating tracks have been developed in the United States. During the last decade, top American skaters have often spent several months of the year competing in Europe, to get used to regulation tracks and to sharpen their skills against top competition.

Most countries have a single supervisory body for both figure and speed skating. In the United States, however, there is a separate body with jurisdiction over speed skating, the Amateur Skating Union of the United States. National men's championships have been conducted since 1891; indoor championships were inaugurated in 1906. The ASU began conducting championships for women, both indoor and outdoor, in 1921.

Types of Competition. Races in the United States often use the pack start; all entrants start together and race each other. In international competition, however, skaters race in pairs, against the clock. They race in lanes and they change lanes each lap, at a crossover point, so that each will travel the same distance.

Races in which skaters actually race each other are becoming increasingly rare. Several of them are patterned after bicycle races. Skaters may, for example, race in pairs, with the winner of each heat going on to further competition, while the loser is eliminated. Or there may be heats for several racers; the winner of each heat, or the top two or three finishers, advance to further competition.

An enjoyable type of race for spectators is the "devil take the hindmost," in which, at the end of each lap, the competitor who is last is eliminated and the skaters keep going until just two of them are left to fight it out at the finish.

Equipment. The speed skate has a long, narrow blade, usually about 18½ in long and from ⅟₃₂ to ⅟₁₆ in wide, reinforced above with steel tubing. The boot is made of very thin leather and has little extra support for the ankle; it is low-cut and looks much more like an ordinary shoe than the figure or hockey skating boot.

The rest of the speed skater's costume combines warmth and lightness of weight, and is tight-fitting to cut down air resistance. Woolen tights, a tight sweater, and a protective plastic helmet make up the usual outfit.

Technique. The speed-skating stride looks deceptively simple, but it takes some time to master because perfect edge control is required. For each stroke, there is a power foot and a gliding foot. The power foot, by pushing back against the ice, gives the skater impetus, and the contestant then glides for a period on the other foot. There is a continuous rolling action involved. The push is made with the inside edge of the blade, while the glide begins on the outside edge. During the glide the skater rolls the gliding skate from the outside edge to the inside edge so that foot, in turn, can become the power foot.

U.S. Outdoor Champions

Men

1891	Joseph Donoghue	1904	Morris Wood
1892	Joseph Donoghue	1905	Morris Wood
1893	John S. Johnson	1906	Morris Wood
1894	John S. Johnson	1907	Morris Wood
1895	John S. Johnson	1908	Edmund Lamy
1896	John Nilsson	1909	Edmund Lamy
1897	John Nilsson	1910	Edmund Lamy
1898–99	No competition	1911	Robert McLean
1900	Leroy See	1912	Robert McLean
1901	Morris Wood	1913	Robert McLean
1902	Morris Wood	1914	Robert McLean
1903	Morris Wood	1915	Russell Wheeler

A speed skater leans sharply inward to round a turn on the Lake Placid, New York, Olympic course. *(F. Kelly MacNeill.)*

1916	Harry Cody	1950	Ken Bartholomew
1917	Arthur Staff	1951	Ken Bartholomew
1918–19	No competition	1952	Ken Bartholomew
1920	Roy McWhirter	1953	Ken Bartholomew
1921	Charles Jewtraw	1954	Ken Bartholomew
1922	Roy McWhirter	1955	Ken Bartholomew
1923	Harry Kashkey	1956	Ken Bartholomew
1924	Charles I. Gorman	1957	Ken Bartholomew
1925	Francis A. Allen		Bobby Snyder
1926	O'Neill Farrell	1958	Gene Sandvig
1927	No competition	1959	Ken Bartholomew
1928	Lloyd Guenther	1960	Ken Bartholomew
1929	Allen Potts	1961	Ed Rudolph
1930	Jack Shea	1962	Floyd Bedbury
1931	No competition	1963	Tom Gray
1932	James Webster	1964	Neil Blatchford
1933	Melvin Johnston	1965	Richard Wurster
1934	James Webster	1966	Richard Wurster
1935	Marvin Swanson	1967	Mike Passarella
1936	Marvin Swanson	1968	Peter Cefalu
1937	Marvin Swanson	1969	Peter Cefalu
1938	Vic Ronchetti	1970	Peter Cefalu
1939	Ken Bartholomew	1971	Jack Walters
1940	Leo Freisinger	1972	Barth Levy
1941	Ken Bartholomew	1973	Mike Woods
1942	Ken Bartholomew	1974	Leigh Barczewski
1943–46	No competition		Mike Passarella
1947	Ken Bartholomew	1975	Bill Lanigan
1948	George Fisher	1976	John Wurster
1949	Ray Blum		

Women

1921	Gladys Robinson	1952	Barbara Marchetti
1922	Gladys Robinson	1953	Pat Gibson
1923	Gladys Robinson	1954	Pat Gibson
1924	Rose Johnson	1955	Pat Gibson
1925	Rose Johnson	1956	Pat Gibson
1926	Lois Littlejohn	1957	Mary Maland
1927	No competition	1958	Jeanne Omelenchuk
1928	Elsie Muller	1959	Jeanne Omelenchuk
1929	Lorette Neitzel	1960	Mary Novak
1930	Leila B. Potter	1961	Jean Ashworth
1931	No competition	1962	Jeanne Omelenchuk
1932	Helen Bina	1963	Jean Ashworth
1933	Kit Klein	1964	Diane White
1934	Dorothy Franey	1965	Jeanne Omelenchuk
1935	Kit Klein	1966	Diane White
1936	Dorothy Franey	1967	Jean Ashworth
1937	Maddy Horn	1968	Helen Lutsch
1938	Mary Dolan	1969	Sally Blatchford
1939	Maddy Horn	1970	Sheila Young
1940	Maddy Horn	1971	Sheila Young
1941–46	No competition	1972	Ruth Moore
1947	Geraldine Scott		Nancy Thorne
1948	Lorraine Sabbe	1973	Nancy Class
1949	Lorraine Sabbe	1974	Kris Garbe
1950	Janice Christopherson	1975	Nancy Swider
1951	Barbara Marchetti	1976	Connie Carpenter
	Gwendolyn DuBois		

SPORTS-CAR RACING—*See* AUTOMOBILE RACING.

SQUASH RACQUETS—About 1850, a group of students at Harrow School, England, had become interested in racquets, but there was only one racquets court available to them. So they began to play on a smaller court—possibly a handball court—and, because the court was smaller, they used a less lively ball. The soft ball made a squashing sound when it hit a wall, so the students called the new sport "squash racquets."

Squash spread rapidly to other English schools. In 1882 it was introduced at St. Paul's (Preparatory) School in Concord, New Hampshire. St. Paul's students probably brought the sport to a number of Eastern colleges; by 1900, squash was being played in private clubs in Philadelphia and Boston, as well as in colleges and schools.

During the 1920s hundreds of squash courts were built throughout the East and Midwest, and a number of larger YMCAs adopted the sport. As the game developed in the United States and Canada, its rules changed somewhat, and squash as played in North America differs a good deal from the English version.

As intersectional competition increased in the United States, a difficulty arose: There were no standardized dimensions for the squash court. In 1930 the U.S. Squash Racquets Association set standard dimensions for courts used in tournament play. However, there are still many courts in the country, built before 1930, which don't conform to standards.

A court was built in 1893 at the Philadelphia Racquets Club, where the first national championships were held in 1907. From that point, many courts were built in colleges, YMCAs, and private clubs. Greatly increased construction costs have now made it difficult for anyone to build more courts. Another obstacle to the game's further growth is the fact that a special, larger court has to be used for doubles play.

However, squash is a good sport for young and old, like many of the indoor court games. It is relatively easy to learn, it offers excellent exercise in a rather short time span, and it is a real challenge to the skilled athelete.

Court and Equipment. The squash-racquets ball is made of hollow black rubber, has a 1¾-in diameter, and weighs about 1 oz. The racquet is approximately the size of a badminton racket, but is more solidly made. Maximum length is 27 in; the strung surface of the round wooden head has a diameter measuring about 6¾ in, and the weight is 8 to 10 oz.

The American singles court is 32 ft long and 18 ft, 6 in wide. A line from front wall to back wall splits the court in half, and there is a "short line," or "service-court line," drawn across the court 18 ft from the front wall. The ceiling is 18 ft or more above the floor, but is out of play A play line on the walls is 16 ft above the floor on the front wall and along each side wall to the service-court line; 12 ft above the floor on the side walls behind the service-court line; and 7 ft above the floor at the back wall. The ball is out of play if it strikes a wall above this line.

A "telltale" of sheet metal, 17 in high, stretches across the base of the front wall. A service line, or cut line, is drawn across the front wall at a height of 6 ft, 6 in. At each side of the court a service box is marked; it is a quarter-circle, with a radius of 4 ft, 6 in, behind the service-court line and drawn from that line to the side wall.

Basic American Rules. Players spin a racquet to determine who will serve the first point. After that, the winner of a point serves the next point; in other words, the server, upon losing a point, also loses service. A player can make the first serve from either service box, right or left, but must then alternate service boxes until service is lost.

The server must have at least one foot completely within the service box until the ball is struck, and may not have either foot over the service-court line. The serve must first hit the front wall, above the service line, and its first contact with the floor must be behind the short line and within the service court on the other side. The ball may hit the side walls or the back wall before landing in the service court. If the first service is a fault, the server gets another try. Two successive faults result in loss of point and service.

All subsequent shots must be played on the fly or on first bounce (from the floor), and must hit the front wall, above the telltale, before striking the floor. The ball may be played off side walls and back wall, but must not hit above the play line. Any shot that hits above the play line, or that hits the telltale, results in loss of point.

A player has to permit an opponent access to the ball, enough space in which to execute a racquet stroke, and free passage for the ball to the front wall and to the side walls near the front wall. Interference with the opponent is called a "hinder"; if intentional, a referee may award a point to the opponent. If the hinder is unintentional, the result is a "let," and the point is played over again. If there is no referee, the player interfered with requests a let, play stops, and the point begins over again.

English Rules. The English court is somewhat wider— 21 ft—and the ball is somewhat smaller and not as lively as the American ball. Only the server can score a point. If the server doesn't score on an exchange, that player merely loses service.

Game consists of 15 points, with a few exceptions. If the score reaches 13-all, the player who lost the last point can "set" the game at 15, 16, or 18 points. If that player sets it at 18, for example, the first player to total 18 points is the winner. If the score reaches 14-all without having been 13-all, the loser of the last point can set the game at 15 or 17.

Doubles. The doubles court is 45 by 25 ft; the play line is 20 ft high on the front wall and on the side walls to a point 31 ft back; 15 ft high on the side walls behind that point; and 7 ft high on the back wall. The service-court line is 30 ft from the front wall; the service boxes are quarter circles with a radius of 9 ft, 6 in; and the service line is 8 ft, 2 in high. The ball is livelier than the singles ball.

The rules of play are the same, except for service. When a team wins service, it retains it until both members of the team have served. In other words, the other team must win two points before gaining service.

Jay Nelson, one of the United States' top squash players, moves to retrieve a shot by Gordon Anderson, one of Canada's best, during a tournament at the New York University Club. *(Bob Lehman, New York City.)*

U.S. Champions

Men's Singles

1907	John A. Miskey	1926	W. Palmer Dixon
1908	John A. Miskey	1927	Myles Baker
1909	William L. Freeland	1928	Herbert N. Rawlins, Jr.
1910	John A. Miskey	1929	J. Lawrence Pool
1911	F. S. White	1930	Herbert N. Rawlins, Jr.
1912	Constantine Hutchins	1931	J. Lawrence Pool
1913	Mortimer L. Newshall	1932	Beekman H. Pool
1914	Constantine Hutchins	1933	Beekman H. Pool
1915	Stanley W. Pearson	1934	Neil J. Sullivan II
1916	Stanley W. Pearson	1935	Donald Strachan
1917	Stanley W. Pearson	1936	Germain G. Glidden
1918–19	No competition	1937	Germain G. Glidden
1920	Charles C. Peabody	1938	Germain G. Glidden
1921	Stanley W. Pearson	1939	Donald Strachan
1922	Stanley W. Pearson	1940	A. Willing Patterson
1923	Stanley W. Pearson	1941	Charles Brinton
1924	Gerald Robarts	1942	Charles Brinton
1925	W. Palmer Dixon	1943–45	No competition

1946	Charles Brinton	1962	Sam Howe
1947	Charles Brinton	1963	Ben Hecksher
1948	Stanley W. Pearson, Jr.	1964	Ralph Howe
1949	Hunter H. Lott, Jr.	1965	Stephen Vehslage
1950	Edward Hahn	1966	Victor Niederhoffer
1951	Edward Hahn	1967	Sam Howe
1952	Harry Conlon	1968	Colin Adair
1953	Ernie Howard	1969	Anil Nayar
1954	G. Diehl Mateer, Jr.	1970	Anil Nayar
1955	Henri Salaun	1971	Colin Adair
1956	G. Diehl Mateer, Jr.	1972	Victor Niederhoffer
1957	Henri Salaun	1973	Victor Niederhoffer
1958	Henri Salaun	1974	Victor Niederhoffer
1959	Ben Heckscher	1975	Victor Niederhoffer
1960	G. Diehl Mateer, Jr.	1976	Peter Briggs
1961	Henri Salaun		

Women's Singles

1928	Eleonora R. Sears
1929	Mrs. William F. Howe, Jr.
1930	Mrs. Hazel Hotchkiss Wightman
1931	Mrs. Ruth Hall Banks
1932	Mrs. William F. Howe, Jr.
1933	Susan Noel
1934	Mrs. William F. Howe, Jr.
1935	Margot Lamb
1936	Anne Page
1937	Anne Page

1938	Cecile Bowes
1939	Anne Page
1940	Cecile Bowes
1941	Cecile Bowes
1942–46	No competition
1947	Mrs. Anne Page Homer
1948	Cecile Bowes
1949	Janet Morgan
1950	Elizabeth Howe
1951	Jane Austin
1952	Margaret Howe
1953	Margaret Howe
1954	Lois Dilks
1955	Janet Morgan
1956	Mrs. Pepper Constable, Jr.
1957	Mrs. Pepper Constable, Jr.
1958	Mrs. Pepper Constable, Jr.
1959	Mrs. Pepper Constable, Jr.
1960	Margaret Varner
1961	Margaret Varner
1962	Margaret Varner
1963	Margaret Varner
1964	Mrs. Charles Wentzel
1965	Joyce Davenport
1966	Mrs. Newton B. Meade, Jr.
1967	Mrs. Newton B. Meade, Jr.
1968	Mrs. Newton B. Meade, Jr.
1969	Joyce Davenport
1970	Nina Moyer
1971	Mrs. Terry Thesieres
1972	Nina Moyer
1973	Gretchen Spruance
1974	Gretchen Spruance
1975	Virginia Akabane
1976	Gretchen Spruance

Bibliography. Danzig, Allison: *The Racquet Game,* Macmillan, New York, 1930; Wood, Peter: *The Book of Squash,* Van Nostrand-Reinhold, New York, 1972.

SQUASH TENNIS—In an effort to get a faster game, students at St. Paul's School in Concord, New Hampshire, began playing squash (squash racquets) with tennis rackets and balls shortly after the game was introduced there in 1882. Then Stephen J. Feron, a squash racquets pro in New York, attempted the tennis version of the game and was not wholly satisfied, because he couldn't get the same amount of spin on the tennis ball that he could on the ordinary squash ball. So he wrapped a piece of netting tightly around the ball.

The first formal squash tennis club was organized at the Tuxedo Club in Tuxedo Park, New York, in 1898. The National Squash Tennis Association was organized in 1910, and the first national championships were played the following year.

During the 1920s and 1930s, squash tennis equaled and perhaps surpassed the racquets version of the sport in popularity. However, it has since declined and is now played primarily in the New York area.

Equipment. The squash tennis ball is similar to a lawn tennis ball, but is somewhat smaller. Its diameter is 2⅜ to 2½ in, its weight is 2 to 2.06 oz. It is inflated to a pressure of 34 lb and is covered with webbing. The racket is similar to a lawn tennis racket, but is slightly smaller.

The court is the same as a squash racquets court. However, the server can stand anywhere behind the service-court line, not in the arc that marks the service box in the racquets version, and the squash tennis service court is the area in front of the service-court line, not behind it.

The service may not be volleyed for return—it must be hit on the bounce—and one fault results in loss of point.

See also SQUASH RACQUETS.

U.S. Men's Singles Champions

1911	Alfred Stillman
1912	Alfred Stillman
1913	George Whitney
1914	Alfred Stillman
1915	Eric S. Winston
1916	Eric S. Winston
1917	Eric S. Winston
1918	Fillmore Van S. Hyde
1919	John W. Appel, Jr.
1920	Auguste J. Cordier
1921	Fillmore Van S. Hyde
1922	Thomas R. Coward
1923	R. Earl Fink
1924	Fillmore Van S. Hyde
1925	William Rand, Jr.
1926	Fillmore Van S. Hyde
1927	Rowland B. Haines
1928	Rowland B. Haines
1929	Rowland B. Haines
1930	Harry F. Wolf
1931	Harry F. Wolf
1932	Harry F. Wolf
1933	Harry F. Wolf
1934	Harry F. Wolf
1935	Harry F. Wolf
1936	Harry F. Wolf
1937	Harry F. Wolf
1938	Harry F. Wolf
1939	Harry F. Wolf
1940	Harry F. Wolf
1941	Joseph J. Lordi
1942	H. Robert Reeve
1943–45	No competition
1946	Frank R. Hanson
1947	Frederick B. Ryan, Jr.
1948	H. Robert Reeve
1949	H. Robert Reeve
1950	H. Robert Reeve
1951	J. T. P. Sullivan
1952	H. Robert Reeve
1953	Howard J. Rose
1954	H. Robert Reeve
1955	H. Robert Reeve
1956	H. Robert Reeve
1957	J. Lenox Porter
1958	J. Lenox Porter
1959	J. Lenox Porter
1960	James Prigoff
1961	James Prigoff
1962	James Prigoff
1963	John Powers
1964	James Prigoff
1965	No competition
1966	James Prigoff
1967	James Prigoff
1968	James Prigoff
1969	Dr. Pedro Bacallao
1970	Dr. Pedro Bacallao
1971	Dr. Pedro Bacallao
1972	Dr. Pedro Bacallao
1973	Dr. Pedro Bacallao
1974	Dr. Pedro Bacallao
1975	Dr. Pedro Bacallao
1976	Dr. Pedro Bacallao

STADIUMS AND ARENAS—The word "stadium" comes from the Greek *stadion,* a unit of measurement which was the length of the first Olympic foot race (606 ft, 9 in). The race was given the same name, and eventually it was applied to the area where the race was run, including the stands from which spectators could watch. The *stadion* at Olympia, where the first Olympic Games were held, was probably the first structure of its kind, although similar amphitheaters were used for religious ceremonies, dramas, and games in other parts of the world during ancient times.

The famous Colosseum of Rome was the second major stadium of ancient times. After the fall of the Roman Empire, formally organized outdoor games and, therefore, stadiums virtually disappeared. They became important again only with the rise of organized sports late in the nineteenth century, although some large stadiums for bullfighting had been built in Spain before that.

The rise of sports also brought the construction of major indoor sports arenas, chief among them Chicago Stadium and the first Madison Square Garden in New York.

The major outdoor stadiums have usually been patterned after those of Greece and Rome. The bowl type of stadium is similar to the Colosseum; the Greek style is represented by the horseshoe-shaped stadium with one open end, which may contain bleacher seats.

During the 1960s there was a trend toward domed, all-purpose stadiums, such as Houston's Astrodome, which has been used for basketball and boxing as well as for football and baseball. However, tremendously increasing construction costs led many cities and counties to opt for simple, single-purpose stadiums instead.

In most cases it is more desirable to build a stadium for just one sport. In football stadiums, seats should be concentrated along the sidelines, although some fans do prefer end-zone seats. For baseball, on the other hand, seats should be concentrated around the diamond area. In a stadium built for both sports, spectators often have to sit rather far from the action.

One of the most controversial of the new stadiums is the Louisiana Superdome in New Orleans. Originally estimated at $35 million, the Superdome actually cost more than $160 million. The unique stadium seats nearly 19,000 for basketball and 75,000 for football, and was constructed for all four major spectator sports—baseball, basketball, football, and hockey—as well as for conventions. The gigantic structure, which is 273 ft high and has a diameter of 680 ft, contains 88 rest rooms, 52 meeting rooms, and parking facilities for 5,000 cars. One of its unusual features is a six-sided screen that offers spectators instant replays on closed-circuit television.

STEEPLECHASE—The steeplechase is a running event, for horses or persons, in which the competitors have to clear a variety of obstacles on their way around the course. (For the human version, *see* TRACK AND FIELD.)

The steeplechase for horses is based on the fox hunt, in which horses follow a pack of dogs, which are in turn following a fox, across fields with such natural and man-made obstacles as stone walls, mounds, hedgerows, fences, and streams. As a sport in itself, the steeplechase originated in Ireland during the eighteenth century. The first races were run across open country to a prominent, visible landmark in the distance—often a church steeple; hence the name.

The first definitely recorded race was run in 1752. Probably most of the early steeplechases were match races involving only two horses. In 1792, however, there was a steeplechase in which several horses raced. The first organized steeplechase was held in 1830, and in 1836 the Grand National was inaugurated at Aintree, near Liverpool, England. The Grand National is the oldest continuously run horse race in the world, and one of the very oldest organized sporting events still in existence.

There are two types of steeplechases: those, like the Grand National, that are run over specially prepared tracks, and point-to-point meetings, in which the race is over natural country from one point to another.

British courses generally use three types of obstacles: brush fences, either natural or artificial, of spruce, fir, or similar material; hurdle fences, only about 3 ft high, patterned after wooden sheep hurdles often seen in fields; and water jumps, which consist of a small fence followed by a stretch of water 8 ft or more in breadth. On some Irish courses there are also stone walls.

In North America. There are reports of a steeplechase held as early as 1834 in Washington, D.C., but apparently it was an isolated phenomenon. The sport didn't come to the United States permanently until 1865, when it was exported from Canada, where it had flourished since 1838. Steeplechasing was introduced at a number of flat tracks: Jerome Park in New York in 1869, Pimlico in 1873, Belmont Park in 1895. However, it has never been a prominent sport in this country. Ironically, one reason is that bettors don't like steeplechasing, despite the fact that jumping horses tend to run much truer to form than flat horses.

In 1972 the first $100,000 steeplechase in this country was run: the Colonial Cup, at Camden, South Carolina. The Colonial Cup is run at 2 mi, 6½ fur over a course that has 17 obstacles. Steeplechasing is also conducted at a number of hunt meetings in Maryland, Virginia, and other mid-Atlantic states. Perhaps the most famous of the events is the Maryland Hunt Cup, run over a 4-mi course near Glyndon, Maryland. This is the only race at the meeting, there is no purse, and no admission is charged. The race annually draws up to 20,000 spectators, who gather along hillsides to watch.

In the United States, obstacles are similar to those used in England, but some steeplechases include timber fences, patterned after the post-and-rail fences common in this country. The Hunt Cup, for example, is run over a 4-mi course that includes 20 timber fences, some of them nearly 5 ft in height.

Steeplechase Horse of the Year

1942	Elkridge	1960	Benguala
1943	Brother Jones	1961	Peal
1944	Rouge Dragon	1962	Barnaby's Bluff
1945	Mercator	1963	Amber Diver
1946	Elkridge	1964	Bon Nouvel
1947	War Battle	1965	Bon Nouvel
1948	American Way	1966	Tuscalee
1949	Trough Hill	1967	Quick Pitch
1950	Oedipus	1968	Bon Nouvel
1951	Oedipus	1969	L'Escargot
1952	Oedipus	1970	Top Bid
1953	The Mast	1971	Shadow Brook
1954	King Commander	1972	Soothsayer
1955	Neji	1973	Athenian Idol
1956	Shipboard	1974	Gran Kan
1957	Neji	1975	Life's Illusion
1958	Neji	1976	Straight and True
1959	Ancestor		

Steeplechase horses and riders go over a jump during a Virginia meet. *(Courtesy of National Steeplechase and Hunt Association, Inc.)*

Leading U.S. Jockeys

1905	Nat Ray	1941	Tom Roby
1906	Nat Ray	1942	E. Roberts
1907	H. Boyle		G. Walker
1908	McKinely	1943	W. Owen
1909	Donohue	1944	W. Owen
1910	J. Lynch	1945	W. Owen
1911	F. Williams	1946	J. Magee
1912	W. Allen		F. D. Adams
1913	W. Allen	1947	T. Field
	J. Kermath	1948	D. Marzani
1914	W. Allen	1949	F. D. Adams
1915	F. Williams	1950	F. D. Adams
1916	F. Williams	1951	F. D. Adams
1917	V. Powers	1952	F. D. Adams
1918	Dolly Byers	1953	F. D. Adams
1919	R. H. Crawford	1954	F. D. Adams
1920	R. H. Crawford	1955	F. D. Adams
1921	Dolly Byers	1956	A. P. Smithwick
1922	R. H. Crawford	1957	A. P. Smithwick
1923	C. Mergler	1958	A. P. Smithwick
1924	L. Cheyne	1959	J. Murphy
1925	R. Haynes	1960	T. Walsh
1926	R. H. Crawford	1961	Joe Aitcheson, Jr.
1927	L. Cheyne	1962	A. P. Smithwick
	C. Smoot	1963	Joe Aitcheson, Jr.
1928	Dolly Byers	1964	Joe Aitcheson, Jr.
1929	H. Jeffcott	1965	D. Small, Jr.
1930	W. Hunt	1966	T. Walsh
1931	F. Bellhouse	1967	Joe Aitcheson, Jr.
1932	W. G. Collins	1968	Joe Aitcheson, Jr.
1933	W. G. Collins	1969	Joe Aitcheson, Jr.
1934	F. Slate	1970	Joe Aitcheson, Jr.
1935	F. Bellhouse	1972	Jerry Fishback
1936	P. McGinnis	1972	Michael O'Brien
1937	A. Bauman	1973	Jerry Fishback
1938	E. Kennedy	1974	Jerry Fishback
1939	J. Penrod	1975	Jerry Fishback
1940	J. McCulloch	1976	Tom Skiffington

STOCK-CAR RACING—*See* AUTOMOBILE RACING.

SULLIVAN AWARD—Formally the James E. Sullivan Memorial Trophy, this award is named for the former secretary-treasurer of the Amateur Athletic Union and is given annually by the AAU "to the amateur athlete who, by performance, example and good influence, did the most to advance the cause of good sportsmanship during the year." The winners:

1930	Robert T. Jones, Jr., golf
1931	Bernard E. Berlinger, track
1932	James E. Bausch, track
1933	Glenn Cunningham, track
1934	William R. Bonthron, track
1935	W. Lawson Little, Jr., golf
1936	Glenn Morris, track
1937	J. Donald Budge, tennis
1938	Donald R. Lash, track
1939	Joseph W. Burk, rowing
1940	J. Gregory Rice, track
1941	T. Leslie MacMitchell, track
1942	Cornelius Warmerdam, track
1943	Gilbert Dodds, track
1944	Ann Curtis, swimming
1945	Felix "Doc" Blanchard, football
1946	Y. Arnold Tucker, football, basketball, track
1947	John B. Kelly, Jr., sculling
1948	Robert T. Mathias, track
1949	Richard T. Button, figure skating
1950	Fred Wilt, track
1951	Robert E. Richards, track
1952	Horace Ashenfelter, track
1953	Maj. Sammy Lee, diving
1954	Malvin Whitfield, track
1955	Harrison Dillard, track
1956	Mrs. Patricia K. McCormick, diving
1957	Bobby Joe Morrow, track
1958	Glenn Davis, track
1959	Parry O'Brien, track
1960	Rafer Johnson, track
1961	Wilma Rudolph, track
1962	James Beatty, track
1963	John Pennel, track
1964	Don Schollander, swimming
1965	Bill Bradley, basketball
1966	James Ryun, track
1967	Randel Matson, track
1968	Debbi Meyer, swimming
1969	Bill Toomey, track
1970	John Kinsella, swimming
1971	Mark Spitz, swimming
1972	Frank Shorter, track
1973	Bill Walton, basketball
1974	Rick Wohlhuter, track
1975	Tim Shaw, swimming
1976	Bruce Jenner, track

SURFING—Although considered by some one of the newest of the new sports, surfing is of unknown antiquity. When Captain James Cook discovered the Hawaiian Islands in 1778, he was astonished to see the natives riding on long narrow boards through the giant surf. Among the Hawaiians, chiefs and kings were the outstanding surfers. Their boards, made of the rather rare wili-wili wood, were 14 to 18 ft long and weighed about 150 lb apiece. Hawaiians of lesser rank used boards of koa wood, which is heavier but more common. Surfing contests for side bets were common among the Hawaiians.

The coming of Western civilization there, however, almost wiped out the sport during the nineteenth century. It began to re-emerge in 1908, with the formation of the Out-Rigger Canoe Club in Hawaii. About the same time, the great Hawaiian swimmer Duke Kahanamoku took up surfing and he helped greatly to popularize the sport. He is credited with introducing it to California and Australia.

The wooden boards used at the time were very heavy and cumbersome, however, and that drawback kept the sport from winning many fans. A young student at the California Institute of Technology, Bob Simmons, brought surfing into its modern era by experimenting with other materials, including balsa wood and plastic foam. His fiberglass-coated balsa boards caught on in the late 1940s. About 1955 the polyurethane-foam boards with fiberglass coatings arrived. They are light, durable, waterproof, and relatively inexpensive, and they have virtually taken over the market now. They have also made surfing much more popular.

The Boards. The surfboard looks like a very simple object, but it is a little more complicated than it looks. It has a deck—the part of the board on which the surfer rides. On either side of the deck is a rail. The front of the board is, of course, the nose, and the rear end is the tail. The board's camber, or "rocker," or "scoop," is the front-to-rear curve. The middle of the board is somewhat lower than the tail, and the nose is somewhat higher than the tail.

The skeg is a fin, underneath the tail, which helps to keep the board on a straight course. The deeper the skeg, the greater the stability. Better boards are built with a stringer, an inset strip of balsa or redwood that runs the length of the board for reinforcement. A board may have two or three stringers.

Boards vary a great deal in size and design, and new designs are being introduced all the time. Some modern, semiexperimental boards have two or three skegs of varying sizes; some are grooved; a few even have holes in them. Generally the nose is slightly rounded and the tail is slightly flattened.

Size is based primarily on the surfer's weight, for beginners. However, larger surfboards are needed for heavier surf, and the design also changes as the surf varies in intensity. The Malibu board, for light to medium surf, is 9 to 10 ft in length and about 22 in wide, and has the general shape and camber described above. The "guns" are for heavy surf; they're long (11 ft or more), narrow in proportion, sharp-nosed, heavier, and have smaller skegs for less drag.

The Surf. The beginning surfer should think of the board as a toboggan, and of the wave as a hill. In essence, this is riding down a hill on a toboggan. The fact that the hill is moving doesn't affect the basic fact that the surfer rides the wave from crest to trough. What is important is the steepness of the hill—and higher surf usually has steeper "hills." However, the type of surf is important, too.

Basically, there are four kinds of surf, caused by four different kinds of bottoms. A shore break is caused by a steep drop near the edge of the water. A surfer wants to get onto the wave at the point where it breaks, and a shore break occurs so close to the shore that the surfer will not get much of a ride.

The multiple break is common on gently sloping beaches: The surf may break three times, at varying distances from the shore, before dying out on the sand.

The beach break, or reef break, occurs where there is a sandy beach and a fairly steep drop-off, or where there is a reef or sandbar some distance from shore. The swell will peak over the offshore sand deposits, sandbar, or reef, and will then break quickly as the incoming water meets the backwash from a wave that has hit the beach and rebounded.

The point break, or peak break, is the best for surfers. It is caused by an underwater finger of land, a large submerged rock, or even a jetty or pier. As the water hits the submerged point, waves bend in around it, and surf builds up and travels in along one or both sides of the point.

Whatever the specific type of surf, the surfer must remember that the idea is to catch the wave at its peak, just as it is about to break, and then ride down its slope. The slope is moving; the surfer wants to be traveling at just about the same speed as the wave upon getting onto the wave, so the slope can neither leave the surfer behind nor lag behind that person.

Basic Techniques

Learning. A surfer should begin, not by surfing, but by paddling; to be a good surfer, a person has to be able to get the board going at the speed of the wave. The board is taken out into the water, perhaps into mild surf, and mounted from the seaward side, so the board won't be shoved against the body by a sudden incoming wave. The body is positioned on the stomach, in the center of the board, with chin up, toes pointed back, and knees a comfortable distance apart. The nose of the board should be about 1 in out of the water—somewhat more in choppy water. If it is too low, the body is moved back; if too high, the body adjustment is forward.

The paddling stroke is similar to swimming's butterfly stroke: Hands are cupped, fingers together, and the arms move back in unison. The arms should be just about straight throughout the stroke, entering the water as far forward as possible, and leaving the water as far back as possible. After practicing the stroke from the prone position, the surfer should try the kneeling position. It is

These surfers are enjoying light surf in Hawaii—where it all began. *(Courtesy of Hawaii Visitors Bureau.)*

basically the same, but the stroke will be shorter and faster. Then the surfer should learn the sitting position, which is used basically in waiting for waves to start coming. This is a relaxed position, with the feet dangling straight down into the water. The feet are used to turn the board toward shore when the proper moment arrives. If the waves are coming in on the right, for example, the board should be turned to the right to get in line. To turn right, the surfer paddles back with the right foot while bringing the left foot forward through the water in a reverse paddling motion.

The next learning step before actual surfing is to ride in on the foamline of waves which have already broken. The beginner brings the board out to an area inside the line of breakers, and lies prone with the nose pointed toward the beach, while watching, over the shoulder, for a wave. When a good one is spotted, the beginning surfer turns the board so it is in line and begins paddling, to try to get the board up to the wave's speed. When it hits, the beginner grabs the rails in order to hold on for the ride. If the connection with the wave is missed, one course is to try to paddle faster to catch up with the wave; another is to "drop out" by ceasing to paddle and, if necessary, by shifting some weight toward the tail of the board.

Riding the foam can give the surfer a good deal of practice in handling the surfboard and in sharpening basic techniques. The beginner can work up to a kneeling position, practice steering, and get the feel of the board and the water.

The Real Thing. Real surfing is done from a standing position. This position, too, can be practiced in the foam. The surfer begins in the prone or kneeling position, waiting for a wave, and then begins paddling to get up speed. At the moment the wave hits, both hands are placed flat on the board and a leap brings the body into a standing position. This is accomplished by swinging both legs under the body and onto the board with the left foot usually slightly ahead; then the body's weight is quickly shifted from the hands to the feet. The front foot should then be positioned at about a 45-degree angle, the rear foot at a 90-degree angle to the direction of travel.

Some surfers keep both feet sideways, with the trunk twisted forward; others have both feet at 45-degree angles; and there are many variations in between. The individual surfer alone can determine the foot position that is most suitable. But neither foot should be pointed directly forward.

For proper balance, the arches of both feet should be over the center line of the board, as drawn from nose to tail. The front foot should be ahead of the center of the board's balance, the rear foot about an equal distance behind it. And the knees should be flexed somewhat, to act as shock absorbers. The arms are out at the sides and used to help maintain balance.

The way to ride a wave properly is to travel diagonally across the front of the wave in the same direction as the break is running; thus the surfer stays constantly in front of the break and, therefore, below the crest of the wave. This affords a long downhill ride. To get such a ride, the surfer has to watch the direction of the break as it moves across the wave. As soon as the wave is caught, the surfer wants to turn in that direction, away from the trough at the bottom. There are several easy ways of turning. The best for beginners is the rear-foot turn: The rear foot is

moved to the left or right, causing more drag on that side of the board, which will make it turn in that direction. An even simpler turn, but one which will not be nearly so sharp, is the leaning turn, in which the surfer merely shifts body weight to the heels, to turn in the direction of the heels, or to the balls of the feet, to turn in the other direction.

A more advanced technique is the kick turn. The surfer steps sharply back with the rear foot, moving it to the side of the turn. This lifts the nose of the board out of the water. At the same time, the upper body is twisted in the direction of the desired turn, which jerks the nose in that direction. Then a balanced stance is resumed.

If the surfer attempts to go straight down a sizable wave, the nose of the board will almost instantly hit the trough, the board will stall, and the cresting wave will then crash down, resulting in a "wipe out." On the other hand, if too sharp a turn is made, the surfer may get out so far that there isn't enough slope to keep a person going at a good speed; when that happens, the surfer has to make a "cutback," turning back toward the peak to give it a chance to catch up.

Another important part of the ride is the end. A runaway surfboard can be dangerous to its owner and to others, and getting off properly, or stopping a ride, involves keeping control of the board. The surfer can stall out by shifting body weight to the rear of the board, slowing it down so the wave runs on ahead. This technique can be used to stay out of a wave, before the ride begins, in hopes that a better one will be along soon. It can also be used at the end of a ride.

"Proning out" is essentially an emergency move. If the crest of a large wave is about to land, the surfer drops into a prone position and heads for the beach, hoping to escape the wave and get into the soup, the churning white water that moves toward the shore when a wave breaks.

The surfer can simply jump off the side of the board, provided care is taken to get an arm on it quickly to keep it under control. A better way is the "nose pullout": The surfer, on jumping off the side, pushes the tail of the board in the other direction, then grabs the nose and holds on. This will make the board pivot so it's facing out to sea again.

A similar move, when the surfer is angling along the face of the wave and gets out—usually because the crest is gaining—is the "island pullout." The surfer moves far forward on the board and crouches, grabbing the rail on the shore side with both hands. Then the surfer leans into and through the wave, dragging along the board. Because of the forward weight, the tail should lift out of the water to make execution of the wave easier, and surfer and board together should go right through the wave and out the back side. In the standing island pullout, the surfer remains upright and uses foot and body action to turn the board back into the wave. As it hits, the surfer jumps off and grabs the nose.

For advanced surfers, there's the "kickout," a method of getting out of a wave that becomes disappointing, or of avoiding a breaking crest that might cause a wipeout. The surfer uses foot and body action to turn into the wave, and then rides up it. The rear foot is moved back and then the surfer kicks hard to lift the nose over the crest. The surfer may also lift the front foot momentarily to get the nose even higher. As the nose goes over the summit, the surfer moves the weight forward by dropping into a prone position or by running forward, so the board slides down the back of the wave.

Hotdogging. In surfing, a "hot dog" is an expert, not a show-off. There are all sorts of tricky maneuvers that can be done on a surfboard, but they are all essentially balancing acts. The important thing to know is that a surfboard, like a bicycle, gains stability as it gains speed. At a certain speed it begins to hydroplane, and the proper trim (front-to-back balance) is not nearly as crucial as at lower speeds. (Proper side-to-side balance is still very important, though.)

The beginner's first steps toward trick surfing are actually shuffles: learning to shift weight toward the front of the board, and back again, by sliding the feet forward, one at a time, starting with the rear foot. Walking is a little more difficult, and it demands a crossover action. The rear foot is picked up, moved forward, and put in front of the front foot, which is then quickly moved forward to its normal position nearer the nose. In walking backward, the front foot moves first.

Upon learning to move to the front of the board, the surfer is ready for some tricks. Draping the toes of the front foot over the nose of the board is known as "hanging five." "Hanging ten"—a feat for an expert—involves getting the other foot alongside the front foot.

Among other surfing tricks frequently seen in competition is the spinner, or turnaround. The surfer turns completely around on the sliding board. If this process of turning around and around is continued for a whole ride, it is called a "roto-moto." In the Quasimodo, the surfer crouches low, facing the side, with one arm stretched directly over the nose of the board and the other straight back toward the tail. In the *el spontaneo* the surfer crouches or squats so low as to be looking backward, between the legs, with hands clasped behind the back. One of the most exciting surfing tricks is called "riding the tube," right up against the face of the wave. The surfer gets into this tube by very precisely stalling the board slightly while angling across the wave. Properly done, this gets the surfer right up against the face of the wave, so water is falling on the body's shoreward side and in fact now surrounds the surfer. Some people consider head-dipping the ultimate in surfing: The surfer "simply" leans over the side of the board while riding the tube, or while just below the break, and dips the head into the water.

Inland Surfing. Until 1964, surfing was strictly an ocean sport. In that year, surfboard manufacturer Hobie Alter came up with a new version of the sport, called "wake surfing." Alter reasoned that a heavy boat's wake is equivalent to surf, and he rode his board for 9 mi in the feather of the wake behind a sport fishing boat. Wake surfing is now practiced at many lakes and ponds.

Competition

Surfing is still young enough, especially as a competitive sport, so that rules may vary considerably from one contest to another. Generally a contest is organized with elimination runs, followed by semifinal and final heats. In each heat a group of surfers (usually five or six) go out together; there is a specific time limit on the heat but, within that time limit, a surfer can ride as many waves as

This surfer has moved well back on his board and is shifting weight to execute a slide turn. *(Courtesy of Hawaii Visitors Bureau.)*

is desired. Each of the rides is scored, on a scale of 1 to 10 or 1 to 20 points. Sometimes the worst score is thrown out; in some competitions only the four or five best rides are counted.

Judges consider a number of factors in scoring a ride. The most important are: making the wave—the surfer's ability to get into the wave at the proper place and time, and to end the ride at the proper time; remaining as close as possible to the breaking white water while keeping the board in good trim and performing maneuvers in this position; riding the full length of the breaking curl, until the wave loses most of its force; making turns and cutbacks appropriate to the type of wave being ridden, and with proper form and grace; and spending time on the nose, the front quarter of the board, which is often painted a different color to simplify judging.

The time spent on the nose may be clocked by judges. In some contests, points scored in nose riding are multiplied by a difficulty factor if the surf is especially difficult during the ride.

If more than one surfer gets on the same wave, the surfer nearest the curl is considered to have possession of the wave, as long as the position is maintained. If another surfer interferes, a penalty is assessed. In some contests a surfer who is on the wave can tag an intruding surfer as a warning to leave. If the intruding surfer doesn't leave, a penalty is again levied. If the first surfer cannot make the tag, the assumption is that there was no real interference.

In tandem competition, the man must usually carry his

female partner in certain compulsory positions before going on to optional tricks. The positions most commonly required are the shoulder swan, the one-legged knee stand, the one-arm lift, and the shoulder stand.

Surfing meets may also include other types of competition, such as paddling races for individuals and relay teams, body surfing, and dory racing.

Glossary

angling the crest—Sliding, right or left, across the top of a wave that is just about to break.

back pedal—To walk backward on the board.

backwash—Water returning to the ocean after a breaker has reached the shore.

bailing out—Jumping or diving off the board to avoid a wipeout.

barge—A large, awkward board.

belly—The bottom of the board.

belly board—A surfboard less than 3 ft long.

big gun—A board for use on big waves; long, with a wide nose and a pointed tail.

bomb—To fall, take a spill, be wiped out.

bomber—A hard-breaking wave.

boomer—A wave that crashes down violently.

break—The point where a wave crests and collapses.

breaker—Any wave with a break.

caught inside—Riding on the shore side of a breaking wave.

chatter—Flexing and bending of the board in rough water.

closed door—A wave that breaks in one piece along the beach, and thus has no shoulder to be ridden.

curl—The concave section of the wave as it breaks.

cut out—To force another surfer out of a wave; or, to pull out of a wave by kicking out.

deck—The top of the board.

dig—To paddle hard.

ding—A dent or hole in the board.

double-ender—A board shaped the same at both ends, with a skeg that can be attached at either end.

drive—To make the board go faster by adjusting trim.

droppers—Large waves.

falls—The tumbling part of a wave.

feather—The fringe of foam on a wave crest.

floater—A large, very buoyant board.

glass-off—A sudden smoothing of the surf.

goofy-foot—Stance with the right foot forward; or, a surfer who consistently uses that stance.

greenback—An unbroken swell.

gremmy—For "gremlin"; an objectionable surfer, because of poor manners or technique.

hairy—Said of surf that is difficult or dangerous.

hamburger—A crash on the rocks.

hero—Said sarcastically of a surfer who isn't as good as he thinks he is.

highway surfer—Someone who rides around with a surfboard on his car but never uses it.

hodad—A derogatory term for a pseudo-surfer, wise guy, or the like.

hump—A large wave; or, the peak of a wave.

hung up—Stuck in a wave, unable to pull out.

kamikaze—A deliberate wipeout.

killer surf—Waves of 15 ft or higher.

left-go-right—To zigzag.

locked in—Riding securely in the curl of a wave.

log—Same as "barge."

mushy—Said of a slow wave.

overstriding—Moving too far forward, causing the nose to dip underwater.

palming the wall—Putting a hand into the face of a wave, for balance or to slow the board.

pearling—Riding straight down a wave, so the nose of the board drops into the water, dumping the rider; from "pearl diving."

peeler—A perfectly curling wave.

pigboard—A board with a narrow nose and broad tail.

proning out—Dropping to a prone position to avoid a wipeout.

Queen Mary—A surfboard too large for the surfer.

roller—A wave that breaks up into white water instead of curling.

scoop—The upcurved nose of the board.

scratch—Same as "dig."

shooting the pier—A dangerous maneuver in which the surfer travels through the pilings of an extended pier; sometimes called "pier roulette."

shore pound—Surf that breaks heavily right on the shore.

skim board—A small board, often circular in shape, used to skim over backwash or other shallow water.

snuffed out—Wiped out while shooting the tube.

spoon—Same as "scoop."

stick—A surfboard.

stoked—Excited.

submarine—A board that's too small for the surfer.

surf hog—An unsportsmanlike, inconsiderate surfer.

switchfoot—A surfer who feels comfortable with either foot forward.

trandem—Three on a board.

trough—The bottom of the hollow between two waves.

turnaround—A 180-degree turn by the surfer, who consequently is riding backward.

turn turtle—To flip the board over deliberately and hang on beneath, for protection.

wired—Completely figured out or checked out.

Bibliography. Kirk, Cameron, and Zack Hanle: *The Surfer's Handbook*, Dell, New York, 1968; Nelson, William D.: *Surfing: A Handbook*, new ed., Mason and Lipscomb, 1973.

SWIMMING—Although it undoubtedly dates to prehistoric times, swimming declined for some centuries during the Middle Ages and didn't regain its popularity, as a recreation, until the late eighteenth century. As an organized competitive sport, it is little more than a century old. However, the "modern" crawl, which revolutionized techniques around the turn of the century, was essentially borrowed from primitive peoples who had to be good swimmers to survive.

Among the ancient Greeks and Romans, swimming was a vital military skill, and Assyrian bas-reliefs from nearly 3,000 years ago show soldiers swimming with an overarm stroke that looks similar to the modern crawl. During the Middle Ages in Europe, however, outdoor bathing was considered dangerous; it was believed to be a cause of the deadly plague and other diseases. Nevertheless, some of the skills seem to have survived, at least in the Mediterranean area. By 1800 swimming was in vogue again, particularly in England, and there was a good deal of experimentation with various strokes.

The earliest stroke was probably the familiar "dog paddle," and it is quite possible that primitive man learned this stroke by imitating animals. But islanders in the South Pacific and other areas long ago developed a crawl stroke, the basis of modern freestyle swimming. Some American Indians may also have developed the crawl. A group of them gave a swimming demonstration in London in 1844, and a contemporary description of their style makes it sound like the crawl. The winning Indian swam a 130-ft pool in 30 sec, roughly equivalent to swimming 100 yd in 70 sec, which would have been a world record as late as 1891.

During the early eighteenth century, a type of breaststroke was most commonly used by English swimmers. This gradually gave way to an underarm sidestroke and to various forms of the backstroke, and then to an overarm sidestroke—a good stroke for distance swimming, still commonly used by marathon swimmers.

It is not known when the first indoor swimming pool was built in England. Reportedly, there were six of them in England by 1837, when the National Swimming Society of England was formed. In 1862 a group called the Associated Swimming Clubs held a meet in the German Gymnasium in London. This was the first known formally organized meet. By 1869, when the Amateur Swimming Association of Great Britain was formed, there were more than 300 swimming clubs in England.

The new emphasis on indoor competitive swimming, necessarily over relatively short distances, led to the need for a new, faster stroke for swimming sprints.

The Crawl. In 1873, J. Arthur Trudgen introduced a "new" stroke to English swimmers. Trudgen had seen South American Indians using the hand-over-hand method of swimming and was impressed by their speed. He began teaching the stroke to his pupils; but the "Trudgen stroke" was combined with the scissors kick already used by most English swimmers.

Another teacher, Frederick Cavill, improved the new stroke through better observation. Cavill went to Australia in 1878, built that continent's first swimming tanks, and taught the sport. Somewhere around 1900, he and his family visited the South Seas and saw natives using the hand-over-hand stroke; but Cavill also noticed that they used a "flutter kick," with the legs moving up and down, alternately, through the water.

Cavill's six sons, all competitive swimmers, learned the new stroke. One of them, Richard, introduced it to England in 1902 and became the first swimmer to break 60 sec for 100 yd. Australians called it the "splash stroke," but a British newspaper account described Cavill as "crawling over the water," and the stroke became known in England as the "Australia crawl."

In 1903, Sydney Cavill arrived at the Olympic Club of San Francisco as swimming coach. One of his students, J. Scott Leary, in 1905 became the first American to swim 100 yd in 60 sec. A rival, Charles M. Daniels, studied Leary's technique and further refined it. Daniels' chief contributions were to emphasize the full leg, from the hips down, in the flutter kick, and to synchronize the kick with the arm action, using six powerful kicks per cycle. In 1906, Daniels tied the world record (57.6 sec) for 100 yd; by 1910 he had lowered the record to 54.8 sec.

Daniels' stroke became known as the American crawl. Ironically, when the great swimmer Duke Kahanamoku arrived in California in 1913, he was using the American crawl, and he explained that Hawaiians had been using it for "generations and generations."

International Competition. The New York Athletic Club pioneered major competitive swimming in the United States, conducting its first national meet in 1883—three years before the first national track and field championships. When the Amateur Athletic Union was organized in 1888, it took over the national meets.

There was enough international interest in swimming that three swimming events were included on the first modern Olympics program, in 1896, and swimming has been a major Olympic event ever since. At the 1896 Olympics, the events were dominated by Middle European athletes, two Hungarians and an Austrian winning the gold medals.

Aside from Olympic competition, the only major international confrontations came in 1973, when the first World Aquatic Championships were held, in Belgrade, Yugoslavia. The championships, conducted by the Fédération Internationale de Natation Amateur (FINA), included swimming, diving, synchronized swimming, and water polo.

Marathon Swimming. The swimming equivalent of a cross-country run is a marathon swim in a natural body of water. Greek legend reports that Leander often swam the Hellespont (now the Dardanelles) to make secret visits to his sweetheart, Hero. The feat was duplicated by the English poet Lord Byron in 1810.

One of the most famous of the marathons is the English Channel swim, first accomplished by Capt. Matthew Webb of England in 1875. (Webb later died while swimming the rapids below Niagara Falls.) No one else accomplished the distance until 1911, when Thomas W. Burgess of England did it. Since then, however, there have been more than 100 successful crossings by about 50 swimmers.

Gertrude Ederle was the first woman to swim the channel, in 1926, and her time of 14 hr, 31 min was a record. Florence Chadwick, also an American, was the first woman to swim the channel in both directions. Since 1948 there have been a number of races across the channel, with sizable groups of swimmers making the crossing at the same time. On August 16, 1951, for example, 18 swimmers made the trip.

In 1965, Edward "Ted" Erikson of Chicago swam the channel in both directions with only a 10-min rest in between. He was the second man to do it, and he established a record of 30 hr, 3 min for the feat.

There have been other notable long-distance swims, though they have won less notice than the channel swim. The longest nonstop swim ever was by John V. Sigmund of St. Louis, who swam 292 mi of the Mississippi River in 89 hr, 42 min in 1940. In 1966, Mihir Sen of India performed four remarkable marathon swims: the Palk Strait, from India to Ceylon (now Sri Lanka); the Straits of Gibraltar, from Europe to Africa; the Dardanelles, from Europe to Asia Minor; and the whole length of the Panama Canal.

There are two annual marathon races held in Canada that are worth noting. The 10-mi marathon in Hamilton, Ontario, is a fairly straightforward distance event. However, the 28-mi Chicoutini, Quebec, Marathon is a grueling event which includes rapids and dangerous tidal channels. Only about 10 percent of the swimmers who enter each year manage to finish.

Competition

The usual swimming meet includes swims of various distances for four different types of strokes: freestyle (the crawl), backstroke, breaststroke, and butterfly. In addition, there are individual medley relays, in which each competitor swims one leg each of freestyle, butterfly, back, and breast; team medley relays, in which there is a different swimmer for each stroke; and freestyle relays.

Diving events are also usually part of a swimming meet. (*See* DIVING.)

In a dual meet, two swimming teams compete against one another for points. A team usually gets 5 points for each first place, 3 for each second place, and 1 for each third place in individual competition, while a relay win counts 7 points.

In triangular meets, a team gets 6 points for first, 4 for second, 3 for third, 2 for fourth and 1 for fifth. Relay winners get 8 points; the second team gets 4 points.

In large meets in which a number of teams and unattached individuals are entered, the point distribution depends on the number of finalists. The first-place winner gets 1 point more than the number of finalists—9

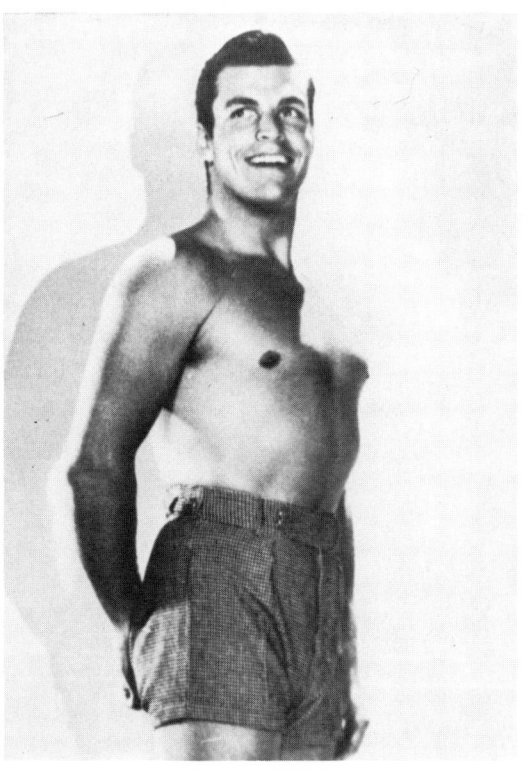

Clarence "Buster" Crabbe was a top middle-distance swimmer of the late 1920s and early 1930s; he won the 400-meter freestyle in the 1932 Olympics. *(International Swimming Hall of Fame.)*

points in an eight-lane final, 5 points in a four-lane final, for example. The second-place finisher gets 2 points less than the winner, and the points are then scaled down to 1 point for the last-place swimmer in the finals.

Preliminary heats are held to select the finalists. Heat times, not orders of finish, are the determining factors; thus, it would be possible for every swimmer in one preliminary heat to get into the finals. When heats result in ties that would place too many swimmers in the finals, a swim-off among the tied swimmers is held.

Courses. There are basically two types of courses in which the FINA recognizes world records, the long course (50 m) and the short course (25 m). In the AAU national championships, the long course is 50 m long and 22.885 m (75 ft) wide, while the short-course pool is 25 yd (22.885 m) long and 25 m (82.108 ft) wide. The NCAA championships are conducted in the short-course pool.

A starting platform, approximately 30 in high, is flush with one end of the pool in each lane. Each platform is about 20 in square. A swimmer is guided by a painted line on the bottom of the pool. The line, at least 10 in wide, is in the middle of the lane. In addition, lines and floating markers at water level mark the divisions between lanes.

Judging and Timing. Most major meets now use completely automatic timing equipment. The timer is started when the starter's gun goes off, through a direct electronic hookup to the gun, and it automatically records the elapsed time in each lane when the swimmer touches a pad at the end of the pool. There are also semiautomatic types of timing equipment. In most cases the timer starts when the starter's gun goes off, but the finishes are recorded by three timers in each lane. If there is no sort of automatic equipment, the three timers start their watches when they see the flash from the starter's gun.

Other officials include the starter, who may also be the referee; two stroke-and-turn judges on either side of the pool, who can disqualify a swimmer for not using the proper stroke or for not touching the end of the pool before turning; two finish judges, who may be called upon to vote, with lane timers, in the event of a close finish; and relay takeoff judges, one for each lane, who may disqualify a relay team if one of the swimmers leaves the starting platform before a preceding teammate has touched.

The Start. For all events but the backstroke, swimmers use a forward start from the starting platform. The starter first directs all swimmers to step into their places. At the command "Take your mark" they prepare to dive; they must be absolutely motionless before the starting signal. The starter fires a gun as the command to start.

If a swimmer starts before the signal, the field is recalled by a second shot on the pistol, a recall whistle, or a recall rope which is dropped across the course. On a short course, the swimmer who started early is charged with a false start, and two false starts in the same event call for disqualification. On a long course, the first two false starts are charged to the field; a swimmer who commits a false start after these first two is disqualified. A false start can also be called if a swimmer delays unnecessarily in taking the starting position upon command.

In the backstroke, the swimmers start in the water, facing the starting end of the pool, with both hands on the end or rail of the pool, on the starting platform, or on starting grips, if they are provided. The feet are placed against the end of the pool; they must be below the surface. At the starting signal, the swimmer pushes off on the back.

The Strokes. "Freestyle" means that a swimmer may use any stroke desired. The universally used stroke is the crawl.

In the backstroke the swimmer must remain on the back throughout the entire race. The contestant may touch to make a turn with the head or the foremost hand or arm. The swimmer must return to a position on the back before pushing off from the wall on making a turn.

In the breaststroke and butterfly there are very strict specifications. In the breaststroke, both shoulders must be kept in line with the surface of the water from the beginning of the first arm stroke after the start and after each turn. The arms must be moved simultaneously, the hands pushed forward together, and brought back on or under the surface of the water. Part of the head must remain above the general water level.

The so-called frog kick must be used. The legs are bent at the knee, and slightly spread; the feet are extended upward; then there is a powerful kick backward, in which the feet turn outward before coming back together. The legs must be moved simultaneously.

In the butterfly both arms must be brought forward over the water and back through the water simultaneously. Shoulders must be kept in the horizontal plane throughout the race, from the beginning of the first arm stroke after the start and after each turn. The "dolphin kick" must be used; this is essentially a flutter kick in which the legs move simultaneously instead of alternately. It is comparable to the action of a fish's tail, except that the fish would have to be swimming on the side. For the downstroke, the legs are lowered into the water, with the knees somewhat bent; then the knees are straightened with a sudden, quick movement that propels the body forward.

In both breaststroke and butterfly, touches must be made simultaneously with both hands at the same level, with the shoulders in line with the water surface. This rule applies to touches before a turn and at the end of a race.

Conduct of Relays. In an individual medley relay, the swimmer uses the strokes in this order: butterfly, backstroke, breaststroke, and freestyle. In the team medley, the order is backstroke, breaststroke, butterfly, freestyle. In team relays, a swimmer must keep the feet on the starting block until the teammate swimming the preceding leg has touched the end of the pool.

See also DIVING; SYNCHRONIZED SWIMMING.

AAU Outdoor Champions—Men

(R denotes meet record)

100-Yard Freestyle

1883	A. F. Camacho	1:28¼
1884	H. E. Toussaint	1:21
1885	Herbert Braun	1:18.4
1886	Herbert Braun	1:29.2
1887	Herbert Braun	1:17.2
1888	Herbert Braun	1:16.2
1889	W. C. Johnson	1:22.4
1890	W. C. Johnson	1:05.2
1891	W. C. Johnson	1:10.6
1892	A. T. Kenney	1:18.2

1893	A. T. Kenney	1:12.4
1894	A. T. Kenney	1:09.6
1895	No competition	
1896	George R. Whittaker	1:13.4
1897	D. B. Renear	1:07.4
1898	S. P. Avery	not available
1899	E. Carroll Schaeffer	1:08.6
1900	E. Carroll Schaeffer	1:05.6
1901	E. Carroll Schaeffer	1:10.0
1902	E. Carroll Schaeffer	1:07.0
1903	Fred A. Wenck	1:09.6
1904	Zoltan de Holomay	1:02.8
1905	Charles M. Daniels	1:03.8
1906	Charles M. Daniels	1:00.0
1907	Charles M. Daniels	1:03.4
1908	Charles M. Daniels	57.2
1909–1915	No competition	
1916	Duke Kahanamoku	53.2
1917	Duke Hakanamoku	54.0
1918	Perry McGillivray	56.2
1919	Perry McGillivray	1:05.8
1920	Duke Kahanamoku	55.4
1921	Pua Kela Kealoha	53.0
1922	John Weissmuller	52.8
1923	John Weissmuller	54.6
1924	No competition	
1925	John Weissmuller	52.0R

110-Yard Freestyle

1940	Otto Jaretz	58.4
1942	Alan Ford	59.4
1943	Alan Ford	59.5
1950	Richard Cleveland	58.2R
1952	Richard Cleveland	58.4

100-Meter Freestyle

1926	John Weissmuller	59.6
1927	John Weissmuller	58.0
1928	John Weissmuller	57.8
1929	Walter Spence	1:02.2
1930	George Kojac	59.2
1931	Manuella Kalili	60.2
1932	No competition	
1933	James Gilhula	1:01.3
1934	Art Highland	1:01.6
1935	Peter Fick	59.6
1936	Peter Fick	58.3
1937	Peter Fick	59.8
1938	Peter Fick	1:00.2
1939	Otto Jaretz	1:00.7
1941	Takashi Hirose	1:00.1
1944	Jerry Kerschner	59.0
1945	Albert Isaacs	1:02.1
1946	Bill Smith	59.0
1947	Walter Ris	58.5
1948	Robert Nugent	58.9
1949	Robert Gibe	58.2
1951	Richard Cleveland	58.0
1953	Richard Cleveland	57.5
1954	Richard Celveland	57.5
1955	Hendrick Gideonse	57.6
1956	Dick Hanley	56.3
1957	Dick Hanley	57.3
1958	Jon Henricks	55.8
1959	Jeff Farrell	56.9
1960	Jeff Farrell	54.8
1961	Steve Clark	54.4
1962	Steve Jackson	54.6
1963	Steve Clark	54.9
1964	Don Schollander	54.0
1965	Don Roth	53.8
1966	Don Schollander	53.5
1967	Don Schollander	53.3

1968	Mark Spitz	53.6
1969	Don Havens	52.5
1970	Frank Heckl	52.4
1971	Mark Spitz	52.4
1972	No competition	
1973	Jim Montgomery	52.95
1974	Tom Hickcox	52.164
1975	Jim Montgomery	51.04
1976	Jonty Skinner	49.44R

220-Yard Freestyle

1897	D. M. Reeder	2:54.7
1898	H. H. Reeder	3:07.6
1899	E. Carroll Schaeffer	2:53.6
1900	E. Carroll Schaeffer	3:07.2
1901	E. Carroll Schaeffer	2:50.8
1902	E. Carroll Schaeffer	2:58.8
1903	Charles Ruberl	3:18.4
1904	Charles M. Daniels	2:44.2
1905	Charles M. Daniels	2:45.0
1906	Charles M. Daniels	2:42.4
1907	Charles M. Daniels	3:13.8
1908	Charles M. Daniels	2:36.8
1909	No competition	
1910	Charles M. Daniels	2:33.0
1911–1920	No competition	
1921	John Weissmuller	2:28.0
1922	John Weissmuller	2:22.4
1923	Harry Glancy	3:36.6
1924–1933	No competition	
1934	James Gilhula	2:18.5
1935	James Gilhula	2:15.0
1936	Tom Haynie	2:14.3
1937	Irving McCaffrey	2:18.8
1938	Adolph Kiefer	2:18.7
1939	Kiyoshi Nakama	2:16.3
1940	Otto Jaretz	2:13.1
1942	Bill Smith	2:10.7
1943	Alan Ford	2:19.4
1950	James McLane	2:10.5R
1952	William Woolsey	2:13.2

200-Meter Freestyle

1941	Bill Smith	2:16.1
1944	Jerry Kerschner	2:12.9
1945	Kiyoshi Nakama	2:18.7
1946	Bill Smith	2:14.4
1947	Bill Smith	2:12.6
1948	Ed Gilbert	2:16.9
1949	Yoshiro Hamaguchi	2:11.0
1951	Wayne Moore	2:08.4
1953	Wayne Moore	2:09.0
1954	Ford Konno	2:10.6
1955	William Woolsey	2:02.2
1956	William Woolsey	2:06.5
1957	Dick Hanley	2:08.4
1958	Jon Henricks	2:05.2
1959	Jeff Farrell	2:06.9
1960	Jeff Farrell	2:03.2
1961	Tsuyoshi Yamanaka	2:00.4
1962	Don Schollander	2:00.4
1963	Don Schollander	1:59.0
1964	Don Schollander	1:57.6
1965	Gary Ilman	1:59.0
1966	Don Schollander	1:56.2
1967	Don Schollander	1:55.7
1968	Mark Spitz	1:57.0
1969	Hans Fassnacht	1:56.5
1970	Mark Spitz	1:54.6
1971	Mark Spitz	1:54.3
1972	No competition	
1973	Rick DeMont	1:53.69

1974	Tim Shaw	1:51.66
1975	Bruce Furniss	1:50.32R
1976	Mark Greenwood	1:52.21

440-Yard Freestyle

1893	A. T. Kenney	6:24.4
1894	P. F. Dickey	7:24.6
1895–96	No competition	
1897	Howard F. Brewer	7:08.4
1898	Paul Neumann	6:51.4
1899	E. Carroll Schaeffer	6:48.6
1900	E. Carroll Schaeffer	6:52.8
1901	E. Carroll Schaeffer	6:26.0
1902	E. Carroll Schaeffer	6:18.2
1903	T. E. Kitching, Jr.	6:31.6
1904	Charles M. Daniels	6:16.2
1905	Budd Goodwin	6:22.0
1906	Charles M. Daniels	6:24.0
1907	Charles M. Daniels	6:26.8
1908	Charles M. Daniels	5:54.2
1909	Charles M. Daniels	5:57.4
1910	Charles M. Daniels	5:59.8
1911	R. M. Ritter	5:52.6
1912	R. E. Frizell	5:56.8
1913	J. C. Wheatley	6:04.6
1914	Harry J. Hebner	6:22.0
1915	Ludy Langer	5:32.2
1916	Ludy Langer	5:38.6
1917	Norman Ross	5:58.6
1918	W. L. Wallen	5:57.8
1919	W. L. Wallen	5:45.0
1920	Norman Ross	5:40.4
1921	Ludy Langer	5:45.0
1922	John Weissmuller	5:16.4
1923	John Weissmuller	5:37.4
1924	No competition	
1925	John Weissmuller	5:22.5
1926	John Weissmuller	5:21.8
1927	John Weissmuller	4:52.0
1928	John Weissmuller	4:58.6
1929	Clarence "Buster" Crabbe	5:04.0
1930	Maiola Kalili	4:56.4
1931	Clarence "Buster" Crabbe	4:49.8
1932	No competition	
1933	Jack Medica	4:52.8
1934	Jack Medica	4:50.9
1935	John Macionis	4:51.6
1938	Ralph Flanagan	4:51.1
1939	Ralph Flanagan	4:50.2
1940	Kiyoshi Nakama	4:50.4
1942	Bill Smith	4:39.6
1943	Eugene Rogers	5:04.2
1950	John Marshall	4:39.3R
1952	Ford Konno	4:48.0

400-Meter Freestyle

1936	Ralph Flanagan	4:48.6
1937	Ralph Flanagan	4:46.0
1941	Bill Smith	4:47.6
1944	Kiyoshi Nakama	4:53.6
1945	Kiyoshi Nakama	5:05.7
1946	James McLane	4:49.5
1947	James McLane	4:41.9
1948	James McLane	4:53.5
1949	Hironoshin Furuhashi	4:33.3
1051	Wayne Moore	4:35.8
1953	Ford Konno	4:39.8
1954	William Woolsey	4:42.3
1955	Ford Konno	4:38.7
1956	George Breen	4:37.6
1957	George Breen	4:35.1
1958	Murray Rose	4:25.5
1959	Alan Somers	4:30.6

Dr. James Counsilman, Indiana University coach who has produced many outstanding swimmers, is shown with two of them: Mark Spitz, at edge of pool, and Gary Hall, in the water. *(International Swimming Hall of Fame.)*

1960	Alan Somers	4:21.9
1961	Tsuyoshi Yamanaka	4:17.5
1962	Murray Rose	4:17.2
1963	Don Schollander	4:17.7
1964	Don Schollander	4:12.7
1965	John Nelson	4:14.1
1966	Don Schollander	4:11.6
1967	Greg Charlton	4:09.8
1968	Ralph Hutton	4:06.5
1969	Hans Fassnacht	4:04.0
1970	John Kinsella	4:02.8
1971	Tom McBreen	4:02.1
1972	No competition	
1973	Rick DeMont	4:00.14
1974	Tim Shaw	3:54.69
1975	Tim Shaw	3:53.31R
1976	Casey Converse	3:54.65

880-Yard Freestyle

1893	W. G. Douglas	15:39.4
1894	T. Carey	15:33.0
1895–96	No competition	
1897	Paul Neumann	15:06.6
1898	Fred A. Wenck	14:08.0
1899	Fred A. Wenck	15:03.0
1900	W. G. Douglas	15:04.6
1901	Budd Goodwin	14:18.8
1902	E. Carroll Schaeffer	13:27.4
1903	Charles Ruberl	13:30.6
1904	Emil Rausch	13:11.6
1905	Charles M. Daniels	12:58.6
1906	Jamison Handy	12:24.0
1907	Budd Goodwin	13:02.4
1908	Budd Goodwin	13:23.0
1909	Charles M. Daniels	12:18.4

1910	Budd Goodwin	13:12.0
1911	Budd Goodwin	14:25.8
1912	Budd Goodwin	12:42.0
1913	Gilbert E. Tomlinson	12:49.6
1914	Budd Goodwin	12:55.6
1915	Ludy Langer	12:08.6
1916	Ludy Langer	12:02.0
1917	W. L. Wallen	13:05.8
1918	W. L. Wallen	11:27.6
1919	W. L. Wallen	12:36.2
1920	Charles Shields	12:48.0
1921	Ludy Langer	12:00.3
1922–24	No competition	
1925	John Weissmuller	11:12.0
1926	Arne Borg	10:38.4
1927	John Weissmuller	10:22.2
1928	Clarence "Buster" Crabbe	10:29.2
1929	Clarence "Buster" Crabbe	10:27.0
1930	Clarence "Buster" Crabbe	10:20.4
1931	Clarence "Buster" Crabbe	10:37.6
1932	No competition	
1933	Jack Medica	10:20.4
1934	Jack Medica	10:16.1
1935	Ralph Flanagan	10:07.6
1937	Ralph Flanagan	10:19.2
1938	Ralph Flanagan	10:11.1
1939	Ralph Flanagan	10:11.9
1940	Kiyoshi Nakama	10:08.6
1942	Bill Smith	9:54.6
1943	Eugene Rogers	10:46.7
1950	John Marshall	9:37.5R
1952	Ford Konno	10:07.8
(Discontinued)		

800-Meter Freestyle

1936	Ralph Flanagan	10:07.0
1941	Kiyoshi Nakama	10:06.2
1944	Kiyoshi Nakama	10:26.9
1945	James McLane	10:33.3
1946	James McLane	10:06.7

1947	James McLane	10:18.1
1948	James McLane	10:17.1
1949	Hironoshin Furuhashi	9:35.5R
1951	Ford Konno	9:39.9
(Discontinued)		

1-Mile Freestyle

(*indicates aided by tide)

1877	R. Weissenborn	45:44¼
1878	J. J. Heath	29:20.0
1879–82	No competition	
1883	R. P. Magee	29:42¼
1884	R. P. Magee	25:41.5*
1885	R. P. Magee	22:38.0*
1886	R. P. Magee	29:02.0*
1887	A. Meffert	35:18.2
1888	Herbert Braun	26:57.0
1889	A. Meffert	27:20.0*
1890	A. Meffert	22:39.4*
1891	J. R. Whitmore	24:11.6*
1892	A. T. Kenney	28:45.4*
1893	George R. Whittaker	28:55.4*
1894	A. T. Kenney	33:34.4
1895	No competition	
1896	B. A. Hart	30:27.6
1897	Paul Neumann	30:24.4
1898	Fred A. Wenck	29:51.6
1899	Fred A. Wenck	30:33.8
1900	George W. Van Cleaf	34:45.6
1901	Otto Wahle	28:52.6
1902	E. Carroll Schaeffer	28:14.6
1903	Charles Ruberl	28:05.6
1904	Emil Rausch	27:15.2
1905	Charles M. Daniels	26:41.8
1906	Jamison Handy	28:43.4
1907	Jamison Handy	29:29.8
1908	Charles M. Daniels	27:20.6
1909	Charles M. Daniels	26:19.6
1910	Budd Goodwin	20:02.4
1911	J. H. Reilly	25:40.4
1912	Budd Goodwin	25:25.0
1913	Budd Goodwin	25:18.4
1914	Budd Goodwin	25:42.2
1915	Ludy Langer	24:59.4
1916	Ludy Langer	23:22.0
1917	Norman Ross	24:10.0
1918	W. L. Wallen	25:08.6
1919	W. L. Wallen	25:37.6
1920	Eugene Bolden	25:26.4
1921	No competition	
1922	Clyde Goldwater	25:02.0
1923	Eugene Bolden	25:06.0
1924	No competition	
1925	Harry Glancy	24:27.8
1926	Arne Borg	21:46.4
1927	Clarence "Buster" Crabbe	22:52.4
1928	Clarence "Buster" Crabbe	21:35.6
1929	Clarence "Buster" Crabbe	22:09.8
1930	Clarence "Buster" Crabbe	21:27.0
1931	Clarence "Buster" Crabbe	22:14.8
1932	No competition	
1933	Ralph Flanagan	21:12.2
1934	Jack Medica	20:57.8
1935	Ralph Flanagan	21:00.3
1936	Ralph Flanagan	20:58.9
1937	Ralph Flanagan	20:42.6
1938	Ralph Flanagan	21:06.3
1939	Ralph Flanagan	21:00.7
1940	Bunmei Nakama	21:31.4
1942	Kiyoshi Nakama	20:29.0
1943	Paul Maloney	23:06.5

| 1950 | John Marshall | 20:08.6R |
| 1952 | Ford Konno | 20:47.1 |

1,500-Meter Freestyle

1941	Kiyoshi Nakama	19:55.8
1944	Kiyoshi Nakama	19:42.6
1945	James McLane	19:49.5
1946	James McLane	19:23.1
1947	James McLane	19:57.5
1949	Hironoshin Furuhashi	18:29.9
1951	Ford Konno	18:46.3
1953	Ford Konno	19:20.0
1954	Ford Konno	19:07.1
1956	George Breen	18:27.6
1957	George Breen	18:17.9
1958	Murray Rose	18:06.4
1959	Alan Somers	17:51.3
1960	George Breen	17:33.5
1961	Roy Saari	17:29.8
1962	Murray Rose	17:16.7
1963	Roy Saari	17:34.6
1964	Murray Rose	17:01.8
1965	Steve Krause	16:58.7
1966	Mike Burton	16:41.6
1967	Mike Burton	16:34.1
1968	Mike Burton	16:29.4
1969	Mike Burton	16:04.5
1970	John Kinsella	15:47.1
1971	Mike Burton	16:09.6
1972	No competition	
1973	Rick DeMont	15:51.02
1974	Tim Shaw	15:31.752
1975	Bobby Hackett	15:32.00
1976	Casey Converse	15:21.03R

110-Yard Backstroke

1940	Adolph Kiefer	1:05.5R
1950	Allen Stack	1:08.2
1952	Yoshinobu Oyakawa	1:05.7

100-Meter Backstroke

1934	Albert Vande Weghe	1:11.0
1935	Adolph Kiefer	1:07.8
1936	Adolph Kiefer	1:06.5
1937	Adolph Kiefer	1:06.3
1938	Adolph Kiefer	1:07.8
1939	Adolph Kiefer	1:06.6
1941	Adolph Kiefer	1:06.3
1942	Adolph Kiefer	1:06.6
1943	Adolph Kiefer	1:07.0
1944	Jack Weeden	1:12.1
1945	Robert E. Cowell	1:10.6
1946	Harry Holiday, Jr.	1:08.0
1947	Allen Stack	1:07.8
1948	Allen Stack	1:07.7
1949	Allen Stack	1:07.1
1951	James Thomas	1:07.4
1953	Yoshinobu Oyakawa	1:06.8
1954	Albert Wiggins	1:07.2
1955	Yoshinobu Oyakawa	1:05.3
1956	Yoshinobu Oyakawa	1:05.9
1957	Frank McKinney	1:04.5
1958	Frank McKinney	1:04.5
1959	Frank McKinney	1:03.6
1960	Tom Stock	1:02.9
1961	Bob Bennett	1:01.3
1962	Tom Stock	1:01.0
1963	Richard McGeagh	1:01.7
1964	Richard McGeagh	1:01.6
1965	Thompson Mann	1:00.5
1966	Charles Hickcox	1:01.0
1967	Charles Hickcox	59.7

1968	Larry Barbiere	1:00.9
1969	Mitch Ivey	1:00.2
1970	Mike Stamm	58.5
1971	Mel Nash	59.2
1972	No competition	
1973	Mike Stamm	59.35
1974	John Naber	58.12
1975	John Naber	57.35
1976	John Naber	56.48R

200-Meter Backstroke

1963	Tom Stock	2:12.4
1964	Robert Bennett	2:15.7
1965	Thompson Mann	2:12.4
1966	Charles Hickcox	2:12.4
1967	Charles Hickcox	2:12.3
1968	Jack Horsley	2:12.2
1969	Gary Hall	2:06.6
1970	Mike Stamm	2:06.3
1971	Charles Campbell	2:07.1
1972	No competition	
1973	John Naber	2:05.67
1974	John Naber	2:03.53
1975	John Naber	2:02.52R
1976	John Naber	2:03.73

110-Yard Breaststroke

1952	Jerry Holan	1:09.3

100-Meter Breaststroke

1951	John Davies	1:08.4
1953	John Dudeck	1:08.4
1954–55	No competition	
1956	Robert Hughes	1:11.2
1957	Robert Hughes	1:12.1
1958	Manuel Sanguilly	1:15.9
1959	Manuel Sanguilly	1:14.6
1960	Chet Jastremski	1:12.4
1961	Chet Jastremski	1:07.5
1962	Chet Jastremski	1:08.2
1963	William Craig	1:10.2
1964	Chet Jastremski	1:10.0
1965	Tom Tretheway	1:08.3
1966	Ken Merten	1:08.9
1967	Ken Merten	1:08.7
1968	Mike Dirksen	1:08.8
1969	Jose Fiolo	1:06.9
1970	Brian Job	1:06.4
1971	Peter Dahlberg	1:06.9
1972	No competition	
1973	John Hencken	1:05.17
1974	John Hencken	1:04.38
1975	Rick Colella	1:05.95
1976	John Hencken	1:04.36

200-Yard Breaststroke

1906	A. M. Goersling	3:01.2
1907	Jamison Handy	3:17.6
1908	A. M. Goersling	2:46.4R
1909	A. M. Goersling	2:49.0

220-Yard Breaststroke

1921	Michael J. McDermott	3:10.4
1922	Robert D. Skelton	3:22.8
1923	Robert D. Skelton	3:06.6
1924–1933	No competition	
1934	John Higgins	2:55.0
1935	John Higgins	2:47.6
1937	Ray Kaye	2:52.2
1938	Jim Werson	2:49.2
1939	James Skinner	3:46.6
1940	James Skinner	2:48.8
1942	Jim Counsilman	2:45.4
1943	Joseph Verdeur	2:53.2

1950	Robert Brawner	2:41.0
1952	Bowen Stassforth	2:34.7R

200-Meter Breaststroke

1936	John Higgins	2:43.3
1941	Jose Balmores	2:45.5
1944	Joseph Verdeur	2:46.3
1945	Dave Seibold	2:55.5
1946	Joseph Verdeur	2:44.2
1947	Joseph Verdeur	2:38.4
1948	Joseph Verdeur	2:48.7
1949	Joseph Verdeur	2:36.3
1951	John Davies	2:35.8
1953	Dave Hawkins	2:37.9
1954	Dick Fadgen	2:49.5
1955	Bob Mattson	2:46.8
1956	Dick Fadgen	2:45.8
1957	Manuel Sanguilly	2:44.0
1958	Norbert Rumpel	2:47.8
1959	Ronald Clark	2:45.6
1960	Peter Fogarasy	2:38.8
1961	Chet Jastremski	2:29.6
1962	Chet Jastremski	2:30.0
1963	Ken Merten	2:34.5
1964	Chet Jastremski	2:31.8
	Bill Craig	2:31.8
1965	Chet Jastremski	2:30.1
1966	Ken Merten	2:31.2
1967	Ken Merten	2:30.8
1968	Brian Job	2:31.2
1969	Mike Dirksen	2:26.9
1970	Brian Job	2:24.1
1971	Rick Colella	2:25.0
1972	No competition	
1973	John Hencken	2:20.52
1974	John Hencken	2:18.93R
1975	Rick Colella	2:21.32
1976	John Hencken	2:21.17

100-Meter Butterfly

1954	Dick Fadgen	1:07.4
1955	No competition	
1956	Al Wiggins	1:04.2
1957	Al Wiggins	1:02.8
1958	Mike Troy	1:02.8
1959	Lance Larson	1:01.1
1960	Lance Larson	58.7
1961	Fred Schmidt	58.6
1962	Ed Spencer	50.9
1963	Walter Richardson	58.8
1964	Walter Richardson	57.5
1965	Luis Nicolao	57.8
1966	Mark Spitz	58.1
1967	Mark Spitz	56.7
1968	Mark Spitz	57.0
1969	Doug Russell	56.0
1970	Mark Spitz	56.1
1971	Mark Spitz	55.3
1972	No competition	
1973	Robin Backhaus	56.81
1974	Mike Bottom	55.50
1975	Steve Baxter	55.29R
1976	Greg Jagenburg	55.73

200-Meter Butterfly

1955	Bill Yorzyk	2:29.1
1956	Bill Yorzyk	2:24.3
1957	Bill Yorzyk	2:22.0
1958	Bill Yorzyk	2:22.5
1959	Mike Troy	2:16.4
1960	Mike Troy	2:13.4
1961	Carl Robie	2:12.6

1962	Carl Robie	2:10.8
1963	Carl Robie	2:08.8
1964	Carl Robie	2:09.2
1965	Carl Robie	2:07.7
1966	Phil Houser	2:09.9
1967	Mark Spitz	2:06.4
1968	Carl Robie	2:08.9
1969	Mike Burton	2:06.5
1970	Gary Hall	2:05.0
1971	Mark Spitz	2:03.8
1972	No competition	
1973	Steve Gregg	2:04.11
1974	Mike Bruner	2:01.69
1975	Greg Jagenburg	2:00.73
1976	Bill Forrester	2:00.03R

200-Meter Individual Medley

1963	Dick Roth	2:16.0
1964	Dick Roth	2:15.5
1965	Dick Roth	2:14.9
1966	Greg Buckingham	2:12.4
1967	Greg Buckingham	2:13.3
1968	Juan Bello	2:14.1
1969	Gary Hall	2:09.6
1970	Gary Hall	2:09.4
1971	Gary Hall	2:10.0
1972	No competition	
1973	Stan Carper	2:08.99
1974	Steve Furniss	2:08.263
1975	Bruce Furniss	2:06.08R
1976	Steve Furniss	2:07.36

300-Yard Individual Medley

1925	Harry Glancy	

330-Yard Individual Medley

1940	Adolph Kiefer	3:58.6
1950	James Thomas	3:55.1
1952	Burwell Jones	3:46.2R

300-Meter Individual Medley

1926	Walter Spence	4:25.4
1927	Walter Spence	4:14.6
1928	Clarence "Buster" Crabbe	4:16.0
1929	Clarence "Buster" Crabbe	4:12.2
1930	Clarence "Buster" Crabbe	4:06.8
1931	Clarence "Buster" Crabbe	4:05.8
1932	No competition	
1933	Ralph Flanagan	4:14.2
1934	No competition	
1935	John Higgins	4:09.7
1936	Paul Wolf	4:02.4
1937	Paul Wolf	4:09.8
1938	Adolph Kiefer	4:02.0
1939	Adolph Kiefer	4:02.2
1941	Jose Balmores	3:56.9
1942	Mike Priano	4:09.1
1943	Adolph Kiefer	4:04.5
1944	Joseph Verdeur	4:07.3
1945	Dave Seibold	4:18.5
1946	Harry Holida	3:58.8
1947	Joseph Verdeur	3:59.2
1948	Joseph Verdeur	4:00.0
1949	Joseph Verdeur	3:53.7
1951	Burwell Jones	3:52.3
1953	Burwell Jones	3:46.2R

400-Meter Individual Medley

1954	Burwell Jones	5:29.0
1955	George Harrison	5:23.3
1956	Bill Yorzyk	5:19.0
1957	Gary Heinrich	5:15.6
1958	Frank Brunell	5:20.6
1959	Bill Barton	5:14.6

The backstroke is the only event that begins with the swimmers already in the water. *(International Swimming Hall of Fame.)*

1960	Dennis Rousavelle	5:04.5
1961	Ted Stickles	4:55.6
1962	Ted Stickles	4:51.5
1963	Ted Stickles	4:55.0
1964	Dick Roth	4:48.6
1965	Dick Roth	4:49.2
1966	Dick Roth	5:47.9
1967	Peter Williams	4:50.8
1968	Gary Hall	4:48.0
1969	Gary Hall	4:33.9
1970	Gary Hall	4:31.0
1971	Gary Hall	4:33.1
1972	No competition	
1973	Rick Colella	4:32.38
1974	Steve Furniss	4:30.56
1975	Dave Hannula	4:31.35
1976	Jesse Vassollo	4:28.34R

330-Yard Medley Relay

1940	Towers Club, Chicago	3:22.0
1950	Coca-Cola S.C., Cincinnati	3:19.4
1952	Ohio State	3:13.5R

300-Meter Medley Relay

1934	Chicago Lake Shore AC	3:32.7
1935	Chicago Lake Shore AC	3:28.4
1936	Detroit AC	3:22.2
1937	Chicago Lake Shore AC	3:25.6
1938	Ohio State	3:30.1
1939	Detroit AC	3:22.2
1941	Towers Club, Chicago	3:29.3
1942	Ohio State	3:24.2
1943	Yale	3:34.5
1944	Philadelphia North YMCA	3:29.4
1945	Michigan State	3:32.4
1946	Ohio State	3:20.7
1947	Michigan	3:15.3R
1948	Brighton-Drake S.C.	3:22.7

1949	Iowa	3:18.8
1951	Ohio State	3:17.4
1953	Cherry Point Marines	3:21.9

400-Meter Medley Relay

1954	North Carolina SC	4:14.7
1955	New Haven SC	4:28.6
1956	New Haven SC	4:26.5
1957	Indianapolis AC	4:21.6
1958	Los Angeles AC	4:24.6
1959	Detroit AC	4:21.9
1960	Indianapolis AC	4:09.2
1961	Indianapolis AC	4:03.0
1962	Indianapolis AC	4:01.6
1963	Indianapolis AC	4:04.9
1964	Verdugo Hills SC	4:03.8
1965	Indianapolis AC	4:01.8
1966	Los Angeles AC	4:02.2
1967	Santa Clara SC	3:59.7
1968	Santa Clara SC	4:00.3
1969	Phillips 66 SC	3:57.5
1970	Santa Clara SC	3:55.6
1971	Santa Clara SC	3:55.2
1972	No competition	
1973	Gatorade SC "A"	3:56.57
1974	Santa Clara SC "A"	3:50.23R
1975	Long Beach SC "A"	3:51.55
1976	Santa Clara SC	3:51.34

400-Meter Freestyle Relay

1964	Santa Clara SC	3:39.4
1965	Santa Clara SC	3:36.1
1966	Santa Clara SC	3:35.4
1967	Los Angeles AC	3:36.4
1968	Los Angeles AC	3:35.3
1969	Los Angeles AC	3:32.8
1970	Los Angeles AC	3:28.7R
1971	Los Angeles AC	3:32.3
1972	No competition	
1973	Huntington Beach Aquatic Club	3:34.96
1974	Gatorade SC "A"	3:30.468
1975	Badger Dolphins	3:28.522
1976	Central Jersey AC	3:27.91R

880-Yard Freestyle Relay

1923	Illinois AC	10:05.4
1924	Los Angeles AC	10:34.0
1925	Illinois AC	NA
1926	Illinois AC	9:43.0
1927	Illinois AC	9:35.0
1928	Illinois AC	9:32.6
1929	Hollywood AC	9:42.9
1930	New York AC	9:27.0
1931	Hollywood AC	9:21.8
1932	No competition	
1933	Los Angeles AC	9:40.4
1934	Los Angeles AC	9:41.9
1935	Detroit AC	9:21.6
1936	Yale	9:22.5
1937	Lake Shore AC	9:20.0
1938	Ohio State	9:51.4
1939	Alexander House AC	9:21.0
1940	Alexander House AC	9:17.3
1942	Ohio State	9:13.4
1943	Yale	9:59.3
1944	Camp Chikopi	10:04.4
1945	Great Lakes Naval Training Station	10:18.6
1946	Hawaii Univ.	9:25.4
1947	Ohio State	9:13.8
1948	New Haven SC	9:21.0
1949	Tokyo SC	9:45.4R

1950	New Haven SC	9:07.0
1952	New Haven SC	9:58.8

800-Meter Freestyle Relay

1941	Alexander House AC	9:14.9
1951	New Haven SC	8:51.0
1953	New Haven SC	9:07.6
1954	New Haven SC	9:07.9
1955	New Haven SC	8:54.2
1956	New Haven SC	8:53.7
1957	New Haven SC	8:53.7
1958	Los Angeles AC	8:42.7
1959	Indianapolis AC	8:35.9
1960	Indianapolis AC	8:17.0
1961	Indianapolis AC	8:17.9
1962	Santa Clara SC	8:12.2
1963	Santa Clara SC	8:07.6
1964	Santa Clara SC	8:09.1
1965	Santa Clara SC	8:04.6
1966	Santa Clara SC	7:56.9
1967	Santa Clara SC	7:52.1
1968	Santa Clara SC "A"	7:55.0
1969	Phillips 66 SC	7:52.7
1970	Phillips 66 SC	7:47.6
1971	Phillips 66 SC	7:48.580
1972	No competition	
1972	Santa Clara SC "A"	7:49.24
1974	Long Beach SC "A"	7:36.62
1975	Long Beach SC "A"	7:30.54R
1976	Mission Viejo "A"	7:34.48

AAU Outdoor Champions—Women

100-Yard Freestyle

1917	Gertrude Artelt	1:18.4
1918	Charlotte Boyle	1:11.6
1919	No competition	
1920	Ethelda Bleibtrey	1:05.2
1921	Ethelda Bleibtrey	1:03.4
1922	Helen Wainwright	1:08.4
1923	Adelaide Lambert	1:13.4
1924	Ethel Lackie	1:06.0
1925	Doris O'Mara	1:07.4

110-Yard Freestyle

1940	Brenda Helser	1:09.6
1949	Thelma Kalama	1:10.9
1953	Judy Roberts	1:07.9
1956	Wanda Werner	1:06.3
1957	Dawn Fraser	1:03.9R
1959	Chris von Saltza	1:04.8

100-Meter Freestyle

1926	Ethel Lackie	1:14.4
1927	Martha Norelius	1:13.8
1928	Eleanor Garratti	1:10.6
1929	Eleanor Garratti	1:09.8
1930	Helene Madison	1:08.2
1931	Helene Madison	1:09.4
1932	Jennie Cramer	1:13.4
1933	Lenore Kight	1:10.8
1934	Olive McKean	1:11.7
1935	Olive McKean	1:10.2
1936	Toni Redfern	1:10.1
1937	Elizabeth Ryan	1:08.0
1938	Virginia Hopkins	1:10.5
1939	Esther Williams	1:09.0
1941	Brenda Helser	1:09.9
1942	Suzanne Zimmerman	1:10.3
1943	Brenda Helser	1:09.3
1944	Ann Curtis	1:09.5
1945	Ann Curtis	1:07.5
1946	Brenda Helser	1:07.2
1947	Ann Curtis	1:07.0

1948	Ann Curtis	1:08.0
1950	Jackie LaVine	1:10.0
1951	Sharon Geary	1:07.6
1954	Jody Alderson	1:06.1
1955	Wanda Werner	1:06.1
1958	Chris von Saltza	1:03.5
1960	Chris von Saltza	1:01.6
1961	Robyn Johnson	1:03.2
1962	Robyn Johnson	1:02.2
1963	Robyn Johnson	1:01.5
1964	Sharon Stouder	1:00.7
1965	Pokey Watson	1:00.7
1966	Pokey Watson	59.9
1967	Janie Barkman	59.8
1968	Janie Barkman	1:00.1
1969	Sue Pedersen	59.7
1970	Cindy Schilling	1:00.3
1971	Linda Johnson	1:00.3
1972	No competition	
1973	Shirley Babashoff	58.77
1974	Kim Peyton	58.22
1975	Shirley Babashoff	57.48
1976	Jill Sterkel	57.20R

200-Meter Freestyle

1963	Robyn Johnson	2:15.6
1964	Jeanne Hallock	2:13.3
1965	Martha Randall	2:12.3
1966	Pokey Watson	2:10.5
1967	Pam Kruse	2:09.7
1968	Eadie Wetzel	2:08.8
1969	Sue Pedersen	2:07.8
1970	Ann Simmons	2:09.6
1971	Linda Johnson	2:08.9
1972	No competition	
1973	Shirley Babashoff	2:04.63
1974	Shirley Babashoff	2:02.947
1975	Shirley Babashoff	2:02.39R
1976	Kim Peyton	2:03.01

440-Yard Freestyle

1916	Claire Galligan	7:43.2
1917	Olga Dorfner	7:53.4
1918	Claire Galligan	7:20.0
1919	Ethelda Bleibtrey	6:30.2
1920	L. Snowgrass	8:24.0
1921	Ethelda Bleibtrey	6:30.0
1922	Gertrude Ederle	6:01.2
1923	Gertrude Ederle	6:35.4
1924	Helen Wainwright	6:10.4
1925	V. Whitenack	6:07.0
1926	Martha Norelius	6:06.0
1927	Martha Norelius	5:57.2
1928	Martha Norelius	5:49.6
1929	Josephine McKim	5:47.4
1930	Helene Madison	5:39.4
1931	Helene Madison	5:42.8
1932	No competition	
1933	Lenore Kight	5:33.6
1934	Lenore Kight	5:40.2
1935	Lenore Kight	5:32.5
1936	Lenore Kight Wingard	5:37.6
1937	Katherine Rawls	5:36.0
1938	Katherine Rawls	5:34.5
1940	Mary M. Ryan	5:30.1
1949	Thelma Kalama	5:41.2
1953	Delia Meulenkamp	5:22.2
1956	Marley Shriver	5:13.8
1957	Lorraine Crapp	5:08.5
1959	Chris von Saltza	4:59.6R

400-Meter Freestyle

1939	Nancy Merki	5:29.6

1941	Betty Bemis	5:23.7
1942	Betty Bemis	5:32.5
1943	Ann Curtis	5:27.8
1944	Ann Curtis	5:32.4
1945	Ann Curtis	5:26.3
1946	Ann Curtis	5:26.7
1947	Ann Curtis	5:21.5
1948	Ann Curtis	5:26.5
1950	Thelma Kalama	5:30.9
1951	Barbara Hobelmann	5:21.6
1954	Carolyn Green	5:14.7
1955	Dougie Gray	5:16.1
1958	Sylvia Ruuska	5:04.1
1960	Chris von Saltza	4:46.9
1961	Carolyn House	4:52.5
1962	Carolyn House	4:45.3
1963	Robyn Johnson	4:46.8
1964	Marilyn Ramenofsky	4:41.7
1965	Martha Randall	4:39.5
1966	Martha Randall	4:38.0
1967	Debbie Meyer	4:29.0
1968	Debbie Meyer	4:26.7
1969	Debbie Meyer	4:26.4
1970	Debbie Meyer	4:24.3
1971	Ann Simmons	4:24.8
1972	No competition	
1973	Keena Rothhammer	4:18.07
1974	Shirley Babashoff	4:15.77
1975	Shirley Babashoff	4:15.63R
1976	Rebecca Perrott	4:17.60

880-Yard Freestyle

1916	Thelma Darby	16:08.8
1917	Claire Galligan	15:35.0
1918	Claire Galligan	13.31.8
1919	Ethelda Bleibtrey	15:26.4
1920	Ethelda Bleibtrey	16:30.0
1921	Ethelda Bleibtrey	14:37.6
1922	Helen Wainwright	13:05.0
1923	Gertrude Ederle	13:19.0
1924	Gertrude Ederle	13:59.0
1925	Ethel McGary	13:06.0
1926	Martha Norelius	12:47.0
1927	Martha Norelius	12:17.8
1928	Martha Norelius	11:56.6
1929	Josephone McKim	12:03.8
1930	Helene Madison	11:41.2
1931	Helene Madison	11:50.4
1932	Katherine Rawls	12:35.6
1933	Lenore Kight	11:44.6
1934	Lenore Kight	11:50.7
1935	Lenore Kight	11:34.0
1936	Lenore Kight Wingard	11:38.6
1937	Katherine Rawls	11:44.2
1938	Katherine Rawls Thompson	11:33.2
1940	Mary M. Ryan	11:26.4
1949	Katherine Kleinschmidt	11:48.1
1953	Carolyn Green	11:15.2
1956	Sylvia Ruuska	10:54.5
1957	Sylvia Ruuska	10:45.8R
(Discontinued)		

800-Meter Freestyle

1939	Nancy Merki	11:19.9
1941	Nancy Merki	11:16.0
1942	Betty Bemis	11:41.0
1943	Ann Curtis	11:19.3
1944	Ann Curtis	11:29.5
1945	Ann Curtis	11:24.1
1956	Ann Curtis	11:26.3
1947	Ann Curtis	11:21.8
1948	Ann Curtis	11:37.4
1950	Carolyn Green	11:28.3
1951	Carolyn Green	11:15.5

1954	Carolyn Green	10:49.9
1955	Carolyn Green	10:45.3R

(Discontinued)

1-Mile Freestyle

1916	Claire Galligan	31:19.6
1917	Claire Galligan	33:08.0
1918	Frances Cowells	33:03.0
1919	No competition	
1920	Ethelda Bleibtrey	32:25.2
1921	Thelma Darby	31:58.0
1922	Helen Wainwright	26:44.8
1923	Olive Holland	29:27.4
1924	No competition	
1925	Ethel McGary	26:27.4
1926	Ethel McGary	26:33.4
1927	Martha Norelius	24:19.4
1928	Josephine McKim	24:49.6
1929	Josephine McKim	25:10.0
1930	Helene Madison	24:32.2
1931	Helene Madison	24:45.0
1932	No competition	
1933	Lenore Kight	24:53.8
1934	Lenore Kight	25:10.5
1935	Lenore Kight	24:20.4
1936	Lenore Kight Wingard	24:07.2
1937	Katherine Rawls	24:19.6
1938	Katherine Rawls Thompson	23:47.4
1939	Mary M. Ryan	24:12.8
1940	Mary M. Ryan	23:15.0
1949	Jean Lutyens	24:34.5
1953	Carolyn Green	23:03.4
1957	Carolyn Murray	22:13.9
1959	Sylvia Ruuska	21:38.9R

1,650-Yard Freestyle

1956	Carolyn Green	21:30.2

1,500-Meter Freestyle

1941	Nancy Merki	22:12.2
1942	Nancy Merki	22:18.2
1943	Florence Schmitt	22:31.3
1944	Ann Curtis	22:13.1
1945	Marilyn Sahner	21:59.3
1946	Ann Curtis	22:08.1
1947	Marilyn Sahner	22:23.1
1948	Joan Mallory	22:58.4
1950	Barbara Hobelmann	22:25.7
1951	Carolyn Green	21:48.3
1954	Carolyn Green	21:08.5
1955	Carolyn Green	21:15.4
1958	Sylvia Ruuska	20:34.6
1960	Carolyn House	19:45.0
1961	Carolyn House	19:46.3
1962	Carolyn House	18:44.0
1963	Ginnie Duenkel	18:57.9
1964	Patty Caretto	18:30.5
1965	Patty Caretto	18:23.7
1966	Patty Caretto	18:12.9
1967	Debbie Meyer	17:50.2
1968	Debbie Meyer	17:38.5
1969	Debbie Meyer	17:19.9
1970	Debbie Meyer	17:28.4
1971	Cathy Calhoun	17:19.2
1972	No competition	
1973	Jo Harshbarger	16:54.14
1974	Jenny Turrall	16:33.947R
1975	Heather Greenwood	16:47.11
1976	Evie Kosenkranius	16:41.97

100-Yard Backstroke

1922	Sybil Bauer	1:17.6

150-Meter Backstroke

1923	Sybil Bauer	2:04.8

110-Yard Backstroke

1940	Gloria Callen	1:18.5
1949	Barbara Jensen	1:20.3
1953	Barbara Stark	1:16.6
1956	Carin Cone	1:14.5
1957	Carin Cone	1:13.6
1959	Carin Cone	1:13.3R

100-Meter Backstroke

1939	Edith Motridge	1:18.9
1941	Gloria Callen	1:17.5
1942	Gloria Callen	1:18.6
1943	Suzanne Zimmerman	1:18.3
1944	Joan Fogle	1:20.2
1945	Marion Pontacq	1:18.7
1946	Suzanne Zimmerman	1:18.0
1947	Suzanne Zimmerman	1:17.6
1948	Suzanne Zimmerman	1:16.4
1950	Maureen O'Brien	1:17.9
1951	Mary Freeman	1:18.8
1954	Shelley Mann	1:15.5
1955	Carin Cone	1:15.6
1958	Carin Cone	1:13.5
1960	Lynn Burke	1:10.2
1961	Nina Harmer	1:11.0
1962	Donna de Varona	1:10.4
1963	Cathy Ferguson	1:09.2
1964	Cathy Ferguson	1:09.2
1965	Christine Caron	1:08.1
1966	Ann Fairlie	1:07.9
1967	Kendis Moore	1:09.2
1968	Karen Muir	1:06.9
1969	Susie Atwood	1:06.0
1970	Susie Atwood	1:06.2
1971	Susie Atwood	1:06.7
1972	No competition	
1973	Melissa Belote	1:05.72
1974	Margie Moffit	1:04.68
1975	Linda Jezek	1:04.70
1976	Linda Jezek	1:04.40R

220-Yard Backstroke

1924	Sybil Bauer	3:09.4
1925	Sybil Bauer	3:11.0
1926	Adelaide Lambert	3:15.0
1927	Adelaide Lambert	3:11.0
1928	Lisa Lindstrom	3:03.4
1929	Eleanor Holm	3:03.6
1930	Eleanor Holm	3:05.0
1931	Eleanor Holm	3:04.4
1932	Eleanor Holm	2:57.8
1933	Eleanor Holm	2:57.2
1934	Alice Bridges	3:06.0
1935	Elizabeth Kompa	2:58.9
1936	Eleanor Holm Jarrett	2:51.8
1937	Erna Kompa	2:57.5
1938	Jeanne Laupheimer	3:02.0
1949	Barbara Jensen	2:54.9
1953	Barbara Stark	2:47.5
1956	Carin Cone	2:43.8
1957	Chris von Saltza	2:40.2
1959	Carin Cone	2:37.9R

200-Meter Backstroke

1946	Suzanne Zimmerman	2:48.7
1947	Suzanne Zimmerman	2:49.0
1948	Suzanne Zimmerman	2:48.3
1950	Maureen O'Brien	2:51.2
1954	Barbara Stark	2:47.9
1955	Carin Cone	2:45.6
1958	Chris von Saltza	2:37.4
1960	Lynn Burke	2:33.5
1961	Nina Harmer	2:35.0
1962	Ginnie Duenkel	2:32.1

1963	Ginnie Duenkel	2:30.8
1964	Cathy Ferguson	2:29.2
1965	Cathy Ferguson	2:28.0
	Judy Humbarger	2:28.0
1966	Karen Muir	2:26.4
1967	Kendis Moore	2:28.1
1968	Karen Muir	2:24.3
1969	Susie Atwood	2:21.5
1970	Susie Atwood	2:22.0
1971	Susie Atwood	2:22.9
1972	No competition	
1973	Melissa Belote	2:20.75
1974	Wendy Cook	2:18.81
1975	Melissa Belote	2:18.169
1976	Linda Jezek	2:17.33R

100-Yard Breaststroke

1922	Edna O'Connell	1:34.2
1949	Carol Pence	1:25.8
1957	Mary Lou Elsenius	1:24.9R

110-Yard Breaststroke

1953	Gail Peters	1:18.0R
1956	Mary Jane Sears	1:22.7
1959	Marianne Hargreaves	1:22.4

100-Meter Breaststroke

1943	Jane Dillard	1:24.3
1944	Jane Dillard Kittleson	1:25.3
1945	Jeanne Wilson	1:26.2
1946	Jeanne Wilson	1:26.2
1947	Nel Van Vliet	1:21.6
1948	Jeanne Wilson	1:28.9
1950	Judy Cornell	1:23.1
1951	Judy Cornell	1:21.0
1958	Susan Ordogh	1:23.8
1960	Ann Warner	1:23.4
1961	Dale Barnhard	1:22.6
1962	Wiltrud Urselman	1:20.6
1963	Jean Dellekamp	1:20.7
1964	Claudia Kolb	1:19.0
1965	Claudia Kolb	1:17.1
1966	Catie Ball	1:16.4
1967	Catie Ball	1:14.6
1968	Catie Ball	1:15.7
1969	Kim Brecht	1:15.7
1970	Linda Kurtz	1:16.6
1971	Diane Nickloff	1:16.7
1972	No competition	
1973	Marcia Morey	1:16.04
1974	Marcia Morey	1:14.19R
1975	Marcia Morey	1:13.55R
1976	Dawn Rodighiero	1:14.64

220-Yard Breaststroke

1923	Ruth Thomas	3:50.6
1924	Agnes Geraghty	3:35.2
1925	Agnes Geraghty	3:32.4
1926	Agnes Geraghty	3:29.4
1927	Agnes Geraghty	3:28.4
1928	Lisa Lindstrom	3:19.4
1929	Agnes Geraghty	3:17.0
1930	Margaret Hoffman	3:20.0
1931	Katherine Rawls	3:13.6
1932	Katherine Rawls	3:18.8
1933	Margaret Hoffman	3:14.6
1934	Ann Govednik	3:18.3
1935	Katherine Rawls	3:17.1
1936	Iris Cummings	3:17.2
1937	Iris Cummings	3:16.9
1938	Iris Cummings	3:18.7
1940	Fujiko Katsutani	3:14.9
1949	Evelyn Kawamoto	3:14.5

1953	Gail Peters	3:01.1
1956	Mary Jane Sears	2:59.0R
1957	Mary Lou Elsenius	3:04.8
1959	Ann Warner	3:02.4

200-Meter Breaststroke

1939	Fujiko Katsutani	3:16.1
1941	Patty Aspinall	3:14.9
1942	Patty Aspinall	3:19.5
1943	Patty Aspinall	3:21.2
1944	Nancy Merki	3:16.5
1945	Clare Lamore	3:18.6
1946	Nancy Merki	3:15.0
1947	Nel Van Vliet	2:58.6
1948	Jeanne Wilson	3:17.7
1950	Marge Hulton	3:10.2
	Evelyn Kawamoto	3:10.2
1951	Carol Pence	3:09.2
1954	Mary Jane Sears	3:07.4
1955	Mary Jane Sears	3:01.4
1958	Susan Ordogh	2:58.6
1960	Ann Warner	2:53.3
1961	Jean Dellekamp	2:56.7
1962	Wiltrud Urselman	2:53.3
1963	Jean Dellekamp	2:53.4
1964	Claudia Kolb	2:49.8
1965	Claudia Kolb	2:48.6
1966	Catie Ball	2:44.4
1967	Catie Ball	2:39.5
1968	Catie Ball	2:40.9
1969	Kim Brecht	2:45.4
1970	Claudia Clevenger	2:44.6
1971	Claudia Clevenger	2:45.7
1972	No competition	
1973	Lynn Colella	2:41.63
1974	Marcia Morey	2:39.90
1975	Marcia Morey	2:38.43R
1976	Dawn Rodighiero	2:39.40

110-Yard Butterfly

1956	Shelley Mann	1:11.8
1957	Nancy Ramey	1:11.3
1959	Becky Collins	1:11.2R

100-Meter Butterfly

1954	Shelley Mann	1:17.0
1955	Betty Mullen	1:15.0
1958	Nancy Ramey	1:10.3
1960	Becky Collins	1:10.8
1961	Susan Doerr	1:08.2
1962	Mary Stewart	1:07.6
1963	Kathy Ellis	1:06.2
1964	Sharon Stouder	1:05.4
1965	Sue Pitt	1:06.2
1966	Sue Pitt	1:07.0
1967	Ellie Daniel	1:05.7
1968	Ellie Daniel	1:06.9
1969	Virginia Durking	1:05.9
1970	Alice Jones	1:04.1
1971	Deena Deardurff	1:05.0
1972	No competition	
1973	Deena Deardurff	1:03.85
1974	Deena Deardurff	1:02.77
1975	Camille Wright	1:02.90
1976	Wendy Boglioli	1:01.76R

220-Yard Butterfly

1956	Shelley Mann	2:44.4
1957	Jane Wilson	2:47.6
1959	Becky Collins	2:37.0R

200-Meter Butterfly

1958	Sylvia Ruuska	2:43.6
1960	Becky Collins	2:36.8
1961	Becky Collins	2:32.8

1962	Sharon Finneran	2:32.1
1963	Sharon Finneran	2:31.8
1964	Sharon Stouder	2:26.4
1965	Kendis Moore	2:26.3
1966	Lee Davis	2:27.2
1967	Toni Hewitt	2:23.6
1968	Toni Hewitt	2:24.2
1969	Lynn Colella	2:21.6
1970	Alice Jones	2:19.3
1971	Ellie Daniel	2:18.4
1972	No competition	
1973	Lynn Colella	2:18.34
1974	Valerie Lee	2:16.52
1975	Valerie Lee	2:15.07R
1976	Alice Browne	2:15.57

200-Meter Individual Medley

1963	Donna deVarona	2:31.8
1964	Donna deVarona	2:29.9
1965	Claudia Kolb	2:30.8
1966	Claudia Kolb	2:27.8
1967	Claudia Kolb	2:25.0
1968	Claudia Kolb	2:27.5
1969	Lynn Vidali	2:26.3
1970	Lynn Vidali	2:26.0
1971	Yoshimi Nishigawa	2:26.0
1972	No competition	
1973	Kathy Heddy	2:25.41
1974	Kathy Heddy	2:22.477
1975	Kathy Heddy	2:19.93R
1976	Kathy Heddy	2:21.54

300-Yard Individual Medley

1922	Hilda James	4:40.8
1923-24	No competition	
1925	Adelaide Lambert	4:38.6R

330-Yard Individual Medley

1940	Chieko Miyamoto	4:35.7
1953	Gail Peters	4:21.7R

300-Meter Individual Medley

1926	Adelaide Lambert	5:01.0
1927	Eleanor Holm	4:57.8
1928	Eleanor Holm	4:56.0
1929	Eleanor Holm	4:49.8
1930	Eleanor Holm	4:57.0
1931	Katherine Rawls	4:45.8
1932	Katherine Rawls	4:52.8
1933	Katherine Rawls	4:35.6
1934	No competition	
1935	Katherine Rawls	4:38.5
1936	Katherine Rawls	4:40.2
1937	Katherine Rawls	4:38.7
1938	Katherine Rawls Thompson	4:33.1
1939	Doris Brennan	4:32.3
1941	Chieko Miyamoto	4:32.7
1942	Joan Fogle	4:43.0
1943	Joan Fogle	4:35.3
1944	Joan Fogle	4:33.1
1945	Joan Fogle	4:34.7
1946	Nancy Merki	4:29.9
1947	Nancy Merki	4:32.9
1948	Barbara Jensen	4:31.3
1949	Evelyn Kawamoto	4:27.5R
1950	Evelyn Kawamoto	4:29.0
1951	Evelyn Kawamoto	4:33.0

440-Yard Individual Medley

1946	Shelley Mann	5:52.5
1947	Sylvia Ruuska	5:43.7
1959	Sylvia Ruuska	5:40.2R

400-Meter Individual Medley

1954	Marie Gillett	6:06.9

1955	Marie Gillett	6:01.5
1958	Sylvia Ruuska	5:43.7
1960	Donna deVarona	5:36.5
1961	Donna deVarona	5:34.5
1962	Sharon Finneran	5:25.4
1963	Donna deVarona	5:24.5
1964	Donna deVarona	5:17.7
1965	Mary Ellen Olcese	5:19.6
1966	Claudia Kolb	5:15.5
1967	Claudia Kolb	5:08.2
1968	Sue Pedersen	5:10.3
1969	Debbie Meyer	5:08.6
1970	Susie Atwood	5:07.3
1971	Jennifer Bartz	5:08.3
1972	No competition	
1973	Jennifer Bartz	5:08.73
1974	Jenni Franks	5:00.51
1975	Jenni Franks	4:53.86R
1976	Donnalee Wennestrom	4:57.74

330-Yard Medley Relay

1940	New York Women's SA	4:01.4
1953	Walter Reed SC	3:47.6R

300-Meter Medley Relay

1934	Miami Beach SC	4:15.0
1935	New York Women's SA	4:09.3
1936	New York Women's SA	4:01.6
1937	New York Women's SA	4:04.1
1938	Los Angeles AC	4:07.8
1939	Los Angeles AC	3:52.8
1941	New York Women's SA	3:53.5
1942	Multnomah AC, Portland, Oreg.	4:02.8
1943	Multnomah AC, Portland, Oreg.	4:00.0
1944	Multnomah AC, Portland, Oreg.	3:58.8
1945	Multnomah AC, Portland, Oreg.	3:54.2
1946	Multnomah AC, Portland, Oreg.	3:59.1
1947	Los Angeles AC	4:00.2
1948	Los Angeles AC	4:01.6
1949	Los Angeles AC	4:02.6
1950	Lafayette, Ind., SC	3:54.8
1951	Lafayette, Ind., SC	3:52.4R

440-Yard Medley Relay

1956	Walter Reed SC	5:05.8
1957	Santa Clara SC	5:06.6
1959	Santa Clara SC	4:59.9R

400-Meter Medley Relay

1954	Walter Reed SC	5:14.0
1955	Walter Reed SC	5:07.0
1958	Santa Clara SC	5:00.9
1960	Santa Clara SC	4:49.1
1961	Vesper Boat Club	4:50.3
1962	Vesper Boat Club	4:47.5
1963	Los Angeles AC	4:44.4
1964	Santa Clara SC	4:40.3
1965	Santa Clara SC	4:38.4
1966	Santa Clara SC	4:37.7
1967	Santa Clara SC	4:34.6
1968	Santa Clara SC	4:33.8
1969	Lakewood, Calif., AC	4:31.4
1970	Lakewood, Calif., AC	4:31.2
1971	Phillips 66 SC	4:32.0
1972	No competition	
1973	Santa Clara SC "A"	4:30.13
1974	Lakewood, Calif., AC "A"	4:24.76
1975	Mission Valley, Calif.	4:24.07
1976	Central Jersey AC	4:22.49R

400-Meter Freestyle Relay

1963	Los Angeles AC	4:13.7
1964	Santa Clara SC	4:08.5
1965	Santa Clara SC	4:08.6
1966	Santa Clara SC	4:04.5
1967	Santa Clara SC	4:03.5
1968	Santa Clara SC	4:02.1
1969	Santa Clara SC	4:02.9
1970	Santa Clara SC	4:06.2
1971	Lakewood AC	4:02.9
1972	No competition	
1973	Huntington Beach AC	4:01.37
1974	Mission Viejo "A"	3:58.10
1975	Mission Viejo, Calif.	3:55.815
1976	El Monte, Calif., AC	3:53.76R

880-Yard Freestyle Relay

1923	New York Women's SA	12:15.2
1924	New York Women's SA	10:48.2
1925	New York Women's SA	12:17.0
1926	New York Women's SA	11:45.6
1927	New York Women's SA	Not available
1928	New York Women's SA	Not available
1929	New York Women's SA	11:22.2
1930	Los Angeles AC	11:15.4
1931	Los Angeles AC	11:20.4
1932	Homestead, Pa., Library	11:17.8
1933	Homestead, Pa., Library	11:10.0
1934	Homestead, Pa., Library	11:13.3
1935	Seattle AC	10:37.8
1936	Seattle AC	10:46.3
1937	Seattle AC	11:10.4
1938	New York Women's SA	10:55.5
1939	No competition	
1940	New York Women's SA	10:58.8
1942	Indianapolis Riviera Club	11:09.5
1943	Indianapolis Riviera Club "A"	10:42.1
1944	Indianapolis Riviera Club	10:52.2
1945	San Francisco Crystal Plunge	10:44.5
1949	Hawaii "A"	10:42.9
1953	Walter Reed SC	10:24.9
1956	Walter Reed SC	10:09.8

800-Meter Freestyle Relay

1941	Indianapolis Riviera Club	10:30.7
1946	San Francisco Crystal Plunge	11:10.0
1947	San Francisco Crystal Plunge	11:02.6
1948	San Francisco Crystal Plunge	11:37.4
1950	Hawaii SC	10:37.4
1951	Lafayette, Ind., SC	10:53.3
1954	Ft. Lauderdale SA	10:18.7
1955	Walter Reed SC	10:10.3
1964	Santa Clara SC	9:08.8
1965	Commerce, Calif., SC	9:00.1
1966	Santa Clara SC	8:55.4
1967	Santa Clara SC	8:53.0
1968	Arden Hills SC	8:46.2
1969	Arden Hills SC	8:42.3
1970	Arden Hills SC	8:49.2
1971	Lakewood, Calif., AC	8:35.5
1972	No competition	
1973	Santa Clara SC "A"	8:37.84
1974	Mission Viejo	8:20.23R
1975	Mission Viejo, Calif.	8:25.60
1976	Central Jersey AC	8:21.40

AAU Indoor Champions—Men

(No meet 1904–05, 1907–08; metric long
course 1976)

100-Yard Freestyle

1901	E. Carroll Schaeffer	1:06.8

1902	H. Lemoyne	1:04.0
1903	Budd Goodwin	1:09.2
1906	Charles M. Daniels	58.0
1909	Charles M. Daniels	56.8
1910	Charles M. Daniels	54.8
1911	Charles M. Daniels	56.8
1912	Duke Kahanamoku	57.8
1913	Harry J. Hebner	55.4
1914	Harry J. Hebner	55.6
1915	A. C. Raithel	54.4
1916	Perry McGillivray	56.2
1917	Ted Cann	55.2
1918	Petty McGillivray	55.4
1919	Perry McGillivray	55.4
1920	Ted Cann	53.6
1921	Norman Ross	58.2
1922	John Weissmuller	54.0
1923	John Weissmuller	54.8
1924	John Weissmuller	53.8
1925	John Weissmuller	52.2
1926	Walter Laufer	52.4
1927	John Weissmuller	51.4
1928	John Weissmuller	50.8
1929	Walter Laufer	51.8
1930	Walter Laufer	52.8
1931	Albert Schwartz	53.7
1932	Maiola Kalili	53.8
1933	Walter Spence	53.6
1934	Walter Spence	51.4
1935	Peter Fick	52.6
1936	Peter Fick	51.4
1937	Peter Fick	51.7
1938	Peter Fick	51.6
1939	Peter Fick	52.3
1940	Otto Jaretz	52.3
1941	Otto Jaretz	51.4
1942	Bill Prew	51.0
1943	Alan Ford	51.8
1944	Bill Smith	51.6
1945	Walter Ris	51.3
1946	Walter Ris	51.1
1947	Walter Ris	50.9
1948	Walter Ris	50.5
1949	Walter Ris	51.4
1950	Clarke Scholes	51.3
1951	Richard Cleveland	50.0
1952	Clarke Scholes	50.2
1953	Reid Patterson	50.6
1954	Richard Cleveland	49.8
1955	John Glover	49.8
1956	Rex Aubrey	49.1
1957	Al Wiggins	50.9
1958	Lance Larson	49.5
1959	Lance Larson	49.2
1960	Jeff Farrell	48.2
1961	Steve Clark	46.8
1962	Steve Jackman	48.3
1963	Steve Jackman	46.5
1964	Steve Clark	47.1
1965	Steve Clark	45.6
1966	Steve Rerych	47.5
1967	Donald Havens	46.0
1968	Donald Havens	45.67
1969	Donald Havens	45.92
1970	Dave Edgar	45.01
1971	Frank Heckl	45.5
1972	Mark Spitz	45.1
1973	Ken Knox	42.269R
1974	Joe Bottom	44.84
1975	Andy Coen	44.501

100-Meter Freestyle

1976	Jim Montgomery	50.77

220-Yard Freestyle

1903	Charles A. Ruberl	2:54.0
1906	Charles M. Daniels	2:33.2
1909	Charles M. Daniels	2:25.4
1910	Charles M. Daniels	2:33.0
1911	Charles M. Daniels	2:26.0
1912	Perry McGillivray	2:34.2
1913	Perry McGillivray	2:20.0
1914	Harry J. Hebner	2:23.4
1915	Perry McGillivray	2:26.6
1916	Herbert Vollmer	2:23.6
1917	Norman Ross	2:22.2
1918	Norman Ross	2:24.4
1919	No competition	
1920	Ted Cann	2:29.8
1921	Norman Ross	2:22.2
1922	John Weissmuller	2:17.4
1923	John Weissmuller	2:22.0
1924	John Weissmuller	2:14.8
1925	Arne Borg	2:18.4
1926	Arne Borg	2:15.8
1927	John Weissmuller	2:10.8
1928	John Weissmuller	2:10.4
1929	Walter Laufer	2:12.8
1930	Clarence "Buster" Crabbe	2:16.8
1931	Albert Schwartz	2:16.2
1932	Maiola Kalili	2:14.8
1933	George Fissler	2:13.6
1934	Walter Spence	2:11.6
1935	Jack Medica	2:10.8
1936	Jack Medica	2:11.6
1937	Charles Hutter	2:11.2
1938	Ralph Flanagan	2:10.9
1939	Jack Medica	2:12.7
1940	Tom Haynie	2:13.4
1941	Otto Jaretz	2:10.3
1942	Alan Ford	2:09.3
1943	Bill Smith	2:09.6
1944	Bill Smith	2:08.0
1945	Eugene Rogers	2:12.5
1946	Walter Ris	2:11.3
1947	Bill Smith	2:08.0
1948	Bill Smith	2:08.5
1949	Robert Gibe	2:10.6
1950	John Marshall	2:05.3
1951	John Marshall	2:06.7
1952	Ford Konno	2:06.4
1953	James McLane	2:07.2
1954	Ford Konno	2:06.5
1955	Ford Konno	2:04.0
1956	Richard Hanley	2:05.9
1957	Richard Hanley	2:05.1
1958	Murray Rose	2:02.5
1959	Murray Rose	2:02.2
1960	Jeff Farrell	2:00.2
1961	Steve Clark	2:00.0
1962	Roy Saari	1:58.6R

200-Yard Freestyle

1963	Don Schollander	1:44.4
1964	Don Schollander	1:42.6
1965	Don Schollander	1:41.7
1966	Don Schollander	1:42.8
1967	Don Schollander	1:41.2
1968	Bill Burrell	1:43.46
1969	Frank Heckl	1:42.30
1970	John Kinsella	1:40.7
1971	Frank Heckl	1:40.5
1972	Steve Genter	1:39.2
1973	Tim McDonnell	1:40.040
1974	Kurt Krumpholtz	1:39.47
1975	Tim Shaw	1:38.357R

200-Meter Freestyle

1976	Jim Montgomery	1:51.41

400-Yard Freestyle

1901	E. Carroll Schaeffer	5:26.2

440-Yd Freestyle

1903	Charles A. Ruberl	6:14.0
1906	Charles M. Daniels	5:50.4
1907–39	No competition	
1940	Tom Haynie	4:50.7
1941	Paul Herron	4:45.5
1942	Kiyoshi Nakama	4:42.4
1943	Bill Smith	4:42.7
1944	Bill Smith	4:42.1
1945	Kiyoshi Nakama	4:44.5
1946	Jack Hill	4:42.7
1947	Bill Smith	4:42.5
1948	Bill Smith	4:44.3
1949	James McLane	4:41.0
1950	John Marshall	4:31.2
1951	John Marshall	4:32.0
1952	Ford Konno	4:34.5
1953	James McLane	4:36.6
1954	Ford Konno	4:28.3
1955	Ford Konno	4:28.2
1956	George Breen	4:30.1
1957	George Breen	4:31.5
1958	Murray Rose	4:21.6
1959	Murray Rose	4:18.8
1960	Alan Somers	4:22.6
1961	Murray Rose	4:18.2
1962	Roy Saari	4:14.6R

500-Yard Freestyle

1963	Roy Saari	4:48.2
1964	Don Schollander	4:44.5
1965	Carl Robie	4:44.1
1966	Greg Buckingham	4:41.1
1967	Mike Burton	4:37.0
1968	Trevor Charlton	4:37.29
1969	Hans Fassnacht	4:32.99
1970	John Kinsella	4:22.1R
1971	John Kinsella	4:28.8
1972	John Kinsella	4:28.2
1973	Jack Tingley	4:26.863
1974	Tim Shaw	4:23.50
1975	Tim Shaw	4:22.570

400-Meter Freestyle

1976	Doug Northway	3:56.48

1,500-Meter Freestyle

1932	Clarence "Buster" Crabbe	19:45.6
1936	Jack Medica	19:06.8
1942	Kiyoshi Nakama	19:35.4
1948	Jack Taylor	20:08.2
1950	John Marshall	18:37.0
1951	John Marshall	18:10.8
1952	Ford Konno	18:47.7
1953	James McLane	18:54.0
1954	Ford Konno	19:07.8
1955	George Breen	18:52.4
1956	George Breen	18:20.2
1957	George Breen	17:34.0
1958	Murray Rose	18:28.5
1959	Murray Rose	18:18.4
1960	George Breen	18:00.8
1961	Murray Rose	17:43.7
1962	Roy Saari	16:54.1
1976	Casey Converse	15:40.04R

1,650-Yard Freestyle

1963	Roy Saari	16:52.1
1964	Roy Saari	16.49.3
1965	Roy Saari	16.40.8
1966	Mike Burton	16:27.3

1967	Mike Burton	16:08.0
1968	Mike Burton	16:04.56
1969	Mike Burton	15:40.1
1970	John Kinsella	15:35.9
1971	John Kinsella	15:42.3
1972	John Kinsella	15:31.3
1973	Jack Tingley	15:19.419
1974	Mike Bruner	15:15.33
1975	John Naber	15:09.510R

100-Yard Backstroke

1951	Jack Taylor	58.5
1952	Richard Thoman	56.9
1953	Richard Thoman	57.5
1954	Yoshi Oyakawa	56.8
1955	Yoshi Oyakawa	57.2
1956	Albert Wiggins	57.0
1957	Charles Krepp	57.8
1958	Frank McKinney	56.5
1959	Charles Bittick	55.5
1960	Charles Bittick	54.4
1961	Charles Bittick	53.4
1962	Bob Bennett	54.1
1963	Charles Bittick	53.3
1964	Bob Bennett	53.7
1965	Thompson Mann	52.5
1966	Rich McGeagh	53.9
1967	Fred Haywood	52.6
1968	Charles Hickcox	52.51
1969	Fred Haywood	52.26
1970	Mike Stamm	51.1
1971	Mike Stamm	51.5
1972	Mike Stamm	51.8
1973	John Naber	51.367
1974	John Naber	50.41
1975	John Naber	50.368 R

100-Meter Backstroke

1976	John Naber	56.99

150-Yard Backstroke

1906	Charles A. Ruberl	2:05.4
1907–09	No competition	
1910	Harry J. Hebner	1:56.4
1911	Harry J. Hebner	1:57.2
1912	Harry J. Hebner	1:55.4
1913	Harry J. Hebner	2:16.8
1914	Harry J. Hebner	1:49.8
1915	Harry J. Hebner	1:54.0
1916	Harry J. Hebner	1:56.8
1917	Norman Ross	1:50.6
1918	Perry McGillivray	1:49.6
1919	No competition	
1920	Perry McGillivray	1:48.8
1921	R. Kegeris	1:49.8
1922	R. Kegeris	1:49.8
1923	John Weissmuller	1:42.0
1924	Oliver Horn	1:47.4
1925	Paul Wyatt	1:47.2
1926	Walter Laufer	1:42.8
1927	George Kojac	1:39.2
1928	Walter Laufer	1:37.6
1929	George Kojac	1:39.0
1930	Walter Laufer	1:40.6
1931	Walter Laufer	1:39.9
1932	George Kojac	1:38.0
1933	Dan Zehr	1:39.5
1934	Albert Vande Weghe	1:36.9
1935	Adolph Kiefer	1:36.1
1936	Adolph Kiefer	1:32.7
1937	Adolph Kiefer	1:33.0
1938	Albert Vande Weghe	1:34.1

1939	Adolph Kiefer	1:33.2
1940	Adolph Kiefer	1:33.3
1941	Adolph Kiefer	1:33.1
1942	Adolph Kiefer	1:30.5
1943	Harry Holiday, Jr.	1:32.8
1944	Adolph Kiefer	1:31.0
1945	Adolph Kiefer	1:33.5
1946	Bob Cowell	1:36.6
1947	Robert De Groot	1:34.8
1948	Allen Stack	1:32.3
1949	Allen Stack	1:30.7R
1950	Allen Stack	1:32.9
1951	Jack Taylor	1:32.5
1952	Richard Thoman	1:30.8
1953	Richard Thoman	1:32.4
1954	Yoshi Oyakawa	1:30.7R
(Discontinued)		

220-Yard Backstroke

1955	Yoshi Oyakawa	2:22.5
1956	Frank McKinney	2:21.7
1957	Frank McKinney	2:19.6
1958	Frank McKinney	2:16.9
1959	Frank McKinney	2:16.1
1960	Charles Bittick	2:13.1
1961	Charles Bittick	2:07.7
1962	Tom Stock	2:09.0R

200-Yard Backstroke

1963	Charles Bittick	1:55.9
1964	Ed Bartsch	1:56.3
1965	Thompson Mann	1:56.8
1966	Charles Hickcox	1:59.9
1967	Mark Mader	1:54.4
1968	Charles Hickcox	1:54.93
1969	Gary Hall	1:52.00
1970	Gary Hall	1:51.4
1971	Mike Stamm	1:52.2
1972	Mike Stamm	1:51.0
1973	John Naber	1:50.485
1974	John Naber	1:49.70
1975	John Naber	1:48.135R

200-Meter Backstroke

1976	John Naber	2:03.25

100-Yard Breaststroke

1951	Charles Moss	59.3
1952	John Davies	59.2
1953	David Hawkins	59.6
1954–55	No competition	
1956	Donald Kutyna	1:03.0
1957	Manuel Sanguilly	1:04.0
1958	Manuel Sanguilly	1:04.2
1959	Norbert Rumpel	1:04.9
1960	Dick Nelson	1:02.4
1961	Chet Jastremski	59.6
1962	Chet Jastremski	59.1
1963	Chet Jastremski	58.5
1964	Bill Craig	1:00.1
1965	Paul Scheerer	1:00.4
1966	Wayne Anderson	1:01.2
1967	Ken Merten	58.9
1968	Ken Merten	58.83
1969	Brian Job	58.11
1970	Brian Job	57.1
1971	Brian Job	57.7
1972	Brian Job	57.5
1973	Mark Chatfield	57.367
1974	John Hencken	55.50R
1975	John Hencken	56.166

200-Meter Breaststroke

1976	David Wilkie	1:04.46

220-Yard Breaststroke

1921	Robert D. Skelton	3:02.6
1922	Donald McClellan	3:10.4
1923	Robert D. Skelton	2:58.6
1924	J. Faricy	2:52.4
1925	Walter Spence	2:51.8
1926	Erich Rademacher	2:46.0
1927	Walter Spence	2:47.6
1928	Walter Spence	2:43.6
1929	Walter Spence	2:47.6
1930	Thomas Blankenburg	2:52.6
1931	Leonard Spence	2:44.6
1932	Leonard Spence	2:43.6
1933	Leonard Spence	2:45.9
1934	Leonard Spence	2:43.5
1935	Leonard Spence	2:43.8
1936	John H. Higgins	2:39.2
1937	John H. Higgins	2:40.5
1938	Jack Kasley	2:40.0
1939	Richard R. Hough	2:39.5
1940	Richard R. Hough	2:40.8
1941	James Skinner	2:41.7
1942	James Counsilman	2:39.4
1943	Charles Gantner	2:42.2
1944	Joseph Verdeur	2:40.3
1945	David Seibold	2:47.9
1946	Joseph Verdeur	2:35.6
1947	Joseph Verdeur	2:35.8
1948	Joseph Verdeur	2:30.5
1949	Keith Carter	2:30.7
1950	Robert Brawner	2:29.3
1951	John Davies	2:34.7
1952	John Davies	2:29.1
1953	Jerry Holan	2:31.0
1954	Dick Fadgen	2:42.9
1955	Robert Gawboy	2:38.0
1956	Dick Fadgen	2:37.1
1957	Manuel Sanguilly	2:37.3
1958	Fred Munsch	2:38.5
1959	Norbert Rumpel	2:36.1
1960	William Mulliken	2:34.8
1961	Chet Jastremski	2:26.8
1962	Chet Jastremski	2:25.3R

200-Yard Breaststroke

1906	A. M. Goersling	2:52.6
1907–09	No competition	
1910	Michael McDermott	2:56.0
1911	Michael McDermott	2:43.2
1912	Michael McDermott	2:38.8
1913	Michael McDermott	2:55.4
1914	Michael McDermott	2:43.0
1915	Michael McDermott	2:43.0
1916	Michael McDermott	2:43.6
1917	Michael McDermott	2:39.8
1918	Michael McDermott	2:41.4
1919	G. H. Taylor	2:44.4
1920	G. H. Taylor	2:44.8
1963	Chet Jastremski	2:09.0
1964	Kenjiro Matsumoto	2:09.7
1965	Ken Merten	2:11.8
1966	Ken Merten	2:12.5
1967	Ken Merten	2:10.4
1968	Brian Job	2:08.00
1969	Brian Job	2:07.34
1970	Brian Job	2:04.00
1971	Brian Job	2:04.4
1972	Brian Job	2:02.3
1973	Rick Colella	2:03.186
1974	Rick Colella	2:01.43
1975	John Hencken	2:00.894R

200-Meter Breaststroke

1976	David Wilkie	2:18.48

100-Yard Butterfly

1954	Dave Hawkins	58.8
1955	No competition	
1956	Albert Wiggins	54.5
1957	Albert Wiggins	55.0
1958	Tony Tashnick	54.3
1959	Frank Legacki	53.6
1960	Mike Troy	53.1
1961	Frank Legacki	51.9
1962	Larry Schulhof	52.1
1963	Walter Richardson	51.5
1964	Walter Richardson	50.8
1965	Luis Nicolao	50.9
1966	Ross Wales	51.3
1967	Mark Spitz	49.9
1968	Mark Spitz	49.72
1969	Ross Wales	50.54
1970	Mark Spitz	49.0
1971	Frank Heckle	49.5
1972	Mark Spitz	48.7R
1973	Bruce Robertson	49.598
1974	Steve Baxter	49.51
1975	Gary Hall	48.863

100-Meter Butterfly

1976	Steve Gregg	55.49

220-Yard Butterfly

1955	Eulalia Rios	2:30.2
1956	Jiro Nagasawa	2:19.4
1957	Jack Nelson	2:25.5
1958	William Yorzyk	2:18.0
1959	Mike Troy	2:18.6
1960	Mike Troy	2:12.4
1961	Mike Troy	2:10.9
1962	Larry Schulhof	2:10.7

200-Meter Butterfly

1963	Fred Schmidt	1:55.2
1964	Fred Schmidt	1:53.8
1965	Carl Robie	1:52.7
1966	Carl Robie	1:54.9
1967	Mark Spitz	1:50.6
1968	Mark Spitz	1:51.50
1969	Gary Hall	1:50.5
1970	Gary Hall	1:50.5
1971	Gary Hall	1:48.4
1972	Mark Spitz	1:49.0
1973	Robin Backhaus	1:49.552
1974	Robin Backhaus	1:47.27R
1975	Greg Jagenberg	1:47.283

200-Yard Butterfly

1976	Mike Bruner	2:02.49

200-Yard Individual Medley

1959	Joe Hunsaker	2:07.0
1960	John McGill	2:03.3
1961	Ted Stickles	2:02.1
1962	Chet Jastremski	1:59.4
1963	Chet Jastremski	1:58.3
1964	Dick Roth	1:58.2
1965	Roy Saari	1:56.2
1966	William Utley	1:57.8
1967	William Utley	1:55.9
1968	Charles Hickcox	1:53.30
1969	Dave Johnson	1:56.22
1970	Gary Hall	1:54.6
1971	Gunnar Larsson	1:53.3
1972	Gary Hall	1:53.1
1973	Steve Furniss	1:51.595
1974	Lee Engstrand	1:51.28
1975	Lee Engstrand	1:50.317R

200-Meter Individual Medley

1976	David Wilkie	2:06.25

300-Yard Individual Medley

1924	Harold Kruger	3:52.0
1925	Walter Spence	3:45.0
1926	Walter Laufer	3:45.6
1927	Walter Spence	3:46.8
1928	Walter Laufer	3:39.8
1929	Walter Spence	3:40.0
1930	Clarence "Buster" Crabbe	3:41.0
1931	Clarence "Buster" Crabbe	3:58.5
1932	Clarence "Buster" Crabbe	3:36.4
1933	Wallace Spence	3:42.3
1934	Leonard Spence	3:35.6
1935	Leonard Spence	3:37.5
1936	John Higgins	3:28.7
1937	John Higgins	3:32.2
1938	Andrew Clark	3:31.5
1939	Andrew Clark	3:30.0
1940	Adolph Kiefer	3:29.6
1941	Adolph Kiefer	3:29.6
1942	Adolph Kiefer	3:28.2
1943	Norman Siegel	3:35.7
1944	Adolph Kiefer	3:23.9
1945	Adolph Kiefer	3:30.4
1946	Joseph Verdeur	3:32.1
1947	Joseph Verdeur	3:26.1
1948	Joseph Verdeur	3:25.1
1949	Joseph Verdeur	3:22.9
1950	Joseph Verdeur	3:25.1
1951	James Thomas	3:24.2
1952	Burwell Jones	3:20.7R
1953	Burwell Jones	3:21.1

400-Yard Individual Medley

1954	Bert Wardrop	4:41.7
1955	Jack Wardrop	4:36.9
1956	Tim Jecko	4:46.6
1957	Tim Jecko	4:39.2
1958	George Harrison	4:41.3
1959	George Harrison	4:35.8
1960	George Harrison	4:28.6
1961	Charles Bittick	4:23.7
1962	Ted Stickles	4:18.1
1963	Roy Saari	4:16.6
1964	Dick Roth	4:13.2
1965	Greg Buckingham	4:08.9
1966	Dick Roth	4:15.5
1967	Dick Roth	4:09.5
1968	Gary Hall	4:10.07
1969	Gary Hall	4:00.80
1970	Gary Hall	3:59.6
1971	Gunnar Larsson	4:01.5
1972	Gary Hall	3:58.0
1973	Thomas Szuba	3:57.780
1974	Rick Colella	3:57.19
1975	Andras Hargitay	3:54.916R

400-Meter Individual Medley

1976	Zoltan Verraszto	4:26.00

300-Yard Medley Relay

1927	Illinois AC	3:06.2
1928	IllinoisAC	3:05.6
1929	Brooklyn Central YMCA	3:11.6
1930	Hollywood AC	3:06.0
1931	Lake Shore AC	3:05.6
1932	New York AC	3:01.2
1933	New York AC	3:03.8
1934	Detroit AC	3:04.2
1935	Lake Shore AC	2:57.7
1936	Lake Shore AC	2:54.9
1937	Lake Shore AC	2:55.1
1938	Princeton U	2:54.2
1939	Princeton U	2:52.5
1940	Princeton U	2:54.6

1941	Chicago Towers Club	2:55.4
1942	Yale U	2:56.0
1943	U of Michigan "A"	2:56.0
1944	Great Lakes Naval Training	2:59.0
1945	Bainbridge Naval Training	2:55.7
1946	Ohio State U	2:56.0
1947	Ohio State U	2:52.4
1948	U of Michigan	2:50.9
1949	New Haven SC	2:52.4
1950	New Haven SC	2:51.6
1951	New Haven SC "B"	2:50.0
1952	New Haven SC "A"	2:47.4R
1953	New Haven SC "A"	2:50.3

400-Yard Medley Relay

1954	New York AC	4:00.9
1955	No. Carolina AC	3:51.5
1956	No. Carolina AC	3:46.0
1957	No. Carolina AC	3:52.2
1958	New Haven SC	3:46.6
1959	New Haven SC	3:47.0
1960	U So. California	3:42.0
1961	No. Carolina AC	3:39.8
1962	No. Carolina AC	3:37.9
1963	Indiana U	3:33.2
1964	Yale U	3:33.7
1965	U So. California	3:31.9
1966	U So. California	3:33.6
1967	Santa Clara SC	3:30.4
1968	Yale U	3:30.41
1969	Yale U	3:30.40
1970	Santa Clara SC	3:24.1
1971	Indiana U	3:24.566
1972	Indiana U	3:24.4
1973	U So. California "A"	3:23.723
1974	U So. California	3:20.87
1975	U So. California	3:19.722R

400-Meter Medley Relay

1976	Gatorade SC "A"	3:52.19

400-Yard Freestyle Relay

1910	New York AC	4:12.0
1911	New York AC	4:10.6
1912	City AC	3:59.6
1913	Illinois AC	3:46.2
1914	Illinois AC	3:52.8
1915	Illinois AC	3:45.6
1916	Illinois AC	3:42.4
1917	Illinois AC	3:42.6
1918	Illinois AC	3:48.4
1919	No competition	
1920	Illinois AC	3:47.8
1921	Illinois AC	3:44.0
1922	Illinois AC	3:43.6
1923	Illinois AC	3:42.0
1924	Illinois AC	3:41.4
1925	Illinois AC	3:45.0
1926	Cincinnati Central YMCA	3:38.0
1927	Chicago AA	3:40.4
1928	Illinois AC	3:32.6
1929	New York AC	3:43.2
1930	Chicago AA	3:39.2
1931	New York AC	3:34.9
1932	New York AC	3:31.8
1933	New York AC	3:38.1
1934	New York AC	3:31.8
1935	New York AC	3:34.6
1936	New York AC	3:34.2
1937	U Michigan	3:31.4
1938	Ohio State U	3:31.5
1939	New York AC	3:31.3
1940	U Michigan	3:35.2
1941	Chicago Towers Club	3:29.6

1942	Yale U	3:28.6
1943	U Michigan	3:34.9
1944	Great Lakes Naval Training	3:29.1
1945	Bainbridge Naval Training	3:38.6
1946	Ohio State U	3:34.6
1947	Yale U	3:27.8
1948	New Haven SC	3:27.3
1949	New Haven SC	3:28.6
1950	New Haven SC	3:26.4
1951	New Haven SC "A"	3:23.0
1952	New Haven SC "A"	3:23.0
1953	New Haven SC "A"	3:23.7
1954	New Haven SC	3:25.0
1955	New Haven SC	3:21.8
1956	New Haven SC	3:22.2
1957	New Haven SC	3:27.9
1958	U So. Calif. Freshmen	3:20.4
1959	U So. California	3:21.1
1960	U So. California	3:16.0
1961	New Haven SC	3:15.9
1962	Santa Clara SC	3:17.4
1963	Yale U	3:08.1
1964	Yale U	3:10.9
1965	U So. California	3:07.4
1966	No. Carolina AC	3:10.9
1967	Yale U	3:06.5
1968	Phillips 66 SC	3:04.70
1969	U So. California	3:05.00
1970	U So. California	3:03.6
1971	U So. California	3:02.86
1972	U So. California	3:03.26
1973	U So. California "A"	3:02.494
1974	U So. California "A"	3:02.16
1975	Indiana U "A"	2:59.340R

400-Meter Freestyle Relay

1976	U of Tennessee "A"	3:26.97

800-Yard Freestyle Relay

1966	Yale U	7:04.1
1967	Yale U	6:56.2
1968	Indiana U	6:55.11
1969	U So. California	6:53.47
1970	U So. California	6:47.2
1971	U So. California	6:42.66
1972	U So. California	6:42.1
1973	U So. California "A"	6:39.241
1974	U So. California	6:41.24
1975	U So. California "A"	6:35.613R

800-M Freestyle Relay

1976	U So. California	7:33.53

AAU Indoor Champions—Women

100-Yard Freestyle

1916	Olga Dorfner	1:08.8
1917	Olga Dorfner	1:07.6
1918	Olga Dorfner	1:10.6
1919	Charlotte Boyle	1:08.6
1920	Ethelda Bleibtrey	1:06.2
1921	Charlotte Boyle	1:07.2
1922	Ethelda Bleibtrey	1:07.0
1923	Helen Wainwright	1:07.2
1924	Helen Wainwright	1:07.6
1925	Ethel Lackie	1:06.0
1926	Ethel Lackie	1:03.4
1927	Martha Norelius	1:04.0
1928	Ethel Lackie	1:03.4
1929	Albina Oisipowich	Not available
1930	Helene Madison	1:06.0
1931	Helene Madison	1:03.2
1932	Helene Madison	1:02.4
1933	Lenore Kight	1:03.4

1934	Olive McKean	1:03.8
1935	Katherine Rawls	1:03.0
1936	Claudia Eckert	1:02.5
1937	Claudia Eckert	1:01.8
1938	Halina Tomska	1:01.3
1939	Dorothy Evans	1:02.0
1940	Halina Tomska Tullis	1:01.0
1941	Patricia McWhorter	1:02.8
1942	Marilyn Sahner	1:01.9
1943	Suzanne Zimmerman	1:02.2
1944	Brenda Helser	1:00.9
1945	Ann Curtis	1:01.9
1946	Brenda Helser	1:00.4
1947	Ann Curtis	1:00.3
1948	Marie Corridon	59.9
1949	Jackie LaVine	1:01.1
1950	Marie Corridon	1:00.1
1951	Jackie LaVine	1:00.5
1952	Jackie LaVine	59.1
1953	Judy Roberts	59.2
1954	Jody Alderson	58.5
1955	Shelley Mann	58.7
1956	Wanda Werner	58.6
1957	Molly Botkin	58.3
1958	Chris von Saltza	56.8
1959	Shirley Stobs	57.7
1960	Chris von Saltza	56.3
1961	Chris von Saltza	55.8
1962	Robyn Johnson	55.5
1963	Terri Stickles	55.3
1964	Sharon Stouder	54.2
1965	Jeanne Hallock	54.5
1966	Martha Randall	53.6
1967	Erika Bricker	53.3
1968	Jane Barkman	52.1
1969	Wendy Fordyce	52.8
1970	Wendy Fordyce	52.8
1971	Sandy Neilson	53.2
1972	Barbara Shaw	52.1
1973	Shirley Babashoff	52.155
1974	Kathy Heddy	50.89R
1975	Shirley Babashoff	50.974

100-Meter Freestyle

1976	Kim Peyton	57.53

220-Yard Freestyle

1916	Claire Galligan	3:15.8
1917	Olga Dorfner	2:59.6
1918	Claire Galligan	3:03.8
1919	Elizabeth Ryan	3:08.4
1920	No competition	
1921	Margaret Woodbridge	2:52.4
1922	Helen Wainwright	2:54.2
1923	Gertrude Ederle	2:50.2
1924	No competition	
1925	Helen Wainwright	2:50.8
1926	Martha Norelius	2:44.6
1927	Martha Norelius	2:41.0
1928	Martha Norelius	2:47.6
1929	Albina Oisipowich	Not available
1930	Helene Madison	2:35.0
1931	Helene Madison	2:36.0
1932	Helene Madison	2:39.4
1933	Lenore Kight	2:35.4
1934	Lenore Kight	2:36.8
1935	Lenore Kight	2:35.5
1936	Mary Lou Petty	2:34.2
1937	Virginia Hopkins	2:37.6
1938	Halina Tomska	2:32.4
1939	Dorothy Leonard	2:35.3
1940	Brenda Helser	2:30.3
1941	Dorothy Leonard	2:33.8

1942	Betty Bemis	2:32.6
1943	Brenda Helser	2:36.9
1944	Ann Curtis	2:29.2
1945	Ann Curtis	2:31.5
1946	Ann Curtis	2:27.3
1947	Ann Curtis	2:23.3R
1948	Ann Curtis	2:26.2
1950	Jackie LaVine	2:32.3

250-Yard Freestyle

1953	Delia Mulenkamp	2:50.4
1954	Carol Tait	2:53.0
1955	Shelley Mann	2:49.4
1956	Dougie Gray	2:45.4
1957	Chris von Saltza	2:42.9
1958	Chris von Saltza	2:42.3
1959	Molly Botkin	2:44.4
1960	Chris von Saltza	2:38.4
1961	Chris von Saltza	2:39.2
1962	Robyn Johnson	2:34.6
1963	Terri Stickles	2:34.7
1964	Terri Stickles	2:32.0R

200-Yard Freestyle

1965	Penny Estes	1:58.2
1966	Martha Randall	1:56.9
1967	Pokey Watson	1:54.1
1968	Debbie Meyer	1:52.1
1969	Linda Gustavson	1:54.4
1970	Wendy Fordyce	1:55.5
1971	Nancy Spitz	1:55.8
1972	Kim Peyton	1:51.4
1973	Keena Rothhammer	1:50.517
1974	Shirley Babashoff	1:48.79R
1975	Shirley Babashoff	1:49.528

200-Meter Freestyle

| 1976 | Shirley Babashoff | 2:02.54 |

440-Yard Freestyle

1939	Halina Tomska	5:29.5
1940	Nancy Merki	5:30.3
1941	Nancy Merki	5:30.1
1942	Nancy Merki	5:31.6
1943	Joan Fogle	5:37.4
1944	Ann Curtis	5:21.7
1945	Ann Curtis	5:27.7
1946	Ann Curtis	5:17.1
1947	Ann Curtis	5:07.9R
1948	Ann Curtis	5:17.9
1949	Joan Mallory	5:27.1
1950	Jackie LaVine	5:28.9

400-Yard Freestyle

| 1951 | Ann Moss | 4:52.3 |
| 1952 | Carolyn Green | 4:49.6R |

500-Yard Freestyle

1953	Carolyn Green	5:59.1
1954	Carol Tait	6:00.6
1955	Carol Tait	6:01.4
1956	Dougie Gray	5:55.8
1957	Sylvia Ruuska	5:47.8
1958	Sylvia Ruuska	5:44.9
1959	Sylvia Ruuska	5:46.6
1960	Chris von Saltza	5:37.7
1961	Chris von Saltza	5:34.5
1962	Robyn Johnson	5:27.2
1963	Sharon Finneran	5:23.4
1964	Terri Stickles	5:19.2
1965	Patty Caretto	5:15.6
1966	Pam Kruse	5:15.5
1967	Pam Kruse	5:06.9

1968	Debbie Meyer	4:54.1
1969	Vicki King	5:00.6
1970	Debbie Meyer	5:00.7
1971	Debbie Meyer	5:03.8
1972	Keena Rothhammer	4:57.4
1973	Keena Rothhammer	4:52.547
1974	Shirley Babashoff	4:47.34R
1975	Shirley Babashoff	4:50.950

400-Meter Freestyle

| 1976 | Shirley Babashoff | 4:15.82 |

1,650-Yard Freestyle

1964	Sharon Finneran	18:31.5
1965	Patty Caretto	18:03.6
1966	Sharon Finneran	18:10.9
1967	Debbie Meyer	17:38.1
1968	Debbie Meyer	17:04.4
1969	Debbie Meyer	17:04.4
1970	Debbie Meyer	16:54.6
1971	Debbie Meyer	17:11.8
1972	Jo Harshbarger	16:59.3
1973	Shane Gould	16:46.659
1974	Karen Hanzen	16:28.37R
1975	Jo Harshbarger	16:27.114

100-Yard Backstroke

1920	Ethelda Bleibtrey	1:17.4
1921	Sybil Bauer	1:21.0
1922	Sybil Bauer	1:17.6
1923	Sybil Bauer	1:15.2
1924	Sybil Bauer	1:14.0
1925	Sybil Bauer	1:15.0
1926	Sybil Bauer	1:15.0
1927	Corinne Condon	1:18.8
1928	Corinne Condon	1:17.4
1929	Joan McSheehy	1:15.4
1930	Eleanor Holm	1:12.0
1931	Eleanor Holm	1:14.4
1932	Eleanor Holm	1:11.6
1933	Joan McSheehy	1:13.6
1934	Eleanor Holm Jarrett	1:10.8
1935	Eleanor Holm Jarrett	1:09.6
1936	Eleanor Holm Jarrett	1:08.4
1937	Dorothy Forbes	1:12.1
1938	Jeanne Laupheimer	1:12.1
1939	Helen Perry	1:09.2
1940	Gloria Callen	1:09.2
1941	Helen Perry	1:09.7
1942	Gloria Callen	1:08.5
1943	Suzanne Zimmerman	1:10.3
1944	Suzanne Zimmerman	1:11.2
1945	Marion Pontacq	1:11.4
1946	Suzanne Zimmerman	1:08.1
1947	Suzanne Zimmerman	1:08.4
1948	Suzanne Zimmerman	1:08.2
1949	Maureen O'Brien	1:08.1
1950	Maureen O'Brien	1:07.4
1951	Maureen O'Brien	1:08.4
1952	Maureen O'Brien	1:09.0
1953	Barbara Stark	1:08.7
1954	Shelley Mann	1:06.4
1955	Carlie O'Connor	1:07.8
1956	Carin Cone	1:07.2
1957	Carin Cone	1:03.8
1958	Carin Cone	1:03.6
1959	Carin Cone	1:04.3
1960	Lynn Burke	1:03.0
1961	Nina Harmer	1:04.2
1962	Donna deVarona	1:04.0
1963	Nina Harmer	1:02.6
1964	Cathy Ferguson	1:01.5
1965	Cathy Ferguson	1:00.9

1966	Elaine Tanner	1:00.7
1967	Kay Hall	1:01.6
1968	Kay Hall	59.3
1969	Susie Atwood	58.80
1970	Susie Atwood	58.7
1971	Susie Atwood	58.2
1972	Susie Atwood	58.7
1973	Linda Stimpson	58.507
1974	Linda Stimpson	57.30R
1975	Tauna Vandeweghe	58.128

100-Meter Backstroke

| 1976 | Linda Jezek | 1:04.45 |

200-Yard Backstroke

1948	Suzanne Zimmerman	2:29.4
1949	Barbara Jensen	2:32.6
1950	Maureen O'Brien	2:29.5
1951	Mary Freeman	2:32.1
1952	Barbara Stark	2:27.5
1953	Barbara Stark	2:27.0
1954	Barbara Stark	2:27.5
1955	Maureen Murphy	2:27.4
1956	Carin Cone	2:26.4
1957	Carin Cone	2:25.2
1958	Carin Cone	2:19.8
1959	Carin Cone	2:20.2
1960	Lynn Burke	2:16.7
1961	Chris von Saltza	2:19.9
1962	Donna deVarona	2:17.9
1963	Ginny Duenkel	2:14.9
1964	Cathy Ferguson	2:12.8
1965	Cathy Ferguson	2:13.2
1966	Judy Humbarger	2:11.8
1967	Kendis Moore	2:10.2
1968	Kay Hall	2:10.8
1969	Susie Atwood	2:07.5
1970	Susie Atwood	2:05.8
1971	Susie Atwood	2:06.0
1972	Susie Atwood	2:04.0
1973	Melissa Belote	2:00.498R
1974	Wendy Cook	2:04.00
1975	Nancy Garapick	2:02.843

100-Meter Backstroke

| 1976 | Cheryl Gibson | 2:18.11 |

100-Yard Breaststroke

1920	Eleanor Smith	1:25.2
1921	Frances Taylor	1:31.8
1922	Ruth Smith	1:23.8
1923–25 No competition		
1926	Agnes Geraghty	1:19.4
1927	Agnes Geraghty	1:22.0
1928	Katherine Mearls	1:22.4
1929	Jane Fauntz	1:21.8
1930	Agnes Geraghty	1:21.4
1931	Margaret Hoffman	1:24.4
1932	Jane Cadwell	1:25.6
1933	Margaret Hoffman	1:21.4
1934	Doris Shimman	1:20.9
1935	Katherine Rawls	1:20.6
1936	Katherine Rawls	1:18.6
1937	Katherine Rawls	1:18.5
1938	Katherine Rawls	1:18.5
1939–42 No competition		
1943	Alice Miller	1:20.6
1944	Patricia Sinclair	1:17.5
1945	Jeanne Wilson	1:15.1
1946	Patricia Sinclair	1:14.6
1947	Clara Lamore	1:13.8
1948	Carol Pence	1:15.2
1949	Marge Hulton	1:16.5

1950	Judy Cornell	1:12.6
1951	Carol Pence	1:12.5
1952	Gail Peters	1:11.7
1953	Gail Peters	1:10.6
1954–55 No competition		
1956	Mary Jane Sears	1:12.2
1957	Patty Kempner	1:15.5
1958	Patty Kempner	1:13.0
1959	Linda Clark	1:13.6
1960	Susan Rogers	1:12.8
1961	Jean Dellekamp	1:12.9
1962	Roby Whipple	1:13.3
1963	Cynthia Goyette	1:11.7
1964	Claudia Kolb	1:09.3
1965	Cynthia Goyette	1:09.0
1966	Catie Ball	1:07.4
1967	Catie Ball	1:06.6
1968	Jan Henne	1:07.0
1969	Sharon Wichman	1:07.6
1970	Kim Brecht	1:06.5
1971	Lynn Colella	1:06.7
1972	Lynn Vidali	1:07.0
1973	Catherine Carr	1:06.106
1974	Marcia Morey	1:05.53
1975	Kim Dunson	1:02.254R

100-Meter Breaststroke

| 1976 | Christine Jarvis | 1:14.70 |

250-Yard Breaststroke

1923	Sarah Freeman	4:01.2
1924	Agnes Geraghty	3:40.2
1925	Agnes Geraghty	3:27.8
1926–38 No competition		
1939	Helene Rains	3:13.3
1940	Patty Aspinall	3:10.1
1941	Patty Aspinall	3:07.8
1942	Helene Rains	3:12.0
1943	June Fogle	3:18.8
1944	Nancy Merki	3:15.5
1945	Patricia Sinclair	3:13.1
1946	Patricia Sinclair	3:07.2
1947	Nancy Merki	3:11.1
1948	Clara Lamore	3:10.5
1949	Nancy Merki Lees	3:12.2
1950	Carol Pence	3:01.4R
1953	Gail Peters	3:27.4
1954	Mary Jane Sears	3:29.0
1955	Mary Jane Sears	3:29.8
1956	Mary Jane Sears	3:22.1
1957	Ivanelle Hoe	3:24.3
1958	Susan Ordogh	3:20.0
1959	Susan Ordogh	3:24.3
1960	Susan Ordogh	3:14.6
1961	Susan Ordogh	3:19.7
1962	Andrea Hopkins	3:15.2
1963	Roby Whipple	3:14.7
1964	Cynthia Goyette	3:09.1

200-Yard Breaststroke

1917	Mable Arklie	3:36.8
1918	Mabel Arklie	3:27.0
1919	Eleanor Smith	3:10.6
1951	Carol Pence	2:45.0
1952	Gail Peters	2:40.1
1965	Cynthia Goyette	2:26.4
1966	Cynthia Goyette	2:25.6
1967	Catie Ball	2:25.2
1968	Sharon Wickman	2:25.2
1969	Kim Brecht	2:24.44
1970	Linda Kurtz	2:23.0
1971	Lynn Colella	2:21.9

1972	Lynn Colella	2:22.3
1973	Lynn Colella	2:20.595
1974	Lynn Colella	2:19.77
1975	Marcia Morey	2:18.775R

200-Meter Breaststroke

1976	Noel Moran	2:39.39

100-Yd Butterfly

1954	Shelley Mann	1:06.5
1955	Betty Mullen	1:05.4
1956	Shelley Mann	1:04.1
1957	Nancy Ramey	1:01.9
1958	Nancy Ramey	1:02.9
1959	Nancy Ramey	1:02.0
1960	Nancy Ramey	1:00.3
1961	Kathy Ellis	1:01.7
1962	Mary Stewart	59.2
1963	Kathy Ellis	59.2
1964	Kathy Ellis	58.8
1965	Sharon Stouder	58.0
1966	Elaine Tanner	58.7
1967	Lee Davis	58.4
1968	Ellie Daniel	58.2
1969	Ellie Daniel	59.3
1970	Lynn Colella	58.0
1971	Deena Deardurff	57.0
1972	Deena Deardurff	57.1
1973	Deena Deardurff	56.449
1974	Peggy Tosdal	55.91
1975	Deena Deardurff	55.708R

100-Meter Butterfly

1976	Wendy Boglioli	1:02.14

200-Yard Butterfly

1956	Shelley Mann	2:26.3
1957	Shelley Mann	2:27.7
1958	Nancy Ramey	2:19.2
1959	Becky Collins	2:16.8
1960	Becky Collins	2:16.9
1961	Becky Collins	2:18.4
1962	Sharon Finneran	2:16.2
1963	Kim Worley	2:15.3
1964	Donna deVarona	2:10.5
1965	Sue Pitt	2:09.6
1967	Lee Davis	2:07.9
1968	Ellie Daniel	2:06.6
1969	Ellie Daniel	2:06.65
1970	Lynn Colella	2:03.9
1971	Calice Jones	2:03.9
1972	Karen Moe	2:03.3
1973	Shane Gould	2:02.720
1974	Valerie Lee	2:00.84
1975	Valerie Lee	2:00.702R

200-Meter Butterfly

1976	Nicole Kramer	2:19.01

200-Yard Individual Medley

1963	Donna deVarona	2:15.0
1964	Donna deVarona	2:12.4
1965	Jeanne Hallock	2:14.2
1966	Jane Barkman	2:13.8
1967	Claudia Kolb	2:09.7
1968	Claudia Kolb	2:08.5
1969	Lynn Vidali	2:09.2
1970	Lynn Vidali	2:10.9
1971	Susie Atwood	2:10.1
1972	Jennifer Bartz	2:08.2
1973	Leslie Cliff	2:06.753
1974	Kathy Heddy	2.05.06
1975	Jenni Franks	2:04.747R

200-Meter Individual Medley

1976	Kathy Heddy	2:23.02

300-Yard Individual Medley

1925	Carin Nilsson	4:34.6
1926	Carin Nilsson	4:36.4
1927	Adelaide Lambert	4:34.4
1928	Eleanor Holm	4:26.2
1929	Eleanor Holm	4:26.4
1930	Eleanor Holm	4:16.0
1931	Eleanor Holm	4:22.4
1932	Eleanor Holm	4:27.2
1933	Katherine Rawls	4:14.8
1934	Katherine Rawls	4:12.4
1935	Katherine Rawls	4:09.2
1936	Katherine Rawls	4:06.3
1937	Katherine Rawls	4:06.4
1938	Katherine Rawls	4:03.2
1939	Doris Brennan	4:04.5
1940	Lorraine Fischer	4:10.2
1941	Helene Rains	4:04.9
1942	Helene Rains	3:59.1
1943	Joan Fogle	4:07.6
1944	Nancy Merki	4:02.1
1945	Clara Lamore	4:04.2
1946	Nancy Merki	4:00.1
1947	Nancy Merki	3:53.4
1948	Nancy Merki	4:04.0
1949	Barbara Jensen	3:57.3
1950	Barbara Jensen	4:00.4
1951	Mary Freeman	4:06.3
1952	Gail Peters	3:53.1R
1953	Mary Freeman	3:55.6

400-Yard Individual Medley

1954	Shelley Mann	5:18.6
1955	Shelley Mann	5:19.7
1956	Sylvia Ruuska	5:14.9
1957	Sylvia Ruuska	5:08.1
1958	Sylvia Ruuska	5:03.5
1959	Sylvia Ruuska	4:58.2
1960	Sylvia Ruuska	4:57.0
1961	Becky Collins	4:55.5
1962	Sharon Finneran	4:52.9
1963	Donna deVarona	4:47.3
1964	Donna deVarona	4:42.9
1965	Sharon Finneran	4:47.4
1966	Sharon Finneran	4:49.4
1967	Sue Pedersen	4:37.0
1968	Claudia Kolb	4:32.2
1969	Lynn Vidali	4:36.7
1970	Debbie Meyer	4:34.2
1971	Susie Atwood	4:34.8
1972	Susie Atwood	4:28.8
1973	Shane Gould	4:27.115
1974	Jenni Franks	4:26.22
1975	Jenni Franks	4:24.516R

400-Meter Individual Medley

1976	Cheryl Gibson	4:57.20

300-Yard Medley Relay

1927	New York Women's SA	3:55.0
1928	New York Women's SA	3:46.2
1929	Illinois Women's AC	NA
1930	New York Women's SA	3:38.8
1931	New York Women's SA	3:45.4
1932	New York Women's SA	3:45.6
1933	New York Women's SA	3:45.4
1934	New York Women's SA	3:42.6
1935	New York Women's SA	3:40.2
1936	New York Women's SA	3:30.0
1937	Washington AC	3:37.4
1938	Los Angeles AC	3:37.5

A relay race: The swimmer in the foreground is already diving into the water, while others wait for their teammates to touch. *(International Swimming Hall of Fame.)*

1939	Los Angeles AC	3:32.9
1940	New York Women's SA	3:28.6
1941	New York Women's SA	3:30.5
1942	New York Women's SA	3:28.7
1943	Multnomah Club, Portland, Oreg.	3:34.9
1944	Multnomah Club, Portland, Oreg.	3:31.2
1945	San Francisco Crystal Plunge	3:30.7
1946	Multnomah Club, Portland, Oreg.	3:27.8
1947	San Francisco Crystal Plunge	3:26.5
1948	Multnomah AC, Portland, Oreg.	3:29.7
1949	Multnomah AC, Portland, Oreg.	3:29.6
1950	Lafayette, Ind., SC	3:25.9
1951	Chicago Town Club	3:21.0R
1952	Lafayette, Ind., SC "A"	3:21.9
1953	Walter Reed SC "A"	3:26.4

400-Yard Medley Relay

1954	Walter Reed SC	4:37.0
1955	Walter Reed SC	4:33.5
1956	Walter Reed SC	4:27.4
1957	Santa Clara SC	4:27.2
1958	Santa Clara SC	4:28.9
1959	Berkeley, Calif., YMCA	4:25.4
1960	Santa Clara SC	4:16.2
1961	Multnomah AC, Portland, Oreg.	4:20.0
1962	Indianapolis Riviera Club	4:17.9
1963	Santa Clara SC	4:09.5
1964	Santa Clara SC	4:07.3
1965	Commerce, Calif., SC	4:06.8
1966	Vesper Boat Club	4:06.0
1967	Santa Clara SC	4:05.4
1968	Santa Clara SC	4:02.4
1969	Santa Clara SC	4:00.6

1970	Lakewood, Calif., AC	4:01.7
1971	Lakewood, Calif., AC	3:58.615
1972	Lakewood, Calif., AC	3:57.4
1973	Santa Clara SC "A"	3:57.131
1974	Santa Clara SC "A"	3:54.24
1975	Santa Clara SC "A"	3:53.709R

400-Meter Medley Relay

1976	Santa Clara SC "A"	4:24.09

400-Yard Freestyle Relay

1920	Illinois AC	4:43.8
1921	New York Women's SA	4:51.0
1922	New York Women's SA	4:38.6
1923	New York Women's SA	4:49.4
1924	No competition	
1925	New York Women's SA	4:43.0
1926	New York Women's SA	4:32.2
1927	New York Women's SA	4:37.4
1928	Illinois AA	4:29.8
1929	Illinois Women's AC	NA
1930	New York Women's SA	4:19.4
1931	Washington AC	4:24.8
1932	Washington AC	4:19.2
1933	No competiton	
1934	Homestead, Pa., Library	4:21.0
1935	Washington AC	4:15.3
1936	Washington AC	4:13.4
1937	Washington AC	4:19.0
1938	Washington AC	4:22.0
1939	New York Women's SA	4:18.9
1940	New York Women's SA	4:14.1
1941	Multnomah Club, Portland, Oreg.	4:12.4
1942	Multnomah Club, Portland, Oreg.	4:12.4
1943	Multnomah Club, Portland, Oreg.	4:15.5
1944	Multnomah Club, Portland, Oreg.	4:09.1
1945	San Francisco Crystal Plunge	4:17.3

1946	Multnomah Club, Portland, Oreg.	4:06.5
1947	San Francisco Crystal Plunge	4:08.3
1948	San Francisco Crystal Plunge	4:13.5
1949	Multnomah AC, Portland, Oreg.	4:13.2
1950	Chicago Town Club	4:07.7
1951	Lafayette, Ind., SC	4:08.7
1952	Chicago Town Club "A"	4:05.3
1953	Chicago Community Builders "A"	4:04.9
1954	Walter Reed SC	3:59.2
1955	Walter Reed SC	4:02.3
1956	Lafayette, Ind., SC	3:56.8
1957	Lafayette, Ind., SC	4:03.8
1958	Santa Clara SC	4:01.8
1959	Berkeley, Calif., YMCA	3:59.6
1960	Multnomah AC, Portland, Oreg.	3:59.5
1961	Multnomah AC, Portland, Oreg.	3:51.6
1962	Cleveland SC	3:52.2
1963	Santa Clara SC	3:43.9
1964	Santa Clara SC	3:41.2
1965	Commerce, Calif., SC	3:40.8
1966	Santa Clara SC	3:37.1
1967	Santa Clara SC	3:37.1
1968	Santa Clara SC	3:32.6
1969	Santa Clara SC	3:35.4
1970	Jack Nelson SC	3:36.1
1971	Phillips 66SC	3:36.67
1972	Santa Clara SC "A"	3:32.801
1974	Mission Viejo	3:29.22
1975	Mission Viejo	3:27.249R

400-Meter Freestyle Relay

| 1976 | El Monte AC "A" | 3:56.06 |

800-Yard Freestyle Relay

1966	Vesper Boat Club	8:00.4
1967	Santa Clara SC	7:53.7
1968	Santa Clara SC	7:42.7
1969	Arden Hills SC	7:44.34
1970	Arden Hills SC	7:51.9
1971	Arden Hills SC	7:50.61
1972	Santa Clara SC	7:36.8
1973	Santa Clara SC "A"	7:36.742
1974	Mission Viejo	7:30.73
1975	Mission Viejo	7:28.779R

800-Meter Freestyle Relay

| 1976 | Central Jersey AC "A" | 8:22.98 |

Halls of Fame

The Citizens Savings Athletic Foundation established its hall of fame for swimming and diving in 1950. The International Swimming Hall of Fame was established in Fort Lauderdale, Florida, in 1965. In the following list, C indicates Citizens, I indicates International. All enshrinees are from the United States, unless otherwise noted.

Swimmers

Greta Anderson (Denmark) I
Susan Atwood C
Catherine Ball C
Walter Bathe (Germany) I
Sybil Bauer C, I
Frank Beaurepaire (Australia) I
Ethelda Bleibtrey C, I
Arne Borg (Sweden) I
George Breen C, I
Michael Buron C
Tedford Cann I

Cavill family (Australia) I
Florence Chadwick I
Andrew "Boy" Charlton (Australia) I
Steve Clark I
Richard Cleveland C
Carin Cone C
Clarence "Buster" Crabbe C, I
Lorraine Crapp (Australia) I
Ann Curtis C, I
Charles M. Daniels C, I
Donna deVarona C, I
Olga Dorfner I
Fanny Durack (Australia) I
Gertrude Ederle C, I
Jeffrey Farrell C, I
Cathy Ferguson C
Peter Fick C
Ralpha Flanagan C
Jennie Fletcher (England) I
Alan Ford C, I
Dawn Fraser (Australia) I
Hironoshin Furuhashi (Japan) I
Claire Galligan I
L. Budd Goodwin C, I
Carolyn Green C
Alfred Hajos (Hungary) I
Gary Hall C
Zoltan de Halmay (Hungary) I
Jamison "Jam" Handy C, I
Karen Harup (Denmark) I
Harry J. Hebner C, I
Brenda Helser C
Jon Hendricks (Australia) I
Charlie Hickcox C
John Higgins I
George Hodgson (Canada) I
Eleanor Holm C, I
Dick Hough I
Ragnhild Hveger (Denmark) I
John Jarvis (England) I
Chester Jastremski C
Duke P. Kahanamoku C, I
Warren Kealoha I
Annette Kellerman (Australia) I
Adolph Kiefer C, I
Barney Kieran (Australia) I
Lenore Kight C
Cor Kint (Holland) I
Kusuo Kitamura (Japan) I
George Kojac C, I
Claudia Kolb C, I
Ford Konno C, I
Ilsa and John Konrads (Australia) I
Ethel Lackie I
Freddy Lane (Australia) I
Ludy Langer C
Walter Laufer I
Helene Madison C, I
Shelley Mann C, I
John Marshall (Australia) I
Hendrika Mastenbroek (Holland) I
Michael "Turk" McDermott C, I
Perry McGillivray C
Frank McKinney C, I
James McLane C, I
Jack Medica C, I
Nancy Merki C
Deborah "Debbie" Meyer C
Kiyoshi Nakama C, I
Sandra Neilson C
Martha Norelius C, I
Novak sisters (Hungary) I

Willy den Ouden (Holland) I
Yoshi Oyakawa C, I
Erich Rademacher (Germany) I
Emil Rausch (Germany) I
Katherine Rawls C, I
Wally Ris C, I
Carl Robie C
Murray Rose (Australia) C, I
Norman Ross C, I
Richard Roth C
Keena Rothhammer C
Sylvia Ruuska C
Roy Saari C
E. Carroll Schaeffer C, I
Clark Scholes C
Don Schollander C, I
Bill Smith C, I
Leonard Spence (England) I
Wallace Spence (England) I
Walter Spence (England-U.S.) C, I
Mark Spitz C
Allen Stack C
Sharon Stouder C, I
Henry Taylor (England) I
David Theile (Australia) I
Mike Troy C, I
John Trudgen (England) I
Yoshiyuki Tsuruta (Japan) I
Nell Van Vliet (Holland) I
Joseph Verdeur C, I
Chris von Saltza C, I
Helen Wainwright C, I
W. L. Wallen C
Lillian Watson C
Matthew Webb (England) I
John Weissmuller C, I
Alic Wickam (Solomon Islands) I
Esther Williams I
William Woolsey C
Mina Wylie (Australia) I
William Yorzyk C, I
Suzanne Zimmerman C

Coaches
Arthur Adamson C
David Armbruster C, I
William Bachrach C, I
Ernst Brandsten C, I
Ma Braun (Holland) I
Stan Brauninger I
Fred Cady C, I
Jack Cody C, I
George Corsan, Sr. (Canada) I
Ray Daughters C, I
Samuel J. Greller C
L. DeB. Handley I
Steve Hunyfadi (Hungary, Italy, U.S.) I
Edward T. Kennedy C, I
Robert Kiphuth C, I
Frederick Lanoue C
E. J. Manley C
Matt Mann II C, I
James McAdoo C
Al Neuschaefer I
Richard Papenguth C
Michael Peppe C, I
James Reilly C
Tom Robinson C, I
Urho Saari C
Soichi Sakamoto I
Charles Sava I
Charles E. Silvia C

Roman Speegle C
Joseph Steinhauer C
Jan Stender (Holland) I
Clyde Swendsen C
Niels Thorpe C
Jack Torney C
Otto Wahle C

Contributors
Carl Bauer C, I
Jacques Yves Cousteau (France) I
Capt. Bert Cummins (England) I
Charlotte Epstein I
Harold Fern (England) I
Benjamin Franklin I
Ellen Fullard-Leo I
Harold Henning C
William Henry (England) I
Beth Kaufman I
Commodore Longfellow I
Fred Luehring I
R. Max Ritter (Germany-U.S.) C, I

Bibliography. *AAU Official Rules*, Amateur Athletic Union, Indianapolis (annual); Armbruster, David A. et al.: *Swimming and Diving*, 6th ed., Mosby, St. Louis, 1973; *Sports Illustrated Book of Swimming*, Lippincott, New York and Philadelphia, 1961.

SYNCHRONIZED SWIMMING—Essentially an outgrowth of the water ballet type of swimming show, synchronized swimming developed during the late 1930s as a kind of stepchild of competitive swimming, but it became a full-fledged competitive sport in its own right in 1950, when the first national AAU championships were held. It has grown into a truly international sport in a very short time; since 1951, synchronized swimming has been on alternate Pan-American Games programs, and it was included in the first World Aquatic Championships in 1973.

Synchronized swimming is patterned basically after other competitive sports involving subjective judging, and is quite similar to gymnastics in many respects. There are 136 recognized figures, divided into four groups and rated in difficulty from 1.1 to 2.2. In figure competition, each competitor must perform six figures, drawn by lot. The figures are performed in a relatively stationary position, except for a few that call for movement through the water. Routine competition is the approximate equivalent of the free-skating portion of figure-skating competition: The competitor performs a routine to music, including five compulsory figures. There is a time limit of 4 min for solo and duet routines, 5 min for team routines.

A panel consists of five to nine judges. In addition there is a referee, who can subtract points or reduce scores for certain violations of the rules. In figures, a perfect score is 10, with 5 points for design (essentially body position) and 5 points for control (essentially movement from one position to another). If there are nine judges, the two highest and two lowest scores for each figure are thrown out; if there are five or seven judges, the highest and lowest are thrown out. The remaining scores for each figure are then added and multiplied by the degree of difficulty. Then these scores are added and divided by 10 to get the final figure score. The same general procedure is followed in judging routines, except that the individual scores are first totaled and then multiplied by the average degree of difficulty—the total of the five degrees of difficulty, divided by five. In team competition, a half-point is added to the routine score for each competitor over four on a team.

AAU Indoor Champions

Solo

1950	June Taylor
1951	June Taylor
1952	June Taylor
1953	June Taylor
1954	Beulah Gundling
	Jo Ann Speer
1955	Joanne Royer
1956	Joanne Royer Maury
1957	Tony Stewart
1958	Tony Stewart
1959	Betty Vickers
1960	Papsie Georgian
1961	Papsie Georgian
1962	Barbara Burke
1963	Roberta Armstrong
1964	Roberta Armstrong
1965	Pam Morris
1966	Margo McGrath
1967	Margo McGrath
1968	Margo McGrath
1969	Kim Welshons
1970	Carol Reynolds
1971	Heidi O'Rourke
1972	Gail Johnson
1973	Teresa Andersen
1974	Kathy Kretschmer
1975	Gail Johnson Buzonas
1976	Robin Curren

Duet

1947	Ruth and Gloria Geduldig
1948	Marilyn Stanley-Alice Micus
1949	Billie and Rosemarie Voelker
1950	Marilyn Stanley-Shirley Simpson
1951	Ellen Richard-Connie Todoroff
1952	Jo Ann Speer-Carla Courter
1953	Jo Ann Speer-Carla Courter
1954	Ellen Richard-Connie Todoroff
1955	Joan and Lynn Pawson
1956	Jackie Brown-Joanne Berthelson
1957	Judy Haga-Sandy Giltner
1958	Mary Jane Gury-Rosalind Calcattera
1959	Sue Laurence-Jackie Vargas
1960	Sue Laurence-Jackie Vargas
1961	Phyllis Firman-Louella Sommers
1962	Claire Vida-Louella Sommers
1963	Claire Vida-Judy Wejak
1964	Margaret Durbrow-Patty Willard
1965	Pam Morris-Patty Willard
1966	Margo McGrath-Carol Redmond
1967	Margo McGrath-Carol Redmond
1968	Nancy Hines-Kim Welshons
1969	Barbara Trantina-Heidi O'Rourke
1970	Barbara Trantina-Heidi O'Rourke
1971	Joan Lang-Heidi O'Rourke
1972	Gail Johnson-Teresa Andersen
1973	Gail Johnson-Teresa Andersen
1974	Kathy Kretschmer-Amy Miner
1975	Robin Curren-Amanda Norrish
1976	Robin Curren-Amanda Norrish

Team

1947	McFadden-Deauville Pool, Miami
1948	St. Claire Recreation Center, Detroit
1949	St. Claire Recreation Center, Detroit
1950	St. Claire Recreation Center, Detroit
1951	KRNT, Des Moines
1952	KRNT, Des Moines
1953	Athens Water Follies, Oakland
1954	Athens Water Follies, Oakland
1955	Athens Water Follies, Oakland
1956	Athens Water Follies, Oakland
1957	Athens Water Follies, Oakland
1958	Athens AC Athenians, Oakland
1959	Athens AC Athenians, Oakland
1960	Athens AC Athenians, Oakland
1961	Merionettes, San Francisco
1962	Merionettes, San Francisco
1963	Merionettes, San Francisco
1964	Merionettes, San Francisco
1965	Merionettes, San Francisco
1966	Merionettes, San Francisco
1967	Merionettes, San Francisco
1968	Aquamaids, Santa Clara, Calif.
1969	Aquamaids, Santa Clara, Calif.
1970	Merionettes, San Francisco
1971	Merionettes, San Francisco
1972	Aquamaids, Santa Clara, Calif.
1973	Aquamaids, Santa Clara, Calif.
1974	Aquamaids, Santa Clara, Calif.
1975	Aquamaids, Santa Clara, Calif.
1976	Aquamaids, Santa Clara, Calif.

AAU Outdoor Champions

Solo

1950	Beulah Gundling
1951	Beulah Gundling
1952	Beulah Gundling
1953	Beulah Gundling
1954	Joanne Royer
1955	Joanne Royer
1956	Linda Ridings
1957	Betty Vickers
1958	Sandy Giltner

Beulah Gundling was the first AAU outdoor solo champion in synchronized swimming, in 1950, and she won three more outdoor titles in consecutive years. *(International Swimming Hall of Fame.)*

1959	Sandy Giltner
1960	Papsie Georgian
1961	Papsie Georgian
1962	Barbara Burke
1963	Roberta Armstrong
1964	Roberta Armstrong
1965	Pam Morris
1966	Margo McGrath
1967	Margo McGrath
1968	Kim Welshons
1969	Kim Welshons
1970	Barbara Trantina
1971	Heidi O'Rourke
1972	Gail Johnson
1973	Gail Johnson
1974	Gail Johnson
1975	Gail Johnson Buzonas
1976	Sue Baross

Duet

1946	Ruth and Gloria Geduldig
1947	Alice Micus-Marilyn Stanley
1948	Alice Micus-Marilyn Stanley
1949	Shirley Simpson-Connie Todoroff
1950	Shirley Simpson-Marilyn Stanley
1951	Ellen Richard-Connie Todoroff
1952	Ellen Richard-Connie Todoroff
1953	Lynn and Joan Pawson
1954	Lynn and Joan Pawson
1955	Jackie Brown-Joanne Berthelson
1956	Judy Haga-Sandy Giltner
1957	Judy Haga McDonald-Sandy Giltner
1958	Mary Jane Gury-Rosalind Calcatera
1959	Sue Laurence-Jackie Vargas
1960	Sue Laurence-Jackie Vargas
1961	Barbara Burke-JoAnne Schaack
1962	Louella Sommers-Claire Vida
1963	Claire Vida-Judy Wejak
1964	Margaret Durbrow-Patty Willard
1965	Pam Morris-Patty Willard
1966	Margo McGrath-Carol Redmond
1967	Margo McGrath-Carol Redmond
1968	Nancy Hines-Kim Welshons
1969	Nancy Hines-Kim Welshons
1970	Barbara Trantina-Heidi O'Rourke
1971	Joan Lang-Heidi O'Rourke
1972	Teresa Andersen-Gail Johnson
1973	Teresa Andersen-Gail Johnson
1974	Gail Johnson-Sue Baross
1975	Robin Curren-Amanda Norrish
1976	Robin Curren-Amanda Norrish

Team

1946	Town Club Team C, Chicago
1947	Town Club, Chicago
1948	Not available
1949	St. Claire Recreation Center, Detroit
1950	St. Claire Recreation Center, Detroit
1951	St. Claire Synchronettes, Detroit
1952	Athens Water Follies, Oakland
1953	Peterborough, Ont., Ornamental Swimming Assn.
1954	Athens Water Follies, Oakland
1955	Athens Water Follies, Oakland
1956	Athens Water Follies, Oakland
1957	Athens AC Athenians, Oakland
1958	Athens AC Athenians, Oakland
1959	Athens AC Athenians, Oakland
1960	Athens AC Athenians, Oakland
1961	Merionettes, San Francisco
1962	Merionettes, San Francisco
1963	Merionettes, San Francisco
1964	Merionettes, San Francisco
1965	Merionettes, San Francisco
1966	Merionettes, San Francisco
1967	Merionettes, San Francisco
1968	Aquamaids, Santa Clara, Calif.
1969	Aquamaids, Santa Clara, Calif.
1970	Aquamaids, Santa Clara, Calif.
1971	Merionettes, San Francisco
1972	Aquamaids, Santa Clara, Calif.
1973	Aquamaids, Santa Clara, Calif.
1974	Aquamaids, Santa Clara, Calif.
1975	Aquamaids, Santa Clara, Calif.
1976	Aquamaids, Santa Clara, Calif.

Halls of Fame

The Citizens Savings Athletic Foundation established its hall of fame for synchronized swimming in 1958. The International Swimming Hall of Fame occasionally recognizes someone from the field. In the list, C indicates Citizens, I indicates International. Married names are in parentheses.

Swimmers
Roberta Armstrong (Gorham) C
Margaret Durbrow C
Carolyn Ann "Papsie" Georgian C
Beulah Gundling I
Nancy Hines C
Margo McGrath C
Pamela Morris (Wiley) C, I
Heidi O'Rourke C
Joan Pawson C
Carol Redmond C
June Taylor (Gregory) C
Barbara Trantina C
Clair Vida C
Kim Welshons C
Patty Willard C

Teams
Athens Club, Oakland, 1958 (Janet Anthony, Loretta Barrows, Sue Laurence, Lynn Pawson, Jackie Vargas)
St. Claire Synchronettes, Detroit, 1950 (Ellen Richard, Shirley Simpson, Marilyn Stanley, Connie Todoroff)

Contributors
Theresa Anderson C
Dawn Pawson Bean C
Ross C. Bean C
Re Calcatera C
Katherine Curtis C
Joy Cushman C
Edna Hines C
Lawrence Johnson C
Frances L. Jones C
Marion Olsen Kane C
Annette Kellerman C
David Clark Leach C
Will Luick C
Lillian MacKellard C
Norma Olsen C
Ike Pierce C
Margaret Swan C
Kay Vilen C

Bibliography. *AAU Official Handbook* (annual), Amateur Athletic Union, Indianapolis.

SYNTHETIC TURF—*See* Artificial Turf.

T

TABLE TENNIS—Oddly enough, although table tennis is a relatively new sport, its exact origin is not known. It apparently developed from a game called "indoor tennis," which was marketed by Parker Brothers in the 1890s. This was actually more like indoor badminton, with miniature rackets, a small ball covered with netting, and a portable net which could be hung across a table.

This game became fairly popular in England. It was generally called "whiff whaff" or "gossima." In 1902 the hollow celluloid ball was introduced, and a wooden paddle with a stippled rubber surface replaced the old, awkward racket, consisting of a frame with a drumhead stretched tightly across it. The sound of the ball on the table led to the popular name "Ping Pong," which was then patented by Parker Brothers.

Ping Pong was a fad in the United States, Great Britain, and much of Europe during the early part of the century. But the fad died quickly, before World War I. It was revived, however, about 1923, in England and Continental Europe. The English Table Tennis Association was formed in that year, and in 1926 the International Table Tennis Federation was organized at a meeting in Germany. World championship play began in 1927.

The sport was then also revived in the United States. The American Ping Pong Association was organized in 1930. Because the sport bore a trademarked name, however, only Parker Brothers equipment could be used in its tournaments. In 1932 the United States Table Tennis Association was formed, and it held its own championships. By 1935 the APPA was defunct and the USTTA became the only governing organization in this country.

Although ordinarily a little-noticed sport in the United States, table tennis has been the indicator of international political trends on a couple of occasions. One of the first signs that a cold war was going on came in 1950, when the United States team wasn't allowed to enter Hungary to take part in the world championships. In 1953 the USTTA didn't send a team to Rumania because that country was a Russian satellite. On the other hand, the first real sign of a relaxation of tensions between the United States and Red China came in 1971, when the Communist Chinese invited an American table-tennis team to visit their country. "Ping Pong diplomacy" was prominent in headlines for months. The Red Chinese had been noted for their outstanding table-tennis players for some years before abruptly withdrawing from the international federation, and therefore from international play.

Rules. Table tennis is played on a table 9 ft long, 5 ft wide, and 2 ft, 6 in high. The table is divided into four equal sections by a 6-in-high net, which runs across its width and extends 6 in beyond the table on either side, and by a white line which runs the length of the table. The table is outlined by a white line, ¾ in wide.

The hollow celluloid ball weighs less than ¹⁄₁₀ oz. There is no limit on the size of the paddle, but it is usually about 12 in long. Paddle surfaces are generally of stippled rubber over a layer of sponge rubber, or of "sandpaper." Many outstanding world-class players, however, use a surface of smooth sponge rubber.

In singles competition, players normally flip a coin to determine who serves first. The other player (receiver) can choose the end of the table he or she wants. If more than one game is played, the person who served first in the first game serves second in the second game, first in the third game, and so on. The server must throw the ball upward from the palm of the hand before striking it; the service must first hit once on the server's side of the table, then clear the net and hit the table on the other side. The receiving player must let the serve bounce on that side of the table before returning it. If the serve isn't proper, or if the player attempts to serve but misses the ball, the server loses the point. If the ball, when served, touches the net before going over and hitting on the other side, it is a let, and the server gets another chance.

A player retains service for five consecutive points; thus, whenever the players' point totals add up to a multiple of five—when the score is 6-4 or 8-7, for example—service changes. If a shot (other than a service) strikes the table on the player's own side, or if a shot fails to hit the table on the other side, the point is lost. The first player to gain 21 points wins the game. However, if the score reaches 20-all, a player must get a 2-point lead to win, and the players alternate in serving, from 20-all, until the game is over. The 2-point lead necessary for winning the game is gained by winning 2 consecutive points.

In doubles, the server must always serve from the right-hand corner, and the serve must hit the right-hand service court on the server's own side of the table, clear the net, and land in the opponents' right-hand service court. Partners alternate shots (that is, returns) in doubles. If player A-1 serves to B-1, player A-2 must return B-1's shot, and player B-2 must then return player A-2's shot. If a player hits the ball when it is not that player's turn, the player's team loses the point.

U.S. Champions

(From 1932 through 1934, two rival associations conducted national championship play.)

Men's Singles

1931	Marcus Schussheim	1952	Louis Pagliaro
1932	Marcus Schussheim	1953	Richard Miles
	Coleman Clark	1954	Richard Miles
1933	James M. Jacobson	1955	Richard Miles
	Sidney Heiter	1956	Erwin Klein
1934	James McClure	1957	Bernard Bukiet
	Sol Schiff	1958	Martin Reisman
1935	Abe Berenbaum	1959	Bob Gusikoff
1936	Sol Schiff (closed)	1960	Martin Reisman
	Viktor Barna (open)	1961	Erwin Klein
1937	Sol Schiff (closed)	1962	Richard Miles
	Laszlo Bellak (open)	1963	Bernard Bukiet
1938	Laszlo Bellak	1964	Erwin Klein
1939	James McClure	1965	Erwin Klein
1940	Louis Pagliaro	1966	Bernard Bukiet
1941	Louis Pagliaro	1967	Manji Fukushima
1942	Louis Pagliaro	1968	Dal Joon Lee
1943	William Holzrichter	1969	Dal Joon Lee
1944	John Somael	1970	Dal Joon Lee
1945	Richard Miles	1971	Dal Joon Lee
1946	Richard Miles	1972	Dal Joon Lee
1947	Richard Miles	1973	Dal Joon Lee
1948	Richard Miles	1974	Kjell Johansson
1949	Richard Miles	1975	Kjell Johansson
1950	John Leach	1976	Dragutin Surbak (open)
1951	Richard Miles		Ray Guillen (closed)

Women's Singles

1933	Jessie Purves	1955	Leah Thall Neuberger
	Fanny Pockrose	1956	Leah Thall Neuberger
1934	Ruth Hughes Aarons	1957	Leah Thall Neuberger
	Iris Little	1958	Susie Hoshi
1935	Ruth Hughes Aarons	1959	Susie Hoshi
1936	Ruth Hughes Aarons	1960	Sharon Acton
1937	Ruth Hughes Aarons	1961	Leah Thall Neuberger
1938	Emily Fuller	1962	Mildred Shahian
1939	Emily Fuller	1963	Bernice Chotras
1940	Sally Green	1964	Valleri Bellini
1941	Sally Green	1965	Patty Martinez
1942	Sally Green	1966	Violetta Nesukaitis
1943	Sally Green	1967	Patty Martinez
1944	Sally Green	1968	Violetta Nesukaitis
1945	Davida Hawthorn	1969	Patty Martinez
1946	Bernice Charney	1970	Violetta Nesukaitis
1947	Leah Thall	1971	Connie Sweeris
1948	Peggy McLean	1972	Wendy Hicks
1949	Leah Thall Neuberger	1973	Violetta Nesukaitis
1950	Reba Kirson Monness	1974	Yuki Ohzeki
1951	Leah Thall Neuberger	1975	Chung Hyun Sook
1952	Leah Thall Neuberger	1976	Kim Soon Ok (open)
1953	Leah Thall Neuberger		In Sock Bhusan (closed)
1954	Mildred Shahian		

Bibliography. Miles, Dick: *The Game of Table Tennis*, Lippincott, Philadelphia-New York, 1968.

TEAM HANDBALL—When team handball became an Olympic sport in 1972, few Americans had heard of it, and it was written that the sport was quite new to the United States, having been introduced as late as 1959 by European immigrants. Actually, team handball—which is called simply "handball" in Europe—has been alive and well in this country for some time, but it has been masquerading under the name "fieldball."

To further complicate the nomenclature problem, the sport was originally called "field handball" when it was developed, probably in Germany, early in this century. It apparently arrived in the United States in 1930 or earlier, and it was then a form of soccer, played with the hands

Ellen Klatt of the Netherlands, left, faces Britta Andersen of Denmark, in braids, in 1973 World championships at Sarajevo, Yugoslavia. (*Courtesy of Malcolm R. Anderson, U.S. Table Tennis Association.*)

instead of the feet. (Which makes the name perfectly "logical," since soccer is called "football" in Europe.) The name was then abbreviated to "fieldball," which has become primarily a sport for girls and women. Meanwhile the Scandinavian countries had developed an indoor version of the game, with a smaller playing area, a smaller ball, and fewer players.

This indoor version of the sport was introduced to the United States about 1959 by a group of European immigrants in the metropolitan New York–New Jersey area. The U.S. Army has adopted it as a camp sport in many areas, and Explorer Scouts, high schools, and some colleges have also begun playing it. In 1971, with the announcement that team handball would become an Olympic sport, and with the selection of a United States team, the sport spread rapidly from the Northeast to the rest of the country, under the leadership of the U.S. Team Handball Federation, which had been organized in 1947.

The indoor version of the sport can be played outdoors, and often is. In many areas of Europe, it is a year-around sport, and some American high schools play the game outdoors in the fall and indoors in winter.

Rules. Team handball is played on a court or field 100 to 166 ft long and 50 to 83 ft in width. (International rules call for 126–147 ft in length, 60–73 ft in width.) There are six players and a goalie on each team; only three substitutes are allowed. At each end of the court is a net, 6 ft, 6¾ in high and 9 ft, 10¼ in wide.

The game resembles a cross between soccer and basketball. A player may take only three steps without dribbling, but there is no limit on the distance the ball may be advanced by dribbling. Once the player stops moving, however, the ball must be disposed of within three seconds. The object is to propel the ball into the opponent's goal net, which scores one point. Any part of the body above the knees may be used in thus propelling the ball. The leather-covered ball has a 7-in diameter and weighs 15 to 17 oz.

Although basically a noncontact sport, team handball can be very rough. Rules pertaining to body contact are similar to those of soccer, and accidental contact, which is not penalized, is very common. Scores are usually quite high. The net is somewhat bigger than a hockey net, and the degree of accuracy attained in propelling the ball is much greater, since the player throws the ball instead of hitting it with a stick.

See also FIELDBALL.

TENNIS—There were several fairly popular games employing rackets, in England during the 1870s, but most of them were played indoors; construction of proper courts was difficult and expensive, so relatively few people were able to play. Badminton, however, was becoming quite popular, and was one of the few sports that women could play. There apparently had been some attempts to develop an outdoor version of court tennis early in the nineteenth century. But nothing much had come of them.

Early Development

Maj. Walter Clopton Winglfield, who had played court tennis and racquets, and who noted the rapid growth of badminton, decided that England needed a good outdoor rackets game that could be played by men and women. Combining elements of court tennis with elements of badminton, he patented a game which he called "Sphairistike, or Lawn Tennis." (*Sphairistike* is a Greek word meaning "to play"; as a command, it is roughly equivalent to baseball's "play ball" and to the French *tenez*, from which the word "tennis" is believed to have derived.) The patent was issued for a diagram, a set of rules, and a package of equipment which the major hoped to market throughout Great Britain. He introduced the game at a lawn party in the Welsh town of Nantclwyd in December 1873.

The major's version of lawn tennis bore little resemblance to the modern sport that we call "tennis," or "lawn tennis." The court was narrower at the net than at the baselines; the net itself was 5 ft high, as in badminton; the server stood approximately in the middle of the side of the court in which the server was stationed; and the service courts were in the back half of the receiver's side. Scoring used the 15-point system of badminton and most other rackets games.

There did indeed seem to be some need for the new sport, but not in that exotic form. Lawn tennis changed rapidly in the first few years after its "invention." The Marylebone Cricket Club issued a new set of rules in 1875, and in 1877 the All-England Croquet Club at Wimbledon converted one of its croquet lawns into a tennis court and wrote another set of rules. It also held the first All-England tournament for the national championship, which still survives as one of the world's most prestigious tournaments, popularly known as "Wimbledon."

Already the court and the scoring system had assumed their present forms, and the net had been lowered somewhat.

Tennis in the United States. The new sport reached the United States in a surprisingly short time. British army officers had brought it to Bermuda early in 1874, and there Mary Ewing Outerbridge of Staten Island (New York) saw tennis being played. When she returned home in February of that year, she brought a set of equipment with her. After some problem with customs officials who didn't know whether she should pay duties or not, she arrived with the equipment, and during the spring a court was laid out at the Staten Island Cricket and Base Ball Club.

Before the end of the century, there were also courts in Nahant and Brookline, Massachusetts; Newport, Rhode Island; and Philadelphia. Unfortunately the rules didn't spread as fast as the general idea of the sport, and every area used different rules and different types of equipment.

In 1881 the U.S. Lawn Tennis Association (USLTA) was organized at a meeting in New York; 34 clubs were represented. The group adopted the rules of the All-England club and decided to hold a national championship tournament at the Newport Casino in August. The first intercollegiate tournament was held just two years later, one of the very first national college championship events held in any sport. (At the time, tennis was still played primarily in the Northeast, and colleges from that region dominated the national championship tournaments until 1921.)

The Davis Cup. In 1900, Dwight F. Davis, then a Harvard tennis player, gave the USLTA the International Lawn Tennis Challenge Trophy, and the British Isles almost immediately sent a team to challenge for it. The Americans successfully—and somewhat surprisingly—beat the challengers and kept the cup, which became a symbol of supremacy in international men's play. Until 1907 the United States and Britain dominated Davis Cup competition; then little Australia suddenly arrived on the scene to win the cup on three consecutive occasions. During the 1920s and early 1930s, France produced some outstanding players and won the cup several times. After World War II, Australia was once again dominant.

As more and more countries discovered tennis, the International Lawn Tennis Federation (ILTF) set up a system of zonal and interzonal matches to select a challenger for the Davis Cup. The defending nation didn't have to take part in any competition until a challenging nation had been chosen. Starting in 1972, however, the defending nation was also required to participate in qualifying rounds.

The format of Davis Cup play is such that one or two outstanding players can often win the cup for their country. Each country has two singles players and a doubles team—which may include one or both of the singles players. There are four singles matches and one doubles match.

Until 1974, only four countries had ever won the cup—the United States, Great Britain, Australia, and France. But in that year the finalist countries were South Africa and India. However, India defaulted, in protest against South Africa's apartheid policies. In 1975, Sweden defeated Yugoslavia in the finals, and Italy beat Chile in 1976.

Growth and Change. During its early years, tennis was basically a "society" sport, played almost entirely on private or club courts. Around the turn of this century, it began to spread rapidly. This was an era when sport was becoming more important to the average person. Public playgrounds were being built across the country, and many of them had tennis courts.

The change was signaled by the victory of Maurice McLoughlin in the 1912 national tournament. McLoughlin had learned the sport on public courts in San Francisco. The increase of public courts brought another change. Lawn tennis had originally been played on grass. But the public courts, for the most part, had surfaces of cement, asphalt, or clay. As part of the national recreation movement during the 1920s, more and more local tournaments were established. In 1923 the Public Parks championships began, and many of the top young players were now learning the game and sharpening their competitive skills on public courts.

Early Stars. The first dominant figure in American tennis was Dick Sears, who won seven consecutive national championships starting in 1881. (Until 1912, the defending champion did not have to compete except in the final round of the tournament, again a single challenger.)

The first Davis Cup star was Malcolm D. Whitman, who won three consecutive national championships. He took all four of his singles matches in the first two Davis Cup challenges, won by the United States, 5-0 and 3-2. One of his victories, over Reggie Doherty in 1902, was considered a major upset because Doherty, along with his brother Laurie, was noted one of the top players in the world.

William Larned won seven national singles titles in an 11-year period starting in 1901. Larned had a good record in Davis Cup play, but got little support; during his heyday the British and Australians owned the cup.

Australia produced the sport's first great lefthander in Norman Brookes. He was the first foreigner to win the men's singles at Wimbledon, in 1907. His Davis Cup partner, Tony Wilding, won that championship four years in a row, and Brookes and Wilding led Australian teams to Davis Cup victories from 1907 through 1911 and again in 1914.

McLoughlin, the redheaded "California Comet," brought a new style into American tennis when he arrived on the national scene in 1909. McLoughlin had a tremendous serve, and he was the first player who consistently rushed the net behind his service. One reason for this style of play was that he had learned the game on speedy concrete surfaces that inspired a fast, aggressive style of play.

Tilden. The 1920s are known as the "Golden Age of Sports," and it seems that every sport had its own hero ready for the decade. In tennis it was William T. "Big Bill" Tilden, a late-bloomer who won his first national title in 1920, at the age of 27—and then proceeded to dominate the sport for a decade, even when he was losing. Tilden was the first American to win the men's singles at Wimbledon, also in 1920, and at the end of the year he and "Little Bill" Johnston won the Davis Cup from Australia. Tilden was a dramatic figure, in action. Tall and broad-shouldered, he could cover the court with deceptive speed. His cannonball serve was, and is, famous; but above all Tilden was a master tactician who could vary his game as necessary to work on an opponent's weaknesses. By the time he became a professional, in 1931, Tilden had won seven U.S. singles titles, including six in a row, and three Wimbledon titles—the last in 1930, when he was 37. And, largely because of his play, the United States had won eight Davis Cup challenge rounds in a row, from 1920 through 1927.

The Women. Tilden was the first American man to win a singles title at Wimbledon. A woman had done it much earlier; May Sutton, at the age of 16, won the 1905 Wimbledon women's singles championship and repeated in 1907.

The women's singles had been initiated at Wimbledon in 1884, and the U.S. women's championship began in 1887. There were those who didn't think tennis was suita-

"Big Bill" Tilden won seven U.S. national singles titles, including six in a row; he was the first American to win the Wimbledon singles, in 1920, and he also won in 1921 and 1930. He won many other major amateur titles and was world professional champion in 1931 and in 1935, when he was 42. (*National Lawn Tennis Hall of Fame.*)

ble for women; certainly the costumes of the day didn't encourage exciting play.

Among the early women's stars were Elisabeth Moore and Juliette Atkinson. In England, Lottie Dod had won her first Wimbledon title at age 14, and she won a total of five, the last in 1893. But Miss Sutton started a minor revolution. She wore less clothing than other women tennis players—although, of course, she didn't come anywhere near the brief outfits of today—and other women began to follow her lead.

The first of the great diminutive women players was Hazel Hotchkiss, another Californian. Just 5 ft tall, she played a great volleying game, using her quickness and speed to beat more powerful rivals. From 1909 through 1911, she won not only the national singles but the women's and mixed doubles as well. Then she got married, temporarily retired from major competition, and returned to win another singles title in 1919. In 1928, when she was 42, she teamed with Helen Wills to win her last national doubles title.

Miss Wills, still another Californian, was the dominant woman during the 1920s, winning six U.S. singles and eight Wimbledon singles titles. Unfortunately she had only one meeting with the great Suzanne Lenglen of France, in a special 1926 match in Cannes. It was a close match, Miss Lenglen winning in two sets. This fiery French star had won five Wimbledon titles in a row and then won one more before turning professional in 1927.

Helen Wills won seven national singles titles in a nine-year period, 1923 through 1931. *(National Lawn Tennis Hall of Fame.)*

Miss Wills (by now Mrs. Moody) did have some classic confrontations with another American star, Helen Jacobs. Miss Jacobs won the 1932 national title, when Mrs. Moody didn't play. In 1933 they met in the national finals, Miss Jacobs winning a close match when Mrs. Moody quit because of a leg injury. In 1935 they met in the Wimbledon finals. Miss Jacobs seemed to have the match won, but Mrs. Moody took five games in a row to win the title. In 1938 they met once again at Wimbledon and once again Mrs. Moody won.

Their successor was Alice Marble, whose career was delayed by a siege of tuberculosis; she won four national titles in five years before turning professional.

The Wightman Cup. Hazel Hotchkiss became Mrs. Wightman in 1912, and in 1919 she donated a cup for international women's play, similar to the Davis Cup competition among men. The first Wightman Cup match was played in 1923, between the United States and England, and it has continued to be an annual event involving only those two countries. More players are involved than in Davis Cup play. Competition consists of five singles and two doubles matches. Since 1930 the United States has completely dominated Wightman Cup play, winning all but four matches.

The Professional Era Begins

C. C. "Cash and Carry" Pyle, the promoter who had signed Red Grange to play professional football, decided in 1926 that tennis could also be a paying proposition. He started by signing Suzanne Lenglen for $50,000 in cash.

Then he signed Mary Browne, a former U.S. singles champion, as Miss Lenglen's opponent, and added four men, chief among them Vince Richards, then ranked third in the world.

The tour was a success. In 1927, Richards formed the U.S. Professional Lawn Tennis Association. Without Pyle's promotional skills, the pro tour wasn't quite as successful. But Bill Tilden joined in 1931. Though past his prime, he was still a great drawing card, and his tour with Czech pro Karel Kozeluh grossed nearly a quarter of a million dollars. Receipts dropped sharply during the next two years, though, and it became obvious that professional tennis, to succeed, would need continual infusions of new blood. In 1934, Ellsworth Vines, the hardest hitter the game had yet produced, turned pro and toured with Tilden. Again the gross was close to a quarter of a million. By 1936, however, the tour was losing money. Then Frederick Perry, who had been a British Davis Cup star, joined Vines. They were well matched. In 1937 they grossed more than $400,000 and in 1938, as promoters of their own tour, they took in $175,000. Then Don Budge, an outstanding American player with a great backhand, became a pro. He beat Vines 22 of 39 times, in a tour that took in more than $200,000.

The tour, nevertheless, was not in good shape as the 1940s began, and World War II ended it. It was to come back after the war; but, like many other sports, professional tennis would have to wait for the advent of television, and television money, before it could become a consistent, unqualified success.

The Amateurs. Since the tour was centered in the United States, it had an adverse effect on America's Davis Cup chances. Budge led the United States to victories in 1937—the first since 1926—and again in 1938. Then he, too, turned pro. But not before becoming the first male player to achieve the "Grand Slam"—the national singles championships of the United States, Australia, England, and France.

It wasn't just professional tennis that hurt; other countries produced some outstanding players. The French had three of them—René Lacoste, Henri Cochet, and Jean Borotra—during the late 1920s and early 1930s, and they showed the way in six straight Davis Cup victories. Then the English had Perry.

Immediately after World War II the United States won the cup four consecutive times. Meanwhile the pro tour was being reorganized. Jack Kramer was one of the American amateurs who helped win back the cup in 1946 and keep it in 1947, with the help of Ted Schroeder. In 1948, Kramer became a pro, but Schroeder and Frank Parker defended the cup. When Parker turned pro, Pancho Gonzales arrived to team with Schroeder in another cup defense. But Gonzales also became a professional.

The Australians. Then came the young Australians, products of a remarkable "tennis factory" system presided over by Harry Hopman. Promising youngsters were recruited at an early age and given intensive training, with an eye to producing top players who could win the Davis Cup for Australia. It worked, and even the inroads made by professional tennis seemed to have little effect.

Frank Sedgman and Kenneth McGregor brought the cup to Australia in 1950 and defended it for two more years. Then they became professionals and were replaced by two 18-year-olds, Lew Hoad and Ken Rosewall, who kept the cup against two experienced Americans, Vic Seixas and Tony Trabert. Trabert and Seixas won the cup for their country in 1954, but Australia won it back in 1955 and defended successfully for two more years.

All told, in the period from 1950 through 1967, Australia won 15 of 18 Davis Cup challenge rounds. Among the great Australian players were Neale Fraser, Tony Roche, Fred Stolle, Roy Emerson, and Rod Laver. Laver, a left-hander, is considered by some the greatest tennis player of all time, by others merely as the greatest since Tilden. In 1969, Laver became the first man to accomplish the "Grand Slam" twice.

The Modern Era

Jack Kramer. The professional tennis tour was reasonably successful in the first several years after World War II. Kramer and Bobby Riggs brought in $353,000 in the United States and abroad in 1948, and in 1949 Gonzales and Kramer also drew well. In 1950, women were added: Gussie Moran, whose lace tennis panties had brought down the wrath of the USLTA, and Pauline Betz Addie.

Kramer had become the tour's promoter, and was aggressive in going after amateur talent. He proved that people were willing to pay to see top-rated Davis Cup stars. His signing of Sedgman and McGregor touched off

Jack Kramer won the Wimbledon singles in 1947 and the U.S. national singles in 1946 and 1947, then joined the pro tour. In 1954, he became a full-time promotor of professional tennis, and his success paved the way for the success of the modern professional circuits. *(National Lawn Tennis Hall of Fame.)*

a furor in Australia, but they brought in spectators in the United States. Like Tex Rickard, the great boxing promoter, Kramer offered written financial guarantees to players, rather than just giving them a share of the receipts. And the guarantees were substantial, especially when compared with salaries in other sports. Sedgman, for example, was guaranteed a minimum of $75,000 in 1953; Hoad was guaranteed $125,000 for 25 months in 1957–1958.

Kramer also built up a stable of players and had them competing in a round-robin tournament, which added spectator interest. No longer were people being asked to buy tickets just to watch two top players in a match that had no more significance than an exhibition.

Modern Women Stars. Although they were rarely asked to become professionals during the 1950s and early 1960s, there were many outstanding women players during the period. Maureen "Little Mo" Connolly came out of California to win the national singles at 16, in 1951; in 1953 she became the first woman to achieve the "Grand Slam." A horseback-riding accident unfortunately ended her competitive career.

Others were Doris Hart, five times runner-up in the national singles before winning titles in 1953 and 1954; Althea Gibson, the first black woman to compete in the national championships, and winner of the U.S. and Wimbledon singles titles in 1957 and 1958; Maria Bueno, from Argentina, who won four U.S. and three Wimbledon titles; and Darlene Hard, twice the U.S. champion.

During the period described, most women stars had relatively short careers in major competition. Two women who changed that trend were Margaret Court of Australia, who became Mrs. Smith, retired for a year to have a baby, and then returned to win more championships; and Billie Jean Moffitt, who became Mrs. King without sacrificing her career, and who was a leader in the militant women's movement in the late 1960s and 1970s.

More Money, More Pros. As more and more young players were being trained and more and more major tournaments were being held, it became harder for a true amateur to remain at the top for very long. Tennis "amateurism" had long been criticized by many who considered it "shamateurism"; the phrase "tennis bum" had been coined during the 1930s by George Lott, describing his own life as an amateur.

A good amateur could virtually play for a living. He might get all his equipment free; his traveling expenses were taken care of, as were his living expenses, during a tournament; and there were undoubtedly many under-the-table cash payments made by tournament promoters who wanted to make sure they had the best players. Despite all this, the tennis establishment, as represented by the USLTA and the ILTF, frowned on professionalism. An amateur could lose his standing by taking part in the same tournament with a professional, even if they never played one another.

During the 1960s, tennis really boomed. More and more people were taking up the sport as a form of recreation; and, as in golf, the weekend player is a potential spectator. Some major tournaments were getting television coverage. The time was ripe for professionalism on a new scale, and the tennis establishment had to make some adjustments.

In 1968 the staid, prestigious Wimbledon tournament

became an open, with amateurs and professionals allowed to compete. The following year, the USLTA set up three player categories: touring pros, under contract to promoters; registered players, allowed to collect prize money in open tournaments; and amateurs. The ILTF went along with the idea; registered players, but not touring pros, were allowed to take part in Davis Cup competition; registered players were allowed to play in tournaments sanctioned by their national associations; and touring pros were allowed to play in all open tournaments. For the first time, the U.S. National Championships at Forest Hills became an open tournament.

The Grand Prix. The professional tour had now become an international circuit of major tournaments, and the Grand Prix was established in 1970. Points were awarded to players for high finishes in major tournaments, with prize money awarded to top point winners at the end of the season. The top players were also given a chance to win more money in a season-ending Masters tournament.

Although the idea was sound enough, the Grand Prix circuit was soon caught up in major warfare with two groups: the World Championship Tennis (WCT) circuit, organized in September 1970, and the Women's Tennis Association (WTA). In 1974 yet another rival came along—World Team Tennis (WTT). Nevertheless, with sponsorship first from Pepsi-Cola and then from the Commercial Union Assurance Company, the Grand Prix circuit kept growing more lucrative. In 1974 it offered $500,000 in bonus money and $100,000 in its Masters tournament.

World Championship Tennis. WCT was the brainchild of H. L. Hunt, millionaire owner of football's Houston Oilers. In essence it was similar to the Grand Prix setup. In the first season, 32 top players from all over the world were invited to play in a series of 20 tournaments, each with a $45,000 prize fund, with the top eight players then competing in a $100,000 world championship final. By 1974 the WCT had attracted so many top players that it had three circuits operating.

"Women's Lobbers." While the Grand Prix and WCT enabled male players to earn $200,000 or more in a single season, the women were not so fortunate. The first militant group was the Women's Tennis Association, which decided to stay away from the Grand Prix in order to concentrate on the Virginia Slims circuit for women professionals. The militant leader among the players was Billie Jean King, who insisted that women should get equal prize money. She won her point in the U.S. Open, which equalized prize money for men and women in 1973. But the Virginia Slims circuit was just what the women needed, and it developed that they were better off on their own, with their own sponsor. The WTA and the Women's International Tennis Federation made peace with the USLTA and ILTF in 1973, but it was an uneasy peace.

In 1971, Mrs. King became the first woman to win more than $100,000, and she did it again in 1972. In 1973, Margaret Court Smith won more than $150,000, and the following year Chris Evert won $157,500. Evert went over the $300,000 mark in 1975.

Women's tennis was fortunate in having some excellent match-ups. Mrs. King and Mrs. Court were challenged by two youngsters, Miss Evert and Evonne Goolagong of Australia. Miss Evert, then 17, and Miss Goolagong, 20,

met for the first time in the 1972 semifinals at Wimbledon. Miss Goolagong, the defending champion, won, but then lost to Mrs. King in the final. In 1974, Miss Evert really emerged. She won at Wimbledon and had a record of 60 consecutive victorious matches before losing at Forest Hills.

The "Chauvinist." One person who disagreed with the "women's lob" movement—or said he did—was Bobby Riggs. A triple winner at Wimbledon in 1939, Riggs had turned professional at a relatively early age, in 1942, and had also competed professionally after the war.

In 1973, at 55, Riggs announced that he was willing to take on the world's best women tennis players to prove that men of his age could play better tennis than women—and therefore should also be allowed to compete for major prizes. On Mother's Day, Riggs demolished Mrs. Court, 6-2, 6-1. And the match's television ratings were far above those for the WCT championship, played on the same day. Mrs. King, who had been bothered by injuries earlier in the year, then accepted Riggs's challenge. The result was the most lucrative tennis match in history, up to that time, thanks largely to prime-time television. Riggs was demolished this time, 6-4, 6-3, 6-3. The audience of 30,492 in the Houston Astrodome was a record for tennis, and millions more watched on TV.

Riggs may or may not have been sincere in his male chauvinism. Certainly his brash approach and flamboyant statements did for tennis what Muhammad Ali had done for boxing. And, ironically, while tennis in general benefited from the Riggs challenge, women's tennis benefited most of all.

Modern Male Stars. Many of the former Australian Davis Cuppers were still going strong as professionalism reached its peak. Rod Laver, for example, earned more than $200,000 in 1970 and more than $160,000 in the first six months of 1971 before a slump, combined with nagging injuries, slowed his pace. Ken Rosewall was the top player of 1972.

The top American men to arrive in the late 1960s were Arthur Ashe and Stan Smith. Ashe was the first black male to win the U.S. singles (in 1968). Smith won the U.S. Open in 1971 and the Wimbledon singles in 1972. In 1973 he dominated WCT competition, winning 6 of 11 tournaments and $154,100.

A brash young American, Jimmy Connors, was the top male player in 1974, even though he avoided the WCT in order to play in the U.S. indoor professional circuit, promoted by his business manager, Bill Riordan. Connors, only 22, won the Australian, Wimbledon, and U.S. Open titles. His chance for a grand slam was prevented by a dispute between World Team Tennis, with which Connors had signed, and European tennis bodies. He was not allowed to play in the French or Italian championships.

Other countries were also turning out some outstanding players. One of the top WCT pros was Ilie "Nasty" Nastase of Rumania. He and Ion Tiriac brought their country into three Davis Cup challenge rounds, but were beaten by the United States all three times, thanks largely to the fine play of Ashe and Smith. One of the top youngsters was Bjorn Borg of Sweden, who won the 1974 French Open at 18. Jan Kodes of Czechoslovakia won the 1973 Wimbledon title, beating Russia's Alex Metreveli in the final. (Most top pros boycotted that tournament because the ILTF had suspended Nikki Pilic of Yugoslavia.) Spain, Mexico, India, and South Africa also produced some fine players, although most of them didn't participate extensively in Grand Prix or WCT play.

World Team Tennis. There is nothing new about the idea of tennis as a team sport. Although major events have always emphasized tournament-style one-on-one play, high-school and college tennis is a team sport, a series of singles and doubles matches in which the team that wins the most matches wins the team match—as in Davis and Wightman Cup play.

World Team Tennis, which began play in the spring of 1974, has a different format. A match consists of one set each of women's singles, women's doubles, men's singles, men's doubles, and mixed doubles. The total of games won decides the winner of the match.

WTT started with franchises in Baltimore, Boston, Chicago, Cleveland, Denver, Florida, Honolulu, Houston, Los Angeles, Minnesota, New York, Oakland, Philadelphia, Pittsburgh, and Toronto-Buffalo. Even the organizers of WTT were surprised at the number of top players who signed with the group. Among them were Jimmy Connors, Ion Tiriac, Cliff Richey, Nancy Gunter, Clark Graebner, Tony Roche, Cliff Drysdale, Roy Emerson, Dennis Ralston, John Newcombe, Billie Jean King, Ken Rosewall, Evonne Goolagong, and Tom Okker. The Denver Racquets, led by player-coach Roche, won the first championship in a play-off with the Philadelphia Freedoms, coached by Billie Jean King.

Rules

Court and Equipment. The tennis court is 78 ft long by 27 ft wide, with an alley 4 ft, 6 in wide on either side for doubles play. The court is divided in half by a net, which is 3 ft, 6 in high at its ends and at least 3 ft high in the center. The net is suspended from posts which are 3 ft outside the court. On either side of the net, and 21 ft from it, is a service line; a center line divides the service area into two service courts, each 13 ft, 6 in wide.

The ball is a hollow rubber sphere, inflated to a high pressure, and covered with rough felt. The diameter is 2½ to 2⅝ in and the ball's weight is 2 to 2¹/₁₆ oz. There is no restriction on the size or construction of the rackets. They usually have frames of laminated wood or steel and are strung with gut or nylon. Dimensions are about 27 by 9 in, and the weight is usually about 14 oz for men, about 13 oz for women.

Progress of Play. Competitors flip a racket to determine who will serve first. Play begins with a player serving from behind the baseline on the right side of the court (to the right of the center line). The ball being served is thrown into the air and hit before it strikes the ground. The serve must clear the net and land in the service court diagonally opposite. The server is given two attempts to make a proper serve. Faulting on both attempts results in loss of the point. After the first point is scored, the server moves to the left side of the court (to the left of the center line); this alternation continues throughout the player's service turn which extends through one game. If a serve touches the net and then lands in the proper service court, it is a "let"; it doesn't count, and the server is allowed to make the serve again. It is a fault if the server changes position by walking or running while in the act of serving, or if either foot touches the baseline or the area on the wrong side of court before the racket touches the ball.

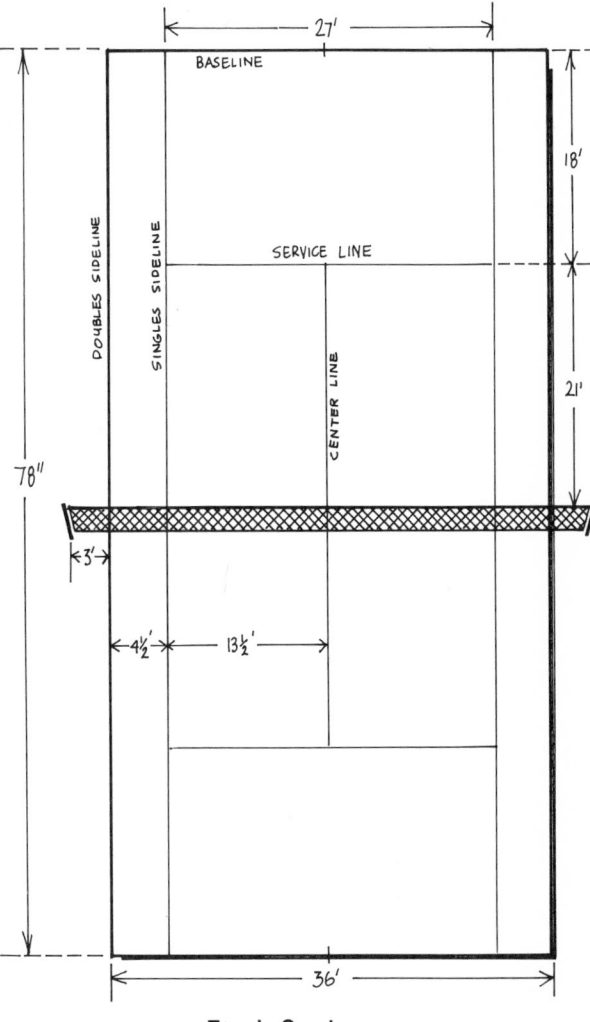

Tennis Court

After the receiver returns service, the two players keep hitting the ball back and forth across the net until one of them loses the point then at stake. The point is lost if a player: fails to return the ball before it strikes the ground for the second time; hits the ball into the net; hits the ball so that it lands outside the opponent's court; hits the net with the racket or with any part of the body; strikes the ball when it is not on the player's side of the net; is struck by the ball; or hits the ball twice. Each of these conditions represents an improper return. Players change sides of the court after the first game and after each odd-numbered game in the match.

Scoring. Essentially, a tennis game is won by the first player to score four points, except that the player must win by two or more points. Scoring is based on the strange system used in court tennis. The progress is: "love" (no score), 15 (one point), 30 (two points), 40 (three points), and game (four points). A (tie) score of 40-all produces a condition called "deuce," and a player must now take two consecutive points to win the game. At deuce, a player who wins the next point is said to have the advantage, or "ad"; "ad in" signifies that it is the server's advantage, "ad out" that it is the receiver's advantage. If then the opposing player scores a point, the score reverts to deuce. The game ends when one of the two players takes two consecutive points after deuce.

A set is won by the first player to take six games, again with the stipulation that the margin of victory must be two games or more. Thus, if the score in games is 5-5, a player must win two consecutive games to win the set. (But see the next section.) Just as a group of games constitutes a set, several sets make up a match. In major men's competition, a match is usually decided by victory in three of five sets; in women's play, a match is determined on a two-of-three basis.

Tiebreakers. In 1964, James Van Alen introduced a scoring system similar to that used in other racket sports. The Van Alen Simplified Scoring System (VASSS) originally had a 31-point set; a player had to win a set by two points or more, and the serve changed hands at five-point intervals.

Van Alen later modified his system to conform more closely with the traditional method, counting points from one through four, with a game going to the first player who wins four. *When a set is tied at 6-all, a tiebreaker goes into effect.* The tiebreaking system was adopted, in many cases, before the rest of VASSS was adopted. Its great advantage is that it makes the time element much more predictable, an important factor for televised matches.

There are two (different) tiebreaking systems. In the nine-point system, the first player to score five out of nine points wins the set. In the 12-point system, the first player to score seven points wins, provided the player leads by two or more. If the score reaches 6-all, the first player to lead by two is the winner. In some cases, a tiebreaker is played only when a set reaches 8-all.

The tiebreaker was adopted for the U.S. Open and some other major tournaments in 1970, and is now used at most major tournaments around the world, including Wimbledon. In 1974 both the NCAA and World Team Tennis adopted the VASSS in its entirety.

Doubles. The rules of doubles are the same as those in singles. The court is 9 ft wider, through addition of the alleys, but service courts remain the same size. The order of service and of receiving service is the only complicating factor.

If team A serves first, either member of the team may serve, and either member of team B may receive the first service. A-1 serves to B-1 in the right service court, then to B-2 in the left service court, then to B-1 in the right service court again, and so on. Throughout the set, B-1 always receives service in the right court, B-2 in the left court. Service alternates between teams. A-1 serves the first game, B-1 the second, A-2 the third, and so forth.

Basic Techniques

The Grip. Most average players use the Eastern grip, which is a simple matter of shaking hands with the racket, which becomes an extension of the arm. It is considered an especially good grip for play on grass, since it is well suited to returning low-bouncing shots.

The Continental grip is used by many top-ranking players because it allows a long reach and requires less time in preparing for a shot. It also requires a very strong wrist. For this grip, the palm of the hand is on top of the handle rather than behind it, and the wrist is set at an angle of about 45 degrees to the handle.

The Western grip seems awkward to most players, at least until they get used to it. The palm of the hand is now under the racket handle. The grip was developed for play on the hard courts of California, because it allows a player to hit a high-bouncing ball well, but it is not very good for low-bouncing shots.

The Western grip doesn't have to be changed for the backhand—the hand is simply turned over so that the palm is on top—but the other grips have to be modified somewhat. In the Eastern, the palm is shifted slightly to the top of the handle with the thumb diagonally across the back. In the Continental, the palm may be shifted just slightly more over the top of the handle, but some players use the same grip for both forehand and backhand.

The Forehand. A shot to the player's racket side is hit with the forehand stroke, and its essentials are, in many ways, the same as the essentials of a good baseball or golf swing. The stroke is made with the hand moving palm-forward. The player turns sideways at approximately a right angle to the direction of the ball's flight. The left foot (for a right-hander) is placed at an angle of about 45 degrees. The feet should be comfortably well apart. The racket is brought back to a point where the shoulders, the arm, and the racket are approximately on a line.

There is usually a slight pause at this point; the weight is well on the back foot, and wrist and elbow are slightly flexed. The forward swing should be timed so that the ball is hit at a point just in front of the left hip. The weight shifts from the back foot to the front foot as the swing takes place. The wrist should be firm at the moment of contact.

The follow-through should carry the racket slightly upward and to a point where the tip of the racket is pointing in the direction the ball has taken. (This is the flat drive; the upward movement of the racket imparts a small amount of top spin.)

The Backhand. It would seem that the backhand is simply a forehand in reverse, but that is not quite true. The grip, as noted, is usually changed somewhat, with the palm moved to the top of the racket handle. The stroke itself is executed with the back of the hand facing outward as the arm moves forward. The player will often turn much farther back than in executing the forehand, so that the body is half-facing away from the net, permitting a longer backswing and therefore a more powerful forward swing. The racket is brought up somewhat on the backswing, and both elbow and wrist may be bent much farther than in execution of the forehand. Then the racket is brought quickly down into the proper plane and "through" the ball. The follow-through may be somewhat more extreme than in the case of the forehand; most beginning players tend to pat the ball on the backhand, using little follow-through, and this tendency must be overcome.

The Service. A good service is of utmost importance in the type of tennis played by top-ranking competitors today. It can not only score points by itself, it can allow a player to establish an offensive immediately. A powerful service can allow the player to go quickly to net to make killing shots.

Most good servers use the Continental grip because it permits the server to impart several different kinds of spin to the ball. Exact techniques vary a good deal from one player to another. Essentially, as the ball is thrown up, the racket is brought down and back, and body weight is shifted to the back foot. The racket moves in a semicircular upward motion to a point behind the head, while the body begins to lean forward. The player should hit the ball at as high a point as possible, while approximately on tiptoe. The procedure is to hit down on the ball, so the racket face is inclined somewhat forward at impact. The follow-through brings the racket down and across the body, the right foot moving forward and slightly in front of the left foot to take the weight of the body again.

This kind of serve, being driven down toward the court, is usually hit at top speed, and the ball will tend to skid somewhat when it hits. At its best, this is the "cannonball" service. But a good server will vary the pace of the serve somewhat, and will also use various kinds of spin, especially on the second service attempt, when it is important to avoid the risk of a double fault.

The American twist is a serve with severe top spin. The ball is thrown up approximately above the left shoulder. As the racket makes contact, it moves sharply up and across the back surface, and the follow-through takes the racket face to the right. This serve will take a high bounce to the receiver's left when it strikes the court.

The sliced serve is the opposite. The ball is thrown somewhat lower and farther to the right, and the racket face cuts down and across the outside surface of the ball. The ball will bounce low and to the receiver's right.

Going to Net. In men's play, and often in women's as well, victory frequently depends on which player can get to the net most often, and on how he or she performs there. When playing near the net, the player has to volley the ball—hit it before it bounces. In volleying a low shot, the player takes little or no backswing, but simply thrusts the racket out, with the arm extended, the wrist locked, and the racket face tipped somewhat upward, to block the ball back over the net.

In returning a ball taken above the level of the net, however, the player should use a full backswing to drive the ball as hard and deep as possible, forcing the opponent well back; or, if the opportunity is there, the player may angle the ball sharply to one side or the other to score a placement, a shot that the opponent cannot reach or cannot return.

To return a very high shot, usually a lob, the player can use an overhead smash (essentially, a serve). A poor lob—one which doesn't go high or deep enough—should prompt a killing smash that wins the point. The player needs exceptional timing for this shot; the procedure is to hit the ball just in front of the head, to get a downward trajectory. If the ball is hit too far back or too far forward, the point has probably been lost.

Two other shots used at net are the drop volley, for which the racket is tilted back just at impact, putting a lot of backspin on the ball so it will not bounce deep; and the drive volley, employed when the ball arrives at just about shoulder height, and the player can hit down on it with a full follow-through, attempting to drive it right to the baseline.

The Lob. This is basically a high, deep defensive shot, meant to get an opponent away from the net. Occasion-

ally it is used as an offensive shot, a change of pace that might disturb the opponent's rhythm. At its best, it is disguised until the last minute; it must be hit from beneath with an open-faced racket, and the player should be able to make the shot look like a drive until the last moment, when the player suddenly opens the face of the racket and hits up on the ball.

Slices and Chops. Another way to change the pace of a match or to catch an opponent off guard is to put unexpected spin on the ball. For the slice, the backswing is somewhat higher and shorter than usual, and the face of the racket is tipped slightly upward, so the strings slide down across the ball, imparting backspin. The player can increase the amount of backspin by using forearm action. This shot should be hit low and deep; the ball will skid when it hits, and often gives the player a good chance to rush to net.

The chop is struck with a chopping motion, which also imparts backspin. Both the backspin and the follow-through are relatively short; the racket begins high, even with or above the right shoulder, and ends up in front of the left leg (on the forehand). The ball will bounce almost straight up. The chop is best used when hitting an angled shot toward a sideline, not when the ball is being hit deep.

The drop shot is similar to the chop, but is hit rather slowly and delicately. The ball should be dropped just over the net, when the opponent is in the backcourt.

Position Play. Tennis is a sport in which proper position is very important. The good player works to get the opponent out of position, to set up the other for a shot that the opponent can't reach. There are some varying theories about position, and the proper position depends to a certain extent on a player's strengths and weaknesses.

The basic aim in positioning oneself and one's shots is to cut down the possible angles of the opponent's return while maximizing one's own possible angles. Suppose you are returning a serve from your left service court, on your backhand. If, from this spot, you hit crosscourt to your opponent's backhand, you are leaving yourself wide open for your opponent to score with a shot right down the line. If, instead, you drive down the line, you can now rush to net, to a point just left of the center. Only two small areas are now available if the opponent wants to try a passing shot. If the opponent fails to pass you, you may now be able to hit the crosscourt shot to the opponent's backhand, angle a shot toward either sideline, hit a drive right at the rival's feet, or even attempt a drop volley or drop shot.

It is also important, however, not to use the same tactics constantly, especially against a skilled player. The opponent will begin to anticipate your moves and, probably, counter effectively.

Doubles. The best doubles partners are those who have played together often enough to know each other's strengths and weaknesses and to understand each other's styles of play. The strategy of doubles is quite different from that of singles. The best shot in doubles is often right down the middle of the court, since the opponents may be confused about which of them should handle it. On the other hand, angled drives to the sidelines are often more effective in doubles than drives to the baseline.

Good doubles partners play side by side. When one goes to the net, the other should also move up, and if one of them has to retreat the baseline, the other should also move back. The reason is that, if one partner is up and the other is back, one whole corner is left unprotected if the opponents can hit an angled shot to that area.

Doubles is also, above all, a game of anticipation because the ball goes back and forth much faster; there are very few long runs made to get to a shot. And one team or the other is almost always at net, so a good deal of volleying takes place.

Finally, it is a team game. Two good players who believe in teamwork can beat two great singles players who just can't coordinate their styles of play and constantly find themselves "poaching" on each other's shots, or attempting grandstand shots that leave the partner vulnerable to a good return.

Glossary

ace—A service that scores a point.

band—The strip of canvas across the top of the net.

baseline—The line that marks the back of the court.

double fault—Two faults on the same service, resulting in loss of point.

backcourt—The area between the service line and the baseline.

fault—An improper service.

foot fault—A fault called because the server had a foot on or across the baseline or on the wrong side of the court, as divided by the center line.

forecourt—The area between the net and the service line.

half-volley—The tennis equivalent of a "trap" in baseball or football; the ball is struck immediately after it touches the court, as it has just begun its bounce.

let—A service that touches the net before landing in the proper service court; also, a play in which a player accidentally interferes with an opponent. The point is replayed.

linesman—An official who rules on whether shots are in the prescribed playing area or not.

lob volley—A volley hit over the opponent's head.

midcourt—A rather indefinite area between the extreme forecourt and extreme backcourt.

net-cord judge—An official whose sole job is to call service lets.

overhead—A shot hit when the ball is above the head; commonly, a smash.

passing shot—A shot hit past an opponent who is at the net or advancing toward it.

rally—An exchange of shots between two players, ending when one of them has scored a point.

referee—The official who is in overall charge of a tournament; an umpire's ruling may be appealed to the referee, if it involves interpretation of the official rules.

umpire—The official with overall responsibility for the match; the umpire's chief duties include calling out the score after every point, informing the players when they should change sides, and seeing that new balls are brought into play as necessary.

See also COURT TENNIS; PADDLE TENNIS; PLATFORM TENNIS.

Wimbledon Champions
(Became open in 1968)

Men's Singles

1877	Spencer W. Gore
1878	P. Frank Hadow
1879	J. T. Hartley
1880	J. T. Hartley
1881	William Renshaw
1882	William Renshaw
1883	William Renshaw
1884	William Renshaw
1885	William Renshaw
1886	William Renshaw
1887	Herbert F. Lawford
1888	Ernest Renshaw
1889	William Renshaw
1890	Willoughby J. Hamilton
1891	Wilfred Baddeley
1892	Wilfred Baddeley
1893	Joshua L. Pim
1894	Joshua L. Pim
1895	Wilfred Baddeley
1896	Harold S. Mahoney
1897	Reginald F. Doherty
1898	Reginald F. Doherty
1899	Reginald F. Doherty
1900	Reginald F. Doherty
1901	Arthur W. Gore
1902	Hugh L. Doherty
1903	Hugh L. Doherty
1904	Hugh L. Doherty
1905	Hugh L. Doherty
1906	Hugh L. Doherty
1907	Norman E. Brookes
1908	Arthur W. Gore
1909	Arthur W. Gore
1910	Anthony F. Wilding
1911	Anthony F. Wilding
1912	Anthony F. Wilding
1913	Anthony F. Wilding
1914	Norman E. Brookes
1915–18	No competition
1919	Gerald L. Patterson
1920	William T. Tilden II
1921	William T. Tilden II
1922	Gerald L. Patterson
1923	William M. Johnston
1924	Jean Borotra
1925	René Lacoste
1926	Jean Borotra
1927	Henri Cochet
1928	René Lacoste
1929	Henri Cochet
1930	William T. Tilden II
1931	Sidney B. Wood, Jr.
1932	H. Ellsworth Vines, Jr.
1933	John H. Crawford
1934	Frederick J. Perry
1935	Frederick J. Perry
1936	Frederick J. Perry
1937	J. Donald Budge
1938	J. Donald Budge
1939	Robert L. Riggs
1940–45	No competition
1946	Yvon Petra
1947	John A. Kramer
1948	Robert Falkenburg
1949	Frederick R. Schroeder, Jr.
1950	Edward "Budge" Patty
1951	Richard Savitt
1952	Frank Sedgman
1953	E. Victor Seixas, Jr.
1954	Jaroslav Drobny
1955	Tony Trabert
1956	Lewis Hoad
1957	Lewis Hoad
1958	Ashley Cooper

Billie Jean King not only established herself as one of the game's greatest players by winning six Wimbledon and four U.S. titles, she struck major blows for women by beating Bobby Riggs in a 1973 challenge match and by leading a boycott of major tournaments that led to "equal pay for equal work." (*U.S. Tennis Association.*)

1959	Alex Olmedo
1960	Neale Fraser
1961	Rodney Laver
1962	Rodney Laver
1963	Charles McKinley
1964	Roy Emerson
1965	Roy Emerson
1966	Manuel Santana
1967	John Newcombe
1968	Rodney Laver
1969	Rodney Laver
1970	John Newcombe
1971	John Newcombe
1972	Stan Smith
1973	Jan Kodes
1974	James Connors
1975	Arthur Ashe
1976	Bjorn Borg

Women's Singles

1884	Maud Watson
1885	Maud Watson
1886	Blanche Bingley
1887	Lottie Dod
1888	Lottie Dod
1889	Blanche Bingley Hillyard
1890	L. Rice
1891	Lottie Dod
1892	Lottie Dod
1893	Lottie Dod
1894	Blanche Bingley Hillyard
1895	Charlotte Cooper
1896	Charlotte Cooper
1897	Blanche Bingley Hillyard
1898	Charlotte Cooper
1899	Blanche Bingley Hillyard
1900	Blanche Bingley Hillyard
1901	Charlotte Cooper Sterry
1902	M. E. Robb
1903	Dorothy K. Douglass
1904	Dorothy K. Douglass
1905	May G. Sutton
1906	Dorothy K. Douglass
1907	May G. Sutton
1908	Charlotte Cooper Sterry
1909	Dorothea Boothby
1910	Dorothy Douglass Chambers
1911	Dorothy Douglass Chambers
1912	Ethel W. Larcombe
1913	Dorothy Douglass Chambers

1914	Dorothy Douglass Chambers
1915–18	No competition
1919	Suzanne Lenglen
1920	Suzanne Lenglen
1921	Suzanne Lenglen
1922	Suzanne Lenglen
1923	Suzanne Lenglen
1924	Kathleen McKane
1925	Suzanne Lenglen
1926	Kathleen McKane Godfree
1927	Helen Wills
1928	Helen Wills
1929	Helen Wills
1930	Helen Wills Moody
1931	Cecile Aussem
1932	Helen Wills Moody
1933	Helen Wills Moody
1934	Dorothy E. Round
1935	Helen Wills Moody
1936	Helen Hull Jacobs
1937	Dorothy E. Round
1938	Helen Wills Moody
1939	Alice Marble
1940–45	No competition
1946	Pauline M. Betz
1947	Margaret E. Osborne
1948	Louise Brough
1949	Louise Brough
1950	Louise Brough
1951	Doris Hart
1952	Maureen Connolly
1953	Maureen Connolly
1954	Maureen Connolly
1955	Louise Brough
1956	Shirley Fry
1957	Althea Gibson
1958	Althea Gibson
1959	Maria Bueno
1960	Maria Bueno
1961	Angela Mortimer
1962	Karen Susman
1963	Margaret Smith
1964	Maria Bueno
1965	Margaret Smith
1966	Billie Jean King
1967	Billie Jean King
1968	Billie Jean King
1969	Ann Haydon Jones
1970	Margaret Smith Court
1971	Evonne Goolagong
1972	Billie Jean King
1973	Billie Jean King
1974	Chris Evert
1975	Billie Jean King
1976	Chris Evert

U.S. Champions

(Became open in 1968; in 1968 and 1969, there was also a national tournament from which contract professionals were barred. In those years, O indicates open, N indicates national, * indicates won both tournaments.)

Men's Singles

1881	Richard D. Sears
1882	Richard D. Sears
1883	Richard D. Sears
1884	Richard D. Sears
1885	Richard D. Sears
1886	Richard D. Sears
1887	Richard D. Sears
1888	Henry W. Slocum, Jr.
1889	Henry W. Slocum, Jr.

1890	Oliver S. Campbell
1891	Oliver S. Campbell
1892	Oliver S. Campbell
1893	Robert D. Wrenn
1894	Robert D. Wrenn
1895	Fred H. Hovey
1896	Robert D. Wrenn
1897	Robert D. Wrenn
1898	Malcolm D. Whitman
1899	Malcolm D. Whitman
1900	Malcolm D. Whitman
1901	William A. Larned
1902	William A. Larned
1903	Hugh L. Doherty
1904	Holcombe Ward
1905	Beals C. Wright
1906	William J. Clothier
1907	William A. Larned
1908	William A. Larned
1909	William A. Larned
1910	William A. Larned
1911	William A. Larned
1912	Maurice E. McLoughlin
1913	Maurice E. McLoughlin
1914	R. Norris Williams II
1915	William Johnston
1916	R. Norris Williams II
1917	R. Lindley Murray
1918	R. Lindley Murray
1919	William Johnston
1920	William T. Tilden II
1921	William T. Tilden II
1922	William T. Tilden II
1923	William T. Tilden II
1924	William T. Tilden II
1925	William T. Tilden II
1926	René Lacoste
1927	René Lacoste
1928	Henri Cochet
1929	William T. Tilden II
1930	John H. Doeg
1931	H. Ellsworth Vines, Jr.
1932	H. Ellsworth Vines, Jr.
1933	Frederick J. Perry
1934	Frederick J. Perry
1935	Wilmer L. Allison
1936	Frederick J. Perry
1937	J. Donald Budge
1938	J. Donald Budge
1939	Robert L. Riggs
1940	Donald McNeill
1941	Robert L. Riggs
1942	Frederick R. Schroeder, Jr.
1943	Joseph R. Hunt
1944	Frank A. Parker
1945	Frank A. Parker
1946	John A. Kramer
1947	John A. Kramer
1948	Pancho Gonzales
1949	Pancho Gonzales
1950	Arthur Larsen
1951	Frank Sedgman
1952	Frank Sedgman
1953	Tony Trabert
1954	E. Victor Seixas, Jr.
1955	Tony Trabert
1956	Ken Rosewall
1957	Mal Anderson
1958	Ashley Cooper
1959	Neale Fraser
1960	Neale Fraser
1961	Roy Emerson
1962	Rod Laver

1963	Rafael Osuna
1964	Roy Emerson
1965	Manuel Santana
1966	Fred Stolle
1967	John Newcombe
1968	Arthur Ashe*
1969	Rod Laver (O)
	Stan Smith (N)
1970	Ken Rosewall
1971	Stan Smith
1972	Ilie Nastase
1973	John Newcombe
1974	Jimmy Connors
1975	Manuel Orantes
1976	Jimmy Connors

Women's Singles

1887	Ellen F. Hansell
1888	Bertha L. Townsend
1889	Bertha L. Townsend
1890	Ellen C. Roosevelt
1891	Mabel E. Cahill
1892	Mabel E. Cahill
1893	Aline M. Terry
1894	Helen R. Helwig
1895	Juliette P. Atkinson
1896	Elisabeth H. Moore
1897	Juliette P. Atkinson
1898	Juliette P. Atkinson
1899	Marion Jones
1900	Myrtle McAteer
1901	Elisabeth H. Moore
1902	Marion Jones
1903	Elisabeth H. Moore
1904	May G. Sutton
1905	Elisabeth H. Moore
1906	Helen Homans
1907	Evelyn Sears
1908	Maude Barger-Wallach
1909	Hazel V. Hotchkiss
1910	Hazel V. Hotchkiss
1911	Hazel V. Hotchkiss
1912	Mary K. Browne
1913	Mary K. Browne
1914	Mary K. Browne
1915	Molla Bjurstedt
1916	Molla Bjurstedt
1917	Molla Bjurstedt
1918	Molla Bjurstedt
1919	Hazel Hotchkiss Wightman
1920	Molla Bjurstedt Mallory
1921	Molla Bjurstedt Mallory
1922	Molla Bjurstedt Mallory
1923	Helen Wills
1924	Helen Wills
1925	Helen Wills
1926	Molla Bjurstedt Mallory
1927	Helen Wills
1928	Helen Wills
1929	Helen Wills
1930	Betty Nuthall
1931	Helen Wills Moody
1932	Helen Hull Jacobs
1933	Helen Hull Jacobs
1934	Helen Hull Jacobs
1935	Helen Hull Jacobs
1936	Alice Marble
1937	Anita Lizana
1938	Alice Marble
1939	Alice Marble
1940	Alice Marble
1941	Sarah Palfrey Cooke
1942	Pauline M. Betz

Although often criticized for brash, even unsportsmanlike behavior, Jimmy Connors, at the age of 22, was recognized as the world's top male player in 1974. He became the fourth American to win the Australian singles title and went on to win the U.S. and Wimbledon titles that year. (*U.S. Tennis Association.*)

1943	Pauline M. Betz
1944	Pauline M. Betz
1945	Sarah Palfrey Cooke
1946	Pauline M. Betz
1947	Louise Brough
1948	Margaret Osborne duPont
1949	Margaret Osborne duPont
1950	Margaret Osborne duPont
1951	Maureen Connolly
1952	Maureen Connolly
1953	Maureen Connolly
1954	Doris Hart
1955	Doris Hart
1956	Shirley Fry
1957	Althea Gibson
1958	Althea Gibson
1959	Maria Bueno
1960	Darlene Hard
1961	Darlene Hard
1962	Margaret Smith
1963	Maria Bueno
1964	Maria Bueno
1965	Margaret Smith
1966	Maria Bueno
1967	Billie Jean King
1968	Virginia Wade (O)
	Margaret Smith Court (N)
1969	Margaret Smith Court*
1970	Margaret Smith Court
1971	Billie Jean King
1972	Billie Jean King
1973	Margaret Smith Court
1974	Billie Jean King
1975	Chris Evert
1976	Chris Evert

Tennis has been one of the fastest-growing recreational sports in
recent years. Here two youngsters work on some of the basics.
(*Hank Seaman,* New Bedford Standard-Times.)

International Team Champions

Davis Cup

1900	U.S. 5, Great Britain 0
1901	No competition
1902	U.S. 3, Great Britain 2
1903	Great Britain 4, U.S. 1
1904	Great Britain 5, Belgium 0
1905	Great Britain 5, U.S. 0
1906	Great Britain 5, U.S. 0
1907	Australia 3, Great Britain 2
1908	Australia 3, U.S. 2
1909	Australia 5, U.S. 0
1910	No competition
1911	Australia 5, U.S. 0
1912	Great Britain 3, Australia 2
1913	U.S. 3, Great Britain 2
1914	Australia 3, U.S. 2
1915–18	No competition
1919	Australia 4, Great Britain 1
1920	U.S. 5, Australia 0
1921	U.S. 5, Japan 0
1922	U.S. 4, Australia 1
1923	U.S. 4, Australia 1
1924	U.S. 5, Australia 0
1925	U.S. 5, France 0
1926	U.S. 4, France 1
1927	France 3, U.S. 2
1928	France 4, U.S. 1
1929	France 3, U.S. 2
1930	France 4, U.S. 1
1931	France 3, Great Britain 2
1932	France 3, U.S. 2
1933	Great Britain 3, France 2
1934	Great Britain 4, U.S. 1
1935	Great Britain 5, U.S. 0
1936	Great Britain 3, Australia 2
1937	U.S. 4, Great Britain 1
1938	U.S. 3, Australia 2
1939	Australia 3, U.S. 2
1940–45	No competition
1946	U.S. 5, Australia 0
1947	U.S. 4, Australia 1
1948	U.S. 5, Australia 0
1949	U.S. 4, Australia 1

1950	Australia 4, U.S. 1
1951	Australia 3, U.S. 2
1952	Australia 4, U.S. 1
1953	Australia 3, U.S. 2
1954	U.S. 3, Australia 2
1955	Australia 5, U.S. 0
1956	Australia 5, U.S. 0
1957	Australia 3, U.S. 2
1958	U.S. 3, Australia 2
1959	Australia 3, U.S. 2
1960	Australia 4, Italy 1
1961	Australia 5, Italy 0
1962	Australia 5, Mexico 0
1963	U.S. 3, Australia 2
1964	Australia 3, U.S. 2
1965	Australia 4, Spain 1
1966	Australia 4, India 1
1967	Australia 4, Spain 1
1968	U.S. 4, Australia 1
1969	U.S. 5, Rumania 0
1970	U.S. 5, W. Germany 0
1971	U.S. 3, Rumania 2
1972	U.S. 3, Rumania 2
1973	Australia 5, U.S. 0
1974	S. Africa beat India by default
1975	Sweden 3, Czeckoslovakia 2
1976	Italy 4, Chile 1

Wightman Cup

1923	U.S. 7, England 0
1924	England 6, U.S. 1
1925	England 4, U.S. 3
1926	U.S. 4, England 3
1927	U.S. 5, England 2
1928	England 4, U.S. 3
1929	U.S. 4, England 3
1930	England 4, U.S. 3
1931	U.S. 5, England 2
1932	U.S. 4, England 3
1933	U.S. 4, England 3
1934	U.S. 5, England 2
1935	U.S. 4, England 3
1936	U.S. 4, England 3
1937	U.S. 6, England 1
1938	U.S. 5, England 2
1939	U.S. 5, England 2
1940–45	No competition
1946	U.S. 7, England 0
1947	U.S. 7, England 0
1948	U.S. 6, England 1
1949	U.S. 7, England 0
1950	U.S. 7, England 0
1951	U.S. 6, England 1
1952	U.S. 7, England 0
1953	U.S. 7, England 0
1954	U.S. 6, England 0
1955	U.S. 6, England 1
1956	U.S. 5, England 2
1957	U.S. 6, England 1
1958	England 4, U.S. 3
1959	U.S. 4, England 3
1960	England 4, U.S. 3
1961	U.S. 6, England 1
1962	U.S. 4, England 3
1963	U.S. 6, England 1
1964	U.S. 5, England 2
1965	U.S. 5, England 2
1966	U.S. 4, England 3
1967	U.S. 6, England 1
1968	England 4, U.S. 3
1969	U.S. 5, England 2
1970	U.S. 4, England 3

1971	U.S. 4, England 3
1972	U.S. 5, England 2
1973	U.S. 5, England 2
1974	England 6, U.S. 1
1975	England 5, U.S. 2
1976	U.S. 5, England 2

Halls of Fame

(The Citizens Savings Athletic Foundation established its hall of fame for tennis in 1949. The National Lawn Tennis Hall of Fame and Museum, in the Newport, Rhode Island, Casino, was sanctioned by the USLTA in 1954 and opened in 1955. In the following list, C indicates Citizens, N indicates National.)

George T. Adee N
Frederick B. Alexander N
Wilmer L. Allison C, N
Juliette P. Atkinson C, N
Maud Barger-Wallach N
Karl Behr N
Pauline Betz (Addie) C, N
Molla Bjurstedt (Mallory) C, N
Jean Borotra N
Louise Brough C
Mary K. Browne C, N
Jacques Brugnon N
J. Donald Budge C, N
Mabel Cahill N
Oliver S. Campbell C, N
Malcolm G. Chace N
Mrs. L. B. Clapp N
Joseph S. Clark N
William J. Clothier
Henri Cochet N
Maureen Connolly (Brinker) C, N
Allison Danzig N
Dwight F. Davis C, N
Victor Denny C
John Doeg N
James Dwight N
Bob Falkenburg N
Shirley Fry (Irvin) C, N
Charles S. Garland N
Althea Gibson (Darben) C, N
Richard "Pancho" Gonzales C, N
Clarence J. "Peck" Griffin N
Harold H. Hackett N
Ellen Hansell (Allerdice) N
Darlene Hard C, N
Doris Hart C, N
Hazel Hotchkiss (Wightman) C, N
Fred B. Hovey N
Joseph R. Hunt N
Francis T. Hunter N
Helen Hull Jacobs C, N
William M. Johnston C, N
Perry T. Jones C, N
John A. "Jack" Kramer C, N
Rene Lacoste N
William A. Larned C, N
Arthur Larsen N
George M. Lott, Jr. C, N
C. Gene Mako C, N
Alice Marble C, N
A. B. Martin N
Charles "Chuck" McKinley C
Maurice E. McLoughlin C, N
W. Donald McNeill N
Billie Jean Moffitt (King) C
Elisabeth Moore C, N

R. Lindley Murray C, N
Julian S. Myrick C
Arthur C. Neilsen N
Margaret Osborne (duPont) C, N
Sarah Palfrey C, N
Frank A. Parker C, N
Theodore R. Pell N
Vincent Richards C, N
Nancy Richey (Gunter) C
Robert L. Riggs C, N
Elizabeth Ryan C
Dick Savitt N
Frederick R. "Ted" Schroeder C, N
Eleanora Sears N
Richard Sears C, N
E. Victor Seixas, Jr. C, N
Frank Shields N
Henry W. Slocum, Jr. N
May G. Sutton (Bundy) C, N
William Talbert N
William T. Tilden II C, N
Bertha Townsend (Toulmin) N
Tony Trabert C, N
James Van Alen N
John Van Ryn N
H. Ellsworth Vines C, N
Marie Wagner N
Holcombe Ward C, N
Watson Washburn N
Malcolm D. Whitman C, N
R. Norris Williams II C, N
Helen Wills (Moody) C, N
Sidney B. Wood, Jr. N
Robert D. Wrenn C, N
Beals C. Wright N

Bibliography. Cummings, Parke: *American Tennis: The Story of a Game*, Little Brown, Boston, 1957; Grimsley, Will: *Tennis: Its History, People, and Events*, Prentice-Hall, Englewood Cliffs, N.J., 1971; *Official USLTA Tennis Guide and Yearbook*, U.S. Lawn Tennis Association, New York (annual); Talbert, Bill et al.: *Sports Illustrated Tennis*, Lippincott, Philadelphia-New York, 1972.

TOBOGGANING—*See* BOBSLEDDING; LUGE.

TOUCH FOOTBALL—Little is known about the origin of this less violent version of American football. It has been claimed that touch football was played in Green Bay, Wisconsin, during the 1890s, but without documentation—and it seems likely that this version of the sport couldn't have developed earlier than 1906, when the forward pass was legalized, since the pass is the primary method of attack in touch football.

Touch football is unusual in that it is a genuine competitive sport with wide popularity, yet its rules have never been codified on a nationwide basis. Even in a single town or city, the rules may vary a great deal from game to game.

There are two main varieties. In friendly, pickup games, passing the ball forward is often permitted at any time and from any place on the field, even from beyond the line of scrimmage. In the more formalized version, as played, for example, by high school and college intramural teams, the passer must be behind the line of scrimmage when throwing the ball.

There are also variations in the touch required to "down" a ball carrier. A one-hand touch anywhere on the body may be sufficient; sometimes, the player must be touched simultaneously with both hands. In flag football the player has a flag or a piece of cloth sticking out of a pocket, and this flag must be removed by a defender. In other versions the touch must be made on a certain part of the body—below the waist, for example, or above the waist but below the neck.

One set of rules drawn up at Michigan State University is widely used in formal play. Under these rules, the field is 70 yd long by 30 yd wide; a team has four linemen and three backs, all of whom are eligible to receive passes; forward passing is permitted from anywhere on the field; and a team is given four downs in which to score. Often a field is divided into two or four zones, and a team is given three or four downs in which to advance the ball from one zone to the next (the equivalent of gaining 10 yd or more in tackle football).

See also FOOTBALL.

TOURNAMENTS—In the ancient jousting tournaments, all the knights competed in the first round, drawing opponents by lot. The winners advanced to the second round and the losers were eliminated.

That is the simplest and most common kind of tournament in sports. There are a couple of complicating factors, though. A true tournament can be organized only if the number of entrants is a power of 2—that is, 4, 8, 16, 32, 64 and so on. If the number doesn't equal a power of 2, some entrants will have to get "byes": during some round, usually the first, they will not have to play and will simply get a free pass to the next round. For example, if 14 teams enter a basketball tournament, 2 of them will get byes, while the other 12 play; then the 6 winners and the teams with byes advance to the second round. The total number of teams is now 8, a power of 2, so the tournament can proceed smoothly.

In the early years of the national lawn tennis championships, the results were often considered unsatisfactory because, by the luck of the draw, outstanding players might meet one another in very early rounds. So in 1922 the U.S. Lawn Tennis Association introduced the concept of seeding, in order to prevent such an occurrence (and early elimination of some standouts).

In seeding, a certain number of entrants are chosen in advance as the cream of the crop, and they are assigned to places in the tournament schedule that will prevent their meeting too early. To choose the simplest example, if there are two seeds, one of them is put in the top half (bracket) of the tournament chart, the other in the lower bracket. If they play one another, it will be in the final game.

In a double-elimination tournament, often used in baseball and softball, where a single good pitcher might win a game for an inferior team, one loss doesn't eliminate an entrant. Losers, in effect, continue their own tournament, in the losers' bracket. Finally, there are only two teams left, one undefeated and one with a single loss. They play for the championship. The unbeaten team needs just one victory to win, while the other team must win two games to take the title.

A round-robin tournament is more time-consuming, and is not commonly seen. In this type of tournament, every team or player meets every other team or player, and the entrant with the best won-lost record is the champion. In some cases the round-robin is used as a preliminary round to select two or more teams to take part in another kind of tournament or play-off to determine the champion.

See also PLAY-OFF; SEEDING.

TRACK AND FIELD—The athletic contests lumped under this heading are measures of the most basic human athletic skills: running, jumping, and throwing. Most of the events undoubtedly originated with primitive man thousands of years ago, when speed and strength were basic to everyday survival. Even an apparently modern sport like discus throwing is centuries old. Perhaps the newest of the track and field events is pole vaulting—and even that is based on an English sport of unknown age.

It is only an accident that all these activities are now grouped. The ancient Greeks did combine races of various distances with the discus throw and other events in their Olympic Games. But the concept of having a number of track and field events held at the same time, in the same place, apparently dates from twelfth-century England, where open areas were set aside in several locations to allow people to run, jump, and throw weights. These were practice grounds, but informal competitions must have taken place there on many occasions.

Most sports, except archery, were banned in England for nearly a century—but the more popular ones survived, and it is likely that the practice of track and field events also continued. In 1834, standards were set for certain events: 60 sec for the quarter-mile run, 5 min for the mile, 10 min for the 2-mi run, 20 ft for the broad jump, and 5½ ft for the high jump. It would appear that these "standards" were, in effect, records—or, at least, standards of exceptionally good performance, like par in golf, since they're quite close to the world records established in the 1860s.

Eton College was an early leader in track and field programs. Evidently the 440-yd event was the shortest race run in formal competition in the early nineteenth century, and long-distance running was much more common. Eton, however, added hurdle races to its interclass track program in 1837, and the steeplechase in 1843. The high jump and broad jump were first formally added to a program in 1851, at Exeter College, England. Until the early 1900s, standing jumps (made without a running start) were common, but they are now obsolete except in competition for youngsters and seniors. The pole vault is believed to have derived from the English custom of using a stick to vault over streams; it was originally a distance event. It became a height event in England during the 1860s.

Weight throwing of one kind or another is certainly an ancient sport. The discus throw, believed to have been the most prestigious event in the ancient Olympics, probably began with competitors sailing large flat stones. The sport was revived in Greece late in the nineteenth century and became an international event when it was placed on the 1896 Olympic program, as a connecting link to the ancient Games. Weight throwing was a particularly popular event in ancient Ireland and Scotland; undoubtedly the weights were originally large stones. The 35- and 56-lb weight throws came directly from Irish games. A cannon ball was also used as a weight in Ireland during the sixteenth century, and from that event came the shot put. The hammer throw also developed in Ireland, where workers actually competed against one another in throwing sledge hammers. Gradually the hammer evolved into the stylized version now seen.

By 1860, "sports programs"—essentially track and field meets—were common throughout England, although many of them were primarily contests for runners. In 1864 the first recorded dual team meet took place, between Oxford and Cambridge Universities, and in 1866 the London Athletic Club sponsored the first national championship meet.

Two years later the New York Athletic Club was organized, and held an indoor meet. In 1876 the Intercollegiate Association of Amateur Athletes of America held its first meet, and the New York AC conducted the first United States national championships. The club continued running the championships until 1879, when the National Association of Amateur Athletes of America was formed. The NAAAA became the Amateur Athletic Union (AAU) in 1887.

The first international meet was a contest between Oxford and Yale in 1894, in London. The following year, the New York AC and London AC held a meet, also in London. The final great thrust to track and field, on the international level, was the establishment of the modern Olympic Games in 1896.

The Track

The outdoor track is an oval, 440 yd or 400 m in total length as measured on a line 1 ft from its inner edge. AAU rules specify that there must be an unbroken border, 2 in high and no more than 2 in wide, of board, cement, or other material, marking the inner edge. Specifications call for eight (sometimes six) lanes, each about 4 ft wide, marked clearly for a distance of at least 220 yd (or 200 m). Also specified is an extended straightaway stretching from one of the long ends of the oval, to permit the 100-yd or 100-m dash to be run straight for the entire distance. The track is covered with finely crushed cinders or with one of the artificial surfaces recently developed for the purpose.

Field events are usually held in the infield area bordered by the track. For major meets, two throwing circles are needed: a 7-ft circle for the shot put, hammer throw, and weight throws, and an 8-ft, 2½-in circle for the discus throw. Each circle is marked by a metal strip, painted white, which is sunk so that it is flush with the ground. The hard-packed earth inside the circle is ½ to 1 in lower than the top of metal strip.

For the javelin throw there is a runway, 98½ to 120 ft long and 13 ft, 1½ in wide, marked by chalk lines. The end of the runway is marked with a strip of wood or metal, the arc of a circle with a radius of 26 ft, 3 in. The strip is painted white and sunk flush with the surface of the earth. From either end of the arc, lines are drawn to a distance of 300 ft, 3 in, marking the sector in which the thrown javelin must fall to be valid. This represents a sector of approximately 29 degrees.

For the hammer, discus, and weight throws, a sector of 45 degrees is marked, and throws must fall within that sector to be valid. The ends of the sector lines are marked with metal flags, measuring approximately 8 by 16 in and set on a standard at least 2 ft high.

A curved board 4 ft long, with an inner edge which fits the inner edge of the shotput circle, is called the stopboard. It is 4½ in wide and 3¼ in above the ground on the outside of the circle. It is painted white, and its purpose is to prevent overstepping of the circle by the contestant.

For major championship events, the AAU requires runways of at least 57 ft, 3 in in length for the high jump, and of at least 147 ft, 6 in for the long jump, pole vault, and triple jump. The same runway may be used for two or more jumps.

For the long jump and triple jump, a takeoff board is required. It is wooden, at least 4 ft long, 7.874 in wide, and 3.937 in deep. The end of the board nearest the landing area is recessed to accommodate another board coated with plasticine, a soft plastic substance capable of recording footprints and therefore of showing whether a competitor fouled in jumping.

A takeoff box is required for the pole vault. It is made of metal or wood with a metal-lined bottom; the AAU specifies a length of 3 ft, 3.337 in, measured on the inside. The bottom tapers in width from 1 ft, 11.622 in at the front to 5.905 in at the stopboard. The box tapers from ground level at the front to a depth of 7.874 in at the stopboard. The stopboard is set at an angle of 105 degrees to the bottom; the sides slope outward at an angle of about 120 degrees.

The AAU specifies minimum dimensions for the high-jump and pole-vault landing pits: 16 ft, 4 in by 13 ft, 1½ in for the high jump; 16 ft, 4 in by 16 ft, 4 in for the pole vault. The pits are filled with sawdust, shavings, chunks of foam rubber, or other suitable material to a minimum height of 12 in above the takeoff for the high jump, and of 18 in for the pole vault. Landing areas for the long jump and triple jump are normally made of deep sand. The landing area should be at least 42 ft from the takeoff board for the triple jump, and 3¼ to 15 ft for the long jump.

Pole vault crossbars should be at least 12 ft, and no more than 14 ft, 2 in, long; for the high jump the range is 12 ft to 13 ft, 2½ in. The crossbars are circular or triangular in cross section; if triangular, the corners should be rounded. If circular, the diameter should be .984–1.181 in; if triangular, each side should measure 1.181 in. In both events, the crossbar is shorter than the distance between the uprights, and is suspended from supports on the inside of the crossbar. In the high jump, the supports are flat, 1.575 in wide and 2.36 in long. In the pole vault they are round pegs, no more than ½ in in diameter and no more than 3 in long.

Indoor Tracks. A few indoor tracks have dirt or cinder surfaces similar to outdoor tracks, but most of them are made of wooden sections, easily fitted together or disassembled, and sharply banked at the curves. The total distance is usually 220 yd or less. The AAU requires lanes of at least 3 ft in width for any indoor race of 300 m or less.

Because of space limitations, generally only five field events are held indoors: the high jump, broad jump, pole vault, shot put, and weight throw. Weight circles are usually painted on the wood surface in the infield; dimensions are the same as in outdoor competition. Landing pits for the high jump and pole vault are usually large canvas containers full of foam-rubber chunks. The shot put and weight are covered with leather or plastic to minimize damage to the wooden floor.

Rules

Running Events. All competitors must be behind the starting line before the starting signal. They may not touch the line, nor may they have any parts of their bodies over the line. The starter gives the commands, "On your mark" and "Get set," and then fires a pistol to start the race. If any runner touches the line or the ground in front of it, or leaves the mark before the starting signal, it is a false start. A competitor is warned after one false start; the second results in disqualification. It is also a false start if a runner delays in assuming the "set" position upon command. If there is a false start, the starter or a special recall starter fires another shot to call the runners back.

Starting blocks are allowed in races of up to 880 yd; in relay races, they may be used only by a team's leadoff runner, if that member's leg of the event is no longer than 880 yd. Starting blocks must be made of rigid materials, and must not contain any springs or similar devices which would give the runner artificial impetus.

All races up to and including 440 yd are run in separate lanes throughout. Since the 220 and the 440, or their metric equivalents, are run around turns, a staggered start is necessary—otherwise the runners in outside lanes would have to travel farther than the runners in the inside lanes.

In longer races, a runner must be at least 2 yd in front of a competitor before that runner may cut in front of the rival. Once a runner enters the final straightaway, the runner has to stay in the same lane unless there is a contestant directly in front, in which case the runner can go around that contestant, to the inside or outside—provided that the runner doesn't interfere with any other contestant. A runner can be disqualified for obstructing a competitor. If there is a foul in a preliminary heat, the runner interfered with can be placed in the next round of races by the referee. If obstruction occurs in a final event, the referee can order a new race, after disqualifying the interfering runner.

The finish is marked both by a line on the track and, for judging purposes, by a string or tape, 4 ft above the ground, suspended between two finish posts, each 4½ ft high. A runner has finished when any part of the torso is across the line, or when one foot touches the ground beyond the line. The runner who breaks the tape is usually, but not necessarily, the winner: It is possible for a runner to touch the ground beyond the line before hitting the tape with the torso. It is also possible for the tape to be broken by someone's arm, and having an arm or hand across the finish line doesn't represent a legal finish—unless it is touching the track beyond the line.

Hurdling. There are basically three hurdle races: at 120 yd or 110 m; 220 yd or 200 m; and 440 yd or 400 m. The hurdles are of different heights: 3 ft, 6 in for the shortest race; 2 ft, 6 in for the middle distance; and 3 ft for the longest distance. Thus the short race is sometimes called the "high hurdles," the middle race the "low hurdles," and the long race the "intermediate hurdles."

There are 10 hurdles in each race. In the high hurdles, the first hurdle is 15 yd from the start; the last is 15 yd from the finish line; and the intervening hurdles are spaced 10 yd apart. In the lows, the hurdles are set at intervals of 20 yd. (In the 200-m event, the interval is 18.29 m, and the last hurdle is 17.10 m from the finish.) In the intermediates, the first hurdle is 49¼ yd (45 m) from the start, the intervening hurdles are 38¼ yd (35 m) apart, and the last hurdle is 46½ yd (40 m) from the finish.

Indoor events are at 50 yd (four hurdles), 60 yd (five hurdles), and 70 yd (six hurdles). All are high-hurdle events.

A competitor can be disqualified for running around, or trailing a foot or leg alongside, a hurdle; for jumping a hurdle not in the competitor's own lane; or for deliberately (in the opinion of the referee) knocking down a hurdle. However, a hurdler may accidentally knock down one or more hurdles without being disqualified.

In women's events, the hurdles are 2 ft, 9 in high for races of up to 100 m, and 2 ft, 6 in high for the 220-yd or 200-m races.

A hurdle is made of wood or metal; it is constructed with two bases and two uprights that support a rectangular frame, 3 ft, 11 in wide. It is counterweighted so that a force of at least 8 lb, and no more than 8 lb, 13 oz, is required to overturn it. The top bar must be striped in black and white for visibility.

The Steeplechase. There are two standard steeplechase distances, 2 mi and 3,000 m. The 3,000-m event has 28 hurdles and 7 water jumps; the 2-mi has 32 hurdles and 8 water jumps.

In the 3,000-m steeplechase, the competitors run 280 m before coming to the first hurdle. The hurdles are 78 m apart, and the distance from the last hurdle to the finish line is 68 m. In the 2-mi, contestants run 90 yd before coming to the first hurdle; the hurdles are 86 yd apart, and the distance from the last hurdle to the finish line is 76 yd. In either event, the water jump is between the third and fourth hurdles.

Hurdles are 3 ft high and 13 ft wide, and the bases are fixed to the ground so the hurdle cannot be knocked over. The water jump is 12 ft square; it is 2 ft, 3⅜ in deep immediately beyond the hurdle and slopes to ground level. The bottom is covered with a mat, at least 12 ft wide and 8 ft long. The hurdle in front of the water jump is the same size as the other hurdles.

Competitors must go over all hurdles and must go over or through the water each time they reach the water jump.

Relays. There are two types of relay races: those in which each runner on a team runs the same distance, and the medley relay, in which the legs, or segments, are of different distances. A relay team consists of four runners. As already noted, the first runner may use starting blocks if that contestant's leg is 880 yd or less. The first runner carries a baton, 12 in long and with a circumference of 4¾ in, which must be passed from one runner to the next throughout the race. The baton has to be carried in the hand; if it is dropped, the runner must recover it.

The 4 × 100- and 4 × 220-yd (or 200-m) relays are run entirely in lanes, requiring a staggered start. In the 4 × 440-yd (or 400-m) relay, the first leg is run entirely in lanes, and the second leg is run in lanes through the end of the first turn.

The baton has to be passed in a takeover zone, marked by two lines across the track, 10 m on either side of the starting line. In races up to and including 4 × 220, a runner can start from a point 10 m outside the takeover zone, but the baton pass must be made within the zone. If a pass is made outside the zone, the team is disqualified.

Throwing. In throwing from a circle, a competitor may touch the inside of the ring or the stopboard, but must not step on or over it. If the contestant does, it is a foul throw, which counts as one attempt but is not measured.

Even after the throw is completed, the competitor is not allowed to step through the front of the circle, but must leave through the rear half. In the javelin throw, the competitor must make the throw from behind the arc, and must leave the runway from behind the arc.

Measurements are made from the mark made by the implement's fall to the inside of the circle's circumference, along a line to the center of the circle; in the javelin competition, the measurement is made to the inside of the arc along a line to the center of the imaginary circle of which the arc is a part.

The shot, hammer, weight, and discus must land in a sector of 45 degrees, marked on the ground. The javelin must land in a marked sector of approximately 29 degrees.

Heavy Weight. The 56-lb weight has a round head of lead or lead-filled brass, connected to a triangular iron or steel handle with a diameter of ½ in. No side of the triangle may be more than 7¼ in, by inside measurement. The connection is made by a steel link with a diameter of ⅜ in. The overall length must not exceed 16 in. The 35-lb weight is the same except, of course, that it is lighter, and the link is an inch longer. The overall length is 16 in. The weight is thrown by the handle, gripped in both hands.

Hammer Throw. The hammer is actually a spherical metal ball, with a handle of spring steel wire connected to a rigid grip. The overall weight is 16 lb; length is just under 4 ft, and the diameter of the head must be between 102 and 120 mm (4.016 and 4.724 in). Like the heavy weight, the hammer is thrown by the handle, with both hands. The head of the hammer may touch the ground before it is released, without penalty.

Shot Put. The shot is a solid sphere of iron, or of brass filled with lead. It weighs 16 lb (8lb, 13 oz for women) and its diameter must be at least 4¹¹/₃₂ in but no more than 5⅛ in (3¾ in to 4¹¹/₃₂ in for women). The shot must be put with one hand, from above the shoulder. The hand and the shot must remain above the level of the shoulder at all times, once the competitor assumes a starting stance.

Javelin Throw. The javelin is a spear with a shaft of wood or metal, a sharp metal point, and a cord grip. Minimum weight is 1 lb, 12¼ oz for men, and 1 lb, 5¼ oz for women. The length must range between 8 ft, 6⅜ in and 8 ft, 10¼ in for men; 7 ft, 2⅝ in and 7 ft, 6½ in for women. The diameter of the shaft at its thickest point must range from 1 to 1¹/₁₆ in for men, ¹³/₁₆ to 1 in for women. Permissible ranges for the width of the grip are 6 to 6⁵/₁₆ in for men, 5½ in to 5⅞ in for women. The grip must be located approximately at the center of gravity.

The cross section of the shaft must be circular throughout, and it must be tapered so the diameter at a point halfway between the grip and either end is no more than 90 percent of the maximum diameter and, at a point 6 in from either end, no more than 80 percent of maximum.

The javelin must be thrown with one hand only, and the hand must remain on the grip until the javelin is released. The throw has to be made overhand, and the competitor may not turn the back of the body toward the throwing area during the run preliminary to making the throw. The javelin's point must strike the ground first; if it doesn't, the throw is a foul.

Discus Throw. The discus is made either of wood, with metal plates set flush into the sides, or entirely of metal. It must be symmetrical. The weight is 4 lb, 6⅔ oz for men, and 2 lb, 3¼ oz for women. Permissible range for the

Marilyn King takes off during broad jump competition in U.S.-U.S.S.R. dual meet. (*W. J. Wallace, Duke University.*)

outer diameter is 8⅝ to 8¹¹⁄₁₆ in for men, 7³⁄₃₂ to 7⁵⁄₃₂ in for women. The center of the discus is a flat circle with a diameter measuring .984 in. From the outside of this circle, the sides taper in a straight line from the circle to the curved edge. The discus must be thrown with one hand.

High Jump and Pole Vault. The same general rules apply to both these events. The bar is set at a starting height, and each competitor is given three chances to clear it. Three misses at a single height eliminate the competitor. A competitor may pass—elect not to attempt—a certain height. The contestant who misses once or twice at a given height can pass and still continue in the competition. However, three successive misses, even at different heights, eliminate the contestant.

The high-jump takeoff must be made from one foot, and knocking off the bar, or touching the ground or the landing area beyond the uprights without having first cleared the bar, constitutes a miss.

The pole used for vaulting may be made of any material, and there are no limitations on its size. If metal is used, the surface must be smooth. The competitor may bind the pole with no more than two layers of adhesive tape; the bottom 12 in of the pole may be bound with more layers of tape, however, to help prevent shattering.

The pole-vault takeoff must be made from the takeoff box. It is a miss if the vaulter or the pole knocks down the crossbar; if the vaulter fails to clear the bar; if the vaulter changes the position of the hands on the pole after leaving the ground; and if any part of the body or the pole touches the ground or the landing area beyond the uprights without the contestant's having cleared the bar.

Measurements for both events are made from the ground to the upper side of the bar.

Long Jump. The takeoff for the long jump must be made from behind the scratch line. It is a foul if the competitor touches the ground beyond the takeoff line with any part of the body; if the takeoff is made from beside the takeoff board; or if the contestant touches the ground, outside the landing area, closer to the takeoff line than the mark made by the jump. Measurement of the jump is made at a right angle from the scratch line to the nearest break in the landing area made by any part of the competitor's body.

Triple Jump. Formerly known as the "hop, step, and jump," the triple jump is governed by basically the same rules as the long jump. The first jump is a hop; takeoff is made from one foot, and the landing must be made on that foot. The competitor then takes a long step to the other foot and long-jumps, taking off from and landing on both feet. If the contestant touches the ground at any time with a trailing foot or leg, it is a foul.

In the long jump and triple jump, each competitor is given three attempts, and the best attempt is the one that counts.

Combined Events. There are five combined events in track and field: the decathlon, the pentathlon, the triathlon, the all-around, and the all-around weight event.

The decathlon is a series of 10 events conducted over a two-day period. On the first day, competitors take part in the 100-m dash, the long jump, shot put, high jump, and 400-m run; on the second day, the 110-m hurdles, the discus, pole vault, javelin, and 1,500-m run. The basic rules of these events apply, except that a competitor is allowed three false starts before disqualification from a running event.

The pentathlon consists of five events, conducted in one day: the long jump, javelin throw, 200-m run, discus throw, and 1,500-m run. (The women's pentathlon consists of the 100-m hurdles, 200-m dash, high jump, long jump, and shot put, and may be conducted over a two-day period.)

The triathlon, for women, consists of the 100-m dash, high jump, and shot put.

In these combined events, points are awarded for performances based on a special scoring table, and the competitor who compiles the highest point total is the winner.

The all-around competition consists of 10 events: 100-yd dash, shot put, high jump, 880-yd walk, hammer throw, pole vault, 120-yd hurdles, 56-lb weight throw, long jump, and mile run. Each event starts five minutes after the preceding event has finished. Scoring is based on the 1893 AAU records; a performance matching the record gets 1,000 points, and other point totals come from a scoring table.

The all-around weight competition consists of the shot put, hammer throw, discus throw, javelin throw and 35-lb weight throw. Each competitor gets three trials in each event, and the best trial is used for scoring. Again special scoring tables are used.

Records. In the broad jump and triple jump, and all races up to and including 220 yd, a record may be set only if the average speed of the wind, in the direction of the competition, does not exceed 2 m a second (4.47 mi an hour) during the event. A wind gauge is set up halfway down the straightaway in the races, 20 m from the takeoff point for the long jump and the triple jump, to record wind speed at the time of competition.

The AAU is responsible for certifying two kinds of records: American records, set by American citizens in any part of the world, and all-comers records, set in the United States by any competitor. World records are maintained by the International Amateur Athletic Federation; if set in the United States or by an American, a world record must first be certified by the AAU, then forwarded to the IAAF for ratification.

See also CROSS-COUNTRY; MARATHON; WALKING.

AAU Outdoor Champions—Men
(*Indicates wind-aided)

100-Yard Dash

1876	F. C. Saportas	10.5
1877	C. C. McIvor	10.5
1878	William C. Wilmer	10.0
1879	B. R. Value	10.6
1880	Lon E. Myers	10.4
1881	Lon E. Myers	10¼
1882	A. Waldron	Not available
1883	A. Waldron	10¼
1884	Maxwell W. Ford	10.8
1885	Maxwell W. Ford	10.6
1886	Maxwell W. Ford	10.4
1887	Charles H. Sherrill	10.4
1888	F. Westing	10.6
1889	John Owen, Jr.	10.4
1890	John Owen, Jr.	9.8
1891	Luther H. Cary	10.2
1892	Harry Jewett	10.0
1893	C. W. Stage	10.2
1894	T. I. Lee	10.2
1895	Bernard J. Wefers	10.0
1896	Bernard J. Wefers	10.2
1897	Bernard J. Wefers	9.8
1898	Frank W. Jarvis	10.0
1899	Alvin C. Kraenzlein	Not available
1900	Maxwell W. Long	10.0
1901	Frank M. Sears	9.8
1902	P. J. Walsh	10.0
1903	Archie Hahn	10.2
1904	Lawson Robertson	10.4
1905	Charles L. Parson	9.8
1906	Charles J. Seitz	10.2
1907	H. J. Huff	10.2
1908	William F. Hamilton	10.2
1909	W. Martin	10.2
1910	J. M. Rosenberger	10.2
1911	Gwinn Henry	10.0
1912	Howard P. Drew	10.0
1913	Howard P. Drew	10.4
1914	Joseph Loomis	10.2
1915	Joseph Loomis	9.8
1916	A. E. Ward	10.0
1917	A. E. Ward	10.2
1918	A. H. Henke	10.2
1919	William D. Hayes	10.2
1920	Loren Murchison	10.0
1921	Charles W. Paddock	9.6
1922	Robert McAllister	10.0
1923	Loren Murchison	10.1
1924	Charles W. Paddock	9.6
1925	Frank Hussey	9.8
1926	Charles Borah	9.8
1927	Chester Bowman	9.6
1929	Eddie Tolan	10.0
1930	Eddie Tolan	9.7
1931	Frank Wykoff	9.5
1953	Arthur Bragg	9.5
1954	Arthur Bragg	9.5
1955	Bobby Morrow	9.4
1957	Leamon King	9.7
1958	Bobby Morrow	9.4
1961	Frank Budd	9.2
1962	Bob Hayes	9.3
1963	Bob Hayes	9.1
1965	George Anderson	9.3
1966	Charlie Greene	9.4
1967	Jim Hines	9.3
1969	Ivory Crockett	9.3
1970	Ivory Crockett	9.3
1971	Delano Meriwether	9.0*
1973	Steve Williams	9.4

100-Meter Dash

1928	Frank Wykoff	10.6
1932	Ralph Metcalfe	10.6
1933	Ralph Metcalfe	10.5
1934	Ralph Metcalfe	10.4
1935	Eulace Peacock	10.2*
1936	Jesse Owens	10.4
1937	Perrin Walker	10.7
1938	Ben Johnson	10.7
1939	Clyde Jeffrey	10.2*
1940	Harold Davis	10.3
1941	Barney Ewell	10.3
1942	Harold Davis	10.5
1943	Harold Davis	10.3*
1944	Claude Young	10.5
1945	Barney Ewell	10.3
1946	Bill Mathis	10.7
1947	Bill Mathis	10.5
1948	Barney Ewell	10.6
1949	Andy Stanfield	10.3
1950	Arthur Bragg	10.4
1951	James Golliday	10.3
1952	Dean Smith	10.5
1956	Bobby Morrow	10.3
1959	Ray Norton	10.5
1960	Ray Norton	10.5
1964	Bob Hayes	10.3

1968	Charlie Greene	10.0
1972	Robert Taylor	10.2
1974	Steve Williams	9.9
1975	Don Quarrie	10.16
1976	Chris Garpenborg	10.39

220-Yard Dash

1877	Edward Merritt	24.0
1878	William C. Wilmer	27⅞
1879	Lon E. Myers	23.6
1880	Lon E. Myers	23.6
1881	Lon E. Myers	23.5
1882	Henry S. Brooks, Jr.	22.6
1883	Henry S. Brooks, Jr.	22.8
1884	Lon E. Myers	24.2
1885	Maxwell W. Ford	23.8
1886	Maxwell W. Ford	23.2
1887	F. Westing	23.2
1888	F. Westing	22.2
1889	John Owen, Jr.	23.6
1890	F. Westing	22.2
1891	Luther H. Cary	22.8
1892	Harry Jewett	21.8*
1893	C. W. Stage	22.2
1894	T. I. Lee	22.0
1895	Bernard J. Wefers	21.8
1896	Bernard J. Wefers	23.0
1897	Bernard J. Wefers	21.4
1898	J. H. Maybury	22.4
1899	Maxwell W. Long	22.4
1900	W. S. Edwards	22.6
1901	Frank M. Sears	22.0
1902	P. J. Walsh	22.8
1903	Archie Hahn	23.2
1904	William Hogenson	22.8
1905	Archie Hahn	22.2
1906	R. L. Young	22.4
1907	H. J. Huff	22.2
1908	W. F. Keating	22.4
1909	W. F. Dawbarn	22.4
1910	Gwinn Henry	22.6
1911	J. Nelson	21.8
1912	Alvin T. Meyer	21.8
1913	Howard P. Drew	22.8
1914	I. T. Howe	22.2
1915	R. F. Morse	21.2*
1916	A. E. Ward	21.6
1917	A. E. Ward	22.2
1918	Loren Murchison	22.4
1919	H. Williams	21.8
1920	Charles W. Paddock	21.4
1921	Charles W. Paddock	21.8
1922	J. Alfred Leconey	22.1
1923	Loren Murchison	22.3
1924	Charles W. Paddock	20.8
1925	Jackson V. Scholz	20.8*
1926	Tom Sharkey	21.4
1927	Charles Borah	21.6
1929	Eddie Tolan	21.9
1930	George Simpson	21.3
1931	Eddie Tolan	21.0
1953	Andy Stanfield	21.2
1954	Arthur Bragg	21.1
1955	Rod Richards	21.0
1957	Ollan Cassell	21.0
1958	Bobby Morrow	20.9
1961	Paul Drayton	21.0
1962	Paul Drayton	20.5
1963	Paul Drayton	20.4
	Henry Carr	20.4
1965	Adolph Plummer	20.6
1966	Jim Hines	20.5
1967	Tommie Smith	20.4

1969	John Carlos	20.2
1970	Ben Vaughan	20.8
1971	Don Quarrie	20.2
1973	Steve Williams	20.4

200-Meter Dash

1928	Charles Borah	21.4
1932	Ralph Metcalfe	21.5
1933	Ralph Metcalfe	21.1
1934	Ralph Metcalfe	21.3
1935	Ralph Metcalfe	21.0*
1936	Ralph Metcalfe	21.2
1937	Jack Weiershauser	20.9
1938	Mack Robinson	21.3
1939	Barney Ewell	21.0
1940	Harold Davis	20.4
1941	Harold Davis	20.4
1942	Harold Davis	20.9
1943	Harold Davis	20.2*
1944	Charles Parker	21.3
1945	Elmore Harris	21.9
1946	Barney Ewell	21.2
1947	Barney Ewell	21.0
1948	Lloyd LaBeach	21.0
1949	Andy Stanfield	20.4
1950	Robert Tyler	21.1
1951	James Ford	20.8
1952	Andy Stanfield	21.1
1956	Thane Baker	20.6
1959	Ray Norton	20.8
1960	Ray Norton	20.8
1964	Henry Carr	20.6
1968	Tommie Smith	20.3
1972	Chuck Smith	20.7
1974	Don Quarrie	20.5
1975	Don Quarrie	20.12
1976	Millard Hampton	20.89

440-Yard Run

1876	Edward Merritt	54.5
1877	Edward Merritt	55¼
1878	F. W. Brown	54⅜
1879	Lon E. Myers	52.4
1880	Lon E. Myers	52.0
1881	Lon E. Myers	49.4
1882	Lon E. Myers	51.6
1883	Lon E. Myers	52⅛
1884	Lon E. Myers	55.8
1885	H. M. Raborg	54.2
1886	J. S. Robertson	52.0
1887	H. M. Banks	51.8
1888	Walter C. Downs	51.0
1889	Walter C. Downs	51.4
1890	Walter C. Downs	50.0
1891	Walter C. Downs	51.0
1892	Walter C. Downs	50.0
1893	E. W. Allen	50.4
1894	Thomas F. Keane	51.0
1895	Thomas E. Burke	49.6
1896	Thomas E. Burke	48.8
1897	Thomas E. Burke	49.0
1898	Maxwell W. Long	50.8
1899	Maxwell W. Long	50.8
1900	Maxwell W. Long	52.6
1901	H. W. Hayes	52.4
1902	Fay R. Moulton	50.8
1903	Harry L. Hillman	52.0
1904	D. H. Meyer	51.2
1905	Frank Waller	49.6
1906	Frank Waller	50.2
1907	John B. Taylor	51.0
1908	Harry L. Hillman	49.6
1909	Edward F. Lindberg	50.4

1910	W. Hayes	52.0
1911	Edward F. Lindberg	49.0
1912	T. J. Halpin	49.4
1913	C. B. Haff	51.2
1914	James E. "Ted" Meredith	50.2
1915	James E. "Ted" Meredith	47.0*
1916	T. J. Halpin	49.8
1917	Frank J. Shea	49.6
1918	C. C. Shaughnessy	49.4
1919	Frank J. Shea	50.2
1920	Frank J. Shea	49.0
1921	William E. Stevenson	48.6
1922	J. W. Driscoll	49.9
1923	Horatio M. Fitch	50.0
1924	James Burgess	49.8
1925	Cecil G. Cooke	49.2
1926	Kenneth Kennedy	48.6
1927	Herman Phillips	49.6
1929	Reginald F. Bowen	48.4
1930	Victor Williams	48.8
1931	Victor Williams	48.8
1953	Jess W. Mashburn	47.1
1954	Jim Lea	46.6
1955	Charles Jenkins	46.7
1957	Reggie Pearman	46.4
1958	Eddie Southern	45.8
1961	Otis Davis	46.1
1962	Ulis Williams	45.8
1963	Ulis Williams	45.8
1965	Ollan Cassell	46.1
1966	Lee Evans	45.9
1967	Lee Evans	45.3
1969	Lee Evans	45.6
1970	John Smith	45.7
1971	John Smith	44.5
1973	Maurice Peoples	45.2

400-Meter Run

1928	Raymond J. Barbuti	51.4
1932	William A. Carr	46.9
1933	Ivan Fuqua	47.7
1934	Ivan Fuqua	47.4
1935	Edward O'Brien	47.6
1936	Harold Smallwood	47.3
1937	Ray Malott	47.1
1938	Ray Malott	47.6
1939	Erwin Miller	48.3
1940	Grover Klemmer	47.0
1941	Grover Klemmer	46.0
1942	Cliff Bourland	46.7
1943	Cliff Bourland	47.7
1944	Elmore Harris	48.0
1945	Herbert McKenley	48.4
1946	Elmore Harris	46.3
1947	Herbert McKenley	47.1
1948	Herbert McKenley	46.3
1949	George Rhoden	46.4
1950	George Rhoden	46.5
1951	George Rhoden	46.0
1952	Mal Whitfield	46.4
1956	Tom Courtney	45.8
1959	Eddie Southern	46.1
1960	Otis Davis	45.8
1964	Mike Larrabee	46.2
1968	Lee Evans	45.0
1972	Lee Evans	45.0
1974	Maurice Peoples	45.2
1975	David Jenkins	44.93
1976	Maxie Parks	44.82

880-Yard Run

1876	H. Lambe	2:10.0
1877	R. R. Colgate	2:04¾

1878	Edward Merritt	2:05¼
1879	Lon E. Myers	2:01.4
1880	Lon E. Myers	2:04.6
1881	William Smith	2:04.0
1882	W. H. Goodwin, Jr.	1:57⅞
1883	T. J. Murphy	2:04.4
1884	Lon E. Myers	2:09.8
1885	H. L. Mitchell	2:02.6
1886	C. M. Smith	2:04.0
1887	G. Tracy	2:01.6
1888	G. Tracy	2:02.2
1889	R. A. Ward	2:06.2
1890	H. L. Dadman	1:59.2
1891	Walter C. Downs	2:04.2
1892	T. B. Turner	1:58.6
1893	T. B. Turner	2:01.8
1894	Charles H. Kilpatrick	1:55.8
1895	Charles H. Kilpatrick	1:56.4
1896	Charles H. Kilpatrick	1:57.6
1897	J. W. Cregan	1:58.6
1898	Thomas E. Burke	2:00.4
1899	H. E. Manvel	1:58.2
1900	Alex Grant	2:04.2
1901	H. H. Hayes	2:02.8
1902	J. H. Wright	1:59.6
1903	Howard V. Valentine	2:02.8
1904	Howard V. Valentine	2:00.8
1905	James D. Lightbody	2:03.6
1906	Mel Sheppard	1:55.4
1907	Mel Sheppard	1:55.2
1908	Mel Sheppard	1:55.6
1909	Clarence Edmundson	1:55.2
1910	Harry Gissing	2:01.8
1911	Mel Sheppard	1:54.2
1912	Mel Sheppard	1:57.4
1913	Homer Baker	2:00.2
1914	Homer Baker	1:57.6
1915	L. Campbell	2:01.0
1916	Don M. Scott	1:54.0
1917	Michael A. Devaney	1:57.0
1918	T. S. Campbell	1:56.8
1919	Joie W. Ray	1:56.0
1920	Earl Eby	1:54.2
1921	Alan B. Helffrich	1:54.8
1922	Alan B. Helffrich	1:56.3
1923	Ray B. Watson	1:57.2
1924	Edward Kirby	1:58.9
1925	Alan B. Helffrich	1:56.6
1926	Alvo Martin	1:53.6
1927	Ray B. Watson	1:53.6
1929	Phil Edwards	1:55.7
1930	Edwin Genung	1:53.4
1931	Edwin Genung	1:52.6
1953	Mal Whitfield	1:51.5
1954	Mal Whitfield	1:50.8
1955	Arnold Sowell	1:47.6
1957	Tom Courtney	1:50.1
1958	Tom Courtney	1:49.2
1961	James Dupree	1:48.5
1962	Jerry Siebert	1:47.1
1963	Bill Crothers	1:46.8
1965	Morgan Groth	1:47.7
1966	Tom Farrell	1:47.6
1967	Wade Bell	1:46.1
1969	Byron Dyce	1:46.6
1970	Ken Swenson	1:47.4
1971	Juris Luzins	1:47.1
1973	Rick Wohlhuter	1:45.6

800-Meter Run

1928	Lloyd Hahn	1:51.4
1932	Edwin Genung	1:52.6

1933	Glenn Cunningham	1:51.8
1934	Ben Eastman	1:50.8
1935	Elroy Robinson	1:53.1
1936	Charles Beetham	1:50.3
1937	John Woodruff	1:50.0
1938	Howard Borck	1:51.5
1939	Charles Beetham	1:51.7
1940	Charles Beetham	1:51.1
1941	Charles Beetham	1:50.2
1942	John Borican	1:51.2
1943	William Hulse	1:53.4
1944	Robert Kelly	1:51.8
1945	Robert Kelly	1:54.1
1946	John Fulton	1:52.7
1947	Reginald Pearman	1:50.9
1948	Herbert Barten	1:51.3
1949	Mal Whitfield	1:50.5
1950	Mal Whitfield	1:51.8
1951	Mal Whitfield	1:52.9
1952	Reginald Pearman	1:53.5
1956	Arnold Sowell	1:47.6
1959	Tom Murphy	1:47.9
1960	James Cerveny	1:48.4
1964	Jerry Siebert	1:47.5
1968	Wade Bell	1:45.4
1972	Dave Wottle	1:47.3
1974	Rick Wohlhuter	1:43.9
1975	Mark Enyart	1:44.87
1976	James Robinson	1:46.6

1-Mile Run

1876	H. Lambe	4:51.2
1877	R. Morgan	4:49¾
1878	T. H. Smith	4:51¼
1879	H. M. Pellatt	4:42.4
1880	H. Fredericks	4:30.6
1881	H. Fredericks	4:32.6
1882	H. Fredericks	4:36.4
1883	H. Fredericks	4:36.8
1884	P. C. Mederia	4:36.8
1885	G. Y. Gilbert	4:41.2
1886	Edward C. Carter	4:33.4
1887	Edward C. Carter	4:30.0
1888	G. M. Gibbs	4:27.2
1889	A. B. George	4:36.0
1890	A. B. George	4:24.8
1891	Thomas P. Conneff	4:30.6
1892	George W. Orton	4:27.8
1893	George W. Orton	4:32.8
1894	George W. Orton	4:24.4
1895	George W. Orton	4:36.0
1896	George W. Orton	4:47.0
1897	J. F. Cregan	4:27.6
1898	J. F. Cregan	4:47.0
1899	Alex Grant	4:28.2
1900	George W. Orton	4:42.4
1901	Alex Grant	4:36.4
1902	Alex Grant	4:35.8
1903	Alex Grant	4:52.0
1904	D. C. Munson	4:41.2
1905	James D. Lightbody	4:48.8
1906	F. A. Rodgers	4:22.8
1907	J. P. Sullivan	4:29.0
1908	H. L. Trube	4:25.0
1909	Joe Ballard	4:30.2
1910	J. W. Monument	4:31.0
1911	Abel R. Kiviat	4:19.6
1912	Abel R. Kiviat	4:18.6
1913	Norman S. Taber	4:26.4
1914	Abel R. Kiviat	⊙25.2
1915	Joie W. Ray	4:23.2
1916	I. A. Myer	4:22.0
1917	Joie W. Ray	4:18.4

1918	Joie W. Ray	4:20.0
1919	Joie W. Ray	4:14.4
1920	Joie W. Ray	4:16.2
1921	Joie W. Ray	4:16.8
1922	Joie W. Ray	4:17.0
1923	Joie W. Ray	4:18.0
1924	Ray Buker	4:24.8
1925	Ray Buker	4:19.4
1926	Lloyd Hahn	4:16.0
1927	Ray Conger	4:23.6
1929	Leo Lermond	4:24.6
1930	Ray Conger	4:19.8
1931	Leo Lermond	4:15.0
1953	Wes Santee	4:07.6
1954	Fred Dwyer	4:09.5
1955	Wes Santee	4:11.5
1957	Merv Lincoln	4:06.1
1958	Herb Elliott	3:57.9
1961	Dyrol Burleson	4:04.9
1962	James Beatty	3:57.9
1963	Dyrol Burleson	3:56.7
1965	Jim Ryun	3:55.3
1966	Jim Ryun	3:58.6
1967	Jim Ryun	3:51.1
1969	Marty Liquori	3:59.5
1970	Howell Michael	4:01.8
1971	Marty Liquori	3:56.5
1973	Len Hilton	3:55.9

1,500-Meter Run

1928	Ray Conger	3:55.0
1932	Norwood P. Hallowell	3:52.7
1933	Glenn Cunningham	3:52.3
1934	William R. Bonthron	3:48.8
1935	Glenn Cunningham	3:52.1
1936	Glenn Cunningham	3:54.2
1937	Glenn Cunningham	3:51.8
1938	Glenn Cunningham	3:52.5
1939	Blaine Rideout	3:51.5
1940	Walter Mehl	3:47.9
1941	Leslie MacMitchell	3:53.1
1942	Gilbert Dodds	3:50.2
1943	Gilbert Dodds	3:50.0
1944	William Hulse	3:54.3
1945	Roland Sink	3:58.4
1946	Lennart Strand	3:54.5
1947	Gerald Karver	3:52.9
1948	Gilbert Dodds	3:52.1
1949	John Twomey	3:52.6
1950	John Twomey	3:51.3
1951	Leonard Truex	3:52.0
1952	Wes Santee	3:49.3
1956	Jerome Walters	3:48.4
1959	Dyrol Burleson	3:47.5
1960	James Grelle	3:42.7
1964	Tom O'Hara	3:38.1
1968	John Mason	3:43.1
1972	Jerome Howe	3:38.2
1974	Rod Dixon	3:37.5
1975	Len Hilton	3:38.26
1976	Eamonn Coghlan	3:42.41

3-Mile Run

1953	Charles Capozzoli	14:28.2
1954	Horace Ashenfelter	14:18.5
1955	Horace Ashenfelter	14:45.2
1957	John Macy	13:55.0
1958	Alex Henderson	13:37.1
1961	Laszlo Tabori	13:50.0
1962	Murray Halberg	13:30.6
1963	Pat Clohessy	13:40.4
1965	Bob Schul	13:10.4
1966	George Young	13:27.4

1967	Gerry Lindgren	13:10.6
1969	Tracy Smith	13:18.4
1970	Frank Shorter	13:24.2
1971	Steve Prefontaine	12:58.6
1973	Steve Prefontaine	12:53.4

5,000-Meter Run

1932	Ralph Hill	14:55.7
1933	John Follows	15:27.0
1934	Frank Crowley	15:18.6
1935	Joseph P. McCluskey	15:14.1
1936	Donald Lash	15:04.8
1937	Joseph P. McCluskey	15:04.1
1938	J. Gregory Rice	15:15.0
1939	J. Gregory Rice	14:50.9
1940	J. Gregory Rice	14:33.4
1941	J. Gregory Rice	14:45.2
1942	J. Gregory Rice	14:39.7
1943	Gunder Hagg	14:48.5
1944	James Rafferty	15:22.3
1945	John Kandl	16:14.4
1946	Francis Martin	15:50.7
1947	Curtis Stone	15:02.7
1948	Curtis Stone	14:49.1
1949	Fred Wilt	14:49.3
1950	Fred Wilt	15:19.4
1951	Fred Wilt	14:47.5
1952	Curtis Stone	15:03.3
1956	Dick Hart	14:47.4
1959	William Dellinger	14:47.6
1960	William Dellinger	14:26.4
1964	Bob Schul	13:56.2
1968	Bob Day	13:50.4
1972	Mike Keogh	13:51.7
1974	Dick Buerkle	13:33.4
1975	Marty Liquori	13:29.00
1976	Dick Buerkle	13:31.2

5-Mile Run

1880	J. H. Gifford	27:51.2
1881	W. C. Davies	27:43.4
1882	T. F. Delaney	27:34.4
1883	T. F. Delaney	26:47.4
1884	G. Stonebridge	27:45.0
1885	P. D. Skillman	27:13.4
1886	Edward C. Carter	27.04.0
1887	Edward C. Carter	25:23.6
1888	Thomas P. Conneff	26:46.4
1889	Thomas P. Conneff	26:42.0
1890	Thomas P. Conneff	25:37.8
1891	Thomas P. Conneff	27:38.4
1892	William D. Day	25:54.4
1893	William D. Day	26:08.4
1894	C. H. Bean	26:53.4
1895–98	No competition	
1899	Alex Grant	28:30.8
	R. Grant	28:30.8
1900	A. L. Newton	27:41.4
1901	F. M. Kanaly	25:44.8
1902	Alex Grant	26:32.0
1903	No competition	
1904	John Joyce	28:25.2
1905	Frank Verner	28:57.6
1906	William Nelson	26:22.6
1907	John J. Daly	26:04.0
1908	Frederick G. Bellars	26:14.8
1909	H. McLean	26:09.6
1910	W. J. Kramer	27:06.4
1911	George V. Bonhag	25:50.4
1912	Hannes Kolehmainen	25:43.4
1913	Hannes Kolehmainen	26:10.6
1914	Willi Kyronen	25:52.4
1915	Hannes Kolehmainen	25:50.2

1916	Joie W. Ray	26:11.6
1917	Charles Pores	26:26.4
1918	Charles Pores	24:36.8
1919	Charles Pores	26:02.0
1920	No competition	
1921	R. Earl Johnson	25:53.4
1922	R. Earl Johnson	25:33.0
1923	R. Earl Johnson	26:52.0
1924	Ilmar Prim	26:20.4
(Discontinued)		

6-Mile Run

1925	George W. Lermond	31:34.6
1926	Philip Osif	31:31.0
1927	Willi Ritola	30:43.4
1929	Louis Gregory	33:47.7
1930	Louis Gregory	31:31.3
1931	Louis Gregory	31:26.4
1953	Curtis Stone	31:18.2
1954	Curtis Stone	31:39.4
1955	Dick Hart	31:58.5
1957	Doug Kyle	29:22.8
1958	John Macy	29:25.6
1961	John Gutknecht	28:52.6
1962	Bruce Kidd	28:23.1
1963	Pete McArdle	28:29.2
1965	Billy Mills	27:11.6
1966	Tracy Smith	28:02.0
1967	Van Nelson	28:18.8
1969	Frank Shorter	29:00.2
1970	J. Bacheler	27:24.0
	Frank Shorter	27:24.0
1971	Frank Shorter	27:27.2
1973	Gordon Minty	27:20.8

10,000-Meter Run

1928	Joie W. Ray	31:28.4
1932	Thomas Ottey	32:18.2
1933	Louis Gregory	32:39.4
1934	Eino Pentti	33:34.2
1935	Thomas Ottey	32:07.3
1936	Donald Lash	31:06.9
1937	Eino Pentti	32:02.0
1938	Eino Pentti	32:15.6
1939	Louis Gregory	33:11.5
1940	Donald Lash	32:29.2
1941	Louis Gregory	33:11.0
1942	Joseph P. McCluskey	32:28.3
1943	Louis Gregory	33:22.0
1944	Norman Bright	33:53.0
1945	Ted Vogel	35:30.7
1946	Edward O'Toole	32:17.5
1947	Edward O'Toole	33:28.3
1948	Edward O'Toole	32:29.7
1949	Fred Wilt	31:05.7
1950	Horace Ashenfelter	32:44.3
1951	Curtis Stone	32:30.7
1952	Curtis Stone	30:33.4
1956	Max Truex	30:52.0
1959	Max Truex	31:22.4
1960	Al Lawrence	30:11.4
1964	Pete McArdle	30:11.0
1968	Tracy Smith	28:47.0
1972	Greg Fredericks	28:08.0
1974	Frank Shorter	28:16.0
1975	Frank Shorter	28:02.17
1976	Ed Leddy	28:46.0

120-Yard High Hurdles

1876	George Hitchcock	19.0
1877	H. E. Ficken	18¼
1878	H. E. Ficken	17¼
1879	J. E. A. Haigh	19.0

1880	H. H. Moritz	19.2
1881	J. T. Tivey	19⅛
1882	J. T. Tivey	16.8
1883	S. A. Safford	19.4
1884	S. A. Safford	18.2
1885	Alexander A. Jordan	17.6
1886	Alexander A. Jordan	16.5
1887	Alexander A. Jordan	16.4
1888	Alexander A. Jordan	16.2
1889	C. Schwegler	17.0
1890	Fred T. Ducharme	16.0
1891	Alfred F. Copeland	16.0
1892	F. C. Puffer	15.4*
1893	F. C. Puffer	16.0
1894	Stephen Chase	15.6
1895	Stephen Chase	15¾
1896	W. B. Rogers	16.2
1897	J. H. Thompson, Jr.	16.0
1898	Alvin C. Kraenzlein	15.2
1899	Alvin C. Kraenzlein	15.8
1900	R. F. Hutchison	16.2
1901	W. T. Fishleigh	16.2
1902	R. H. Hatfield	17.8
1903	Frederick W. Schule	16.6
1904	F. Castleman	16.2
1905	Hugo Friend	16.2
1906	W. M. Armstrong	16.0
1907	Forrest Smithson	15.6
1908	Arthur B. Shaw	15.2
1909	Forrest Smithson	15.2
1910	J. Case	15.8
1911	Arthur B. Shaw	15.6
1912	John P. Nicholson	15.8
1913	Frederick W. Kelly	16.4
1914	H. Goelitz	16.2
1915	Fred Murray	15.0*
1916	Robert Simpson	14.8
1917	Harold E. Barron	15.0
1918	Earl J. Thomson	15.2
1919	Robert Simpson	15.2
1920	Harold E. Barron	15.2
1921	Earl J. Thomson	15.0
1922	Earl J. Thomson	15.3
1923	Karl W. Anderson	15.1
1924	Ivan H. Riley	15.4
1925	George Guthrie	14.6*
1926	Leighton Dye	14.6
1927	C. D. Werner	14.6
1929	Stephen E. Anderson	14.9
1930	Stephen E. Anderson	14.4
1931	Percy Beard	14.2
1953	Jack Davis	13.9
1954	Jack Davis	14.0
1955	Milt Campbell	13.9
1957	Lee Calhoun	14.2
1958	Hayes Jones	13.8
1961	Hayes Jones	13.6
1962	Jerry Tarr	13.4
1963	Hayes Jones	13.4
1965	Willie Davenport	13.6
1966	Willie Davenport	13.3
1967	Willie Davenport	13.3
1969	Willie Davenport	13.3
	Leon Coleman	13.3
1970	Tom Hill	13.3
1971	Rod Milburn	13.1
1973	Tom Hill	13.2

110-Meter High Hurdles

1928	Stephen E. Anderson	14.8
1932	Jack Keller	14.4
1933	John Morriss	14.3
1934	Percy Beard	14.6
1935	Percy Beard	14.2*
1936	Forrest Towns	14.2
1937	Allan Tolmich	14.5
1938	Fred Wolcott	14.3
1939	Joe Batiste	14.1
1940	Fred Wolcott	13.9
1941	Fred Wolcott	13.7
1942	Bill Cummins	14.1
1943	Bill Cummins	14.3
1944	Owen Cassidy	14.9
1945	Charles Morgan	14.9
1946	Harrison Dillard	14.2
1947	Harrison Dillard	14.0
1948	William Porter	14.1
1949	Craig Dixon	13.8
1950	Richard Attlesey	13.6
1951	Richard Attlesey	13.8
1952	Harrison Dillard	13.7
1956	Lee Calhoun	13.6
1959	Lee Calhoun	14.0
1960	Hayes Jones	13.6
1964	Hayes Jones	13.8
1968	Earl McCulloch	13.5
1972	Rod Milburn	13.4
1974	Charles Foster	13.4
1975	Gerald Wilson	13.38
1976	Tom Hill	13.64

220-Yard Low Hurdles

1887	Alfred F. Copland	27.0
1888	Alfred F. Copland	26.8
1889	Alfred F. Copland	26.6
1890	Fred T. Ducharme	25.8
1891	H. H. Morrell	25.2
1892	F. C. Puffer	25.8
1893	F. C. Puffer	25.4
1894	F. C. Puffer	25.6
1895	S. A. Syme	28.2
1896	J. Buck	25.4
1897	Alvin C. Kraenzlein	25.0
1898	Alvin C. Kraenzlein	25.4
1899	Alvin C. Kraenzlein	26.2
1900	Henry Arnold	27.4
1901	Henry Arnold	26.0
1902	Harry L. Hillman	27.2
1903	M. Bockman	26.0
1904	J. S. Hill	25.2
1905	Frank Waller	25.8
1906	Harry L. Hillman	25.2
1907	John J. Eller	25.2
1908	John J. Eller	24.8
1909	Joe Malcolmson	25.0
1910	John J. Eller	25.2
1911	John J. Eller	24.8
1912	John J. Eller	25.2
1913	C. Cory	25.6
1914	Joseph Loomis	24.8
1915	Feg Murray	23.6*
1916	Feg Murray	24.0
1917	Frank F. Loomis	24.8
1918	Frank F. Loomis	24.2
1919	Robert Simpson	24.4
1920	No competition	
1921	Earl J. Thomson	24.6
1922	J. S. Taylor	24.6
1923	Charles R. Brookins	24.5
1924	Herbert Meyer	24.3
1925	Charles R. Brookins	23.4*
1926	Kenneth Grumbles	24.0
1927	Robert Maxwell	24.2
1929	Stephen E. Anderson	24.1
1930	Robert Maxwell	24.1
1931	Robert Maxwell	23.5

Robin Campbell, left, and Mary Decker lead around the final turn of the 800-m run; Russia's Valentina Gerasimova is on the inside. *(W. J. Wallace, Duke University.)*

1953	Jack Davis	23.7
1954	Jack Davis	23.2
1955	Charles Pratt	23.5
1957	Elias Gilbert	22.5
1958	Fran Washington	23.1
1961	Don Styron	23.2
1962	Jerry Tarr	22.6
(Discontinued)		

200-Meter Low Hurdles

1928	Frank J. Cuhel	23.6
1932	George Saling	23.6
1933	Heye Lambertus	23.5
1934	Philip Good	24.5
1935	Dale Schofield	23.2*
1936	James H. Hucker	23.8
1937	Allan Tolmich	23.3
1938	Fred Wolcott	23.6
1939	Fred Wolcott	22.9
1940	Fred Wolcott	22.6
1941	Fred Wolcott	22.8
1942	Bob Wright	23.5
1943	Bill Cummins	22.8
1944	Elmore Harris	24.1
1945	Ronald Frazier	24.0
1946	Harrison Dillard	23.3
1947	Harrison Dillard	23.3
1948	Madill Gartiser	23.9
1949	Craig Dixon	22.6
1950	William Fleming	23.6
1951	Jack Davis	23.2
1952	Ralph Person	22.5
1956	Charles Pratt	22.8
1959	Charles Tidwell	22.6
1960	Richard Howard	23.3
(Discontinued)		

440-Yard Intermediate Hurdles

1914	William H. Meanix	54.8
1915	William H. Meanix	52.6*
1916	W. A. Hummel	54.8
1917	Floyd Smart	55.6
1918	D. Hause	59.0
1919	Floyd Smart	55.6
1920	Frank F. Loomis	55.0
1921	August Desch	53.4
1922	Joseph Hall	56.5
1923	Ivan H. Riley	55.4
1924	F. Morgan Taylor	54.5
1925	F. Morgan Taylor	53.8*
1926	F. Morgan Taylor	55.0
1927	John A. Gibson	52.6
1929	Gordon Allott	54.3
1930	Richard Pomeroy	53.1
1931	Victor Burke	54.2
1953	Josh Culbreath	52.5
1954	Josh Culbreath	52.0
1955	Josh Culbreath	52.0
1957	Glenn Davis	50.9
1958	Glenn Davis	50.9
1961	Clifton Cashman	50.9
1962	Willie Atterbury	50.5
1963	Rex Cawley	50.4
1965	Rex Cawley	50.3
1966	Jim Miller	50.1
1967	Ron Whitney	50.3
1969	Ralph Mann	50.1
1970	Ralph Mann	49.8

1971	Ralph Mann	49.3
1973	Jim Bolding	49.2

400-Meter Intermediate Hurdles

1928	F. Morgan Taylor	52.0
1932	Joseph Healy	53.5
1933	Glenn Hardin	52.2
1934	Glenn Hardin	51.8
1935	Thomas Moore	53.5
1936	Glenn Hardin	51.6
1937	Jack Patterson	52.3
1938	Jack Patterson	52.8
1939	Roy V. Cochran	51.9
1940	Carl McBain	51.6
1941	Arky Erwin	54.5
1942	J. Walter Smith	52.0
1943	Arky Erwin	53.1
1944	Arky Erwin	54.0
1945	Arky Erwin	53.7
1946	Arky Erwin	55.5
1947	J. Walter Smith	52.3
1948	Roy V. Cochran	52.3
1949	Charles Moore, Jr.	51.1
1950	Charles Moore, Jr.	53.6
1951	Charles Moore, Jr.	51.4
1952	Charles Moore, Jr.	51.2
1956	Glenn Davis	50.9
1959	Richard Howard	50.7
1960	Glenn Davis	50.1
1964	Billy Hardin	50.1
1968	Ron Whitney	49.6
1972	Richard Bruggeman	50.0
1974	Jim Bolding	48.9
1975	Ralph Mann	48.74
1976	Tom Andrews	48.55

2-Mile Steeplechase

1889	Albert B. George	11:17.4
1890	William T. Young	10:50.4
1891	Ernest W. Hjertberg	11:34.6
1892	Ernest W. Hjertberg	13:10.0
1893	George W. Orton	12:02.0
1894	George W. Orton	12:38.8
1895	No competition	
1896	George W. Orton	10:58.6
1897	Geoge W. Orton	12:08.4
1898	George W. Orton	11:41.8
1899	George W. Orton	11:44.6
1900	Alex Grant	12:19.4
1901	George W. Orton	11:58.0
1902	A. L. Newton	12:28.8
1903	No competition	
1904	John J. Daly	10:51.8
1905	Harvey Cohn	12:05.2
1906–15	No competition	
1916	Michael A. Devaney	10:48.0
1917–18	No competition	
1919	Michael A. Devaney	10:17.4
1921	Michael A. Devaney	11:34.0
1922	Michael A. Devaney	11:10.2
1923	Willi Ritola	10:45.6
1924	Marvin Rick	10:43.2
1925	Russell Payne	10:40.8
1926	Willi Ritola	10:34.2
1927	Willi Ritola	10:19.4
1929	David Abbott	10:59.1
1930	Joseph P. McCluskey	10:44.2
1931	Joseph P. McCluskey	10:11.6
1953	Horace Ashenfelter	10:02.5
1954	William Ashenfelter	10:08.2
1955	Ken Reiser	10:20.7
1957	Charles Jones	9:49.6
1963	Pat Traynor	8:51.2

1965	George Young	8:50.6
1966	Pat Traynor	8:40.6
1967	Pat Traynor	8:42.0

3,000-Meter Steeplechase

1920	Paty Flynn	9:58.2
1928	William O. Spencer	9:35.8
1932	Joseph P. McCluskey	9:14.5
1933	Joseph P. McCluskey	9:38.5
1934	Harold Manning	9:15.1
1935	Joseph P. McCluskey	9:30.3
1936	Harold Manning	9:15.1
1937	Floyd Lochner	9:26.6
1938	Joseph P. McCluskey	9:23.3
1939	Joseph P. McCluskey	9:23.1
1940	Joseph P. McCluskey	9:16.6
1941	Forest Efaw	9:13.7
1942	George DeGeorge	9:16.5
1943	Joseph P. McCluskey	9:39.7
1944	Forest Efaw	9:39.6
1945	James Wisner	10:00.6
1946	James Rafferty	10:01.0
1947	Forest Efaw	9:32.5
1948	Forest Efaw	9:32.9
1949	Curtis Stone	9:31.0
1950	Warren Druetzler	9:33.6
1951	Horace Ashenfelter	9:24.5
1952	Robert McMullen	9:25.3
1956	Horace Ashenfelter	9:04.1
1958	Charles Jones	8:57.3
1959	Philip Coleman	9:19.3
1960	Philip Coleman	8:55.6
1961	Charles Jones	8:48.0
1962	George Young	8:48.2
1967	Pat Traynor	8:42.2
1968	George Young	8:30.5
1969	Mike Manley	8:36.6
1970	Bill Reilly	8:34.8
1971	Sid Sink	8:26.4
1972	James Dare	8:33.7
1973	Doug Brown	8:26.8
1974	Jim Johnson	8:28.8
1975	Randall Smith	8:28:16
1976	Randall Smith	8:26.71

High Jump

1876	H. E. Ficken	5-5
1877	H. E. Ficken	5-4
1878	H. E. Ficken	5-5
1879	W. Wunder	5-7
1880	A. L. Carroll	5-5
1881	C. W. Durand	5-8
1882	A. L. Carroll	5-7
1883	Maxwell W. Ford	5-8½
1884	J. T. Rindhart	5-8
1885	William B. Page	5-8⅞
1886	William B. Page	5-9
1887	William B. Page	6-½
1888	I. D. Wester	5-8½
1889	R. K. Pritchard	5-10½
1890	H. L. Hallock	5-10
1891	Alvin Nickerson	5-8⅛
1892	Michael F. Sweeney	6-0
1893	Michael F. Sweeney	5-11
1894	Michael F. Sweeney	6-0
1895	Michael F. Sweeney	6-0
1896	C. U. Powell	5-9½
1897	Irving K. Baxter	6-2¼
1898	Irving K. Baxter	6-0
1899	Irving K. Baxter	6-0
1900	Irving K. Baxter	6-1
1901	Samuel S. Jones	6-2
1902	Irving K. Baxter	5-7½

1903	Samuel S. Jones	6-0
1904	Samuel S. Jones	5-9
1905	H. W. Kerrigan	6-1½
1906	J. Neil Patterson	5-11½
1907	Con Leahy	6-1
1908	Harry F. Porter	5-11¼
1909	Egon Erickson	5-11⅗
1910	Walter Thomassen	6-2
1911	Henry Grumpelt	6-3
	Harry F. Porter	6-3
1912	J. O. Johnstone	6-3
1913	Alma W. Richards	6-1⅜
1914	Joseph Loomis	6-1⅞
1915	George Horine	6-¾
1916	Wesley Oler, Jr.	6-2
1917	Clinton Larsen	6-2½
1918	Carl Rice	6-1
1919	John Murphy	6-3 3/16
1920	John Murphy	6-4¼
1921	D. V. Alberts	6-4
1922	D. V. Alberts	6-5⅛
1923	LeRoy Brown	6-5⅝
1924	R. L. Juday	6-4
1925	Harold M. Osborn	6-7
1926	Harold M. Osborn	6-4½
1927	Robert W. King	6-2⅝
1928	Charles E. McGinnis	6-5
	Robert W. King	6-5
1929	Henry Lasallette	6-3⅝
1930	Anton B. Burg	6-4⅞
1931	Anton B. Burg	6-5⅜
1932	Robert Van Osdel	6-6⅝
	George Spitz	6-6⅝
	Cornelius C. Johnson	6-6⅝
1933	Cornelius C. Johnson	6-7
1934	Cornelius C. Johnson	6-8⅝
	Walter Marty	6-8⅝
1935	Cornelius C. Johnson	6-7
1936	Cornelius C. Johnson	6-8
1937	David Albritton	6-8⅝
1938	Melvin Walker	6-7
1939	Les Steers	6-8⅛
1940	Les Steers	6-8¾
1941	William Stewart	6-9¾
1942	Adam Berry	6-7
1943	Peter Watkins	6-7¾
1944	Fred Sheffield	6-7
	Willard Smith	6-7
1945	David Albritton	6-5¾
	Joshua Williamson	6-5¾
	Richard Schnacke	6-5¾
	Leslie Howe	6-5¾
1946	David Albritton	6-6⅞
1947	David Albritton	6-6
1948	Tom Scofield	6-7⅝
	William A. Vessie	6-7⅝
1949	Richard Phillips	6-6⅞
1950	John Heintzmann	6-5½
	David Albritton	6-5½
	Virgil Severns	6-5½
	Jack Rapazzo	6-5½
1951	J. Lewis Hall	6-8
1952	Walter Davis	6-10½
1953	Walter Davis	6-11½
1954	Ernie Shelton	6-9¾
1955	Ernie Shelton	6-10
	Charles Dumas	6-10
1956	Charles Dumas	6-10
1957	Charles Dumas	6-10¼
1958	Charles Dumas	6-9¾
1959	Charles Dumas	6-9
1960	John Thomas	7-2
1961	Robert Avant	7-0
1962	John Thomas	6-10
1963	Gene Johnson	7-0
1964	Ed Caruthers	7-1
1965	Otis Burrell	7-0
1966	Otis Burrell	7-2
1967	Otis Burrell	7-¼
1968	Ed Hanks	6-11
1969	Otis Burrell	7-1
1970	Reynaldo Brown	7-1
1971	Reynaldo Brown	7-2
1972	Barry Schur	7-2
1973	Dwight Stones	7-5
1974	Dwight Stones	7-3⅗
1975	Tom Woods	7-5½
1976	Dwight Stones	7-4¼

Long Jump

1876	I. Frazier	17-4
1877	W. T. Livingston	18-9½
1878	William C. Wilmer	18-9
1879	F. J. Kilpatrick	19-6¾
1880	J. S. Voorhees	21-4
1881	J. S. Voorhees	21-4¾
1882	J. F. Jenkins, Jr.	21-5¾
1883	Maxwell W. Ford	21-7½
1884	Maxwell W. Ford	21-1½
1885	Maxwell W. Ford	21-1½
1886	Maxwell W. Ford	22-¾
1887	Alexander A. Jordan	22-3½
1888	W. Halpin	23-0
1889	Maxwell W. Ford	22-7½
1890	Alfred F. Copland	23-3⅛
1891	C. S. Reber	22-4½
1892	Eugene W. Goff	22-6½
1893	C. S. Reber	23-4½
1894	Eugene W. Goff	22-5
1895	E. B. Bloss	22-2
1896	E. B. Bloss	22-0
1897	E. B. Bloss	21-10½
1898	Myer Prinstein	23-7
1899	Alvin C. Kraenzlein	23-5
1900	H. P. McDonald	22-0
1901	H. P. McDonald	22-7
1902	Myer Prinstein	21-5½
1903	P. Molson	22-2½
1904	Myer Prinstein	22-4¾
1905	Hugo Friend	22-10⅛
1906	Myer Prinstein	22-4
1907	Dan Kelly	23-11
1908	Platt Adams	21-6½
1909	Frank Irons	22-5
1910	Frank Irons	23-5⅛
1911	Platt Adams	23-⅖
1912	Platt Adams	22.44
1913	P. Stiles	22-0
1914	Platt Adams	23-2
1915	H. T. Worthington	23-10
1916	H. T. Worthington	23-2½
1917	Joseph Irish	22-4¾
1918	D. Politzer	22-4
1919	Floyd Smart	22-7¼
1920	Sol Butler	24-8
1921	Edward O. Gourdin	23-7¾
1922	DeHart Hubbard	24-5⅛
1923	DeHart Hubbard	24-7¾
1924	DeHart Hubbard	24-0
1925	DeHart Hubbard	25-4⅜*
1926	DeHart Hubbard	25-2½
1927	DeHart Hubbard	25-8¾
1928	Edward B. Hamm	25-11⅛
1929	Edward I. Gordon, Jr.	24-4¼

1930	Alfred H. Bates	24-3¾
1931	Alfred H. Bates	24-7
1932	Edward Gordon	25-3⅜
1933	Jesse Owens	24-6⅜
1934	Jesse Owens	25-7⅘
1935	Eulace Peacock	26-3
1936	Jesse Owens	26-3
1937	Kermit King	25-1½
1938	William Lacefield	25-3³⁄₁₀
1939	William Lacefield	25-5½
1940	William Brown	25-1⅛
1941	William Brown	25-4½
1942	William Brown	24-3½
1943	William Christopher	24-4⅝
1944	William Lund	23-3½
1945	Herbert Douglas	24-⅛
1946	William Steele	24-0
1947	William Steele	24-9¼
1948	Fred Johnson	25-4½
1949	Gay Bryan	25-1½
1950	James Holland	25-9
1951	George Brown	25-8½
1952	George Brown	25-9
1953	George Brown	25-10¾
1954	John Bennett	24-10¼
1955	Gregory Bell	26-½
1956	Ernie Shelby	26-1¼
1957	Ernie Shelby	25-2½
1958	Ernie Shelby	25-10¼
1959	Gregory Bell	26-1¼
1960	Henck Visser	25-2
1961	Ralph Boston	26-11¼
1962	Ralph Boston	26-6
1963	Ralph Boston	26-10
1964	Ralph Boston	26-7½
1965	Ralph Boston	26-3½
1966	Ralph Boston	26-3¼
1967	Jerry Proctor	26-¾
1968	Bob Beamon	27-4
1969	Bob Beamon	26-11
1970	J. E. Moore	26-2¾
1971	Arnie Robinson	26-10¾
1972	Arnie Robinson	26-5¼
1973	Randy Williams	26-1
1974	J. E. Moore	26-5¾
1975	Arnie Robinson	26-5
1976	Arnie Robinson	27-3½

Pole Vault

1877	C. McNichol	9-7
1878	A. Ing	9-4
1879	W. J. Van Houten	10-4¾
1880	W. J. Van Houten	10-11
1881	W. J. Van Houten	10-6
1882	B. F. Richardson	10-0
1883	Hugh H. Baxter	11-½
1884	Hugh H. Baxter	10-6
1885	Hugh H. Baxter	10-3
1886	Hugh H. Baxter	10-1½
1887	T. Ray	11-¾
1888	L. D. Godshall	10-0
1889	E. L. Stone	10-0
1890	W. S. Rodenbaugh	10-6
1891	T. Luce	10-6½
1892	T. Luce	11-0
1893	C. T. Buchholz	10-6
1894	C. T. Buchholz	11-0
1895	H. Thomas	10-0
1896	F. W. Allis	10-5
1897	J. L. Hurlburt, Jr.	11-1
1898	Raymond G. Clapp	10-9
1899	Irving K. Baxter	10-9

1900	Bascom Johnson	11-3
1901	Charles E. Dvorak	11-3
1902	A. G. Anderson	10-9
1903	Charles E. Dvorak	11-0
1904	H. L. Gardner	10-5¼
1905	E. C. Glover	11-6
1906	LeRoy Samse	11-6
1907	Edward T. Cooke, Jr.	12-3
1908	W. Happenny	11-9
1909	R. Paulding	11-0
1910	Harry S. Babcock	12-1
1911	Edward T. Cooke, Jr.	12-6
	H. Coyle	12-6
	S. Bellah	12-6
1912	Harry S. Babcock	12-0
1913	S. B. Wagoner	13-0
1914	K. R. Curtis	12-3
1915	S. Bellah	12-9
1916	S. Landers	12-9
1917	Ed Knourek	12-9
1918	C. Buck	12-3
1919	Frank K. Foss	12-9
1920	Frank K. Foss	13-1
1921	Ed Knourek	12-7½
1922	Ed Knourek	13-0
1923	E. E. Meyers	13-1
1924	E. E. Meyers	13-0
1925	Harry Smith	12-11½
1926	Paul Harrington	13-0
1927	Lee Barnes	13-0
1928	Lee Barnes	13-9
1929	Fred Sturdy	13-9¼
1930	Fred Sturdy	13-6
1931	Jack Wool	13-4½
1932	William Graber	14-4⅜
1933	Matt Gordy	14-0
	Keith Brown	14-0
1934	Keith Brown	13-11⅜
	William Graber	13-11⅜
	Wirt Thompson	13-11⅜
1935	Earle Meadows	13-10⅜
	William Sefton	13-10⅜
1936	George Varoff	14-6½
1937	William Sefton	14-7⅝
1938	Cornelius Warmerdam	14-5½
1939	George Varoff	14-4
1940	Cornelius Warmerdam	15-1⅛
1941	Cornelius Warmerdam	15-0
1942	Cornelius Warmerdam	15-2½
1943	Cornelius Warmerdam	15-0
1944	Cornelius Warmerdam	15-0
1945	A. Richmond Morcom	13-6
	Robert Phelps	13-6
1946	Irving Moore	14-4¾
1947	A. Richmond Morcom	14-0
1948	A. Richmond Morcom	14-6
	Robert Richards	14-6
1949	Robert Richards	14-4
1950	Robert Richards	14-8
1951	Robert Richards	14-4
1952	Robert Richards	14-8
	Donald Laz	14-8
1953	Donald Laz	14-1
	George Mattos	14-1
1954	Robert Richards	15-3½
1955	Robert Richards	15-½
1956	Robert Richards	15-0
1957	Robert Richards	15-1½
1958	Ron Morris	14-9
1959	Donald Bragg	15-3
1960	Aubrey Dooley	15-3¾
1961	Ron Morris	15-8

1962	Ron Morris	16-¼
1963	Brian Sternberg	16-4
1964	Fred Hansen	17-0
1965	John Pennel	17-0
1966	Bob Seagren	17-0
1967	Paul Wilson	17-7¾
1968	Dick Railsback	17-¼
1969	Bob Seagren	17-6
1970	Bob Seagren	17-2
1971	Jan Johnston	17-0
1972	Dave Roberts	18-¼
1973	Mike Cotton	17-4
1974	Dave Roberts	17-6
1975	Don Baird	17-6
1976	Earl Bell	17-10¼

Triple Jump

1893	E. B. Bloss	48-6
1894–1905	No competition	
1906	J. F. O'Connell	45-3¾
1907	Platt Adams	44-9
1908	Platt Adams	45-4
1909	Frank Irons	44.19
1910	Daniel F. Ahearn	48-¼
1911	Daniel F. Ahearn	48.16
1912	Platt Adams	45.70
1913	Daniel F. Ahearn	50-0
1914	Daniel F. Ahearn	48-6⅛
1915	Daniel F. Ahearn	50-11⅛
1916	Daniel F. Ahearn	46-½
1917	Daniel F. Ahearn	47-8
1918	Daniel F. Ahearn	46-3¾

1919	S. G. Landers	47-8½
1920	S. G. Landers	48-7⁹⁄₁₀
1921	K. Geist	46-3
1922	DeHart Hubbard	48-1½
1923	DeHart Hubbard	47-½
1924	Homer Martin	45-8¾
1925	Homer Martin	47-11¼
1926	Levi Casey	49-4¼
1927	Levi Casey	48-4¾
1928	Levi Casey	48-10⅛
1929	Robert Kelley	48-6¾
1930	Levi Casey	47-11⅝
1931	Robert Kelley	47-7½
1932	Sidney Bowman	48-11¼
1933	Nathan Blair	47-3
1934	Dudley Wilkins	48-2¼
1935	Roland Romero	50-4⅞
1936	William Brown	49-2
1937	William Brown	49-7¼
1938	Herschel Neil	48-5⁹⁄₁₀
1939	Herschel Neil	47-9⅞
1940	William Brown	50-2⅝
1941	William Brown	50-11½
1942	William Brown	48-11½
1943	William Brown	45-8
1944	Don Barksdale	47-2⅞
1945	Burton Cox	45-10⅜
1946	Ralph Tate	47-11¼
1947	Bob Beckus	45-11¼
1948	Gaylord Bryan	47-11½
1949	Gaylord Bryan	49-1
1950	Gaylord Bryan	47-11
1951	Gaylord Bryan	46-11½
1952	Walter Ashbaugh	50-8¾

Peter Shmock follows through in the shotput. *(W. J. Wallace, Duke University.)*

1953	George Shaw	47-8
1954	Claudio Cabrejas	47-3
1955	Victor Paredes	50-4
1956	Willie Hallie	49-6
1957	William Sharpe	50-4¼
1958	Ira Davis	50-8¼
1959	Ira Davis	50-6½
1960	Ira Davis	53-4½
1961	William Sharpe	52-4¾
1962	William Sharpe	52-1¼
1963	Kent Floerke	51-7¾
1964	Chris Mousaides	53-1
1965	Art Walker	53-1
1966	Art Walker	53-8
1967	Charlie Craig	53-1½
1968	Art Walker	53-9¼
1969	John Craft	52-9¼
1970	Milan Tiff	53-0
1971	John Craft	54-7
1972	John Craft	54-10
1973	John Craft	55-8¾
1974	John Craft	54-4¾
1975	Anthony Terry	54-9¾
1976	Tommy Haynes	55-9¾

Shot Put

1876	Henry E. Buermeyer	32-5
1877	Henry E. Buermeyer	37-2
1878	Henry E. Buermeyer	37-4
1879	A. W. Adams	36-3⅛
1880	A. W. Adams	36-4⅞
1881	Frank L. Lambrecht	37-5½
1882	Frank L. Lambrecht	39-9⅞
1883	Frank L. Lambrecht	43-0
1884	Frank L. Lambrecht	39-10½
1885	Frank L. Lambrecht	42-2⅜
1886	Frank L. Lambrecht	42-1¼
1887	George R. Gray	42-3
1888	George R. Gray	42-10¼
1889	George R. Gray	41-4
1890	George R. Gray	43-9
1891	George R. Gray	46-5¾**
1892	George R. Gray	43-3¾
1893	George R. Gray	47-0
1894	George R. Gray	44-8
1895	William O. Hickok	43-0
1896	George R. Gray	44-3⅛
1897	Charles H. Hennemann	42-7¾
1898	Richard Sheldon	43-8⅝
1899	Richard Sheldon	40-½
1900	Dennis Horgan	46-1¼
1901	F. G. Beck	42-11¼
1902	George R. Gray	46-5
1903	L. E. J. Feuerbach	42-11⅝
1904	Martin J. Sheridan	40-9½
1905	W. W. Coe	49-6
1906	W. W. Coe	46-10½
1907	Ralph Rose	49-6½
1908	Ralph Rose	49-½
1909	Ralph Rose	50.26
1910	Ralph Rose	49-1
1911	Patrick J. McDonald	47-9
1912	Patrick J. McDonald	48.51
1913	L. A. Whitney	46-2⅝
1914	Patrick J. McDonald	46-3½
1915	Arlie Mucks	48-11¾
1916	Arlie Mucks	47-2⅛
1917	Arlie Mucks	45-10⅝
1918	A. Richards	42-3¾
1919	Patrick J. McDonald	45-8
1920	Patrick J. McDonald	47-¼

**Shot only 15½ pounds

1921	Clarence Houser	46-11¾
1922	Patrick J. McDonald	46-11⅞
1923	O. Wanzer	47-⅝
1924	Ralph G. Hills	46-5¾
1925	Clarence Houser	50-1
1926	Herbert Schwarze	49-10⅞
1927	John Kuck	48-5
1928	Herman Brix	50-11¾
1929	Herman Brix	50-2½
1930	Herman Brix	52-5¾
1931	Herman Brix	50-8¼
1932	Leo J. Sexton	52-8
1933	Jack Torrance	51-4⅞
1934	Jack Torrance	55-5
1935	Jack Torrance	51-6¼
1936	Dmitri Zaitz	50-7⅝
1937	James Reynolds	51-7⅛
1938	Francis Ryan	52-1½
1939	Lilburn Williams	53-7
1940	Alfred C. Blozis	55-⅜
1941	Alfred C. Blozis	54-⅝
1942	Alfred C. Blozis	53-8⅜
1943	Earl Audet	52-11⅜
1944	Earl Audet	52-8
1945	Wilfred Bangert	52-10
1946	Wilfred Bangert	52-2½
1947	Francis Delaney	52-9½
1948	Francis Delaney	53-8¼
1949	James Fuchs	57-2⅛
1950	James Fuchs	57-2⅛
1951	Parry O'Brien	55-9¼
1952	Parry O'Brien	57-4⅜
1953	Parry O'Brien	57-11¼
1954	Parry O'Brien	58-5¾
1955	Parry O'Brien	58-5¾
1956	Ken Bantum	59-1½
1957	Bill Neider	61-6½
1958	Parry O'Brien	61-11¼
1959	Parry O'Brien	62-2¼
1960	Parry O'Brien	62-6¼
1961	Dallas Long	62-2
1962	Garry Gubner	63-6½
1963	Dave Davis	62-5¾
1964	Randy Matson	64-11
1965	John McGrath	63-0
1966	Randy Matson	64-2½
1967	Randy Matson	66-11
1968	Randy Matson	67-5
1969	Neil Steinhauer	67-4
1970	Randy Matson	67-10¼
1971	Karl Saab	67-2¾
1972	Randy Matson	69-6½
1973	Al Feuerbach	68-1
1974	Al Feuerbach	70-9¾
1975	Al Feuerbach	68-10¾
1976	Terry Albritton	69-4¾

Discus

1897	Charles H. Hennemann	118-9
1898	Charles H. Hennemann	108-8⅝
1899	Richard Sheldon	not available
1900	Richard Sheldon	114-0
1901	Martin J. Sheridan	111-9½
1902	Martin J. Sheridan	113-7
1903	J. H. Maddock	113-0
1904	Martin J. Sheridan	119-1½
1905	Ralph Rose	117-5
1906	Martin J. Sheridan	129-10
1907	Martin J. Sheridan	129-5¾
1908	M. F. Horr	132-9
1909	Ralph Rose	131-8
1910	M. H. Giffin	135-6¼
1911	Martin J. Sheridan	133-9½

1912	E. Muller	130.22
1913	E. Muller	132-7⅛
1914	E. Muller	137-½
1915	Arlie Mucks	146-9¼
1916	Arlie Mucks	145-4½
1917	Arlie Mucks	140-1½
1918	E. Muller	136-0
1919	Arlie Mucks	143-9¾
1920	August R. Pope	146-5
1921	August R. Pope	144-0
1922	August R. Pope	145-11
1923	Thomas J. Lieb	151-3¾
1924	Thomas J. Lieb	144-7¼
1925	Clarence Houser	156-6
1926	Clarence Houser	153-6½
1927	Eric C. W. Krenz	146-10
1928	Clarence Houser	153-6¼
1929	Eric C. W. Krenz	157-2
1930	Paul B. Jessup	169-8⅞
1931	Paul B. Jessup	152-5¼
1932	John Anderson	165.54
1933	John Anderson	165-1½
1934	Robert Jones	155-11
1935	Kenneth Carpenter	158-11½
1936	Kenneth Carpenter	166-2
1937	Phil Levy	163-7⅞
1938	Peter Zagar	167-3¼
1939	Phil Fox	172-4½
1940	Phil Fox	170-4½
1941	Archie Harris	167-9½
1942	Robert Fitch	166-10
1943	Hugh Cannon	161-2
1944	Hugh Cannon	162-1
1945	Jack Donaldson	151-2
1946	Robert Fitch	179-⅛
1947	Fortune Gordien	174-1½
1948	Fortune Gordien	168-5
1949	Fortune Gordien	174-5⅜
1950	Fortune Gordien	173-2½
1951	Dick Doyle	175-6½
1952	Jim Dillon	175-3⅝
1953	Fortune Gordien	183-9½
1954	Fortune Gordien	182-2
1955	Parry O'Brien	175-7
1956	Ron Drummond	180-3
1957	Al Oerter	181-6
1958	Rink Babka	187-10
1959	Al Oerter	186-5
1960	Al Oerter	193-9½
1961	Jay Silvester	195-8
1962	Al Oerter	201-½
1963	Jay Silvester	198-11½
1964	Al Oerter	201-1½
1965	Ludvik Danek	205-7
1966	Al Oerter	193-9
1967	Gary Carlsen	205-10
1968	Jay Silvester	203-9
1969	Jon Cole	208-10
1970	Jay Silvester	205-4
1971	Tim Vollmer	208-4
1972	Jay Silvester	213-0
1973	Mac Wilkins	211-11
1974	John Powell	214-11
1975	John Powell	208-10
1976	Mac Wilkins	230-0

Javelin

1909	Ralph Rose	141.7
1910	B. Brodd	163-1
1911	O. F. Snedigar	165-2/10
1912	H. Lott	162.65
1913	B. Brodd	161-3
1914	George A. Bronder, Jr.	166-8½

1915	George A. Bronder, Jr.	177-7¾
1916	George A. Bronder, Jr.	190-6
1917	George A. Bronder, Jr.	184-½
1918	George A. Bronder, Jr.	169-10½
1919	George A. Bronder, Jr.	176-6
1920	Milton S. Angier	192-10¾
1921	Milton S. Angier	189-3¼
1922	Flint Hanner	193-2¼
1923	Howard Hoffman	194-7½
1924	John Leyden	181-0
1925	Henry Bonura	213-10½
1926	John Kuck	199-7
1927	Charles Harlow	193-3¾
1928	Creth B. Hines	202-1¾
1929	Jesse P. Mortensen	204.975
1930	James DeMers	222-6¾
1931	James DeMers	211-5¼
1932	Malcolm Metcalf	219.66
1933	Lee Bartlett	209-6¾
1934	Ralston Legore	216-9⁶⁄10
1935	Horace O'Dell	217-1⅝
1936	John Mottram	214-7⅜
1937	William Reitz	224-9⅜
1938	Nick Vukmanic	218-7¾
1939	Boyd Brown	215-10¾
1940	Boyd Brown	223-1⅜
1941	Boyd Brown	218-3
1942	Boyd Brown	216-7½
1943	Martin Biles	202-5
1944	Martin Biles	211-0
1945	Earl Marshall	215-4
1946	Garland Adair	213-7
1947	Stephen Seymour	248-10
1948	Stephen Seymour	230-5
1949	Franklin Held	232-2½
1950	Stephen Seymour	228-10⅞
1951	Franklin Held	241-¾
1952	Bill Miller	236-1
1953	Franklin Held	242-7
1954	Franklin Held	249-8½
1955	Franklin Held	260-3
1956	Cy Young	247-11½
1957	Bob Voiles	251-5½
1958	Franklin Held	252-½
1959	Al Cantello	246-9
1960	Al Cantello	271-9
1961	John Fromm	249-11½
1962	Dan Studney	246-6
1963	Larry Stewart	255-3
1964	Frank Covelli	253-7
1965	Bill Floerke	258-7
1966	John Tushaus	260-8
1967	Delmon McNabb	268-3
1968	Frank Covelli	269-6
1969	Mark Murro	284-3
1970	Bill Skinner	276-7
1971	Bill Skinner	267-2
1972	Fred Luke	277-5
1973	Cary Feldmann	265-3
1974	Sam Colson	280-8
1975	Richard George	272-11
1976	Fred Luke	280-8

Hammer Throw

1876	William B. Curtis	76-4
1877	G. D. Parmly	84-0
1878	William B. Curtis	80-2
1879	J. G. McDermott	85-11½
1880	William B. Curtis	87-4¼
1881	Frank L. Lambrecht	89-8
1882	Frank L. Lambrecht	93-½
1883	W. L. Coudon	93-11
1884	Frank L. Lambrecht	92-5

Mamie Rallins is just behind going over this hurdle, but she went on to win—as she usually does. *(W. J. Wallace, Duke University.)*

1885	Frank L. Lambrecht	96-10
1886	W. L. Coudon	95-3
1887	C. A. J. Queckberner	102-7
1888	William J. M. Barry	127-9
1889	James S. Mitchel	127-7½
1890	James S. Mitchel	130-8
1891	James S. Mitchel	136-1
1892	James S. Mitchel	140-11
1893	James S. Mitchel	134-8
1894	James S. Mitchel	135-9½
1895	James S. Mitchel	139-2½
1896	James S. Mitchel	134-8¾
1897	John J. Flanagan	148-5
1898	John J. Flanagan	151-10½
1899	John J. Flanagan	155-4½
1900	Martin J. Sheridan	138-2
1901	John J. Flanagan	158-10½
1902	John J. Flanagan	151-4
1903	James S. Mitchel	140-1
1904	Alfred D. Plaw	162-0
1905	Alfred D. Plaw	163-4
1906	John J. Flanagan	166-6½
1907	John J. Flanagan	171-¾
1908	Matthew J. McGrath	173-0
1909	Lee Talbott	165.8
1910	Matthew J. McGrath	168-4½
1911	Cornelius Walsh	177-6½
1912	Matthew J. McGrath	174.67
1913	Patrick J. Ryan	177-7¾
1914	Patrick J. Ryan	183-3¾
1915	Patrick J. Ryan	176-2¾
1916	Patrick J. Ryan	174-8
1917	Patrick J. Ryan	168-7½
1918	Matthew J. McGrath	173-11¼

1919	Patrick J. Ryan	175-5¾
1920	Patrick J. Ryan	169-4
1921	Patrick J. Ryan	170-7½
1922	Matthew J. McGrath	155-9
1923	Frederick D. Tootell	173-6⅝
1924	Frederick D. Tootell	173-11½
1925	Matthew J. McGrath	172-½
1926	Matthew J. McGrath	162-10¼
1927	Jack Merchant	170-7½
1928	Edmund Black	166-4¼
1929	Jack Merchant	170-6
1930	Norwood G. Wright	163-9¼
1931	Edward F. Flanagan	158-8
1932	Frank Conner	170.90
1933	Patrick O'Callaghan	161-3⅜
1934	Donald Favor	163-5¾
1935	Henry F. Dreyer	168-8½
1936	William Rowe	175-7
1937	Irving Folswarthny	173-7⅝
1938	Irving Folswarthny	179-3
1939	Chester Cruikshank	174-1½
1940	Stanley Johnson	182-6⁷⁄₁₆
1941	Irving Folswarthny	175-6⅛
1942	Chester Cruikshank	173-8½
1943	Henry F. Dreyer	164-6¾
1944	Henry F. Dreyer	166-6½
1945	Henry F. Dreyer	166-11½
1946	Irving Folsworth	169-8
1947	Robert Bennett	180-11
1948	Robert Bennett	175-7
1949	Samuel M. Felton, Jr.	176-10
1950	Samuel M. Felton, Jr.	187-3¾
1951	Samuel M. Felton, Jr.	184-2¾
1952	Thomas Bane	179-11½
1953	Martin Engel	186-9
1954	Robert Backus	189-3
1955	Harold Connolly	199-8

Reynaldo Brown is one of the world's outstanding high jumpers. (*W. J. Wallace, Duke University.*)

1956	Harold Connolly	205-10½
1957	Harold Connolly	216-3
1958	Harold Connolly	225-4
1959	Harold Connolly	216-10
1960	Harold Connolly	224-4½
1961	Harold Connolly	213-6½
1962	Al Hall	219-3
1963	Al Hall	214-11
1964	Harold Connolly	226-5½
1965	Harold Connolly	232-1
1966	Ed Burke	220-0
1967	Ed Burke	235-11
1968	Ed Burke	217-2
1969	Tom Gage	228-5
1970	George Frenn	230-0
1971	George Frenn	230-1
1972	Al Schoterman	228-1
1973	Ted Bregar	215-4
1974	Steve DeAutremont	226-6
1975	Boris Djerassi	222-10
1976	Larry Hart	225-10

Decathlon

1915	Alma Richards
1916-19	No competition
1920	Brutus Hamilton
1921	Dan Shea
1922	S. Harrison Thomson
1923	Harold M. Osborn
1924	Anthony J. Plansky
1925	Harold M. Osborn
1926	Harold M. Osborn
1927	Fait Elkins
1928	J. Kenneth Doherty
1929	J. Kenneth Doherty
1930	Wilson Charles
1931	Jess Mortensen

1932	James A. Bausch
1933	Bernard E. Berlinger
1934	Robert Clark
1935	Robert Clark
1936	Glenn Morris
1937	No competition
1938	Joseph Scott
1939	Joseph Scott
1940	William Watson
1941	John Borican
1942	William Terwilliger
1943	William Watson
1944	Irving Mondschein
1945	Charles Beaudry
1946	Irving Mondschein
1947	Irving Mondschein
1948	Robert Mathias
1949	Robert Mathias
1950	Robert Mathias
1951	Robert Richards
1952	Robert Mathias
1953	Milton Campbell
1954	Robert Richards
1955	Robert Richards
1956	Rafer Johnson
1957	Charles Pratt
1958	Rafer Johnson
1959	Chuang-Kwang Yang
1960	Rafer Johnson
1961	Paul Herman
1962	Chuang-Kwang Yang
1963	Steve Pauly
1964	Chuang-Kwang Yang
1965	Bill Toomey

1966	Bill Toomey
1967	Bill Toomey
1968	Bill Toomey
1969	Bill Toomey
1970	J. Warkentin
1971	Rick Wanamaker
1972	Jeff Bennett
1973	Jeff Bennett
1974	Bruce Jenner
1975	Fred Samaro
1976	Bruce Jenner

AAU Outdoor Champions—Women
(No meet in 1934)

50-Yard Dash

1923	Marion R. McCartie	6.6
1924	Christine Pylick	6.2
1925	Elta Cartwright	6.1
1926	Elta Cartwright	6.1
1927	Elta Cartwright	6.2
1928	Elta Cartwright	6.6
1929	Betty Robinson	5.8
1930	Mary Carew	6.2
1931	Alice Monk	6.4
1932	Dorothy Nussbaum	6.3
1955	Isabel Daniels	6.0
1957	Barbara Jones	6.2
1958	Barbara Jones	6.0

50-Meter Dash

1933	Louise Stokes	6.6
1935	Louise Stokes	6.7
1936	Ivy Wilson	6.7
1937	Claire Isicson	6.8
1938	Claire Isicson	6.6
1939	Gertrude Johnson	6.7
1940	Jean Lane	6.6
1941	Lucy Newell	6.6
1942	Jeannette Jones	6.7
1943	Alice Coachman	6.5
1944	Alice Coachman	6.4
1945	Alice Coachman	6.5
1946	Alice Coachman	6.5
1947	Alice Coachman	6.8
1948	Mabel Walker	6.7
1949	Juanita Watson	6.5
1950	Dolores Dwyer	6.7
1951	Mary McNabb	6.6
1952	Catherine Hardy	6.4
1953	Mabel Landry	6.6
1954	Mabel Landry	6.5
1956	Isabel Daniels	6.4

100-Yard Dash

1923	Frances Ruppert	12.0
1924	Frances Ruppert	12.0
1925	Helen Filkey	11.4
1926	Rosa Grosse	11.8
1927	Elta Cartwright	11.4
1929	Betty Robinson	11.2
1930	Stella Walsh	11.2
1931	Eleanor Egg	11.4
1932	Wilhelmina von Bremen	12.3
1955	Mae Faggs	10.8
1957	Barbara Jones	10.9
1958	Margaret Matthews	11.1
1961	Wilma Rudolph	10.8
1962	Wilma Rudolph	10.8
1963	Edith McGuire	11.0
1965	Wyomia Tyus	10.5
1966	Wyomia Tyus	10.5
1969	Barbara Ferrell	10.7

1970	Chi Cheng	10.1
1973	Iris Davis	10.3
1974	Renaye Bowen	10.4

100-Meter Dash

1928	Elta Cartwright	12.4
1933	Annette Rogers	12.2
1935	Helen Stephens	11.6
1936	Helen Stephens	11.7
1937	Claire Isicson	12.8
1938	Lula Hymes	12.4
1939	Olive Hasenfus	12.6
1940	Jean Lane	12.0
1941	Jean Lane	12.4
1942	Alice Coachman	12.1
1943	Stella Walsh	11.6
1944	Stella Walsh	12.0
1945	Alice Coachman	12.0
1946	Alice Coachman	12.3
1947	Juanita Watson	13.1
1948	Stella Walsh	12.9
1949	Jean Patton	12.1
1950	Jean Patton	13.3
1951	Mary McNabb	12.2
1952	Catherine Hardy	12.3
1953	Barbara Jones	11.9
1954	Barbara Jones	12.0
1956	Mae Faggs	11.7
1959	Wilma Rudolph	12.1
1960	Wilma Rudolph	11.5
1964	Wyomia Tyus	11.5
1967	Barbara Ferrell	11.1
1968	Margaret Johnson Bailes	11.1
1971	Iris Davis	11.2
1972	Alice Annum	11.5
1975	Rosalyn Bryant	11.6
1976	Chandra Cheeseborough	11.34

200-Yard Dash

1926	Frances Keddie	28.6
1927	Ellen Brough	26.8
1928	Florence Wright	27.4
1929	Maybelle Gilliland	27.4
1930	Stella Walsh	25.4
1931	Stella Walsh	26.4
1932	Olive Hasenfus	26.5
1955	Mae Faggs	25.1
1957	Isabel Daniels	24.7
1958	Lucinda Williams	24.3
1961	Lacey O'Neill	24.1
	Vivian Brown	24.1
1962	Vivian Brown	24.1
1963	Vivian Brown	24.4
1965	Edith McGuire	23.6
1966	Wyomia Tyus	23.8
1969	Barbara Ferrell	23.8
1970	Chi Cheng	22.7
1973	Mabel Ferguson	23.4
1974	Alice Annum	23.1

200-Meter Dash

1933	Olive Hasenfus	26.2
1935	Helen Stephens	24.6
1936	Beverly Hobbs	26.6
1937	Gertrude Johnson	26.0
1938	Fanny Vitale	26.7
1939	Stella Walsh	25.5
1940	Stella Walsh	26.1
1941	Jean Lane	25.2
1942	Stella Walsh	25.4
1943	Stella Walsh	26.3
1944	Stella Walsh	24.6
1945	Stella Walsh	26.6

1946	Stella Walsh	26.3
1947	Stella Walsh	26.2
1948	Stella Walsh	25.5
1949	Nell Jackson	24.2
1950	Nell Jackson	25.0
1951	Jean Patton	25.4
1952	Catherine Hardy	25.5
1953	Dolores Dwyer	24.4
1954	Mae Faggs	24.5
1956	Mae Faggs	24.6
1959	Isabelle Daniels	24.1
1960	Wilma Rudolph	22.9
1964	Edith McGuire	23.6
1967	Diana Wilson	23.6
1968	Wyomia Tyus	23.5
1971	Raelene Boyle	23.1
1972	Alice Annum	23.4
1975	Debra Armstrong	23.0
1976	Brenda Morehead	22.94

400-Yard Run

1958	Christine McKenzie	1:01.6
1961	Jackie Patterson	59.5
1962	Suzanne Knott	58.1
1963	Suzanne Knott	57.0
1964	Janell Smith	54.7
1965	Janell Smith	55.1
1966	Charlette Cook	53.4
1969	Kathy Hammond	54.4
1970	M. Laing	52.9
1973	Mabel Ferguson	54.1
1974	Debra Sapenter	52.2

400-Meter Run

1959	Kimberly Polson	59.0
1960	Irene Robertson	59.1
1967	Charlette Cook	52.5
1968	Jarvis Scott	52.9
1971	Mabel Ferguson	53.3
1972	Kathy Hammond	52.3
1975	Debra Sapenter	51.6
1976	Lorna Forde	52.30

880-Yard Run

1958	Florence McArdle	2:26.7
1961	Pat Daniels	2:19.2
1962	Leah Bennett	2:12.3
1963	Sandra Knott	2:12.5
1965	Marie Mulder	2:11.1
1966	Charlette Cooke	2:05.0
1969	Madeline Manning	2:11.1
1970	Cheryl Toussaint	2:05.1
1973	Wendy Koenig	2:04.7
1974	Mary Decker	2:05.2

800-Meter Run

1959	Grace Butcher	2:21.2
1960	Pat Daniels	2:17.5
1964	Sandra Knott	2:10.4
1967	Madeline Manning	2:03.6
1968	Doris Brown	2:05.1
1971	Cheryl Toussaint	2:04.3
1972	Carole Hudson	2:06.7
1975	Madeline Manning Jackson	2:00.5
1976	Madeline Manning Jackson	2:0.1.0

1,500-Meter Run

1965	Marie Mulder	4:36.5
1966	Doris Brown	4:20.2
1967	Natalie Rocha	4:29.0
1968	Jane Hill	4:46.5
1969	Doris Brown	4:27.3
1970	Francie Larrieu	4:20.8

1971	Kathy Gibbons	4:19.2
1972	Francie Larrieu	4:18.4
1975	Julie Brown	4:13.5
1976	Francie Larrieu	4:09.93

1-Mile Run

1973	Francie Larrieu	4:40.3
1974	Julie Brown	4:45.1

2-Mile Run

1971	Doris Brown	10:07.0
1973	Eileen Claugus	10:19.4
1974	Lynn Bjorklund	10:11.1

3,000-Meter Run

1972	Tena Anex	9:46.2
1975	Lynn Bjorklund	9:10.6
1976	Jan Merrill	8:57.17

60-Yard Hurdles

1923	Hazel Kirk	9.6
1924	Hazel Kirk	9.0
1925	Helen Filkey	8.3
1926	Helen Filkey	8.7
1927	Helen Filkey	8.2
1928	Helen Filkey	8.4

80-Meter Hurdles

1929	Helen Filkey	12.6
1930	Evelyn Hall	13.0
1931	Mildred Didrikson	12.0
1932	Mildred Didrikson	12.1
1933	Simone Schaller	12.1
1935	Jean Hiller	13.0
1936	Anne O'Brien	12.0
1937	Cora Gaines	12.8
1938	Marie Cotrell	13.0
1939	Marie Cotrell	12.5
1940	Sybil Cooper	13.1
1941	Leila Perry	13.2
1942	Lillie Purifoy	12.6
1943	Nancy Cowperthwaite	12.3
1944	Lillie Purifoy	12.8
1945	Lillie Purifoy	12.5
1946	Nancy Cowperthwaite	12.2
1947	Nancy Cowperthwaite	12.6
1948	Bernice Robinson	12.1
1949	Bernice Robinson	11.9
1950	Evelyn Lawler	11.9
1951	Nancy C. Phillips	12.2
1952	Constance Darnowski	12.1
1953	Nancy C. Phillips	12.2
1954	Constance Darnowski	12.2
1955	Bertha Diaz	11.5
1956	Bertha Diaz	11.2
1957	Shirley Crowder	12.4
1958	Bertha Diaz	11.4
1959	Shirley Crowder	11.7
1960	Jo Ann Terry	11.4
1961	Cherie Parrish	11.5
1962	Cherie Parrish	11.3
1963	Rosie Bonds	11.3
1964	Rosie Bonds	10.8
1965	No competition	
1966	Cherie Parrish Sherrard	10.7
1967	Mamie Rallins	10.9
1968	Mamie Rallins	10.6

100-Meter Hurdles

1969	Chi Cheng	13.7
1970	Mamie Rallins	13.4
1971	Pat Van Wolvelaere Johnson	13.5
1972	Mamie Rallins	13.5
1973	Pat Van Wolvelaere Johnson	12.9

1974	Pat Van Wolvelaere Johnson	13.2
1975	Jane Frederick	13.8
1976	Jane Frederick	13.29

200-Meter Hurdles

1963	Sally Griffith	29.5
1964	Sally Griffith	28.2
1965	Jennifer Wingerson	27.6
1966	Pat Van Wolvelaere	27.6
1967	Pat Van Wolvelaere	27.8
1968	Pat Van Wolvelaere	27.3
1969	Pat Hawkins	27.4
1970	Pat Hawkins	26.1
1971	Pat Hawkins	26.1
1972	Pat Hawkins	26.3

400-Meter Hurdles

1973	Gale Fitzgerald	1:01.1
1974	Andrea Bruce	59.7
1975	Debbie Esser	57.3
1976	Arthurine Gainer	57.24

440-Yard Relay

1923	Meadowbrook Club	52.4
1924	Meadowbrook Club	57.0
1925	Pasadena AC	52.8
1926	Toronto Ladies AC	51.0
1927	Pasadena AC	52.6
1928	No. California AC	52.2
1929	Millrose AA	51.2
1930	Millrose AA	49.4
1931	Illinois Women's AC	51.0
1932	Illinois Women's AC	49.4
1946	Malvernette, Canada, AC	50.0
1955	Tennessee State	49.1
1957	Tennessee State	47.0
1958	Tennessee State "A"	46.9
1961	Mayor Daley YF	47.0
1962	Tennessee State	46.0
1963	Tennessee State	46.7
1965	Tennessee State	46.5
1966	Tennessee State	45.7
1969	Mayor Daley YF	46.4
1970	Tennessee State	45.2
1971	Tennessee State	44.8
1972	Sports International	45.4
1973	Tennessee State	45.5
1974	Texas Women's Univ.	45.6
1975	Tennessee State	45.8
1976	Tennessee State	44.97

400-Meter Relay

1933	Illinois Women's AC	49.5
1935	St. Louis AC	51.0
1936	Illinois Catholic WC	48.4
1937	Mercury AC	51.2
1938	Tuskegee Institute	52.0
1939	Tuskegee Institute	49.4
1940	Tuskegee Institute	49.3
1941	Tuskegee Institute	50.0
1942	Tuskegee Institute	50.7
1943	Toronto Laurel Ladies' AC	50.6
1944	Toronto Laurel Ladies' AC	52.8
1945	Toronto Laurel Ladies' AC	51.4
1947	Tuskegee Institute	50.5
1948	Tuskegee Institute	50.3
1949	Tuskegee Institute	50.0
1950	Tuskegee Institute	50.2
1951	Tuskegee Institute	49.8
1952	Police Athletic League	52.5
1953	Chicago CYO	49.7
1954	Chicago CYO	49.0
1956	Tennessee State	47.1
1959	Tennessee State	47.5

1960	Tennessee State	46.1
1964	Compton TC	47.2
1967	Texas Southern	46.3
1968	Mayor Daley YF	45.4

880-Yard Medley Relay (220-110-110-440)

1961	San Mateo, Calif.	1:49.0
1962	Mayor Daley YF	1:47.1
1963	Mayor Daley YF	1:46.9
1964	Oakettes AC	1:45.5
1965	Cleveland Recreation	1:44.3
1966	Cleveland Recreation	1:44.3
1969	Tennessee State	1:42.4
1970	Mayor Daley YF	1:43.1
1971	Angels TC	1:43.5
1972	Sports International	1:40.6
1973	West Coast Jets	1:43.2
1974	Sports International	1:38.5
1976	Los Angeles Mercurettes	1:38.69

800-Meter Medley Relay (200-100-100-400)

1960	Tennessee State	1:47.3
1967	Tennessee State	1:41.7
1968	Los Angeles Mercurettes	1:41.7
1975	Sports International	1:40.0

1-Mile Relay

1969	Angels TC	3:47.8
1970	Atoms TC	3:41.3
1971	Atoms TC	3:38.8
1972	Canton, Oh., TC	3:45.3
1973	Albuquerque Olympics	3:47.0
1974	Sports International	3:39.6
1975	Atoms TC	3:37.9
1976	Prairie View A&M	3:33.85

2-Mile Relay

1972	San Jose Cindergals	9:07.3
1973	San Jose Cindergals	8:58.0
1974	San Jose Cindergals	8:49.1
1975	Blue Ribbon, Wycliff, Oh.	8:46.4
1976	Los Angeles TC	8:34.44

High Jump

1923	Catherine Wright	4-7½
1924	No competition	
1925	Elizabeth Stine	4-10
1926	Catherine Maguire	4-11¼
1927	Catherine Maguire	5-½
1928	Mildred Wiley	4-11¾
1929	Jean Shiley	4-9⅞
1930	Jean Shiley	5-1
1931	Jean Shiley	5-2
1932	Jean Shiley	5-3³⁄₁₆
	Mildred Didrikson	5-3³⁄₁₆
1933	Alice Arden	5-3¼
1935	Barbara Howe	4-11
1936	Annette Rogers	5-2½
1937	Margaret Bergmann	4-11½
1938	Margaret Bergmann	5-2
1939	Alice Coachman	5-2
1940	Alice Coachman	4-11
1941	Alice Coachman	5-2¾
1942	Alice Coachman	4-8
1943	Alice Coachman	5-0
1944	Alice Coachman	5-1⅝
1945	Alice Coachman	5-0
1946	Alice Coachman	5-0
1947	Alice Coachman	5-1
1948	Alice Coachman	5-0
1949	Gertrude Orr	5-0
1950	Dorothy Chisholm	4-8¼
1951	Marion Boos	4-9¾
1952	Marion Boos	4-11⅝

Rick Wohlhuter, winner of the 1974 Sullivan Award as the U.S. amateur athlete of the year, is all alone as he crosses the finish line in a 1,500-m run. *(W. J. Wallace, Duke University.)*

1953	Mildred McDaniel	5-1½
1954	Jeannette Cantrell	5-¼
	Verneda Thomas	5-¼
1955	Mildred McDaniel	5-6½
1956	Mildred McDaniel	5-4
1957	Verneda Thomas	4-10
	Neomia Rodgers	4-10
	Hazel Ulmer	4-10
1958	Barbara Brown	5-2½
	Rose Robinson	5-2½
1959	Lis Josefsen	5-4
1960	Lis Josefsen	5-5¼
1961	Lis Josefsen	5-1
1962	Kinuko Tsutsumi	5-3
1963	Eleanor Montgomery	5-8
1964	Eleanor Montgomery	5-8
1965	Eleanor Montgomery	5-7
1966	Eleanor Montgomery	5-7
1967	Eleanor Montgomery	5-6¼
1968	Teresa Thrasher	5-6
1969	Eleanor Montgomery	5-11
1970	A. Plihal	5-8
1971	Linda Iddings	5-8
1972	Audrey Reid	6-½
1973	Deanne Wilson	5-9
1974	Joni Huntley	6-0
1975	Joni Huntley	6-0
1976	Joni Huntley	6-2

Long Jump

1923	Helen Dinnehey	15-4
1924	Dorothy Walsh	15-3
1925	Helen Filkey	17-0
1926	Nellie Todd	16-7⅜
1927	Eleanor Egg	17-1¾
1928	Elta Cartwright	16-10¾
1929	Nellie Todd	17-3¼
1930	Stella Walsh	18-9⅜
1931	Mildred Didrikson	17-11½

1932	Nellie Todd	17-6⅛
1933	Genevieve Valvoda	17-2¾
1935	Etta Tate	16-6
1936	Mabel Smith	18-0
1937	Lula Hymes	17-8½
1938	Lula Hymes	17-2
1939	Stella Walsh	19-4.8
1940	Stella Walsh	17-7½
1941	Stella Walsh	18-6¾
1942	Stella Walsh	17-11
1943	Stella Walsh	19-1
1944	Stella Walsh	17-11⅛
1945	Stella Walsh	18-3
1946	Stella Walsh	17-¾
1947	Lillie Purifoy	17-6
1948	Stella Walsh	17-8½
1949	Mabel Landry	17-5
1950	Mabel Landry	17-5⅞
1951	Stella Walsh	17-3
1952	Mabel Landry	18-1½
1953	Mabel Landry	18-7½
1954	Mabel Landry	17-11
1955	Nancy C. Phillips	17-5¾
1956	Margaret Matthews	19-4
1957	Margaret Matthews	19-5½
1958	Margaret Matthews	20-1
1959	Margaret Matthews	19-4½
1960	Willye White	19-1½
1961	Willye White	19-11½
1962	Willye White	20-3
1963	Edith McGuire	19-4¾
1964	Willye White	21-7
1965	Willye White	20-5½
1966	Willye White	20-7½
1967	Pat Winslow	20-8¼
1968	Willye White	20-11¼
1969	Willye White	19-8¾
1970	Willye White	21-1
1971	Kim Attlesey	20-8¾

1972	Willye White	20-6¼
1973	Martha Watson	21-4¾
1974	Martha Watson	21-3½
1975	Martha Watson	21-3
1976	Kathy McMillan	22-3

Shot Put

1923	Bertha Christophel	30-10½
1924	Esther Behring	30-1½
1925	Lillian Copeland	32-10⅝
1926	Lillian Copeland	38-3¾
1927	Lillian Copeland	39-6⅛
1928	Lillian Copeland	40-4¼
1929	Rena McDonald	42-3
1930	Rena McDonald	38-11½
1931	Lillian Copeland	40-2⅜
1932	Mildred Didrikson	39-6¼
1933	Catherine Rutherford	38-11
1935	Rena McDonald	38-3⅞
1936	Helen Stephens	41-8½
1937	Margaret Bergmann	37-6¾
1938	Catherine Fellmeth	38-5¾
1939	Catherine Fellmeth	41-1¾
1940	Catherine Fellmeth	38-3⅝
1941	Catherine Fellmeth	37-⅜
1942	Ramona Harris	37-10½
1943	Frances Gorn	37-11
1944	Dorothy Dodson	36-¼
1945	Frances Kaszubski	37-9⅞
1946	Dorothy Dodson	38-10¾
1947	Dorothy Dodson	37-11
1948	Frances Kaszubski	40-5⅞
1949	Amelia Bert	39-8¼
1950	Frances Kaszubski	39-3⅞
1951	Amelia Bert	41-3
1952	Amelia Bert	37-9
	Janet Dicks	37-9
1953	Amelia Bert	40-2½
1954	Lois Testa	41-11¾
1955	Wanda Wejzgrowicz	37-4⅝
1956	Earlene Brown	45-0
1957	Earlene Brown	43-½
1958	Earlene Brown	47-5½
1959	Earlene Brown	46-4¾
1960	Earlene Brown	49-8½
1961	Earlene Brown	47-8½
1962	Earlene Brown	48-10¾
1963	Sharon Shepherd	48-3½
1964	Earlene Brown	46-11
1965	Lynn Graham	47-7
1966	Lynn Graham	47-11¾
1967	Maren Seidler	46-10
1968	Maren Seidler	50-3¾
1969	Lynn Graham	48-11¾
1970	Lynn Graham	49-10
1971	Lynn Graham	52-0
1972	Maren Seidler	52-9
1973	Maren Seidler	51-8¼
1974	Maren Seidler	54-3
1975	Maren Seidler	53-2½
1976	Maren Seidler	54-4

Discus Throw

1923	Babe Wolbert	71-9½
1924	Roberta Ranck	70-0
1925	Maybelle Reichardt	87-2¾
1926	Lillian Copeland	101-1
1927	Lillian Copeland	103-8⁵⁄₁₆
1928	Maybelle Reichardt	116-9¼
1929	Rena McDonald	113-4
1930	Evelyn Farrara	111-6
1931	Evelyn Farrara	108-10⅝
1932	Ruth Osborn	133-¾
1933	Ruth Osborn	123-¼
1935	Margaret Wright	113-9½
1936	Helen Stephens	121-6½
1937	Elizabeth Lindsey	107-11
1938	Catherine Fellmeth	126-¼
1939	Catherine Fellmeth	113-7½
1940	Catherine Fellmeth	114-11
1941	Stella Walsh	113-10⅜
1942	Stella Walsh	110-11¾
1943	Frances Gorn	109-6¼
1944	Hattie Turner	101-7¾
1945	Frances Kaszubski	103-¼
1946	Dorothy Dodson	102-6
1947	Frances Kaszubski	110-4¾
1948	Frances Kaszubski	124-3⅜
1949	Frances Kaszubski	123-9
1950	Frances Kaszubski	113-4¾
1951	Frances Kaszubski	121-⅛
1952	Janet Dicks	114-7½
1953	Janet Dicks	123-2
1954	Marjorie Larney	120-11½
1955	Alejandra Harra	117-8
1956	Pamela Kurrell	140-11
1957	Olga Connolly	147-8
1958	Earlene Brown	152-5½
1959	Earlene Brown	153-8
1960	Olga Connolly	159-6½
1961	Earlene Brown	149-4½
1962	Olga Connolly	172-2
1963	Sharon Shepherd	150-6
1964	Olga Connolly	158-4
1965	Lynn Graham	157-9
1966	Carol Moeske	159-8
1967	Carol Moeske	152-5
1968	Olga Connolly	170-10
1969	Carol Frost	167-3
1970	Carol Frost	172-3
1971	Josephine Dela Vina	175-6
1972	Josephine Dela Vina	172-9
1973	Jean Roberts	173-3
1974	Joan Pabelich	173-11
1975	Jean Roberts	159-7
1976	Lynn Winbigler	174-1

Javelin Throw

1923	Roberta C. Ranck	59-7¾
1924	Esther Spargo	72-5¾
1925	Aloa Silva	105-8
1926	Lillian Copeland	112-5½
1927	Margaret Jenkins	127-3½
1928	Margaret Jenkins	112-5⅝
1929	Estelle Hill	100-5
1930	Mildred Didrikson	133-3
1931	Lillian Copeland	116-1½
1932	Mildred Didrikson	139-3
1933	Nan Gindele	130-2¼
1935	Sylvia Broman	102-7⅝
1936	Martha Worst	125-¼
1937	Rose Auerbach	123-5½
1938	Rose Auerbach	121-6¾
1939	Dorothy Dodson	130-9½
1940	Dorothy Dodson	126-1
1941	Dorothy Dodson	128-7⅛
1942	Dorothy Dodson	122-10½
1943	Dorothy Dodson	111-3
1944	Dorothy Dodson	123-1½
1945	Dorothy Dodson	124-10
1946	Dorothy Dodson	120-2
1947	Dorothy Dodson	122-5
1948	Dorothy Dodson	125-10⅜
1949	Dorothy Dodson	123-1
1950	Amelia Bert	115-1¾
1951	Frances Licata	120-½
1952	Marjorie Larney	126-3⅞
1953	Amelia Wershaven	124-7

1954	Karen Anderson	127-1
1955	Karen Anderson	150-1¼
1956	Karen Anderson	159-1
1957	Marjorie Larney	187-8
1958	Marjorie Larney	153-7½
1959	Marjorie Larney	152-9½
1960	Marjorie Larney	151-10½
1961	Frances Davenport	157-8
1962	Karen Mendyka	158-5
1963	Frances Davenport	158-5
1964	RaNae Bair	166-7½
1965	RaNae Bair	175-½
1966	RaNae Bair	174-10
1967	RaNae Bair	196-3
1968	Barbara Friedrich	178-10
1969	Kathy Schmidt	177-4
1970	Sherry Calvert	184-9
1971	Sherry Calvert	175-7
1972	Sherry Calvert	184-0
1973	Kathy Schmidt	194-6
1974	Kathy Schmidt	203-2
1975	Kathy Schmidt	209-7
1976	Kathy Schmidt	218-3

Halls of Fame

(The Citizens Savings Athletic Foundation established its hall of fame for track and field in 1949. Its inductees are listed in three categories: athletes, coaches, and noteworthy contributors. The National Track and Field Hall of Fame, in Charleston, West Virginia, and the U.S. Track and Field Hall of Fame, in Angola, Indiana, both held their first induction ceremonies in 1974. In the following list, C denotes Citizens, N denotes National, and U.S. denotes the U.S. Track and Field Hall of Fame.)

Athletes

Platt Adams C
Daniel F. Ahearn C
David Albritton C
Horace Ashenfelter C, U.S.
Richard Attlesey C
Robert Backus C
Raymond Barbuti C
Lee Barnes C
Robert Beamon C, U.S.
Gregory Bell C
Alfred C. Blozis C
George V. Bonhag U.S.
John Borican C
Ralph Boston C, N
Donald Bragg C
Herman Brix C
Earlene Brown C
T. E. Burke C
Lee Q. Calhoun C, N, U.S.
Milton Campbell C
Kenneth Carpenter C
Sabin Carr C
William Carr U.S.
Alice Coachman C
Roy V. Cochran C
Thomas Conneff C
Harold Connolly C, U.S.
J. B. Connolly U.S.
Olga Connolly C, U.S.
Lillian Copeland C
Tom Courtney C
Ralph Craig C
Glenn Cunningham C, N, U.S.
Willie Davenport
Glenn Davis C, N, U.S.

Harold Davis C, N
Jack Davis C
Ron Delany C
Clarence DeMar C
Mildred "Babe" Didrikson C, N, U.S.
Harrison Dillard, C, N
Gilbert Dodds C
Dorothy Dodson C
James Donahue C
Henry F. Dreyer C
Charles Dumas C
Ben Eastman C
Barney Ewell C
Ray C. Ewry C, N, U.S.
Mae Faggs C
J. J. Flanagan C
Maxwell W. Ford C
Fortune Gordien C
Edward Gordon C
Alex Grant C
George R. Gray C
Louis Gregory C
Archie Hahn C
Evelyne Hall C
Edward Hamm C
Kathy Hammond U.S.
Glenn Hardin C
Bob Hayes C
Franklin Held C
George Horine C
Clarence Houser C
DeHart Hubbard C
Cornelius Johnson C
Rafer Johnson C, N
Hayes Jones C
John Paul Jones C
Frances Kaszubski C
John A. Kelley C
John J. Kelley C
Abel R. Kiviat C
Alvin C. Kraenzlein C, N
Richard Landon U.S.
Mabel Landry C
Marjorie Larney C
Michael Larrabee C
Donald Lash C, U.S.
James C. Lightbody C
Dallas Long C
Madeline Manning U.S.
Robert Mathias C, N. U.S.
Randy Matson C
Peter McArdle C
Joseph P. McCluskey C
Mildred McDaniel C
Patrick J. McDonald C
Matthew McGrath C
Edith McGuire C
Leslie MacMitchell C
Earle Meadows C
J. E. "Ted" Meredith C, U.S.
Ralph Metcalfe C, U.S.
Billy Mills, C, U.S.
J. S. Mitchel C
Charles Moore, Jr. C
Glenn Morris C
Ronald Morris C
Bobby Morrow C
Loren Murchison C
Lawrence E. "Lon" Myers C, N
William Nieder C
Parry O'Brien C, N, U.S.
Alfred Oerter C, N, U.S.
George W. Orton C
Harold M. Osborn C, N

Unidentified U.S. pole vaulter clears the bar during 1974 U.S.-U.S.S.R. dual meet. *(William J. Wallace, Duke University.)*

Jesse Owens C, N, U.S.
Charles Paddock C, U.S.
Melvin Patton C
Eulace Peacock C
Myer Prinstein C
Joie W. Ray C, U.S.
George Rhoden C
J. Gregory Rice C
Alma Richards C
Robert Richards C
Betty Robinson C, U.S.
Ralph Rose C
Wilma Rudolph C, N, U.S.
Patrick Ryan C
James Ryun C
Jackson V. Scholz C
Robert Seagren C
Melvin Sheppard C
Martin Sheridan C
Jean Shiley C
Robert Simpson N
Jay Silvester C
Arnold Sowell C
Andrew Stanfield C
Lester Steers C, N
Helen Stephens C
Curtis Stone C
F. Morgan Taylor C
John Thomas C
Wilbur Thompson C

Jim Thorpe U.S.
Eddie Tolan C
William Toomey C
Jack Torrance C
Forrest Towns C
Wyomia Tyus C
Stella Walsh C
Cornelius Warmerdam C, N
Bernard J. Wefers C
Willye White C, U.S.
Malvin Whitfield C, N
Fred Wilt C
Fred Wolcott C
John Woodruff C
Frank Wykoff C
C. K. Yang C
"Cy" Young U.S.

Coaches
Harry Adams C
Frank Anderson C
Weems Baskin C
George Bresnahan C
Emmett Brunson C
Michael Butler C
Walter Christie C
Mack Clark C
Boyd Comstock C
Dean Cromwell C, U.S.
J. Kenneth Doherty C
Harold Drew C
Clarence Dussault C
Bill Easton C
Clarence Edmundson C
James F. Elliott C
Edward Farrell C
Stephan Farrell C
Robert Fetzer C
Keane Fitzpatrick C
Ivan Fuque C
Matthew Geis C
John Gibson C
Harry L. Gill C
George Griffin C
Brutus Hamilton C
J. Flint Hanner C
Billy Hayes C, U.S.
Ward Haylett C
William Hayward C
Oscar Hedlund C
Ralph Higgins C
Frank Hill C
Harry Hillman C
Charles Hoyt C
Ward Hutsell C
John Jacobs C
Chester Jenkins C
Leo T. Johnson C
Thomas Jones C
Payton Jordan C
Thomas Keane C
James Kelly C
Leland P. Lingle C
Clyde Littlefield C
John Magee C
John Moakley C
Bernie Moore C
Jesse Mortensen C
Michael Murphy C
Winton E. Noah C
Joseph Pipal C
Anthony Plansky C
Archie Post C

Dale Ranson C
George L. Rider C
Lawson Robertson C
Jack Rourke C
Michael Ryan C
Jack Ryder C
Karl Schlademan C
Harry Schulte C
Arthur Smith C
Larry Snyder C
Bart Sullivan C
Robert Templeton C
Earl J. Thomson C
Fred Tootell C
Emil Von Elling C
A. Heath Whittle C
Alex Wilson C
Lloyd "Bud" Winter C

Contributors
Emil Breitkrutz C
Donald Canham U.S.
William B. Curtis C
Daniel Ferris C
John J. Griffith C
James B. Haralson C
Lawrence Houston C
Hilmer Lodge C
Harry McMillian C
Thomas P. Rosandich C
Fred Schmertz C
W. R. "Bill" Schroeder U.S.
Amos Alonzo Stagg C
James E. Sullivan C
Kenneth L. "Tug" Wilson U.S.

Bibliography. *AAU Official Handbook* (biennial), Amateur Athletic Union, Indianapolis; Doherty, J. M.: *Modern Track and Field,* Prentice-Hall, Englewood Cliffs, N.J., 1953.

TRAMPOLINE AND TUMBLING—Formerly conducted as gymnastics events, trampoline and tumbling have now become separate sports, controlled by the International Trampoline Federation. The chief governing body in the United States is the Amateur Athletic Union.

Tumbling is actually an offshoot of gymnastics; routines are performed on a mat, 60 ft long, 5 to 6 ft wide, and 1½ to 4 in thick.

Trampoline, oddly, comes from the Italian word for "stilt," and the original trampolinists were circus acrobats who performed their stunts on stilts during the Middle Ages. The trampoline as we know it is a net or sheet of strong canvas stretched tightly over a frame, acting as a large springboard for tumbling routines. Similar apparatus was also used in circuses, but the device was perfected and named by George Nissen of the United States in 1926; he patented it in 1939, and the sport became fairly popular after World War II, when trampolines were introduced into many gymnasiums.

Trampoline Rules. The rules for trampoline competition originated from gymnastics, and are somewhat similar. The ITF specifies a trampoline 1 m (39.36 in) high, ranging from 3.60 to 4.30 m in length and 1.80 to 2.15 m in width. The AAU specifies a frame 10 by 17 ft with a bed—the part of the net actually used in competition—of 7 by 14 ft. Height is 41 in.

Each competitor performs one compulsory and one optional routine in preliminaries. The top 10 finishers then

The trampoline reached sudden heights of popularity during the 1950s and is now used in competitive sport, based on gymnastics. *(Courtesy of Nissen Co.)*

advance to the finals, where each does another optional routine, which may or may not be the one done in preliminaries. The compulsory routine is a test of 10 basic movements or skills, demonstrated in the course of 10 bounces on the trampoline. Judges base their scoring on form, execution, body control, and height of bounce, giving a maximum of 1 point for each skill performed. Points are deducted for such faults, following the tenth bounce, as taking steps after landing, touching the cloth with the hands, landing on the knees, sitting, or landing on the stomach or back. If a competitor touches the frame or suspension system or falls off the trampoline at any point, the routine is considered ended at that point and the contestant is scored only for demonstration of completed skills. The optional routine also consists of 10 exercises. A skill may be performed twice. If performed more than twice, no points are awarded for the additional repetitions.

There are four aesthetic judges. The highest and lowest scores are thrown out, and the middle scores are averaged and then doubled to get the contestant's final score in the compulsory routine. In the optional routine, there is a fifth judge, who scores only on the basis of difficulty involved, according to a specific table which awards .1 to .4 points for somersaults, twists, and other difficult maneuvers. After the two middle judges' scores are averaged and doubled, the difficulty score is added to get the contestant's final score in the optional routine.

Synchronized trampoline is an event in which two teammates perform identical routines on side-by-side trampolines. The same general procedure is used as in single trampoline: a compulsory routine followed by an optional one. Scoring is the same as in single trampoline except that there are also two synchronization judges who deduct fractions of a point for unsynchronized landings. Their deductions are averaged and subtracted from the score given by the two middle judges. Then, in the optional, the difficulty points are added.

Team scores are based on the top three raw scores of team members in compulsory competition and the top three raw scores in the first optional competition; scores from the final optional routine do not count.

Tumbling Rules. As in trampoline, tumblers first perform a compulsory and an optional routine, and then 10 finalists do their second optionals. AAU rules call for a compulsory routine consisting of three passes, with five movements per pass. Each pass begins with a run from off the mat and ends with the competitor standing stationary for three seconds. The exact sequence of movements is prescribed by specific regulations, and may change from year to year.

The optional routine also consists of three passes in major meets, and the routine may be composed of up to 20 parts (15 in those competitions in which only two passes are allowed). One pass must be predominantly forward, one predominantly backward, and the third mixed. The maximum number of points given for an optional routine in the first phase of judging is 8.5, based on form, execution, control, rhythm, and height. Values ranging from 0.1 to 1.0 point are deducted for various flaws; deductions of 0.5 point are also made for each part exceeding the limit of 20 or for failure to have three different kinds of passes.

After the deductions are made, judges may add up to 1.5 points, for a possible total of 10, on the basis of risk, virtuosity, and unusual difficulty in the routine as a whole. "Risk" implies not so much physical danger as the willingness to attempt a difficult move or difficult combination of moves that could result in serious loss of points if performed badly. "Virtuosity" implies the demonstration of a wide range of difficult skills.

High and low scores are thrown out and the two middle scores added; then difficulty points are added.

See also GYMNASTICS.

World Trampoline Champions
(Competition biennial since 1968)

Men

1964	Danny Millman, U.S.
1965	Gary Irwin, U.S.
1966	Wayne Miller, U.S.
1967	Dave Jacobs, U.S.
1968	Dave Jacobs, U.S.
1970	Wayne Miller, U.S.
1972	Paul Luxon, England
1974	Richard Tison, France
1976	Eugeni James, U.S.S.R.
	Richard Tison, France

Women

1964	Judy Wills, U.S.
1965	Judy Wills, U.S.
1966	Judy Wills, U.S.
1967	Judy Wills, U.S.
1968	Judy Wills, U.S.
1970	Renee Ramson, U.S.
1972	Alexandra Nicholson, U.S.
1974	Alexandra Nicholson, U.S.
1976	Svetlana Levina, U.S.S.R.

Bibliography. *AAU Official Handbook* (biennial), Amateur Athletic Union, Indianapolis.

TRAPSHOOTING—We have almost forgotten how this sport got its name; some even think the trap is the target rather than a device for launching the target. But the cruel fact is that, in its original form, trapshooting was a form of practice, using live birds as targets. The birds, usually pigeons, were held in traps. At the shooter's command, a string was pulled to remove the lid, the bird would take flight, and the shooter would get his practice.

The earliest known reference to trapshooting was in a 1793 English magazine, where it was already referred to as "a well established recreation." One reason for the sport's popularity in England was the shortage of public hunting grounds, because the aristocrats had set up private game preserves on large areas of land. It spread to the United States as a form of practice for the hunter, whereas in England it was basically a replacement for real hunting. The first known trapshooting in this country was carried on at the Sportsmen's Club in Cincinnati, beginning in 1831. In 1840 a Long Island Club was established.

As birds became scarcer, substitutes were sought. The English developed the idea of shooting at glass balls, but the traps they used were troublesome, and the sport never really caught on. In 1866, Charles Portlock of Boston invented a better trap for launching the glass balls, whose diameter was 2½ in, and this time the sport did catch on. Feathers were sometimes glued to the balls to give some semblance of realism.

There were other, less popular substitutes: a 2-in balloon enclosed in a cardboard collar, like the planet Saturn and its rings; a gyrobird, which resembled a child's rudimentary helicopter; the artificial "live" bird, which was shaped something like a pigeon and which ran along a

A recent development is this unusual dual "minitrampoline." *(Courtesy of Nissen Co.)*

wire; and the tin pigeon, which had a small disc in the center that would be knocked loose by a direct hit.

Clay pigeons were developed during the 1860s, but a Cincinnatian, George Ligowsky, developed the first really good one in 1880. According to one story, Ligowsky saw some youngsters skipping shells over the water, and decided the shape would be ideal for a flying target. (Actually, however, it appears that saucer-shaped targets had been used previously.) Ligowsky's targets were made of real clay, baked to hardness, and they didn't break easily. He began experimenting with other materials, but an Englishman named McCaskey invented the modern clay pigeon, made from a mixture of river silt and pitch. McCaskey also developed a much improved trap for launching his targets, and his two inventions helped to standardize the sport and bring it worldwide popularity.

The sport's first governing body in the United States was the Interstate Manufacturers' Trapshooting Association, organized in the 1880s. The IMTA, as the name implies, was controlled by manufacturers of guns and ammunition. The name was changed to the American Trapshooting Association in 1922. In 1924 the Amateur Trapshooting Association (ATA), controlled by the shooters instead of the manufacturers, was organized, and that association still governs the sport in the United States. The ATA has permanent headquarters at Vandalia, Ohio, on a 97-acre site that has 53 traps stretching over a mile and a quarter. The site is now the permanent home of the North American championship event, the Grand American Tournament.

The Grand American. The first national trapshooting tournament was held in 1885 in New Orleans. The first Grand American was held in 1893 at Dexter Park, Long Island, and it was conducted at various sites until it got its permanent home in Vandalia in 1924. About 4,000 competitors shoot it out in Vandalia every year, for a number of different championships. The best-known and most prestigious is the Grand American Handicap.

The Trap Field. The trap is located in a house 16 yd from a line on which five shooting stations are marked, numbered 1 to 5 from left to right. The stations are 3 yd apart. A round of trap consists of five shots from each of the five positions, a total of 25 shots.

The trap has to throw the target, which has a diameter of 4½ in, a distance of between 48 and 52 yd, requiring an initial speed of about 60 mph. The trap also throws the target at an angle, determined at random by an oscillating motor that drives the trap. Traps are usually set to throw the target at any angle up to 22 degrees left or right of center. The general direction of the target is away from the shooter.

Types of Competition. The basic trapshoot is the 16-yd event, in which shooters are grouped into classes according to past performance, and all shots are taken from the 16-yd line. More popular is handicap shooting, in which each shooter is placed a certain distance from the trap, depending on ability—the better shooters, of course, farther away. Distance ranges from 16 to 27 yd, in ½- or 1-yd increments. In this type of competition there are no classes; all shooters compete against one another, and the best score wins.

The most difficult type of shooting is doubles, in which two targets are released simultaneously. The flight of the targets is fixed: One is thrown at an angle 22 degrees left

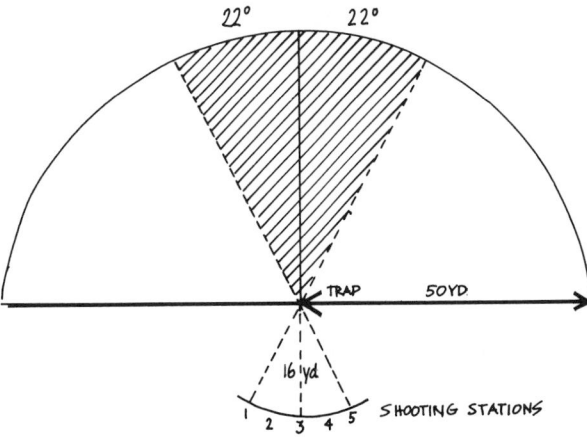

Trap field: Shaded section represents area in which targets will travel at most ranges. Note that extreme right path is almost a straightaway shot for shooter at position 1.

of center, the other at 22 degrees right of center.

Progress of Competition. A shooter begins at Station 1, fires at five targets from there, then moves on to Station 2, and so on. The shooter may call for the target when he wants. The command is "pull"—a relic of the days when someone pulled a string to open the trap. Today the "puller" pushes a button to release the target. At some fields the release is effected by the shooter's voice.

If the target is released too quickly or too slowly, the shooter doesn't have to take a shot. Instead, the contestant must say "slow" or "fast" and lower the gun. A referee then rules on whether the refusal was justified. If it was, the shooter gets another chance. If the refusal is disallowed—a rare occurrence—it counts as a missed shot.

If the gun malfunctions, the shooter must call in an official to examine it. If the gun is at fault, the contestant gets another chance at the target. If the shooter clears up the malfunction without official inspection, a miss is recorded. If there are more than two malfunctions in a single event, the shooter is disqualified.

International Trap. On the international level, trap is very different, and much more difficult, than the American version. International trap, sometimes called Olympic trench shooting, uses 15 traps, set in a trench below ground. The traps are arranged in five groups of three each. The shooting line is 15 m (about 16½ yd) behind the trench.

The target must be hurled at least 71 m (about 77½ yd), so the initial speed is greater than in American trap, and the targets have to be smaller in diameter to travel that distance. Although 25 targets still constitute a round, a shooter takes just one target at a station before moving on to the next one; consequently it is necessary to make five circuits of the stations to complete a round. There are three traps at each station, and any one of the three might release the target. In addition, the traps throw the targets at a great variety of angles; some will travel just a few feet above the ground and others will go almost straight up.

The shooter gets a second shot at a target, if necessary, and is scored on the number of targets hit, regardless of the total number of shots taken. Thus a perfect round of 25 may actually represent 50 shots.

Modified Clay Pigeon. As a kind of training for Americans interested in international competition, the National Rifle Association has established a similar kind of shooting, called modified clay pigeon. The trap field layout is similar to that used in ordinary American competition, but the smaller targets are used, and a special trap can duplicate nearly all the variations in angle produced by the three traps used in the international sport. Shooters take five targets per station, as in American trap, but they are allowed two shots at each target.

Equipment. Trapshooting has been described as "rifle shooting with a shotgun," and a trap gun is therefore quite different from a field gun. In shooting at live game, 40 yd is generally considered the greatest effective range for a shotgun. However, the average trapshooter will break a target at a distance of 36 yd, from the 16-yd mark, and, of course, at an even greater distance if the contestant shoots with a handicap.

To get accuracy at that range, a trap gun has to be choked considerably more than an ordinary field gun. (The "choke" of a shotgun is the constriction of the bore; the fuller the choke, the smaller the opening through which the shot passes, and the tighter the resulting pattern.) Trap guns at one time almost always had a full choke—meaning 70 to 90 percent of the shot would be placed in a 30-in circle at a range of 40 yd—but somewhat looser chokes are now commonly used.

The trap gun resembles a rifle in much of its design. It has a straighter, longer stock than an ordinary shotgun, and is designed to shoot high—above the apparent sighting level—since the trap target is always rising. The butt plate has a heavily cushioned recoil pad, often of nonskid material. And a trap gun, unlike a field gun, has a pistol grip for consistent alignment and minimum recoil.

Ammunition loads are regulated by ATA rules; the charge is the equivalent in smokeless powder of 3 drams of black powder, and the maximum amount of shot is $1\frac{1}{8}$ oz. The largest shot permitted is $7\frac{1}{2}$. Most shooters actually use 8 or $8\frac{1}{2}$ shot, depending on wind conditions. (A higher number indicates smaller shot, and therefore more pellets per shell. The $1\frac{1}{8}$-oz load of $7\frac{1}{2}$ shot represents about 480 pellets, while $8\frac{1}{2}$ would represent about 640 pellets.)

Trapshooters also usually use earplugs or special earmuffs, and shooting vests that offer cushioning against recoil and have pockets for such things as shells and scoring pads.

Technique. The basic difficulties of trap are that the shooter doesn't know at what angle the target will be traveling, and that the range of the target is constantly increasing, so a fairly quick shot is essential. The advantages over field shooting are that the shooter does know when the target will be released, and also knows the area that must be covered—the area between the two most extreme possible angles.

From Station 1, for example, the most extreme angle to the right would give the shooter a straightaway shot; the most extreme angle to the left would require a great deal more horizontal lead. The shooter has to take a stance that will permit a relaxed shooting position at either of these extremes. The shooter should face halfway between them, toes about 12 in apart and heels more closely together.

Gun positioning should also be started about halfway between the two possible extremes. The gun is raised to shooting position and sighted before the target is called for. To hit the target, the shooter must lead it to a certain extent, depending on the exact angle at which it is traveling.

There are two methods of establishing the lead. The first is to determine the path of the target, swing the gun ahead of it to the correct interval, and fire. The second is known as the "blot-out" method: The shooter swings the gun along the target's path from behind and, when the muzzle catches up to and blots out the target, fires. Here the lead is established by the fact that the gun muzzle is moving faster than the target. In either method, the swing must be very smooth and steady, and the shooter must follow through with the swing even after firing.

The most important thing is to lead the target enough. Too much lead can result in a hit, because the scattered shot forms a column several feet long, and trailing pellets may hit the target after the leading pellets have missed it.

The most difficult shots are presented from Stations 1 and 5, since a great deal of horizontal lead may be called for. Shots from Stations 2, 3, and 4 are closer to straightaway, at whatever angle the target is traveling.

In handicap shooting from greater distances, the necessary lead on any shot is smaller, since the angle is reduced. However, there is much less margin for error—the greater distance involved magnifies an error of 1 degree into nearly 2 degrees at 27 yd, for example—and an optical illusion makes the angles look greater than they really are. In establishing lead, the shooter must swing the gun more slowly as the handicap distance increases.

Doubles shooting calls for great speed, above all else, especially on the first shot. A doubles shooter will normally take the most nearly straightaway shot first, since it is somewhat easier and the target is moving rapidly away. Then the more severe angle shot will be taken after the lead has been established. From Stations 1 and 2, and usually from 3, the contestants will shoot first at the target on the right and then at the target on the left.

The best gun for doubles trap is an over-under. The lower barrel will usually be bored for a wide pattern, so that first quick shot at the straightaway target doesn't have to be perfect, and the second barrel will be choked much more tightly, since the second target will be a greater distance away.

Handicap Classes. Trapshooters, for handicap purposes, are classified according to their shooting percentages at 16 yd. Classes range from AA down to D, and percentages must be based on at least 2,000 shots from the 16-yd distance. The classes, percentages, and handicap distances are

AA—96.5 percent and better—24–27 yd

A—94 to 96 percent—22–23 yd

B—91 to 93 percent—20–21 yd

C—88 to 90 percent—18–19 yd

D—Below 88 percent—16 yd

A handicap committee determines the exact distance at which shooters will be placed in a specific meet, based not only on classes but on previous prizes won. A shooter who hasn't taken the minimum 2,000 shots in registered competition is placed at 22 yd. To prevent "sandbagging''—deliberately keeping the average low in order to compete in a lower class—a committee can place a shooter at a greater distance than the designated class would call for, if the contestant has won a great deal of prize money.

See also HUNTING; SHOOTING; SKEET.

Grand American Handicap Winners

Men

1900	Rolla O. Heikes	91
1901	E. C. Griffith	95
1902	C. W. Floyd	94
1903	M. Diefenderfer	94
1904	R. Guptil	96
1905	R. R. Barber	99
1906	F. E. Rogers	94
1907	J. J. Blanks	96
1908	Fred Harlow	92
1909	Fred Shattuck	96
1910	R. Thompson	100
1911	Harvey Dixon	99
1912	W. E. Phillips	96
1913	M. S. Hootman	97
1914	W. Henderson	98
1915	L. B. Clarke	96
1916	L. E. Wulf	99
1917	C. H. Larson	98
1918	J. D. Henry	97
1919	G. W. Lorimer	98
1920	A. L. Ivins	99
1921	E. F. Haak	97
1922	J. S. Frink	96
1923	Mark Arie	96
1924	H. C. Deck	97
1925	E. C. Starner	98
1926	Charles A. Young	100
1927	Otto Newlin	98
1928	I. Andrews	95
1929	M. Newman	98
1930	Alfred R. King	97
1931	Garfield Roebuck	96
1932	A. E. Sheffield	98
1933	Walter Beaver	98
1934	L. G. Dana	98
1935	J. B. Royall	98
1936	B. F. Cheek	98
1937	F. G. Carroll	100
1938	O. W. West	99
1939	D. L. Ritchie	99
1940	E. H. Wolfe	98
1941	Walter Tulburt	99
1942	J. F. Holderman	93
1943	Jasper Rogers	97
1944	L. C. Jepson	97
1945	Don Englebry	99
1946	F. J. Bennett	98
1947	H. H. Crossen	99
1948	John W. Schenk	99
1949	Pete Donat	100
1950	Oscar Scheske	100
1951	Mike Wayland	99
1952	Orval Voorhees	98
1953	Raymond A. Williams	98
1954	Nick Egan	99
1955	Logan Bennett	99
1956	C. W. Brown	99
1957	Carmi Russell Crawford	98
1958	Emerson Clark	99
1959	Clyde Bailey	99
1960	Roy Foxworthy	100
1961	Steven Foxworthy	99
1962	Milton Young	99
1963	ALbert Kees	100
1964	W. E. Duggan	99
1965	Daniel C. Pautler, Jr.	99
1966	Delbert Grim	100
1967	Herman Welch	100
1968	Denton Childers	100
1969	Bernard Bonn, Jr.	99
1970	Charles Harvey	98
1971	Ralph Davis	98
1972	George Mushrush	99
1973	Dennis Taylor	99
1974	John Steffen	99
1975	Wayne Heywood	99
1976	Frank Crevatin	99

Women

1967	Mary Lou Huizdos	97
1968	Rosemary Miller	98
1969	JoAnn Nelson	94
1970	Carol Harmon	97
1971	Leona Powers	97
1972	Charlotte Wells	99
1973	JoAnn Nelson	96
1974	Mrs. Georgie McCown	99
1975	Ann Kisner	99
1976	Judith Whittenberger	97

TRIATHLON—A women's combined event in track and field, consisting of the 100-m dash, the high jump, and the shot put.

See also TRACK AND FIELD.

TRIPLE CROWN—Originally, winning the "triple crown" meant winning three major horse races, the Kentucky Derby, Belmont Stakes, and Preakness. The term is now also applied to other major achievements involving three championships. A triple crown winner in baseball leads a league in batting average, home runs, and runs batted in. Harness racing has two triple crowns, for trotters and for pacers, and there are also so-called triple-crown events in horse racing for fillies, mares, two-year-olds, and other categories.

TRIPLE JUMP—A track and field event, formerly known in this country as the hop, step, and jump, a term that pretty well describes it.

See also TRACK AND FIELD.

TUMBLING—*See* TRAMPOLINE AND TUMBLING.

U-V

UNIONS—*See* PLAYER ASSOCIATIONS.

VOLLEYBALL—Like James W. Naismith, who invented basketball in 1891, William G. Morgan felt that a new indoor game was needed. Morgan, director of the Holyoke, Massachusetts, YMCA, knew about basketball, but he wanted a somewhat slower game, one that would be suited to older men who didn't want to run up and down a court. In 1895 he came up with a kind of overgrown version of badminton—indeed, the original name, "mintonette," was undoubtedly derived from "badminton." Morgan suspended a lawn tennis net high above the floor and used the bladder of a soccer ball as the first ball for his invention. The new sport was demonstrated at a YMCA directors' conference in Springfield, Massachusetts, where basketball had been invented. At that conference Dr. A. T. Halsted suggested the name should be "volleyball," since the ball was volleyed back and forth across the net.

Volleyball didn't spread as dramatically as basketball, but formal rules were drawn up for YMCA play in 1897, and the game did catch on at YMCAs across the country and in other parts of the world. In 1922 the YMCA held the first national tournament. By 1928 many schools and colleges had discovered volleyball, the sport had moved outdoors to a large number of playgrounds, and there were many enthusiastic women players. The U.S. Volleyball Association was organized to govern the sport. Since 1928 the USVA has conducted its own national championships; the major event is the U.S. Open. The AAU has conducted national championships since 1925, and the NCAA in 1970 added a volleyball tournament to its championship schedule.

Internationally the sport got a tremendous boost during World War II, when American servicemen introduced it to many countries. Volleyball became especially popular in the Orient, particularly in Korea and Japan. The International Volleyball Federation was organized in 1947 and now has more than 60 member countries. The first IVF world championships were held in 1949, and volleyball became an Olympic sport in 1952.

Rules

Court and Equipment. The volleyball court is 60 ft long and 30 ft wide, divided in the center by a net and a center line. The top of the net is 8 ft above the floor for men's play, 7 ft, 4¼ in for women's play. On each side of the center line and 10 ft from it is a "spiking line."

The ball has a circumference of 25 to 27 in and weighs 250 to 280 g (about 9 to 10 oz). It is inflated to 7 to 8 lb of pressure if leather-cased, 5 to 7 lb if rubber-cased.

Teams. A team is made up of six players: left, center,

and right forwards, and left, center, and right backs. When the ball is served, each player must be within the general area denoted by the position played; all forward-line players must be in front of all back-line players, and no back-line player may be in front of the spiking line. Players may move from their positions after the server's hand has come into contact with the ball, but a back may never spike the ball from above net level while in front of

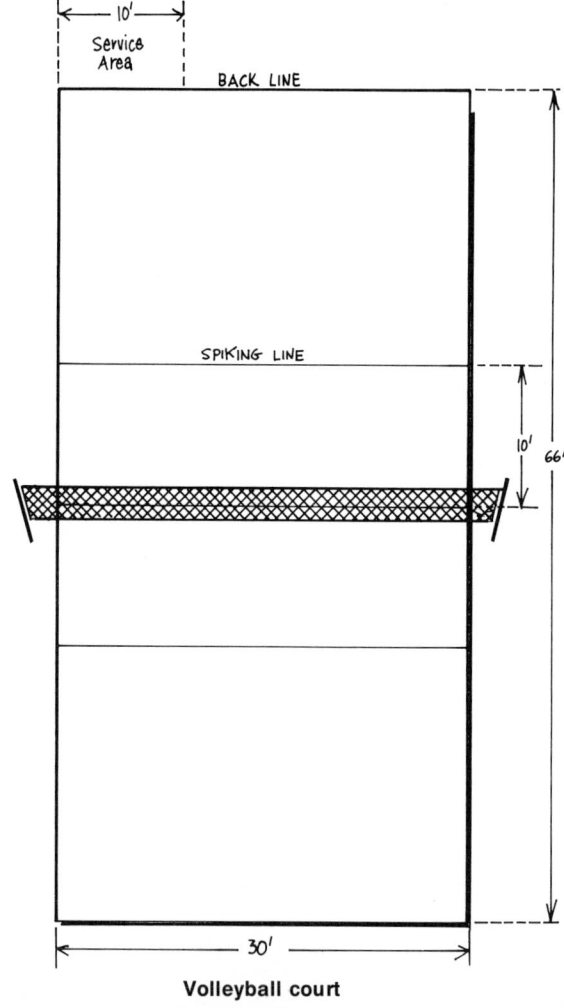

Volleyball court

the spiking line. (Spiking, the act of driving the ball into the opponent's court by leaping before the net and then striking the ball, is described in a section of this article under the heading "Basic Techniques.")

The player in the right-back position is the server; every time a team wins service, the players rotate clockwise, so the right-front player becomes the server, the left-back player moves to the left-front position, and so forth. A squad may consist of up to 12 players. Substitutions may be made any time the ball is dead, but a player may enter the game no more than three times. A substitute must take the position of the player being replaced, and any time a player re-enters the game the returnee must take the same position played earlier, in relation to other players on the team.

Service. The serve must be made from the service area—behind the end line and within 10 ft of the right sideline. The ball must carry over the net on the fly; if not touched by the receiving team, it must land within the boundary lines of the receiving team's court to be a legal serve. The same player continues serving until that player's team loses service.

Only the serving team can score a point. If the serving team makes an error or commits a foul, no point is scored, but the serve goes to the other team.

Progress of Play. The teams continue hitting the ball back and forth across the net after service until one team makes an error or commits a foul. A team is allowed only three touches of the ball in the process of returning it to the other side of the net (the ball, that is, may be touched three times by members of that team).

No player may touch the ball twice in succession unless: On one of the contacts, the player and a teammate or the player and an opponent have touched the ball simultaneously; the player is blocking the ball at the net, in which case, if the ball is blocked into the air, the player may touch it again; or the player is attempting to play a hard-driven spiked ball, in which case two successive contacts may be made.

If two opposing players make contact with the ball simultaneously at the net, it doesn't count as one of the allowed touches for either team. Any contact of the ball with part of a player's body is considered a touch; if the ball bounces off a player's head, for example, that is one of a team's three allowed touches. Kicking the ball is an error. And the ball must be clearly hit—that is, when hit with a hand, the ball must definitely bounce off the hand; it may not be thrown or held for a fraction of a second before it starts on its course.

It is a foul when: A player is out of position when the ball is served; a player serves out of turn or from outside the serving area; a player touches the net or crosses the center line while the ball is in play; a player reaches over the net (unless the player's hand goes over the net on the follow-through after that player has clearly hit the ball on his or her own side of the net); a player interferes with an opponent from a position under the net; a back-line player spikes the ball while in front of the spiking line (although the player can land in front of the line if it is clear that contact with the ball was made behind it); and a player comes into the game in the wrong position, or comes into the game for the fourth time. If each team commits a foul on the same play, the fouls offset each other and the point is replayed.

Game is usually 15 points, but a team must win by a

A Japanese player spikes as two Americans try to block. (*U.S. Volleyball Association.*)

margin of 2 or more points. In some cases—usually in the early rounds of a tournament with a large number of teams—8 or 10 min of playing time is allotted for a game, and the team that is ahead when the time has elapsed is the winner.

A match consists of three games, if necessary; the first team to win two games wins the match. The team that wins the initial coin flip wins the right to serve in the first and third games, if desired. Teams change courts between games. If there is a third game, they change courts again after one team has scored 8 points or, in a timed game, the first time the ball is dead after half the playing time has elapsed, if that comes before one team has scored 8 points.

Officials. The referee, who is in overall charge of the game, sits on a high platform or ladder at one end of the net. The referee calls most fouls, can overrule other officials, and signals with a whistle when the ball becomes dead. An umpire is basically responsible for watching the position of the players, and also keeps track of time-outs. In major games there are four linesmen, near the corners of the court, who watch for foot faults by the server and also signal whether the ball is in the playing area or out when it touches the floor near a boundary.

Beach Volleyball. Remarkably popular in Southern California, beach volleyball follows the regular rules of the sport, except that the net is 7 ft, 10 in high when the game is played on hard-packed sand and an inch lower on loose sand, and the boundaries are marked by ropes. Teams change sides after every 5 points, to equalize disadvantages caused by sun, wind, and other factors related to the setting.

Doubles. In doubles volleyball, there are only two players on each team; the playing area is 30 by 50 ft, and game is 11 points or 5 min of actual play.

Basic Techniques and Strategy

Volleyball is a team game. In most cases a team should use all three of its allowed hits in making a successful return. A team is usually made up of four spikers and two setters, whose responsibility it is to get the ball in the air near the net so that one of the spikers can drive the ball into the opponent's court. (If the alignment were three and three, the time would have to come when two spikers would be in the back line and only one in the front line, as a result of player rotation.) A good team will usually switch positions once the ball is in play to get one setter into the center-front position; from there, that player can set the ball up to either side of the court. The player's movement, however, makes it necessary for teammates to adjust somewhat to keep all parts of the court covered. Whenever possible, a player receiving the ball should give it to a setter, who can then set up a spiker for the kill. The setter is usually nearer the net than the spiker—front-center, if the setter can get there, and the first player to hit the ball, in the process of returning it, should attempt to get it to that area.

Since serves usually go deep, the team returning service often uses the "crescent formation," in which five players drop back, positioning themselves in the form of a crescent while the setter nearest front-center moves quickly to that spot as soon as the serve is in the air.

Teams also use definite (defensive) systems to cover the court when the other team is setting up a spike. When one player moves quickly to the net to try to block the spike, other players have to move to cover areas behind the blocker. In the "center man cover" system, if the left-front player has to move up to block, the center back moves into the vacated area behind that player; the right back then has to move toward the center to fill the newly vacated area. In the "wing man cover" system, the left back moves forward, the center back moves left, and the right back again moves somewhat toward the center.

Serving. The serve usually used by skilled players is the overhand, which greatly resembles the tennis serve. The server faces the net with the left foot forward, tosses the ball about 3 ft above the head and slightly in front of it, then strikes the ball with the heel of the hand or with the closed fist. The serving arm should be fully extended at impact, so that the ball is at its greatest possible height when struck. The server can control the direction of the ball by varying the angle at which it is struck, and can also put spin on the ball by cutting the hand across the ball in one direction or the other as the serve is made.

A more difficult serve, both to execute and to return, is the roundhouse. The server's left shoulder is toward the net; the ball is tossed slightly behind the right shoulder and is struck approximately at head level. The follow-through should bring the hand around and down almost to where it started, and the player should be facing the net almost squarely when service is completed. The proper action gives the ball a lot of top spin, and the resultant serve is a virtual line drive that will sink sharply after crossing the net.

Passing. It isn't as easy to pass a volleyball as it looks. A very delicate touch is required for soft, accurate passes. In most cases the passer should get directly under the ball, like a baseball catcher going after a pop foul. The hands are above the face; the elbows are extended out so there is a diamond-shaped aperture between the hands, through which the player can see. The knees should be flexed somewhat, and the wrists relaxed. When the ball arrives, contact is made with the fingertips; then the arms and legs are straightened to get the necessary upward follow-through.

The setter uses that basic form. But whereas an ordinary pass calls for the ball to be played from just about the level of the upturned chin, the setter's pass is made from above the forehead, and contact with the ball is made somewhat higher, since the setup pass is normally a high, short pass. This position also allows the setter to make a back set—to a player behind—by bending the hands back sharply at the wrists as contact with the ball is made.

To return serves and hard shots, a player often uses the underhand pass, also known as the "bump." The basic idea is to get the arms in the way of the ball and simply let it bounce off in the direction desired. In executing such a pass, the player must get down very low, in a crouch, with arms straight out and hands clasped together. The ball should hit the forearms just above the wrists. The player then straightens up somewhat and follows through gently, more to control the flight of the ball than to give it any additional impetus.

Spiking. The beginner thinks of the spiker as a player who stands at the net and waits for a high pass, so that the ball can be slammed to the floor on the other side of the net by the spiker. Actually, the spiker usually starts from well behind the net and then moves to the spot where the ball is being set. This provides momentum which can be transferred to the ball, and it also allows the opposition less time to prepare for a block.

A good spiker should jump to a maximum height and hit the ball at the top of the leap, which requires precise timing. Starting from perhaps 10 ft back, the spiker takes two long strides toward the net, positions the feet together, and then takes off. (A two-foot takeoff is employed so that the player can get as close as possible to the net without touching it with a foot or leg on the way up.) This leap requires strong arm action; both arms swing upward to add momentum to the jump. The ball is hit with the heel of the cupped hand or, occasionally, with the fist. Much momentum must come from a forward snap of the wrist at the moment of impact, or the spiker may face a penalty for throwing the ball.

There are three basic types of spikes. When right at the net, the spiker should make contact slightly behind the top of the ball, to drive it downward. When stationed a little farther back, up to some 5 ft from the net, the spiker hits the ball slightly above center; this gives it a slight downward direction but permits clearing the net. From 5 ft and more behind the net, the spiker should hit the ball squarely in the center, to drive it forward.

At the very top of the leap, the expert spiker can quickly size up the defense in seeking an opening. If confronted by blockers, the spiker may lob the ball deep or "dink" it—tap it just over the net or just over the blockers. In any event, good strategy calls for hitting in the direction of an uncovered area, from which a return will be impossible or at least difficult.

Blocking. The block is the basic defense against the spike, and a good blocker needs the same good timing that a spiker has. The blocker should get into position directly opposite the spiker, and leap a little bit later than the spiker does, while extending the arms fully above the head, with the fingers spread and the thumbs just an inch or two apart. The hands should be slightly in front of the head and bent slightly forward at the wrists so that, when the ball rebounds, it will be traveling downward.

Glossary

ace—A point scored on an unreturned serve.

change of pace—A serve or spike hit at less than usual speed.

cross set—A set that travels a long distance, parallel to the net.

dig—A save made near the floor on a hard-hit ball, usually with the forearms or with the heel of one hand.

double foul—When both teams commit fouls on the same volley, a double foul is the result.

double hit—When a player illegally hits or touches the ball twice in succession, the infraction is so called.

foot foul—Stepping on or across the end line before hitting the ball when serving.

held ball—When the ball is not cleanly hit, but momentarily rests in a player's hands or arms, it is said to be "held."

kill—Usually a spike; sometimes, another hard shot that results in a point.

side-out—Loss of service through an error or foul.

tip—Similar to a "dink"; a short shot to an uncovered area.

U.S. Volleyball Association Open Champions

Men

1928	Germantown, Pa., YMCA
1929	Hyde Park YMCA, Chicago
1930	Hyde Park YMCA, Chicago
1931	San Antonio YMCA
1932	San Antonio YMCA
1933	Houston YMCA
1934	Houston YMCA
1935	Houston YMCA
1936	Houston YMCA
1937	Duncan YMCA, Chicago
1938	Houston YMCA
1939	Houston YMCA
1940	Los Angeles AC
1941	North Ave. Larrabee YMCA, Chicago
1942	North Ave. Larrabee YMCA, Chicago
1943-44	No competition
1945	North Ave. Larrabee YMCA, Chicago
1946	Pasadena YMCA
1947	North Ave. Larrabee YMCA, Chicago
1948	Hollywood YMCA
1949	Downtown YMCA, Los Angeles
1950	Long Beach YMCA
1951	Hollywood YMCA
1952	Hollywood YMCA
1953	Hollywood YMCA
1954	Stockton, Calif., YMCA
1955	Stockton, Calif., YMCA
1956	Hollywood YMCA
1957	Hollywood YMCA
1958	Hollywood YMCA
1959	Hollywood YMCA
1960	Los Angeles West Side JCC
1961	Hollywood YMCA
1962	Hollywood YMCA
1963	Hollywood YMCA
1964	Hollywood YMCA
1965	Los Angeles West Side JCC
1966	Long Beach Sand & Sea Club
1967	Fresno Volleyball Club
1968	Los Angeles West Side JCC
1969	Downtown YMCA, Los Angeles
1970	Chart House, San Diego
1971	Santa Monica, Calif., YMCA
1972	Chart House, San Diego
1973	Chuck's Steak House, Santa Monica, Calif.
1974	U of Calif.-Santa Barbara
1975	Chart House, San Diego
1976	Maccabi Union, Los Angeles

Women

1949	Houston
1950	Santa Monica, Calif.
1951	Houston Eagles
1952	Voit No. 1, Santa Monica
1953	Voit No. 1, Santa Monica
1954	Houston Houstonettes
1955	Santa Monica Mariners
1956	Santa Monica Mariners
1957	Santa Monica Mariners
1958	Santa Monica Mariners
1959	Santa Monica Mariners
1960	Santa Monica Mariners
1961	Long Beach Breakers
1962	Long Beach Aherns
1963	Long Beach Aherns
1964	Los Angeles Ahern Shamrocks
1965	Los Angeles Ahern Shamrocks
1966	Los Angeles Renegades
1967	Long Beach Shamrocks
1968	Long Beach Shamrocks
1969	Long Beach Shamrocks
1970	Long Beach Shamrocks
1971	Los Angeles Renegades Red
1972	South Texas, Houston
1973	E Pluribus Unum, Houston
1974	Los Angeles Renegades
1975	Adidas VC, Anaheim, Calif.
1976	Pasadena, Texas

Citizens Savings Volleyball Hall of Fame

Players

Spartico Anzuini	Zoann Neff (McFarland)
Holly Brock	Michael O'Hara
Wilbur Caldwell	William Olsson
Lou Sara Clark (McWilliams)	Nancy Owen
Rolf Engen	Carl Owens
Jean K. Gaertner	Pedro Velasco
Carolyn Gregory (Conrad)	James Ward
Lois Ellen Haraughty	Jane Ward
A. H. Massopust	Samuel M. Ward
James Montague	John Weible
Linda Murphy	Harold Wendt
Sidney Nachlas	James Wortham

Contributors

George J. Fisher	A. H. Massopust
A. Provost "Pop" Idell	William G. Morgan

Bibliography. Hartman, P. F.: *Volleyball: Fundamentals*, Merrill, Columbus, Ohio, 1968; Robison, Bonnie et al.: *Sports Illustrated Volleyball*, Lippincott, Philadelphia–New York, 1972.

WALKING—During the middle of the nineteenth century, walking had something like the position that jogging has today: It was considered an excellent outdoor exercise, especially for older men who might not want to compete in more vigorous sports. As a sport, it won some public attention through individual endurance efforts, first in England and then in the United States. During the 1870s, walking races were remarkably popular in the United States—especially the "six-day" races at Gilmore Gardens in New York, which were eventually supplanted by the better-known bicycle races.

Because a distinct line had to be drawn between fast walking and slow running, the kind of walking seen in competition is not the kind we are used to seeing on the street. In race walking, at least one foot must be in contact with the ground at all times. Specifically, the advancing foot must touch the ground before the rear foot leaves the ground. In addition, for a moment during each step the leg must be straightened—that is, the knee must be unbent for that moment.

Rules pertaining to the start, progress, and finish of a walking race are the same as those for running events, except that starting blocks are never used in walking races. In races of more than 20 km or 12 mi, competitors are allowed to stop at official refreshment stands every 5 km or 3 mi, starting at the 10-km or 6-mi mark.

A competitor is warned upon committing a first violation of the rules and disqualified for a second violation.

Walking events are on the Olympic program, and shorter walks are conducted as part of the AAU national track and field meets.

AAU Outdoor Champions

3,000 Meters

1920	William Plant	13:08.0
1921–34	No competition	
1935	Harry Hinkel	13:43.3
1936	Harry Hinkel	13:36.8
1937	Max Beutel	14:15.0
1938	Henry Cieman	13:39.9
1939	Otto Kotraba	14:04.7
1940	Otto Kotraba	13:53.0
1941	Joseph Megyesy	14:37.9
1942	John Connolly	14:16.3
1943	James Wilson	14:16.9
1944	Fred Sharaga	14:08.5
1945	Sam Bleifer	14:27.5
1946	Ernest Weber	13:51.8
1947	Ernest Weber	14:10.1
1948	Henry H. Laskau	13:17.9
1949	Henry H. Laskau	13:34.0
1950	Henry H. Laskau	13:09.6
1951	Henry H. Laskau	13:13.2
1952	Henry H. Laskau	12:52.7
1956	Henry H. Laskau	12:39.0
1959	Elliott Denman	13:52.2
1960	Rudy Haluza	13:22.1
1964	Ronald Zinn	13:48.6
1968	Don DeNoon	12:37.9

2 Miles

1953	Henry H. Laskau	14:23.4
1954	Henry H. Laskau	14:23.3
1955	Henry H. Laskau	15:09.4
1957	Henry H. Laskau	14:28.3
1958	John Humcke	15:07.5
1961	Ronald Zinn	15:46.8
1962	Ronald Zinn	14:35.8
1963	Ronald Zinn	14:03.6
1965	Ron Laird	14:04.2
1966	Ron Laird	13:52.6
1967	Ron Laird	13:41.4
1969	Ron Laird	13:31.6
1970	Tom Dooley	13:44.0
1971	Larry Young	13:49.6

3 Miles

1972	Larry Young	21:39.8
1973	John Knifton	21:36.4

5,000 Meters

1974	John Knifton	22:23.0
1975	Ron Laird	22:08.6
1976	Ron Laird	21:09.32

AAU Indoor Champions

1,500 Meters

1933	William Carlson	6:15.8
1934	Charles Eschenback	6:14.8
1935	Henry Cieman	6:07.3
1936	Charles Eschenback	6:18.1
1937	Nathan Jaeger	6:20.2
1938	Otto Kotraba	6:21.8
1939	Otto Kotraba	6:23.0

1 Mile

1897	Harry Ladd	7:23.0
1898–1906	No competition	
1907	Sam Leibgold	7:41.2
1908	Sam Leibgold	7:19.8
1909	Sam Leibgold	7:13.6
1910–19	No competition	
1920	J. B. Pearman	6:39.8
1921	R. F. Remer	6:29.0
1922	William Plant	6:40.6
1923	William Plant	6:55.8
1924	William Plant	6:43.4
1925	Alexander Zeller	7:04.8
1926	Harry Hinkel	7:03.6

1961	Ronald Zinn	6:38.8
1962	Ronald Zinn	6:36.0
1963	Ronald Zinn	6:42.6
1964	Ron Laird	6:22.7
1965	Ronald Zinn	6:25.7
1966	Rudy Haluza	6:39.2
1967	Don DeNoon	6:28.0
1968	Ron Laird	6:16.9
1969	Dave Romansky	6:21.9
1970	Dave Romansky	6:14.0
1971	Ron Laird	6:24.9
1972	Dave Romansky	6:13.4
1973	Ron Daniel	6:22.0

2 Miles

1974	Larry Walker	13:24.0
1975	Ron Daniel	13:36.8
1976	Ron Laird	13:37.0

Hall of Fame

(Citizens Savings Athletic Foundation has elected the following race walkers to its Track and Field Hall of Fame.)

John Deni	William Mihalo
Harry Hinkel	William Plant
Henry H. Laskau	Ronald Zinn

WATER POLO—The name seems unlikely, but there was a reason for it when water polo was first played in England about 1870: The players rode on floating barrels, painted to resemble horses, and the ball was hit with a stick. Other versions soon developed in swimming-crazy England, among them water football, water basketball, and water handball. Modern water polo probably derived primarily from water football.

The sport arrived in the United States some time during the 1880s, and in 1897 Harold Roeder of the Knickerbocker Athletic Club in New York drew up the first formal set of rules. In 1900 water polo was on the Olympic program.

In the meantime, softball water polo had been developed in the United States. In this version the ball is slightly deflated, and the rules allow holding the ball while swimming with it. Such a provision makes it a very rough sport, since swimmers are "tackled" and held under water until they release the ball. In the softball version, a goal is scored by the player upon touching the ball to a small outlined area at one end of the pool.

Softball water polo was on the 1904 Olympic program in St. Louis, but other countries refused to enter. The AAU, which took control of the sport in 1906 and held the first national championship in that year, banned the softball game in 1910. Nevertheless, it lingered on in some clubs until the 1930s.

Water polo has grown greatly in popularity in the United States since World War II. One major reason is probably its adoption, in 1952, as a permanent Olympic sport. Another is the extremely competitive nature of swimming in this country. An excellent swimmer who may be a couple of seconds too slow to place in the national championships can gain some measure of satisfaction by playing for a good water-polo team.

The YMCA began national invitational championship play in 1963. The NAIA held its first national tournament

Fred Spector leads Elliott Denman (25) in walking race. (*Jack Boitano, AAU.*)

1927	William Plant	6:34.8
1928	Harry Hinkel	6:35.4
1929	Harry Hinkel	6:40.4
1930	Michael Pecora	6:43.4
1931	William Carlson	6:47.8
1932	Michael Pecora	6:27.2
1940	Charles Eschenback	6:51.7
1941	Nathan Jaeger	7:12.1
1942	Albert Cicerone	7:13.9
1943	Sune Carlson	7:20.4
1944	Joseph Megyesy	7:10.5
1945	Joseph Megyesy	7:13.9
1946	Joseph Megyesy	7:11.4
1947	Ernest Weber	6:44.2
1948	Henry H. Laskau	6:43.8
1949	Henry H. Laskau	6:29.5
1950	Henry H. Laskau	6:43.4
1951	Henry H. Laskau	6:27.0
1952	Henry H. Laskau	6:28.0
1953	Henry H. Laskau	6:20.6
1954	Henry H. Laskau	6:31.7
1955	Henry H. Laskau	6:30.4
1956	Henry H. Laskau	6:44.5
1957	Henry H. Laskau	6:39.7
1958	John Humcke	6:55.5
1959	John Humcke	6:42.2
1960	Frank Sepos	6:27.4

in 1968, and the NCAA followed suit in 1969. In addition, high school leagues exist in a number of states. It is estimated that there are now more than 1,000 college and club teams in this country.

The United States has become competitive internationally, but has yet to win an Olympic medal in the sport. The best finish was fourth, in 1952.

Rules

Pool and Equipment. Championship-level games are played in an all-deep pool (at least 6½ ft deep), 30 m long, and 20 m wide. At each end of the pool is a goal, a cage with a sloping back, 10 ft wide, 3 ft high from water surface to the top, and at least 18 in deep.

The ball has a circumference measuring 27 to 28 in. It weighs 14 to 16 oz and is inflated to 15 lb of pressure. It is yellow, for visibility, and has an unusually rough surface, for easy gripping when wet.

Players are required to wear caps as a means of team identification. The home team wears white, the visiting team caps of a color that will not be mistaken for white or for the yellow of the ball. (In international play the visitors' caps are always blue-black.)

Teams and Players. A team consists of seven players: three forwards, three guards, and a goalie. Except for the goalie, designations of position mean little or nothing in the modern game, in which every player is expected to cover the entire pool.

In international and AAU tournament play, a squad may consist of no more than 11 players. Substitutes may enter the game only during the interval after a goal or before overtime, or to replace players who have been expelled.

Time and Timeouts. Time limits vary from 5 min per quarter, under international rules, to 8 min per quarter in intercollegiate championship play. AAU rules call for 7 min per quarter. There are no timeouts under international or AAU rules. In AAU women's competition, one timeout is allowed per half. There are three allowable timeouts per game under NCAA rules.

The goalie rises in the water as the ball hovers in the goal area. *(Water Polo Scoreboard.)*

Progress of Play. When the game begins, the ball is placed in the center of the pool and members of both teams sprint for it from their own goal lines. A player may move the ball by passing or by "dribbling"—swimming with the head up and the ball between the arms so that it bobs along on the wave created by the swimmer's head. No player, except the goalie, may touch the ball with more than one hand at a time, nor touch the bottom or sides of the pool while touching or holding the ball.

Defensive players may not hold, sink, or pull a player back unless the opponent is holding the ball, and they may not interfere in any way with a player's free limb movement unless that player is touching the ball.

The object of the game is to score points by throwing the ball into the opponent's goal. Teams generally maneuver offensively in an attempt to get a player free in the center-forward position—in front of the goal and as close to it as possible, ideally about 2 yd away. A team is given 45 sec after gaining possession of the ball in which to make a scoring attempt. If time expires before a shot is taken, the other team is awarded a free throw.

The goalie must remain within the team's own goal area, marked by a 4-yd (4-m) line, at all times. The goalie may handle the ball with both hands, but may never throw it beyond the center line.

If regulation play ends in a tie, two overtime periods of 3 min each, with a 1-min interval, are played; if necessary thereafter, overtime periods continue until there is a decision.

Out of Play. The ball is out of play when it hits the side of the pool above the water line, or goes entirely out of the pool, or completely crosses a goal line. In the first two cases, the ball is put back into play from the spot where it went out, by the nearest opponent. If an attacker is responsible for the ball's going over the goal line, the opposing goalie puts the ball in play with a throw from the goal line, between the goal posts. If a defender is responsible, the nearest attacker puts the ball in play with a corner throw from the 2-yd (2-m) line on the side of the pool where the ball went out. No player except the defending goalie may be within the 2-m area.

Fouls and Penalties. Intercollegiate and international rules pertaining to fouls and penalties differ in many respects.

In international competition, major fouls include holding, pushing, and sinking a player, and committing a minor foul, inside the goal area, that directly prevents the scoring of a goal. The penalty is a 1-min eviction to the penalty box, with no substitution allowed.

A major foul in intercollegiate play is a foul that endangers an opponent—attacking, striking, or kicking—or the act of refusing to obey a referee or interfering with a penalty shot or free throw. The player is ejected from the game but may be replaced by a substitute after 1 min.

Holding, pulling, pushing, and sinking a player are called personal fouls in intercollegiate play; after five personal fouls, a player is out of the game permanently, as in basketball. If a team commits 10 personal fouls, the opposing team is given a penalty shot.

A penalty shot is also awarded, in intercollegiate and international play, for certain fouls committed directly in front of the goal, inside the goal area, that prevent scoring of a goal. For a penalty shot, the player is given the ball at the 4-yd mark, with only the goalie defending, and must

A player looks for an open teammate to pass to as a defender approaches to force his hand. *(Water Polo Scoreboard.)*

1941 Los Angeles AC
1942–46 No competition
1947 Los Angeles AC
1948 No competition
1949 Whittier, Calif., Swimming Club
1950 Whittier, Calif., Swimming Club
1951 Illinois AC
1952 Los Alamitos, Calif., Naval Air Station
1953 El Segundo, Calif., Swimming Club
1954 New York AC
1955 Illinois AC
1956 New York AC
1957 San Francisco Olympic Club
1958 Illinois AC
1959 San Francisco Olympic Club
1960 Toronto Water Polo Club
1961 New York AC
1962 Commerce, Calif.
1963 Inland-NuPike
1964 Inland-NuPike
1965 New York AC
1966 Commerce, Calif.
1967 Mayor Daley YF, Chicago
1968 Phillips 66, Long Beach, Calif.
1969 DeAnza Aquatic Foundation
1970 DeAnza Aquatic Foundation

shoot the ball immediately at the goal upon a signal from the referee.

In international play a player is expelled from the game after a third major foul. The player may be replaced immediately if a penalty shot is awarded for the foul, or after 1 min if no penalty shot is awarded.

Minor fouls include many lesser violations, such as holding or punching the ball, touching it with both hands, deliberately impeding an opponent who doesn't have the ball, jumping up from the bottom of the pool, and pushing off the sides of the pool. The other team is awarded a free throw from the point of the offense. The player taking the free throw may throw the ball or drop it and dribble it. At least two players must touch the ball after a free throw before a goal can be scored.

Officials. Because of the general European belief that an official runs a game absolutely, and shouldn't have to divide authority, there is only one referee under international rules. Intercollegiate and AAU rules, however, call for two referees, who are basically independent of each other, like basketball officials. In the AAU national tournament, there is just one referee, since the champion will enter international competition. There are usually to two goal judges, as in hockey, and a timekeeper.

AAU Champions

Outdoor—Men
1906 New York AC
1907 New York AC
1908 New York AC
1909 New York AC
1910–28 No competition
1930 New York AC
1931 New York AC
1932 No competition
1933 New York AC
1934 New York AC
1935 New York AC
1936 No competition
1937 New York AC
1938 New York AC
1939 New York AC
1940 No competition

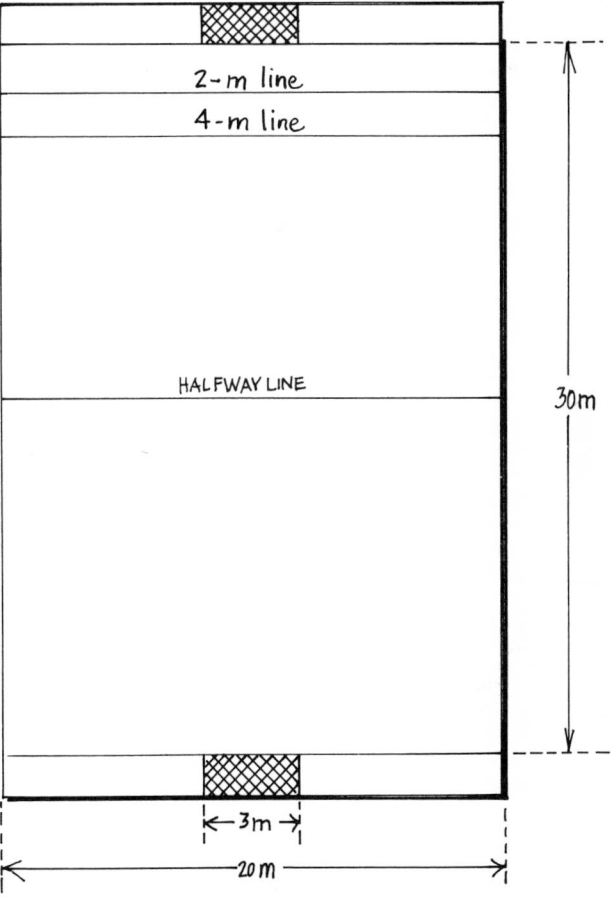

Water polo field

1971   New York AC
1972   Concord, Calif., Swim Club
1973   Concord, Calif., Swim Club
1974   Fullerton, Calif.
1975   Concord, Calif., Swim Club
1976   Concord, Calif., Swim Club
Outdoor—Women
1975   North Miami Beach, Fla.
1976   Fullerton, Calif.

WATERSKIING—There are several different versions of how waterskiing came into existence. One story is that snow skiers visiting the French Riviera during the 1920s began using their skis on the water. Another is that, in 1922, a Minnesotan named Ralph Samuelson made the first water skis of two long pine planks. A third is that Fred Waller of Long Island was the inventor, in 1925.

There may be some truth in all three stories. It may also be true, as has been written, that Waller got the water-ski idea during a visit to the Riviera, and improved on it by producing special skis, about twice as wide as ordinary snow skis. It is certain that Waller in 1925 patented a water ski.

Waterskiing, however, didn't make such progress until the 1930s, when a particularly enthusiastic pioneer came along. Bruce Parker learned to water-ski in 1935, using two planks pulled from the side of a barn. In 1938, Parker got some publicity for the new sport by skiing at 90 mph while towed by an airplane.

Another early enthusiast was John H. Andresen, Jr. In a 1936 meet of aquaplanists, Andresen demonstrated trick riding techniques, including a jump over a ramp more than 3 ft high—a breath-taking accomplishment at the time. His demonstration convinced many that riding on skis would be more fun that riding an aquaplane—essentially a surfboard towed by a boat.

The demonstration also spurred Dan B. Hains to set up a national organization for the sport. The American Water Ski Association (AWSA) was formed in 1939, with Hains as its first president, and Parker won the association's first national tournament that year.

Like many other participant "thrill sports," waterskiing has boomed tremendously since World War II, although interest has apparently leveled off somewhat as other sports—surfing, skin diving, skydiving, for example—have proliferated. The World Water Ski Union, established in 1949, holds world championships every two years.

The Skis. In competition, water skis must be at least 4 ft long and no more than 8 in wide, and the skier is towed on a 75-ft line. Any type of binding is allowed. Like snow skis, water skis are made of a variety of materials, including woods, aluminum, fiber glass, and wood fiberglass combinations.

Conventional water skis look like ordinary planks, rounded at the tips, which curl up slightly. Length ranges from 5 ft to 6 ft, 3 in, width from 5 ½ to 6 ½ in. The most popular bindings are two-piece units of molded rubber, one piece for the front part of the foot, one piece to fit over the heel.

Jumping skis are similar to conventional skis; however, they are slightly heavier and stronger, because of metal reinforcement at the tips and, usually, wooden blocks glued flush to the heel of the ski. Length for men is about 6 ft, with a width of 6½ in; women's skis are about 5 ft long and 6 to 6½ in wide. At the bottom of each ski is a small fin, or keel, about 1 in deep, tapered to allow an easy ride over a ramp.

There are two types of slalom skis, single and double. The single slalom ski is sharply tapered in the rear, and it has two sets of bindings; the rear set has no heel piece, to permit the skier to pivot the foot for better balance. The double slalom ski is similar to a conventional ski. Both types of slalom skis have large, deep fins, to prevent skidding on fast, sharp turns.

Trick skis are quite short (only 4 to 5 ft) and wide (up to the maximum of 8 in). They are slightly curved up, both in front and back, so that they look somewhat like chair rockers in profile. Some skiers like a squared-off heel; others prefer the "banana" shape, with a curved taper both front and back.

Other Gear. The line should be strong, light in weight, and resistant to stretching. Manila is still popular as a fiber, but synthetic fibers, especially polyethylene, are also used. The line is connected to both ends of a tow bar, which may be nothing more than a simple wooden dowel that the skier can grip with both hands.

The simplest attachment to the boat is a shackle-ring combination. Two rings are bolted about 3 in below the

Carl Lyman performs a one-ski ramp flip during his trick run at the 1974 national championships. *(Courtesy of American Water Ski Association.)*

top of the boat's transom and about 8 in apart, and shackles, spliced to each end of the V-shaped bridle, snap on the rings. Another type of attachment is the pylon, a triangular device of pipe, mounted inside the boat, just aft of midships. The AWSA requires that the top of the pylon must be 3 to 5 ft above water level.

The best boat for towing a skier has a shallow-draft V-bottom, a wide transom, and a well-flared bow; this type of boat will leave a minimum of wake to trouble the skier, and will accelerate quickly. Skiing at less than 15-20 mph is difficult; for the slalom and jumping events, a speed of about 35 mph is necessary for top performance.

Basic Techniques. To get started, the skier sits back in the water, with the ski tips above the surface and the line between the tips. The boat should idle into position, taking up all the slack in the line. Then the skier gives the signal to "hit it." The skier's arms are kept straight out in front, parallel to the water's surface; the knees are bent and the body relaxes as the boat does the work. At slower speeds the skis will be tilted up at an angle of as much as 45 degrees, but as the speed increases they will flatten out naturally, until they begin to plane over the surface.

The skier's proper position, once speed is up, is almost vertical; the back should be straight and the skier should be leaning backward slightly, arms straight in line with the tow bar. The knees should be flexed, to act as independent shock absorbers. At first, a beginning skier will ride in the trough between the two waves of the wake. There's better riding in the smoother water outside the wake, though.

To get there, the skier has to know how to turn, a fairly simple matter. To turn right, the skier leans to the right, banking the skis in the same direction. If the skier wants to get outside the wake to the right, the first move is to swing as far as possible to the left, staying in the trough. Then the skier turns as sharply right as possible; the closer the turn approaches a right angle, the easier it will be to get across the wake.

Landing is largely a matter of timing; it takes practice. The boat should travel parallel to the beach, and the skier should head for the beach at an angle, never straight in. Until the skier learns at just what point to let go of the towline, it may be necessary to execute the snowplow in order to slow down without crashing. In the snowplow, as on snow skis, the tips of the skis are brought nearly together while the heels are spread wide apart. Both inside edges should be dug in. A good snowplow gives very effective braking action.

Every water-skier is going to fall from time to time, and beginners can expect to fall fairly often. The first rule is to let go the towline when a fall is coming; the second is to bail out to one side or the other, covering the head with the arms to keep from hitting or being hit by a ski.

Types of Competition

National and regional tournaments must include competition in jumping, slalom, and trick riding; mixed-doubles competition is optional. In addition there is an overall championship based on the total number of points accumulated in the three major events.

Jumping. As in snow skiing, jumpers are judged both on distance and form. The jumper starts with 30 points, and then points and half-points are deducted for specific flaws.

The winner of a long string of national championships, Liz Allan Shetter is shown setting a new women's jumping record of 125 ft at the 1974 national championships. *(Courtesy of American Water Ski Association.)*

The standard ramp is 20 ft long and 6 ft high at the jumping end; it has a waxed, wooden surface. Boat speed is optional with the skier, up to a maximum of 35 mph for men. Each skier gets three jumps.

Points scored on form are added to the jump distance to get the total score for each jump, and the total scores for the top two jumps are added to determine the winner.

Slalom. The skier is allowed to ride on either one or two skis in the slalom, which requires maneuvering along a sinuous course through a series of gates marked by buoys. The skier has to pass outside each buoy. Speed is specified for the run, and scoring is based on points awarded. The skier gets one point for each buoy negotiated. A run consists of four trips along the course, two in each direction. The first set of runs usually brings a number of perfect scores, and competition continues with more runs at increasingly higher speeds until a champion has emerged.

Tricks. In water skiing, each trick is assigned a specific point value. Speed is generally about 20 mph. Judges can deduct up to 20 percent of the listed value for poor form. If a trick is repeated, it doesn't count the second time. If the skier falls, the run is terminated.

Mixed Doubles. Basically a spectator event, mixed doubles calls for two skiers to create an act on skis, from a comedy skit to a pantomimed story done in full costume. Judging is on the basis of continuity, originality, and skiing form.

U.S. Champions—Men

Overall

1939	Bruce Parker
1940	Bruce Parker
1941	Chuck Sligh
1942–45	No competition
1946	Lew Withey
1947	Bob Sligh
1948	Dick Pope, Jr.
1949	Dick Pope, Jr.
1950	Dick Pope, Jr.
1951	Skillman Suydam
1952	Emilio Zamudio
1953	Warren Witherell
1954	Butch Rosenberg
1955	Butch Rosenberg
1956	Alfredo Mendoza
1957	Chuck Stearns
1958	Chuck Stearns
1959	Michael Osborn
1960	Chuck Stearns
1961	Michael Amsbry
1962	Chuck Stearns
1963	Larry Perracho
1964	Michael Osborn
1965	Chuck Stearns
1966	Paul Merrill
1967	Chuck Stearns
1968	Mike Suyderhoud
1969	Mike Suyderhoud
1970	Mike Suyderhoud
1971	Mike Suyderhoud
1972	Mike Suyderhoud
1973	Wayne Grimditch
1974	Ricky McCormick
1975	Ricky McCormick
1976	Chris Redmond

U.S. Champions—Women

Overall

1939	Esther Yates
1940	Virginia Pfoff
1941	Lynda Mae Helder
1942–45	No competition
1946	Willa Worthington
1947	Willa Worthington
1948	Willa Worthington
1949	Willa McGuire
1950	Willa McGuire
1951	Willa McGuire
1952	Marguerite Williams
1953	Leah Marie Rawls
1954	Willa McGuire
1955	Willa McGuire
1956	Elaine Roper
1957	Leah Marie Atkins
1958	Nancie Lee Rideout
1959	Nancie Lee Rideout
1960	Norine Bardill
1961	Janell Kirtley
1962	Jenny Hodges
1963	Barbara Clack
1964	Dicksie Ann Hoyt
1965	Dicksie Ann Hoyt
1966	Barbara Clack
1967	Weslie Walker
1968	Liz Allan
1969	Liz Allan
1970	Liz Allan
1971	Liz Allan Shetter
1972	Liz Allan Shetter
1973	Liz Allan Shetter
1974	Liz Allan Shetter
1975	Liz Allan Shetter
1976	Cindy Todd

Bibliography. Hardman, Thomas C. and William D. Clifford: *Let's Go Water Skiing,* Hawthorn, New York, 1969.

WEIGHTLIFTING—In a sense, weightlifting is probably an ancient sport—it is easy enough to imagine one primitive man challenging another to try lifting a heavy rock. But in its present form, it is a very modern sport which, like gymnastics, originated as a method of training for other sports.

Dumbbells, barbells, and other types of weights were used by traveling strong men to demonstrate their strength to audiences during the early nineteenth century. Weight training began to be taken seriously, especially for wrestlers, about 1885 in Europe, and a national organization to supervise weightlifting and wrestling was organized in Germany in 1891.

Stage performances by such outstanding strong men as Louis Cyr, Eugen Sandow (Frederick Mueller), and George Hackenschmidt, also famous as a wrestler, helped increase interest in the sport in the United States around the turn of the century.

Cyr, a Canadian, was billed as the strongest man in the world, and at one time *The Police Gazette* offered a $5,000 prize to anyone who could duplicate one of his feats of strength. His greatest fame came from his back lift—he once lifted 18 men, standing on a platform that weighed approximately 500 lb, on his back—but he also handled barbells and dumbbells.

Sandow was not as strong as Cyr—he was not nearly as big—but he was an outstanding showman. He stood about 5 ft, 8 in and weighed about 186 lb. Under the management of Flo Ziegfeld in this country, Sandow performed such feats as "jumping rope" with a 125-lb barbell, chinning himself with a single thumb, and doing a backward somersault over a chair while holding a 35-lb dumbbell in each hand. Front-row seats at his performance sometimes brought as much as $250 apiece. After retiring in 1905, Sandow opened an Institute of Physical Culture in London.

Hackenschmidt, who was born in Estonia, was perhaps the most popular and the strongest of the triumvirate. He was known in this country as a professional wrestler, but it was also well known that he had given weightlifting exhibitions and that weightlifting was part of his training routine. "Hack" lingered in legend long after retiring. When the Chicago Cubs held a contest among baseball fans to choose a nickname for their young power hitter, Lewis R. Wilson, the winning entry was "Hack" for Hackenschmidt—14 years after Hackenschmidt had retired to London.

The major promoter of weightlifting as a sport in the United States was Alan Calvert, who founded the Milo Barbell Company in Philadelphia in 1902. Calvert sold much of his equipment by mail order, and he publicized the sport and his company through a magazine, *Strength.* Shortly afterward, Bob Hoffman founded the York Barbell Company, and he also published his own magazine, *Strength and Health.* Both men contributed greatly to the growth of weightlifting in this country.

Nevertheless, weightlifting was rather slow to catch on

In the clean and jerk, the weightlifter first pulls the weight to his chest, then raises it above his head, arms fully extended. This is Vasily Alexeev of Russia. *(Bruce Klemens.)*

in the United States. The AAU conducted the first national championships in 1929. The sport had been on the Olympic program permanently since 1920, and there were two weightlifting events at the first modern Olympic Games in 1896. Despite the late start, the United States quickly became dominant in international competition, starting in the late 1930s, and the domination continued until the 1956 Olympics, when Russia came to the forefront.

One reason for the comparative American decline has perhaps been the development of a new form of the sport in this country and Canada (and, to a lesser extent, in England). The classical weightlifting events—snatch, clean and jerk, and press—are replaced, in "powerlifting," by the two-hand bench press, the squat, and the two-hand dead lift. These lifts put much less emphasis on form and balance, and correspondingly more emphasis on sheer strength. Another element in powerlifting is the judging of physique—the "Mr. America" contests, for example, are primarily contests among exponents of powerlifting. The Amateur Athletic Union took over nationwide supervision of the sport in 1967, and the International Powerlifting Federation was formed in 1972, with 13 member nations. Powerlifting has also become a popular collegiate sport.

Competitive Events

Several different kinds of lifts have, at one time or another, been the basis for competition. By 1936, how-

ever, three lifts had been adopted as the standard ones, and they remained unchanged until 1973.

The Press. Pressing a weight consists of raising it from the chest or shoulders over the head and, in formal competition, holding it there for 2 sec with the arms fully extended. The legs must not be used to assist.

There are two recognized kinds of pressing. In the military press, the lifter must remain in a military position of attention throughout the lift, body perfectly erect and heels together, and with no backward bend at the waist.

In international competition, the actual event was the clean and press, in which the weight is first lifted in a single continuous movement (cleaned) from the floor to the chest, then pushed upward above the head. The weight must not touch the chest. The "Olympic press," which permits a certain amount of back bend, also is used; feet may be comfortably spaced. After the 1972 Olympics the clean and press was dropped from formal competition because it was considered too difficult to judge—the amount of back bend permitted was subject to wide interpretation—and because the press puts undue strain on the back muscles.

Clean and Jerk. In this event a competitor can lift a good deal more weight than in either of the other Olympic events. It begins, as the name implies, with a clean lift of the weight to the chest; then the weight is thrown overhead with combined leg and arm thrust. There are two different methods of "jerking" the weight overhead; either the lifter squats and then restraightens the knees with a snap, or the legs are split, one extended far behind, in order to get under the weight.

Snatch. The snatch is similar to the clean, except that the lifter must bring the weight over the head in one continuous movement. Either a squat or a split may be employed in order to get leg power into the lift, and to decrease the total distance the weight must be raised.

In all three lifts, the weight must be held overhead for 2 sec. Competition is held in weight divisions, and the champion in each division is the contestant who has lifted the greatest total weight.

Bench Press. In this event the contestant lies on a bench and lifts a weight from the chest to locked arms above the chest. AAU rules specify a bench 10 to 12 in wide and 14 to 18 in high; it is generally about 4 ft long. The lifter usually lets the feet hang to the floor. The barbell is on a support above the lifter; the contestant takes it on straight arms, lowers it to the chest for 2 sec, then presses it over the chest again. No bridging of the back is allowed.

Dead Lift. This is considered the basic test of overall body strength. The lifter simply picks up a barbell from the ground and raises it while getting to an erect position, then holds it there for 2 sec.

Squats. Also called the "deep knee bend," this event is a common training method for weightlifters, wrestlers, and other athletes who want to develop leg strength. The lifter first supports a barbell across the shoulders, usually with the help of two or more assistants, then bends the knees as far as possible and straightens up again. The feet must be kept flat on the heels throughout the lift, and the lifter must bend the knees far enough so that the tops of the thighs are at least parallel to the floor.

AAU Champions

(Usually 3 lifts through 1972; 2 lifts since then)

112 lb

1932	Lucian LaPlante	470
1933	Lucian LaPlante	485½
1934	Robert K. Knodle	693
1935	David Rothman	638
1936	John Fritshe	456½
1937	A. Hutchinson	515
1938	Americo Lemma	561
1939	Americo Lemma	530

Flyweight (114½ lb)

1970	Eugene Casasola	605
1971	Dave Moyer	584¼
1972	John Yamauchi	595½
1973	Donald Warner	391¼
1974	Joel Widdel	430
1975	Forrest Felton	363.8
1976	Joel Widdell	424.4

118 lb

1929	Robert Knodle	682
1930	Robert Knodle	715
1931	Robert Knodle	715
1932	Joseph Fiorito	485
1933	Joseph Fiorito	496½
1934	Ralph Vieria	731½
1935	Joseph Fiorito	718
1936	Joseph Fiorito	533½
1937	Ed Heffernan	535

1938	B. Leardi	520
1939	B. Leardi	525

Bantamweight (123½ lb)

1929	Al Gaukler	665½
1930	J. Arthur Levan	819½
1931	J. Arthur Levan	852½
1932	J. Arthur Levan	540
1933	J. Arthur Levan	568
1934	J. Arthur Levan	830½
1935	J. Arthur Levan	841½
1936	J. Arthur Levan	588½
1937	Mike Mungioli	685
1938	Mike Mungioli	600
1939	Elwood P. Cauffman	560
1940	Joseph Fiorito	550
1941	Wesley Cochrane	616½
1942	Joseph De Pietro	565
1943	Joseph De Pietro	585
1944	Emerick Ishikawa	630
1945	Emerick Ishikawa	635
1946	Joseph De Pietro	646
1947	Joseph De Pietro	615
1948	Joseph De Pietro	675
1949	Joseph De Pietro	620
1950	Joseph De Pietro	635
1951	Joseph De Pietro	640
1952	Richard Tom	628½
1953	Jack Hughes	615
1954	Charles Vinci	690
1955	Charles Vinci	690
1956	Charles Vinci	690
1957	Angel Famiglietti	640
1958	Charles Vinci	715
1959	Charles Vinci	700
1960	Charles Vinci	700
1961	Charles Vinci	740
1962	Dick Krell	670
1963	Shiro Ichinosaka	700
1964	Gary Hanson	700
1965	Gary Hanson	665
1966	Lennell Sheppard	630
1967	Gary Hanson	690
1968	Fernando Baez	740
1969	Fernando Baez	745
1970	Salvador Dominguez	650
1971	Salvador Dominguez	667
1972	Salvador Dominguez	672½
1973	Dwight Tamanaka	452
1974	Salvador Dominguez	485
1975	John Yamauchi	468½
1976	John Yamauchi	479½

Featherweight (132 lb)

1929	Richard Bachtell	852½
1930	Richard Bachtell	847
1931	Richard Bachtell	852½
1932	Anthony Terlazzo	570
1933	Michael Fontana	579
1934	Richard Bachtell	896½
1935	Richard Bachtell	935
1936	Anthony Terlazzo	693
1937	Richard Bachtell	635
1938	John Terry	640
1939	John Terry	660
1940	John Terry	665
1941	John Terry	665
1942	Joseph Mills	635
1943	Richard Bachtell	630
1944	Fred Curry	660
1945	Joseph De Pietro	615
1946	Emerick Ishikawa	641
1947	Emerick Ishikawa	670

1948	William Lowrance	675
1949	Richard Tomita	665
1950	Richard Greenawalt	640
1951	George Yoshioka	650
1952	Richard Tomita	661
1953	Mitz O'Shima	680
1954	Yaz Kuzuhara	685
1955	Isaac Berger	705
1956	Isaac Berger	720
1957	Isaac Berger	760
1958	Isaac Berger	800
1959	Isaac Berger	740
1960	Isaac Berger	810
1961	Isaac Berger	790
1962	Walter Imahara	720
1963	Yoshinobu Miyako	800
1964	Isaac Berger	795
1965	Walter Imahara	790
1966	Walter Imahara	765
1967	Walter Imahara	775
1968	Walter Imahara	795
1969	Gary Hanson	770
1970	Fernando Baez	750
1971	Enrique Hernandez	766
1972	Philip Sanderson	744
1973	Roy Moore	518
1974	Roman Mielec	512½
1975	Dane Hussey	534.6
1976	Dane Hussey	534.6

Lightweight (148¾ lb)

1928	Arnie Sundberg	570
1929	Max Rohrer	891
1930	Max Rohrer	935
1931	George Horn	935
1932	Arnie Sundberg	632
1933	Anthony Terlazzo	667
1934	Robert M. Mitchell	990
1935	Anthony Terlazzo	1,006½
1936	John Terpak	737
1937	Anthony Terlazzo	780
1938	Anthony Terlazzo	765
1939	Anthony Terlazzo	805
1940	Anthony Terlazzo	770
1941	Anthony Terlazzo	800
1942	Anthony Terlazzo	760
1943	Anthony Terlazzo	800
1944	Anthony Terlazzo	800
1945	Anthony Terlazzo	760
1946	Peter George	716
1947	Joseph Pitman	705
1948	Joseph Pitman	730
1949	Joseph Pitman	735
1950	Joseph Pitman	765
1951	Joseph Pitman	775
1952	Tommy T. Kono	798
1953	Joseph Pitman	745
1954	Joseph Pitman	755
1955	Joseph Pitman	765
1956	Joseph Pitman	785
1957	Joseph Pitman	770
1958	Kenzie Onuma	795
1959	Paul Goldberg	780
1960	Tony Garcy	780
1961	Paul Goldberg	745
1962	Tony Garcy	800
1963	Tony Garcy	805
1964	James Massai Bu	775
1965	Homer Brannum	820
1966	Larry Mintz	805
1967	Homer Brannum	835
1968	Steve Mansour	820
1969	Steve Mansour	860

1970	James Benjamin	860
1971	James Benjamin	859¾
1972	Dan Cantore	931½
1973	Dan Cantore	600¾
1974	Dan Cantore	633¾
1975	Dan Cantore	606.3
1976	Dan Cantore	628¼

Middleweight (165 ¼ lb)

1928	B. McDowell	570
1929	A. Faas	902
1930	Arnie Sundberg	968
1931	Arnie Sundberg	940½
1932	Stanley Kratkowski	680
1933	Walter Zagurski	694½
1934	Stanley Kratkowski	1,039½
1935	Stanley Kratkowski	1,095
1936	Stanley Kratkowski	748
1937	John Terpak	805
1938	John Terpak	785
1939	John Terpak	800
1940	John Terpak	800
1941	John Terpak	815
1942	John Terpak	800
1943	James Manning	750
1944	John Terpak	800
1945	John Terpak	775
1946	Frank Spellman	831
1947	Stanley Stanczyk	825
1948	Frank Spellman	855
1949	Peter George	830
1950	Peter George	835
1951	Peter George	860
1952	Peter George	860
1953	Tommy T. Kono	915
1954	Bert Elliott	765
1955	Dick Giller	800
1956	C. Warner	835

In the snatch, the lifter has to pick up the weight in one continuous movement, holding it over his head for 2 sec. He is allowed to split or to squat under it, as Christo Plachkov of Bulgaria is doing here. *(Bruce Klemens.)*

1957	Peter George	885
1958	Tommy Kono	890
1959	Tommy Kono	905
1960	Tommy Kono	865
1961	Frank Spellman	800
1962	Joseph Puleo	875
1963	Hitoshi Ouchi	895
1964	Joseph Puleo	905
1965	Tony Garcy	880
1966	Tony Garcy	940
1967	Russell Knipp	955
1968	Russell Knipp	955
1969	Fred Lowe	950
1970	Fred Lowe	960
1971	Russell Knipp	1,008½
1972	Fred Lowe	992
1973	Fred Lowe	694¼
1974	Fred Lowe	672½
1975	Fred Lowe	655.9
1976	Fred Lowe	672¼

Light-Heavyweight (181¾ lb)

1928	Al Bevan	605
1929	Albert Manger	957
1930	William L. Good	1,017½
1931	William L. Good	1,056
1932	William L. Good	715
1933	William L. Good	733
1934	Gino Quilici	1,012
1935	S. Weisch	1,023½
1936	John H. Miller	761
1937	William L. Good	800
1938	Stanley Kratkowski	805
1939	John Davis	815
1940	John Davis	855
1941	Frank Kay	850
1942	Frank Kay	860
1943	John Terpak	800
1944	Bill Bush	755
1945	Harold Vinkin	770
1946	Frank Kay	836
1947	John Terpak	840
1948	Stanley Stanczyk	880
1949	Stanley Stanczyk	915
1950	Stanley Stanczyk	910
1951	Stanley Stanczyk	885
1952	Clyde Emrich	864
1953	Stanley Stanczyk	915
1954	Tommy T. Kono	930
1955	Tommy T. Kono	940
1956	Jim George	875
1957	Tommy T. Kono	970
1958	Jim George	880
1959	Jim George	900
1960	Jim George	915
1961	Tommy Kono	980
1962	Tommy Kono	945
1963	Tommy Kono	970
1964	Gary Cleveland	955
1965	Gary Cleveland	985
1966	Joe Puleo	935
1967	Joe Puleo	955
1968	Joe Puleo	1,025
1969	Michael Karchut	1,035
1970	Michael Karchut	1,055
1971	Michael Karchut	1,008¾
1972	Michael Karchut	1,041¾
1973	Michael Karchut	694¼
1974	Tom Hirtz	762½
1975	Peter Rawluk	689.9
1976	Sam Bigler	705¼

Middle-Heavyweight (198 lb)

1951	Norbert Schemansky	915
1952	Norbert Schemansky	886
1953	Norbert Schemansky	900
1954	Dave Sheppard	975
1955	Dave Sheppard	965
1956	Clyde Emrich	955
1957	Clyde Emrich	910
1958	Fred Schutz	925
1959	Clyde Emrich	945
1960	John Pulskamp	990
1961	Bill March	950
1962	Bill March	975
1963	Bill March	1,000
1964	Bill March	1,010
1965	Bill March	1,020
1966	B. Bartholomew	985
1967	Phil Grippald	1,035
1968	Phil Grippaldi	1,055
1969	Frank Capsouras	1,080
1970	Phil Grippaldi	1,090
1971	Rick Holbrook	1,097
1972	Rick Holbrook	1,130
1973	Phil Grippaldi	716½
1974	Phil Grippaldi	755¼
1975	Michael Karchut	749.6
1976	Lee Jones Jr.	782½

Heavyweight (242 lb)

1928	Tom Tyler	760
1929	William Rohrer	1,045
1930	Albert Manger	1,001
1931	William Rohrer	784½
1932	Albert Manger	704
1933	John Mallo	760½
1934	William L. Good	1,210
1935	William L. Good	1,205
1936	John Grimek	786½
1937	David Mayor	835
1938	Steve Stanko	850
1939	Steve Stanko	895
1940	Steve Stanko	950½
1941	John Davis	1,009¾
1942	John Davis	905
1943	John Davis	940
1944	Frank Schofro	850
1945	H. G. Curtis	855
1946	John Davis	918
1947	John Davis	900
1948	John Davis	1,025
1949	Norbert Schemansky	885
1950	John Davis	1,010
1951	John Davis	1,062
1952	John Davis	1,002
1953	John Davis	990
1954	Norbert Schemansky	1,050
1955	Paul Anderson	1,145
1956	Paul Anderson	1,175
1957	Norbert Schemansky	990
1958	David Ashman	1,000
1959	David Ashman	1,040
1960	James Bradford	1,085
1961	James Bradford	1,070
1962	Norbert Schemansky	1,140
1963	Sid Henry	1,125
1964	Norbert Schemansky	1,160
1965	Norbert Schemansky	1,155
1966	Gary Gubner	1,170
1967	Bob Bednarski	1,175
1968	Joe Murry	1,035
1969	Bob Bednarski	1,215

1970	Bob Bednarski	1,185
1971	Gary Deal	1,157¼
1972	Frank Kapsoures	1,175½
1973	Bob Bednarski	749¼
1974	Allan Feuerbach	760½
1975	Mark Cameron	804.7
1976	Mark Cameron	848¾

Super-Heavyweight (over 242 lb)

1968	Bob Bednarski	1,280
1969	Ken Patera	1,195
1970	Ken Patera	1,285
1971	Ken Patera	1,306¼
1972	Ken Patera	1,329¼
1973	Jacob Stefan	776¼
1974	James Gaigano	760½
1975	Bruce Wilhelm	766.1
1976	Bruce Wilhelm	848¾

Citizens Savings Hall of Fame

Weightlifters

Paul Anderson—AAU heavyweight champion 1955–56; world champion 1955, Olympic champion 1956.

Dick Bachtell—AAU featherweight champion 1929–1931, 1934–1935, 1937, 1943.

David Berger—A native of the United States, Berger moved to Israel in 1970 and was a member of the 1972 Olympic team, one of the nine athletes killed after being kidnapped by Arab terrorists.

Isaac Berger—AAU featherweight champion 1955–1961, 1964; world champion 1958, Olympic champion 1956.

Dan Cantore—AAU lightweight champion 1969, 1972–1976.

John Davis—AAU heavyweight champion 1941–1943, 1946–1948, 1950-1953; world champion 1946–1952; Olympic champion 1948, 1952.

Joe De Pietro—AAU bantamweight champion 1942–1943, 1946–1951, featherweight champion 1946; world bantamweight champion 1947, Olympic champion 1948.

Clyde B. Emerich—AAU light-heavyweight champion 1952, middle-heavyweight 1956-1957, 1959.

James George—AAU light-heavyweight champion 1956, 1958–1960.

Peter George—AAU lightweight champion 1946, middleweight 1949–1952, 1957; world lightweight champion 1947, 1953, middleweight 1952, 1954-55; Olympic middleweight champion 1952.

John C. Grimek—AAU heavyweight champion 1936.

Gary Gubner—AAU heavyweight champion 1966.

Walter Imahara—AAU featherweight champion 1962, 1965–1968.

Michael Karchut—AAU light-heavyweight champion 1969–1973, middle-heavyweight champion 1975.

Russell Knipp—AAU middleweight champion 1967–1968, 1971.

Tommy Kono—AAU lightweight champion 1952, middleweight champion 1953, 1958–1960, light-heavyweight champion 1954–1955, 1957,1961–1963; world middleweight champion 1953, 1957–1958, light-heavyweight 1954–1955; Olympic lightweight champion 1952, middleweight champion 1956.

Bill March—AAU middle-heavyweight champion 1961–1965.

Joe Mills—AAU featherweight champion 1942.

Michael Mungioli—AAU bantamweight champion 1937–1938.

Ken Patera—AAU super-heavyweight champion 1969–1972.

Joseph Puleo—AAU middleweight champion 1962, 1964, middle-heavyweight 1966–1968.

Norbert Schemansky—AAU middle-heavyweight champion 1951–1953, heavyweight champion 1949, 1954, 1957, 1962, 1964–1965; Olympic middle-heavyweight champion 1952; world middle-heavyweight champion 1952–1953, heavyweight 1954.

David Sheppard—AAU middle-heavyweight champion 1954–1955.

Frank Spellman—AAU middleweight champion 1946, 1948; Olympic middleweight champion 1948.

Stanley Stanczyk—AAU middleweight champion 1947, light-heavyweight champion 1948–1951, 1953; world lightweight champion 1946, middleweight 1947, light-heavyweight 1949–1951; Olympic light-heavyweight champion 1948.

Stephen Stanko—AAU heavyweight champion 1938–1940.

Anthony Terlazzo—AAU featherweight champion 1932, 1936, lightweight 1933, 1935, 1937–1945; world lightweight champion 1938-1939; Olympic featherweight champion 1936.

John Terpak—AAU lightweight champion 1936, middleweight 1937–1942, 1944–1945; world middleweight champion 1937.

John Terry—AAU featherweight champion 1938–1941.

Contributors

Gordon Andrews	Jim Messer
Jack Ayars	Joe Paul
Frank Bates	Peary Rader
Romera Bergeron	Joseph Raymond
Lawrence Bernholth	Rudolph Sablo
Mark Berry	Robert Samuels
Bob Crist	John Schubert
Charles E. Eising	Adam Swirz
Fraysher Ferguson	John Terlazzo
Charles I. Geschwind	John Terpak
Don J. Haley	James Toth
Bob Hise	Morris Weissbrot
Bob Hoffman	Karo Whitfield
Clarence Johnson	Arch Williams
Herbert Lucy	Dietrich Wortmann
David A. Matlin	Dr. Richard You
David Mayor	

WINTER OLYMPICS—The Winter Olympics had their seed in the English love of figure skating early in this century. When the summer games were held in London in 1908, the British exercised the host country's prerogative of selecting one sport by choosing figure skating, a choice made possible by the relatively recent development of indoor, refrigerated ice rinks. (This also marked the first Olympic event of any kind in which women competed.) There was no follow-up to this move in the 1912 games, but in the next Olympics, in Antwerp in 1920, figure skating was again on the program, along with ice hockey.

The exposure given those two sports by their temporary inclusion in the Olympics led advocates of other winter sports to urge the establishment of a regular Winter Olympics. Skating could take place indoors during the warm months, but skiing could not, for obvious reasons. In 1924 the Alpine town of Chamonix, France, planned a winter sports festival, and the Marquis de Polignac, one of the French members of the International Olympic Committee, proposed that the festival be given IOC sanction as a Winter Olympics. Baron Pierre do Coubertin, the founder of the modern Olympic movement, was opposed, but the IOC voted in favor of de Polignac's plan, and the Winter Olympics began.

The 1920 games, which included figure skating, speed skating, four-man bobsledding, ice hockey, and Nordic skiing events, were successful by almost any standards. There were 293 athletes representing 16 nations in Chamonix; the IOC was given credit; and the winter sports got what they wanted, international publicity. The first hero of the Winter Olympics was Thorleif Haug of Norway, who won three gold medals, for the 18-km and 50-km cross-country skiing events and the Nordic combined.

The 1928 Olympics introduced a genuine phenomenon: Sonja Henie. As an 11-year-old at the 1924 games—the youngest competitor in the history of the Olympics—she had finished an unhappy last in figure skating. In 1928 she was 15 and already the world champion in her event. She won the first of three consecutive gold medals that year, at St. Moritz, Switzerland, and she made an unforgettable contribution to figure skating, to the Winter Olympics as a whole, and to the tentative acceptance of women in sports. For the first time in history, a woman won international sports headlines—in competition with men as well as other women.

The United States had not fared notably well in the first two games, but 1932 was to be this country's Olympic year. The summer competition was held in Los Angeles, and the Winter Games were awarded to Lake Placid, New York. Because of the preparations for those Olympics, the United States had, for the first time, a real winter sports complex, complete with a bobsledding run and ski trails. The weather was warm and unsuitable, but 80,000 spectators turned out. American athletes rewarded them by winning all four speed-skating medals, and both the two-man and four-man bobsledding events.

The winter program was substantially expanded for the 1936 games, held in Garmisch-Partenkirchen, Germany. Alpine skiing events were added (these included women skiers for the first time), along with a cross-country relay race. There were also demonstrations of a number of offbeat winter sports, including curling. Again, Sonja Henie was the great star; total attendance reached 500,000.

The next Olympiad was to begin in 1940, but World War II canceled the 1940 games. Despite the fact that Europe was still struggling to recover from the devastation of the war, the program—winter and summer—went on in 1948. St. Moritz again was host to the Winter Games, which drew record numbers of athletes (almost 900) and participating countries (24). The women's slalom was an Olympic event for the first time—in 1936 the slalom had been run only as part of the Alpine combined—and Gretchen Fraser surprised the world by winning that event's gold medal for the United States. This country's postwar domination of figure skating was signaled by Dick Button's smashing performance in the

men's singles. Another significant victory was that of France's Henri Oreiller in the downhill ski event; France was to produce many more world and Olympic winners in Alpine competition during the next two decades.

One of the first major controversies in Olympic history occurred at the 1948 Winter Games, and it threatened to force cancellation of the games. It all began when the United States sent two hockey teams to Switzerland. The AAU team had the sanction of the U.S. Olympic Committee. The rival Amateur Hockey Association team, however, was recognized by the international federation, Ligue Internationale Sur Glace. The International Olympic Committee compounded the problem by first ruling that neither American team could compete and that hockey would be played as a non-Olympic event. The LISG complained, and the Swiss organizing committee decided to allow the AHA team to compete. The IOC then decided that hockey would be an Olympic event after all, that the American team could compete, but that none of its games would count in the results! This incredibly tortuous solution saved the games, but left a bitter taste in many mouths.

There were virtually no problems in 1952 in Oslo. Although snow was astonishingly scarce just a few days before the games, a sizable storm arrived just in time. The program was expanded somewhat, by the addition of women's cross-country skiing and the giant slalom, for men and women.

The United States had remarkable success in 1952. Andrea Mead Lawrence won gold medals in the slalom and giant slalom, Dick Button repeated his victory in men's figure skating, Ken Henry won the 500-m speed-skating event, and the American hockey team surprised Canada with a 3-3 tie to gain a silver medal. The big medal winner, though, was Norway's own Hjalmar Anderson, who won the other three speed-skating events, setting a world record in one and an Olympic record in another. More than 750,000 people saw the 1952 Winter Games in Norway, and a record number of countries, 30, competed.

Russia, which had entered the summer Olympic competition for the first time in 1952, didn't get into the winter Games until 1956, in picturesque Cortina d'Ampezzo, an Italian resort town in the Dolomite Alps. They immediately dominated the events, winning three of four gold medals in speed skating, two cross-country ski events, and the hockey gold medal. The United States again finished second in hockey; Hayes Alan Jenkins and Tenley Albright won the figure-skating golds. The individual hero was Austria's Toni Sailer, who became the second triple winner in Winter Olympic history by winning all three Alpine ski events.

The United States was host to the Winter Games for a second time, in 1960, at Squaw Valley, California. For the first time, enormous amounts of money were spent to prepare a site—which had been standard operating procedure for the summer competition since 1932. Squaw Valley was, before 1960, a largely undeveloped resort area. By the time the games opened, it was a remarkable winter sports complex, built at a cost of more than $9 million. Russians again dominated the scoring tabulation. They won three gold medals in women's speed skating (on the program for the first time), three more in men's speed skating, and one in the women's cross-country. The United States scored a major upset in hockey, beating both Canada and Russia to win the gold medal. American figure skaters continued to dominate their events; David Jenkins and Carol Heiss won gold medals.

Innsbruck, Austria, a long-time ski resort, was the site of the 1964 games. There was one problem: no snow. Snow was trucked down from the mountains, and was dissolved by rain. More snow was trucked down from the mountains. A British tobogganist and an Australian skier were killed in practice runs. But the games went on; nearly a million people attended, a record number. And a woman emerged as the first competitor to win four gold medals: Russia's Lydia Skoblikova, who won every speed-skating event and set three Olympic records in the process. (She had won two golds in 1960.) The United States could manage only one gold, by Terry McDermott in the 500-m men's speed-skating event. (This country's entire figure-skating team had been killed in a plane crash in 1961, en route to the world championships.) Russia also won golds in pairs figure skating, hockey, all three women's Nordic ski events, the individual biathlon, and one event in men's speed skating.

In 1968, however, Soviet dominance ended, at least temporarily—not because the Russians had slipped, but because other countries had improved greatly, particularly Norway, Sweden, and the Netherlands. Norwegian skiers won four gold medals in Nordic events, and Norway also added golds in the individual biathlon and one men's speed-skating event. Toini Gustafsson of Sweden won upset victories in both women's cross-country ski events, and was a member of the silver-medal relay team. The Netherlands, where speed skating had been invented, reclaimed some glory with three gold medals in that sport.

The individual heroes, though, were from none of these countries. Jean-Claude Killy of France scored the Alpine triple, with victories in the downhill, slalom, and giant slalom. And Eugenio Monti, of Italy, who had won nine world championships but never an Olympic gold medal, piloted two-man and four-man bobsled teams to victory, then announced his retirement at age 39. Peggy Fleming, with an exquisite performance in the women's figure-skating finale, won the only gold medal for the United States.

The 1968 games were held in Grenoble, France—a surprising choice because, although Grenoble is in the Alps, it was known as an industrial city with few facilities for winter sport. The French spent $240 million getting the area ready. The choice of a 1972 site was even more surprising: Sapporo, Japan. Few people had heard of it before. But Sapporo, with a population of about 1 million, was the biggest city ever to stage the Winter Games, and the Japanese prepared for them with close attention to detail.

For a time the 1972 Winter Games were seriously threatened by the intransigence of the president of the International Olympic Committee, Avery Brundage. A staunch believer in simon-pure amateurism, Brundage has long felt that amateur Alpine skiing was virtually nonexistent, and that most top "amateur" skiers were really professionals, paid by equipment companies—a charge never seriously denied by anyone from the world of Alpine skiing. Brundage threatened to ban most of the world's top Alpine skiers from the 1972 games. The Japanese, however, complained. Brundage gave in, part way—but Austria's top Alpine skier, Karl Schranz, was banned. Schranz was, in effect, chosen as a scapegoat and as a warning. He had been openly contemptuous of the Olympic idea, and ideal, of amateurism, and reportedly made as much as $50,000 a year by skiing.

Schranz was welcomed back to Austria as if he were a conquering hero, but at Sapporo the whole incident was quickly forgotten in the heroics of Ard Schenk of the Netherlands, who won three speed-skating gold medals; Marie-Therese Nadig of Switzerland, who scored astounding upsets in the downhill and giant slalom; and Yukio Kasaya, who won the ski jumping gold for the host country and became an instant national hero. The United States failed to win a single gold medal in figure skating for only the second time since World War II, but Barbara Cochran won the women's slalom, the first American gold medal in skiing since Andrea Mead Lawrence's double victory in 1952.

The 1976 Winter Olympics, meanwhile, were running into problems even before the 1972 games were held. Denver had originally been selected as the site of the games, which would coincide with the two hundredth anniversary of the American Revolution. A new revolution began to brew in Colorado, however. Increasingly concerned about the headlong growth of Denver and other communities, Coloradans focused on the Olympics as a threat that could damage the environment and spur further real-estate development and too-rapid growth without proper planning. In addition, cost estimates had been far too low, and it became evident by 1972 that the State of Colorado was going to have to put up a lot more money than had been originally estimated. In November, 1972, Colorado voters overwhelmingly approved a referendum barring further expenditures of public money for development of the site. The IOC quickly decided to move the 1976 Winter Games to reliable Innsbruck.

Extensively televised in North America, the Innsbruck games went off virtually without a problem. U.S. speed skaters did exceptionally well, winning six medals in eight events—led by Sheila Young, who won a gold, a silver and a bronze. Dorothy Hamill returned the women's figure skating championship to the United States, and Vermonter Bill Koch won a surprising silver medal in the 30-k cross-country ski race. U.S. Alpine skiers won only a single medal, but a popular heroine emerged, for the host Austrians and many television spectators as well: 25-year-old Rosi Mittermaier, of West Germany, who won gold medals in the downhill and slalom and a silver medal in the giant slalom. And those who root for the underdog could delight in the fact that tiny Liechtenstein, population 23,000, won two medals.

See also OLYMPIC GAMES.

Winter Olympic Champions

Biathlon

Individual
1960   Klas Lestander, Sweden
1964   Vladimir Melanin, USSR
1968   Magnar Solberg, Norway

1972 Magnar Solberg, Norway
1976 Nikolai Kruglov, USSR

Team Relay
1968 USSR
1972 USSR
1976 USSR

Bobsledding

Four-Man
1924 Switzerland
1928 United States
1932 United States
1936 Switzerland
1948 United States
1952 Germany
1956 Switzerland
1960 No competition
1964 Canada
1968 Italy
1972 Switzerland
1976 East Germany

Two-Man
1932 United States
1936 United States
1948 Switzerland
1952 Germany
1956 Italy
1960 No competition
1964 Great Britain
1968 Italy
1972 West Germany II
1976 East Germany

Figure Skating

Men
1908 Ulrich Salchow, Sweden
1920 Gillis Grafstrom, Sweden
1924 Gillis Grafstrom, Sweden
1928 Gillis Grafstrom, Sweden
1932 Karl Schaefer, Austria
1936 Karl Schaefer, Austria
1948 Richard Button, U.S.
1952 Richard Button, U.S.
1956 Hayes Jenkins, U.S.
1960 David Jenkins, U.S.
1964 Manfred Schnelldorfer, Germany
1968 Wolfgang Schwarz, Austria
1972 Ondrej Nepela, Czechoslovakia
1976 John Curry, Great Britain

Women
1908 Madge Syers, Great Britain
1920 Magda Julin, Sweden
1924 Herma Szabo-Planck, Austria
1928 Sonja Henie, Norway
1932 Sonja Henie, Norway
1936 Sonja Henie, Norway
1948 Barbara Ann Scott, Canada
1952 Jeannette Altwegg, England
1956 Tenley Albright, U.S.
1960 Carol Heiss, U.S.
1964 Sjoujke Dijkstra, Holland
1968 Peggy Fleming, U.S.
1972 Trixi Schuba, Austria
1976 Dorothy Hamill, U.S.

Pairs
1908 Anna Huebler-Heinrich Burger, Germany
1920 Ludowika and Walter Jacobsson-Eilers, Finland
1924 Helene Englemann-Alfred Berger, Austria
1928 Andree Joly-Pierre Brunet, France

1932 Andree and Pierre Brunet, France
1936 Maxi Herber-Ernst Baier, Germany
1948 Micheline Lannoy-Pierre Baugniet, Belgium
1952 Ria and Paul Falk, Germany
1956 Elizabeth Schwarz-Kurt Oppelt, Austria
1960 Robert Paul-Barbara Wagner, Canada
1964 Ludmilla Belousova-Oleg Protopopov, USSR
1968 Ludmilla Belousova-Oleg Protopopov, USSR
1972 Irina Rodnina-Alexi Oulanov, USSR
1976 Irina Rodnina-Alexander Zaitsev, USSR

Ice Dancing
1976 Ludmila Pakhomova-Alexander Gorshkov, USSR

Hockey

1920 Canada
1924 Canada
1928 Canada
1932 Canada
1936 Great Britain
1948 Canada
1952 Canada
1956 USSR
1960 United States
1964 USSR
1968 USSR
1972 USSR
1976 USSR

Luge

Men's Singles
1964 Thomas Koehler, Germany
1968 Manfred Schmidt, Austria
1972 Wolfgang Scheidel, E. Germany
1976 Detlev Guenther, E. Germany

Women's Singles
1964 Ortrun Enderlein, Germany
1968 Erika Lechner, Italy
1972 Anna M. Muller, E. Germany
1976 Margitt Schumann, E. Germany

Men's Doubles
1964 Josef Pfiestmantl-Manfred Stengl, Austria
1968 Klaus Bonsack-Thomas Koehler, E. Germany
1972 Paul Hildgartner-Walter Plaikner, Italy
1976 Horst Hornlein-Reinhard Bredow, E. Germany

Skiing—Men

15-Km Cross-Country
1956 Hallgeier Brenden, Norway
1960 Haakon Brusveen, Norway
1964 Eero Maentyranta, Finland
1968 Harald Groenningen, Norway
1972 Sven-Ake Lundback, Sweden
1976 Nikolai Bayukov, USSR

18-Km Cross-Country
1924 Thorleif Haug, Norway
1928 Johan Grottumsbraaten, Norway (19,700 m)
1932 Sven Utterstrom, Sweden (18,214 m)
1936 Erik-August Larsson, Sweden
1948 Martin Lundstrom, Sweden
1952 Hallgeier Brenden, Norway

30-Km Cross-Country
1956 Veikko Hakulinen, Finland
1960 Sixten Jernberg, Sweden
1964 Eero Maentyranta, Finland
1968 Franco Nones, Italy
1972 Vyacheslav Vedenin, USSR
1976 Sergei Saveilev, USSR

40-Km Cross-Country Relay
1936 Finland
1948 Sweden
1952 Finland
1956 USSR
1960 Finland
1964 Sweden
1968 Norway
1972 USSR
1976 Finland

50-Km Cross-Country
1924 Thorleif Haug, Norway
1928 Per Erik Hedlund, Sweden
1932 Veli Saarinen, Finland
1936 Elis Viklund, Sweden
1948 Nils Karlsson, Sweden
1952 Veikko Hakulinen, Finland
1956 Sixten Jernberg, Sweden
1960 Kalevi Hamalainen, Finland
1964 Sixten Jernberg, Sweden
1968 Ole Ellefsaeter, Norway
1972 Paul Tyldum, Norway
1976 Iver Formo, Norway

Jumping—70-M Hill
1924 Jacob T. Thams, Norway
1928 Alfred Andersen, Norway
1932 Birger Ruud, Norway
1936 Birger Ruud, Norway
1948 Petter Hugsted, Norway
1952 Arnfinn Bergmann, Norway
1956 Antti Hyvaarinen, Finland
1960 Helmut Recknagel, Germany
1964 Veikko Kankkoen, Finland
1968 Jiri Kaska, Czechoslovakia
1972 Yukio Kasaya, Japan
1976 Hans-Georg Aschenbach, E. Germany

Jumping—80-M Hill
1964 Toralf Engen, Norway

Jumping—90-M Hill
1968 Vladimir Beloussov, USSR
1972 Wojciech Fortuna, Poland
1976 Karl Schnabl, Austria

Nordic Combined

(18-km race and jumping through 1952; 15-km race and 70-m jumping since 1956)

1924 Thorleif Haug, Norway
1928 Johan Grottumsbraaten, Norway
1932 Johan Grottumsbraaten, Norway
1936 Oddbjorn Hagen, Norway
1948 Haikki Hasu, Finland
1952 Simon Slattvik, Norway
1956 Sverre Stenersen, Norway
1960 Georg Thomas, Germany
1964 Tormod Knutsen, Norway
1968 Franz Keller, W. Germany
1972 Ulrich Wehling, E. Germany
1976 Ulrich Wehling, E. Germany

Downhill
1948 Henri Oreiller, France
1952 Zeno Colo, Italy
1956 Toni Sailer, Austria
1960 Jean Vuarnet, France
1964 Egon Zimmerman, Austria
1968 Jean-Claude Killy, France
1972 Bernard Russi, Switzerland
1976 Franz Klammer, Austria

Slalom
1948 Edi Reinalter, Switzerland
1952 Othmar Schneider, Austria
1956 Toni Sailer, Austria
1960 Ernst Hinterseer, Austria
1964 Josef Stiegler, Austria
1968 Jean-Claude Killy, France
1972 Francisco Fernandez, Spain
1976 Piero Gros, Italy

Giant Slalom
1952 Stein Eriksen, Norway
1956 Toni Sailer, Austria
1960 Roger Staub, Switzerland
1964 Francois Bonlieu, France
1968 Jean-Claude Killy, France
1972 Gustavo Thoeni, Italy
1976 Heini Hemmi, Switzerland

Alpine Combined (Downhill and Slalom)
1936 Franz Pfnur, Germany
1948 Henri Oreiller, France

Skiing—Women

5-Km Cross-Country
1964 Claudia Boyarskikh, USSR
1968 Toini Gustafsson, Sweden
1972 Galina Kolukova, USSR
1976 Helena Tukkalo, Finland

10-Km Cross-Country
1952 Lydia Wideman, Finland
1956 Lyubov Kozyreva, USSR
1960 Marija Gusakova, USSR
1964 Claudia Boyarskikh, USSR
1968 Toini Gustafsson, Sweden
1972 Galina Kolukova, USSR
1976 Raisa Smetanina, USSR

15-Km Cross-Country Relay
1956 Finland
1960 Sweden
1964 USSR
1968 Norway
1972 USSR
1976 USSR

Downhill
1948 Hedi Schlunegger, Switzerland
1952 Trude Jochum-Beiser, Austria
1956 Madeleine Berthod, Switzerland
1960 Heidi Beibl, Germany
1964 Christl Haas, Austria
1968 Olga Pall, Austria
1972 Marie-Therese Nadig, Switzerland
1976 Rosi Mittermaier, W. Germany

Slalom
1948 Gretchen Fraser, U.S.
1952 Andrea Mead Lawrence, U.S.
1956 Renee Colliard, Switzerland
1960 Anne Heggtveit, Canada
1964 Christine Goitschel, France
1968 Marielle Goitschel, France
1972 Barbara Cochran, U.S.
1976 Rosi Mittermaier, W. Germany

Giant Slalom
1952 Andrea Mead Lawrence, U.S.
1956 Ossi Reichert, Germany
1960 Yvonne Ruegg, Switzerland
1964 Claudia Boyarskikh, USSR
1968 Toini Gustafsson, Sweden
1972 Marie-Therese Nadig, Switzerland
1976 Kathy Kreiner, Canada

Alpine Combined

1936	Christel Cranz, Germany	
1948	Trude Beiser, Austria	

Speed Skating—Men

500 Meters

1924	Charles Jewtraw, U.S.	44.0
1928	Clas Thunberg, Finland	43.4
	Bernt Evensen, Norway	43.4
1932	John A. Shea, U.S.	43.4
1936	Ivar Ballangrud, Norway	43.4
1948	Finn Helgesen, Norway	43.1
1952	Ken Henry, U.S.	43.2
1956	Yevgeni Grishin, USSR	40.2
1960	Yevgeni Grishin, USSR	40.2
1964	Terry McDermott, U.S.	40.1
1968	Erhard Keller, W. Germany	40.3
1972	Erhard Keller, W. Germany	38.4
1976	Yevgeni Kulikov, USSR	39.17

1,000 Meters

1976	Peter Mueller, U.S.	1:19.32

1,500 Meters

1924	Clas Thunberg, Finland	2:20.8
1928	Clas Thunberg, Finland	2:21.1
1932	John A. Shea, U.S.	2:57.5
1936	Charles Mathisen, Norway	2:19.2
1948	Sverre Farstad, Norway	2:17.6
1952	Hjalmar Andersen, Norway	2:20.4
1956	Yevgeni Grishin, USSR	2:08.6
	Yuri Mikhailiov, USSR	2:08.6
1960	Yevgeni Grishin, USSR	2:10.4
	Roald Aas, Norway	2:10.4
1964	Ants Antson, USSR	2:10.3
1968	Kees Verkerk, Netherlands	2:03.2
1972	Ard Schenk, Netherlands	2:02.96
1976	Jan Egil Storholt, Norway	1:59.38

5,000 Meters

1924	Clas Thunberg, Finland	8:39.0
1928	Ivar Ballangrud, Norway	8:50.5
1932	Irving Jaffee, U.S.	9:40.8
1936	Ivar Ballangrud, Norway	8:19.6
1948	Reidar Liaklev, Norway	8:29.4
1952	Hjalmar Andersen, Norway	8:10.6
1956	Boris Shilkov, USSR	7:48.7
1960	Viktor Kosichkin, USSR	7:51.3
1964	Knut Johannesen, Norway	7:38.4
1968	Fred Maier, Norway	7:22.4
1972	Ard Schenk, Netherlands	7:23.6
1976	Sten Stensen, Norway	7:24.48

10,000 Meters

1924	Julien Skutnabb, Finland	18:04.8
1928	No decision (ice thawed)	
1932	Irving Jaffee, U.S.	19:13.6
1936	Ivar Ballangrud, Norway	17:24.3
1948	Ake Seyffarth, Sweden	17:26.3
1952	Hjalmar Andersen, Norway	16:45.8
1956	Sigge Ericsson, Sweden	16:35.9
1960	Knut Johannesen, Norway	15:46.6
1964	Johnny Nilsson, Sweden	15:50.1
1968	Johnny Hoeglin, Sweden	15:23.6
1972	Ard Schenk, Netherlands	15:01.35
1976	Piet Kleine, Netherlands	14:50.59

Speed Skating—Women

500 Meter

1960	Helga Haase, Germany	45.9
1964	Lidiya Skobilkova, USSR	45.0
1968	Ludmila Titova, USSR	46.1
1972	Anne Henning, U.S.	43.44
1976	Sheila Young, U.S.	42.76

1,000 Meters

1960	Klara Guseva, USSR	1:34.1
1964	Lidiya Skobilkova, USSR	1:33.2
1968	Carolina Geilson, Netherlands	1:32.6
1972	Monika Pflug, Germany	1:31.40
1976	Tatyana Averina, USSR	1:28.43

1,500 Meters

1960	Lidiya Skobilkova, USSR	2:25.2
1964	Lidiya Skobilkova, USSR	2:22.6
1968	Kaija Mustonen, Finland	2:22.4
1972	Dianne Holum, U.S.	2:20.85
1976	Galina Stepenskaya, USSR	2:16.58

3,000 Meters

1960	Lidiya Skobilkova, USSR	5:14.3
1964	Lidiya Skobilkova, USSR	5:14.9
1968	Johanna Schut, Netherlands	4:56.2
1972	Stien Baas-Kaiser, Netherlands	4:52.14
1976	Tatyana Auerina, USSR	4:45.19

WOMEN IN SPORTS—There are Egyptian wall paintings that show women taking part in a kind of sport, a sacred ball ritual, more than 3,500 years ago. Women were not even allowed to watch the ancient Olympic Games but, in the sixth century B.C., they had their own version of the Olympics, the Heraean Games, and they were later admitted to some Olympic events as well.

Organized competitive sports virtually disappeared from the Western world after classical times, and when they began to revive, they were almost exclusively the province of males—and, at first, of upper-class males. Mary Queen of Scots did play golf on occasion, and Queen Anne of England was an accomplished horsewoman, but they had royal prerogatives.

Sport on the collegiate level has long been more important in the United States than in most other countries. When women's colleges were first being organized in this country—over the protests of many who insisted that women were not physically or mentally fit for long hours of study—regular physical exercise of one sort or another was part of the collegiate program. The first women's college, Vassar, included among physical activities such outdoor, nonathletic diversions as flower gardening; but it also had a well-equipped gym and facilities for bowling, horseback riding, boating, swimming, and skating. Unfortunately, public coeducational colleges did not often offer much in the way of physical exercise for their female students, with a couple of notable exceptions.

During the 1880s the picture began to change somewhat. Tennis and golf had become popular upper-class sports, and women were participating along with men. The national women's outdoor tennis tournament was established in 1887, the national women's amateur golf tournament in 1895. Tennis, archery, and other sports were adopted for women, often in coeducational schools as well as in women's colleges. (The University of California even had a football—probably soccer—club for women in 1877.)

Another important development in terms of women's right to exercise was the safety bicycle, which was doubly important. There were people who thought it improper for a women to ride a bicycle. But the number of women who wanted to ride, and did, overcame that objection. It was almost impossible to ride a bike in the "proper" costume of the day; so women who rode bikes did away with corsets and cut down on underskirts. Some women even wore knickers and bloomers, or the era's equivalent of the pantsuit, for cycling.

1890 to 1920. This was an important period for sports and for women. Physical education, often in the form of organized sports, was being adopted as part of the college curriculum. Women were winning the right to vote, and they were also winning the right to physical education in their colleges. Competitive team sports were part of physical-education programs, and two team sports, though invented specifically for YMCAs, were also enthusiastically taken up by many young women: basketball and volleyball.

Although Vassar had had a baseball program as early as 1876, basketball was the first real team sport for women. Invented in 1891, it was quickly introduced to women by the man who conceived it, Dr. James A. Naismith himself. One of the players in the first women's game later became Mrs. Naismith. By 1900 it was being played at several women's colleges. As a matter of fact, in 1910 it was considered primarily a women's sport on the West Coast.

Sheer exercise, in the form of calisthenics, was rapidly being abandoned in favor of organized sports activity. Tennis and golf were being widely played by women. Field hockey, previously rejected by male students as being too rough, was reintroduced for women. Swimming was also becoming important as a form of required exercise at many colleges, and many women's colleges went along with the trend by building swimming pools.

The movement spread beyond the colleges. The New York Fencers Club began classes for women. And some Olympic sports were also added for women, though not always permanently. Tennis became an Olympic sport in 1900, and there was a women's singles championship. Archery and fencing were added in 1904, figure skating in 1908, swimming and diving in 1912.

1920 to World War II. During the "Golden Age of Sports," genuine female stars emerged in the United States and elsewhere: Glenna Collett Vare in golf; Martha Norelius, Eleanor Holm, Helene Madison in swimming; Helen Meany and Georgia Coleman in diving; Suzanne Lenglen, Helen Wills, Helen Hull Jacobs, and Alice Marble in tennis; Stella Walsh, Helen Filkey, and Lillian Copeland in track and field. Gertrude Ederle proved a woman could swim the English Channel, and Amelia Earhart proved a woman could be a pretty good aviator.

The best-known woman athlete to emerge before World War II was probably Mildred "Babe" Didrikson. (Norway's Sonja Henie, with three Olympic gold medals in skating and her subsequent movie career, was probably better known to more people, but her sport was not always highly regarded as a sport.) Babe Didrikson, it was said, was as good as a man in a lot of sports. She starred with an outstanding women's basketball team, and she excelled at softball and baseball. She won national track and field championships in the hurdles, the broad jump, the high jump, the shot put, the javelin throw, and the discus throw. She won Olympic gold medals in 1932 in the 80-m hurdles and the javelin, and should have won one in the high jump, but was disqualified for using the Western roll, a fairly common American technique at the time. She played tennis quite well, but never in serious competition; she took up golf instead. The major portion of her golf career belongs to the post-

Shooting was perhaps the first sport in which women competed directly with men. Annie Oakley's name is still synonymous with shooting skill. *(Amateur Trapshooting Association Hall of Fame.)*

war period, but by the mid-1930s Babe Didrikson was already a legend in her own time.

But some unhappy things happened to women's sport during the period. The attitude that would today win the "male chauvinist pig" label for a man was, during the 1920s, the attitude of many of the women who were in charge of women's sports. The Athletic Conference of American College Women (ACACW), organized in 1917, was opposed to intercollegiate competition, and favored the adoption of special women's rules for basketball.

Those rules turned an active sport into a dull, static exercise.

In 1923, 22 percent of the women's and coeducational colleges in the United States had varsity sports for women. Largely as a result of the women's movement, the figure was down to 12 percent by 1930.

The ACACW and a couple of similar groups—the Committee on Women's Athletics of the American Physical Education Association and the Women's Division of the National Amateur Athletic Federation—were also opposed to women's participation in international athletics, and they fought against the formal inclusion of women in the 1928 U.S. Olympic team. (While women had competed previously, they had been more or less on their own, not official members of a national team.)

These were, by and large, the women who controlled women's sports on the collegiate level and, to a lesser extent, on the high school level. Outstanding women athletes could, and often did, find other places to compete. They could play "real" basketball under AAU auspices in industrial leagues, and there were also industrial softball leagues for women. Women from fairly well-to-do families could swim, golf, or play tennis at private clubs. And they could bowl.

But most women of average means, deprived of any real training or competition at the interscholastic and intercollegiate levels, had little chance to find out whether they could, or might want to, participate seriously in sports.

World War II to 1960. The necessities of war began the gradual emancipation of women. They worked in factories and shipyards because there weren't enough men to do the work that had to be done. The gradual emancipation continued after the war, with sudden prosperity and the conversion of new technologies to peacetime uses. Labor-saving devices for the home began to appear in the marketplace, and women gained more leisure time.

The end of the war also marked the beginning of the sports explosion that has continued right up to this moment, and women got in on some of it. The 1948 Olympics had more women's events than any previous Olympics, and many women were headliners, along with men. Fanny Blankers-Koen of Holland won three gold medals in track and field, and her name, if not quite a household word, became well known among sports followers. Ann Curtis, already a well-known swimmer, was the only American woman to win a gold medal in swimming. And Gretchen Fraser became the first American woman to win a gold medal in skiing.

The women's professional golf tour was founded before the war was even over, and the first Women's Open was played in 1946. Patty Berg, Babe Didrikson Zaharias, and Louise Suggs became fairly well known, even among male-chauvinist sports fans. And Florence Chadwick swam the English channel four times between 1950 and 1955.

The 1960s and 1970s. Sports had been booming ever since the end of World War II. About 1960 they entered a new kind of boom because of a major new source of money: television. And television brought yet another kind of boom, in communications. These influences all had an impact on women's sports.

Still another important factor was the Olympic cold war between the West and the Iron Curtain countries—especially between the United States and the Soviet Union. The Russians, who entered Olympic competition for the first time in 1952, had outstanding women athletes, and their medals in track and field, gymnastics, and fencing were a major reason for apparent Russian superiority.

Olympic events were televised nationally for the first time in 1960, and the outstanding American performer in those games was Wilma Rudolph, who won three gold medals. Her exploits, and those of America's women swimmers, must have made many young girls realize that they too might someday become Olympic heroes.

Attitudes were changing among women's physical-education leaders as well. The women's intercollegiate golf tournament had been founded in 1940 by Gladys Palmer of Ohio State, and had become the responsibility of a committee with representation from three different groups: the Division for Girls' and Women's Sports of the National Association for Health, Physical Education, and Recreation; the National Association for Physical Education of College Women; and the Athletic and Recreation Federation of College Women. The cooperation among those three groups led to the formation of the National Joint Committee on Extramural Sports for College Women, which restudied the question of intercollegiate women's sports and established standards for intercollegiate competition in some sports.

In 1966 the Division for Girls' and Women's Sports adopted guidelines for intercollegiate sports, and the Commission for Intercollegiate Athletics for Women was formed to supervise in this area. The CIAW took over the intercollegiate golf tournament and, in 1969, inaugurated

Mildred "Babe" Didrikson Zaharias is generally considered the greatest all-around women athlete in history. Largely because of her skills and fame, the Ladies' Professional Golf Association tour was organized. *(U.S. Golf Association.)*

national gymnastics and track and field championships. In 1970, championships were added in badminton, swimming and diving, and volleyball. Basketball was added to the national championship program in 1972.

Intercollegiate competition was by now growing so rapidly that a real supervisory body was needed, especially since the NCAA, despite all its programs for men, had never set up women's programs. The Association for Intercollegiate Athletics for Women (AIAW) was organized in the 1971–1972 school year, with nearly 300 members.

Meanwhile, professional sports were getting more and more money, not only from television but, in the cases of golf and tennis, from tournament sponsors. In those two sports—the major professional sports for women—some women began complaining that they weren't receiving as much money as the men.

One of the leaders of the militant women's movement was tennis star Billie Jean King, who was adamant in her belief that women should get equal money when playing in the same tournament as men. She led a group of women tennis players who boycotted a 1970 United States Lawn Tennis Association tournament to play in a more lucrative Virginia Slims tournament that was not sanctioned by the USLTA. They then proceeded to set up their own tournament circuit, with assistance from *World Tennis* magazine and major sponsorship from Virginia Slims, the "you've-come-a-long-way-baby" cigarettes. Ultimately a truce was reached. The USLTA agreed to pay equal money to women in the U.S. Open, and the Virginia Slims circuit was sanctioned. In 1971, Mrs. King became the first women athlete ever to win more than $100,000 in a single year.

Women golfers didn't have quite the same bone of contention, since their tour had always been separate from the men's; equal pay for the same tournaments was not an issue. However, many of them were unhappy about the amount of prize money available to them, and several sponsors were willing to listen. The first major sponsors were Sears, Sealy, and Eve cigarettes. Then Colgate-Palmolive entered the picture in 1973 with the richest tournament of all—and national television sponsorship. For the first time a women's golf tournament was carried on network television.

One other major professional sport that began to attract women—and the only one in which they could compete against men directly—was horse racing. In 1969, Diane Crump became the first professional woman jockey, and in 1973, Robyn Smith became the first woman to ride the winner in a stakes race.

Minor moves toward professionalism were made in other sports. Plans were announced for a women's pro basketball league, and professional football for women began to receive some attention (more as a novelty than as a genuine sport).

More important, though, was the increasing pressure for girls and women to get into organized sports—either with males or on their own separate but equal teams. In 1974, girls were allowed to play baseball in Little Leagues, after several court suits. And a number of colleges acted, more or less unilaterally, to increase competitive sports programs for women.

Title IX. As far as coeducational colleges are concerned, the biggest women's-lib problem came when the U.S.

A revolt let by Billie Jean King, and sponsorship from Virginia Slims, greatly increased women's tennis purses. A major benefactor was Chris Evert, who won more than $300,000 in 1974 and more than $400,000 in 1975. *(U.S. Tennis Association.)*

Department of Health, Education, and Welfare drew up regulations pertaining to Title IX of the Education Amendments Act of 1972. Essentially, Title IX made discrimination by reason of sex unlawful in schools receiving federal aid—meaning virtually every school of higher education in the country. The HEW regulations regarding sports were more stringent than most colleges—or, at least, most college athletic directors—had expected them to be. The regulations called for equal expenditure on women's sports and equal access, for women, to sports and physical-education facilities on campuses.

Oddly, while so many athletic directors and (male) coaches were up in arms about Title IX and the HEW regulations, college administrators did not necessarily attack them by reflex. The 1975 NCAA convention, as a matter of fact, attracted more college presidents than any previous convention, and most of the presidents were there because they were concerned about the hard-line attitude toward Title IX being taken by the NCAA.

During that convention, the NCAA announced plans to begin conducting intercollegiate championship events for women, a move attacked by the AIAW, which, as noted, was already conducting such championships in many sports. The AIAW saw the NCAA move as an attempt to take over, for purely expedient considerations, an area that it had previously, and deliberately, ignored.

Underlying Questions. Both the defenders of the status quo and the supporters of women's liberation in sports seem to be contradicting themselves at times; at other times, they are obviously talking at cross purposes.

The problem is that there are underlying questions about the role of sports in our society that need to be

Many women have been attracted to the "thrill sports," such as sky-diving, in recent years. This is Jeanni McComb of San Francisco. (Parachutist *Photo by Jerry Irwin*.)

answered. One question is: Do we encourage sports among youngsters and in educational institutions to develop outstanding athletes, or because the activity is beneficial to those who take part in it? An extension of that question: If we decide that athletic activity can benefit all, or most, youngsters, do we still feel that the superior athlete is entitled to special encouragement and perhaps even special programs and facilities so that he (or she) can develop his (or her) skills to the utmost? And how does professionalism fit into the picture? Why is an athlete paid for performing? Because the athlete brings in more money, ultimately, than the same athlete costs? Or simply because superior skills deserve reward, in whatever field?

Those who favor "big" college sports are apt to say, on the one hand, that football scholarships are good because they allow young men to attend college and, on the other hand, that scholarships for women athletes are not good because women's sports don't bring in enough box-office money to justify the scholarships. If the first argument is valid, then obviously women should have equal rights to athletic scholarships; if the second argument is valid, then the first argument is destroyed.

Many men who opposed girls' participation in Little League baseball argued that it would deprive some boys of the training that would help develop skills that might make possible careers in the major leagues; these men also said that girls' playing would destroy softball leagues

that allow many girls to participate in organized sport. But if the goal of Little League and other such organizations is to help children develop athletic skills to a very high level, it is precisely the talented girl who needs most help and most exposure to higher-level competition. Providing such needed help means, at that age level, at least, the chance to compete against boys, not against the talented girl's supposed (exclusively female) peers. And if the goal is wide participation, there should be no concern about trying to develop major-league players.

The Billie Jean King approach ("equal pay for equal work") also has some pitfalls, especially since she has coupled it with the argument that women attract at least as many spectators as men. Carried to the ultimate extreme, the "equal pay" argument might mean that every tournament should have the same amount of prize money. If, however, players are to be paid on the basis of their box-office appeal, then paying money on the basis of a player's finish in a tournament is the wrong approach. The unpopular idea of paying guaranteed "appearance money" to certain players, regardless of their finish, would be more to the point.

Another difficulty is that many of the people most ardently in favor of women's participation in intercollegiate sports are the same ones who dislike "big-time" college competition, because of the pressure it places on student-athletes and because of what these critics regard as the hypocrisy of supposed amateurism. Yet there are already some signs that the pressure, at least, is creeping into women's sports, along with the scholarships.

There is no question that girls and women are entitled to fuller participation in organized athletics, at every level, at least through college. But it would seem that the reasons that their fuller participation is desirable should be carefully thought out and well defined, so that new programs and expanded programs really do accomplish the goals sought.

Bibliography. Hoepner, Barbara J. (ed.): *Women's Athletics: Coping with Controversy*, American Association for Health, Physical Education and Recreation, Washington, D.C., 1974.

WORLD CUP—There are several World Cups, each emblematic of international supremacy in a specific sport. The best-known and most important of them is awarded in soccer and is probably the most prized sports trophy in the world. The soccer trophy is awarded every four years. World Cups are also awarded in golf, tennis (for competition between United States and Australian pros), field hockey, and other sports. *See* individual sports for lists of winning countries.

WORLD TROPHY—The Helms Athletic Foundation (now Citizens Savings Athletic Foundation) in 1948 set up a plan to honor the outstanding amateur athlete of the year on each of six continents: Africa, Asia, Australia, Europe, North America, and South America. Through intensive research, selections for Australia, Europe, and North America were dated back to 1896, the year of the first modern Olympic Games. Selections for the other three continents were dated back to 1920. The huge World Trophy, in the Citizens Savings-Helms Hall of Fame, bears the names of all the recipients. Each athlete honored is given a silver plaque.

World Trophy Winners

North America

(Winners are from U.S., unless otherwise noted; Can.-Canada)

1896	Robert S. Garrett		
1897	Robert D. Wrenn	1937	J. Donald Budge
1898	Juliette P. Atkinson	1938	Angelo "Hank" Luisetti
1899	T. Truxton Hare	1939	Alice Marble
1900	Alvin C. Kraenzlein	1940	J. Gregory Rice
1901	Charles Daly	1941	Robert L. Riggs
1902	William A. Larned	1942	Cornelius Warmerdam
1903	Walter J. Travis	1943	Gilbert Dodds
1904	John D. Lightbody	1944	Ann Curtis
1905	May Sutton	1945	Glenn Davis
1906	Walter Eckersall	1946	Pauline Betz
1907	Martin J. Sheridan	1947	John A. "Jack" Kramer
1908	Melvin Sheppard	1948	Robert Mathias
1909	Charles M. Daniels	1949	Melvin Patton
1910	Fred C. Thomson	1950	Richard Attlesey
1911	Hazel Hotchkiss	1951	Robert Richards
1912	James Thorpe	1952	Horace Ashenfelter
1913	Maurice E. McLoughlin	1953	Malvin Whitfield
1914	Francis Ouimet	1954	Wes Santee
1915	Jerome D. Travers	1955	Patricia McCormick
1916	J. E. "Ted" Meredith	1956	Parry O'Brien
1917	Molla Bjurstet	1957	Robert Gutowski
1918	Avery Brundage	1958	Rafer Johnson
1919	William Johnston	1959	Ray Norton
1920	Charles W. Paddock	1960	Wilma Rudolph
1921	William T. Tilden II	1961	Ralph Boston
1922	Thomas Hitchcock, Jr.	1962	Terry Baker
1923	John Weissmuller	1963	Brian Sternberg
1924	Harold "Red" Grange	1964	Alfred Oerter
1925	Ernest Nevers	1965	Michael Garrett
1926	Robert T. Jones	1966	James Ryun
1927	Benjamin Oosterbaan	1967	J. Randel Matson
1928	Percy Williams (Can.)	1968	Robert Beamon
1929	Helen Wills	1969	Bill Toomey
1930	Glenna Collett	1970	Gary Hall
1931	Helene Madison	1971	Pat Matzdorf
1932	H. Ellsworth Vines	1972	Mark Spitz
1933	Glenn Cunningham	1973	Keena Rothhammer
1934	W. Lawson Little	1974	Tim Shaw
1935	Jesse Owens	1975	Shirley Babashoff
1936	Glenn Morris	1976	Bruce Jenner

WRESTLING—One of the most ancient of all sports, wrestling developed independently in many parts of the world. A statue of two wrestlers coming to grips, found in Iraq, is believed to be nearly 5,000 years old, and tomb paintings in Egypt, from about 1850 B.C., show a series of wrestling holds almost identical to some of those used today.

The ancient Greeks adopted the Egyptian style of wrestling, with some changes, and by the time wrestling became an event in the ancient Olympics, there were already two different forms, anticipating the two modern forms, Greco-Roman and freestyle (catch-as-catch-can). The early counterpart of Greco-Roman was "upright" wrestling, in which the object was to throw an opponent off his feet. That was the major style used in the ancient Olympics. The other type, "ground" wrestling, usually took place on muddy earth, and the match continued until one wrestler gave up. This style was used in the Olympic *pankration,* which combined wrestling, boxing, and kicking.

When the Romans conquered Greece and took over supervision of the Olympics, they combined their own type of wrestling with Greek upright wrestling, to create something like the style now known as Greco-Roman.

Wrestling was one of the few sports that survived during the Middle Ages. France and England staged a number of international matches before royal audiences. The French practiced, essentially, Greco-Roman wrestling, but both styles were popular in various parts of Britain. Greco-Roman, probably introduced by Roman soldiers, was the style in Cumberland-Westmoreland and Cornwall-Devon; the less artificial catch-as-catch-can style was particularly popular in Lancashire, and the Scots and the Irish had similar styles.

Both types of wrestling were also popular in the United States by the late nineteenth century. Abraham Lincoln, as a young man, took part in catch-as-catch-can matches. As an organized sport, however, wrestling was Greco-Roman wrestling, which was on the first modern Olympic program, in 1896. But a modified form of catch-as-catch-can, which became known as freestyle wrestling, became more popular in most parts of the world in the early part of the century.

Professional Wrestling. Among the first great American wrestlers was Martin "Farmer" Burns. Though he weighed only about 170 lb, Burns won the professional heavyweight championship in 1895 by beating the original "Strangler" Lewis. He lost the title in 1897 to Tom Jenkins, a rolling-mill worker from Cleveland. In matches all over the country, Jenkins helped make freestyle wrestling a popular spectator sport; so did a number of traveling carnival wrestlers who took on all comers.

Meanwhile, Burns had discovered and trained a young 200-pounder, Frank Gotch. Gotch challenged Jenkins in 1903 and was beaten, but in 1904 he threw Jenkins to win the championship. The two men had eight matches during their careers, Gotch winning five of them. In all, Gotch won 154 of 160 professional matches and ruled as champion until 1913, when he retired. He beat George Hackenschmidt, the European champion, twice, once on a disputed decision and once when Hackenschmidt was suffering from a severe knee injury. Many observers felt that Hackenschmidt was the better wrestler, since he had beaten Jenkins rather easily in two matches.

After Gotch retired, the American championship passed rather quickly from one wrestler to another. Between 1914 and 1917, Henry Ordeman, Charles Cutler, Dr. Benjamin Roller, Joe Stecher, and Earl Caddock all held the title at one time or another. Stecher won it in 1915, lost it to Caddock in 1917, and then won it back from Caddock in 1920, after both men had returned from service in World War I.

The outstanding wrestlers of the postwar era were Stecher and the second "Strangler" Lewis, whose real name was Robert H. Friedrich. Lewis won the title from Stecher late in 1920, lost it to Stanislaus Zbyszko in 1921, and won it back in 1922. Then he held it until 1925, when Wayne "Big" Munn defeated him. The title again changed hands quickly, Munn losing to Zbyszko, who in turn lost to Stecher. Then, in 1928, the 38-year-old Lewis won back his title by beating Stecher, two falls to one.

That virtually marked the end of real professional wrestling in the United States. The better wrestlers became self-proclaimed champions, organized their own barnstorming tours, and avoided wrestling one another, for the most part. Gus Sonnenberg, a former Dartmouth and professional football player, beat Lewis twice in 1929. Sonnenberg's "flying tackle" was the first of the show-business gimmicks that have turned wrestling, on the professional level, from sport into staged exhibition. During the 1930s a promoter named Jack Pfeffer introduced such gimmicks as wrestling in mud and in cages; he also introduced women's wrestling and various man-versus-animal matches.

During World War II, Pfeffer invented Australian tag-team wrestling, in which partners wrestle as teams. One wrestler, upon getting tired, can be relieved by a partner—if the partner can tag the other without leaving the assigned corner of the ring. The main reason for the new version of the sport was that, with most able-bodied men in military service, the wrestlers who remained were overage and out of shape, and they needed the relief, but tag-team wrestling is still very popular.

With the coming of televised wrestling after World War II, the professional version became even less of a sport. The ring became a stage and the wrestlers became stock characters. The most famous was "Gorgeous George," whose real name was Raymond Wagner. He bleached and marcelled his hair, borrowed his name from Georges Carpentier, the French boxer who had been known as the "Orchid Man" because of his elegance and taste, and had a valet as a handler. At the peak of his career, Gorgeous George earned $250,000 a year.

Villains were needed. In the early postwar years, they were usually Germans or Japanese, like Hans Schmidt and Mr. Moto. When the Cold War began, there were also Russian villains, among them "Ivan Koloff, the Commissar." The masked villain was also introduced, for economic reasons: By changing trunks and the type of mask he wore, the masked villain could wrestle twice or more on a single card, cutting down on the number of wrestlers needed on tour.

Professional bouts are not, as some people think, choreographed down to the last detail. But the winner and the time when the bout will end are known in advance, and usually the way in which the end will come is also planned. Blood is usually produced by breaking small capsules of the kind also used on the stage and in movies. And though pro wrestling has many fans, and pro wrestlers are, in many cases, skilled athletes who really can wrestle, their sport is no longer a sport.

The Amateurs. Wrestling was one of the first amateur sports taken over by the AAU, in 1889. Freestyle wrestling was already the style in this country. There was only one freestyle event on the 1896 Olympic program, and it didn't appear again until 1904, when the Olympics were held in St. Louis. In 1906, Greco-Roman wrestling alone was on the program, and remained the only style of Olympic wrestling until 1920, when freestyle again appeared.

Since 1920, both types of wrestling have been permanent Olympic sports. The AAU, however, didn't begin holding national Greco-Roman championships until 1953. Although the rules are quite different, a number of wrestlers have been quite adept at both styles.

The NCAA began conducting national collegiate freestyle wrestling championships in 1928, but has no Greco-Roman championships. However, the U.S. Wrestling Federation, organized in 1969, sponsors national championships in both styles. In 1973, the USWF replaced the AAU as the representative United States body in international wrestling. The sport is under the worldwide jurisdiction of the Amateur Wrestling Federation, which was organized in 1921.

Rules

Freestyle. Under international rules, the wrestling mat is 12 m (about 39¼ ft) square; the contest circle is 9 m (about 29½ ft) in diameter, and its center is a 1-m (39.36-in) circle.

A match consists of three rounds of 3 min each. It begins with the wrestlers in their corners; at the starting whistle, they approach each other and grapple.

Wrestling continues if one competitor is brought to the mat. If that competitor goes off the mat, the bout is stopped and resumed in the center circle, with the wrestler who was on the bottom in a kneeling position, hands and knees at least 20 cm (about 8 in) apart. The wrestler who was on top takes a position with both hands touching the back of the kneeling wrestler. When the referee's whistle sounds, action resumes. The wrestler on top must not jump on the kneeling opponent. The wrestler on the bottom is off the mat when the head and shoulders are off, or when the head touches the mat outside the limit.

A wrestler is said to be in danger of a fall when in a horizontal position, with back to the mat, forming a bridge or using the elbows to keep the shoulders from touching; or when the wrestler's chest or stomach is in contact with the mat so that, if the body were turned over, the shoulders would be touching the mat.

It is a fall when both shoulders are held to the mat for 3 sec.

Dangerous holds and maneuvers are fouls. Among the fouls are tripping, gripping the opponent's throat, forcing a knee or elbow into the opponent's abdomen, using a two-hand head hold or a headlock, touching the opponent's face between the eyebrows and the mouth, forcing the opponent's arm behind the back or bending it more than 90 degrees, and using a leg scissors on the opponent's head or body.

Greco-Roman. The general rules and progress of the bout are the same in Greco-Roman wrestling, but use of the legs is severely restricted. It is illegal to grab the opponent's legs, to grip the opponent with the legs, or to use the legs to push, lift, or exert pressure when they are touching any part of the opponent's body.

Cautions. A wrestler is expected to be aggressive, and "passive obstruction" is penalized severely. Basically, passive obstruction is purely defensive wrestling: continually obstructing an opponent's holds, deliberately lying on the mat or running off the mat, or holding an opponent's hands or arms merely to prevent the opponent from getting a hold.

After one warning, the referee may give a wrestler a caution, signaled by holding the offender's wrist with one hand and raising the other arm into the air. A caution is also given for a foul or other rules infringement, or for arguing with the referee or a judge. If no points are scored in a round as a result of inaction, both wrestlers may be cautioned.

Three cautions result in loss of the bout.

Scoring. A wrestler wins a bout upon pinning an opponent for 5 sec (a fall), or if the opponent is given three cautions. Otherwise the winner is determined on the basis of points awarded.

A wrestler gets 3 points for keeping an opponent in danger for 5 consecutive sec; 2 points for using a correct hold to keep an opponent in danger for less than 5 sec, or for pinning an opponent for less than 3 sec; 1 point for bringing an opponent to the mat and holding the opponent in control, or for moving from the underneath position to the uppermost position, in control. One point is also awarded if the opponent is cautioned.

If neither wrestler leads by more than 1 point at the end of a bout, it is a draw.

Tournament Scoring. A major tournament, with a sizable number of entrants in each weight class, is conducted as a round robin, with wrestlers eliminated on the basis of penalty points. Penalty points are determined by the outcome of each bout, based on this table:

Win by a fall, or by 12 or more points—0
Win by 8 to 11 points—½
Win by less than 8 points—1
Win by passivity, opponent given two cautions—2
Loss by a fall or by less than 8 points—3
Loss by 12 or more points or disqualification—4

A wrestler is eliminated upon accumulating 6 penalty points. The round robin continues until only three wrestlers are left in the weight class; they enter the finals. If any finalists haven't opposed each other in earlier rounds, they must wrestle in a final bout; in the case of those who have wrestled earlier, penalty points for those bouts are carried into the finals, and they do not wrestle again.

After such finals bouts as are necessary, the winner is the finalist with the fewest penalty points. If two of them are tied, the winner is the one who defeated the other. If three of them are tied, the wrestler with the most wins on falls or on points is the winner. If there is still a tie, the winner is the one with the fewest cautions in the finals. If this method doesn't break the tie, the result is a draw.

AAU Freestyle Champions

(The present method of identifying divisions by name, such as "bantamweight," was adopted only recently; previously each division was simply classified by its weight limit, and the limits varied a great deal through the years. In the lists below, I have lumped together roughly equivalent weight divisions, under the names currently used. The present weight limit is listed in parentheses. For example, the division classified below as "light flyweight" now has a limit of 105½ lb; the divisions grouped under this heading have varied from 105 to 112 lb through the years.)

Light Flyweight (105½)

1889	J. B. Reilly	1902	W. Karl
1890	J. B. Reilly	1903	Robert Curry
1891	F. Bertsch	1904	Robert Curry
1892	No competition	1905	J. Heins
1893	C. Monnypenny	1906	W. Lott
1894	R. Bonnett	1907	G. Taylor
1895	J. Hiliah	1908	R. Schwartz
1896	H. Cotter	1909	G. Taylor
1897	G. W. Owen	1910	G. Taylor
1898	No competition	1911	H. Donaldson
1899	G. W. Nelson	1912	G. Taylor
1900	G. W. Nelson	1913	G. Taylor
1901	W. Karl	1914	R. Goudie

1915	R. Goudie	1934	R. Johnson
1916	G. Taylor	1935	R. Myers
1917	C. Benson	1936	C. E. Ritchie
1918	J. Meagher	1937	Charles Peterson
1919	J. Meagher	1938	Charles Peterson
1920	C. Benson	1939	H. Farrell
1921	C. Benson	1940	J. Leeman
1922	No competition	1941	H. Farrell
1923	R. Rowsey	1942–68	No competition
1924	R. Rowsey	1969	Dale Kestel
1925	Harold DeMarsh	1970	Bob Orta
1926	L. Lupton	1971	Wayne Holmes
1927	L. Pfeiffer	1972	Dale Kestel
1928	G. Rosenberg	1973	David Range
1929	G. Shoemaker	1974	David Range
1930	H. Phillips	1975	David Range
1931–33	No competition	1976	Bill Rosado

Flyweight (114½)

1889	F. Mueller	1933	W. Frederick
1890	F. Mueller	1934	E. Thomas
1891	E. Beck	1935	Rex Perry
1892	No competition	1936	Joe McDaniel
1893	J. Holt	1937	M. Croft
1894	F. Bertsch	1938	J. Speicher
1895	M. Kervin	1939	T. Imoto
1896	R. Bonnett	1940	Casey Fredericks
1897	R. Bonnett	1941	Joe McDaniel
1898	No competition	1942	W. Curtis
1899	R. Bonnett	1943	F. Preston
1900	J. Renzlard	1944	C. Parks
1901	G. Owens	1945	Grady Peninger
1902	George Mehnert	1946	Arlie Curry
1903	George Mehnert	1947	Grady Peninger
1904	George Mehnert	1948	Malcolm McDonald
1905	G. Bauer	1949	Arnold Plaza
1906	G. Bauer	1950	John Harrison
1907	G. Bauer	1951	George Creason
1908	George Mehnert	1952	Sidney Nodland
1909	G. Bauer	1953	Richard Delgado
1910	J. Hein	1954	Richard Delgado
1911	N. Chapman	1955	Katsutoshi Yokoyama
1912	W. Strohback	1956	Richard Delgado
1913	J. Hein	1957	Takashi Hirata
1914	J. Vorees	1958	Tsukuhisa Torikura
1915	F. Glahe	1959	Dick Wilson
1916	K. Borsits	1960	Gil Sanchez
1917	L. Servais	1961	Dick Wilson
1918	V. Vosen	1962	Hiroyaka Harada
1919	M. Gans	1963	Takashi Hirata
1920	S. Pammow	1964	Hiroaki Aoki
1921	J. Troyer	1965	Ray Sanchez
1922	V. Vosen	1966	Ray Sanchez
1923	L. Servais	1967	Noriyuki Suzuki
1924	No competition	1968	Arthur Chavez
1925	G. Campbell	1969	Yusuo Katsumura
1926	C. Mitchell	1970	John Morley
1927	L. Lake	1971	John Morley
1928	No competition	1972	John Morley
1929	T. McCrary	1973	Dale Kestel
1930	Robert Pearce	1974	Sergio Gonzales
1931	Joseph Sapora	1975	John Marley
1932	L. Conti	1976	Jim Haines

121–123

1924	B. Hines	1940	Dale Hanson
1928	R. Hewill	1941	Harold Byrd
1932	Joseph Sapora	1942	R. Barber
1936	Ross Flood	1943	P. McDaniel
1937	W. Duffy	1944	Malcolm MacDonald
1938	Joe McDaniel	1945	Bill Klein
1939	Ed Collins	1946	Dick Hauser

1947 Charles Ridenour	1951 John Lee
1949 John Harrison	(Discontinued)
1950 Arnold Plaza	

Bantamweight (125½)

1893 W. Troelsch	1933 M. Andes
1894 W. Reilly	1934 J. Gott
1895 W. Reilly	1935 Ross Flood
1896 E. Harris	1936–41 No competition
1897 A. Meanwell	1942 S. Marks
1898 No competition	1943 Charles Ridenour
1899 M. Wiley	1944 F. Barkovich
1900 A. Kurtzman	1945 Richard Dickerson
1901 Isaac Niflot	1946 Ed Collins
1902 Isaac Niflot	1947 Louis Kachiroubas
1903 Isaac Niflot	1948 Robert Kitt
1904 Isaac Niflot	1949 Russell Bush
1905 George Mehnert	1950 Richard Hauser
1906 George Mehnert	1951 Gene Lybbert
1907 Louis Dole	1952 Jack Blubaugh
1908 Louis Dole	1953 Richard Hauser
1909 L. Ruggiero	1954 Jack Blubaugh
1910 M. Himmelhock	1955 Etsuma Iwano
1911 G. Bauer	1956 Bill Carter
1912 G. Bauer	1957 Terry McCann
1913 V. Vosen	1958 Terry McCann
1914 S. Vorees	1959 Terry McCann
1915 S. Vorees	1960 Carmen Molino
1916 C. Liljehult	1961 Usaki Imaizumi
1917 C. Liljehult	1962 Dave Auble
1918 J. Felios	1963 Norio Tominaga
1919 M. Gans	1964 Gary Simons
1920 A. Callas	1965 Rich Sanders
1921 Robin Reed	1966 Richard Sofman
1922 A. Callas	1967 Rich Sanders
1923 A. Callas	1968 Richard Sofman
1924 No competition	1969 Toshio Nakano
1925 Buell Patterson	1970 Rich Sanders
1926 H. Boyvey	1971 Michi Tanaka
1927 Arthur Holding	1972 John Miller
1928 No competition	1973 Don Behm
1929 G. Campbell	1974 Richard Sofman
1930 J. Reed	1975 Mark Massery
1931 Robert Pearce	1976 Jan Gitcho
1932 No competition	

Featherweight (136½)

1889 M. Luttbeg	1915 O. Runchey
1890 No competition	1916 W. Hallas
1891 A. Ullman	1917 P. Metropoulos
1892 No competition	1918 S. Vorees
1893 C. Clark	1919 B. Johnson
1894 A. Lippman	1920 G. Metropoulos
1895 J. McGrew	1921 J. Hummerich
1896 A. Ullman	1922 Robin Reed
1897 H. Wolff	1923 J. Vorees
1898 No competition	1924 Robin Reed
1899 M. Wiley	1925 L. Brigham
1900 M. Wiley	1926 Allie Morrison
1901 M. Wiley	1927 Allie Morrison
1902 F. Cook	1928 Allie Morrison
1903 Benjamin Bradshaw	1929 J. Erickson
1904 Benjamin Bradshaw	1930 Z. Letowt
1905 Isaac Niflot	1931 L. Morford
1906 A. Rubin	1932 J. Fickel
1907 Benjamin Bradshaw	1933 E. Stout
1908 George Dole	1934 E. Stout
1909 S. Fleischer	1935 R. Rasor
1910 S. Kennedy	1936 F. Parkey
1911 P. Kranzke	1937 G. Hanks
1912 E. Helikman	1938 F. Millard
1913 A. Anderson	1939 B. Renfo
1914 H. Jenkins	1940 Ray Cheney

1941 Doug Lee	1959 Jerry Hoke
1942 Doug Lee	1960 Linn Long
1943 Merle Jennings	1961 Lee Allen
1944 V. V. Cronhardt	1962 Osamu Watenabe
1945 Clifford McFarland	1963 Harno Abe
1946 Lowell Lange	1964 Mitsuo Hara
1947 Lowell Lange	1965 Chikara Murane
1948 Lee Thomson	1966 Nobuyuki Motokawa
1949 Lowell Lange	1967 Bob Buzzard
1950 Lowell Lange	1968 Masamitsu Ichiguchi
1951 Bill Armstrong	1969 Dan Gable
1952 Josiah Henson	1970 Mike Young
1953 Jim Sinadinos	1971 Rich Sanders
1954 Shozo Sasahara	1972 Testu Ikeno
1955 Motoichi Motohashi	1973 Dave Pruzhansky
1956 Alan Rice	1974 Don Behm
1957 Masashi Kokubo	1975 Doug Moses
1958 Naboru Ikeda	1976 Kiyoshi Abe

Lightweight (149½)

1897 W. Riggs	1934 F. Stout
1898 No competition	1935 A. Tomlinson
1899 M. Wiley	1936 L. Fegg
1900 M. Wiley	1937 E. Bruno
1901 M. Wiley	1938 B. Hanson
1902 N. Nelson	1939 D. Taylor
1903 M. Yokel	1940 E. Viskocil
1904 Otto Roehm	1941 C. Soukas
1905 R. Tisney	1942 David Arndt
1906 C. Clapper	1943 William Maxwell
1907 Richard Jaeckel	1944 L. Cowell
1908 M. Wiley	1945 Gale Miklos
1909 C. Johnson	1946 James Miller
1910 C. Johnson	1947 James Miller
1911 W. Milchewski	1948 Newton Copple
1912 G. Petterson	1949 Keith Young
1913 C. Johnson	1950 Keith Young
1914 H. Jenkins	1951 Bob Hoke
1915 D. Burns	1952 Newton Copple
1916 L. Nelson	1953 Newton Copple
1917 H. Jenkins	1954 Tommy Evans
1918 A. Forst	1955 Joe Scandura
1919 G. Smith	1956 Tommy Evans
1920 W. Tikka	1957 Tommy Evans
1921 Russell Vis	1958 Newton Copple
1922 Russell Vis	1959 Newton Copple
1923 Russell Vis	1960 Frank Betucci
1924 Russell Vis	1961 Gerald Grenier
1925 K. Truckemuller	1962–68 No competition
1926 R. Myers	1969 Fumiaki Nakamura
1927 R. Prunty	1970 Dan Gable
1928 C. Berryman	1971 Gene Davis
1929 A. Tomlinson	1972 Mike Young
1930 O. Kapp	1973 Lloyd Keaser
1931 A. Tomlinson	1974 Gene Davis
1932 Ben Bishop	1975 Gene Davis
1933 G. Sappington	1976 Lloyd Keaser

Welterweight (163)

1888 Dr. Shell	1902 J. Schmicker
1889 M. Lau	1903 W. Beckman
1890 G. Haskin	1904 Charles Erickson
1891 Z. Von Bockman	1905 W. Schaefer
1892 No competition	1906 J. McAfee
1893 W. Osgood	1907 F. Marganes
1894 F. Ellis	1908 C. Anderson
1895 C. Reinicke	1909 F. Marganes
1896 A. Ullman	1910 F. Marganes
1897 D. Chesterman	1911 C. Gesek
1898 No competition	1912 J. Smith
1899 A. Mellinger	1913 J. Smith
1900 M. Wiley	1914 B. Reubin
1901 J. Schmicker	1915 B. Reubin

1916	W. Americus
1917	C. Johnson
1918	Stephenson
1919	G. Tragos
1920	E. Leino
1921	C. Johnson
1922	E. Wolff
1923	E. Leino
1924	P. Martter
1925	R. Hammonds
1926	R. Hammonds
1927	Fendley Collins
1928	L. Appleton
1929	B. Sherman
1930	Jack Van Bebber
1931	O. Kapp
1932	Jack Van Bebber
1933	G. Belshaw
1934	E. Kielhorn
1935	Frank Lewis
1936	G. Belshaw
1937	Walter Jacobs
1938	Walter Jacobs
1939	Walter Jacobs
1940	E. Blanke
1941	H. Faucett
1942	Vernon Logan
1943	R. Roberts
1944	E. Tomick
1945	Douglas Lee
1946	Robert Roemer

165–168

1931	Jack Van Bebber
1933	Robert Hess
1934	O. England
1935	O. England
1942	J. Scarpello
1943	Melvin Northrup
1944	E. Blake
1945	Melvin Northrup

Middleweight (180½)

1913	J. Varga
1914	Earl Caddock
1915	Earl Caddock
1916	N. Pendleton
1917	D. Verga
1918	K. Kunert
1919	K. Kunert
1920	K. Kunert
1921	F. Myer
1922	Paul Berlenbach
1923	Paul Berlenbach
1924	W. Wright
1925	O. Stuteville
1926	F. Bryan
1927	George Rule
1928	R. Hammonds
1929	K. Krough
1930	Glenn Stafford
1931	Conrad Caldwell
1932	J. Schutte
1933	A. Sweet
1934	George Martin
1935	L. Ricks
1936	Richard Voliva
1937	A. Crawford
1938	A. Crawford
1939	No competition
1940	Henry Wittenberg
1941	Henry Wittenberg
1942	G. Inman

1947	Orville Long
1948	Leland Merrill
1949	Bill Nelson
1950	Bill Nelson
1951	Keith Young
1952	James LaRock
1953	James LaRock
1954	Jay Holt
1955	Melvin Northrup
1956	Bill Fischer
1957	Doug Blubaugh
1958	Larry Ten Pas
1959	Fritz Fivian
1960	Doug Blubaugh
1961	Steven Friedman
1962	Kazuo Abe
1963	Greg Ruth
1964	Greg Ruth
1965	Jim Burke
1966	Werner Holzer
1967	Bobby Douglas
1968	Bobby Douglas
1969	Lee Detrick
1970	Wayne Wells
1971	Gary Bell
1972	Wayne Wells
1973	Carl Adams
1974	Stan Dziedzic
1975	Carl Adams
1976	Stan Dziedzic

1946	Doug Lee
1947	Doug Lee
1948	No competition
1949	William Smith
1950	William Smith
1951	William Smith
(Discontinued)	

1943	Dale Thomas
1944	Melvin Northrup
1945	James Dernehl
1946	Frank Bissell
1947	Dale Thomas
1948	Dale Thomas
1949	Shuford Swift
1950	Charles Swift
1951	Louis Holland
1952	Shuford Swift
1953	Dan Hodge
1954	Dan Hodge
1955	Wenzel Hubel
1956	Dan Hodge
1957	Meb Turner
1958	Wenzel Hubel
1959	Jim Ferguson
1960	Jim Ferguson
1961	Jim Ferguson
1962	Jim Ferguson
1963	Dean Lahr
1964	Len Kauffman
1965	Russ Camilleri
1966	Steve Combs
1967	Pat Kelly
1968	Mike Gallego
1969	Len Kauffman
1970	Jay Robinson
1971	Russ Camilleri
1972	Jay Robinson

1973	John Peterson
1974	Greg Hicks

Light Heavyweight (198)

1922	F. Myer
1923	No competition
1924	Charles Strack
1925–27	No competition
1928	E. Edwards
1929–31	No competition
1932	L. Putrin
1933–35	No competition
1936	Lloyd Ricks
1937	W. Norton
1938	J. Harrell
1939	V. Cavagnaro
1940	Ed Valorz
1941	G. Frei
1942	S. Santo
1943	Henry Wittenberg
1944	Henry Wittenberg
1945	Robert Wilson
1946	No competition
1947	Henry Wittenberg
1948	Henry Wittenberg
1949	Vern Gagne
1950	David Whinfrey
1951	Henry Lanzi
1952	Henry Wittenberg

Heavyweight (220)

1904	B. Hansen
1905	B. Hansen
1906	M. McAfee
1907	J. Gundersen
1908	J. Gundersen
1909	E. Payne
1910	F. Motis
1911	H. Grim
1912	A. Kaino
1913	J. Gundersen
1914	A. Minkley
1915	Earl Caddock
1916	S. Schwartz
1917	D. Very
1918	K. Kunert
1919	S. Czarnecke
1920	N. Pendleton
1921	F. Myers
1922	F. Myers
1923	K. Leppanen
1924	R. Flanders
1925	R. Krouse
1926	Charles Strack
1927	R. Flanders
1928	E. George
1929	E. George
1930	Earl McCready
1931	R. Jones
1932	L. Hammack
1933	G. Ellison
1934	Ralph Teague
1935	Ralph Teague
1936	R. Dunn
1937	Richard Vaughn
1938	C. Gustafson
1939	M. Sims
1940	W. Nead

Unlimited

1963	Larry Kristoff
1964	Jim Raschke
1965	Larry Kristoff

1975	John Peterson
1976	Brady Hall

1953	Dale Thomas
1954	Dale Thomas
1955	Tim Woodin
1956	Peter Blair
1957	Tim Woodin
1958	Frank Rosenmayr
1959	Frank Rosenmayr
1960	Frank Rosenmayr
1961	Don Brand
1962	Shunichi Kawano
1963	Russ Camilleri
1964	Russ Camilleri
1965	Wayne Baughman
1966	Dean Lahr
1967	Bill Harlow
1968	Russ Camilleri
1969	Buck Deadrich
1970	Wayne Baughman
1971	Wayne Baughman
1972	Wayne Baughman
1973	Ben Peterson
1974	Peter Leiskau
1975	Russ Hellickson
1976	Ben Peterson

1941	L. Maschi
1942	Leonard Levy
1943	R. Metzger
1944	Richard Vaughn
1945	Richard Vaughn
1946	Mike DeBiase
1947	Ray Gunkel
1948	Ray Gunkel
1949	Robert Maldegan
1950	Fred Stoeker
1951	Carl Abell
1952	Richard Clark
1953	Bill Kerslake
1954	Bill Kerslake
1955	Bill Kerslake
1956	Bill Kerslake
1957	Bill Kerslake
1958	Bill Kerslake
1959	Bill Kerslake
1960	Bill Kerslake
1961	Dale Lewis
1962	Jiro Seki
1963	Dan Brand
1964	Dan Brand
1965	Jerry Conine
1966	Ken Johnson
1967	Henk Schenk
1968	Henk Schenk
1969	Jess Lewis
1970	Larry Kristoff
1971	Dominic Carollo
	Henk Schenk
1972	Buck Deadrich
1973	Russ Hellickson
1974	Greg Wojchiechowski
1975	Greg Wojchiechowski
1976	Russ Hellickson

1966	Larry Kristoff
1967	Larry Kristoff
1968	Larry Kristoff

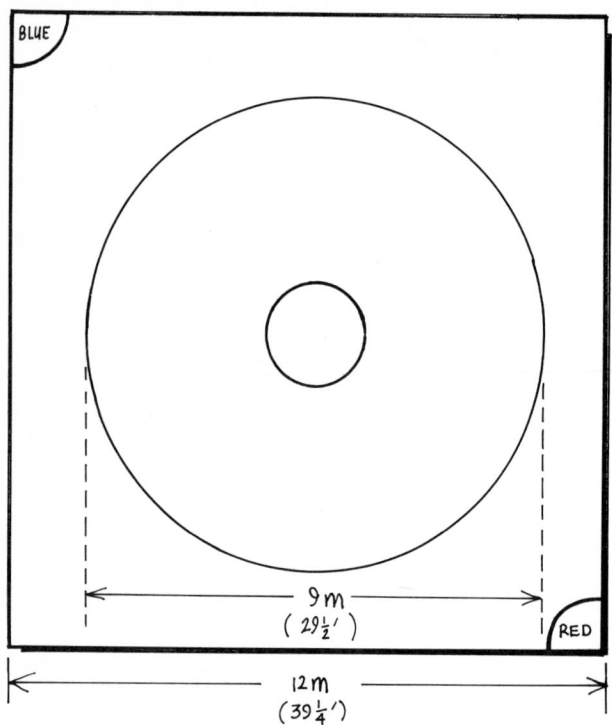

Mat used in international wrestling. Inner circle is 1 m (3ft 3.36 in) diameter.

1969	Dale Stearns	1973	Chris Taylor
1970	Greg Wojchiechowski	1974	Mack McCready
1971	Greg Wojchiechowski	1975	Mack McCready
1972	Greg Wojchiechowski	1976	Mack McCready

Citizens Savings
Hall of Fame

Wrestlers

Charles Ackerly
David Arndt
Richard W. Baughman
Peter Blair
Ned Blass
Douglas Blubaugh
Glenn Brand
Conrad Caldwell
Newton Copple
Richard DiBattista
George S. Dole
Edward Eichelberger
Ross Flood
Dan Gable
Vern Gagne
Anthony Gizone

William Kerslake
William H. Koll
Lowell Lange
George Layman
Frank Lewis
Hardie Lewis
Vernon Logan
Lawrence Mantooth
Wayne Martin
Terrence McCann
Earl McCready
Charles McDaniel
Joseph McDaniel
George M. Mehnert
Peter Mehringer
Allie Morrison

Larry Hayes
Stanley Henson, Jr.
Robert Hess
Dan Hodge
Dick Hutton
Burl Jennings
Merle Jennings
Alan D. Kelley
Robin Reed
Jack Riley
Joseph Sapora
Joe Scarpello
Elliott Simons
Virgil Smith
William Smith
John Spellman
Harry Steele
Ralph Teague

Norvard Nalan
William J. Nelson
Gene Nicks
Melvin A. Northrup
Edwin Peery
Hugh Peery
Ben Peterson
Arnold Plaza
Yojiro Uetake
Jack Van Bebber
Russell Vis
William Weick
Wayne Wells
Alfred Whitehurst
Shelby Wilson
Henry Wittenberg
Keith Young

Coaches

Leroy Alitz
Richard L. Barker
Joseph Begala
Fendlev Collins
Finn Ericksen
Tom Evans
Casey L. Fredericks
Edward C. Gallagher
Frank Gardner
Arthur Griffith
John W. Hancock
Marvin Hess
Vaughan Hitchcock
Harold Howard
Briggs Hunt
Hubert Jack
Wallace T. Johnson
Clifford Keen
Paul V. Keen
Harold E. Kenney
Karl Kitt
Everett Lantz
Gerald E. Leeman
Rometo Macias
George Martin
William Martin
Archie Mathis

Charles W. Mayser
David McCuskey
Mike Milkovich
Bernard Mooney
Raymond Murdock
Harold Nichols
Hugo Otopalik
Charles Parker
Buell Patterson
Rex Peery
Grady Peninger
Claude Reeck
Port Robertson
Myron Roderick
Joseph Scalzo
Raymond Schwartz
William Sheridan
Bob Siddens
Raymond Sparks
Charles Speidel
Henry Stone
Dale O. Thomas
W. H. "Billy" Thom
Arnold W. Umback
Richard Voliva
Julius F. Wagner
Arthur J. Weiss

Contributors

Stephen M. Archer
W. Austin Bishop
Henry Boresch
Wilfred E. Cann
Raymond G. Clapp
Albert DeFerrari
Bob Dellinger
John H. Drummond
John Engel
William Farrell
Manuel Gorriaran
Josiah Henson

Jess Hoke
Ken Kraft
Thomas M. Lumly
Erich Pohl
Neal F. Quimby
G. D. Richardson
Clay Roberts
Raymond V. Roberts
Donald Sayenga
C. W. Streit
Dr. William Thomas
T. Ralph Williams

Bibliography. Gallagher, Edward C.: *Wrestling*, Ronald, New York, 1951; Umback, Arnold W., and Warren R. Johnson, *Successful Wrestling*, 2nd ed., William C. Brown, Dubuque, Ia., 1972.

Y

YACHTING—The Dutch word *jaght* means "to put on speed," and the original *jaghtschips* were small, fast cargo boats used on Dutch canals. By the early seventeenth century they often took part in informal races.

King Charles II was presented with a yacht by the Dutch when he left the Netherlands to assume the British throne in 1660. The king skippered his yacht *Jamie* to a victory over the Duke of York's *Anne* in 1662 to win a 100-pound bet, and yacht racing had begun in England. It grew slowly during the late seventeenth and early eighteenth centuries. The first yacht club, the Water Club of Cork Harbor, Ireland, was organized in 1720. There is a record of a sailing match on the Thames River in 1749, and on June 28, 1775, the first full-scale regatta was held on the Thames. A short time later, on July 13, the Duke of Cumberland presented a cup for another Thames regatta.

The United States was a seafaring country throughout the nineteenth century, but yachting arrived here rather late. Of course, the yachts of the day were large, expensive vessels and neither the money nor the leisure time for the sport was available until almost the middle of the century. The first recorded yacht race in American waters was an informal affair, in 1835, when Robert Bennett Forbes of Boston, sailing his *Sylph* near Nantucket, challenged John C. Stevens' *Wave*.

It was aboard another Stevens yacht, *Gymcrack*, that the New York Yacht Club (NYYC) was formed in July 1844. The club held its first regatta in 1845—shortly after the first American regatta was held in Massachusetts Bay—and a year later the club invented the "Corinthian" regatta, in which no paid hands were allowed in racing crews, only club members.

The NYYC virtually ruled yachting in this country for many years, and made many contributions to the development of competitive sailing. In 1847 the club developed a handicap system, based on size, and this system was further revised through the years, forming the basis for handicap races throughout the country and other parts of the world.

The America's Cup. The British were having a world's fair in 1851, and they hoped an American yacht would take part in a fair regatta. Stevens and other members of the NYYC formed a syndicate and hired George Steers to design a schooner. Launched on May 3, 1851, she was named *America,* and on June 21 she set sail for Le Havre, France. After being repainted and outfitted with racing sails, she then set sail for Cowes, England.

En route, *America,* skippered by Dick Brown, was engaged in an informal race by a fast English cutter, *Laverock*. *America* won easily, and after word of the victory got around, British yachtsmen lost all interest in racing the speedy Yankee craft.

Stevens and friends finally decided to enter the vessel in a Royal Yacht Squadron race around the Isle of Wight for a trophy known as the Hundred Guineas Cup. The race began at 10 A.M. on August 22; at 8:37 P.M., *America* crossed the finish line 8 min ahead of her nearest competitor. The Americans then sold their schooner for $25,000—she was to start a new trend in British yacht design—and came home with their trophy.

In 1857 they gave the trophy to the New York Yacht Club as a challenge cup for foreign yachts. The first challenge didn't come until 1868, when James Ashbury of England offered to bring his schooner *Cambria* over to race against an American vessel. The NYYC insisted, however, that *Cambria* would have to race against a whole club fleet, since *America* had won the cup against a fleet. Ashbury finally agreed, and the race took place on August 8, 1870, with *Cambria* against 14 American yachts. The American schooner *Magic* won the race; *Cambria* finished eighth.

Ashbury wasn't ready to give up, however. He had a new schooner, *Livonia,* especially built for his next challenge, and the NYYC agreed to some concessions: The cup would go to the winner of a four-out-of-seven series of races, and in each race *Livonia* would go against a single American vessel. But the American defender in each race would be named the morning of the race, permitting the club to switch vessels, if necessary, because of wind conditions or poor performance. *Columbia* beat *Livonia* twice, but her steering gear broke and she lost the third race. *Sappho* was then substituted, and beat *Livonia* twice more.

The ground rules for America's Cup racing have changed many times since then, often as the result of acrid controversy. Since 1920 the competition has been won by the first vessel to score four victories, and just one defending vessel meets one challenging vessel in the series. America's Cup yachts have become progressively smaller through the years, reflecting an overall trend in yachting. Time allowances, based on the sizes of the yachts involved, were used up until 1930.

In the 1930, 1934, and 1937 races, yachts of the J class were specified. Since the series resumed in 1958, the yachts have had to be of the 12-m class. Each vessel must be designed and built in the country she represents, and must also be completely outfitted in that country, insofar as possible. However, the NYYC will entertain requests that a challenger be allowed to obtain certain items—sails, for instance—in another country.

Since 1930 the races have been conducted off Newport, Rhode Island, at an area well away from the harbor, so local knowledge is no longer an important factor, as it was when matches took place in the mouth of New York

Harbor. The "Olympic" course has been used since 1964: a six-leg course totaling 24.3 mi. If neither vessel finishes the course in 6 hr, the race doesn't count.

The most persistent challenger in the America's Cup series was Sir Thomas Lipton, the English merchant and yachtsman, who challenged with five different vessels, each named *Shamrock*, between 1899 and 1930. Five of the last six challenges have come from Australia; in three of those years, France also challenged, but lost to Australia in the elimination series to select the challenging country. Since 1881, elimination trials have also been held to select the defending vessel.

Ocean Racing. At first, yacht racing was confined to bays and harbors, inland lakes, and coastal waters. The big schooners that represented yachting after the Civil War, however, were quite capable of sailing on the open ocean. The first major ocean race was a really major one—the transatlantic race of 1866, the result of a bet between two NYYC members. A third, James Gordon Bennet, also got into the act, and his *Henrietta* won the historic race, from Sandy Hook Lightship to the Isle of Wight, in 13 days, 21 hr, and 45 min.

The next major "ocean" race was actually sailed on Lake Michigan, from Chicago to Mackinac Island, a 333-mi journey. The first event in this series, held in 1898, also grew out of a bet among yacht owners. The competition wasn't held again until 1904. It is now conducted annually under the auspices of the Chicago Yacht Club.

The Bermuda race was originally held in 1906, and was repeated in 1907 and 1910, then dropped owing to lack of interest. It was revived, however, in 1923 and is now held every two years. Since 1924 the starting point has been Newport; the total distance is 635 mi.

The transpacific race also began in 1906 and was held every other year through 1912. It, too, was revived in 1923 and has become a more or less biennial event. The race covers more than 2,200 mi, from Los Angeles to Hawaii.

A major series of ocean races is held annually by the Southern Ocean Racing Conference (SORC). This began with a St. Petersburg–Havana race in 1930. There are now six races run by the conference, five of which count toward the overall championship. The two most important are the St. Petersburg–Fort Lauderdale, a 403-mi race around the Florida peninsula, and the Miami-Nassau, a three-leg, 184-mi race.

Smaller Boats. Although yachting was long identified with large boats and wealth, small pleasure boats gained some popularity as early as the 1830s. The first of them was the "sandbagger," a shallow sloop ballasted with sandbags, which were shifted from one side of the boat to the other, as necessary to get proper trim. The sandbagger, developed in New York Harbor, spread all over the continent by the turn of the century.

Another early small boat was the catboat, developed on Narragansett Bay, Rhode Island, in the 1870s. Originally a workboat, the cat soon became a pleasure vessel throughout New England waters.

W. P. Stephens, a canoe enthusiast, developed a sailing canoe during the 1870s. In 1895 the Seawanhaka International Challenge Trophy was established for competition among sailing canoes, essentially double-ended, 15-ft boats with twin masts. Stephens' *Ethelwynn* defeated *Spruce IV*, skippered by J. Arthur Brand of England, three races to two, in the first series.

The real beginnings of small-boat sailing, however, lay in development of the "one design," a whole set of sailboats built to the same specifications. The one-design idea came into being about 1900, but didn't have much impact on sailing at first. Then in 1911 the famous, and still popular, Star was designed by Francis Sweisguth. By 1922 enough people owned the Star—a 22-ft, 7½-in sloop—so that the Star Class Association of America was formed. The class soon had its own regatta, its own yearbook, and even its own monthly magazine.

The one-design sailboat has two great advantages. First, if all the boats in a race are virtually identical, the race is a real test of skippers, not of designs, and no handicapping is necessary. Second, one-design boats are a good deal cheaper than custom-made boats. Other one-design classes soon followed the Star. Two early designs that are still popular are the Snipe, a 15½-footer developed in 1931, and the Comet, a 16-footer developed in 1932.

The popularity of sailing rose even further after World War II, not only because of the increase in leisure time and discretionary income, but because of the proliferation of one-design boats and the development of the fiberglass hull. Unlike a wooden hull, a fiberglass hull can be molded in large quantities, making mass production possible, and it requires very little maintenance.

It is estimated that there are nearly a half-million sailboat owners in the United States today, and that about 3 million people take part in sailing.

Sailboats and Gear

Types of Hulls. Hulls are classified, first, according to whether they have keels or centerboards, and second, by their cross-sectional shapes when viewed from the bow.

A keel is a relatively narrow downward extension of the hull which keeps the boat from sliding sideways through the water. The deep, or full, keel is generally triangular, as viewed from the side, and extends from the bow to near the stern. The fin keel is a much smaller projection which goes almost straight down into the water from a point approximately halfway between bow and stern. It usually has a longer, cigar-shaped bottom for ballast.

The centerboard performs the same function as the keel. It is shaped like a fin keel, without the ballast attachment, and it is adjustable; it is hinged so that it can easily be raised or lowered through a slot in the bottom of the boat. A variation is the daggerboard, which is simply thrust straight down into the water without hinging; it can be lifted entirely out of the boat.

A keel boat is more stable, but it cannot be sailed in water shallower than the keel; it is difficult to transport, and it will sink when swamped. The deep-keeled boat is also more difficult to turn. The centerboard boat can be sailed in fairly shallow water, but must be relatively broad in the beam for stability; if it strikes an underwater object, the centerboard will usually swing up, allowing the boat to keep moving. The daggerboard requires less cockpit space, but will not give way when it strikes an underwater object.

The most stable hull shape is the V-bottom, which also gives good speed. The round-bottom is stronger, but not quite so stable; it's also a fast hull shape. The arc-bottom is a V in which both sides are concave; it is at least as fast and as stable as the V, but it is considerably more expensive to build. Least expensive of all is the flat-bottom, but it is also the least suited for sailing; it can be sailed only on well-protected waters.

There are also many types of bow and stern shapes, which affect a boat's speed and performance.

Planing Hulls. A rather recent development is a very lightweight hull, which, when it reaches the right speed under the right conditions, will begin to hydroplane— ride up on its own bow wave so that there is less surface area going through the water and, therefore, less friction to reduce its speed.

To hydroplane, a boat must be kept upright, or nearly upright. To accomplish this, it is often necessary to have one or more crew members actually hanging out of the boat, to windward, to keep the boat from heeling in the other direction. Special gear used for this purpose are trapezes, hiking straps, and hiking seats.

Multihulls. The catamaran is a two-hulled vessel developed centuries ago in the Polynesian islands. It was probably developed from the outrigger canoe, which is attached to a log for stability. The Polynesians realized they could substitute another canoe for the log.

The first sailing catamaran was designed by Nathanael Herreshoff in the late nineteenth century. It was a fast boat—so fast that it was banned from NYYC competition—but it lacked maneuverability. The modern catamaran was developed in England in the early 1950s. The hulls were U-shaped instead of V-shaped, and centerboards greatly improved maneuverability. Since then, the trimaran, with three hulls, has also entered the picture.

The multihulls are faster than single-hulled vessels of the same size, once the size gets big enough, and they are also more stable. Even with improved hull design, however, they aren't quite as maneuverable, and they are much more severely affected by rough water than the single hulls.

Rigs. The rig of a yacht is the general configuration of her masts and sails. The most common type of small sailboat is the sloop, which has a single mast with a large mainsail and one or more other sails in front of the mast. These foresails are called jibs.

The catboat is the simplest of sailboats; it has just the mast and the mainsail. The mast is stepped (placed) very far forward.

The cutter is similar to the sloop, but its mast is nearly in the middle of the boat, between bow and stern, and she always carries at least two foresails and sometimes more.

The yawl has two masts, one near the bow and one, the mizzenmast, well astern. The mainmast carries a mainsail and one or more foresails; the mizzenmast may carry only one sail, the mizzen, or a variety of sails, including a staysail aft and a backstay aft. The mizzen rides aft of the mast.

The ketch is similar, except that the mizzenmast is farther forward and the mainmast is usually a little farther aft. This means that the mainsail is smaller and the mizzen is larger.

Sails. The ideal sail cloth would be quite strong but lightweight, resistant to stretching, and tightly woven so that little wind can "leak" through it. Until recently the sailor had to settle for various compromises, but man-made fabrics, specifically Dacron polyester, have changed that. Dacron, first produced in 1953, is a virtually ideal

Two small boats engage in a match race on Narragansett Bay.

sail material, and almost all sails are made of it today. Nylon, which stretches a good deal but is lighter in weight, is often used for spinnakers, where light weight is a definite advantage and stretchability not much of a disadvantage.

Mainsails and mizzens can be rigged in either of two ways. The jib-headed sail is basically triangular in shape, and it is raised and lowered up and down the mast. The gaff-headed sail is basically rectangular, and it calls for the use of a spar which projects upward from the mast, across the top ("head") of the sail.

The bottom of the sail is its foot; the side attached to the mast is its luff; the third side, which is attached to neither mast nor boom, is the leech. The head, in the case of a jib-headed sail, is the corner at the top of the mast; in the case of a gaff-headed sail, it is the side which is rigged to the spar. The corner between the foot and the luff is the tack; the corner between the foot and the leech is the clew.

On a gaff-headed sail, the corner between head and leech is the peak, and that between head and luff is the throat.

Rigging. There are two types of rigging. Standing rigging supports masts and remains in place while the mast does, at least on larger boats. Running rigging is used to raise and lower sails.

A mast has two stays, the headstay, which runs to the bow of the boat, and the backstay, which runs to the stern. Shrouds are stays that run from the mast to the side of the boat. As a mast gets larger, the number of stays increases.

Any rope used to hoist, set, or trim a sail is called a line. A halyard is a line that hoists the head of the sail to the top of the mast. A sheet is a line used to trim a sail. It is attached to a boom or to a corner of the sail.

Fundamentals of Sailing

A sailboat obviously is propelled by the wind. But, at its fastest, it is propelled in two different ways. When the boat is sailing exactly in the direction the wind is blowing, there is only the push, and the boat can travel no faster than the wind. However, when the boat is sailing across the wind, its sail acts as an airfoil, like the wing of an airplane. A partial vacuum is created on the leeward side of the sail (the side away from the wind), and the boat is thus pushed by the wind and sucked along by the vacuum effect, enabling it, under ideal conditions, to travel faster than the wind.

Points of Sailing. A boat is said to be running, or running before the wind, when she is sailing with, or nearly with, the wind—when the wind is coming from directly astern or a point or two to either side of the stern. (A "point," in sailing terminology, is 11¼ degrees of angle.)

She is said to be reaching when she is sailing across the wind. It is a beam reach if the wind is blowing approxi-

Intrepid passes the committee boat during the 1970 America's Cup series, in which she defeated the Australian challenger, *Gretel II.* (*Milt Silvia,* New Bedford Standard-Times.)

mately at right angles to her course; a broad reach if the wind is coming from somewhat behind; and a close reach when the wind is coming from somewhat in front. A boat usually reaches her top speed on a close reach.

When sailing almost against the wind, a vessel is said to be beating, or sailing on the wind. When beating, she can't proceed directly to her objective, but must make a series of tacks—zigzagging back and forth across the line of the wind—to get there.

Racing Sails. On most points of sailing, the mainsail does most of the work of driving the boat. The main purpose of the jib is to guide air over the leeward side of the mainsail, to prevent turbulence, which could cause the sail to flap. This is particularly important when sailing close to the wind.

When the vessel is running, the jib is often replaced by a spinnaker, a balloonlike, triangular sail made of very light cloth. In racing, the Genoa jib is often used. It is a relatively large sail, long at the foot, which overlaps the mainsail; this gives it a very powerful driving effect.

Steering. A boat is steered by a rudder, which is controlled by a tiller in smaller boats, by a steering wheel in large boats. Steering with a tiller is like steering a car in reverse: To turn right, the tiller is pushed to the left. The rudder is effective only when the boat is moving; the greater the speed, the more effective the rudder.

The sails can also be used to steer. This is often done in shallow water, before the rudder is in the water, or when the boat is just getting under way and the rudder is relatively ineffective. Sheeting in the jib will make the boat turn toward the direction in which the wind is blowing; sheeting in the mainsail and letting off the jib will make her turn into the wind.

The crew can also help in the steering process by shifting their weight from one side or the other to make the boat heel in that direction. When heeling to one side, the boat will tend to turn in the other direction.

Running. Oddly, the most difficult, and least pleasurable, kind of sailing is with the wind. The boat simply doesn't go very fast, and therefore doesn't respond as well to the helm.

The mainsheet, which controls the mainsail, should be let out until the sail is approximately at right angles to the boat's center line. This may prevent the wind from getting to the jib; if so, the jib may be spread out on the opposite side. (The boat is then sailing "wing to wing.")

Actually, a boat is rarely sailed in exactly the same direction as the wind; usually, the wind will be a point or so off the stern, in one direction or the other. The mainsail should then be swung out to the opposite side, and the helmsman should "work to leeward." When the wind puffs up strongly, the helmsman should turn slightly toward the wind; when it dies, the helmsman should turn somewhat in the other direction.

When the wind really is from dead astern, or nearly so, the wise sailor will tack back and forth across the direction of the wind. The increased speed will usually more than make up for the increased distance.

Reaching. When sailing is more or less across the wind, little maneuvering is necessary to travel a straight line to a destination. But it is important to study wind direction to take the greatest possible advantage of a reach. Sheets should be let out until the sails begin to luff; then they should be hauled in a bit. When the wind draws ahead, sails will begin to luff; when it draws behind, the boat will heel and lose speed.

Beating. A boat cannot sail against the wind; the best she can do, ordinarily, is to sail within 45 degrees of the wind. Sailing to windward is the opposite of running: The boat should be turned slightly away from the wind when it puffs up, or slightly away from it when it dies down.

The helmsman's job is most important during a beat, because the margin for error is very small. There are many signs that might signal a slight change in course. Now and then, the helmsman should turn a little into the wind to see if the boat slows down. If she does, the helmsman should bring her back a little, away from the wind, to see if she gains speed. Continual testing of this sort is vital when the boat is beating. Beating is more difficult when the boat is going against waves, or when the wind is very light, and the helmsman also must keep those factors in mind when beating.

Tacking. Since a boat can't sail against the wind, it is necessary to tack when the wind is blowing in the wrong direction. For a short time, the boat is headed at an angle, away from the mark; then she is swung back, across the wind, in the other direction.

Changing direction from one tack to another, when the wind comes directly across the bow at one point in the change, is called "coming about." A boat is said to be on a starboard tack when she is in a broad reach, with the wind coming over the starboard side. To change to a port tack, the boat is brought around by rudder, and the jibsheet is released. When the boat is pointed into the wind, the sails will shake, or luff; the boat also is said to be luffing. As the boat swings around somewhat more, the jib should be trimmed, so it will fill with wind and swing the boat more rapidly.

Jibing. A jibe is essentially a tack, except that the boat is sailing before the wind, not into it. It happens much more rapidly, however; instead of luffing, the sails suddenly fill with wind on the lee side and swing across the boat, and extreme care must be taken that no one is hit by the rapidly moving boom.

Rules of Racing

There are basically two kinds of courses for a yacht race: point-to-point, in which the boats proceed from one place to a destination, and closed-circuit, in which they travel around a course.

Point-to-point races are generally long ocean races: the transatlantic or Newport-Bermuda, for example. Closed-circuit races are shorter, and the course is usually laid out so the boats have to spend some time beating, reaching, and running. Triangular courses are very common. Less common are windward-leeward courses, in which the boats spend equal amounts of time running and beating. Variations of the triangular course are the Gold Cup course, in which the boats beat, run, and beat again before sailing the other two sides of the triangle; the modified Gold Cup, in which they travel three sides of the triangle, then beat and run along one side; and the Olympic course, in which they sail the triangle, then beat, run, and beat again along one side.

The course is established by three kinds of marks: line marks, which mark the ends of the starting and finishing lines; rounding marks, which a boat must sail around during the race; and guide marks, which establish the outer boundaries of the course.

Crews. The rules of the North American Yacht Racing Union limit the number of crewmen allowed, based on the boat's sail area: two crew members (including skipper) for less than 100 ft²; three for 100 to 199 ft²; and three crew members, plus one for each 250 ft² of sail area, or fraction thereof, for boats with 200 ft² or more. Many classes have their own crew limitations.

Right of Way. A yacht can be disqualified from a race for infringing the right-of-way rules; a yacht that has the right of way can also be disqualified for making no attempt to avoid a collision resulting in serious damage.

The basic right-of-way rules are:

A boat on the port tack must keep clear of a boat on the starboard tack.

When yachts are on the same tack, the windward boat must keep clear of the leeward boat, and a boat that is clear astern must keep clear of a yacht that is clear ahead. If neither yacht is clear astern of the other, there is said to be an overlap. When one boat has established an overlap on another to leeward, from having been clear astern, she must give the windward yacht an opportunity to keep clear. The leeward yacht must not sail above her proper course during the overlap.

When a boat is tacking or jibing, she must keep clear of a yacht that is on a tack. A boat may not tack or jibe into a right-of-way position unless she is far enough from a yacht on a tack to allow that yacht to keep clear without having to alter course until the tack or jibe is completed. If two boats are tacking or jibing at the same time, the boat on the other's port side must keep clear.

Rounding Marks. If a boat touches a mark, or causes a mark vessel to shift to avoid being touched, she should retire from the race immediately, unless she claims that she was forced into it by the action of another boat, in which case she must protest. However, if the mark is surrounded by navigable water, the yacht can correct her error by sailing completely around it, provided she leaves it on the required side.

If a boat rounds or passes a mark on the wrong side, she can make up for it by turning back and rounding or passing it properly.

Some special right-of-way rules apply when boats are about to pass or round a mark. An outside yacht that is overlapped must, in most cases, give the overlapping boat room on the inside to round or pass the mark. A yacht clear astern must keep clear, in anticipation of a round or passing maneuver and during the maneuver. She is not entitled to room for passing if she establishes an inside overlap when the boat ahead is already within two lengths of the mark, or if the boat ahead cannot give the required room. The boat claiming the inside overlap has the responsibility of satisfying the race committee that the overlap was established properly.

Starts. The customary method of starting a race is to give three signals. Ten minutes before the start, a warning signal is given, by hoisting a flag, usually accompanied by a whistle or gunshot. The warning signal is hauled down 4½ min later, and 30 sec after that—5 min before the start—a preparatory signal is given, again by hoisting a flag, accompanied by an audible signal. This also comes down 4½ min later and, 30 sec after that, the start is signaled by another flag with audible signal.

If a boat is already over the starting line when the starting signal is given, she is notified, and she must turn back and recross the line, and she must remain clear of all boats that are starting, or have started, correctly, until she has completely recrossed.

It is usually permissible for a boat to cross the starting line before the signal, and then attempt to work her way back across the line in order to recross it in the proper direction when the signal is given. In many cases, however, there is a time limitation. Specific race rules often state that a boat must not be across the line less than a minute before the starting signal.

If a number of boats are across the starting line when the starting signal is given, the race committee may make a general recall of all boats for a new start.

Special Rules. It is illegal for a boat to release into the water any substance meant to reduce the skin friction of the hull as it goes through the water.

The boat must be propelled only by the natural action of the wind and the water. It is illegal to "pump" the sails by frequent rapid trimming, except to promote hydroplaning. Rocking the boat from side to side and "ooching"—lunging forward and stopping abruptly—are also forbidden.

An oar, paddle, or similar object may be used for steering in an emergency, but not for propelling the boat.

A boat is required to render all possible assistance to a person or a vessel in peril. If a boat is delayed by rendering such assistance, or through being disabled by another boat that should have kept clear, the race committee may cancel or abandon the race, or assign that boat to a finish higher than her actual finish.

Handicaps. There are many different systems of handicapping yacht races when boats of different sizes and sail areas are involved. Generally a formula is used, based on sail area, displacement, and other factors. Some of the formulas are quite complicated. The result is usually a rated length, in feet or meters, which doesn't necessarily have anything to do with the boat's actual length.

The rated length is then applied to a table which gives a time allowance for that boat. The boat that should be the fastest is called the "scratch boat"; she gets no time allowance at all, and her normal time allowance is deducted from the normal time allowances of the other boats in the race to give their specific allowances for that race.

There are two kinds of time allowance. One is based on the time of the race, the other on the distance. When a boat finishes, her elapsed time is recorded, and her time allowance is then subtracted to give her corrected time. The winner is the boat with the best corrected time.

Scoring Systems. A champion is often determined, not by one race but by a series of races, and a scoring system is then used to select a winner. There are several systems.

The simplest is the low-point system, in which a boat gets a number of points corresponding to its finish in each race; that is, the first place boat gets 1 point, the second-place boat 2 points, and so forth. If a boat doesn't finish, it gets one point more than it would have for finishing last. A disqualified boat gets 2 points more than it would have for finishing last. The boat with the lowest total wins the series.

The high-point system gives 1 point for finishing, 1 point for each yacht defeated, and ¼ point for finishing first. For example, a boat that won a 12-boat race would be given 12¼ points: 1 for finishing, 11 for defeating 11 other boats, and the ¼-point bonus for winning.

Other scoring systems are more complicated. Olympic yacht racing uses a low-point system in which the first-place boat gets no points, the second-place boat 3 points, the third-place boat 5.7 points, the fourth-place boat 8 points, the fifth-place boat 10 points, and the sixth-place boat 11.7 points.

Protests. If a yacht breaks a rule or a sailing instruction, she is supposed to retire from the race immediately. If she does not, another boat is entitled to protest. A protest should be signaled as soon as possible, so the crew of the boat being protested against is aware of the incident and can remember the circumstances. The protest is signaled by hoisting a special flag into the rigging; it must be kept flying until the protester finishes the race. (A single-handed competitor can simply wave the flag to alert the protested boat, and then wave it again to alert the race committee upon crossing the finish line.)

Immediately after the race, the protest must be drawn up in writing; it must explain when, where, and how an alleged violation occurred, with a statement of facts and, usually, a diagram. The race committee then holds a hearing, which should be conducted very much like a trial, and makes a decision. If the protest is upheld, the guilty boat is usually disqualified. A boat can also be disqualified without protest, if the committee members saw an infringement, or if a witness not taking part in the race reports an infringement.

Racing Tactics

Starts. Quite often the boat that gets ahead at the start goes on to win the race. Even if it isn't won at the start, a race can be hopelessly lost there. In the ideal start, the boat hits the line at top speed just as the starting signal is hoisted. There are several ways of trying to do this. An important factor is determining which end of the line is preferable, a matter that depends partly on the best tack for the boat to take after crossing the line: If a starboard tack, the windward end of the line is best; if a port tack, the leeward end is best. If the line isn't square to the wind, the skipper can determine the best end by heading the boat directly into the wind. The bow will then point closer to the best end.

There are various methods of trying to hit the line at the right place and time. In the timed start, the boat starts at the line perhaps 5 min before the starting signal; sails away from the line for approximately half that time, less the amount of time it will take to come about; and then comes about and sails back to the line.

A boat can also sit on the line, luffing, and sheet in just before the gun in order to cross at the right moment. A similar technique is to run along the line, starting to the windward of the starting spot, until just before the gun, then trim sails and head toward the line on the proper course.

In the dip start, the boat is kept above the line—on the starting side—until 2 min or so before the signal. Then the skipper looks for an opening; upon seeing one, the skipper dips into the opening just a few seconds before the start, and turns back to cross the line at the gun.

The least subtle and most dangerous kind of start is the

barging start, in which the skipper hopes to be able to squeeze across the starting line between the mark and another boat. The risk is that the boat may not be able to squeeze through without fouling.

Blankets and Wind Shadows. In most kinds of racing, a vehicle tends to pull another vehicle along behind it, because the vehicle in back encounters less air and therefore less air resistance. With sailboats, however, the opposite effect may occur: If the boats are close enough together, the sails of the windward boat (ordinarily the lead boat) will "blanket" the leeward boat, depriving it of wind.

When boats are running, however, it is the boat in back that is to windward; if close enough to the leading boat, the boat in back will deprive it of wind.

"Wind shadow" is turbulent air that spills around the lee side of a boat's sails. The turbulence from one boat's sails can seriously hinder another boat; and it is the boat to windward that is affected. Furthermore, the effect of wind shadow extends farther than the effect of a wind blanket, which is a cone never wider than the boat's length. Wind shadow extends as far back as two boat-lengths, and gets wider as it gets farther from the boat. Thus, when two boats are within two boat-lengths of each other, and the leeward boat's abeam the windward boat, or even farther aft, the leeward boat's wind shadow will hinder the windward boat—unless they are so close together that the windward boat's blanket is affecting the leeward boat.

Covering. A boat is said to cover another boat when it stays between that boat and the next mark, or between that boat and the wind. It is a vital tactic in a match race, or in a fleet race where two boats are well ahead of the pack.

However, covering should be used with care; covering too closely after getting ahead may deprive a boat of the advantage gained by a good start. The boat behind may go off on the wrong tack, simply to get "clear air," and if it is a poor tack the leading boat will only lose ground by covering.

Nevertheless, it is a rule of thumb in racing to cover the boat astern, staying between her and the mark—not necessarily to blanket her, but to insure getting to the mark first—and it is a rule that should be broken only for a good reason.

Breaking Cover. A common technique for getting out of a close cover is to make several tacks in rapid succession. This will lose ground but, if the leading boat doesn't follow the tacks, the trailing boat will end up on an opposite tack, winning clear air and a chance to get to windward of the lead boat.

Another method, more commonly used in match racing, is the false tack. The trailing boat makes several tacks, allowing the lead boat to cover each time, then begins to come about as if for another tack. The lead boat should respond quickly. If she does, the trailing boat, after luffing, swings back onto her original course.

Sailing to Windward. When in a sizable fleet, a skipper is probably best off sailing the race he thinks he should sail, following the quickest route to the lay line (the line that will take him around the mark) without worrying much about the other boats in the race. The first leg is usually a windward leg, and this leg can easily decide the outcome of the race. The skipper should have the course well

Sailing, including racing, is fun for many youngsters; these three are being given a lesson. (*Hank Seaman,* New Bedford Standard-Times.)

planned beforehand and, insofar as possible, should stick to that course, being careful to avoid boats to his leeward and trying to stay to leeward himself.

Running and Reaching. On running and reaching legs, the best thing a skipper can do, ordinarily, is to sail as straight as possible between marks. A boat will sail faster when higher (closer to the wind), but sailing lower will result in a shorter course that will usually get the boat to the mark sooner, and in better position to round the mark. The best course is to stay slightly below (to windward of) the straight line to the mark, so the boat will head up more into the wind when near the mark; the additional burst of speed will give her a good opportunity to get in ahead of boats that have been sailing higher but now have to sail on a broad reach to round the mark.

Tactics for sailing downwind depend on the position in which the boat is placed. Again, following a straight line is advisable, because most of the other boats are likely to be sailing higher; staying away from them will prevent them from blanketing. If the boat is ahead, however, with a large number of boats close behind, sailing high is usually better, to avoid being blanketed.

When behind several boats, it may be possible to approach them one at a time, blanket them with a spinnaker, and then pass them. However, care should be taken not to pass close, either to leeward or to windward. The proper way to pass is to cut across behind the boat being passed, traveling rapidly to windward, and getting away from the other boat as rapidly as possible, to be well out of the way before turning back onto the proper course.

Another important consideration on a running leg is the amount of time it takes to get a spinnaker up and to get it down again. Leaving it up too long can waste a great amount of time, getting around the mark; taking it down too early can be equally disastrous.

Rounding Marks. Like any other kind of race, a yacht race can be won in the turns. A boat that saves space, and therefore time, by getting to the inside in rounding a mark can move up many places in the standings.

A turn must be made gradually and smoothly; the larger the boat, the more gradual a turn must be. Generally it is best to begin a turn some distance from the mark, and to come close to it as the turn is being completed. However, going too wide at the beginning may enable another boat from behind to sneak to the inside; a skipper always has to keep such possibilities in mind when deciding precisely how to round a mark.

A clear understanding of the overlap rule is vitally important. When trying to overtake another boat to the inside while rounding a mark, the skipper has to realize that if he can get to the inside position in time, he has a good chance of rounding the mark ahead. However, if he can't establish the overlap in time, he has to choose other tactics. It will often be to his advantage to stay close astern of the boat in front, especially if it will be necessary to tack soon after rounding the mark. The lead boat may not be able to tack safely if the trailing boat is close behind; this will enable the trailing boat to get on the desired tack first, thus gaining time.

Glossary

afterguard—Members of a large crew who compose the "brain trust" rather than doing physical work; helmsman, navigator, and so forth.

amidships—The center of a vessel.

apparent wind—The forward motion of the sailboat, combined with the direction of the actual wind, produces an apparent wind somewhere between the two directions.

back—The wind is said to back when it shifts in a counterclockwise direction.

balloon sail—Large, light sails used when reaching or running, such as the balloon spinnaker.

batten—A strip of some stiff material that is put in a pocket in the sail to help hold its shape.

beam—The widest part of a vessel.

bear down—To approach from windward.

bear off—To turn farther to leeward; or, to keep clear of something.

bend—To fasten a sail into place on boom and mast.

boom—A spar to which the sail's foot is attached.

bowsprit—A spar that extends forward from the bow.

bunt—The middle of a sail.

close-hauled—Sailing close to the wind.

cruiser—A boat with living arrangements on board.

day sailer—A boat with no living accommodations.

draft—The minimum depth of water in which a boat can sail.

flying jib—A jib fastened only by its corners.

foremast—On a boat with two or more masts, the mast farthest forward.

heel—A boat is said to heel when it leans or lists to one side or the other.

high—To windward.

kite—A spinnaker.

lay line—The course that would bring the boat, when close-hauled, straight to the mark.

lee—The side away from the wind.

length overall—The longest measurement of a boat.

midships—The widest part of a boat.

offshore wind—A wind blowing from the shore.

off the wind—With the wind astern.

on the wind—Sailing close-hauled.

outpoint—To sail closer to the wind than a racing rival.

overhaul—To gain on.

overstand—To sail past a mark without rounding it.

parachute—A balloon spinnaker.

pinch—To hold a boat too much into the wind.

privileged vessel—The boat with the right of way.

regatta—A meet that includes a number of races.

short-tacking duel—What takes place when a trailing boat goes through a whole series of tacks in an attempt to break cover.

spanking breeze—A good wind from astern, or nearly astern.

stand in—To approach.

stand off—To keep away.

stiff—Stable; said of a boat.

tender—Opposite of stiff.

trick—A turn at the helm.

trim—To adjust a sail so it is at the most effective angle to the wind.

underlay—To head for a point below the mark, so that another tack will be necessary before rounding it.

up—Toward the wind's direction.

America's Cup Results

Year	Winning Boat, Skipper	Losing Boat, Country	Score
1851	*America*, R. Brown	19 British vessels	1-0
1870	*Magic*, A. Comstock	*Cambria*, England	1-0
1871	*Columbia*, N. Comstock *Sappho*, S. Greenwood	*Livonia*, England	4-1
1876	*Madeleine*, J. Williams	*Countess of Dufferin*, Canada	2-0
1881	*Mischief*, N. Clark	*Atalanta*, Canada	2-0
1885	*Puritan*, A. Crocker	*Genesta*, England	2-0
1886	*Mayflower*, M. V. B. Stone	*Galatea*, England	2-0
1887	*Volunteer*, H. C. Haff	*Thistle*, Scotland	2-0
1893	*Vigilant*, W. Hansen	*Valkyrie II*, England	3-0
1895	*Defender*, H. C. Haff	*Valkyrie III*, England	3-0
1899	*Columbia*, Chas. Barr	*Shamrock*, N. Ireland	3-0
1901	*Columbia*, Chas. Barr	*Shamrock II*, N. Ireland	3-0
1903	*Reliance*, Chas. Barr	*Shamrock III*, N. Ireland	3-0
1920	*Resolute*, C. F. Adams II	*Shamrock IV*, N. Ireland	3-2
1930	*Enterprise*, H. S. Vanderbilt	*Shamrock V*, N. Ireland	4-0
1934	*Rainbow*, H. S. Vanderbilt	*Endeavor*, England	4-2

1937	*Ranger,*		
	H. S. Vanderbilt	*Endeavor II,*	
		England	4-0
1958	*Columbia,*		
	B. S. Cunningham	*Sceptre,* England	4-0
1962	*Weatherly,*		
	E. Mosbacher, Jr.	*Gretel,* Australia	4-1
1964	*Constellation,*		
	R. N. Bavier, Jr.	*Sovereign,* England	4-0
1967	*Intrepid,*		
	E. Mosbacher, Jr.	*Dame Pattie,*	
		Australia	4-0
1970	*Intrepid,* W. Ficker	*Gretel II,* Australia	4-1
1974	*Courageous,* "Ted" Hood	*Southern Cross,*	
		Australia	4-0

Congressional Cup

(Winner of round-robin match-race competition)

1965 Gerry Driscoll
1966 Gerry Driscoll
1967 Scott H. Allan
1968 Robert E. Allan III
1969 Henry Sprague III
1970 Argyle Campbell
1971 Thomas Pickard
1972 Argyle Campbell
1973 Dennis Conner
1974 Bill Ficker
1975 Dennis Conner
1976 Dick Deaver

Adams Cup

(North American women's championship)

1924 Ruth Sears
1925 Ruth Sears
1926 Jessie Bancroft
1927 Lorna Whittelsey
1928 Lorna Whittelsey
1929 Frances Williams
1930 Lorna Whittelsey
1931 Lorna Whittelsey
1932 Clair Dinsmore
1933 Ruth Sears
1934 Lorna Whittelsey
1935 Frances McElwain
1936 Frances McElwain
1937 Frances McElwain
1938 No competition
1939 Sylvia Shethar
1940 Sylvia Shethar
1941 Lois MacIntyre
1942–45 No competition
1946 Virginia Weston Besse
1947 Sylvia Shethar Everdell
1948 Aileen Shields
1949 Jane Smith
1950 Allegra Knapp Mertz
1951 Jane Smith

1952 Pat Hinman
1953 Judy Webb
1954 Allegra Knapp Mertz
1955 Toni Monetti
1956 Glen Hill Lattimore
1957 Jane Pegel
1958 Nancy Underhill Meade
1959 Allegra Knapp Mertz
1960 Pat Duane
1961 Timothea Schneider
1962 Susan W. Sinclair
1963 Allegra Knapp Mertz
1964 Jane Pegel
1965 Timothea Schneider Larr
1966 Jerie Clark
1967 Betty Weed Foulk
1968 June Methot
1969 Jan O'Malley
1970 Jan O'Malley
1971 Romeyn "Rusty" Everdell
1972 Sally Lindsay
1973 Timothea Schneider Larr
1974 Deborah Freeman
1975 Cindy Batchelor
1976 Ellen Gerloff

Mallory Cup

(North American men's championship)

1952 Cornelius Shields
1953 Eugene H. Walet III
1954 Eugene H. Walet III
1955 William Buchan, Jr.
1956 Fred E. Hood
1957 George D. O'Day
1958 Robert Mosbacher
1959 Harry C. Melges, Jr.
1960 Harry C. Melges, Jr.
1961 Harry C. Melges, Jr.
1962 James S. Payton
1963 James DeWitt
1964 G. Shelby Fredrichs, Jr.
1965 Cornelius Shields
1966 William S. Cox, Jr.
1967 Clifford W. Campbell
1968 James M. Hunt
1969 Graham M. Hall
1970 Dr. John Jennings
1971 John Kolius
1972 Edwin Sherman
1973 Dr. John Jennings
1974 Vann Wilson
1975 Chris Pollock
1976 David Crockett

Bibliography. *Encyclopedia of Sailing,* editors of *One Design and Offshore Yachtsman,* Harper and Row, New York, 1971; Robinson, Bill: *World Yachting,* Random House, New York, 1967.

Directory of Sports Organizations and Associations

(NOTE: In the case of many smaller organizations the address is actually the home address of an officer, and is therefore subject to rather sudden change. Addresses listed were correct as of January 1, 1975.)

PROFESSIONAL RACE PILOTS
ASSOCIATION
Lyle Shelton, President
16644 Roscoe Blvd.
Van Nuys, CA 91406

AMATEUR ATHLETIC UNION OF
THE UNITED STATES
Richard E. Harkin, Secretary
3400 West 86th St.
Indianapolis, IN 46268

NATIONAL ARCHERY
ASSOCIATION
1951 Geraldson Drive
Lancaster, PA 17601

NATIONAL FIELD
ARCHERY ASSOCIATION
Rt. 2, Box 514
Redlands, CA 92373

PROFESSIONAL ARCHERS
ASSOCIATION
77 McLean St.
Ballston Spa, NY 12020

AUTOMOBILE COMPETITION
COMMITTEE FOR THE UNITED
STATES
330 Vanderbilt Motor Parkway
Hauppauge, NY 11787

INTERNATIONAL MOTOR CONTEST
ASSOCIATION
1925 Park Ave.
Des Moines, IA 50315

INTERNATIONAL MOTOR SPORTS
ASSOCIATION
P.O. Box 805
Fairfield, CT 06430

NATIONAL ASSOCIATION FOR
STOCK CAR AUTO RACING
1801 Volusia Ave.
Daytona Beach, FL 32015

SPORTS CAR CLUB OF AMERICA
P.O. Box 22476
Denver, CO 80222

UNITED STATES AUTO CLUB
4910 W. 16th St.
Indianapolis, IN 46224

AMERICAN BADMINTON ASSN.
Mrs. Waldo Lyon, Secretary
1330 Alexandria Drive
San Diego, CA 92107

SPORT BALLOON SOCIETY OF THE
UNITED STATES
c/o Menlo Oaks Balloon Field
Menlo Park, CA 94025

AMERICAN LEAGUE (Baseball)
280 Park Ave.
New York, NY 10017

COMMISSIONER OF BASEBALL
680 Fifth Ave.
New York, NY 10019

NATIONAL LEAGUE (Baseball)
220 Montgomery St.
San Francisco, CA 94104

NATIONAL ASSOCIATION OF
PROFESSIONAL BASEBALL
LEAGUES
P. O. Box A
St. Petersburg, FL 33731

U.S. BASEBALL FEDERATION
Lee Eilbracht, Secretary
University of Illinois
Champaign, IL 61820

NATIONAL BASKETBALL
ASSOCIATION
2 Pennsylvania Plaza
New York, NY 10001

BASKETBALL FEDERATION OF THE
UNITED STATES
Norvall Neve, Executive Director
4215 Tallwood
Greensboro, NC 27410

U.S. MODERN PENTATHLON AND
BIATHLON ASSOCIATION
123 Brittany Drive
San Antonio, TX 78212

BILLIARD CONGRESS OF AMERICA
717 N. Michigan Ave.
Chicago, IL 60611

BILLIARD PLAYERS ASSOCIATION
OF AMERICA
Joe Jancik, Executive Secretary
Cue Club Billiard Academy
Johnston City, IL 62951

AMERICAN BOWLING CONGRESS
5301 S. 76th St.
Greendale, WI 53129

BOWLING PROPRIETORS'
ASSOCIATION OF AMERICA
P.O. Box 5802
Arlington, TX 76011

WOMEN'S INTERNATIONAL
BOWLING CONGRESS
5301 S. 76th St.
Greendale, WI 53129

WORLD BOXING ASSOCIATION
Jack Cohen, Executive Secretary
1 S. Calvert St.
Baltimore, MD 21202

WORLD BOXING COUNCIL
P.O. Box 3990
Manila, Philippine Islands

NATIONAL PADDLING
COMMITTEE, AMERICAN CANOE
ASSOCIATION
Mrs. Eileen Fox, Secretary
1709 N St., NW
Washington, DC 20036

AMERICAN WHITEWATER
AFFILIATION
P.O. Box 321
Concord, NH 03301

AMERICAN CASTING ASSOCIATION
P.O. Box 158
Jackson, KY 41339

WORLD CHAMPIONSHIP CUTTER
AND CHARIOT RACING
ASSOCIATION
Box 84
Pocatello, ID 83201

NATIONAL ASSOCIATION OF
INTERCOLLEGIATE ATHLETICS
1205 Baltimore Ave.
Kansas City, MO 64105

NATIONAL COLLEGIATE ATHLETIC
ASSOCIATION
P.O. Box 1906
Shawnee Mission, KS 66222

AMERICAN ROQUE LEAGUE
(Croquet)
4205 Briar Creek Lane
Dallas, TX 75214

U.S. MEN'S CURLING ASSOCIATION
119 Monona Ave.
Madison, WI 53703

U.S. WOMEN'S CURLING
ASSOCIATION
Mrs. C. Frank Pollen, President
410 Grove St.
Glencoe, IL 60022

AMATEUR BICYCLE LEAGUE OF
AMERICA
Ernest Seubert, President
137 Brunswick Rd.
Cedar Grove, NJ 07009

AMERICAN GREYHOUND TRACK
OPERATORS ASSOCIATION
1632 DuPont Building
Miami, FL 33131

NATIONAL HOT ROD ASSOCIATION
10639 Riverside Drive
North Hollywood, CA 91602

NATIONAL DUCKPIN BOWLING
CONGRESS
711 Fourteenth St., NW
Washington, DC 20005

AMATEUR FENCERS LEAGUE OF
AMERICA
Irwin Bernstein, Secretary
249 Eton Place
Westfield, NJ 07090

FIELD HOCKEY ASSOCIATION OF
AMERICA (Men)
1160 Third Ave.
New York, NY 10021

U.S. FIELD HOCKEY ASSOCIATION
(Women)
107 School House Lane
Philadelphia, PA 19144

U.S. FIGURE SKATING
ASSOCIATION
575 Boylston St.
Boston, MA 02116

INTERNATIONAL GAME FISH
ASSOCIATION
3000 E. Las Olas Blvd.
Ft. Lauderdale, FL 33316

NATIONAL FOOTBALL LEAGUE
410 Park Ave.
New York, NY 10022

NATIONAL FOX HUNTERS
ASSOCIATION
P.O. Box 1806
Jackston, TN 38301

LADIES PROFESSIONAL GOLF
ASSOCIATION
1776 Peachtree St.
Atlanta, GA 30309

PROFESSIONAL GOLFERS
ASSOCIATION OF AMERICA
P.O. Box 12458
Lake Park, FL 33403

U.S. GOLF ASSOCIATION
Far Hills, NJ 07931

U.S. GYMNASTICS FEDERATION
Frank Bare, Executive Director
P.O. Box 4699
Tucson, AZ 85717

U.S. HANDBALL ASSOCIATION
4101 Dempster St.
Skokie, IL 60076

U.S. TROTTING ASSOCIATION
750 Michigan Ave.
Columbus, OH 43215

AMATEUR HOCKEY ASSOCIATION
OF THE UNITED STATES
7901 Cedar Ave., S
Bloomington, MN 55420

NATIONAL HOCKEY LEAGUE
922 Sun Life Building
Montreal, Quebec, Canada

WORLD HOCKEY ASSOCIATION
4299 MacArthur Blvd.
Newport Beach, CA 92660

THOROUGHBRED RACING
ASSOCIATIONS OF THE UNITED
STATES
5 Dakota Drive, Suite 210
New Hyde Park, NY 11040

NATIONAL HORSESHOE PITCHERS
ASSOCIATION
819 Eye St.
Eureka, CA 95501

AMERICAN HORSE SHOWS
ASSOCIATION
527 Madison Ave.
New York, NY 10022

U.S. AMATEUR JAI ALAI PLAYERS
ASSOCIATION
100 SE Second Ave.
Miami, FL 33131

U.S. INTERCOLLEGIATE LACROSSE
ASSOCIATION
Edward L. Athey, Secretary
Washington College
Chestertown, MD 21620

U.S. WOMEN'S LACROSSE
ASSOCIATION
20 E. Sunset Ave.
Philadelphia, PA 19118

AMERICAN LAWN BOWLS
ASSOCIATION
10337 Cheryl Drive
Sun City, AZ 85351

AMERICAN MOTORCYCLE
ASSOCIATION
P.O. Box 141
Westerville, OH 43081

NATIONAL ALL-TERRAIN VEHICLE
ASSOCIATION
342 Broad St.
New Bethlehem, PA 16242

U.S. OLYMPIC COMMITTEE
Olympic House
57 Park Ave.
New York, NY 10016

U.S. PADDLE TENNIS ASSOCIATION
189 Seeley St.
Brooklyn, NY 11218

NATIONAL PADDLEBALL
ASSOCIATION
Sports Building, University of
Michigan
Ann Arbor, MI 48104

AMERICAN PLATFORM TENNIS
ASSOCIATION
Robert A. Brown, President
235 Madison Rd.
Scarsdale, NY 10683

U.S. POLO ASSOCIATION
Suite 706, 1301 W. 22nd St.
Oak Brook, IL 60521

AMERICAN POWER BOAT
ASSOCIATION
22811 Greater Mack
St. Clair Shores, MI 48080

INTERNATIONAL RACQUETBALL
ASSOCIATION
4101 Dempster St.
Skokie, IL 60076

RODEO COWBOYS ASSOCIATION
2929 W. 19th Ave.
Denver, CO 80204

U.S. ROLLER SKATING
CONFEDERATION
7700 A St.
Lincoln, NE 68510

INTERCOLLEGIATE ROWING
ASSOCIATION
Robert M. Whitelaw, Secretary-
Treasurer
c/o Royal Manhattan Hotel
New York, NY 10036

NATIONAL ASSOCIATION OF
AMATEUR OARSMEN
4 Boathouse Row
Philadelphia, PA 19130

U.S. REVOLVER ASSOCIATION
59 Alvin St.
Springfield, MA 01104

NATIONAL RIFLE ASSOCIATION
1600 Rhode Island Ave., NW
Washington, DC 20036

NATIONAL SHUFFLEBOARD
ASSOCIATION
10418 NE Second Ave.
Miami, FL 33138

NATIONAL SKEET SHOOTING
ASSOCIATION
P.O. Box 28188
San Antonio, TX 78228

U.S. SKI ASSOCIATION
1726 Champa St.
Denver, CO 80202

U.S. PARACHUTE ASSOCIATION
P.O. Box 109
Monterey, CA 93940

INTERNATIONAL SLED DOG
RACING ASSOCIATION
P.O. Box 144
Ontario, NY 14519

SOARING SOCIETY OF AMERICA
P.O. Box 66071
Los Angeles, CA 90066

NORTH AMERICAN SOCCER
LEAGUE
101 Park Ave.
New York, NY 10017

U.S. SOCCER FOOTBALL
ASSOCIATION
350 Fifth Ave.
New York, NY 10001

AMATEUR SOFTBALL ASSOCIATION
OF AMERICA
P.O. Box 11437
Oklahoma City, OK 73111

AMATEUR SKATING UNION OF THE
UNITED STATES
4423 W. Deming Place
Chicago, IL 60639

U.S. SQUASH RACQUETS
ASSOCIATION
211 Ford Road
Bala-Cynwyd, PA 19004

U.S. FRONTON ATHLETIC
ASSOCIATION
15 W. 43rd St.
New York, NY 10036

NATIONAL STEEPLECHASE AND
HUNT ASSOCIATION
P.O. Box 308
Elmont, NY 11003

U.S. TABLE TENNIS
ASSOCIATION
c/o Jack Carr, Executive Vice President
5 Roberta Drive
Hampton, VA 23366

U.S. TEAM HANDBALL
FEDERATION
10 Nottingham Road
Short Hills, NJ 07078

U.S. LAWN TENNIS
ASSOCIATION
51 E. 42nd St.
New York, NY 10017

U.S. TRACK AND FIELD
FEDERATION
1225 N. 10th Ave.
Tucson, AZ 85705

AMATEUR TRAPSHOOTING
ASSOCIATION OF AMERICA
P.O. Box 246
Vandalia, OH 45377

U.S. VOLLEYBALL
ASSOCIATION
557 Fourth St.
San Francisco, CA 94107

AMERICAN WATER SKI
ASSOCIATION
7th St. and Ave. G, SW
Winter Haven, FL 33880

NATIONAL ASSOCIATION FOR
GIRLS AND WOMEN IN SPORT
1201 16th St., NW
Washington, DC 20036

U.S. WRESTLING FEDERATION
Steve Combs, Executive Director
4000 W. 19th St.
Stillwater, OK 74074

NORTH AMERICAN YACHT RACING
UNION
37 W. 44th St.
New York, NY 10036

Bibliography

The following are general reference books. After many entries for major sports, the reader will find bibliographies applicable to those specific topics.

Associated Press: *Sports Almanac, 1974,* Dell, New York, 1974.

Bass, Howard: *Winter Sports,* A. S. Barnes, New York, 1968.

Burton, Bill (ed.): *The Sportsman's Encyclopedia,* Varsity, New York, 1971.

Cummings, Parke: *The Dictionary of Sports,* Ronald, New York, 1949.

Diagram Group: *Rules of the Game,* Paddington, New York, 1974.

Jessup, Harvey M. (ed.): *The Little Known Olympic Sports,* American Association for Health, Physical Education, and Recreation, Washington, D.C., 1972.

Koppett, Leonard: *The New York Times Guide to Spectator Sports,* Quadrangle Books, New York, 1971.

Menke, Frank: *The Encyclopedia of Sports,* 2nd rev. ed., A. S. Barnes, New York, 1960.

Pratt, John Lowell and Jim Benagh: *The Official Encyclopedia of Sports,* Watts, New York, 1964.